ROLEX

Presents

The World of
Professional Golf

Founded by
Mark H. McCormack

2010

sports · entertainment · media

Editor: Bev Norwood
Contributors: Andy Farrell, Doug Ferguson, Donald (Doc) Giffin, Marino Parascenzo

First published 2010
© IMG Operations, Inc. 2010

Designed and produced by Davis Design

ISBN-13: 978-1-878843-59-3
ISBN-10: 1-878843-59-1

Printed and bound in the United States.

Contents

Rolex Rankings 1

Official World Golf Ranking 6

World's Winners of 2009 14

Multiple Winners of 2009 22

World Money List 23

World Money List Leaders 30

Career World Money List 31

Women's World Money List 32

Senior World Money List 35

1   The Year In Retrospect 39

THE MAJOR CHAMPIONSHIPS

2   Masters Tournament 54

3   U.S. Open Championship 61

4   The Open Championship 70

5   PGA Championship 79

6   Women's Major Championships 87

WORLDWIDE TOURS

7   American Tours 102

8   European Tours 155

9   Asia/Japan Tours 185

10   Australasian Tour 220

11   African Tours 230

12   Women's Tours 250

13   Senior Tours 301

APPENDIXES

U.S. PGA Tour 336

Special Events 399

Nationwide Tour 402

Canadian Tour 418

Tour de las Americas (South America) 426
European Tour 434
Challenge Tour 476
Asian Tour 490
OneAsia Tour 509
Omega China Tour 512
Japan Tour 514
Australasian Tour 529
African Tours 539
U.S. LPGA Tour 560
Ladies European Tour 580
Japan LPGA Tour 593
Australian Ladies Tour 612
Champions Tour 616
European Senior Tour 635
Japan Senior Tour 644

Introduction

Rolex has done so many things over the years that were and are good for golf. Sponsorship of this publication is a prime example. My friends at Rolex, recognizing the historic and research value *The World of Professional Golf* has provided to the game continuously since the middle 1960s, stepped up in 2005 with the support necessary to continue its existence and the service it extends to the world of golf.

I well remember my conversations with my close friend and business manager, the late Mark McCormack, when he outlined his concept of filling a written gap in the game's history with an annual book carrying detailed stories and statistics covering every organized national and international tournament during that particular calendar year. The idea made complete sense to me and I encouraged him to proceed. He did, recruiting a group of talented golf journalists to work with him in producing the first edition that covered the 1966 season worldwide. Its publication has continued and grown in size and scope ever since, keeping pace with the tremendous growth of the game throughout the world.

Mark McCormack passed away in 2003, but his contribution to the historical record of golf did not die. Credit for this goes to IMG executives and others within the organization who considered the book an important continuing tribute to Mark and to Patrick Heiniger and his executive associates at Rolex, whose support has kept the literary chain intact.

Arnold Palmer
Orlando, Florida

Foreword
(Written in 1968)

It has long been my feeling that a sport as compelling as professional golf is deserving of a history, and by history I do not mean an account culled years later from the adjectives and enthusiasms of on-the-spot reports that have then sat in newspaper morgues for decades waiting for some patient drudge to paste them together and call them lore. Such works can be excellent when insight and perspective are added to the research, but this rarely happens. What I am talking about is a running history, a chronology written at the time, which would serve both as a record of the sport and as a commentary upon the sport in any given year—an annual, if you will....

When I embarked on this project two years ago (the first of these annuals was published in Great Britain in 1967), I was repeatedly told that such a compendium of world golf was impossible, that it would be years out of date before it could be assembled and published, that it would be hopelessly expensive to produce and that only the golf fanatic would want a copy anyway. In the last analysis, it was that final stipulation that spurred me on. There must be a lot of golf fanatics, I decided. I can't be the only one. And then one winter day I was sitting in Arnold Palmer's den in Latrobe, Pennsylvania, going through the usual motions of spreading papers around so that Arnold and I could discuss some business project, when Arnold happened to mention that he wanted to collect a copy of each new golf book that was published from now on, in order to build a golf library of his own. "It's really too bad that there isn't a book every year on the pro tour," he said. "Ah," I thought. "Another golf fanatic. That makes two of us." So I decided to do the book. And I have. And I hope you like it. If so, you can join Arnold and me as golf fanatics.

Mark H. McCormack
Cleveland, Ohio
January 1968

Mark H. McCormack
1930 – 2003

In 1960, Mark Hume McCormack shook hands with a young golfer named Arnold Palmer. That historic handshake established a business that would evolve into today's IMG, the world's premier sports and lifestyle marketing and management company —representing hundreds of sports figures, entertainers, models, celebrities, broadcasters, television properties, and prestigious organizations and events around the world. With just a handshake Mark McCormack had invented a global industry.

Sean McManus, President of CBS News and Sports, reflects, "I don't think it's an overstatement to say that like Henry Ford and Bill Gates, Mark McCormack literally created, fostered and led an entirely new worldwide industry. There was no sports marketing before Mark McCormack. Every athlete who's ever appeared in a commercial, or every right holder who sold their rights to anyone, owes a huge debt of gratitude to Mark McCormack."

Mark McCormack's philosophy was simple. "Be the best," he said. "Learn the business and expand by applying what you already know." This philosophy served him well, not only as an entrepreneur and CEO of IMG, but also as an author, a consultant and a confidant to a host of global leaders in the world of business, politics, finance, science, sports and entertainment.

He was among the most-honored entrepreneurs of his time. *Sports Illustrated* recognized him as "The Most Powerful Man in Sports." In 1999, ESPN's Sports Century listed him as one of the century's 10 "Most Influential People in the Business of Sport."

Golf Magazine called McCormack "the most powerful man in golf" and honored him along with Arnold Palmer, Gerald Ford, Dwight D. Eisenhower, Bob Hope and Ben Hogan as one of the 100 all-time "American Heroes of Golf." *Tennis* magazine and *Racquet* magazine named him "the most powerful man in tennis." Tennis legend Billie Jean King believes, "Mark McCormack was the king of sports marketing. He shaped the way all sports are marketed around the world. He was the first in the marketplace, and his influence on the world of sports, particularly his ability to combine athlete representation, property development and television broadcasting, will forever be the standard of the industry."

The London *Sunday Times* listed him as one of the 1000 people who influenced the 20th century. Alastair Cooke on the BBC said simply that "McCormack was the Oracle; the creator of the talent industry, the maker of people famous in their profession famous to the rest of the world and making for them a fortune in the process … He took on as clients people already famous in their profession as golfer, opera singer, author, footballer, racing car driver, violinist—and from time to time if they needed special help, a prime minister, or even the Pope."

McCormack was honored posthumously by the Golf Writers Association of America with the 2004 William D. Richardson Award, the organization's highest honor, "Given to recognize an individual who has consistently made an outstanding contribution to golf."

Among McCormack's other honors were the 2001 PGA Distinguished Service Award, given to those who have helped perpetuate the values and ideals of the PGA of America. He was also named a Commander of the Royal Order of the Polar Star by the King of Sweden (the highest honor for a person living outside of Sweden) for his contribution to the Nobel Foundation.

Journalist Frank Deford states, "There have been what we love to call dynasties in every sport. IMG has been different. What this one brilliant man, Mark McCormack, created is the only dynasty ever over all sport."

Through IMG, Mark McCormack demonstrated the value of sports and lifestyle activities as effective corporate marketing tools, but more importantly, his lifelong dedication to his vocation—begun with just a simple handshake—brought enjoyment to millions of people worldwide who watch and cheer their heroes and heroines. That is his legacy.

ROLEX

© ROLEX/Jess Hoffman

Rolex is pleased to present *The World of Professional Golf*, a review of the highlights of what proved to be another thrilling year on the professional golf circuits.

The brand's commitment to contributing to the growth of golf worldwide and encouraging the advancement of talented young golfers continues undiminished. Rolex especially congratulates its Testimonee Lorena Ochoa, fourth-time Rolex Player of the Year, who in 2009 retained her position as number one in women's golf.

Rolex is proud to be Official Sponsor of the fourth tournament of the World Golf Championship series. The WGC-HSBC Champions, held at Shanghai's Sheshan International Golf Club and fittingly won in 2009 by Rolex Testimonee Phil Mickelson, is the only WGC tournament to be held outside the United States. The elevation of the competition to WGC status indicates the growing importance of golf in Asia and the exponential growth opportunities for the game in China, whose top player, Liang Wenchong, Rolex welcomed as a Testimonee during the year.

Believing strongly in the great potential and talent of Indian golfers, the brand has expanded its activities on the subcontinent through its association with India's finest player and Rolex Testimonee, Jeev Milkha Singh, and new partnerships with both the Professional Golf Tour of India and the Indian Golf Union.

In the Middle East, Rolex has strengthened its presence in golf through its partnership with the Dubai World Championship, the last event in the season-long Race to Dubai, in which the top 60 players compete for the highest prize money on the European Tour.

This edition of *The World of Professional Golf* promises to be an exciting reminder of many of the splendid moments of the 2009 golf season.

Bruno Meier
Chief Executive Officer
Rolex SA

Rolex and Golf

Rolex's association with golf dates from 1967 when Andre Heiniger presented Arnold Palmer with a gold Oyster Perpetual to honor his achievements on the golf course. This marked the beginning of a loyal and privileged relationship, not only with Arnold Palmer and afterwards with two other golfing greats, Gary Player and Jack Nicklaus, but also many of the great talents who have followed them. Rolex has also established relationships with the major organizating bodies of the game.

Ai Miyazato is presented with a Rolex watch by Rolex CEO Bruno Meier at the Evian Masters.

ROLEX/Fadil Berisha

Gary Player, Arnold Palmer and Jack Nicklaus

ROLEX/Chris Turvey

M. Bertrand Gros presents a watch to European Ryder Cup team captain Colin Montgomerie.

The Rolex Rankings' Top 10

1. Lorena Ochoa (Mexico) 11.75 points

2. Jiyai Shin (Korea) 9.04 points

3. Suzann Pettersen (Norway) 7.49 points

4. Cristie Kerr (USA) 7.20 points

Michael Cohen/Getty Images

5. Yani Tseng (Taiwan) 7.13 points

Chris Graythen/Getty Images

6. Paula Creamer (USA) 7.04 points

Andy Lyons/Getty Images

7. Anna Nordqvist (Sweden) 7.00 points

Stuart Franklin/Getty Images

8. Ai Miyazato (Japan) 6.61 points

Hunter Martin/Getty Images

9. Angela Stanford (USA) 6.49 points

Kevin C. Cox/Getty Images

10. Michelle Wie (USA) 6.28 points

Rolex and Sport

Since 1927, Rolex has been associated with the quest for excellence in sport, when it placed a Rolex Oyster on the wrist of a young swimmer, Mercedes Gleitze, as she swam across the English Channel. In 1933, Rolex began to sponsor Himalayan and polar expeditions, including the first successful ascent of Everest by Sir Edmund Hillary in 1953.

Today Rolex supports top sporting and cultural events all over the world. It is present at more than 150 events in the realms of golf, yachting, tennis, equestrian events, motor sports, exploration, culture and the arts, as well as philanthropic awards programs. Because of the commitment and continuity of these relationships, Rolex is seen not only as a sponsor … but as a real partner.

Lorena Ochoa at the Evian Masters

ROLEX/Chris Turvey

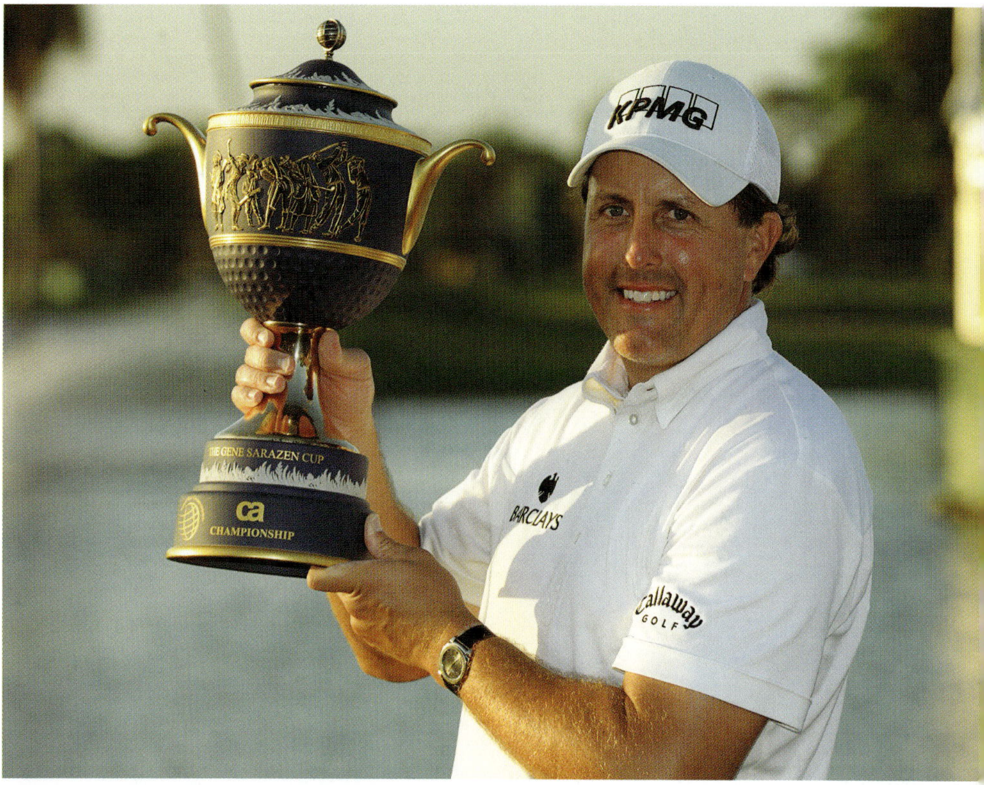

Phil Mickelson at the CA Championship

ROLEX/Chris Turvey

Adam Scott

ROLEX/Chris Turvey

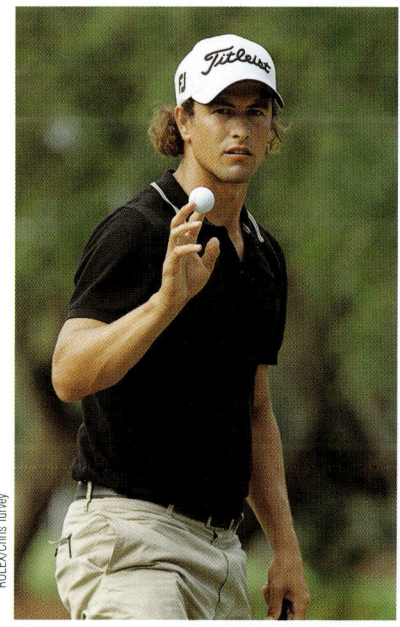

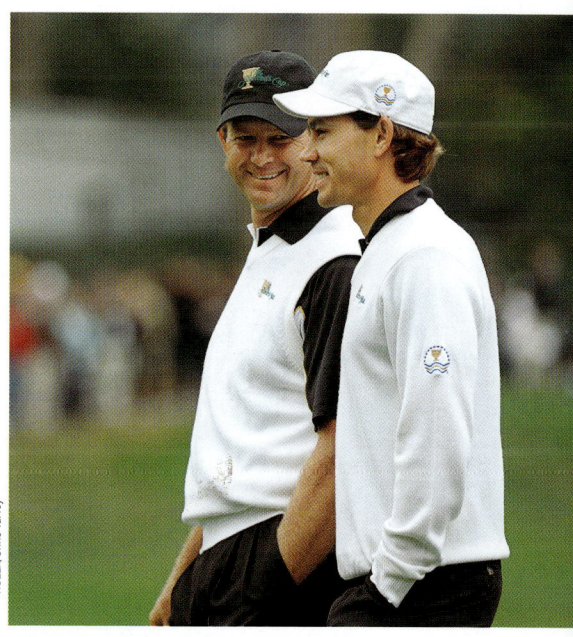

Retief Goosen and Camilo Villegas

ROLEX/Chris Turvey

Jeev Milkha Singh

ROLEX/Chris Turvey

Martin Kaymer

ROLEX/Chris Turvey

Liang Wen-chong

Rolex Rankings

The Rolex Player of the Year for 2009, Lorena Ochoa of Mexico maintained her No. 1 place on the Rolex Rankings as her two closest rivals did not pose challenges to her position. Ochoa, who had a points average of 15.64 at the close of 2008, finished the year with a points average of 11.75, but was well ahead of No. 2 Jiyai Shin of South Korea, with a 9.04 average, after Shin led the LPGA money list and was Rolex Rookie of the Year. Ochoa had three victories for the year and finished fourth on the LPGA money list.

The No. 2 player finishing 2008 was Taiwan's Yani Tseng, with a 9.31 average. She slipped to No. 5 with a 7.13 average. Annika Sorenstam of Sweden, the No. 3 player, retired from professional golf after 2008.

The new No. 3 player was Suzann Pettersen of Norway, with a 7.49 average, including a victory in the Canadian Women's Open. Pettersen had been No. 5 in 2008. Cristie Kerr of the United States, second to Shin on the LPGA money list, was ranked No. 4 with a 7.20 average, up from No. 7 the previous year, then Tseng completed the top five in the world.

Paula Creamer of the United States, ninth on the LPGA money list, slipped two positions to No. 6 with a 7.04 average, then came Anna Nordqvist of Sweden, the McDonald's LPGA champion, at No. 7 with an even 7.00 average. Ai Miyazato of Japan, who was third on the money list and won the Evian Masters, was No. 8 with a 6.61 average, up from No. 36 in 2008. Angela Stanford of the United States was No. 9 with a 6.49 average, her same position as last year.

Michelle Wie of the United States was No. 10 with a 6.28 average after achieving her long-awaited first professional victory in the Lorena Ochoa Invitational in Mexico.

In addition to Sorenstam, those dropping out of the top 10 in the Rolex Rankings after 2009 were Helen Alfredsson of Sweden, who fell from No. 8 to No. 25, and Karrie Webb of Australia, who went from No. 10 to No. 13.

The Rolex Rankings—which was developed at the May 2004 World Congress of Women's Golf—is sanctioned by the five major women's professional golf tours: the Ladies Professional Golf Association (LPGA), Ladies European Tour (LET), Ladies Professional Golfers' Association of Japan (JLPGA), Korea Ladies Professional Golf Association (KLPGA), Australian Ladies Professional Golf (ALPG), and the Ladies' Golf Union (LGU).

The five major golf tours and the LGU developed the rankings and the protocol that governs the ranking while R2IT, an independent software development company, was retained to develop the software and to maintain the rankings on a weekly basis. The official events from all of the tours are taken into account and points are awarded according to the strength of the field, with the exception of the four major championships on the LPGA Tour schedule and the Futures Tour events, which have a fixed points distribution. The players' points averages are determined by taking the number of points awarded over a two-year rolling period and dividing that by the number of tournaments played, with a minimum divisor of 35.

The Rolex Rankings are updated and released following the completion of the previous week's tournaments around the world.

Rolex Rankings
(As of December 31, 2009)

Rank	Player	Country	No. of Events	Average Points	Total Points
1	Lorena Ochoa	Mexico	44	11.75	517.16
2	Jiyai Shin	Korea	63	9.04	569.56
3	Suzann Pettersen	Norway	48	7.49	359.36
4	Cristie Kerr	USA	51	7.20	366.98
5	Yani Tseng	Taiwan	57	7.13	406.65
6	Paula Creamer	USA	50	7.04	351.80
7	Anna Nordqvist	Sweden	23	7.00	245.08
8	Ai Miyazato	Japan	58	6.61	383.47
9	Angela Stanford	USA	48	6.49	311.41
10	Michelle Wie	USA	29	6.28	219.75
11	In-Kyung Kim	Korea	54	6.03	325.86
12	Na Yeon Choi	Korea	58	6.01	348.78
13	Karrie Webb	Australia	44	5.84	257.06
14	Song-Hee Kim	Korea	54	4.82	260.50
15	Sakura Yokomine	Japan	69	4.81	331.83
16	Catriona Matthew	Scotland	35	4.45	155.70
17	Shinobu Moromizato	Japan	68	4.13	280.58
18	Sophie Gustafson	Sweden	53	4.08	216.08
19	Eun-Hee Ji	Korea	59	3.94	232.74
20	Chie Arimura	Japan	71	3.91	277.58
21	Kristy McPherson	USA	50	3.89	194.35
22	Mi-Jeong Jeon	Korea	64	3.87	247.51
23	Morgan Pressel	USA	51	3.70	188.84
24	Maria Hjorth	Sweden	45	3.65	164.06
25	Helen Alfredsson	Sweden	47	3.59	168.75
26	Brittany Lang	USA	54	3.57	192.78
27	Momoko Ueda	Japan	60	3.56	213.81
28	Lindsey Wright	Australia	50	3.52	175.95
29	Ji-Hee Lee	Korea	59	3.29	194.28
30	Brittany Lincicome	USA	44	3.23	142.34
31	Seon-Hwa Lee	Korea	55	3.21	176.77
32	Bo-Bae Song	Korea	55	3.19	175.42
33	Yuri Fudoh	Japan	46	3.14	144.23
34	Sun Young Yoo	Korea	56	3.13	175.27
35	Katherine Hull	Australia	63	3.12	196.66
36	Hee Young Park	Korea	58	2.99	173.22
37	Candie Kung	Taiwan	54	2.93	158.33
38	Yuko Mitsuka	Japan	64	2.83	181.34
39	Miho Koga	Japan	68	2.76	187.44
40	Hee-Won Han	Korea	54	2.75	148.75
41	Ji Young Oh	Korea	56	2.58	144.38
42	Inbee Park	Korea	56	2.56	143.23
43	Se Ri Pak	Korea	44	2.55	112.38
44	Hee Kyung Seo	Korea	52	2.54	132.04
45	M.J. Hur	Korea	45	2.52	113.43
46	Jee Young Lee	Korea	54	2.45	132.48
47	Stacy Lewis	USA	33	2.26	79.00
48	Jeong Jang	Korea	35	2.25	78.81
49	Christina Kim	USA	56	2.23	125.12
50	Juli Inkster	USA	39	2.20	85.98

Rank	Player	Country	No. of Events	Average Points	Total Points
51	Michele Redman	USA	39	2.19	85.40
52	Amy Yang	Korea	48	2.17	104.28
53	Akiko Fukushima	Japan	55	2.16	118.95
54	Angela Park	Brazil	45	2.08	93.58
55	Eunjung Yi	Korea	42	2.06	86.43
56	Eun-A Lim	Korea	59	1.98	116.66
57	Karen Stupples	England	48	1.96	94.14
58	Natalie Gulbis	USA	42	1.91	80.23
59	So Yeon Ryu	Korea	46	1.89	86.78
60	Mika Miyazato	Japan	26	1.85	64.62
61	Yukari Baba	Japan	68	1.81	122.99
62	Vicky Hurst	USA	37	1.78	66.02
63	Mayu Hattori	Japan	67	1.78	119.42
64	Pat Hurst	USA	49	1.77	86.66
65	Nicole Castrale	USA	51	1.72	87.64
66	Miki Saiki	Japan	62	1.71	106.19
67	Meena Lee	Korea	55	1.67	91.98
68	Wendy Ward	USA	43	1.66	71.54
69	Sun Ju Ahn	Korea	39	1.64	64.08
70	Ayako Uehara	Japan	64	1.63	104.08
71	Kyeong Bae	Korea	51	1.62	82.86
72	Shi-Hyun Ahn	Korea	38	1.62	61.46
73	Sandra Gal	Germany	45	1.58	70.88
74	Nikki Campbell	Australia	63	1.56	98.34
75	Hyun-Ju Shin	Korea	52	1.55	80.66
76	Teresa Lu	Taiwan	50	1.50	74.94
77	Laura Diaz	USA	48	1.47	70.54
78	Jane Park	USA	46	1.44	66.18
79	Stacy Prammanasudh	USA	47	1.37	64.22
80	Jeong-Eun Lee	Korea	33	1.34	46.90
81	Meaghan Francella	USA	46	1.32	60.64
82	Shiho Oyama	Japan	45	1.31	59.00
83	Akane Iijima	Japan	73	1.31	95.56
84	Janice Moodie	Scotland	46	1.31	60.07
85	Giulia Sergas	Italy	50	1.30	64.80
86	Rui Kitada	Japan	69	1.29	88.87
87	Bo-Mee Lee	Korea	24	1.25	43.60
88	Mi Hyun Kim	Korea	31	1.24	43.53
89	Hiromi Mogi	Japan	64	1.24	79.46
90	Laura Davies	England	61	1.22	74.51
91	Ah-Reum Huang	Korea	54	1.21	65.41
92	Young Kim	Korea	48	1.21	58.06
93	Shanshan Feng	China	49	1.20	58.87
94	Soo-Yun Kang	Korea	49	1.18	58.01
95	Jimin Kang	Korea	53	1.16	61.67
96	Li-Ying Ye	China	28	1.16	40.53
97	Tamie Durdin	Australia	61	1.13	68.68
98	Erina Hara	Japan	72	1.12	80.46
99	Allison Fouch	USA	46	1.11	51.08
100	Rikako Morita	Japan	42	1.07	45.12

Rank	Player	Country	No. of Events	Average Points	Total Points
101	Mikaela Parmlid	Sweden	39	1.07	41.62
102	Hye Jung Choi	Korea	57	1.05	59.83
103	Becky Brewerton	Wales	42	1.05	43.93
104	Michie Ohba	Japan	60	1.01	60.72
105	Maiko Wakabayashi	Japan	70	1.00	69.87
106	Midori Yoneyama	Japan	65	1.00	64.79
107	Yuko Saitoh	Japan	65	0.99	64.08
108	Gwladys Nocera	France	49	0.99	48.27
109	Ha Neul Kim	Korea	48	0.98	47.14
110	Kaori Aoyama	Japan	48	0.98	47.07
111	Saiki Fujita	Japan	60	0.98	58.67
112	Anna Grzebien	USA	35	0.96	33.71
113	Il Mi Chung	Korea	53	0.96	50.85
114	Paige MacKenzie	USA	33	0.95	33.10
115	Minea Blomqvist	Finland	54	0.95	51.03
116	Marianne Skarpnord	Norway	38	0.94	35.67
117	Ran Hong	Korea	45	0.94	42.17
118	Ji-Woo Lee	Korea	65	0.91	58.87
119	Sarah Lee	Korea	39	0.90	35.29
120	Becky Morgan	Wales	47	0.90	42.50
121	Irene Cho	USA	41	0.90	37.06
122	Tania Elosegui	Spain	36	0.88	31.74
123	Heather Young	USA	45	0.87	39.24
124	Kumiko Kaneda	Japan	35	0.84	29.30
125	Jin-Joo Hong	Korea	44	0.82	35.86
126	Carin Koch	Sweden	41	0.81	33.18
127	Karine Icher	France	50	0.81	40.28
128	Melissa Reid	England	32	0.80	27.83
129	Katie Futcher	USA	42	0.79	32.98
130	Yun-Jye Wei	Taiwan	60	0.78	47.01
131	Amy Hung	Taiwan	36	0.78	27.95
132	Na-Ri Lee	Korea	59	0.77	45.27
133	Jennifer Rosales	Philippines	37	0.76	28.17
134	Julie Lu	Taiwan	53	0.76	40.14
135	Ae-Ree Pyun	Korea	38	0.75	28.36
136	Leta Lindley	USA	39	0.74	28.85
137	Beth Bader	USA	44	0.73	32.31
138	Nicole Gergely	Austria	32	0.73	25.69
139	Taylor Leon	USA	37	0.73	26.99
140	Alena Sharp	Canada	48	0.71	34.15
141	Hiromi Takesue	Japan	55	0.70	38.74
142	Harukyo Nomura	Korea	2	0.69	24.21
143	Moira Dunn	USA	44	0.69	30.19
144	Ha Na Jang	Korea	6	0.68	23.97
145	Russy Gulyanamitta	Thailand	33	0.68	23.70
146	Allison Hanna-Williams	USA	31	0.67	23.49
147	Esther Lee	Korea	66	0.67	44.12
148	So-Hee Kim	Korea	67	0.66	44.37
149	Reilley Rankin	USA	43	0.66	28.46
150	Amanda Blumenherst	USA	13	0.66	23.10

Rank	Player	Country	No. of Events	Average Points	Total Points
151	Haeji Kang	Korea	39	0.66	25.72
152	Yuki Ichinose	Japan	62	0.66	40.64
153	Hyun-Ji Kim	Korea	33	0.65	22.74
154	Chella Choi	Korea	35	0.65	22.67
155	Maria Iida	Brazil	33	0.64	22.53
156	Kris Tamulis	USA	39	0.64	25.01
157	Tomomi Hirose	Japan	45	0.63	28.39
158	Felicity Johnson	England	43	0.63	26.88
159	Jimin Jeong	Korea	33	0.62	21.63
160	Louise Stahle	Sweden	33	0.61	21.48
161	Anja Monke	Germany	47	0.61	28.84
162	Anna Rawson	Australia	45	0.61	27.46
163	Rachel Hetherington	Australia	45	0.61	27.39
164	Bomi Suh	Korea	38	0.60	22.89
165	Tomoko Kusakabe	Japan	59	0.60	35.50
166	Jill McGill	USA	49	0.60	29.27
167	Yui Kawahara	Japan	66	0.60	39.42
168	Hye-Yong Choi	Korea	48	0.60	28.63
169	Seul-A Yoon	Korea	35	0.59	20.81
170	Linda Wessberg	Sweden	48	0.59	28.52
171	Mika Takushima	Japan	37	0.59	21.86
172	Karin Sjodin	Sweden	40	0.59	23.62
173	Louise Friberg	Sweden	48	0.59	28.29
174	Sarah Kemp	Australia	44	0.59	25.86
175	Beatriz Recari	Spain	29	0.59	20.56
176	Mie Nakata	Japan	63	0.59	36.88
177	Iben Tinning	Denmak	31	0.58	20.44
178	Mindy Kim	Korea	33	0.58	20.37
179	Azahara Munoz	Spain	5	0.58	20.34
180	Ji-Na Lim	Korea	45	0.55	24.88
181	Julieta Granada	Paraguay	49	0.55	26.87
182	Nobuko Kizawa	Japan	68	0.55	37.26
183	Yunhee Cho	Korea	33	0.53	18.58
184	Wendy Doolan	Australia	38	0.52	19.67
185	Jin Young Pak	Korea	37	0.51	18.95
186	Bo-Kyung Kim	Korea	39	0.51	19.74
187	Yayoi Arasaki	Japan	61	0.51	30.83
188	Jade Schaeffer	France	41	0.50	20.69
189	Sarah Jane Kenyon	Australia	46	0.50	22.77
190	Maria Jose Uribe	Colombia	8	0.47	16.62
191	Nari Kim	Korea	28	0.47	16.58
192	Hiroko Yamaguchi	Japan	65	0.47	30.50
193	Eun-Hye Lee	Korea	58	0.46	26.88
194	Virginie Lagoutte-Clement	France	23	0.46	15.97
195	Ikue Asama	Japan	45	0.45	20.45
196	Junko Omote	Japan	65	0.44	28.68
197	Veronica Zorzi	Italy	32	0.44	15.40
198	Mayumi Nakajima	Japan	63	0.44	27.65
199	Yumiko Yoshida	Japan	23	0.43	15.22
200	Diana Luna	Italy	35	0.43	15.16

Official World Golf Ranking
(As of December 31, 2009)

Ranking		Player	Country	Points Average	Total Points	No. of Events	2009 Points Lost	2009 Points Gained
1	(1)	Tiger Woods	USA	14.67	586.68	40	-496.57	604.54
2	(3)	Phil Mickelson	USA	8.26	363.20	44	-348.47	367.29
3	(15)	Steve Stricker	USA	6.67	300.17	45	-207.52	333.57
4	(10)	Lee Westwood	Eng	6.60	343.09	52	-212.00	299.54
5	(4)	Padraig Harrington	Ire	5.55	294.30	53	-275.16	215.02
6	(13)	Jim Furyk	USA	5.53	276.43	50	-199.34	265.05
7	(41)	Paul Casey	Eng	5.36	235.64	44	-170.30	282.86
8	(8)	Henrik Stenson	Swe	5.33	250.44	47	-226.87	234.25
9	(39)	Rory McIlroy	NIre	4.86	277.15	57	-108.94	283.06
10	(14)	Kenny Perry	USA	4.72	245.48	52	-200.01	247.21
11	(2)	Sergio Garcia	Sp	4.67	242.85	52	-301.43	122.94
12	(26)	Ian Poulter	Eng	4.63	235.95	51	-157.54	226.68
13	(25)	Martin Kaymer	Ger	4.48	233.02	52	-164.05	225.58
14	(12)	Geoff Ogilvy	Aus	4.45	222.51	50	-218.92	228.29
15	(59)	Sean O'Hair	USA	4.22	210.86	50	-145.12	241.54
16	(16)	Stewart Cink	USA	4.20	197.31	47	-183.98	192.59
17	(9)	Ernie Els	SAf	4.13	218.84	53	-228.35	189.91
18	(29)	Ross Fisher	Eng	4.03	205.62	51	-133.96	188.34
19	(45)	Retief Goosen	SAf	3.94	228.35	58	-142.49	239.10
20	(177)	Lucas Glover	USA	3.84	203.66	53	-84.82	234.68
21	(27)	Robert Allenby	Aus	3.84	230.40	60	-152.52	196.20
22	(46)	Zach Johnson	USA	3.63	188.86	52	-139.55	214.36
23	(7)	Camilo Villegas	Col	3.52	182.92	52	-189.85	128.01
24	(11)	Anthony Kim	USA	3.51	182.28	52	-182.47	137.91
25	(42)	Angel Cabrera	Arg	3.49	174.69	50	-146.28	195.39
26	(5)	Vijay Singh	Fiji	3.30	151.93	46	-281.00	67.42
27	(6)	Robert Karlsson	Swe	3.14	131.75	42	-193.08	55.22
28	(31)	Luke Donald	Eng	3.09	129.97	42	-124.60	139.23
29	(44)	Hunter Mahan	USA	3.07	162.82	53	-136.71	165.09
30	(60)	Ryo Ishikawa	Jpn	3.04	164.18	54	-51.84	133.13
31	(478)	Y.E. Yang	Kor	3.00	176.69	59	-44.87	203.03
32	(203)	Nick Watney	USA	2.93	158.22	54	-86.60	197.43
33	(389)	Yuta Ikeda	Jpn	2.87	114.79	40	-17.23	114.15
34	(17)	Adam Scott	Aus	2.76	129.91	47	-159.82	118.58
35	(50)	Soren Kjeldsen	Den	2.71	146.41	54	-114.15	128.67
36	(21)	Mike Weir	Can	2.66	135.88	51	-150.41	115.48
37	(28)	Tim Clark	SAf	2.65	148.42	56	-133.26	126.11
38	(79)	Francesco Molinari	Ity	2.58	144.21	56	-76.25	128.93
39	(33)	Graeme McDowell	NIre	2.57	141.28	55	-126.22	109.63
40	(89)	Anders Hansen	Den	2.57	128.44	50	-87.60	139.83
41	(40)	Oliver Wilson	Eng	2.56	133.21	52	-113.83	108.14
42	(116)	David Toms	USA	2.55	119.96	47	-77.58	142.26
43	(129)	Simon Dyson	Eng	2.43	143.06	59	-72.09	139.85
44	(312)	Michael Sim	Aus	2.40	96.01	40	-35.00	107.94
45	(23)	Justin Leonard	USA	2.40	124.65	52	-157.62	107.09
46	(111)	Brian Gay	USA	2.37	142.33	60	-97.86	155.39
47	(47)	Soren Hansen	Den	2.36	127.61	54	-114.67	116.54
48	(653)	Edoardo Molinari	Ity	2.34	116.78	50	-16.43	123.94
49	(22)	Miguel A. Jimenez	Sp	2.33	130.36	56	-152.96	102.60
50	(24)	Ben Curtis	USA	2.26	99.30	44	-111.47	63.99

( ) Ranking in brackets indicates position as of December 31, 2008.

Ranking		Player	Country	Points Average	Total Points	No. of Events	2009 Points Lost	2009 Points Gained
51	(158)	Ryan Moore	USA	2.26	117.30	52	-61.57	121.89
52	(73)	Alvaro Quiros	Sp	2.25	123.68	55	-75.96	127.02
53	(143)	Dustin Johnson	USA	2.22	121.96	55	-62.19	139.31
54	(55)	Peter Hanson	Swe	2.20	116.67	53	-96.69	91.64
55	(97)	Alexander Noren	Swe	2.20	107.76	49	-65.36	93.89
56	(32)	Shingo Katayama	Jpn	2.14	117.51	55	-122.87	83.52
57	(37)	Stephen Ames	Can	2.13	100.19	47	-113.12	86.22
58	(91)	Thongchai Jaidee	Tha	2.12	125.32	59	-81.79	116.43
59	(35)	Jeev Milkha Singh	Ind	2.11	138.92	66	-150.20	85.20
60	(63)	Scott Verplank	USA	2.09	102.26	49	-93.18	99.15
61	(135)	Matt Kuchar	USA	2.08	108.19	52	-60.49	104.53
62	(65)	Chad Campbell	USA	2.07	111.66	54	-102.46	104.55
63	(76)	Gonzalo Fdez-Castano	Sp	2.06	108.91	53	-87.30	104.55
64	(83)	Hiroyuki Fujita	Jpn	2.04	99.92	49	-64.15	88.44
65	(68)	Charl Schwartzel	SAf	2.01	114.76	57	-90.60	98.05
66	(597)	Jason Dufner	USA	2.00	100.08	50	-24.20	112.42
67	(34)	Rory Sabbatini	SAf	1.99	109.41	55	-155.97	116.29
68	(198)	Ross McGowan	Eng	1.98	108.97	55	-50.85	106.76
69	(233)	Kevin Na	USA	1.96	108.02	55	-65.66	131.38
70	(19)	Justin Rose	Eng	1.96	101.98	52	-163.07	100.39
71	(100)	Heath Slocum	USA	1.88	110.77	59	-74.66	103.72
72	(139)	Koumei Oda	Jpn	1.83	91.44	50	-43.72	78.94
73	(172)	Kenichi Kuboya	Jpn	1.83	89.43	49	-34.75	75.47
74	(194)	Chris Wood	Eng	1.82	72.68	40	-29.78	65.93
75	(188)	Yasuharu Imano	Jpn	1.80	72.06	40	-29.57	57.77
76	(106)	John Senden	Aus	1.80	113.44	63	-86.98	114.82
77	(53)	Brendan Jones	Aus	1.78	76.46	43	-81.92	56.88
78	(58)	Mathew Goggin	Aus	1.76	102.34	58	-94.88	71.71
79	(80)	Davis Love	USA	1.75	87.30	50	-66.32	80.42
80	(102)	Jerry Kelly	USA	1.70	98.79	58	-90.09	103.36
81	(72)	James Kingston	SAf	1.69	91.27	54	-82.02	73.01
82	(107)	Liang Wen-chong	Chn	1.68	80.57	48	-57.20	62.26
83	(110)	Anthony Wall	Eng	1.67	91.63	55	-69.98	81.76
84	(51)	Kevin Sutherland	USA	1.65	87.34	53	-92.98	65.07
85	(126)	Gregory Bourdy	Fra	1.64	91.56	56	-56.59	79.98
86	(109)	Stephen Marino	USA	1.63	105.84	65	-83.23	102.35
87	(175)	John Rollins	USA	1.60	88.08	55	-68.37	100.45
88	(18)	K.J. Choi	Kor	1.58	77.63	49	-183.71	62.84
89	(134)	Louis Oosthuizen	SAf	1.56	82.66	53	-80.33	101.56
90	(82)	Pat Perez	USA	1.54	77.04	50	-91.42	80.38
91	(117)	Scott Strange	Aus	1.54	83.01	54	-63.98	73.04
92	(56)	Rod Pampling	Aus	1.51	95.15	63	-105.18	70.60
93	(43)	Richard Sterne	SAf	1.50	73.64	49	-89.82	35.28
94	(52)	Prayad Marksaeng	Tha	1.48	94.69	64	-112.14	62.71
95	(84)	David Smail	NZ	1.47	73.65	50	-67.82	61.54
96	(64)	Brandt Snedeker	USA	1.47	79.52	54	-107.30	67.92
97	(125)	Bubba Watson	USA	1.46	77.47	53	-71.34	79.25
98	(217)	Marc Leishman	Aus	1.46	87.54	60	-29.35	82.56
99	(49)	Lin Wen-tang	Twn	1.46	58.31	40	-60.77	25.29
100	(131)	Tomohiro Kondo	Jpn	1.46	68.41	47	-47.17	60.16

( ) Ranking in brackets indicates position as of December 31, 2008.

Ranking		Player	Country	Points Average	Total Points	No. of Events	2009 Points Lost	2009 Points Gained
101	(98)	Paul Goydos	USA	1.46	75.65	52	-58.67	67.39
102	(101)	Ben Crane	USA	1.45	75.46	52	-60.54	78.81
103	(119)	Mark Wilson	USA	1.45	82.48	57	-69.87	83.01
104	(268)	Martin Laird	Sco	1.44	80.88	56	-31.40	72.08
105	(38)	Stuart Appleby	Aus	1.44	80.77	56	-121.58	53.09
106	(382)	Bryce Molder	USA	1.42	75.30	53	-24.83	75.87
107	(151)	Thomas Levet	Fra	1.42	72.27	51	-52.62	75.11
108	(175)	Fred Couples	USA	1.41	56.54	40	-45.34	62.58
109	(69)	Azuma Yano	Jpn	1.41	74.66	53	-58.71	41.00
110	(265)	Kim Kyung-tae	Kor	1.40	67.35	48	-22.32	61.89
111	(78)	Nick Dougherty	Eng	1.40	72.83	52	-85.77	72.00
112	(30)	Andres Romero	Arg	1.40	66.98	48	-129.01	46.96
113	(70)	Darren Clarke	NIre	1.38	77.24	56	-79.04	51.63
114	(613)	Ryuichi Oda	Jpn	1.37	65.74	48	-10.96	66.54
115	(171)	John Mallinger	USA	1.36	76.04	56	-63.08	80.15
116	(48)	Boo Weekley	USA	1.33	63.64	48	-116.83	52.95
117	(161)	Richie Ramsay	Sco	1.33	70.24	53	-31.74	56.79
118	(178)	Jason Bohn	USA	1.32	52.89	40	-37.73	51.74
119	(1353)	Tom Watson	USA	1.32	52.82	40	-7.38	60.00
120	(67)	Fredrik Jacobson	Swe	1.32	64.64	49	-73.09	52.43
121	(245)	Charley Hoffman	USA	1.31	74.47	57	-61.27	91.10
122	(95)	Nick O'Hern	Aus	1.31	73.07	56	-76.45	66.76
123	(170)	Johan Edfors	Swe	1.30	70.12	54	-57.08	73.15
124	(90)	Gareth Maybin	NIre	1.30	66.03	51	-41.33	45.78
125	(61)	Richard Green	Aus	1.29	60.45	47	-75.04	44.32
126	(112)	Steve Webster	Eng	1.29	62.96	49	-64.01	58.95
127	(75)	J.B. Holmes	USA	1.28	65.16	51	-93.62	67.88
128	(57)	Woody Austin	USA	1.27	68.80	54	-113.11	58.54
129	(260)	Shigeki Maruyama	Jpn	1.27	68.71	54	-36.98	62.06
130	(254)	Rafael Cabrera Bello	Sp	1.27	74.78	59	-34.28	67.76
131	(86)	Peter Hedblom	Swe	1.26	67.01	53	-60.21	50.07
132	(1194)	Nicolas Colsaerts	Bel	1.26	50.25	40	-4.98	54.33
133	(20)	Trevor Immelman	SAf	1.26	53.96	43	-144.58	18.32
134	(216)	Raphael Jacquelin	Fra	1.24	70.42	57	-47.46	73.64
135		Shane Lowry	Ire	1.23	49.23	40	-8.82	58.04
136	(140)	George McNeill	USA	1.22	68.38	56	-61.77	62.84
137	(120)	Toshinori Muto	Jpn	1.21	55.84	46	-37.95	33.77
138	(616)	Danny Willett	Eng	1.18	47.32	40	-15.33	54.32
139	(36)	Aaron Baddeley	Aus	1.17	57.46	49	-123.33	50.33
140	(224)	Jason Day	Aus	1.17	53.58	46	-42.28	58.41
141	(388)	Thomas Aiken	SAf	1.16	61.65	53	-26.97	68.96
142	(141)	Charles Howell	USA	1.16	69.66	60	-73.61	77.32
143	(618)	Danny Lee	NZ	1.15	45.94	40	-20.60	58.32
144	(200)	Greg Chalmers	Aus	1.15	67.71	59	-48.87	64.45
145	(339)	Rhys Davies	Wal	1.14	63.87	56	-18.93	61.35
146	(332)	Webb Simpson	USA	1.14	50.16	44	-23.80	52.09
147	(114)	Charlie Wi	Kor	1.14	63.75	56	-68.66	55.54
148	(155)	Jonathan Byrd	USA	1.14	59.20	52	-59.08	64.63
149	(244)	Robert Rock	Eng	1.14	59.17	52	-34.63	54.81
150	(137)	Graeme Storm	Eng	1.13	61.26	54	-59.84	57.76

( ) Ranking in brackets indicates position as of December 31, 2008.

Ranking		Player	Country	Points Average	Total Points	No. of Events	2009 Points Lost	2009 Points Gained
151	(286)	Daisuke Maruyama	Jpn	1.13	63.43	56	-29.95	53.51
152	(173)	John Merrick	USA	1.11	62.23	56	-61.76	65.40
153	(77)	Hideto Tanihara	Jpn	1.11	55.44	50	-66.90	34.02
154	(154)	Robert-Jan Derksen	Hol	1.11	57.47	52	-55.10	52.36
155	(370)	Toru Suzuki	Jpn	1.10	50.67	46	-16.90	46.20
156	(197)	Bae Sang-moon	Kor	1.10	43.96	40	-28.82	36.78
157	(250)	Bo Van Pelt	USA	1.09	67.71	62	-49.26	72.28
158	(93)	Toru Taniguchi	Jpn	1.09	49.01	45	-71.90	40.89
159	(179)	Peter Lawrie	Ire	1.09	60.86	56	-50.00	54.53
160	(446)	David Drysdale	Sco	1.09	66.26	61	-25.82	71.75
161	(205)	Brian Davis	Eng	1.09	72.73	67	-59.26	75.09
162	(239)	Ricardo Gonzalez	Arg	1.08	51.95	48	-29.89	46.08
163	(157)	Bradley Dredge	Wal	1.07	53.65	50	-47.91	51.60
164	(261)	Jamie Donaldson	Wal	1.06	55.16	52	-36.53	51.84
165	(231)	Jeff Klauk	USA	1.05	58.81	56	-43.95	58.98
166	(353)	Chris Tidland	USA	1.05	44.11	42	-21.99	42.66
167	(362)	Tetsuji Hiratsuka	Jpn	1.05	56.65	54	-29.23	61.14
168	(603)	Gaganjeet Bhullar	Ind	1.05	41.82	40	-12.91	45.92
169	(773)	Blake Adams	USA	1.03	41.29	40	-8.24	44.73
170	(280)	Tim Petrovic	USA	1.03	64.81	63	-40.60	63.06
171	(545)	Chad Collins	USA	1.03	50.21	49	-13.59	50.18
172	(384)	Christian Nilsson	Swe	1.02	40.93	40	-17.30	38.15
173	(66)	Ryuji Imada	Jpn	1.02	54.06	53	-100.99	40.24
174	(187)	Gary Orr	Sco	1.01	41.34	41	-31.08	35.08
175	(731)	James Nitties	Aus	1.01	40.29	40	-16.64	51.40
176	(196)	Scott Piercy	USA	1.01	49.26	49	-33.89	47.01
177	(242)	Kaname Yokoo	Jpn	1.00	50.18	50	-28.33	41.54
178	(74)	D.J. Trahan	USA	1.00	58.11	58	-91.06	46.85
179	(174)	Damien McGrane	Ire	0.98	60.87	62	-56.84	55.97
180	(222)	Brett Quigley	USA	0.98	52.92	54	-45.73	58.48
181	(517)	Kazuhiro Yamashita	Jpn	0.98	45.92	47	-8.78	43.50
182	(185)	Troy Matteson	USA	0.97	58.30	60	-46.77	52.48
183	(341)	Christian Cevaer	Fra	0.97	49.54	51	-32.60	52.81
184	(113)	Briny Baird	USA	0.97	56.34	58	-75.28	50.68
185	(477)	Cameron Percy	Aus	0.96	47.25	49	-13.91	48.35
186	(247)	Jeff Overton	USA	0.95	57.20	60	-42.35	57.36
187	(282)	D.A. Points	USA	0.95	54.29	57	-36.71	53.47
188		Josh Teater	USA	0.93	37.22	40	-2.30	39.53
189	(538)	Tom Gillis	USA	0.92	36.92	40	-11.50	37.83
190	(427)	Jose-Filipe Lima	Por	0.92	45.74	50	-19.01	43.35
191	(360)	Masaya Tomida	Jpn	0.91	42.91	47	-21.24	40.84
192	(133)	Matt Bettencourt	USA	0.90	55.90	62	-35.22	41.53
193	(802)	David Duval	USA	0.90	37.81	42	-9.79	43.33
194	(439)	Ricky Barnes	USA	0.90	44.91	50	-21.87	45.93
195	(241)	Scott McCarron	USA	0.90	43.97	49	-27.16	41.54
196	(186)	Katsumasa Miyamoto	Jpn	0.89	43.73	49	-36.06	32.88
197	(191)	Tano Goya	Arg	0.88	44.98	51	-33.52	41.61
198	(71)	Rocco Mediate	USA	0.88	43.20	49	-69.11	24.14
199	(252)	Bill Haas	USA	0.88	52.78	60	-43.56	52.47
200	(301)	Bob Estes	USA	0.88	44.74	51	-37.14	47.71

( ) Ranking in brackets indicates position as of December 31, 2008.

Age Groups of Current Top 100 World Ranked Players

Under 25	25-28	29-32	33-36	37-40	Over 40
		Casey			
		Garcia			
		Ogilvy		Mickelson	
		R. Fisher	Woods	Harrington	
	Kaymer	Glover	Westwood	Furyk	
	O'Hair	Donald	Stenson	Els	
	Villegas	Scott	Poulter	Goosen	
	Mahan	McDowell	Cink	Allenby	
	Watney	O. Wilson	Z. Johnson	Cabrera	
	F. Molinari	Dyson	Kjeldsen	Karlsson	
	Sim	Curtis	T. Clark	Y.E. Yang	
	E. Molinari	P. Hanson	S. Hansen	Weir	Stricker
	Moore	Kuchar	Katayama	A. Hansen	Perry
	Quiros	Fdez-Castano	C. Campbell	Leonard	V. Singh
	D. Johnson	Dufner	Sabbatini	Gay	Toms
	Noren	Rose	Slocum	Jaidee	Jimenez
	Schwartzel	K. Oda	Imano	J.M. Singh	Ames
	McGowan	W.C. Liang	B. Jones	Fujita	Verplank
McIlroy	Na	Marino	Goggin	Kuboya	Love
A. Kim	Bourdy	Strange	Wall	Senden	Kelly
Ishikawa	Oosthuizen	Snedeker	Rollins	K.J. Choi	Kingston
Ikeda	Sterne	B. Watson	Perez	Pampling	Sutherland
C. Wood	Lieshman	Kondo	W.T. Lin	Smail	Marksaeng

2009 World Ranking Review

Major Movements

Upward				Downward			
	Net Points	Position			Net Points	Position	
Name	Gained	2008	2009	Name	Lost	2008	2009
Rory McIlroy	174	39	9	Vijay Singh	213	5	26
Y.E. Yang	158	478	31	Sergio Garcia	178	2	11
Lucas Glover	149	177	20	Robert Karlsson	137	6	27
Steve Stricker	126	15	3	Trevor Immelman	126	20	133
Paul Casey	112	41	7	K.J. Choi	120	18	88
Nick Watney	110	203	32	Andres Romero	82	30	112
Tiger Woods	107	1	1	Carl Pettersson	74	62	212
Edoardo Molinari	107	653	48	Aaron Baddeley	73	36	139
Yuta Ikeda	96	389	33	Stuart Appleby	68	38	105
Retief Goosen	96	45	19	Jeev Milkha Singh	65	35	59
Sean O'Hair	96	59	15	Boo Weekley	63	48	116
Jason Dufner	88	597	66	Justin Rose	62	19	70
Lee Westwood	87	10	4	Camilo Villegas	61	7	23
Ryo Ishikawa	81	60	30	Ryuji Imada	60	66	173
Dustin Johnson	77	143	53	Padraig Harrington	60	4	5
Zach Johnson	74	46	22				
Michael Sim	72	312	44				
Ian Poulter	69	26	12				
Simon Dyson	67	129	43				
Kevin Na	65	233	69				
Jim Furyk	65	13	6				
David Toms	64	116	42				

Highest-Rated Events of 2009

	Event	Top 5	Top 15	Top 30	Top 50	Top 100	World Rating Points
1	PGA Championship	4	14	28	48	97	801
2	The Open Championship	4	14	28	45	82	751
3	Masters Tournament	5	15	30	49	68	737
4	U.S. Open Championship	5	14	29	45	70	719
5	The Players Championship	5	15	28	45	75	759
6	WGC - CA Championship	5	15	30	50	70	747
7	WGC - Accenture Match Play	5	15	30	50	64	731
8	WGC - Bridgestone Invitational	5	15	29	49	65	722
9	The Barclays	3	11	23	34	61	596
10	Deutsche Bank Champ.	4	11	23	33	59	581
11	Quail Hollow Championship	4	10	19	30	53	551
12	BMW Championship	4	10	22	31	53	538
13	WGC - HSBC Champions	4	12	20	28	47	509
14	BMW PGA Championship	1	3	11	17	33	305
15	Shell Houston Open	4	12	20	24	44	477
16	Memorial Tournament	3	10	17	25	48	467
17	Northern Trust Open	3	7	15	28	49	457
18	Arnold Palmer Invitational	4	5	12	26	51	433
19	Crowne Plaza Colonial	1	8	15	23	45	395
20	The Tour Championship	3	9	17	23	29	379
21	Dubai World Championship	1	8	14	23	38	349
22	Commercialbank Qatar Masters	1	6	10	18	38	329
23	Barclays Scottish Open	0	2	10	22	41	336
24	FBR Open	1	5	11	18	40	337
25	Dubai Desert Classic	1	5	10	16	34	306
26	AT&T National	2	6	8	13	32	295
27	Abu Dhabi Championship	2	3	8	14	28	266
28	European Open	2	3	10	15	25	257
29	Chevron World Challenge	3	9	14	17	18	266
30	Verizon Heritage	0	3	9	15	35	269
31	Transitions Championship	0	3	6	14	36	262
32	AT&T Pebble Beach Pro-Am	3	5	7	11	25	247
33	Barclays Singapore Open	1	2	6	11	25	213
34	Alfred Dunhill Links	0	2	7	14	26	217
35	Honda Classic	1	3	8	13	29	248
36	St. Jude Classic	2	5	7	11	23	233
37	Portugal Masters	0	2	6	13	24	201
38	Mercedes-Benz Championship	1	7	12	14	20	217
39	Sony Open	0	4	9	14	28	233
40	HP Byron Nelson Champ.	0	2	6	13	31	221

World Golf Rankings 1968-2009

Year	No. 1	No. 2	No. 3	No. 4	No. 5
1968	Nicklaus	Palmer	Casper	Player	Charles
1969	Nicklaus	Player	Casper	Palmer	Charles
1970	Nicklaus	Player	Casper	Trevino	Charles
1971	Nicklaus	Trevino	Player	Palmer	Casper
1972	Nicklaus	Player	Trevino	Crampton	Palmer
1973	Nicklaus	Weiskopf	Trevino	Player	Crampton
1974	Nicklaus	Miller	Player	Weiskopf	Trevino
1975	Nicklaus	Miller	Weiskopf	Irwin	Player
1976	Nicklaus	Irwin	Miller	Player	Green
1977	Nicklaus	Watson	Green	Irwin	Crenshaw
1978	Watson	Nicklaus	Irwin	Green	Player
1979	Watson	Nicklaus	Irwin	Trevino	Player
1980	Watson	Trevino	Aoki	Crenshaw	Nicklaus
1981	Watson	Rogers	Aoki	Pate	Trevino
1982	Watson	Floyd	Ballesteros	Kite	Stadler
1983	Ballesteros	Watson	Floyd	Norman	Kite
1984	Ballesteros	Watson	Norman	Wadkins	Langer
1985	Ballesteros	Langer	Norman	Watson	Nakajima
1986	Norman	Langer	Ballesteros	Nakajima	Bean
1987	Norman	Ballesteros	Langer	Lyle	Strange
1988	Ballesteros	Norman	Lyle	Faldo	Strange
1989	Norman	Faldo	Ballesteros	Strange	Stewart
1990	Norman	Faldo	Olazabal	Woosnam	Stewart
1991	Woosnam	Faldo	Olazabal	Ballesteros	Norman
1992	Faldo	Couples	Woosnam	Olazabal	Norman
1993	Faldo	Norman	Langer	Price	Couples
1994	Price	Norman	Faldo	Langer	Olazabal
1995	Norman	Price	Langer	Els	Montgomerie
1996	Norman	Lehman	Montgomerie	Els	Couples
1997	Norman	Woods	Price	Els	Love
1998	Woods	O'Meara	Duval	Love	Els
1999	Woods	Duval	Montgomerie	Love	Els
2000	Woods	Els	Duval	Mickelson	Westwood
2001	Woods	Mickelson	Duval	Els	Love
2002	Woods	Mickelson	Els	Garcia	Goosen
2003	Woods	Singh	Els	Love	Furyk
2004	Singh	Woods	Els	Goosen	Mickelson
2005	Woods	Singh	Mickelson	Goosen	Els
2006	Woods	Furyk	Mickelson	Scott	Els
2007	Woods	Mickelson	Furyk	Els	Stricker
2008	Woods	Garcia	Mickelson	Harrington	Singh
2009	Woods	Mickelson	Stricker	Westwood	Harrington

(The World of Professional Golf 1968-1985; World Ranking 1986-2009)

Year	No. 6	No. 7	No. 8	No. 9	No. 10
1968	Boros	Coles	Thomson	Beard	Nagle
1969	Beard	Archer	Trevino	Barber	Sikes
1970	Devlin	Coles	Jacklin	Beard	Huggett
1971	Barber	Crampton	Charles	Devlin	Weiskopf
1972	Jacklin	Weiskopf	Oosterhuis	Heard	Devlin
1973	Miller	Oosterhuis	Wadkins	Heard	Brewer
1974	M. Ozaki	Crampton	Irwin	Green	Heard
1975	Green	Trevino	Casper	Crampton	Watson
1976	Watson	Weiskopf	Marsh	Crenshaw	Geiberger
1977	Marsh	Player	Weiskopf	Floyd	Ballesteros
1978	Crenshaw	Marsh	Ballesteros	Trevino	Aoki
1979	Aoki	Green	Crenshaw	Ballesteros	Wadkins
1980	Pate	Ballesteros	Bean	Irwin	Player
1981	Ballesteros	Graham	Crenshaw	Floyd	Lietzke
1982	Pate	Nicklaus	Rogers	Aoki	Strange
1983	Nicklaus	Nakajima	Stadler	Aoki	Wadkins
1984	Faldo	Nakajima	Stadler	Kite	Peete
1985	Wadkins	O'Meara	Strange	Pavin	Sutton
1986	Tway	Sutton	Strange	Stewart	O'Meara
1987	Woosnam	Stewart	Wadkins	McNulty	Crenshaw
1988	Crenshaw	Woosnam	Frost	Azinger	Calcavecchia
1989	Kite	Olazabal	Calcavecchia	Woosnam	Azinger
1990	Azinger	Ballesteros	Kite	McNulty	Calcavecchia
1991	Couples	Langer	Stewart	Azinger	Davis
1992	Langer	Cook	Price	Azinger	Love
1993	Azinger	Woosnam	Kite	Love	Pavin
1994	Els	Couples	Montgomerie	M. Ozaki	Pavin
1995	Pavin	Faldo	Couples	M. Ozaki	Elkington
1996	Faldo	Mickelson	M. Ozaki	Love	O'Meara
1997	Mickelson	Montgomerie	M. Ozaki	Lehman	O'Meara
1998	Price	Montgomerie	Westwood	Singh	Mickelson
1999	Westwood	Singh	Price	Mickelson	O'Meara
2000	Montgomerie	Love	Sutton	Singh	Lehman
2001	Garcia	Toms	Singh	Clarke	Goosen
2002	Toms	Harrington	Singh	Love	Montgomerie
2003	Weir	Goosen	Harrington	Toms	Perry
2004	Harrington	Garcia	Weir	Love	Cink
2005	Garcia	Furyk	Montgomerie	Scott	DiMarco
2006	Goosen	Singh	Harrington	Donald	Ogilvy
2007	Rose	Scott	Harrington	Choi	Singh
2008	Karlsson	Villegas	Stenson	Els	Westwood
2009	Furyk	Casey	Stenson	McIlroy	Perry

World's Winners of 2009

U.S. PGA TOUR

Mercedes-Benz Championship	Geoff Ogilvy
Sony Open	Zach Johnson
Bob Hope Classic	Pat Perez
FBR Open	Kenny Perry
Buick Invitational	Nick Watney
AT&T Pebble Beach National Pro-Am	Dustin Johnson
Northern Trust Open	Phil Mickelson
WGC - Accenture Match Play Championship	Geoff Ogilvy (2)
Mayakoba Golf Classic	Mark Wilson
Honda Classic	Y.E. Yang
WGC - CA Championship	Phil Mickelson (2)
Puerto Rico Open	Michael Bradley
Transitions Championship	Retief Goosen (2)
Arnold Palmer Invitational	Tiger Woods
Shell Houston Open	Paul Casey (2)
Masters Tournament	Angel Cabrera
Verizon Heritage	Brian Gay
Zurich Classic	Jerry Kelly
Quail Hollow Championship	Sean O'Hair
The Players Championship	Henrik Stenson
Valero Texas Open	Zach Johnson (2)
HP Byron Nelson Championship	Rory Sabbatini
Crowne Plaza Invitational	Steve Stricker
Memorial Tournament	Tiger Woods (2)
St. Jude Classic	Brian Gay (2)
U.S. Open Championship	Lucas Glover
Travelers Championship	Kenny Perry (2)
AT&T National	Tiger Woods (3)
John Deere Classic	Steve Stricker (2)
U.S. Bank Championship	Bo Van Pelt
RBC Canadian Open	Nathan Green
Buick Open	Tiger Woods (4)
WGC - Bridgestone Invitational	Tiger Woods (5)
Legends Reno-Tahoe Open	John Rollins
PGA Championship	Y.E. Yang (2)
Wyndham Championship	Ryan Moore

PGA TOUR PLAYOFFS FOR THE FEDEXCUP

The Barclays	Heath Slocum
Deutsche Bank Championship	Steve Stricker (3)
BMW Championship	Tiger Woods (6)
The Tour Championship	Phil Mickelson (3)

PGA TOUR FALL SERIES

Turning Stone Resort Championship	Matt Kuchar
The Presidents Cup	United States
Justin Timberlake Shriners Hospitals Open	Martin Laird
Frys.com Open	Troy Matteson
Children's Miracle Network Classic	Stephen Ames

SPECIAL EVENTS

Tavistock Cup	Lake Nona
CVS/Caremark Charity Classic	David Toms/Nick Price (2)
PGA Grand Slam of Golf	Lucas Glover (2)
Kiwi Challenge	Anthony Kim
Callaway Golf Pebble Beach Invitational	Mark Brooks
Chevron World Challenge	Jim Furyk
The Shark Shootout	Jerry Kelly (2)/Steve Stricker (4)

NATIONWIDE TOUR

Panama Digicel Championship	Vance Veazey
Chitimacha Louisiana Open	Bubba Dickerson
Stonebrae Classic	Michael Sim
Athens Regional Foundation Classic	Patrick Sheehan
South Georgia Classic	Garth Mulroy
BMW Charity Pro-Am	Michael Sim (2)
Rex Hospital Open	Kevin Johnson
Melwood Prince George's County Open	Mathias Gronberg
Knoxville Open	Kevin Johnson (2)
Fort Smith Classic	Jason Enloe
Nationwide Tour Players Cup	Tom Gillis
Ford Wayne Gretzky Classic	Roger Tambellini
Cox Classic	Rich Barcelo
Nationwide Children's Hospital Invitational	Derek Lamely
Preferred Health Systems Wichita Open	Chris Tidland
Price Cutter Charity Championship	Justin Bolli
Christmas in October Classic	Michael Sim (3)
Northeast Pennsylvania Classic	Gary Christian
Mexico Open	Troy Merritt
Utah Championship	Josh Teater
Albertsons Boise Open	Fran Quinn
WNB Golf Classic	Garrett Willis
Soboba Classic	Jerod Turner
Chattanooga Classic	Chris Baryla
Miccosukee Championship	Chad Collins
Nationwide Tour Championship	Matt Every

CANADIAN TOUR

Corona Mazatlan Classic	Maurico Molina
Times Colonist Open	Byron Smith
City of Surrey Invitational	Mike Grob
ATB Financial Classic	Graham DeLaet
Telus Edmonton Open	James Hahn
Saskatchewan Open	Andres Gonzales
Canadian Tour Players Cup	Graham DeLaet (2)
Roxul Jane Rogers Championship	Ryan Yip
Desjardins Montreal Open	Stuart Anderson
Seaforth Country Classic	Brian Unk
Canadian Tour Championship	James Love
Iberostar Riviera Maya Open	Rafael Gomez
Riviera Nayarit Classic	James Hahn (2)

TOUR DE LAS AMERICAS (SOUTH AMERICA)

Abierto Internacional de Antioquia	Peter Gustafson
Club Colombia Masters	Alan Wagner
Campeonato Abierto del Centro	Fabian Gomez
TLA Players Championship Alcapulco	Eduardo Herrera
Copa Mitsubishi Tres Diamantes	Paulo Javier Pinto

Venezuela Open Canal I	Daniel Barbetti
Abierto Internacional Ciudad de Bucaramanga	Oscar Alvarez
Abierto Internacional de Golf Copa Sura	Jose Manuel Garrido
Abierto de Chile	Agustin Jauretche
Abierto Hacienda Chicureo Copa BCI	Luciano Giometti
Carlos Franco Invitational	Agustin Jauretche (2)
Roberto de Vicenzo Classic	Fabian Gomez (2)
Torneo de Maestros	Tom Lehman (2)
Visa Open de Argentina	Cesar Agustin Costilla

EUROPEAN TOUR

Abu Dhabi Golf Championship	Paul Casey
Commercialbank Qatar Masters	Alvaro Quiros
Dubai Desert Classic	Rory McIlroy
Madeira Islands Open BPI - Portugal	Estanislao Goya
Open de Andalucia	Soren Kjeldsen
Estoril Open de Portugal	Michael Hoey
Open de Espana	Thomas Levet
BMW Italian Open	Daniel Vancsik
The 3 Irish Open	*Shane Lowry
BMW PGA Championship	Paul Casey (3)
European Open	Christian Cevaer
Celtic Manor Wales Open	Jeppe Huldahl
Saint-Omer Open	Christian Nilsson
BMW International Open	Nick Dougherty
Open de France ALSTOM	Martin Kaymer
Barclays Scottish Open	Martin Kaymer (2)
The Open Championship	Stewart Cink
SAS Masters	Ricardo Gonzalez
Moravia Silesia Open	Oskar Henningsson
KLM Open	Simon Dyson
Johnnie Walker Championship	Peter Hedblom
Omega European Masters	Alexander Noren
Mercedez-Benz Championship	James Kingston
Austrian Golf Open	Rafael Cabrera-Bello
The Vivendi Trophy with Seve Ballesteros	Great Britain & Ireland
Alfred Dunhill Links Championship	Simon Dyson (2)
Madrid Masters	Ross McGowan
Portugal Masters	Lee Westwood
Castello Masters Costa Azahar	Michael Jonzon
Volvo World Match Play	Ross Fisher
Dubai World Championship	Lee Westwood (2)

CHALLENGE TOUR

Tusker Kenya Open	Gary Boyd
Moroccan Classic	Robert Coles
Allianz Open Cotes d'Armor Bretagne	Lee S. James
Piemonte Open	Edoardo Molinari
Telenet Trophy	Francois Calmels
Karnten Golf Open	Christoph Gunther
Challenge of Ireland	Robert Coles (2)
The Princess	Andrew Butterfield
Credit Suisse Challenge	Peter Baker
Allianz EurOpen de Lyon	Alexandre Kaleka
SWALEC Wales Challenge	Rhys Davies
Scottish Hydro Challenge	Jamie McLeary
SK Golf Challenge	Nicolas Colsaerts
Trophee du Golf de Geneve	Julien Quesne
DHL Wroclaw Open	Eric Ramsay

Fred Olsen Challenge de Espana	Rhys Davies (2)
Dutch Futures	Nicolas Colsaerts (2)
Kazakhstan Open	Edoardo Molinari (2)
ECCO Tour Championship	Jose-Filipe Lima
Allianz Golf Open Grand Toulouse	John Parry
Italian Federation Cup	Edoardo Molinari (3)
Apulia San Domenico Grand Final	Peter Whiteford

ASIAN TOUR

The Royal Trophy	Asia
Asian Tour International	James Kamte
Maybank Malaysian Open	Anthony Kang
Enjoy Jakarta Indonesia Open	Thongchai Jaidee
Singha Thailand Open	Jyoti Randhawa
SAIL Open	Chapchai Nirat
Black Mountain Masters	Johan Edfors
Ballantine's Championship	Thongchai Jaidee (2)
GS Caltex Maekyung Open	Bae Sang-moon
Indonesia President Invitational	Gaganjeet Bhullar
Brunei Open	Darren Beck
Worldwide Holdings Selangor Masters	Rick Kulacz
Queen's Cup	Chinnarat Phadungsil
Macau Open	Thaworn Wiratchant (2)
Mercuries Taiwan Masters	Lin Wen-tang
Hero Honda Indian Open	C. Muniyappa
Iskandar Johor Open	K.J. Choi
Barclays Singapore Open	Ian Poulter
WGC - HSBC Champions	Phil Mickelson (4)
UBS Hong Kong Open	Gregory Bourdy
Johnnie Walker Cambodian Open	Marcus Both
Omega Mission Hills World Cup	Italy
The King's Cup	Chan Yih-shin

ONEASIA TOUR

Volvo China Open	Scott Strange
Kolon-Hana Bank Korea Open	Bae Sang-moon (2)
Midea China Classic	Liang Wen-chong

OMEGA CHINA TOUR

Dell Championship	Wu Wei-huang
Sofitel Zhongshan IGC Open	Kurt Barnes
Luxehills Golf Championship	Chen Jian
Dongfeng Nissan Teana Open	Thaworn Wiratchant

JAPAN TOUR

Token Homemate Cup	Koumei Oda
Tsuruya Open	Masaya Tomida
The Crowns	Tetsuji Hiratsuka
Mitsubishi Diamond Cup	Takashi Kanemoto
UBS Japan Golf Tour Championship	Yuji Igarashi
Japan PGA Championship	Yuta Ikeda
Mizuno Open Yomiuri Classic	Ryo Ishikawa
Nagashima Shigeo Invitational	Hiroyuki Fujita
Sun Chlorella Classic	Ryo Ishikawa (2)
Kansai Open Golf Championship	Hiroyuki Fujita (2)
Vana H Cup KBC Augusta	Yuta Ikeda (2)
Fujisankei Classic	Ryo Ishikawa (3)
ANA Open	Toru Taniguchi

Asia-Pacific Panasonic Open	Daisuke Maruyama
Coca-Cola Tokai Classic	Ryo Ishikawa (4)
Canon Open	Yuta Ikeda (3)
Japan Open Championship	Ryuichi Oda
Bridgestone Open	Yuta Ikeda (4)
Mynavi ABC Championship	Toru Suzuki
The Championship by Lexus	Toshinori Muto
Mitsui Sumitomo Visa Taiheiyo Masters	Yasuharu Imano
Dunlop Phoenix	Edoardo Molinari (4)
Casio World Open	Koumei Oda (2)
Golf Nippon Series JT Cup	Shigeki Maruyama

AUSTRALASIAN TOUR

Subaru Victorian Open	Ashley Hall
Cellarbrations Victorian PGA Championship	Andre Stolz
Johnnie Walker Classic	*Danny Lee
Moonah Classic	Alastair Presnell
HSBC New Zealand PGA Championship	Steven Alker
Michael Hill New Zealand Open	Alex Prugh
John Hughes Geely WA Open	Michael Curtain
Laurance Scrap Metals WA PGA Championship	Andrew Bonhomme
Cellarbrations Queensland PGA Championship	Steven Bowditch
JBWere Masters	Tiger Woods (7)
Cellarbrations NSW PGA Championship	Aaron Townsend
NSW Open	Leigh McKechnie
Australian Open	Adam Scott
Australian PGA Championship	Robert Allenby (2)

AFRICAN TOURS

Joburg Open	Anders Hansen
Africa Open	Retief Goosen
Dimension Data Pro-Am	Deane Pappas
Nashua Masters	Darren Fichardt
Vodacom Championship	Anders Hansen (2)
Telkom PGA Championship	Jaco Van Zyl
Vodacom Business Origins - Bloemfontaine	Trevor Fisher, Jr.
SAA Pro-Am Invitational - Prince's Grant	Adilson da Silva
Samsung Royal Swazi Sun Open	Jaco Van Zyl (2)
Nashua Golf Challenge	Doug McGuigan
Vodacom Business Origins of Golf - Pretoria	Brandon Pieters
Lombard Insurance Classic	Peter Karmis
Vodacom Business Origins of Golf - Fancourt	Brandon Pieters (2)
Suncoast Classic	Louis de Jager
Vodacom Business Origins of Golf - Erinvale	Jaco Ahlers
Telkom PGA Pro-Am	Jaco Van Zyl (3)
Zambia Open	Jbe' Kruger
SAA Pro-Am Invitational - Randpark	Ryan Tipping
Vodacom Business Origins of Golf - Selborne	Darren Fichardt (2)
SAA Pro-Am Invitational - Paarl	Prinavin Nelson
Vodacom Business Origins of Golf - Final	Brandon Pieters (3)
BMG Classic	Graham DeLaet (3)
Highveld Classic	Lindani Ndwandwe
Platinum Classic	Darren Fichardt (3)
MTC Namibia PGA Championship	Hennie Otto
Coca-Cola Championship	Christiaan Basson
Gary Player Invitational	Angel Cabrera (2)/Tony Johnstone (2)
Nedbank Affinity Cup	Jake Roos
Nedbank Golf Challenge	Robert Allenby
Alfred Dunhill Championship	Pablo Martin
South African Open Championship	Richie Ramsay

U.S. LPGA TOUR

HSBC LPGA Brasil Cup	Catriona Matthew
SBS Open	Angela Stanford
Honda LPGA Thailand	Lorena Ochoa
HSBC Women's Champions	Jiyai Shin
MasterCard Classic Honoring Alejo Peralta	Pat Hurst
J Golf Phoenix LPGA International	Karrie Webb
Kraft Nabisco Championship	Brittany Lincicome
Corona Championship	Lorena Ochoa (2)
Michelob Ultra Open	Cristie Kerr
Sybase Classic	Ji Young Oh
LPGA Corning Classic	Yani Tseng
LPGA State Farm Classic	In-Kyung Kim
McDonald's LPGA Championship	Anna Nordqvist
Wegmans LPGA	Jiyai Shin (2)
Jamie Farr Owens Corning Classic	Eunjung Yi
U.S. Women's Open	Eun-Hee Ji
The Solheim Cup	United States
Safeway Classic	M.J. Hur
CN Canadian Women's Open	Suzann Pettersen
P&G Beauty NW Arkansas Championship	Jiyai Shin (3)
Samsung World Championship	Na Yeon Choi
CVS/pharmacy LPGA Challenge	Sophie Gustafson
Navistar LPGA Classic	Lorena Ochoa (3)
Hana Bank-Kolon Championship	Na Yeon Choi (2)
Lorena Ochoa Invitational	Michelle Wie
LPGA Tour Championship	Anna Nordqvist (2)

LADIES EUROPEAN TOUR

Comunitat Valenciana European Nations Cup	Netherlands
Deutsche Bank Ladies Swiss Open	Marianne Skarpnord
HypoVereinsbank Ladies German Open	Jade Schaeffer
ABN AMRO Ladies Open	Tania Elosegui
Ladies Open de Portugal	Johanna Westerberg
AIB Ladies Irish Open	Diane Luna
SAS Ladies Masters	Diane Luna (2)
Open de Espana Femenino	Becky Brewerton
Evian Masters	Ai Miyazato
Ricoh Women's British Open	Catriona Matthew (2)
S4/C Wales Ladies Championship of Europe	Karen Stupples
Finnair Masters	Beatriz Recari
UNIQA Ladies Golf Open	Linda Wessberg
Randstad Open de France	Nicole Gergely
Tenerife Ladies Open	Felicity Johnson
Madrid Ladies Masters	Azahara Munoz
Casta Si Ladies Italian Open	Marianne Skarpnord (2)
Suzhou Taihu Ladies Open	Bo Mi Suh
Daishin Securities Korean Ladies Masters	Hyun-Ji Kim
Omega Dubai Ladies Masters	In-Kyung Kim (2)

JAPAN LPGA TOUR

Daikin Orchid Ladies	Yuko Mitsuka
Yokohama Tire PRGR Cup	Ayako Uehara
Yamaha Ladies Open	Ah-Reum Hwang
Studio Alice Ladies Open	Sakura Yokomine
Life Card Ladies	Ji-Hee Lee
Fujisankei Ladies Classic	Tamie Durdin
Crystal Geyser Ladies	Chie Arimura
World Ladies Championship Salonpas Cup	Shinobu Moromizato

Vernal Ladies	Yuko Saitoh
Chukyo TV Bridgestone Ladies	Eun-A Lim
Kosaido Ladies Golf Cup	Sakura Yokomine (2)
Resort Trust Ladies	Mi-Jeong Jeon
We Love Kobe Suntory Ladies Open	Shinobu Moromizato (2)
Nichirei PGM Ladies	Sakura Yokomine (3)
Promise Ladies	Shinobu Moromizato (3)
Meiji Chocolate Cup	Mi-Jeong Jeon (2)
Stanley Ladies	Chie Arimura (2)
AXA Ladies	Momoko Ueda
NEC Karuzawa 72	Chie Arimura (3)
CAT Ladies	Shinobu Moromizato (4)
Yonex Ladies	Mi-Jeong Jeon (3)
Golf 5 Ladies	Shinobu Moromizato (5)
Japan LPGA Championship Konica Minolta Cup	Shinobu Moromizato (6)
Munsingwear Ladies Tokai Classic	Sakura Yokomine (4)
Miyagi TV Cup Dunlop Ladies Open	Chie Arimura (4)
Japan Women's Open	Bo-Bae Song
Sankyo Ladies Open	Ai Miyazato (2)
Fujitsu Ladies	Nikki Campbell
Masters Golf Club Ladies	Jiyai Shin (4)
Hisako Higuch IDC Otsuka Ladies	Mi-Jeong Jeon (4)
Mizuno Classic	Bo-Bae Song (2)
Itoen Ladies	Sakura Yokomine (5)
Daioseishi Elleair Ladies Open	Chie Arimura (5)
Japan LPGA Tour Championship Ricoh Cup	Sakura Yokomine (6)
The Kyoraku Cup	Korea

AUSTRALIAN LADIES TOUR

Peugeot Kangaroo Valley ALPG Classic	Karen Lunn
Xstrata Coal Branxton Golf Club Pro-Am	Rachel Bailey
LG Bing Lee Women's NSW Open	Sarah Oh
New Zealand Women's Open	Gwladys Nocera
ANZ Ladies Masters	Katherine Hull
Women's Australian Open	Laura Davies

CHAMPIONS TOUR

Mitsubishi Electric Championship	Bernhard Langer
Allianz Championship	Mike Goodes
ACE Group Classic	Loren Roberts
Toshiba Classic	Eduardo Romero
AT&T Champions Classic	Dan Forsman
Cap Cana Championship	Keith Fergus
Outback Steakhouse Pro-Am	Nick Price
Liberty Mutual Legends of Golf	Bernhard Langer (2)/Tom Lehman
Regions Charity Classic	Keith Fergus (2)
Senior PGA Championship	Michael Allen
Principal Charity Classic	Mark McNulty
Triton Financial Classic	Bernhard Langer (3)
Dick's Sporting Goods Open	Lonnie Nielsen
3M Championship	Bernhard Langer (4)
U.S. Senior Open	Fred Funk
JELD-WEN Tradition	Mike Reid
Boeing Classic	Loren Roberts (3)
Walmart First Tee Open	Jeff Sluman
Greater Hickory Classic	Jay Haas
SAS Championship	Tom Pernice, Jr.
Constellation Energy Senior Players	Jay Haas (2)
Administaff Small Business Classic	John Cook

| AT&T Championship | Phil Blackmar |
| Charles Schwab Cup Championship | John Cook (2) |

EUROPEAN SENIOR TOUR

Aberdeen Brunei Senior Masters	Mike Cunning
DGM Barbados Open	Sam Torrance
Son Gual Mallorca Senior Open	Mark James
Irish Seniors Open	Ian Woosnam
Jersey Seniors Classic	Delroy Cambridge
Ryder Cup Wales Seniors Open	Bertus Smit
De Vere Collection PGA Seniors Championship	Carl Mason
The Senior Open Championship	Loren Roberts (2)
Bad Ragaz PGA Seniors Open	John Bland
Cleveland Golf/Srixon Scottish Senior Open	Glenn Ralph
Travis Perkins plc Senior Masters	Tony Johnstone
Casa Serena Open	Peter Mitchell
Benahavis Senior Masters	Carl Mason (2)
OKI Castellon Senior Tour Championship	Mike Harwood
Mauritius Commercial Bank Open	Kevin Spurgeon

JAPAN SENIOR TOUR

Fancl Classic	Tateo Ozaki
Komatsu Open	Tomohiro Maruyama
Japan PGA Senior Championship	Kiyoshi Murota
Fujifilm Senior Championship	Hajime Meshiai
Japan Senior Open Championship	Tsukasa Watanabe
Handa Cup Philanthropy Senior Open	Ian Woosnam (2)

Multiple Winners of 2009

PLAYER	WINS	PLAYER	WINS
Tiger Woods	7	Brian Gay	2
Shinobu Moromizato	6	Lucas Glover	2
Sakura Yokomine	6	Fabian Gomez	2
Chie Arimura	5	Retief Goosen	2
Yuta Ikeda	4	Jay Haas	2
Ryo Ishikawa	4	James Hahn	2
Mi-Jeong Jeon	4	Anders Hansen	2
Bernhard Langer	4	Thongchai Jaidee	2
Phil Mickelson	4	Agustin Jauretche	2
Edoardo Molinari	4	Kevin Johnson	2
Jiyai Shin	4	Zach Johnson	2
Steve Stricker	4	Tony Johnstone	2
Paul Casey	3	Martin Kaymer	2
Graham DeLaet	3	Jerry Kelly	2
Darren Fichardt	3	In-Kyung Kim	2
Lorena Ochoa	3	Tom Lehman	2
Brandon Pieters	3	Diane Luna	2
Loren Roberts	3	Carl Mason	2
Michael Sim	3	Catriona Matthew	2
Jaco Van Zyl	3	Ai Miyazato	2
Robert Allenby	2	Anna Nordqvist	2
Bae Sang-moon	2	Koumei Oda	2
Angel Cabrera	2	Geoff Ogilvy	2
Na Yeon Choi	2	Kenny Perry	2
Robert Coles	2	Nick Price	2
Nicolas Colsaerts	2	Marianne Skarpnord	2
John Cook	2	Bo-Bae Song	2
Rhys Davies	2	Lee Westwood	2
Simon Dyson	2	Thaworn Wiratchant	2
Keith Fergus	2	Ian Woosnam	2
Hiroyuki Fujita	2	Y.E. Yang	2

World Money List

This list of the 350 leading money winners in the world of professional golf in 2009 was compiled from the results of men's (excluding seniors) tournaments carried in the Appendixes of this edition. This list includes tournaments with a minimum of 36 holes and four contestants and does not include such competitions as skins games, pro-ams and shootouts.

In the 44 years during which World Money Lists have been compiled, the earnings of the player in the 200th position have risen from a total of $3,326 in 1966 to $676,899 in 2009. The top 200 players in 1966 earned a total of $4,680,287. In 2009, the comparable total was $490,240,639.

The world money list of the International Federation of PGA Tours was used for the official money list events of the U.S. PGA Tour, PGA European Tour, PGA Tour of Japan, Asian Tour, Southern Africa Tour and PGA Tour of Australasia. The conversion rates used for 2009 for other events and other tours were: Euro = US$1.39; Japanese yen = US$0.01; South African rand = US$0.13; Australian dollar = US$0.65; Canadian dollar = US$0.93.

POS.	PLAYER, COUNTRY	TOTAL MONEY
1	Tiger Woods, USA	$10,998,054
2	Steve Stricker, USA	7,087,636
3	Jim Furyk, USA	6,646,515
4	Phil Mickelson, USA	6,600,757
5	Lee Westwood, England	5,594,136
6	Zach Johnson, USA	5,344,813
7	Sean O'Hair, USA	5,336,749
8	Kenny Perry, USA	4,972,228
9	Ian Poulter, England	4,813,935
10	Lucas Glover, USA	4,642,580
11	Paul Casey, England	4,530,777
12	Retief Goosen, South Africa	4,522,576
13	Rory McIlroy, N. Ireland	4,485,248
14	Henrik Stenson, Sweden	4,468,059
15	Geoff Ogilvy, Australia	4,426,479
16	Padraig Harrington, Ireland	4,345,064
17	Y.E. Yang, Korea	4,215,311
18	Robert Allenby, Australia	4,112,125
19	Nick Watney, USA	4,012,507
20	Anthony Kim, USA	3,963,333
21	Martin Kaymer, Germany	3,810,296
22	Graeme McDowell, N. Ireland	3,759,935
23	Stewart Cink, USA	3,596,537
24	Ross Fisher, England	3,587,356
25	Angel Cabrera, Argentina	3,498,913
26	Hunter Mahan, USA	3,461,349
27	Brian Gay, USA	3,412,861
28	Ernie Els, South Africa	3,344,024
29	David Toms, USA	3,197,198
30	Dustin Johnson, USA	3,069,151
31	Jerry Kelly, USA	2,974,154
32	Rory Sabbatini, South Africa	2,887,194

POS.	PLAYER, COUNTRY	TOTAL MONEY
33	Tim Clark, South Africa	2,746,771
34	Matt Kuchar, USA	2,738,706
35	Kevin Na, Korea	2,724,825
36	Camilo Villegas, Colombia	2,705,656
37	Mike Weir, Canada	2,704,422
38	Justin Leonard, USA	2,694,044
39	Luke Donald, England	2,684,449
40	Ryan Moore, USA	2,652,948
41	Francesco Molinari, Italy	2,575,709
42	John Senden, Australia	2,426,317
43	Jason Dufner, USA	2,322,682
44	John Rollins, USA	2,269,475
45	Scott Verplank, USA	2,253,780
46	Steve Marino, USA	2,203,687
47	Simon Dyson, England	2,203,067
48	Heath Slocum, USA	2,195,565
49	Stephen Ames, Canada	2,131,538
50	Ryo Ishikawa, Japan	2,003,101
51	Chad Campbell, USA	1,971,903
52	Sergio Garcia, Spain	1,969,017
53	Ross McGowan, England	1,966,880
54	Bo Van Pelt, USA	1,945,307
55	Charley Hoffman, USA	1,894,925
56	Soren Kjeldsen, Denmark	1,888,514
57	Brian Davis, England	1,874,318
58	Charles Howell, USA	1,854,460
59	Adam Scott, Australia	1,842,698
60	Mark Wilson, USA	1,838,414
61	Pat Perez, Uruguay	1,819,950
62	Marc Leishman, Australia	1,817,737
63	Justin Rose, England	1,814,072
64	Edoardo Molinari, Italy	1,795,974
65	Anders Hansen, Denmark	1,753,762
66	Oliver Wilson, England	1,744,152
67	John Mallinger, USA	1,717,140
68	Yuta Ikeda, Japan	1,700,852
69	Davis Love, USA	1,676,151
70	Ben Crane, USA	1,667,085
71	Gonzalo Fernandez-Castano, Spain	1,645,506
72	Paul Goydos, USA	1,619,918
73	Thongchai Jaidee, Thailand	1,616,581
74	Soren Hansen, Denmark	1,599,347
75	Tim Petrovic, USA	1,551,866
76	George McNeill, USA	1,511,842
77	John Merrick, USA	1,502,892
78	Jeev Milkha Singh, India	1,500,348
79	Brett Quigley, USA	1,492,751
80	Miguel Angel Jimenez, Spain	1,489,894
81	Brandt Snedeker, USA	1,483,557
82	Martin Laird, Scotland	1,482,502
83	Bryce Molder, USA	1,480,248
84	Nathan Green, Australia	1,476,239
85	Troy Matteson, USA	1,466,070

POS.	PLAYER, COUNTRY	TOTAL MONEY
86	Peter Hanson, Sweden	1,464,339
87	Charlie Wi, Korea	1,439,096
88	Charl Schwartzel, South Africa	1,438,089
89	Alexander Noren, Sweden	1,432,150
90	J.B. Holmes, USA	1,431,200
91	Bubba Watson, USA	1,430,244
92	Bill Haas, USA	1,425,418
93	Alvaro Quiros, Spain	1,416,071
94	D.A. Points, USA	1,345,021
95	Jonathan Byrd, USA	1,316,771
96	Robert Karlsson, Sweden	1,294,963
97	Vijay Singh, Fiji	1,289,723
98	Hiroyuki Fujita, Japan	1,283,460
99	Koumei Oda, Japan	1,282,825
100	Boo Weekley, USA	1,281,062
101	Rod Pampling, Australia	1,275,604
102	Greg Chalmers, Australia	1,266,327
103	Jason Day, Australia	1,251,219
104	Webb Simpson, USA	1,249,674
105	Nick O'Hern, Australia	1,248,217
106	Jeff Klauk, USA	1,243,696
107	Thomas Levet, France	1,234,555
108	Shingo Katayama, Japan	1,229,263
109	Kevin Sutherland, USA	1,220,805
110	Fred Couples, USA	1,208,396
111	Jeff Overton, USA	1,193,346
112	Liang Wen-chong, China	1,192,364
113	Fredrik Jacobson, Sweden	1,189,995
114	Briny Baird, USA	1,186,982
115	Ben Curtis, USA	1,180,390
116	Vaughn Taylor, USA	1,178,282
117	Shigeki Maruyama, Japan	1,175,341
118	Mathew Goggin, Australia	1,174,471
119	J.J. Henry, USA	1,164,241
120	Jason Bohn, USA	1,159,936
121	Robert Rock, England	1,155,074
122	Nick Dougherty, England	1,152,757
123	Woody Austin, USA	1,137,331
124	K.J. Choi, Korea	1,127,006
125	Johan Edfors, Sweden	1,107,623
126	Raphael Jacquelin, France	1,106,235
127	Alex Cejka, Germany	1,100,564
128	Louis Oosthuizen, South Africa	1,097,261
129	Scott Strange, Australia	1,094,557
130	Bob Estes, USA	1,079,929
131	D.J. Trahan, USA	1,078,256
132	Stuart Appleby, Australia	1,039,256
133	Scott Piercy, USA	1,032,716
134	Anthony Wall, England	1,028,973
135	James Nitties, Australia	1,009,779
136	Kevin Streelman, USA	1,007,444
137	Kenichi Kuboya, Japan	996,794
138	Rafael Cabrera-Bello, Spain	994,134

POS.	PLAYER, COUNTRY	TOTAL MONEY
139	Gregory Bourdy, France	988,604
140	Scott McCarron, USA	980,819
141	Ryuichi Oda, Japan	969,829
142	Daniel Chopra, Sweden	965,831
143	James Kingston, South Africa	947,170
144	Michael Sim, Australia	946,643
145	David Drysdale, Scotland	935,364
146	Kevin Stadler, USA	925,514
147	Peter Hedblom, Sweden	921,160
148	Darren Clarke, N. Ireland	918,719
149	Kim Kyung-tae, Korea	912,140
150	Aaron Baddeley, Australia	906,457
151	Graeme Storm, England	902,363
152	Chris Wood, USA	897,584
153	Michael Letzig, USA	896,478
154	Steve Webster, England	890,683
155	Jamie Donaldson, Wales	881,978
156	Ryuji Imada, Japan	874,075
157	Lee Janzen, USA	871,187
158	Mark Calcavecchia, USA	864,846
159	Thomas Aiken, South Africa	864,191
160	Niclas Fasth, Sweden	863,349
161	Peter Lawrie, Ireland	861,714
162	Bradley Dredge, Wales	838,982
163	Ted Purdy, USA	838,707
164	Bill Lunde, USA	835,691
165	Danny Willett, England	830,537
166	Andres Romero, Argentina	827,293
167	Daisuke Maruyama, Japan	823,613
168	Prayad Marksaeng, Thailand	821,557
169	James Driscoll, USA	816,825
170	Brendan Jones, Australia	804,564
171	Stephen Dodd, Wales	797,457
172	Richard Sterne, South Africa	784,780
173	Yasuharu Imano, Japan	778,206
174	Toru Suzuki, Japan	772,607
175	Matt Bettencourt, USA	771,550
176	Chris DiMarco, USA	766,575
177	Greg Owen, England	763,517
178	Steve Flesch, USA	759,302
179	Tomohiro Kondo, Japan	751,733
180	Gareth Maybin, N. Ireland	742,687
181	Harrison Frazar, USA	738,615
182	Chris Stroud, USA	735,019
183	Ignacio Garrido, Spain	733,787
184	Cameron Beckman, USA	733,005
185	Christian Cevaer, France	728,858
186	Michael Bradley, USA	727,788
187	Jeppe Huldahl, Denmark	727,343
188	Damian McGrane, Ireland	724,576
189	Jeff Quinney, USA	718,950
190	Tetsuji Hiratsuka, Japan	712,369
191	Richard S. Johnson, Sweden	701,873

POS.	PLAYER, COUNTRY	TOTAL MONEY
192	Ricky Barnes, USA	697,913
193	Richie Ramsay, Scotland	692,788
194	Michael Jonzon, Sweden	691,823
195	Robert-Jan Derksen, Netherlands	685,561
196	Rickie Fowler, USA	684,490
197	Roland Thatcher, USA	681,631
198	Fabrizio Zanotti, Paraguay	678,759
199	Nicholas Thompson, USA	678,078
200	Rich Beem, USA	676,899
201	David Smail, New Zealand	674,371
202	Azuma Yano, Japan	669,091
203	Jimmy Walker, USA	662,683
204	Will MacKenzie, USA	662,254
205	Robert Garrigus, USA	657,204
206	Jeff Maggert, USA	651,384
207	Pablo Martin, Spain	635,636
208	Ricardo Gonzalez, Argentina	633,581
209	Richard Green, Australia	632,721
210	Oskar Henningsson, Sweden	632,193
211	Chris Riley, USA	630,417
212	David Duval, USA	623,824
213	Tim Herron, USA	619,843
214	Matt Jones, Australia	619,713
215	Joe Ogilvie, USA	613,700
216	Kazuhiro Yamashita, Japan	611,918
217	Toshinori Muto, Japan	606,639
218	Shiv Kapur, India	605,619
219	Todd Hamilton, USA	605,225
220	Toru Taniguchi, Japan	596,808
221	Rafael Echenique, Argentina	580,745
222	Kaname Yokoo, Japan	574,350
223	Carl Pettersson, Sweden	564,605
224	Marcel Siem, Germany	557,421
225	Danny Lee, New Zealand	556,268
226	Mathias Gronberg, Sweden	556,203
227	Takashi Kanemoto, Japan	554,060
228	Bae Sang-moon, Korea	549,800
229	Jyoti Randhawa, India	548,840
230	Matt Weibring, USA	542,066
231	Brendon de Jonge, Zimbabwe	540,366
232	Spencer Levin, USA	539,893
233	Daniel Vancsik, Argentina	537,944
234	Gary Orr, Scotland	528,672
235	Trevor Immelman, South Africa	526,018
236	Anthony Kang, USA	525,783
237	Masaya Tomida, Japan	519,688
238	Marc Warren, Scotland	517,423
239	Jose Manuel Lara, Spain	509,672
240	Paul Broadhurst, England	508,214
241	Paul Lawrie, Scotland	507,765
242	Aron Price, Australia	506,489
243	Felipe Aguilar, Chile	506,456
244	Tommy Armour, USA	505,356

POS.	PLAYER, COUNTRY	TOTAL MONEY
245	Chapchai Nirat, Thailand	502,728
246	Estanislao Goya, Argentina	501,725
247	Christian Nilsson, Sweden	499,614
248	David Horsey, England	497,638
249	Michael Hoey, N. Ireland	497,036
250	Corey Pavin, USA	490,285
251	Rocco Mediate, USA	486,717
252	Mikko Ilonen, Finland	484,960
253	Chez Reavie, USA	482,016
254	Marcus Fraser, Australia	481,877
255	Charles Warren, USA	475,726
256	Hirofumi Miyase, Japan	474,935
257	Thomas Bjorn, Denmark	468,854
258	Katsumasa Miyamoto, Japan	465,323
259	Maarten Lafeber, Netherlands	464,768
260	Cliff Kresge, USA	464,401
261	Martin Erlandsson, Sweden	463,104
262	Ryan Palmer, USA	454,510
263	Jamie Lovemark, USA	453,872
264	Brett Rumford, Australia	451,773
265	Brandt Jobe, USA	450,776
266	Alastair Forsyth, Scotland	447,707
267	Hideto Tanihara, Japan	447,265
268	Colin Montgomerie, Scotland	447,188
269	Yuji Igarashi, Japan	446,691
270	Glen Day, USA	445,720
271	David Lynn, England	443,175
272	Dean Wilson, USA	442,600
273	Patrick Sheehan, USA	442,103
274	Garrett Willis, USA	434,761
275	Johnson Wagner, USA	434,571
276	Derek Lamely, USA	433,186
277	Francois Delamontagne, France	425,823
278	Cameron Percy, Australia	422,310
279	Leif Olson, USA	421,297
280	Mark Foster, England	420,173
281	Paul McGinley, Ireland	417,285
282	Kim Hyung-sung, Korea	416,637
283	Chad Collins, USA	415,114
284	Jason Gore, USA	415,080
285	Han Lee, USA	413,991
286	Jose Maria Olazabal, Spain	413,528
287	Rich Bland, England	403,353
288	Markus Brier, Austria	403,117
289	David Mathis, USA	400,659
290	Blake Adams, USA	399,749
291	Sam Little, England	396,297
292	Garth Mulroy, South Africa	395,296
293	Billy Mayfair, USA	393,853
294	Yusaku Miyazato, Japan	393,516
295	Gary Lockerbie, England	390,813
296	Brad Adamonis, USA	387,721
297	Ken Duke, USA	382,826

POS.	PLAYER, COUNTRY	TOTAL MONEY
298	Andrew McLardy, South Africa	377,408
299	Casey Wittenberg, USA	376,076
300	Lin Wen-tang, Taiwan	370,912
301	Kenneth Ferrie, England	368,731
302	Tag Ridings, USA	366,997
303	Tom Gillis, USA	366,829
304	Scott Hend, Australia	359,622
305	Paul Waring, USA	358,421
306	Kiradech Aphibarnrat, Thailand	357,877
307	Shane Lowry, Ireland	357,487
308	Chris Tidland, USA	354,510
309	Rhys Davies, Wales	348,994
310	Michio Matsumura, Japan	348,310
311	David Dixon, England	345,411
312	Tim Wilkinson, New Zealand	343,200
313	Chris Baryla, Canada	341,925
314	Seve Benson, England	340,945
315	Kris Blanks, USA	340,119
316	Taichi Teshima, Japan	339,715
317	Jonathan Kaye, USA	338,914
318	Andrew Coltart, Scotland	335,748
319	Simon Khan, England	334,978
320	Peter Lonard, Australia	333,825
321	Gaganjeet Bhullar, India	333,441
322	Scott Sterling, USA	331,797
323	Pablo Larrazabal, Spain	331,196
324	Steve Lowery, USA	329,114
325	Alejandro Canizares, Spain	328,303
326	Mark Brooks, USA	326,716
327	Bart Bryant, USA	326,590
328	Tadahiro Takayama, Japan	326,502
329	Josh Teater, USA	326,438
330	Gary Murphy, Ireland	321,098
331	Jarrod Lyle, Australia	320,919
332	Alessandro Tadini, Italy	318,873
333	Scott Drummond, Scotland	318,738
334	Mark Brown, New Zealand	318,111
335	Richard Finch, England	315,081
336	Benn Barham, England	313,316
337	Bob Heintz, USA	312,699
338	Tetsuya Haraguchi, Japan	312,696
339	Michael Lorenzo-Vera, France	312,039
340	Jean-Francois Lucquin, France	310,809
341	Steven Conran, Australia	309,397
342	Roger Tambellini, USA	307,482
343	Matt Every, USA	303,136
344	Pelle Edberg, Sweden	302,372
345	Kent Jones, USA	301,879
346	J.P. Hayes, USA	300,102
347	Shaun Micheel, USA	298,905
348	Darron Stiles, USA	298,457
349	Marcus Both, Australia	298,343
350	Justin Bolli, USA	287,137

World Money List Leaders

YEAR	PLAYER, COUNTRY	TOTAL MONEY
1966	Jack Nicklaus, USA	$168,088
1967	Jack Nicklaus, USA	276,166
1968	Billy Casper, USA	222,436
1969	Frank Beard, USA	186,993
1970	Jack Nicklaus, USA	222,583
1971	Jack Nicklaus, USA	285,897
1972	Jack Nicklaus, USA	341,792
1973	Tom Weiskopf, USA	349,645
1974	Johnny Miller, USA	400,255
1975	Jack Nicklaus, USA	332,610
1976	Jack Nicklaus, USA	316,086
1977	Tom Watson, USA	358,034
1978	Tom Watson, USA	384,388
1979	Tom Watson, USA	506,912
1980	Tom Watson, USA	651,921
1981	Johnny Miller, USA	704,204
1982	Raymond Floyd, USA	738,699
1983	Seve Ballesteros, Spain	686,088
1984	Seve Ballesteros, Spain	688,047
1985	Bernhard Langer, Germany	860,262
1986	Greg Norman, Australia	1,146,584
1987	Ian Woosnam, Wales	1,793,268
1988	Seve Ballesteros, Spain	1,261,275
1989	David Frost, South Africa	1,650,230
1990	Jose Maria Olazabal, Spain	1,633,640
1991	Bernhard Langer, Germany	2,186,700
1992	Nick Faldo, England	2,748,248
1993	Nick Faldo, England	2,825,280
1994	Ernie Els, South Africa	2,862,854
1995	Corey Pavin, USA	2,746,340
1996	Colin Montgomerie, Scotland	3,071,442
1997	Colin Montgomerie, Scotland	3,366,900
1998	Tiger Woods, USA	2,927,946
1999	Tiger Woods, USA	7,681,625
2000	Tiger Woods, USA	11,034,530
2001	Tiger Woods, USA	7,771,562
2002	Tiger Woods, USA	8,292,188
2003	Vijay Singh, Fiji	8,499,611
2004	Vijay Singh, Fiji	11,638,699
2005	Tiger Woods, USA	12,280,404
2006	Tiger Woods, USA	13,325,949
2007	Tiger Woods, USA	12,902,706
2008	Vijay Singh, Fiji	8,025,128
2009	Tiger Woods, USA	10,998,054

Career World Money List

Here is a list of the 50 leading money winners for their careers through the 2009 season. It includes players active on both the regular and senior tours of the world. The World Money List from this and the 43 previous editions of the annual and a table prepared for a companion book, *The Wonderful World of Professional Golf* (Atheneum, 1973) form the basis for this compilation. Additional figures were taken from official records of major golf associations, although shortcomings in records-keeping outside the United States in the 1950s and 1960s and a few exclusions from U.S. records during those years prevent these figures from being completely accurate, although the careers of virtually all of these top 50 players began after that time. Conversion of foreign currency figures to U.S. dollars is based on average values during the particular years involved.

POS.	PLAYER, COUNTRY	TOTAL MONEY
1	Tiger Woods, USA	$111,356,267
2	Vijay Singh, Fiji	75,381,713
3	Ernie Els, South Africa	70,925,441
4	Phil Mickelson, USA	61,880,755
5	Jim Furyk, USA	53,346,574
6	Davis Love III, USA	48,024,986
7	Padraig Harrington, Ireland	42,720,916
8	Retief Goosen, South Africa	42,256,042
9	Sergio Garcia, Spain	40,945,608
10	Colin Montgomerie, Scotland	40,733,741
11	Hale Irwin, USA	35,651,409
12	Bernhard Langer, Germany	35,532,163
13	Kenny Perry, USA	34,594,406
14	Nick Price, Zimbabwe	34,362,386
15	David Toms, USA	34,143,965
16	Lee Westwood, England	32,542,259
17	Justin Leonard, USA	32,455,450
18	Fred Couples, USA	31,877,248
19	Stewart Cink, USA	30,987,516
20	Mark Calcavecchia, USA	29,253,209
21	Robert Allenby, Australia	29,251,267
22	Mike Weir, Canada	28,865,702
23	Tom Kite, USA	28,864,442
24	Darren Clarke, Northern Ireland	28,628,652
25	Adam Scott, Australia	28,087,191
26	Fred Funk, USA	27,884,014
27	Jay Haas, USA	27,720,371
28	Stuart Appleby, Australia	27,453,400
29	Tom Lehman, USA	27,182,666
30	Scott Hoch, USA	26,891,659
31	Jose Maria Olazabal, Spain	26,556,245
32	Gil Morgan, USA	26,497,695
33	Steve Stricker, USA	26,171,015
34	Greg Norman, Australia	25,915,285
35	Tom Watson, USA	25,796,034
36	Scott Verplank, USA	25,477,011
37	Loren Roberts, USA	25,368,867

POS.	PLAYER, COUNTRY	TOTAL MONEY
38	Chris DiMarco, USA	25,165,734
39	Jeff Sluman, USA	24,619,767
40	Geoff Ogilvy, Australia	23,860,586
41	K. J. Choi, South Korea	23,813,143
42	Mark O'Meara, USA	23,643,986
43	Luke Donald, England	23,328,778
44	Miguel Angel Jimenez, Spain	22,999,152
45	Rory Sabbatini, South Africa	22,807,086
46	Jerry Kelly, USA	22,268,679
47	Masashi Ozaki, Japan	21,913,015
48	Henrik Stenson, Sweden	21,669,516
49	Craig Stadler, USA	21,619,532
50	Brad Faxon, USA	21,593,622

These 50 players have won $1,680,886,167 in their careers.

Women's World Money List

This list includes official earnings on the U.S. LPGA Tour, Ladies European Tour, Japan LPGA Tour and Australian Ladies Tour, along with other winnings in established unofficial events when reliable figures could be obtained.

POS.	PLAYER, COUNTRY	TOTAL MONEY
1	Jiyai Shin, Korea	$2,179,908
2	Ai Miyazato, Japan	1,986,946
3	Sakura Yokomine, Japan	1,785,536
4	Shinobu Moromizato, Japan	1,689,252
5	Cristie Kerr, USA	1,519,722
6	Lorena Ochoa, Mexico	1,489,395
7	Chie Arimura, Japan	1,446,241
8	Na Yeon Choi, Korea	1,371,078
9	Suzann Pettersen, Norway	1,369,717
10	Mi-Jeong Jeon, Korea	1,366,824
11	Yani Tseng, Taiwan	1,308,721
12	In-Kyung Kim, Korea	1,268,396
13	Paula Creamer, USA	1,253,864
14	Angela Stanford, USA	1,081,916
15	Song-Hee Kim, Korea	1,032,031
16	Yuko Mitsuka, Japan	992,003
17	Karrie Webb, Australia	981,595
18	Eun-Hee Ji, Korea	967,284
19	Anna Nordqvist, Sweden	962,544
20	Michelle Wie, USA	918,659
21	Ji-Hee Lee, Korea	893,798
22	Sophie Gustafson, Sweden	855,077
23	Momoko Ueda, Japan	829,604

POS.	PLAYER, COUNTRY	TOTAL MONEY
24	Kristy McPherson, USA	816,182
25	Bo-Bae Song, Korea	759,249
26	Lindsey Wright, Australia	743,322
27	Miho Koga, Japan	736,084
28	Brittany Lincicome, USA	700,897
29	Morgan Pressel, USA	684,063
30	Brittany Lang, USA	675,065
31	Hee Young Park, Korea	666,305
32	Sun Young Yoo, Korea	644,874
33	Yukari Baba, Japan	615,611
34	Ji Young Oh, Korea	558,316
35	Katherine Hull, Australia	543,707
36	Candie Kung, Taiwan	539,853
37	Akiko Fukushima, Japan	523,290
38	Nikki Campbell, Australia	521,392
39	Eun-A Lim, Korea	507,678
40	Catriona Matthew, Scotland	492,589
41	Yuri Fudoh, Japan	491,847
42	Ayako Uehara, Japan	488,000
43	Maria Hjorth, Sweden	484,577
44	Seon Hwa Lee, Korea	458,316
45	Yuko Saitoh, Japan	458,283
46	Hee-Won Han, Korea	450,197
47	Miki Saiki, Japan	448,276
48	Se Ri Pak, Korea	447,683
49	M.J. Hur, Korea	445,022
50	Mayu Hattori, Japan	444,809
51	Helen Alfredsson, Sweden	444,020
52	Rui Kitada, Japan	430,050
53	Akane Iijima, Japan	426,350
54	Tamie Durdin, Australia	413,357
55	Ah-Reum Hwang, Korea	400,878
56	Erina Hara, Japan	390,797
57	Meena Lee, Korea	386,335
58	Natalie Gulbis, USA	376,392
59	Amy Yang, Korea	373,433
60	Pat Hurst, USA	370,873
61	Jee Young Lee, Korea	358,711
62	Christina Kim, USA	344,055
63	Wendy Ward, USA	326,395
64	Stacy Lewis, USA	325,605
65	Kyeong Bae, Korea	324,460
66	Hiromi Mogi, Japan	323,454
67	Juli Inkster, USA	318,089
68	Becky Brewerton, Wales	316,919
69	Michele Redman, USA	316,533
70	Eunjung Yi, Korea	314,600
71	Vicky Hurst, USA	305,773
72	Rikako Morita, Japan	303,950
73	Laura Davies, England	302,864
74	Sandra Gal, Germany	298,763
75	Meaghan Francella, USA	292,266
76	Michie Ohba, Japan	290,001

POS.	PLAYER, COUNTRY	TOTAL MONEY
77	Marianne Skarpnord, Norway	288,705
78	Mika Miyazato, Japan	284,788
79	Na-Ri Lee, Korea	282,937
80	Maiko Wakabayashi, Japan	281,607
81	Tania Elosegui, Spain	280,474
82	Inbee Park, Korea	271,303
83	Ji-Woo Lee, Korea	270,440
84	Midori Yoneyama, Japan	269,099
85	Hyun-Ju Shin, Korea	264,141
86	Saiki Fujita, Japan	263,789
87	Kaori Aoyama, Japan	260,471
88	Diana Luna, Italy	257,487
89	Nicole Castrale, USA	257,299
90	Li-Ying Ye, China	255,653
91	Angela Park, Brazil	253,391
92	Teresa Lu, Taiwan	242,546
93	Karen Stupples, England	236,665
94	Melissa Reid, England	233,717
95	Gwladys Nocera, France	223,541
96	Stacy Prammanasudh, USA	217,971
97	Jimin Kang, Korea	214,942
98	Soo-Yun Kang, Korea	212,352
99	Janice Moodie, Scotland	208,396
100	Giulia Sergas, Italy	207,628
101	So-Hee Kim, Korea	207,384
102	Shi Hyun Ahn, Korea	202,624
103	Julie Lu, Taiwan	200,712
104	Jane Park, USA	194,856
105	Yuki Ichinose, Japan	192,060
106	Jade Schaeffer, France	181,302
107	Young Kim, Korea	181,166
108	Nobuko Kizawa, Japan	178,089
109	Hiromi Takesue, Japan	175,906
110	Becky Morgan, Wales	174,768
111	Karine Icher, France	173,965
112	Laura Diaz, USA	168,688
113	Yui Kawahara, Japan	167,194
114	Anna Grzebien, USA	166,905
115	Junko Omote, Japan	165,619
116	Mie Nakata, Japan	165,212
117	Tomoko Kusakabe, Japan	165,037
118	Maria Iida, Brazil	164,756
119	Kuniko Maeda, Japan	157,469
120	Hye Jung Choi, Korea	154,984
121	Yun-Jye Wei, Taiwan	153,213
122	Natsu Nagai, Japan	150,551
123	Tomomi Hirose, Japan	148,275
124	Haeji Kang, Korea	148,048
125	Johanna Westerberg, Sweden	144,885
126	Nicole Gergely, Austria	143,325
127	Mika Takushima, Japan	142,770
128	Yayoi Arasaki, Japan	142,040
129	Paige Mackenzie, USA	140,671

POS.	PLAYER, COUNTRY	TOTAL MONEY
130	Mikaela Parmlid, Sweden	137,355
131	Allison Fouch, USA	131,856
132	Felicity Johnson, England	130,182
133	Katie Futcher, USA	128,702
134	Shiho Oyama, Japan	128,280
135	Beth Bader, USA	126,441
136	Il Mi Chung, Korea	126,168
137	Shanshan Feng, China	123,694
138	Mayumi Nakajima, Japan	122,489
139	Amy Hung, Taiwan	122,442
140	Alena Sharp, Canada	122,345
141	Iben Tinning, Denmark	122,064
142	Christel Boeljon, Netherlands	121,038
143	Ursula Wikstrom, Finland	119,938
144	Kumiko Kaneda, Japan	119,589
145	Ikue Asama, Japan	119,560
146	Sarah Lee, Korea	119,507
147	Irene Cho, USA	118,302
148	Minea Blomqvist, Finland	117,705
149	Moira Dunn, USA	116,529
150	Mikiyo Nishizuka, Japan	116,120

Senior World Money List

This list includes official earnings from the world money list of the International Federation of PGA Tours, U.S. Champions Tour, European Senior Tour and Japan Senior Tour, along with other winnings in established unofficial events when reliable figures could be obtained.

POS.	PLAYER, COUNTRY	TOTAL MONEY
1	Bernhard Langer, Germany	$2,218,583
2	Loren Roberts, USA	2,011,870
3	John Cook, USA	1,801,964
4	Jay Haas, USA	1,758,395
5	Fred Funk, USA	1,600,736
6	Tom Watson, USA	1,531,275
7	Jeff Sluman, USA	1,498,494
8	Nick Price, Zimbabwe	1,366,952
9	Mark O'Meara, USA	1,344,532
10	Andy Bean, USA	1,313,217
11	Dan Forsman, USA	1,207,888
12	Tom Lehman, USA	1,172,275
13	Mark McNulty, Zimbabwe	1,163,625
14	Michael Allen, USA	1,143,727
15	Joey Sindelar, USA	1,124,437
16	Gene Jones, USA	1,120,812
17	Larry Mize, USA	1,050,077

POS.	PLAYER, COUNTRY	TOTAL MONEY
18	Keith Fergus, USA	1,004,340
19	Brad Bryant, USA	936,110
20	Russ Cochran, USA	903,996
21	Tom Pernice, Jr., USA	851,598
22	Tom Kite, USA	848,871
23	Mark Wiebe, USA	817,048
24	Lonnie Nielsen, USA	710,203
25	Tom Jenkins, USA	683,801
26	Eduardo Romero, Argentina	682,212
27	Mike Goodes, USA	675,717
28	Mike Reid, USA	668,807
29	Phil Blackmar, USA	658,313
30	Ian Woosnam, Wales	648,165
31	Gil Morgan, USA	636,864
32	Don Pooley, USA	629,476
33	David Eger, USA	615,278
34	Mark James, England	500,625
35	Tim Simpson, USA	497,484
36	Craig Stadler, USA	451,762
37	Tateo Ozaki, Japan	445,481
38	Hal Sutton, USA	443,982
39	Jim Thorpe, USA	441,663
40	Scott Hoch, USA	441,034
41	Fulton Allem, South Africa	433,093
42	Olin Browne, USA	428,770
43	Kiyoshi Murota, Japan	424,898
44	Morris Hatalsky, USA	421,305
45	Ronnie Black, USA	420,951
46	Bruce Fleisher, USA	416,506
47	Bob Tway, USA	383,808
48	Bruce Vaughan, USA	378,872
49	David Frost, South Africa	375,467
50	Larry Nelson, USA	374,522
51	Joe Ozaki, Japan	364,575
52	Tsukasa Watanabe, Japan	353,876
53	Ben Crenshaw, USA	352,057
54	Denis Watson, USA	344,654
55	Scott Simpson, USA	335,579
56	Tom Purtzer, USA	332,921
57	James Mason, USA	326,135
58	Bob Gilder, USA	312,294
59	Sandy Lyle, Scotland	299,414
60	Dana Quigley, USA	298,572
61	Hale Irwin, USA	297,161
62	Jerry Pate, USA	294,853
63	Bobby Wadkins, USA	291,786
64	R.W. Eaks, USA	279,696
65	Hajime Meshiai, Japan	276,354
66	Sam Torrance, Scotland	273,598
67	Tommy Nakajima, Japan	267,808
68	Gary Hallberg, USA	267,160
69	John Morse, USA	258,225
70	Fuzzy Zoeller, USA	246,040
71	Des Smyth, Ireland	228,774

POS.	PLAYER, COUNTRY	TOTAL MONEY
72	Greg Norman, Australia	224,905
73	Masahiro Kuramoto, Japan	219,448
74	Carl Mason, England	217,137
75	Glenn Ralph, England	212,153
76	Tomohiro Maruyama, Japan	209,585
77	Jay Don Blake, USA	208,933
78	Angel Franco, Paraguay	207,408
79	Robert Thompson, USA	206,996
80	Chip Beck, USA	199,404
81	David Edwards, USA	197,490
82	Gohei Sato, Japan	194,330
83	Katsunari Takahashi, Japan	193,629
84	Mike McCullough, USA	191,492
85	D.A. Weibring, USA	187,145
86	Yoshinori Mizumaki, Japan	184,316
87	Peter Mitchell, England	180,971
88	Katsuyoshi Tomori, Japan	175,597
89	Bob Cameron, England	175,365
90	Peter Senior, Australia	174,514
91	Allen Doyle, USA	172,137
92	Mike Harwood, Australia	172,131
93	Tony Johnstone, Zimbabwe	171,863
94	Bertus Smit, South Africa	162,837
95	Masami Ito, Japan	158,586
96	Steve Thomas, USA	157,549
97	Bruce Lietzke, USA	153,934
98	Tom McKnight, USA	148,648
99	John Harris, USA	146,321
100	Roger Chapman, England	142,825
101	Ross Drummond, Scotland	141,598
102	David Merriman, Australia	139,921
103	Nick Job, England	137,739
104	Bob Boyd, USA	133,554
105	Gordon J. Brand, England	132,059
106	Kevin Spurgeon, England	127,769
107	Gordon Brand, Jr., Scotland	126,503
108	Ken Green, USA	123,906
109	Jerry Bruner, USA	119,807
110	Wayne Levi, USA	118,755
111	David Ishii, USA	115,716
112	Chris Williams, South Africa	115,477
113	Boonchu Ruangkit, Thailand	111,917
114	Yutaka Hagawa, Japan	110,936
115	Hiroshi Ueda, Japan	107,530
116	Tom Wargo, USA	106,522
117	Robin Freeman, USA	105,110
118	Ikuo Shirahama, Japan	104,559
119	John Jacobs, USA	103,642
120	Jose Rivero, Spain	102,996
121	John Bland, South Africa	102,509
122	Eamonn Darcy, Ireland	99,455
123	Bobby Lincoln, South Africa	99,088
124	Seiji Ebihara, Japan	97,591
125	Nobumitsu Yuhara, Japan	97,252

1. The Year in Retrospect

The same question that captivated golf when the 2009 season began still lingered 346 days later when it officially ended: When will Tiger Woods return to competition? The only difference were the circumstances surrounding his absence.

The world's No. 1 player was on the mend from reconstructive knee surgery after his epic U.S. Open victory at Torrey Pines in June 2008. He stayed largely out of the news, except to announce after the final round of the Buick Invitational, which he did not defend, that his wife had given birth to their second child. And to say during the first round of the Northern Trust Open that he was ready to return and that he would defend his title in the Accenture Match Play Championship. No one was desperate to see Woods in public because they figured he was at home in Isleworth rehabilitating his knee and slowly working his game into form. Apparently, that wasn't a problem. Woods won seven of the 19 tournaments he played. And then he vanished again.

As for those 346 days of golf? Memorable in ways no one could have predicted.

Golf around the world already was under the enormous cloud of economic uncertainty. PGA Tour commissioner Tim Finchem sent his players a video message encouraging them to add a tournament or two to their schedules to help the sponsors, even as some of them — Geoff Ogilvy, Anthony Kim, Camilo Villegas, Rory Sabbatini and others — joined the European Tour to take part in the new "Race to Dubai," which was to offer $10 million in bonus money at the end of a $10 million Dubai World Championship. The European Tour even changed its logo for the first time since 1996, featuring the iconic figure of Harry Vardon and a skyline of landmarks around the world. So much enthusiasm, however, was tempered by the global financial crisis that was hitting real estate particularly hard, especially in Dubai.

The top two tours managed to cope with a recession, although it was a different story one notch below on the LPGA Tour. As marketing dollars began to dry up, it was the women's circuit that first began to feel the sting of an economic meltdown. They lost tournaments in Hawaii, then Arizona, longtime stops such as the Corning Classic in New York, and new tournaments like the Ginn Open in Florida. LPGA commissioner Carolyn Bivens remained bullish about the future, yet she was losing the support of her players. It came to a head in July, when a player revolt eventually forced Bivens to resign, and a retired Naval admiral, Marsha Evans, tried to straighten the ship.

Optimism ran high inside the ropes, yet more surprises awaited. With Woods still out of action, Sergio Garcia was presented his best opportunity to take over as No. 1 in the World Ranking. Padraig Harrington, coming off his historic feat of becoming the first European to capture consecutive major championships in the same season, was looking ahead to the Masters and a chance to join Woods and Ben Hogan as the only players to win three in a row since the Masters was created in 1934. No one could have imagined they would both go an entire season without winning. Nor could anyone have guessed that Phil Mickelson would match a career-high with four victories while missing a large part of the summer as he coped with cancer, first detected in his wife, then in his mother.

Woods and Mickelson were all the rage during the majors, just not during the trophy presentation. They were paired together in the final round at Augusta National for the first time in eight years. Mickelson set a record with his fifth runner-up at the U.S. Open. Woods missed the cut in the Open Championship for the first time in his career, then lost a 54-hole lead at the PGA Championship, the first time he had ever done that in a major. The winners? They collectively made history, for this was the first time since the Official World Golf Ranking began in 1986 that none of the major champions — Angel Cabrera, Lucas Glover, Stewart Cink and Y.E. Yang — were ranked among the top 30. Only when the season began did it look like golf as we know it.

Woods swept all the awards on the PGA Tour. Lee Westwood ended the decade the way it began, by holding off a player from Northern Ireland — Darren Clarke in 2000, Rory McIlroy in 2009 — to win the money title on the European Tour. He finished the year at No. 4 in the World Ranking, matching his high from a decade ago. "The most satisfying thing is coming back from that massive low, the disappointment of losing form and then getting it all back," Westwood said. "I felt like I had to work a lot harder to get back then when I got through the first time."

Even more satisfied was Woods, even though it was only the fourth time in his 13 full seasons as a professional that he failed to win a major. Woods used to say that winning a major is all it takes to turn a good year into a great year. There was an asterisk on this season, however, for no one knew how he would return from such a serious surgery, not even the man himself. "I'm as curious as you, too," Woods said in February upon announcing his return. "Getting out there and competing again, and feeling the adrenaline and feeling the rush of competition and playing again — all of that, I haven't done in a while."

The eight months away from golf was the longest break of his life. Skepticism was aimed more at the future. This was the fourth time Woods had surgery on his left knee, dating to 1994 when he was in college at Stanford, and it was the most extensive surgery. He only had missed two months in his previous two surgeries as a pro, and both times he won in his first tournament back. The high desert of Arizona was filled with as much anticipation as saguaro cactus plants, and more than 50 photographers were camped out around the parking lot, clubhouse and practice range. When he played a practice round on Tuesday of tournament week, it was the first time he had walked 18 holes since winning the U.S. Open the previous summer. And it was the only time he walked 18 holes all week. The sacrificial lamb in the opening round was Brendan Jones of Australia, the No. 64 seed. Woods looked as though he had never been gone. Taking five practice swings with his three wood, he fired his opening drive down the right side of the fairway and dropped an eight iron to five feet for birdie. Then came a three iron that settled four feet from the cup for eagle. He closed out Jones, 3 and 2, and the PGA Tour was back to normal. One day later, however, Tim Clark made six birdies and eliminated Woods in the second round, 4 and 2. It wasn't a long week, but it was a start.

Perhaps it was only a coincidence, but the day Woods announced he was returning to competition, Phil Mickelson shot 63 at Riviera to take the lead at the Northern Trust Open, which he would go on to win. Woods learned quickly what kind of competition he faced when he played his first stroke-play event since the U.S. Open at another World Golf Championship, the CA Championship at Doral. Woods was never in the hunt on a Blue Monster course where he had won three straight times and had not finished worse than fifth in a decade. He was 10 shots behind going into the weekend, and only a 68-68 finish allowed him to sneak into the top 10. Mickelson captured his first World Golf Championship, and there was a growing sense of urgency for Woods when he made his third start at the Arnold Palmer Invitational two weeks later.

There were signs of progress, but Woods still faced a five-shot deficit going into the final round. He at least managed to get into the final group with Sean O'Hair, the 54-hole leader, and former Masters champion Zach Johnson. Woods caught up at the turn, both players made a mistake over the closing stretch and, because of a rain delay, it came down to one putt on the 18th hole as darkness neared. Woods had been there before. A year ago, he made a 25-foot birdie on the final hole to win at Bay Hill. This putt was only 15 feet up the hill, yet everyone knew it was going in — even the tournament host, Arnold Palmer, standing beside the green. Woods holed the putt, turned for a fist pump and ran into the arms of his caddie, Steve Williams. It was more emotion than he typically shows at a regular PGA Tour event because this felt like a major victory. He proved to himself and to the golfing world — if anyone really doubted — that he was back. "It feels good to be back in contention, to feel the rush," Woods said. "It's been awhile, but God, it felt good."

So began a most peculiar season for Woods — not how many times he won, but when he won.

The Arnold Palmer Invitational was his tune-up for the Masters, and that one putt made him a heavy favorite at Augusta National. It had taken him only three tournaments to win, and Woods was excited about finally having a stable left leg. He was far from consistent, however, and was seven shots behind after three rounds at the Masters, so disgusted that he headed to the range with swing coach Hank Haney to hit balls and to vent. He was uncertain of his swing, yet certain of the attention he would get in the final round while being paired with Mickelson for the first time at Augusta National since 2001, when Woods won his fourth consecutive major. Augusta National set up the course for fireworks, and the world's top two players delivered, both raising hopes they could storm from behind to win, both running out of holes. Woods wound up in a tie for sixth, four shots behind.

Woods competed in the same group against Jack Nicklaus for the first time since the 2000 PGA Championship, this occasion a skins game that replaced the pro-am at the Memorial Tournament, with Kenny Perry and Stewart Cink along for the ride. Woods left his mark at Muirfield Village when it mattered, storming from four shots back in the final round for his second victory of the year, and his first at the Memorial in eight years. Woods won in style, as often is the case at Jack's place. First came a nine iron on the 17th hole that landed softly on the top tier of a firm green for a birdie putt just inside 10 feet. Woods wrapped up the title with a seven iron from 183 yards that stopped about a foot from the hole. It was his final tune-up before a major — does that sound familiar? — and the way Woods won, by controlling his driver and playing out of the fairway, made believers out of everyone, the tournament host included.

All week long, Nicklaus had entertained questions about Woods at 14 majors, and how much longer before he reached the Nicklaus benchmark of 18 professional majors. "I suspect No. 15 will come for Tiger Woods in about two weeks," Nicklaus said at the trophy presentation, looking ahead to Bethpage Black and the U.S. Open. "If he drives the ball this way and plays this way, I'm sure it will. And if not, it will surprise me greatly."

Alas, the U.S. Open was full of surprises. Not only did Glover win his first major and deny a fairytale week for Mickelson and David Duval, Woods had never hit the ball that well at a U.S. Open without winning, and winning big. This time, he couldn't get a putt to fall and wound up in the same spot as he did in the Masters — a tie for sixth, four shots behind.

The next stop was the AT&T National at Congressional, where Woods achieved a rare hat trick by winning all three PGA Tour events where a player is the official host — the Arnold Palmer Invitational, the Memorial hosted by Nicklaus and this one hosted by Woods himself. Anthony Kim had won the AT&T National the previous year when Woods was laid out on the couch in the weeks following knee surgery. They were tied going into the final round, and while Kim surged ahead early, Woods won more out of consistency. The highlight came when it was over and the tournament host presented the trophy to himself. "I've always wanted to do this, so bear with me," Woods told a thousand or so fans surrounding the 18th green. He then interviewed himself. "So, Tiger, how did you play today?" Woods asked.

Again, he was riding high going to a major championship, and felt his game was in good shape for links golf at Turnberry. But for the third straight time, he went into a major fresh off a victory then failed to win. This was the worst of all, as Woods played an atrocious stretch along the back nine, dropping seven shots in six holes, and missed the cut for the first time in golf's oldest championship. "I kept compounding my problems out there," Woods said.

After winning the Buick Open, Woods headed to Firestone for his final tune-up before the final major, and he got a familiar result. With some help from Harrington, who took a triple-bogey eight on the 16th hole, Woods came from three shots behind to win the Bridgestone Invitational, giving him at least one World Golf Championship each year since the series began in 1999. It was his fifth victory of the year, and the third time he had to rally from at least three shots back on the final day. And once again, he was the betting favorite at the PGA Championship.

Even though he had said the year would be a success without a major because of his return from knee surgery, Woods looked determined to make sure that wouldn't happen. He was on his way to a wire-to-wire victory, leading by four shots going into the weekend and still two shots clear of Yang going into the final round. But when the putts stopped falling, Woods finally looked human. Yang chipped in for eagle and rallied to win by two, the first time Woods has ever lost a major when leading going into the last round. Greg Norman was famous for the "Saturday Slam" in 1986 when he was atop the leaderboard after the third round of all four majors and won only one of them. Call this one the "Premature Slam," for Woods won all four tournaments he played before the majors, and didn't win any of the Grand Slam events that he covets. "Tiger's good, but he could always have a bad day. Guess this is one of those days," Yang said.

The majors were over. Woods's season was not. He paid the PGA Tour a big favor by playing in all four FedExCup Playoff events for the first time. He won the BMW Championship at Cog Hill outside Chicago with a 62-68 weekend on a course that had been beefed up with hopes of attracting a U.S. Open. Woods won by eight strokes to take over the No. 1 seed in the FedExCup finale, and while more players had a mathematical chance of the $10 million prize, Woods finished ahead of all his challengers to win the cup. Mickelson wound up winning The Tour Championship, and it was rare to see golf's biggest rivals sharing the stage, each with a trophy, on the 18th green.

Woods finished the year with just over $10.5 million (not including his FedExCup bonus of $10 million), along with another Vardon Trophy, the player of the year from the PGA of America, PGA Tour and Golf Writers Association of America. In the absence of a major, he made the record books as the first American to go 5-0 in the Presidents Cup with only one partner, teaming with Steve Stricker in four matches.

Woods ended his year on a high, not only winning the JBWere Australian Masters at Kingston Heath, but drawing record crowds along the way. Ticket sales were limited to about 25,000, and they were scooped up long before the opening tee shot. The $3 million in appearance money — half of it paid for by the government — was no longer an issue when officials measured Woods's value on the economy at $31 million. For Woods, it was the final frontier. He now has won on every continent where golf is played. "I haven't played the Antarctica Four-Ball yet," he joked. "But to have won on every playable continent, it's something I've always wanted to do." That was the lasting image of Woods on the golf course. His final stroke was tapping in for par, wearing the gold jacket awarded to the winner, joking at how much money his mother, Kultida, had spent shopping in Australia.

Woods left behind what had been shaping up as a renewed rivalry with Mickelson, a surprise only considering how bleak Mickelson's future looked in the summer. The game of the San Diego southpaw was never better. It was his plight off the course that left him feeling frightened, uncertain and at times weeping during such simple tasks as driving his car. Mickelson won twice during the spring just weeks apart, starting with the Northern Trust Open at Riviera. He opened with a 63, regained control with a 62 in the third round, then overcame some sloppy play in the final round with consecutive birdies late in the round for a one-shot victory. Then came his victory at Doral, despite playing the final round with food poisoning. And while he didn't win the Masters, he lit up Augusta National with a thrilling charge on Sunday, derailed only by a tee shot into the water at No. 12. Even so, Mickelson felt healthy and happy. He played poorly at The Players Championship, but his wife, Amy, walked with him on the last day and they headed off to celebrate Mother's Day. Upon returning home to San Diego, his wife had tests that revealed breast cancer.

Few other wives are more popular than Amy Mickelson, a vivacious blonde whom Mickelson met at Arizona State when she knew nothing about him or the sport he played. She treats friends and strangers alike. She is a familiar figure behind the ropes and on the 18th green with their three children when Mickelson wins. Devastated by the news, Mickelson announced an indefinite leave as she went through a battery of tests, and he feared for the worst. "I've never been this emotional, where if I'm driving along or what have you, I'll just start crying," Mickelson said. "We're scared. I think a lot of it is the unknown." Early tests all brought positive results, and Mickelson returned to golf in time for one tune-up at the St. Jude Classic, followed by the U.S. Open at Bethpage Black. The New York fans embraced Mickelson when he so gallantly tried to make up a four-shot lead against Woods in 2002 and finished runner-up. That he even showed up on Long Island when facing such a serious issue at home made Mickelson more popular than ever. And his golf sent fans over the top.

His wife remained home in San Diego, instructing Mickelson to bring the U.S. Open trophy with him to Houston, where Amy would undergo a series of tests that would prove critical to the recovery. Surely, he was in no shape to contend at a tournament, much less a U.S. Open. And yet there he was, smiling and giving thumbs-up signs to his adoring gallery at every turn, ready to flood a rain-soaked course with tears from every corner. Instead, Mickelson make history with his record fifth runner-up finish, done in yet again by a balky putter. He missed a short par putt on the 15th, one from about 10 feet on the 17th, and he wound up two shots behind. There was no need to go to the 18th green to collect his silver medal; Mickelson already has enough of those.

The U.S. Open behind him, next came a part of the year that suddenly was far more important. While keeping the details private, Mickelson learned that his wife's breast cancer recovery was going as well as it could at every turn. He still skipped the British Open, then returned in time for the Bridgestone Invitational and the PGA Championship. He was never a factor at Hazeltine, and it was clear he was severely distracted. His year looked as though it would end with two victories, including his first World Golf Championship, and hope that his wife's recovery would be successful.

Only his year wasn't over. It started with a phone call from his caddie, Jim "Bones" Mackay, after the BMW Championship and another lackluster performance. Mackay called a reporter looking for the phone number of Dave Stockton, the former PGA champion revered as one of the top instructors with a putter. Mackay arranged for them to meet, and Stockton encouraged Mickelson to go back to being a "feel" putter. Mickelson put that to use immediately, winning The Tour Championship at East Lake by rallying from four shots behind Kenny Perry — and two shots behind Woods — to close with a 65 and win the final meaningful tournament of the year. "Now I feel like I've got the right track, the right direction that I wanted," Mickelson said.

But he still wasn't done. He was among the Americans who traveled to Shanghai for the HSBC Champions, which was converted to a World Golf Championship. Mickelson was paired with Woods in the final round (Mickelson had a two-shot lead) and one of them had a meltdown on the front nine at Sheshan International. This time, it was Woods. He went out in 40 and watched the coronation for Mickelson. It gave Mickelson four victories, matching his most wins in a single season. He was a solid No. 2 behind Woods, and 2010 couldn't arrive soon enough.

In between The Tour Championship and HSBC Champions, Mickelson played a quiet but starring role at Harding Park. He didn't lose a match, going 4-0-1, yet his record was remarkable considering he had three partners during the team play. Never before had Mickelson looked so capable of strapping someone to his back and taking them along for the ride. "Going into 2010, not only am I excited about it, but I have very high expectations," he said.

If the Woods-Mickelson rivalry began its renewal late in the year in the FedExCup — Woods winning the BMW Championship, Mickelson at The Tour Championship — it would be worth noting a player who took on a supporting role. Stricker finished the year at No. 3 in the World Ranking, narrowly ahead of Westwood, closer to the top than he was to the rest of the Americans. His revival first gained attention in 2006 when he went from having no status on the PGA Tour to Ryder Cup consideration. Stricker then won a stroke-play tournament for the first time in 11 years in 2007 and made his first Ryder Cup team in 2008.

Was this remarkable resurgence about to end? It sure looked that way in Palm Springs, when Stricker wasted a three-shot lead by making a triple bogey and a quadruple bogey. In Los Angeles, he had a chance to catch Mickelson until missing a short birdie putt. And he looked as though he might waste another chance at Colonial when he missed short putts down the stretch. That changed with a chip-in on the 17th, a victory in a playoff and more tears. Stricker has never won a PGA Tour event without crying in celebration, and he had more opportunities to do that. He won the John Deere Classic and capped off the best season of his career with a comeback victory at the TPC Boston to win the Deutsche Bank Championship. It was his first victory with Woods in the field, and briefly moved him to No. 2 in the world. "It's been a blast, and I want to keep riding it out," Stricker said. About the only thing he hasn't done is win a major, and based on the World Ranking over the last three years, one could make a case for Stricker being on the list of "best to have never won a major."

His presence in the same conversation with Woods and Mickelson also speaks to the FedExCup, which is gaining traction after three years of packaging big tournaments at the end of the PGA Tour season and awarding big money. The four Playoff events were won by the top three players in the World Ranking — Woods, Mickelson and Stricker — along with Heath Slocum, the stunner in the group who narrowly qualified for the 125-man

Playoffs, then won at The Barclays over a Sunday leaderboard that featured Woods, Harrington, Stricker and Ernie Els. That earned him a spot in the four majors, yet after beating a group like that, it was hard to argue that Slocum didn't earn it.

The FedExCup points had changed every year as the PGA Tour tried to figure out how to get the best players to the final round and still keep it dramatic, not an easy task with a guy like Woods around. A year after Harrington and his two majors were left out of The Tour Championship, the FedExCup went about as well as could be expected. The points were not reset until the last event at The Tour Championship, meaning Woods had the highest seed and best odds, yet four players (Woods, Stricker, Jim Furyk and Sean O'Hair) had a chance to win the $10 million bonus on the back nine at East Lake. Mickelson played too poorly — or maybe he waited too long before calling Dave Stockton — to win the cup. Even so, it led to a peculiar moment on the 18th green as Finchem handed trophies to his two best players. The checks were deposited directly, which probably was a good thing. "Let me see if I get this straight," Mickelson said. "I shot 65 and he shot (70), and he gets a check for $10 million and I get a check … no, I'm just kidding. I didn't play well in the first three events to give myself a chance."

Others had no chance at all, and there was a reason for that. Eight players from the top 15 in the World Ranking at the end of last year failed to win a single tournament in 2009. Robert Karlsson, who captured the 2008 Order of Merit on the European Tour, suffered an eye injury and wound up missing the entire summer, including three majors. Of those eight players who failed to win, he was the only one who did not have joint membership on the PGA Tour and only cares about FedEx when shipping a package. The others were Harrington, Garcia, Furyk, Els, Kim, Camilo Villegas and Vijay Singh.

The most surprising name in this group was Harrington. The Irishman was coming off the greatest season of his career, the first European in more than a century to win the Open Championship in consecutive years, and the first European ever to win consecutive majors in the same season when he captured the PGA Championship. He climbed as high as No. 3 in the World Ranking during the early part of his encore, yet there were warning signs. Harrington narrowly made the cut in the Buick Invitational, missed the next two cuts on the PGA Tour and was eliminated in the first round of the Accenture Match Play Championship. Harrington had spent some four months tackling questions about the pressure that awaited him at Augusta National. He finished the previous year with two straight majors, and he would be going for three in a row at the Masters. Was it really that far-fetched that Harrington could match Woods and make it four in a row? But by the time he drove down Magnolia Lane, the talk was about Woods returning from surgery and Harrington's poor form. It only got worse, for at one point, Harrington missed five consecutive cuts. This wasn't a case of a player becoming a multiple major champion and trying to look like one with a picture-perfect swing. Rather, winning three majors in a two-year span allowed Harrington patience as he searched for the mystery of his swing at impact. He was sliding laterally and cupping his wrist, and he tried to fix both at the same time. He found the answer, finally, right around Turnberry, with no regrets how long the search lasted.

"I have to be honest, I have spent the last two and a half years, probably three years, trying to do this," Harrington said. "The only difference is that I had not succeeded in the first two years. So in the last eight months, I kind of dived headfirst into it." Sure enough, results — scores, not trophies — soon followed. He was on the cusp of winning the Bridgestone Invitational until he became rattled by being put on the clock on the 16th hole, leading to a triple bogey. He was one shot behind at the PGA Championship until a quintuple-bogey eight on the par-three eighth hole of the final round. He had top 10s in all four FedExCup Playoff events. For all his strife, Harrington kept a happy face and wound up at No. 5 in the world, one spot lower than where he had started the season. Strange year.

Garcia's injury was not as easy for the world to see. He confided to British journalists that he was suffering from a broken heart over the breakup with Morgan Leigh Norman, the daughter of two-time major champion Greg Norman. Garcia also was afflicted with poor putting, which was far more easy to detect. Either way, he finished his last season in his 20s on a dour note. Coming off a year in which he won three times, the Spaniard went 10 consecutive tournaments without a top 10. It was a wasted opportunity, for sure, because Garcia went to the CA Championship at Doral in March with a mathematical chance to become No. 1 in the world. He would have needed a victory, and for Woods to finish 27th or worse. Garcia didn't crack the top 30 that week, and Woods won his next tournament. That was that. The one time Garcia had a chance to win was at the Wyndham Championship, and he lost a Sunday lead.

Equally mysterious were the plights of Anthony Kim and Camilo Villegas, regarded as two hip, young players who had the kind of appeal that might help during Woods's absence early in the year. Villegas went 15 straight tournaments out of the top 10, a stretch that included the four majors, while Kim opened the year with a runner-up finish in Hawaii and played the next 14 tournaments without a top 10. Few will question the work ethic of Villegas, a Colombian who is meticulous in his preparations. The same isn't true for Kim, who conceded to not working hard enough at the end of the year. His reputation, created in the Ryder Cup team room celebration, followed him in tougher times, to the point that Robert Allenby accused him of being out until 4 a.m. on the eve of their Presidents Cup singles match — and this after Kim handily defeated the Australian. Just their luck, the two were paired again at the Volvo World Match Play Championship, their next tournament, and Kim drummed him again. The young Californian was runner-up in Spain, his best finish of the year. He vowed better times.

Of the older set, Furyk did everything right except win, which explains why he had a chance to win the FedExCup on the final day despite having not won any tournament since the 2007 Canadian Open. The 46-year-old Singh showed signs of his body finally breaking down. He returned early from knee surgery and never was the same. The reigning FedExCup champion, Singh failed to win a tournament for the first time since 1996. The other drought belonged to Els, who missed consecutive cuts in a major for the first time since 1995, and failed to win a tournament anywhere in the world since 1991. At least he ended the season on a high note, closing with a 63 to finish second in the HSBC Champions. Then again, he hit into the water and made bogey on the 18th hole, or he might have won.

Another race was playing out in Shanghai that was among the most fascinating of the year, a true generational clash among players under the same management. Rory McIlroy, the 20-year-old from Holywood — Northern Ireland, not California, hence the spelling — had already won the Dubai Desert Classic and acquitted himself nicely in the majors, finishing in a tie for third at the PGA Championship along with Westwood. But it was a 63 in the final round of the HSBC Champions that put McIlroy, with his mop of brown hair and endless energy, atop the Race to Dubai going into the final two weeks of the season. He was trying to become the youngest player to lead Europe since 1979, last achieved by a dashing young Spaniard named Seve Ballesteros.

Unlike the points-driven FedExCup in America, the Race to Dubai kept it simple. It was all about money, simple as that, and it concluded with the Dubai World Championship, which replaced the Volvo Masters at Valderrama as the season-ending event in Europe. The Race to Dubai was enticing enough to attract several U.S.-based players, although only Ogilvy managed to stay in the hunt for the bonus based on his play in the majors and World Golf Championships. Other players, like Boo Weekley and John Daly, fared so poorly they didn't put in the minimum 12 events required, and while Kim qualified for the Dubai World Championship, he was so worn out by his travels that he elected not to play the finale.

The only hitch in the inaugural Race to Dubai was the economy, for it battered corporate owner LeisureCorp to the extent that the prize money was reduced 25 percent — $7.5 million for the purse at the tournament and $7.5 million from the bonus pool paid to the top players. "Not disappointed, not surprised," Westwood said. "I think it's a reality check for everybody that in times like this when there's a credit crunch, people are struggling financially, that nobody is immune. That's still a massive prize when you think about it. I think we're lucky to be playing for that kind of money."

Unlike the first two years of the FedExCup, when Woods and Singh had the prize essentially wrapped up when they arrived at the season finale, McIlroy held a slim lead over Westwood entering the final tournament, with a handful of other players having an outside chance. By the end of the week, Westwood made sure they had no chance at all. The Englishman opened with rounds of 66-69-66 to build a two-shot lead in the tournament and stay five shots clear of McIlroy, his most important competition. With everything to lose on the final day, Westwood was as good as ever. He closed with a 64 to set the course record on the Earth Course and won by six shots to become Europe's No. 1 golfer.

Westwood earned $1.25 million to finish nearly $1 million ahead of McIlroy, and along with the $1.5 million bonus, took home the largest payday in European Tour history. In a peculiar coincidence, Westwood last won Europe's money title in 2000 by holding off another player from Northern Ireland, longtime friend Darren Clarke. "Rory is only 20. I can't even remember what it was like to be 20. And he will have many more chances ahead of him to win the money list. But this is my moment."

It was the revival that brought Westwood so much emotion. He had climbed to as high as No. 4 in the world when his competition was Woods, Els and David Duval. Then came a slump into the abyss, and Westwood worked his way out of trouble and back to the top of his game. The key thought in the final round came from his caddie, Billy Foster. "Billy told me to go out and bully other people, to make them take notice of me, rather than the other way round," Westwood said.

The Race to Dubai proved to be troublesome in a freakish way to those who courted the big prize. Paul Casey won the Abu Dhabi Championship, his first PGA Tour victory at the Shell Houston Open, then captured the BMW PGA Championship at Wentworth, the flagship event in Europe, to rise to world No. 3 and lead the Race to Dubai. A month later, Casey injured his rib while at Turnberry, and the pain never left him. He withdrew from the Bridgestone Invitational, didn't start at the PGA Championship, and didn't play another round of golf until the Volvo World Match Play, at which point his hopes for the Race to Dubai were fading. Then there was Martin Kaymer, the exciting young German, who won consecutive weeks at the French Open and Scottish Open. He moved to No. 2 in the Race to Dubai behind Casey with his victory at Loch Lomond, then had the bad fortune of injuring his foot while riding a miniature motor cart. He missed 10 weeks, returned to a runner-up finish in Spain, but by then was well off the pace.

It was about time that Westwood took center stage again. He began his turnaround in 2007 with victories in Spain and England. He thrust himself into major championship contention a year later at Torrey Pines, when he stood over a 15-foot putt at the last to join Woods and Rocco Mediate in the U.S. Open playoff, only to see it turn away. Then came Turnberry, a major he viewed with mixed emotions. The nine iron he played from a pot bunker in the 18th fairway — the most club he could hit and carry the lip, which he cleared by inches — was as pure as can be. The ball barely reached the green. Looking behind him to see Watson in the fairway, Westwood figured he had to make the putt to have any chance, and he rammed the 70-footer by the cup, leading to a three-putt bogey. Alas, Watson took bogey on the 18th and Westwood missed the playoff by one shot. Even so, it was another sign that he was getting closer to an elusive major. Perspective came from his eight-year-old son who was waiting for him behind the 18th. "I was pretty deflated," Westwood said. "He said, 'Dad, you did really well. You finished third.' So there you go."

McIlroy, indeed, seems to have it all. He first made a worldwide splash at Carnoustie, reputed to be the toughest of all links courses, in the 2007 Open when he shot 68 as an 18-year-old amateur. He earned his European Tour card that year by finishing second at the Dunhill Links Championship, only his second tournament as a pro, then proved he belonged right away. Even after winning the Dubai Desert Classic for his first European Tour victory, he continued a steady march to top 10 in the world. McIlroy really turned heads in the Arizona desert when he made his World Golf Championship debut with a quarter-final loss to Ogilvy, the eventual winner of the Accenture Match Play Championship. McIlroy rose to No. 15 in the week. "This will be the worst ranking he's got for the next 10 years," Ogilvy said. "It's only going to go up because he's very impressive. He's the real deal." By year end, McIlroy was No. 9 in the world, joining Garcia as the only player at age 20 to reach the top 10 in the world.

McIlroy, however, was not the only rising star. Equally impressive was the teenager from the land of the Rising Sun — Ryo Ishikawa of Japan — who had long ago made history at age 15 when he won the Munsingwear Open KSB Cup on the Japan Golf Tour when he was a freshman in high school. That made him the youngest winner on a tour recognized by the Official World Golf Ranking. He turned pro a year later and won the mynavi ABC Championship. The teenager with rock star looks and a massive following was fifth on the money list.

They call him the "Bashful Prince," and his play got the attention of The King. Arnold Palmer offered Ishikawa an exemption to Bay Hill, and others soon followed — the Northern Trust Open at Riviera, where he made his PGA Tour debut, and the Transitions Championship outside Tampa, Florida. He brought a huge media contingent with him, mainly photographers, which caused tournaments to expand the media centers and print instructions in Japanese and English. Ogilvy is among those who saw it coming, for he played in the Taiheiyo Masters on the Japan Golf Tour years ago when he noticed a swarm of photographers coming over a hill. He asked which player they were after. "It's the kid," they told him. Ogilvy had not seen so much attention on one player since the early days of Woods, and Els heaped more praise on Ishikawa at the Presidents Cup, where the 18-year-old became the youngest player ever in those matches. "I think Ryo is one of the most exciting players in the world today," Els said.

It wasn't just hype, either. Ishikawa struggled initially away from home soil, missing the cut in the Masters, failing to qualify for the U.S. Open, missing the cut again at Turnberry while playing with Woods. He made the cut at the PGA Championship, yet continued to star in Japan. He won four times and won the Order of Merit, becoming the youngest player to ever lead a tour's money list. And with such an enormous fan base, Ishikawa had a sense of responsibility to his tour. Toward the end of an amazing year, the Bashful Prince was not the least bit shy about signing up to play. He competed 17 consecutive weeks, with seven top 10s and two victories. That included his week at Harding Park for the Presidents Cup, when he went 3-2-0. He capped off an amazing week by beating 49-year-old Kenny Perry, who has three children older than Ishikawa. He finished the year at No. 30 in the world, and it might be only a matter of time before he joins Garcia and McIlroy as the next 20-year-old to reach the top 10 in the world.

More examples of youth: Matteo Manassero of Italy became the youngest winner of the British Amateur at age 16, while the U.S. Amateur crowned 17-year-old Byeong-Hun An of South Korea as its youngest champion in history.

Golf needed all the media coverage it could get, especially in America, where a downturn in the newspaper business led to layoffs, and golf writers were among the first to go. It was noticeable at the Open Championship, when only six U.S. newspapers sent a golf writer across the Atlantic to cover golf's oldest championship — three from New York, two from Washington and *USA Today*. Not having Woods for the first two months, and not knowing when he was going to return at the end of the year, only added to the economic worries.

The PGA Tour felt the sting of a financial downturn when General Motors filed for bankruptcy, ending sponsorship of the Buick Invitational at Torrey Pines and the Buick Open. Another sponsor, U.S. Bank, pulled out of Milwaukee, while FBR said it would not renew its deal in Phoenix, reputed to have the largest gallery among PGA Tour events. Another popular stop, Hilton Head, said its title sponsor (Verizon) would not renew after the contract expired in 2010. Finchem found a replacement for the Buick Open outside Detroit with a new tournament at The Greenbrier in West Virginia, and he renewed deals for two of the World Golf Championships (Bridgestone and Accenture), along with stops in Connecticut, New Orleans and a new title sponsor for the season opener in Hawaii.

The changing economy was more obvious with two other developments. The PGA Tour joined in with other tours that sanctioned the HSBC Champions by turning it into a World Golf Championship. Even though the PGA Tour did not recognize it as an official event, it allowed Finchem his first entry into China. He later announced a new tournament in Malaysia with a $6 million prize fund. Europe, meanwhile, twice had two tournaments the same week — the JBWere Australian Masters and UBS Hong Kong Open, and the Volvo Match Play Championship in Spain was the same week as the Barclays Singapore Open.

And perhaps the biggest sign that the PGA Tour was thinking globally was its push to put golf back in the Olympics. Finchem had been lukewarm toward the idea earlier in the decade, but gave this a full-court press. He helped secure video testimony from the likes of Woods, Nicklaus, Annika Sorenstam and even Michelle Wie. They cashed in when the International Olympic Committee voted to make golf an Olympic sport in 2016, right after awarding the Summer Games to Rio de Janeiro.

No one felt the punch of the economy quite like the LPGA Tour. This was to be the year Bivens, appointed commissioner in 2005, was going to install her business plan that required tournaments to pay higher fees with hopes of helping the women get a retirement plan and higher purses. Her determination worked against her, however, as tournaments opted instead to close shop. Gone was the Hawaii swing that once started the LPGA season, with the SBS Open instead signing up to sponsor a PGA Tour event. Stanford Financial signed up to sponsor the LPGA Tour Championship until it ran into legal problems with an alleged ponzi scheme. The Kapalua Classic in Hawaii asked for a year off to find a title sponsor, only to be told by the LPGA it was being sued.

A short time later, players met at a dinner to discuss the LPGA future and decided that it was time to find a new commissioner. Under increasing pressure, Bivens resigned. "Carolyn did a lot of great things. She tried to stand up for the LPGA, which no one has done in a long time," said Juli Inkster, a member of the LPGA board and Hall of Famer. "I just think her delivery on the whole thing was not the best." By the end of the year, the

LPGA hired Michael Whan, a surprising choice with a strong background in marketing.

On the course, there were signs of a changing of the guard. Lorena Ochoa finished the year at No. 1 in the Rolex Women's World Ranking, and she won the Rolex LPGA Player of the Year. But the Mexican star failed to so much as contend in a major, and the money title went to Jiyai Shin of South Korea, who played her first year on the LPGA Tour. Neither of them factored in the majors, which again proved to be as exciting as ever.

It started with the Kraft Nabisco Championship and a dramatic finish at the par-five 18th hole that is surrounded by water. Brittany Lincicome was one shot behind when she pounded a 275-yard drive, leaving her a tough decision. The big-hitter from Florida pulled hybrid from the bag and hit it perfectly. The ball cleared the water and landed on the upper tier of the green, then curled back down the slope and settled some four feet from the cup. She made the eagle for a one-shot victory. "If I had to make anything further than that ... my hands were shaking so bad, I was almost crying," Lincicome said.

Anna Nordqvist, an unheralded Swede, won the McDonald's LPGA Championship at Bulle Rock in Maryland. More drama awaited at Saucon Valley in Pennsylvania, site of the U.S. Women's Open, where another South Korean stole the show. Eun-Hee Ji made a 20-foot birdie on the 72nd hole to capture the biggest prize in women's golf — this despite starting the final round with two bogeys on the opening four holes and a double bogey on the 10th. She closed with three birdies over the final six holes and became the third South Korean in five years to capture the U.S. Women's Open. There wasn't much drama at Royal Lytham & St. Annes for the Ricoh Women's British Open, although it was no less amazing. Catriona Matthew, the quiet but efficient Scot, birdied three straight holes on the back nine to seize control. She won her first major just 10 weeks after giving birth to her second child.

Still, it was a peculiar year. Most telling about the LPGA Tour year is that none of its major champions finished among the top 12 on the money list. Perhaps the biggest winner — for her and the tour — was Wie, the Hawaii teen who some thought had played her best golf while still in high school. Wie came into her own, first by leading the American team to victory in the Solheim Cup, then by capturing her first professional victory in Mexico. For so much angst about Wie turning pro right before her 16th birthday, she seemed to have it all — a career on the LPGA Tour, a student at Stanford, where she exchanged Twitter messages with Stanford football coach Jim Harbaugh and sweated over exams while playing in Dubai. She never looked happier.

Australia wound up having a banner year at home, starting with Woods's appearance at Kingston Heath for the JBWere Masters. The course was lined with thousands of fans throughout the week, and some abandoned their cars in traffic some two miles before the parking lot because they didn't want to miss a shot. Three weeks later, Adam Scott ended the worst slump of his career when he won the Australian Open, his first professional victory on native soil. Allenby, the only player to win the "Triple Crown" of Australian majors, was going to skip all of them until Singh pulled out of the Australian PGA Championship with an injury. Allenby took his place and won at Coolum to end his season with consecutive victories. He also won the Nedbank Challenge in South Africa.

As much as golf began to look younger, with the likes of McIlroy, Ishikawa, the U.S. and British Amateur champions and 21-year-old American Rickie Fowler nearly winning a PGA Tour event and breezing through the qualifying tournament, one of the best celebrations belonged to Arnold Palmer, who celebrated his 80th birthday in September. The King threw out the first pitch at a Pittsburgh Pirates baseball game, then retreated to his famous home course, Latrobe Country Club, for golf with friends. He later was awarded a Congressional Gold Medal. "He never stopped playing the game for the love of it, like an amateur," Dow Finsterwald told *Golf Digest* magazine. "Sure, he liked making a nice living. But he loved to play. Still does."

2. Masters Tournament

Tiger Woods was the focal point of golf from the instant he turned professional in 1996, but never more so than when he arrived at Augusta National Golf Club for the 2009 Masters Tournament. This was his first major championship since he won the 2008 U.S. Open Championship on a damaged left knee, and he required ligament reconstruction that kept him out of golf for nine months. Rarely in sports had the return of a star been awaited so intently. Woods had tested the knee in three PGA Tour events leading up to the Masters and won one of them, the Arnold Palmer Invitational. He was ready to go after his fifth green jacket.

As things turned out, Woods had to share center stage. First, there was Augusta National. It was playing like its old self, its pre-Tiger-proofing days. The other was an amiable, barrel-chested Argentine named Angel Cabrera, 39, who came from nowhere to win the 2007 U.S. Open, and who had done very little since. He also came out of nowhere to win this Masters. All it took was for Kenny Perry, everyone's Mr. Nice Guy, to fold over the last two holes and fall back into a tie with Cabrera and Chad Campbell, and then for Cabrera to win it with a par on the second playoff hole. He was the first Argentine to win the Masters — ring down the echoes of the star-crossed Roberto de Vicenzo — and it brought out the poet it him.

"This," Cabrera said, "is the Masters. A lot of magical things can happen."

First Round

Masters week arrived windy and chilly, but heated by a long dispute. The subject was the "Tiger-proofing" of Augusta National, the renovations designed to guard the course from the predations of modern technology, a fear brought on by Tiger Woods and his 12-stroke victory in 1997.

The net result: The great roars from the gallery weren't thundering over the hills and down the hollows any more, following the birdies and eagles as they shaped the great tournament.

Just before the start of the 2009 tournament, Augusta chairman Billy Payne said that rainy, windy weather was principally to blame for the higher scores in the last few Masters. And then the 96 competitors had arrived from around the world for the 2009 Masters, and in the cold and windy practice rounds, they suffered, but not in silence. The complaints kept raining down. At which Payne grinned and said, "I'll keep blaming the weather."

As if the weather gods were in Payne's corner, the weather turned sunny and warm, with a bit of wind. Through the four rounds the course gave up the greatest number of under-par scores in years — 977 birdies, well above the 919 of 2001, and 34 eagles, above the 30 of 2004. Like the swallows to Capistrano, the roars had returned to Augusta.

The good times began rolling with the first round on Thursday. Fully 38 of the 96 starters broke par, led by Chad Campbell and his seven-under-par 65, one ahead of the 66s by Hunter Mahan and Jim Furyk, who shot the only bogey-free round of the day. Furyk hit all 18 greens in regulation.

"That's probably something I'll never replicate again," he said.

Could Payne have been right about the weather? Or had the course been set up to allow for good scoring? Or a bit of both?

And the headliners? Woods matched his best-ever start with a lukewarm 70 on a burst of three birdies from the 13th and a bogey at the 18th on an eight-iron approach that ended up three rows deep behind the green. Woods was surprised by the scoring. "I didn't expect scores to be that low," he said. "The greens are fast, but they're soft, so you can go ahead and be somewhat aggressive." Phil Mickelson, a two-time Masters winner, said the course was "as easy as I've seen it." The thumbnail of his 73: "I drove it terrible. I played terrible. Putted terrible."

Cabrera hadn't won since the 2007 U.S. Open. In the young 2009 season, he missed the cut three times in six starts, and a tie for 13th was his best finish. His Masters record was equally unimpressive. In nine previous visits he missed the cut three times, and two top-10s were his best finishes. But his spirits and his prospects brightened with the opening 68 that tied him with Kenny Perry and seven others. Perry birdied four of his first six holes on the back nine and bogeyed the 16th. "I don't know if I was ever out of the fairway," he said.

Cabrera also had a great day. "I shot the ball very well all around, and my putting was with me," Cabrera said. "I made a few putts ... within 10 feet, and they gave me confidence." He made six birdies, four of them at the par-fives — Nos. 2, 8, 13 and 15 — and was slowed by bogeys at Nos. 9 and 11. As to his chances: "Well, winning a major is very difficult, but the most difficult one is the first one (the U.S. Open)," he said.

Chad Campbell, who hadn't won since 2007, set a Masters record with birdies on the first five holes. He then birdied four straight from the 12th on putts of five, 10, 12 and one feet, getting to nine under with the course-record 63 in his sights. "It entered my mind," Campbell said. Maybe a bit too soon. He bogeyed the last two holes for a 65 and one-stroke lead.

Away from the leaderboard, there came more of the stuff of the Masters legend.

As if underlining that the old Augusta National was back, three members of the senior class shot their best starting rounds since the mid-1990s. Bernhard Langer, 51, a two-time champion, shot 70, and Larry Mize, 50, also a former champion, shot 67. Greg Norman, 54, shot 70. (Langer and Norman would miss the cut, and Mize would finish tied for 30th.)

The three teen whizzes, all in their Masters debuts, kept the pot bubbling. Ireland's Rory McIlroy, 19, shot 72; Japan's Ryo Ishikawa, 17, a 73 — both professionals — and New Zealand's Danny Lee, 18, the U.S. Amateur champion, 74. Trevor Immelman, the defending champion, recovered from a four-bogey front nine and shot 71.

England's Ross Fisher, 28, in his first Masters, got to five under par, then bogeyed the last two holes and observed, "If you can walk off Augusta National disappointed with a 69, you're obviously doing something right."

It was the beginning and the end for two golfers. Dutch amateur Reinier Saxton, 21, the British Amateur champion, was nervous before his Masters debut. "I think I saw every hour of the clock," he said. He shot

75. Gary Player, 73, playing in his 52nd Masters in order to break Arnold Palmer's record, was delighted with his 78. Said Player: "I think I retired too soon."

First-Round Leaders: Chad Campbell 65, Hunter Mahan 66, Jim Furyk 66, Shingo Katayama 67, Larry Mize 67, Tim Clark 68, Angel Cabrera 68, Mike Weir 68, John Merrick 68, Todd Hamilton 68, Aaron Baddeley 68, Sean O'Hair 68, Kenny Perry 68

Second Round

Strong winds shaped play in the second round, and no one told the story better than Hunter Mahan. "In wind like this, you've got to be very committed," Mahan said, and the rest of the thought was in his score, a 75 that included a double bogey at No. 3 and a triple bogey at No. 12, where he watched a good tee shot hold up and drop into the water in front. "It's perfect conditions for head-scratching," he said. Tell it to Ireland's Padraig Harrington. He was set for a short birdie putt at the 15th when a gust blew his ball a few inches away. The penalty stroke gave him a 73.

All of which made Kenny Perry's five-under 67 amazing. It was the only bogey-free round of the day. "I just didn't have any nerves," he said. It tied him for the halfway lead at 135 with Chad Campbell, who shot 70.

"I don't think I've lost anything from my mid-20s to now," said Perry, approaching age 49. "I think I have more experience than the young guys," he added. But Perry's experience at Augusta National hadn't been all that great. In eight previous Masters, he missed the cut five times, and his best finish was a tie for 12th. For all of his power — and he did have power — only two of his five birdies came at par-five holes: No. 2, off a bunker shot to four feet, and No. 15, on a five iron to a foot. At the 18th, he hit an eight-iron approach to three feet and birdied to tie Campbell.

Campbell was off and running with four birdies over the first 10 holes, then cooled off. Almost wind-free early, he birdied the second hole from three feet, and the demanding par-three fourth, playing at 162 yards instead of 240, with a seven iron to five feet. Birdies at the eighth and 10th put him 11 under. Then came two of the toughest holes on the course, and they weren't any easier in the wind. He missed the green at the 11th and bogeyed, and he three-putted the par-three 12th for another. A bogey-birdie finish gave him a 70 and a tie with Perry. "Birdieing the last hole definitely gives me a good attitude going into tomorrow," he said.

Cabrera took third place with another 68, thanks to every golfer's miracle cure. "The thing that was missing was … my confidence," he said. "I've been working very hard to bring it back." There's nothing like a good short game to rev up a guy's confidence. Four of his five birdies were on one-putts of seven, six and 12 feet and a tap-in at the 13th. He had one bogey, a "good" one, at the par-five 15th — a bad tee shot, a bad second, then a bad club selection. So after all those bads, "a good bogey," Cabrera said.

And then there was Anthony Kim, 23, in his first Masters, running off a record 11 birdies for a 65 and a 140 total. His chances at matching or breaking the course-record 63 disappeared in two bogeys and a double bogey. In his birdie feast, he ran off four straight from No. 5, and four straight from No. 12. "I really don't know what happened," Kim said. Perhaps a dash of brutal reality helped. There was that newspaper story on a young major league baseball player killed by a drunk driver. Kim was numbed by the thought. "There's no reason to pout about a bogey or a three-putt," Kim said. "So I went out to have some fun."

Todd Hamilton, who hadn't won since the 2004 Open Championship in Britain, matched his all-time Masters low with a 70 and was in fourth place. Tim Clark, the gritty South African who did everything but win, recovered from a front-nine 40 with a 31 on the back — which included an eagle at the 13th — to sit in fifth place with a 71.

Tiger Woods had the kind of day that reduced him to one-word answers. Tough day? "Yeah." Wind difficult? "Yeah." Frustrated? "Yeah." And could he come back from a seven-stroke deficit? "Yeah." All that from a three-birdie, three-bogey 72 that left him tied for 19th. Could he come back? Well, he came from nine behind once to win, and from seven behind four times. The biggest Masters comeback after 36 holes was by Jack Burke, Jr., from nine behind to beat Ken Venturi in 1956.

Lefty Phil Mickelson turned righty to get out from behind a tree to save par at the first, then pulled back from the brink of missing the cut with a furious close — five under over the last seven holes off three birdies and an eagle at the 13th, where he hit a 345-yard drive and a nine iron to two feet. "I was thinking, walking up 12, I've done this before, I've shot five under the last seven," Mickelson said. "Let's go do it again." And he did, for a 68 to sit six off the lead.

Of the three young amigos, two didn't make the cut. New Zealand's Danny Lee, the only amateur, had a nightmarish six-putt for a Masters record nine at No. 10 and shot 81, and Japan's Ryo Ishikawa shot 77. Northern Ireland's Rory McIlroy survived, thanks to what many considered a truly generous decision by the rules committee. At the 18th, he failed to get his first shot out of the bunker, and pawed the sand with his foot. Was he smoothing it (no penalty) or kicking at it in frustration, which would constitute testing it (two-shot penalty)? He triple-bogeyed the hole for a 73 to make the cut right on the number, 145, which didn't include the two-stroke penalty he would have gotten for testing, and so he would have been disqualified. But McIlroy convinced the committee that he was smoothing the sand, and so he made the cut in his first Masters.

For all of the fireworks at the top of the leaderboard, there were some amazing duds at the bottom. The cut came in at one-over 145, and among those not making it: Ernie Els (71) missed the cut for the third straight time; 2007 Masters champion Zach Johnson, after opening with a 70, posted an 80; Stewart Cink double-bogeyed twice and shot 78, leaving with such veterans as Retief Goosen (71), Adam Scott (75) and Justin Leonard (73).

One golfer departed with gratitude — Gary Player, 73, three-time Masters champion. He said goodbye after playing in a record 52 Masters. After his opening 78, he made his way to an 83 through standing ovations, and when he reached the 18th, he dropped to one knee and clasped his hands to say thanks. "I'll never forget this as long as I live," Player said. "The Masters has meant an awful lot to me..."

Second-Round Leaders: Chad Campbell 70–135, Kenny Perry 67–135,

Angel Cabrera 68–136, Todd Hamilton 70–138, Tim Clark 71–139, Anthony Kim 65–140, Rory Sabbatini 67–140, Shingo Katayama 73–140, Jim Furyk 74–140, Sergio Garcia 67–140

Third Round

Kenny Perry and Chad Campbell started the third round tied for the lead, but three other scenarios were the focus of golf fans: Could Tiger Woods make up seven shots and win his fifth Masters? If not, could Phil Mickelson come from six behind for his third? Or could Padraig Harrington, winner of the Open Championship and PGA Championship in 2008, win his third straight major at Augusta?

Harrington got his answer like a kick in the belly in the form of a brutal nine at the par-five No. 2, one of the easiest holes on the course. It came out of a hooked tee shot, a twice-hit tree, an azalea patch and a ditch. He re-grouped and shot 73, but it was over. Hearts went out to the pleasant and unassuming Irishman. If he had birdied, as 25 others had in the round, he would have been in the hunt. He found the capacity for a little self-deprecating humor. "There wasn't too much stress after that," he said. (He would finish tied for 35th.)

Woods's chances took a body blow coming out of the starting gate. At No. 1, he hooked his tee shot into the trees and double-bogeyed. After two bogeys and a birdie, he salvaged a 70 with birdies at Nos. 13, 15 and 17 to sit at four under and trail by seven going into the final round. Could he make up that kind of ground? "It depends," he said. "If they go any lower, it's going to be hard for us to get them."

Mickelson likewise didn't make up ground. He feasted on the par-fives, birdieing all four, and that was it. But bogeys at the 10th, 11th and 16th gave him a 71 and a 212, tying with Woods at four under. Mickelson said a 64 or 65 Sunday would give him a chance. Was that realistic? someone wondered. Said Mickelson: "A lot of things happen on Sunday at Augusta."

The field was pulling itself together for a big push. Jim Furyk matched the day's-best 68 and moved to fourth place, three off the lead. "I actually didn't have the best warm-up session, but I got my rhythm on the golf course," said Furyk. Steve Stricker ran his bogey-free stretch to 35 holes in a four-birdie 68, moved up to fifth, four behind, and had broken an abysmal Masters record — five missed cuts in eight previous starts. "I'm usually not here on Saturday," he said.

Still in the hunt, five behind:

Rory Sabbatini (70): "If I can get something going on the front nine, anything's possible."

Japan's Shingo Katayama (70): "I am chasing, and I can be as aggressive as I want to."

Todd Hamilton (72): "If you're within five shots, as long as conditions aren't silly, you'll probably have a chance."

And youth will be served. Said Anthony Kim, 23, trailing by seven after a 72 that gave him a record 16 birdies in consecutive rounds: "If I get the ball rolling, I'm still not counting myself out of it."

Chad Campbell was one of 28 who parred the 11th, the toughest hole on the course (it gave up no birdies this day), but the par-three 16th knocked him out of the lead. After two birdies on the first nine, Campbell was 11 under coming to the 16th. He hit a six iron that mystified him, and his explanation was also mystifying. "It was a really great shot, but it was the wrong club," Campbell said. His ball ended up in a bunker. It took him two to get out, and he double-bogeyed. A birdie-bogey finish gave him a 72 that left him two off the lead going into the final round.

Perry touched recent history when he dropped an eight-foot birdie putt at the 10th. It put him at 12 under par — the first time anyone got to 12 under in the Masters since 2002. It also gave him the lead briefly. Then he bogeyed the 11th, three-putting from off the front of the green, then fell out of the lead with another bogey at the 12th after missing the green. He got a stroke back at the 13th, hitting a four-iron second to 25 feet and two-putting for a birdie, then parred in for a 70, and sat at 11 under. It was a tough day.

"The first two days felt like I was on vacation," Perry said. "Today felt like a job."

Cabrera's 69 made him only the 11th player in Masters history to open with three rounds in the 60s, but he started poorly, with a three-putt bogey at No. 1. "I was able to be patient and keep the concentration going," he said. He birdied Nos. 3, 8 and 10 on putts of nine, five and 15 feet. The bunker-free 14th slowed him with a bogey, and then he birdied the 15th, chipping close, and the 17th, hitting a wedge to 12 feet. Then came the big question: If he were to win this Masters, would the people back in Argentina be more excited for it or for his 2007 U.S. Open?

"For me," Cabrera said, "majors are all the same. They are all big."

Third-Round Leaders: Angel Cabrera 69–205, Kenny Perry 70–205, Chad Campbell 72–207, Jim Furyk 68–208, Steve Stricker 68–209, Rory Sabbatini 70–210, Shingo Katayama 70–210, Todd Hamilton 72–210, Tim Clark 72–211, Sean O'Hair 68–212, Ian Poulter 68–212, Lee Westwood 70–212, Tiger Woods 70–212, Phil Mickelson 71–212, Nick Watney 71–212, Stephen Ames 71–212, Hunter Mahan 71–212, Anthony Kim 72–212

Fourth Round

The Associated Press summed up the final round of the 2009 Masters with wonderful economy: "The Masters delivered the show everyone wanted and a champion no one expected."

The champion no one expected was Angel Cabrera — unexpected because he had gone quiet for almost two years, since winning the 2007 U.S. Open, and he had done nothing to recommend him in his previous nine Masters.

The show everyone wanted was the pairing of Tiger Woods and Phil Mickelson, a head-to-head battle of the top two players in the world.

Mickelson had the better of this one by a little, finishing fifth with a 67 and a nine-under 279 total, to Woods's 68–280 and a tie for sixth. Mickelson started in a fury, birdieing six of the first eight holes. "I just felt if I could shoot under par on the back nine, I would have a very good chance to win," Mickelson said. He was right, but at the wicked par-three 12th, he put his nine-iron tee shot into Rae's Creek and double-bogeyed. His bid was done for. He finished fifth, one behind Japan's Shingo Katayama (68–278).

Woods also crept close and thought he still had a chance. "Yeah, when I birdied 16, I was right there," he said. An eagle at the eighth and four birdies got him to 10 under. But bogeys at the 17th and 18th (the latter for the third time) turned him away. "I fought my swing all day," Woods said.

Masters rookie John Merrick birdied four straight from the 13th and shot the day's-best 66 and tied for sixth. "I can't wait to come back," Merrick said. Sergio Garcia didn't share his enthusiasm. He tied for 38th, still struggling after 11 Masters. "I don't like the course," he said. "It's too tricky. I don't think it's fair."

Perry and Cabrera were co-leaders from the start. Then Perry, grinding out pars on the first 11 holes, edged ahead, thanks to erratic play by Cabrera and Campbell. Then Perry dropped the gift the gods had offered, Campbell couldn't find the spark, and Cabrera needed a miracle to stay alive in the playoff. A Masters that began with a roar on Thursday ended with a whimper on Sunday.

While Perry was parring away, Cabrera birdied No. 3, then bogeyed three times through the 10th. Campbell, playing in the group ahead, had two birdies and two bogeys. The drama took a leap at the par-three 12th. Perry birdied and stayed one ahead of Campbell, who also had birdied, and went up by three on Cabrera, who parred. Perry then birdied the 15th and 16th and was 14 under. Cabrera matched those birdies, and Campbell birdied only the 15th. So Perry led both by two with two holes to play. He had a virtual lock. But it quickly came unlocked.

Unbelievably, Perry bogeyed the 17th after a bad chip and the 18th off a bunkered tee shot. That was a 71, and Cabrera (71) and Campbell (69) parred both, and the three were tied at 12-under 276. Then came Cabrera's miracle. The playoff began at the 18th. Cabrera drove into the trees on the right. He tried to hit through a slot and hit a tree, and aghast, looked back and forth. Where did it go?

In fact, the ball had caromed out into the fairway. He lifted a 70-yard wedge shot to the green, eight feet from the flag, and made the putt, matching Perry's routine par. Campbell bunkered his second, came out to four feet, two-putted for bogey and was out.

At the second playoff hole, the 10th, Perry missed the green badly and bogeyed, and Cabrera parred and had the Masters.

"I had the tournament to win, I lost the tournament," said Perry. "I may never get this opportunity ever again, but I had a lot of fun being in there. Angel hung in there. I was proud of him."

"This is something every player would want to have," Cabrera said. "It's the end of the world."

Indeed — for the Argentine who had come from poverty, a magical thing had happened at the Masters.

The Final Leaders: Angel Cabrera 71–276 (won on second hole of playoff), Kenny Perry 71–276, Chad Campbell 69–276, Shingo Katayama 68–278, Phil Mickelson 67–279, John Merrick 66–280, Steve Flesch 67–280, Tiger Woods 68–280, Steve Stricker 71–280, Hunter Mahan 69–281, Sean O'Hair 69–281, Jim Furyk 73–281

3. U.S. Open Championship

In early September of 2008, Lucas Glover was so dissatisfied and frustrated with his golf game that he took the next four months off. He had finished 105th on the PGA Tour money list and had earned less than $1 million for the first time in his four years on the circuit.

"Last year, he pretty much hit the wall and realized he needed a new attitude and to get off his own case," said Jimmy Glover, Lucas's stepfather. "He had gotten to the point where it was almost relentless."

"He was frustrated all the time. I knew he wasn't happy," said Glover's wife, Jennifer. "His work ethic was never in question. He works so hard, but he was taking things hard when he didn't see the results that he thought he should be having. When he took the time off, I knew it would be great for him."

A player who could be hard on himself learned how to be patient. It is patience that tends to be the most valuable commodity in the United States Open Championship.

Glover, who had one victory on the PGA Tour, in 2005 at Walt Disney World in Orlando, and who had missed the cut in all three of his previous U.S. Open starts, outlasted foul weather and a strong field by submitting a four-under-par 276 total, two strokes better than David Duval, Phil Mickelson and third-round leader Ricky Barnes.

This was the second U.S. Open played on the Black Course at Bethpage State Park, on Long Island in Farmingdale, New York. Tiger Woods, who won the first in 2002, shot 280 this year and tied for sixth place.

On Thursday, the first day of the championship, play was suspended because of rain after little more than three hours of play, and continued precipitation resulted in the championship being carried to a Monday finish.

Entering the week ranked No. 71 in the world, Glover, age 29, of Greenville, South Carolina, probably was overdue for the sort of breakthrough he realized at Bethpage Black. The Clemson All-American and U.S. Walker Cup player seemed on his way to a more celebrated professional career after his Disney triumph and subsequent participation on the winning U.S. Presidents Cup team in 2007.

But more consistent performance never materialized, and so Glover took that break. When Glover returned at the Bob Hope Classic in late January, he was a new man. His caddie, Don Cooper, noticed, and not simply because Glover posted a pair of top-three finishes in his 14 starts leading up to the U.S. Open, including runner-up at the Quail Hollow Championship.

"If he made a mistake, he shook it off better. He didn't stare at the ground counting blades of grass," Cooper said. "He was a lot more patient with himself, and I think that has really helped his game."

It helped him immensely at Bethpage Black. There are always interludes in the U.S. Open where a bad run can turn into a championship-killing nosedive. It is the nature of America's Open golf championship, which demands not only shot-making excellence, but also strength of mind and character.

Glover went through one of those tenuous stretches during Sunday's third round when he fell six shots behind Barnes after going four over par in a three-hole stretch. Instead of continuing the slide, however, Glover pulled himself together, and he ended the third round where he started, at seven under and one stroke behind Barnes. By the seventh hole Monday, his sixth hole of the day, Glover was in the lead. He never relinquished it, though Mickelson and Duval each had a share of the top spot briefly only to fall back.

"If I can win this one, I guess I can play all right," Glover said as he cradled the sterling silver prize. "It's going to be a big confidence boost."

First Round

Mike Weir was not hesitant to recognize the luck of the draw in the first round. The former Masters champion seized the lead with 64, six under par at Bethpage Black, the lowest score in the U.S. Open in six years and one stroke off the championship record. Eight birdies, including two to close his round, gave the left-handed Canadian a two-stroke lead over Sweden's Peter Hanson.

"It's about as easy as this course will ever play," Weir said on a sunny Friday afternoon after leading a birdie barrage unusual for a U.S. Open. "Our side definitely had a big advantage. For us to be able to play in nice conditions all day like this is huge."

Scheduled to tee off in the first round at 1:58 p.m. Thursday, Weir did not strike his first shot until close to 12 noon Friday.

The championship began at 7:00 a.m. Thursday under gloomy skies that soon gave way to rain. With the course already saturated by weeks of precipitation, any significant rain was going to threaten play. Sure enough, when the rain came, casual water soon enveloped the fairways, and the greens became so filled with water that officials were forced to suspend play at 10:15 a.m. Play was never resumed. USGA officials announced at 1:55 p.m. that play was suspended for the rest of the day.

Jeff Brehaut, Johan Edfors, Andrew Parr and Ryan Spears shared the lead at one under par, but only Brehaut had played more than four holes. He was through 11 holes. Ian Poulter and Justin Leonard, playing in the same group, were at even par through seven holes, and 2009 Masters champion Angel Cabrera had the same score through six.

Play was resumed at 7:30 a.m. Friday, but it was the second wave of players starting out, which embarked at 10 a.m., that got a chance to hit the pliable ground running — and they gleefully ran over the earlier groups.

Weir led the way, which should not have been a surprise to those who know his record. The last time a major championship was washed out in the first round was at the 2003 Masters. Weir thrived at soggy Augusta National Golf Club, due mainly to an uncanny week with his putter.

Just as in his Masters performance, Weir's scoring was largely dependent on how effectively he navigated the benign Bethpage greens, which hadn't been cut since the day before, although they had been rolled.

Weir, whose best U.S. Open finish came in 2003 when he tied for third at Olympia Fields, hit 13 greens in regulation and cleaned up nicely on the greens with only 25 putts. Beginning his round on No. 10, he had six birdies over his first 13 holes and his iron play was sharp. Five of his six birdie attempts were from two feet or less. The other was seven feet.

"I was just in one of those days where I was so focused on what I was doing, had a great feel with all my irons and just wanted to kind of let it ride," Weir said, adding, "It's nice but it doesn't mean a whole lot. It's such a long week."

Weir led a group of 25 men who shot par or better over the opening 18 holes. After Hanson and his 66, former Open Championship winners David Duval and Todd Hamilton were at 67, along with former U.S. Amateur champion Ricky Barnes. Hamilton and Barnes escaped with just one bogey each. Rocco Mediate, the runner-up to Tiger Woods in the 2008 U.S. Open, was at 68. A group at 69 included former British Amateur champion Drew Weaver, former U.S. Walker Cup player Lucas Glover and sentimental favorite Phil Mickelson.

Four times a runner-up in the U.S. Open, which shared the championship record, Mickelson was carrying an emotional burden of trying to win for wife Amy, who was home in California after being diagnosed with breast cancer the month before.

"I thought I played pretty well," Mickelson said. "I didn't putt as well as I would have liked. Even though the greens were soft and they were not as fast as normal, they were tough to make, because there were some little impressions and so forth, but still that's no excuse."

He wasn't alone among that satisfied second wave, which included 18 of the 25 players who broke par 70. The course played almost two strokes harder in the morning — averaging 74.8 strokes against 72.9 for the afternoon players.

"We got the good end of the tee times," Mickelson said. "We had some great conditions to play golf and make birdies."

Unfortunately for the reigning major championship winners, they couldn't take advantage. Cabrera bogeyed three of his last holes to come in with 74. The defending champion, Woods also finished with 74, his highest start in a major championship since a 76 in the 2006 U.S. Open. Padraig Harrington, winner of the 2008 Open Championship and PGA Championship, had 76.

First-Round Leaders: Mike Weir 64, Peter Hanson 66, David Duval 67, Todd Hamilton 67, Ricky Barnes 67, Rocco Mediate 68, Drew Weaver 69, Graeme McDowell 69, David Toms 69, Lucas Glover 69, Adam Scott 69, Phil Mickelson 69, Sean O'Hair 69

Second Round

A scoring record was produced in the second round by a player who had never finished better than 59th in the U.S. Open and by a PGA Tour rookie who had never won a professional event and had never been able to score that low in any of the previous 12 tournaments he had played this year.

The 2002 U.S. Amateur champion, Ricky Barnes took advantage of the ideal scoring conditions from the previous day and seized the lead over another upstart, Lucas Glover. Barnes followed an opening 67 with a bogey-free, five-under-par 65 — in his second round but the third day of the championship — for a 132 total to break the U.S. Open 36-hole scoring record and come in one stroke ahead of Glover, who just missed a record of his own.

If Glover could have had a 20-foot birdie putt to fall at No. 9, his last hole of the round, he would have tied the all-time U.S. Open record of 63. Instead, he settled for a share of the course record set by Mike Weir in the first round.

"I thought about it," said Glover, who had one PGA Tour title to his credit, when asked about the record. "Then I (chickened) out and left it short. But, yeah, I had a good read, right-edge read. (I thought it) would be pretty cool, but I wasn't going to run it five feet past either."

Barnes fashioned a piece of history by covering the final nine holes of his second round in a brilliant shade of red on Saturday morning, going three under par, including a 10-foot birdie at the par-three eighth to take the lead. His eight-under 132 score broke the 36-hole mark set in 2003 by Vijay Singh and Jim Furyk at Olympia Fields and that Glover tied earlier Saturday when he coupled his bogey-free 64 with his first-round 69.

Hitting 31 of 36 greens, Barnes posted his first sub-70 scores in 12 U.S. Open rounds. He had missed the cut in three of his four previous appearances, and he tied for 59th in the other. On the PGA Tour this year, Barnes had missed six of 12 cuts, and his best finish had been a tie for 47th the previous week in Memphis.

"Could I have predicted I would shoot 132? No. Did I know I had it in me? Yes," Barnes said. "I'm starting to play well."

After Glover, the field was spread out. Weir was another stroke back thanks to a scrambling 70 that left him at 134. Another three shots back at 137 were three players, including David Duval, the former Open Championship winner ranked No. 882 in the world, who backed up his opening 67 with 70. Sweden's Peter Hanson, who shot 71, and Japan's Azuma Yano, who posted 65, joined Duval.

Not yet fully in the mix near the top of the leaderboard were two favorites and highest-ranking players in the world. No. 2 Phil Mickelson was at one-under 139 after his 70, while world No. 1 Tiger Woods bogeyed the ninth hole, his final hole of the round, for 69 to make the cut with a stroke to spare at 143, which left him 11 strokes behind Barnes.

"Unfortunately, my score doesn't reflect how I've been playing," Woods said. Only one player in U.S. Open history, Lou Graham, had ever overcome a deficit so large, rallying to catch John Mahaffey in the 1975 championship at Medinah before winning in a playoff.

"It is what it is. But you never know. I've got 36 more holes over the next probably three days," Woods said, drawing laughs from the media over his estimate of the days remaining. "It's one of those things where if I keep plugging along just like any U.S. Open, just keep plugging along, make a birdie here and there, and we'll see where it ends up."

While Woods managed to gather himself enough to stay in the championship, some other prominent names weren't as fortunate. The current Open Championship and PGA Championship winner, Padraig Harrington, was the biggest name in that group. Harrington shot his second six-over 76 and missed the cut by eight strokes. Others who missed the cut included two-time U.S. Open champion Ernie Els, who shot 155, and former PGA champion David Toms at 145.

On the other hand, senior player Fred Funk, just days after his 53rd birthday, birdied the final hole to make the cut with 74–144. That birdie eliminated 11 players at five over par, because they were no longer within 10 strokes of the lead. Funk wasn't the only Champions Tour player sticking around. Tom Lehman, a former U.S. Open runner-up, also advanced at 144, but reigning U.S. Senior Open champion Eduardo Romero was sent packing with 147.

Three of the 15 amateurs advanced, led by Canadian Nick Taylor, playing in his second U.S. Open. Taylor, a quarterfinalist at the 2007 U.S. Amateur, fired a five-under 65, matching the U.S. Open record for low score by an amateur. James McHale set the mark in 1947 at St. Louis Country Club and Jim Simons tied it in 1971 at Merion.

"I knew I had some birdies in me," said Taylor, age 21, who tied for seventh at 138. Former British Amateur champion Drew Weaver shot 71 to finish at 141, and Kyle Stanley shot 74 to come in on the number at 144.

Once again, the subject of the draw was a prominent topic. Golfers who never had to venture on the golf course Thursday continued to flourish as they got right back out Friday afternoon and completed their rounds Saturday morning, while Woods and others had to wait. More rain was forecast for Saturday but it didn't come until later, and the second round made it into the books.

Lee Westwood was the only golfer from the original Thursday morning wave to break into the top 10 after 36 holes. He shot 66 to be at 138, tied for seventh.

Second-Round Leaders: Ricky Barnes 65–132, Lucas Glover 64–133, Mike Weir 70–134, Azuma Yano 65–137, David Duval 70–137, Peter Hanson 71–137, Lee Westwood 66–138, Nick Taylor 65–138, Sean O'Hair 69–138, Ross Fisher 68–138, Todd Hamilton 71–138

Third Round

Ricky Barnes, who had never led a PGA Tour event after any round, seemed unfazed by the pressure of leading a U.S. Open when the third round finally got into full swing on Sunday afternoon.

The third round had been postponed into Sunday after rain clouds opened over Bethpage Black in the early evening Saturday, with another inch of precipitation.

Barnes got off to a fast start with a birdie and an eagle on the first four holes. When he sank a 20-foot eagle putt at the par-five fourth hole, Barnes jumped to 11 under par for the championship and established a three-shot lead over Lucas Glover. He became just the fourth player in U.S. Open history to reach double digits under par, joining Gil Morgan at Pebble Beach in 1992, Tiger Woods at Pebble Beach in 2000 and Jim Furyk at Olympia Fields in 2003. Woods and Furyk went on to win. Only Woods remained in double digits until the end.

With bogeys on two of his last four holes, Barnes shot an even-par 70 for a 202 total, eight under par, and backed up to where he started — one ahead of Glover, who also shot 70. But Barnes had kept himself out front with one round to play, stealing headlines from the stars in the field and the dreary skies overhead.

"I'm in a good place," said Barnes, who not only held his first 54-hole lead but was enjoying his third professional tournament in which he was as close as 10 strokes with 18 holes to play. "I'm going to take my shoes off and say I shot even par (in the third round) at the Open with the lead, and that's pretty good."

Near the midpoint of the round, Barnes led Glover and Mike Weir by six strokes and seemed to be cruising. But Glover, after making two bogeys and a double bogey in a three-hole stretch ending at the eighth, somehow gathered himself and shot an inward 32 to return the gap to a single stroke entering the final round.

Glover turned the tide with two solid shots at the ninth, then he went on a tear starting with a five-iron shot to within three feet at the 10th — which he called "a bonus," and it was given that the 508-yard par-four was ranked the hardest on the course in the third round. Short irons at the 11th and 16th holes also yielded short birdie tries that he converted. "I felt like I had to attack to get back in it," said Glover, who through three rounds had played the best on the inward nine at six under par. "I reeled it back in and got some momentum."

Momentum was scarce at Bethpage Black. After the second round ended around 4 p.m. Saturday, with 60 players making the cut at four-over 144, the third round began at 5:30 p.m. with groups of two off both tees. Play was suspended at 6:55 p.m. when anticipated heavy rains finally arrived.

After steady overnight rain, the resumption of the championship was further delayed Sunday from 7:30 a.m. to 11:54 a.m., and that meant there was no chance of a Father's Day finish. The U.S. Open was going to be forced into a regulation Monday completion for just the third time in its history, the first since 1983, when Larry Nelson defeated Tom Watson at Oakmont.

Tiger Woods joked that he had lost track of what day it was. "I think it is more mentally challenging," he said. "Physically, you're fine. You can get back up. That's not a problem. You have plenty of time. You know, it's just mentally gearing up, gearing down, gearing up, gearing down."

Woods covered his last 11 holes of the third round in three under par for 68 to complete 54 holes at one-over 211, but his bid for back-to-back U.S. Open titles was growing darker. He had never come from behind in any of his 14 major victories, but more daunting was that he trailed Barnes by nine strokes and there were 14 players ahead of him on the leaderboard.

David Duval, with 70, and England's Ross Fisher, after 69, were tied for third place at three-under 207 after each birdied the last hole. The group tied for fifth at two-under 208 featured former Masters champions and left-handers Mike Weir and Phil Mickelson, along with Hunter Mahan. Weir slid to 74, but Mickelson birdied four of his last six holes to post a spirited 69, and Mahan shot 68. Two-time U.S. Open champion Retief Goosen shot his second consecutive 68 to get in at 209 along with three others: Todd Hamilton, Sean O'Hair and Bubba Watson.

Glover was asked if the final round was shaping up as a two-man race.

"No. There's too many great players, and the golf course is too good," Glover said. "You know, somebody is going to make a run. Greens are still soft and they are rolling perfect. So I fully expect a handful of guys to make a run. You have Phil sitting there and everybody that's playing is a great player, so, no, you can't think that at all."

How right he would be.

Third-Round Leaders: Ricky Barnes 70–202, Lucas Glover 70–203, David Duval 70–207, Ross Fisher 69–207, Mike Weir 74–208, Hunter Mahan 68–208, Phil Mickelson 69–208, Sean O'Hair 71–209, Retief Goosen 68–209, Bubba Watson 67–209, Todd Hamilton 71–209

Fourth Round

Lucas Glover, whose patience finally caught up to his potential, emerged from a scramble of players in the fourth round of the U.S. Open to capture his first major championship and just his second professional victory. He did it by converting a five-foot birdie putt at the 70th hole — his only birdie of the final round — to go in front, and then he registered two solid pars to close out the weather-plagued championship.

"I'm honored and gratified to have won. It's pretty sweet," said Glover, whose three-under-par 67 and four-under 276 total provided a two-stroke victory and all the validation he wanted to assume. "I dreamed about it as a kid and pulled it off and executed some pretty good golf shots. Here I stand."

The last man standing as it turned out.

No fewer than seven players, including Phil Mickelson, David Duval and defending champion Tiger Woods, were in the mix in the final 90 minutes. But Glover, whose only other victory came in 2005 at Walt Disney World in Orlando, was in the end clutching the silver trophy that bore the names of Bob Jones, Byron Nelson, Ben Hogan, Arnold Palmer and Jack Nicklaus, among many other greats in the game's history.

"It's an honor to be on the trophy with names such as that. I hope I don't downgrade it or anything with my name on there," Glover said.

The outcome in no way diminished the three runners-up he vanquished. Mickelson, Duval and Ricky Barnes, who submitted two-under 278 totals, could leave with something less tangible but perhaps more meaningful than their second-place medals.

Barnes, age 28, the former U.S. Amateur champion who had led the second and third rounds, opened the door to the wild scramble when he bogeyed five of his first eight holes in the final round, including four straight starting at the fifth hole. But Barnes steadied himself and played the final six holes in one under par despite slipping to 76.

"It was a great week," Barnes said. "If you told me I would have been two under, if you would have told me I was second, bridesmaid isn't too bad," Barnes said. "When you are right there, it's a tough one to swallow, but I would say a lot more good came out of this week than bad."

Duval, once the top-ranked player who seemed destined never to find his form again, responded to a disastrous triple bogey early in the round with perhaps the gutsiest golf anyone displayed. He played on to four birdies and a share of the lead with three holes to go before settling for 71 and his best finish since winning the 2001 Open Championship at Royal Lytham & St. Annes.

"It's what I want. It may be arrogance, but it's where I feel I belong," said the 37-year-old Duval.

Then there was Mickelson. No one could possibly know the emotional stress under which he was operating all week. His wife, Amy, was due to have surgery for breast cancer after a family vacation that was postponed by the championship spilling into Monday.

Just as he put one hand on the trophy with an inspirational surge, Mickelson lost the grip yet again with two bogeys to finish with 70. But his perspective remained intact, even as he collected his fifth runner-up finish, breaking the record he shared with Jones, Palmer, Nicklaus and Sam Snead.

"(It was) kind of an emotional four days or five days, a lot of ups and downs," Mickelson said "Certainly, I'm disappointed, but now that it's over, I've got more important things going on."

At the turn, Glover was four under par, one stroke ahead of Barnes and two ahead of Mickelson, Ross Fisher and Hunter Mahan. Woods was around even par, not out of it until he suffered a bogey at the 15th. His closing 69 gave him even-par 280, tied with Mahan and Soren Hansen for sixth place.

Duval was the one who appeared done. He bogeyed the first hole late Sunday, then had a terrible break Monday morning on his first swing at the par-three third hole. His tee shot came up short and buried under the lip of a bunker, resulting in a triple bogey. He was then seven shots behind, but he didn't quit.

The last nine holes were filled with key putts. Mickelson saved par at the 10th, then he struck, holing a 40-footer for birdie at the 12th followed by a six iron from 212 yards to within three feet to set up an eagle at the 550-yard, par-five 13th. When he holed it, Mickelson was tied for the lead with Glover, two holes behind at four under par.

Before Mickelson's putt, Fisher, playing in just his second U.S. Open, holed a 10-footer for his own eagle, set up by a three iron from 240 yards, to jump to three under par. Barnes, once flying so high at 11 under par, took himself out of the running when he bogeyed the 11th and 12th holes. That gave him seven bogeys in 12 holes and 11 bogeys in a stretch of 21 holes. A two-putt birdie at the 13th returned him to two under, where he remained.

It looked like it was coming down to Glover and Mickelson. Lefty tripped first when he three-putted from 25 feet at the 15th. Glover, however, also took three putts, and suddenly the two men had company. Amazingly, it was Duval. He hit a wedge close to the hole at the par-three 14th to ignite a run of three straight birdies. He hit a six iron to 14 feet at the 15th and capped the run with an eight-iron approach to the 16th, then a downhill putt from eight feet that brought him a share of the lead.

"I don't quit. I truly believed at that point I was going to win the championship," Duval said.

Mickelson had his own designs until his fortunes turned sour again. A five-iron shot on the par-three 17th landed in thick grass short of the green, he chipped to five feet and missed the par attempt. It was the fourth time he had at least a share of the lead in the U.S. Open with two holes to go and lost the lead. Minutes later, Duval was guilty of the same mistake, missing the green short and two-putting for bogey.

Just before that, Glover was sizing up a four-foot birdie putt at the 16th that was on the same line as Duval's. He had hit a drive in the fairway and then struck an eight iron from 173 yards. The putt was true, and Glover's lead was now two strokes.

"I couldn't have had an easier putt. It was straight and downhill," Glover said. "It was all you could ask for under pressure."

But the pressure was still building. "I'd be lying to say I wasn't nervous," Glover said. "I had the knees knocking pretty good on 16, 17 and 18."

Glover was up to the challenge, however, playing the last two holes impeccably to close out the two-stroke victory.

The Final Leaders: Lucas Glover 73–276, Phil Mickelson 70–278, David Duval 71–278, Ricky Barnes 76–278, Ross Fisher 72–279, Tiger Woods 69–280, Soren Hansen 69–280, Hunter Mahan 72–280, Henrik Stenson 68–281, Rory McIlroy 68–282, Matt Bettencourt 69–282, Sergio Garcia 70–282, Ryan Moore 71–282, Stephen Ames 72–282, Mike Weir 74–282

4. The Open Championship

This was an Open Championship with as much drama as Turnberry's first in 1977. There were more challengers involved this time than then, when Tom Watson and Jack Nicklaus dueled alone. Six players held the lead during the final afternoon, and Stewart Cink was the sixth and last of them. Timing was everything. But not before Watson, as 32 years earlier, had birdied the 71st hole to go one up with one to play.

Back in 1977, Nicklaus birdied the last hole and Watson followed him in. Here it was Cink who claimed a 72nd hole birdie, from 16 feet, while others — first Chris Wood, then Lee Westwood, and finally Watson — bogeyed it. "It will be the most crucial putt I've ever struck in my life," Cink said.

The putt got Cink into a four-hole playoff with Watson, and Cink took control then, finishing six strokes ahead, by 14 strokes to Watson's 20, when they completed the 18th hole for the second time. The playoff was uncomfortable to watch, the deflation following Watson's dribbled attempt at an eight-foot, championship-winning putt at the 72nd hole was as acute as most observers had ever experienced.

While Watson, who at the age of 59 might have tied Harry Vardon's record with a sixth Open victory, proved himself as a champion of links golf for all years, the champion golfer for this year was the 36-year-old Cink.

"It would have been a hell of a story, wouldn't it?" Watson said. "It wasn't to be. And, yes, it's a great disappointment. It tears at your gut, as it has always torn at my gut. It's not easy to take. I put myself into position to win and didn't do it on the last hole. I knew I was playing well coming in and I could have dreamed it, yes. And it was almost. Almost. The dream almost came true."

Watson had marched down the 18th fairway to the acclaim of the gallery with victory in sight. Doing the same walk an hour later was even more emotional, the reception from the crowd even more heartfelt. "The memories are hard to forget," he said. "Coming up in the amphitheater of the crowd and have them cheer you on like they do here for me. As I've said before, the feeling is mutual but that warmth makes you feel human. It makes you feel so good. I'll take those memories from this week and sense of spirituality. There was something out there helping me along. I still believe that. It's Turnberry."

Cink also received a generous ovation when he removed his cap to salute the crowd, smiled and accepted the Claret Jug with such evident joy. "I'm filled with pride and honor," he said. "Having outlasted the field on this golf course with the way the weather beat us down the last three days, it's something I'll never forget. It's great to be the one left."

"And to play against Tom Watson in the playoff, it was with mixed emotions, to be honest. I have watched him with such admiration this week. And going way back, I could never have dreamed of going head-to-head against Tom Watson in a playoff for a major championship. That would be beyond even my mind's imaginative capabilities. But then after playing with him in practice at the Masters this year, I would have told you I really don't ever want to have to go head-to-head against him because he hits it so well. The same Tom Watson that won this tournament in 1977 showed up here this week and he just about did it. He beat everybody but one guy. And it was really special."

First Round

On a sunny and calm day at Turnberry this was about as joyful a start to the Open as could be imagined. Tom Watson was dominating the challenge once again. After opening with a 65, Watson said: "There was something slightly spiritual about today. I feel inspired playing here again."

No one in the first half of the draw, which included world No. 1 Tiger Woods, could match Watson, and so Watson's name was at the top of the leaderboard for most of the afternoon. Finally 2003 champion Ben Curtis, with four birdies in the last six holes, and Japan's Kenichi Kuboya joined Watson with their 65s, then shortly before 7 p.m., Miguel Angel Jimenez posted the day's best score of 64 after birdies at the last two holes.

Even Jimenez recognized that his round was not the main story of the day. "What a legend," Jimenez said of Watson. "He was a legend before, he was a legend today, and he will be a legend tomorrow. We have to feel proud to play with him."

The 65 was a fitting number for Watson. It was the fourth time he had that score in four Opens here. He did so in the second round of 1994, when he had another run at the title but was let down by his putting, and, of course, in the third and fourth rounds in 1977, when he defeated Jack Nicklaus by one stroke in what will always be known as the Duel in the Sun.

Watson had also played in two Senior Opens at Turnberry, winning in 2003. "This is my sixth championship here and you do get to know the course," he said. "Experience helps. There are certain shots out here that the kids are unfamiliar with, that people who haven't played here before are unfamiliar with."

Newcomers to Turnberry, which had not hosted the Open since 1994, included Woods and double defending champion Padraig Harrington.

Watson showed all of his old expertise in playing his way around the links. He drove the ball superbly, hit his irons as crisply as ever, and gave anyone who had missed his supremacy of links golf — he won five Opens within nine years between 1975 and 1983 — a masterful lesson in how golf can be an art rather than being reduced to the science of modern engineering.

At the first hole Watson hit a nine iron to eight feet and holed the putt for a birdie. He missed from 12 feet at the second but made a putt from 20 feet at the third to go two under par. "She was defenseless today," Watson said of the course. "It gave you some opportunities with the lack of wind. After the practice rounds I felt good about the way I was hitting the ball and the first few holes were a nice continuation of that. I hit a lot of quality shots."

He did not drop a shot to par all day. He went to the turn in 33 and then hit a six iron to 12 feet at the 10th and holed from eight feet at the 12th for birdies. He saved par from a bunker at the 14th and then made two good putts at the last two holes. He was successful from eight feet for his fifth birdie at the 17th and then saved par from six feet at the 18th hole.

Playing an hour and a half behind Watson, Stewart Cink came in with 66 which included twos at both the fourth and sixth holes as well as a second bogey of the day at the 18th. No one managed fewer than his 26 putts, a welcome boost for his confidence after ditching the long putter a couple of months earlier. Cink had prepared for the Open with a trip to Ireland the previous week. The only other time he had made such preparation was 2007, when he tied for sixth at Carnoustie.

Tied for fifth with Cink after their 66s was John Senden, an Australian based in Dallas who was the seventh reserve and only got in the championship on Tuesday. He parred his first 12 holes and then collected four birdies in the last six holes. He was the first to post 66 and was joined by Steve Stricker, Camilo Villegas, who birdied the last three holes, and Mathew Goggin, another American-based Australian.

But all eyes on the opening morning were on the 9:09 a.m. group of Woods, Lee Westwood and Ryo Ishikawa, the 17-year-old Japanese sensation. A great cavalcade of officials, photographers and reporters went off with them. If Westwood felt any lack of attention alongside two players whose every move was being monitored in minute detail, then three birdies in the first three holes put that right. Westwood shot 68 which might have been better, while Woods shot 71 which could have been worse. He had to continually save himself after going offline, usually to the right. Ishikawa matched Westwood with 68.

Harrington got off to a modest start with 69.

Jimenez was out in 31 and built on that with birdies at the 17th and 18th, where he holed from over 50 feet. The popular Spaniard got a rousing reception at the last hole, a sign there were no hard feelings about him displacing Watson at the top of the leaderboard. "I like very much the Scottish people, the British people," Jimenez said. "They are understanding this sport very well. They appreciate what we are doing. It feels like home."

First-Round Leaders: Miguel Angel Jimenez 64, Tom Watson 65, Ben Curtis 65, Kenichi Kuboya 65, John Senden 66, Steve Stricker 66, Camilo Villegas 66, Stewart Cink 66, Mathew Goggin 66

Second Round

After the calm of Thursday, Friday dawned rainy and cool, with the wind picking up and coming from the north. Suddenly, the examination for the Open Championship was even more severe in the second round.

Ben Curtis, after a birdie at the first hole to tie for the lead, then dropped eight strokes in the next eight holes to be out in 42. Ian Poulter, Paul Casey and Geoff Ogilvy all went to the turn in 41. Miguel Angel Jimenez, the first-round leader, bogeyed the second, third, fourth and sixth holes. During the first round, the front nine was the marginally easier of the two. On Friday it played over a stroke harder than the second nine.

Two players with the initials TW both had fives beside their names at the end of the day. One was five under par and sharing the lead, the other was five over and sharing a departure with all who missed the cut. Surprisingly, it was world No. 1 Tiger Woods who was packing his bags, while Tom Watson was once more on top of the leaderboard.

Besides Watson, the other surprise leader was Steve Marino, an American on his first visit to the British Isles. Including practice days, Marino had played four rounds of links golf in his life, while Woods was missing the cut for the first time in 14 appearances (two as an amateur) in the Open.

Watson shot even-par 70 for his 135 total while Marino shot 68. Mark Calcavecchia was in third place at 136 following his 69.

Peter Dawson, the Chief Executive of the R&A, was intent at Turnberry on putting more of an emphasis on driving the ball well. After two rounds it was obvious this requirement, not always a high priority on tour courses, was essential for any potential Open contender.

"The one thing I'm doing very well is putting the ball in the fairway," Watson said. "I'm getting the ball in play off the tee and that's what you have to do here. The players that are struggling are the people that are not finding the fairway. I've played links golf when I'm not playing well and it's a struggle. You add a little wind like we had today and it's even more of a struggle."

Over the two rounds, Watson had found 21 of the 28 fairways and was ranked ninth in that category, which was led by Ross Fisher with 24 fairways. Fisher, who shot 68 with three birdies in a row from the 15th, was tied for fourth place at 137 with Jimenez, Kenichi Kuboya, Retief Goosen and Vijay Singh.

Woods, on the other hand, had hit only 15 fairways, which had a lot to do with him being tied for 74th place after rounds of 71 and 74, and one stroke outside the cut line, which fell at four over par. Since Woods was playing alongside Lee Westwood, the contrast was sharp. Westwood was playing steady golf and his 70 left him in good shape at 138, two under. He was tied for ninth with Stewart Cink, J.B. Holmes, James Kingston and Mathew Goggin.

For the second year running, the Open would be without the world No. 1 player on the weekend. The man who benefited in 2008, when Woods had his knee operation, was Padraig Harrington, winning for the second successive time. A hat-trick of titles became highly unlikely when the Irishman struggled to 74 and was three over par at 143. Paul Casey, who entered the championship with high expectations as the world No. 3, had 76 and at 144 only just squeezed through.

Among those joining Woods in an early exit were Adam Scott, Anthony Kim and David Duval, who could not repeat his form from the U.S. Open, where he was a runner-up. Golf's newest knight, Sir Nick Faldo, also missed the cut, along with 2008 Open runner-up Greg Norman, Geoff Ogilvy and Ian Poulter.

Ben Curtis was the first of those high up on the first day to play on Friday and went from tied for second to missing the cut after 80, 15 strokes higher than on Thursday. Jimenez managed to steady himself on the back nine and came home in 34 to be three under. Kuboya began well on Friday with birdies on the first and fourth holes and briefly led by two strokes. He finished with 72 to be three under.

Fisher, who finished fifth in the U.S. Open, was continuing his good form at Turnberry despite the fact his wife, Jo, was overdue with their first child. He was prepared to leave at any minute if his wife went into labor.

The clubhouse leader virtually all day after going out in the fourth group was Marino, age 29, who was in his third season on the PGA Tour. No one could match Marino's 22 putts of the round, but at times he didn't even need to get the putter out of his bag. At the third, after finding the rough off the tee, he holed out a wedge shot for a birdie, and at the short sixth, he holed out from a bunker short of the green for a two. He birdied the fifth, the hardest hole of the day, and made eagle-three on the 17th with a putt from 20 feet.

Watson followed his 65 with 70 to remain at five under. "Lady Turnberry took her gloves off today," he said. "She had some teeth." Although he birdied the first and the ninth, Watson made five bogeys going out but was four under par for the last 11 holes as he came home in 32, matching the best last nine of day.

Second-Round Leaders: Steve Marino 68–135, Tom Watson 70–135, Mark Calcavecchia 69–136, Ross Fisher 68–137, Retief Goosen 70–137, Miguel Angel Jimenez 73–137, Kenichi Kuboya 72–137, Vijay Singh 70–137, J.B. Holmes 70–138, James Kingston 71–138, Lee Westwood 70–138, Stewart Cink 72–138, Mathew Goggin 72–138

Third Round

Could Tom Watson really do it? There were a lot more believers at the end of the third round when the 59-year-old Watson took sole possession of the lead and was only 18 holes away from a record-equaling sixth Open title.

As the round unfolded, challengers came and fell back again while Watson slipped behind then rallied, birdieing the 16th and 17th holes. On another difficult day for scoring, Watson's 71 left him at four-under-par 206 and one stroke ahead of Mathew Goggin, an Australian yet to win in Europe or America, and England's Ross Fisher, who had become another sentimental favorite due to the dilemma of his wife about to give birth. One stroke further behind were Retief Goosen, a two-time former U.S. Open champion, and England's Lee Westwood.

Only seven players were left under par — there had been 50 on the first day — and at one under were Jim Furyk, the 2003 U.S. Open champion, and Stewart Cink, who had won at the World Golf Championships level, but no higher. At even-par 210 were Thongchai Jaidee and Bryce Molder, a 30-year-old former American Walker Cup player, who returned the best score of the day, a 67 with five birdies after two early bogeys. Molder jumped from a tie for 53rd place to a tie for eighth.

There were only four rounds of 69, moving those players up the leaderboard, particularly Goggin, who made the biggest move within the top 10. Going in the opposite direction were Steve Marino, the co-leader after 36 holes, who had a 76 to fall into a tie for 10th, and Mark Calcavecchia, whose 77 dropped the former Open champion to a tie for 27th.

Watson and Marino did not tee off until 3 p.m., and Watson made productive use of the morning by watching the television coverage to get a feel for the course conditions. Marino bogeyed the second hole to leave

Watson alone in the lead, and the younger American proceeded to drop five shots in four holes before rallying with an eagle on the seventh.

Watson made five straight pars before bogeying the sixth. Goosen was briefly tied for the lead but only while in the process of taking a double-bogey at the par-five seventh. Watson got back to five under with a four at the seventh, but three-putted from the back of the ninth green and also three-putted at the 12th. Suddenly Watson was tied with Goggin, who had just birdied the 17th to get to under par for the round and to three under par for the championship. He set the clubhouse lead at 207.

"The turning point of the round was the eighth, where I looked like making a double after birdieing the seventh," Goggin said. "But I knocked in a good putt there for a bogey and played the last 10 holes really solid."

In the pairing ahead of Goggin were Cink and Westwood. The American was prepared for the Englishman to get the crowd's attention, and Westwood rewarded the faithful with a superb four-iron shot at the 12th hole which ran up to less than three feet from the hole. The putt went in, and Westwood was back to even par for the round, having earlier bogeyed the third hole. He made a birdie-four with two putts from just off the green to get to three under and a tie for lead. A bogey on the last hole left him with a 70 and 208 total.

Westwood believed he was ready to win a major championship. "I've put myself in position a few times and I've learned from those experiences," he said.

Cink was still flying under the radar. He did have a scare to report, however. "Pretty sure I've got swine flu," Cink reported on Twitter. "I thought if you like BBQ as much as I do that your antibodies would be built up against it." It turned out he did not have swine flu but he was not feeling great. "It was a worry," he said. "I was feeling really bad and I've been on medication all week."

He had his second successive round over par, but a 71 left him at one under and still in touch. He bogeyed the fifth and seventh holes, but got a two at the 11th and finished with seven fours, including a bogey at the 15th and a birdie at the 17th.

"It's funny over here," Cink said. "The weather dictates what your score is. I feel like I played the same every day. I've hit the ball well and kept it in play and avoided the bunkers for the most part. I shot four under the first day then shot over par the next two. A little bit of wind and it gets a lot trickier.

"But links golf and I really like each other. These weather conditions are absolutely ideal for this kind of golf. Nothing goofy, just the right amount of wind to challenge everybody and see what everybody has. It was a test out there. Everybody stumbles and it's a question of how much you picked yourself up. It wasn't a day where I got everything out of the round, but I think there is still hope."

Back at the 14th, Watson holed a 20-footer for par, but then found the back bunker at the 15th and dropped a shot to fall out of the lead. But at the 16th, where he had holed an outrageous putt on Friday, he did so again, making a 40-footer before claiming a four at the 17th to get back into the lead by one.

Marino was not having such a good time with sixes at the 15th and 16th before closing with two birdies, but it was quite an experience. "It was a combination of the good, the bad and the ugly," he said. "But it was awesome playing with Tom. I told him he could be the King of Scotland. These people love him. It was super special to watch him and, you know, there's a reason he has won five Claret Jugs."

If Watson could make it six, he would equal a record set by Harry Vardon back in 1914.

"I don't know what is going to happen," Watson said. "But I do know one thing. I feel good about what I did today. I feel good about my game plan, the number of birdies and bogeys I can make. I didn't feel real nervous out there. I felt serene. Even though I messed up a couple of times, it didn't bother me. The crowd was wonderful on every tee, every green, and the feeling is mutual. So, who knows, it might happen."

Third-Round Leaders: Tom Watson 71–206, Mathew Goggin 69–207, Ross Fisher 70–207, Lee Westwood 70–208, Retief Goosen 71–208, Jim Furyk 70–209, Stewart Cink 71–209, Bryce Molder 67–210, Thongchai Jaidee 69–210, Richard S. Johnson 69–211, Boo Weekley 72–211, Angel Cabrera 72–211, Steve Marino 76–211

Fourth Round

Ross Fisher took the early spotlight in the fourth round. He holed from 18 feet for a birdie at the first hole and chipped in for another birdie at the second. With Tom Watson dropping a shot at the first, missing the green with a six iron, chipping then taking two putts from 10 feet, Fisher now led the Open by two strokes. He missed the green on the fourth and dropped a shot, but with Watson making a bogey at the third, missing the green again, this time with a five iron, Fisher was still two strokes clear.

Then came Fisher's disaster at the fifth. His drive at the fifth went right and he barely moved the ball with his second shot. His third, still from the rough, went over the fairway and now things were going from bad to worse. He had to take an unplayable and eventually holed out for an eight, a quadruple bogey. Two more bogeys followed at the seventh and eighth holes. Even though he finished with 10 straight pars for a 75, Fisher was out of the picture with a two-over 282.

"It's a shame but I fought all the way," Fisher said. "It was just one bad swing on the fifth. It's been a great week and I'm just glad I was here for the four days. Fingers crossed, in a couple of days I'll become a dad."

The lead was now back to Watson and Chris Wood. The 21-year-old from Bristol, in his rookie season on the European Tour, had rounds of 70, 70, and 72 and was now going superbly. He eagled the seventh from 12 feet and birdied the ninth from 10 feet to get under par for the championship and holed from 25 feet for a three at the 10th. As he walked off the 12th green he was tied for the lead, although he was not sure of this because his caddie had told him not to look at the leaderboards.

Wood promptly dropped shots at the 13th and 14th holes and it was now Westwood who made his charge. Playing alongside Fisher, Westwood had bogeyed the fifth while Fisher was having his troubles. Then Westwood holed from 20 feet for a two at the sixth, and hit a three iron to 15 feet at the seventh and holed that for eagle-three. Now Westwood was ahead by two, although Watson got a birdie at the seventh but then bogeyed the ninth.

Out in 33, Westwood drove into the rough at the 10th and took a five. When Watson's playing partner, Mathew Goggin, had a three at the hole moments later, Westwood and Goggin were now tied at three under. At the par-three 11th Watson holed another of his long putts, from 40 feet, and now there was a three-way tie.

Up ahead, Wood had recovered his composure and soon also the shots he had lost. A seven iron to 12 feet at the 15th gave him a two, and he made a four at the 17th to get back to two under and one off the lead. At the 18th Wood had 210 yards to the hole and took a nine iron, but the ball bounded on through the green. "I've never hit a nine iron that far in my life," he said.

Chipping from the rough, Wood ran the ball 20 feet past the hole and took a five. He finished with a 67 and was at one-under 279, the leader in the clubhouse. Only later would it become obvious that a par at the last hole would have put the youngster in a playoff.

Cink got within one stroke of the lead for the third time during the afternoon with a birdie at the 15th hole on a eight-iron shot to six feet. His had been a stop-start round — bogey at the fifth, birdie at the seventh, bogey at the 10th, birdie at the 11th, birdie at the 13th. The pattern continued as he flared a five iron right of the 14th green and bogeyed before claiming another two, this time at the short 15th.

The roller coaster continued. Three putts from 45 feet for a bogey at the 16th dropped Cink two behind Westwood, who now led on his own after Watson and Goggin bogeyed the 14th. The Australian bogeyed three of the last five holes and drifted out of the picture.

Westwood now had his best chance ever of winning a major championship. What he did not want to do was bogey three of the last four holes. He could not get up and down for pars at either the 15th or 16th holes. Watson, who had bogeyed the 14th, parred the 15th and 16th and was back in the lead on his own for the first time since teeing off.

Cink said he felt remarkably calm, but he could not birdie the 17th, missing a putt from eight feet. A two iron off the 18th tee left him in the fairway with 190 yards to the green, and Cink debated whether to use an eight or nine iron next. It was a decision that Watson behind him would soon also consider. Certain that an eight-iron shot would be over the green, Cink played short with a nine iron, and his judgment was proven correct as his shot rolled pin-high, 16 feet from the hole.

"I don't remember knowing exactly what I needed to do, but I just knew I wanted to try and make that putt," Cink said. "I've been working really hard on my putting and my mental approach and this was another test. I had a good solid routine going and I hit that putt without a care in the world of whether it went in or it missed. A blank mind like that is the best way to approach a pressure-packed situation and I was proud of the way I handled that."

Cink was the new clubhouse leader at 278, two under par after a 69, and for the first time in the afternoon he was tied for the lead with Watson out on the course. Westwood joined them after a birdie on the 17th after an exquisite five iron finished 15 feet short of the hole. His eagle attempt very nearly dropped.

Following behind, Watson also birdied the 17th, reaching the fringe in two with a two hybrid, to go back in front by one. Westwood's drive on the 18th ran into a bunker by the corner of the dogleg, but he recovered with a nine iron that found the green, 45 feet from the hole. He ran the putt 10 feet past the hole and could not hole the par-saver. After a 71 Westwood was at 279, tied with Wood, one behind Cink and two behind Watson.

"I thought I had to hole that putt, to be perfectly honest," Westwood admitted. "I didn't see Tom bogeying the last from the fairway, since he's such an experienced player. I shouldn't have got ahead of myself." When it turned out that the final bogey meant he had missed the playoff, Westwood said: "I've gone from frustration to sickness now. I played great all week. Third place is not to be sniffed at in a major championship, but I'm disappointed, really."

In the middle of the 18th fairway 32 years ago, Alfie Fyles, Watson's caddie, advised taking a seven iron instead of a six, and Watson put his approach to two feet. Now Watson considered a nine iron but went with an eight — the opposite of Cink's choice. He hit the shot he as he intended but the ball took a hard bounce and wouldn't stop on the green. "That eight iron will always live with me," he said. "I hit the shot I wanted to hit and it had the whole length of the green to stop and it never did."

Watson had an awkward lie just off the fringe and decided to putt, but the ball ran eight feet past. That putt was short and right, leaving Watson with a 72 and tied with Cink at 278. Suddenly he had nothing left. Cink saved par on the first playoff hole (the fifth) to be one ahead, and Watson's double bogey on the next (the sixth) handed Cink a four-shot advantage.

"The playoff was just one bad shot after another," Watson said. "I didn't give Stewart much competition. It looked like I ran out of gas, didn't it, but I didn't feel that."

Watson summed up the mood in his press conference with his opening words: "This ain't a funeral, you know." He was, as ever, gracious in defeat.

The Final Leaders: Stewart Cink 69–278 (14), Tom Watson 72–278 (20), Chris Wood 67–279, Lee Westwood 71–279, Luke Donald 67–280, Retief Goosen 72–280, Mathew Goggin 73–280, Soren Hansen 67–281, Justin Leonard 68–281, Ernie Els 68–281, Thomas Aiken 69–281, Richard S. Johnson 70–281

5. PGA Championship

It's hard to imagine an upset bigger than Y.E. Yang beating Tiger Woods in the 2009 PGA Championship. David over Goliath, perhaps.

To measure the magnitude and the surprise of Yang's victory — he was the first Asian ever to win a major championship — consider that Woods led through the first three rounds and was 14-0 from that position in majors, and that he was on a hot streak, winning five of 12 PGA Tour starts since returning from knee surgery nine months earlier.

Yang, 37, a South Korean — his full name is Yong-eun Yang — was in his second year on the PGA Tour. He took up golf at 19, much to the chagrin of his father, a farmer. "Golf is for rich people," his dad would say. But Yang persisted. He had one win on the PGA Tour, in the 2009 Honda Classic. Before that, he'd won some Japan Tour events, and then secured his place in golf trivia in the Asian-European Tour's HSBC Champions tournament in 2006, in which he beat none other than Tiger Woods by two shots. Those tempted to cry "Fluke!" should know that the field also included Retief Goosen, Paul Casey, Padraig Harrington and Jim Furyk, among others.

"This is such a big thing that's happening to me right now," Yang said then, "that it's really hard for me to explain it in words how I feel."

But this was 2009, and Woods had long been aiming at Jack Nicklaus's record of winning 18 majors. Woods was up to 14, No. 14 being the 2008 U.S. Open on a damaged knee that required surgery. His sat out the last two of 2008 and struck out on the Masters, U.S. Open and the Open Championship in 2009.

Woods was, of course, the huge favorite for all the usual reasons, and also because Hazeltine National, near Minneapolis, was the longest course for a major championship, at 7,674 yards. The 10 par-fours would be grinders. Just one is under 400 yards, No. 14, at 352, but adjustable to about 290 to tempt players to drive the green. The four par-fives ranged from 572 to 642 yards.

In short, a hot Woods and Hazeltine were made for each other, and somebody named Y.E. Yang was just another face in a starting field of 156.

First Round

Though everyone knew better, there was a certain romantic temptation to believe that this PGA Championship was over in the first round. After all, Tiger Woods had been on a rampage since coming back from the knee surgery — five wins in 12 starts, including his last two — then shot a bogey-free 67 for the first-round lead. Thus all that remained was the formality of three more rounds. Or so the sentiment was going. Where would anyone get such an absurd idea? Well, a confident Tiger Woods is a dangerous Tiger Woods.

"When I'm playing well, I usually don't make that many mistakes," Woods said.

Woods led by one over Padraig Harrington, the man he beat in the

Bridgestone Invitational the week before. Harrington thought he noticed a change in Woods's game. "I think he's put a little bit of conservatism on his game," he said. "It's nice. And he's very much in control of it."

Indeed he was. Woods hit 12 of the 14 driving fairways, hit 15 greens, and needed just 29 putts. He birdied three of the four par-fives. His putter was working. So were his miracles. At the par-five No. 3, 633 yards (his 12th hole), he nicked a tree with his second shot, put his third at the back of the green, and holed the 30-footer for a birdie. His other one-putts were from two, 20 and 20 feet.

"It's just one of those things where I just keep plodding along," Woods insisted. "Tomorrow, the weather's not supposed to be very good. I've got to go out there and just be consistent."

Of course, no one was conceding this PGA to Tiger Woods, and foremost among them was Padraig Harrington, the winsome Irishman, whose crash at the 16th the week before opened the door to Woods.

At all events, Harrington picked up where he left off and shot 68 Thursday and trailed Woods by a stroke. Harrington, going after his third major, after the Open Championship and PGA of 2008, was in the midst of mysterious swing changes, and spoke mysteriously about them. "About six weeks ago, I got clarity in that," he said. "It doesn't mean I got it in my swing at the moment, but I had clarity." He didn't elaborate.

Harrington, starting on the back nine, birdied his third, the formidable par-four 12th at 518 yards, and then the 16th, matching Woods at two under through the turn. Their third, Rich Beem, the 2002 PGA champion, matched them with a bogey and three birdies. He double-bogeyed his 12th, the par-five No. 3, and a later birdie gave him an opening 71. Coming in, Woods birdied Nos. 2, 3 and 7, while Harrington bogeyed his 10th, then birdied his 11th, 12th and 15th for his 68.

Anyone ready to hand this PGA to Woods would do well to keep an eye on Alvaro Quiros, the Spaniard with the thunderous length. He opened with a three-under 69, and in the process caught everyone's eye at the 606-yard 11th, his second hole. Playing into the wind, he hit his driver off the tee and then hit it again off the fairway, from about 290 yards. His ball rolled up on the green, catching Woods, Harrington and Rich Beem by surprise. Quiros was sheepish. He didn't realize he could reach in the wind.

"Good shot," said Harrington.

Woods smiled and gave a thumbs-up.

Phil Mickelson, in just his second start after his wife Amy's cancer surgery in June, fought a cool putter for a 74. "Off the tee didn't feel too bad," Mickelson said. "But on the greens, I missed a lot of ones that you don't even think about missing."

For all of its record length, Hazeltine proved quite playable. Twenty-six players broke par and 17 others were at par 72.

"It's not going to play any easier than it did today," said former PGA champion Paul Azinger (74).

Two other former champions — David Toms (2001) and Vijay Singh (1998, 2004) were in a group at 69, two behind, thanks to obedient putters. "I thought the pins were very difficult to get close, so your lag-putting had to be good, and mine was today," Toms said. Said Singh, currently switching back and forth from short putter to long putter: "I came in with a positive attitude. It's all about confidence."

Y.E. Yang did nothing to call attention to himself. He made three birdies, two bogeys and a double bogey in his 73.

Most observers might have conceded this PGA to Woods, but there weren't any in a field that had 97 of the world's top 100 players (98 until Paul Casey withdrew with an injury).

"I assure you," said former U.S. Open champion Geoff Ogilvy, "that 95 percent of the guys don't see Tiger on top of the leaderboard and think, 'Oh, God, I've got no shot.'"

First-Round Leaders: Tiger Woods 67, Padraig Harrington 68, Robert Allenby 69, Mathew Goggin 69, Hunter Mahan 69, Alvaro Quiros 69, Vijay Singh 69, David Toms 69, Paul Goydos 70, Thongchai Jaidee 70, Graeme McDowell 70, Lee Westwood 70, Michael Bradley 70, Gonzalo Fernandez-Castano 70, Soren Kjeldsen 70, Ben Crane 70

Second Round

On a hot, windy Friday, Y.E. Yang did nothing to suggest that he was just two days from the biggest moment of his life. He started the second round with a small disaster — a bogey at No. 1, then three more in succession from No. 3. Then he showed what he's made of. He birdied No. 6, eagled No. 7, and then birdied Nos. 10, 13 and 14 for a 70. At 143, he was six off the lead at the halfway point.

Tiger Woods, on the other hand, did nothing to dispel the notion that this was his PGA Championship. He increased his lead to four shots, his biggest halfway lead in a major since the 2005 Open Championship, with a hard-way 70 that was the only under-par score among the top 16 of the first round. But the competition did get a bit more threatening, thanks to an old adversary.

Vijay Singh, 46, a two-time PGA Championship winner, had fallen on quiet times in 2009, but he seemed bent on making a fight out of this one. He shot 72 and joined a five-way tie for second place. Singh blamed putting for his sag after three victories in 2008. Starting on the second nine, he had two birdies and a bogey, but reversed that coming in. "My back nine, it was really blowing," he said. He'd been alternating between a short putter and a long one. For now, he was using the short one. And the long one? "It's not too far away," he said.

Brendan Jones, a 34-year-old Australian who hates stress, hates practice and plays the Japan Tour ("I'm just very, very relaxed"), shot an easy 70 that included an eagle at the reachable par-four 14th. He faced the pressure of further success calmly. "I'm happy where I am in the golfing world," Jones said. "I never had the ambition to be No. 1."

Lucas Glover, 29, who won the U.S. Open in June, also shot a 70 and so made himself a candidate to become only the sixth player to win two majors in the same season while still in his 20s. He offered that his aggressive play cost him. "My defense wasn't as good as my offense," said Glover. "But 10 birdies in two rounds — I'll take."

England's Ross Fisher (68), who finished fifth in the U.S. Open and tied for 13th in the Open Championship, came charging into the picture with a six-birdie run through the 16th and found himself tied with Woods at five under at that point. "I thought, come on, let's nick a couple more," Fisher said. "Unfortunately, I didn't manage to do that."

It was looking like another Tiger Woods-Padraig Harrington shootout, after the Bridgestone Invitational the week before. Woods started the second round Friday — a hot day with brisk winds — leading Harrington by one. Then Harrington broke down for three straight bogeys from the 11th and shot 73, and Woods broke out for three straight birdies, starting at the 290-yard 14th, where he bombed a three wood to 20 feet and narrowly missed an eagle. A bogey at the 18th gave him a 70–137 and a plump four-stroke lead.

Harrington had the shot of the day at the par-five 15th, coming out of a fairway bunker with a three wood from 301 yards, leaving himself a 12-foot putt for an eagle.

Said Woods in admiration: "It was definitely worth the price of admission." Said Harrington: "He did say to me he would have paid to have seen it. So I asked him for 50 bucks."

Harrington birdied, matching Woods there, then bogeyed the 18th and shot 73 to join the tie for second at 141.

The halfway cut came at four-over 148, leaving 80 players for the last two rounds. They would not include Adam Scott, 29, once considered the next challenger to Woods but now looking like a faded promise. He'd missed eight cuts in 15 PGA Tour events, and this was his ninth miss. He shot 82-79–161 and was separated from dead last by only five club pros. Also missing: Sergio Garcia, Justin Rose, Steve Stricker, Darren Clarke and former PGA champion Mark Brooks.

Among those spared: Phil Mickelson, the 2005 PGA champion, was unimpressive but effective, making the cut right on the number with 74-74–148. "I'm not going to beat many putting the way I am," said Mickelson, noting the three-footer he missed for par at No. 1, and the missed birdie at the par-three No. 4, where he fitted a five iron through a crosswind to eight feet.

Also just surviving was Japan's Ryo Ishikawa, at 17 the youngest player ever to compete in the PGA, with 74-74–148. He had six birdies over the first two rounds. Northern Ireland's Rory McIlroy, 20, was the best of the youth corps, shooting 71-73–144, seven off the lead. It was a rocky 73. He bogeyed the first two holes, birdied three straight from the sixth, birdied the 14th and 15th, then bogeyed the 16th and double-bogeyed the par-three 17th. "It was quite a bad tee shot, so five was probably what I deserved," McIlroy said.

Looking ahead to the final two rounds, Harrington put the accepted read on things. "More and more tucked pin positions, with the greens getting a little bit firmer — all in all, probably playing well into Tiger's hands," he said. "But we'll have to put up with that."

Second-Round Leaders: Tiger Woods 70–137, Vijay Singh 72–141, Brendan Jones 70–141, Lucas Glover 70–141, Ross Fisher 68–141, Padraig Harrington 73–141, Ian Poulter 70–142, Lee Westwood 72–142, Soren Kjeldsen 73–143, Ernie Els 68–143, Y.E. Yang 70–143, Martin Kaymer 70–143

Third Round

Y.E. Yang, who had beaten Tiger Woods in the HSBC Champions in 2006, considered his chances of beating him again, here in the PGA Championship. He put the odds at 70-1. His reasoning: Well, he had won once on the PGA Tour and Woods had won 70 times. As handicapping systems go, Yang's would never play in Las Vegas.

The matter was entertaining, nonetheless. Yang, coming from nowhere, had shot 67 in the third round, matching Woods's tournament-low from the first round and tying Padraig Harrington going into the final round two strokes behind Woods, thus earning the right to be co-sacrificial lamb.

In the media interview room just after his third round, Harrington smiled when someone asked how he felt about Woods losing half of his lead. "The narrower the gap, the better," said Harrington.

Woods had started the third round leading by four and finished leading by only two. This came to pass when Woods, after making 10 birdies in the first two rounds with his usual game, suddenly turned quiet. "With my lead, I erred on the side of caution most of the time," Woods explained. "If I did have a good look at it (the flag), a good number (yardage), I took aim right at it. Otherwise, I was just dumping the ball on the green and two-putting."

In other words, Woods turned conservative to protect his lead. It's an old golf story. The result: a birdie at No. 2, a bogey at No. 4 and a birdie at the short No. 14. At three of the par-fives, he missed the fairway and so couldn't go for the green. Then at the par-five 15th, he left his pitch 40 feet short and thus wasted another birdie chance. It all led to a pedestrian one-under 71 and an eight-under 208 total and the two-stroke lead. Was Woods in trouble? Perish the thought.

Rich Beem, the man who beat Woods in the PGA Championship at Hazeltine in 2002, waved off the notion. "It's effortless for him right now," Beem said. "He's controlling his golf ball like nobody I've ever seen. This tournament is his."

Not so fast, came the chorus.

"You could feel there's a real championship going on around you," Ernie Els said. "It's not a runaway deal. It looks like the guys are really set to give Tiger a go." Els himself was giving Woods a go, closing to within a stroke before he bogeyed the last three holes for a 70 and fell five behind.

Harrington seconded the motion with four birdies in eight holes, the last on a seven-foot putt at the 14th that tied him with Woods. But a bogey from over the green at the 18th gave him a 69 and dropped him two behind. "Obviously you've got to beat him by three tomorrow," Harrington said. "That's a tall order. But we have nothing to lose."

Others shared his sentiments. U.S. Open champion Lucas Glover shot a three-birdie 71 and didn't count himself out at four behind. "We all know how Tiger is in the last round, so it's going to take something crazy," he said. "I made a bunch of birdies this week. I just need to put a bunch together in one round." Henrik Stenson, who won The Players Championship, shot 68 and was also four back, and had a modest outlook. "You can play a little bit more aggressively," he said. "But if I can be up there within three when we turn into the back nine, it's time to make a couple of good putts."

Prospects had finally faded for a shootout with Woods and two great opponents. Phil Mickelson ended his hopes with a 76 that put him eight over. "I didn't hit the ball very well, I didn't make very many putts," he said, and he refused to alibi the turmoil over his wife's and mother's breast cancer. "I'm disappointed in my performance. Regardless of what's going on, on and off the course, I still have high expectations." A showdown with Vijay Singh evaporated with a breakdown in his game. He missed several putts from inside five feet, stumbled to three bogeys and a double bogey from the 10th to the 16th, and shot 75 and was eight behind.

Northern Ireland's Rory McIlroy was winning the battle of the youth, even after running afoul of Hazeltine's bunkers. "I felt as if I've played better than a 71," he protested, after getting stuck under the lips of two bunkers, getting a plugged lie at the 13th and a buried lie at the 15th. "I couldn't even see my ball," he said. "Instead of making three or four there, I made six." He finished seven behind. Japan's Ryo Ishikawa shot 76 and was just five strokes from last as the PGA headed into the final round.

And when the third round was put into the record books, one fact still was echoing through Hazeltine: When Tiger Woods led in a major going into the final round, he won it.

Third-Round Leaders: Tiger Woods 71–208, Y.E. Yang 67–210, Padraig Harrington 69–210, Henrik Stenson 68–212, Lucas Glover 71–212, Soren Kjeldsen 70–213, Ernie Els 70–213, Alvaro Quiros 69–214, John Rollins 68–214, Martin Kaymer 71–214, Ross Fisher 73–214, Brendan Jones 73–214

Fourth Round

No disrespect intended, they said, but based on credentials, Y.E. Yang — ranked 110th in the world, one career victory — would be the odd man out in the fourth round. Tiger Woods was in the lead, and Yang and Padraig Harrington were tied, two shots behind. Harrington, the defending champion, playing just ahead, would be the one to challenge Woods. But with this reminder: Woods was 14-0 in majors, and overall 36-1, in which he led or shared the lead going into the final round.

First, Harrington wasn't halfway into the round before he was out of the picture. At the par-three No. 8, he crashed to a colossal eight that involved a tee shot into the water, a chip over the green and another watered shot coming back the other way.

"I hit a bad shot," Harrington said. "Such is life. Some days they don't come off, some days they do."

Harrington went on to shoot 78, matching his worst score ever in a PGA Championship.

The No. 3 surprise — after the principals — was Rory McIlroy, the prince of the youth movement, playing in his first PGA. He rocketed from a tie for 13th to finish tied for third with a 70, and there's no telling what might have happened if he'd stayed out of Hazeltine's sands.

And so this PGA Championship finished in a two-man battle, but not the one anyone could have dreamed of, except Yang himself.

"I've sort of visualized this," Yang said, through an interpreter. "Playing against the best player ... playing with him in the final round of a major championship."

Yang might have been awed by this wish-fulfillment, but he wasn't dumbstruck. This was a classic mano-a-mano battle. Yang, showing solid nerves and a gentle touch, birdied No. 3 with a 10-foot putt, while Woods flew his third shot to the back of the green and parred. Yang had picked up his first stroke.

Woods's problems were pretty much characterized by his bogey at the par-three fourth. His tee shot was 40 feet below the hole, his first putt four feet short, and then he missed the par putt. Yang two-putted from 25 feet and they were tied at seven under. Woods regained the lead with a par at No. 5 after Yang nicked a tree with his approach and bogeyed. Then they were tied again at No. 8 when Yang parred and Woods bogeyed out of a bunker.

They made the turn tied at six under, Woods with 38, Yang 36. Everyone was waiting for Yang to crack. But he was still smiling.

Woods got his first birdie of the day at the par-five 11th, reaching in two and two-putting against Yang's par. But at the par-four 12th, Woods went from rough off the tee to rough behind the green and took his third bogey. Yang tied with a par.

Then came the 14th, the enticing par-four, playing about 313 yards. It would be the signature of this PGA.

Woods bunkered his tee shot and Yang was about 20 yards short of the green. Woods came out to eight feet, marked his ball. Yang took his 52-degree wedge and chipped, trying to get close. The ball hopped twice and rolled in for the eagle. Yang exploded in fist pumps, high-fives and a huge grin. Woods knew what a knockout punch looked like, but he never flinched. He coolly holed his birdie putt. But he was out of the lead for the first time.

Woods saw daylight one final time. Yang made his second bogey at the par-three 17th, after a tee shot to the front edge. Woods went right at the flag but ended up off the back of the green. His pitch was poor, leaving him 10 feet for par. He two-putted for a bogey, and Yang led by one going to the last.

At the 18th, a 475-yard par-four, Yang hit one of the great shots of golf history, one that ranked with Corey Pavin's four wood at the final hole when he won the 1995 U.S. Open. Woods boomed his drive down the middle. Yang pulled his tee shot to the left, into the first cut of rough. Woods hit his second into the collar, about 15 feet from the pin. Yang had 210 yards to the green and a view obstructed by trees. After a moment's study, he took a hybrid three iron and hit a soaring shot that settled softly 12 feet from the hole. There was pandemonium all around.

Yang waited. Woods was chipping for birdie.

"I think only Tiger chipping," said Yang. "Miss the chipping. And thinking, 'Just please.'"

He didn't need an interpreter for that one.

Woods missed the birdie chip and, worse, ran the ball six feet past. Then he two-putted from there for another bogey and a 75. Yang could now comfortably two-putt for his par and the win. Instead, he holed the 12-footer for a birdie, a 70 and a three-stroke win over the mighty Tiger Woods.

"I did everything I needed to do, except for getting the ball in the hole," said Woods, who needed 33 putts. "I didn't putt well enough to win." As for Yang: "I think he played beautifully," Woods said.

When Yang finally settled down, he turned to his interpreter. "Tiger's good, but he could always have a bad day," Yang said. "Guess this is one of those days." And then he added: "This might be my last win as a golfer, but it sure is a great day."

The Final Leaders: Y.E. Yang 70–280, Tiger Woods 75–283, Lee Westwood 70–285, Rory McIlroy 70–285, Lucas Glover 74–286, Martin Kaymer 73–287, Ernie Els 74–287, Soren Kjeldsen 74–287, Henrik Stenson 75–287, John Merrick 70–288, Dustin Johnson 70–288, Zach Johnson 71–288, Francesco Molinari 72–288, Graeme McDowell 72–288, Padraig Harrington 78–288

6. Women's Major Championships

Kraft Nabisco Championship

When seen at work, the golfer looks composed, determined and calculating in pursuit of the maddening craft. But how does the golfer really feel inside, especially at those times when victory hangs in the balance and the mind is stretched like a violin string?

This was Brittany Lincicome as she was making that last, desperate effort to win the Kraft Nabisco Championship: "My hands were shaking so bad. I was almost crying."

So much for the composed, determined, calculating golfer. But Lincicome kept enough control of herself so that moments later, in one of the most electrifying finishes in LPGA Tour history, she had the victory, her first in a major championship and the third win in her five years on the tour.

In the last round, the final threesome of Lincicome, her good friend Kristy McPherson, in her third season and seeking her first victory, and Cristie Kerr, an 11-time winner in her 13th year, battled nose-to-nose in as tight and intense a battle as the tour had seen. Lincicome trailed all the way, even by as much as three strokes, and labored to catch up. She led only once, and that's when it counted — at the final hole, where she authored a bold, brilliant, spectacular eagle to win. Then it was time to celebrate.

"Celebrate?" Lincicome said. "After this, I'm going to go hang out. I guess the tournament office is having a little party, so I'll definitely go there. Probably hang out with my friends. And then if I'm not golfing, I'm either fishing or hanging out with friends, watching movies. Anything but golf, really."

By winning the Kraft Nabisco, the first of the LPGA's four major championships of the season, Lincicome merely fulfilled predictions heaped on her from her bright days in junior golf. She had won twice in her five years on the tour, the 2006 HSBC World Match Play and the 2007 Ginn Open, and she'd had three top-10 finishes in the majors, her best a tie for second in the 2007 Kraft Nabisco. But now, in early April, she had missed the cut in her first outing, tied for 65th in her second, and tied for 39th in her third. Next, she's a winner.

The Kraft Nabisco got under way with two surprises.

The first was Lincicome taking the first-round lead with a six-under-par 66. She would add 74, 70 and 69 for a 279 total, nine under par, and a one-stroke win over McPherson and Kerr. Interestingly enough, the 66 surprised even Lincicome. "If you would have told me that this morning, I would have taken it and ran," she said. "It's a major, so it's going to be playing long. The rough is going to be thick. Even par, or one or two under, I would have been completely satisfied."

Her 66 was a classic. She had seven one-putt greens, on putts ranging from eight to 20 feet, and she also shook off two bogeys, for a one-stroke lead over Angela Stanford, Brittanny Lang and South Korean Ji Young Oh. It was practically a head-to-head battle with Oh. Both started on the 10th. Lincicome hit 16 greens, Oh 14. Lincicome made four birdies going out, Oh three, and after making the turn, they matched scores for five holes, going birdie-birdie-bogey-birdie-birdie. "It was like match play, nine holes straight," Lincicome said. "She would make a 30-footer for birdie and I would top it. I would make one and she would come on top of mine. So it was really just a fun day."

The other surprise was Lorena Ochoa, defending champion and the Rolex No. 1 in the world. She'd won her season start in the Honda LPGA Thailand and had two other top-10 finishes in her five starts. So her opening 73 lifted eyebrows. Her driver was driving her bonkers. She hit only four fairways. "I got in trouble from the tee," Ochoa said. She started at the 10th and was two under at the turn. Then she made three bogeys and no birdies coming home. "I think it was a good way to start, a couple under," she said. "And then I'm pretty upset that I didn't take advantage of that." She shot another 73 in the second round, and then in the third, she birdied the last hole for a par 72. "Well," she said, resigned to having one of those weeks, "it was a better score." Ochoa closed with a flourish, a chip-in eagle at the 18th, but by then all it meant was 69 that lifted her to a tie for 12th. It was her worst finish in the Kraft Nabisco since 2005.

Michelle Wie, 19 and a sophomore at Stanford University, cobbled together an admirable one-under 71 in a day of rescuing her stray tee shots. She holed a number of putts in the eight-foot range, and logged three birdies and two bogeys. "It was a little sketchy in the beginning," Wie said. "You always get that same jittery feeling when you play in the majors." She was still smarting from the 2006 Kraft Nabisco when she muffed a chance to win, chopping up the last hole, turning a 25-foot eagle chance into a three-putt par that kept her out of a playoff. This time, she never got close. She followed her opening 71 with two 81s and finished tied for 67th, third from last.

Heavy winds cropped up in the second round, but before they did, McPherson had posted 70 and Christina Kim 69 for 138 totals that would hold up for the halfway lead when play was completed Saturday morning. "Yeah," McPherson said, "I was counting my blessings." Lincicome finished in the strong winds and shot 74, falling two shots off the lead. "I survived," she said. But there were some unhappy golfers. Said Angela Stanford (75): "I don't really know what unplayable is. I think if balls are rolling off greens, it probably is unplayable." Ochoa, after another 73, had similar sentiments. "With so much wind," the slightly built Mexican said, "I kept losing my balance." Ji Young Oh became the victim of one of the game's unkindest penalties. She had hit the green in regulation at the par-five 18th, some 30 feet from the flag. After she had marked and then replaced her ball, a gust blew it off the green and into the water in front, costing her a one-stroke penalty. She three-putted for a double bogey and shot 78 and was out of the running.

Paula Creamer, another pre-tournament favorite, stayed in the running through the second round, but broke down for 77 in the third round, thanks largely to a stubborn mysterious stomach ailment that had left her weak and unable to eat much more than pasta and ice cream. "I don't know what's wrong with me," Creamer said. "It's not something you want to have hanging over your shoulders." She persevered and closed with 69 and tied for 17th.

They lined up 1-2-3 in the third round, all three shooting 70 — McPherson leading by one at 208, Kerr at 209 and Lincicome at 210. It was, by coincidence, an all-American top of the leaderboard, a rarity these days. "I'm hoping that a lot of Americans are having a solid week," said McPherson, perhaps smarting from criticism American players had come into in recent years. Said Kerr: "Things go in cycles. I think the Americans are back. It's a Solheim Cup year. I think they are getting ramped up to play the Solheim."

After starting the third round with a birdie at No. 1, McPherson bogeyed twice, then headed home with three straight birdies from the 10th, on putts of six, 10 and four feet. Kerr had a bogey and three birdies, the last a tap-in after a near ace at the par-three 17th. Lincicome parred the front, then birdied the 10th from six feet and 13th from 25, and after a three-putt bogey at the 14th, she rolled in a 40-footer for a birdie at the 15th.

McPherson narrowly missed having a two-stroke lead. She pulled her birdie putt just left of the flag and got her 70. "It's a tough leaderboard up there," she said. "You've got a lot of girls that can do a lot of good things out there. I know that I have to play really solid golf."

Kerr didn't seem to have any severe doubts. With her seasoning and her victory in the 2007 U.S. Women's Open, she all but picked herself to win. "I definitely think it's an advantage knowing what it's not only like to win a tournament, but a major, and how to handle the emotions and how you feel," she said. Lincicome didn't really look ahead. "It's really cool to see my name up there," she said. "It's been so long since I've been in contention."

And truth be told, it would actually be 17 more holes before Lincicome would be in contention here.

The three made up the final grouping, and McPherson, who started leading by one, and Kerr more or less played tag while Lincicome tagged along. The lead flip-flopped at the second hole where Kerr jumped ahead on a 20-foot birdie putt to McPherson's two-putt bogey. And Kerr went up by three on her birdie at the fourth and McPherson's watery bogey at the fifth.

McPherson caught up with three powerful birdies on Nos. 7, 9 and 10 on two 20-foot putts bracketing a 40-foot chip-in. After they matched bogeys at the 13th, Kerr moved ahead on a birdie at the 14th, dropping a seven-foot putt. Then she made a crippling error. At the par-four 15th, she knocked her tee shot out of bounds and double-bogeyed.

Lincicome, meanwhile, was just about the forgotten third. She birdied No. 8 from 10 feet and No. 9 from five and pulled to within one of Kerr and McPherson heading through the turn. She fell two behind with a bogey out of a plugged lie in a bunker at the 12th. Her prospects had just dimmed considerably. Lincicome parred the next five holes, a silent partner to the duel going on beside her. She was at seven under, tied with Kerr after that double bogey at the 15th, and McPherson was one up, at eight under.

She parred in for her 72 and 280 total, and Kerr tied her with an 18-foot birdie putt from the fringe at the 18th for a 71. Meanwhile, a stunning drama was unfolding.

"It just came down to the 18th, and luckily my length is a strong point, and I bombed it out there," said Lincicome, also known as "Bam-Bam." About 275 yards, in fact, into the fairway. She had 210 yards left. She picked her club nervously.

"The hybrid is in my hands, my hands are shaking and my heart is racing," she said. "I'm trying to calm myself down by breathing or singing or whatever I can possibly do, and right when I hit it, it came off the clubface exactly where we wanted to hit it, and it took the slope like I wanted it to and came really close."

The ball obediently curled to a stop, four feet from the cup.

"If I had to make anything further than that...," Lincicome said. "My hands were shaking so bad, I was almost crying."

And then she holed the putt for an eagle, a 69, a nine-under 279, and her first major.

"I can't even describe it," Lincicome said. "It's surreal, really."

McDonald's LPGA Championship

The front page of the Swedish newspaper *Svenska Dagbladet*, for Monday, July 15, was fairly shouting out the story of a young Swedish woman who had played in a golf event in the United States. The story was in Swedish, of course, but the writer had sprinkled in some quotes from American stories: "splendid fashion," "no kidding," "the steely nerved rookie from Sweden," "frozen in thought."

You didn't need a translator to get the drift of that story. The Swedish woman, Anna Nordqvist, newly 22, had done something remarkable. Namely — in field loaded with the best female golfers in the world — she came from nowhere and won the McDonald's LPGA Championship, one of the tour's coveted major championships, for her first win as a professional. In only her fifth start. And by four shots. That's worth shouting about in any language.

Every major has its newcomer or no-name who barges into the spotlight, stirs up some excitement, and then nervously leaves the stage to the bona fide contenders. That figured to be the role for Anna Nordqvist at the start. Nordqvist had a nice résumé for a young rookie. She was from Eskilstuna, a small town in Sweden; took up golf at the age of 10 under the encouragement of her brothers; became impatient with it and quit, and didn't take it up again until she was 13, and before long said: "I refused to be the worst golfer in the family." From there, she went through the famed Swedish National program. She was the Swedish Junior Player of the Year in 2004 and the Swedish Amateur of the Year in 2005. She soon became the next Swedish standout to get recruited by an American university — Arizona State, in this case, where she was a two-time All-American before leaving after a couple years to turn pro.

But coming to Bulle Rock Golf Course in Maryland, all she had was that outstanding amateur record and the usual dreams. As a pro, she'd had only four starts, and had done nothing out of the ordinary, tying for 60th, 17th, 49th and 40th, and winning $31,246. So Nordqvist had the makings of a great story at Bulle Rock. She would fill in the rest herself before the week was out. But first, she would have to spend some time in the supporting cast.

Nordqvist played Bulle Rock in 66-70-69-68–273, 15 under par, and went into the books as the winner of the final McDonald's LPGA Championship. McDonald's, the fast-food chain, longtime title sponsor, announced they would withdraw after this 2009 edition.

With the field facing a rain-softened course, and with greens receptive and true, Nicole Castrale broke into the first round like a drag racer. She birdied six of the first nine holes and added two more at the 14th and 15th. She had eight one-putt greens, including the big three, from 25, 20 and 18 feet. A missed fairway at the par-four 18th cost her her only bogey in a seven-under-par 65.

Did you get to the point where you said, okay, I got it now?

"No," Castrale said. "That's the thing with golf. You can never say you've got it. Once you say you've got it, I don't think you have it."

Nordqvist was a surprising second at 66, thanks to a devastating iron game. She made seven birdies, all on one-putts, and six of those ranged from only three to six feet, and her longest was a 15-footer at the par-three 17th. She also bogeyed once, at the par-four sixth when she drove into a bunker. The rookie felt at home high on the leaderboard.

"This is where I want to be," said Nordqvist. And she said she was having fun.

The part that wasn't fun yet was the pro life. "Coming up from college and going straight to the tour, I think you've got to learn to live this lifestyle," she said. "Traveling that much, not being home, you play week after week — that's something new to me."

China's Shanshan Feng was at least as much a surprise as Nordqvist. Feng was in third place with a 67, just two off Castrale's lead, and had found herself in the awkward position of being unknown in a threesome with two noted players, Michelle Wie and Christina Kim. The gallery started to rush away at one tee, after Wie and Kim had hit. "Then Christina said to the crowd that we still had one left, talking about me," Feng said. "That made me feel good."

A lot of eyes were on Wie, who shot 70 and who was expecting much of herself this season as a full fledged member of the LPGA Tour. "I'm having so much fun playing almost every week and traveling to different places," she said. "The main goal for me is to have a lot of fun, play my hardest, try my hardest. Win, for sure. Get on the Solheim Cup team."

There was little stirring among the big names. Defending champion Yani Tseng, Juli Inkster and Jiyai Shin had 73s, and Paula Creamer 74. Brittany

Lincicome, winner of the first major, the Kraft Nabisco, had five bogeys and a double bogey and shot 75.

Lorena Ochoa, the Rolex World No. 1, shot a grudging par 72 and of course intended to do better. "I just need to go out there and play my game," Ochoa said. But she wouldn't be a factor in this championship. She got as close as five off the lead at the halfway point, and finished at one-under 287, 14 shots back.

Fans of golf trivia would offer that Anna Nordqvist, now just five events into her pro career, was best known for making the cut in the last two Women's British Opens as a 20-something amateur. Such things tend to stamp the author as someone to watch. Except that Nordqvist wasn't feeling that she was someone to watch. Not yet. This championship was just one grand learning experience to her.

"I'm a rookie and I haven't played that much this year, but I'm here to learn and just have fun," she said. "I'm just going to focus on my game, and if I'm ready, I'm ready."

Concentration has to be especially difficult for a rookie, but Nordqvist wasn't in the least fazed by the pressure of a major. And the week had been a confusing jumble of storms, delays and overlapping rounds. In the second round, she was a prime example of a winner waiting to happen. While Castrale was working on a rocky par 72, Nordqvist slipped a stroke ahead of her with a 70–136. She had just five bogeys in the four rounds, one each in three of them and two in this second round, but she had four one-putt birdies, the last of them a 36-footer at her final hole, No. 9, on a day of slow play. "I really had to pace myself because there was a lot of waiting," she said. "You have to make the best of it."

Castrale was one behind with her 72, which included a watery double bogey at the par-three 12th. "I hit one bad shot that really cost me at the wrong time," Castrale said. "I'm not going to dwell on that." Australians Katherine Hull (69) and Lindsey Wright (68) moved to within two at 138.

The cut, at three-over 147, eliminated some of the biggest names on the LPGA, notably Suzann Pettersen, Brittany Lincicome, Morgan Pressel and Christina Kim. Shanshan Feng was a stunning victim. She soared from a 67 in the first round to an 81 and was the only one of 14 who opened in the 60s to miss the cut.

The issue for Nordqvist, at least in the minds of observers, was pressure. When was the rookie going to feel it and crack? Well, not in the third round, either. In the rain-fragmented round, she dropped a 20-foot putt for a birdie at the 15th as play was called because of darkness. The birdie got her to 10 under and gave her a one-stroke lead over Wright. "Finishing with a birdie brings me some good momentum for Sunday," Nordqvist said. She and Wright were two of eight players who couldn't finish play Saturday in the falling darkness. Said Wright: "There's a disadvantage for not finishing today. I would love to be sleeping in, but it's going to be a big day, regardless."

The big day started at 7:30 a.m. Sunday, with the completion of the third round. Nordqvist bogeyed the 17th and shot 69, taking a two-stroke lead over Wright into the final round a few hours later. Nordqvist was five up on Jiyai Shin, who bogeyed the 18th for a 69 before darkness fell on Saturday. "The last hole, my second shot was not good," she said. "But I am glad that I finished."

Nordqvist wasted no time when after some rest she came back out Sunday afternoon for the final round. If she was feeling any pressure, it didn't show in her game. At the first hole, a par-four of 358 yards, she had just a pitching wedge left to the green, and this she flipped to two feet for the first of five birdies. Then came the sixth, a 387-yard par-four, and this time it was an eight iron to 15 feet and another birdie. Then Wright bogeyed the par-three seventh on a three-putt after missing the green with her tee shot. Nordqvist was leading by five.

Wright is a fighter. Since April, she already had a fourth in the Kraft Nabisco and a tie for third in the Michelob Ultra, and wouldn't let this one slide if she could help it. She turned up the heat with her putter and bounced back with birdies at Nos. 8, 9 and 12 from 35, 15 and 10 feet, and she got to within a stroke when Nordqvist bogeyed the 13th on a three-putt.

Nordqvist never flinched. She came right back with a birdie at the 14th on a 12-foot putt and then stretched her lead to three with another birdie at the par-five 15th, rolling in a 30-footer. Wright birdied the 16th but bogeyed the 17th, and Nordqvist locked it up with a breathtaking birdie at the 422-yard, par-four 18th. With a four-shot cushion, she could have played it safe. But rather than lay up with her second, she took her hybrid and went for the green, and got there — to three feet — for her last birdie and the four-stroke win.

Wright marveled. "That shot on 18," she said. "If that was me, I think I probably would have wedged it up around the green."

Then Wright added what a lot of people were thinking about Nordqvist's performance: "It was amazing. Under that amount of pressure, not being in that position before and in a major and being a rookie? You can't get any better than that. She didn't show any nerves at all."

It was inevitable that the name of Annika Sorenstam would come up.

"I got the opportunity to meet Annika a couple of times," Nordqvist said. "It was a great experience. Just sharing some thoughts about her career. Before the round, I got a few words from her through some friends. She said just try and take one shot at a time and enjoy it. Annika has always been my role model."

It was pointed out to Nordqvist that rookies, and especially those in their fifth start, aren't supposed to win majors.

"Well," she said, smiling, "I think I haven't realized I won a major yet. It's a great feeling, and I think it's going to take a couple of days to realize that I actually won. It's just been an incredible week. I've had so much fun. I just tried to focus on what I can do. I mean, this time — it was my time."

U.S. Women's Open

The U.S. Women's Open, the biggest tournament in women's golf, dawned with the usual high anticipations, only to be upstaged by an issue that had nothing to do with actually hitting a golf ball. This was the rebellion on the LPGA Tour seeking the dismissal of Commissioner Carolyn Bivens, a controversial figure since taking the chair some four years earlier.

The matter came to a rolling boil early in July, shortly before the Women's Open, when some of the biggest names on the tour met in emergency session and issued a call for her to step down. There had been nothing like it in women's golf, probably not in any golf. Word then leaked out of tour headquarters that Bivens would resign, but not until after the Women's Open, in order not to detract from it.

It was just as well, because when it came to stealing shows, Eun-Hee Ji, 24, another in a host of talented South Koreans, stole the show and the U.S. Women's Open along with it. But not until the absolute end. Ji, in only her second Women's Open, rolled in a long birdie putt on the final hole to win by a stroke with an even-par total of 284 at Saucon Valley in Bethlehem, Pennsylvania.

Ji, who had one other LPGA Tour win, the 2008 Wegmans, had visited Saucon Valley shortly before the Open, contemplated the tight fairways and undulating greens, and concluded that she had no chance. "Wow, I didn't even dream about winning this tournament," said Ji, through an interpreter, after winning. "I think this is going to be one of the most memorable moments in my life."

Cristie Kerr, however, would probably prefer to forget it. Kerr, the 2007 Open champion and a 12-time winner on the LPGA Tour, led through the middle rounds but couldn't hold on. It was also memorable for Candie Kung. She climbed the leaderboard over the last two rounds then came up empty when Ji's last putt left her the runner-up by a stroke.

That was the climax of a tough week on a tough course that began with another South Korean becoming the talk of the championship. Na Yeon Choi, 21, runner-up in the rookie of the year chase in 2008, started on the back nine and birdied her first three holes and shot 68. "I just wasn't very intimidated by this course," said Choi.

Lorena Ochoa, the Rolex Ranking's No. 1, seeking her first U.S. Women's Open, and Kerr tied for second at 69, along with qualifier Jean Reynolds, the leading money winner on the developmental Futures Tour. Ochoa, starting on No. 10, balanced two bogeys with two birdies heading out, then holed a long, bending birdie putt at No. 2, her 11th, then birdied her 12th. Had she left some shots out on the course? "No," Ochoa said. "I'm happy with what I have."

Kerr hit 10 fairways and 15 greens, and made three birdies on putts of 15, 12 and eight feet, and took one bogey. "Today I did about as well as anybody is going to do," Kerr said. Paula Creamer, another of the pre-tournament favorites, got away with a 72. "I had some not-so-smart decisions," Creamer said. "Overall, I'll take where I'm at."

The leaderboard had two surprise visitors. Reynolds just missed a share of the lead when her birdie putt at the last lipped out. She shrugged it off. "Coming in under the radar and leading the U.S. Open in the first round is pretty awesome," she said. The biggest surprise was Alexis Thompson, only 14, the reigning U.S. Girls' Junior champion, who shot 71.

Some players hurt their chances with sluggish starts, among them Suzann Pettersen and Morgan Pressel (74s) and defending champion Inbee Park (75). Others killed their hopes with fatal starts. Two-time champion Juli Inkster, in her 30th straight Women's Open, shot 78, as did Angela Stanford. Sophie Gustafson and 2005 champion Birdie Kim had 81s.

First-round leaders: Na Yeon Choi 68, Lorena Ochoa 69, Cristie Kerr 69, Jean Reynolds 69

Developments in the second round cleared a path for Kerr, and she grabbed her chance. Her biggest obstacle was Ochoa, but after that encouraging first round, she mysteriously backslid into the indifferent play that had kept her winless since April. An eight-over 79 knocked her out of the running. She would finish tied for 26th.

Choi's resolve remained strong after that opening 68, but her game weakened. A 74 knocked her back and she couldn't recover. Ji, among others, was just holding her own against the demanding course. A 72 put her at one-over 143, four behind Kerr. At this point, Kerr clearly was the most likely to succeed.

It didn't look that way early in Kerr's second round. Starting on the back nine, she bogeyed her first two holes, then got the shots back immediately with two straight birdies. A bogey at her eighth (No. 17) left her one over going out, and a bogey at her 10th (No. 2) put her two over. Then she caught fire, making three straight birdies from her 15th on putts of nine, three and eight feet for a 70, one of only six rounds under par for the day. It gave her a one-stroke lead on Creamer.

Creamer, coming off a thumb injury, posted five birdies and two bogeys for 68 and second place alone, her best position after two rounds in a Women's Open. Reynolds, still the surprise of the championship, hit only nine of the 14 driving fairways but managed a 72 for third place. The Open would take on a view of the past and the future with the celebrated veteran Laura Davies and 14-year-old amateur Alexis Thompson. Davies shot 75 for a 149 total and Thompson 73 for 144. Thompson made the cut for the first time in three tries, Davies for the first since 2007. (Davies would tie for 17th, Thompson for 34th.)

It all made for a very interesting final two rounds. Said the confident Kerr: "My mindset for the weekend is you have to be focused on every shot. It feels great. It's great to know that I've won one, and I know I can do it on the weekend."

Second-round leaders: Cristie Kerr 70–139, Paula Creamer 72–140, Jean Reynolds 72–141, Na Yeon Choi 74–142, Giulia Sergas 67–142

The third round was marked by the steady play of Kerr, the rise of Ji and the amazing fall of Creamer. It was a compelling sequence of events. Kerr shot 72 to expand her lead to two strokes, but not over Creamer. Creamer, a stroke back to start the round, suffered a stunning collapse, an eight-over 79 that killed her chances. Reynolds, the Futures Tour star, two behind to start, drifted back another two with a 74.

Up came Ji, with four birdies and three bogeys for 70 that lifted her from four back to second place, two behind Kerr. "Every time I look up at the leaderboard and see my name up there, it gives me excitement," Ji said, through an interpreter. "It makes me a little nervous, but in a good way, where you can maybe compete a little harder."

Creamer was the talk of the day. Her troubles were many and mixed. At No. 1, she missed the green from 65 yards. At No. 8, her tee shot was a weekender's low slice that went about 150 yards. The killer came at the par-four 10th, which officials set up at 253 yards to tempt players into trying to drive the green. Creamer took the bait, drove into a bunker, flew her bunker shot 20 yards over the green, hit her return into greenside rough, barely got the next on the green, and then two-putted for a triple-bogey seven. "I don't know what happened there," Creamer said. The 79 knocked her back eight strokes.

Reynolds stayed close until a stumbling finish — three bogeys over the last four holes — gave her a 74, four behind Kerr and tied with Taiwan's Teresa Lu (70). "I love being in the hunt," Reynolds said. "And if I stumble, I try not to let it get to me."

Kerr bogeyed Nos. 2 and 9 and birdied No. 4 to make the turn at one over, then had a birdie-bogey exchange in a par trip home for her 72 and her two-stroke lead. At 211, she was the only player under par.

"There really isn't a better place for me," said Kerr, a 12-time winner on the LPGA Tour. "I'm sure there's going to be some nerves in the morning. But I've been there. I know I can handle it."

Third-round leaders: Cristie Kerr 72–211, Eun-Hee Ji 70–213, Jean Reynolds 74–215, Teresa Lu 70–215

Saucon Valley's par-four 10th, that temptress with the reachable green which ruined Creamer in the third round, nearly claimed another victim in the fourth. It was playing at 242 yards this time. Ji, deep in the hunt, pulled out her driver. She found a bunker short of the green, chunked her next into another bunker and double-bogeyed. It was the kind of small disaster that usually unnerves a player. But it had the reverse effect on Ji.

"Actually, it gave me an opportunity to calm myself down," Ji said. "Up until that point, Cristie was so far ahead and I just didn't think anyone was going to be able to catch up with her, and in my mind I said, 'Let's go and play the rest of the round.' I think that was one of the factors of winning the tournament."

It would all come down to Ji's clutch birdie putt on the last hole.

At one point on the final nine there was a four-way tie for the lead among Ji, Kerr, Taiwan's Candie Kung and South Korea's In-Kyung Kim.

Kerr bogeyed the first, birdied the third, then bogeyed the fifth and sixth. A three-putt bogey at the 16th sealed her fate. Her closing 75 dropped her to a tie for third, two strokes back, with Kim (70). "Not playing the way I did the last three days, this golf course is pretty much all I can handle," said Kerr, who needed 35 putts.

Kung bogeyed the par-three 17th out of a bunker, and it haunted her.

"That's pretty much the only thing I was thinking about," a disappointed Kung said. "But it's over. I had a lot of very good breaks, made some very good putts coming in. Nothing I can do."

Ji certainly didn't look like a champ for the first 10 holes. She bogeyed the second, fourth and seventh holes, birdied the sixth and eighth, then came the nearly fatal double bogey at the 10th and the calm that followed. Ji birdied the 13th and 14th. Kung had finished with the clubhouse lead and was on the practice green, anticipating a playoff. It never came.

The 18th had been set at 388 yards, down from the original 444. Ji drove into the fairway, then hit the green, pin-high, 20 feet to the left of the cup. Then she had another of those strange, calming moments.

"Right before I hit the putt, I was nervous to the point where my hands were shaking," said Ji. "I knew the worst possible scenario was the playoff, so I cleared my mind and thought, you know, let's give it a try."

She rolled in the putt for the birdie that made her the U.S. Women's Open champion.

Final leaders: Eun-Hee Ji 71–284, Candie Kung 69–285, In-Kyung Kim 70–286, Cristie Kerr 75–286

Ricoh Women's British Open

Catriona Matthew, a 39-year-old mother of two, won the Ricoh Women's British Open. Every part of that sentence is remarkable. For most mothers of multiple young children, simply making sure the right number are washed and fed and back in bed each night is achievement enough. To become the first Scot to win the Women's British Open and only the fourth Briton to win a major championship in women's golf gave Matthew a place in the history of the game even without the remarkable circumstances that surrounded her victory at Royal Lytham and St. Annes. For it came just 11 weeks after the birth of her second daughter, Sophie, and in only her second tournament after returning to competitive golf after a five-month maternity break.

But that is not all. On the eve of her comeback tournament in France, Matthew and her husband, Graeme, escaped a rampant fire in their small hotel and raised the alarm. A week later, in the second round of the last major championship of the season, Matthew made successive eagles, including a hole-in-one at the 12th. She came home in 30 strokes, the first time that score has ever been achieved on the back nine at Lytham by man or woman. Matthew owned the homeward stretch, and after a poor start to the final round, sealed her victory with three birdies in a row from the 13th hole.

She finished as the only player under par for the week, and after a 73 to be three under, won by three strokes over Karrie Webb, who made a gallant charge with a closing round of 68. Four players shared third place:

Ai Miyazato, Paula Creamer, Christina Kim and Hee-Won Han. Such were the difficulties encountered on the Lancashire links Creamer took a double bogey at the last hole, Miyazato at the 17th. Matthew avoided such disasters and strode up the 18th fairway to a rapturous reception, the crowd egged on by Matthew's exuberant playing partner, Kim, who added her own applause.

"I've never felt a feeling like that before," Matthew said. "It was absolutely fantastic, but I had a tear in my eye and had to get myself up for the last two putts. It was only after my drive at the last found that fairway that I let myself believe it was going to happen. If you get in one of those bunkers anything can still happen. Playing with Christina was great because she really kept me relaxed over the last few holes. She couldn't have been more supportive."

Kim and Matthew are veritable opposites. The Scot is hardly the most demonstrative person, but waved her hat to the crowd in pure joy. "I can't quite believe what I have achieved," she said. "It was amazing and unbelievable, but it has not sunk in yet."

This was Matthew's sixth career victory, but her last in Europe had been in 2007 and her last in America in 2004. But right at the start of the year she won the Brasil Cup, an unofficial event. It was around five weeks after the birth of Sophie, a younger sister to Katie, that Matthew started practicing and playing again. "I just started slowly and built it up," she said. "After a while it felt pretty much back to normal. It was a good chance to practice, as during the season it is difficult to have that much time, five weeks, just to work on the same things. I'm probably hitting my irons the best I have done in a couple of years, so the break's done me beautifully."

She admitted being nervous before the first round of her comeback event at the Evian Masters the week before the Open. But that may also have had something to do with the events of the previous evening. At around 10:30 p.m., Matthew was in bed but her husband was still working on his computer on the balcony of their hotel room. Hearing an ever increasing noise, Matthew said: "Oh, it's heavy rain out." Graeme came in and said: "What on earth are you talking about?" "Eventually we opened the door and it was just flames and smoke outside the door," Matthew explained. "It was very scary. We just ran out of the room and out of the hotel. We kind of panicked and forgot to put on any shoes and Graeme got his feet burnt. Then we kind of ran around shouting fire and getting other people out."

Another player, Amy Yang, and her father were on a higher floor but could not escape through the hotel. They threw the mattresses from their beds over the balcony and jumped down. They were uninjured. Matthew was just thankful that their daughters were not with them in France but were being cared for at home by Graeme's parents. "If we had had the kids with us we would probably have been exhausted and asleep already. It was fortunate it was just the two of us."

Matthew won the British Women's Amateur Championship at Lytham in 1993, but her record in the Women's Open was better away from the links courses. She led with a round to play at Sunningdale in 2001 and finished third. The halfway leader at St. Andrews in 2007, she fell away over the weekend. Her best result in a major championship had come at the Kraft

Nabisco Championship in 2007 when she was second. But her goals were not exactly high. "Coming back to play last week and this I was just hoping to make two cuts," she said.

Doing that at Lytham was no mean feat. The first phase of toughening up the links in preparation for the 2012 men's Open meant a number of new bunkers and some new mounding. After a wet summer the rough was long, and after a few days of steady downpours, was wet. "It was hellacious," said Karen Stupples, the 2004 champion who had an 82.

Defending champion Jiyai Shin had a 77 which included double bogeys at the last two holes. After that the South Korean put up a fine defense of her title until another six at the 18th on Sunday dropped her out of a tie for third place. She had recorded a charity record in Korea and had promised to sing at the prize giving if she won, but the vocals were not required. Webb also opened with a 77, but Laura Davies had a 79 and European No. 1 Gwladys Nocera a 91.

At the other end of the leaderboard five players did break par despite the strong wind which was particularly difficult on the second nine. Hee Young Park and Yuko Mitsuka had 71s, Song-Hee Kim and Angela Stanford 70, and Sandra Gal a 69, three under par. Gal, out in the penultimate group, birdied the 17th to take the lead as dusk was descending. The German, now based in America, also holed a good putt on the last for her par.

But in many ways the round of the day came from Stanford, whose form had been trailing off since her mother was diagnosed with breast cancer. She also did not have the best record in the British Open, so, after the Evian, planned a mini vacation in Rome to see the sights and offer up the odd prayer in the Sistine Chapel. She arrived in Lancashire only on Wednesday afternoon and played just the one practice round. "Given my form in this event in recent years I think the trip made me much more relaxed and I think this justifies it," Stanford said.

Matthew opened with a 74, which included a double bogey at the 17th hole where she thinned her second shot into a hillock covered in some of the worst rough on the course. She had to declare a lost ball and reload, making a good six in the end. On Friday, the wind was still gusting, but now helping more on the back nine. She was out in 37, two over par, and her chances were dwindling, but then she holed a good putt on the 10th green for a par and that turned everything around. The last six holes at Lytham represent one of the strongest finishing stretches on the Open rota, and although the 15th becomes a par-five for the women, making the inward par 37, it is no less difficult.

But Matthew's run started at the par-five 11th where she hit a rescue club from 218 yards to six feet and holed the putt for an eagle. At the next hole, the 160-yard 12th, she hit an eight iron into the hole. "I knew it was a good shot, but I was just relieved that I had hit the green and turned away. It was only when Graeme shouted 'Get in the hole' that I looked up, but I missed it going in."

Matthew's efforts on Friday meant 1010 trees were planted under a scheme for the environment supported by the sponsors, Ricoh. Jeong Jang also had a hole-in-one, at the first on Sunday, to make the total contribution significantly in excess of the 2008 tally.

Matthew punched a seven iron to 10 feet at the 13th for a birdie, chipped to three feet for a birdie-four on the 15th, and hit a gap wedge from 100 yards to a matter of inches to go seven under for her last six holes. She dropped a shot at the 17th, but then holed from 10 feet at the last for a closing birdie and a round of 67, equaling the best of the week. Her inward 30 had never been achieved at Lytham. "Of course it's got to be one of my best nines ever," she said.

Matthew shared the halfway lead with Giulia Sergas of Italy, who also had 67, at three under par. The only other players in red figures were Yuko Mitsuka, who was two under after two rounds of 71, and Song-Hee Kim, who was one under. Cristie Kerr was at three over, with Shin, Creamer, Webb at four over and Michelle Wie at five over after a double bogey at the 18th. Among those missing the cut at 10 over were Suzann Pettersen, Helen Alfredsson and Natalie Gulbis, while Becky Brewerton was 11 over, Stupples and Melissa Reid 15 over.

While Sergas fell away with a 78 in the third round, Matthew held firm despite bogeys at the third and fourth holes. She responded with a two at the fifth and did not drop another shot. She birdied the 10th and 13th in an inward 35 and hardly missed a green. She owned the back nine and after a 71 was at four under and leading by three over Christina Kim, who also had a 71. With a 68 Shin moved up to even par alongside Miyazato, the Evian Masters winner, while Creamer was at two over. "There are a lot of good players up there, so I can't afford to let up," Matthew said.

Matthew's opening tee shot ran through the green at the par-three first and she could not get up and down. She dropped another shot at the third and missed a short birdie chance at the fifth. This was not going to plan. Graeme Matthew, her husband and caddie, told her: "You're still in the lead, keep going." Matthew admitted: "I was getting a little anxious and a bit down on myself, but his words really helped."

Up ahead, Webb, who started eight shots back at four over, had birdied the sixth and then chipped in for an eagle at the 15th and holed from four feet for a birdie at the 16th. The Australian, a three-time former winner, set the clubhouse target at even par but still trailed Matthew by one and was not hopeful of getting in a playoff, but was not going anywhere either.

Matthew's troubles continued at the 10th where she had to take an unplayable from a bush beside the green. She holed a good putt to save her bogey and then she was into her back nine mode again. She saved par with another good putt at the 12th before hitting a brilliant second from the rough at the 13th and holing from 18 feet. At the next she holed from 40 feet and now had an inkling that things really were going to go her way. "Right, you are never going to have a better chance than this," she said to herself. At the par-five 15th she got up and down for a third successive birdie, and what had been a crowded leaderboard suddenly had an obvious winner, and a bogey at the 17th could not change that, especially as Miyazato and Creamer ran into trouble on the closing holes.

Matthew was inside the qualifying positions for the European Solheim Cup team, but part of her returning to action so soon was to ensure her place in the match in Illinois a few weeks later. This was the last qualifying event for both teams and the victory not only secured her place on the team but meant Europe would travel with two major champions, Matthew and Anna Nordqvist, the LPGA champion who was one of Alison Nicholas's three wild card picks. The others were Janice Moodie and Becky Brewerton. The American qualifying positions did not change and Beth Daniel selected Inkster and Wie for her two picks.

Nicholas said: "What Catriona has achieved is phenomenal, not just coming back after having the baby, but also considering the situation with the fire in France last week. She really deserves it and it has been a great boost for the whole team. We have certainly helped her celebrate in the clubhouse."

After her first child, Matthew finished second and third in her first two events. Here she went one better. Perhaps more children were on the agenda? "No, we decided two was going to be enough, but perhaps we should have started earlier," Matthew said. "At 39, it sounds old, but I don't feel that old," Matthew reflected. "Hopefully I've got a few years left in me yet. I feel as if I'm playing as well as ever."

7. American Tours

Historians trying to decide what was the top golf story of 2009 shouldn't have much trouble settling the debate. The nearest coin ought to do nicely. Call it:

For thrills, there was the return of Tiger Woods after eight months recuperating from knee ligament surgery. For those wondering whether he would still be himself on a repaired knee, the answer was six victories in 17 starts.

For inspiration, there was Phil Mickelson, trying to play golf after his wife Amy, 37 and the mother of two, underwent surgery for breast cancer. And in a cruel twist, his mother was also diagnosed with breast cancer and had surgery about the same time. In a fragmented season, he somehow managed three victories.

And for gloom, doom and impact, there was the damaged economy, hitting the PGA Tour right where it lived — in the upper levels of finance and business. Some mighty financial institutions were swept away like a house of cards, and some other sponsors were badly hurt. Buick, for example, ended a 51-year connection with the tour, wiping out the Buick Invitational and the Buick Open.

Woods hadn't played since winning the 2008 U.S. Open Championship with a torn anterior cruciate ligament and two stress fractures of the left knee. He underwent surgery, and in his absence the all-powerful TV ratings fell. The golf world fretted. After some eight months, he returned in March. He was ousted in the second round of the WGC - Accenture Match Play Championship and tied for ninth in the WGC - CA Championship. "I hit the ball a lot better than my scoring indicates," he said. Phil Mickelson got out of a hospital bed to win the CA Championship, dehydrated and shaking, and had only one regret. "I would love the opportunity to play head-to-head (against Woods)," Mickelson said. He would get that wish at the other end of the most difficult year of his career.

Woods hit his stride late in March, winning the Arnold Palmer Invitational at Bay Hill for the sixth time, then Jack Nicklaus's Memorial Tournament in early June. Then mark them off: the AT&T National, Buick Open, WGC - Bridgestone Invitational and finally the BMW Championship in September. Six victories in 17 starts.

"It's one of my best years," Woods said. "It's just been a matter of making a couple of putts." But it was a down year in his primary goals. He came up empty in the four majors.

• Masters: Angel Cabrera won it on the second playoff hole after tying with Chad Campbell and a faltering Kenny Perry, who let it slip away with bogeys on the last two holes.

• U.S. Open: Lucas Glover, firing great tee shots at demanding Bethpage Black, won his first major. "I dreamed about it as a kid," said Lucas. "Here I stand."

• The Open Championship: It fell one hole short of being one of the greatest stories in golf history. Tom Watson, 59, incredibly came within the 72nd hole of winning his sixth claret jug. When he faltered, Stewart Cink tied him and beat him in a playoff. Tiger Woods missed the cut for only the second time as a professional in a major championship.

• PGA Championship: It became a landmark event when the largely unknown Y.E. Yang, of South Korea, holed a chip-shot eagle at the 14th and birdied the 18th off a brilliant hybrid out of the rough to end Woods's record — 14-for-14 — of winning when he shared or held the lead after 54 holes.

Woods won the Player of the Year award, and Australian Marc Leishman, thanks to a second in the BMW Championship and two other top-10s, finished 47th on the money list and won the Rookie of the Year award. Woods headed a list of eight multiple winners in 2009. Mickelson and Steve Stricker won three each on the tour (Mickelson had a fourth, the WGC - HSBC Championship in Shanghai), and Zach Johnson, Geoff Ogilvy, Brian Gay, Kenny Perry and Y.E. Yang won two each.

Mickelson won three tour events and $5.3 million in 18 starts in his painful and disjointed season. He won the Northern Trust Open and the WGC - CA Championship early on, then missed much of the season after his wife's illness was diagnosed in May. He tied for second in the U.S. Open, and returned full-time at the Bridgestone Invitational in August. He went on to beat Woods head-to-head in The Tour Championship, when Woods won the FedExCup bonus. "I like the way today went," Mickelson said. "I was two back of him, I beat him by three. He gets the $10 million check, and I get the $1 million." Mickelson beat Woods again — adding Ernie Els to his bag — in the HSBC Champions in Shanghai.

In any other year, Stricker might have shared top billing. A journeyman pro since joining the tour in 1994, he had what amounted to a breakout year in 2009 — three victories, No. 2 on the money list with $6.3 million, and a smashing partnership with Woods in the Presidents Cup.

There were seven first-time winners, the fewest since 2003: Pat Perez, in the Bob Hope Classic; South Korea's Y.E. Yang, the Honda Classic (he then would beat Woods in the PGA Championship); England's Paul Casey, Shell Houston Open; Bo Van Pelt, U.S. Bank Championship; Australia's Nathan Green, RBC Canadian Open; Ryan Moore, Wyndham Championship; Scotland's Martin Laird, Justin Timberlake Shriners Hospitals for Children Open.

Northern Ireland prodigy Rory McIlroy, 20, who made the cut in all four majors and rose to No. 17 in the World Ranking, said he would join the PGA Tour for 2010. "I just feel that I will become a better golfer if I also play in America," he said.

McIlroy would fit the tour perfectly. A total of 16 countries were represented among the final top 125, and international players won 12 times in 2009.

And finally this statistical tidbit from the 2009 tour: No player in the top 10 in hitting greens in regulation won a tournament, but the top putters won six times, and the lead scramblers won five times.

U.S. PGA Tour

Mercedes-Benz Championship
Maui, Hawaii
Winner: Geoff Ogilvy

In retrospect, it was quite an amazing admission from a runaway winner. "I had never had a six-shot lead before," Geoff Ogilvy said. "That's quite an uncomfortable feeling, really." But that was Ogilvy after taking the Mercedes-Benz Championship, the 2009 season opener, in an exclusive field of 33 winners from 2008.

It seemed that Ogilvy, who won the 2006 U.S. Open in a clutch finish, had something of a cruise in the tournament at the par-73 Plantation Course at Kapalua Resort, Hawaii. Ogilvy shot 67-68-65-68–268, a robust 24 under par in beating Anthony Kim (67) and Davis Love (67) by six shots. He joined Ernie Els and Vijay Singh as the only wire-to-wire winners since the event moved to Kapalua in 1999.

Things aren't always as simple as they seem, and that certainly was the case here. First off, Ogilvy led by two strokes in the first round and by one after the second round. Then he raced to a six-stroke lead in the third round on a bogey-free 65 that included three straight birdies on the second nine and also three missed birdies on the closing holes.

Ogilvy was six strokes up on Justin Leonard (65) and D.J. Trahan (70). Camilo Villegas double-bogeyed the first hole, then made eight birdies over 10 holes for 66. Leonard was the most frustrated golfer in the field. He birdied eight of his last 14 holes, then checked the leaderboard at the 18th and saw, to his surprise, that Ogilvy was 19 under. "It was a little deflating, to say the least," Leonard said. But Ogilvy was not especially impressed with his position. "It's never over until the last hole," he said.

Ogilvy turned out to be closer to the truth than he wanted to be. After going the first 54 holes with just one bogey, he began the final round with four bogeys in his first eight holes. He missed the fairway at No. 1 and bunkered his tee shot at No. 2, and before long his six-shot cushion was down to three over Anthony Kim, who made four birdies on the first nine. Then Ogilvy was short of the seventh green and bogeyed, then missed the eighth green by 20 yards and bogeyed again. His lead was down to one. "It felt like a normal tournament again," he said. "I just told myself, 'It's a great spot to be in after 63 holes — get on with it.'" And he did so, immediately.

The par-five ninth was the turning point. Kim birdied it for a first-nine 32, but Ogilvy eagled it, hitting a two iron off the tee and a three iron from 230 yards to 21 feet and holing the putt. He was back to three up.

"From then on, I was a different person," Ogilvy said. He birdied the 10th hole with a 20-foot putt, the 12th from five, then made four consecutive birdies from eight feet or less and chalked up his fifth PGA Tour victory.

Sony Open
Honolulu, Hawaii
Winner: Zach Johnson

Zach Johnson was sounding like a travel guide. "The worst part of Hawaii," he said, toasting the natives with champagne, "is leaving." But this time it wouldn't be too hard. He was taking the Sony Open title with him.

This was the PGA Tour's first full-field event of the 2009 season, in mid-January at Waialae, and it was really two shows in one. There was the tournament proper, which ended up in something of a real match-play battle won by Johnson, the 2007 Masters champion, and then there was the strong subplot that occupied the home fans, and that was the diminutive Tadd Fujikawa, an 18-year-old Honolulu high school boy in a thrilling try to become the youngest winner in tour history. The riveting final-round duel among Johnson, David Toms, Adam Scott and Charles Howell played second banana for the huge home galleries. They were escorting Fujikawa's inspired effort. Fujikawa, who opened with 71-69, shook the Sony Open in the third round with an eight-under-par 62, rocketing to within two strokes of the lead, then held by Johnson. "Two years ago, I just went out there to have fun," said Fujikawa, who tied for 20th as a 16-year-old amateur. This time, drawing the gallery with him, he struggled to 73 in the final round and tied for 32nd. "I just couldn't get anything going," said Fujikawa. And then he was headed back to school on Monday.

"What he did this week should be inspiring, not only to himself, but to others," Johnson said.

Johnson had to work his way up the leaderboard. His opening 69 left him four behind Japan's Shigeki Maruyama, trying to shake off a gloomy 2008. In the wind and the rain Friday, Tom Pernice needed a driver and a three wood to get within 92 yards of the par-five 18th, and then punched a wedge for a hole-out eagle, a score of 63 and a share of the lead with Nathan Green (66) at 132. The chase was on. A dozen players were within four of the lead, led by Johnson, who exploded home with a birdie-birdie-eagle finish for 65, two off the lead. Then 66 in the third round sent Johnson into the fourth with a one-stroke lead.

It ended up as a final-nine duel between Johnson and Toms. When Toms birdied the ninth, they headed home tied at 11 under. They matched birdies at the 10th, then Johnson edged ahead at the 11th with a five iron to four feet for a birdie. He added another on an eight-footer at the 14th and two-putted the par-five 18th from 40 feet for his final birdie.

Bob Hope Classic
La Quinta and Bermuda Dunes, California
Winner: Pat Perez

The name was the same — Pat Perez. But the golfer was a whole new man. The old Pat Perez would have lost his temper, his game and the tournament on making a double bogey. The new Pat Perez kept his head for all five rounds, shook off a crucial double bogey, and with a huge boost from the unfortunate Steve Stricker, made the 50th Bob Hope Classic his first PGA Tour victory.

"I got tired of getting upset all the time," Perez explained. "I learned how the best guys do it. They put stuff behind them. Before, if I made a double ... the tournament was over. I look at that as a speed bump now."

Perez did double-bogey No. 5 in the fifth and final round after hitting a shot in the water. By this point, the tournament had taken a dramatic turn against him. Perez led for the first three rounds: by only one on his opening 61 at the PGA West Palmer course, one of four used in a rotation, and all four took a beating. Perez won by three strokes at 33 under par, and Brenden de Jonge, who finished 74th and dead last, was 10 under.

In the second round, a flawless nine-birdie 63 put Perez up by two on Briny Baird (63), who aced the 14-yard seventh. Perez's putting was extraordinary. He made birdies on putts of 15, 20 and 40 feet, and others from 10 feet and in. He needed just 25 putts for the second straight day.

Perez still led by two through the third round with 67–191, over Stricker, who closed fast with 61. Stricker then shot 62 in the fourth round to take a three-stroke lead on Perez (67–258) into the final round. It looked like a Perez-Stricker shootout in the finale.

Not so. Stricker crashed horribly — a triple-bogey seven out of the water at No. 7, then a quadruple-bogey eight at No. 10. He shot 77. John Merrick, eight behind at the start of the final round, took the lead briefly on the last nine. Merrick, starting his third full year on the PGA Tour, had his best finish, second place, thanks in large part to an incredible break. At the 16th, his fairway shot was wide right, heading for a canal, but the ball bounced off the concrete lining all the way back onto the green, 10 feet from the pin. He two-putted en route to 67–330 and a second-place finish by three.

Perez, playing in the last group, might have been expected to protect his lead down the 18th. Not so. Instead, he went right at a dangerous pin sitting behind a fronting pond, a tremendous six-iron shot from 200 yards to three feet. That set up his 69–327, 33 under par.

"I don't lay up," Perez said. "I mean, how hard is it? It's a six iron. I was going to hit it." And so the new, controlled Pat Perez found out what he'd been missing.

FBR Open
Scottsdale, Arizona
Winner: Kenny Perry

Kenny Perry, the amiable Kentucky boy who became the unlikeliest story of 2008, wrote another chapter of the tale early in 2009 in the FBR Open, emerging from the pack in the last two rounds, shaking off a bogey at the final hole, then beating Charley Hoffman on the third hole of a playoff.

"The playoff was ugly," Perry said. "We were hitting it everywhere, having to scramble from all over the place." But if it didn't win any style points, the playoff did give Perry his 13th PGA Tour win and his first following three victories in 2008.

Perry came roaring into the picture in the third round when he made up a four-stroke deficit over the last five holes, the last on a 33-foot putt at the 18th. It gave him a five-under-par 66 and a one-stroke lead over rookie Scott Piercy. The rally capped a long climb that began in the first round when he was four over with four to play. It started at the par-five 15th, where he boomed a three-wood second shot from 275 yards, setting up a birdie. "It's amazing what one shot can do for you," Perry said.

The same could be said for Piercy, but in reverse, also in the third round. Piercy roared off to eight birdies in the first 13 holes and was leading Perry by four. "The hole looked like a five-gallon bucket," he said. Then came the shot, a fluffed chip at the 14th. It led to the first of three bogeys. Said Piercy, "I look at it as eight birdies." But he was trailing Perry by one.

In the final round, Piercy backed up with 71 (he tied for sixth), but Perry still had his pursuers. Kevin Na, for one, came from six behind and would have joined the playoff but for a narrowly missed eight-footer at the 18th. Charley Hoffman shot 67 for a 270, leaving Perry needing only a par at the last to win. But he bogeyed out of a fairway bunker for 69 and a tie.

The playoff was rather messy, as Perry said. At the first extra hole, No. 18, both bunkered their tee shots and bogeyed. At the second, the par-four 10th, Hoffman bounced his tee shot off a cart path and over the green, and chipped to 13 feet. Perry drove into the left rough, then came out to 20 feet. Both two-putted for pars, and it was on to the third, the 17th. There, Perry drove to the right of the green and chipped poorly, to 22 feet. Hoffman buried his drive in a bunker and could only chip to the fringe. He managed a par from there, and Perry holed his 22-footer for the win, becoming, at 48, the oldest ever to win the FBR Open.

"It feels kind of funny," said Perry, "playing with all these young kids."

Buick Invitational
San Diego, California
Winner: Nick Watney

Nick Watney didn't lead the Buick Invitational for long — just long enough. That is, just at the final hole. "If you're going to lead for one hole," Watney said, "this is the time to do it."

That would be the 72nd hole, the 18th at the Torrey Pines South Course, the tougher of the two courses, holing a short birdie putt that had to feel like the ol' dagger in the heart to John Rollins. Rollins had the championship at his fingertips, leading by three strokes with just five holes to play. Then Rollins stumbled coming in, and Watney, 27, birdied the last two holes for his second PGA Tour victory in the tournament Tiger Woods had won for the previous four years. Woods, who also won the 2008 U.S. Open at Torrey Pines, missed this one, recovering from knee surgery the previous June.

Rollins had come a long way in the tournament. He opened with a two-under-par 70 on Torrey Pines North and was seven behind Camilo Villegas (62). A 64 on the South Course then lifted him to within one of Villegas at the halfway point. The third round started with a jolt when Charlie Hoffman, who had moved into contention, moved right back out when he got stung weirdly. He hit his opening tee shot into a tree and the ball didn't come back down. The lost-ball penalty sent him to a triple bogey and he was out of the running.

Rollins started the third round a shot off the pace and surged into a five-stroke lead. Maybe it was a sign of things to come when Rollins tripped twice coming in, shot 70 and was down to a three-stroke lead through the third round over Villegas (74) and Watney (71).

Rollins started the last round with bogeys at the first two holes, but he stayed ahead of the pack. Watney got a glimmer of encouragement when he birdied the par-five 15th, but the glimmer faded fast when Rollins eagled it and was back up by three. But not for long. At the par-four 14th, Rollins missed both the fairway and the green and bogeyed. He also bogeyed the par-three 16th out of a plugged lie in a bunker. Watney then holed a 40-foot birdie putt at the 16th, and they were tied at 10 under. Finally, at the par-five 18th, Watney was on in two, hitting a hybrid club from 235 yards to 60 feet. Rollins hit his second into a greenside bunker, then came out to 12 feet. Watney lagged his 60-footer down to three feet and then holed that for his first lead — and his last.

Villegas (72) and Lucas Glover (68), who started the final round seven strokes back, tied for third, and Padraig Harrington tied for 24th. If Watney was a surprise winner, Phil Mickelson was a surprise flop. Mickelson, who missed the cut in his season start, tied for 42nd at two-over 290.

AT&T Pebble Beach National Pro-Am
Pebble Beach, California
Winner: Dustin Johnson

A funny thing happened to Dustin Johnson on his way to breakfast that morning. He won a golf tournament.

This was the awkward end to the rain-plagued AT&T Pebble Beach National Pro-Am. Johnson, age 24, a rookie and a one-time winner, led by four strokes through the third round, and then a severe storm forced officials to postpone Sunday's play. So it was Monday morning that Johnson was going to breakfast before the final round when his telephone rang. He wouldn't have to play. "It was Michael Letzig, one of my buddies out here," Johnson said. "He called to congratulate me, and I didn't know what he was talking about."

Letzig was calling to say that Monday's play also had been scratched, and that Johnson had been declared the winner after 54 holes. Johnson said he would have preferred to win in four rounds. But, he said, "A win is a win."

Johnson, who won the Turning Stone Resort Championship back in October, made a big statement right out of the blocks in this one. Starting at Pebble Beach in the three-course tournament, he holed a nine iron from 151 yards for an eagle at No. 1 and went on to a bogey-free 65 and a share of the first-round lead with Robert Garrigus. Johnson then shot 69 at

Spyglass Hill and 67 at Poppy Hills, and then the heavy weather wiped out the final round. Johnson finished with a 15-under-par 201 total and won by four strokes over Mike Weir. The big names, meanwhile, were not factors. Mickelson made the cut right on the number, and Vijay Singh and Padraig Harrington both missed the cut.

While no one was really paying attention, the efficient Johnson was 12 under par for his first 29 holes, had a stretch of 33 holes in 12 under, and he had just one bogey and one double bogey through his three rounds. After sharing the lead with Garrigus in the first round, he slipped behind at Spyglass Hill in the second. He opened with four birdies in his first six holes, but double-bogeyed the 17th from the trees and settled for 69–134, two behind Retief Goosen (64–132).

Johnson went largely unnoticed in the third round, playing Poppy Hills, the least of the three courses, and after a birdie-bogey exchange at Nos. 4 and 8, he birdied the next four and added the 18th for his 67 and his four-stroke margin.

The victory, the second in his last nine starts, lifted Johnson to No. 45 in the World Ranking, and it left him and Anthony Kim the only players under age 25 with more than one win.

PGA Tour Commissioner Tim Finchem provided a subplot to the tournament. He made a rare appearance in a tournament, playing in a pro-am team with Davis Love. "It makes you nervous to go out and play with these great players," Finchem said, "and being nervous is kind of fun."

Northern Trust Open
Pacific Palisades, California
Winner: Phil Mickelson

Phil Mickelson added a new verb to the language, the infinitive of which was "to heart." As he said after taking the Northern Trust Open in a wild finish, "To be able to heart it out on 16 and 17 with birdies, then to make that par on 18 when two years ago I didn't, that meant a lot to me."

Once the convolutions were smoothed out, one had a concise account of how Mickelson, defending champion, squandered an early five-stroke lead, trailed by two with three holes to play, and then won by one.

It was his 35th career win and 17th on the western portion of the PGA Tour. He became the fourth, after Ben Hogan, Corey Pavin and Mike Weir, to score back-to-back victories at Riviera.

Mickelson had a wild time at Riviera, playing the famed par-71 course near Los Angeles in 63-72-62-72–269, 15 under. He led by four going into the final round and bumped that to five with an eagle at No. 1 for the third straight day, getting to 18 under. Then he began crumbling — a chunked chip shot and a bogey at No. 2, a hooked tee shot into a tree and a bogey at No. 3, and then he bogeyed the 12th and 14th and was at 13 under.

Through Mickelson's travails, Fred Couples and Andres Romero, two close pursuers, couldn't grab the advantage. But Steve Stricker could. Playing ahead of Mickelson, Stricker birdied three of his first six holes, bogeyed No. 8, then birdied Nos. 9, 11 and 12, the last on a six-foot putt that gave him the lead for the first time over the sagging Mickelson. A birdie at the par-five 17th might have locked up the win for him, but he missed on the 12-foot try, and then he suffered a fatal bogey at the 18th. He finished with 67 and a 270 total and was about to get ready for a playoff when he heard the dooming roar from the 18th.

Mickelson was just finishing. He had come to the par-three 16th trailing by two and picked up a shot with a birdie off a nine iron to five feet. Then he birdied the 17th, knocking a three wood to 70 feet and two-putting. Then he remembered costing himself the tournament two years earlier, blowing the lead at the 18th. So bracing himself, he found the last fairway confidently, hit his second to 70 feet and two-putted for par, the winner from a nerve-wracking six feet. That triggered the roar that stopped Stricker on his way to warm up for a playoff.

"It's just a little disappointing when you don't finish it off ... and I didn't," said Stricker, also remembering how the Bob Hope Classic had gotten away from him a month earlier.

Said Mickelson: "I'm pleased to be sitting here as the champion. Even though I didn't have my best stuff, I was able to fight through it. I'll take a lot out of this."

Including some deep breaths.

WGC - Accenture Match Play Championship
Marana, Arizona
Winner: Geoff Ogilvy

Of the 64 players in the field for the World Golf Championships - Accenture Match Play Championship, 63 knew that no matter what happened, this was Tiger Woods's week. This was the long-awaited return of Woods, eight months since surgery after he won the 2008 U.S. Open with a torn anterior cruciate ligament and two small stress fractures of his left knee. Interest in the PGA Tour had fallen in Woods's absence. Now he was back, proclaimed by publications as the one who would save golf.

Woods's return overshadowed even the tournament itself. The Accenture attracted 500 media members and 175 media outlets — both figures up considerably from the 2008 tournament — to the Ritz-Carlton Golf Club in Marana, Arizona.

So it was Tiger Woods's week, all right, but it was Geoff Ogilvy's tournament. Ogilvy, the No. 8 seed, made his way through the six rounds, defeating Paul Casey (23rd) by 4 and 3 in the 36-hole final for his second Accenture Match Play title and his third WGC victory.

The top-seeded Woods, in his first competitive golf since the 2008 U.S. Open, ousted nervous Australian Brendan Jones, 3 and 2, without incident in the first round. "I've been nervous ever since I found out I was playing him," Jones said. But in the second round, South Africa's diminutive Tim Clark (5-foot-7, 165 pounds), also nervous ("I just tried to calm myself down"), went 16 holes without a bogey and beat Woods, 4 and 2. "I knew I had to play out of my mind to beat him," Clark said.

Said Woods, on his way out, "I was really pleased ... I hit the ball well the last two days." For example, against Jones, at the 574-yard No. 2, he fired a three iron to four feet, setting up a conceded eagle.

Back at the tournament, Vijay Singh was the only other of the four No. 1 bracket seeds to advance through the first round, beating Soren Kjeldsen, 2 and 1. The other two No. 1s were dumped 1 up — Padraig Harrington by Pat Perez and Sergio Garcia by Charl Schwartzel. Singh was ousted in the second round by Luke Donald in 19 holes.

Ogilvy made his way through to the final by beating Kevin Sutherland, Shingo Katayama, Camilo Villegas, Northern Ireland whiz kid Rory McIlroy (age 19) and Stewart Cink. Casey defeated Aaron Baddeley, Matthew Goggin, Peter Hanson, Sean O'Hair and Ross Fisher.

Ogilvy, running his match play record to 18-3, was a machine. He didn't trail over the last 62 holes and didn't make a bogey over the last 57. "The best thing I can say is that I enjoy the format," Ogilvy said. "Generally, when you enjoy something, you do it well."

Casey himself was no slouch at match play, not with a 16-3-1 record coming into the final. But Ogilvy had him three down after the morning match, and after Casey birdied three of the first eight holes in the afternoon, he found himself five down. Ogilvy then holed a six-foot birdie putt at the 15th for the win.

"I have no excuses right now," Casey said.

The win left Ogilvy, who won the season-opening Mercedes-Benz Championship, facing questions about rising to No. 4 in the World Ranking. "That's not really for me to decide," he said, and then he conceded, "I think I'm a pretty decent player."

Mayakoba Golf Classic
Riviera Maya, Mexico
Winner: Mark Wilson

Winning the Mayakoba Golf Classic — the PGA Tour's lone stop in Mexico, played opposite the WGC - Accenture Match Play — was largely a matter of playing the percentages for Mark Wilson. His putting had soured so much that he had to make an emergency stop to see his guru just before the tournament. The guru observed that he was getting about 70 percent of his weight on his right foot and only 30 on his left. It also didn't help that he was lined up wrong. Corrections were made.

Then during the Tuesday pro-am, Wilson — who had missed three cuts and finished so-so twice in five events — found that he would be more accurate if he geared back to about 80 percent power on his tee shots. "All of a sudden," said Wilson, "the ball started curving a little to the left, which I like. I just kind of went from there."

That is, from there to his second PGA Tour victory, his first since 2007. He shot 66-64-69-68 for a 13-under 267 total, two ahead of J.J. Henry.

And he wrapped it up in the final round in the teeth of blustery February-March winds that made frustrating work of the par-70 El Camaleon at Playa del Carmen.

Wilson's win denied two guys who had visions of finally getting that first win. Bo Van Pelt led the first round with 63 and tied Wilson for the third-round lead. Then in the fourth round, he doubled-bogeyed four straight holes from the 14th and blew to a 79. Kevin Na got his hopes up with 62 that tied Wilson in the second round, then tapered off and finished fifth.

Overall, Wilson, armed with his newly reduced power, made life easier for himself first by hitting fairways. "It's not a bomber's course," said Wilson, who's not a bomber. And second, by solving the tricky greens with his newly corrected putting.

Wilson, co-leader through the second and third rounds, took the lead for good at No. 2 in the final round. But his victory wasn't a lark. Wilson was leading Henry by three, but was down to one when he bogeyed the 14th. Then he bogeyed the 16th as well. But Henry couldn't cash in the opportunity. He bogeyed the 16th and 17th, then saw a birdie chance at the 18th die when the winds turned his approach shot aside.

"Extremely difficult," Henry said. "But it was the same for everybody."

Wilson's three-wood approach to the 18th, through the treacherous wind and onto the green, was a thing of beauty, and it helped him survive a tense moment. "You know, you're just so nervous, and (then) you somehow pull off one of the best shots of the week," he said. "It's just pure joy ... that you don't get overwhelmed by the situation and you hit a good shot."

Honda Classic
Palm Beach Gardens, Florida
Winner: Y.E. Yang

It doesn't get any more obscure than this: Coming into the Honda Classic, early in March, South Korea's Y.E. Yang, age 37, with seven victories in various places, was ranked 460th in the world. He was best remembered, if at all, for beating Tiger Woods by two strokes in the HSBC Champions tournament in Shanghai in 2006. It wasn't exactly a flukish accomplishment. Woods wasn't alone. Yang finished three ahead of Retief Goosen and Michael Campbell, and scattered back through the field were such world stage performers such as Paul Casey, Padraig Harrington, Jim Furyk and Luke Donald.

In the Honda Classic, at PGA National in Palm Beach Gardens, Florida, Yang pulled away in the second round and took a one-stroke win over John Rollins with a nine-under-par 271 at the par-70 Champion Course.

Yang, with two-under-par 68 in the first round, was easily upstaged by Robert Allenby, Erik Compton and Mathias Gronberg, all for different reasons. Allenby solved the heavy winds for a one-stroke lead on 66. "I just took one or two clubs more, tried not to force it," he said. Compton, who opened with 69, was celebrated as the man who underwent a second heart transplant in 2008. Then there was Gronberg and his disaster. He was one over through six holes, then made three triple bogeys in four holes and shot 89. Said Gronberg: "That's a record for me."

Yang was dynamite with the putter in the second round in a bogey-free 65. He needed just 25 putts and one-putted 11 times for a one-stroke lead on Will MacKenzie (67), Jeff Overton (67) and Allenby (68). Those expecting Yang to fall back would be disappointed in the third round. Six different players had at least a share of the lead, but Yang posted a one-birdie, one-bogey 70 to keep his one-stroke lead, this time over Overton (70) and Jeff Klauk (67). Which would he like better if he won, the $1,008,000 first prize or the two-year exemption on the PGA Tour? "Both would be nice," Yang said.

And both is what he got. Far from folding, as might be expected, Yang tightened his grip with three straight birdies on the front nine that carried him to a four-stroke lead. But he wasn't safe yet. Rollins birdied four of five holes around the turn, then birdied the 18th while Yang bogeyed the par-three 17th from a bunker and led by only a shot. Yang faced his moment of truth at the 18th, where from only 117 yards he put his approach 50 feet from the flag. But he braced himself and got his first putt to two feet, then holed out for the victory. And then he pumped his fist, high-fived the gallery and cried — a reaction totally out of character with the classical notion of the stoic Asian. "Pure emotion," Yang explained.

WGC - CA Championship
Miami, Florida
Winner: Phil Mickelson

In classical boxing lore, the contender gets up off the canvas to win by a knockout. How about Phil Mickelson's version in the WGC - CA Championship — getting out of a hospital bed?

Mickelson, after holding or sharing the lead through the first three rounds, ended up in a hospital bed wracked by a stomach ailment that left him shaking, sweating and dehydrated. "It took a lot out of me," Mickelson said. "I haven't eaten much in three days. ... I'm very excited to have finished it off."

This he did — after starting 65-66-69 — by closing with a three-under-par 69 to hold off an error-prone Nick Watney by a stroke with his 19-under 269 total at Doral's Blue Monster in Miami. It was Mickelson's second victory in three starts, after the Northern Trust Open, and his first in the World Golf Championships. Jim Furyk (67) finished third, and India's Jeev Milka Singh (70), co-leader in the first round, was a solo fourth, his best finish on the PGA Tour. Tiger Woods, making his second start since returning from knee surgery, was never a factor and tied for ninth. "I didn't get anything out of my rounds," he said. "I hit the ball a lot better than my scoring indicates."

It was in the first round, by the way, that Sweden's Henrik Stenson stripped down to his undershorts to hit a shot out of the water at No. 3, thereby gaining instant fame, courtesy of an alert photographer.

Mickelson's opening 65, tying him for the lead, was the work of his amazing short game. After a watery double bogey at No. 3, he watered his tee shot at the par-three No. 4 and chipped in to save par. He almost drove the 355-yard 16th, and pitched tight and birdied, then chipped in at the 18th. In the second round, he birdied the seventh with another chip-in, and birdied the par-five eighth spectacularly, curving a 245-yard three wood around the trees, over water and to within 15 feet of the hole. His 66 gave him a two-stroke lead on Watney (67), the Buick Invitational winner.

Mickelson had hoped for a head-to-head meeting with Woods and got it instead with Watney in the third round. Watney tied him with 67 that included three straight birdies from No. 2 and his first bogey of the tournament. Mickelson bogeyed the 17th out of the bushes and shot 69.

In the fourth round, there were seven lead changes through the 11th. Watney birdied the ninth with a chip-in, then eagled the 10th. But he hurt himself with three bogeys out of bunkers, the last at the 12th. Mickelson, still fighting his illness, bogeyed after hitting an inverted eight-iron shot right-handed from under a bush but kept the lead when Watney bogeyed out of a bunker. Mickelson closed with 69 and the one-stroke win, and had just one regret: Woods wasn't really in it.

"I would love the opportunity to play head-to-head," Mickelson said.

Puerto Rico Open
Rio Grande, Puerto Rico
Winner: Michael Bradley

Everybody quotes that threadbare golf cliché, "You drive for show and you putt for dough." But in case anyone had forgotten, Michael Bradley was only to happy to drag it out, dust it off, and hang it on his victory in the Puerto Rico Open.

"My short game was good this week," said Bradley, notching his third PGA Tour victory, but first since 1998. "It cured some ills off the tee and some in iron play, so I have to credit this (victory) to chipping and putting."

Especially at the final hole. Bradley reached the par-five 18th in two, but badly misread his lengthy eagle putt and left himself a dicey 11-footer for a birdie and the victory. He rolled it in like a veteran winner.

It didn't take the edge off his glow that the high-ranked players were at the WGC - CA Championship at Doral, in Florida. It was worth $630,000, a two-year exemption on the tour and berths in the 2009 PGA Championship and the 2010 Mercedes-Benz Championship.

It was a victory crafted out of a week in nagging March winds and constant pressure at Trump International. Bradley, never more than two strokes off the lead, shot 67-69-68-70–274, 14 under par, to win by one over Brett Quigley and Jason Day, 21, the promising Australian who shared the lead through the first three rounds. He had a chance to tie Bradley on the final hole, but missed his birdie from seven feet.

Day and Monday qualifier Derek Lamely shared the first-round lead at 66. Bradley was a shot back, and pleased. "Kept it out of the wind when need be, and I'm definitely happy with 67," Bradley said. Day (68) then shared the second-round lead with Matt Jones, who tied the course record with 64, amazing considering the wind.

Then it was Day (70) and Bradley (68) tied at 12 under in heavy winds through the third. "You're aiming 30, 40, 50 feet left of where you want the ball to go," Bradley said.

In the final round, Day suffered a near-fatal double bogey at the par-five second hole, but pulled his game back together. Bradley salvaged a birdie at the 12th. He missed the green long, then pitched in from behind. Then came the 18th. Bradley, after goofing on the long eagle putt, sank the 11-footer for his birdie. Day bunkered his approach, came out to seven feet, and missed the putt. It was a case of nerves. "I tell you, my whole body was shaking over that putt," he admitted.

All wins are important, but this was more so to Bradley. "I'm almost 43, and you don't know really how many opportunities you're going to have," Bradley said. "I'm not Tiger Woods. So when I do have an opportunity ... to win, it's probably a little more special."

Transitions Championship
Tampa Bay, Florida
Winner: Retief Goosen

Standing on the final green of the Transitions Championship, Retief Goosen needed only to two-putt from 25 feet to win. When he rapped his first putt five feet past the cup, then he had his choice of memories — the nightmare at Southern Hills, where he missed a short putt and nearly blew the 2001 U.S. Open, or the thrill of Shinnecock Hills, where he won the 2004 U.S. Open in a putting frenzy. The greens at the Copperhead Course at Innisbrook, in Florida, had become crusty and swift, and they bedeviled the field all week. And it was the ugly memory of Southern Hills that rushed in on him when he ran that first putt five feet past. "I didn't want to have another U.S. Open," Goosen was to say. "It was great to see that putt go in," he said, after rapping the thing home for a one-stroke win, his seventh PGA Tour victory but his first in almost four years. "The greens got scary. Down those last few holes, they were definitely getting like Shinnecock was. You just cannot hit them soft enough."

The putt gave Goosen a 70 and a one-stroke win over Brett Quigley (68), who was now 0-for-342 in 13 years on the tour, and Charles Howell (69), who was tied for the lead with four holes to play, then bogeyed two straight. "If Retief's five-footer had lipped out, I wouldn't have cried," Howell said. He needed a victory to get into the Masters, and time was running out. Now he had only two chances left — the Arnold Palmer Invitational and the Shell Houston Open.

Jim Furyk, who had skipped the first five weeks of the season, led the first round with a six-under 65. "I was a little nervous about being rusty," he said. Perhaps he was. He shot 78 in the second.

The Transitions looked like the rebirth of Tom Lehman in the third round. He'd just turned 50 and had recovered from elbow tendonitis and was Champions Tour-bound. But he wanted another crack at the PGA Tour. A burst of four straight birdies from the 12th produced a 68, a one-stroke lead over Goosen (69) and a rare flash of temper. TV commentator Johnny Miller suggested that Lehman had chunked the delicate short chip from deep grass that rolled up to tap-in range at the par-three 17th. "That's one of the best shots I hit all week," Lehman said. "Gosh, that makes me mad."

As to Goosen's scary five-footer to win, it seems his worry was wasted. For the tournament, he made all 55 putts he had from that range and 62 out of 64 from 10 feet and in.

Arnold Palmer Invitational
Orlando, Florida
Winner: Tiger Woods

In sports parlance, an athlete who has great success at a particular venue is said to own it. So Tiger Woods owns Bay Hill, Arnold Palmer's golf course in Orlando. In winning the 2009 Arnold Palmer Invitational, Woods ran his record to six victories in 13 visits. And it was the third time he won with a birdie on the 72nd hole. If that's not a deed signed, sealed and delivered, what is it?

To complete the drama, it was Woods's third tournament and first victory on returning from reconstructive knee surgery eight months before. "It feels good to be back in competition, to feel the rush," said Woods. "It's been awhile, but God, it felt good."

Woods came from five strokes behind in the final round — with astonishing help from Sean O'Hair — to win by one. He shot 68-69-71-67–275, five under par.

"It's like Stevie was saying out there," Woods said, speaking of his caddie, Steve Williams. "This feels like we hadn't left. You just remember how to do it."

It had to be a crushing blow for O'Hair, 26, a two-time winner in his four years on the PGA Tour. He was dominating the tournament from the second round when his five-under-par 65 gave him a three-stroke lead over Jason Gore (70). "The rough is very penal," O'Hair said, "but if you're in the fairway all day, you don't have to worry about it."

Said Woods: "You can make bogeys in a heartbeat because the greens are not accepting shots very well." A 69 left him five behind O'Hair.

The winds vexed everyone in the third round. O'Hair, leading by six, made three bogeys in his last four holes. "Sometimes," he said, "you have to hang on for dear life." He shot 71 and still led by five over Woods, who also could only manage 71. "I thought I played better than that," Woods said.

The final round was a nightmare for O'Hair. His touch failed. He hit greens but left himself long putts and didn't hit a fairway in the first six holes. Woods picked up three strokes on the front nine with three birdies and a bogey to O'Hair's two bogeys and his only birdie of the round. O'Hair's lead was down to one through the 10th, and Woods caught him with a birdie at the 15th. O'Hair squandered a good chance. At the 16th, Woods was in the rough, but O'Hair hit his seven-iron approach into the water and bogeyed to fall behind. But they were tied again when Woods bogeyed the 17th.

So it came down to the 18th — Woods's territory. He faced a 15-foot putt for a birdie and the win. Down it went.

"It's just a little bit disappointing that I couldn't close it," O'Hair said.

Said Woods: "You just have that feel of what to do. And it's a matter of getting it done."

Shell Houston Open
Humble, Texas
Winner: Paul Casey

England's Paul Casey, a nine-time winner on the European Tour and a Ryder Cup standout, had been knocking around on the PGA Tour for six years, and in early April, at the Shell Houston Open at Redstone Golf Club, was finally beginning to feel comfortable. But for that truly warm, cozy feeling, nothing beats watching the other guy hit it into the water. That was J.B. Holmes, hooking his tee shot at the first playoff hole. Casey stepped through for his first PGA Tour win.

"I'm finally getting to ... have belief in myself," said Casey, a former Arizona State University star. The win lifted him to No. 6 in the World Ranking.

Casey opened with a sparkling 66 — a bogey at No. 3, then seven birdies over the final 13 holes, including the last four straight. He went the rest of the way in 70-69-72 and was about to win in regulation play, but bogeyed the final hole to tie at 11-under 277 with Holmes, who had finished three hours earlier. After Holmes's drive at the first playoff hole, Casey carefully jumped at his chance. He hit a three wood off the tee, away from the water, and caught a fairway bunker. He laid up from there, pitched on, and two-putted from 27 feet for a bogey and the victory.

"I'll forget about it tomorrow," said Holmes, who shot 69 after starting the day three behind Casey. Casey had a huge gift earlier. Fred Couples, on the verge of his first victory since the 2003 Houston Open, led for much of the final round, then he bogeyed his last three holes and tied for third.

The tournament had plenty of other moments. The first round, for example, was delayed because of wind gusts that moved balls on the green. Phil Mickelson, hoping for a good pre-Masters tune-up after a layoff, shot 77-76 and missed the cut. "Stuff like that I needed to get out of my system after a couple of weeks off," Mickelson said. Greg Norman closed with 81 and tied for 70th, and Sergio Garcia closed with 74-81 and tied for 77th and last.

The final round, played in a buffeting wind, was a real shootout. In the biggest 54-hole traffic jam since 1970, fully 11 players, including Casey and Couples, were tied for the lead after the delayed third round ended Sunday morning. Couples moved ahead, but Casey tied him, birdieing the 12th from 10 feet and the par-five 13th from two. With Couples stumbling down the last three holes, Casey missed his chance to win outright, bogeying the 18th to tie Holmes. Then he added the playoff win to go with his European Tour victory at Abu Dhabi and his runner-up finish in the WGC - Accenture Match Play.

"I just took a little while to get used to things and feel comfortable," Casey said. "Now I feel comfortable out here."

Masters Tournament
Augusta, Georgia
Winner: Angel Cabrera

See Chapter 2.

Verizon Heritage
Hilton Head Island, South Carolina
Winner: Brian Gay

There was a decided flavor of stockcar racing in Brian Gay's victory in the Verizon Heritage. This was your basic pedal-to-the-metal, a-pox-on-the-rear-view-mirror dash to the finish line with a five-lap lead. Conventional golf says Gay should have throttled back coming down the stretch, but no. Gay, 37, a one-time winner, played as though he felt the seething breath of the devil himself on his neck.

The short version: Gay began the final round up by three shots and stretched that to six with a birdie-eagle start. But instead of playing conservatively, as he had in the 2008 Mayakoba Golf Classic — the first win in his 293 starts on the PGA Tour — this time he kept pouring it on. In the Mayakoba, he finished 16 under par and won by two, and in this one he was 20 under and won by an absurd 10 strokes, playing the Harbour Town course in Hilton Head Island, South Carolina, in 67-66-67-64–264.

"Once he started like that, it was almost like playing for second," said Tim Wilkinson, his playing partner, who slipped to a tie for sixth.

Gay had drawn some criticism for protecting his lead in the Mayakoba, played opposite the exclusive WGC - Accenture Match Play. He didn't want a repeat performance, so he jumped at his chances and started the final round birdie-eagle — a 10-foot putt at No. 1 and a huge, bending 57-footer at the par-five No. 2 — and was up by six, then by seven with a birdie at the par-five fifth.

"I told myself to keep my head down and keep plugging along," Gay said. "I didn't watch any (leader) boards, I didn't watch anything." It was an exercise in tunnel vision. Gay reached the final green and turned to his caddie: "I said, 'Who's in second?' He said, 'I don't know.' I said, 'How far ahead am I?' And he said, 'I don't know.'"

It became a question of records: Gay's 20-under total broke Loren Roberts's 19 under in the 1996 Verizon Heritage, and his 10-stroke victory buried Davis Love's margin of seven strokes in 1998.

It was Gay's tournament once he moved past first-round leader Alex Cejka, whose seven-under 64 was highlighted by a birdie on a 47-foot putt at the 17th. Gay bolted into the lead in the second round, posting six birdies on the front nine, including a burst of five straight from No. 4 on putts of 18, 25, five, 10 and 20 feet. "Heck, I was as surprised as anybody," Gay said. At No. 10, he took his first bogey of the tournament, then parred in. He would make only one other bogey, that at the 12th in the final round.

Gay was reminded that many of the top golfers had taken the week off, leaving only six of the top 20 in the field, the obvious suggestion that this was a watered-down win. "Who else is playing doesn't really matter," Gay said. "I think (the victory) will be a validation of winning last year."

Zurich Classic
Avondale, Louisiana
Winner: Jerry Kelly

There was yet another New Orleans parade that April Sunday evening, and strutting right out in front of the Dixieland jazz band was the parade marshal draped in his fancy tasseled sash, with parasol held on high. Only this parade wasn't in the French Quarter. It was at the 18th green at the TPC Louisiana, and the man out front was Jerry Kelly, who had just snatched the paraphernalia from the real parade marshal and was leading his own celebration.

"It's been a long time," said the good-natured Kelly, much relieved after taking the Zurich Classic. Kelly, 42, had just ended a victory drought that went back seven years and 200 starts. "I sometimes doubted if it was ever going to happen again."

It wouldn't have happened this time if Charles Howell had held himself together. He caught fire late, and from the 13th in the third round to the 11th in the fourth round — a span of flawless 17 holes — he was 10 under par on 10 birdies, racing into a two-stroke lead. Then he bogeyed twice down the home stretch, pulling his tee shot at the 15th and three-putting the par-three 17th. "It's frustrating," said Howell. "I got up to (No.) 15 and had every chance to do it. I just couldn't finish it off."

Kelly, playing behind Howell, said he wasn't troubled when Howell was leading by two at the 11th hole. "I knew what the back side had been doing to everybody all week," Kelly said. "And I had actually been playing the back side better."

Kelly bogeyed the eighth and 10th holes, birdied the 11th, then holed an eight-footer at the par-three 14th for another birdie and parred in, completing a card of 68-66-69-71—274, 14 under par, to win by one over Howell (68), Charlie Wi (68) and Rory Sabbatini (67).

After trailing Wi (66) in the first round, Kelly led the rest of the way, taking command with a strong 66 in the second round. He was six under through the 15th, made his second bogey of the tournament at the 16th, and birdied the 18th. Kelly made peace with his swing. "It wasn't completely on, but it was helping me get in there," he said. Troy Matteson (64) and Charley Hoffman (66) were a stroke back at 135. Kelly got some breathing room in the third round, his 69–203 putting him three up on Steve Marino (206). Kelly was leading that parade, and 18 holes later, he was leading another, off the 18th green.

The Zurich Classic was notable for another reason. Danny Lee, the reigning U.S. Amateur champion fresh from the Masters, was making his professional debut. It was predictably inauspicious for an 18-year-old. He shot 76-75, making four birdies, a bogey, two double bogeys and a triple bogey in the first round and three birdies and six bogeys in the second. Maybe someday history would have reason to know this was Danny Lee's start.

Quail Hollow Championship
Charlotte, North Carolina
Winner: Sean O'Hair

It was something like an old cowboy story. Sean O'Hair got thrown hard at Bay Hill, but he got right back on the horse at Quail Hollow and rode off with the championship. Not to carry the analogy too far.

"Losing stank at Bay Hill," the much embarrassed O'Hair said. And well it might have. Five weeks earlier, he blew a five-shot lead over Tiger Woods in the final round of the Arnold Palmer Invitational, leaving Woods with the victory. This time, in the Quail Hollow Championship, against a powerful field and even with Woods breathing down his neck, O'Hair raced home in the fourth round and, despite two closing bogeys, won by one over Lucas Glover and Bubba Watson and by two over Woods. It was O'Hair's third PGA Tour victory.

Note that the Quail Hollow Championship, taking its name from its site, the club in Charlotte, North Carolina, is the former Wachovia Championship. After the Wachovia Bank was taken over by Wells Fargo during the 2008 financial crisis, Wells Fargo removed its name from the event.

O'Hair tagged along with solid golf through the first three rounds, shooting 69-72-67 at the par-72 course. In the fourth round, he fell four behind with a bogey at No. 1, then went on a tear with birdies at Nos. 5, 8, 10, 12, 15 and 16. He caught Watson and Glover with the birdie at the 12th and grabbed the lead at the par-five 15th, two-putting from 70 feet. Then came perhaps his shot of the tournament at the 16th, pretty much a forced eight iron to eight feet. "I hit it as hard as I could and tried to flight it," O'Hair said, "and hit really a perfect golf shot." The birdie gave him the cushion he needed when he bogeyed the last two — a missed green at the 17th and a three-putt at the 18th — for a 69 and an 11-under 277 total.

The pursuit failed. Zach Johnson, leading by two strokes going into the final round, triple-bogeyed No. 2. Watson, leading for much of the back nine, missed a six-foot birdie try at the 15th and a six-foot par save at the 16th. Glover missed a five-footer for birdie at the 15th and bogeyed the 17th.

Woods, who led the first round on 65, labored through the fourth round. He bogeyed the first and sixth holes, birdied the fifth and eighth, and parred the last 10 holes. Woods blew a great opportunity at the par-four 14th. He thrilled the crowd by driving the green and had just under 25 feet for eagle. But he three-putted for par. "I made a mistake there," Woods said. "I knew the green was baked out. It was downwind, and I didn't heed my own warning, and ended up putting too hard."

And so O'Hair enjoyed a kind of redemption from the Bay Hill disaster.

The Players Championship
Ponte Vedra Beach, Florida
Winner: Henrik Stenson

Henrik Stenson was amazed that he was famous for having stripped to his underwear to hit a shot out of the water and not for his golf. "I guess," said the naive Swede, "I got as much attention off that thing as from my results the last 10 years." Well, not that anyone will ever forget the scene, but Stenson did take a giant step toward correcting the imbalance with a rousing come-from-behind victory in The Players Championship, playing the daunting TPC Sawgrass course like his personal violin in a grinding finish.

Think of starting the final round trailing by five strokes, then winning by four. He shot a bogey-free 66 on the Pete Dye masterpiece that was hard and running like a highway in the hot weather. It was his 10th career win, his second on the PGA Tour.

"It just seems to bring the best out of me ... playing the best players," Stenson said. He finished at 12-under-par 276 and won by four over Ian Poulter. It was a frustrating time for the big names. Jim Furyk tied for fifth, and Tiger Woods, never a threat, finished eighth. Padraig Harrington tied for 49th and Phil Mickelson for 55th.

The tournament turned on a tough third round. There were only five scores in the 60s, with a low of 68. Alex Cejka, who took the lead at 36 holes, shot par 72 and led by five, the biggest 54-hole margin in The Players' 36 years. It also got him paired with Woods in the final round, which is generally regarded as a death sentence. "I've got to play well tomorrow to win here," Cejka said. But he didn't.

Stenson was trailing by only two strokes, then bogeyed three of the last five holes for 73 and tied for second.

In the final round, the unfortunate Cejka saw his five-shot lead evaporate in the first four holes. He shot 79 and tied for ninth. "I hit good shots, but I got bad breaks, bad lies," he said. "I'm still happy."

The expected charge from Woods never materialized. He missed three fairways on the front nine, bogeyed all three holes, shot 73 and finished seven behind. "When you're playing a golf course like this and you don't have it, you can shoot some pretty high numbers," Woods said.

Stenson, meanwhile, went on a tear, making six birdies over 10 holes: the seventh from 15 feet, the par-five ninth on two putts from 55 feet, a bunker shot to six feet at the 11th, a 10-footer at the 13th, a two-footer at the 15th and a tap-in at the par-five 16th. Then he faced possibly the scariest hole in golf, the watery 137-yard 17th.

"Once I hit the 17th green, I pretty much knew I was going to win," Stenson said. Which he did. He parred in for a flawless 66, the only bogey-free finish, a 276 total and the four-shot victory, thus giving golf something else to remember him for.

Valero Texas Open
San Antonio, Texas
Winner: Zach Johnson

Zach Johnson had it pegged exactly right. "It just kind of went my way," he said, and that pretty well explained how he picked off his second straight Valero Texas Open and his sixth PGA Tour victory. Not that anybody simply handed it to him, though. Consider, for example, that tidy 10-under-par 60 he posted in the third round. Then there was the matter in the final round when seven players were scrambling within a stroke of the lead with four holes to play.

It came down to a playoff between Johnson, the former Masters champion, and James Driscoll, who wasn't even in the running when the final round began, not from eight shots off the lead. But Driscoll raced in with an eight-under 62, then had to wait more than an hour to see where he stood.

The way the challengers were taking themselves out of the running, it had to be in the cards for Johnson. First there was Paul Goydos, 44, the sentimental favorite after the tragic death of his ex-wife. He graciously accepted the sympathies. "We're all going to go through difficult times," the much admired Goydos said. Goydos shared the first-round lead at 63 with Justin Leonard, who was in the hunt for a record fourth Texas Open. Then Goydos took the solo lead by three with 65 in the second round. In the fourth round, he retook the lead briefly, dropping a 13-foot birdie putt at the 16th. Then came Johnson's first big edge. Goydos bogeyed the last two holes.

Next, Bill Haas, who had charged with five birdies in six holes from No. 11, fell just short when he two-putted from six feet and bogeyed the par-three 17th. Haas tied for third with Goydos, a stroke off the lead. Leonard, a definite factor, fell two strokes short with 69.

Johnson had edged into the race with 67 in the second round, getting to within seven of Goydos's lead. "Maybe a little polishing on the weekend, and hopefully we can make a push," he said. And what a push he made. In the third round, he posted eight birdies and crowned his day with an eagle, a hole-out from 84 yards at the par-four seventh for the 60 that erased his seven-stroke deficit. His chance for 59 slipped away at the 18th when his birdie try from 17 feet pulled up two feet short. He tapped in 18 seconds after the horn ended play in the deep twilight after a five-hour rain delay.

In the final round, Driscoll was already in with his 62–265 and the challengers were stepping aside when Johnson tied him with a 70. At the first playoff hole, Johnson fired a six-iron approach to 10 feet and holed the birdie putt, and that was it. Then Johnson told of how he felt about it all. "I feel very lucky," Johnson said.

HP Byron Nelson Championship
Irving, Texas
Winner: Rory Sabbatini

Rory Sabbatini, breaking through for his first victory since 2007, took the HP Byron Nelson Championship with a tournament record 19-under-par 261 total, and out of those 261 shots, which one would stand out most in his mind? One of his 26 birdies? One of his seven bogeys? None. A par.

It came on a bunker shot at his 12th hole in the second round. Sabbatini had driven into the water, taking a penalty drop, and then hit his third into a greenside bunker and was looking at a bogey or worse. And then he holed the bunker shot, a 96-footer, for his par. True, it would be two days and 42 holes before he would win, but for Sabbatini, it was the par on the bunker shot that did it. "My par on No. 3 (his 12th)," he said, "was better than any of the birdies."

The shot not only saved him from more trouble, it triggered a string of four straight birdies from his 13th hole on putts of nine feet, 13, nine again, and two putts from 65 at the par-five No. 7 that carried him to his season-low of 64 and a share of the halfway lead with John Mallinger at eight-under 132. Sabbatini had missed the cut at the Quail Hollow Championship and The Players Championship. "I made a bad choice of playing while I was sick," he said. "A few bad things crept into my swing. ... Luckily, I've worked that out a little bit."

Mallinger kept pace with a rather wild 65 — three bogeys, four birdies and eagles at both par-fives — a 45-foot bunker shot at No. 7 and a 14-foot putt at No. 16. Mallinger was sinking until a birdie-eagle-birdie stretch from No. 6 righted him. "It was kind of slipping away," he said. "Now we're in a perfect spot."

They stayed tied for the lead through the third round, both shooting 65s. Then Mallinger stumbled to two bogeys and two birdies coming out of the gate in the final round, but Sabbatini was off and running, and so was England's Brian Davis, looking for his first win. Davis had a blistering run, birdieing Nos. 7, 9, 10 and 11, and then making eagle at the 17th but falling short with a bogey-free 64. "I'm disappointed I didn't win, but all you can do is put yourself in position," he said. "I played great, stuck in there..."

Sabbatini went birdie-birdie-bogey from No. 4, then made seven birdies in 11 holes from No. 7. The critical point came when Davis eagled No. 16, cutting Sabbatini's lead from three to one. But Sabbatini tapped in for birdie there, then got his third straight birdie on an eight-footer at the 17th. A bogey at the 18th merely cut his winning margin to two.

It was an emotional victory for Sabbatini. First, there were ever-present thoughts for Phil Mickelson's wife, Amy, recently diagnosed with breast cancer. And then a personal friend, battling cancer. "It really puts everything we do out here into perspective," Sabbatini said.

Crowne Plaza Invitational
Fort Worth, Texas
Winner: Steve Stricker

It's the first commandment of the ubiquitous mind gurus of modern golf: "Thou shalt take something positive away from even the worst situation." But this time Tim Clark couldn't follow the doctor's orders. Said Clark, after leading the Crowne Plaza Invitational by two strokes with five holes to play, "I can't take anything positive from today."

Thus the tale of how Steve Stricker won a tournament he shouldn't have won, and how Clark lost a tournament he shouldn't have lost. Throw in Steve Marino crashing a party of errors, and it all ended up with Stricker winning on the second hole of a three-way playoff.

"I've been on the other end a couple times this year, where you feel you're going to win and end up losing," said Stricker, survivor of a long slump. "This feels very good."

Marino, winless in 81 tries, also felt pretty good. "I'm excited about playing golf and I feel good about my game," he said.

Clark, on the other hand, felt lousy. He was still trying for his first win. But he would leave Colonial Country Club in Fort Worth, Texas, with an 0-for-184 stretch and stuck with the tag as the man who won the most money — over $13 million — without winning a tournament.

Stricker and Clark nearly matched each other from the start, shot for shot. They shared the first-round lead with Woody Austin at seven-under-par 63. Clark had a three-foot birdie putt on the final hole for a 62 and the solo lead, but he missed it. Stricker played the benign Colonial course in another 63 in the second round for a tournament record 14-under 126 total. Clark (64) then leapfrogged into the lead in the third round with 66–193, to lead Stricker (69), Jason Day (65) and Marino (62) by two. Then the scramble was on.

In the final round, Stricker re-took the lead with birdies at Nos. 5 and 6, then bogeyed the next two holes. He seemed out of it when he missed a four-foot par putt at the 16th, but then chipped in for a birdie at the 17th and shot 68, matching Marino. Clark, who was tied for the tournament record and leading by two with five holes to play, suddenly turned erratic. He hit two tee shots into trouble, bogeyed the 14th, and finally missed a nine-foot par putt for the win at the last hole, and shot 70. On to the playoff.

On the first extra hole, Clark had a seven-footer to win. He missed. The second extra hole was the 17th, which Stricker had birdied three times already. Marino was wild off the tee and out of the running. Clark's approach hit the pin and ended up 20 feet away. He missed that birdie try. Stricker knocked his approach to three feet, and he didn't miss.

"You need breaks to win," Stricker said. "That's why winning is so hard to do."

Said Clark: "I have a lot of work to do when it comes to closing tournaments."

Memorial Tournament
Dublin, Ohio
Winner: Tiger Woods

The 2009 U.S. Open was pretty much awarded in advance to Tiger Woods by various and sundry media people, by fans, possibly by soothsayers looking for a sure thing, and also by no less an authority than Jack Nicklaus. What precipitated this cascade of deference or resignation, depending on one's point of view, was Woods snatching the Memorial Tournament that first week of June.

The usually cautious Nicklaus was inspired by Woods's performance at his golf course, Muirfield Village, near Columbus, Ohio, and so ventured, "I suspect that No. 15 will come to Tiger Woods in two weeks." Meaning that Woods, pursuing Nicklaus's record of 18 wins in majors, would get his 15th at the U.S. Open at Bethpage Black on Long Island.

Not that Woods dominated this Memorial. He trailed all the way and didn't really get a grip on it until the final two holes, with two great birdies. At the par-four 17th, he put a towering nine-iron approach to within nine feet, and at the par-four 18th, an uphill, dogleg right, he hit a seven iron to within inches. After tagging along on rounds of 69-74-68, Woods closed brilliantly with 65 for a 12-under-par 276 total, taking his fourth Memorial title by a stroke and leaving Jim Furyk (69–277) with his 21st runner-up finish in 400 PGA Tour starts.

"I knew I could do this," said Woods, notching his second victory in seven starts since returning from his 2008 knee surgery. "I was close to winning, but the game wasn't quite there. I rectified that."

One thing Woods rectified was his driver. He went up a half degree to 10 degrees of loft, and if that was for accuracy, he got it. Not known for his sharpness off the tee, he hit 49 of 56 driving fairways for the tournament, including a perfect 14-for-14 in the final round.

Woods was comparatively quiet at first. Luke Donald was center stage in the first round with a 64 that included just 20 putts. "Just really got on a hot streak," he said. Said defending champion Kenny Perry, starting later: "That's rough when you walk to the first tee and you're already eight behind."

In the second round, Woods shot his worst score in almost two years, 74, despite missing only two fairways. Furyk (70) and Jonathan Byrd (68) shared a one-shot lead at 137, with Woods six behind. A 68 in the third round left him four behind Matt Bettencourt (68), a 34-year-old rookie, and Mark Wilson (70) at 207.

Woods made his way up the leaderboard in the final round. He took a giant step at the par-five 11th, chipping in for an eagle. A bogey out of a bunker at the 16th dropped him into a tie with Furyk, Byrd and Davis Love. Then he broke free with the birdie at the 17th, and clinched it with another at the 18th.

"This is how you have to hit it to win U.S. Opens," Woods said.

Nicklaus couldn't have put it better himself.

St. Jude Classic
Memphis, Tennessee
Winner: Brian Gay

Brian Gay, best known for blitzing the Heritage by 10 shots just two months ago, this time led wire-to-wire and won by five at the St. Jude Classic, and in the process he locked up a berth in the U.S. Open the following week. Impressive as Gay's showing was, the St. Jude was Phil Mickelson's tournament, start to finish.

Not that Gay or anyone else minded. This was Mickelson's first week back after he announced a month earlier that his wife Amy had been diagnosed with breast cancer. An outpouring of sympathy and support from fans and players engulfed a worn-looking Mickelson all the way. "It's pretty flattering," Mickelson said. "The people here have been terrific." He entered the St. Jude to tune up for the U.S. Open the following week. No matter what else was happening in the St. Jude, the crowds were following Mickelson, cheering and offering words of encouragement, trying desperately, it seemed, to will him to victory. Mickelson did his best, but the circumstances showed in his game, and he tied for 59th, along with John Daly, making his first PGA Tour appearance after a six-month suspension for questionable conduct.

Gay, meanwhile, worked in comparative quiet and forged a wire-to-wire victory, playing the TPC Southwind course in Memphis, Tennessee, in 64-66-66-66–262, 18 under par, beating David Toms and former college star Bryce Molder by five. But the victory wasn't quite that decisive. Gay led by only one through each of the first three rounds. Then he pulled away in the fourth round. He birdied the second hole from six feet, the fourth from 16 and the sixth from 30. Later, after two bogeys and a birdie through the 10th, Gay had a tap-in birdie at the par-three 11th.

Said Molder, on his way to his best PGA Tour finish, "I didn't even get close to catching him."

Gay parred the next six holes, then played the 18th boldly — unnecessarily so, truth be known — going at the pin from 163 yards. The shot left him a five-foot putt. He got his final birdie, his third straight 66 and his second victory in five starts. The secret was in the putter. If this wasn't his best week on the greens, what was? He needed just 100 putts for the tournament. By round, that was 26, 23, 24 and 27.

And the win forced him into a sudden change of schedule. He hadn't counted on playing his way into the coming U.S. Open, and so he planned on taking the next week off. But the win got him in. It caught him unprepared. And so he was on his way to Bethpage Black on Long Island.

"Right now, I don't know if we're going home first or what we're going to do," Gay said. "Get to work on Tuesday, I guess."

U.S. Open Championship
Farmingdale, New York
Winner: Lucas Glover

See Chapter 3.

Travelers Championship
Cromwell, Connecticut
Winner: Kenny Perry

If Kenny Perry was damaged by his collapse at the Masters, it sure didn't show in the turkey shoot called the Travelers Championship some three months later.

"Everyone kind of asks about that Augusta hangover deal," Perry said. "I guess I kind of shoved that aside a little bit."

No question that the two tournaments were light years apart in terms of pressure and prestige, but Perry did what he had to do when he had to do it in the Travelers, retaking the lead in the final round and rushing off with a three-stroke victory. It was his second victory of the year and fifth in 13 months, and what a record he would have had if he hadn't stumbled to two closing bogeys at the Masters.

Perry looked like a runaway winner at the start, opening with a bogey-free 61 at the par-70 TPC River Highlands in Cromwell, Connecticut. "I was looking for the magical number," said Perry. But two closing pars kept him from getting down to 59. Paul Goydos and Charles Warren shot 63s, four others were at 64, including Boo Weekley, who birdied his first six holes, and Australian Greg Chalmers, who birdied six of his last eight and offered, "Sometimes on this course, you can get on a roll." All told, over 100 broke par the first day. The turkey shoot was on.

TPC River Highlands, though softened by rain, could stand as a lab test for the case that technology was outstripping the game. The halfway cut came at two-under 138. Of the 72 finishers, 22 shot all four rounds in the 60s, 69 were under par, and Vaughn Taylor was 72nd and dead last at only two over.

Perry had already posted 68 in the second round when thunderstorms forced 73 players to finish on Saturday, and from there, the Travelers Championship turned into a battle in the third. Goydos birdied five holes coming home to take a one-stroke lead over Perry. "I was turning lemons into lemonade," Goydos said. He included his "circus putt" at the 16th, a 28-footer from off the green that helped him to his second 63 against Perry's 66.

In the final round, Perry regained the lead in a duel with Goydos. Goydos holed a 40-foot putt at the seventh, but suffered a two-stroke swing when he bogeyed the par-three eighth and Perry birdied it from three feet. Goydos eagled the 15th from 20 feet, birdied the 16th, but missed a birdie at the 17th. Perry birdied the 15th, then locked up the tournament at the 17th, dropping an eight-footer for birdie after a 164-yard approach, and parred the last for 63 and the three-stroke win that helped ease the pain of Augusta.

"I knew that I had to keep making birdies," Perry said. "I wasn't going to play defensive golf. I learned something from that mistake."

AT&T National
Bethesda, Maryland
Winner: Tiger Woods

It's the classical tale of the young hopeful dreaming of beating his hero for the title someday. And so it was for Anthony Kim, age 24, a rising talent on the PGA Tour, who dreamed of beating Tiger Woods. And there he was, paired with his hero and tied for the lead in the final round. This is where Kim's dream crashed into reality. Kim, the defending champion, dropped four strokes over the first four holes, and Woods went on to win his own tournament, the AT&T National, at Congressional Country Club near Washington, D.C., early in July.

Woods had some shaky moments down the stretch, but held firm for a one-stroke victory over Hunter Mahan, who had finished an hour earlier with a sizzling 62, tying the course record Kim had set in the first round.

Taking his third victory of the year, Woods played Congressional in 64-66-70-67–267, 13 under par, and the key was the third round, when he had to scramble for a par 70 to tie Kim.

"It was a tough day," Woods said. "One of those, you just had to grind it out and get through it."

Woods opened the third round with a tee shot into the gallery and deep rough, and later squandered a three-shot lead over two holes. He ran afoul of the 11th, catching rough, a bunker, another bunker and then two-putting for a double bogey that cost him the lead. He finally did birdie, tapping in at the 16th, and two closing pars tied him with Kim at 10-under 210.

Kim also made a few errors, but steadied himself and birdied the 16th to tie Woods. Both had to share the stage with Michael Allen, who had won the Senior PGA Championship in his over-50 debut in May. Allen shot 65 and suddenly was in position to break his 0-for-336 winless drought on the PGA Tour. And if he did it? "Champagne for everyone," he said.

Kim's quick four-stroke stumble in the last round would have left the tournament pretty much to Woods, except along came Hunter Mahan and his outburst — a rush of six birdies on the back nine, and the last of them at the 18th for the 62. But he would have to wait about an hour to see whether it would beat or tie Woods, still on the course.

Woods had to scramble twice to save par and stay tied with Mahan. Then, as he so often did, he found a way to get the clincher. At the par-five 16th, he chipped weakly out of the rough and left himself a 20-foot putt for birdie. He rolled it in for the lead and parred in for the win.

It was after that shaky third round that Woods learned Kim held him up as a hero and wanted to beat him. Did it mean anything to him?

"I'm aging," Woods said, grinning. "That's what it means."

John Deere Classic
Silvis, Illinois
Winner: Steve Stricker

Steve Stricker put it this way: "I warmed up very poorly on the range this morning. I made a lot of great putts. I wasn't very aggressive at times, but I hit the ball very well and gave myself some opportunities."

That's a thumbnail description of a golfer's so-so day at the office, except this was Stricker explaining his 61.

For all its electricity, the 61 merely lifted Stricker to within three of Darren Stiles's halfway lead in the John Deere Classic. But it did get him rolling, and with a 68-64 double-round Sunday finish to the storm-wracked tournament, Stricker survived some hot pursuit for a three-stroke win, his second victory of the year and career sixth. Stricker shot 71-61-68-64 for a robust 20-under-par 264 on the benign, par-71 TPC Deere at Silvis, Illinois.

"I didn't see it coming," said Stricker, after tying both his personal low and the tournament record with that 61. He had 11 threes on his card and needed just nine putts on the second nine and 22 overall. Starting on the back, he birdied the first two holes, then the 14th and 15th. At the par-five 17th, he holed a 93-yard wedge for an eagle (there would be an echo the next day). Coming home, he birdied the first two, and thoughts of a 59 began to creep in, but a bogey at his 12th (No. 3) cooled things off. Then he birdied the fourth and sixth.

Said Scott Verplank, "I shot three under on the back, and I'm getting run over."

Stricker was humming along quite nicely Sunday afternoon in the fourth round (his second round of the day) when he came to his 24th hole of the day, the par-four sixth. He had 98 yards to the green, with a waiting bunker in his way. He made that smooth, untroubled swing. The ball took off, cleared the bunker and disappeared into the cup for one of golf's greatest joys, a hole-out eagle. That eagle was a message if he ever saw one.

"I kind of felt this could be my week," Stricker said later. "I did that twice this week, holing out from the fairway (No. 17 in the second round). When that went in, it felt like this could be the day."

It was the day, for a fact. Stricker wrapped up that double-round Sunday for a three-stroke victory that wasn't quite as comfortable as the final margin suggested. Stricker did not have a walk in the park, but his biggest threat came from Tim Petrovic, a playing partner. Petrovic was just two behind coming to the 36th and final hole, then hit into the water and double-bogeyed, leaving Stricker to win by three over Brandt Snedeker (68-65), Brett Quigley (62-67) and Zach Johnson (64-66).

"I've given myself a lot of chances to win," Stricker said. "Some didn't go my way and some have."

The Open Championship
Ayrshire, Scotland
Winner: Stewart Cink

See Chapter 4.

U.S. Bank Championship
Milwaukee, Wisconsin
Winner: Bo Van Pelt

While one dream almost came true at the Open Championship — 59-year-old Tom Watson came within a whisker of winning it — another did in the U.S. Bank Championship in Milwaukee.

Bo Van Pelt, 34, the epitome of frustration and persistence, had gone some 10 years and 229 PGA Tour starts without winning. Finally — and he would mark this — on Sunday, July 19, 2009, at Brown Deer Park — Van Pelt got that first victory. But he scared himself up to the very end.

On the second playoff hole, the par-five 18th, John Mallinger hit his approach into a greenside bunker and parred. Van Pelt put his approach on the green, 20 feet from an eagle. Then the drama began. He mocked himself. "Twenty feet, two putts to win," Van Pelt said. "I'd get that done — no problem. Like that'd be the easiest thing. And sure enough, I leave it three feet short."

He had seen pros on television missing clutch three-footers. Now he feared he might join them. But he braced himself and knocked it in. Ironically, his first win might have been in the tournament's last stand. The word at the time was that U.S. Bank, citing the poor economy, would end its sponsorship. Whether this would end the Milwaukee stop as well after 42 years was the question at that time. It didn't help that the tournament was played opposite the Open Championship and so attracted few name players.

Australian Greg Chalmers, tying for the first-round lead at 64 with Jeff Klauk, turned prophetic on that point, on what a "fantastic story" an opposite event could produce without the big names around. "It could be a first-time winner, someone who goes from nowhere to somewhere very quickly," said Chalmers. Leaving room for himself, of course. And that would be precisely the case. After Chalmers led the second round and Frank Lickliter the third, the final round ended up with two players seeking that first win — Van Pelt and Mallinger, who just hung around in contention for three rounds.

Mallinger started 70-66-66, and in the final round eagled the par-five 15th and birdied the 16th and 18th for a 65. Van Pelt, after posting 67-68-68, closed with a bogey-free round capped by a four-foot birdie putt at the last for a 64. They tied at 13-under 267, one ahead of local favorite Jerry Kelly.

In the playoff at the par-five 18th, both birdied on the first try. On the second visit, after Mallinger parred, Van Pelt faced down that fearful three-footer. He received a $720,000 check and a crystal trophy.

"We don't have a whole lot of crystal in the house," Van Pelt said. "I have a feeling at some point, there's going to be some (beer) drunk. A lot of that."

RBC Canadian Open
Oakville, Ontario, Canada
Winner: Nathan Green

For Australian Nathan Green it was like coming home when he showed up for the RBC Canadian Open — by definition, in Canada.

"This is where I started my pro career," said Green, 34, a former Canadian Tour player. "I love coming up here." The occasion was a Canadian Tour victory in 2000. Then there were the victories in the Queensland PGA in Australia in 2000 and the European Tour's New Zealand Open in 2006. But the big one kept slipping away. Such as in the 2006 Buick Invitational, when he came as close as a playoff and then was ousted by eventual winner Tiger Woods. Green once admitted he thought he might never win.

Finally, his patience was rewarded. In a Canadian Open battered and delayed by five inches of late July rain, Green parred the second playoff hole, beating South Africa's Retief Goosen for — at last — his first victory in 112 starts on the PGA Tour.

"It's just been a bizarre week — a long week," Green said. The win was no fluke. The par-72 Glen Abbey course at Oakville, Ontario, was wet and receptive for everyone. He played it in 18 under par on rounds of 68-65-69-68. Goosen, two-time U.S. Open champion, shot 65-69-67-69.

Kevin Na, also seeking his first win, and with seven top-10 finishes in 18 events this season, birdied the last five holes and nine of his last 12 for a convincing 63 and a two-stroke lead over Goosen in the first round. The soft conditions were helping. "The greens are holding, so you can get aggressive with the irons," Na said.

As Mark Calcavecchia demonstrated with a tour-record nine straight birdies in a second-round 65.

With the tournament played under the lift-clean-place format all week, 58 players finished under par.

A variety of challengers stepped forward through the delays, among them Camilo Villegas, who matched Na's 63 the next morning, playing the last six holes in six under. He birdied the par-three 15th from an inch, then chipped in from 15 feet for an eagle at the par-five 18th. "What a great way to finish a round," said Villegas.

Finally, what a way to finish a tournament. Goosen birdied the par-five 13th to take the lead, then bogeyed the next two holes. Green scrambled to a par at the par-five 16th, getting up and down from 38 yards for a two-stroke lead. Goosen, two groups ahead, eagled the 18th on a 15-foot putt to tie Green.

In the playoff, Goosen's big chance evaporated when he missed a six-foot birdie putt at the first hole. At the second, the par-four 17th, Goosen missed fairway and green and bogeyed on two putts from eight feet. Green fired a four iron from 195 yards to 12 feet and two-putted for his first victory.

What a relief. Talk about great winning speeches. Said Green: "It's a huge surprise to finally win."

Buick Open
Grand Blanc, Michigan
Winner: Tiger Woods

Tiger Woods tossed a golf ball to the fans at the 17th, the next-to-last hole — literally — of the Buick Open. Then approaching the green at the 18th, the last hole — literally — he turned and threw a ball back down the fairway to the fans.

"I never do that, but today was different," Woods said. "We aren't coming back here, and I wanted to thank all these people."

Shortly after the tournament the PGA Tour and Buick announced that the event, the longest running at 51 years, had come to an end. It was another victim of the troubled economy. It would be replaced by the Greenbrier Classic at the West Virginia resort in 2010.

Woods, having trailed by eight strokes back in the first round, proceeded to polish off a three-stroke victory. It was his third victory in nine Buick Opens at friendly Warwick Hills at Grand Blanc, Michigan. It was also his fourth victory of the season and his career 69th.

Woods arrived at the Buick Open not in the highest of moods, having just missed the cut in the Open Championship. He began the Buick Open with a one-under 71, eight behind Steve Lowery's nine-under 63 on the benign Warwick Hills course. He was delighted with the start. "But if you don't follow it up the rest of the week," Lowery said, "it ain't going to hang around." (Unfortunately, he didn't and it didn't.)

Woods took the reverse of that view. "I not only have to play well to make the cut, I have to play well to get myself back into contention," he said. He did, and he did.

He shot a 63 of his own in the second round, triggering it with a blazing birdie-birdie-eagle-birdie-birdie start from No. 10. He eagled his third hole (the par-four 12th) with a big tee shot and a 40-yard hole-out. Then he made a sensational birdie at the par-five 13th, cutting a five-iron second from behind a big tree to within 50 feet of the green, chipped to 10 feet and made the putt. But the 63 only cut his deficit in half, leaving him four behind halfway leader John Senden (66–130).

Woods then took the lead in the third round with 65 cobbled together from such things as twice hitting tee shots into adjacent fairways and another that hit a cup of beer in a fan's hands. He was pleased with the 65, but scolded himself for all the scrambling. "This course is pretty short," he said. "You have to take advantage, and I did, but unfortunately, I didn't do it the correct way."

Not to look a gift horse in the mouth, but the 65 gave him a 199 total and a one-stroke lead on Michael Letzig, who playing earlier had double-bogeyed the 18th for 68.

Woods all but coasted in the final round to a bogey-free 69 and a three-stroke win over Greg Chalmers (68), Roland Thatcher (64) and John Senden (70). The only real drama was Woods tossing the farewell golf balls, saluting the fans.

WGC - Bridgestone Invitational
Akron, Ohio
Winner: Tiger Woods

Tiger Woods has had help from some unusual outside sources — fans moving a big rock out of his line, a spectator smacking a stray shot back into play, things like that. This one was new: A stopwatch aimed at Padraig Harrington.

Woods, the emperor of Firestone, took the World Golf Championships - Bridgestone Invitational, his seventh win in 11 visits to the course. And he was the first to say that the clock on Harrington had as much to do with it as his own play, which was, at times, dazzling. Woods contended that Harrington, nervous at being timed, rushed his play and committed huge errors at the 16th that changed the course of the tournament.

"I don't know if you guys know it or not," Woods told the media, "but we got put on the clock. I don't think Paddy would have hit the pitch shot that way if he was able to take his time, look at it, analyze it. But he was on the clock, had to get up there quickly and hit it — yeah, and hit it in the water."

At the monster 667-yard 16th in the final round, Harrington, leading Woods by a stroke, seemed nervous and hurried. He drove into the right rough, hit his second across into the left rough, and his third from an awkward uphill lie onto a downslope in heavy grass just behind the green. Then, as Woods noted, Harrington was quick to hit. The ball bounced off the green and into the pond in front. He had to go back up into the fairway for his penalty drop, and from there he made a triple-bogey eight.

Of course, it didn't help Harrington that Woods had lobbed his eight-iron third to within inches for a tap-in birdie. Woods went on to close with a five-under 65 for a 12-under 268 and a four-stroke win over Harrington (72) and Robert Allenby (66). It was his fifth win of the year.

"I'm sorry that John (Paramour, rules official) got in the way of a great battle," Woods said. "I don't understand why we got put on the clock." Woods and Harrington were the last pairing.

"We had no choice but to put them on the clock," Paramour said. And PGA Tour official Slugger White noted, "We're just doing our job."

Harrington declined to blame Paramour. "I had an awkward fourth shot," he said. "I had to go after it and probably rushed it a bit."

Harrington had led all the way, shooting 64-69-67, and led Woods (68-70-65) by three going into the final round. This was a revitalized Harrington, who had been working on his game for the past eight months. He wouldn't speak in terms of results. "Has no relevance in the overall scheme of things," Harrington said. The relevance surfaced at the 16th.

Woods was asked, did you win because of your brilliant eight iron or the stopwatch? Said Woods: "Both."

Legends Reno-Tahoe Open
Reno, Nevada
Winner: John Rollins

Golf is an 18-hole game. Thank goodness for that, John Rollins was saying at the Legends Reno-Tahoe Open. Or to put it more to the point, "Luckily, we ran out of holes," Rollins said.

Much of the golf world was focused on the WGC - Bridgestone Invitational at Firestone, in Ohio, that early August week, but at the Montreux Golf and Country Club at Reno, Nevada, the eyes were on one man. Rollins, 34, had entered the final round leading by four strokes and was up by six through the final turn. But Rollins, a two-time winner on the PGA Tour, was runner-up twice in 2009, at the Buick Invitational and the Honda Classic. He was on the verge of blowing victory No. 3. It would be a cruel fate for a man who had tied the course-record 62 in the second round.

"After I bogeyed 15," he said, "I sort of kicked myself in the butt and told myself I'm not going to let this tournament get away from me." Rollins, who tied for second at Reno in 2008, birdied the 17th and logged a three-stroke victory over Jeff Quinney and Martin Laird.

Rollins took a big grip on the tournament with that 62 in the second round. He lit up the course with a spectacular eagle at the 616-yard, par-five No. 9. He hit his second 284 yards to 34 feet and rolled in the putt for a 30 on the first nine. He backed that up with birdies at the next two holes — on a 14-foot putt at the 10th, then a tap-in at the par-five 11th after just missing an eagle from nine feet. He parred the next five holes, then birdied the par-five 17th, getting up and down from a bunker, and finally holed a 22-foot putt at the 18th for his eighth birdie of the round. The 62 included a furious streak of birdie-birdie-eagle-birdie-birdie.

"It was just one of those days, I guess," Rollins said. "I hit a lot of good shots and made a lot of putts. That's really all it is — you just make putts."

Rollins, leading by two going into the third round, shot 67 to take a four-stroke lead over his good pal, Ryan Palmer, into the final round.

He double-bogeyed the fourth, birdied the fifth, then got another great eagle at the par-five 11th — a 351-yard drive, a 212-yard second and a 40-foot chip-in to get to 19 under. Then the alarm went off. He bogeyed the 12th, 13th and 15th, and led by only two with three holes to play.

But a calming par at the 16th, and then a two-putt birdie at the 17th restored order and his lead to three. And he got home safe and sound. "It was a hang-on kind of day," Rollins said. "I'm proud I managed to come out on top."

PGA Championship
Chaska, Minnesota
Winner: Y.E. Yang

See Chapter 5.

Wyndham Championship
Greensboro, North Carolina
Winner: Ryan Moore

"It felt like an uphill battle," Ryan Moore was saying. The problem was, his hill felt like Mt. Everest.

He had come out of the amateur ranks with huge promise, having won the U.S. Amateur, the U.S. Amateur Public Links, the Western Amateur and the NCAA Championship, all in 2004. Things like that will stamp a guy "can't-miss." But Moore kept on missing. Then, finally, came the 2009 Wyndham Championship.

"I was able to stay patient, really," Moore said, after his playoff victory. "That's what won this one."

When Moore, 26, arrived at the Wyndham, at Sedgefield Country Club in Greensboro, North Carolina, in August, he was 0-for-111 and runner-up four times on the PGA Tour since turning pro in 2005.

He tied for the lead for the first two rounds, on 64-65, and slipped behind with a 70 in the third round, when Sergio Garcia (64) took the lead. But Garcia let another one get away in the final round. He seemed well on course to his eighth victory, then took three bogeys in a five-hole stretch from No. 8 and was gone again. He'd held at least a share of the third-round lead seven times but converted only twice. He finished fourth this time. "I felt like I was fighting myself," Garcia said.

Moore went racing up the leaderboard in the final round with a 65 and tied with Jason Bohn (62) and Kevin Stadler (66) at 264, 16 under on the par-70 course.

In a tournament of woulda's and coulda's, Jason Bohn had a wild ride. He started the final round seven strokes off the lead, birdied seven of his first 14 holes and eagled the 15th for the 62 and the clubhouse lead at 16 under. "I wasn't even thinking I would get into a playoff," Bohn said.

Stadler had a five-birdie round going, then got too bold at the 18th. Stadler had thought he was trailing by three. "But the next leaderboard I saw, I was only one back," he said. His bid to close the gap ended up in a bogey and a 66. Moore, after a one-under front nine, caught fire on the back and made five straight birdies from the 12th. Then with that first victory at his fingertips, he bogeyed the 18th and slipped back into a three-way tie.

In the playoff, Bohn was axed at the first extra hole when his first try out of a greenside bunker rolled back in and he bogeyed. At the third extra hole, Stadler knocked his second off the back of the green. He chipped back to 20 feet, then missed the putt.

Moore put his approach to six feet and, after Stadler missed, rolled it in for the winning birdie. And about time, he figured.

"I just haven't been healthy, haven't felt like myself again over the golf ball," Moore said. "And (I'm) just kind of getting some confidence back in the putter and every aspect of the game. That's really carried through to this week."

PGA Tour Playoffs for the FedExCup

The Barclays
Jersey City, New Jersey
Winner: Heath Slocum

If Tiger Woods, Padraig Harrington, Steve Stricker and Ernie Els all tied for second, who in the world was left to win The Barclays?

Try short-hitting Heath Slocum, 5-foot-8, 150 pounds, best known as an old down-home school chum of Boo Weekley and Bubba Watson and winner of two PGA Tour "opposite-field" events played when the cream of golf was off playing somewhere else. To further build the case of least-likely-to-succeed, note that Slocum was No. 197 in the World Ranking, and also that of the 125 golfers who qualified for the FedExCup Playoffs, he was 124th, and by that tiny margin got into The Barclays, the Playoffs opener.

"I was sweating it out last week," Slocum said. "I didn't even know if I'd be here. I came in with the attitude that I had nothing to lose."

And, of course, everything to gain, which he did — a $1.35 million check and a berth in the season-ending Tour Championship after his 66-72-70-67–275, nine under par at Liberty National Golf Club near Jersey City, New Jersey, for a one-stroke win.

For the first three rounds, Slocum was back near where the 124s usually are. Paul Goydos, Steve Marino and Sergio Garcia led the first round with 65s, and rookie Webb Simpson led the second (68–134), with Tiger Woods eight back with 70-72–142.

Goydos and Marino went into the final round leading by two over Fredrik Jacobson (72) and Simpson (72), three over Stricker, by four over Slocum, five over Woods and Harrington, and six over Els. It was shaping up into a dandy finish.

Goydos and Marino both tripped over No. 3 and were on their way out of contention. Els shot 66 and was encouraged. Harrington birdied four of the last seven holes for a 67. Stricker had a 10-foot par putt to tie at the 18th, but missed and shot 69.

Woods lost some ground at No. 4 when his three-foot par putt rimmed out. But he birdied Nos. 5, 7 and 8, and then No. 14 on a 10-footer and No. 16 from two feet. That set up a crucial moment. At the 18th, he hit a six iron from 189 yards to seven feet for a birdie. But he missed and shot 67. "We misread it by almost a cup," Woods said.

Slocum exploded out of the gate. He rolled in a 25-footer for a birdie at the second, then holed a 157-yard seven iron for an eagle at the par-four fifth to tie for the lead. He birdied the sixth, took his only bogey at the seventh, and added a final birdie at the 13th. Like Woods, he came to a crucial moment at the 18th. Except he was facing a par putt and from 20 feet. Make it and he wins. Miss, and he slips into a tie with four of the best golfers in the world. He made it.

Deutsche Bank Championship
Norton, Massachusetts
Winner: Steve Stricker

Steve Stricker was explaining his improved play of late. "It's getting closer to hunting season," he said. "I see the light at the end of the tunnel." If that seemed obtuse, well, this was a man eager to get on with things. This was right after he bagged the Deutsche Bank Championship, second of the four FedExCup Playoff tournaments.

But it wasn't like finding a bird on the ground. It took two closing birdies to carry him to a one-stroke victory, his third win of the season.

Stricker staked a lightning claim to the TPC Boston course with a burst of five straight birdies to open the tournament. He raced on to an eight-under-par 63 and a share of a two-stroke lead with Jim Furyk, who birdied five of his first six holes. Tiger Woods posted a so-so 70 and noted: "I didn't feel real good over any shot today." He didn't feel much better the rest of the way, until a closing 63 lifted him to a tie for 11th.

The tournament turned into a free-for-all in the second round. On a day when nearly half of the starting 99 players shot in the 60s, Stricker fell five behind with a 72 while Sean O'Hair erupted over eight middle holes for six birdies and an eagle and shot 64, tying at 12 under with Furyk, who had six birdies in a 67. They led by two over Marc Leishman (62) and Retief Goosen (67).

The Deutsche Bank Championship was played on Labor Day weekend, but it was a frolic at TPC Boston. It took one-under 141 to make the cut. Stricker returned in the scrambling third round and was among eight who held at least a share of the lead. He made it a three-way lead on the par-five 18th with a bold 230-yard hybrid that was a little out of his range and into the wind. His ball just cleared the stream and ended up five feet from the cup. He made the eagle for 65 to tie Goosen (68) and O'Hair (70).

"I maxed that one out, and it turned out good," Stricker said. "I needed a day like this to get back into it."

The final round was up for grabs. Stricker's chances grew dimmer. He was only grinding out nine straight pars through the 16th. At the par-four 17th, facing a 15-foot putt, he was one behind Scott Verplank and Jason Dufner, both in at 268. He made the birdie and tied them. Then at the 18th, he drove into the fairway, hit his hybrid from 245 yards to just off the green, and pitched to a foot. The tap-in birdie gave him 67, a 17-under 267 total and his third win of the year. It also lifted him to No. 2 in the world behind Woods.

There was a little work left to do — the BMW Championship, the third FedExCup Playoff event, and then The Tour Championship. Then it was on to hunting season.

BMW Championship
Lemont, Illinois
Winner: Tiger Woods

It got rather silly in the BMW Championship. Tiger Woods opened this third leg of the Playoffs for the FedExCup with 68-67, trailing by two strokes in the first round, then tying for the lead in the second. And then he blew up the entire tournament in the third with a course-record 62. It gave him a seven-shot lead at Cog Hill, the Chicago course where he had won four times before.

"Looks like Tiger is making it difficult on us," said Brandt Snedeker, who closed with four straight birdies, shot 66, and found himself in second place and needing a miracle to hope for better. Woods was practically foolproof when leading through 54 holes. But with him leading by seven, the final round would amount to an academic exercise for the rest of the field.

"It's one of my best years," said Woods, scoring his sixth victory since returning from an eight-month absence after knee surgery in June 2008. Woods completed the formality with a closing 68 for a 19-under 265 total and an eight-stroke win over Jim Furyk and Marc Leishman. It was the 10th time that Woods had won on the PGA Tour by eight strokes or more.

"I felt like we had a tournament within a tournament," said Furyk, who closed with a 66. "Tiger was kind of running away. It was a tournament for second place."

Woods's recipe for that 62? First, you start with a bogey ...

For his opening tee shot in the third round, Woods used a three wood, which he dropped in disgust with that certain look on his face. The ball landed in a fairway bunker to the left. He bogeyed.

"After I got past the first hole, I was doing all right," Woods said. "It was one of those days that kind of built upon itself." But Woods, who started the final round tied for the lead, was trailing by three through five holes. The challengers were moving. Padraig Harrington birdied three straight early holes, and Leishman birdied four straight in the middle of the front nine. Woods's rampage started with a birdie at third. He was trailing by three coming to the par-three sixth. He birdied it, and the eighth as well. At the par-five ninth, he hit a sensational three wood from 300 yards to 10 feet and holed the putt for an eagle and took the lead.

Woods made the turn in 31, and birdies at Nos. 11, 13, 14 and 17 gave him another coming in for the 62 and the seven-stroke lead. In the last round, his 68 seemed routine. Except, perhaps, for the sensational birdie at No. 9 — a three iron through trees and a hooked nine iron to the green for a birdie. It seems it was all so simple.

"It's just been a matter of making a couple of putts," Woods said. "And lo and behold — boom! And that's how it happens."

The Tour Championship
Atlanta, Georgia
Winner: Phil Mickelson

Neither Shakespeare nor PGA Tour Commissioner Tim Finchem could have written a better ending. There was Tiger Woods, wrapping up a year that proved there is life after knee surgery. And there was Phil Mickelson, after a summer of anguish in which both his wife and his mother underwent cancer surgery. And there they were, the best player in the world and the second-best, battling it out in the final round. That's pure box office.

The setting was the PGA Tour's sort-of-season-ending Tour Championship at East Lake, at Atlanta late in September, with a field of only 30 who qualified through a points system and three playoff tournaments. (The 2009 season would actually end with the "Fall Series.")

The crucial point of the tournament actually came the week before, when Mickelson consulted putting whiz Dave Stockton for a tune-up. It sure worked. Mickelson came from behind on scores of 73-67-66-65–271, to win by three strokes over Woods.

Woods, the favorite as usual, was in or near the lead for the first three rounds. Mickelson, who played little since the U.S. Open — when news of wife Amy's cancer broke — trailed through the first three rounds. He didn't show much potential. In fact, his opening three-over-par 73 — which included a crushing quadruple-bogey eight at the 14th — tied him for 26th out of the 30. But the rejuvenated Mickelson had yet to surface while others took center stage in what became the tournament of putting tips.

Sean O'Hair got a tip from Woods — open the putter face on the backswing. O'Hair then shot a four-under 66 for the first-round lead by one over, of course, Woods, and Padraig Harrington and Stewart Cink. "I'm going to go chew him out right now," said Woods, who then shot 68 and took a one-stroke lead over O'Hair (70) and Harrington (69) in the second round. Kenny Perry raced into the third-round lead with a 64, two up on Woods (69) and four on Mickelson (66). But Perry wilted in the fourth, weakened by dehydration, leaving the tournament and golf with a classic battle.

Woods, strangely enough, couldn't get moving. He bogeyed the first and 13th, then birdied the 15th and 16th, and finished with a par 70 and a six-under 274.

Stockton advised Mickelson to widen his stance, put the ball back in his stance, square his feet and use a forward press. In the final round, Mickelson was off and running. He birdied the third and fourth from 15 and 30 feet, tapped-in at the eighth for a share of the lead, then birdied the ninth from 12. He added his fifth birdie in a bogey-free round with a 15-foot pitch at the 16th, and shot 65 for a nine-under 271 to beat Woods by three. Woods, who had won six times this season since returning from knee surgery, got quite a consolation prize. With his point total, he won the FedExCup and the $10.1 million bonus. Mickelson, taking his third title, won $1.35 million. No matter.

"I like the way today went," Mickelson said. "I was two back of him, I beat him by three. He gets the $10 million check, and I get the $1 million. I've got no problem with that."

PGA Tour Fall Series

Turning Stone Resort Championship
Verona, New York
Winner: Matt Kuchar

Matt Kuchar was the amateur kid with the big, radiant smile in the 1997 Masters. And now, 12 years later, Kuchar was a professional but still the kid with the radiant smile as he hoisted the trophy at the Turning Stone Resort Championship.

"It's hard to describe the feeling," said Kuchar, 31, who turned professional in 2000 and scored his only other win in 2002, his first full season on the PGA Tour. "They're so difficult to win. If you don't win, there's not a whole lot of rewards. The game beats you up."

Kuchar shot 67-68-67-69 at the par-72 Atunyote Golf Club in Verona, New York, and tied with Vaughn Taylor at 17-under-par 271, then won on the sixth hole of a playoff that started Sunday evening and ended Monday morning. Kuchar won with an 18-inch par putt.

Kuchar trailed by a stroke for the first two rounds, then tied for the lead in the third round with Scott Piercy at 202. Kuchar made four birdies over a seven-hole stretch for his 67, while Piercy (66) made four in a five-hole span. "If you look at conditions out there," Kuchar said, "you'd be really disappointed to make bogeys." He was speaking of a course made vulnerable by so much rain that for the first two rounds officials permitted lift and drop even in the rough to allow golfers relief from standing water. The first round was especially tough, with both rain and temperatures under 50.

Piercy had an interesting ambition for the final round. "If I can hit 17 greens tomorrow, I like my chances for winning," he said. Taylor, the solo leader in the second round, shot 71 in the third and tied for sixth. But he bounced back with a 66 to tie Kuchar (69) in the fourth.

"There certainly were a lot of nerves on that opening (playoff) hole," Kuchar said. The playoff was staged over the 12th and 18th, both par-fives, and the par-four 13th. They tied one hole with birdies, another with pars, before darkness ended play Sunday.

On Monday morning, at the third playoff hole, Kuchar lipped out a three-footer for par and they tied with bogeys. At the 18th, Kuchar holed a 20-footer for birdie and Taylor matched him from seven feet. At the 12th, Taylor's 21-footer for birdie pulled up just short and Kuchar saved par from a greenside bunker to tie him. Then at the sixth extra hole, No. 13, a light rain began to fall. Taylor hit his tee shot into the water hazard to the right and had to take a penalty drop. "Just a bad swing," he said. Kuchar hit his second to the right of the green and pitched to about 18 inches for the par that won for him.

"I was nervous on that putt," Kuchar said. "It felt great to hear it hit the back of the hole."

The Presidents Cup
San Francisco, California
Winners: United States

The eighth Presidents Cup turned into a veritable fountain of story lines. You had Tiger Woods, at last finding peace and happiness in team match play (the secret was in the partner, in this case, Steve Stricker). There was the flowering of Phil Mickelson, no matter who his partner was, and Fred Couples, discovering the secret to being a successful captain (pair 'em up and get out of the way), and another big step for Japanese teenage prodigy Ryo Ishikawa. But it ended up as the same old story. The Americans rolled again, taking a 19½-to-14½ victory and running their record to 6-1-1.

It was no surprise that Woods was the centerpiece of the 34 matches spread over those four October days at Harding Park Golf Course in San Francisco. He posted a perfect 5-0-0 record, becoming only the third player ever to play in and win all of the matches. Four of those victories came with Stricker (4-1-0), a pairing that almost seemed enchanted. How did Couples happen on it? He didn't. They had asked him.

They had two dynamite, pivotal matches. They were in trouble only once, in the Saturday foursomes, with Mike Weir and Tim Clark leading one up going to the 17th. There, Stricker left Woods a 23-foot putt for birdie. Woods dropped it to square the match. At the 18th, Stricker put Woods in the fairway, and Woods faded a three iron from 229 yards to nine feet. The Internationals ended up conceding the birdie and thus the match. Woods and Stricker went to 4-0 in a surreal four-ball against Ishikawa and Y.E. Yang in the afternoon, when Stricker birdied six of their first 10 holes.

Said Woods: "I helped out on … three holes all day. Otherwise, I was cheerleading all day." Someone cracked that Stricker had to carry Woods. Said Stricker: "I didn't carry him."

International captain Greg Norman also found a strong pairing in Ernie Els and Weir. They ran their four-ball record to 4-0 in two Presidents Cups.

Mickelson, coming off the difficult summer in which his wife and mother had breast cancer surgery, continued with the strong play that won him The Tour Championship two weeks earlier. Rejuvenated by Dave Stockton's putting tip, Mickelson went 4-0-1, losing in one team match.

Norman had no qualms about playing the rookie Ishikawa in all five matches and was rewarded with a 3-2-0 showing. Kenny Perry, 49, put Ishikawa's performance into perspective. "He sent me into retirement, that kid," Perry said. "He beat me three matches."

The United States took a three-point lead into the singles, and Woods clinched the Cup with his 6-and-5 romp over South Korea's Y.E. Yang, and then revealed he hadn't felt comfortable at times during the week. "But when you have Stricker making everything from everywhere, that certainly carried us," he said. Woods then volunteered a position paper. "For me," Woods said, "it was a pleasure and an honor to play with Stricks."

Had Woods ever spoken about another golfer so loftily before? And guess who future Ryder Cup and President Cup captains would pair with Woods?

Justin Timberlake Shriners Hospitals for Children Open
Las Vegas, Nevada
Winner: Martin Laird

Martin Laird got it backwards. In the Justin Timberlake Shriners Hospitals for Children Open in Las Vegas, he was a bundle of nerves coming down the final stretch. But then in the playoff, he was calm. The result? His first victory on the PGA Tour.

The four-round assault on the TPC Summerlin ended up in a three-way tie among Laird, who closed with a 68, George McNeill (67) and Chad Campbell (69), all at 19-under-par 265. Campbell bowed out at the second extra hole, and at the third, the par-four 18th, McNeill came out of a greenside bunker to 18 feet and lipped out his birdie try. Laird had put his approach to 11 feet and calmly rolled it in for a birdie and his breakthrough win.

Laird, 26, a Scot who played at Colorado State University and joined the tour in 2007, said he was nervous over the last few regulation holes. "Once I got in the playoff, I relaxed more," he said. "And when I stood up there on the first playoff hole and struck the ball down the middle, it was the perfect way to start the playoff."

The early challengers set a hot pace, then eventually vanished. Tom Pernice, Jr., Troy Matteson and Spencer Levin shared the first-round lead with nine-under 62s. Pernice finished tied for seventh, Matteson for 27th and Levin for 54th.

In the second round, Campbell eagled his final hole, the par-five ninth, for a 62 and a share of the halfway lead with Matteson (67). In the third, Campbell eagled the par-four 12th and birdied the 13th and 15th, but double-bogeyed the 16th and tied Scott Piercy (65) for a one-stroke lead.

Laird, one stroke out of the lead through the first three rounds, finally took over in the fourth. After a bogey at the second hole, he made four birdies through the turn, parred the next six, birdied the 16th, bogeyed the 17th and parred the 18th for his 68. Campbell birdied the 16th and parred in for a 69, and McNeill birdied the 16th and 18th for his 67.

All three parred the first playoff hole, the par-four 18th. Campbell left with a bogey at the second, the par-three 17th. Then the calmer, cooler Laird birdied the third, the 18th. He would take a lot of memories from his first win, but none more warming than his second shot at the 16th in the fourth round, setting up his final birdie. For a nervous golfer, he was remarkable.

"It was probably the best shot I ever hit," said Laird. The wind was coming from the left, a scary thing for a player who hits a fade, with water on the right. "It was a tough shot for me to start out left and not lose it too far right," he said. "It was a do-or-die shot. To pull it off was a big moment."

Frys.com Open
Scottsdale, Arizona
Winner: Troy Matteson

On winning the Frys.com Open, Troy Matteson took the opportunity to issue one of the great self-evident statements ever in golf. Said Matteson: "That's as well as I can play. I really don't have to worry about playing better than that, because that's it." He was speaking of his 61-61 in the middle rounds, merely a PGA Tour record of 122 for the lowest score in consecutive rounds. Also a great relief. He had opened with a 72, but the course was taking such a beating he feared he still would miss the cut. The win was also a great relief for a man who by late October had made only 19 cuts in 30 starts, and who had no top-10 finishes for the season coming into the tournament.

This was at Grayhawk Golf Club's par-70 Raptor Course, which contrary to its name was more like the prey than the predator. The scoring onslaught was impressive.

Ironically, after that huge surge, Matteson squandered his opportunity, stumbled to a closing 68, and had to win in a playoff. He hit his approach at the second extra hole to nearly gimme range for a birdie to beat Jamie Lovemark and upstart Rickie Fowler, who both finished with their second 64s of the tournament, the three tying at 18-under 262. It was Matteson's second PGA Tour win. The first, confusingly enough, was also a Frys.com Open in 2007, but a different one.

Fowler, 20, was challenging in just his second PGA Tour event since tuning pro after the Walker Cup. "What you're seeing is pretty much how I feel," said Fowler, after tying for the second-round lead. "I just feel like I'm going around and having fun."

Matteson went largely unnoticed with his 61 in the second round, and then despite taking the lead with another 61 in the third, he was nearly upstaged by Nicholas Thompson's amazing burst. Thompson double-eagled the par-five 11th, holing out a three-wood second from 261 yards, then aced the 199-yard par-three 13th with a six iron en route to a 65. That was five under on two holes. What did it mean to him? Said Thompson: "I didn't have to putt."

Matteson led by three going into the final round and didn't let up — for a while. He eagled the fourth and birdied the sixth, and after a bogey at the seventh, he birdied the 11th and 12th. Fowler led briefly in the round, but a bogey at the 18th cost him the win. Lovemark made seven birdies, five of them coming home. They had already finished, and what still looked like a rosy situation for Matteson turned sour at the end when he bogeyed the 17th and 18th and slipped into the tie. All three parred the first playoff hole, and at the second Matteson hit his approach to 21 inches, setting up his winning birdie.

"I know I stumbled down the stretch," Matteson said. "I just can't believe it ended up like this. I'm still beside myself."

Children's Miracle Network Classic
Lake Buena Vista, Florida
Winner: Stephen Ames

What a way to end the year.

Golfers like to say they never have a "number" in mind, a score they're shooting for. Stephen Ames was different at the Children's Miracle Network Classic in mid-November, the final PGA Tour event of the year.

"I wished for 64," Ames said, "and I got 64."

And he needed it. Coming from three shots off the lead at the start of the final round, Ames closed with that eight-under gem at the Magnolia Course at Disney World for the clubhouse lead at 13-under-par 270. Justin Leonard and George McNeill, among the co-leaders at the start, finished with 67s behind him to force a playoff.

Ames needed a great finish to hit that 64 on the nose. After four birdies and a bogey on the front nine, he breezed home with birdies at Nos. 12, 13, 14, 16 and 17. McNeill, who had two eagles in the third round, went birdie-par-eagle-birdie from the second hole, and coming in had three birdies and two bogeys and parred his way home from the 15th for his 67. That matched Leonard, who birdied five of his first 11, then parred home, and was shocked at the 18th to see what would have been a winning birdie putt from 16 feet lip out. "To be this close and not be able to pull it out is disappointing," Leonard said.

Leonard was ousted on the first playoff hole, while McNeill made an excellent par save from a tee shot that landed among the trees. At the second, McNeill missed a short par putt, and Ames, 45, had his victory. It was Ames's second win in three years in this tournament, his first win of the year and fourth of his career.

The Children's was also the last chance for players to crack the top 125 on the money list, for its all-exempt status for the 2010 season. Nicholas Thompson and Jimmy Walker were the only two players who were outside the top 125 and who shot their way in. Thompson birdied the 16th and 17th, then needed a nine-foot putt for bogey at the 18th. He holed it for a 66 and a 275 total, tying for 11th and winning $103,400. That lifted him to No. 123 on the final money list with $675,178.

Walker cut it much closer. After making double bogey on the 17th out of a hazard, he parred the 18th for a 69–276, tying for 15th place. He won $72,850 and finished right on 125, $2,997 ahead of Will MacKenzie at 126th. Among others who fell outside the 125 — former major championship winners David Duval, Todd Hamilton and Trevor Immelman.

The victory forced Ames to change his plans for early 2010. Ames liked to take the family on vacation to Hawaii to start the year. Now he was in the field for the season-opening SBS Championship there. "Golf always gets in the way," Ames cracked. "I don't want to play golf. I want to sit on the beach and relax."

Special Events

Tavistock Cup
Orlando, Florida
Winners: Lake Nona

It was the annual Tavistock Cup, the bragging-rights special between PGA Tour golfers from two high-profile Orlando, Florida, communities in March. The host Lake Nona team, down two points to Isleworth after the first round, were looking for something to get them going in the second. Up stepped Ben Curtis shooting a 68 and Trevor Immelman a 69 in the lead-off match, beating Mark O'Meara and John Cook. Nona was on its way. In all, six of Lake Nona's 10 players shot in the 60s in the second round, locking up a 17-13 victory.

"It's about time we won this thing again," said Lake Nona captain Ernie Els, who contributed a 69.

In the first round, Isleworth, captained by Tiger Woods, led 6-4. Woods and Cook shot 63, beating Henrik Stenson and Chris DiMarco in the opening match. "I made some nice putts," Woods said. "Keep working at it." Two Lake Nona wins came with the best scores of the day. Graeme McDowell and Retief Goosen shot a 60 and won by four over J.B. Holmes and Daniel Chopra, and Justin Rose and Ian Poulter shot 62 to edge Stuart Appleby and Robert Allenby. Appleby chipped in for a birdie to tie the match, but Rose answered with a birdie on a 12-foot putt for the win.

In the second round, Woods and Charles Howell each shot 69 and picked up three points, but Lake Nona had already locked up the cup.

CVS/Caremark Charity Classic
Barrington, Rhode Island
Winners: David Toms and Nick Price

David Toms figured he owed one to his partner, Nick Price. Actually, that he owed him a bunch. And that was the story in a nutshell of the CVS/Caremark Charity Classic at the Rhode Island Country Club in June.

Toms was referring to Price's brilliant first round, getting six birdies in their five-under-par 66. Toms repaid him with eight birdies in the second round for an 11-under 60 and a 36-hole 126 total, 16 under. They finished three ahead of Matt Kuchar and Laura Diaz (the event was played under coed format for the first time).

Price, a member of the Champions Tour, added to his record as the most successful player in the CVS's history. He won with Mark Calcavecchia in 2001 and with Tim Clark in 2006.

"We both played really well the last 27 holes," said Toms, getting his first win in the event. "The way my partner played on the back nine Monday,

I'll remember that for a long time. He shot 29 and kind of carried me around."

Said Price: "I missed a couple of short putts, but David just played so well today. I was just going along for the ride. I said to him, 'Now I know how you felt yesterday.'"

PGA Grand Slam of Golf
Southampton Parish, Bermuda
Winner: Lucas Glover

The PGA Grand Slam of Golf is a summit meeting of the winners of the four majors each year. Lucas Glover, the U.S. Open champion, turned the 2009 gathering in Bermuda into a learning experience and a $600,000 lark.

Learning experience? "I brought new irons with the new grooves just to try and see how they work," Glover said. This was a test run with the U.S. Golf Association's mandated new grooves that go into effect in 2010.

The lark? Glover played the Port Royal Golf Course in 65-66 for an 11-under-par 131 total, beating Masters champion Angel Cabrera (70-66) by five strokes, Open champion Stewart Cink (67-70) by six and PGA champion Y.E. Yang (71-70) by 10.

Glover made 13 birdies and one eagle over the two days. In the second round, he streaked with birdies at Nos. 5, 7, 9, 10, 11, 15 and 17. The 12th hole was pivotal. "I had it going, and then the wheels fell off," Cink said, after a bogey at the 12th. Cabrera said he lost there when Glover made a long putt for par and he missed a short one for birdie.

Kiwi Challenge
Hawke's Bay, New Zealand
Winner: Anthony Kim

It's not often that a golfer can stumble to a bogey at a par-five hole and still pick up a winning check for $1 million, but that was the bonanza for Anthony Kim in a playoff at the Kiwi Challenge. It also was the measure of Sean O'Hair's problems in the four-man, 36-hole event at New Zealand's Cape Kidnappers Golf Resort in November.

"I did what I had to do to win, and fortunately I made a couple putts," said Kim. In the playoff at the 650-yard 15th hole, Kim needed four shots to get to the green, then two-putted for a bogey. O'Hair, who had birdied the 18th in regulation to tie Kim, drove into the trees on the left and double-bogeyed. "That tee shot just doesn't appeal to my eye," said O'Hair. "I probably should have hit a five wood, but at 650 yards you feel like you have to hit driver."

Kim shot 71-66 and O'Hair 68-69 to tie at five-under-par 137. O'Hair won $500,000. Hunter Mahan, the defending champion, shot 73-67–140 and won $300,000, and Camilo Villegas (69-72–141) won $200,000.

Callaway Golf Pebble Beach Invitational
Pebble Beach, California
Winner: Mark Brooks

The Callaway Golf Pebble Beach Invitational is something of an end-of-season version of the old Bing Crosby Clambake on California's Monterey Peninsula, but showed signs of turning into the Mark Brooks Member-Guest. With three victories, a guy stamps his name on things.

"I believe I had only four bogeys the entire week, and two of those were on short putts," said Brooks, after picking off that record third title, a two-stroke victory over D.A. Points and Rickie Fowler, the late-season surprise on the PGA Tour. The tournament, in its 38th year, drew a field from the three men's tours, the LPGA Tour, club pros and amateurs playing Del Monte, Spyglass Hill and Pebble Beach.

"I kept the ball in the fairway, and that's always been what I do best," said Brooks, who shot 70-70-69-67–276, 12 under par. Brooks took a share of the lead in the third round, tying Fowler at 209. "I just played pretty solid," Brooks said. "I wasn't really in a lot of trouble."

In the final round, Fowler trailed Brooks by two through No. 4. They exchanged the lead until the 16th, where Brooks moved ahead for good with one of three birdies across the last four holes. He punctuated the run with a 16-footer at the 18th. Points closed with a 65 and Fowler with a 69 to tie for second place.

Mina Harigae, who would join the LPGA Tour in 2010 and the only one of four women in the field to make the cut, closed with a 68 for a 282 total.

Chevron World Challenge
Thousand Oaks, California
Winner: Jim Furyk

Jim Furyk, he of the quirky swing with the loop at the top, had gone nearly two years without a win. Then on a Sunday afternoon early in December, he dropped key putts on the last two holes to win the Chevron World Challenge by a stroke. It wasn't an official PGA Tour event but it felt just as good against an 18-man invitational field at Sherwood Country Club in Thousand Oaks, California. And the $1.35 million first prize would spend beautifully. "It bothered me," Furyk said of his long dry spell. "That's your goal — to go out and win, and I haven't been able to do that. Hopefully, this will be a stepping stone."

Six players had a share of the lead at some point in the final round, until Furyk birdied the 10th and was ahead to stay. He made a sensational save at the par three 17th, where he came out of a bunker to 35 feet past the flag, and then holed the putt. And at the 18th, he floated a 146-yard nine-iron shot to five feet and holed the putt for a birdie, wrapping up a 67 and a 13-under-par 275 for a one-stroke win over Graeme McDowell.

The Shark Shootout
Naples, Florida
Winners: Jerry Kelly and Steve Stricker

Anyone handicapping Greg Norman's Shark Shootout — he sat out because of elbow surgery — would have to give very long odds against golf's noted Wisconsinites, Jerry Kelly and Steve Stricker, with that weak start in the third and final round. They were limping along while, for example, Kenny Perry and J.B. Holmes were torching Tiburon Golf Club at Naples, Florida — an eagle at No. 1, then birdies on 11 of the next 13 holes to get to 25 under par. "It was in cruise control," Perry said.

Stricker and Kelly tied for the first-round lead with 66 in the modified alternate shot; shot 65 in the second-round better ball for a one-stroke lead, and a 59 in the last-round scramble to win by a stroke at 26 under. "We came here to have fun and to play well at the same time," said Stricker, "and we did that."

While Perry and Holmes were lighting up the course, Stricker and Kelly struggled through pars early in the final round. In a scramble, pars are not good. Then they caught fire. They made five straight birdies, parred twice, and from the 14th went birdie-birdie-birdie-eagle and finished at 26 under, winning by a shot over three pairs — Perry and Holmes, Justin Leonard and Scott Verplank, and Chad Campbell and Tim Clark.

"One of us always seemed to step up," Kelly said.

Nationwide Tour

If pure determination and performance are just a peek at the future, then one of the toughest Australians since Greg Norman will be plying his craft on the PGA Tour in 2010. This would be Michael Sim, 6 feet, 170 pounds, and age 25 when he finished dismantling the Nationwide Tour in 2009. Sim, many said, was the greatest player ever in the 20 years of the Nationwide Tour.

Of course, a lot of golfers, Aussies and non-Aussies, have raised great expectations and never blossomed, but it is reasonable to say that Sim was the most dominating player ever on the Nationwide Tour. He scored three victories — getting the "battlefield promotion" that went with them — and finished runner-up twice. All told, he made the cut in 12 of his 14 starts, had nine top-10 finishes, and won a record $644,142.

This will be Sim's second crack at the PGA Tour. A tie for seventh was his best finish in his 29 starts the first time around. "My goal next year is to win a PGA Tour event," he said. "In 2007, I didn't give myself a good shot at it. I was coming off an injury. I feel like I'm a better player now."

Kevin Johnson was the only other multiple winner in the parade of the top 25 Nationwide Tour money winners who took the reserved spots on the PGA Tour.

This Nationwide Tour graduating class, like most others, was top-heavy with players who have played the PGA Tour but lost their cards. (Been there, done that — but not nearly well enough.) That group ranged from Garth Mulroy and Josh Teater, who played just once, to such vets as Mathias Gronberg, who played in 170 events, Garrett Willis (161) and Jeff Gove (141). Only three graduates will be hitting the PGA Tour for the first time — Blake Adams, Jerod Turner and Alex Prugh.

Sim showed the benefit of seasoning. He had good power, averaging 292 yards off the tee. He hit 78 percent of his fairways, which was 10 points higher than the Nationwide Tour average, and hit 74 percent of greens in regulation (five points higher). And he averaged 28 putts per round, one putt below the average.

Sim ran away with the Stonebrae Classic by six shots, thanks to a pair of 64s. "I had a really good feeling that I was going to win," he said. He showed resiliency at the BMW Charity Pro-Am. He shot a 62 in the third round, with eight birdies, an eagle and one bogey, then in the final round, shook off a double bogey at No. 1 and bounced back with four birdies for a 69 to tie Fabian Gomez and beat him in a playoff. And in his third win, at the Christmas in October Classic, he made just two bogeys, one in each of the first two rounds, and was bogey-free in his 65-67 finish for a two-stroke win.

Matt Every, a former Walker Cup player, was on the verge of wrapping up his second winless season when he held off Sim and won the season-ending Nationwide Tour Championship. The win lifted him from 49th to

10th on the money list and into the Promised Land, the PGA Tour. "I've always felt I'm talented enough to win," Every said. "I couldn't have waited any longer to do it, I'll tell you that."

Brendan Todd, already a member of the PGA Tour, stopped by long enough to make a bit of history. In the Athens Regional Foundation Classic, he aced the same hole twice, the par-three 17th, with an seven iron in the first round and an eight iron in the second. "It was a stroke of good luck twice in a row," said Todd, who tied for 50th.

Kevin Johnson brought a touch of irony to his success. Johnson, 42, was there when the Nationwide Tour began. He won the Rex Hospital Open and the Knoxville Open and rejoiced. "The last two years were just dismal," Johnson said. "I needed to make a change or quit playing." So he found himself a coach. "I think I went searching for a new golf swing and a new Kevin Johnson," he said.

Six of the 25 got a spot without winning, led by Blake Adams, 34, who took the prize as the most intriguing. He finished third on the money list and set a record of earning the most money, $399,749, without winning. He did this with two seconds and overall eight top-10 finishes in 21 starts. "I think the thing I'm looking forward to most is playing the courses I saw the pros play on TV back when I was a kid," Blake said.

Henrik Bjornstad, 30, the first Norwegian to play the PGA Tour, earned his second try on six top-10s that put him 18th on the Nationwide list with $218,652. "In 2006, I wasn't ready," Bjornstad said. An impressive statistic — at 5-feet-8 and about 165 pounds, he averaged 298 yards on his drives.

Fran Quinn, 44, who played 47 times on the PGA Tour, won the 25th and last spot, plus the hearts of the fans. He took the Albertsons Boise Open, beating the unfortunate Blake Adams on the final hole with an eight iron to four feet, setting up his winning birdie. "I had to hit that shot at that time," Quinn said. "All the chips were on the table." Then he won his tour spot with his gritty finish in the Nationwide Tour Championship in October. He came out of a hospital bed for the last two rounds. "Worst pain I've ever been in," he said. "I had the shakes. I had brutal cramps. My back hurt. I was really breaking into vicious sweats." He closed with 75-74 to tie for 46th and grab the final berth by $5,000.

Canadian Tour

The year 2009 clearly was the year of his life for Canada's Graham DeLaet, from winning two tournaments on the Canadian Tour to topping the money list to getting a berth on the PGA Tour. A note on his website said it best, exclamation points and all: "I did it! I qualified for the PGA Tour!"

This was early in December, after he'd wrapped up a rich season on the Canadian Tour, then finished eighth in the PGA Tour's qualifying tournament. Not far behind came James Hahn, another two-time winner but who fell cruelly short in trying to qualify.

DeLaet, who had won once before on the Canadian Tour, got his second late in June when he raced off with the ATB Financial Classic by four shots at Sirocco Golf Club in Calgary. In the final round, DeLaet parred the first hole then birdied six of the next seven, and one-putted his first seven holes. "I'm a little bit speechless," DeLaet said. Riding the crest, he rolled in a twisting 30-footer for his seventh birdie and shot 64 for the four-stroke win over Byron Smith.

DeLaet got his second win of the season some three weeks later in the Canadian Tour Players Cup at Pine Ridge in Winnipeg. DeLaet shook off a couple early bogeys, birdied the eighth, then birdied three of four holes from the 12th and won by a shot when Smith bogeyed the last.

Hahn, a Californian, closed hard to catch Jim Rutledge with birdies at the 15th and 17th, then beat him on the first playoff hole for the Telus Edmonton Open at Glendale Golf Club. Rutledge, hitting first, pushed his drive into a hazard. "I was able to relax a bit," said Hahn, who hit a two iron to the middle of the fairway, then his approach to two feet, and two-putted for the victory, which was something of a surprise for the former shoe salesman. "I came over here last year and gave myself two or three years before I would even start contending," said Hahn. "I didn't expect a win to come so soon."

Hahn wrapped up his best year by winning the season-ending Riviera Nayarit Classic at Punta Mita in Nayarit, Mexico, late in September. And he did it in dramatic fashion, without a chance to practice because he was late in arriving from the Nationwide Tour qualifier. Hahn closed with a 69 for a 19-under 269 and a one-stroke win over Eduardo Herrera, a former PGA Tour player. "This is a huge win and a real confidence booster," Hahn said, and therein lay a golf tragedy. Hahn came to the final hole of the qualifying tournament needing a two-putt par from 65 feet to win a berth, but four-putted and missed by two. The story was not all bad, however. Hahn did get a berth on the Nationwide Tour, one of a record 15 Canadian Tour players who made it.

Mauricio Molina took the season-opening Corona Mexican PGA Championship with a classic storybook finish. In the final round, he was standing on the 18th tee, trailing Andy Matthews by two strokes. "I didn't think I could catch him," said Molina, who was hoping to finish second. "I just wanted to make a birdie." Matthews three-putted the last from 30 feet for a bogey, and Molina birdied, and they tied at 11-under 277. At the first playoff hole, Molina won easily when Matthews's tee shot hung up in a tree and he had to return to the tee.

In the Time Colonist Open at Victoria's Upland Golf Club, Byron Smith, the 2007 Player of the Year, shared an interesting moment with the gallery at the 12th tee in the final round. "I told the spectators, this is where it starts," Smith said. He proceeded to eagle the 12th and birdie three of the next four holes, pulling away for a three-stroke win. It was his third Canadian Tour win.

The veteran Mike Grob, 45, showed the value of experience in the Surrey Invitational when he fired a bunch of birdies and led by six in the final round, then comfortably parred in for a 67 and his sixth tour win, a two-stroke decision over DeLaet. Andres Gonzales closed with fireworks in the Saskatchewan Open for his first Canadian Tour win. After four birdies on the front side, and birdies at Nos. 13, 14 and 16, he hit his second over the green at the par-five 18th and chipped in for an eagle, a bogey-free 63 and a one-stroke win at 14-under 274.

It seemed little went uncontested on the tour, and that was the case in the Jane Rogers Championship at Milton's Greystone Golf Club, where Ryan Yip birdied the third playoff hole for the win.

Stuart Anderson figured he'd need 20 under to win the Desjardins Montreal Open at Saint-Raphael, but he went one better with a closing 63 and a 21-under 263 for his third tour victory. In the Seaforth Country Classic at Seaforth Country Club in Ontario, Brian Unk set three tour records in his three-stroke victory. He closed with a bogey-free 64 for a record 28-under 256, the lowest cumulative score and lowest score in relation to par. And he set a 54-hole record for a cumulative score.

James Love scored his first tour win in the Canadian Tour Championship with a par on the first playoff hole, and Rafael Gomez took the Iberostar Rivera Maya Open by a shot, despite blowing a six-stroke lead and lurching home with a four-over 76.

DeLaet, with two victories in nine starts, topped the money list with $94,579, nearly $13,000 more than No. 2 Byron Smith ($73,842). Hahn was a close third with $73,417.

Ryan Yip was the top birdie-getter with 207 in his 44 rounds. Scott Gibson was second with 199, while Hahn had 36 in 155 and DeLaet 32 in 148. Andres Gonzales led in eagles with nine in 36 rounds, and Hahn tied for 13th with six in 36.

Tour de las Americas (South America)

The 2009 Tour de las Americas season was marked by two double winners, a one-time winner who topped the Order of Merit, and a successful visit by American star Tom Lehman.

The Order of Merit was taken by Sweden's Peter Gustafsson, who had one victory and enough other high finishes to amass $40,934, nearly $13,000 more than runner-up Julio Zapata. Gustafsson, a former European Tour player, got his win in the season-opening Abierto Internacional de Antioquia at the Deportivo Club in Medellin, Colombia. He was trailing by three going into the final round and made up the deficit with a four-under-par 66. He took the lead for good at the par-five 16th, hitting two five woods to the green and sinking a 20-foot putt. He won by one over Argentina's Daniel Altamirano, then saluted the field. "There are many great players all over the world, and South America is no exception," said Gustafsson, who picked up $31,000 for the win.

The Campeonato Abierto del Centro, at Cordoba Golf Club in Argentina, was also a celebration for native son Angel Cabrera, fresh from winning the Masters. He received a hero's welcome. "I really felt the warmth of my people," said Cabrera. He finished third, and it became a family affair when his son Federico, 19, shot 68 and finished sixth in his best start as a pro. Another Argentine standout, Andres Romero, finished fifth and would be defending his Zurich Classic title on the PGA Tour the next week. They only made Fabian Gomez's victory all the sweeter. The quiet-spoken Gomez didn't sit on the three-stroke lead he carried into the final round and authored a three-under 68 to win by three over Ricardo Gonzalez, who shot a day's-best 65.

Gomez added his second win of the season and his career fourth with a sensational final nine in the Roberto de Vicenzo Classic at San Eliseo Golf Club in Buenos Aires. Tied with nine to play, Gomez raced to four birdies in five holes from the 11th, shot 69, and won by two strokes. "This is a very special tournament," Gomez said. "You know, you don't get to be presented with a trophy by De Vicenzo that often."

Argentina's Agustin Jauretche, 31, had been looking for his first win since 2006 and then he had two in 26 days. In mid-October, Jauretche charged from five strokes off the lead to win the Abierto de Chile at Santiago's Los Leones Golf Club. He closed with a 69 to edge local junior whiz Matias Dominguez by a stroke. "This was a huge experience that will increase my confidence for the national amateur season," said Dominguez, whose 67-69 finish was the best of the field. The win also did wonders for Jauretche's confidence. "I was coming off a poor week at the European Tour's qualifying school," Jauretche said, "but now I'm thinking I can do this all over this weekend."

Not the next weekend, but 26 days later, in early November, Jauretche took the Carlos Franco Invitational. This time he led by one going into the final round and won by that margin with a 69 at the Carlos Franco Country

Club in Asuncion, Paraguay, when Fabrizio Zanotti (69) bogeyed the last hole. Zanotti was tied for second when Argentina's Rodolfo Gonzalez put on a furious finish with two birdies and an eagle over the last five holes for a 68.

Argentina's Alan Wagner, a mere 19, scored the second win of his young career but the most important one in the Club Colombia Masters in Bogota. He parred the 18th for a 68 to nip Italy's Edoardo Molinari by one with a 13-under 275. The victory was all the sweeter because the tournament was co-sanctioned by the European Challenge Tour, giving Wagner a berth on that circuit as well. "Now I'm just looking forward to playing all the Challenge Tour events," said Wagner, who took the lead for good with an eagle at the 13th. He bogeyed the 14th and parred in.

Colombia's Eduardo Herrera, a former PGA Tour player, holed a 12-foot birdie putt at the 18th for a 67 to force a playoff, then dropped a 16-footer at the second extra hole to take the TLA Players Championship over countryman Jaime Clavijo. Herrera, turning 44, found high hopes in the victory at Acapulco's Fairmont Pierre Marques. "I believe I still have the game, and it might even take me back to the PGA Tour," he said. "Why not?"

Lehman, 50, a former Open champion, closed with a 70 and rolled to a five-stroke victory in the Argentina Masters at Buenos Aires' Olivos Golf Club. Lehman, only the fifth foreigner to win at Olivos, said the future was bright for Latin American golf, and especially for Argentina. "There's a lot more in your future — way beyond Cabrera and the two Romeros," said Lehman, referring to players such as amateur Emiliano Grillo, 17, who finished 11th. And then there was Julian Etulain, whose two third-place finishes and five top-10s in 12 starts won him the Rookie of the Year award.

Argentine golfers dominated the TLA for 2009, taking eight of the 13 events. Also joining the parade: Daniel Barbetti won the Canal I Venezuela Open, Luciano Giometti the Abierto Hacienda Chicureo, and Cesar Agustin Costilla the season-ending Visa Open de Argentina.

8. European Tours

If the premise was that someone would play outstandingly well and have a putt to win the inaugural Dubai World Championship and with it the Race to Dubai, otherwise known as the Order of Merit, as well as an awful lot of money, then the restyled grand finale to the European Tour worked out almost perfectly. The only thing that went awry was that Lee Westwood played so outstandingly well that he had six putts for it on the 72nd green. Westwood played so brilliantly at the new Greg Norman-designed venue of the Earth Course at Jumeirah Golf Estates that he overcome a six-figure deficit to Rory McIlroy on the money list and claimed his second Order of Merit title nine years after the first.

It was a stunning performance from Westwood, who scored the lowest round of the week, a 64, on the Sunday, played the weekend in 130 strokes with no bogeys in the last 46 holes and finished at 23 under par, six ahead of Ross McGowan and eight ahead of McIlroy, who hardly gave up the No. 1 spot without a fight by finishing in third place. McIlroy, at age 20, was hoping to become the youngest winner of the Order of Merit since Seve Ballesteros in 1976 when the Spaniard was just 19. It was the season when the young Northern Irishman established himself as one of the finest talents in the world game. He won the Dubai Desert Classic at the start of the year and was a perennial threat on the leaderboard. His last four events produced results of tied for fifth, fourth, second and third.

But Westwood's season was built on firmer foundations than simply the last event. From the French Open in July, where he was the runner-up, he finished in the top 10 in 11 of his last 13 events. With five events to play he realized he might have to win twice to win the inaugural Race to Dubai and promptly claimed the Portugal Masters for his first win for two years. If there was a turning point for his season, it was the Open Championship at Turnberry, where he led during the final round but three-putted the final green to miss out on the Stewart Cink-Tom Watson playoff by a stroke. It was "as disappointing a moment as I've had in my career," he said. After earning his first Order of Merit title in 2000, after a number of seasons of seemingly winning at will, Westwood's career slumped and he drifted out of the world's top 250.

Now he was fitter, stronger, more consistent, a better recovery player — his shot over trees from a bare lie to a tap-in at the 71st hole with water threatening behind won him the Portugal Masters — and, at 36, more experienced. But it was by rekindling the spark of ruthlessness, of being aggressive at the right time, that characterized his early career that got him over the line. Knowing that he had more victories and more years on tour than all his rivals for the Order of Merit — McIlroy, Martin Kaymer and Ross Fisher — put together only made him stronger. He appeared on the final day in red, in homage to his favorite football team, Nottingham Forest, rather than Tiger Woods.

The victory put Westwood back at No. 4 on the World Ranking, his highest previous ranking back in early 2001, and following the Dubai World Championship Europe had six golfers in the world's top 10 for the first time ever. Paul Casey, whose three wins included the BMW PGA Championship and his first win in the United States, Padraig Harrington, Henrik Stenson, The Players champion, Sergio Garcia and McIlroy were the others. McIlroy became only the second player aged as young as 20 to join the top 10, the other being Garcia. Kaymer, who won the French and Scottish Opens, was 12th and Ian Poulter 13th, while Fisher was 20th.

With 10 months to go until the Ryder Cup at Celtic Manor, European captain Colin Montgomerie might have purred with delight that Monday morning when the rankings appeared. While much would change in the interim, it seemed obvious that McIlroy, Kaymer and Fisher would be making their Ryder Cup debuts and others were queuing up to make a case, such as Simon Dyson, Alvaro Quiros, McGowan and Francesco Molinari (or perhaps his elder brother Edoardo who stepped up as the Challenge Tour No. 1 to win the Dunlop Phoenix in Japan). There might also be a case for Chris Wood, who again performed miracles at the Open Championship — tied for third at Turnberry after tying for fifth as an amateur at Birkdale — on the way to being the Rookie of the Year.

What was clear across the tour was the breadth of talent willing to step up and perform if others would not or could not — Casey missed most of the second half of the season with a rib injury, Robert Karlsson, the former No. 1, was out for most of the year with an eye problem, and Kaymer missed over two months due to broken toes suffered in a go-karting accident. Going low was the order of the day. Rafael Cabrera-Bello scored 60 to win the Austrian Open and McGowan took the Madrid Masters after 60 in the third round. Then there was McIlroy, who was still 19 when he won the Dubai Desert Classic, and Danny Lee, the New Zealand amateur who broke a 38-year-old record when he became the youngest ever winner at the Johnnie Walker Classic at the age of 18 years and 213 days. Lee was not the only amateur to win; Ireland's Shane Lowry won his national Open amid stirring scenes at Baltray.

McIlroy announced late in the year that he would be taking up his PGA Tour card in 2010. It was not unexpected, but he said his schedule would not change too much, just a few more in the United States rather than a full-time residency. His intention was to play against the best players as often as possible. While catching up with Tiger Woods and Phil Mickelson a little more often in America would help that cause, the World Ranking suggested that when all Europe's best are in the same place those tournaments feature among the strongest available. The European Tour deserves credit for setting up an exciting finish to the season, taking advantage of the PGA Tour ending its main proceedings early in September, and extending its own circuit deep into the autumn.

It was not without problems, with the prize fund for the Dubai World Championship and the bonus pool for the Race to Dubai being cut by 25 percent. Westwood still took home US$2.75 million for doing the double, but the collapse of the property market in Dubai meant serious problems for sponsor Leisurecorp. George O'Grady, the chief executive of the European Tour, was confident they would see out their five-year contract, but amid the world financial downturn, pulling together a tour schedule was proving far from an easy task.

Joburg Open
Johannesburg, South Africa
Winner: Anders Hansen

See African Tours chapter.

The Royal Trophy
Bangkok, Thailand
Winners: Asia

See Asia/Japan Tours chapter.

Abu Dhabi Golf Championship
Abu Dhabi, United Arab Emirates
Winner: Paul Casey

Paul Casey had to wait exactly two years for a victory, and even after it looked assured with eight holes to play, the job was not completed until safely two-putting on the 18th green. Triumph at the Abu Dhabi Golf Championship was Casey's ninth on the European Tour but the first since he won the same event in 2007. For a player of his undoubted quality it was a strange drought and he was in danger of slipping outside the world's top 50. But back in Abu Dhabi, Casey showed his brilliance again to reclaim the falcon trophy from the defending champion, Martin Kaymer, who tied as runner-up with Louis Oosthuizen.

After an opening 69, Casey added 65 in the second round to get within one of the lead. It was a stunning 63 on the third day, with nine birdies and no bogeys, that put Casey four ahead of Kaymer and back on center stage. Early in the final round Casey played with characteristically fearless abandon. He birdied the first two holes, the sixth and the eighth to be out in 32. Kaymer was out in 33 and lost ground. When Casey birdied the 10th he was six ahead. A dropped shot at the 11th appeared insignificant. At the 13th he had a birdie putt from six feet but, unsettled by an errant camera click, he three-putted. A third bogey in four holes followed at the 14th.

Now his lead was down to two, although Casey had adopted the policy of not looking at the leaderboards so managed not to scare himself further. Oosthuizen birdied the 18th to close out a rampaging 64 to get to 20 under and one behind Casey. Kaymer eagled the 18th for 67 to tie with Oosthuizen, but by then Casey had steadied himself and closed with four solid pars, including after the last despite driving into the rough and having to lay up. He closed with 70, one ahead of a quality field that included Padraig Harrington, who tied for fifth with Rory McIlroy, while Sergio Garcia, after a closing 64, tied for eighth with Danny Willett.

"That was a bit of a nervous one," admitted Casey. "I started off great, but it was tricky coming in. The greens were exceptionally difficult to read and there were a couple of camera clicks which put me off. It feels very satisfying to get my hands on the trophy again. It felt great two years ago to win so early, and then I really didn't follow it up with anything. But it feels very different this time, a bit of a weight off my shoulders."

The victory was Casey's first since marrying Jocelyn Heffner in December.

Commercialbank Qatar Masters
Doha, Qatar
Winner: Alvaro Quiros

Alvaro Quiros has something of the showman about him. At 6-foot-3 he hits the ball miles and with his sideburns and wide-brimmed hat has a look that suggests he is not to be trifled with. Henrik Stenson and Louis Oosthuizen tried it at the Commercialbank Qatar Masters, but Quiros proved a winner by three strokes at the Doha Golf Club.

The Spaniard celebrated his 26th birthday on the eve of the tournament and at the end had the perfect present as he jumped 48 places on the World Ranking to 28th place. That guaranteed him starts in the upcoming World Golf Championships and the Masters. "At the beginning of the year we were trying to get into the top 50 in the world," Quiros said. "After Abu Dhabi, my game was good, but it was just waiting and keep going and now very close to the majors and everything. The most important thing is I'm qualified for the Match Play and it's the first World Golf Championships I will play, but to play in the Masters would be great, I've watched that tournament on television so many years."

In ranking-point terms, Quiros was helped by this being one of the strongest tournaments ever staged on the European Tour outside the majors, WGCs and the BMW PGA at Wentworth. This was the biggest of his three victories, coming just three months after taking the Portugal Masters the previous October. Stenson was one of the first-round leaders after 66. Oosthuizen, after rounds of 67 and 65, led at halfway, but Quiros was two over with a round to play after scores of 69, 67 and 64. His closing 69, taking him to 19 under par, was a tense affair, but he rallied brilliantly after a shaky start despite the James Bond fan having relaxed in the morning by watching *Tomorrow Never Dies*.

Out in 37, he fell behind Stenson when the Swede, who was four behind at the start, eagled the 10th. But from the ninth Quiros produced four birdies in five holes before admitting going for the impossible at the 15th. His six iron from the rough never made the carry over the water, yet at the vital moment of the day, he holed a left-to-righter from 15 feet to make a bogey. He was tied with Stenson, but the Swede had missed out on a birdie at the short par-four 16th. Quiros, driving just short of the green, did not and also birdied the 17th after a fine tee shot and suddenly the pressure was off. Stenson, a runner-up for the second year running after winning in 2006, three-putted the last to fall into a tie for second with Oosthuizen, second for the second week running.

Dubai Desert Classic
Dubai, United Arab Emirates
Winner: Rory McIlroy

Living up to the greatest of compliments, and in golf that means a favorable comparison with Tiger Woods, is not always easy, nor is hanging onto a big lead over the closing few holes. But Rory McIlroy managed to do both despite a nervous wobble down the stretch to claim his maiden victory at the Dubai Desert Classic. At 19 years of age, the Northern Ireland teenager became the seventh youngest winner on the European Tour after just 16 months as a professional.

Woods did not even turn pro until he was 20. But after McIlroy opened with 64 at the Emirates Golf Club, his playing partner Mark O'Meara, who mentored the young Tiger, said: "Ball-striking–wise, Rory is probably better than Tiger at that age. His technique is better. Certainly, Tiger has developed his swing over the years, but Rory is a step ahead. He has all the tools. It's hard to compare anyone with Tiger because of his mind and heart, but Rory shot eight under today and made it look pretty easy."

McIlroy went on to lead wire-to-wire with further rounds of 68, 67 and 70 for 19-under-par 269 total, but the last bit was definitely not easy. Six ahead with six holes to play, McIlroy won by only one over Justin Rose. The Englishman closed with 67 to be one ahead of Henrik Stenson. McIlroy, two ahead starting the final round, birdied the first three holes, but double-bogeyed the fifth and dropped another shot at the eighth. From the ninth he responded with maturity beyond his years, claiming five birdies in a row. The last of them came at the 13th where Rose eagled to get back to five behind.

Then the shots started drifting away. At the short 15th he took the wrong club, hit it heavy and missed the green. At the 16th he swung poorly off the tee and his ball found the trees in the desert scrub. At the next a camera click on the tee led to another wayward drive. Three shots gone in three holes and he led Rose, who birdied the 17th, by only one. At the par-five last he was in the back bunker in three, but played a superb recovery to three feet. Rose had a chance to force a playoff, but missed from 15 feet for a birdie, while a relieved McIlroy holed out for the victory.

"It would have been tough to take to lose a lead like that, but I got it done," he said. "You see guys coming down the stretch with a four- or five-shot lead and it looks easy, but it isn't. I had to fight back and held it together with a great up-and-down at the last. To hold off a field like this with Rose, Casey, Stenson, Garcia, Kaymer, that makes it even more satisfying."

Maybank Malaysian Open
Kuala Lumpur, Malaysia
Winner: Anthony Kang

See Asia/Japan Tours chapter.

Johnnie Walker Classic
Perth, Australia
Winner: Danny Lee

See Australasian Tour chapter.

Madeira Islands Open BPI - Portugal
Porto Santo, Portugal
Winner: Estanislao Goya

Estanislao Goya continued his rapid rise in professional golf by winning his sixth event on the European Tour at the Madeira Island Open BPI - Portugal. The event was played for the first time at the Seve Ballesteros-designed course on the tiny island of Porto Santo, just off Madeira and renowned for its famous beach. Fittingly, on the new layout, two rookies ended up in contention for the title, although Callum Macaulay thought he was always too far behind.

The Scot, playing in only his fifth event as a professional, only just made the cut at six over par, but then produced a 67 in the third round and equaled the course record with 64 on the last day. The 25-year-old from Falkirk became the Scottish champion at Carnoustie and helped Scotland to its first Eisenhower Trophy in 2008 before earning his card at the qualifying tournament. He came home in 28 with eight birdies, only failing to birdie the par-five 12th. As he flashed up the leaderboard, with six birdies at the last six holes, the pressure turned on Goya.

Goya, 20, from Cordoba in Argentina, won his place on the main circuit by finishing fifth on the Challenge Tour Rankings in 2008. The same season he won the Order of Merit on the Tour de las Americas, just a year after winning the qualifying tournament by nine strokes and breaking Johnny Miller's 32-year-old course record at Bonaventure with 61. He won twice on the Challenge Tour, including the season-ending San Domenico Grand Final with four birdies in the last five holes.

Here he was leading by three strokes after rounds of 68, 68 and 69, but a closing 73 and 278 total meant he won by one over Macaulay. He had two double bogeys, at the third and 16th holes, the latter leaving him no margin for error. He safely parred the last two holes to take the title. Damien McGrane and Wil Besseling, of the Netherlands, tied for third place, two behind the winner.

"It's great for me. I am so happy to have made one of my dreams come true," said Goya. "I want to be one of the best players in the world and this is one of the steps that I have to take to do that. It's amazing that I have my Tour card for the next two years and a win here in Madeira. It was just over a year ago that I was thinking how much I would love to play in Europe and here I am now having won."

Open de Andalucia
Seville, Spain
Winner: Soren Kjeldsen

At the start of the Open de Andalucia, Colin Montgomerie celebrated play-ing in his 500th European Tour event with a cake from promoter Miguel Angel Jimenez and an opening round of 67. But as the Ryder Cup captain faded, Soren Kjeldsen enjoyed a superb weekend to win his third title. The 33-year-old Dane scored 62 in the third round, a course record at the Jose Maria Olazabal-designed Real Club in Seville and a career best. There were nine birdies, seven of them in a row, and an eagle in a brilliant display of approach play and putting.

When Kjeldsen finished his third round he was six ahead, but the leaders still had many holes to play and an eagle-birdie-birdie finish from David Drysdale got the Scot within one. The final round was a duel between the two, and although Drysdale twice drew level with Kjeldsen, he could never get in front. When Kjeldsen bogeyed the 15th, the pair was tied with three to play. Then Kjeldsen went in the water with his second shot at the par-five 16th.

But the turning point was when the Dane holed from 20 feet for a par. It kept him on even terms and then a two-shot swing at the short 17th went in his favor. Drysdale found a bunker and dropped a shot, while Kjeldsen holed another 20-footer. At the last, the drama suddenly fizzled as Drysdale's approach spun back into the water. His double bogey meant Kjeldsen could three-putt and still win by three strokes. Drysdale's closing 74, however, meant that he matched his best finish on the European Tour and, after 10 visits to the qualifying tournament, the probability of retain-ing his card this year.

Kjeldsen, who finished on 14-under 274 after a 72, won his biggest title at the Volvo Masters in 2008, just five months earlier, and after a slow start to the season a second victory in Spain came after finishing seventh at the CA Championship and just ahead of his Masters debut.

"I was very nervous all day," he said. "I knew it was going to be a tough day and it was. But I never lost patience and belief. I felt like I was giving it away after a horrific shot on 16, but I had to grit my teeth and it was great to make that putt there and play 17 the way I did."

Estoril Open de Portugal
Cascais, Portugal
Winner: Michael Hoey

Between Darren Clarke and Rory McIlroy, Northern Ireland had produced another fine player, one who won the British Amateur Championship in 2001 and that year played in the same Walker Cup-winning team at Sea Island with the likes of Luke Donald and Nick Dougherty. But Michael Hoey's career as a professional had not gone as he would have hoped. Until now, at the age of 30, when he won the Estoril Open de Portugal at the exposed Oitavos Dunes. It was a maiden win on the European Tour and inflicted a first playoff defeat, at the fourth attempt, on Gonzalez Fernandez-Castano.

Hoey was on the European Tour in 2006 but lost his card, won from the Challenge Tour, immediately. In 2008 he won for the third time on the Challenge Tour and then got through qualifying for the first time in six attempts.

The up-and-down times did not stop this week. He had a 66 in the first round but a 76 in the second round. A 69 on Saturday left him five behind Paul Broadhurst with a host of others in between. But a five-under 66 on Sunday put him in the clubhouse at seven-under 277 and the leaders were struggling, Broadhurst dropping three shots in the first five holes in the wind and later double-bogeying the 13th. Fernandez-Castano came in with a 67 to tie Hoey, but no one else could join them in the playoff.

The Spaniard had won three of his four titles in playoffs and never lost one. But twice at the 18th and then back to the 17th, he found his match in Hoey who got up and down every time, holing his third six-footer in a row to take the title after Fernandez-Castano chipped poorly at the 17th and two-putted.

"I didn't really think about winning, but I had all the breaks and it really was my day," said Hoey. "It's totally a life changing moment, it's amazing really. If I can keep this mentality going it's definitely the way forward. It's not going to sink in yet. It's a bit of a dream that I will cherish for a long time, and I'd just like to thank all those people who have supported me over the years."

Volvo China Open
Beijing, China
Winner: Scott Strange

See Asia/Japan Tours chapter.

Ballantine's Championship
Jeju Island, South Korea
Winner: Thongchai Jaidee

See Asia/Japan Tours chapter.

Open de Espana
Girona, Spain
Winner: Thomas Levet

At the age of 40 Thomas Levet simply gets better and better. The Frenchman needed to be at his best to hold off a strong mix of opponents and conquer the fine test of golf that is the Stadium Course at PGA Golf Catalunya near Girona. The course, tree-lined and more reminiscent of northern European tracks than those in southern Spain, was received well by players and spectators alike, but Levet emerged a winner of the Open de Espana by two strokes over Fabrizio Zanotti.

Levet immediately paid tribute to a man who won the Spanish Open three times, Seve Ballesteros. "I always think about Seve, he is having a hard time at the moment," Levet said. "The thing I most admired about him was his fight, and I had to fight today."

Levet led after both the second and third rounds, having compiled scores of 64 — Soren Hansen had an opening 63 — 67 and 71. A closing 68 gave him a total of 18-under-par 270 and the fifth victory of his career on the European Tour. It was the first time he had won in consecutive years on tour, having also won in Spain at the Andalucia Open in 2008.

But it was not easy. Early on, Levet trailed after two bogeys in the first four holes and only one birdie, while Stuart Davis birdied the first three holes to go two ahead after four. Davis, 35, is a rookie on the European Tour and his lack of experience showed after he took a double bogey at the fifth. His dream of a maiden win turned into a nightmare when he came home in 42 to fall to a tie for 15th place.

Levet re-established the lead with three birdies in a row from the sixth. Zanotti, the 25-year-old Paraguayan, closed with a 65, having gone out in 31, but could not get within two of the Frenchman. But Thomas Bjorn, showing a welcome return to form with 66, and Peter Lawrie, trying to become the first player since Max Faulkner in 1953 to successfully defend the title, still pushed the leader hard. Lawrie finished with a 69 to tie with Bjorn for third place. Levet was only one ahead before he birdied the 15th from eight feet, and he sealed the win with another birdie at the 17th.

BMW Italian Open
Torino, Italy
Winner: Daniel Vancsik

Not even the sight of John Daly's garishly colored trousers and his charge up the leaderboard to second place could distract Daniel Vancsik from a runaway six-stroke victory at the BMW Italian Open at Royal Park I Roveri in Torino. If Daly is unpredictable, then Vancsik can also produce surprising results. This was a second victory on the European Tour for the 32-year-old from Argentina. His first came at the 2007 Madeira Island Open by seven strokes, his 50th event on the circuit, having never had a top-10 finish. In the year prior to this tournament, he also had not registered a top-10 and his best result of the season to date was 42nd place the previous week in Spain.

But here he was superb, posting rounds of 68, 65, 69 and 65 to finish at 17-under-par 267. He led from the second round, and although only one ahead going into the last day, he went out in 32 to a comfortable advantage and then birdied the 10th, 13th and 14th before only his second dropped shot of the day at the 15th. England's Robert Rock and France's Raphael Jacquelin shared second place with Daly on 11 under after they closed with 68s, while Daly had a 66 with birdies on the back nine at the 11th, 14th, 16th and 17th.

Before the Spanish Open, where he was 31st, Daly, 43, had not played for over four months, having been suspended by the PGA Tour. Having lost weight after having a gastric band fitted and working on his game with coach Rick Smith, it was good to see Daly playing fine golf again.

But Vancsik would like to take his game to a new level by playing in a major championship for the first time. "My putting was fantastic," he said. "I played more aggressive and thought if I got to six or seven under on the day, the tournament is for me. Now my goal is to get into a major."

The 3 Irish Open
Baltray, Drogheda, Ireland
Winner: Shane Lowry

On one of the most amazing days in the history of the European Tour, Shane Lowry, a 22-year-old amateur from Clara, won The 3 Irish Open at County Louth in Baltray after a three-hole playoff with Robert Rock. Rock, as the leading professional, took the €500,000 first prize, but Lowry the trophy and the glory in front of a huge and excited gallery that included Irish Prime Minister Brian Cowen. Lowry became the third amateur to win on the circuit, following Pablo Martin in 2007 and Danny Lee at the Johnnie Walker Classic earlier in the season. But this was the first time an amateur had won on his very first appearance and also to win his national championship.

Martin and Lee were relatively well known compared to Lowry, the 2007 winner of the Irish Close Amateur title. He partnered Rory McIlroy in team golf before the latter turned professional and was ranked 16th on the World Amateur Golf Rankings. By the end of the tournament he was ranked 168th on the Official World Golf Ranking. The weather all week was cold, wet and windy, yet Lowry knew the links at Baltray extremely well, and despite liberal curses following wayward shots, he knew exactly how to cope with the conditions.

Lowry took the halfway lead after a 62 in the second round, the lowest ever score by an amateur on the European Tour. It would have been a course record had not Graeme McDowell scored a 61 earlier in the day. McDowell improved on his first-round 77 by 16 strokes, but had to withdraw the following day with shin splints. While Padraig Harrington missed the cut and McIlroy drifted down the leaderboard on the weekend, Lowry kept going, a five-hour weather delay on Saturday overcome as he shared the third-round lead with Rock.

Although Marc Warren had 68 on Sunday and Nick Dougherty a 69 to tie for fourth on 13 under, the final day belonged to the final threesome, who all shot 71s, leaving Sweden's Johan Edfors, the most experienced of the trio, two strokes behind. Rock and Lowry tied at 17-under 271, but the home player pitched to four feet at the par-five 18th only to miss for the victory, much to the agony of the gallery and himself.

Playing the 18th again and again, Lowry drove into a fairway bunker on the first extra hole but both men parred. Next time Lowry hit a superb fairway wood from 269 yards onto the green and made a birdie, but Rock got up and down from a greenside bunker to match it. But on the third extra hole, Rock was over the back for three and could not match Lowry's par, leaving Rock with a third runner-up finish of the season and the second in successive weeks.

"I can't believe it. This is going to take a long time to sink in," said Lowry. "I know my life is about to change forever. I'm feeling shock more than anything. I got an invite here, it's my first tournament and I would have been happy to make the cut. But then I shot the 62 and after that I thought 'this is my week — I can win.' And I did!" A Walker Cup squad member, Lowry turned professional later the following week to claim his two-year exemption on the European Tour.

BMW PGA Championship
Virginia Water, Surrey, England
Winner: Paul Casey

Paul Casey was introduced to golf by the junior foundation at Foxhills. Ross Fisher joined a similar foundation at Wentworth, just next door to Foxhills. On the final day of the BMW PGA Championship they put on quite a show in front of huge crowds supporting their local heroes. Casey squeezed home, just, after a 69 for 17-under-par 271 total, despite Fisher firing a low-round of the week 64 at him.

Fisher, who shot a final-round 84 on his home course two years previously, made eight birdies and did not drop a shot. His only slip — it was not even an error — was not to convert a birdie chance on the tricky 15th. Casey did to get his nose in front again and then covered Fisher with birdies at the last two holes, holing from eight feet on the 17th and five feet on the 18th after coming out of the bunker. "It was a tough day," Casey said. "I always knew someone would come at me, and 64 by Ross was a fantastic round of golf. I knew he would keep being aggressive to the end and I needed to keep making the birdies. Thank God I holed that putt on the last."

Casey said he could not remember when he first watched golf on the West course, but it may have been as far back as 1987 when Bernhard Langer won. "There is something special about this course," Casey said. "This is where I caught the bug for golf. I remember sneaking in and watching the great players, Seve and Faldo and the rest, and seeing all the great shots. That's where I got the ambition to be out here. It is so weird. I used to be outside the ropes watching as the ball whistled past my nose. Now I'm the one hitting the shots."

It was Casey's third win of the season, following a two-year drought before Abu Dhabi and including his first win in the States in Houston. The win put him at No. 3 in the world. "Wow," he said, "that's exciting." Only Nick Faldo, Sandy Lyle, Ian Woosnam and Colin Montgomerie have achieved a top-three ranking from Britain.

"It is flattering to be in that sort of company, but I still have a lot of work to do to feel I can match their achievements," he said. "I'm my own harshest critic and I was not satisfied with the last couple of years. I'm not interested in the money, I want to get my name on the trophies."

He also joined an elite group who have won the PGA and the World Match Play on the West Course — Seve Ballesteros, Faldo, Woosnam and Monty.

European Open
Ash, Kent, England
Winner: Christian Cevaer

Christian Cevaer discovered a brilliant time to recover winning form as he won the European Open at the London Club after a wild weekend in which there were almost 50 changes of lead. The last two days saw sunshine but strong winds on the exposed Jack Nicklaus-designed Heritage course, but Cevaer, one of the shorter hitters on tour, put on a superb display of battling golf. He used a utility club to good effect off both tees and fairways and got up and down on numerous occasions.

The 39-year-old Frenchman from the island of New Caledonia went into the tournament ranked 449th in the world and placed 196th in the Race to Dubai. But with a round to play he was tied for the lead with Jeev Milkha Singh with the pair three ahead of the field. While the Indian slumped to 76, Cevaer found that 74, the highest winning final-round score of the season, was good enough.

He went out in three over par and his only birdie of the day came at the 15th. But the crucial stretch was the last three holes and Cevaer produced three pars to finish while others faltered. Steve Webster and Alvaro Quiros both bogeyed the last hole when tied for the lead, with the Spaniard hitting spectators with both his first and second shots. They tied for second place with Gary Orr, one back at 282. Stephen Dodd was six under for his round before bogeying the last two holes and dropping back to a share of fifth place with Singh and Chris Wood, the leading amateur at the 2008 Open Championship.

The par-four 18th hole proved a beast all week, averaging 4.7 and recording 26 scores of seven or worse. But Cevaer played it in one under for the week with a birdie in the third round and pars the other three days, including in the final round with the tournament on the line. He finished at seven-under-par 281, which was 13 strokes higher than Ross Fisher's winning total in 2008.

"I'm not a long player, but I used my utility club and it worked out great," Cevaer said after being showered with champagne by his compatriots as is the tradition with French players. It was the second win of his career and came five years after taking the Spanish Open. "I made a point that no matter what happened to just enjoy my golf, enjoy my skills and hang in there."

Celtic Manor Wales Open
Newport, Wales
Winner: Jeppe Huldahl

As befitting the scene of the 2010 Ryder Cup, both captains were play-ing in the Celtic Manor Wales Open. For the record, Colin Montgomerie "beat" Corey Pavin by a shot, but the Scot was back in 37th place so it was not exactly relevant to anything. While the American was getting his first view of the resort near Newport, Montgomerie was urging his potential team members to play at the venue in 2010 — in 2009 only Miguel Angel Jimenez from the 2008 Ryder Cup team was present. Monty also stated that the winner would be in a strong position, either in qualifying or if he needed to seek a wild card.

The first winner over the new layout in 2008 was Scott Strange, who is Australian, so he will not be in Montgomerie's thinking, but the 2009 winner was a European but would certainly have not been on the Scot's radar prior to this week. Jeppe Huldahl had never previously finished in the top 10 on the European Tour. He made the circuit in 2004 but then lost his card and only got back for the 2009 season.

The 26-year-old from Denmark was tied for the lead after three rounds, but instead of leaving the stage gracefully, the newcomer played like a veteran in compiling a 67 with four birdies and no bogeys. He won by one over Niclas Fasth, with another former Ryder Cup player, Ignacio Gar-rido, in third place. Fasth drew level before bogeys at the 16th and 17th and before a birdie at the par-five 18th. Garrido was also tied for the lead before a double bogey at the 16th. Yet Huldahl kept his head and parred the last seven holes to claim victory.

"It feels amazing," Huldahl said. "I don't know what to say to be hon-est. I didn't even dream of this coming into this week. I couldn't feel my hands on the last three holes. I knew I was doing well, but I didn't know how well until I asked my caddie on the 18th tee. He told me I needed a par — and it's nice to have a par-five and have a chance to lay up. But I couldn't put winning out of my head and it was quite emotional."

Saint-Omer Open
Lumbres, France
Winner: Christian Nilsson

Christian Nilsson is coached by Henri Reis, the man behind the rise of Annika Sorenstam, the Swede who became the best player in the women's game. "I would love to do just half of what she has done," Nilsson said. "She is an amazing player and someone Sweden can be very proud of." Every great career has to start with a maiden victory and Nilsson's came at the Saint-Omer Open at Aa Saint-Omer Golf Club in northern France.

With rounds of 68, 69 and 65, Nilsson built a four-stroke lead with a round to play and never faltered during the final round. He made eight pars, then birdied the ninth and 10th holes, then finished with eight pars again. It was a resolute performance and the 69 for a 13-under-par 271 total meant the 30-year-old from Karlstad won by six strokes over Jose-Felipe Lima. The Portuguese player, who was brought up in France, won the tournament in 2004 and made six birdies in a final round of 68, but could not close the gap on Nilsson.

Nilsson played on the European Tour in 2006 and 2007, but went back to the Challenge Tour in 2008 and it was a runner-up finish in the co-sanctioned event at Saint-Omer that helped the Swede regain his card for the main tour. His form had hardly suggested a win was imminent, but victory gave him an exemption through the 2010 season.

"It feels great, although I'm still in shock at the moment, I think," Nilsson said. "It's obviously a massive win for me, so it might take awhile to realize just what it means. I was very nervous this morning and I didn't sleep that well last night either. I was just trying to focus on how I was going to play, but so many thoughts were going round my head at the same time. So I was extremely pleased with how I handled the pressure today. I'm just so, so happy."

BMW International Open
Munich, Germany
Winner: Nick Dougherty

An emotional Nick Dougherty looked to the heavens and blew a kiss to his late mother after winning the BMW International Open at Eichenried near Munich. Dougherty, 27, lost his mother in May 2008 and his form collapsed. This was the Liverpool man's third win on the European Tour, all two years apart, but after the second at the Alfred Dunhill Links Championship in 2007 he was looking for a Ryder Cup place the following year.

But by the start of 2009 he was out of the major championships and had recorded only one top-10 finish before arriving in Germany. A final-round slump at the Wales Open meant a chance had slipped away, but he made no mistake here, coming from three behind Retief Goosen with a brilliant eight-under 64 to finish at 22-under 266.

Three birdies in the first three holes put him level with Goosen, who was the leader after each of the first three days. The South African needed to eagle the ninth to stay even, but then his challenge stumbled, while the third member of the final group, Bernhard Langer, never got into contention. Still looking for his first win at the BMW after five runner-up finishes, the 51-year-old slipped to ninth place.

Dougherty birdied the 10th, 13th, 14th and 15th holes. Victory looked assured, but ahead Spain's Rafa Echenique birdied the short 17th and then had an albatross at the 18th to finish two-two. He holed a three iron from 243 yards and was suddenly at 21 under par and Dougherty was only one ahead. He managed to par the last three holes, but at the last needed to hit a five wood to avoid the water he found with a driver the previous evening and then laid up, pitched on and two-putted.

"It's no secret that the last year has been tough for me," Dougherty said. "There have been times I haven't felt like playing golf, but I've come through it and this means so much. To go and beat two major champions you're playing with and fend off a very exciting finish from Rafa, that really caught me by surprise a little bit. I kind of thought I had done the deal once I hit the green on 16. But I'm delighted with what I did and the way I went about my business."

Open de France ALSTOM
Paris, France
Winner: Martin Kaymer

The danger awaiting on the closing holes on the Albatross Course at Le Golf National, near Paris, was amply demonstrated as overnight leader Rafa Echenique — a week after finishing second at the BMW International Open with a closing albatross — suffered triple bogeys at the 15th and 18th holes. The Argentinean dropped to 13th place, but the battle for the title had already turned towards Martin Kaymer, who equaled the course record with 62 on the opening day and was one behind with a round to go, and Lee Westwood, who was four back.

Westwood and Ian Poulter were the men to make the biggest charges. Poulter finished with 67 that was spoilt by bogeys at the 15th and 18th holes. At the former, he was disturbed by a photographer's click on his downswing on the second shot and he found the water. Upset, he said later he would not return to the tournament.

Westwood, searching for his first win in two years, was out in 32 and then posted three more birdies in a row from the 11th. His only blemish was a six at the par-five 14th, but the turnaround in his game that produced a 65 was a putting tip from his caddie, Billy Foster, the previous night. But Kaymer had a strange day on the greens, holing from almost 80 feet on the ninth to go out in 33, holing another long one at the 10th, but missing birdie chances at the 15th, 16th and 17th holes.

After tying at 13-under 271, Kaymer and Westwood went to a playoff at the tricky 18th, where both men found the rough off the tee. Kaymer missed the green, but also just missed the water with his second shot, but Westwood was not so lucky, coming up a foot short of solid land. Westwood could not get down in less than six, but Kaymer chipped to 20 feet and then holed that for a par and the third victory of the 24-year-old German's career.

"This is obviously very special for me," Kaymer said. "I had some good chances, but finally I won it, so it's good." Of his second shot in the playoff, he said: "It was an okay lie and I thought that I could easily get it over the water. I had 170 meters with a six iron, but I pulled it a little bit, which probably turned out to be a good thing. I carried the water by about a meter or so."

Barclays Scottish Open
Glasgow, Scotland
Winner: Martin Kaymer

Martin Kaymer continued his brilliant form with a second victory in successive weeks at the Barclays Scottish Open. At the age of 24 the German became the youngest-ever winner of the tournament in finishing two ahead of Gonzalo Fernandez-Castano and Raphael Jacquelin. Adam Scott, returning to form a week before the year's third major championship, finished tied for fourth, with Retief Goosen and Nick Watney sharing sixth place.

Picking up at Loch Lomond where he left off at Paris National, Kaymer produced rounds of 69, 65, 66 and 69 for a 15-under-par total of 269. He was one behind Fernandez-Castano going into the final round and dropped a shot at the second hole, but was quickly level with the Spaniard by the fourth. Fernandez-Castano, whose wife was at home expecting their first child and also dealing with their lost dog, closed with a one-over 72 and could not put any pressure on the German. Jacquelin finished impressively with four birdies in the last six holes, but by then Kaymer was looking comfortable. He was helped by the putting woes of Goosen, who dropped six strokes in five holes from the seventh. Goosen had an up-and-down week. He topped his first tee shot in the second round, but after that mishap was virtually flawless in a 63 that gave him the halfway lead.

Kaymer birdied the 13th and 15th holes to go three ahead, and a dropped shot at the 16th was nothing to worry about. With the Open Championship the following week at Turnberry, Kaymer could not have found form at a better time.

"This week was very special, because I think if you win in the home of golf in Scotland, it's always something special, and I really enjoyed the last two days," said Kaymer. "It was amazing, the spectators, they were supporting us, it was unbelievable. ... Everybody asks me about the third win in a row, but we are playing a major next week, and the field is going to be the best we have all year long. But, of course, I'm really looking forward to next week, but it's going to be really, really difficult, which is always good — if you play majors, they should be difficult."

With four career wins in only his third year on the European Tour, Kaymer is now tied with Alex Cejka in second place behind Bernhard Langer in the list of German winners on tour.

The Open Championship
Ayrshire, Scotland
Winner: Stewart Cink

See Chapter 4.

SAS Masters
Malmo, Sweden
Winner: Ricardo Gonzalez

After a week chopping down trees on his farm just south of Buenos Aires — he had not qualified for the Open Championship — Ricardo Gonzalez returned to swinging a golf club and claimed his first victory on the European Tour in five years. It was the Argentinean's fourth victory on the circuit and was sealed with some breathtaking shots over the closing holes. Gonzalez was trailing clubhouse leader Jamie Donaldson, who closed with a 68 for eight-under-par 284, and the man making the running out on the course, Denmark's Jeppe Huldahl, when Gonzalez birdied five of the last six holes. A blip of 77 in the third round, after earlier twin efforts of 68, did not matter after a closing 69 gave him a 10-under-par 282 total to win the SAS Masters at Barseback, which was revamped in its 40th year and at 7,665 yards was the longest ever played on the European Tour.

Huldahl, from just across the Oresund from Malmo, was aiming for his second win of the season, but bogeys at the 10th and 11th opened up the tournament. It was Gonzalez who took advantage. He birdied the 13th and 14th holes, but the really spectacular stuff came at the closing three holes. He played a very fine chip over a bunker at the 16th to set up a tap-in birdie at the par-five, but at the last two holes was even more brilliant. At the 17th he faced a plugged lie in a greenside bunker but holed the shot, saying later that he routinely practiced from such lies at home. Then at the last his drive finished in the left trees, but he struck a nine iron through a small gap to five feet and holed that as well.

"Incredible," said Gonzalez, who had not had a top-10 finish in 2009 until this victory. "It's been a hard year, but I was fighting, fighting, fighting. I had the feeling that you can always make it if you work hard and never lose faith. I don't know whether the shot on the last was luck or just brilliant."

Donaldson finished in second place, two behind, with Huldahl two further back after a 74. American Nathan Smith finished tied for fourth after starting the tournament with a triple bogey after a two-stroke penalty for being late on the tee after a rain delay. He sprinted from the putting green to the tee after getting a phone call on his mobile from a tournament official and arrived just one minute before being disqualified.

Moravia Silesia Open
Celadna, Czech Republic
Winner: Oskar Henningsson

By winning the Moravia Silesia Open, Oskar Henningsson became only the third player to win a tournament in his rookie season on the European Tour after winning the qualifying tournament to get his card. Gordon Brand, Jr., and Jose Maria Olazabal were the only other two to have achieved the feat. The 23-year-old Swede followed his best finish of the season at the SAS Masters the previous week, where he tied for fourth, with a maiden victory by two strokes over Steve Webster, the overnight leader, and Sam Little.

Henningsson, who started the tournament with a double-bogey seven in the first round, came from three behind Webster with 67 for a 13-under 275 total at Prosper Golf Resort in the Czech Republic. Little closed with 70 and Webster a 72 after dropping three shots in the first seven holes. Zimbabwe's Marc Cayeux, England's Graeme Storm and Spain's Ignacio Garrido — who led for much of the day before four bogeys in a row from the 10th — were tied for fourth at 10 under.

Henningsson took advantage of Webster's slip with a outward 32 which included birdies at the first and the fourth before a four-footer at the eighth put him in a tie for the lead. Further birdies followed at the ninth, 13th and 16th, and a dropped shot at the last did not matter.

"It feels great. I'm overwhelmed by it," Henningsson said. "I had no expectations that I would win this week, it feels strange but good. I'm very happy but I'm tired at the moment — I've not realized what I have done yet. I've a 10-hour trip home by car, so I will have a lot of time to think about it and what I have done.

"Of course it would be fantastic if I could have a career like those of Olazabal and Brand. Hopefully this is the starting point for me to achieve similar things to what they have done," he added. "I felt the game was really good last week and I was trying to keep the same game as in Sweden. It's been really good the last few weeks. I know I can contend as I've been there before. I was hoping to win this year, but I didn't expect to this soon."

KLM Open
Zandvoort, Netherlands
Winner: Simon Dyson

History repeated itself for Simon Dyson as he won the KLM Open in a playoff at Kennemer. It was the 31-year-old Englishman's third victory on the European Tour but his first in three years, since winning the same title at the same venue. Then, Dyson recalled, he hardly felt like celebrating as it was the day that Darren Clarke's wife Heather died from breast cancer. This time Clarke, the defending champion, was among those Dyson overtook to take the title. Clarke had a couple of putts finish on the lip and, as a result, finished two strokes behind, tied for fifth place.

Damien McGrane showed what was possible with a last-round charge of 64 to take fourth place, just one shot outside the three-way playoff. But it was Dyson who really set the Dutch links alight by equaling the course record with a 63 to post the clubhouse target at 15 under par with a total of 265. He then had to wait until the final twosomes of Peter Hedblom, who led by two overnight, and Peter Lawrie tied his score with closing efforts of 69 and 67 respectively.

Dyson came from six strokes behind starting the final day, the best recovery of the season since Richard Sterne won the South African Open late in 2008. He went out in 32 before adding further birdies at the 10th, 12th and 17th on a bogey-free day. "When I birdied the seventh and ninth

I thought back to doing the same when I won," said the York golfer. "Then I birdied the 12th like I did then." The crucial moment of the round was when he holed a 35-footer at the 17th. "It was traveling," he admitted. "It's funny when you see the line, you're not thinking about the pace. That was a bonus."

Lawrie took the lead with his sixth birdie of the day at the 12th, but dropped a shot at the 16th to fall back to 15 under. Hedblom, after a slow start, birdied the 15th and 17th holes to get into the playoff. Playing the 18th again, both Lawrie and Hedblom missed the green, with the Irishman facing a five-footer for par and the Swede over the green and in for a bogey when Dyson holed from 18 feet for a winning birdie.

Dyson, who also won in a playoff in 2006, said: "I had the best day of my life by far three years ago and this has gone miles past it. I've played probably my best golf ever this week and I've only just won it in a playoff. It just shows it's not easy to win."

Johnnie Walker Championship
Perthshire, Scotland
Winner: Peter Hedblom

A week after losing in a playoff at the KLM Open, Peter Hedblom took advantage of his revived form to win the Johnnie Walker Championship at the PGA Centenary course at Gleneagles, venue for the 2014 Ryder Cup. The 39-year-old Swede claimed his third title on the European Tour but his first in Europe after victories in Malaysia and Morocco. Having taken the lead after 54 holes from Paul Lawrie, the former Open champion who topped the leaderboard on the first two days, Hedblom was himself overtaken while still playing the front nine.

Compatriot Martin Erlandsson had the round of his life with a 62 that would have been a course record but for the fact that preferred lies were in operation. Erlandsson racked up 10 birdies and no bogeys, with seven of the birdies coming in a row from the sixth, one short of the European Tour record. Erlandsson was three ahead when he set the clubhouse target at 276, 12 under par, but Hedblom responded with birdies at the seventh, eighth, ninth and 10th to go back in front by one. He dropped a shot at the 15th, but got it back with a birdie at the next and then parred the last two holes. Lawrie and defending champion Gregory Havret tied for third place, two behind Erlandsson.

Hedblom said: "That was so tough. I thought last week was, but this was harder. It feels unbelievable. I had to dig down so deep, but I am so happy. What a round Martin played — I couldn't believe it and he should have won. I just had to plug on. I hit a great shot into 16, but making two pars was even harder. This year has been unbelievable. I played so poorly (not a single top-30 finish) until last week. I want to play in the big tournaments, but I keep taking one step back. Hopefully this is two steps forward."

Erlandsson admitted he has struggled with the mental side of the game. As a result, his psychologist, a former international hurdler, advised turning his mind to other things when under pressure. "I was looking at my thumb and wondering how it looked," he said to a quizzical media. "I was also trying to look at a tree or somebody in the audience to keep my mind at peace. I got off to a good start and that helped my confidence and I really enjoyed it and played free and that was the key."

Omega European Masters
Crans Montana, Switzerland
Winner: Alexander Noren

Buzz Aldrin, former NASA astronaut and the second man to walk on the moon, was on hand to present the Omega European Masters trophy to Alexander Noren, a Swede claiming his first title on the European Tour. The 27-year-old made the perfect start to the 2010 Ryder Cup qualifying as the win put him on top of the standings. Early days, but Noren said: "I will just have to try and stay there."

Noren's third full season on the European Tour had not been going to plan as he suffered wrist and knee injuries, but he had long been a promising player to watch, one for whom positions of 88th on the Race to Dubai money list and 130th in the world starting the week did not do him justice. A third round of 63 at the par-71 Crans-sur-Sierre course put Noren two in front of Charl Schwartzel and three clear of Bradley Dredge.

Schwartzel three-putted the first two greens while Noren birdied the opening two holes to go four strokes clear of Dredge. The Welshman had also had a poor season, but the thought of representing Europe in the Ryder Cup on home soil in 2010 gave him the feeling that, "the season starts here." He eagled the ninth, holing out from 63 yards, and then birdied the next two while Noren bogeyed the eighth and birdied the 10th, so they were even. They were level again after they exchanged bogeys at the 12th and 13th holes, but then Noren birdied the 14th to go one clear again.

It was at the par-five 15th that the Swede clinched the victory with a brilliant bunker shot that rolled into the hole for an eagle. Dredge birdied but was now two behind and both men parred home. "I was so happy when that bunker shot went in," Noren said. "I've never felt this good about my game, and to win was just brilliant."

Noren closed with a 66 for a 20-under total of 264 with Dredge's 65 putting him at 18 under, one ahead of Ross McGowan, who also closed with a 65. Miguel Angel Jimenez was fourth and Thongchai Jaidee fifth in the first European-based event to be co-sanctioned with the Asian Tour.

Mercedes-Benz Championship
Cologne, Germany
Winner: James Kingston

James Kingston went from not even thinking he would be playing the Mercedes-Benz Championship at Gut Larchenhof to ending the week with his second victory on the European Tour. The 43-year-old South African had not won since claiming his own national championship at the end of 2007. Because that event counted on the 2008 European Tour, Kingston made it into the elite, no-cut tournament after finishing 17th on the Order of Merit. But his recent form had not been good — he had missed his last four cuts and had not earned a check since the Open Championship in July two months earlier. Yet Kingston produced rounds of 67, 69, 70 and 69 for 275 total to tie with Anders Hansen and then win the playoff at the first extra hole.

Kingston was a stroke behind Peter Hanson overnight with Hansen two further back. But the Dane holed a bunker shot at the opening hole and closed with a 67 to set the target at 13 under par. Soren Hansen, no relation, was also involved on the final day and ended up tied for third place with Hanson and Simon Dyson, who had a chance from 20 feet at the last to join the playoff but came up just short.

Kingston holed from 12 feet at the 15th to take the lead as Anders Hansen three-putted the 16th to fall two behind. But the Dane then birdied the 17th from eight feet while Kingston would later three-putt the same hole. But at the 18th in the playoff Hansen found a greenside bunker and came out to six feet. His par effort lipped out, but Kingston, who had lagged up from the back of the green, still had to hole from almost four feet for the win.

"A week ago I didn't even know I was in the event," said Kingston. "I got in through last year's rankings, so to come out and win a championship like this on a golf course like this makes it more special. I would probably have spent a few more days at home this week, but it shows how things can change. It's like the South African Open. I was injured a couple of days beforehand and didn't think I could play and I went on to win that. Two wins and both of them unexpected."

Austrian Golf Open
Vienna, Austria
Winner: Rafael Cabrera-Bello

Starting the final round eight strokes out of the lead, Rafael Cabrera-Bello nevertheless completed his maiden victory on the European Tour with a stunning closing round of 60. The 11-under-par effort, in which he did not drop a stroke to par, could have been even lower had the 25-year-old Spaniard holed from 30 feet on the 18th green for an eagle. Although he did not become the first player to score a 59 on the European Tour, Cabrera-Bello was able to tap in for what would be a one-stroke victory over Benn Barham.

Cabrera-Bello had 12 one-putt greens in the final round and began his charge with three birdies in a row from the third. Out in 30, he made four birdies in a row around the turn from the eighth hole. He then birdied the 13th and 14th, the 16th and again at the 18th. After rounds of 71, 67 and 66, Cabrera-Bello was at nine under, but adding the 60 left him at 20-under-par 264 at Fontana, in the village of Oberwaltersdorf, in the outskirts of Vienna.

Barham had been the leader for the first three rounds after opening with 63 and then adding 66 and 67 to be 17 under par. Barham needed to win to give himself a chance of retaining his card, but bogeyed the third hole and could not make a birdie until the 11th. He also birdied the 12th and kept in touch with the new leader by birdieing the 16th, but drove into the rough at the last before missing from 18 feet for a birdie to force a playoff.

Cabrera-Bello, whose sister Emma plays on the Ladies European Tour, grew up beside a golf course on the island of Gran Canaria and won at every age-group level in Spain. Twice having graduated from the Challenge Tour, he had missed eight of his previous 10 cuts and had never scored better than a 64 on the European Tour. He became the 13th player to score a 60 on the circuit, but only the third to do it in the final round.

"It's just amazing. I played the best golf of my life and I can't believe it," he said. "I was so far back I wasn't thinking about winning. I just tried to play a shot at a time and today it worked out really, really good."

The Vivendi Trophy with Seve Ballesteros
Paris, France
Winners: Great Britain & Ireland

With a new name, sponsors and venue at St. Nom-la-Breteche, Great Britain & Ireland won The Seve Trophy for the fifth consecutive year — the Continent of Europe has only won the inaugural match in 2000 — and by the same score of 16½ to 11½ as for the last two matches. It was another convincing victory with Rory McIlroy and Graeme McDowell winning at the top of the singles order to confirm the inevitable. After Anthony Wall pulled out with a shoulder injury suffered during the second day's play, which meant a half in his match with Alvaro Quiros, Europe needed to win 8½ points out of nine, and apart from the first two matches fought a strong rearguard action but could only win the singles 6-4.

Europe had the advantage in terms of world rankings, but GB&I — missing six big names in Padraig Harrington and Luke Donald (playing in The Tour Championship), Paul Casey (injured) and Lee Westwood, Ian Poulter and Justin Rose (resting) — proved too strong on the first three days. They won the fourballs 3-2 on both the Thursday and Friday and then had a superb Saturday, taking the greensomes 3-1 and the foursomes 3½-½.

McIlroy and McDowell led the way, winning three points out of four together and then both won their singles, McIlroy sneaking a tight match against world No. 5 Henrik Stenson at the last and McDowell beating Robert Karlsson, in his first tournament after months out with an eye problem, 3 and 2. The only player to have a better record than the two Northern Irishmen was Chris Wood, the young Englishman who finished third at the Open Championship and halved his singles with Peter Hanson to finish with 4½ points out of five.

The performance of the week came from Anders Hansen who was 10 under for 12 holes in beating Nick Dougherty 7 and 6. It was a rare moment of joy for European captain Thomas Bjorn, who said: "There's a lot of talent on our side — they just didn't get it done this week. There's nobody on my team that can't be in the next Ryder Cup team."

With Colin Montgomerie, the European Ryder Cup captain for 2010, taking an observer's role, GB&I were captained by Paul McGinley, who was as impressive as his team. "I've just done what I believe in and what I've learned from experience over the years," McGinley said. He added: "We've talked a lot about Seve every day, in all our meetings. I think we really played with his spirit."

Alfred Dunhill Links Championship
St. Andrews & Fife, Scotland
Winner: Simon Dyson

For a player who gained his initial successes in Asia, Simon Dyson is showing himself to be a more than accomplished player at the traditional bump-and-run game. Confirmation came at the Alfred Dunhill Links Championship where he conquered not just the Old Course at St. Andrews but Carnoustie and Kingsbarns as well. It was the biggest win of the 31-year-old's career and not just because he collected a first prize of €540,440. Starting the final round one stroke behind Luke Donald and alongside Rory McIlroy, Dyson left his more illustrious challengers for dead with six birdies in the first seven holes on the Old Course and came home with a 66 to beat McIlroy and Oliver Wilson by three strokes.

Dyson was a member of the Great Britain & Ireland team that won the Walker Cup in 1999. The following year, as a rookie, he won three times on the Asian Tour, and when his first European Tour victory arrived in 2006 it was also out east. But that year he also won the KLM Open on a seaside course in the Netherlands and in August this year won there again — with another blistering final round. His rise was illustrated here by his jump from 92nd to 44th on the World Ranking, entering the top 50 for the first time.

Playing in rotation for the first three days in the pro-am style event, Dyson had 68 at Carnoustie, then 66 at St. Andrews and 68 at Kingsbarns before another 66 on the Old Course — delayed until Monday due to Saturday's play being cancelled on account of high winds — for a total of 20-under-par 268.

"This is like our fifth major, a massive tournament at the Home of Golf and I've shot 66 to win it," said Dyson after what he described as the best round of his career. "I'm absolutely buzzing. Darren Clarke has just said to me 'Take your time and enjoy it — it does not get any better than winning at St. Andrews.'"

In the team event, Soren Hansen and Kieran McManus set a new record of 44 under par after a 59 in the final round, as Irish stud farmer McManus followed in the footsteps of his father J.P., twice a winner with Padraig Harrington.

Madrid Masters
Madrid, Spain
Winner: Ross McGowan

Playing in the final threesome of the Madrid Masters was a trio that perhaps represents the future of the European Tour. All were looking for their maiden victories, but Ross McGowan and France's Michael Lorenzo-Vera were old rivals from the Challenge Tour and Danny Willett a tour rookie. Both McGowan and Willett were English Amateur champions. But it was not quite a fair fight given that McGowan had a seven-stroke lead over his two challengers, and despite the odd wobble along the way, ended up with a three-stroke victory over Finland's Mikko Ilonen.

McGowan really won the event on the third day when he shot a round of 12-under 60 at Centro Nacional. Helped only marginally by preferred lies being in operation, he had two eagles, including from 18 feet at the last, 10 birdies and two bogeys. He finished birdie, birdie, birdie, eagle and did not have a par on the back nine. Even more impressively, McGowan was playing alongside the best player in the field, Sergio Garcia. The Spaniard was the joint halfway leader but bogeyed four of the last seven holes, and weekend scores of 71 and 71 saw him fall to a tie for 17th place.

McGowan, who was third and sixth in his previous two outings, started with a bogey-six at the first on the final day and dropped another shot at the fourth before responding immediately with two birdies and another at the ninth. He dropped a shot at the 11th and then with four holes to play saw that Ilonen, who closed with a 66, had got within two shots. The 27-year-old, who lost a two-shot lead with six to play at the Johnnie Walker Classic in Australia earlier in the year, hit his approach to 10 feet at the 15th for a birdie. There was a final moment of drama at the par-five 18th when his second shot was heading for the water but stopped on some greenery growing through the wooden sleepers on the bank of the lake.

"It means a lot to win," McGowan said. "That's another goal out of the way and hopefully from here I can progress and move on to bigger things. I came here this week in form and it's lovely to come away with the trophy."

Portugal Masters
Vilamoura, Portugal
Winner: Lee Westwood

For a man who was a prolific winner a decade earlier, Lee Westwood was playing some of the most consistent golf of his career but could not win. At the start of the week, at a function marking just under a year to go to the 2010 Ryder Cup, European captain Colin Montgomerie said he was pleased with how his team was shaping up, early days though it was, but would like to see some wins from Padraig Harrington, Sergio Garcia and Lee Westwood. The first two had not won for a year; Westwood had not won for two years.

Yet in that time the 36-year-old from Worksop had 26 top-10 finishes, had lost out in three playoffs and come close to winning two major championships. He was fitter, his long game among the best in the world, and his recovery skills much improved. Finally, his 19th European Tour win and the 30th of his career arrived at the Portugal Masters at the Oceanico Victoria course at Vilamoura. Westwood came from three behind Retief Goosen to win by two over Francesco Molinari after a bogey-free final round of 66. A consistent week saw Westwood post three scores of 66 and a 67 for a 23-under-par 265 total.

"Winning is a habit, but I got out of that habit," Westwood said. "I have been very consistent and been getting into contention, but it is nice to finish it off. You never know when the next win will come and you start to question yourself."

Westwood went to the top of the Order of Merit and fifth on the World Ranking. He birdied the first four holes as Goosen, who had a 62 in the third round, fell away with a 75, and although Harrington had his own 62 on Friday, a final round of 67 was only good enough for third place. Molinari was the leader after the first two rounds, with an opening 63, and kept up the pressure despite a double bogey at the seventh. The Italian drew even at the 11th and both he and Westwood birdied the 12th.

But as Westwood escaped brilliantly for a birdie at the par-five 17th, Molinari missed a three-foot par putt at the short 16th to fall two behind. Westwood went over the green at the 17th but got a free drop from a cart path. He still faced a delicate shot with large bushes immediately in front of him and the lake the other side of the green. "All I could see were trees and water, and I had a tight lie," Westwood said. Yet he almost holed his third shot and tapped in for the four. Moments later Molinari missed from five feet for his four, lipping out for the second hole running.

Castello Masters Costa Azahar
Castellon, Spain
Winner: Michael Jonzon

Michael Jonzon had already entered the second stage of the qualifying process, but a ninth visit to the final stage could be forgotten after the 37-year-old Swede won the Castello Masters Costa Azahar at Mediterraneo. Jonzon, whose only previous win was at the 1997 Portuguese Open, started the season's last full-field event on European soil at 158th on the money list, but a first top-10 of the year meant he not only kept his card — he needed to finish first or second — but at 65th on the Race to Dubai gave himself a chance of qualifying for the season-ending championship.

Jonzon was ranked 482nd in the world and in the final round was playing with the world No. 10, Sergio Garcia, also the tournament host, and the world No. 12, Martin Kaymer. The pair had scored 63s in the first round to take the lead, but Jonzon, with rounds of 64, 68 and 65 took the lead with a round to play. Although Garcia started fast, the local hero soon faded, and Jonzon was out in 31 with three birdies and an eagle to take a comfortable lead.

His nearest challenger became fellow Swede Christian Nilsson, the bearded wonder who rolled in six birdies in a row around the turn. Nilsson closed with 65 to set the target at 19 under, and Jonzon slipped back to that mark with a double bogey at the 15th, when his drive finished next to the root of a tree and his second ended deeper in the trees, and a bogey at the 17th.

Kaymer, who was playing for the first time, but still limping, nine weeks after breaking toes in his left foot in a go-karting accident, took a double-bogey seven at the 13th to be six back with five to play, but three birdies in the next four holes brought him level with Jonzon and Nilsson. The German put his approach at the 18th to just under 10 feet, but Jonzon, who was 18 feet away, holed first and then Kaymer missed for the tie.

"It's been desperate for me and I am kind of speechless at the moment," Jonzon said. "I'm just so thrilled to have a playing status for next year and I'm so proud of myself the way I handled these days. I'm on the moon."

Barclays Singapore Open
Singapore
Winner: Ian Poulter

See Asia/Japan Tours chapter.

Volvo World Match Play
Casares, Spain
Winner: Ross Fisher

Ross Fisher's victory at the Volvo World Match Play , after beating Anthony Kim 4 and 3 in the final, kept alive Wentworth's association with the tournament that was played at the famous Surrey venue in England for 44 years. After a year's hiatus, and under new sponsors who lost the Volvo Masters under the Race to Dubai restructuring of the European Tour, the event moved to a new Spanish venue at Finca Cortesin. But Fisher, 28, was able to take the trophy back to Wentworth, where he learned the game on a scholarship scheme and remains the club's touring professional.

Fisher used to watch the event and even helped out on the driving range, so it was a special victory, the biggest of his three wins on tour and his first since the European Open in 2008. After near misses at the U.S. Open and the Open Championship, where he endured an eight while leading in the final round, Fisher became a father for the first time, but now rejoined the winner's circle. Having reached the semi-finals at the Accenture Match Play in February, Fisher survived 126 holes here on a physically demanding course, where the hills meant players were often worn out from green to tee and even tee to fairway.

Fisher also became the first player to win the title despite losing a match under the event's new round-robin format with the 16 players in four groups. Fisher beat Camilo Villegas, lost to Lee Westwood, but then beat Jeev Milkha Singh to top his group, although only thanks to Westwood, who had earlier lost by six holes to Singh, claiming a half with Villegas.

In the group stage, matches continued to the 18th with "hole difference" proving decisive. Kim, having beaten Retief Goosen and Paul Casey, was losing to Scott Strange and at four down with one to play was heading out of the event. But his five wood to five feet at the par-five 18th meant he lost by only three holes and allowed him to advance at the expense of Strange.

In the semi-finals, over 36 holes, Kim beat Robert Allenby, who had suggested the young American had been out drinking ahead of their contest in the singles of the Presidents Cup. The rematch was a cool affair with the American winning again. Fisher beat Masters champion Angel Cabrera at the 39th hole, with the 18th being played three extra times. Cabrera also suffered at the hole in the consolation final, when Allenby won the 18th to force extra holes and then eagled it to win at the 19th. With a hole-in-one at the 230-yard sixth hole, with a five wood, Allenby was 10 under for the 19 holes.

In the 36-hole final, Fisher won the first and never trailed. He was one up at lunch and eagled the short par-four fourth to go two up. A birdie at the next extended the lead, and although Kim got one hole back at the sixth, his three-putts at the next two let Fisher off the hook.

"I'm absolutely ecstatic," Fisher said. "It's been a long, grueling week, but obviously very worthwhile. This course was very physically demanding and I don't think I am the fittest of blokes out here. I know I need to work a lot more in the gym, but the only thing that's been missing this year was a win. I think this format suits me. I'm quite an aggressive player and sometimes it's caught me out in the past, but the best player in the world is an aggressive player and he hasn't done too badly. That's where I draw inspiration from — try to be aggressive, but smart as well."

JBWere Masters
Melbourne, Australia
Winner: Tiger Woods

See Australasian Tour chapter.

UBS Hong Kong Open
Fanling, Hong Kong
Winner: Gregory Bourdy

See Asia/Japan Tours chapter.

Dubai World Championship
Dubai, United Arab Emirates
Winner: Lee Westwood

With the most scintillating performance at the brand new Greg Norman-designed Earth Course at Jumeirah Estates, Lee Westwood provided the perfect finish to the inaugural Race to Dubai by winning the new season-ending Dubai World Championship and the new-style Order of Merit title. Westwood started the week behind Rory McIlroy, who had regained the top position the previous week in Hong Kong. But even though the 20-year-old finished in third place here, McIlroy was no match for his more experienced opponent who took the victory by six strokes over Ross McGowan.

It was Westwood's 20th win on the European Tour and the second time he had claimed the Order of Merit. The first was in 2000, after which his lengthy winning streak promptly ended. He fell from fourth in the world to outside the top 250. Here he completed the long climb back up to fourth in the world again. But here was no disputing he was the best in Europe with rounds of 66, 69, 66 and 64, the lowest score of the week and hence a course record. He made only two bogeys all week and none in the last 46 holes. On Sunday he hit every fairway and every green in regulation.

McIlroy, aiming to be the youngest winner of the Order of Merit since the 19-year-old Seve Ballesteros in 1976, was uncomfortable playing with Westwood on the first day but clung on with a 68. He then added two rounds of 69, but on Saturday he bogeyed the last three holes. Trying to recovery those shots on Sunday he parred the first eight holes and by then Westwood was out of sight. McIlroy bravely battled on to close with a 67 but finished eight behind. Westwood, in Sunday red as in Portugal the previous month, birdied five of the first seven holes to be out in 31, and although McGowan briefly got within four shots with five birdies in a row on the back nine, Westwood calmly kept on producing superb shots one after the other. His only problem on this day was raising the huge new Race to Dubai trophy above his head, a struggle even for someone now as fit and strong as Westwood.

"It's hard to imagine playing better," Westwood said. "I think that's about as good as I've ever played under this pressure, and not just today but all week and especially 66-64 over the weekend. It's definitely the biggest moment of my golfing life to date. I knew that before I set out and it gives me a lot of confidence that I was able to hold myself together. Winning the Order of Merit in 2000 meant a lot, but to fall into obscurity a bit and then to get back into the top 10 in the world and now to crown it all by winning this means ever more."

Challenge Tour

Edoardo Molinari took immediate advantage of winning the Challenge Tour for 2009 by taking up an invitation to play in the Dunlop Phoenix tournament in Japan and winning that too. There Molinari won in a play-off over Robert Karlsson, the former European No. 1 whose season was blighted by an eye injury, and earned the biggest prize of his career to date, a huge $444,000 first-place check. That dwarfed the €242,980 that the Italian earned in topping the Challenge Tour Rankings, but it was such a dominant performance that, even allowing for inflation, it was thought likely that his record tally might last for some years to come.

Molinari finished over €100,000 clear at the top of the money list after winning three times and claiming 12 top-10 finishes. While younger brother Francesco was also enjoying a career-best season on the European Tour and jumping into the world's top 50, Edoardo, at 28 two years the elder, started the season at 653rd in the world and after winning in Japan was at 63rd.

Twice the Italian Foursomes champion with his brother, Edoardo won the Italian Amateur in 2001 and the U.S. Amateur in 2005. He turned professional a year later and won twice on the Challenge Tour in 2007, but his 2008 season on the European Tour ended with him losing his card. Molinari made up for it with a fine string of results on the junior circuit in 2009, winning the Kazakhstan Open and twice on home soil at the Piemonte Open and the Italian Federation Cup. He had already sealed top spot on the Rankings by the time of the Apulia San Domenico Grand Final, where he was seventh.

"I made a lot of technical changes over the winter, because last year when I was playing well on the European Tour, I could compete. But if I wasn't playing well, I was struggling to make the cut. This season I've shown I can still compete even when I'm not playing my best. My goal at the start of the season was to finish in the top 10 in the Rankings, but I've had to keep setting new goals all the time.

"So now I feel much more ready to compete with the guys on the main tour, including my brother. We are competitive, as all brothers naturally are. But we're also very happy when the other brother plays well. In the main we have a very good relationship, because we were very close when we were young and growing up together. Because I was older I was probably hitting the ball a bit farther and playing a bit better, so he was always trying to catch me up. But now it's the other way round!"

Portugal's Jose-Filipe Lima also returned to the European Tour after finishing second in the Rankings, as did Belgium's Nicolas Colsaerts, who won his card as an 18-year-old at the 2000 qualifying but whose form and enthusiasm for the game had waned so much over the years that he started the 2009 without official status on either the European or Challenge Tours. Colsaerts won the SK Challenge and the Dutch Futures event to finish third on the Rankings, while Rhys Davies, of Wales, and England's Robert

Coles also won twice each to be fourth and 10th respectively. Scotland's Peter Whiteford was fifth after winning the Grand Final in a playoff over Australia's Andrew Tampion, who had the consolation of jumping from 39th to 15th on the Rankings and earning his card.

The others to claim their cards were: Andrew Butterfield, Gary Boyd, Richard McEvoy, former Ryder Cup player Peter Baker, Chris Gane, John Parry and James Morrison, all of England; France's Julien Quesne, former British Amateur champion Julien Guerrier and Francois Calmels; Spain's Carlos Rodiles; Andrew McArthur, of Scotland, and Wales' Sion Bebb.

9. Asia/Japan Tours

It seemed turmoil was the theme of golf in 2009, and Asia was hardly exempt. Enter the OneAsia Tour.

The OneAsia Tour was formed by the China Golf Association, the Korea Professional Golf Tour, the Korea Golf Association and the PGA Tour of Australia. The Japan Tour had been part of the group, but withdrew, citing reservations.

OneAsia not only formed as a competitor of the Asian Tour but took three of its five inaugural tournaments from the Asian schedule, the other two coming from the Australian PGA. This, of course, drew an exchange of sharp words from the two camps.

Australian Scott Strange became the first OneAsia champion, winning the Volvo China Open, and he dedicated it to his late sister. "If my sister was here now, I'm sure she would be proud of me," he said. South Korea's Bae Sang-moon ignored his mother's advice, and the move won him the Kolon-Hana Bank Korea Open. "I am pleased I laid up today," he said. And for Liang Wen-chong, winning the Midea China Classic was a matter of national pride. "I see it as a win for Chinese professionals," he said.

It wasn't true turmoil on the Japan Tour, merely the game marching on.

A clear-cut changing of the guard occurred on the Japan Tour in 2009 as Ryo Ishikawa, golf's brightest new young star, dominated the headlines and led the money list. Beyond that, the 18-year-old's most serious challenger for that title was another newcomer, Yuta Ikeda, just 23 and playing his first full season on the circuit.

Meanwhile, Shingo Katayama and Toru Taniguchi, the No. 1 champions six of the previous seven seasons, managed just one 2009 victory between them, Taniguchi's in the ANA Open in September. Katayama was shut out for the first time since 1997, but still finished fourth on the money list.

Ishikawa, who has attracted international attention since he won a Japan Tour event when he was a 15-year-old schoolboy, shattered a record as youngest money leader that stood since 1973 when Masashi "Jumbo" Ozaki, then 26, finished No. 1. On the other hand, Ikeda's emergence came out of the blue. He had only one top-10 showing in his debut 10 events in 2008. Ikeda was one of just five first-time winners in 2009, not counting Italian Edoardo Molinari, the victor in the Dunlop Phoenix, who was the only non-Japanese winner of the season.

Edoardo and brother Francesco made history on the Asian Tour when they won the World Cup. It was the first time that Italy won the cup, and the first time that a team of brothers won.

The Asian Tour had 27 events worth a total of $37 million, and some things remained steady. Like Thailand veteran Thongchai Jaidee, who won twice in 10 starts, taking the Enjoy Jakarta Indonesian Open and the Ballantine's Championship for a tour record 12 victories. He also topped the Order of Merit for a record third time with $779,580, and played all over the world.

"It's never easy playing against the best in the world," Thongchai said, "but I've shown that it's possible, and this is good for golf in Asia."

Among the memorable moments:

Thailand's Chapchai Nirat set the world record, winning the SAIL Open at 32 under par. Said Chapchai: "My goal was to win the title. I was not thinking of the world record."

Could there be a rising young star on the Asian Tour horizon? Thailand's Chinnarat Phadungsil, 20, came from behind and won the inaugural Queen's Cup by three shots. It was the third win of his young career. Said Chinnarat: "I can't believe that I won three times before my 21st birthday." He wasn't alone.

Some first-time winners grabbed the spotlight, none more so than South Africa's James Kamte, who scored a trio of firsts — first start, first win, and in the Asian Tour's first tournament of 2009, the Asian Tour International. "I've always wanted this to happen," Kamte said.

India's Gaganjeet Bhullar, 21, echoed Kamte's sentiments when he got his first win in the Indonesia President Invitational. "I've been waiting for this for the past two years," Bhullar said.

Australia's Darren Beck got his first win in the Brunei Open the hard way. He trailed by six entering the final round, shot 65, and thought "there'll be no way I could put myself in a playoff." But he did, and beat Bhullar and Boonchu Ruangkit for his first victory.

Not only did a personable Indian get his first win, he also won Name of the Year — Chinnaswamy Muniyappa. Just call me "C," he said. Trying to keep his tour card, he surprised himself by winning the Hero Honda Indian Open. "I don't know what I will do with the prize money," he said. "Maybe rent a house."

And then there was the remarkable Danny Lee, 18, New Zealand amateur and the 2008 U.S. Amateur champion. He won the Johnnie Walker Classic and noted, "This is a pro event, and all I wanted to do was make the cut..."

No one was happier with the final money standings than Malaysia's Shaaban Hussin. Said Hussin, on learning that he'd kept that precious final spot on the tour's top 65 exempt list despite missing the cut in the season-ending King's Cup: "Oh, my gosh — I want to cry."

Asian Tour

The Royal Trophy
Bangkok, Thailand
Winner: Asia

After taking a commanding five-point lead through the first two days, Asia entered the singles needing only two points against Europe for their first Royal Trophy after two losses, and to the delight of the home crowd at Bangkok's Amata Spring County Club, Thailand's Prayad Marksaeng did his share. Prayad guaranteed a tie with his 5-and-4 victory over Spain's Pablo Larrazabal, and then Japan's Toru Taniguchi clinched the 10-6 victory with his relentless 7-and-6 crushing of Sweden's Niclas Fasth.

Prayad fed off a big boost at the first hole, when he scrambled to a half, holing a 20-footer after Larrazabal hit it close. "I tried to maintain my composure throughout the day," Prayad said, "and I outlasted him to get the win." Taniguchi got the winning point with a 15-foot birdie putt at the 12th, giving Asian captain Naomichi "Joe" Ozaki his revenge over Jose Maria Olazabal and the Europeans. "When I was here in 2007, I was very nervous as a captain and I didn't know what to do," Ozaki said. "I think all my team members felt what I was thinking and they realized how I wanted them to play. This win means a lot to me." And for a reward, his players tossed him into the lake near the ninth green. Asia won the foursomes, 3-1, and the fourballs, 3½-½, then lost the singles, 3½-4½, but won the match.

Olazabal congratulated the Asian team, then turned his thoughts to tournament founder Seve Ballesteros, who was home recovering from brain cancer surgery. "I might not be the captain next year," Olazabal said, "and I can assure you he is going to be tougher than I was!"

Asian Tour International
Bangkok, Thailand
Winner: James Kamte

Some dreams come true faster than others. For South Africa's James Kamte, it couldn't have been any faster. The scenario couldn't have been more perfect. It was the Asian Tour's season opening Asian Tour International, and Kamte was a tour rookie, making his debut. And he charged down the final stretch to win it.

"I've always wanted this to happen, and hopefully this is not going to be my last one," said Kamte, who finished fourth in the tour's qualifying tournament. "I knew I was hitting the ball really well the whole week and I just needed to make the putts." And that Kamte did through scores of 71-63-68-66, a 16-under 268 total at Bangkok's par-71 Suwan Golf and Country Club. He won by two over Japan's Tetsuji Hiratsuka.

Kamte trailed by eight strokes in the first round, by three through the second round and by two going into the final round. He opened the last round with birdies on his first two holes, then lost the lead when he bogeyed the fifth, letting Australia's Unho Park slip ahead. Then he raced out of the turn with a most un-rookie-like burst under the pressure, birdieing the 11th, 13th and 16th holes.

Hiratsuka, who led Park by one through the third round, gave Kamte the help he needed with his erratic play. He bogeyed the first two holes, then the 14th, and three birdies coming home only got him back to even par. Thailand veteran Prom Meesawat made a strong move with birdies on the first three holes, but cooled soon enough and tied for third.

The big jump of the day came from China's Wu Ashun. With a nine-birdie 63 he zoomed from a tie for 30th to a tie for seventh.

Maybank Malaysian Open
Kuala Lumpur, Malaysia
Winner: Anthony Kang

The cliché about the dream coming true was real for Anthony Kang. "I actually dreamt last night that I won the tournament," said Kang, after taking the Maybank Malaysian Open, co-sanctioned by the Asian and European Tours. But then Kang added, "I have those sort of dreams quite often," so maybe it wasn't quite the exercise in precognition it seemed.

That being the case, this was only the third time in his career and the first time since 2001 that his dream paid off. This one came on a rally in the final round and a clutch birdie on the final hole that delivered a one-stroke decision over a host of pursuers. It also came in a surprise finish. Kang was nowhere in the race for most of the tournament.

South Korean teenager Noh Seung-yul opened with a sizzling 62, 10 under at the Saujana Golf and Country Club at Kuala Lumpur. Then Danny Chia, trying to become the first native son to win the tournament, took the halfway lead with 65. Australia's Adam Blyth then led the third round after 66. This is when Kang entered the race, shooting 64.

Kang started the final round two shots off the lead, and long birdie putts at Nos. 6 and 8 had him out in 33 and one ahead at the turn with seven players in hot pursuit. A watery bogey at the 15th left him needing a birdie at the par-five 18th to win. He reached the green in two and two-putted from 45 feet to wrap up a card of 74-66-64-67 for a 17-under 271 total and a one-stroke win.

"It feels great to have beaten a strong field here," Kang said. "To finally win this event, I'm speechless."

Johnnie Walker Classic
Perth, Australia
Winner: Danny Lee

See Australasian Tour chapter.

Enjoy Jakarta Indonesia Open
Bali, Indonesia
Winner: Thongchai Jaidee

Thai standout Thongchai Jaidee discovered that Bali, famed resort island, was indeed a touch of paradise — but not for the usual reasons. Thongchai took command in the third round, faltered a bit late in the fourth, then came through in the clutch to take the co-sanctioned Enjoy Jakarta Indonesia Open, thereby taking a record 11th Asian Tour victory and his first European Tour title in four years.

"It's my first time in Bali, and I've been enjoying myself," Thongchai said, and then added, if redundantly, "I'm very happy to win here."

Thongchai took the lead in the third round, posting six birdies and a bogey for a five-under-par 67 at the New Kuta Golf Resort course. "My irons were good and consistent, except for one hole," Thongchai said. He was one up on Sweden's Alexander Noren as the earlier leaders faded. The Philippines' Angelo Que took a huge four-stroke lead over six others in the first round with 64 in which he needed just 20 putts. He might have done that before, "...in a computer game," Que conceded. Thongchai, at No. 88 the highest ranked player in the field, was well back in the crowd at one-under 71.

Thongchai, who led by one stroke heading into the final round, was threatening to run away with the tournament in the final round. He notched three straight birdies from No. 3 and led by four. But his grip started to weaken. Bogeys at the eighth and 14th cut his edge to one over England's Steve Webster. A birdie at the 16th padded his edge and he went on to close with 69 and a 12-under 276 total and a two-stroke win over Webster (68), Noren (70) and Simon Dyson (69).

Singha Thailand Open
Phuket, Thailand
Winner: Jyoti Randhawa

Just when the world figured the path to success came with bleeding hands on the practice tee, along came Jyoti Randhawa in the Singha Thailand Open at the Laguna Phuket resort.

"I swam, I went scuba diving, and I enjoyed myself," said Randhawa, "and here I am — I won a golf tournament." It was his eighth Asian Tour win, a two-shot decision over Welshman Rhys Davies.

"I need to do this more often," Randhawa said. So much for hitting balls until your hands bleed.

It didn't look that simple at first. Randhawa opened with a two-under-par 68, five behind fellow Indian Digvijay Singh and Australian Mitchell Brown, and three behind Thailand's Boonchu Ruangkit, who at age 52 stole the show with 65. "The Thailand Open means a lot to me," Boonchu said. "It is in my heart."

Another 68 in the second round dropped Randhawa to eight shots behind India's S.S.P. Chowrasia, who blasted the resort course with a score of 62 that included only 25 putts. Then the good times paid off for Randhawa. With 14 one-putt greens, he shot 62 to tie Chowrasia (70) and Davies (69) at 192.

Randhawa then got some help in the final round. Chowrasia eagled the first hole, then faded. Davies bogeyed the par-five 17th, shot 67 and finished two behind. Taiwan's Lu Wei-chih was closing in, but also bogeyed the 17th. "I tensed up with the tee shot," he said, and he finished third.

So Randhawa wrapped it up. He birdied Nos. 1, 4 and 5, then Nos. 12 and 15 for a flawless 65 and a 17-under 263 total. And then he revealed the rest of his secret. "You don't practice and work hard during the tournament," Randhawa said. "You do it before."

SAIL Open
New Delhi, India
Winner: Chapchai Nirat

The trivia question from the 2009 SAIL Open will be — who finished second? The answer is Australia's Richard Moir and India's Gaganjit Bhullar, tied for second at 267, a whopping 21 under par. They were trivia status because they were second by an equally whopping 11 strokes after Thailand's Chapchai Nirat destroyed the record book in a stunning 32-under 256 at the Classic Golf Resort outside New Delhi, India. Chapchai led all the way, shooting 62-62-65-67 and smashing records along the way.

"My goal was to win the title," Chapchai said. "I was not thinking of the world record." But records are what he got.

First Round: Chapchai shot a course-record 62, making five birdies on each side, among them a chip-in at the 17th and a tap-in at the par-three 11th. He needed just 26 putts overall.

Second Round: He made 11 birdies and one bogey for another 62, setting the Asian Tour halfway-point record at 20-under 124. He led by four over tour rookie Mark Purser (63) of New Zealand. "The course is very suitable to my game," said Chapchai. "I can reach all the par-fives in two strokes. The par-four holes present birdie opportunities because they are pretty open, and my putting has been fantastic."

Third Round: Chapchai birdied the last five holes for 65–189, moving to 27 under par, the Asian Tour record, for an eight-stroke lead over Bhullar. Said Chapchai: "I'm a little disappointed that I couldn't shoot another 62."

Fourth Round: Chapchai finished like a champion, making birdie on the final hole for 67 to set the Asian Tour record of 32-under-par 256. It broke Ernie Els's Asian Tour record of 29 under in the 2003 Johnnie Walker Classic, and also his U.S. PGA Tour record of 31 under at the 2003 Mercedes-Benz Championship. Not bad for a warm-up. Said Chapchai: "I entered this tournament to get some good practice for the European Tour, where I'm going to play for the next few months."

Black Mountain Masters
Hua Hin, Thailand
Winner: Johan Edfors

It went into the book as a wire-to-wire win for Sweden's John Edfors in the inaugural Black Mountain Masters, but that neat little entry doesn't show the bumps, bruises and scary close calls. There was, for example, that near killer at the 16th hole in the final round, when he drove next to a tree and double-bogeyed, thus blowing a two-stroke lead.

"I guess I made it too exciting," said Edfors, grinning with relief. "I made a couple of poor shots and bad decisions, and then had to really fight for it at the end."

Edfors's fight at the end consisted of brilliant clutch birdies on the last two holes. He dropped a 10-foot putt at the 17th to retake the lead and then a 15-footer at the 18th for a card of 64-68-71-68–271, 17 under par at Thailand's Black Mountain Golf Club, and a two-stroke win over Thailand's hard-charging Prayad Marksaeng (64) and England's Chris Rodgers (68).

Prayad, the huge home crowd favorite, credited his putting for rocketing him from six off Edfors's lead in the final round. And then came the anxiety. "Now I'll have to wait to know if I will qualify for the Masters through the World Ranking," he said. (The answer was yes.) A putting glitch cost Rodgers his big chance. "The killer for me was not making birdie on 16 when Johan made double," said Rodgers, who three-putted the hole. "That was the moment for me to seize, but I didn't."

Edfors could chart his success across Black Mountain's par-fives, especially the 18th, which he played in four under — eagle-bogey-birdie-birdie.

Ballentine's Championship
Jeju Island, South Korea
Winner: Thongchai Jaidee

Thongchai Jaidee's timing was perfect. "When we got to the playoff, I knew that I would stand a good chance as I had just finished playing that hole about 15 minutes ago." The hole was the 18th at Pinx Golf Club on South Korea's Jeju Island, and Thongchai, the veteran Thai star, had just finished with a two-under-par 70 to tie Spain's Gonzalo Fernandez-Castano and South Korea's Kang Wook-soon at four-under 284 in the Asian-European Tour co-sponsored event.

In the playoff, Fernandez-Castano, who finished with 69, missed his birdie chip from the back of the green. Kang, who had three-putted the 18th for a bogey and 68, missed an eight-footer for birdie in the playoff. Thongchai then holed a five-footer for a birdie and the win.

The late-April tournament found golfers in knitted caps and long-sleeved garb in weather so chilly and windy in the middle rounds that the Netherlands' Robert-Jan Derksen, who took the lead in the second round, held on to it in the third with 75. "I think it was unfair and unplayable," Derksen said. Thongchai himself was a casualty in the second round, when the strong wind moved his ball on the green and cost him a penalty stroke.

Only an awkward twist sent the tournament into a playoff. Kang had taken the lead with a hole-out eagle at the 16th, but then muffed the outright victory when he three-putted the 18th for a bogey.

And Fernando-Castano's third time in a playoff wasn't so charming. "This is my third playoff in the last three weeks, and it really hurts," he said. He was now 0-for-3 in playoffs.

GS Caltex Maekyung Open
Seoul, South Korea
Winner: Bae Sang-moon

It was more good news for South Korea's Bae Sang-moon, but more bad news for Ted Oh in the GS Caltex Maekyung Open at Seoul's Nam Seoul Country Club.

For the frustrated Oh, failure came down to a shaky third round and then a missed short putt at the 18th in the final round, and there went that first Asian Tour victory for the California-based Korean. Together, these opened the door to Bae. Not one to turn down an opportunity, Bae stepped through and took his third Asian Tour victory on the second hole of a playoff.

"It's unbelievable," said Bae. "I've never played in a playoff before, and to win this way is always something special."

Oh had good reason to be disappointed. With his opening 68, he was just one stroke off the lead shared by Kim Jong-duk and S.K. Ho. Another 68 got him a one-stroke lead at the halfway point, with Bae (71-70) back in the pack, five behind. But the May rains in the third round were Oh's downfall. He lurched to five bogeys and got only one birdie on the first nine, but he rallied for birdies at the 11th, 14th and 15th to get home with 75 and a tie for a one-stroke lead with Bae (70) and Kim Dae-hyun (69) going into the final round, with six others within two strokes.

Victory continued to dangle just out of Oh's reach. He came to the 18th needing a five-foot birdie putt for that elusive first win. But he missed, shot 70, and tied with Bae (70) at seven-under-par 281. Oh then three-putted the second playoff hole for a bogey, and Bae won with a par.

"It's disappointing, but I guess that's golf," said Oh. "I hope it'll be my week to win next time."

Indonesia President Invitational
Jakarta, Indonesia
Winner: Gaganjeet Bhullar

For Gaganjeet Bhullar, 21, a rising Indian hopeful, this was worth the wait — not just for the anxious closing moments in the clubhouse, but from two years earlier. The prize was nothing less than his first victory on the Asian Tour, and it came in the Indonesia President Invitational.

Bhullar had finished the weather-interrupted third round in the morning, took a one-stroke lead into the fourth round — when it finally got under way — and finished with a bogey-free 67 and the clubhouse lead. Then came the wait to see what would happen on the Bumi Serpong Damai course at Jakarta. When the challengers fell short, Bhullar had his first win by two strokes, and a sigh of relief to go with it.

"I've been waiting for this for the past two years," said Bhullar, who was stung in the 2007 tournament when the Philippines' Juvic Pagunsan finished birdie-eagle. Nobody came up with the magic this time, and Bhullar's 22-under-par, one-bogey 266 total stood up, leaving Australia's Adam Blyth (68–268) still looking for his first win. "I gave it all I could," Blyth said. "I putted well but they just weren't dropping."

The key came in the third round. Bhullar had opened with 69-68, chasing Darren Beck, Thaworn Wiratchant and other front-runners. Then he blistered Damai with a flawless 62. The last of his 10 birdies came in near darkness, thanks to storm delays. He couldn't see his tee shot or his approach, yet was on in two, 15 feet from the flag, and two-putted.

Bhullar kept rolling in the final round, birdieing four of his first six holes to go up by four. He scored his fifth and last birdie at the 13th, shot 67, then sat back for the longest wait of his career.

Brunei Open
Bandar Seri Begawa, Brunei
Winner: Darren Beck

Australia's Darren Beck had never won on the Asian Tour, and so in the Brunei Open, having finished the final round, he had pretty much convinced himself that couldn't win this time, either.

"I was sitting in the locker room and cooling off, as I thought that there'll be no way I could put myself in a playoff," he said. But he did, and he'd earned his way. He opened the final round with two birdies, and after par-ring to the turn, he birdied the 10th, 14th, 15th and 16th holes, coming home for 65. Then he scored that first victory in a three-way playoff.

Actually, Beck's situation had looked hopeless. He trailed by six going into the final round, chasing Thai veteran Boonchu Ruangkit, who led by a stroke starting the round, and India's Gaganjeet Bhullar, who was two behind him. Beck closed strong with the 65 and was in the Brunei's Empire Hotel and Country Club clubhouse at 271, 13 under par, and leading the field by one.

Bhullar, 21, who scored his first win at Jakarta the week before, needed a closing birdie to become the Asian Tour's first back-to-back winner of the season. But he missed the 18-footer and shot 69. "I clearly misread the line," he said.

Then came Boonchu, who at 53 years and 82 days would have become the tour's oldest winner. But he bogeyed the last for a 71, slipping into the tie. In the playoff, all three tied on the first hole. Boonchu departed on a bogey at the second, and then Beck won at the third, holing a 10-foot putt for a birdie.

"It was very nerve-wracking, but it's definitely great to make it to six under and to win in the playoff," said Beck.

Worldwide Holdings Selangor Masters
Kuala Lumpur, Malaysia
Winner: Rich Kulacz

Golf-wise, Australian Rick Kulacz figured to have no chance in the Worldwide Holdings Selangor Masters. Shooting 68-71-71 in the first three rounds, he trailed, respectively, by four, four, and then by six going into the final round.

"To get a win from out of nowhere is really enjoyable," said Kulacz, who had won once before, "because the year has been pretty average." He had missed eight cuts in the first half. But there was nothing average about his final round — an eight-under-par 63, tying the course record at Seri Selangor, in Malaysia, and lifting him to a one-stroke victory over rookie Kiradech Aphibarnrat, seeking his first Asian Tour win. He led through the middle rounds and by two going into the final round, but stalled out on 17 pars and a birdie for a 70, and finished second by a stroke. "This is my first time leading on the Asian Tour," he said, "and I felt a bit of pressure."

Kiradech trailed by one in the first round, behind Danny Chia (64), and led through the middle rounds, and by two going into the fourth. But then the pressure set it, and Kulacz came rushing on.

Kulacz notched six birdies for a front-nine 30 to tie Kiradech. Two more birdies after the turn put him two up going to the 18th. His six-foot birdie putt lipped out, leaving him with the 63 and the chancy clubhouse lead by two. Kiradech cut the lead to one with a birdie at the 17th. But at the 18th, his nine-iron approach was 30 feet short of the cup, and he missed the birdie try. Kulacz had his second win.

"I'll probably enjoy this one a little bit more than the last," Kulacz said.

Queen's Cup
Koh Samui, Thailand
Winner: Chinnarat Phadungsil

One win by a teenager might have been lucky, a second a fluke. But a third win, now at age 20, means Asian golf might have found itself a rising star in the person of Thailand's Chinnarat Phadungsil.

"I can't believe that I won three times before my 21st birthday," said Chinnarat, after taking the inaugural Queen's Cup at Santiburi Samui Country Club in Thailand. Nobody's saying he's the next Tiger Woods, but his accomplishments have been remarkable in their own right.

Chinnarat was in the thick of the Queen's Cup from the start. Shooting 66-65-70-67, he had to come from behind as well as hold a lead, and he won by three with a 16-under-par 268 total.

Along the way, he raced by another rising talent, fellow Thai Kiradech Aphibarnrat, 20, who fell just short of winning the Selangor Masters the week before. Kiradech opened the Queen's Cup with a six-under 65, with a maturing, reined-in game. "If you miss your driver here, you can shoot a five, six or seven," he said. He would finish five behind Chinnarat.

Chinnarat took a three-stroke lead in the second round with 65 that included seven birdies from inside eight feet. And he missed two chances from three feet. "It's okay," he said. "I feel confident of winning this tournament."

His confidence proved to be well-founded. After trailing Japan's Yoshinobu Tsukada by a stroke in the third round, and after a bogey at No. 3 in the fourth, he was off and running. He birdied three straight from the fifth, bogeyed the 12th, then birdied the 14th, 16th and 18th.

"At the turn, I knew I could win," Chinnarat said. "I aimed for pars and then went for birdies over the closing few holes."

Macau Open
Macau
Winner: Thaworn Wiratchant

Thailand's Thaworn Wiratchant, a solid veteran of 42, left a lot of frustrated young pursuit in his wake at the Macau Open. Chief among them would be India's Gaganjeet Bhullar, who had to be wondering what one had to do to beat him. Bhullar started the final round birdie-eagle-birdie, shot 66, and all it got him was the runner-up spot by six strokes.

The story was in the card. Thaworn, just back from a tie for 11th in the Omega European Masters, played the par-71 Macau Golf and Country Club in 67-68-66-68–269, 15 under par, for the easy six-stroke win. He took control with the third-round 66, which he completed on the morning of the final round of the stormy tournament.

"I didn't take my lead for granted, because, on this course, anything can happen," said Thaworn, who had five birdies and two bogeys in his closing 68. "The other players were also very close and I was playing it safe until the back nine, where I was more confident of winning."

Said Bhullar: "I was having a look at Thaworn's score, but I didn't think I could catch him." Bhullar rode that hot start to a 275 total, three better than South Africa's Keith Horne, who fought a balky putter for 70, and Australia's Matthew Griffin, who sparked his 66 at the second hole with a three wood from 250 yards to 10 feet.

Thaworn's victory was his 11th, one behind the Asian Tour record of fellow Thai Thongchai Jaidee. Was there a race here?

"I try to win every tournament," said Thaworn, "but the thought of overcoming Thongchai's victories on the Asian Tour is not my main objective, as I only strive to do my best. But if I am fit enough, I think breaking his record would not be a problem."

Asia-Pacific Panasonic Open
Kyoto, Japan
Winner: Daisuke Maruyama

See Japan Tour section.

Mercuries Taiwan Masters
Taipei, Taiwan
Winner: Lin Wen-tang

It definitely was an ill wind that blew no good for Thailand's Udorn Duangdecha, but it was just what the doctor ordered for Taiwan's Lin Wen-tang. Typhoon Parma was just about to crash the party, hurling strong winds and rain at the Mercuries Taiwan Masters. The unfortunate Udorn, 38, seeking his first Asian Tour win, led for the first three rounds, then stumbled through the storm to a closing 77. Lin, who advanced steadily up the leaderboard, solved the turbulence and delighted the home crowds by taking his fifth Asian title. After climbing on rounds of 71-66-71 at the Taiwan Golf and Country Club, Lin battled the weather on even terms for a closing par 72, an eight-under-par 280 total and a three-stroke win over countryman Lu Wen-teh (73), the defending champion.

"It was tough," Lin said. "I kept believing in myself in these wet and windy conditions."

Benign conditions greeted the first round, and Udorn leaped at his chance, logging five birdies and an eagle for a 65 and a two-stroke lead. Lin was six behind. "I'm very lucky that the good weather played a part in my solid play," Udorn said, "and I hope this can stay with me throughout the week." It would, but only for two more rounds. Then the front edges of the typhoon arrived, making club selection and accuracy more difficult and lifting scores.

Udorn was about to add to his lead in the third round when gusty winds cost him a triple bogey at the 18th. Lin then mastered the powerful winds in the final round. After two early bogeys, he birdied three straight from the sixth. Then he passed Udorn with birdies at the 14th and 15th. A bogey at the 17th merely cut his winning margin to three.

Hero Honda Indian Open
New Delhi, India
Winner: C. Muniyappa

He goes by C. Muniyappa, and the revelation of his first name shows why he prefers just the initial. It's Chinnaswamy. The question of his name came up when this 32-year-old Asian Tour rookie, who taught himself the game with two clubs, put on a remarkable performance in the Hero Honda Indian Open, holding tight through four rounds then beating South Korean veteran Lee Sung in a playoff.

"I only came here to try and keep my Asian Tour card," said Muniyappa, who was as surprised as anyone by his success. Reality dawned slowly. "It was only when I got to the playoff," he admitted, "that I thought, let's go for the win."

It took one extra hole. Muniyappa holed a 10-foot birdie putt after Lee missed from 12 feet. They had tied at 12-under-par 276 at New Delhi's DLF Golf and Country Club. They had battled it out from the start. Lee shot 65 in the first round, Muniyappa 66, behind leader Adam Blyth (64).

From there, Muniyappa shot 69-71-70, Lee 70-72-69, either holding or sharing the lead all the way.

It was touch-and-go in the final round. Muniyappa birdied the seventh and ninth going out, then had two birdies and two bogeys coming home for his 70. Lee had got to three under on the front, but bogeyed the 12th and 16th, then birdied the par-five 18th to tie, setting up the final drama for Muniyappa, who once caddied as a seven-year-old.

"I learned the game watching members at the club," said Muniyappa, who turned pro in 1996. "My first clubs were a seven iron and a two iron."

Now victory presented him with a new problem. "I don't know what I will do with the prize money," said Muniyappa, who won nearly US$200,000. "Maybe rent a house."

Iskandar Johor Open
Johor, Malaysia
Winner: K.J. Choi

South Korea's K.J. Choi, who had fallen on relatively lean times on the PGA Tour, returned to his golfing roots and enjoyed some home cooking. And "enjoyed" would be the correct word for going 20 under par for three rounds and winning the rain-shortened Iskandar Johor Open in Malaysia.

Choi, who learned his golf on the Asian Tour before heading for the United States, sat just off the lead in the first two rounds with his 68-64 at the par-72 Royal Johor. In the third round, Choi was off in a rush, birdieing the first three holes. On a roll, he added birdies at Nos. 6 and 7, then 11, 12 and 18 coming in. He had only one brush with trouble. At the 15th, he watered his tee shot, then saved par by chipping in from 30 feet, keeping his card bogey-free.

"I was not really concerned about my shot at the 15th," Choi said. "Even if I had made bogey, I knew that the next few holes were difficult holes and I had some space between Himmat and me, so I kept myself calm."

But India's Himmat Kai, the second-round leader, shot 70 and slipped to joint third. Choi's nearest challenger was Thailand's Chapchai Nirat, who chipped in for birdies at three of the last four holes for a 66 to finish second, four behind Choi.

The fireworks of the day came from South Africa's Retief Goosen, who started eight shots off the lead. "As I said yesterday," Goosen said, "I had no chance of winning. I just came out to improve my position." Which he did, grandly, with a 10-under 62 to tie for third.

Barclays Singapore Open
Singapore
Winner: Ian Poulter

Free-spirited Ian Poulter began the Barclays Singapore Open by messaging his fans on Twitter and ended it by delighting them with his first victory in two years. England's Poulter, Ryder Cup standout, survived heavy rains, long delays and overlapping rounds for a wire-to-wire victory, his eighth on the European Tour. (The tournament was co-sanctioned for the first time by the European and Asian Tours.)

But Poulter had to survive a serious case of the wobbles in the final round to complete a card of 66-64-72-72 for a 10-under 284 total at the par-71 Sentosa Golf Club. It gave him a scary one-stroke victory over China's Liang Wen-chong. The big test for Poulter came in the final round Sunday, after he'd played 12 holes in the morning to complete the third round.

"Getting off to the start I did, getting out of the blocks pretty quick, surprised me a little, as I was mis-hitting some shots," he said. He had opened the fourth round with birdies at Nos. 1 and 4. Then the mis-hitting started — bogeys at Nos. 7, 9, 11 and 12. During the stretch, Poulter and Graeme McDowell traded the lead. Poulter saved himself by dropping a 30-foot putt for a birdie at the 13th to tie McDowell. Then McDowell opened the door with three straight bogeys.

Poulter parred the last five holes for the one-stroke edge that beat the waiting Liang, who could only shrug. "I tried my best, but Lady Luck was eluding me," he said.

"The birdie on 13 pumped me up," Poulter said. "I played so well in spells … and it was just so annoying to let easy holes slip."

WGC - HSBC Champions
Shanghai, China
Winner: Phil Mickelson

The drama couldn't have been higher. The World Golf Championships - HSBC Champions was in China for the first time, early in November, and Phil Mickelson was out-dueling a struggling Tiger Woods, but faltering behind a charging Ernie Els in the final round. Mickelson would beat Els by a stroke, but first, a pause for some low comedy that would warm the hearts of every weekender.

Els, with eight birdies and an eagle, was 10 under par for the day, but at the par-five 18th he dumped his five-wood second into the middle of the fronting pond and bogeyed. "I basically duffed it," said Els. He tied Sheshan International Golf Club's course record of 63 and finished at 16-under 272, then began a nervous wait.

Mickelson, tied with Els, and Woods, barely alive, both missed the green at the 16th, a driveable par-four. Mickelson was visibly shaken when his try for a flop shot slid under the ball. He just got his next on, but holed the 20-foot putt to save par. Woods then chunked his a few yards into a bunker. He also saved par, but the lost birdie finished him.

The mercurial Mickelson birdied the 17th, then barely held on at the 18th. He drove into the heavy left rough, hit rough again with his second shot, and put his third on, but about 45 feet from the pin. But he easily got down in two for his par and beat Els by a stroke, shooting Sheshan in 69-66-67-69–271, 17 under.

Woods, not a factor after the second round, started the last round with a double bogey and two bogeys, shot 72, and tied for sixth.

So Mickelson, his mind always on his cancer-stricken wife, ended an anxious 2009 season with his fourth win. "I didn't hit it great, the putts weren't falling, and yet I hung in there," he said. "It feels terrific."

UBS Hong Kong Open
Fanling, Hong Kong
Winner: Gregory Bourdy

Of all the players and fans at the UBS Hong Kong Open, there was only one who didn't know that Rory McIlroy, the young phenomenon, was on a tear. That would be France's Gregory Bourdy, who was playing the last round with tunnel vision.

"I wanted to play my game, stay focused on my game," said Bourdy, going after his third European Tour win in the European-Asian Tour co-sanctioned event. "I knew if I played minus-three or minus-four, it was okay to win this tournament." Good thinking. Bourdy, co-leader in the second round and leader in the third, put together a three-under-par 67 in the final round without knowing that McIlroy had come within a whisker of derailing him.

"I went out with the mindset that if I went lower than 65, I might have a chance," said McIlroy, 20, playoff runner-up in the 2008 Hong Kong. He almost pulled it off. He birdied twice on the front, eagled the 13th and birdied the 15th and 16th. But he missed a short putt at the 17th, and in disgust, tossed his ball into the gallery. His 64–263 left him a runner-up again, two behind Bourdy's 19-under 261.

Bourdy opened with 64-67, then broke away in the third round with a flawless 63 — four birdies on the front, three on the back. McIlroy posted a wild 65, with six birdies, an eagle, a bogey and a double bogey. He started the final round five behind Bourdy but couldn't quite close the gap.

Thai veteran Thongchai Jaidee, 40, tied for 11th in the mid-November tournament and locked up a record third Asian Tour Order of Merit title. Said Thongchai: "The competition is always getting tougher, and to win it again shows that my game is improving each year, as well."

Johnnie Walker Cambodian Open
Siem Reap, Cambodia
Winner: Marcus Both

Marcus Both entered the Johnnie Walker Cambodian Open with his eye fixed on ending a victory drought that by mid-November had stretched to six years. The problem was, as the tournament rolled on, a win drifted farther and farther into the distance, until finally it was out of sight.

Both opened with a 70, two under par at Phokeethra Country Club and three behind the leader, fellow Australian David Gleeson. Both added a 69 in the second round and was four behind Welshman Craig Smith, who shot 66 for 135 at the halfway point. Then a 73 in the third put Both fully six strokes back with eight men between him and Smith (71–206).

On to the final round. "I thought I needed to shoot six under to get close," Both said. "But I guess I'm just fortunate that everything fell my way."

Indeed. Smith blew to a 76. The other contenders melted away. And Both was already in the clubhouse with a 67 and a nine-under 279 total. Malaysia's Shaaban Hussin could still tie him with a birdie at the 18th, but he couldn't get it done, and Both had his career second victory and his first since the 2003 Sanya Open.

Both, hardly thinking about winning, started his drive with birdies at Nos. 2, 6 and 8. Then he ran off three straight birdies from the 11th. A bogey at the 14th left him with a lot to think about after he parred in for his 67 and sat down for a nervous wait. He dedicated his win to his mother for her birthday, and she had been willing to settle for less. "She told me a top-10 would be a good present," Both said. "So I guess this win is the icing on the cake."

Omega Mission Hills World Cup
Shenzhen, China
Winners: Italy (Edoardo Molinari and Francesco Molinari)

History struck twice in the Omega Mission Hills World Cup — the first victory by Italy and the first victory by brothers, namely Edoardo and Francesco Molinari. They won by a stroke over the strong Irish team, the veteran Graeme McDowell and the brilliant, young Rory McIlroy, and also the defending champions, veteran Swedes Robert Karlsson and Henrik Stenson at Mission Hills, at Shenzhen, Southern China. But for three rounds, the Italians tagged along.

First Round (Four Ball/Better Ball): Ireland finished with an eagle and four straight birdies for a 14-under-par 58 and a three-stroke lead over Argentina (Tano Goya and Rafa Echenique). The Italians were six shots off the lead at 64.

Second Round (Foursomes/Alternate Shot): Ireland doubled-bogeyed the 15th but birdied the next two for a 68–126, keeping their lead at three, this time over the Swedes (65). The Italians (66) trailed by four.

Third Round (Four Ball/Better Ball): McDowell and McIlroy shot a 64–190, but their lead shrank to one over both the Swedes (62) and the Italians (61).

The moment of truth for the Italians came at the 18th tee in the final round. They were leading by a shot, with the Irish and the Swedes pressing hard. Francesco split the fairway with his drive, but Edoardo bunkered his approach.

"When I saw the ball in the bunker, it was lying okay," Edoardo said, "and I just said, 'Francesco, just knock it on the green anywhere, and I'm going to hole the putt.'"

Francesco simplified his brother's task, blasting to three feet. Edoardo dropped the putt for a 68 and a 29-under 259 total. The World Cup was theirs by a stroke.

"I think we deserved it," said Francesco said. "We attacked from the first day."

The King's Cup
Khon Kaen, Thailand
Winner: Chan Yih-shin

Everything clicked into place just in time for Taiwan's Chan Yih-shin in The King's Cup in December, a late addition to the Asian Tour schedule to mark the birthday of the king of Thailand. After leading all the way, Chan felt his first tour victory slipping through his fingers, and so for him, a high finish would be a thing of beauty. Then fate — or something — came to his rescue just in time, and he took that first win in a three-way playoff.

"I'm feeling ecstatic," said Chan, who went through Thailand's Khon Kaen Golf Club in 64-73-67-70–274, to tie Scotland's Simon Yates and England's Nick Redfern. Chan birdied the second playoff hole for the victory.

"When I was trailing by a few shots with a few holes to play, I thought I didn't have a chance to win," Chan said, "and I just wanted to finish as high as possible."

Redfern's sizzling performance would lower any opponent's aim. Redfern racked up eight birdies and took a two-shot lead with two holes to play. Then he plugged his tee shot in a bunker at the par-three 17th. It took him two shots to escape, and he double-bogeyed, shot 66, and slipped back into a tie with Chan and Yates (68), who was doing well, considering his recent injury.

Come the playoff and all three parred the first playoff hole. At the second, Chan holed a five-footer for birdie, and Yates stepped up to a three-footer to tie him — and missed. Chan had his win.

The key to his win had come earlier, he said, after Redfern doubled the 17th. "I made a crucial birdie on 17 to draw level," Chan said. "That was an important moment."

Followed, to be sure, by another important moment on the second playoff hole that brought the 2009 season to a ringing finish.

OneAsia Tour

Volvo China Open
Beijing, China
Winner: Scott Strange

The OneAsia Tour, another step in the global developments in golf, made its debut in mid-April with the Volvo China Open, a fixture on the Asian Tour since 1995 and the first of five tournaments in 2009.

As a point of history, then, it was Australian Scott Strange who won OneAsia's inaugural tournament at the Beijing CBD International Golf Club. But it was more than a win for him. It was a bittersweet moment and a kind of dedication. "If my sister was here now, I'm sure she would be proud of me," Strange said. He lost his sister to cancer the previous June.

Strange tagged along through the first three rounds in 70-73-69 and trailed, respectively, by three, five and four strokes. He broke away in the final round with long birdie putts at the 14th, 15th and 17th for a 68 and an eight-under 280 total to win by one over Spain's Gonzalo Fernandez-Castano.

Fittingly, with such a mixed field, the tournament had a different leader, from a different country, in each round. Austria's Markus Brier led the first round with 67, followed by South Korea's Choi Ho-sung (68–138) and England's Richard Finch (66–208).

The tournament was still anyone's in the final round, and no one squandered an opportunity as did New Zealand's Mark Brown. He made four birdies on the front nine, two bogeys and a double bogey over the next five holes, then birdied three of the last four, all for a 69 to finish at 282 and tie for third.

"It's not a course you can tear apart," said a sympathetic Strange. "There are so many holes that you can't attack. I managed to bring it home today."

Kolon-Hana Bank Korea Open
Cheonan, South Korea
Winner: Bae Sang-moon

South Korea's Bae Sang-moon thinks it's generally a prudent idea to listen to his mother. For example: "My mom," he said, "has been telling me all week to be more aggressive with my second shot at the 18th." After all, the par-five 18th at Woo Jeung Hills was within his reach. And was he obedient? "She has been mad with me all week about that," Bae said. "But I am pleased I laid up today after Kim hit that shot."

Bae, defending champion in the Kolon-Hana Bank Korea Open, went against his mother's advice at a critical time — the last hole. Kim Dae-sub, two-time winner of the tournament as a teenage amateur, forced Bae's hand. Bae had a lock on the tournament, leading by three in the 18th fairway. Then Kim holed out his third from 100 yards for an eagle and a 69. Suddenly, aggressive wasn't smart. So Bae laid up, hit his third comfortably on, two-putted for par and won by a stroke at 10-under 274 total, on a card of 71-71-65-67.

Lost in Bae's tense finish was the fact that he had trailed by nine at the halfway point, and had to fight through a field that included such other young talent as Northern Ireland's Rory McIlroy, 20, and Japan's Ryo Ishikawa, 17.

Ishikawa, fresh from his fifth victory in Japan, tied for 15th. McIlroy, after tying Kim for the third-round lead, then slipped to a 72 and finished tied for third. Bae raced from nine behind to one off the third-round lead. His next big move came in the final round, a burst of three consecutive birdies as McIlroy stumbled to bogeys at the 11th and 14th. That left the stage to Bae and Kim at the 18th.

Midea China Classic
Guangzhou, China
Winner: Liang Wen-chong

For Liang Wen-chong, winning the Midea China Classic was more than a personal triumph. It was a matter of national pride in the developing geo-politics of golf as China was growing fast in the game. "The win is a lot more than a trophy and a paycheck," Liang said. "This means so much at this time, and I see it as a win for Chinese professionals."

The Midea was the third of five events in the inaugural season of the OneAsia Tour, and the first won by a Chinese. Liang found the Royal Orchid International Golf Club to his liking — a comparatively short course at some 6,900 yards that required skill as much as power. Liang shot it in 69-65-68-68—270, and won by four over China's first outstanding player, Zhang Lian-wei.

"I played as well as Liang, but he putted better," said Zhang, who won the event in 2006.

Liang made his point about accuracy in the second round, hitting all 18 greens in regulation and sharing a two-stroke lead at eight-under-par 134 with Australia's Andrew Martin. "I decided with my coach (Kel Llewellyn) that the aim was to hit every green in regulation," Liang said. He started with a birdie on his first hole, No. 10, then holed a 35-foot birdie putt at his sixth, No. 15, that triggered a run of five birdies in six holes.

Liang took a one-shot lead into the final round, then birdied Nos. 1, 3, 8 and 10. He bogeyed No. 9 — only his second bogey of the week — then rolled from there to a 68 and a win that was almost too comfortable.

"I felt a lot of pressure," Liang said. "But when I was a few strokes ahead, I had to concentrate hard to maintain my game and stay in front."

Australian Open
Sydney, New South Wales
Winner: Adam Scott

See Australasian Tour chapter.

Australian PGA Championship
Coolum Beach, Queensland
Winner: Robert Allenby

See Australasian Tour chapter.

Omega China Tour

The Omega China Tour, the country's developmental circuit, entered its fifth year in 2009, but smaller instead of larger, as was announced at its debut. The tour opened in 2005 with four three-round tournaments, and reached eight four-round events in 2008. But the 2009 tour was down to four tournaments, presumably the effect of the new OneAsia Tour, of which China was a charter member.

Kurt Barnes, a beefy Australian, won the Sofitel Zhongshan IGC Open, and went on to top the Order of Merit with RMB 264,750 (about US$38,500). Two rising Chinese players took the next two spots — Wu Wei-huang, RMB 215,638 ($31,432), and Chen Jian, RMB 212,338 ($30,951).

The Omega China Tour, meanwhile, at whatever size, remained a showcase for the increase in the numbers of golfers and the quality of play as the game continued to grow in the land.

Dell Championship
Xiamen
Winner: Wu Wei-huang

Wu Wei-huang, 40, a former martial arts champion, added golf to his trophy case in taking the Dell Championship on the Omega China Tour in March. Wu, who took up golf in 1995, led wire-to-wire on a card of 66-67-70-71–274, 14 under par at the Orient Golf Club in Xiamen.

"When I holed the part putt on 18, I just felt so relieved that I'd finally done it," said Wu, who got into trouble once, when he double-bogeyed the par-five No. 5, letting Wu Ashun to get within a stroke. "At the start, I was watching Wu Ashun and C.J. Gatto too much and focusing on their game," Wu said. "However, after No. 5 I realized I had to play my own game. I started to believe I would win when I birdied No. 13, and I held my nerve on the way in."

Sofitel Zhongshan IGC Open
Nanjing
Winner: Kurt Barnes

The big question for Kurt Barnes was whether he would survive Zhongshan International's 16th hole. He played it in a whopping six over par for the week. The question was answered at No. 18 in the final round when he holed a short par put for the win in the Sofitel Zhongshan IGC Open in Nanjing in April. It was a great debut on the tour for the big Aussie, who shot 69-70-73-72–284, four under, edging Thailand's Wisut Arjanawat by a stroke.

"This is awesome — it's a huge weight off my shoulders," said Barnes, one of 10 Australians invited. But it wasn't a smooth win. Barnes bogeyed the sixth, eagled the par-five seventh, then four-putted the par-three eighth for a double bogey. "I dodged a lot of bullets today," Barnes admitted.

Luxehills Golf Championship
Chengdu
Winner: Chen Jian

It's in the records that Chen Jian won the Luxehills Golf Championship in mid-June, the first Omega China Tour to be televised live, on the second hole of a playoff. Put another way, the playoff went the entire last round, until Chen holed a short par putt at the "20th" hole to beat Australia's Rowan Beste. Chen seemed comfortable entering the final round, leading by three. Then came one of the tour's great battles.

Chen opened with birdie-double bogey-birdie. Beste tied him with a birdie at the fourth, had three more birdies and a bogey, and led by one through the turn. Beste bogeyed the 14th, then both birdied the 16th. Chen closed with a 70, Beste 69 and they tied at 11-under 277. Beste then missed a five-foot par putt on the second playoff hole, and Chen holed a two-footer for his first victory.

Dongfeng Nissan Teana Open
Hangzhou
Winner: Thaworn Wiratchant

It was young vs. old in the Dongfeng Nissan Teana Open late in June, and this time youth wasn't served. That's because the "old" was Asian Tour star Thaworn Wiratchant, 42, making his Omega China Tour debut and leaving with a win and a record. "Everything was great this week," Thaworn said.

Thaworn played the Anji King Valley Golf Club in 70-68-63-67–268, a tour record 20 under par. Thaworn started the final round tied with South Korea's Eom Jae-woong, a mere 18. Both shot 33 on the first nine. Coming in, Thaworn birdied the 11th for the lead, then went two ahead on an eight-foot birdie putt at the 15th. Eom cut his lead to one with a birdie at the 18th. "Eom was very good and he's only 18," Thaworn said. "He has a bright future."

Japan Tour

Token Homemate Cup
Nagoya, Mie
Winner: Koumei Oda

Koumei Oda picked up at the start of the 2009 Japan Tour season where he left off at the end of the 2008 campaign. Oda, who scored his maiden victory in the Casio World Open, the final full-field event of the 2008 season, opened 2009 with a playoff win in the Token Homemate Cup, the traditional starting tournament on the Japan Tour calendar.

The victor himself conceded that his game, particularly his driving, was rather ragged in the final round at Nagoya's Token Tado Country Club. "I played the golf of a loser but got lucky at the end," he said after a par-saving three-foot putt on the second hole of the playoff gave him the victory over 47-year-old South Korean Kim Jong-duck.

Oda shared the third-round lead with Australian Brendan Jones, an eight-time winner in Japan, at seven-under-par 206, as he birdied the last two holes for 68 after Jones posted a 67. Jones had begun the tournament with a 66, trailing leader Tetsuya Haraguchi by a stroke, then slipped three behind Australian veteran Craig Parry, Michio Matsumura (67) and Tadahiro Takayama (68) at 135. Oda was at 139.

Shaky tee shots led to two early bogeys Sunday, but again Oda birdied the 17th and 18th for 68 to tie Kim, who won his fourth title in Japan in 2004. Both players were through the green on the second overtime hole and the South Korean missed his six-foot par putt before Oda converted his shorter one for the victory.

Tsuruya Open
Kawanishi, Hyogo
Winner: Masaya Tomida

Masaya Tomida gave little advance notice that he was about to become a winner when the Tsuruya Open went on stage in late April. The 31-year-old pro had finished the previous season 39th on the money list and had not placed higher than 34th in the last five seasons.

He had played solidly the first two days at Yamanohara Golf Club, but was four strokes off the lead at 134 (68-66) going into the third and final round of the Tsuruya when play resumed after a Saturday weather cancellation. Sunday was all his. He put together a blistering seven-under-par 64 and rolled to a two-stroke victory.

Tomida's main victim was Yui Ueda, who had begun the tournament with a sizzling 63 and a four-shot lead and remained on top after Friday's round with 67–130. Australia's David Smail scored a rare double eagle, shot 64 and took over second place at 133, a stroke ahead of Tomida and 2008's No. 1 Shingo Katayama (68-66).

Tomida came out firing Sunday after the 24-hour delay. He chopped Ueda's lead down to one with a birdie at the 10th hole after an outgoing 32. He added two more birdies, then eagled the 17th hole to go eight under for the round before taking a bogey at the final hole for the 64 and the winning 198. Smail shot 67 to finish second, a stroke in front of Ueda (71) and Tomohiro Kondo (66).

The Crowns
Togo, Aichi
Winner: Tetsuji Hiratsuka

Tetsuji Hiratsuka did a complete turnaround in the silver anniversary of The Crowns. After missing cuts in the first two tournaments of the season, the 37-year-old Hiratsuka rolled to a seven-stroke victory, his fifth in the last seven years on the circuit. He put up four solid rounds in the 60s en route to his 17-under-par 263.

Hiratsuka took the lead in the second round and never looked back. His first-round 67 positioned him in a nine-way tie for fifth place, three shots behind Hiroyuki Fujita's leading 64, and his second-round 66 jumped him in front by a stroke. His 133 gave him the one-shot margin over Takao Nogami (65-69) with Fujita (71), Kenichi Kuboya and Naoya Sugiyama (both with 68-67) at 135.

Hiratsuka was flawless Saturday on Nagoya Golf Club's Wago course, running off six birdies and taking no bogeys for 64–197. That stationed him four strokes in front of Fujita (66) and six ahead of Nogami (69), Toru Suzuki and Taichi Teshima, who posted 66s. Comfortable with the four-stroke cushion, Hiratsuka breezed home with a six-birdie, two-bogey 66 for the 263 and his first win since the 2007 Mitsubishi Diamond Cup tournament. Kuboya nailed the runner-up spot with a closing 65–270 and Teshima (69) shared third place with Prayad Marksaeng (64) at 272.

Mitsubishi Diamond Cup
Oarai, Ibaraki
Winner: Takashi Kanemoto

The waiting was over for Takashi Kanemoto. After 16 winless seasons on the Japan Tour, the 38-year-old Kanemoto finally broke the ice in the Mitsubishi Diamond Cup. But it wasn't easy. He had to duel Australian Brendan Jones, an eight-time winner in Japan, through three extra holes before capturing the title at long last.

Much like winner Tetsuji Hiratsuka in the most recent event nearly a month earlier, Kanemoto came to Ibaraki Prefecture's Oarai Golf Club after a feeble start of the season — two missed cuts and a tie for 44th in the Tsuruya Open. Nor were matters very promising for him after the first 36 holes. He opened with a par 72, six behind leader Kim Kyung-tae, and followed with a 76 on a day in which a lone 72 was the best score. Thailand's Chawalit Plaphol had that par round and it gave him the lead at 143, leaving Kanemoto still five back.

Conditions improved drastically Saturday. Jones had the day's best round this time — an eagle, five birdies and two bogeys — and the 67 boosted him into first place. His 214 gave him a two-stroke lead over Kanemoto (68), 54-year-old Tsuneyuki (Tommy) Nakajima (69) and Chawalit, who faltered with a 73. Kanemoto shot 67 Sunday to overtake Jones (69) at five-under-par 283 and bring about the playoff. The two matched pars on the first two extra holes before Kanemoto nailed an approach from a fairway bunker to five feet on the par-four 18th and dropped the birdie putt. He became the season's second first-time winner, joining Masaya Tomida (Tsuruya Open).

UBS Japan Golf Tour Championship
Kasama, Ibaraki
Winner: Yuji Igarashi

Talk about duplication. The result of the major UBS Japan Golf Tour Championship nearly matched what had happened the previous week in the Mitsubishi Diamond Cup. Yuji Igarashi, a winless 40-year-old journeyman, was finally victorious in the Tour Championship just as 38-year-old circuit veteran Takashi Kanemoto was in the Diamond Cup.

Igarashi didn't have to work overtime for his win, but it didn't come easily. He was two strokes off the pace of Yuta Ikeda entering the final round of the year's first major and prevailed with the unwilling help of Ikeda, Australia's David Smail and South Korea's Jang Ik-jae, who shared the second-round lead at 134 with Igarashi (67-67) with the help of a hole-in-one that led to a 64.

Ikeda fell apart Sunday and shot 78. Smail started fast with three birdies on the first four holes, but fell back when he took bogeys on four of the next seven holes. Yang, who also led by two on the back nine before taking bogeys at the 15th and 17th, had the best shot at Igarashi. When Jang reached the final hole, Igarashi was already in with an eight-under-par 70–276. Yang only needed a par to force a playoff, but he bogeyed the hole for 72–277, joining Smail (72) and Toru Suzuki (70) in the runner-up spot. Thus, the tour had its third new winner in its first five events.

Japan PGA Championship
Eniwa, Hokkaido
Winner: Yuta Ikeda

The parade of first-time winners continued at the venerable Japan PGA Championship, but this one had different consequences. While the first three maiden victors — Masaya Tomida, Takashi Kanemoto and Yuji Igarashi — had mediocre seasons subsequently, Yuta Ikeda, the PGA champion, went on to greater glory and nearly won the year's money title.

The 23-year-old Ikeda, playing his first full season on the Japan Tour after making nine starts in 2008, romped to a seven-stroke victory at rain-swept Eniwa Country Club in Hokkaido, shooting rounds of 69 and 65 in a 36-hole finale brought about by the weather-forced postponement of Thursday's opening round. He posted a 14-under-par 266, and Mitsuhiro Tateyama, at 273, was the only player within nine strokes of him. It soothed a wound left when Ikeda blew a victory chance the previous Sunday in the Japan Tour Championship with a final-round 78.

Ikeda's rebound began when play got underway Friday, scoring a 65 and sharing first place with Norio Shinozaki and Shintaro Domoto. He was the solo leader the rest of the way. He shot 67 Saturday and at 132 was four strokes in front of Shintaro Kai (68-68) and Tetsuji Hiratsuka (66-70), the Crowns winner in May.

His lead slipped to two after the third round Sunday morning with the one-under 69, but he dominated the field that afternoon. After a one-under front nine, Ikeda birdied the 11th and 12th holes — "I thought I would go all the way after getting those birdies" — and two more coming home to clinch the victory. Interestingly, Masashi (Jumbo) Ozaki launched his remarkable career with victory in a 36-hole finish of the 1971 PGA Championship.

Gateway to the Open Mizuno Open Yomiuri Classic
Nishinomiya, Hyogo
Winner: Ryo Ishikawa

Ryo Ishikawa, Japan's teenaged phenom, hadn't given his enormous galleries much to cheer about in the early stages of the Japan Tour's 2009 season, not finishing any higher than 29th in any of his six starts and missing two cuts. The seventh event — Gateway to the Open Mizuno Open Yomiuri Classic — was the turning point of a record-setting year.

Ishikawa showed the poise of a veteran on his way to his third tour victory, a three-stroke win with his 13-under-par 275 at Yomiuri Country Club in Hyogo Prefecture. The popular young man had carried a three-stroke lead over Prayad Marksaeng and Kim Hyung-sung into the final day after posting rounds of 69-65-68 for 202 and was sailing along with a five-stroke lead Sunday afternoon when disaster struck. He knocked two tee shots out of bounds at the par-four 12th, took a nine and fell back into a tie with David Smail and Kim, who led after the first two rounds with his 67-66–133.

Ishikawa steadied himself, the others couldn't take advantage of the situation, and he restored three strokes of his lead with a 30-yard eagle chip-in at the par-five 16th and a birdie at the home hole for 73. Smail wound up with 72–278, his third runner-up finish of the season. Ishikawa, Smail and third-place-finishers Kenichi Kuboya and Tomohiro Kondo qualified for the Open Championship in Britain along with Yuta Ikeda and Koumei Oda, first and second on the money list.

Nagashima Shigeo Invitational Sega Sammy Cup
Chitose, Hokkaido
Winner: Hiroyuki Fujita

Playing with "a do-or-die spirit" in the final round, Hiroyuki Fujita came from three shots off the lead to capture the Nagashima Shigeo Invitational Sega Sammy Cup when the Japan Tour resumed action after an unusual month-long break in the heart of the summer. Fujita birdied three of his last four holes for a six-under-par 66 and a one-stroke win with his 272.

"Golf is really difficult when you get to 40 years old," said Fujita after scoring his seventh career victory. Perhaps that is why 47-year-old Kouki Idoki couldn't finish off a victory himself and had to settle for 70–273. He came that close to his first win in 16 years.

Both pros were close to the top in the early going at the North Country Golf Club. Idoki was one back and Fujita two behind as Kim Jong-duck and Jang Ik-jae of South Korea and Paul Sheehan of Australia led with 67s. Katsumasa Miyamoto took over first place Friday with 68-66–134, a shot ahead of Idoki. Fujita was one of five players at 137.

Idoki, whose second career win was in the 1993 NST Niigata Open, emerged with a three-shot lead over Fujita (69) and three others when he registered a 68–203. Fujita was flawless with his winning, six-birdie 66 Sunday.

Sun Chlorella Classic
Otaru, Hokkaido
Winner: Ryo Ishikawa

Ryo Ishikawa learned how difficult it is to lead a tournament from start to finish when he did it in the Sun Chlorella Classic. Picking up his second victory of the season, the then 17-year-old had to drop an eight-foot birdie putt to eke out a one-stroke triumph over Australian veteran Brendan Jones.

"I never had a neck-to-neck battle like this," said Ishikawa, who became the circuit's first double winner of the year. "I felt the difficulty of starting the final round with the lead. I'm proud of today's great duel."

Jones was in the picture from the start. He trailed Ishikawa (65) by a stroke the first day, but dropped three shots off the pace Friday when Ishikawa shot 68 for 133 and a one-stroke lead over Kazuhiro Yamashita. Ishikawa's third round was shaky — five birdies and four bogeys — but the 71 actually widened his margin to two over Yamashita (72). Jones shot 71 and was just three back entering the final round.

The Aussie closed the gap to one on the front nine Sunday and the two battled it out for the title the rest of the way until Ishikawa's eighth birdie of the day for 67–271 provided the final margin. Jones shot 65–272, recording his second runner-up finish of the season. Yuta Ikeda took third place with his 275.

Kansai Open Golf Championship
Takarazuka, Hyogo
Winner: Hiroyuki Fujita

Course-record rounds played a big part in the main storyline and in Hiroyuki Fujita's second victory of the season in the Kansai Open Golf Championship, an official event on the circuit for the first time in 17 years. Fujita was 20 under par at 264, two strokes ahead of Tetsuji Hiratsuka and Tomohiro Kondo, at the end.

Until faltering in the final round, Masaya Tomida was tracking toward a second 2009 win himself. That was primarily because of his sizzling, nine-under-par 62 in the first round. That gave the Tsuruya Open winner a three-stroke lead over Koumei Oda, Kiyoshi Miyazato and Hiratsuka. He had 10 birdies and a bogey as he set a new course record at Takarazuka Golf Club in Hyogo Prefecture.

Tomida made six more birdies Friday, but four bogeys brought his card back to 69–131 and his lead down to one over Kunihiro Kamii, who shot 65–132. Fujita was four shots off the lead with 69-66–135, then shattered the two-day-old course record with a splendid 61, the product of an eagle and eight birdies. Tomida shot 65 and went into the final round tied with Fujita at 196.

Tomida ran out of gas Sunday, slumping to 74 and a sixth-place finish. Hiratsuka and Tomohiro Kondo gave Fujita a run for his money, but his closing 68 — four birdies and a bogey — gave him the victory.

Vana H Cup KBC Augusta
Shima, Fukuoka
Winner: Yuta Ikeda

What's going on in Japan? On the heels of the sensational play of teenager Ryo Ishikawa the last three years came 14-year-old Masamichi Ito, who shot 72-69–141 in the Vana H Cup KBC Augusta and became the youngest player ever to make the cut in a Japan Tour competition. That became a fascinating sidebar to an exciting battle involving Ishikawa and Yuta Ikeda, his strongest challenger for the top spot on the money list.

Ishikawa, gunning for his third win of the season, took over first place from Tetsuya Haraguchi, the first-round leader at 64, when he put up rounds of 65-66 for 131 and a two-stroke lead over veteran star Toru Taniguchi. Ikeda was then four shots behind. Ishikawa clung to the top spot despite a 71 Saturday. At 202, he led by one over Jun Kikuchi and Hiroyuki Fujita, coming off his second 2009 victory in the Kansai Open. Ikeda was among six players at 204

Two brilliant rounds Sunday left Ishikawa on the outside looking in. Ishikawa shot a fine 66, but it wasn't quite enough to get him into a playoff as Yasuharu Imano and Ikeda matched the course record with 63s, Ikeda with birdies on seven of his final eight holes, for 17-under-par 267s. In the subsequent playoff, Ikeda birdied the second hole for his second win of the year and the money lead.

Fujisankei Classic
Fujikawaguchiko, Yamanashi
Winner: Ryo Ishikawa

It wasn't going to happen again to Ryo Ishikawa. For the second week in a row, Ishikawa held the third-round lead in a Japan Tour tournament. Despite a 66 in the final round the previous Sunday in the KBC Augusta, he lost to a pair of 63s. In the following Fujisankei Classic, one of the circuit's oldest events, he led by two prior to Sunday's finale.

This time the 17-year-old star put on a four-birdie finishing kick and raced to 272 and a five-stroke victory, his third of the season and fifth overall.

Ishikawa took over first place in the second round from Kouki Idoki, who aced his second hole with a seven wood and birdied his last three holes for 65 in the opening round, which had to be finished Friday when heavy fog delayed the start that morning. Ishikawa shot a bogey-free 65 Friday for 134 and took a one-stroke lead over Kenichi Kuboya as Idoki shot 71–136.

He widened the gap to two strokes Saturday, but was somewhat erratic. He shot 68 in a round that saw him bogey three holes early on the back nine and follow with three straight birdies. Kuboya shot 69 but held onto second place, two behind Ishikawa's 202. Ishikawa didn't have a birdie until the 12th hole Sunday, but nobody took advantage. He then added birdies at the 14th, 15th and 17th before a bogey at the final hole. Kuboya plunged to 78 and Daisuke Maruyama slipped into second place with 69–277.

ANA Open
Kitahiroshima, Hokkaido
Winner: Toru Taniguchi

The longest dry spell of his fine career finally ended in Hokkaido when Toru Taniguchi marched to an impressive, four-stroke victory in the ANA Open against a field that sported a strong cast of current and past winners on the Japan Tour. Long considered one of Japan's most talented players, Taniguchi had not been a serious victory contender since he won the 2007 Japan Open Championship, his 14th tour victory that led him to his second money-winning title.

The 41-year-old Taniguchi had his eyes on his 15th victory from the start on the Wattsu course of Sapporo Golf Club in the mid-September tournament. He trailed only the first day and then by only a shot behind Koumei Oda, Kenichi Kuboya and Azuma Yano, who opened with 66s. Taniguchi repeated his 67 Friday and moved two strokes in front of veteran Tsuneyuki (Tommy) Nakajima, who owns four ANA titles, the most recent in 1993.

Taniguchi put himself on easy street Saturday and expressed confidence about victory when he fashioned a six-birdie 66 for 200 and moved five shots ahead of Nakajima (69) and Kazuhiro Yamashita (67). "I believe I can hold on to win tomorrow as long as I play like I have in the first three rounds," he exclaimed.

He really didn't play as well Sunday, settling for a par 72 and 272. But nobody mounted a charge on the windy day and, despite two bogeys on the front nine, Taniguchi posted the four-stroke triumph. The 54-year-old Nakajima (71) tied for second with Yamashita (71) and Kim Kyung-tae (69) at 276.

Asia-Pacific Panasonic Open
Joyo, Kyoto
Winner: Daisuke Maruyama

When Daisuke Maruyama won the Fujisankei Classic in 2005, he was encouraged to take a shot at the PGA Tour in America, conquered the rigors of the qualifying process that fall, and played on the big stage for two seasons with mediocre success. Back in his element on the Japan Tour in 2009, Maruyama savored victory in the Asia-Pacific Panasonic Open in late September at Joyo Country Club in Kyoto. "I had completely forgotten what victory tastes like," said a happy Maruyama after putting the finishing touches on a four-stroke win.

A second-round 66 propelled the 38-year-old into the lead and he didn't let it slip away the rest of the way. With the 66–135, he took first place away from the unlikely first-day leaders — Tetsuya Haraguchi, a non-winner in 12 seasons on the circuit, and Lam Chih Bing of Singapore — who opened with 66s. Maruyama then cushioned his margin to four strokes with a four-under-par 67 Saturday. His closest pursuer was South Korean Kim Kyung-tae, a runner-up the previous Sunday in the ANA Open.

Gusty winds inflated the scoring Sunday. Although he could do no better than 74, Maruyama still was able to maintain his four-stroke lead and finished eight under par at 276 in the season's joint venture with the Asian Tour. The victory gives Maruyama a choice of tours as an exempt player for the next two years. Kim also shot 74 and shared second place with Liang Wen-chong (73) and Yuta Ikeda (72), the money runner-up who moved closer to leader Ryo Ishikawa.

Coca-Cola Tokai Classic
Miyoshi, Aichi
Winner: Ryo Ishikawa

His handling of the final holes of the Coca-Cola Tokai Classic illustrated why Ryo Ishikawa, though just 18 years old, has become the bright star of the Japan Tour. Locked in a stretch battle in the last round at Miyoshi Country Club, Ishikawa stumbled badly when he absorbed his second double bogey of the day at the 14th. Instead of folding as many players would in such circumstances, Ishikawa bounced back immediately with an eagle at the par-five 15th.

When he reached the 17th hole, he was a stroke off the lead. He birdied there to tie for the lead, then knocked his pressure approach at the 18th inside two feet as Yuta Ikeda put his second shot in the water and Takeshi

Kajikawa, the other contender, left himself a monster putt he didn't make. The result: Ishikawa, with his 69 and 14-under-par 274, won his fourth tournament of the season and strengthened his No. 1 position on the money list. Kajikawa's par gave him the runner-up slot with 69–275. Ikeda, Ishikawa's money list challenger, dropped two shots further back with his 71, tying for third with Shingo Katayama.

Ikeda, already a two-time winner this season, had started the tournament with a 64 and a two-stroke lead, then yielded the top spot to Daisuke Maruyama, the Panasonic Open winner, in the rain-interrupted second round. Maruyama posted his 68-68–136 before play was called for the day. Ishikawa slipped into first place with 66–205, a stroke ahead of Kajikawa (65) and Ikeda (68), setting the stage for the raucous finish Sunday.

Canon Open
Yokohama, Kanagawa
Winner: Yuta Ikeda

This time in the Canon Open a 64 start paid off with a victory for Yuta Ikeda and tightened his challenge of Ryo Ishikawa for the season championship on the Japan Tour. Ikeda had begun the previous week's Tokai Classic with the same score, but couldn't convert it into a win.

Actually, Ikeda shot 64 twice in the Canon Open, the first one coming on Friday after Typhoon Melor raked through the island of Honshu, forcing cancellation of the Thursday round to allow crews to get Yokohama's Totsuka Country Club back into tournament shape. He produced the other one in the final round Sunday as he spurted to a four-stroke victory at 16-under-par 200.

It was the third win for the surprise star of 2009, playing in his first full season on the circuit after making just 10 starts in 2008. He nearly caught Ishikawa with the ¥22.5 million winner's check, since Ishikawa was playing on the International team in the Presidents Cup in San Francisco that week.

Ikeda entered the final round three strokes behind leader Kenichi Kuboya (65-68–133) after following his first-day 64 with an even-par 72. He took command early Sunday, running off three consecutive birdies starting at the second hole, went out in 30 and scored eight birdies in all in his no-bogey 64. Tomohiro Kondo (66) and Han Lee (69) tied for second at 204.

Japan Open Championship
Iruma, Saitama
Winner: Ryuichi Oda

"Unbelievable!" That was Ryuichi Oda's assessment of his playoff victory in the Japan Open Championship. "I had felt frustration for not being able to win a tournament," said the 32-year-old, a long-time winless campaigner on the Japan Tour.

What made Oda's victory particularly impressive was his final-day performance. After three rounds at Musashi Country Club at Iruma, Saitama Prefecture, he sat in a three-way tie for fifth place, four strokes behind the exciting Ryo Ishikawa, who was just back from a fine showing in the Presidents Cup in America and seemingly headed for victory in the venerable national championship.

Ishikawa had rebounded from a second-round 76–146 with a blistering 65 Saturday that overcame his five-shot deficit against Friday co-leaders Hiroyuki Fujita, already a two-time winner in 2009, and American Han Lee. Both had 69-72–141 cards. At 211, Ishikawa entered the final round a shot in front of Yasuharu Imano. A strong back nine boosted Oda into contention Sunday. His eighth birdie of the day came at the 18th, giving him a 67, the best score of the final round, and the six-under-par 282 knotted Oda with Imano (70) and Ishikawa, who had to work hard to overcome a bogey and double bogey on the front nine.

The playoff went two holes, Oda winning with a seven-foot birdie at the par-four 18th hole after his opponents missed birdies from longer range.

Bridgestone Open
Chiba
Winner: Yuta Ikeda

Yuta Ikeda took full advantage of his opportunity to show his hometown fans in Chiba why he was having such a successful season on the Japan Tour when the Bridgestone Open was played in his neighborhood in late October. To the delight of the friendly galleries at familiar Sodegaura Country Club, Ikeda overcame a two-stroke deficit the last day and rolled to his fourth victory of the season.

"I watched this tournament live when I was a schoolboy," said Ikeda, who jumped into the lead of the money race with the ¥30 million first prize. "I especially wanted to win this one. I wasn't thinking too much about the money rankings, but it's a nice feeling to be on top." He supplanted Ryo Ishikawa, who tied for 20th place.

Ikeda was in contention all week. He and two others trailed first-round leader Tatsunori Nukaga by a stroke with their 67s, and when Ikeda repeated the 67 Friday, he joined Koumei Oda (68-66), the Token Homemate Cup winner in April, atop the standings.

Kaname Yokoo, winless for three years, sparkled on Saturday. His eight-birdie 64–203 carried him from five back to one shot in front of Shingo Katayama, the tour's brightest star this decade but winless in 2009. Ikeda shot 71–205, then soared Sunday with an eight-birdie, one-bogey 65 for 270, two better than Kenichi Kuboya (67) and three ahead of Katayama (69). Yokoo stumbled with a 74, dropping into a tie for seventh at 277.

Mynavi ABC Championship
Kato, Hyogo
Winner: Toru Suzuki

Toru Suzuki ended a five-year victory drought on the Japan Tour with a decisive win in the Mynavi ABC Championship. Winless since the 2004 Acom International, Suzuki seized a big lead in the third round at Kato's ABC Golf Club and rode it to a 71–274 and a five-stroke triumph. It was the eighth win in a long career for the 43-year-old, whose first victory came in 1993 in the Gene Sarazen Jun Classic.

Suzuki got his game in high gear Friday after opening with a modest 70 that left him four strokes off the pace. Azuma Yano, Kim Hyung-sung and Hidemasa Hoshino led with 66s. Scores were generally higher the next day and a three-under-par 69 enabled Hoshino to grab a two-shot lead with 135. The runner-up position was occupied by multiple 2009 winners Ryo Ishikawa (68-69) and Hiroyuki Fujita (69-68) and Suzuki (70-67).

Suzuki capped his takeover round Saturday with an eagle at the 18th hole for a 66 and the five-shot advantage over Fujita (71). Ishikawa shot 72, slipping seven off the lead with South Korea's Kim, and his concluding 73–282 dropped him into a tie for sixth place. He missed the chance to regain the No. 1 position on the money list with leader Yuta Ikeda on the shelf nursing a sore wrist.

Suzuki had four birdies and three bogeys in his mediocre but effective 71 close.

The Championship by Lexus
Bando, Ibaraki
Winner: Toshinori Muto

A blazing, seven-under-par 64 finish propelled Toshinori Muto to a three-stroke victory in The Championship by Lexus in early November. The win overshadowed Shigeki Maruyama's strong bid for his first victory since returning to the Japan Tour fulltime after nine seasons on the PGA Tour in America.

Muto and Maruyama hovered on or near the top of the standings all week at the Otone Country Club in Bando, Ibaraki Prefecture. Maruyama, 40, whose last win in Japan was in the 1999 Bridgestone Open, shared the first-round lead with South Korea's Kim Kyung-tae and Kim Hyung-sung and Australia's Wayne Perske at 66. Muto was two behind, but came up with a 65 to take a share of the lead with Kim Kyung-tae at 133. Maruyama shot 68 for 134.

Maruyama regained a piece of the lead with a 68–202 to match Kim Kyung-tae's 69–202, as Muto dropped two off the pace with 71–204, tied with Perske (69). Muto's charge Sunday began somewhat slowly with two front-nine birdies, then he racked up five more on the back nine for the winning 64–268, 16 under par. Kim shot 69–271 to edge Maruyama (70–272) for second place. It was the 31-year-old Muto's third career victory.

The tournament went without the tour's three leading money winners

— Yuta Ikeda, Ryo Ishikawa and Shingo Katayama — who were playing in the WGC - HSBC Champions, a new international event in Shanghai.

Mitsui Sumitomo Visa Taiheiyo Masters
Gotemba, Shizuoka
Winner: Yasuharu Imano

An aching Yasuharu Imano wiped out "a long four years" when he made a final-round, one-over-par 73 stand up for his seventh tour victory. The sixth one had been the Nippon Series title at the end of 2005. The seventh victory surprised Imano. "I never thought I would be able to win," he said. "I started to feel pain in my elbow and neck."

It was also a long final day on the Taiheiyo Club's Gotemba course, since all but a few players had to complete their third rounds Sunday morning after a three-hour rain delay Saturday. Imano was one of them and his eventual 68 gave him a three-stroke lead at 202 going into the fourth round. He had taken a two-shot lead Friday with 69-65–134. After 54 holes, little-known Masao Nakajima was at 205 with Kenichi Kuboya, Kaname Yokoo and Taigen Tsumagari at 206.

Imano absorbed a bogey and a double bogey in shooting the final 73 for 275 total. Kuboya, a frequent contender all season but winless in 2009, shot 71 and shared second place with Han Lee, who closed with 69 for his 277.

Ryo Ishikawa also posted 69 Sunday, tied for fourth, and regained the No. 1 spot on the money list as Yuta Ikeda had a bad week and tied for 45th place.

Dunlop Phoenix
Miyazaki
Winner: Edoardo Molinari

The Dunlop Phoenix, which usually attracts a goodly number of prominent international players, was not exactly star-studded in 2009, but, as is the case more often than not at the Dunlop Phoenix, the winner of one of the season's richest tournaments still came from overseas. Italy's promising Edoardo Molinari kept that pattern intact with a playoff victory over Sweden's Robert Karlsson, the European Tour's leading money winner in 2008. The most recent Japanese winner of the Dunlop was Kaname Yokoo in 2002.

In the early going, it appeared that Kenichi Kuboya might break the visitors' spell and end his seven-year victory drought. Fifth on the Japan Tour money list without collecting a first-place check, Kuboya was at the top of the standings for three days before falling away with a 75 on Sunday. The 37-year-old led with 65 after the first round, shared the lead at 70–135 with Yudai Maeda (70-65) and Tetsuji Hiratsuka (69-66), and slipped a stroke behind Molinari into a tie with Karlsson with a 71 Saturday.

Molinari, who led Europe's Challenge Tour with record earnings, and

Karlsson distanced themselves from the field in the early going Sunday and wound up tied at 271, Karlsson shooting 65 and Molinari 66. The playoff went to the second hole, where the Italian dropped a three-foot birdie putt on the par-five 18th hole for the victory.

Ryo Ishikawa strengthened his hold on the money list when he tied for 22nd, and Yuta Ikeda, still bothered by a sore right wrist, tied for 46th. Vijay Singh, the biggest "name" in the field, was never in contention.

Casio World Open
Geisei, Kochi
Winner: Koumei Oda

Koumei Oda finished the full-field season just as he started it — with a victory. In the process of winning the Casio World Open to go with his season-opening triumph in the Token Homemate Cup, Oda became the only player during the 2009 Japan Tour season to successfully defend a title. This year's victory in the Casio had a much different scenario, though. Instead of leading wire to wire as he did in 2008 when he gathered his first tour victory, Oda broke from a three-way tie with a final-round 65 to win the tournament by three strokes. He was 21 under par with his 267.

The ingredients for the finish took shape in the second round when Oda and Maruyama, both with rounds of 67-65, shared the lead and Ryo Ishikawa, attempting to clinch the money title, trailed by two shots with 68-66–134. It became a three-way deadlock at 14-under 202 Saturday when Ishikawa shot 68 and the co-leaders scored 70s.

Oda had the hot hand Sunday. He broke away in the middle of the round with birdies on four of five holes beginning at the sixth and "tried to go as low as I could." Ishikawa shot 68 to finish second and stretch his money lead to more than ¥24 million over Yuta Ikeda, who tied for 19th. Maruyama shot 72 and dropped into a tie for seventh.

Golf Nippon Series JT Cup
Tokyo
Winner: Shigeki Maruyama

It took longer than most golf followers anticipated and came the hard way, but veteran Shigeki Maruyama finally put a 2009 victory into the books in the season-ending Golf Nippon Series JT Cup. Back in Japan full-time after nearly a decade on the U.S. PGA Tour, Maruyama had mixed in four top-10 finishes with five missed cuts and several other weak showings in 19 starts prior to the Nippon Series and its limited field of 27 comprised of 2009 winners and money leaders.

Finally, victory came at Tokyo Yomiuri Country Club, but only after Maruyama overcame a four-stroke deficit in the final round to tie South Korea's Kim Kyung-tae and then go four extra holes before chalking up his 10th win on the Japan Tour. He won three times during his years in America.

Despite a tie-for-19th performance in the finale, Ryo Ishikawa secured the season's money-winning championship with earnings of ¥183,524,051, some ¥25 million ahead of Yuta Ikeda, who also had a stellar season. Both young men had four victories during the year. The 18-year-old Ishikawa is by far the youngest to ever win the money title. Masashi (Jumbo) Ozaki was 26 when he led the standings in 1973.

Maruyama seized a one-stroke lead in Friday's second round with 70-67–137, but fell four shots off the pace Saturday, when Kim, 23, four times a runner-up earlier in the season but winless in Japan, fired a six-under-par 64 and jumped two shots in front with his seven-under 203. The 40-year-old Maruyama responded with a 64 of his own Sunday to match Kim's 68–271 and force the playoff. A short par putt at the fourth extra hole gave Maruyama the triumph as the South Korean bogeyed the par-three 18th hole.

10. Australasian Tour

The emergence of talent from Australasia continued with Danny Lee and Michael Sim leading the way in 2009. Lee, who won the U.S. Amateur in 2008, followed up that triumph by becoming the second player on the European Tour to win as an amateur. He achieved the feat at the Johnnie Walker Classic and also broke a longstanding record held by South Africa's Dale Hayes by becoming the youngest-ever winner on the European circuit at the age of 18 years and 213 days. The triumph brought Lee into a trio of sensational youngsters in the game along with Northern Ireland's Rory McIlroy and Japan's Ryo Ishikawa, and after playing in the Masters Lee joined them as a professional.

Sim had a double triumph, winning the money lists on both the Australasian Tour and the Nationwide Tour in America. Sim, the 25-year-old born in Aberdeen but who moved to Perth at age five, won three times on the latter circuit, although not in time to earn a battlefield promotion to the PGA Tour. Nevertheless he will start his campaign on the PGA Tour in 2010 in better shape than three years earlier after also qualifying from the Nationwide Tour. But then he was suffering from back pain, later diagnosed as a stress fracture.

At home Sim took the Von Nida Medal for winning the Order of Merit with consistent performances. The tour was expanded to include events previously only included on the Von Nida developmental circuit, but many of the bigger names who returned home during the season did not complete the minimum qualification of four events.

The year ended with a pair of reviving victories for Adam Scott and Robert Allenby. Scott had suffered a poor season on the PGA Tour and was a surprise wild card pick for the International Presidents Cup team by captain Greg Norman. But the faith shown in him by his mentor gave Scott such a boost that his form returned in time for him to claim his first win in Australia at his national Open.

Allenby's year started with the death of his mother from breast cancer, but at the Nedbank Challenge in South Africa he won for the first time in four years and a week later he won the Australian PGA Championship for the fourth time. The third leg of the circuit's big three events, the JBWere Masters, was won by Tiger Woods.

Back in America, Marc Leishman, 26, was voted as the Rookie of the Year on the PGA Tour after three top-10 finishes and a runner-up spot at the BMW Championship. Geoff Ogilvy finished the year as the only Australian in the world's top 20, but did not quite follow up after a brilliant start to the season when he won the opening event on the PGA Tour at the Mercedes-Benz Championship and then the following month the Accenture Match Play, his third World Golf Championship title.

Off course, politics were never far away during the year with the creation of the OneAsia circuit. In 2009 there were five events, finishing with the Australian Open and PGA. The initial event was the Volvo China Open, won by Scott Strange, who would claim the money list title from the circuit's five events. The series was backed by the China Golf Association, the Korean Golf Association and the PGA of Australia with the aim of bringing all tours in the Asia-Pacific region under one umbrella. But the Japanese Tour decided not to continue their involvement and the Asian Tour protested that the new circuit was taking their events. Indeed the China Open switched allegiance from the Asian Tour to OneAsia at only weeks' notice, much to the concern of the European Tour who were co-sanctioning the event. The Asian Tour kept their stance of not negotiating with OneAsia, who announced a series of nine events in 2010 but promised an expanded tour in subsequent years.

Subaru Victorian Open
Clayton, Victoria
Winner: Ashley Hall

Ashley Hall won the Subaru Victorian Open to claim his home state Open two years after his only other Australasian Tour victory at the Victorian PGA Championship. Hall, 25, closed out the win with a final round of 69, after earlier efforts of 68, 65 and 72 to finish at 10-under-par 274 and two strokes ahead of Scott Laycock and Craig Scott. Hall and Laycock shared the lead overnight and swapped the lead during a windy final day at Spring Valley. Laycock finished with 71 while Scott closed with a 70 of two halves, playing himself out of contention on the front nine but charging back by playing the back nine in six under.

Laycock, a former winner of the event but returning from a wrist injury which forced him off the Japanese Tour after eight years, edged one in front of Hall early on the back nine but then bogeyed three holes out of four. Hall took advantage to build a four-stroke lead, but a two-stroke swing at the 17th after Hall's birdie meant his lead was cut to two. But he calmly parred the last to claim the victory.

"It gives me the confidence that I wasn't just a 'one hit wonder' and that I can do it again," said Hall. "To be honest I just came into this event to get myself ready for the Johnnie Walker Classic and the bigger events, but this is the best possible start to the year I could have hoped for. It means a lot to me, I played in every team for the VGA... juniors, colts and seniors, so it is really special. I'm a little bit relieved. A four-shot lead turned into two pretty quickly at 17, but I figured if I just hit it into the middle of the green on the last I was always going to make par."

Cellarbrations Victorian PGA Championship
Melbourne, Victoria
Winner: Andre Stolz

Nine months after returning to competitive golf after a wrist injury that kept him out of action for three years, Andre Stolz won the Cellarbrations Victorian PGA Championship at Sanctuary Lakes. It was the 38-year-old's fourth win in Australia but his first anywhere since claiming the Michelin

Championship in Las Vegas on the PGA Tour in 2004. Stolz returned rounds of 68, 67, 69 and 67 to finish at 17-under-par 271 and two ahead of Stuart Bouvier, while Adam Bland and Cameron Percy shared third place a further shot behind.

The event was played out in extreme weather conditions that led to some of the worst bush fires in Victoria and other southern states of Australia for many years. During the third round the temperature reached over 110°F, while the wind was gusting to 30 mph. While Stolz shot his 69 to take a two-shot lead, Luke Hickmott, who led for the first two days after an opening course-record 61, slumped out of contention with a 78.

Conditions were easier on Sunday and Stolz maintained his advantage with a brilliant 67. "It's been an amazing week, the weather threw everything at us, but it feels good to have won a four-round event again," said Stolz. "When I play well, I play really well, and when I play bad I'm horrendous, so things haven't really changed. I either win or miss the cut a lot of the time. I can't explain it. It used to annoy me but now I just go with it."

Johnnie Walker Classic
Perth, Western Australia
Winner: Danny Lee

An alarming trend of late has been for players to win the U.S. or British Amateurs and, rather than await their exemptions for majors like the Masters and the Open Championship, to turn professional and get cracking on their new career. Not so Danny Lee. The South Korean who moved to New Zealand at the age of eight became the youngest winner of the U.S. Amateur in 2008. In no hurry to play for the money, Lee opted to stay amateur until after the Masters, but in the meantime earn some experience from playing in professional events.

At the Johnnie Walker Classic, a tri-sanctioned event by the Australasian, Asian and European tours, Lee's only aim was to be still playing at the weekend at the Vines Resort in Perth. He made the cut easily with rounds of 67 and 68, was two strokes off the lead of John Bickerton and Ross McGowan after a third round of 69, and claimed victory with a closing 67. At 17-under-par 271, Lee won by one over McGowan, Felipe Aguilar and Hiroyuki Fujita. At 18 years and 213 days he also became the youngest-ever winner on the European Tour, beating the record of South African Dale Hayes from 1971. He was only the second amateur to win on the European circuit, following Pablo Martin in 2007, and the second teenager to win in a matter of weeks after Rory McIlroy took the Dubai Desert Classic.

Lee's win looked unlikely after he bogeyed the 12th hole to fall four behind with six to play. McGowan's eagle at the ninth took him two ahead and a birdie at the 12th put him at 17 under. But Lee birdied the 13th and the 14th, while McGowan, playing just behind, bogeyed the latter. Lee almost found the water at the short 16th and holed a vital par putt of 12 feet before he birdied the 17th from six feet. At the par-five 18th, he very nearly holed a 25-footer for an eagle, but the brilliant effort left him with only a tap-in for his fourth birdie in six holes. McGowan, also trying to claim his maiden title, bogeyed the 16th and then birdied the last to join the tie for second place.

"It still feels like I'm in dreamland," Lee said. "Hopefully no one wakes me up. I was dreaming about winning but my goal was to make the cut after two rounds and to try to get into the top 20 or top 10. I played extremely well the last few days, and yeah, here I am. You know winning a European Tour event, it's pretty amazing what I've done." Looking back at the 16th hole, Lee added: "I was at 15 under and the leader was at 16, so I was thinking, this is the putt if you want to win the tournament. I was really focused on the putt and I made it."

Moonah Classic
Fingal, Victoria
Winner: Alistair Presnell

Alistair Presnell kept the dream alive by winning the Moonah Classic at Moonah Links in his home state of Victoria. The 29-year-old Australian was contemplating giving up tournament golf, but the victory put him on top of the Australasian Order of Merit and earned him a two-year exemption on the Nationwide Tour in America. In 2008 Presnell went to the United States to try to Monday-qualify at four Nationwide Tour events, but failed on each occasion and returned home. During the month he shared a camper van with another player. "I was not living the dream, I was chasing it," he said.

Presnell's improved form started with a fifth place at the Victorian PGA. "These four weeks were about it for me," he said. "If I couldn't get anything done to make enough for another trip over to the States, I might have had to call my old boss and see if I could get my old job back as an air conditioning apprentice. America is where I'd love to get to. I'm really looking forward to it. It certainly wasn't on the plans at the start of the year. The money is great, but the win opens a big door for me."

With overnight leader Miguel Carballo falling away with a 78, it was Peter O'Malley who led for much of the final day. Presnell kept in touch and survived with no worse than a bogey at the 16th after visiting two bunkers, while he saved par from off the green at the 17th. As Presnell headed up the par-five 18th, O'Malley three-putted the 17th to fall back into a tie. Presnell hit his third to 15 feet at the 18th and holed the putt, while O'Malley later missed from similar range. Presnell's closing birdie gave him a 68 and 279 total, with O'Malley one back after a 70.

HSBC New Zealand PGA Championship
Christchurch, New Zealand
Winner: Steven Alker

Not since Frank Nobilo in 1987 had a home player won the HSBC New Zealand PGA Championship. It might have been dormant for 15 years before being revived in 2002, but in its current incarnation at Clearwater in Christchurch there had not been even a sniff of a chance for a Kiwi to take the title. But in 2009 Steven Alker led a one-two-three for the home nation as the 37-year-old won by two strokes over Josh Geary and David Smail with 273 total. Alker, who started the final day one behind overnight leader Steve Friesen, closed with 67, as did Geary, while Smail had a 68. Friesen, from Nebraska, closed with an even-par 72 but was overtaken in the rush of low scoring and finished tied for seventh, alongside amateur sensation Danny Lee, the Johnnie Walker Classic winner, who bogeyed the last two holes to end four back. Michael Sim, Henrik Bjornstad and Ryan Hietala all shared fourth place.

This was Alker's ninth victory and his second on the Nationwide Tour, the first coming in Louisiana in 2002. But most importantly it was Alker's first win in New Zealand. "It's pretty special to win here," said Alker, who was the touring pro for the Clearwater Resort for three years starting in 2002. "It's great to come back here and see all the members and staff. It's really been a fun week for me." Alker quit the Nationwide Tour after the 2006 season to play in Europe, where he lived in London, but still has a home in Arizona and suggested he would take up his exemption to return to the States.

Alker finished at 15 under par after rounds of 69, 70 and twin 67s, his weekend improvement he put down to his strategy of trying to hit more fairways and greens in regulation. As the turn approached, the leaderboard was still crowded, but Alker swept ahead with three birdies in a row from the ninth. He then birdied the 15th to go three ahead, and although he dropped a shot at the short 16th, none of the other contenders finished strongly.

Michael Hill New Zealand Open
Queenstown, New Zealand
Winner: Alex Prugh

Alex Prugh produced a brilliant burst of scoring to win the Michael Hill New Zealand Open, which for the first time was co-sanctioned with the Nationwide Tour. Prugh, who started the final round at The Hills Golf Club amid the amazing scenery of Queenstown one behind overnight leader Martin Piller, was even par for the day after seven holes. Then, from the right rough at the par-four eighth hole, Prugh holed out with a pitching wedge for an eagle-two. "That really kick-started my round," Prugh said. "I thought, now we can really go. Before that, it felt like I was being lapped by everybody."

Prugh birdied the 11th, 12th and 14th holes to draw level with Piller. But he had not finished there. He birdied the short 16th and then claimed his second eagle of the day at the 17th where he holed from 15 feet. The 24-year-old from eastern Washington, where hilly scenery is similar to the amazing views from Queenstown on New Zealand's South Island, compiled rounds of 65, 71, 69 and 64 for a 19-under-par 269 total and a three-stroke win over Piller, with Jim Herman making it a one-two-three for the States. It was Prugh's first win in his second season on the Nationwide Tour and

America's first victory in the championship since Corey Pavin won back-to-back titles in 1984-85. Richard Johnson produced only the second hole-in-one at a par-four on the Nationwide Tour when he aced the 347-yard 15th, but then bogeyed the next two holes to fall back to 10th place.

John Hughes Geely WA Open
Swanbourne, Western Australia
Winner: Michael Curtain

After suffering a poor rookie season on the European Tour and having to go back through the qualifying tournament, where he got his card for 2009, Michael Curtain returned to Australia to claim his first full Australasian Tour victory on the revamped circuit which includes events from the old Von Nida Tour. Curtain, the co-leader overnight, produced a bogey-free final round of 67 with five birdies to win the John Hughes Geely WA Open at Cottesloe Golf Club by four strokes with 272 total. Kim Felton finished as the runner-up after a 68, while Michael Hendry, who shared the lead with Curtain with a round to play, Anthony Brown, Steve Jones and Adam Blyth all tied for third place.

Curtain claimed places in the Australian Masters and the Australian Open, although his participation depended on his progress at the European Tour qualifying, but he would be returning to Spain with renewed confidence. "It has been a tough slog," said the 30-year-old Victorian. "I feel as if I've been close for so many years but not been able to finish off when I've been in contention. This means so much to me. I thought of winning so many times throughout the round but kept telling myself not to think about it."

Laurance Scrap Metals WA PGA Championship
Clifton Park, Western Australia
Winner: Andrew Bonhomme

While his closest challengers each played the last four holes in even par, Andrew Bonhomme finished with four birdies in a row to win the Laurance Scrap Metals WA PGA Championship at Bunbury in the south of the state. Bonhomme thought he would be in a playoff with his 281 total, but New Zealand's Hamish Robertson failed to get up and down from a bunker at the last, missing a short par effort, and fell into a tie for second place with David Diaz.

Bonhomme, 37, from the Sunshine Coast in Queensland, broke his hand in 2008 and spent much of 2009 on the Nationwide Tour in the States in an unsuccessful attempt to make it to the PGA Tour. "I hung in with a lot of good shots, but nothing seemed to drop for me until the final few holes," he said. "I was really proud of myself and the way I hung in mentally when things weren't going my way. You become more accepting of yourself when you get older and that has been one of my strengths over the last few years."

Cellarbrations Queensland PGA Championship
Toowoomba, Queensland
Winner: Steven Bowditch

Steven Bowditch lived up to his promise of scoring 20 under par around the City Golf Club in Toowoomba and in the process won the Cellarbrations Queensland PGA Championship by six strokes. Bowditch had gone eight ahead after three rounds of 64, 64 and 63 at the par-70 layout and was able to coast home with a closing 69 for 260 total. Clint Rice took second place after a final round of 64, while Michael Hendry was third after a 68.

It was Bowditch's first win since taking the Jacob's Creek Open in 2005, an event co-sanctioned with the Nationwide Tour and which helped Bowditch onto the PGA Tour. However, his career stalled after periods of depression.

"The course played a little tougher today and I was thankful to go into today eight in front," Bowditch said. "My putting today was probably the best it's been all week. I holed some nice putts when I needed them to help me out of a bit of trouble. Around 20 to 25 under was my target and it was nice to be able to come here and shoot that. I drove the ball really well all week, and although the fairways are narrow and a little short, you can get rewards here for playing attacking golf. I just hope I can hold that form now heading to Melbourne next week."

JBWere Masters
Melbourne, Victoria
Winner: Tiger Woods

Such was the interest in Tiger Woods playing in Australia for the first time in 11 years that around 7,000 people turned up at the airport when he arrived and daily crowds of 25,000 swarmed over Kingston Heath during the JBWere Masters.

The world No. 1 lived up to his end of the bargain by winning the tournament, his seventh victory of the season and his first Down Under. "I've never won down here, so now I have won on every continent, except for Antarctica," Woods said. "I haven't played the Antarctica Fourball yet. But to have won on every playable continent, it's something I've always wanted to do. And now I've done that." Australia is the 13th country in which Woods has won an individual event, but his only success in Africa was the shared Presidents Cup in 2003.

Woods, who had not been to Melbourne since the 1998 Presidents Cup, opened with 66 to share the lead, then pulled clear with a 68. But a poor third round of 72, when he struggled with his driving and on the greens, meant he was back in a tie for the lead with Greg Chalmers and James Nitties. But three birdies in the first six holes of the fourth round put him clear again, and his only blemish was a bogey at the 13th. Birdies at the 12th and 15th helped him to a 68 for 14-under-par 274 total. Chalmers finished two shots back, with Francois Delamontagne sharing third place to retain his European Tour card.

"I got a 'W,' that was the goal this week," said Woods. "It was a great day today. All the guys have raved about this golf course and I understand why. I enjoy all the sandbelt courses, really, because it brings back shot-making, something that we don't see enough of in the States. It was one of those things where you had to make some birdies early, and I was able to do that and I kept it going for most of the day."

Cellarbrations NSW PGA Championship
Wollogong, New South Wales
Winner: Aaron Townsend

Aaron Townsend became one of the few players to hold both of the main titles in New South Wales when he won the Cellarbrations NSW PGA Championship at Wollongong almost exactly a year after claiming the NSW Open, then a Von Nida Tour event. Townsend went into the defense of that crown with the boost of a three-stroke victory over Scott Arnold and Michael Wright. Townsend came from one behind Wright with a closing round of 66 to finish at 21-under-par 259, while Wright finished with 70 and Arnold a 66.

Townsend holed a string of important putts, just as he had done in the second round when he equaled the course record with a nine-under 61. Twice the round was interrupted by weather delays, the first after the 28-year-old had started with six birdies in a row, the second when he faced a 35-foot eagle putt at the 17th. He returned to the course and two-putted for a birdie and then parred the last.

"To go into the defense of my NSW Open title after this win certainly gives me plenty of confidence. I feel my game is solid and I played well all week here so I'm looking forward to it," said Townsend, who had focused on playing in Japan over the previous two years. "Winning events at home certainly shows that you have the game to do well overseas. I really enjoyed myself this week, the course was playing well and it was a great tournament."

NSW Open
Hunter Valley, New South Wales
Winner: Leigh McKechnie

Leigh McKechnie, 36, won the NSW Open to claim his first title on the PGA of Australasia at the Vintage Golf Resort, Hunter Valley. With rounds of 70, 72, 70, 69 for three-under-par 281, McKechnie finished one stroke ahead of James Nitties. "I am just delighted," he said. "With the conditions the way they were today I knew I had a chance, but to actually win is unbelievable. I had no idea of what was happening. I saw my name on the leaderboard when I was on the 15th, but I didn't see any numbers."

Overnight leader Jason Norris, the 2007 champion, struggled in the difficult conditions, dropping eight shots on the front nine to throw the tournament wide open. He finished with 79. Beginning the final round seven shots in arrears, McKechnie made a steady start before making birdie on the toughest hole on the course, the par-three eighth, by holing his shot from the greenside bunker. With birdies on three of the last six holes, including on the 18th, McKechnie posted the score to catch, and Nitties, with a 76, fell one short. Scott Arnold fired the day's low round with a five-under 66 to finish third.

Australian Open
Sydney, New South Wales
Winner: Adam Scott

Adam Scott won for the first time on home soil after surviving a late scare to win the Australian Open by five strokes at the NSW Club and ending a poor season on a high note. So poor was the 29-year-old's form in 2009 that he missed 10 of 19 cuts on the PGA Tour in America and was a surprise wild card selection for the International Presidents Cup team by captain Greg Norman. After lifting the Stonehaven Cup on the 18th green, Norman, a five-time winner, was the first person Scott sought out for a congratulatory hug.

Stuart Appleby was the runner-up after opening with two rounds of 66. Scott, six behind before embarking on 29 holes on Saturday, had rounds of 68, 66 and 67 to lead by two going into the final round. The advantage was wiped out at the first, but then Scott led by seven with six holes to play. However, bogeys at the 13th, 14th and 16th let Appleby back into it, but a par-birdie finish saw Scott home safely. He closed with a 72 for 15-under 273, Appleby with 75–278.

"I'm so proud to be a national champion of your own country," Scott said. "It's the pinnacle really. Just thinking of the names on that trophy, I'm so happy to be on there. It's something I will treasure forever.

"Over the last few years there was a lot of coverage about me not winning down here but playing so well everywhere else. I always thought I'd get my chance. It's so bizarre this game, off the back of such a bad year I finally play good enough to win down here. It's a crazy game.

"This week was really good. I stuck with it and worked hard today. I made some great putts through the round which gave me a bit of a buffer, which I needed coming in. I feel like I've been working really hard and it pays off. You've got to stick with it.

"Greg and I have a fairly close relationship and obviously he's a big supporter of mine and I wish I could have played this well for him at the Presidents Cup. He's my hero. I've said that all along and he's been so generous to me with so many things and countless bits of advice on the game."

Australian PGA Championship
Coolum Beach, Queensland
Winner: Robert Allenby

A late decision to play in the Australian PGA Championship, which required a sponsor's invitation, was vindicated as Robert Allenby took the Kirkwood Cup for the fourth time. It was his second victory in successive weeks after Allenby skipped the Australian Open to win the Nedbank Golf Challenge in South Africa, which ended a four-year victory drought.

Allenby had two rounds of 66 over the weekend at the revamped Coolum course as the 37-year-old converted a one-stroke lead with a round to play into a four-stroke victory over Scott Strange and John Senden. Allenby was flawless on the final day, with birdie-twos coming at the second and sixth holes, birdie-fours at the 12th and 15th holes, and a birdie-three at the 17th as he finished on 14-under 270.

Allenby was again wearing a pink shirt on Sunday in honor of his mother, Sylvia, who died of breast cancer at the start of the year. "It's nice to win with the pink shirt on, that's for sure," Allenby said. "This year pink was always my last-day shirt and it was always in honor of my mother. Throughout the year I've had a couple of chances to win tournaments in America and in Europe and just haven't come through because I've let too many emotions get in the way of things. It's been a very tough year, but to come out on top last week and this week has been absolutely fantastic. It's definitely going to be fantastic for my career, it's just the little bit that's been missing.

"I did what I had to do, from the first hole to the last hole. I knew I had some very, very tough competitors behind me and I had a lot of respect for them. So I tried to just pace myself, I tried to hit as many fairways as I could, I tried to hit as many greens as I could. And that's what I did all day, I just felt totally in control on every shot."

11. African Tours

Anders Hansen became the first European to win the Order of Merit on the Sunshine Tour with an impressively consistent campaign on his visits to the southern hemisphere. It helped that the Dane won the opening event of the year at the Joburg Open, despite only just making the cut, for his third victory on the European Tour. Previously, Hansen's successes had both come at Wentworth as a double winner at the PGA Championship.

But having got a taste for victory away from the headquarters of the European Tour, Hansen returned to South Africa and won the Vodacom Championship to give himself a virtually unassailable lead on the money list. The 39-year-old made sure with third-place finishes in both of the big end-of-season events at the Alfred Dunhill Championship and the South African Open. Given that he was sixth in his only other appearance on the Sunshine Tour, his consistency across the year was remarkable, while back in Europe he finished the inaugural Race to Dubai in 24th place on the money list.

Charl Schwartzel, a former three-time winner of the Order of Merit, was the runner-up, ahead of Darren Fichardt and Jaco Van Zyl, both of whom won three times during the year, as did Brandon Pieters. Another successful visitor was Canada's Graham DeLaet, who took rookie of the year honors. Schwartzel did not win in 2009, having won in Europe the year previously, but he too showed consistent form but was too often let down on the greens. At the Alfred Dunhill Championship it almost all came together as five birdies in the last seven holes took him one behind Pablo Martin.

The two European Tour events at the end of the year brought victories for two more Europeans, but both Martin and Richie Ramsay, like Schwartzel before them, showed how a great amateur career could be converted to professional success. Martin was the first amateur to win on the European Tour at the Portuguese Open in 2007 but had then suffered as a professional before a 63 in the second round at the Alfred Dunhill at Leopard Creek. The 23-year-old Spaniard hung on over the weekend and was in contention the following week at the South African Open, but had to give way to Ramsay, who became the first Scot to win the U.S. Amateur Championship for 108 years in 2006.

Internationally there were victories for Rory Sabbatini at the Byron Nelson Classic in America, for James Kingston at the Mercedes-Benz Championship in Germany and for James Kamte at the Asian Tour International. Three South Africans made the International team for the Presidents Cup but there were questions marks against each of Ernie Els, Retief Goosen and Tim Clark, who finished the year at 17th, 19th and 37th on the World Ranking. Els missed out on a victory somewhere in the world for the first time since 1990. He went into the last round of his last event just two behind the unheralded Martin at Leopard Creek, but closed with a 77 and again found water at the notorious 18th, which had destroyed his hopes in the same event two years earlier.

Goosen, who turned 40, won the inaugural Africa Open early in the year and produced a brilliant putting display on treacherous greens at Innisbrook to win the Transitions Championship on the PGA Tour. But too often during the year he struggled with his putting despite some superb form from tree-to-green, a frustrating combination. For Clark, that maiden win in America again proved agonizingly elusive, particularly when losing a playoff at the Crowne Plaza Invitational at Colonial.

Joburg Open
Johannesburg, South Africa
Winner: Anders Hansen

Anders Hansen's third victory on the European Tour was the first not to be achieved at the tour's headquarters at Wentworth. The 38-year-old Dane, who won the prestigious PGA Championship in both 2002 and 2007, started 2009 in fine form by winning the Joburg Open, an event co-sanctioned with the Sunshine Tour. After a slow start on the first day, Hansen eventually birdied the final hole to win by one stroke over Andrew McLardy at Royal Johannesburg and Kensington.

Hansen's first hole of the year ended with a double bogey. After a bogey at the next he was three over par, and an opening round of 71 left him eight strokes off the lead. But a 68 and then a 64 in the third round left Hansen one behind the trio of leaders, McLardy, David Drysdale and Charl Schwartzel. Playing in the penultimate group on the final day, Hansen played a brilliant front nine of 31 strokes to take the lead. After a birdie at the third, four followed in a row from the sixth.

A dropped shot at the 12th was his only blip, but otherwise the birdies dried up. McLardy put together a run of three birdies in a row from the start of the back nine and the pair were tied at 14 under par as Hansen arrived at the 18th. There he hit his second shot at the par-five to 25 feet. Though he missed the eagle putt, Hansen holed out for birdie from three feet. McLardy, in the group behind, then needed a birdie to tie but drove into the trees and could only make a five. McLardy closed with a 68 to Hansen's 66 which left the Dane at 15-under 269. Drysdale's 69 left the Scot in third place, two strokes behind, with English rookie Danny Willett sharing fourth place with Schwartzel and Tyrone van Aswegen.

Defending champion Richard Sterne could not quite make it three victories in a row after winning the Alfred Dunhill Championship and the South African Open at the end of 2008, while Retief Goosen enlivened the final day with an albatross at the 18th, holing a three iron from 216 yards in an otherwise disappointing round of 74.

"I think it means a lot to win," Hansen said, "especially after the first day, where the first two holes I started double bogey-bogey and was thinking, 'what is this?' But I turned that round around and got off to a flying start on the second day. Today I played really nice on the front nine and on the last I hit a great second shot. The two-putt was enough, so it's great."

Africa Open
East London, South Africa
Winner: Retief Goosen

About the only thing Retief Goosen did wrong on the final day of the Africa Open at East London was to three-putt the 18th green for a closing bogey. But it was not to prove a costly mistake as Goosen simply won the tournament by one stroke instead of two. Sharing second place were Darren Clarke, Darren Fichardt, Michael Hoey and Branden Grace. "I hit a fairly good putt, good line, the first time and it came up short," said Goosen of the events on the 18th green.

"I thought the next one was a right-edge putt, but it didn't turn and lipped out, and then I knew I was going to have a playoff. I was very surprised that none of the other guys got to 21 under, so I was lucky with that mistake."

Goosen's putting has often concerned him of late, but for 17 holes of the final round that was not the case. Four birdies on the front nine took him into the lead ahead of the James Kingston and Clarke, who had topped the leaderboard with a round to play. Early on the back nine putting was the least of Goosen's worries as he twice nearly holed out from the fairway to tap-in birdies. The bogey at the last meant a closing 65, after earlier efforts of 66, 70 and 66, and a total of 21-under-par 267.

Grace, the 21-year-old South African, charged into contention with a 65, while Hoey achieved a 66. Fichardt compiled a 68 and Clarke, pressing for victory, a 70, just missing a chip shot he needed to hole to force a playoff. Kingston, after a triple bogey at the 14th, slipped to a 73 and sixth place.

It was Goosen's 10th victory on the Sunshine Tour and his first in his homeland since winning the South African Open in 2005. "This year I feel I am a little more prepared for the game than over the last couple of years," he said. "I'm probably the fittest now that I've been in the last five years."

Dimension Data Pro-Am
Sun City, South Africa
Winner: Deane Pappas

With lightning in the air, Deane Pappas rushed up the 18th hole at the Gary Player Country Club at Sun City and got off the course as quickly as possible by holing a 20-foot downhill putt for a birdie. The putt made no difference to the result of the Dimension Data Pro-Am other than to confirm an eight-stroke victory for the 41-year-old South African. It did, however, clinch victory in the team event for Pappas and his amateur partner, Murray Winckler, a former international squash player. "It was a good thing we ran up the 18th," Pappas said. "I didn't have time to over-think anything."

It was only the second victory on the Sunshine Tour for Pappas, who now lives in Florida. His only other triumph came at the South African

PGA Championship in 2001. Brilliant early rounds of 65, 66 and 69 had put Pappas six ahead going into the final round. A closing 68, including a birdie at the 16th as well as at the last, left him at 20-under-par 268. Defending champion James Kamte made a brave bid to retain his title with a closing 67 to finish at 12 under, but was always too far behind. Dawie Van der Walt also had a 67 to take third place, but Martin Maritz fell from second to a tie for fifth after a 74.

Pappas survived an early scare at the fifth when he drove into trouble, but a two iron, a wedge to six feet and a single putt helped him save par. "Around this course, things can go badly wrong," he said. "You stand on every tee box knowing you must hit the fairway, because often from the rough you have no shot at all." Pappas paid tribute to a fellow player for help with his game. "I got a lesson from Hendrik Buhrmann at last week's Africa Open for my irons, and that really transformed my game," said Pappas.

Nashua Masters
Port Edward, Natal
Winner: Darren Fichardt

Going into the final round of the Nashua Masters at the Wild Coast Sun Country Club, Darren Fichardt lamented: "I really must try and close the deal." After two close misses in the previous two weeks, including a runner-up spot at the Africa Open, the 33-year-old from Pretoria did just that. Fichardt came from one behind the overnight leader and defending champion, Marc Cayeux, to win by one after holing from 15 feet on the final green.

Fichardt compiled rounds of 66, 67, 65 and 65 to finish at 17-under 263 compared to Cayeux's efforts of 66, 66, 65 and 67. The pair were tied until the 14th where the Zimbabwean suffered a double bogey. But he hit back with birdies at the next two holes, while Fichardt had to birdie the 16th to stay one ahead. At the 18th, Cayeux kept the pressure up by putting his approach to two feet, which would have forced a playoff but for Fichardt converting his birdie effort from 15 feet.

"It felt like a 20-meter putt," said Fichardt, who claimed his seventh Sunshine Tour victory and his first since the 2006 Highveld Classic. "The short stick finally started working. I actually started losing my putting stroke three years ago, and the rest of my swing went with it. But I made some changes, took a bit more time over my putts, drew a line on the ball to line it up properly, and it's slowly been coming back."

Fichardt and Cayeux separated themselves from the field with Branden Grace, after a 62, Tyrone van Aswegen and Jaco Van Zyl sharing third place, four strokes behind Cayeux.

Vodacom Championship
Pretoria, South Africa
Winner: Anders Hansen

Anders Hansen collected his second title of the season in South African by winning the Vodacom Championship at Pretoria. After winning in Johannesburg at the start of the year, the Dane returned here to win by four strokes over Charl Schwartzel and Canada's Graham DeLaet. Hansen started slowly with scores of 69 and 70 but then got himself into contention with a 66 in the third round. He went into the final round two strokes behind DeLaet and one behind Schwartzel, and a closing 65, seven under par, left him clear at 18-under 270.

Hansen established a lead on the front nine but saw his advantage trimmed when he could only save par on the 13th while his challengers claimed birdies. However, Hansen responded with birdies at the next two holes, hitting approaches to two feet and three feet respectively. He polished off the day with birdies at the last two holes. "I had a bit of a hiccup at the 12th, with a terrible drive and a terrible second shot," Hansen said. "It was one of those holes I expected to birdie but saved par, and then the next, which is a difficult hole, I birdied, and got another at 14, so then things were going my way."

Having established a large lead on the Order of Merit, Hansen added: "It is an achievement to win any order of merit, so I would be stupid not to try and win this one." Schwartzel closed with 70 and DeLaet with 71 to finish one ahead of Charl Coetzee and Titch Moore.

Telkom PGA Championship
Johannesburg, South Africa
Winner: Jaco Van Zyl

Jaco Van Zyl visited some unusual parts of the Woodmead course at the Country Club of Johannesburg, but still managed to win the Telkom PGA Championship, the last main event of the summer season on the Sunshine Tour. Van Zyl found water at the 17th but managed to hit his third shot close and save par. At the par-five 18th, he hardly finished in champion style. He approached the hole at 17 under, alongside the clubhouse leaders Graham DeLaet, who closed with 64, and Trevor Fisher, Jr., who finished with 65. Van Zyl needed a birdie for a 66 to win by one stroke, but his second shot faded to the right and ended up in a bed of roses.

"That final hole was a real tester for me," he said. "The wind was behind us for the first three days, but I knew I couldn't make it in two today. I just told myself to hit it anywhere but right. I had no idea how bad it was until my caddie said he hoped it hadn't gone into the roses." When Van Zyl got up to his ball, he found there was still a route to the green. "I knelt down and saw there was a V-shape in the hedge in front of me," he said, "but I would have to keep the ball low or it would get caught in a rose bush." His recovery came out fast but checked on the third bounce and left him with a 15-footer for the victory. "I practice those 15-footers all the time," said Van Zyl. "Ernie Els said he practiced them to win majors; I practiced them to win the Telkom PGA."

DeLaet was one of the first players to congratulate the man from Pretoria. "That was a hell of an up-and-down," he said. It was the third victory for Van Zyl but the biggest of his career and the last on the summer schedule. It also came just one day before his 30th birthday.

Vodacom Business Origins of Golf - Bloemfontein
Bloemfontein, South Africa
Winner: Trevor Fisher, Jr.

A fortnight after swapping his clubs for caddieing duties in America at a World Golf Championship event, Trevor Fisher, Jr. collected his fourth title on the Sunshine Tour by winning the opening event of the winter season at the Vodacom Business Origins of Golf at Bloemfontein. Fisher, 29, tied for second place in the last event of the summer swing at the Telkom PGA Championship, but his duties in March were to caddie for Thomas Aiken at the CA Championship at Doral where his compatriot was thrilled with a top-10 finish.

Fisher returned home for this three-day event but entered the final round six behind Jaco Van Zyl, who was looking for back-to-back Sunshine wins. But a few early bogeys let others into the championship, including Willie van der Merwe, who equaled the tournament-best with a 64 to post 14 under. He would finish tied for second, his best ever finish, alongside Jean Hugo, who closed with 70. Van Zyl was fourth after a disappointing 73, but Fisher finished at 15-under 201 after a 65.

There were birdies at the third, fourth and fifth holes to get Fisher into contention. Then he birdied the 10th and 13th holes but then nearly blew it with a double bogey at the 15th. Others were stumbling, too, as van der Merwe double-bogeyed the 17th and Van Zyl, who had got himself back into the lead with three to play, found water at both the 16th and 17th holes. Fisher still needed to produce some dramatics at the 18th, hitting his second at the par-five to 18 feet and then holing for an eagle. "I just knew I had to sink it," said Fisher. "When I caddied for Thomas Aiken in Florida it really helped my thought process this week. The top players mean business every time they play, and I went out there with that focus this week."

SAA Pro-Am Invitational - Prince's Grant
KwaZulu-Natal, South Africa
Winner: Adilson da Silva

Adilson da Silva won his first Sunshine Tour event in two years when he took the SAA Pro-Am Invitational at the Prince's Grant Golf Estate. He birdied four of the last nine holes to pull one shot clear of his pursuers, his final-round four-under 68 giving him a 13-under total of 203 and his first victory since the Vodacom event at Fancourt in 2007. It was a fifth

Sunshine Tour victory in all for the 37-year-old Brazilian. He beat Anton Haig and overnight leader Darren Fichardt into second place, while Jbe' Kruger and Keith Horne shared fourth, one stroke further back on 205.

Despite a slow start, once he got things rolling, there was no stopping da Silva, a former resident of Prince's Grant and very familiar with all the course's twists and turns. "After nine holes, I was very disappointed, especially with a bogey on the first," he said. "And when I got to the back nine, I was really down on myself. But somehow, I got myself together again. I know the course, and I know I can go low on it.

"When I holed a birdie putt on the 10th, it gave me a bit of confidence," he added. He also birdied the 11th and 15th too, and when he got another on the 16th, he hit the front. "Although it's two years since I've won anything, I've been working pretty hard now, and with the support of my coaching team, my sponsors, and my wife, it's paying off," he said.

Kruger raced home on the back nine in 31 for a 64 to break the two-day-old course record set by Darryn Lloyd in the first round.

Samsung Royal Swazi Sun Open
Mbabane, Swaziland
Winner: Jaco Van Zyl

Jaco Van Zyl outpaced the opposition with nine birdies in his final round of the Samsung Royal Swazi Sun Open to finish with 65 points, with Zimbabwe's T.C. Charamba and Tyrone van Aswegen sharing second with 53 at the Royal Swazi Spa Country Club course. Titch Moore finished in fourth with 47 points, while Tyrone Ferreira was fifth with 46.

The tournament was played in a modified-Stableford format in which players earn eight points for an albatross (double eagle), five for an eagle, and two for a birdie and pars count for nothing, but one point is deducted per bogey and three for a double bogey or worse. But had it been played as a stroke-play event, he would have finished at 31 under par, having made just three bogeys all week — two in the second round and one in the third.

It was Van Zyl's fourth win on the Sunshine Tour and his second of the year after taking the Telkom PGA Championship. "My last couple of wins have always been a grind towards the end, and I have managed to pull it through by one, or win in a playoff, or with a 20-foot putt on the last," he said. "I've always wondered what if it went the other way. So this was the first really convincing win and it really is a good feeling."

Although he did not claim an eagle all week, Van Zyl did chalk up the birdies relentlessly. On the last day he began with three birdies in his first four holes, and five in the opening nine, before easing home with four more on the way in, including an eight-footer on the 18th. The win came after missing the cut the previous week. "This game bites you as soon as you think you're on top," he said.

"It was the first cut I missed in years. So I have to come out again next week and do my best and compete. I'm making a point of being in the gym every day, being out on the range, working on the short game. Now, if I get over a shot, I know I have been working on it for a lot of hours, whereas before, I'd much rather go hang-gliding or fly model airplanes and just pitch up at the tournament and play."

Nashua Golf Challenge
Sun City, South Africa
Winner: Doug McGuigan

Doug McGuigan kept calm on a difficult final day at the Nashua Golf Challenge to claim victory by two strokes over Tyrone van Aswegen. It was the 38-year-old's fourth victory on the Sunshine Tour and began with a 66 over the Gary Player Country Club course at Sun City. It was his first bogey-free round on the track in over 20 years and "probably the round of my life," he said. He then added a 70 on the Lost City course in the second round to share the lead with Christiaan Basson and Neil Schietekat, who had a 63 at Lost City.

But conditions were not good on the Gary Player course for the final round. Schietekat had a 76 and Basson 77, while McGuigan's 73, one over par, kept him in front, while van Aswegen had a 74. The only player to break par was Jaco Van Zyl, who hit six birdies on the front nine in a 69. Van Zyl shared third place with Schietekat, James Kamte and Oliver Bekker.

McGuigan had three birdies and four bogeys, including back-to-back drops at the 14th and 15th, but kept his nerve. "I've been playing nicely the past few weeks. I just haven't been putting it together, and my frustration levels have been more than I can handle," said McGuigan. "This week, I've managed to keep it together and made a conscious effort not to get upset after a bogey, and it helps. On this golf course, anything around level par is obviously well played. I figured if I could get it to level for the day, then anyone was going to struggle to catch me."

Vodacom Business Origins of Golf - Pretoria
Pretoria, South Africa
Winner: Brandon Pieters

Brandon Pieters suffered all day in pursuit of his maiden victory on the Sunshine Tour, but with a nervous two-foot birdie putt at the 18th the 33-year-old South African won the Vodacom Business Origins of Golf at Pretoria Country Club. This was Pieters's 16th season in professional golf, but he could not have played better as he achieved a wire-to-wire win.

Two eagles in three holes helped Pieters to an opening 65 and he followed up with a 67 on the second day, in which he did not drop a shot. He led by three overnight and extended that lead to five after three holes. But then he missed from three feet for a birdie on the fifth and from five feet for another on the sixth. At the next he went over the green, chipped and three-putted for a double bogey as a wobble set in. At the ninth he needed to scramble for a par, but he still lost the lead to Darren Fichardt's eagle.

But Fichardt took a triple bogey at the 11th, and although Pieters dropped a shot there, he was back in the lead. He birdied the 12th and then reeled off five pars as the tension mounted. Fichardt was not finished and chipped in for an eagle at the 18th, leaving Pieters having to get his birdie-four, which he did. A 72 left Pieters at 12-under 204, one ahead of Fichardt and three ahead of Dean Lambert.

"I told myself that it was just another round, and to just play one shot at a time, but it's not that easy," Pieters said. "I think I got a number in my head, and I made the mistake of trying to chase the number. There I was thinking that I had two putts for the win at the last, and then Darren sank that chip. I really battled with my putting out there, but it was great to hole that one at the end."

Lombard Insurance Classic
Mbabane, Swaziland
Winner: Peter Karmis

Peter Karmis became the first player ever to score 59 on the Sunshine Tour, and in the process, naturally enough, won the Lombard Insurance Classic at Royal Swazi Sun Country Club. Karmis celebrated his 28th birthday a few days early with his second career victory, the first coming in the same tournament two years earlier. Rounds of 65 and 74 left Karmis four behind second-round leader Bradford Vaughan. But after eagling the fifth hole in the third and final round, Karmis was on a charge to victory.

He had three eagles in all, the others coming at the 12th and 13th, holing out from the fairway at the latter to help keep his putting stats down to 23 for the day. His only long putt of the round was a 20-footer at the 15th for a birdie, which was followed by two more at the 16th and 17th holes to get to 13 under par for the round. At the 17th he very nearly holed out from a greenside bunker for what would have been a fourth eagle of the round. He then held his nerve to par the last, the shakes only setting in when he tried to sign his card.

"I'm speechless right now, I don't know what to say," Karmis said. "I tried not to think about shooting 59, but when I got the eagle on five, I knew there was a special round happening. I tried to play it a little bit conservatively, because that's the way I need to play in order to shoot a good round. In the end, I just hit it close so many times, that I couldn't help scoring low."

The 59 put Karmis at 18-under-par 198 total and four ahead of Jaco Van Zyl, who closed with 66, while Jbe' Kruger was third a further three strokes adrift.

Playing partner Shaun Norris, who finished tied for fourth, said: "I played pretty decently, but that was just phenomenal. He never looked like faltering, and there were no fluke shots in the round either."

Vodacom Business Origins of Golf - Fancourt
George, South Africa
Winner: Brandon Pieters

Brandon Pieters claimed a second consecutive victory on the Vodacom Business Origins of Golf Tour when he won the Fancourt leg of the series by a single stroke. Pieters closed with 69 to win the shortened event on three-under-par 141, one clear of Clinton Whitelaw, who also signed for a final round of 69. Pieters's win followed his maiden victory as a professional the previous month in Pretoria.

"This was a lot easier than the first one," said Pieters, who started the final round two strokes off the shared lead of Attie Schwartzel and Callie Swart. Schwartzel closed with a 75 to finish tied fifth on one over par, while Swart signed for a 73 to claim third on one under. Pieters started well with two birdies in his first four holes and then opened his back nine with two birdies in three holes from the 10th.

That gave him a one-shot cushion playing the par-five 18th. Playing ahead of him, Whitelaw birdied the last to make a bid for a first victory since his triumph in the 1997 Moroccan Open. But Pieters was afforded a comfortable par putt at the 18th for the title in a week in which the tournament had to be reduced to 36 holes because of some extreme weather.

"You know, we had a bit of everything this week, even snow. So it was good to finish with a win," said Pieters. "I had set myself a target of 68 today, and I missed a couple of five-footers for birdie, which upset me a bit. But if three under was good enough to win, then so be it. My Pretoria win was still fresh in my mind, so I know I can compete at this level. I've set a goal for myself for the next two years, and hopefully I can reach that."

Suncoast Classic
Durban, South Africa
Winner: Louis de Jager

Louis de Jager won both the stroke play and match play South African Amateur titles in 2007, but had to wait until the Suncoast Classic in 2009 to win for the first time as a professional. Even then he had to sweat a little on the final hole as his tee shot landed against a building in an unplayable position, but he held it together to win by two strokes. He got relief from his position, but the free drop was unplayable and he had to take another drop with a penalty to get it onto the green for three.

But with Chris Swanepoel three shots behind him in second, he had the luxury of knowing he could double bogey and still win. He made sure of his two-putt for bogey and punched the air in delight. Thanks to a 71 he finished on nine-under 207, two clear of Swanepoel (71) and three ahead of Adilson da Silva (69), Titch Moore (71), T.C. Charamba (71) and Jean Hugo (73). "It was something I was aiming for this year," said de Jager, "to get a win, and now that it's come, it feels great."

His victory was the product of some steady putting throughout the tournament and calmness in the face of the pressure of leading a tournament on his own for the first time in his young career. "I was nervous all day," he said, "because it's been some time since I have been in a position to win anything."

He was playing with Hugo and Ryan Cairns, who started the day one behind him, but Cairns had to endure a horrible start to his round and finished with a three-over 75 in a share of ninth. It certainly helped de Jager that his playing partners were not putting him under any more pressure: "I was looking at the leaderboards, though, to make sure I knew what was happening around me."

Vodacom Business Origins of Golf - Erinvale
Somerset West, South Africa
Winner: Jaco Ahlers

Advice from double defending Open champion Padraig Harrington on the practice range at Turnberry helped Jaco Ahlers to his first victory as a professional at the Erinvale leg of the Vodacom Business Origins of Golf Tour. After hearing the 26-year-old South African curse one wayward shot after another, Harrington told him: "One shot at a time." It was a way of saying Ahlers needed to keep his temper under control, to stay cool under pressure. After doing just that to beat Ulrich van den Berg in a playoff, he admitted the Irishman's intervention "definitely helped."

After day one's play was washed out due to torrential rain, reducing the event to 36 holes, Ahlers posted rounds of 64 and 71 for a nine-under-par 135 that was matched by van den Berg's 67-68. It was van den Berg who took control on the second and final day and birdied the 15th to go two ahead. But there was a two-shot swing at the 17th as van den Berg failed to get up and down from short of the green to take a bogey and then Ahlers holed from 25 feet for a birdie. "I just tried to get it close and I'm glad the hole jumped up in front of it," he said.

In the playoff Ahlers hit his approach to three feet and van den Berg to 12 feet but could not convert the birdie putt, leaving Ahlers to claim his first win after four years on tour.

Telkom PGA Pro-Am
Pretoria, South Africa
Winner: Jaco Van Zyl

Jaco Van Zyl completed his third win of the season and the double of winning the Telkom PGA Pro-Am to go with the Telkom PGA Championship, the biggest of his five career wins to date. Van Zyl cruised to a five-stroke victory with rounds of 68, 70 and 66 for a 12-under-par 204 total. He made seven birdies at Centurion on the final day and only dropped one shot, arriving at the 18th with the comfort of a four-shot cushion before collecting one final birdie.

Zimbabwe's T.C. Charamba finished in second place after a 68, while Jbe'

Major Champions

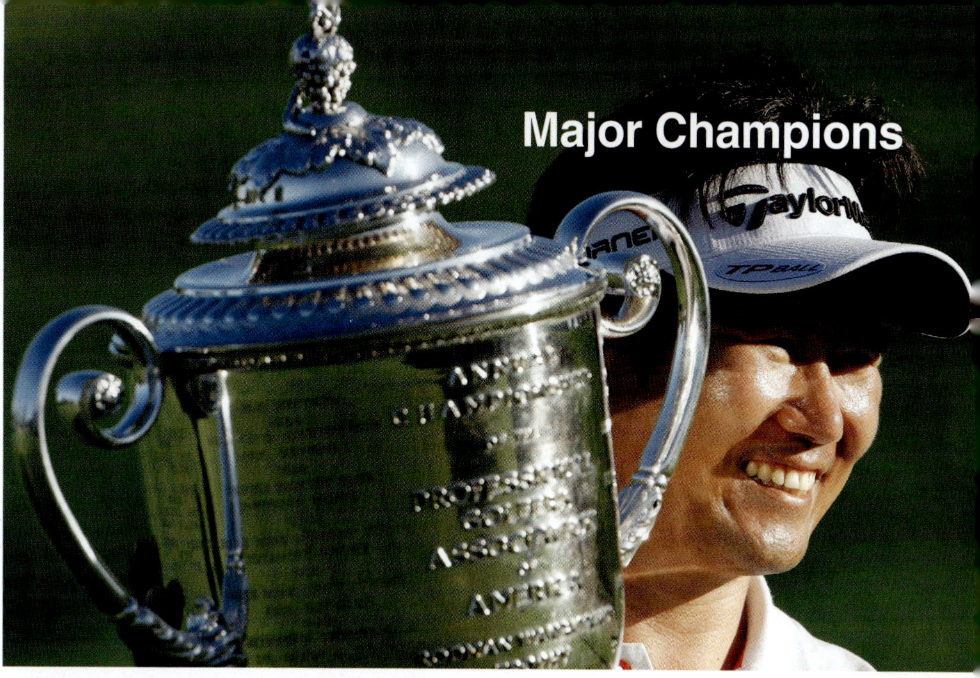

Streeter Lecka/Getty Images

Y.E. Yang overtook Tiger Woods to win the PGA Championship.

Andy Lyons/Getty Images

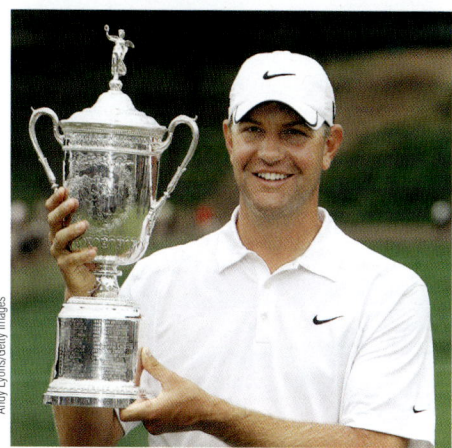

Lucas Glover, U.S. Open Championship

Jamie Squire/Getty Images

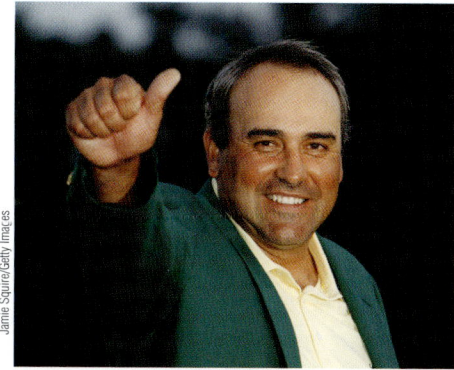

Angel Cabrera, Masters Tournament

David Cannon/Getty Images

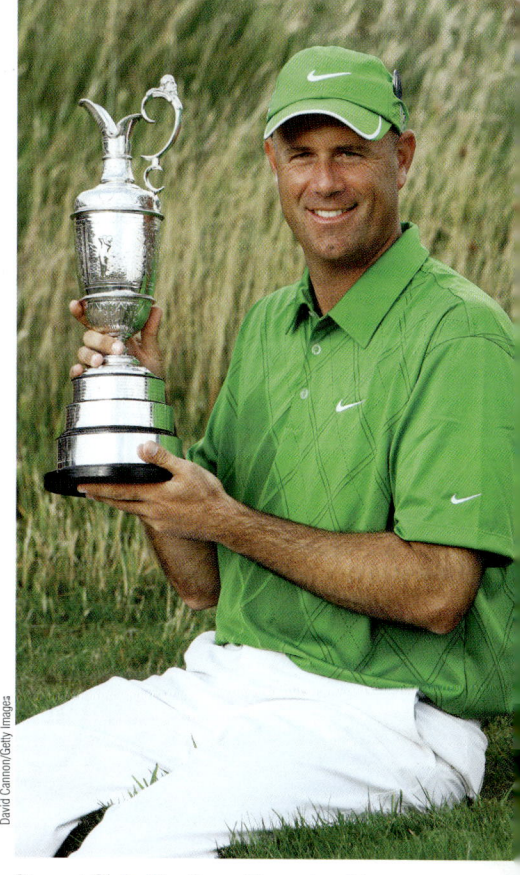

Stewart Cink, The Open Championship

Angel Cabrera won a playoff to became the first Argentine winner of the Masters Tournament.

Kenny Perry missed this chip on the first playoff hole.

Chad Campbell missed an 18-footer to win.

Phil Mickelson took fifth after his closing 67.

Shingo Katayama finished fourth.

A birdie on the 70th hole and two solid pars gave Lucas Glover a two-stroke victory.

David Duval shared the lead as late as the 16th.

Phil Mickelson had an eagle on the 13th.

Ricky Barnes's miss on 18 cost him second alone.

Ross Fisher missed on No. 18 to place fifth.

Caddie Frank Williams congratulated Stewart Cink after Cink won a four-hole playoff.

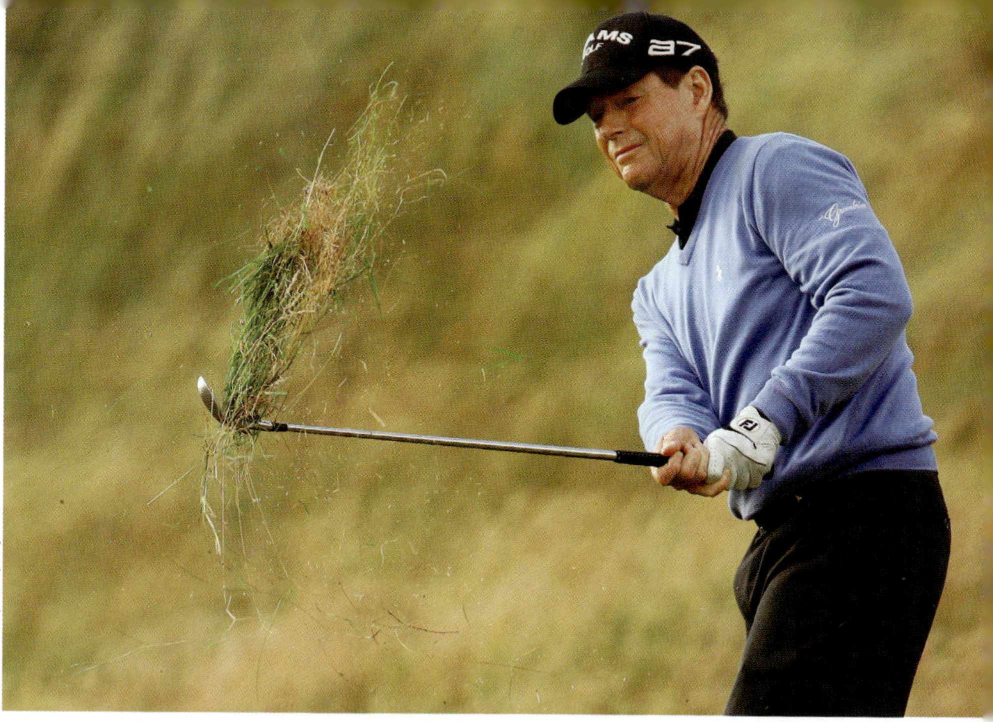

Andrew Redington/Getty Images

Tom Watson drove in the rough on the third playoff hole, taking seven to Cink's four.

Stuart Franklin/Getty Images

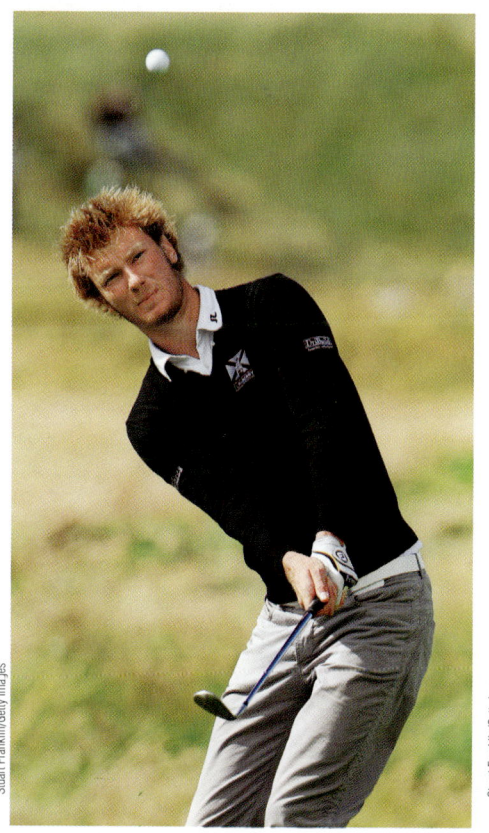

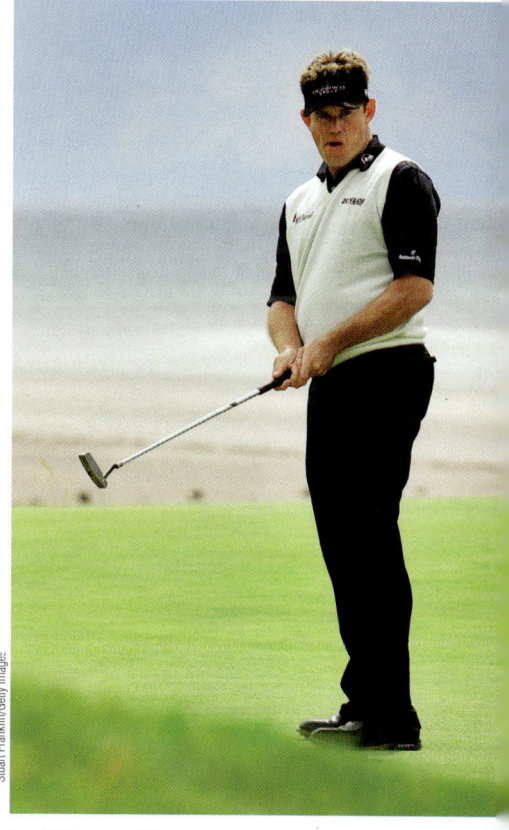

Chris Wood finished birdie-bogey to tie for third.

Stuart Franklin/Getty Images

Lee Westwood bogeyed three of the last four.

PGA Championship

Y.E. Yang became the first major championship winner from South Korea.

Tiger Woods shot 75 to place second.

Lee Westwood contended again.

Rory McIlroy shared third place.

Lucas Glover was fifth alone.

Presidents Cup

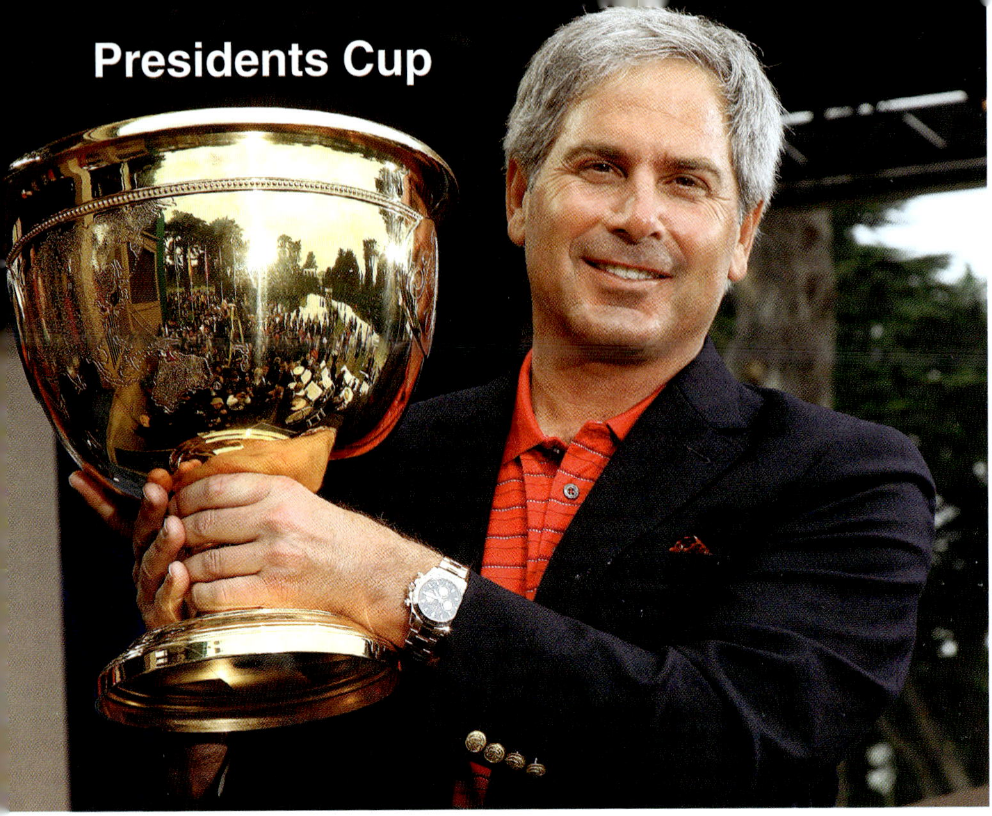

David Cannon/Getty Images

United States captain Fred Couples raised the Presidents Cup after a 19½ points to 14½ victory.

Harry How/Getty Images

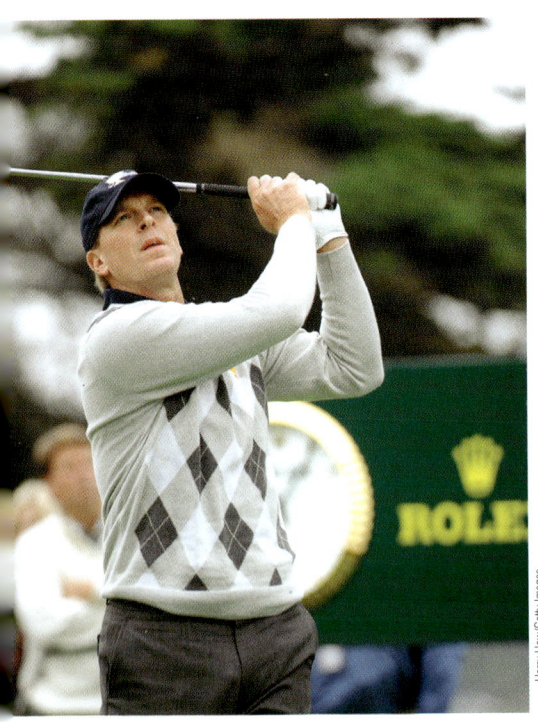

Steve Stricker was 4-1 after losing in singles.

Chris Condon/PGA TOUR

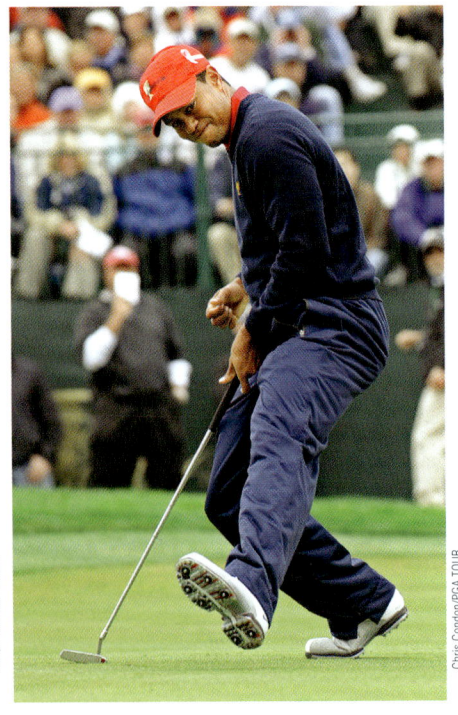

Tiger Woods had a perfect 5-0-0 record.

David Cannon/Getty Images

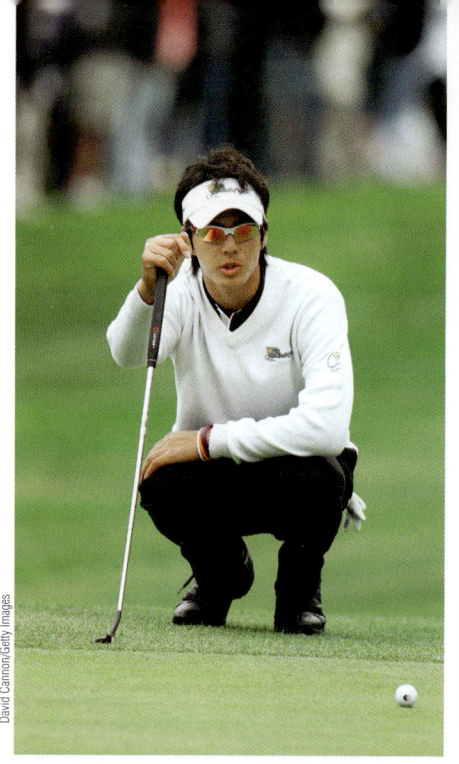

Ryo Ishikawa was an International star.

Chris Condon/PGA TOUR

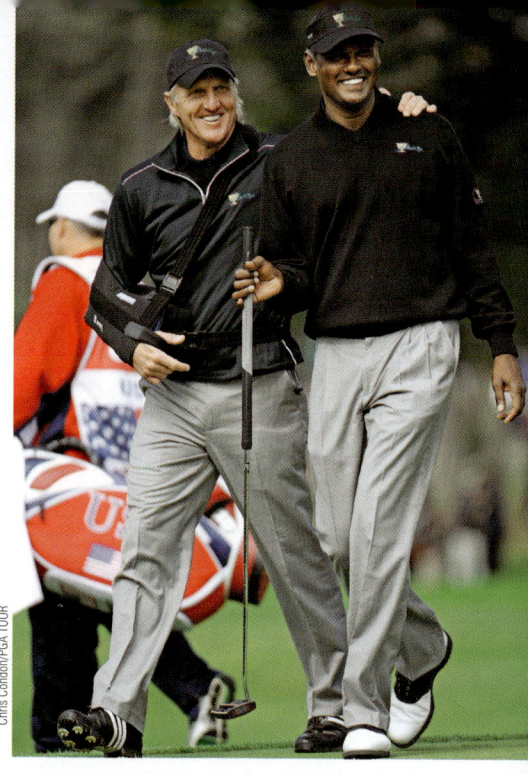

Greg Norman and points leader Vijay Singh.

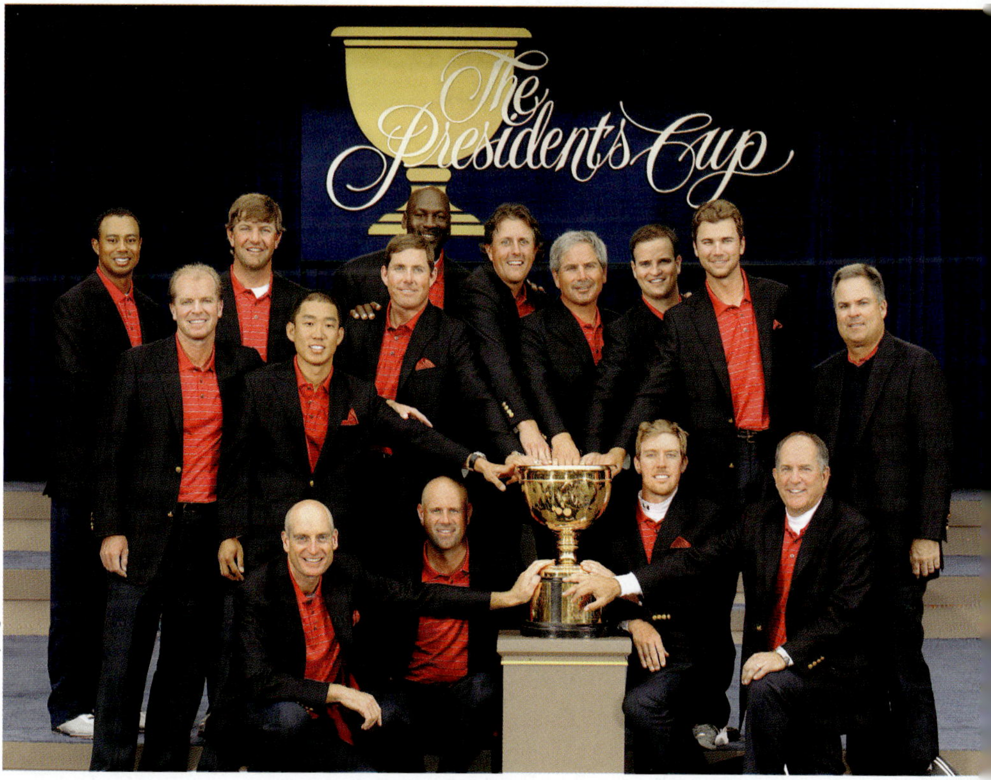

David Cannon/Getty Images

The American team won its third consecutive Presidents Cup against the Internationals.

Six victories on the PGA Tour left Tiger Woods in his customary place on top of the money list.

Scott Halleran/Getty Images

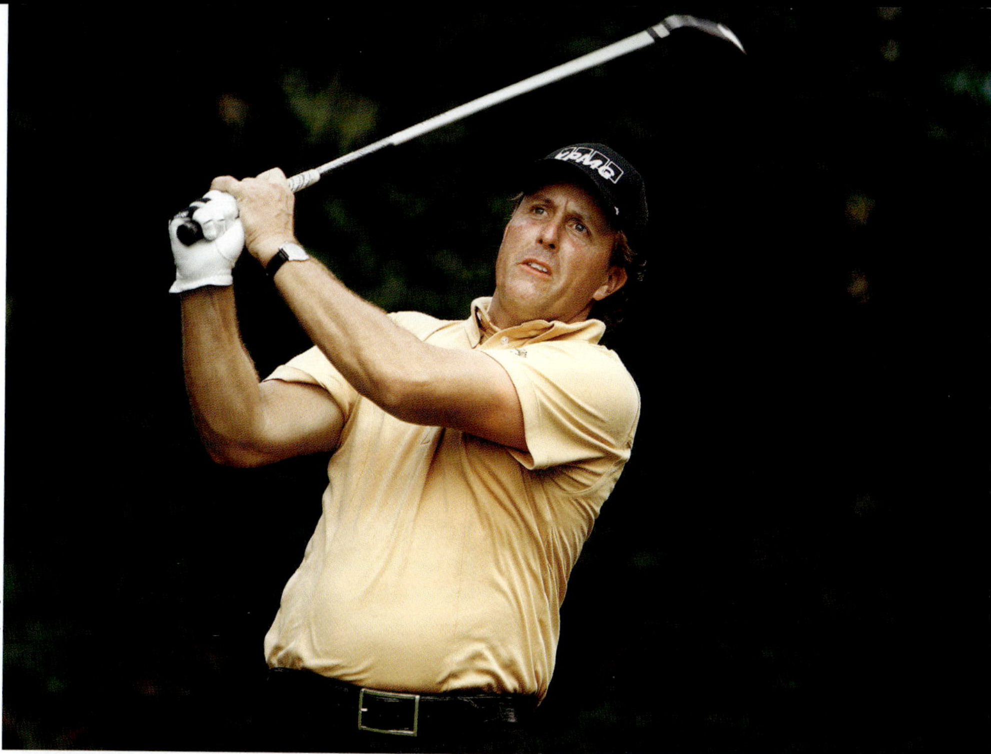

Phil Mickelson claimed his third victory of the year in The Tour Championship.

Michael Cohen/Getty Images

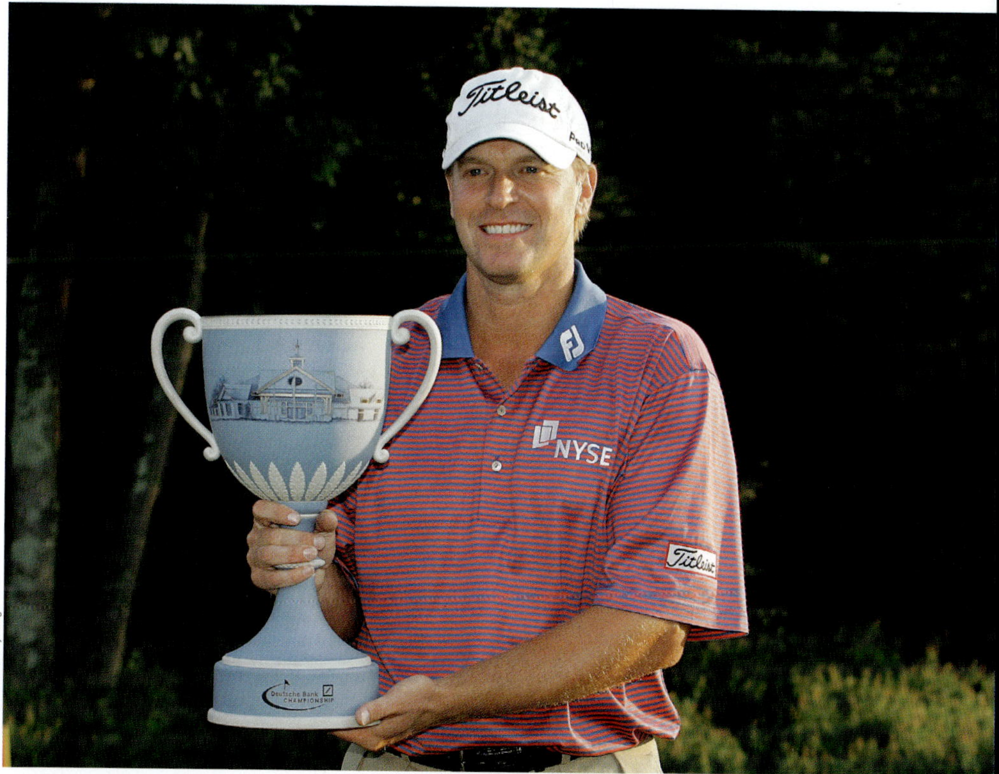

Steve Stricker earned his third 2009 victory in the Deutsche Bank Championship.

Sean O'Hair won at Quail Hollow.

Jim Furyk was seventh on the money list.

Paul Casey's three wins included the BMW PGA.

Zach Johnson claimed the Sony Open.

Geoff Ogilvy started with a win in Hawaii.

David Cannon/Getty Images

Lee Westwood won the Dubai World finale.

Richard Heathcote/Getty Images

Retief Goosen was 11th on the U.S. money list.

Junko Kimura/Getty Images

Ryo Ishikawa won four in Japan.

Ian Walton/Getty Images

Padraig Harrington was No. 6 in the world.

Martin Kaymer won in France and Scotland.

Henrik Stenson claimed The Players trophy.

Rory McIlroy was second in Europe.

Ross Fisher won the Volvo World Match Play.

Thongchai Jaidee won the Indonesia Open.

Kruger and second-round leader Tyrone Mordt shared third on six-under 210, with Desvonde Botes and Christiaan Basson sharing fifth on five-under 211.

"My last win was in Swaziland, which I pretty much wrapped up on 17, and it's not always great playing 16, 17 and 18 with a one-shot lead," Van Zyl said of the advantage he had built up by the stretch. His playing partners, Mordt and Louis Moolman, fell away with rounds of 73 and 74 respectively. Although Moolman finished nine strokes adrift, he had the consolation of a hole-in-one with an eight iron at the 17th hole.

"With due respect to the guys I was playing with, I knew they were less experienced than I am," said Van Zyl, "and I knew if I put the pedal to the metal early on, I could hold the upper hand. I've been in this position dozens of times. I might only have won four times before this, but I have learned how to handle myself and how to cope with the emotions."

Zambia Open
Ndola, Zambia
Winner: Jbe' Kruger

In a season in which he had collected five of his career 16 top-10s, Jbe' Kruger finally posted his maiden victory on the Sunshine Tour at the Zambia Open. Kruger produced a final round of six-under-par 67 at Ndola Golf Club to win by three over Titch Moore. "It's a big relief to finally win," he said, "because it feels as if I have been hanging on for such a long time."

Kruger turned in even-par 37 on the outward nine, but he sprinted away from the opposition with four birdies and an eagle-three on the way home to finish at 15-under-par 204. "The big thing on that inward nine was my putting," said Kruger. "When the putts started dropping, things started going my way."

His eagle came on the par-five 13th, which he also eagled in his first round. "I hit what was probably my best drive of the day, and then I had a five iron which I hit to about 10 feet," he said. "The putt was fast, downhill and left to right. The good thing about those is you don't have to hit them, and it went in on the inside right."

His final round was the best of the day and it put paid to the chances of overnight leader Neil Schietekat, who started out two shots clear of Kruger but battled his way to a four-over-par 77 for a share of 10th. "When I turned even for the day," said Kruger, "I knew I needed to make three or four under. And I started to sink putts: eight-footers on 10 and 11, and the eagle on 13 and another birdie on 14. That put the pressure on the other guys," he said.

Moore also finished fast, his four-under 69 lifting him into second place on his own, with Mark Murless's five-under 68 (which included a hole-in-one on the eighth) putting him in a share of third place with Ryan Tipping and Desvonde Botes. Defending champion Tyrone Ferreira finished with a two-under 71 to share sixth place with Jean Hugo, Bradford Vaughan and Merrick Bremner.

But it was all about Kruger, who credited his time this year on the Asian

Tour for his win. "It definitely made me mentally stronger," he said. "I learnt on those greens where it's difficult to putt to be patient."

SAA Pro-Am Invitational - Randpark
Johannesburg, South Africa
Winner: Ryan Tipping

Ryan Tipping, wearing black as he did in winning the club championship at Randpark before he turned professional in 2004, earned his maiden Sunshine Tour victory at his home club after a two-hole playoff against Chris Swanepoel. Tipping, 28, eagled the 18th hole just to make the playoff. "I told my caddie as I teed off for the 18th that I'd had dozens of eagles on this hole, so I was going to get another one," he said. Then at the second extra hole, and a third go at the 18th, Tipping gave himself another eagle chance from 25 feet while Swanepoel had a 10-footer for a birdie. It did not go in this time, but he needed only a one-foot tap-in for the birdie, and Swanepoel could not convert for his four.

It was tough on Swanepoel, who had set the target at eight-under-par 208 after a flawless 64 with six birdies and an eagle. He finished an hour ahead of the leaders and had to wait around for Tipping to tie him right at the end of regulation as he posted a closing 69.

"It's like a story to win in my home course," he said. "I never thought I'd get my first pro win here, and it's unbelievable. I wasn't nervous yet, although I had got a few shakes when I stood over that eagle putt in regulation play. I don't know how guys putt for majors."

Vodacom Business Origins of Golf - Selborne
KwaZulu-Natal, South Africa
Winner: Darren Fichardt

Darren Fichardt eased his way to a record-equaling biggest victory margin in the history of the Vodacom Business Origins of Golf Tour at Selborne. On a wet and windy final day, the Pretoria professional distanced himself from the rest of the field with a seven-stroke triumph in the KwaZulu-Natal tournament, closing with a 67 to win on 18-under-par 198 after earlier rounds of 65 and 66. Jbe' Kruger and Keenan Davidse finished second with 11-under-par 205s. Fichardt tied Thomas Aiken, who won the Final at The Links in 2004 by seven strokes, for the biggest victory margin in the series. "I wanted to pip Thomas by one, but it's a nice bonus to achieve something like that," said Fichardt, who went into the final round with a three-stroke lead and was never challenged.

But several players did their best to make a fight of it on the final day. Defending champion Jean Hugo charged through the field with four consecutive birdies in his first five holes to climb to 10 under. But he fell away with a double bogey on the par-four eighth. Kruger birdied three of his first four holes and then added back-to-back birdies early on the back nine to climb to 11 under, which is where he remained. And Davidse collected four consecutive birdies from the ninth to surge to 13 under before a double bogey on the par-three 15th stopped his charge.

But no one had the answer for how to catch a man with seven Sunshine Tour and two European Tour victories and who knows exactly how to close out a tournament. An early birdie on the third hole settled Fichardt. But his dominance was at its most impressive over the turn, where he sprinted away from his challengers with five straight birdies from the eighth hole. And the healthy lead allowed him the luxury of two bogeys in his final four holes. "I lost a bit of focus near the end because I had such a big margin. But I just tried to keep myself in the present and pulled it through."

Fichardt said he was finally over the tendonitis which plagued him during the season. One of his goals for 2010 would be to play his way back onto the European Tour. "I've been practicing hard, working hard in the gym, and been getting committed again. I've got some big goals to achieve and it was nice to get a win under the belt, especially by this kind of margin."

SAA Pro-Am Invitational - Paarl
Paarl, Western Cape, South Africa
Winner: Prinavin Nelson

A graduate of the Ernie Els Foundation, Prinavin Nelson claimed his maiden title with victory at the SAA Pro-Am Invitational at Paarl. The 22-year-old from Scottburgh, in his second season on the Sunshine Tour, was tied for the lead after 36 holes and started the final round with five birdies in the first six holes. Out in 31, Nelson then parred his way to the 18th tee and could afford a three-putt bogey at the last and still win by one stroke over Desvonde Botes. Nelson recorded rounds of 68, 69 and 68 for an 11 under total of 205. Botes set the target for Nelson to beat at 10 under after closing with a 67 to finish one ahead of a group that included Trevor Fisher, Jr., who shared the overnight lead with Nelson but faded to a 70, as well as Chris Swanepoel and Jacques Blaauw. Clinton Whitelaw finished in sixth place a further shot back.

"I was feeling the pressure a little bit, but I was confident in my swing," Nelson said of the back nine. "My putting wasn't up to standard. But I made a good save on 16 when I made about a 15-footer. I had a look at the leaderboard on 16 and I saw I was leading by three, so I knew that level par from there should do it. I was a bit nervous on the last green, but to get my first win feels really great. I hope that everything feels a lot easier from the next tournament onwards."

Vodacom Business Origins of Golf - Final
Kysna, Southern Cape, South Africa
Winner: Brandon Pieters

Brandon Pieters became only the second golfer to win three tournaments in one year on the Vodacom Business Origins of Golf Tour when he claimed the final event of the series at Simola Golf Estate. Pieters closed with a

69 for a total of eight-under-par 208, finishing one stroke clear of Doug McGuigan and Jaco Van Zyl.

Van Zyl stepped up the pressure with a final round of 67 to set the clubhouse mark at seven under. Pieters parred his way into the clubhouse on eight under, using his putter to devastating effect. "I wouldn't say my putter was that hot, but rather that I made some crucial putts at the right times, and that made the difference," he said. Then it was the turn of McGuigan to add to a tense finish when he stood over a seven-foot putt on the 18th for birdie and to force a playoff with Pieters. But McGuigan missed his putt, handing Pieters the victory. Only Thomas Aiken in the inaugural series in 2004 had won three times.

"Doug is a great player and I was getting ready for the playoff. Unfortunately he missed and here I stand as the winner," said Pieters. "It's like a dream come true for me. I've got a goal before the end of 2011, and I don't mind making a habit of this. This is a wonderful feeling.

"For me to win three out of the six is an unbelievable achievement. I have to thank my family for the support they have given me this season. I really want to perform well in the summer tournaments, particularly those co-sanctioned with the European Tour. I want to get my card on one of the big tours, and this is great preparation for that."

BMG Classic
Gauteng, South Africa
Winner: Graham DeLaet

Canada's Graham DeLaet continued a superb rookie season in South Africa by winning the BMG Classic in only his fifth appearance on the Sunshine Tour. DeLaet closed with a 68 after rounds of 68 and 69 for 11-under-par 205 and a one-stroke win over England's Jeff Inglis, who put in a brilliant charge with a 64 at Glendower. Third place was shared by Jacques Blaauw, Louis de Jager and Brandon Pieters.

DeLaet first came down to the Sunshine Tour at the start of the year and was 12th at both the Joburg Open and the Africa Open, then had runner-up finishes at the Vodacom Championship and the Telkom PGA. The three-time winner on the Canadian Tour, with two of those in 2009, returned in October to take a maiden win on the Sunshine Tour. "I loved each one of the five weeks I have spent playing here," he said, "and look at the sun shining on my face," he added as he received his trophy.

A birdie at the 16th, set up yet again by his long and straight driving, gave the 27-year-old a slight cushion and came in handy when he bogeyed the 17th. At the 18th he left himself with a four-foot par putt but confidently rolled that one home.

Highveld Classic
Witbank, South Africa
Winner: Lindani Ndwandwe

Lindani Ndwandwe made a dramatic birdie on the first playoff hole to win the Highveld Classic and claim his second title on the Sunshine Tour. It was his first victory for eight years but was worth the wait as the 34-year-old, who is based at the Durban Country Club, tied with Alex Haindl at Witbank. Playing the 18th hole again, where Haindl had missed from 15 feet for victory in regulation, Ndwandwe was in the trees but managed to get his second out to 35 feet from the hole. He then rolled in the putt for a three, while Haindl could not match him from a similar distance.

Ndwandwe had rounds of 62, 66 and 69 but dropped two shots on the back nine on Sunday as he was caught by Haindl, who closed with a 67, at 19-under-par 197. Doug McGuigan charged into contention with a 64 but finished one stroke behind the playoff.

Ndwandwe had previously won the Western Cape Classic in 2001. "Ironically, winning seems to put more pressure on me," he said, "because now I feel as if I have to go out and do it again."

Platinum Classic
Rustenburg, South Africa
Winner: Darren Fichardt

Darren Fichardt took advantage of Titch Moore's demise on the 16th hole at Mooinooi to make the Platinum Classic his third win of the season and the ninth of his career on the Sunshine Tour. Moore was three ahead with three to play, but his nine-iron second shot at the 16th caught a flier and went behind some trees over the green. He took two more to find the green and two putts for a double-bogey six. Suddenly Fichardt had birdied the 17th and had drawn even. Playing the 18th first, Fichardt holed from the fringe, 12 feet away, and set the target at 15-under-par 201. His inward 32 sealed a 66, after earlier efforts of 70 and 65. Moore had a chance from 25 feet at the last to tie, but it just slipped by.

Fichardt had already won the Nashua Masters and the Vodacom Business Origins of Golf event at Selborne to join Jaco Van Zyl and Brandon Pieters as three-time winners this season. It was a welcome boost before heading back to Europe for the qualifying tournament. "I've been hitting the ball unbelievably this whole week, and it was just a question of making putts," he said. "In the end, though, I was lucky, with Titch making double there on 16 and a par on 17 where I would have expected him to make a birdie, and that left the door open for me on the 18th. There was a little bit of mud on my ball ahead of that putt on 18, so I didn't quite know what was going to happen. But it went in, and that was awesome."

MTC Namibia PGA Championship
Swakopmund, Namibia
Winner: Hennie Otto

Concerned by a back injury and returning home after a poor campaign on the European Tour, where he won the Italian Open in 2008, Hennie Otto produced a strong Sunday finish to win the MTC Namibian PGA Championship at Rossmund Golf Club. Otto beat Titch Moore at the first extra hole after he started the day five strokes behind the third-round leaders.

But the 35-year-old produced a brilliant final round of 66 to set the target at eight-under-par 280, where he was joined by Moore after a 69. Both men got to nine under but then bogeyed the 18th after poor drives. At the same hole in the playoff, Otto was out of position both off the tee and with his approach, but then chipped close to save his par. But Moore was also in trouble off the tee and faced a par putt from 18 inches to continue the playoff but saw it drift wide.

"I was out of the tournament at the beginning of the day, and I played my way back into it. To shoot 66 in this wind, I can take my hat off to myself," said Otto after his eighth Sunshine Tour victory and his first for two years. Of the back injury, he added: "It was serious, and there were times I didn't think I would play again. When I got here this week, I wasn't sure I'd play, but I decided to take it easy and not hit too many balls, and the back held up nicely."

Coca-Cola Championship
George, South Africa
Winner: Christiaan Basson

Christiaan Basson played nerveless golf to win the Coca-Cola Championship hosted by Gary Player played over 54 holes at The Montagu at Fancourt and take his first Sunshine Tour victory. He shot a flawless four-under 68 on the Gary Player-designed course for a total of 13-under 203 to defeat Louis Oosthuizen and Andrew Curlewis by four shots. "I had a look at the leaderboard on the 15th," he said, "and I saw that Louis was on eight under with three to play, so I knew I had to play solid golf all the way in."

It was more than solid, as he birdied the 16th and 18th to put an exclamation point on a win which has been coming for a while. "Any time is a good time to get the first win," he said, "but it's amazing to have won this and to have got my trophy from Gary Player."

He started the day one behind Curlewis and put down a marker early on with a birdie-three on the first. It gave him a share of the lead, and when he birdied the ninth, he took the lead on his own and never relinquished it.

Oosthuizen, recovered from the tiredness brought on by the dash from the Dubai World Championship the previous weekend to South Africa to play in this tournament, had the round of the day in his attempt to chase down the leaders. His 66, which included a bogey-five at the third, lifted him into a share of second place, but his first-round 74 was too big a hurdle to overcome.

Gary Player Invitational
George, South Africa
Winners: Angel Cabrera and Tony Johnstone

Angel Cabrera, on his debut in the event, and Tony Johnstone won the professional fourball section of the Gary Player Invitational at The Links at Fancourt. The pair collected six birdies and an eagle on each of the two days, a bogey in the first round meaning they recorded scores of 66 and 65 for a 15-under-par 131 total. They won by three shots over the team of John Bland and Tjaart van der Walt and that of Bill Longmuir and Omar Sandys.

Cabrera, the Masters champion, and Johnstone, the British Senior Masters champion, birdied the last five holes to secure their victory, while Bland and van der Walt crashed to a double bogey at the 14th. "We dovetailed superbly," Johnstone said. "Angel is a pleasure to play with because he is so relaxed. You feel like he might just start yawning at any moment during the round."

The charity event raised a record-breaking R5 million for underprivileged children. The pro-am section was won by the team of D.J. Spoony, a British broadcaster, UAE businessman Abdullah Al Naboodah, plus professionals Vincent Tshabalala and Thomas Aiken on countback at 22 under par.

Nedbank Affinity Cup
Sun City, South Africa
Winner: Jake Roos

Returning to play in South Africa for the first time after a six-month spell in America, Jake Roos enjoyed immediate success by winning the Nedbank Affinity Cup at the Lost City course at Sun City. Roos beat Mark Murless and Albert Pistorius in a playoff after the trio finished at 12-under-par 204. Pistorius found water on the first playoff hole while Roos and Murless birdied, so they returned to the 18th once more. Roos had already birdied the hole at the end of regulation, but this time it was Murless who made the mistake by pulling his tee shot into the bush and having to escape sideways.

"It was nice to come back home and win," Roos said. "I definitely feel like I have gained a lot of experience over there. I started off slowly with a 71 in the first round, but the last few days, I've hit the ball really well and given myself a lot of chances. I felt like I was very composed and in control of my swing. I've worked hard on my swing over the last two months. I've made a couple of changes and I feel like it held up nicely."

Roos, 29, claimed his second Sunshine Tour title with closing rounds of 66 and 67. Both he and Pistorius, who also shot a 67 on the last day, started the final round five shots behind Murless and Des Terblanche, who closed with scores of 72 and 74 respectively.

Nedbank Golf Challenge
Sun City, South Africa
Winner: Robert Allenby

Robert Allenby became the first Australian to win the Nedbank Golf Challenge and claimed his first victory anywhere in the world for four years. But it took three extra holes for Allenby to win, although that bit was of little surprise since his playoff record now reads 11 successes in 12 attempts.

Allenby outlasted Henrik Stenson, the defending champion. While the Swede had won both the World Cup and the Nedbank in successive weeks a year earlier, this year he had to settle for runner-up finishes at both events. But Stenson's closing round of 69 did put the pressure on the Australian, whose 71 was good enough to leapfrog overnight leader Retief Goosen. The local hero, who was two in front of Allenby and Angel Cabrera, dropped back with a 75. Tim Clark and Ross Fisher, who missed from 20 feet at the last to join the playoff, shared third place after scores of 69 and 70 respectively.

Allenby, 38, had four birdies, the last of them at the 17th which put him one ahead of Stenson, who was by now in the clubhouse with 277 total. But where the Swede had finished birdie-bogey, so did Allenby, and then the pair went back to the 18th three more times. The first two times they both parred the hole, but by now Allenby had played the 18th six times during the week and never hit the green in regulation. On the first playoff hole he had to hole from five feet to stay alive and the next time he recovered from driving into a bunker.

On the seventh time of asking, with Stenson missing the green on the right and hard by a grandstand with a horrid chip to follow, Allenby did make the green, hitting a superb six iron to seven feet. While Stenson failed to get up and down, Allenby safely two-putted.

"I'm glad that's over," said Allenby. "After bogeying the 72nd I knew I had a second chance and my record in playoffs is pretty good. I did think we were going to be here all night at one stage, but once I saw Henrik hit it out right I knew he had a difficult shot. The only thing in my mind then was hitting my six iron straight at the pin and I hit it absolutely perfectly. I'm proud to be the first Australian to win this title."

Alfred Dunhill Championship
Malelane, South Africa
Winner: Pablo Martin

Two and a half years after becoming the first amateur to win on the European Tour, Pablo Martin became the first to win as an amateur and a professional by claiming the Alfred Dunhill Championship at Leopard Creek. The 23-year-old Spaniard won the Portuguese Open in 2007 but then struggled after turning professional, at one point missing 20 of 22 cuts. He was in danger of losing his playing rights on the European Tour, but finished 118th on the Order of Merit in 2009, with the top 120 keeping their cards.

Here, at the first event of the 2010 European Tour season, Martin was partly enjoying a holiday with his sister by visiting the neighboring Kruger

National Park. Until, that is, he scored a 63 in the second round, with eight birdies and an eagle, to lead by four strokes. His advantage was cut to two with a round to play, but his main challenger proved not to be Ernie Els, who closed with a 77 that included going in the water at the last hole, where he collapsed spectacularly in 2007. It meant an end of Els's run of winning every year, which started in 1991.

The island green at the par-five 18th always causes problems, and Sion Bebb, who was one behind after eagling the 13th, had an 11 after tangling with trees and twice finding the water to fall from fifth to 17th. Martin got to 17-under 271 by birdieing the 12th and 13th holes and then parred in, but came under pressure from Charl Schwartzel, who made five birdies, but also three bogeys, in the last eight holes. At the 18th Martin hit a huge drive, but was persuaded by his caddie to lay up before hitting his approach and two-putting for a one-stroke victory.

Martin closed with 69, while Schwartzel had 68, and Anders Hansen was third two behind the South African. "It's an unbelievable feeling," Martin said. "I am so happy and there was so much emotion today. It's probably the most nervous I've been, with Charl making birdies at the end." He added: "My sister can't go home now, because she was with me at both tournaments I have won."

South African Open Championship
Paarl, Western Cape, South Africa
Winner: Richie Ramsay

Describing the final day of the South African Open Championship as a time for "fearless golf," Richie Ramsay produced exactly that to claim his first victory as a professional. Ramsay scored a day's best 65 with seven birdies and then beat India's Shiv Kapur at the first extra hole. The 26-year-old from Aberdeen became the first Scot for 108 years to win the U.S. Amateur in 2006, but he only made sure of keeping his card on the European Tour in his rookie season of 2009 when he finished fourth at the Alfred Dunhill Links Championship.

Building on that confidence, Ramsay put behind him a round of 75 on the second day and overcame a five-stroke deficit to third-round leader Pablo Martin. The Spaniard was hoping to make it two wins in a row, but fell back with a 73 for a tie for sixth place. Instead it was Ramsay who led the way, making back-nine birdies at the 10th, 12th, 15th and 17th holes before missing another chance at the last.

Kapur matched the Scot at 13-under 275 with a round of 67, while Anders Hansen finished one shot back to clinch the Sunshine Tour Order of Merit title. Edoardo Molinari finished in joint fourth place with Fredrik Andersson Hed, and the Italian moved up into the world's top 50 alongside his brother Francesco to guarantee a start at the 2010 Masters.

In the playoff at the par-five 18th, Kapur, straight and steady off the tee all day, pulled his drive into the sandy rough and could not go for the green. Ramsay certainly could and smashed a fairway wood to 15 feet, from where he two-putted for a winning birdie.

12. Women's Tours

A national golf magazine late in 2008 blared out the question from its cover: "Can Wie Save The LPGA?"

Had the LPGA Tour fallen into such ruin that it could only be rescued by a 20-year-old who had finally fulfilled at least part of the promise she had showed from her early teens? Not really. But the fact that the question was even raised shows how deeply the LPGA Tour had been damaged. There was the sagging economy, which wiped out some tournaments, and also, according to published reports, damaged relationships with other tournament sponsors. And then came a rebellion in which players forced controversial Commissioner Carolyn Bivens out of office in mid-July.

Meanwhile, back at the golf course:

Wie was in her first season on the LPGA Tour as a full member. She won her playing card through the qualifying tournament. Her accomplishments in 2009 were relatively modest. But compared to the expectations since she was about 13 years old, Wie had taken off like a rocket. Her long-anticipated breakthrough came in the Solheim Cup. Wie entered the Solheim Cup as a captain's pick and came out the Americans' leading point-getter in their 16-12 victory over Europe, their third straight win and eighth overall. Wie may also have come out a different person. At 19, after some six years of being the pampered teenage prodigy out on the fringe, she found herself just one of the girls. She was welcomed and accepted by her teammates. "I think this was the most fun I've ever had playing golf," Wie said. Said captain Beth Daniel: "There were times I thought she was walking on air." Had Wie finally arrived?

Wie finally broke through on her own in November, winning the Lorena Ochoa Invitational. She did it in style, blasting out of a bunker to six inches at the final hole and tapping in for a birdie and a two-stroke victory. "It's definitely off my back," Wie said. "I think that, hopefully, life will be a lot better, but I still have a lot to do."

The battle for awards came down to Ochoa and South Korea's Jiyai Shin. Shin had the chance to become the first player since Nancy Lopez in 1978 to win both the Rolex Rookie of the Year and the Rolex Player of the Year awards. Shin had already locked up the rookie award, and by late in the season the race came down to decimal points. Ochoa and Shin had both won three events. Ochoa had more seconds and Shin had more thirds, and both had eight top-five finishes. It came down to the top-10 finishes. Ochoa had 13, Shin 12. Shin won more money than Ochoa, topping the money list with $1.807 million to $1.489 million, but she also played in three more tournaments.

And so Ochoa was the Rolex Player of the Year, Shin the Rolex Rookie of the Year.

Ochoa, who dominated the tour for the past four years, had a rare dry spell. She won the Honda LPGA Thailand and the Corona Championship in the spring and the Navistar LPGA Classic six months later, in October. Shin had a more balanced season. She won the HSBC Women's

Champions in March, the Wegmans LPGA in June and the P&G Beauty in September.

Brittany Lincicome authored one of the best shots of the year in the Kraft Nabisco Championship, the first of the four majors. Playing in the final threesome, Lincicome seemed lost in the battle between Cristie Kerr and Kristy McPherson. Then at the par-five 18th, Lincicome hit a hybrid club some 200 yards to the green, to within four feet of the cup, and holed the putt for an eagle and a one-stroke win, her first win in a major and third win overall. "That absolutely was the best shot of my life," Lincicome said.

In the majors, Sweden's Anna Nordqvist, a rookie in her first major, won the McDonald's LPGA Championship in only her fifth start (then added the season-ending LPGA Tour Championship). South Korea's Eun-Hee Ji holed a 20-foot birdie putt on the final hole to take the U.S. Women's Open, and Scotland's Catriona Matthew won the Ricoh Women's British Open.

South Korea's Na Yeon Choi was one of only four players to win more than once in 2009 — Shin, Ochoa and Anna Nordqvist were the others. Choi closed strong, winning the Samsung World Championship in September and the Hana Bank-Kolon Championship in November.

For all of the exciting golf, the 2009 season was played under a cloud following the firing of Bivens in mid-July. Rear Admiral (Retired) Marsha Evans was appointed acting commissioner to finish the season. Then Michael Whan, 44, a former marketing executive in golf and hockey equipment, was named the new commissioner in October, to take the post in January 2010. Whan described himself as passionate about golf. "I was the crazy high school kid cutting grass at 5:30 in the morning so he could play free golf in the afternoon, and caddieing on Sundays," he said. The golf world would be watching to see whether he could turn that passion to restoring the LPGA.

Young players dominated the victory rolls on the 2009 Japan LPGA Tour. Twenty-three-year-old Sakura Yokomine finished No. 1 on the money list by winning the season's final tournament, her sixth victory of the year. She nosed out Shinobu Moromizato, 22, who also posted six wins, and 21-year-old Chie Arimura parlayed five titles into a third-place finish. Those three captured exactly half of the season's 34 tournaments.

South Koreans also made their mark on the season with 10 victories. Mi-Jeong Jeon racked up four and Bo-Bae Song was the other multiple winner, capturing the Japan Women's Open and the prestigious Mizuno Open. Jiyai Shin picked up one of the four wins of her outstanding season in the Masters Golf Club tournament.

On the other hand, the long-dominant Yuri Fudoh failed to add to her 46-win total, the first time she went without a victory in a season since 1998.

U.S. LPGA Tour

HSBC LPGA Brasil Cup
Rio de Janeiro, Brazil
Winner: Catriona Matthew

In a field of fast-rising youths and established players, who would clearly be the least likely to succeed? Try a woman who was not only age 39, but also five months pregnant with her second child.

Meet Scotland's Catriona Matthew, who put together rounds of 69-69–138, six under par, to run away with the inaugural HSBC LPGA Brasil Cup, an exhibition event in January at Rio de Janeiro's Itanhanga Golf Club. She dominated the 15-player field, leading by two strokes in the first round and winning by five.

"I'm feeling fine, actually," Matthew said, after the first round. "I got a little tired toward the end, but it's not really affecting me just yet." She took a grip on the tournament out of the starting gate with birdies on four of the first six holes. Kristy McPherson birdied the last two holes for 71, and Brazil's Angela Park was disappointed in her 72 before the home folks. "But I really didn't play badly at all," she said.

Matthew opened the second round birdie-bogey, then raced ahead with birdies on Nos. 5, 6 and 14, moving a whopping five ahead of McPherson. And what would Matthew be telling her new baby some day? "When you play well," Matthew said, "you don't feel tired."

SBS Open
Kahuku, Oahu, Hawaii
Winner: Angela Stanford

Angela Stanford was the winner, but Michelle Wie was the story at the LPGA Tour's season-opening SBS Open at Turtle Bay in Hawaii.

Wie, the former girl phenomenon (from age 12), was now a 19-year-old multi-millionaire veteran making her 49th start on the tour but her first as a full-fledged member. Only a late stumble kept her from starting with her first victory.

Going head-to-head all the way against the veteran Stanford, 31, Wie double-bogeyed the 11th hole in the final round, and Stanford whizzed on by to a three-stroke victory, the fourth win of her career and the third in seven starts, dating back to 2008.

"Standing on the green at 10, I thought, I don't know if I can make up three shots in this wind," Stanford said. "She was going to need (to make) a mistake." And Wie did. At No. 11, she hit her three-wood tee shot into the marsh, then left a chip shot in the rough and double-bogeyed. Stanford birdied three straight, starting with a five iron to 15 feet at No. 13 for a

70 and a 10-under 206 total, and won by three. Wie missed a short birdie try at the 16th and bogeyed the 17th after hitting into the sand twice and shot 73–209. Angela Park and Na Yeon Choi tied for third at 212.

"Missing the trophy by a little bit is going to motivate me to work even harder," Wie said.

It was a Stanford-Wie shootout from the start. Stanford was brilliant with a bogey-free 65 in the first round. She hit 17 greens, birdied the first two holes and two of the last three. Wie started birdie-bogey-birdie and ended with three straight birdies for 66. Wie caught Stanford in the second round in 30 mile-an-hour winds. Starting on the second nine, Wie birdied three straight from her 11th (No. 2) en route to 70–136. Stanford, still bogey-free, shot 71 and ended up impressed by Wie.

"Once she figures things out, she is going to be just fine," Stanford said.

Said Wie: "I had just one bad hole. Things just didn't go my way, unfortunately."

Honda LPGA Thailand
Chonburi, Thailand
Winner: Lorena Ochoa

Lorena Ochoa, No. 1 in the world, was making her 2009 debut in the Honda LPGA Thailand early in March, and speaking of the third round she said: "Sometimes when you start off bad, you get angry and motivated at the same time." She could have said that about the entire tournament. Ochoa started the tournament with a one-under-par 71, five off the lead, and trailed all the way, but closed with a rush for her first victory of the new season and the 25th of her career.

"I'm pleased — I played exceptionally well," said Ochoa, sitting pretty on a card of 71-69-68-66–274, 14 under at Siam Country Club, and winning by three over South Korea's Hee Young Park (65–277). Paula Creamer, who led entering the final round, closed with 73 and finished third at 278.

Ochoa had trouble on the firm greens in the first round, and her 71 left her five behind South Korea's Jin Joo Hong, a surprise leader in a field that held the top 10 ranked golfers. Brittany Lang took advantage of her length to edge ahead by a stroke in the second round with a bogey-free 69 and a 137 total. Ochoa closed to within three at 69–140. "I like where I am," she said. "I still have the chance to win."

But not a convincing one. Ochoa shot 68 in the third round, but Creamer birdied three straight on the second nine for 67–205 and led by three going into the final round. The edge disappeared fast, with a birdie-bogey exchange at the par-five second, then Creamer's bogey at the par-three third.

Then came the decisive stretch. Ochoa birdied Nos. 6, 8, 11 and 13, bogeyed the 16th, then birdied the 17th for her 66.

Said a disappointed Creamer: "I started on the wrong foot. It wasn't my day."

Said Ochoa: "It's been a great week. My goal was to win the tournament, and here I am with the trophy. I'm pleased."

HSBC Women's Champions
Singapore
Winner: Jiyai Shin

South Korea's Jiyai Shin, only 20 years old, already had the nickname "Final-Round Queen" back home, and she showed why in the HSBC Women's Champions in Singapore. She was out of contention, six strokes off the lead entering the final round, then came charging back, closing with a second straight 66 for a 277 total, 11 under par at Tanah Merah Country Club, to take a two-stroke win over a faltering Katherine Hull. It was her fourth LPGA title in eight months.

Canada's Hull had taken the lead in the third round with a 66, going two up on Angela Stanford (66), and she was six ahead of Shin. "I'm liking the fact that I have a two-shot lead," said Hull, who won the ANZ Ladies Masters a month earlier and the Canadian Women's Open the previous summer. "So, game on," she said.

But unfortunately, the game was off for her. Hull was leading by four strokes with nine holes to play and then collapsed. She bogeyed the 10th, double-bogeyed the par-five 13th and bogeyed the par-three 14th.

Shin, meantime, opened the round with four straight birdies — a nine-foot putt at No. 1, then a 12-foot putt, a 45-foot chip-in and a 15-foot putt. Said Shin, "She starts leader and she looks at score (board), she gets more, I think, pressure." Shin also birdied the par-five 15th on a 12-foot putt and parred in for the 66–277.

Shin was a surprise winner, even to herself. "I am thinking I had a chance for top 10, not for win," she said. She had started 72-73 and in the first round trailed Paula Creamer, Jane Park and Angela Park by five strokes, then trailed Creamer and Jane Park by seven through the second round.

World No. 1 Lorena Ochoa opened with 69 and noted, "I think I need to be a little more aggressive." But she couldn't quite manage it and tied for sixth place.

MasterCard Classic Honoring Alejo Peralta
Mexico City, Mexico
Winner: Pat Hurst

They weren't calling her "Pat the Giant Killer," but that's who veteran Pat Hurst was in the MasterCard Classic Honoring Alejo Peralta near Mexico City. Hurst, then No. 44 on the Rolex Rankings, finished birdie-birdie, and not only scored her career sixth LPGA Tour win and her first since 2006, she also beat the world's top two players in the process — No. 1 Lorena Ochoa and No. 2 Yani Tseng.

"The 17th and 18th holes coming in were very exciting," said Hurst. "I just tried not to get ahead of myself out there." Hurst, who had dropped four shots over the last three holes in the second round, this time holed 10-footers for birdies at the 17th and the par-five 18th for a one-stroke win on a card of 68-70-68–206, 10 under par at rugged BosqueReal Country Club, a course that had frustrated Ochoa for four years.

Ochoa got at least a sense of satisfaction in the first round and also thrilled her adoring home fans by tying the course record with a seven-under-par 65 for the lead. But a 73-69 close thwarted her again. She tied for second place with Tseng (69-71), who was crushed over letting the title get away with a three-putt bogey at the final hole. Tseng was 30 feet short of the cup with her approach, knocked her first putt 15 feet past, and needed two more to get down.

That left Hurst facing a 10-footer for the win. "I wasn't thinking about a playoff or anything," Hurst said. "Just about making the putt." Which she did.

"I just feel really sad," Tseng said. "I just don't know what to say."

Ochoa was in it to the very end. She overhit a seven wood from 226 yards at the 18th hole, and the ball caromed off the lip of a back bunker and onto the green and stopped 15 feet from the hole. A tying eagle was waiting.

"But unfortunately, I didn't make the putt," said Ochoa, now 0-for-5 at BosqueReal. "We'll try again next year."

J Golf Phoenix LPGA International
Phoenix, Arizona
Winner: Karrie Webb

Golf had become a question-and-answer game for Karrie Webb. For Webb, one of the most prolific winners in the history of the LPGA Tour, the question was: "Would I ever win again?" The answer was: "Yes — finally," at the J Golf Phoenix LPGA International in March. After all the painful doubt, Webb broke free in the fourth round for her first victory since 2006 and her 36th career triumph.

"You know you still have the ability," Webb said, "but you're just not putting (up) the scores. Even less than a month ago, I was still questioning that."

Webb, trailing until the final nine, put up scores of 70-68-69-67–274, 14 under par at Papago Golf Course, a toughened municipal course in Phoenix, Arizona. Her doubt hung over her from the start. In-Kyung Kim took a one-stroke lead with 68 off a chip-in eagle at the par-five 18th. Webb was two behind. Defending champion Lorena Ochoa struggled through the wind for 72, and Michelle Wie, in her first start since the season-opener, shot 73. Neither would be a threat.

Kim fought off a stomach ache for another 68 and after 36 holes led by two over Suzann Pettersen (69) and Webb, who tied her with a birdie at the 18th for 68. Kerr got more encouragement in the third round with 69 that tied her for second place, a stroke behind Jiyai Shin, who surged into the lead with 66–206. Webb had to restrain herself. "The problem now is that I want it too badly," she said.

In the final round, Webb nosed into the lead at the par-five sixth, holing a 20-foot putt for an eagle. But Kim retook the lead with three straight birdies from No. 6, then double-bogeyed the par-five 10th off a watered shot, and Webb moved two ahead of Shin with birdies at the 10th and 11th.

Webb wrapped it up at the par-five 18th, reaching in two and two-putting from 10 feet for a birdie, 67 and a two-stroke win that justified her faith in herself.

Kraft Nabisco Championship
Rancho Mirage, California
Winner: Brittany Lincicome

See Chapter 6.

Corona Championship
Morelia, Michoacan, Mexico
Winner: Lorena Ochoa

Golf tournaments can go by various picturesque names. But the Lorena Ochoa-Suzann Pettersen battle at the Corona Championship in April, that was a slugfest. These were heavyweights slugging it out in the final round. And when the air cleared at Tres Marias Country Club at Morelia, Mexico, Ochoa — thrilling her home fans — had as tough a one-stroke victory as she was likely to have in her World No. 1 career.

In a furious exchange of birdies, Pettersen caught Ochoa three times in the final round but just couldn't bring her down, and Ochoa had her second win of the season and 26th of her career. "I had a one-stroke lead over her after the 15th," Ochoa said. "She missed her putt and I knew that, with a birdie, I was going to take a two-stroke lead with two holes left to play, so I made the decision to go for it. I had a good putt, a little bit soft, but it fell. ... That was beautiful." Ochoa played the par-73 Tres Marias course in 65-65-69-68–267, 25 under par.

Ochoa was one stroke ahead starting the final round. Pettersen tied her with a birdie at the third, on a 25-foot putt. Ochoa topped her with a birdie from 15 at the fourth, but Pettersen tied again with a short birdie putt at the fifth. Ochoa birdied Nos. 7 and 8 and was up by two, and they halved the 10th in birdies. They were tied again when Ochoa bogeyed the 11th, three-putting, and Pettersen birdied the 12th from 10 feet. Then came Ochoa's two decisive birdies, on a 12-foot putt at the 15th and an 18-footer at the 16th, and she was up by two, and had the win when Pettersen finished par-birdie.

"My putter just went cold for a little while on the back nine," said Pettersen, who had just one bogey in the tournament.

Someone noted that Ochoa had won the 2008 Corona Championship by 11 and this one by only one. "In a golf tournament, where one is enough to win," she pointed out, "there is no difference."

Michelob Ultra Open
Williamsburg, Virginia
Winner: Cristie Kerr

Cristie Kerr was praising her mind guru, and maybe Lorena Ochoa was hoping to get an appointment with him.

Those were the two extremes at the Michelob Ultra Open at Kingsmill, in Williamsburg, Virginia — Kerr pulling away down the stretch to win it, and thanking her guru, and Ochoa, after threatening to run away with it in the first two rounds, suddenly sliding back with a rare case of un-Ochoa golf over the last two rounds. Ochoa shot 64-65 in the first two rounds for a tournament-record 13 under par at the halfway point. She led by three. Then came the slide, a 74-74 finish. What went wrong? "Pretty much everything," Ochoa said. "I just didn't feel comfortable out there."

Kerr opened with 69 and jumped to within three of Ochoa with a second-round 63. That put her almost head-to-head with the world No. 1 woman golfer. Kerr shrugged. "Nobody has a perfect game," she said. "It's not a given that she's going to win."

Sure enough, Ochoa faded in the third round, and Kerr (66) and Lindsey Wright (64), who had only one bogey in 54 holes, tied for the lead, and then the tournament was locked in a four-way jam coming down the closing holes. Then South Korea's Song-Hee Kim double-bogeyed the 16th, and Kerr, in the group behind, made a gallery-rocking birdie at the par-five 15th. She went for the green from 220 yards. "Come on, be right!" she urged. "Come on!" The ball rolled to the back fringe, and she two-putted for a birdie and a one-stroke lead.

In the same stretch, South Korea's In-Kyung Kim bogeyed the 16th and fell two behind. And coming up just behind, Wright, Kerr's playing partner, also fell two back when she missed the green and bogeyed the 16th.

Kerr, with two birdies and a bogey, closed with 70 and credited her 12th career victory to the Zen approach to golf she learned from her guru. "I was surprised," Kerr said. "I was even calm at 18. I guess that mental training is paying off."

Sybase Classic
Clifton, New Jersey
Winner: Ji Young Oh

For one brief moment, it was a return to an earlier day. Helen Alfredsson, one of the first of the Swedes to join the LPGA Tour, now age 44, opened the Sybase Classic with a scorching 10-under-par 62. Alas, the dream ended the next day on a 76, leaving the Sybase to evolve into a three-way battle of South Korea's Ji Young Oh, Norway's Suzann Pettersen and America's Brittany Lincicome. In the end, it was Oh zipping past the field for a comfortable four-stroke win, her second LPGA title.

"Today, I did everything so right," said Oh, after a final-round 70 and a 14-under-par 274 total at Upper Montclair Country Club in Clifton, New Jersey.

"There were so many chances on the back nine," Pettersen said. "I need to make putts to win tournaments." She had a share of the lead in the fourth round until she hit a stray drive at the 12th and bogeyed. Then came a crushing bogey-bogey finish for 74. And Lincicome soared to 77.

Michelle Wie, 19, and Paula Creamer shot 73s and also fell short, tying for third at 280. It was Wie's third top-10 finish by mid-May. "It was a struggle out there, but I learned a lot of things for next week," she said. Said Creamer: "I felt like I shot six over par, but I really shot one over. It was really tough."

The real showdown took shape in the second round, with Lincicome (69–133) taking a two-stroke lead over Pettersen (70) and Oh (69). Then Pettersen and Oh took the lead in the third with 69s, tying at 204.

Oh made her move down the final stretch. After a bogey at the 10th, she ground out seven straight pars, and in that stretch took the lead on Pettersen's bogey at the 12th. Then, for a sign-off, she holed a seven-foot birdie at the 18th for the four-stroke win. This was the final measure of her success: She was the only player of the top four to break par.

LPGA Corning Classic
Corning, New York
Winner: Yani Tseng

It was a victory speech nearly four months in the giving. "I wrote my (winner's) speech in January," Yani Tseng was saying. "(But) every time I get so close, and I don't win. This week, I just let it go."

Tseng, 20, who won the 2008 McDonald's LPGA Championship as a rookie, came to the LPGA Corning Classic sounding like anything but a winner. "I'm just not comfortable with my game," she said. "And I have no confidence for the last couple years. ... And this week, I didn't practice that much." But something clicked in. She played the agreeable Corning Country Club course in 68-70-62-67–267, a generous 21 under par, and won by one over Paula Creamer and Soo-Yun Kang. Tseng's 62 — and Mika Miyazato's — had to be viewed in context. The halfway cut was at the lowest figure in tournament history, three-under-par 141.

Tseng withstood the test well, trailing by four in the first round, eight in the second and then by only one going into the fourth. And then came her rousing finish. She started the final round with a bogey, then eagled the par-five second on a 14-foot putt, and added four birdies, including a spectacular one at the 310-yard, par-four 16th. She drove the green and two-putted from 12 feet. Then came a tense moment at the 18th. Tseng two-putted from 16 feet for par and her 67, and then was afraid to watch as Kang stood up to the four-foot par putt that would force a playoff. Then relief. "I didn't even know she missed the putt," Tseng said. "My head was down."

Kang (69) tied for second with Paula Creamer, who parred the final three holes — the 18th on a 60-foot putt — for 65.

It seemed the victory would be Tseng's first and last in the LPGA Corning Classic. After 31 years, $17.8 million in prize money and over $5.3 million raised for charity, the tournament was no more.

LPGA State Farm Classic
Springfield, Illinois
Winner: In-Kyung Kim

The LPGA State Farm Classic was working out as a classic battle between a Hall of Famer, Se Ri Pak, the trailblazer for South Koreans, against a ripening major talent, Angela Stanford. But while they were thus engrossed, an enterprising young lady with a surprisingly pressure-proof game slipped in and made off with the prize.

South Korea's In-Kyung Kim, who tagged along just behind the leaders for the first three rounds, birdied two of the last three holes to take a one-stroke victory over Pak for her second LPGA Tour victory and deny Pak her first win in two years.

"This tournament means a lot to me, playing with all the great players that all played this week," Kim said. Only No. 1 Lorena Ochoa was missing from the top 50 players at Panther Creek Country Club, at Springfield, Illinois. "I feel really special," Kim added.

Pak had the win almost in her grasp from the start. She birdied three of her last four holes to tie Jee Young Lee at 66 in the first round. Pak shot 68 in the second and tied with Suzann Pettersen (66) and still hadn't made a bogey. The picture took an odd twist in the third round. Cristie Kerr (66) and Kristy McPherson (69) matched a pair of late bogeys and tied for the lead at 12 under. Pak (72), Stanford (69) and Kim (69) were in a seven-way tie, two shots back.

The final round was a scramble. Stanford got to 16 under through the 13th but bogeyed the next two. Pak reached 16 under with a birdie at the par-five 16th. Meanwhile, Kim had got to 15 under, then birdied the 16th and 17th. Her putt for a third straight birdie, a 13-footer at the 18th, stopped on the lip. The tap-in par gave her 65, a 17-under 271 total and a one-stroke win over Pak (66). Stanford (67) was two back, tied for third.

The win was Kim's great birthday gift to herself. She would turn 21 the following week.

McDonald's LPGA Championship
Havre de Grace, Maryland
Winner: Anna Nordqvist

See Chapter 6.

Wegmans LPGA
Pittsford, New York
Winner: Jiyai Shin

The Wegmans LPGA had reached the halfway point when the big news hit the wires: Cheyenne Woods, age 18, niece of Tiger Woods, making her first visit to the LPGA Tour (on a sponsor's exemption), missed the cut. Woods, just out of her freshman year in college, shot 75-74—149. "I'm happy," she said. "Three more years at Wake Forest, and then hopefully, I'll be back out here."

Meantime, South Korea's Jiyai Shin was beating up on Locust Hill, near Rochester, New York, for a breezy seven-stroke victory. It was her fifth victory on the tour in 11 months, the first three coming before she was a member.

"This year my goal was to win one time," Shin said. "But I've already won two times. Maybe I'll try to win more."

Shin, technically still a rookie, posted an untroubled 65-68-67-71–271, an impressive 17 under par, leaving Kristy McPherson (66) and Yani Tseng (66) to share a distant second place. Shin was out of the lead in the first round, by a stroke, when Germany's Sandra Gal birdied five straight holes from the 11th en route to what she called "a really fun day," a 64. The next round was no fun, a 73.

Shin came to the top with 68 in the rain-delayed second round Friday and was at 11-under 133 at the halfway point, then went to 16 under with a third-round 67.

Morgan Pressel was the one with the best chance to overtake Shin in the final round, trailing by four and playing with her. But Pressel, clad in rain gear against the weather, played her final nine with four bogeys and a triple-bogey seven at the 13th and plummeted on a 78.

Shin was tense when she started the final round. Then at No. 1 she lofted a nine-iron second inside 10 feet and holed the putt. "That birdie changed my feeling," Shin said. "I got my confidence back." Then, with bogeys here and birdies there, she closed with a 71 and the luxurious victory.

Jamie Farr Owens Corning Classic
Sylvania, Ohio
Winner: Eunjung Yi

For the folks in Temecula, California, the place to be that Sunday evening of the Jamie Farr Owens Corning Classic in July was Kyung Su's Minong Korean Barbecue. When his daughter Eunjung Yi took the lead in the third round, she promised that if she won, she would set up the house. "Everything, for whoever comes — all free," she said, and after she holed that 10-foot birdie putt on the first playoff hole for her first LPGA Tour victory, she called her dad.

Yi's birdie ended a terrific rush by Morgan Pressel, who made up a four-stroke deficit with three holes to play, capping it with a stunning hole-out eagle. Pressel, playing ahead of Yi, shot 67 to tie Yi (71) at 18-under-par 266 at the par-71 Highland Meadows course, near Toledo, Ohio.

But it had seemed so easy for Yi just a short while earlier. After opening with 68-66, she rocketed to the top with a 10-under 61 in the third round. "I'm the leader?" she said. "Really? I didn't know that. By four strokes?"

Yi had started three behind Laura Diaz and Sarah Kemp. She birdied four holes on the front side, holed a 110-yard wedge for an eagle at the 10th, then birdied the 12th, 13th, 16th and 17th for the 61 and a four-stroke lead over Pressel (67) and Song-Hee Kim (64).

Yi went up by six with birdies on two of the first three holes, then led by four down the home stretch. But that was cut in half by her bogey against Pressel's birdie at the 16th. And then Pressel caught her, holing out from 70 yards for an eagle at the 17th. On the first playoff hole, the 18th, Pressel was short with her approach, and Yi put hers 10 feet from the flag. Pressel parred, and Yi birdied for the victory.

Then Yi grabbed her cell phone and called home, saying something like, "Dad, guess who's coming to dinner!"

U.S. Women's Open
Bethlehem, Pennsylvania
Winner: Eun-Hee Ji

See Chapter 6.

Evian Masters
Evians-les-Bains, France
Winner: Ai Miyazato

See Ladies European Tour section.

Ricoh Women's British Open
Lancanshire, England
Winner: Catriona Matthew

See Chapter 6.

The Solheim Cup
Sugar Grove, Illinois
Winners: United States

What started out as another exercise in beating the Europeans in the Solheim Cup also turned into what some regarded as the coming-of-age of that unfulfilled and often forlorn teen phenomenon, Michelle Wie. United States captain Beth Daniel used one of her two captain's picks to select Wie, 19. Wie rewarded her confidence with an outstanding performance at Rich Harvest Farms, leading the Americans to a 16-12 victory that was nowhere near as cushy as the margin suggests. This was Wie's first Solheim Cup, and she not only played in four of the five matches, she led the Americans with a 3-0-1 record.

"I think this is the most fun I've ever had playing golf," said Wie, who for the first time found herself accepted and welcomed by other golfers. "It was just unbelievable."

The Americans pulled this one out in the singles, going 8-4 after the two sides deadlocked at 8-8 through two days of team matches. It was their third straight Solheim Cup win and stretched their record in the series to 8-3.

On paper, Europe was badly outgunned. Four of their players were 125th and lower on the Rolex Rankings. But they didn't play that way. "They played their hearts out," said a tearful Euro captain Alison Nicolas. "Unfortunately, the Americans birdied a few more holes than we did."

Paula Creamer won with Cristie Kerr in the opening fourball match and again with Juli Inkster (Daniel's other pick) in the foursomes to lead the U.S. to a 4½-3½ edge Friday. Gwladys Nocera, the top European point-getter with 3-0-1, led her side to an 8-8 tie Saturday, winning with Maria Hjorth in the fourball and with Becky Brewerton in foursomes. Then came the American surge in the singles, starting with a sweep of the first three matches.

Angela Stanford got the first point, beating Brewerton; then Creamer, who went 3-1-0, defeated Suzann Pettersen, and Wie beat Helen Alfreds-son. Morgan Pressel clinched it with her win over Anna Nordqvist.

Daniel could finally breathe. "Most of the day," she said, "I didn't think it was going to happen."

And had Michelle Wie finally arrived? That, of course, remained to be seen.

Safeway Classic
North Plains, Oregon
Winner: M.J. Hur

"I don't know what she has done this year," said a frustrated Suzann Pet-tersen. "I do know that she shot seven under today."

She was speaking of M.J. Hur, a 19-year-old South Korean, who con-founded just about everybody at the Safeway Classic. Hur won her LPGA card by finishing fourth on the Futures Tour money list in 2008. But in 2009, in her debut season on the LPGA Tour, she didn't have much of a record. By the time she arrived at Pumpkin Ridge, near Portland, Oregon, late in August, she had missed the cut seven times in 14 starts, and a tie for 13th was her best showing by far. All of which translated into a dra-matic finish.

Hur opened with a 69, five behind Beth Bader's 64 in the first round. Another 69 in the second round left her four behind rookie Anna Nordqvist (69), winner of the McDonald's LPGA Championship in June. So Hur was doing okay, but she was hardly a threat. Then came that explosion in the third round. Hur birdied the eighth and ninth, eagled the par-five 10th, and birdied the 11th, 12th and 14th. That was seven under in seven holes. She finished with a seven-under 65 and a 13-under 203 total.

Out on the course, Pettersen, winless since her five-win 2007, birdied four straight from the ninth and was leading by three. Then she shot 67 the hard way. She bogeyed the 14th and double-bogeyed the 15th, birdied the 17th and got up-and-down from the fairway at the 18th to tie Hur. Michele Redman, who last won in 2000, also shot 67 and tied.

Redman bowed out of the playoff with a three-putt bogey at the first playoff hole. Pettersen two-putted from 12 feet for a par, and Hur matched her with an up-and-down. At the second hole, No. 17, Pettersen missed her birdie putt and Hur rolled in a six-footer for a birdie and her first victory.

"It's not pressure," Hur said. "I just want it to happen already."

CN Canadian Women's Open
Calgary, Alberta, Canada
Winner: Suzann Pettersen

Suzann Pettersen might have been wondering what else could go wrong. She'd last won in 2007 — five times — and since then had six second places, the latest in the Safeway Classic, where she led by three in the final round and let it get away and lost in a playoff to M.J. Hur.

That was just a week ago and, still smarting, she was again in position to win in the CN Canadian Women's Open at Priddis Greens in Calgary. This time, she was determined not to let it slip.

"You've got to believe you can do it," she said. "Don't fear anything." She fought her way through a small crisis in the final round. Her five-stroke lead had shrunk to three over Karrie Webb and she missed the green at the 10th. But then she holed the chip shot, closed with a 70 for a 15-under-par 269 total and a five-stroke victory over a fivesome that included Webb, Morgan Pressel and Angela Stanford.

Pettersen opened with 65, one off Anna Rawson's lead, then inched ahead with 68. Then came a strong move. In the winds of the third round, when only 19 players broke the par of 71, she shot 66, which sent her into the final round with a five-stroke lead.

Pettersen put her return in solid perspective. "This is obviously not a major win on paper," she said, "but for me, this means as much."

Meanwhile, the strange story of No. 1 Lorena Ochoa rolled on. She started in good shape, 66-68, but slipped to 72-71 to finish tied for 10th, her first top-25 in five starts and only her second top-10 since mid-May.

Michelle Wie expected more after a strong Solheim Cup and a tie for fourth in the Safeway Classic, but things turned sour. She bogeyed five of her last 11 holes for an opening 76, then shot 69 and missed her first cut of the season.

P&G Beauty NW Arkansas Championship
Rogers, Arkansas
Winner: Jayai Shin

It didn't look like much at the time, but it was the beginning of the end for everyone else at the P&G Beauty NW Arkansas Championship. South Korea's Jayai Shin, a rookie and the hottest player on the LPGA Tour, was just starting the third and final round. She had a wedge left to the 320-yard first hole. She lofted the shot gently to within nine feet of the flag, and she made the birdie. But she had started the round seven strokes off the lead.

As things worked out, that opening birdie was her first step in the climb out of that deep hole and to her third victory of the season, the most on the tour. Her final test was a three-way playoff with sister Korean Sun Young Yoo and Angela Stanford. They had tied at 204, nine under par at the Pinnacle Country Club at Rogers, Arkansas. All three birdied the first playoff hole. At the second, Yoo missed her birdie chip shot, and Stanford missed a long birdie putt. Unfortunately for them, Shin's putt was about on Stanford's line. "Angela's ball broke to the right," Shin said. "I trusted Angela's putt." It was a faith well rewarded. Shin rolled her 12-footer right in for the win.

Shin, well back with her 70-70 start, had finished two hours before the others with a bogey-free 64. She got two birdies on the front nine, off the wedge to No. 1 and then a seven iron to three feet at No. 3. Then she caught fire coming in, getting birdies at Nos. 10, 11, 14, 16 (that on a 45-foot putt) and 18. "My putting," she said, in understatement, "was really, really good today."

The victory put Shin atop the tour money list, made her almost a shoo-in for the Rolex Rookie of the Year Award, and also made her a candidate for the Rolex Player of the Year Award. Nancy Lopez, in 1978, was the last to take both awards in the same year.

"I have a chance," Shin said. "So now I want to focus (on) the whole thing."

Samsung World Championship
San Diego, California
Winner: Na Yeon Choi

South Korea's Na Yeon Choi set what might well have been an LPGA Tour record by winning, then losing, then winning a tournament, all in the same round. Well, that's stretching a point, but not by much.

Choi entered the final round leading by one, quickly built her margin to a huge seven, then melted down and squandered it all. She finally had to come from behind, and thanks to her own birdie and Ai Miyazato's error at the final hole, she took her first tour victory, and by one stroke.

"I can't believe that I won," Choi said. "Throughout the second half (back nine), I thought I was going to lose it again."

All signs certainly pointed that way. Choi started 71-67, then scorched Torrey Pines for a nine-under-par 63 in the third round and took a two-stroke lead into the fourth. She birdied two of the first four holes, then holed a 10-foot putt for an eagle at No. 6, and was leading by seven with 12 to play. Then it all started to come undone. Miyazato, playing in the group in front of Choi, cut her lead to five with birdies at Nos. 7 and 8. Next came a decisive stretch. Choi bogeyed Nos. 9, 10, 11 and 15. "Mentally, I felt very weak," she said. Miyazato, just ahead of her, took the lead with a birdie at the 16th, dropping a four-foot putt.

Choi got a reprieve at the end. Miyazato, who had watered her five-wood approach at the 18th in the second round, opted to use it again in the last, again at just over 200 yards — and watered the shot again. It cost her a fatal bogey. "I did what I had to do," Miyazato said, "so I felt really good."

Choi hit a hybrid from 193 yards to the front fringe and two-putted from 36 feet for a birdie and a 71 for a 16-under 272 total to win by a stroke. Said Choi: "I felt like I had just turned professional today."

CVS/pharmacy LPGA Challenge
Danville, California
Winner: Sophie Gustafson

The pun was too obvious to ignore: The CVS/pharmacy LPGA Challenge was just what the doctor ordered for Sophie Gustafson. It had been six long years since she last knew the sweet smell of victory. Had she feared whether she would ever win again?

"Yes — absolutely," Gustafson said, after hammering out a four-stroke victory over Lorena Ochoa that was nowhere near as luxurious as it might seem. Gustafson led wire-to-wire but couldn't relax.

The tournament was an excellent test of Gustafson's nerves under pressure, and she held up completely. She was 20 under par on a score of 65-69-66-68–268 at Blackhawk Country Club. She held the solo lead for the first two rounds and shared it in the third with Rolex World No. 1 Ochoa. Ochoa kept the pressure on all the way, from sitting three behind in the first round, closing in to one back in the second, and finally tying her in the third. Gustafson's six-year drought suggested she would finally fold in the heat of the fourth round. But she didn't. Instead, it was Ochoa who couldn't keep pace.

Gustafson was on fire starting the final round, going four under through the first five holes — a birdie from 10 feet at the first hole, another at the par-five third off an eight iron to five feet, and an eagle at the par-five fifth, on a six iron to six feet. She cooled and bogeyed Nos. 6 and 8, and birdied the par-five No. 9, hitting a wedge to five feet.

The outburst caught Ochoa's attention. "I thought maybe the back nine was mine," Ochoa said. But that wasn't to be, either. "I gave myself birdie chances on Nos. 10, 12, 13 and 14, and none of them dropped," she said. "Everything looked like it was her day." She closed with 72.

Gustafson parred her way home for a 68 to end that long drought with her fifth LPGA Tour victory with a four-stroke decision over Ochoa and a huge smile.

"I had my moments," Gustafson said. "I'm just happy it's over."

Navistar LPGA Classic
Prattville, Alabama
Winner: Lorena Ochoa

The future of the LPGA Tour may have been on display earlier in the Navistar LPGA Classic — in the person of amateur Alexis Thompson, age 14 — but the present reasserted itself in the person of Lorena Ochoa.

Ochoa, the Rolex No. 1, in a puzzling downtime (if not slump), scored her first victory since late April, winning by four shots and breaking a string of 11 starts without a win. It was her third win of the season and the 27th on the tour. And it was her second straight at the Senator Course in Prattville, Alabama.

"There are places where you feel comfortable and you feel a good vibe and you like the course," said Ochoa, after shooting 66-68-66-70–270, 18 under at the par-72 course.

Ochoa was two behind Janice Moodie (64) in the first round and in a five-way tie for the lead in the second. She led Sandra Gall by three going into the final round and squandered that cushion with a bogey and a double bogey in the first five holes. She was undaunted.

"I told myself, 'Forget it, you have many holes to play and just be patient,'" she said. Then the old Ochoa showed up. She birdied the par-five eighth with two putts from 20 feet, the 11th from 10 feet, the 14th on a wedge to three feet and the par-five 17th with two putts from 50 feet, and the brief drought was over.

"I have a lot of emotions because it hasn't been easy," Ochoa said. She won by four over Michelle Wie, who birdied five holes coming home for a 66, and Brittany Lang, with a three-birdie 70.

Thompson, a ninth-grader from Coral Springs, Florida, shot her way into the tournament as a Monday qualifier. She lasted for two rounds as a contender, shooting 65-69-74-74, tying for 27th.

"I wasn't expecting to do that bad," Thompson said. "The last two days seems like I haven't hit a ball for, like, ever."

Hana Bank-Kolon Championship
Incheon, South Korea
Winner: Na Yeon Choi

The Hana Bank-Kolon Championship opened in wet but otherwise agreeable weather, and Anna Grzebien and Meaghan Francella each shot six-under-par 66 to share the lead. But for the last two rounds, the question was, who could handle the really nasty weather?

Enter Na Yeon Choi, 22, who was at home both in South Korea and in its early November winds and cold. Choi handled both well enough for a one-stroke victory over Sweden's Maria Hjorth and Taiwan's Yani Tseng after a three-way chase through the last two rounds.

Choi, who scored her first LPGA Tour victory in September, made her move in the second round with four birdies on the front nine before weather forced a suspension of play. "It was hard to focus as the wind and rain got stronger on the back nine," she said. She bogeyed the 17th for a one-under 71 and tied with Tseng (70) for the lead at five under. Hjorth, a three-time winner, was a stroke back with 72.

The championship was in doubt down to the final hole. Choi and Hjorth came to the par-five 18th tied. Both drove into the fairway, down the left side. Then Hjorth, from 226 yards, watered her four-iron second. She saved her par beautifully, but her penalty drop turned out to be the decisive stroke too many. She tied for second with Tseng (68), one off the lead after Choi chipped her third tight and tapped in for a birdie, a 67 and a 10-under 206 total.

Ironically, Choi had to eagle the final hole to win the Samsung. "This time, I was able to play the last hole comfortably," she said. "I went in thinking birdie."

The weather left some surprising casualties far back in the pack. Lorena Ochoa, World No. 1, opened with a 72, then followed it with 77-73. Cristie Kerr shot 70-76-76, Christina Kim 69-74-80, and Morgan Pressel 70-77-80.

Mizuno Classic
Shima, Mie
Winner: Bo-Bae Song

See Japan LPGA Tour section.

Lorena Ochoa Invitational
Guadalajara, Mexico
Winner: Michelle Wie

The future that was predicted for Michelle Wie when she was 12 or so finally arrived when she was 20, in the next-to-last tournament of the 2009 LPGA Tour schedule, the Lorena Ochoa Invitational. She won. She had finally won.

What words would be appropriate to the occasion? In this case, words that come from the heart would do nicely.

"It's definitely off my back," said Wie. "I think that life, hopefully, will be a lot better." Meaning more wins? Of course. But surely she was also thinking that this was at last the end of all those questions about not winning, that inevitably follow a prodigy. She turned professional in 2005, had one second place in 2006, and didn't come close again until her two seconds and two thirds in this 2009 season.

Wie won by two strokes at Guadalajara Country Club in Mexico, in a field of 36 players, but she had to anguish over this finish, too. After trailing through the first two rounds and tieing with Cristie Kerr in the third round, she could almost taste the title in the fourth round. Dueling with Creamer and Kerr, Wie birdied the first and third from 10 feet, three-putted the sixth for a bogey, then birdied the seventh and 11th from 15 feet, the latter giving her the lead.

Then came the embarrassing episode at the par-four 12th. After a stray drive, she hit squarely with her second, only to see the ball carom 50 yards backward. "Oh, this is not good," Wie told herself. "I just felt kind of stupid."

She scrambled a bogey out of the mess, then got some real boosts. Creamer bogeyed the 14th and 17th, and Kerr bogeyed the 15th and 16th. Wie then put on her own heroics. At the par-five 18th, she came out of a greenside bunker to six inches and made the birdie, wrapping up a card of 70-66-70-69–275, 13 under, for a two-stroke win over Creamer.

"Right now, it feels fantastic," Wie said. "It's a great year."

LPGA Tour Championship
Richmond, Texas
Winner: Anna Nordqvist

A rookie winning two of the LPGA Tour's biggest events in the same season: Was there a message in there?

It sure looked that way. Anna Nordqvist, surprise winner of the McDonald's LPGA Championship in June, might well have stamped herself as the next Swedish Terror when she outran world No. 1 Lorena Ochoa and took the season-ending LPGA Tour Championship.

With her dynamite finish, Nordqvist bore a distinct resemblance to Annika Sorenstam. In the final round — the tournament was cut to three rounds because of heavy November rains — Nordqvist warmed up with a birdie at No. 2, then ran off five straight at Nos. 8, 9, 10, 11 and 12. After a bogey at the 13th, she birdied the 14th and 15th for a seven-under-par 65 for a two-stroke win over Ochoa.

"It was pretty tight up on the leaderboard, so you were really going to have to shoot low in order to pull it off," Nordqvist said. "I definitely tried to be aggressive today."

Said Ochoa: "It really surprised me when I looked up at the leaderboard and Anna had already made two, three birdies. That was not a good feeling."

Nordqvist shot a 13-under 203 total at the Houstonian Golf and Country Club, near Houston. She opened with a two-under 70 that included five birdies, a bogey and a double bogey, then turned in a bogey-free 68, and then posted the sparkling 65.

The anticipated battle for the Rolex Player of the Year award, between Ochoa and Jiyai Shin, fizzled out. Shin, the Rolex Rookie of the Year, was bidding to become the first since 1978 to hold both titles in the same year. But a closing 73 dropped her to a tie for eighth. Ochoa, with three victories and 13 top-10 finishes, won her fourth consecutive Player of the Year award.

"It's a great year for me because it's been tough in many ways," said Ochoa, who struggled at times. "I always … want to stay at the top … so this is just a great year for me." It would get greater. Ochoa was going home to get married early in December.

Ladies European Tour

ANZ Ladies Masters
Ashmore, Australia
Winner: Katherine Hull

See Australian Ladies Tour section.

Women's Australian Open
Melbourne, Australia
Winner: Laura Davies

See Australian Ladies Tour section.

Comunitat Valenciana European Nations Cup
Alicante, Spain
Winners: Netherlands (Christel Boeljon/Marjet van der Graaff)

With France, in the form of Gwladys Nocera and Anne-Lise Caudel, taking the lead after 54 holes, the result of the second Comunitat Valenciana European Nations Cup at La Sella Golf Resort looked clear cut. But on a surprising final day, that was not the case. The Netherlands, who started two strokes behind, came through to win by four, leaving France to tie for second with Italy and Australia. While there were two days of traditional fourballs, there were also two rounds, including the last, played under the Valencia Cup format, a variation of greensomes. The teams play two balls on a par-three, or two balls hit alternately for two shots on a par-four and three on a par-five, before picking one ball.

Italians Veronica Zorzi and Giulia Sergas showed what could be done with a 62 on the last day, but its complications were exposed on day two when Austria were penalized 28 strokes for hitting the wrong ball on the greens. Two early birdies from the Netherlands team and then two bogeys from the French changed the complexion of the last day. The Netherlands claimed a fine birdie at the eighth, and despite a two-shot swing back on the 12th, France bogeyed the 13th and the winners birdied the last two to clinch the victory.

The Netherlands were represented by the unheralded pairing of Marjet van der Graaff, 26, in her second season on the tour, and 21-year-old Christel Boeljon, who showed herself a player of fine potential. This was only her third event, but she had already finished well at the Australian Open. "It's a great start. I don't think I could have asked for a better one, so I'm very happy," Boeljon said. "My putter was working quite well this week, so I made a lot of good birdies and good pars. I don't know what the key was. We both played solid and well, so we worked well as a team."

Defending champions England finished fourth, while America, along with Australia a guest team, were seventh after Meg Mallon and Beth Daniel held the halfway lead.

Deutsche Bank Ladies Swiss Open
Ticino, Switzerland
Winner: Marianne Skarpnord

Norway's Marianne Skarpnord celebrated her country's national day with her maiden victory in the Deutsche Bank Ladies Swiss Open. The 23-year-old's special day came in her fifth season on tour as the circuit hit Europe for the first time. Skarpnord held off a strong challenge from England's Melissa Reid, also looking for her first victory, to win by one at 16-under-par 276 at Golf Gerre Losone.

A seven-under 66 in the third round, after scores of 69 and 71, put Skarpnord ahead by one over Reid starting the final round. But Reid immediately jumped ahead with an eagle at the third. Skarpnord responded with three birdies in a row from the fifth to re-take the lead, but then dropped behind again after three-putting the ninth, where Reid hit her approach to two feet to go out in 32 with three birdies and the eagle. But Reid then faltered with three bogeys in a row from the 11th and Skarpnord birdied the 16th to go three ahead. Yet the drama was not over. Reid birdied the 17th, and after both players hit the green in two at the par-five 18th, seemed to have lost her chance when she missed an eagle putt. But having thought victory was comfortable, Skarpnord three-putted for a par to squeeze home by one.

"To get a win this early in the season is just great and now I can play the Evian Masters," she said. "It was hard work at the end, three-putting there. The first putt I didn't think was so fast, but it was. I thought it didn't matter if I make it or not, I can just put it close."

HypoVereinsbank Ladies German Open
Munich, Germany
Winner: Jade Schaeffer

France's Jade Schaeffer won her maiden title on tour with a fine comeback to beat Paula Marti in a playoff at the HypoVereinsbank Ladies German Open at Golfpark Gut Hausern, near Munich. Schaeffer started the final round six strokes behind Marti. The Spaniard was trying to win for the first time in Europe since she won twice in her rookie season in 2001.

But Marti could only manage a closing 73, while Schaeffer came out of the pack with a brilliant 67. She birdied six of the first eight holes, and despite bogeys at the ninth and 10th, another birdie at the 12th put her into the lead. She finished with six pars and then had to wait as the leaders closed in, but despite numerous chances, Marti could not get ahead of Schaeffer. The pair finished at 13-under-par 275, one ahead of Melissa Reid and Germany's Martina Eberl, who was helping to host the event.

Trish Johnson finished a further stroke behind. The playoff ended at the first extra hole when Schaeffer holed from three feet for a birdie. It was the first time she had made a cut this season.

Schaeffer, 22, is from Strasburg, but now lives in Paris and is the younger sister of former LET player Fany Schaeffer. Her previous best finish was a third place in 2007. While she waited for a possible playoff she was given a pep talk over the phone by her boyfriend, Francois Calmels, who plays on the European Challenge Tour. He told her: "You're fun, you're happy, it's good. You played good and today you will win. Come on Jade, you can do it."

ABN AMRO Ladies Open
Valkenswaard, Netherlands
Winner: Tania Elosegui

When Tania Elosegui finished as runner-up to Laura Davies at the Australian Open early in 2009 it was her fifth second place on the Ladies European Tour. A maiden victory was overdue and finally came on a rainy day at Eindhovensche in the Netherlands at the ABN AMRO Ladies Open. The 27-year-old from Spain, in her fourth season on the tour, came from two strokes behind overnight leader Diana Luna with a closing 69 to finish at nine-under-par 207 for 54 holes. She won by only one stroke over Luna after an exciting duel from the Italian. Still tied for the lead going to the last hole, Luna got up and down from a bunker for a par but could do nothing about Elosegui holing from eight feet for a birdie to take the title.

"Once she (Luna) holed her putt I told myself, 'You have to hole this — you're not going to finish second again,'" Elosegui said. "I feel very, very happy because five times I've finished second already." Luna was second after a 72, while Norway's Marianne Skarpnord was third, three behind the winner, with Jade Schaeffer and Becky Brewerton sharing fourth place.

Ladies Open de Portugal
Rio Maior, Portugal
Winner: Johanna Westerberg

Helped by her caddie — an international tennis star — Johanna Westerberg earned her maiden victory with a stroke of brilliance at the first hole of a playoff. The 31-year-old Swede, who found sand both off the tee and with her second shot, holed out from a greenside bunker for a birdie at the 18th to bring the playoff to an abrupt halt. Westerberg became the fourth player in a row to claim her first victory, but denied Spain's Tania Elosegui from recording a second win in successive weeks.

Elosegui started the third and final round among a group one stroke behind overnight leader Lotta Wahlin, who birdied the first hole but then fell away to a 76 and a tie for 14th place. Elosegui, who closed with a 70, led for much of the day, but Westerberg, who was five behind at the start of the day, put in a superb charge to come in with a 67 and set the clubhouse target at three-under-par 213. She compiled six birdies and dropped only one shot, as twos as the 12th and 16th holes and a four at the par-five 15th took her into the lead.

Elosegui produced a rare three at the 18th to tie, but Westerberg produced another moments later in the playoff. "To hole that to win, I couldn't ask for more," said Westerberg, who had been a runner-up twice in seven years on tour. "To win finally is fantastic, I played really well on the back nine."

Her caddie was her fiancé, Joachim Johannson, otherwise known as "Pim-Pim." A shoulder injury had been keeping him off the tennis tour and available for caddie duties. "He's a great comfort on the course and as he's a top athlete himself he knows what it's all about. That helped keep me calm when the pressure was on."

AIB Ladies Irish Open
Portmarnock, Co. Dublin, Ireland
Winner: Diana Luna

Five years after winning her only other LET title and three weeks after finishing runner-up in Holland, Diana Luna overcame two fog delays at Portmarnock Links to win the AIB Ladies Irish Open by four strokes. Luna was bogey-free on the third and final day and left the experienced duo of Gwladys Nocera and Sophie Gustafson sharing second place with England's Florentyna Parker, who recorded her best ever result, as did Scotland's Krystle Caithness, who was fifth.

Having started the day with a one-shot lead, Luna finished at 11-under-par 205 and victory never looked in doubt. She carded three birdies going out, on the sixth, seventh and ninth holes, for an outward total of 33 before heading back in 35 after a final birdie at the par-five 13th. "I am very happy with the way I played. I hit 18 greens and was always putting. I never had to chip the whole way round so it was a great day for me," said the 2004 Tenerife Ladies Open champion.

After working hard on technique with her coach Roger Damiano at Cannes Mougins in France, Luna estimated that she had put 20 meters on her driving distance. "I could fly more of the bunkers easily this year, so it was like a different course," she added. Identical twins Leona and Lisa Maguire, who even at 14 have both won the Irish Close title, both missed the cut, but on the opening day Leona's 74 out-scored playing partner Laura Davies by a stroke.

SAS Ladies Masters
Larvik, Norway
Winner: Diana Luna

After waiting five years for her second victory, Italy's Diana Luna had to wait less than a week for her third as the 26-year-old won the SAS Ladies Masters at Larvik in Norway. Luna started the third and final round three behind overnight leader Veronica Zorzi, who slipped to 75 as Luna compiled 70 to finish on 12-under-par 207. She won by one over Spain's Laura Cabanillas, who recorded her best ever finish after seven seasons on tour.

Luna had five birdies, four bogeys and an eagle at the ninth hole. Her run to the finish started with a two at the par-three 15th, where she had a hole-in-one on the first day. At the three par-fives from 16 home she had a bogey and a birdie and then three-putted for a par, which she thought would prove disaster. But Zorzi, who gave herself a chance by eagling the 17th, bogeyed the last and tied for third place at 10 under alongside Iben Tinning, Felicity Johnson, Stephanie Na, Beth Allen, Tania Elosegui and Lisa Holm Sorensen, who opened with 62 to become the third player to score that number on the Ladies European Tour.

"I cannot believe it," Luna said after collapsing to her knees and holding her face in her hands. "It's incredible because, honestly, I really didn't expect that, especially after three putts on the 18th. I was really sure that I needed a birdie or even an eagle, because there were no leaderboards. I didn't know that she (Zorzi) was 11 under. I thought she was 12 under. It was very surprising. I thought I had lost, actually, on 18 when I missed my putt."

Open de Espana Feminino
San Jordi, Castellon, Spain
Winner: Becky Brewerton

With only three events left to try to qualify for the European Solheim Cup team, Becky Brewerton's problem was that she was not actually playing in all of them. But the 2007 team member sorted that out and boosted her points tally by winning the Open de Espana Feminino at Panoramica in Castellon. Brewerton shared the first-round lead with a 65, then led by three and then five strokes with rounds of 69 and 66, and finally a 70 gave her an 18-under-par 270 total and a six-stroke victory over Welshwoman Breanne Loucks, Italian Diana Luna and Spaniards Tania Elosegui and Emma Cabrera-Bello.

It was Brewerton's second title following the 2007 Ladies English Open and she earned a first prize of €41,250 as well as a place in the following week's lucrative Evian Masters in France. She was six strokes ahead of Elosegui after four birdies in her first nine holes, but stumbled to a double bogey at the par-three 12th, when she hit her tee shot into the water short of the green. A bogey at the 15th was countered by a closing birdie at the last hole.

"I'm so, so happy. To have such a big lead at the start was nice, because it was a little bit nervy at the end when the wind was gusting up. It was a brilliant week," Brewerton said. "It was an absolute must that I had to win here to get some Solheim points, to get into the Evian, to give myself a better chance of making that team, and it paid off."

Evian Masters
Evians-les-Bains, France
Winner: Ai Miyazato

Winning came easily for Ai Miyazato in Japan, but in her fourth full season on the LPGA Tour, the 24-year-old claimed her first victory on that circuit or on the Ladies European Tour at the Evian Masters which is co-sanctioned by both tours. The 5-foot-2 Miyazato defeated one of the biggest hitters in women's golf in Sophie Gustafson at the first extra hole of a playoff at the 18th hole. Earlier both women had birdied the 18th, with Miyazato holing from 10 feet and Gustafson just tapping in. They finished at 14-under-par 274 after rounds of 69 and 70 respectively and finished one ahead of South Korea's Meena Lee, who closed with the lowest round of the week with a 65, and Cristie Kerr, who had 70.

In the playoff, Miyazato's first on the LPGA Tour, Gustafson drove into the rough and could only reach the green at the par-five in three shots. Miyazato hit a great drive and could go for the green but found a bunker. However, she came out to three feet, and after Gustafson missed from 10 feet for her birdie, Miyazato holed out for the victory. She became the second Japanese winner of the Evian Masters 12 years after Hiromi Kobayashi won the event in a playoff in 1997. Miyazato, who earned a first prize of $487,500, said: "I didn't watch the scoreboard until the end of the final round. I was just trying to make birdies and I tried to control myself."

Miyazato won as an amateur in Japan before turning professional in 2003. In 2005 she helped Japan win the World Cup and at the end of the year won the LPGA qualifying tournament by a record 12 strokes. But then she had to wait for this win. "When I had a good success in Japan I was still very young," she said. "I was just going for it, not scared of anything. When I came to the States, I had to adjust to many things, like the culture, the language. I feel the four years it took me was very valuable."

Gustafson, who struggled with her putter on the weekend, had shared the 54-hole lead with In-Kyung Kim and Becky Brewerton. After winning the Spanish Open, Brewerton had led or shared the lead for seven successive rounds but crashed to a 76 to finish 13th.

Catriona Matthew and Amy Yang had a lucky escape on the night before the tournament when their hotel caught fire. Matthew's husband was treated for burns on his feet, while Yang and her father escaped by jumping out of a window.

Ricoh Women's British Open
Lancashire, England
Winner: Catriona Matthew

See Chapter 6.

S4/C Wales Ladies Championship of Europe
Harlech, Wales
Winner: Karen Stupples

Karen Stupples made up for a disappointing season, culminating in missing out on a wild card pick for the European Solheim Cup team the week before, by winning the S4/C Wales Ladies Championship of Europe at Royal St. David's in Harlech.

At home on the great, traditional links course, Stupples, who grew up playing at Royal Cinque Ports in Deal, Kent, came from two strokes behind Amy Yang with a 70 to win by one over the South Korean despite dropping shots at two of the last three holes. It was the third win of Stupples's career, during which she has mainly been based in America, and her first since becoming the British Open champion in 2004. Stupples birdied the first two holes to tie Yang and then forged ahead with birdies at the fourth and eighth to be three in front at the turn. Yang closed with a 73, while Australian Katherine Hull took third place with a 69, one ahead of home favorite Becky Brewerton.

During 2009, Stupples had missed seven of 14 cuts on the LPGA circuit and missed a month's action after having her appendix removed. She also had a problem with the veins in her legs which restricted her practice. "It's been quite a traumatic year, physically and mentally," Stupples said. "I was very, very disappointed at not being in the Solheim Cup. It was always a big goal of mine to be there and I think, to be perfectly honest, I tried too hard to get in. I've come here free of the burden of trying to be selected or trying to prove how good I am or what form I'm in, and I think the real Karen Stupples showed up this week."

The Solheim Cup
Sugar Grove, Illinois
Winners: United States

See LPGA Tour section.

Finnair Masters
Tali, Finland
Winner: Beatriz Recari

Forced into a playoff after starting the day five strokes ahead of the field, Spain's Beatriz Recari at least found the quickest way to put an end to the tournament and claim her maiden victory. Recari holed her four-iron approach shot from 177 yards at the 18th on the first extra hole and walked up the fairway taking the applause of the gallery and leaving Iben Tinning without the chance to continue.

It was the only eagle all week at the 18th of the Helsinki Golf Club, which has become a favorite venue for the 22-year-old from Pamplona. Her only top-10 finish in four years on tour had come in the Finnair Masters the previous year when she led after the first round and eventually finished tied for third place.

This time Recari led the event every day after rounds of 65 and 64, a new course record, and compiling 13 birdies, an eagle and only two bogeys for the first 36 holes. But on the final day she managed only one birdie and three bogeys in a 73 as she came under pressure from Tinning. The experienced Dane closed with a 68, but Recari held firm to hole from five feet on the 18th to join the playoff.

But extra time did not last long, thanks to the help of her boyfriend and caddie, Andreas Thorp. "That was definitely the shot of my life," Recari said, "one to talk about to the grandchildren. To be honest, I owe a lot to my caddie, because I hit a four iron in the round and it was so short, so I told him, 'hybrid.' He said, 'We'll stick to the club,' and it went in, so I owe him some percentage for that. I was talking to him and he was telling me to just enjoy and have fun. I visualized the shot and he chose the club. It was the only iron I hit well all day."

UNIQA Ladies Golf Open
Neustadt, Austria
Winner: Linda Wessberg

Laura Davies saw her hopes of a third successive victory in the UNIQA Ladies Golf Open drowned in the pond at the 18th hole at Fohrenwald when she twice hit into it on the second hole of a playoff. Davies took a seven, and despite a bogey-six herself, victory went to Sweden's Linda Wessberg.

Wessberg, one of three overnight leaders, claimed her third victory on the tour and her first for two years. After three seasons in America, the 28-year-old from Gothenburg returned to Europe and a few months later saw her game come around. A double bogey at the 10th hole in the final round looked to have played her out of contention, but when she birdied the 12th she was one of seven co-leaders. Wessberg then birdied the next three holes for four in a row, and despite a bogey at the 16th, closed with 71 to join Davies at nine-under-par 279 after the 45-year-old Englishwoman birdied the 16th and 18th holes to come from two behind with a 69.

At the first extra hole Wessberg needed to get up and down from a bunker to survive, but at the next, on the 18th, Davies found a wet lie in the rough as the rain poured down. Twice she attempted to reach the green and came up short. "I had a 50/50 lie in the rough and I went for it, because you go for it in a playoff. It came out a little bit right and went into the water because it was wet, I suppose. The next shot was a shocker."

Wessberg, whose mother Elizabeth was caddieing, said: "I'm just so happy that I can actually show myself that I am able to win again. I had been struggling with a shoulder injury and stuff, but I still played and I probably shouldn't have. Mentally it was really hard."

Randstad Open de France
Nord-Pas de Calais, France
Winner: Nicole Gergely

Nicole Gergely managed to upstage her compatriot Markus Brier, who tied for 17th as the leading home player in the Austrian Open on the men's European Tour, by becoming the first woman from her country to win on the Ladies European Tour. Gergely came from three strokes off the lead to win the Randstad Open de France in its last year at Le Golf d'Arras before the event moves to Paris for 2010. Gergely made a slow start, finding the water at the second for a bogey, but was then faultless in producing a 67 to win at 13-under-par 275 by two strokes over Finland's Ursula Wikstrom. Starting on the same mark as the Austrian, Wikstrom closed with a 69 to finish one ahead of Becky Brewerton, who had a double-bogey six at the last, and Anja Monke.

Gergely, the 24-year-old from Judenburg, leapt into contention with three birdies in a row from the fourth hole and then made crucial birdies at the 10th, 13th and 14th. Gergely was the ninth first-time winner on the circuit in 2009, while Austria became the 12th country to be represented by the winners during the season.

"It's awesome. I can't believe it. It was always a dream," she said. "I played so well this year. Today I thought, 'Okay, I won't put myself under pressure. I'll just see whenever it comes, it comes.' It's really unexpected here; it's unbelievable. I got a mail yesterday from Golf-Live.at, who always does the live scoring for us. Marcus Brier is playing in Austria and he was seventh. They said it would be really cool if you can win it and just put him in the shadow. I thought, 'That's some kind of pressure, but why not.'"

Tenerife Ladies Open
Tenerife, Spain
Winner: Felicity Johnson

After winning the Spanish Open earlier in the season, Becky Brewerton was in line for a double on Spanish soil when she held a three-stroke lead at both halfway and after 54 holes of the Tenerife Open at Costa Adeja. But the Welshwoman was denied by a powerful finish from Felicity Johnson who had five birdies and two bogeys in the last seven holes. It was Johnson's first win in her third season on the tour after four third-place finishes.

The 22-year-old from Birmingham, England, got within one shot of Brewerton with a two-under front nine. Both players birdied the 12th and then twice Johnson caught up before both bogeyed the 16th. Brewerton had birdie chances on the last two holes but could not take them, while Johnson certainly did. She holed from 25 feet at the 17th and then at the 18th she hit a rescue club to six feet for a two-putt birdie. She closed with a 67, compared to Brewerton's 72, to finish on 14-under-par 274 and win by two strokes. Bettina Hauert of Germany finished a distant third, five behind Brewerton, with Melissa Reid and Tania Elosegui tying for fourth.

"It's all a bit surreal at the moment really, but I've worked so hard for this, so it's just fantastic that it's finally come together for me," said Johnson. "I hit a lot of fairways and a lot of greens and made a couple of good up-and-downs early on which kept the pars on the card. I just hit one bad shot on 14 and made a bogey there, but apart from that I played really solid golf again. I hit a really good shot into 15 which hit the flag, so that was pleasing. I holed a really good putt on 17 from 25 feet or so, which gave me the boost I needed at the last."

Madrid Ladies Masters
Madrid, Spain
Winner: Azahara Munoz

Confirmation of the great talent emerging on the Ladies European Tour came at Casino Club de Golf Retamares as Spain's Azahara Munoz won the Madrid Ladies Masters in her first professional tour event. Munoz, a month short of her 22nd birthday, had only previously played in the first stage of the LPGA qualifying in America, where she finished second. Any need of attending the European equivalent later in the year was removed along with the €50,000 check for first place.

Munoz won in spectacular fashion with a final round of 64 and then winning a playoff at the 18th hole with an eagle. She defeated Anna Nordqvist, herself a rookie after winning the qualifying at the start of the season and then becoming a major winner at the McDonald's LPGA Championship. That was in June when Munoz won the British Ladies Amateur Championship by beating compatriot Carlota Ciganda in the final.

Munoz started six behind overnight leader Veronica Zorzi, while Nordqvist was seven back and set the target in the 54-hole event at 16-under-par 203 after a career best of 63, featuring five birdies on each nine. Munoz dropped a shot at the second hole, but after a birdie at the fourth, played the last 13 holes in nine under. Out in 33, she eagled the 10th then holed from inside six feet at the 11th and the 15th before hitting her approaches to tap-in range at the 16th and 18th holes.

"I can't believe I won. It's like a dream come true," said Munoz, who is from Malaga and was a teammate of Nordqvist for two years at Arizona State University. "This is just the beginning. I'm going to keep on practicing and trying to get better. I've been putting well all week, but I've been hitting the ball pretty bad. Today I hit the ball much better and I hit it much closer and I kept on making putts. That was the key."

Carta Si Ladies Italian Open
Milan, Italy
Winner: Marianne Skarpnord

Marianne Skarpnord, despite falling six strokes behind with eight holes to play, beat Laura Davies in a playoff to win the Carta Si Ladies Italian Open at Rovedine Golf Club in Milan. Skarpnord won her second title of the season at the third extra hole when she holed from six feet for a birdie-four at the 18th. But earlier the Norwegian had holed a 35-foot uphill eagle putt at the last to tie Davies, who led by three with two holes to play but bogeyed the 17th and could only par the 18th.

Both Davies and Skarpnord, who shared the 36-hole lead, finished with rounds of 69 to be at 12-under-par 204, but had very different routes to get there. Skarpnord was out in 39, and when Davies birdied the 10th, she was six ahead of her playing partner. But Skarpnord rattled off four birdies and an eagle as she came home in 30 thanks to the help of her caddie and boyfriend.

"I played good on the back nine every day. Petter said when we turned at the ninth and I was three over, 'Okay the back nine is your host; we can play great there.' I like the holes and I did," she explained.

Davies had a chance of winning with an eagle putt on the second extra hole, but could not secure a first win of the season on European soil. "I played great today. I hit one bad shot. I hit a bad eight iron on No. 6 and had a double bogey. After that I played great again," said Davies. "That eagle putt in the playoff could have won it. It's a cruel loss to be honest with you. It's very disappointing. The whole year has been very disappointing to be honest with you, but what can you do."

Suzhou Taihu Ladies Open
Shanghai, China
Winner: Bo Mi Suh

Eleven years after giving up the piano and taking up golf instead, Bo Mi Suh won her maiden title at the Suzhou Taihu Ladies Open. The 28-year-old South Korean, a professional for five years, converted a two-stroke overnight lead into a one-stroke win at six-under-par 210 with rounds of 69, 69 and 72. Her closest challenger was Gwladys Nocera, the European No. 1 in 2008, whose hopes of a first win of 2009 were thwarted by a retrospective two-stroke penalty for being late on the first tee on the first day. It was only the following morning that Nocera's delayed arrival was reported to officials and at that point her opening 68, which tied for the lead with Pornanong Phutlum, was changed to a 70.

The Frenchwoman fell three behind with a 71 on Saturday, but on a closing day that was cold and windy her 70 matched the best of the day but left her one short. Nocera put in a fine effort on the back nine, which she played in three under with birdies at the 10th, 16th and 18th. After stumbling with bogeys at the 10th and 11th, Suh settled her nerves with a birdie at the 12th, but came to the last even with Nocera's clubhouse target. But Suh hit an approach to 20 feet at the par-five, and although she raced the eagle putt four feet past, she made the one back for the victory.

Not that she realized it at the time. "I didn't know. The other players came to me and said congratulations," she said. "I'm very happy. It's a dream come true. Today was very windy so it was difficult to concentrate. I tried to control my game."

Daishin Securities Tomato Tour Korean Ladies Masters
Jeju Island, South Korea
Winner: Hyun-Ji Kim

Hyun-Ji Kim returned on Monday morning to win the Daishin Securities Tomato Tour Korean Ladies Masters and pitched to three feet at the 18th to set up her victory over So Yeon Ryu at the second extra hole. The playoff had been interrupted by darkness the night before after the final round was suspended twice for thunderstorms. Ryu had pitched to eight feet at the par-five 18th but missed her birdie chance, and Kim completed her first victory on the KLPGA and LET circuits at the co-sanctioned event.

Both Kim, 21, and Ryu, 19, were in their second seasons on the KLPGA, but Ryu had already won four times on her home circuit. The pair were joined in the playoff by the London-born South Korean Sarah Lee, who was eliminated on Sunday night when she failed to birdie the 18th on the first playoff hole.

Earlier all three had birdied the 18th to reach the playoff at one-under-par 215 in the difficult conditions at the Cypress Resort on Jeju Island. Kim closed with a 73, Lee had a 74, but Ryu came home in 33 for a 70. Defending champion Hee-Kyung Seo, the leader after 36 holes, finished in fourth place after a 74, while Rebecca Coakley and Anna Rawson shared fifth place with local amateur Se-Young Kim.

Omega Dubai Ladies Masters
Dubai, United Arab Emirates
Winner: In-Kyung Kim

Two players who received invitations to play in the Omega Dubai Ladies Masters, the closing event on the Ladies European Tour, dominated at the Emirates Golf Club, with South Korea's In-Kyung Kim beating Michelle Wie by three strokes. Wie, who spent the week not just getting over jetlag but spending her evenings doing university exams via the internet, finished with a 65 to put the pressure on the leader.

But at the par-five 18th, Wie's second shot found the water and she did well to get up and down for a par to finish on 15 under. Kim, who led Anna Nordqvist by three with a round to play, later birdied the hole to finish at 18-under 270. She had rounds of 70, 65, 67 and 68. Her final round started shakily with a bogey at the first, but then she birdied the next two holes. She also birdied the 10th and 15th, as well as the last, during a highly impressive back nine where she hit every green in regulation.

Kim, 21, moved to America at the age of 16 and had won twice in her three years on the LPGA Tour. This victory also gave her the option of taking up her LET card. "I'm very excited to win this week," said Kim. "Michelle had a great turn. She had six birdies until 13 and was very impressive. But I tried to keep playing my game, and I think, yeah, I did a good job." Although playing in Dubai for the first time, Kim was assisted by her caddie Terry McNamara, who won twice with Annika Sorenstam over the same course.

By finishing 14th, Sophie Gustafson clinched her fourth Henderson Money List title and said she would be looking to play more in Europe in 2010. Catriona Matthew was the runner-up and was also voted the Players' Player of the Year following her victory at the Ricoh Women's British Open, just 11 weeks after giving birth to her second daughter. Nordqvist was the Rookie of the Year.

Japan LPGA Tour

Daikin Orchid Ladies
Nanjo, Okinawa
Winner: Yuko Mitsuka

Yuko Mitsuka's superb 66 in driving rain set the stage for her third victory on the Japan LPGA Tour in the Daikin Orchid Ladies, the traditional season opener on the island of Okinawa in early March. She went on to win by two strokes with her eight-under-par 208.

The six-birdie 66 in the damp second round enabled Mitsuka to take over the lead from Sakura Yokomine and Bo-Bae Song, the defending champion at Ryukyu Golf Club. They shot 68s in the opening round to lead Ayako Uehara, Australia's Tamie Durdin and Okinawa native Shinobu Moromizato by one. Mitsuka was two back with Erina Hara and South Korea's Mi-Jeong Jeon. Her 136 gave Mitsuka a two-shot advantage over Uehara (69) and four or more over the rest of the drenched field.

Her play Sunday contrasted greatly with that second round. She had five birdies and five bogeys on the first 15 holes, then parred home with a 72. Uehara matched the 72 and tied for second with Hara (69).

Yokohama Tire PRGR Cup
Konan, Kochi
Winner: Ayako Uehara

Rainy weather followed the Japan LPGA Tour to its second stop and eventually led tournament officials to shorten the Yokohama Tire PRGR Cup to 36 holes. Ayako Uehara was the beneficiary of the final-round cancellation, winning by five strokes with a nine-under-par 135.

Coming off a runner-up finish two weeks earlier in the Daikin Orchid tournament, Uehara established that five-shot margin in the first round at Tosa Country Club. She ripped off eight birdies and rolled to an eight-under 64 despite windy weather to finish five in front of little-known Yayoi Arasaki. Only four others broke par in the tough conditions. Uehara followed with a 71 Saturday and maintained the big lead, then over Midori Yoneyama (68) and South Korean Ah-Reum Hwang.

She never teed off Sunday as heavy rains eventually made the course unplayable for the day and the round was cancelled. It gave the 25-year-old Uehara a second title to go with her 2008 victory in the Fujisankei Ladies Classic.

Yamaha Ladies Open
Fukuroi, Shizuoka
Winner: Ah-Reum Hwang

Getting her first victory on the Japan LPGA Tour in the Yamaha Ladies Open, the third tournament of the season, surprised Ah-Reum Hwang and overwhelmed the field.

"It came much quicker than I expected," exclaimed the 21-year-old South Korean, who exploded with a seven-under-par 65, the best score of her competitive career, in the final round at Katsuragi Golf Club for an 11-under-par 205 and an eight-stroke victory.

What added to the surprise was her start in the tournament. Hwang, co-runner-up a week earlier in the Yokohama Tire event, shot 73 in the opening round and was tied for 18th place, three behind co-leaders Midori Yoneyama, a seven-time winner on the circuit, and two non-winners, Ikue Asama and Yuka Shiroto. But Hwang bolted into the lead Saturday, making five birdies on her last eight holes for a five-under 67–140, a shot ahead of Erina Hara (68) and Mie Nakata (70).

Five front-nine birdies virtually ensured the victory Sunday. Left far behind in second place were Julie Lu, Ji-Woo Lee and Hara, who shot 72. Nakata, the other Saturday runner-up, tumbled with a 77.

Studio Alice Ladies Open
Miki, Hyogo
Winner: Sakura Yokomine

Sakura Yokomine launched her drive to the No. 1 spot on the money list with a playoff victory in the Studio Alice Ladies Open. In an exciting finish, Yokomine birdied the 54th hole to overtake Mi-Jeong Jeon, then defeated her with a three-foot par putt on the second extra hole.

The Studio Alice got a special boost when Ai Miyazato, Japan's world-class star on the U.S. LPGA Tour, took advantage of a break in that circuit, entered the tournament and made a strong run at the title. The 23-year-old opened with a three-under-par 69 on the Yokawa course of Hanayashiki Golf Club in Miki and shared the first-round lead with Rui Kitada and Jeon.

Miyazato and Jeon followed with 72s for 141 and remained on top. At that point, Yokomine trailed by three after rounds of 71-73–144. Miyazato fell from contention with five bogeys in the middle of the final round. Yokomine made her move with three early birdies, but was a shot behind Jeon until she birdied the last hole for 68 and the tying 212. Kitada finished with a par to miss the playoff by a shot.

Life Card Ladies
Kikuyo, Kumamoto
Winner: Ji-Hee Lee

Ji-Hee Lee, one of the most successful of the recent South Koreans on the Japan LPGA Tour, exhibited the grit that had made her an 11-time winner over the previous six seasons when she made it an even dozen in the Life Card Ladies tournament at the Kumamoto Airport Country Club at Kikuyo.

Locked in a battle with several contenders after carrying a one-stroke lead into the final round, Lee seemed to have taken herself out of the picture when she suffered her fifth straight bogey at the 11th hole. That dropped her three behind Sakura Yokomine, who was gunning for her second win in a row. A par save at the 12th turned things around. Lee then birdied the 14th, 15th and 16th to catch Yokomine, matched her with a par at the 17th, and two-putted for a final birdie at the 18th for the win when Yokomine could only muster her 16th straight par there.

Both players had final-round 73s, Lee's for the winning three-under-par 213.

Fujisankei Ladies Classic
Ito, Shizuoka
Winner: Tamie Durdin

For the second time in little more than a month, bad weather interfered with a Japan LPGA tournament. Heavy winds made the Kawana Hotel Golf Course unplayable early in the final round of the Fujisankei Ladies Classic Sunday afternoon. The round was cancelled after just a few holes were played and Australia's Tamie Durdin was declared the winner, her first in five seasons on that circuit.

Durdin, 32, a collegiate golfer in America at Pepperdine University who spent three years on the U.S. LPGA Tour before going to Japan in 2005, had taken a three-shot lead when she finished her second round that morning with a round of 69 and a 36-hole score of 137. Jiyai Shin, the highly successful young South Korean, had a pair of 70s and secured second place.

Chie Arimura had a spectacular first round, holing a 235-yard three wood for an albatross (double eagle) en route to a 65 and the lead by two over Ami Shiozaki and by three over Sakura Yokomine, amateur Makoto Takemura and Durdin. However, Arimura collapsed in the second round's tough playing conditions and skied to an 80 and a tie for 10th place.

Crystal Geyser Ladies
Chiba
Winner: Chie Arimura

Talk about taking disaster in stride. A week after leading a tournament and then absorbing a crushing 80 in the final round, Chie Arimura put her second victory on the Japan LPGA Tour into the books at the Crystal Geyser Ladies tournament.

The 21-year-old, who picked up her first title in the 2008 Promise Ladies, began her recovery with a first-round 67 at Chiba's Keiyo Country Club and trailed only Akane Iijima's 66. Arimura followed with a two-under-par 70 Saturday that elevated her into a tie for the lead with veteran Yuko Saitoh (68-69) at 137, two in front of Mi-Jeong Jeon and Mie Nakata.

Arimura broke away from Saitoh and Sakura Yokomine on the back side of Sunday's final round. She trailed Saitoh by a stroke through 11 holes, but with birdies at the 12th and 15th and a fine par save at the 14th, she led both players by three strokes and maintained that margin to the finish. She posted another 70 for nine-under-par 207. Yokomine took solo second place with 69–210 as Saitoh shot 75 and tied Nakata (73) for third at 212.

World Ladies Championship Salonpas Cup
Tsukubamirai, Ibaraki
Winner: Shinobu Moromizato

Shinobu Moromizato had her hands full as she drove toward her first victory of 2009 in the World Ladies Championship Salonpas Cup, the season's first major. She carried a two-stroke lead into the final round of the 72-hole championship with the likes of multiple winners Akiko Fukushima, Mi-Jeong Jeon and Chie Arimura right on her heels and Sakura Yokomine and American star Paula Creamer within striking distance.

Moromizato held them all off, just barely, as she registered a one-stroke victory, her fourth and second major to go with the 2007 Japan Women's Open. Her three-under-par 69 gave her a 275, 13 under par.

Moromizato put herself in the midst of the contenders in the first two rounds on Ibaraki Golf Club's West course. Fukushima, the winner of 23 tournaments on the tour during her long career and most recently the 2008 Salonpas Cup, led for two days. She was knotted with Ji-Hee Lee, Hyun-Ju Shin and Jeon at 68 Thursday, then repeated that score Friday to move a shot ahead of Jeon. Creamer, Lee and Moromizato were three back.

The 22-year-old Moromizato then produced a 67–206 to push Fukushima two behind and Jeon three off the pace. Creamer, who teed off in the third-to-last group Sunday, fired a potent 65 to lead in the clubhouse at 276. One stroke too many, as it turned out. Jeon, with 67, tied her for second place.

Vernal Ladies
Asakura, Fukuoka
Winner: Yuko Saitoh

It was time for a veteran to wind up in the winner's circle. Yuko Saitoh had those honors in mid-May as the 41-year-old produced a solid wire-to-wire victory in the Vernal Ladies tournament at Fukuoka Century Golf Club, just the second win in her 18-year tour career.

Saitoh began with a five-under-par 67 and shared the first-round lead with South Korea's So-Hee Kim. Eun-A Lim, the defending champion, shot 68, as did Sakura Yokomine and Yuko Mitsuka. Saitoh's 70–137 Saturday gave her sole possession of first place, but just a stroke ahead of the great Yuri Fudoh, who shot 67 for her 138 in a bid for her first win of the season and 47th of her marvelous career.

Bad weather continued to plague the tour, moving in on Sunday and affecting the scoring. The best scores of the day were the 71s of Miho Koga and Saiki Fujita, so Saitoh's 74 for 211 gave her a three-stroke victory margin. Fudoh shot 76 and tied for second at 214 with Koga and Lim.

Chukyo TV Bridgestone Ladies
Toyota, Aichi
Winner: Eun-A Lim

Eun-A Lim came close to a successful defense of her only title on the Japan LPGA Tour in the Vernal Ladies, finishing second to Yuko Saitoh. Her strong play carried over to the next tournament on the schedule and rewarded her with her second tour victory in the Chukyo TV Bridgestone Ladies. The feat required three playoff holes after she overtook Yuko Mitsuka in the final round.

Mitsuka, who won the season-opening Daikin Orchid tournament, had led all the way until then. She started with a 67 and a two-stroke margin over Lim and three others — Chie Arimura, Maiko Wakabayashi and Kumiko Kaneda. Mitsuka managed to maintain that two-shot edge Saturday despite a wild 71–138. She recorded seven birdies but gave back six of those strokes with four bogeys and a double bogey. Lim and Wakabayashi matched the 71 to remain in the runner-up slot.

Lim rallied late in the final round with three birdies in a four-hole stretch starting at No. 13 for a three-under-par 69 and the deadlock at 209 with Mitsuka. Lim landed the victory with a short par putt on the third extra hole after Mitsuka overshot the green and failed to rescue her par.

Kosaido Ladies Golf Cup
Ichihara, Chiba
Winner: Sakura Yokomine

On the last day of May, the Japan LPGA Tour finally had a multiple 2009 winner. Appropriately, it was Sakura Yokomine, who had finished in the top

10 in eight of nine previous starts, which included her win in the Studio Alice tournament.

An eight-under-par 64 in the second round of the Kosaido Ladies Golf Cup at Chiba Kosaido Country Club keyed the victory. The eight-birdie, no-bogey score equaled her career low round and enabled her to pass first-round leader Chie Arimura (67) and establish a three-stroke margin over her with a 132. Yokomine and So-Hee Kim had trailed Arimura by a shot Friday.

Yokomine had a mundane 71 Sunday with two birdies and a bogey, but was never threatened by Arimura (70) or Maiko Wakabayashi (70) as she won her 11th tournament by two over Arimura with her 13-under-par 203. Shinobu Moromizato made a run Sunday, but her 66 merely tied her for third with Wakabayashi (70) at 206.

Resort Trust Ladies
Koga, Shiga
Winner: Mi-Jeong Jeon

South Korea's Mi-Jeong Jeon, perhaps the best of the overseas players competing regularly on the Japan LPGA Tour, took the first big step of another successful season with a runaway victory as she defended the title in the Resort Trust Ladies tournament. With consecutive 65s in the final two rounds at Koga's The Country Club, Jeon compiled a 14-under-par 202 and rolled to a seven-stroke victory.

Before annexing that 10th tour victory, she had made runs earlier in the season and already had two runner-up finishes, including a playoff loss to Sakura Yokomine in the Studio Alice tournament. Just in her fifth season in Japan, Jeon won nine times in the previous three campaigns and placed sixth or better on those three money lists.

Only eight players broke par in the first round of the Resort Trust, Yuko Mitsuka leading the way with a three-under-par 69. Then, Jeon, who had two double bogeys and a 72 the first day, took over Saturday with the first of her two 65s. The 137 put her four strokes ahead of China's Li-Ying Ye and Akiko Fukushima, who gave up three strokes on the last three holes for 70 and her 141.

After an early bogey Sunday, Jeon birdied eight of her last 12 holes for the second 65 and 14-under-par 202. Fukushima had five birdies on her last six holes for 68 to secure second place.

We Love Kobe Suntory Ladies Open
Kobe, Hyogo
Winner: Shinobu Moromizato

The race was on. Two weeks after Sakura Yokomine became the first double winner of the season, Shinobu Moromizato picked up her second win in the We Love Kobe Suntory Ladies Open. This back-and-forth between the two young stars was to continue to the final event of the season.

Moromizato had to stage a late rally and go extra holes to defeat China's Li-Ying Ye in the Suntory Open, the season's second 72-hole tournament, and land her fifth title on the Japan LPGA Tour.

After two indecisive rounds, Maiko Wakabayashi emerged with a 67 Saturday and went a stroke in front of Moromizato and three ahead of Ye. The Chinese pro got the upper hand in the early going Sunday, but Moromizato birdied the 15th and 16th holes to catch her. She shot 68 and Ye 66 for 276s. Moromizato tapped in a short par putt on the second playoff hole after Ye bunkered her approach and failed to save par.

Nichirei PGM Ladies
Miho, Ibaraki
Winner: Sakura Yokomine

Bad weather may have given Sakura Yokomine a lift when she won her third tournament of the season. For the third time this year, the Japan LPGA was forced to abort a round and declare a 36-hole leader the official winner.

This time it was the Nichirei PGM Ladies event and Yokomine was the title recipient. Torrential rain swamped Miho Golf Club in Ibaraki Prefecture that Sunday morning, leaving the course unplayable.

Yokomine had assumed the lead Saturday, coming from two strokes behind first-round leaders Chie Arimura, the Crystal Geyser winner, and non-winners Mai Arai and 19-year-old Rikako Morita with a five-under-par 67 for 136. Arimura fell two behind with 71–138, with Miho Koga, Mi-Jeong Jeon and Morita another shot back. But those contenders never got a chance to catch Yokomine.

"I was just lucky," said the 23-year-old star, who ran her six-year career win total to 12 with the victory.

Promise Ladies
Kato, Hyogo
Winner: Shinobu Moromizato

Back came Shinobu Moromizato with a powerhouse performance in the see-saw battle of victories with Sakura Yokomine. With eight-under-par 64s on the front and back ends of the Promise Ladies tournament, Moromizato blasted to a five-stroke victory at Madame J Golf Club at Kato, Hyogo Prefecture, and matched Yokomine's three 2009 titles.

With the first-place purse for her sixth career win, Moromizato pulled within ¥3 million of Yokomine in the money race.

Moromizato never trailed in the Promise tournament. The first 64 staked her to a two-stroke lead over Yui Kawahara and she was three ahead of South Korean Ji-Hee Lee and Taiwan's Yun-Jye Wei. Moromizato's margin dwindled to a single stroke over Lee (67-68) Saturday when she settled for a two-under-par 70 for 134.

Scoring was generally quite low Sunday, but Moromizato went lowest as she birdied five of the last seven holes for her second course-record-tying

64 of the week to finish 18-under-par at 198. Lee posted 68–203 and arch-rival Yokomine shot a final round 65 for 204.

Meiji Chocolate Cup
Kita-Hiroshima, Hokkaido
Winner: Mi-Jeong Jeon

Mi-Jeong Jeon had fond memories in mind as she moved toward her 11th win in four seasons on the Japan LPGA Tour in the Meiji Chocolate Cup tournament in mid-July. Jeon's run began with her victory in the Meiji Chocolate Cup in 2006 and "today I played with my previous win here in mind."

Whatever the inspiration, she broke away from her closest pursuers early in the final round and rolled to a six-stroke victory on the Shimamatsu course at Sapporo International Country Club in Hokkaido, finishing with a four-under-par 68 and 207. Bunched at 213 were Midori Yoneyama, a first-round co-leader; Yuko Mitsuka, the Daikin Orchid winner, and Miho Koga, the leading money winner in 2008 making her best showing of the current season.

Jeon started with a 71, two behind Yoneyama, Mayu Hattori and Ai Nishikawa in the rain-interrupted first round, then moved a shot ahead of Yoneyama Saturday with a 68–139, tied with Saiki Fujita, who put together a brilliant 63. After an early bogey Sunday, the 26-year-old South Korean played solidly with five birdies over the last 14 holes and won easily as Fujita wasted her brilliant round with a 76 finish.

Stanley Ladies
Susono, Shizuoka
Winner: Chie Arimura

The Japan LPGA Tour season seemed cursed by the weatherman. Three times during the first four months, heavy rains forced shortening tournaments to 36 holes. The Stanley Ladies faced a different problem — heavy fog on Sunday — and officials wound up limiting play to nine holes; hence, a 45-hole tournament victory for Chie Arimura, who fashioned a two-under-par 34 and won by four strokes with the unusual total of 168.

It was Arimura's second victory of the season following her Crystal Geyser triumph, as she became the fourth multiple winner of the year. The 21-year-old had scored her maiden victory in 2008.

Arimura put 67s back to back in the first two rounds at Tomei Country Club at Susono to establish a three-stroke lead over Yuko Saitoh going into the Sunday round after trailing by one to Hiromi Mogi's 66 Friday. Saitoh had been Arimura's closest challenger when she won the Crystal Geyser. The best she could do Sunday was 35, but she held onto second place with 172.

AXA Ladies
Tomakomai, Hokkaido
Winner: Momoko Ueda

Although not enjoying much success in her two years on the U.S. LPGA Tour, Momoko Ueda showed in a brief return to Japan that she still has her winning talent. Back home during a two-week break on the American circuit, Ueda landed her eighth victory on the Japan LPGA Tour in the AXA Ladies tournament. She had to survive a three-way playoff after finishing regulation in a deadlock with Chie Arimura and Ji-Hee Lee at 11-under-par 205 at Mitsui Kanto Tomakomai Golf Club in Hokkaido.

"I feel like I've finally found my golf," she remarked after the win. "I'd like to take this mental state to the U.S."

The field was bunched up at the top all week. Yuko Mitsuka, Hyun-Ju Shin and Lee shared the first-round lead at 66, and Shin was joined in the lead Saturday by Sakura Yokomine (70-66) and So-Hee Kim (69-67) with five players, including Ueda, Lee, Jiyai Shin and Miho Koga, one behind.

Ueda birded three of her last five holes Sunday for 68 to reach the playoff. Arimura bowed out with a bogey on the first extra hole, and Ueda finished it off spectacularly when she hit the flagstick with her approach on the next hole and tapped in the winning birdie putt.

NEC Karuizawa 72
Karuizawa, Nagano
Winner: Chie Arimura

It easily could have been three in a row for Chie Arimura when she won the NEC Karuizawa 72 in mid-August. The newest star on the Japan LPGA Tour lost in a playoff the previous week in the AXA Ladies after chalking up a four-stroke victory in the Stanley Ladies.

Still, the Karuizawa win, her third of the season, put Arimura right on the heels of Sakura Yokomine and Shinobu Moromizato, also three-time winners, at the top of the money list and came against one the year's strongest fields.

Arimura was in charge from the start on the North course of Karuizawa 72 Golf Club. She followed her leading 66 Friday with a one-under 71 — two birdies, one bogey — Saturday and led Yuko Mitsuka (69-69) by a stroke, Mi-Jeong Jeon (67-72) by two entering the final round. Arimura started slowly with an early bogey Sunday and slipped behind Mitsuka, but bounced back with four consecutive birdies in the middle of the round and went on to 69–206, winning by two over Moromizato, who closed with a 66.

CAT Ladies
Hakone, Kanagawa
Winner: Shinobu Moromizato

Shinobu Moromizato set another standard for her pursuers in the money race when she was the first to register a fourth victory. She did it in a hard-fought final round, edging Miho Koga, the defending champion and 2008 No. 1 money winner, by a stroke with her 11-under-par 208 in the CAT Ladies at Hakone, Kanagawa Prefecture.

The two players were in the thick of things from the opening shots. Both shot 69s on the par-73 Daihakone Country Club course to share the first-round lead with Akane Iijima and top eight others by a stroke. Koga inched a stroke in front Saturday with 70–139. Moromizato shot 71–140, tied with Eun-A Lim, the Bridgestone champion, and storied veteran Akiko Fukushima.

Moromizato, tied for the lead with Fukushima after a 15th hole birdie, parred in for her winning 208. Koga failed to pick up a birdie in the stretch to finish at 209, and Fukushima bogeyed the last two holes to tie Yukari Baba at 210. The ¥12.6 million, first-place money not only extended Moromizato's lead over Sakura Yokomine in those standings, but in passing the ¥300 million mark in her 104th start she became the third fastest behind Ai Miyazato and Yokomine to reach that total.

Yonex Ladies
Nagaoka, Niigata
Winner: Mi-Jeong Jeon

When Mi-Jeong Jeon won on the 2009 Japan LPGA Tour, she won big. On top of her seven-stroke victory in the Resort Trust and her six-shot triumph in the Meiji Chocolate Cup, Jeon stacked up a five-stroke win in the Yonex Ladies when the circuit moved to Niigata Prefecture in late August.

It was the 12th victory in less than four full seasons in Japan for the 26-year-old South Korean, one more than compatriot Ji-Hee Lee has posted. The two have represented their country very well there.

Money leader Shinobu Moromizato and four others had a one-stroke edge on Jeon when they shot 67s the first day. That was the last time Jeon had any heat on her. She had eight birdies and an 18th hole bogey as she fired a seven-under-par 65 Saturday to take a four-stroke lead over Miho Koga. Although seven others were five back, Jeon's closing 66 for 199 was eight or more strokes better than everybody except Yukari Baba, who matched the 66 to take the runner-up spot.

Golf 5 Ladies
Mizunami, Gifu
Winner: Shinobu Moromizato

Shinobu Moromizato continued her torrid play in the Golf 5 Ladies tournament, kiddingly suggesting that she had to keep winning "so I am not outdone by Ryo Ishikawa." Actually, with her victory in the Golf 5 being her fifth of the year, she topped the four scored by the teenaged phenom in his 2009 season.

The big names dominated play at Mizunami Country Club from start to finish. Sakura Yokomine, slipping further behind Moromizato in the money race, got things started in the right direction with a first-round 65. She led Moromizato, Miho Koga and Kurumi Dohi by two.

Mi-Jeong Jeon, fresh from her Yonex triumph the previous Sunday, put herself in position for two in a row with 68-68–136, but so did four others — Yokomine (65-71), Moromizato and Koga (67-69s) and Yui Kawahara (68-68).

Moromizato stepped away to her eighth career title Sunday with a seven birdie-one bogey 66 for 202, 14 under par. Yokomine shot 68 and tied for second with Miki Saiki (65) and Chie Arimura (66).

Japan LPGA Championship Konica Minolta Cup
Seki, Gifu
Winner: Shinobu Moromizato

There was no stopping the remarkable run of Shinobu Moromizato, not even the pressure of playing in one of the Japan LPGA Tour's major championships. Winner of two of the previous three tournaments with a third-place finish sandwiched in between, the 23-year-old Okinawan etched the Japan LPGA Championship onto her increasingly impressive record, collecting the Konica Minolta Cup with a six-stroke victory.

Moromizato also won the first major — the World Championship Salonpas Cup in May, the first of her earlier five 2009 victories.

Ayako Uehara, the Yokohama Tire winner in March, led the first day with 68 as only five players broke par at Gifuseki Country Club. Moromizato took over the lead Friday with 67–139, two ahead of Uehara, who shot 73–141 that day. Six players were then under par.

Moromizato remained two in front with a 70–209. Yukari Baba, with 69, took over the runner-up spot, a shot ahead of Bo-Bae Song. Moromizato got off to a poor start Sunday with bogeys on two of the first three holes and dropped into a tie with Baba, temporarily. She followed with birdies on No. 4 and No. 6 as Baba began a backward slide with a pair of bogeys. Even though winding up with a one-over 73 and 282 total, Moromizato was never challenged. Mi-Jeong Jeon came from well back to grab second place with a final 69.

Munsingwear Ladies Tokai Classic
Minama, Aichi
Winner: Sakura Yokomine

No longer the dominant player on the Japan LPGA Tour, Yuri Fudoh made her first serious run at a 2009 title in the Munsingwear Ladies Tokai Classic, but she fell one stroke short. Instead, the victory went to Sakura

Yokomine, who emerged from a brief slump that had cost her the No. 1 spot on the money list. It was her fourth victory of the season and 13th overall.

The loss was particularly disappointing for the 32-year-old Fudoh after setting a new record on the Mihama course of Minami-Aichi Country Club with a nine-under-par 63 in the opening round. That gave her a two-stroke lead over Yukari Baba, Erina Hara and Maiko Wakabayashi and three over Yokomine, who followed with a 65–131 that lifted her a stroke into the lead. Fudoh took a 69 for 132.

Fudoh was gunning for her 47th career win, but could only match Yokomine's 68 Sunday and had to settle for second place despite a 16-under-par 200. Yokomine had five birdies and took her lone bogey of the week. Her ¥14.4 million winner's check pumped her career earnings over the ¥500 million mark in her 149th start, the fastest any player reached that total. Ironically, Fudoh had held that distinction; it had taken her 171 tournaments to reach that mark.

Miyagi TV Cup Dunlop Ladies Open
Rifu, Miyagi
Winner: Chie Arimura

While the Shinobu Moromizato-Sakura Yokomine money race was attracting much of the attention, Chie Arimura was also churning along at a high octane pace. Her fourth victory of the year in the Miyagi TV Cup Dunlop Ladies Open came at the end of an eight-tournament stretch during which she had three of those wins and was out of the top four only once.

Arimura's main challenge came from Momoko Ueda, who returned from the U.S. LPGA Tour to defend the Dunlop title and tune up for the following week's Japan Women's Open. Ueda got off fast with a 67 on the Rifu Golf Club course and shared the first-round lead with Taiwan's Yun-Jye Wei. Arimura established her bid Saturday when, on a tough playing day that yielded just 10 red numbers, she shot 65 for 135. Ueda had the next-best score, a 69, for 136, with Yokomine tied for third with Yuki Ichinose at 140.

Arimura shot a steady 71 Sunday with two birdies and a bogey for 10-under-par 206, two better than Ueda (72). Yokomine shot 71 to place third at 211. The ¥10.8 million check made Arimura the third ¥100 million player of the year, joining Yokomine and Shinobu Moromizato.

Japan Women's Open
Abiko, Chiba
Winner: Bo-Bae Song

Unaccustomed to the pressure that comes with leading a major championship in the final round, Mika Miyazato let her chances of becoming the youngest winner of the Japan Women's Open fritter away in a sea of bogeys. South Korea's Bo-Bae Song took advantage of her collapse and won the prestigious title by defeating Sakura Yokomine with a birdie on the first playoff hole.

Song shot 68 for 11-under-par 277, and Yokomine forced the overtime with an excellent 65 to tie her. An array of stars dotted the leaderboard right behind them. Ai Miyazato third at 280, Shinobu Moromizato at 281, Yuri Fudoh at 282, and Miho Koga and Akiko Fukushima among four at 283 that also included the crestfallen Mika Miyazato after her 78 finish.

Miyazato, at 19 the youngest of the Japanese players on the U.S. LPGA Tour, built a four-stroke lead in the two middle rounds at Abiko Golf Club after winless Mayumi Shimomura surprised with a first-round-leading 66. Miyazato added a 68 to her opening 67 to move three strokes in front of Yokomine (70-68), Song (69-69) and Fukushima (68-70) Friday.

Giving perhaps a hint of what was to come, Miyazato mixed seven birdies with five bogeys for 70–205 Saturday, but still extended her lead to four over Song and Fukushima, who both shot 71s. Yokomine dropped seven behind Miyazato with a 74, yet made it to the losing playoff Sunday.

Sankyo Ladies Open
Kiryu, Gunma
Winner: Ai Miyazato

Ai Miyazato has devoted most of her attention to the American LPGA Tour, playing only a few events each year in Japan. So it was not so surprising that, when she won the Sankyo Ladies Open in October, it had been three years since she had won in her homeland.

Miyazato came from five strokes off the lead in the final round to win the Sankyo Open at Akagi Country Club in Gunma Prefecture. Her closing 68, the best score posted Sunday, played a big part in the victory, but so did the shocking, final-holes collapse of Mi-Jeong Jeon, the leader the first two days.

Jeon grabbed a three-stroke lead Friday with a six-under-par 66 and still had a one-shot margin over Akane Iijima after a 73–139 Saturday. Miyazato, who had started weakly with a 74, rebounded with a 70–144, five off the pace. Then, with a three-stroke lead over Miyazato and just two holes remaining, Jeon fell apart. She double-bogeyed the 17th and 18th holes for 74 and 213, dropping into a tie for second with Mayu Hattori.

The win was a nice added touch to Miyazato's fine season on the U.S. LPGA Tour, where she won for the first time in the Evian Masters and finished in the top 10 in 12 events.

Fujitsu Ladies
Chiba
Winner: Nikki Campbell

Nikki Campbell, Australia's most successful regular on the Japan LPGA Tour, sank an unlikely 50-foot putt to end the season's longest playoff and pick up her second title on the circuit in the Fujitsu Ladies tournament in

Chiba. With that, Campbell prevented Ai Miyazato from landing her second win in a row in her brief fall return from America.

Campbell's only previous victory during her seven seasons in Japan came in the 2006 Suntory Open. Miyazato won the previous week's Sankyo Open.

The two matched three-under-par 69s in all three rounds at the Tokyu Seven Hundred Club, but they didn't lead until the end of the final round. Yukari Baba and Yuko Shinsakaue were on top with 68s the first day, and Miki Saiki and Akane Iijima took over Saturday with 70-65–135 rounds. Campbell and Miyazato were three back at that point. In a tight finish Sunday, bogeys pushed Campbell back into a tie with Miyazato and cost Iijima a spot in the playoff. It went four holes before Miyazato missed her birdie try from the fringe and Campbell holed her long one.

Masters Golf Club Ladies
Miki, Hyogo
Winner: Jiyai Shin

Jiyai Shin may have surprised herself as she said when she won the Masters Golf Club Ladies tournament, but considering her brilliant season on the U.S. LPGA Tour in 2009, it would be hard to find anybody else who would be surprised by anything she accomplishes.

Playing in just her fifth tournament of the year in Japan, the 21-year-old South Korean, who led the 2009 money list in America, acquired her third title on the circuit. She did it in a playoff with a two-putt par on the first extra hole against Akiko Fukushima and Yuko Mitsuka, the Daikin Orchid victor in March.

Shinobu Moromizato (67) and Sakura Yokomine (68), one-two on the Japan Tour money list, topped the field the first day. Fukushima replaced Moromizato Saturday when she shot 70-65–135 and Moromizato went 67-69–136. Yokomine fell back with 73.

Shin fired 68, Sunday's best round, with a birdie on the last hole, and Mitsuka had a 69 against Fukushima's 73 to forge the playoff deadlock at 208. Fukushima made a brave bogey on the 18th hole, one-putting after driving out of bounds, but she and Mitsuka took bogeys in the playoff.

Hisako Higuchi IDC Otsuka Ladies
Hanno, Saitama
Winner: Mi-Jeong Jeon

Mi-Jeong Jeon gave herself a birthday present on the first of November. On the day she turned 27, Jeon took the fourth victory of her fine 2009 season with a come-from-behind effort in the Hisako Higuchi IDC Otsuka tournament, winning by a stroke over Chie Arimura and veteran Michie Ohba.

The fourth player to notch at least four wins in the 2009 season, the South Korean put herself into a long-shot position in the tight money race, though some ¥32 million behind leader Shinobu Moromizato.

A mediocre middle-round 71 sent Jeon into Sunday's finale two strokes behind Arimura after she had opened the week at Musashigaoka Golf Course with birdies on the first four holes. She went on to a seven-under-par 65, tied for the lead with Maiko Wakabayashi. Arimura had the 65 Saturday that, coupled with her first-round 69, gave her a one-shot edge on Ohba, who was trying for her first win in eight years.

A hot front nine was the key to Jeon's victory Sunday. She assumed a two-stroke lead with birdies on four of the last five holes going out. Arimura came to life on the back nine, overtaking Jeon with her third birdie at the 14th hole. But Arimura bogeyed the 17th to fall back into a second-place tie with Ohba at 204, as Jeon parred in from the 13th hole for 67–202.

Mizuno Classic
Shima, Mie
Winner: Bo-Bae Song

Bo-Bae Song twice rose to the important occasion during the 2009 Japan LPGA Tour season. In early October, the South Korean beat the talented Sakura Yokomine in a playoff in the Japan Women's Open Championship. Then, when the U.S. and Japan LPGAs had their annual rendezvous for the Mizuno Classic at Shima in Mie Prefecture, she chalked up an impressive, three-shot victory against the strongest field of the year.

One of the visiting Americans, Brittany Lang, got in front the first day with a six-under-par 66, a stroke in front of Nobuko Kizawa and South Korea's Hee Young Park. Song started comfortably with 68, then moved in front Saturday with a sparkling 65–133. Akane Iijima and In-Kyung Kim were at 134, with Ai Miyazato and Jiyai Shin within striking distance at 136.

Song was solid Sunday. She ran off five birdies over the first 13 holes to build a six-stroke lead. Lang, the long-hitting ex-Duke University star who has yet to win after four seasons on the U.S. LPGA Tour, made a run with three back-nine birdies, and Lorena Ochoa, the world's top-ranked woman, came up with a course-record-tying 64, but it wasn't enough. She wound up in a runner-up tie with Lang and Hee Young Park (68s) at 204. Song also shot 68 for her winning 15-under-par 201.

Itoen Ladies
Chonan, Chiba
Winner: Sakura Yokomine

Unbeknownst at the time, history was being repeated at the Itoen Ladies tournament. In 2008, Miho Koga began her late surge to the top of the Japan LPGA Tour money list by winning the Itoen Ladies. A year later, Sakura Yokomine, trying to overtake Shinobu Moromizato, started her run to that No. 1 position with a wire-to-wire victory, her fifth of the season and 14th of her career.

Yokomine got things started in the right direction Friday with a five-under-par 67 that gave her a one-stroke lead over Mi-Jeong Jeon and two over Ayako Uehara and Australian Tamie Durdin. Rain caused a two-hour delay and an overnight postponement at Chonan's Great Island Club, but Yokomine still had her one-shot margin over Jeon (70–138) when she completed her second round Sunday morning with 70–137. Uehara remained third with 70–139.

Yokomine set the tone right out of the box a few hours later with a birdie on the first hole of the final round. She racked up three more and took a single bogey en route to a 69 and 10-under-par 206. The ¥16.2 million first-place money hiked Yokomine within ¥20 million, as Moromizato finished with 75 to tie for 17th place.

Daioseishi Elleair Ladies Open
Mitoyo, Kagawa
Winner: Chie Arimura

Chie Arimura injected herself into the torrid money race with an overwhelming victory in the Daioseishi Elleair Ladies Open, the final full-field event of the year. Oddly enough, just as Mi-Jeong Jeon had done three weeks earlier, she did it on her birthday, in her case the 22nd.

The prize money for Arimura's fifth win of the season raised her total high enough that, if she won the final LPGA Tour Championship the next week and both Shinobu Moromizato and Sakura Yokomine faltered badly, she could seize the money title.

A tour-record-tying 62 — 10 birdies — in the second round was the springboard to Arimura's victory at Mitoyo's Elleair Golf Club. Only South Korea's Ok-Hee Ku in 2003 and Akane Iijima in 2008 had produced 62s on par-72 circuit courses over the years. It gave Arimura a 129 and a four-stroke lead over 16-year-old amateur Harukyo Nomura, and she doubled that margin with a 67 to Nomura's 71 Sunday.

The 20-under-par 196 was the lowest winning score of the season and the eight-shot advantage matched the year's biggest.

Japan LPGA Tour Championship Ricoh Cup
Miyazaki
Winner: Sakura Yokomine

The outcome of the Japan LPGA Tour Championship Ricoh Cup and the fascinating money race came down to the final strokes of the season and the winner was Sakura Yokomine. In a dramatic finish at Miyazaki Country Club, the 23-year-old Yokomine capped a huge rally in the final round to win the tournament by a single stroke over four other contenders with a six-under-par 282 and win the earnings title by ¥10 million.

Yokomine started and finished the championship with 69s. She shared the first-round lead with Momoko Ueda, then fell five strokes off the pace the next two days with 71-73. Ueda had first place to herself Friday with 69-70–139 before a 75 took her out of contention. Akane Iijima, with 65, the week's low round, took a commanding, three-stroke lead Saturday at 208, with money leader Shinobu Moromizato at 212 and Yokomine at 213.

Sunday's showdown came down to the final hole. Yokomine was first in with her six-under score. Behind her in the final groups came Moromizato, Iijima, Hattori and Ji-Hee Lee, all needing birdies on the 18th hole. None of them converted, and Yokomine, who finished fourth, third, second and third the previous four seasons, acquired her first money title with her must-win sixth victory. Her winnings of ¥175,016,384 was a record amount.

The Kyoraku Cup
Nanjo, Okinawa
Winner: South Korea

South Korea increased its victory margin to 5-3-1 in the post-season Kyoraku Cup with a 29-19 win in the two-day event, played in 2009 at the par-73 Ryukyu Golf Club in Okinawa after the 2008 match in South Korea was snowed out.

The visiting team got off to an overwhelming 20-4 start in the first round, losing only two of 12 matches. Shinobu Moromizato and Miki Saiki were the only Japanese winners, as Hee-Kyung Seo defeated Sakura Yokomine in the headline match between the No. 1 money winners on the two tours.

Japan could not make up the deficit the final day. Notable wins for Japan that Saturday included Ai Miyazato's 64-71 triumph over Eun-A Lim and Yokomine's bounce-back victory over Mi-Jeong Jeon. Bo Bae Song, who lives in Japan but plays for South Korea, won both of her matches and was named the Cup's best performer.

Australian Ladies Tour

Peugeot Kangaroo Valley ALPG Classic
Kangaroo Valley, New South Wales
Winner: Karen Lunn

Karen Lunn, the 1993 Women's British Open champion who has been plagued by injuries in recent years, held off a strong field to claim the Peugeot Kangaroo Valley ALPG Classic, the richest event of the ALPG Club Car Series. Lunn, who won on two-under-par 140, began the second and final day in a share for second place behind South Australia's Susie Mathews and scored a second consecutive 70 to turn a two-shot deficit into a two-shot win as Mathews slipped to 74.

Lunn, 42, has over 20 years' experience of winning around the world, but her playing schedule has been curtailed of late and she is currently the chairman of the Ladies European Tour. "I was quite nervous today and I really felt it coming down the stretch," she said. "Despite the wear and tear (of body), I am playing some of the best golf of my career. ... Putting has never been my strength, but I have been working very hard on it, and right now my short game is the best it has ever been."

Xstrata Coal Branxton Golf Club Pro-Am
Hunter Valley, New South Wales
Winner: Rachel Bailey

Rachel Bailey, a former contestant on the "Big Break" on the Golf Channel in the U.S., won the Xstrata Coal Branxton Golf Club Pro-Am and with it the Club Car Series. Bailey finished the 36-hole event on two-under-par 142 after rounds of 70 and 72. The 28-year-old from New South Wales won by a stroke over English star Laura Davies and Canada's Nancy Harvey on the nine-hole layout. Davies fell back with a final round of 74 which included a double bogey at the ninth.

It's was Bailey's second win of the series, which she won over Susie Matthews. "Winning the Club Car Series is huge for me," said Bailey, who won a A$7,500 bonus as the No. 1. "The money will really help me out with paying for some of my costs on tour, both here and in the U.S. The bonus pool is a great incentive for me, as I have no sponsors, every dollar counts."

LG Bing Lee Women's NSW Open
Sydney, New South Wales
Winner: Sarah Oh

Sarah Oh, only 20 and in her second season as a professional, won the biggest event of her career by claiming the three-round LG Bing Lee Women's

NSW Open by three strokes over Katherine Hull. Oh, playing in front of her home state gallery at Oatlands, was in superb form from an opening 65 and then added scores of 67 and 69 for a total of 15-under 201. Hull put pressure on the youngster with a closing 68, but Oh responded with birdies at the 10th, 13th and the long 17th. Susie Matthews finished alone in third place, four behind Hull, while Nikki Campbell and Nikki Garrett shared fourth place.

Oh was the rookie of the year on the ALPG in 2007-08 and won for the first time at a 36-hole event. She was also second at the NSW Open after playing with Hull and Laura Davies in the final group.

"This was a big tournament to win, but I was confident and believed in myself all day," Oh said. In an emotional speech, she thanked her parents, her mother having watched her play for the first time in the final round.

Hull's final round was enlivened when her drive at the eighth hit Campbell, who was playing the 10th, on the backside, the ball leaving a clear mark and the player needing assistance from the St. Johns Ambulance.

New Zealand Women's Open
Christchurch, New Zealand
Winner: Gwladys Nocera

After claiming five victories and the Order of Merit title in Europe in 2008, Nocera took her first victory "down under" at the New Zealand Women's Open at Clearwater Resort. Nocera won by six strokes over a group of four players after rounds of 71, 68 and 69 for eight-under-par 208 total. Katherine Hull, closing with 76, shared second place with Nikki Garrett, Sarah Kemp and Bobea Park, while Sarah Oh, the winner the previous week, tied for sixth after crashing out of the lead with a closing 80.

The problem on the final day was the wind that got up as the players approached the turn. Oh led by three overnight over Hull and by four over Nocera and was still one in front of the Frenchwoman after eight holes. But Oh came home in 44 as the wind played havoc with everyone but Nocera, who was five under after 11 holes and kept the damage to a minimum on the way to the clubhouse.

"I like the wind, I enjoy it blowing because it pushes me to play even better," Nocera said. "Sometimes I play too easy and make stupid mistakes and the wind makes me concentrate. ... I knew I was going to make bogeys and so was everybody else, but it didn't really matter as long as I didn't make more than bogeys."

ANZ Ladies Masters
Ashmore, Queensland
Winner: Katherine Hull

Katherine Hull produced a superb performance to become only the third Australian to win the ANZ Ladies Masters. One of the big two events down under with the Australian Open, Hull, a 26-year-old from Queensland, was delighted to join Jane Crafter, twice, and Karrie Webb, six times, as a champion at Royal Pines. She also left a quality field in the distance as she converted a three-stroke overnight lead into a five-stroke victory.

Hull, who won the 2008 Canadian Open for her first victory on the LPGA Tour, compiled rounds of 69, 67, 68 and 68 for 16-under-par 272, with her only dropped shot of the final day coming at the last when it did not matter. Se Yeon Ryu birdied the last four holes to tie for second with Tamie Durdin, while world No. 2 Yani Tseng and European No. 1 Gwladys Nocera were among those in fourth place and British Open champion Jiyai Shin tied for seventh.

"I dreamt about this as a kid," Hull said. "It hasn't quite sunk in yet. There are so many great names on the trophy and you walk past the framed pictures of the winners and you wish you had your picture up there. Now I'm going to be up there, so I'm just stoked. I couldn't have written the story any better this week. If anyone would have said to me that I would shoot four rounds in the 60s I would have been absolutely ecstatic."

Women's Australian Open
Melbourne, Victoria
Winner: Laura Davies

At the start of the week Laura Davies was made an honorary member of the ALPG Tour for her support of the game in Australia. The affection is mutual. "If I ever had to live anywhere else than England, it would be Australia. I love everything about this country, except the spiders," she said. By the end of the week Davies had won the Women's Australian Open for the second time, but her main problem on the final day at Metropolitan Golf Club was the wind. Her closing 68, five under, was the best score of the day, but her one-stroke victory was only possible after Tania Elosegui three-putted at the last.

Davies did not look like adding to her 2004 victory, or a 72nd career title, after rounds of 74 and 76, the latter including seven bogeys in eight holes. She was then 11 shots behind, but a 67 in the third round left her three behind, and a flurry of birdies followed by an eagle at the 14th put her into the lead. She finished with a mixture of two birdies and two bogeys, missing a par at the last to finish on seven-under 285 and thinking her chance had gone. Elosegui arrived at the 18th one ahead, but after finding sand raced her long par putt thinking she needed to hole it to tie. But she missed the four-footer back and double-bogeyed to fall back to six under, one ahead of Melissa Reid, He Yong Choi and Chang Hee Lee.

"This has made the whole trip absolutely fantastic," Davies said. "When I walked off the course on Friday I was very disappointed and I thought I was out of it. On a normal course you would say that was too far back, but on a course like this it wasn't too far. That's what makes this such a good win, is because it's such a good course. I thought I'd blown it at the last, but I'm pretty happy now."

13. Senior Tours

Bernhard Langer is not really, really good at any one aspect of golf, and for this surprising assertion we have the word of — well, the wonderfully successful Bernhard Langer himself.

"I think you attribute it in my case," said Langer, speaking of his success, "to just being a fairly good driver of the ball, fairly good iron player, not having a real weakness."

So Langer's not really, really good at anything, unless you count winning. When the 2009 Champions Tour season had come to an end, there was Langer again, front and center. Or rather, at the top, stacking up a king's ransom of Player of the Year credentials. He won four times and had 15 top-10 finishes in 20 starts. He topped the money list for the second straight year, this with $2.1 million, leading a 2009 season that was brisk with four other multiple winners, Nick Price's breakthrough, and the spread of five different winners of the majors.

Langer started the 2009 Champions Tour with a victory in the season-opening Mitsubishi Electric Championship. Someone mentioned that he performed like a machine. Langer didn't see that as a compliment. Said Langer: "I am definitely not a machine."

Langer won again at the Liberty Mutual Legends of Golf in April, helping teammate Tom Lehman win his Champions debut. In the Triton Financial Classic, Langer rolled to a six-stroke victory over the frustrated Mark O'Meara, still winless on the tour and runner-up for the third time in the season. Said Langer: "Winning never gets old." Said O'Meara: "I guess second is better than third or fourth."

Langer got his fourth in the 3M Championship and was a heartbreaker in the process, chipping in on the final hole for an eagle to beat Andy Bean by a stroke. Lucky shot? Not quite. Before he hit the chip, Langer told his son (and caddie), Stefan, "I'm going to make this."

The ubiquitous Loren Roberts crowned his three-win season with the Senior Open Championship, his career fourth senior major, in a playoff over Fred Funk and Mark McNulty. He sandwiched it between the ACE Group Classic and the Boeing Classic. Keith Fergus and Jay Haas also won twice, Haas, shaking off an injury, posted his third career major with the Constellation Energy Senior Players Championship, handing Tom Watson his second disappointment of the season (after his breathtaking close call in the Open Championship). Fred Funk raced through the final round and won the U.S. Senior Open, his second major, by six strokes.

John Cook also won two events, the Administaff Small Business Classic and the season-ending Charles Schwab Cup, but true to the golfers' code, it was the one that got away that stuck with him. Interestingly, a new John Cook might have emerged from the disappointment. It was in the JELD-WEN Tradition, one of the tour's majors, in August.

"Congrats to Mike Reid," the amiable Cook said, "but it was mine and I let it go. I screamed at myself for a month after that." Cook was leading going to the final hole and needed only a par to win his first major. But he bunkered his tee shot and bogeyed and slipped back into a tie with the mild-mannered Reid, who won the playoff for his second Champions victory and also his second major, after the 2005 Senior PGA Championship.

Cook, saying his lack of confidence had cost him in the past, vowed to be more aggressive, to go after more pins. Two months later he scored his two wins and took the Schwab Cup by five shots with a tournament-record 22-under-par performance.

The season introduced six other first-time winners (in addition to Lehman):

• Mike Goodes won the Allianz Championship by a stroke. "In any dreams I had of this, I feel better than I thought it would," he said.

• Dan Forsman came from five behind in the final round and beat Don Pooley in a playoff at the AT&T Champions Classic. "I'm at a loss for words," Forsman said.

• Nick Price, 52, the most celebrated of the non-winners, who joined the tour in 2007, had to overcome three double bogeys to win the Outback Steakhouse Pro-Am by two, which ended an 0-for-38 streak. "I think the golf gods are testing me," Price said

• Michael Allen, newly 50 and in the Senior PGA Championship field on a special invitation, boldly went after the final hole with his driver and birdied to win by two. And then, with the door to the Champions Tour now open, he returned to the PGA Tour, where he was 0-for-334. Said Allen: "I'm going to be the first guy ever to win his first senior tournament before he wins a PGA Tour event."

• Tom Pernice, Jr., also newly 50, holed a 30-foot birdie putt on the final hole to win the SAS Championship. And then he headed back to the PGA Tour. "I think there's still something left in the tank to compete against the best," Pernice said.

• Phil Blackmar, five off the lead to start the final round, birdied five of his first six holes, came out of a bunker to birdie the 18th and won the AT&T Championship.

The European Senior Tour spread its titles around in 2009 with Carl Mason, the three-time Order of Merit leader, the only player to win more than once. Despite his two victories — the De Vere PGA Seniors Championship and the Benahavis Senior Masters — Mason fell short of another season title. That went to Sam Torrance, his third, matching Mason. Torrance's only win was in Barbados at the start of the 14-tournament season. Four of those events were captured by first-time winners.

Loren Roberts won the Senior Open Championship for a second time in a three-man playoff with Fred Funk and Mark McNulty at Sunningdale.

Champions Tour

Mitsubishi Electric Championship
Ka'upulehu-Kona, Hawaii
Winner: Bernhard Langer

When the 2009 Champions Tour season dawned with the Mitsubishi Electric Championship in Hawaii in mid-January, Bernhard Langer hardly broke stride — or a sweat — in picking up right where he left off.

Langer had a smashing 2008, winning both the Player of the Year and the Rookie of the Year awards. Then he started 2009 by winning the Mitsubishi event, playing the vulnerable Hualalai Resort Golf Club in Hawaii in 64-66-68, 18-under-par 198, for a one-stroke win over Andy Bean.

So Langer started 2009 with his fifth victory in 26 starts since joining the Champions Tour late in 2007. He also had two seconds, a third and 17 top-10s in that stretch. Someone noted he was performing with machine-like efficiency. He took exception to that. "I am not a machine," Langer said. "Don't say that. I am definitely not a machine."

Langer wouldn't have won this one without a final-round collapse by Brad Bryant. Bryant and Langer shared the lead at 64 in the first round, and then Bryant inched ahead in the second. Bryant birdied six of his first 10 holes and shot a seven-under 65 for a 129 and a one-stroke lead on Langer, who birdied four of his last six holes for 66.

In the final round, Bryant birdied two of the first three holes and led Langer by two strokes with 14 holes to play. Then he took a staggering seven at the par-three No. 5, hitting two balls in the water. He completed the fold with three straight bogeys from the 11th. Meantime, Bean had taken up the chase with three birdies on the first nine and an eagle at the 10th. They were tied at 17 under par when Langer bogeyed the 13th and Bean birdied the 14th.

Langer took the lead for good at the par-five 14th, two-putting from 40 feet. Bean still had a chance. He needed the 10-foot birdie putt at the 18th to tie. But he lipped it out, and Langer had started 2008 all over again.

Allianz Championship
Boca Raton, Florida
Winner: Mike Goodes

Golfers vary in degrees of religious belief and devotion, but Mike Goodes might have been the first to detect divine intervention in a bunch of squawking seagulls. The noise forced him to back away from what would be his winning putt on the final hole of the Allianz Championship. "I was thinking the Good Lord was saying, 'You're going to make a birdie here,'" Goodes said. Then he made the putt, and at age 52 and in only his second year as a professional, he had his first Champions Tour victory.

The closing birdie wrapped up a card of 67-68-66–201, 15 under par at Broken Sound in Boca Raton, Florida, for a one-stroke win over his pal Fulton Allem.

Goodes, who gave up his plastics recycling business to turn pro, opened with the 67, three behind co-leaders Bernhard Langer and Jerry Pate (64s). Gil Morgan (65) and Tom Jenkins (67) shared the second-round lead after Langer collapsed down the stretch. Langer was leading at 11 under, then suffered two bogeys and a double bogey and shot 73, and fell three behind. Goodes (68) was one off the lead, and his outlook wasn't encouraging, not against this field.

"You look at the field — Hall of Famer, Hall of Famer, Masters winner, Open winner, British Open winner — they're everywhere out here, and it's pretty cool," Goodes said. "I get to eat lunch with them, breakfast sometimes, and play with them." And also beat them.

Goodes had made six birdies in the final round and came to the 18th hole needing one more birdie to win. He put his second shot on the edge of the green, 25 feet from the flag, and two-putted for his seventh birdie and the victory. Allem, a Monday qualifier, closed with 66 and was second by a stroke. Morgan and Jenkins shot 71s and tied for fourth.

"In any dreams I had of this," said Goodes, "I feel better than I thought I would."

ACE Group Classic
Naples, Florida
Winner: Loren Roberts

When that short putt dropped, Loren Roberts scrinched up his face and jammed both arms up into the air. For him, that was an outburst. This win was special.

"I felt like I went out and won it, birdieing three out of the last four," Roberts said. "Sometimes you win because you get help from somebody else. I felt like I went out and won it. I had to let out some emotion there."

Roberts did get some help when Gene Jones barely missed a 12-foot birdie try at the final hole. Roberts, who had played a 102-yard wedge to three feet, then stepped up and knocked in the putt for a birdie — his third over the last four holes — for 68 and a 209 total at the TPC Treviso Bay in Naples, Florida, to nip Jones by one shot.

But first, Roberts looked like another also-ran. Don Pooley, off four straight birdies, and Argentina's Vicente Fernandez, holing a 60-foot birdie putt at the 18th, tied for the first-round lead at four-under 68. Jay Haas would have had the lead, but he checked with a rules official about accidentally brushing some pine straw in a hazard on his backswing. The two-stroke penalty knocked him back to 69.

Jones got his turn at the 18th in the second round, dropping a 15-foot birdie putt for a 70–140 total and a one-stroke lead over Roberts (71), Pooley (73) and James Mason (67). Roberts got to four under with birdies at Nos. 11, 14 and 17, but three-putted the 18th for a bogey, falling one behind Jones.

The final round was a dogfight. Six players led or shared the lead, then slipped. Ben Crenshaw bogeyed the 13th, Jones bogeyed the 14th, and Pooley doubled-bogeyed the 13th. Roberts birdied the 15th and 16th — the latter on a two iron to a foot — and he and Jones were tied coming to the final hole. Jones hit his approach to 12 feet, and Roberts got well inside, to three feet. Moments later, Roberts was having a victory celebration.

Toshiba Classic
Newport Beach, California
Winner: Eduardo Romero

Not to stretch a point, but you could call him Eduardo the Magnificent, and you might notice that his magic wand looks suspiciously like a belly putter. He waved it over the Toshiba Classic, and voila! there was his fifth career Champions Tour victory.

"The putter changed my life," said Argentina's Eduardo Romero, who took up the belly putter three years ago. "I play like this all my life, but my putting cost me a lot of money and a lot of strokes. But (not) now."

Romero, who won four times in 2008, trailed until the final nine. Starting out, it was Bernhard Langer with a first-round 65 in which he played the first 11 holes in one under par and then the last seven in five under for a one-stroke lead over Romero, Jim Colbert and Bob Gilder.

In the second round, Mark O'Meara, looking for his first win in his 34 Champions Tour starts, had reason to think this would be his week. He hit 13 of the 14 fairways and 16 greens and shot 66 and tied for the lead with Langer, who birdied three of the last four holes for a frustrating 68. He had missed only five greens through 36 holes, but was tied for 60th in putting. "I played well off the tee, but I couldn't make any putts," Langer said.

The final round had an interesting twist. Joey Sindelar, not previously in the hunt, began the day seven off the pace, then closed with 63 for the early clubhouse lead. "So (at) eight under, I would have expected top 10 for sure, and probably around fifth," Sindelar said. Actually, it was good for a tie for second with O'Meara (70).

Romero broke out of a traffic jam through the turn, with three straight birdies from No. 10, and shot 68 for an 11-under 202 total, winning by two over Sindelar and O'Meara.

"I won the tournament on the back nine," Romero said. "I played okay on the front, but I lost concentration. I got more focused on the back nine and changed things around."

AT&T Champions Classic
Valencia, California
Winner: Dan Forsman

"I'm at a loss for words right now," Dan Forsman was saying, just after he won the AT&T Champions Classic. The same might be said for Don

Pooley, who thought he had it won, and for Joey Sindelar, who almost had it won. There are some painful distinctions here.

The March drama at Valencia Country Club in Santa Clarita, California, played out this way:

Sindelar, seeking his first Champions victory in 23 starts, opened with 64-70 and led by one stroke in both rounds. "I'll be excited on the first tee (Sunday), and in four hours I'll know the result," Sindelar said. Unfortunately, the result was 73 and a tie for fourth.

Pooley, who had been chasing Sindelar, suddenly found himself with a chance to win at the last hole. "I hit an incredible bunker shot to six feet," said Pooley, who last won in 2003. "The putt was right, and I aimed left edge. I thought I won right there." But the birdie try just missed, and he tapped in for a par and 70. This tied him with Forsman, who was unnoticed until he came racing up the leaderboard from five strokes off the lead.

Forsman birdied three of the last five holes, then just ducked in with his closing 66 with a scary escape at the par-five 18th. He went for the green in two, then swallowed hard when his hybrid second shot sailed to the right and flirted with the out-of-bounds.

"I had officials at first wave it out of bounds, but then they told me it was right on the string, which means it was in bounds," a relieved Forsman said. He pitched on, but missed a 25-foot birdie putt for the win, and Pooley tied him at 11-under 205. The playoff went back to the 18th, and both had birdie putts. Forsman putted first and rolled in his 12-footer. Then Pooley lipped out his five-footer, leaving the speechless Forsman with his first Champions Tour win in 12 starts.

Cap Cana Championship
Cap Cana, Dominican Republic
Winner: Keith Fergus

The Cap Cana Championship was just one long traffic jam from the start until Keith Fergus unsnarled things with one swing of his wedge at the 17th hole of the final round.

"I knew it was my week when I hit that shot," Fergus said. "It worked out just the way my caddie and I planned. We wanted to hit it just past the hole and have it come back, and it did just that." It was a 95-yard shot that didn't merely "come back," it rolled right into the hole for an eagle that paid off in Fergus's second Champions Tour victory and his first since the 2007 Ginn Championship.

It also yanked the rug out from under Andy Bean and Mark O'Meara. Bean, already in at 12-under 204 at the Dominican Republic's Punta Espada Golf Club, and O'Meara were tied with one-shot leads until Fergus's wedge shot abruptly dropped them one behind. It was especially painful for O'Meara, who was on the verge of his first win since joining the Champions Tour in 2007.

"I had my chances and just didn't do it," O'Meara said. "But all power to Keith. There's a lot of luck involved in a shot like that, but there's also a lot of skill, too."

The tournament was a three-round dogfight. Dave Eger took the first-round lead with 67, and Nick Price, Eduardo Romero, Tim Simpson, Tom Jenkins and Fergus were jammed at 68. Price and Fergus were tied for the lead until they bogeyed the 18th. In the second round, O'Meara (65), Romero (68) and Fergus (68) tied for the lead at 136, and five others were packed in two behind. Fergus let a two-shot solo lead get away when he double-bogeyed the 18th. In the final round, O'Meara got caught from behind, and then blocked his own road at the 18th when he hit a poor tee shot and could only par. And Fergus, after the eagle at the 17th, two-putted the last for a par to win by one.

Outback Steakhouse Pro-Am
Lutz, Florida
Winner: Nick Price

Nick Price, the ever-popular winner of three major championships, stepped forward and solved one of the great mysteries in modern golf. It was a vintage Agatha Christie whodunit titled, "Why hasn't Nick Price won on the Champions Tour?" Price cracked the case through the simple expedient of going out and winning the Outback Steakhouse Pro-Am. Finally.

"I am spent and done," Price said, meaning he was exhausted by the effort. But he might well have been referring to that nagging question: "Why haven't you won?"

"I'm not tired (of the question)," Price had said, earlier in the week, acknowledging that it was perfectly reasonable. Price, age 52, winner of two PGA Championships, an Open Championship and 15 PGA Tour events, joined the Champions Tour in 2007. With his reputation, he was expected to win early and often. Instead, he went winless in 38 starts coming into the TPC Tampa Bay in Florida in April. He also was 0-for-111 since his last win on the PGA Tour in 2002.

Price gave no early sign that this would be his week. He opened in second place, a stroke behind Larry Nelson. His 65 included four straight birdies on his last nine. "I'm playing solidly and I'm hitting the ball where I'm aiming," Price said. "So I'm happy to be where I am."

If Price could have answered that persistent question earlier, he would have won earlier. He solved the mystery with what he considered probably the strangest round of his career. He came into the final round leading by three strokes, and proceeded to make seven birdies but also three double bogeys for scores of 66-67-71–204, nine under par. He won by two over first-round leader Larry Nelson, who stumbled to four bogeys coming home for 70–206.

"I never played golf like that in my life," Price said. "I am absolutely dumbfounded by this round. I might make some bogeys, but not three double bogeys like that. But that, without a doubt, is the toughest win I've ever had."

Liberty Mutual Legends of Golf
Savannah, Georgia
Winners: Bernhard Langer and Tom Lehman

The gang gathered again for the annual party known as the Liberty Mutual Legends of Golf, and then this one, late in April at the Westin Savannah Harbor Resort in Georgia, turned into a party for Tom Lehman, making his Champions Tour debut. Or rather Lehman turned it into a party for himself, teaming with Bernhard Langer to win the better-ball scoring derby best described by Nick Price. "If you shoot 67," Price said, "you might have to shoot 59 or 58 to get back in it."

"It's a great event to kind of break into the tour with," said Lehman, who turned 50 in March. It fit the occasion nicely when Lehman was the man to lock it up, knocking in a short par putt on the second playoff hole against Jeff Sluman and Craig Stadler, thus becoming the 13th player to win his Champions debut.

It started easy. "It was a pretty stress-free round," Lehman said, after he and Langer tied for the first-round lead with Fuzzy Zoeller and John Jacobs at 11-under-par 61. Lehman got their final birdie with a four iron to within three feet at the par-three 17th. The second round promised to be a beauty. "Oh," cracked Zoeller, "I imagine Langer and Lehman will probably be intimidated. They probably won't sleep tonight."

Loren Roberts and Mark Wiebe took the second-round lead on a strong finish, Wiebe birdieing the 17th from 25 feet and Roberts the 18th from 30 for 61–125. In the final round, Stadler and Sluman birdied four straight from the 13th en route to 61. Langer and Lehman birdied the first five holes coming in and shot 62 to tie at 27-under 189.

On the first playoff hole, Langer's approach hit Stadler's ball on the green and ended up 45 feet away. Langer drained the huge putt for a birdie, and Stadler replaced his ball and followed him from long range. On the second extra hole, Sluman missed a four-footer for par, and Lehman holed from inside him to make it a memorable combination birthday and coming-out party.

Regions Charity Classic
Hoover, Alabama
Winner: Keith Fergus

It's said there are courses for horses, but Ross Bridge, at Hoover, Alabama, wasn't the one for Keith Fergus, not after all that rain hit the Regions Charity Classic. "I'm not a real good mudder," Fergus was saying. "I'm from Texas. I like warm weather. But I came out and played extremely well."

Well enough, in fact, to put up a pair of 66s for a 12-under-par 132 total before officials called an end to it all, leaving Fergus a three-stroke winner over Gene Jones after two rounds. It was his second win in four starts, and in terms of drama, 180 degrees away from the Cap Cana Championship in March, where he holed out a wedge shot from 95 yards for an eagle at the 17th.

Dan Forsman was the quick first-round leader with a 65 fueled briskly by three straight birdies on both the front and back nines. Fergus was in a trio a stroke back at 66, five others were at 67. The second round was hit by a four-hour rain delay in the morning and later suspended for the day, leaving Fergus and Jones leading at 10 under through No. 8 when play would resume Sunday morning.

Jones, looking for his first Champions Tour win, eagled the par-five No. 6 for the second straight time with his new sand wedge, this time holing out from 20 yards. "I just fell in love with that darn thing," he cracked.

Jones's final statement wasn't so cheery. Fergus was on a hot streak. He would bogey the 17th, but that only cut into his margin. He made seven birdies over the first 16 holes, the last of which put him at 13 under.

"At that point," Jones said, "there was something inside me (saying) take this second place and move on."

"I wish we could have played 54 holes," Fergus said, grinning, "but we didn't and I'm sitting up here with the trophy and I'm not giving it back."

Senior PGA Championship
Beachwood, Ohio
Winner: Michael Allen

No matter how you counted, it had been a long, long time for Michael Allen to go winless — some 20 years or 0-for-344 on the PGA Tour, either of which would guarantee a golfer a high degree of obscurity. So Allen, newly 50, was surprised to receive an invitation to play in the Senior PGA Championship at Canterbury Country Club in Beachwood, Ohio, a Cleveland suburb. The next surprise was on everyone else. Allen, playing in his first senior event, won it.

"I always thought I was good enough to win," said Allen, one of 13 to receive the special invitation. "It has been a struggle, but it's a struggle I enjoy every day."

Allen opened with a four-over-par 74, then went 66-67-67, 10 under for his last 54 holes, which was six better than anyone else. His six-under 274 gave him a two-stroke win over Larry Mize. "I can't compliment Michael Allen enough," Mize said. "To play the 18th hole the way he did is very impressive."

Allen started the final round one ahead of Tom Kite and Jeff Sluman, and after running off eight straight pars, he was two behind when Mize birdied the seventh and eighth. He birdied No. 9, then regained the lead at the 12th with a short birdie putt against Mize's bogey off a bad drive. Allen bogeyed the 14th, birdied the 15th and parred the next two, and came to the demanding 18th leading by one. There was a pause on the tee.

"I think my caddie wanted me to hit three wood, but I just told him, 'I got this,'" said Allen, ignoring caution. He slugged a 314-yard drive into the fairway and then hit a sand wedge to 10 feet and coolly holed the birdie putt, becoming the 14th player to win in his Champions Tour debut.

The victory gave Allen a berth on the Champions Tour, but he said he would stick with the PGA Tour for now. "I'm going to be the first guy ever to win his first senior tournament before he wins a PGA Tour event," he said.

Then Allen realized his name would be on the trophy along with Arnold Palmer's. "And I thought the only thing Arnold and I had in common," he said, "was we love wine."

Principal Charity Classic
West Des Moines, Iowa
Winner: Mark McNulty

The Principal Charity Classic opened with one of the Champions Tour's bigger traffic jams, three players tying for the lead and 11 just a stroke behind. So it was a fitting finish, a three-man playoff — Nick Price, Fred Funk and Mark McNulty.

Price, who scored his first Champions win in the Outback Steakhouse Pro-Am in April, exited on a par at the second extra hole. Then it was McNulty, getting his seventh Champions win with a bending 30-foot birdie putt at the fourth extra hole after Funk missed his try.

"Mark won it," Funk said. "Nobody gave it to anyone."

McNulty played the Glen Oaks Country Club in West Des Moines, Iowa, in 68-69-66, tying with Funk and Price at 10-under 203. The three had started out in a tie, part of the logjam at 68 in the first round, a stroke behind Olin Browne, Lonnie Nielsen and Bruce Vaughan.

Price seemed headed for his second victory when he took the second-round lead by a stroke with 67. "But it's going to be a shootout tomorrow," he said. "This field is so bunched up." Right he was. In the final round, seven different players had at least a share of the lead at various times.

Funk (66) birdied four of the last six holes on the first nine to take a one-stroke lead over McNulty, who bogeyed the 15th to fall two behind. Price (68) bogeyed three of his first six holes, then birdied three straight, and finally birdied the 18th. McNulty (66) birdied the 16th and 17th to join the tie.

All three birdied the first playoff hole (No. 18), and McNulty and Funk played on with birdies at the second (still the 18th). They parred the third (No. 17). Back at the 18th, Funk missed his long birdie try, and McNulty rolled in the left-to-right 30-footer for the win.

McNulty pooh-poohed any notion of pressure on that 30-footer. "Fred had already putted, and I knew the line, I had the pace," McNulty said. "It's not like I had a six-footer. There's more pressure on a six-foot putt."

Triton Financial Classic
Austin, Texas
Winner: Bernhard Langer

You'd think they would have gotten the hint. Anyone paying attention to the Thursday pro-am would have noticed that Bernhard Langer had birdied the last seven holes and 12 overall. That should have told someone what kind of week it was going to be at the Triton Financial Classic. Mark O'Meara, still hunting for that first Champions Tour win and runner-up for the third time this season, shrugged and put it best. "I guess," O'Meara said, "second is better than third or fourth."

Langer led by a stroke through the first two rounds, then romped through the last, playing Hills Country Club, near Austin, Texas, in 65-69-67–201, a robust 15 under par, to win by six over O'Meara.

"This is what we work and practice for," Langer said. "Winning never gets old." It was his third win of the year and his seventh since he joined the tour in 2007.

Langer, playing the Triton for the first time, rolled from his hot start in the pro-am and didn't let up in the first round, posting eight birdies and a bogey for his 65 and a one-shot lead on David Eger, who birdied the last two holes for 66.

The challenges kept coming. Next it was Gene Jones, seeking his first tour win, shooting 66 to move to within one in the second round. "He's the best we have out here," said Jones, who birdied the par-three 18th after a six iron to three feet, "but if you are going to win for the first time, you might as well beat the best."

Good attitude, but what were Jones's chances? Langer laid it out. "If we play decent, it will be hard for somebody to catch us," he said. "If we play garbage, then anything can happen."

What happened was that Langer shot 32 on the front and was up by five when he made the turn.

"I didn't really look at a scoreboard until I got to 15," Langer said. "Then I realized that if I didn't do anything silly, I would win." He did nothing silly.

Dick's Sporting Goods Open
Endicott, New York
Winner: Lonnie Nielsen

Through the first two rounds of the Dick's Sporting Goods Open, Fred Funk had hit 25 of 28 fairways and 30 of 36 greens. Noted as an accurate player, he felt right at home at the En-Joie Golf Club in Endicott, New York, a straight hitter's fun park. He shot 64-65 and had a three-stroke lead going into the final round. "I've got to keep the pedal to the metal," Funk said. "I've got to keep making birdies or somebody's going to catch me." Thus he became his own best prophet, but a failed one.

Funk shot 69 in the final round, and Lonnie Nielsen went whizzing by to a sensational finish to take his second Champions title.

Nielsen's start was stunning. "I never dreamed I would start like that," Nielsen said. "You wouldn't dare dream that," Funk would say. Funk was right. Dreams like that one are called fantasies. Nielsen started like a rocket — birdie-birdie-eagle-birdie-birdie, six under par on the first five holes. He went on to 63 and a 21-under-par 195 total and won by three over Funk (69) and Ronnie Black (66).

"I had a lot of breaks go my way," Nielsen said, and so he did. At No. 1, his 25-foot putt swung back about a foot and dropped for his first birdie. "That ball had no reason to do what it did," an amazed Nielsen said. "I was off and running." At the par-five No. 3, his 60-foot eagle putt was dangerously too hard, but hit the back of the cup and dropped in. At the par-three 17th, he saved par when his stray tee shot bounced out of the rough and onto the green. And at the 18th, his tee shot glanced off a tree and back into the fairway, and he went on to his last birdie.

"I never had a week like that," Nielsen said.

Nielsen won $247,500, but his success also cost him. He donates $50 for each birdie and $500 for each eagle to the Golf for Injured Veterans Everywhere. With 24 birdies and an eagle, that came to a tidy $1,700.

3M Championship
Blaine, Minnesota
Winner: Bernhard Langer

The scenario was that of a father offering words of wisdom to his son, but not exactly the classical fireplace variety. This came at the 3M Championship, and dad was facing a chip shot from 20 feet off the back fringe of the green, at the final hole of the tournament. Bernhard Langer turned to his son Stefan, his caddie, and said, "I'm going to make this."

Wise man. Langer gave the ball a gentle pop and then watched it roll right into the cup for an eagle, giving him 65 and a one-stroke victory, his second straight win, fourth of the season — by mid-July — and eighth in his 37 Champions Tour starts. Langer played the TPC Twin Cities, in Minnesota, in 67-68-65–200, 16 under par, leaving Andy Bean a frustrated runner-up.

Langer put on an accomplished show. He hit 34 of 42 fairways, 43 of 54 greens and averaged 28 putts.

Langer came from behind in the final round, having trailed Bean and Nick Price by two strokes in the first and Price by two in the second. In the third, after two birdies on the front nine, he birdied three straight from the 10th to take the lead. Then, as Price faded, Bean birdied the 14th to tie Langer.

"Then," said Langer, "I didn't see the leaderboard until 17, when I was tied for the lead." But not for long. At the par-five 18th, Langer hit a hybrid second from 216 yards, slicing the shot over the lake. The ball rolled just off the back of the green, 20 feet from the flag. Then came the fatherly chip shot.

"It came out a little hot, but right on line, hit the back of the cup, and popped up an inch or two and disappeared," Langer said. Taking Bean's dreams with it. Bean, two back, birdied the 18th behind Langer, then took his hat off to him.

"To eagle the last hole to win, you've made a couple great shots, and he certainly came through with that," Bean said.

The Senior Open Championship
Berkshire, England
Winner: Loren Roberts

See European Senior Tour section.

U.S. Senior Open
Carmel, Indiana
Winner: Fred Funk

Fred Funk had some extra baggage heading home from the U.S. Senior Open, no small matter with air travel at the time. An official had offered to ship it to him. Funk declined. It was the U.S. Senior Open trophy, and Funk wasn't about to let it slip through his hands — not back at the course, and not now.

Funk had just finished making Crooked Stick, the crafty Pete Dye layout at Carmel, Indiana, his personal playground, a six-stroke victory being a lark by any measure. And this by the man who just the week before lost in a three-way playoff at the Senior British Open because of defensive play, which he wouldn't repeat.

"I don't want to hit any defensive shots," Funk had said. "I want to stay aggressive."

It was an aggressive Funk who took the lead in the scrambled third round. Funk, Greg Norman, Joey Sindelar and amateur Tim Jackson all led, then slipped back. Norman birdied the par-five 11th, eagled the par-five 15th, took a bogey and shot 68 and was at 12 under, tying Sindelar, who got into and out of trouble for 70. Funk got to 12 under on the first nine with three birdies, and after a birdie-bogey exchange from the 13th, took the lead at the 16th. He rolled in a 20-foot birdie putt while Norman was making bogey from the rough. Funk, who trailed by two with his 68-67 start, was at 13 under and leading by one after 54 holes.

In the last round, Funk pulled away on the first nine with birdies at Nos. 2, 5 and 9, and got help when Norman, after two pars, missed the next five greens and was three over through No. 7. Funk closed with a 65, and there was a secret hidden in his championship-record, 20-under 268. For a supposedly short-hitting man with a bad knee and shoulder, Funk had played the par-fives in 11 under.

Jackson, a real estate developer, was the early star of the show. With a 66-67 start, he tied for the first-round lead and led by one after 36 holes, over Sindelar. Closing with 73-76, Jackson tied for 11th and was low amateur. As he had said, "This will be something we'll talk about for a long time, I'm sure."

JELD-WEN Tradition
Sunriver, Oregon
Winner: Mike Reid

Mild-mannered Mike Reid, now 55, still carries the nickname "Radar," for a coin-toss of reasons, but this time it's what he came in under at the JELD-WEN Tradition. Which is to say, Reid came in under the radar to pick off the fourth of the Champions Tour's five major championships.

For most of the week, at the Crosswater Club in Sunriver, Oregon, Reid was practically unnoticed. The tournament belonged to Brad Bryant for the first three rounds — starting with 62 in the first round — then to John Cook with a hole to play. But it belonged to Reid when it counted.

Bryant faltered in the fourth round, just enough to let Reid (69) and Cook (68) sneak by and tie. Then Reid dropped a 12-foot birdie putt on the first extra hole. He raised his arms in relief.

"I felt," Reid said, "like I'd just climbed Mount Everest."

It was only his second Champions Tour victory in 112 starts, but also his second in a major, after the 2005 Senior PGA Championship.

The most disappointed man in the field was Bryant, who started with an 11-birdie, one-bogey 62 for a three-stroke lead. "Just played really great," he said. He followed with 72-67 and led by one stroke, then by two going into the final round, then lost his edge and closed with 73 and finished third.

Reid birdied the 18th in the third-round 66 and closed within one going into the fourth round. Cook shot 68 and was two behind. In the fourth round, Cook birdied the par-three 17th and led by one with a hole to play. At the 18th, he hit into a bunker and bogeyed for 68, and Reid parred for 69, and they tied at 16-under 272.

"I didn't play like a champion," Cook said.

The playoff went back to the 18th. Cook put his approach to 15 feet, and his downhill birdie try just missed. He parred. Reid's 12-footer wobbled uncertainly, but dropped for the winning birdie. It was almost beyond his comprehension.

"It got to the point," Reid said, "where it was hard for me to paint that picture of holding a trophy."

Boeing Classic
Snoqualmie, Washington
Winner: Loren Roberts

Loren Roberts struck again, and it almost seemed like cruel and unusual punishment for the frustrated Mark O'Meara. Roberts, the wizard of the putter, put on a display that verged on the superhuman — or supernatural, some would contend — and sneaked away with the Boeing Classic, leaving a most hopeful O'Meara grasping at straws.

It came down to the painful end, with Roberts birdieing the last two holes, leaving O'Meara, who had already finished, waiting for the playoff that never came.

"I had the hot hand with the putter," Roberts said, "and I was making some putts you usually don't even think about making."

Roberts, who trailed only in the first round, won with scores of 68-65-65–198, 18 under par at the TPC Snoqualmie Ridge near Seattle. O'Meara (64) was second by a stroke, runner-up for the eighth time and 0-for-46 on the Champions Tour. "I'm tired of silver," O'Meara said. "To get that close and not break through..."

O'Meara took some early hope from his strong start. He capped his first round with an eagle at the par-five 18th, a three iron from 205 yards to 17 feet, for 66 and a two-shot lead on a group that included Mark McNulty, who went out in 30 and cooled to 68. McNulty matched 65s with Roberts to share the second-round lead at 11 under, with a host of challengers in tight for the final round. "I think it's going to be a shootout," Roberts said.

But it wasn't, thanks to Roberts and his magic putter erasing O'Meara's 64. O'Meara was leading by a stroke until he bunkered his approach at the 16th and bogeyed. He got his ninth birdie at the 17th, but at the 18th a shot into a fairway bunker held him to a par and 64. Playing behind him, Roberts holed a five-foot birdie putt at the 17th, and at the 18th his 50-yard pitch stopped three feet from the hole. That's what he needed for a birdie and the win, and that's what he got.

Walmart First Tee Open
Monterey Peninsula, California
Winner: Jeff Sluman

Going into the final round of the Walmart First Tee Open, there were two sure things: Loren Roberts, fresh from finessing a neat victory the week before, could not lose a two-stroke lead in the final round. And Jeff Sluman, the defending champion, could not come from six behind and win.

And, of course, in one of the most amazing twists of the season, both things happened.

Roberts didn't merely squander the lead, he bogeyed three of four holes on the front nine, then bogeyed three straight on the back and shot 78. And while Roberts was unraveling that early September weekend, Sluman, the first-round leader, got back up to speed and with the help of a hole-in-one, rolled to a two-stroke victory over Gene Jones (70). Roberts slipped to a tie for fifth.

"I don't think I've come back from two, certainly not from six," said Sluman, notching his first win of the season and third on the Champions Tour. He opened with a flawless 65 at Del Monte, for a one-stroke lead on Roberts and Olin Browne. Moving to Pebble Beach, Sluman fell six off the lead with a 73 in the second round. It would take a variety of circumstances to bring him back, and that's what he got. Against the backdrop, of course, of Roberts's blow-up.

In the final round, Jones made a big move on the front with three birdies and pulled to within one of the lead with another at the 10th. But he backslid with bogeys at the 11th and 14th.

Sluman's first big statement was an ace at the 187-yard No. 5, with an eight iron. "Being 52, I never saw it go in," Sluman said. The ace tied him with Mark O'Meara for the lead. Sluman took the lead with a birdie at the ninth, bogeyed the 11th, then birdied the 14th and wrapped up 68 at Pebble Beach for a 10-under 206 total.

"All of the years of playing Pebble under so many different conditions helped me out there," Sluman said.

Greater Hickory Classic
Conover, North Carolina
Winner: Jay Haas

They were wondering whatever became of Jay Haas. Haas answered in mid-September at the Greater Hickory Classic, where he opened with a smashing 62 and rolled on to a two-stroke victory.

"I didn't see this coming — and certainly not a couple weeks ago," said the personable Haas, 55, who was off the Champions Tour for a month with tendonitis of the right elbow.

Despite being out of action for that long, he was able to break away from a tie with Nick Price going into the final round and to stay ahead of Russ Cochran and Andy Bean and win by two. It was Haas's 13th tour win and his first of the season, ending a 26-tournament drought dating back to 2008. Haas shot 62-71-65–198, 18 under par at Rock Barn, in Conover, North Carolina, taking the tournament for the second time.

The restless Haas — "I was anxious to play, for sure" — opened the tournament with four straight birdies. After two more on the front nine, he logged four more coming home for a 10-under 62 and a two-stroke lead on Gil Morgan. Haas and Nick Price (67) shared the second-round lead.

Haas was under pressure in the final round, with 31 players within six strokes of the lead on the rain-softened course. Price bogeyed the first two holes, and Haas didn't make a birdie until the fifth, then got his second at the seventh. Up stepped Cochran, in just his 11th start, who made four birdies on the front nine, then took the lead with birdies at the 12th and 13th. Bean, tied for third at the start, birdied twice on the front, then after a big stumble coming in he eagled the 18th to tie Cochran. Both shot 65–200.

Haas sprinted to the win with birdies on five of the last six holes and four straight from the 13th for his own 65 and a tournament-record, 18-under 198.

Said a relieved Haas: "A couple weeks ago ... I didn't know if my shot was going to work. But today, it felt great — no pain at all."

SAS Championship
Cary, North Carolina
Winner: Tom Pernice, Jr.

It was the SAS Championship in late September, and Tom Pernice, Jr., just recently turned 50, was making his Champions Tour debut, rejoining some of the players he'd played against in his years on the PGA Tour. "It's like a family out here," Pernice said. "The guys out here have been wonderful. It's a great experience to get such a warm welcome from the guys." Then he set about wearing out his welcome.

Just that fast, Pernice had joined 14 other players — Arnold Palmer, Jack Nicklaus and Gary Player among them — who won in their Champions debut. Pernice trailed only in the first round at Prestonwood Country Club in Cary, North Carolina, shooting 67-67-69–203, 13 under par, for a one-stroke victory over Nick Price (68) and David Frost (67).

Pernice was likely to remember two shots best, both in the final round. One was his tee shot into the water at No. 9, his 45th hole. It cost him his only bogey of the tournament. The other was the 30-foot birdie putt at the final hole. When it dropped, he was the winner.

But first, the debut: It was instant encouragement when he finished his first round just a stroke behind leaders Denis Watson and Russ Cochran, himself a rookie seeking his first win. Cochran was thwarted by his approach game in the second round, slipping behind with 69. Another 67 moved Pernice into the lead in the second round. "Everything's been pretty solid," he said. "All in all, I'm very thrilled."

The final round was far from a snap, what with Cochran, Watson, Olin Browne, Dan Forsman and Andy Bean all in the hunt. Pernice started hitting stray tee shots after the bogey at No. 9 and suddenly fell behind. Both Price (68) and Frost (67) birdied three of the last five holes. Then came Pernice facing that 30-footer at the 18th.

Perhaps he wouldn't be playing the Champions Tour full time. "I think there's still something left in the tank to compete against the best," Pernice said.

Constellation Energy Senior Players Championship
Timonium, Maryland
Winner: Jay Haas

For Tom Watson, at age 59, having the 2009 Open Championship snatched away from him at the last minute had to be the most crushing blow of his great career. Having the same thing happen three months later in the Constellation Energy Senior Players Championship wasn't nearly in the same class, but it still hurt.

This time, Watson led through the middle rounds, and then it was Jay Haas roaring around him in the final round to pick off the Champion Tour's final major championship by a stroke. It was also his second win of the season and his third major Champions title.

There were no huge mistakes by Watson. He simply played a lukewarm final round for a par 70, while Haas came from deep in the pack and rushed by with a bogey-free 64 and a 267 total at Baltimore Country Club for the one-stroke win over Watson. Mark Wiebe and Loren Roberts tied for third six shots back.

The tournament was tight for the first round, with Lonnie Nielsen, at 65, leading Watson and Haas by one, and others stacked close behind. Watson led by two in the second with a 68, and by four in the third with a 64. Haas slipped behind with his 70-67 in the middle rounds, and was a most unpromising five behind Watson going into the final round. He shrugged.

"I just felt like playing as hard as I can," Haas said. That attitude produced birdies at the third and fourth. "And when I birdied 10, I looked up and saw he was 11 under through the ninth and I was 10 (under). So it made me feel like at least I had a chance." He then birdied the 14th, 17th and — in a great climax — the 18th, off a six-iron approach to three feet.

"With a four-shot lead, the best thing to do is try to make it five, six and seven," Watson said. "I played tentative golf."

Haas was just the opposite. "I was just trying to shoot at the flags and make birdies wherever I could," he said.

Administaff Small Business Classic
The Woodlands, Texas
Winner: John Cook

It sounded like what used to be the old broken record to John Cook — patience, patience, patience, he told himself. And it finally clicked in, in the last round, just in time for him to pull ahead of a sagging Dan Forsman and outrun a host of chasers to win the Administaff Small Business Classic, his third victory on the Champions Tour.

"I've had trouble finishing events," Cook said, still smarting from the playoff loss to Mike Reid at the Tradition and then finishing fifth at the Senior Players Championship two weeks before. "I was getting ahead of myself. Today, I just didn't do that."

Cook opened with 65-72, trailing Forsman by one in the first round and two in the second. A 68 in the third and final round gave him a 205, 11 under par at The Woodlands, near Houston, and a two-stroke win over Bob Tway (70) and Jay Haas (71).

The man with the big disappointment was Forsman. In the first round, he rang up six straight birdies and shot 64, finishing with a six-inch putt. "At that point, I just took a breath and said, good job," Forsman said. He still led by one after a 71 in the second round, and in the third was still on track for his third Champions victory, 11 under through the 13th. Then he hit his tee shot into the water at the 14th and triple-bogeyed. He shot 73 and tied for fourth.

Cook, meanwhile, had started the final round birdie-bogey, then birdied Nos. 5, 9, 12 and 17, the last being the edge he needed. But first he had to wait and sweat. Haas, trying to win his third straight start and hurt by an early double bogey, needed a birdie at the 18th to tie Cook. Haas drove into the rough and hit his approach to the back fringe of the green. He needed that putt for the tie. But he missed.

Said Cook: "One of my friends says, 'Finish like a champion.' I think I did that today."

AT&T Championship
San Antonio, Texas
Winner: Phil Blackmar

The adage says something about music having charms to soothe the savage breast. But there was sure something different about the music Phil Blackmar was listening to on the practice tee before the final round of the AT&T Championship. "I could feel my demeanor change," Blackmar said. "I was ready to fight someone." Happily, golf isn't a contact sport, so Blackmar channeled his fire into his game and won his first Champions Tour title, coming from far behind a top-heavy leaderboard to win the AT&T by a stroke at Oak Hills in San Antonio, Texas.

"I was very nervous, but I was able to hang in there," said Blackmar, a three-time winner on the PGA Tour who joined the Champions Tour late in 2007. Tagging along with a 72-67 start, Blackmar came rushing up from five strokes off the lead to close with a seven-under-par 64 and a 10-under 203 total to edge Tom Kite (68), Andy Bean (70) and Jay Haas (69).

The AT&T Championship, late in October, was the final full-field event of the season, and it was up for grabs. Keith Clearwater and Russ Cochran, both tour rookies, shared the first-round lead at 66. In the second round, Cochran, after three straight birdies from the 15th, was a hole from the solo lead when he bogeyed the par-three 18th and tied with Bean (67). Blackmar was too far back to be considered a contender.

That is, until he birdied five of his first six holes in the final round, incredibly sticking his ball about 10 feet from the flag each time. The nerves hit when he went through the turn, but he held together and tied for the lead with a birdie at the par-five 15th, blasting from a bunker to tap-in range, then took the lead on a 15-foot birdie at the 16th. Still, he had to close with a flourish to lock up the win. At the 18th, he blasted out of a bunker to four feet and holed the birdie putt for his 64.

"I was so nervous," Blackmar said, "I couldn't feel my hands."

Charles Schwab Cup Championship
Sonoma, California
Winner: John Cook

It isn't often that a five-shot win would rank no better than second in the mind of the winner, but that was the case with John Cook, in the Champions Tour's season-ending Charles Schwab Cup Championship. Cook was tearing up Sonoma Golf Club, but the thing on his mind was that his old pal and fellow pro Joey Sindelar was in the hospital with a pulmonary embolism.

"That kind of shocks you when one of your compadres goes down," Cook said. "That's serious stuff. I was thinking of him all day."

Sindelar was stricken during the third round Saturday and taken to the hospital about the time Cook was expanding his lead to an absurd six strokes. Before teeing off that Sunday, Cook received a text message from Sindelar. "He said he was fine and to go finish the deal," Cook said. Comforted by Sindelar's message, Cook could have coasted home. He closed with a bogey-free 69 and a tournament-record 266 total, 22 under par for the five-stroke win over tour rookie Russ Cochran.

As battles go, this one wasn't much, but Cochran tried. He closed within five strokes with a birdie at the eighth, but Cook rolled in a long birdie putt at the par-four 12th. Cook birdied the par-three 17th and tapped in for par at the 18th for his second Champions Tour win of the year, after the Administaff Small Business Classic two weeks earlier, and his fourth overall. His 266 total broke the record 268 shared by Jim Thorpe and Andy Bean. Cook's tournament-record 62 in the second round was nicely balanced. In his 10 birdies, he birdied the first three holes and the last three. He had only two bogeys all week — one in the first round, one in the third.

Loren Roberts, a three-time winner for the season, finished with a second straight 66 to tie for sixth at 275 and take the Schwab Cup points title for the $1 million annuity for the second time in three years.

European Senior Tour

Aberdeen Brunei Senior Masters
Brunei
Winner: Mike Cunning

When his logical first choice didn't pan out, Mike Cunning took full advantage of the alternative and won his first start as a senior in the Aberdeen Brunei Senior Masters, the European Senior Tour's opening tournament of the 2009 season.

The American, who had enjoyed most of his earlier success on the Asian Tour, where he led the money list in 1997, turned to Europe after failing to qualify for the U.S. Champions Tour in the fall of 2008 after turning 50. He hadn't had much luck when the Asian Tour visited Brunei in previous years, but he had plenty of game when the European Seniors went there at the end of February. A shot off the lead after 36 holes at the Empire Hotel and Country Club, Cunning pulled off a two-stroke victory with a closing 70 and a seven-under-par 206.

Englishman Bob Cameron, seeking his first victory on the circuit since his pair of wins in 2004, began his seventh season with a four-under-par 67 and a one-stroke lead over Ross Drummond of Scotland and American Pete Oakley. Cameron yielded the top spot Saturday to Australia's David Merriman, who rode an eagle to a six-under-par 65 and a 135. Cameron shot 69 and shared second place with Cunning (69-67), a shot behind Merriman, winless on the European Senior Tour since he led the 2006 qualifying tournament.

Three birdies in a four-hole stretch in the middle of the final round gave Cunning a cushion that enabled him to post the final two-stroke margin over Northern Ireland's Jimmy Heggarty, the leading qualifier for the 2009 tour, who closed with a 67 for his 208. Cameron shot 73 and slipped into a third-place tie with Giuseppe Cali of Italy and Katsuyoshi Tomori of Japan at 209.

DGM Barbados Open
St. James, Barbados
Winner: Sam Torrance

Sam Torrance salvaged a frustrating 2008 season with a victory in the season-ending Senior Tour Championship - OKI Castellon Open Espana. He quickly made sure he didn't have to have that experience in 2009 by picking off a four-stroke victory in the DGM Barbados Open, the season's second event.

The 55-year-old Scot came up with a tremendous performance in racking up his 11th victory early in his sixth season on the tour. He led from start to finish and set new records for 36 holes for the tour and for 18 holes at Royal Westmoreland Golf Club, the tournament's regular venue on the Caribbean island.

Torrance started with a bang in the mid-March event, firing a bogey-free, seven-under-par 65 to take a three-stroke lead over England's Gordon J. Brand and Australian Mike Harwood. He said the round "was about as good as it gets," then went two strokes better in Thursday's second round, opening an awesome nine-stroke margin over runner-up Angel Franco of Paraguay. The 63 and 128 both set records, the 63 at Royal Westmoreland and the 128 on the tour. His nine-shot margin matched Tommy Horton's 36-hole margin in the 1997 Scottish Seniors Open as the biggest in circuit history. Torrance eagled his fourth hole of the round and ran off seven birdies as he remained without a bogey for the distance.

Torrance cooled off in Friday's final round, absorbing four bogeys to go with a pair of birdies for 74 and the winning 202 total. Franco shot 69 but still fell four shots short with his second-place finish. Harwood was another four back in third place.

Son Gual Mallorca Senior Open
Palma, Mallorca, Spain
Winner: Mark James

Mark James continues to enjoy senior golf success on both sides of the Atlantic. James, the 1999 European Ryder Cup captain, who splits his time between the Champions Tour in the United States and the European Senior Tour, landed his second title on the latter circuit when it resumed action with the Son Gual Mallorca Senior Open in Spain in early May.

James's victory came in a playoff at the expense of the luckless Eamonn Darcy after the two former Ryder Cup teammates produced scintillating final rounds on the Son Gual Golf Club course. Darcy was in first with an error-free, seven-under-par 65 only to be overhauled by James. James had begun the final round in second place with Bobby Lincoln, two strokes behind Englishman Roger Chapman, who was only nine days beyond his 50th birthday and playing in his first senior event. James shot 66 for his 10-under-par 206.

He and Darcy played the 18th hole three times in overtime before James sank a five-foot birdie putt for the win and headed back to the U.S. and the Champions Tour, on which he owns three victories, including the major Senior Players Championship. His miss from 15 feet in the playoff left Irishman Darcy, winless on the European senior circuit, with eight runner-up finishes.

Chapman, who started 68-70–138 to take the front spot away from Florida-based, first-round leader Delroy Cambridge, shot a respectable 71 despite a first-hole bogey and a ball in the water at No. 12. He finished third at 206, failing to tie the all-time tour record for the youngest winner, set by John Bland in 1995.

Irish Seniors Open
County Kerry, Ireland
Winner: Ian Woosnam

Although he's a Welshman, perhaps the country's most successful golfer ever, Ian Woosnam nonetheless feels right at home when he plays in Ireland. With two Irish Open titles on his fine record and his captaincy of the winning 2006 European Ryder Cup team at The K Club near Dublin, the stocky little Woosnam added the Irish Seniors Open to his credits when the tour resumed action in early June.

The victory of the 2008 Order of Merit champion at famed Ballybunion Golf Club came in impressive fashion as he overcame a six-stroke deficit in the final round and outlasted American Bob Boyd in the subsequent three-hole playoff. Interestingly, it was the third consecutive victory by a former Ryder Cup captain in the first four events of the season. Sam Torrance won in Barbados and Mark James at Mallorca.

Woosnam's third European Senior Tour victory took the stage away from Roger Chapman, the former tour official who nearly won in his first start as a 50-year-old in the previous event at Mallorca. Coming off that third-place finish, Chapman led for two days at Ballybunion. He carded two eagles en route to a 67 and a two-stroke lead over five others in the first round. He followed with a 71 for 138 on a blustery Saturday and retained the two-shot margin, then over Boyd (72-68).

Woosnam was six back at 144 in a week which started when his clubs failed to arrive when he did at the airport and an 18th hole double bogey cost him a first-round 74. He put up a fine 67 Sunday as Boyd matched his two-under-par 211 with a 71 to bring about the playoff, as Chapman faltered with 74 ("I played rubbish all day") and finished third again, tied at 212 with Tony Johnstone.

Woosnam and Boyd played the 18th three times in the playoff. Boyd, who won in Spain in 2005 and missed the next two seasons while successfully battling leukemia, made a fine sand save on the first extra hole, but Woosnam dropped a four-foot birdie putt at the third for the win after the American missed from five feet.

Jersey Seniors Classic
Jersey, Channel Isles
Winner: Delroy Cambridge

Jolet Cambridge had it figured out and husband Delroy listened. The result: The Jamaican fixture on the European Senior Tour ended a seven-year title drought with an overtime victory in the Jersey Seniors Classic.

"My wife kept telling me that if I got my putting sorted out I would win again. I'm glad I listened to her," said the 59-year-old Cambridge, who won four times in his first two seasons on the circuit and, though a top-10 finisher 18 times since, had not triumphed again until he topped Australian Mike Clayton on the third extra hole at La Moye Golf Club. It was the tour's third straight three-hole playoff.

Clayton, 52, playing only on a short-term basis because of the recession-induced sag in his course design business, never trailed until he lost the playoff to Cambridge's third straight overtime par, an up-and-down four from a bunker. Clayton blistered La Moye the first day with an eight-under-par, nine-birdie 64, jumping off to a three-stroke lead over second-placed Nick Job.

Although he shot 73 Saturday, Clayton retained a share of first place. Kevin Spurgeon of England (68-69) and Angel Franco of Paraguay (72-65) joined him at 137 with seven players within two shots, including Cambridge (69-70) at 139. One of Cambridge's victories in 2002 also was at La Moye and he recalled Saturday night he was five under par going into the final round and shot 68 to win. That's exactly what he did Sunday and his 207 total overtook 70-shooting Clayton and led to the playoff victory.

Ryder Cup Wales Seniors Open
Mid Glamorgan, Wales
Winner: Bertus Smit

The odds were stacked again South African Bertus Smit as he entered the 2009 season on the European Senior Tour. He had to survive the qualifying tournament just to get into the events, having gone through two fruitless seasons after suffering a stroke that left him with only partial vision in his right eye.

Things hadn't gone well at the first five stops either, a tie for 31st his best finish. It looked baleful after 18 holes in the Ryder Cup Wales Seniors Open, too, as he opened with a 74 and trailed leader Bob Cameron by five strokes at Royal Portcawl Golf Club. Two days later, the 56-year-old Smit, an amateur until 2000, had his first professional victory.

He followed the 74 with rounds of 68 and 69 for a five-under-par 211 and a four-shot victory over Australia's David Merriman. Smit was the second first-time winner of the season, joining Mike Cunning, the Aberdeen Brunei victor.

Going into the final round, all signs pointed to a popular home victory at Royal Portcawl as Ian Woosnam, the country's long-time golf hero, had moved into a share of the lead with Smit and American Jerry Bruner at two-under-par 142. Woosnam's 67 — the day's best round — made up for a 75 start that included an early double bogey.

It was not to be. Woosnam bogeyed the first three holes in the final round and never fully recovered, shooting 74 to tie for third at 216. Bruner shot 76. Smit, on the other hand, ran off six birdies for his winning 69, remarking afterward: "My putting was good and my irons were superb. I didn't miss many greens."

De Vere Collection PGA Seniors Championship
Northumberland, England
Winner: Carl Mason

Not surprisingly, Carl Mason made his first big statement of 2009 in the European Senior Tour's first major championship and at one of his favorite venues. A non-contender in his first three starts, the circuit's leading player scored his first win of the season and 21st of his senior career in the De Vere Collection PGA Seniors Championship at Northumberland's Slaley Hall, where he had victories in 2004 and 2005.

Mason's three-stroke victory in the season's first 72-hole event moved him within two of Tommy Horton, the tour's all-time winner with 23 titles. It marked the seventh straight year that the 56-year-old Mason has won at least one victory.

He started the week four shots behind leaders Gordon Brand, Jr., the playoff loser in the 2008 PGA Senior; American John Benda, South African Jeff Hawkes and Paraguay's Angel Franco, who three-putted the 18th green. Franco followed up with a 72 in the rain after a long fog delay and kept the lead with his 141, a shot in front of Brand and Christopher Williams of South Africa. Mason moved into a five-way tie for fourth with 70–143, joined there by Englishman Kevin Spurgeon, Scot John Chillas, Ulsterman Jimmy Heggarty and American Bob Boyd, the playoff loser at the Irish Seniors.

Despite another lengthy fog delay, Mason produced his A-game on the greens with an eagle and five birdies and surged three strokes in front of Brand and Williams with his 67–210. His steady final round of 69 Sunday maintained the three-shot margin as he finished nine under par at 279. Franco, with a closing 68, placed second with Williams (70) at 282.

The Senior Open Championship
Berkshire, England
Winner: Loren Roberts

Major titles eluded Loren Roberts during his fine career on the PGA Tour, but he has made up for the void during his five years in senior golf on the Champions Tour. Roberts landed his fourth senior major when he outplayed Fred Funk and Mark McNulty in a playoff for the Senior Open Championship at the prestigious Sunningdale Golf Club in Berkshire, England.

It was Roberts's second Senior Open triumph, his first one at Turnberry in 2006 sandwiched by the 2005 JELD-WEN Tradition and the 2007 Senior Players on the Champions Tour.

"When I won back in '06, it was probably the greatest thrill of my life," he recalled. "Then to come here, to a golf course I've never seen before. I absolutely fell in love with this golf course."

Roberts lingered just off the lead all week on Sunningdale's Old Course as Funk ran in front at a record pace over the first two rounds. He opened with a stunning 64, the lowest Senior Open first round ever, ripping off five birdies on his back nine. It put him two strokes ahead of four runners-up, including Roberts. Funk followed with a 65 Friday and widened his margin to three shots, then over Sam Torrance, who also shot 65. The 129 is a 36-hole record for the event. A 68 put Roberts in third place at 134.

Greg Norman, making a rare senior appearance, entered the picture Saturday. He blew past everybody into the lead with a 64–200 as Funk struggled to a two-over-par 72 with two bogeys and a double bogey on his card after widening his lead to four strokes early in the round. That left Funk at 201 with Roberts, who shot 67.

McNulty nearly stole the title Sunday as he finished well ahead of the established contenders with yet another 64, even with missing fairly short birdie putts on the last two holes, finishing at 268. Norman faltered early and Funk regained command with an outgoing 32, but had all pars coming in for 67 and his 268. Roberts also shot 67, getting to 12 under with a fine birdie at the 17th.

Funk couldn't match the birdies of Roberts and McNulty on the first extra hole. Two holes later, McNulty drove into an unplayable lie in a bush and took a bogey, and Roberts wrapped up the title with a routine two-putt par from 12 feet.

Bad Ragaz PGA Seniors Open
Bad Ragaz, Switzerland
Winner: John Bland

John Bland set, and still holds, the record as the youngest winner on the European Senior Tour when he won the 1995 London Masters nine days after he turned 50. Nearly 16 years later, Bland became the oldest winner on the circuit in seven years and second oldest ever when he captured the Bad Ragaz PGA Seniors Open in a playoff against hard-luck American Bob Boyd. Thirteen years and 313 days elapsed between Bland's two victories, as the South African played full-time on the Champions Tour in America rather than in Europe until 2007.

Chivalrously, Bland credited the victory to his wife, Sonja. "She told me to slow down because I was swinging too fast and it seemed to do the trick," he noted after handing Boyd his second playoff loss of the season when he birdied the second extra hole.

The two men had finished at 199, 11 under par, Bland with a sparkling, five-under 65 produced by an eagle and four birdies. Boyd, a blood cancer survivor whose only tour win came in 2005 before he came down with leukemia, sported a three-stroke lead (65-65–130) over Gordon Brand, Jr. entering the final round. He made a sizeable putt on the 18th green, just his second of the day, for the tying 69.

Bland, Boyd and Brand were in the mix throughout the longstanding Swiss tournament. The trio trailed Australian Mike Harwood (64) after the first round before Boyd shot a 65 Saturday to take the three-shot lead over Brand, Harwood and Doug Johnson. Bland was another stroke back at the 36-hole mark.

Cleveland Golf/Srixon Scottish Senior Open
Fife, Scotland
Winner: Glenn Ralph

Glenn Ralph was the third first-time winner in 2009 and his victory in the Cleveland Golf/Srixon Scottish Senior Open was so special to him that "I could have cried on the last hole."

For good reason. "Any victory would have been big. I just wanted to win," said the 53-year-old Englishman. "I'd never won on tour in my life." What he didn't mention was that he had just returned to action at the start of the season after being shelved for 14 months with a broken ankle. Ralph had just two top-10s and was 30th on the money list when he arrived at fabled St. Andrews' Fairmont course.

He didn't attract much attention until his second-round 67–138 jumped him into a deadlock with Argentina's Luis Carbonetti, a stroke behind leader Bob Cameron (69-68–137), who had been a frequent contender on the circuit but winless since two victories in 2004. Cameron had shared the first-round lead at 69 with Carbonetti and Scot Ross Drummond, a non-winner.

Ralph climbed to the top of the leaderboard Sunday when he eagled the par-five sixth and birdied the par-four seventh. He bogeyed the 12th, then parred in for 70 and the winning eight-under-par 208. Carbonetti kept pace with Ralph on the back nine until he bogeyed the 17th and carded 71–209. Cameron finished with 72 for a matching 209, his victory bid spoiled by a double bogey at the 11th hole.

Mike Cunning (Brunei) and Bertus Smit (Wales) were the earlier first-time winners of 2009, not counting Michael Allen, the U.S. Senior PGA champion, and Fred Funk, the U.S. Senior Open victor.

Travis Perkins plc Senior Masters
Milton Keynes, England
Winner: Tony Johnstone

The heart-warming saga of Tony Johnstone on the European Senior Tour added another chapter at the Travis Perkins plc Senior Masters. Faced with a diagnosis of multiple sclerosis in 2004 that might have ended his golfing career, Johnstone decided nonetheless to venture onto the senior circuit in 2006 and amazed everybody when he won the Jersey Seniors in 2008.

He did it again at the Travis Perkins tournament on Woburn Golf Club's Duke's Course, "one of my four favorites anywhere in the world," coming from four strokes behind in the final round to edge Peter Senior, a leader for two days, by a stroke. Johnstone, who lost a playoff and had several other high finishes over the years on the Duke's course, has "always had the feeling that I would win a tournament round here."

The difference Sunday clearly was the putting. Senior, playing in just his second senior event, shared the first-round lead with Johnstone and Costantino Rocca at 69 and moved four shots ahead of Johnstone the second day when he shot 67 for 136. He continued to play well Sunday, hitting all 18 greens, but managed only a 71–207. Johnstone's putter, on the other hand, "was seriously hot." He raced to a 66 for the winning 206.

The timing of Johnston's win was ideal. He hosted a pro-amateur fund-raiser for MS at Woburn the next day.

Casa Serena Open
Prague, Czech Republic
Winner: Peter Mitchell

It hadn't been much of a year for a man who won three tournaments and finished third on the 2008 Order of Merit in his rookie season. Preoccupied through much of 2009 by work establishing a series of golf academies in England and Europe, Englishman Peter Mitchell hadn't been in contention all season and "had been playing so poorly" that he was ready to pack it in.

In fact, he teed it up in the Casa Serena Open in Prague primarily because he fell in love with the course and setting when he nearly won a fourth title there in 2008. When he turned things around and walked off with a three-stroke victory this time, he jumped from 48th to fifth place on the money list.

Mitchell went into the final round a stroke behind Peter Senior, the Australian newcomer who blew a four-shot lead in the Travis Perkins Masters, the last previous event. Senior, playing in just his third tournament on the tour, went in front by two with a 64 Friday and, sparked by a birdie and chip-in eagle on his last two holes Saturday, added 69 for 133 and a one-stroke lead over Mitchell and countryman Noel Ratcliffe.

Determined not to repeat his fatal final round at Casa Serena in 2008, Mitchell came out of the blocks flying Sunday. He birdied the first three holes, added two more at the sixth and ninth holes for an outgoing 31, and breezed to a six-under-par 66 and a 200 total. Senior challenged with three consecutive back-nine birdies, but a bogey at the 17th led to a 70 and a second-place tie with Glenn Ralph, who closed with 65.

Mitchell said a putting lesson at Woburn from American friend Doug Johnson "made the difference, so I guess I owe him a bit of thanks and a beer at least."

Benahavis Senior Masters
Marbella, Spain
Winner: Carl Mason

There it was the middle of October and nobody on the European Senior Tour had managed to win more than a single tournament all season. Appropriately, Carl Mason, the circuit's most successful player, broke the spread-them-around pattern in the Benahavis Senior Masters, the final full-field tournament of the year. Mason, the three-time Order of Merit champion, pulled off a playoff victory over Scotland's Gordon Brand, Jr. in the event at Marbella, Spain's La Quinta Golf and Country Club to go with his earlier win in the De Vere PGA Seniors Championship in June.

The triumph, which denied 51-year-old Brand a first senior victory for a second time in a playoff in his 14 months on tour, was Englishman Mason's 22nd in his seven seasons and moved him within one of Tommy Horton, the all-time record-holder.

Mason staged an extraordinary comeback in the back half of his final round to force the playoff. Nursing a heavy cold, Mason nonetheless had begun with a five-under-par 66, then yielded the lead Saturday when Ross Drummond, also in less than the pink of health with an aching back, shot 69 for 136. A 72 dropped Mason into a fourth-place tie behind Bob Cameron and Tony Johnstone, both with 68-69 rounds.

The Englishman slipped further off the pace when he went one over par on the front nine Sunday, then caught fire. He birdied the 10th and 14th, but still trailed Brand by three shots. Cameron and Eamonn Darcy had fizzled after fast starts. Brand's bogey at the 15th and Mason's birdie at the 16th narrowed the gap, and Mason caught up with a 15-foot birdie putt on the 18th. They matched 68s for their 206 totals.

Brand missed a 10-footer for the win on the first extra hole before Mason canned the winner from 25 feet at the next.

OKI Castellon Senior Tour Championship
Castellon, Spain
Winner: Mike Harwood

In the absence of dominant players over the season, eight men arrived at Castellon, Spain, for the OKI Senior Tour Championship with shots at the John Jacobs Trophy as the Order of Merit champion of 2009. Australian Mike Harwood was not one of them. A rookie on the tour who had been out of the game for a decade, Harwood outshone all of those contenders by rolling to a three-stroke victory at Club de Campo del Mediterraneo in the rich season finale in early November.

The fourth first-time winner of 2009 carved out a splendid 66 on a windy Sunday afternoon to wind up at 203, as Paraguay's winless Angel Franco, the leader for two days (64-70), managed only a par 72 to drop into second place at 206. It was his third runner-up posting of the year.

The third-place finish of Sam Torrance, the former Ryder Cup player and captain, enabled him to climb past Ian Woosnam and Glenn Ralph in the standings and annex his third Order of Merit award, matching the record of Carl Mason. Both are two titles behind Tommy Horton, the star of the circuit's early years.

"My short game today was unbelievable on the front nine," said Harwood, who came to Spain full of confidence just after winning the Australian Senior Open. "And I holed some fantastic four- and five-footers on the back nine, too."

Harwood moved ahead of Franco with a birdie at the 11th hole and widened the gap to the final three-shot margin as the Paraguayan bogeyed there and at the next two holes.

"I hoped I would win this year but thought it might be unrealistic after being out of the game so long. There must be something about Spain and the wind, because my Volvo Masters win (in 1990 at Valderrama) came in exactly the same conditions."

With the victory and several other strong performances during the year, Harwood passed Roger Chapman to become the tour's Rookie of the Year.

Mauritius Commercial Bank Open
Constance Belle Mare Plage, Mauritius
Winner: Kevin Spurgeon

The European Senior Tour found a new time and place to start its 2010 season and Kevin Spurgeon couldn't be happier about the change. The Englishman ended five years of frustration with his initial win as a senior when officials decided to launch the new season in December with the Mauritius Commercial Bank Open on the Indian Ocean island of Mauritius.

Spurgeon, 54, took a two-stroke lead into the final round and survived a very shaky finish to land a one-shot victory over Gordon J. Brand. He shot an even-par 72 on the Constance Belle Mare Plage's Legends course despite four bogeys on the front nine and a double bogey at the 11th that dropped him four strokes behind Nick Job.

However, Job promptly absorbed a quadruple-bogey eight at the next hole, while Spurgeon birdied there and twice more on the way home to snatch the victory. "This is huge for me," said the teary-eyed winner, who had to qualify for the 2008 tour and finished 31st on the Order of Merit in 2009.

Job didn't recover from his disaster and wound up in a 14th-place tie, six strokes behind Spurgeon's 210. Brand fired a 69 to jump into the runner-up slot. Sam Torrance (67) and Angel Franco (70) shared third place at 212.

Japan Senior Tour

Fancl Classic
Susono, Shizuoka
Winner: Tateo Ozaki

Even with 15 victories, Tateo (Jet) Ozaki found himself in the shadow of his even more successful younger brothers Masashi (Jumbo) and Naomichi (Joe) during their regular tour days. That has not been the case on the Japan PGA Senior Tour. The 55-year-old Tateo chalked up his fourth senior win in the belated season-opening Fancl Classic in August. It was a forerunner to a series of strong performances that eventually took him to the Order of Merit title.

Ozaki snatched the Fancl victory with a final-round 67 after hovering just off the lead the first two days. Atsushi Murota seized a huge first-round lead when he shot a nine-under-par 63, five strokes better than the runner-up 68s of Ozaki and Norikazu Kawakami. Murota remained in front Saturday with a 70–133. Ozaki pulled two shots closer with another 68, staying in second place, then with Tsuneyuki (Tommy) Nakajima (69-67).

Murota ran out of gas Sunday, shooting 73 and dropping into a fourth-place tie with Nakajima at 206. Ozaki's 67 for 203 gave him a three-shot victory over Tsukasa Watanabe and Masahiro (Massy) Kuramoto, who both closed with 66s.

Komatsu Open
Komatsu, Ishikawa
Winner: Tomohiro Maruyama

It took a playoff birdie in the Komatsu Open to do it, but Tomohiro Maruyama scored his first victory on the Japan PGA Senior Tour, his first win since he took the NST Niigata Open on the regular Japan Tour in 1995.

Maruyama faced a hard battle throughout the tournament at Ishikawa's Komatsu Country Club in mid-September. The lead was crowded with five players — Tommy Nakajima, David Ishii, Masami Ito, Yuji Takagi and Katsuyoshi Tomori — with 68s in the opening round.

Maruyama added a 67 to his first-round 70 and moved into a tie for the lead Saturday with Ishii (68-69), the Hawaiian who was the leading money winner on the Japan Tour in 1987. They had two shots on Ito and Thailand's Boonchu Ruangkit. Maruyama and Ishii both posted par 72s Sunday for 209 totals and were joined in the playoff by Ito and Boonchu, who both shot 70s. Maruyama ended the playoff with his birdie on the first extra hole.

Japan PGA Senior Championship Tamahome Cup
Fukuoka
Winner: Kiyoshi Murota

Kiyoshi Murota, one the premier players on tour in recent seasons, landed his second Japan PGA Senior Championship in a runaway. Murota, a six-time winner on the Japan Tour between 1991 and 2003, when he won the rich Taiheiyo Masters, left the opposition far behind when he closed with a five-under-par 66 and raced to a six-stroke victory at Fukuoka's Ito Golf Club with his 15-under 269. It was his fifth win on the senior circuit, his first being the Senior PGA Championship in 2005.

Tateo Ozaki dueled with Murota for three rounds before Murota iced matters the last day. The two tied for the lead with opening 68s, then Ozaki, the Fancl winner in August, went in front Friday with 66–134 as Murota shot another 68. The two men swapped places in the third round, Murota firing a 67–203 to Ozaki's 71–205.

Ozaki could only muster a 71 in the final round as Murota's 66 carried him to the six-stroke victory.

Fujifilm Senior Championship
Chiba
Winner: Hajime Meshiai

Hajime Meshiai, the defending Order of Merit champion, who had not done much in the first three events, came to life in the Fujifilm Senior Championship at Chiba's Hirakawa Country Club. The 55-year-old, who won 14 times in Japan during his regular tour career, posted a one-stroke victory in the weather-shortened Fujifilm Senior Championship with his 67-72–139.

Meshiai, one of the Japan's international players over the years, led Tateo Ozaki and Katsuyoshi Tomori by a stroke with the first-round 67. When Sunday's final round had to be cancelled, Meshiai's 139 became the winning score and gave him his fourth senior victory. Ozaki (68-72) had his second runner-up finish to go with his Fancl victory in his three starts in 2009. He shared the runner-up slot with Masami Ito (69-71).

Japan Senior Open Championship
Shiga
Winner: Tsukasa Watanabe

Tsukasa Watanabe has picked up three victories since joining the Japan PGA Senior Tour in 2007 and two of them are major titles. Watanabe followed up his two-win 2008 season that included victory in the Senior PGA Championship with a tight triumph in the 2009 Japan Senior Open Championship. Although slipping with a final-round 73, he finished a stroke in front of Tateo Ozaki and Kiyoshi Murota, two winners earlier in the season.

Watanabe, who scored two victories in his long career on the Japan Tour, was not a serious contender on the Ritto/Mikami course of Shiga's Biwako Country Club until he jumped into the lead in the third round. He started with 73, well off the pace set by Katsunari Takahashi, the tour's leading career titlist with 12 victories. Takahashi started with 67.

Murota took over Friday, adding 69 to his opening 70 to lead Takahashi (73–140) and Yoshinori Mizumaki (69-71–140) by a shot. Watanabe began his move that day with 68 and established a three-stroke margin when he fired a six-under-par 66 Saturday for 207. Murota (71) and Takahashi (70) were at 210, Ozaki (70) and Tsuneyuki Nakajima (68) at 211.

Watanabe's bookend 73s and eight-under-par 280 total stood up as Murota and Takahashi shot final-round 71s and Ozaki, with a third runner-up finish to go with his Fancl win, had 70 for their 281s.

Handa Cup Philanthropy Senior Open
Chiba
Winner: Ian Woosnam

Ian Woosnam, the highly successful Masters champion and Ryder Cup captain, traveled to Japan in mid-November to play in the Handa Cup Philanthropy Senior Open, the final event of the season, and he returned to Wales with his second victory of the year. The Welshman had won the Irish Seniors Open in June.

The tournament attracted a rare international field, but Woosnam was the only visitor to make a strong showing. Not at the start, though. Woosnam opened with 75 and was four strokes off the lead, held jointly by Yutaka Hagawa, Toyotake Nakao and Masahiro Kuramoto at one-under-par 71 at Skyway Country Club in Chiba.

Kuramoto forged a stroke in front with another 71 Friday. Gohei Sato, Yoshinori Mizumaki, Hagawa and Nakao were at 143 and Woosnam with 70 was at 145. Then, on Saturday, Woosnam fired a 68, the lowest round posted all week, and with 213 advanced into a tie for the lead with Mizumaki (70). Woosnam's 71 Sunday for 284 established a three-stroke victory over Sato, who also shot 71.

Although he finished well off the pace at 297, Tateo Ozaki was the easy winner of the season's Order of Merit with Watanabe finishing as runner-up for the second year in a row. Ozaki finished with a ¥5 million margin over Watanabe.

APPENDIXES

American Tours

Mercedes-Benz Championship

Kapalua Resort, Plantation Course, Maui, Hawaii
Par 36-37–73; 7,411 yards

January 8-11
purse, $5,600,000

	SCORES				TOTAL	MONEY
Geoff Ogilvy	67	68	65	68	268	$1,120,000
Anthony Kim	71	68	68	67	274	523,500
Davis Love	69	70	68	67	274	523,500
Sean O'Hair	69	70	71	65	275	312,000
Justin Leonard	74	67	65	70	276	261,000
Ernie Els	68	69	73	67	277	189,250
Zach Johnson	71	75	64	67	277	189,250
Kenny Perry	68	71	68	70	277	189,250
D.J. Trahan	70	66	70	71	277	189,250
Johnson Wagner	68	71	70	69	278	162,000
Dustin Johnson	72	72	68	67	279	152,000
Will MacKenzie	72	70	69	69	280	132,000
Chez Reavie	75	70	68	67	280	132,000
Camilo Villegas	74	67	66	73	280	132,000
K.J. Choi	71	71	66	73	281	107,000
Boo Weekley	70	70	69	72	281	107,000
Carl Pettersson	72	72	70	68	282	92,000
Brian Gay	72	70	70	71	283	77,666.67
Adam Scott	73	67	73	70	283	77,666.67
Ryuji Imada	69	70	74	70	283	77,666.66
Trevor Immelman	72	74	69	69	284	71,000
Richard S. Johnson	72	72	71	69	284	71,000
Cameron Beckman	76	73	66	70	285	68,000
Stewart Cink	74	67	71	74	286	64,000
Steve Lowery	69	75	70	72	286	64,000
Parker McLachlin	77	69	69	71	286	64,000
Daniel Chopra	79	69	67	72	287	59,500
Vijay Singh	73	73	71	70	287	59,500
J.B. Holmes	74	75	72	67	288	57,500
Greg Kraft	72	73	68	75	288	57,500
Ryan Palmer	78	75	72	66	291	56,000
Andres Romero	78	74	71	72	295	55,000
Marc Turnesa	79	73	70	74	296	54,000

Sony Open

Waialae Country Club, Honolulu, Hawaii
Par 35-35–70; 7,060 yards

January 15-18
purse, $5,400,000

	SCORES				TOTAL	MONEY
Zach Johnson	69	65	66	65	265	$972,000
Adam Scott	71	66	66	64	267	475,200
David Toms	70	66	65	66	267	475,200
Charles Howell	67	68	67	66	268	259,200
Brian Gay	66	67	68	68	269	205,200
Kevin Na	72	65	66	66	269	205,200
Steve Marino	68	67	70	66	271	174,150
George McNeill	69	68	65	69	271	174,150

	SCORES				TOTAL	MONEY
Bill Haas	68	71	65	68	272	145,800
Webb Simpson	66	68	70	68	272	145,800
Boo Weekley	66	69	67	70	272	145,800
K.J. Choi	68	69	70	66	273	87,970.91
Tim Clark	71	70	68	64	273	87,970.91
Bob Estes	72	67	68	66	273	87,970.91
Nathan Green	66	66	69	72	273	87,970.91
Tim Herron	68	71	68	66	273	87,970.91
Jeff Klauk	69	69	66	69	273	87,970.91
Marc Leishman	72	66	70	65	273	87,970.91
Sean O'Hair	71	68	66	68	273	87,970.91
Scott Piercy	67	72	69	65	273	87,970.91
Rory Sabbatini	68	70	70	65	273	87,970.91
Shigeki Maruyama	65	68	68	72	273	87,970.90
Briny Baird	69	67	69	69	274	43,380
Cameron Beckman	72	66	67	69	274	43,380
Luke Donald	67	70	68	69	274	43,380
Ryuji Imada	71	70	66	67	274	43,380
Jerry Kelly	67	72	69	66	274	43,380
Cliff Kresge	69	69	69	67	274	43,380
Troy Matteson	71	67	69	67	274	43,380
Chez Reavie	70	70	66	68	274	43,380
Steve Stricker	70	68	67	69	274	43,380
Bart Bryant	71	69	71	64	275	29,237.15
Stewart Cink	71	65	72	67	275	29,237.15
Tadd Fujikawa	71	69	62	73	275	29,237.14
Geoff Ogilvy	66	69	68	72	275	29,237.14
Greg Owen	71	67	70	67	275	29,237.14
D.J. Trahan	71	67	66	71	275	29,237.14
Jimmy Walker	73	66	68	68	275	29,237.14
Ernie Els	72	69	68	67	276	21,600
Michael Letzig	69	70	69	68	276	21,600
Arron Oberholser	68	73	69	66	276	21,600
Scott Sterling	71	69	71	65	276	21,600
Hideto Tanihara	72	65	73	66	276	21,600
Brendon Todd	69	71	66	70	276	21,600
Michael Allen	72	68	70	67	277	15,444
Wil Collins	69	67	69	72	277	15,444
Brian Davis	69	68	68	72	277	15,444
Glen Day	70	68	72	67	277	15,444
Chris Stroud	67	70	71	69	277	15,444
Azuma Yano	71	70	70	66	277	15,444
Alex Cejka	72	69	70	67	278	12,879
Harrison Frazar	69	70	66	73	278	12,879
Ted Purdy	69	69	70	70	278	12,879
Tim Wilkinson	68	70	68	72	278	12,879
Tommy Gainey	71	70	66	72	279	12,258
Steve Lowery	71	68	70	70	279	12,258
Kevin Streelman	70	69	67	73	279	12,258
Casey Wittenberg	71	70	68	70	279	12,258
Matt Bettencourt	73	68	69	70	280	11,718
Joe Durant	73	68	70	69	280	11,718
Richard S. Johnson	70	71	69	70	280	11,718
David Mathis	68	68	71	73	280	11,718
Tom Pernice, Jr.	69	63	75	73	280	11,718
Kenny Perry	69	69	68	74	280	11,718
Arjun Atwal	69	71	72	70	282	11,178
Troy Kelly	71	66	75	70	282	11,178
Jarrod Lyle	70	69	70	73	282	11,178
John Merrick	70	70	72	70	282	11,178
Paul Azinger	68	73	71	71	283	10,800
Jeff Overton	71	69	71	72	283	10,800
Andres Romero	73	68	71	71	283	10,800

	SCORES				TOTAL	MONEY
Spencer Levin	71	69	70	74	284	10,584
Tim Petrovic	69	72	71	73	285	10,368
Jeff Quinney	71	70	72	72	285	10,368
Tag Ridings	71	69	72	73	285	10,368
D.A. Points	68	73	74	71	286	10,152
Matthew Borchert	73	67	73	75	288	10,044
Junpei Takayama	71	69	74	75	289	9,936

Bob Hope Classic

PGA West, Palmer Course: Par 36-36–72; 6,950 yards
PGA West, Nicklaus Course: Par 36-36–72; 6,951 yards
Bermuda Dunes CC: Par 36-36–72; 7,017 yards
SilverRock Resort: Par 36-36–72; 7,578 yards
La Quinta and Bermuda Dunes, California

January 21-25
purse, $5,100,000

	SCORES					TOTAL	MONEY
Pat Perez	61	63	67	67	69	327	$918,000
John Merrick	68	65	67	63	67	330	550,800
Mike Weir	62	70	67	66	67	332	295,800
Steve Stricker	65	67	61	62	77	332	295,800
Stephen Ames	71	63	70	66	63	333	179,138
Bo Van Pelt	66	65	68	67	67	333	179,138
Tim Clark	66	69	63	66	69	333	179,138
Webb Simpson	68	66	64	66	69	333	179,138
Brad Adamonis	67	62	71	69	65	334	127,500
Chad Campbell	66	71	68	65	64	334	127,500
John Senden	67	70	65	64	68	334	127,500
Tom Pernice, Jr.	65	63	68	69	69	334	127,500
Richard S. Johnson	63	65	67	69	70	334	127,500
Bill Lunde	67	68	62	69	69	335	86,700
Rich Beem	66	65	65	68	71	335	86,700
D.J. Trahan	65	67	65	68	70	335	86,700
Chris Stroud	65	63	67	69	71	335	86,700
Robert Garrigus	67	65	64	66	73	335	86,700
Lucas Glover	65	68	68	67	68	336	59,670
Brian Gay	65	70	72	63	66	336	59,670
John Huston	69	70	64	64	69	336	59,670
Scott Piercy	66	66	70	65	69	336	59,670
Charley Hoffman	72	66	64	65	69	336	59,670
Mathew Goggin	66	70	62	67	71	336	59,670
David Toms	68	65	68	67	69	337	36,493
Steve Marino	65	69	64	70	69	337	36,493
Chris DiMarco	64	68	69	66	70	337	36,493
Bill Haas	68	68	67	67	67	337	36,493
Colt Knost	69	68	70	63	67	337	36,493
John Mallinger	66	67	65	68	71	337	36,493
Nick Watney	66	71	72	63	65	337	36,493
Bubba Watson	62	69	68	63	75	337	36,493
Matt Kuchar	66	67	71	69	64	337	36,493
Ryuji Imada	67	65	69	67	70	338	24,671
Charlie Wi	68	67	61	71	71	338	24,671
Casey Wittenberg	69	66	64	68	71	338	24,671
Scott McCarron	66	68	63	69	72	338	24,671
Jason Dufner	63	65	67	71	72	338	24,671
David Mathis	66	66	69	65	72	338	24,671
David Berganio, Jr.	63	64	68	70	73	338	24,671
Vaughn Taylor	63	67	64	68	76	338	24,671
Briny Baird	63	63	70	72	71	339	17,340
Woody Austin	66	68	68	67	70	339	17,340

		SCORES				TOTAL	MONEY
Justin Leonard	72	67	63	68	69	339	17,340
Jerry Kelly	66	71	65	68	69	339	17,340
Ken Duke	68	68	64	71	68	339	17,340
Cameron Beckman	68	67	70	68	66	339	17,340
Dean Wilson	67	71	66	65	71	340	12,818
Kevin Sutherland	64	67	67	69	73	340	12,818
Ryan Palmer	70	65	66	66	73	340	12,818
Cliff Kresge	68	63	67	73	69	340	12,818
Joe Ogilvie	70	73	67	62	68	340	12,818
Joe Durant	73	66	65	69	67	340	12,818
Rick Price	64	70	66	69	72	341	11,679
Heath Slocum	65	67	73	65	71	341	11,679
Martin Laird	67	68	68	68	70	341	11,679
Ben Crane	63	70	70	69	69	341	11,679
Nicholas Thompson	66	70	68	68	70	342	11,373
Alex Cejka	68	67	68	70	69	342	11,373
Peter Lonard	65	67	68	69	74	343	10,965
Jason Bohn	66	70	65	67	75	343	10,965
Jeff Klauk	67	67	67	69	73	343	10,965
Fred Couples	68	72	64	68	71	343	10,965
Chris Couch	67	63	69	66	78	343	10,965
Michael Allen	68	71	66	68	70	343	10,965
Chez Reavie	66	66	68	69	75	344	10,455
Dustin Johnson	68	71	67	66	72	344	10,455
Bob Estes	66	69	66	71	72	344	10,455
Tim Petrovic	68	69	65	71	71	344	10,455
Kirk Triplett	67	69	69	65	75	345	10,098
Steve Lowery	67	65	71	68	74	345	10,098
Michael Letzig	66	68	68	71	72	345	10,098
Glen Day	65	68	71	67	77	348	9,894
Brendon de Jonge	67	70	65	70	78	350	9,792

FBR Open

TPC Scottsdale, Scottsdale, Arizona
Par 35-36–71; 7,216 yards

January 29-February 1
purse, $6,000,000

		SCORES			TOTAL	MONEY
Kenny Perry	72	63	66	69	270	$1,080,000
Charley Hoffman	66	68	69	67	270	648,000
(Perry defeated Hoffman on third playoff hole.)						
Kevin Na	67	70	66	68	271	408,000
James Nitties	65	69	70	68	272	264,000
David Toms	69	68	67	68	272	264,000
Brian Gay	68	68	67	70	273	194,250
Matt Kuchar	67	67	70	69	273	194,250
Ryan Moore	69	67	68	69	273	194,250
Scott Piercy	69	67	66	71	273	194,250
Cliff Kresge	68	69	68	69	274	156,000
Jeff Maggert	70	68	66	70	274	156,000
Zach Johnson	71	66	68	70	275	117,600
Michael Letzig	70	67	69	69	275	117,600
Rod Pampling	72	69	69	65	275	117,600
Rory Sabbatini	72	65	69	69	275	117,600
Nick Watney	70	63	72	70	275	117,600
Parker McLachlin	68	71	69	68	276	87,000
Geoff Ogilvy	70	69	65	72	276	87,000
John Senden	68	70	72	66	276	87,000
D.J. Trahan	68	74	69	65	276	87,000
Woody Austin	69	72	69	67	277	64,800

		SCORES			TOTAL	MONEY
J.J. Henry	69	71	68	69	277	64,800
Brandt Jobe	72	69	69	67	277	64,800
Kevin Sutherland	68	71	69	69	277	64,800
Luke Donald	76	65	68	69	278	44,828.58
Jonathan Byrd	72	69	67	70	278	44,828.57
Brendon de Jonge	71	67	69	71	278	44,828.57
Jonathan Kaye	68	71	69	70	278	44,828.57
Sean O'Hair	69	69	69	71	278	44,828.57
Carl Pettersson	71	68	69	70	278	44,828.57
Bubba Watson	68	70	69	71	278	44,828.57
David Berganio, Jr.	66	71	72	70	279	35,500
Chad Campbell	70	70	72	67	279	35,500
Chris DiMarco	73	69	70	67	279	35,500
Jarrod Lyle	71	69	69	71	280	28,328.58
Aaron Baddeley	69	73	66	72	280	28,328.57
Hunter Mahan	73	67	69	71	280	28,328.57
Troy Matteson	70	68	69	73	280	28,328.57
Rocco Mediate	68	70	67	75	280	28,328.57
Ted Purdy	71	68	65	76	280	28,328.57
Kevin Streelman	73	69	69	69	280	28,328.57
Briny Baird	67	74	72	68	281	20,400
Cameron Beckman	68	67	75	71	281	20,400
Lucas Glover	65	72	75	69	281	20,400
Brett Quigley	69	71	75	66	281	20,400
Kirk Triplett	70	70	70	71	281	20,400
Bob Tway	71	71	69	70	281	20,400
Steve Flesch	69	72	68	73	282	15,264
Nathan Green	73	69	67	73	282	15,264
Jeff Klauk	74	66	72	70	282	15,264
Pat Perez	69	73	70	70	282	15,264
Mark Wilson	70	72	71	69	282	15,264
Steve Elkington	70	69	71	73	283	13,890
Dudley Hart	71	71	70	71	283	13,890
Scott McCarron	70	72	66	75	283	13,890
Vaughn Taylor	69	69	73	72	283	13,890
Charlie Wi	73	68	71	72	284	13,560
Fredrik Jacobson	72	65	74	74	285	13,440
*Rickie Fowler	73	66	72	74	285	
John Merrick	72	70	70	74	286	13,080
Joe Ogilvie	71	70	73	72	286	13,080
Jeff Overton	70	72	68	76	286	13,080
Ryan Palmer	73	67	68	78	286	13,080
Gary Woodland	70	71	67	78	286	13,080
Webb Simpson	68	67	77	75	287	12,720
Ben Curtis	71	71	74	72	288	12,540
Dean Wilson	69	73	76	70	288	12,540
Jason Bohn	71	71	74	73	289	12,300
Nicholas Thompson	72	68	77	72	289	12,300
Brad Adamonis	68	70	75	77	290	12,060
John Rollins	71	71	74	74	290	12,060

Buick Invitational

Torrey Pines Golf Course, San Diego, California
South Course: Par 36-36–72; 7,569 yards
North Course: Par 36-36–72; 6,874 yards

February 5-8
purse, $5,300,000

		SCORES			TOTAL	MONEY
Nick Watney	69	69	71	68	277	$954,000
John Rollins	70	64	70	74	278	572,400

	SCORES				TOTAL	MONEY
Lucas Glover	69	73	69	68	279	307,400
Camilo Villegas	63	70	74	72	279	307,400
Matt Jones	70	73	74	64	281	212,000
Mathew Goggin	69	70	73	70	282	190,800
Ben Crane	69	74	70	70	283	159,662.50
Luke Donald	70	69	71	73	283	159,662.50
Charley Hoffman	71	66	74	72	283	159,662.50
Bubba Watson	71	68	77	67	283	159,662.50
Aaron Baddeley	66	76	70	72	284	108,650
Bill Haas	72	70	72	70	284	108,650
J.J. Henry	70	71	71	72	284	108,650
Jeff Klauk	71	73	69	71	284	108,650
Hunter Mahan	74	70	74	66	284	108,650
Charles Warren	74	69	68	73	284	108,650
Paul Goydos	72	66	72	75	285	82,150
Nicholas Thompson	75	70	70	70	285	82,150
Harrison Frazar	69	70	75	72	286	64,236
Ryuji Imada	70	72	75	69	286	64,236
Dustin Johnson	74	71	72	69	286	64,236
Webb Simpson	72	73	71	70	286	64,236
Dean Wilson	71	73	71	71	286	64,236
Padraig Harrington	71	74	74	68	287	48,760
Scott Sterling	69	72	75	71	287	48,760
Jason Dufner	70	70	75	73	288	36,069.45
Robert Garrigus	68	74	73	73	288	36,069.45
Retief Goosen	71	71	73	73	288	36,069.45
Jonathan Kaye	70	73	73	72	288	36,069.45
Tommy Gainey	77	69	73	69	288	36,069.44
J.B. Holmes	73	70	71	74	288	36,069.44
Marc Leishman	74	68	72	74	288	36,069.44
Ted Purdy	74	71	70	73	288	36,069.44
Tag Ridings	71	72	77	68	288	36,069.44
Lee Janzen	74	72	70	73	289	25,023.58
Jason Day	69	76	70	74	289	25,023.57
Davis Love	66	77	74	72	289	25,023.57
George McNeill	71	70	71	77	289	25,023.57
Rod Pampling	72	74	73	70	289	25,023.57
Aron Price	72	72	73	72	289	25,023.57
Kevin Sutherland	77	68	74	70	289	25,023.57
Nathan Green	70	72	72	76	290	17,052.75
Charles Howell	72	71	77	70	290	17,052.75
Jarrod Lyle	71	74	70	75	290	17,052.75
David Mathis	75	71	74	70	290	17,052.75
Phil Mickelson	70	72	73	75	290	17,052.75
Jesper Parnevik	71	74	72	73	290	17,052.75
Tom Pernice, Jr.	75	68	76	71	290	17,052.75
Brandt Snedeker	75	68	73	74	290	17,052.75
Ben Curtis	76	66	73	76	291	13,038
Carl Pettersson	77	69	74	71	291	13,038
John Senden	76	70	73	72	291	13,038
Arjun Atwal	72	74	74	72	292	12,269.50
Ricky Barnes	69	73	75	75	292	12,269.50
Bart Bryant	73	69	77	73	292	12,269.50
Glen Day	72	74	73	73	292	12,269.50
Stuart Appleby	68	74	78	73	293	11,713
James Driscoll	73	73	74	73	293	11,713
James Nitties	79	67	73	74	293	11,713
Pat Perez	73	73	73	74	293	11,713
Rick Price	72	73	75	73	293	11,713
Y.E. Yang	77	69	73	74	293	11,713
Matt Bettencourt	74	72	75	73	294	11,130
Fred Couples	74	70	74	76	294	11,130
Jason Gore	70	69	80	75	294	11,130

	SCORES				TOTAL	MONEY
John Huston	71	71	79	73	294	11,130
Kent Jones	70	71	77	76	294	11,130
Parker McLachlin	74	71	72	79	296	10,759
D.A. Points	70	72	79	75	296	10,759
*Gregor Main	70	75	72	80	297	
Johnson Wagner	76	70	75	80	301	10,600
Michael Allen	71	75	76		222	10,282
Woody Austin	74	71	77		222	10,282
David Berganio, Jr.	76	70	76		222	10,282
Colt Knost	73	73	76		222	10,282
Tim Petrovic	73	71	78		222	10,282
Brian Bateman	69	77	77		223	9,805
Alex Cejka	73	72	78		223	9,805
Greg Owen	70	75	78		223	9,805
Chris Stroud	73	68	82		223	9,805
Courtland Lowe	71	72	81		224	9,434
Jeff Overton	68	78	78		224	9,434
Gary Woodland	76	70	78		224	9,434
Scott McCarron	74	72	79		225	9,169
Jay Williamson	72	71	82		225	9,169

AT&T Pebble Beach National Pro-Am

Pebble Beach GL: Par 36-36–72; 6,816 yards
Poppy Hills: Par 36-36–72; 6,833 yards
Spyglass Hill GC: Par 36-36–72; 6,858 yards
Pebble Beach, California
(Final round cancelled—rain.)

February 12-15
purse, $6,100,000

	SCORES			TOTAL	MONEY
Dustin Johnson	65	69	67	201	$1,098,000
Mike Weir	67	69	69	205	658,800
Retief Goosen	68	64	74	206	414,800
Mark Calcavecchia	67	69	71	207	268,400
Bob Estes	68	72	67	207	268,400
Kevin Chappell	68	72	68	208	197,487.50
Bill Lunde	67	70	71	208	197,487.50
Chris Stroud	69	69	70	208	197,487.50
D.J. Trahan	67	73	68	208	197,487.50
Mark Brooks	68	69	72	209	146,400
Shigeki Maruyama	69	73	67	209	146,400
Sean O'Hair	71	68	70	209	146,400
Kenny Perry	71	70	68	209	146,400
Jason Day	67	75	68	210	94,550
Charley Hoffman	66	70	74	210	94,550
Matt Kuchar	71	71	68	210	94,550
Spencer Levin	71	70	69	210	94,550
Ted Purdy	68	72	70	210	94,550
Kevin Stadler	71	71	68	210	94,550
Vaughn Taylor	66	75	69	210	94,550
Charlie Wi	68	69	73	210	94,550
Tim Clark	71	71	69	211	49,742.73
Derek Fathauer	71	71	69	211	49,742.73
Tim Herron	72	68	71	211	49,742.73
Len Mattiace	69	72	70	211	49,742.73
Jeff Overton	69	70	72	211	49,742.73
Jeff Quinney	68	73	70	211	49,742.73
Nick Watney	75	69	67	211	49,742.73
Y.E. Yang	69	70	72	211	49,742.73
Michael Allen	67	71	73	211	49,742.72

	SCORES			TOTAL	MONEY
Richard S. Johnson	71	70	70	211	49,742.72
Davis Love	69	72	70	211	49,742.72
Arjun Atwal	68	73	71	212	32,228.34
Jeff Klauk	73	72	67	212	32,228.34
Jim Furyk	71	70	71	212	32,228.33
Steve Lowery	70	69	73	212	32,228.33
John Mallinger	72	71	69	212	32,228.33
Aron Price	68	69	75	212	32,228.33
Rich Beem	66	75	72	213	19,329.38
Glen Day	73	70	70	213	19,329.38
Scott Gutschewski	71	72	70	213	19,329.38
Michael Letzig	69	73	71	213	19,329.38
Frank Lickliter	72	71	70	213	19,329.38
David Mathis	71	75	67	213	19,329.38
James Oh	73	72	68	213	19,329.38
Pat Perez	73	71	69	213	19,329.38
Robert Garrigus	65	71	77	213	19,329.37
Charles Howell	72	70	71	213	19,329.37
Troy Matteson	73	71	69	213	19,329.37
Greg Owen	68	73	72	213	19,329.37
Peter Tomasulo	71	70	72	213	19,329.37
Charles Warren	74	69	70	213	19,329.37
Jay Williamson	70	75	68	213	19,329.37
Mark Wilson	70	73	70	213	19,329.37
Brad Adamonis	71	72	71	214	13,237
K.J. Choi	69	75	70	214	13,237
Brendon de Jonge	69	74	71	214	13,237
Jason Dufner	75	68	71	214	13,237
David Duval	73	72	69	214	13,237
Mathew Goggin	70	73	71	214	13,237
J.J. Henry	71	72	71	214	13,237
J.B. Holmes	74	68	72	214	13,237
Matt Jones	71	71	72	214	13,237
Marc Leishman	72	73	69	214	13,237
Phil Mickelson	72	71	71	214	13,237
Rick Price	70	72	72	214	13,237
Chris Smith	70	75	69	214	13,237
Jimmy Walker	71	73	70	214	13,237
Eric Axley	72	72	71	215	11,651
Ricky Barnes	69	75	71	215	11,651
James Driscoll	73	70	72	215	11,651
John Ellis	69	74	72	215	11,651
Todd Fischer	72	69	74	215	11,651
Bob Heintz	71	69	75	215	11,651
Chris Kirk	73	73	69	215	11,651
Jarrod Lyle	72	73	70	215	11,651
Hunter Mahan	72	71	72	215	11,651
Brian Vranesh	68	74	73	215	11,651
Matt Weibring	70	70	75	215	11,651
Dean Wilson	68	71	76	215	11,651

Northern Trust Open

Riviera Country Club, Pacific Palisades, California
Par 35-36–71; 7,298 yards

February 19 22
purse, $6,300,000

	SCORES				TOTAL	MONEY
Phil Mickelson	63	72	62	72	269	$1,134,000
Steve Stricker	68	66	69	67	270	680,400
K.J. Choi	66	69	67	69	271	327,600

	SCORES				TOTAL	MONEY
Fred Couples	67	70	65	69	271	327,600
Andres Romero	66	70	65	70	271	327,600
Mark Calcavecchia	70	69	64	69	272	203,962.50
Luke Donald	66	69	69	68	272	203,962.50
J.B. Holmes	73	67	64	68	272	203,962.50
Rory Sabbatini	68	67	67	70	272	203,962.50
Brendon de Jonge	69	70	67	67	273	157,500
Dustin Johnson	66	70	67	70	273	157,500
Scott McCarron	64	68	70	71	273	157,500
Rich Beem	68	69	69	68	274	118,125
Angel Cabrera	72	68	68	66	274	118,125
Tim Clark	68	72	66	68	274	118,125
Chris DiMarco	68	72	66	68	274	118,125
Robert Allenby	70	67	68	71	276	79,695
Brian Davis	69	69	68	70	276	79,695
Richard S. Johnson	70	68	67	71	276	79,695
Hunter Mahan	69	69	68	70	276	79,695
Kenny Perry	70	68	69	69	276	79,695
Kevin Sutherland	72	67	68	69	276	79,695
Bubba Watson	69	71	68	68	276	79,695
Dean Wilson	66	72	67	71	276	79,695
Tommy Armour	67	67	72	71	277	49,140
Jason Bohn	73	66	68	70	277	49,140
Ben Curtis	68	69	69	71	277	49,140
Kevin Na	67	69	72	69	277	49,140
Jeff Quinney	69	71	70	67	277	49,140
Woody Austin	68	70	69	71	278	35,840
Briny Baird	67	70	68	73	278	35,840
Charley Hoffman	68	72	70	68	278	35,840
Bill Lunde	69	67	71	71	278	35,840
Geoff Ogilvy	68	67	71	72	278	35,840
Pat Perez	69	66	75	68	278	35,840
D.J. Trahan	67	72	72	67	278	35,840
Marc Turnesa	69	68	71	70	278	35,840
Bo Van Pelt	68	71	74	65	278	35,840
Bob Estes	72	65	73	69	279	27,720
Jeev Milkha Singh	69	70	71	69	279	27,720
Brad Adamonis	70	70	72	68	280	20,386.80
Cameron Beckman	70	71	71	68	280	20,386.80
Jim Furyk	66	71	75	68	280	20,386.80
Soren Hansen	70	69	72	69	280	20,386.80
Jerry Kelly	72	68	69	71	280	20,386.80
Jeff Klauk	67	72	68	73	280	20,386.80
John Mallinger	70	68	73	69	280	20,386.80
Graeme McDowell	70	71	66	73	280	20,386.80
Rocco Mediate	70	68	70	72	280	20,386.80
Joe Ogilvie	70	70	69	71	280	20,386.80
Aaron Baddeley	71	70	72	68	281	14,826
Bart Bryant	74	67	71	69	281	14,826
Ernie Els	71	67	73	70	281	14,826
Brandt Jobe	68	72	70	71	281	14,826
Carl Pettersson	68	71	72	70	281	14,826
Kirk Triplett	67	70	73	71	281	14,826
Chad Campbell	72	68	69	73	282	14,175
Matt Kuchar	70	68	75	69	282	14,175
David Duval	70	69	71	73	283	13,734
Charles Howell	72	67	75	69	283	13,734
Ryuji Imada	67	73	71	72	283	13,734
Nick Watney	71	68	73	71	283	13,734
Charlie Wi	70	71	74	68	283	13,734
Stephen Ames	71	70	71	72	284	13,104
Stuart Appleby	71	68	73	72	284	13,104
Michael Letzig	70	71	71	72	284	13,104

	SCORES				TOTAL	MONEY
John Merrick	66	71	72	75	284	13,104
Scott Verplank	71	70	71	72	284	13,104
Retief Goosen	68	71	71	75	285	12,726
Jimmy Walker	69	70	70	77	286	12,600
Ryan Moore	68	71	77	71	287	12,474
Daniel Chopra	73	67	74	74	288	12,285
Mike Weir	70	71	70	77	288	12,285
Jason Gore	69	70	75	75	289	12,096

WGC - Accenture Match Play Championship

Ritz-Carlton Golf Club, Dove Mountain, Marana, Arizona   February 25-March 1
Par 36-36–72; 7,466 yards   purse, $8,500,000

FIRST ROUND

Tiger Woods defeated Brendan Jones, 3 and 2.
Tim Clark defeated Retief Goosen, 3 and 2.
Rory McIlroy defeated Louis Oosthuizen, 2 and 1.
Hunter Mahan defeated Mike Weir, 1 up.
Geoff Ogilvy defeated Kevin Sutherland, 19 holes.
Shingo Katayama defeated Trevor Immelman, 3 and 2.
Camilo Villegas defeated Rod Pampling, 7 and 6.
Miguel Angel Jimenez defeated Rory Sabbatini, 2 and 1.
Vijay Singh defeated Soren Kjeldsen, 2 and 1.
Luke Donald defeated Ben Curtis, 19 holes.
Ernie Els defeated Soren Hansen, 4 and 2.
Steve Stricker defeated Dustin Johnson, 2 and 1.
Phil Mickelson defeated Angel Cabrera, 19 holes.
Zach Johnson defeated Graeme McDowell, 3 and 1.
Lee Westwood defeated Prayad Marksaeng, 2 and 1.
Stewart Cink defeated Richard Sterne, 19 holes.
Charl Schwartzel defeated Sergio Garcia, 1 up.
Ian Poulter defeated Jeev Milkha Singh, 4 and 3.
Boo Weekley defeated Justin Rose, 1 up.
Sean O'Hair defeated Adam Scott, 1 up.
Peter Hanson defeated Robert Karlsson, 3 and 2.
Stephen Ames defeated Alvaro Quiros, 1 up.
Matthew Goggin defeated Kenny Perry, 2 and 1.
Paul Casey defeated Aaron Baddeley, 1 up.
Pat Perez defeated Padraig Harrington, 1 up.
Ross Fisher defeated Robert Allenby, 1 up.
Jim Furyk defeated Anders Hansen, 2 and 1.
Martin Kaymer defeated Stuart Appleby, 1 up.
Davis Love defeated Henrik Stenson, 21 holes.
Justin Leonard defeated Andres Romero, 2 and 1.
Anthony Kim defeated Lin Wen-tang, 7 and 5.
Oliver Wilson defeated K.J. Choi, 3 and 1.

(Each losing player received $45,000.)

SECOND ROUND

Mickelson defeated Johnson, 1 up.
Cink defeated Westwood, 23 holes.
Leonard defeated Love, 1 up.
Wilson defeated Kim, 2 and 1.
Ogilvy defeated Katayama, 19 holes.
Villegas defeated Jimenez, 5 and 4.
Hanson defeated Ames, 2 and 1.
Casey defeated Goggin, 6 and 4.

Donald defeated Singh, 19 holes.
Els defeated Stricker, 3 and 2.
Fisher defeated Perez, 6 and 5.
Furyk defeated Kaymer, 4 and 2.
Clark defeated Woods, 4 and 2.
McIlroy defeated Mahan, 1 up.
Poulter defeated Schwartzel, 1 up.
O'Hair defeated Weekley, 2 and 1.

(Each losing player received $95,000.)

THIRD ROUND

McIlroy defeated Clark, 4 and 3.
Ogilvy defeated Villegas, 2 and 1.
Els defeated Donald, who conceded due to injury.
Cink defeated Mickelson, 1 up.
O'Hair defeated Poulter, 2 and 1.
Casey defeated Hanson, 4 and 2.
Fisher defeated Furyk, 4 and 3.
Leonard defeated Wilson, 19 holes.

(Each losing player received $140,000.)

QUARTER-FINALS

Ogilvy defeated McIlroy, 2 and 1.
Cink defeated Els, 2 and 1.
Casey defeated O'Hair, 4 and 3.
Fisher defeated Leonard, 2 and 1.

(Each losing player received $270,000.)

SEMI-FINALS

Ogilvy defeated Cink, 4 and 2.
Casey defeated Fisher, 2 and 1.

PLAYOFF FOR THIRD-FOURTH PLACE

Cink defeated Fisher, 1 up.

(Cink earned $600,000; Fisher earned $500,000.)

FINAL

Ogilvy defeated Casey, 4 and 3.

(Ogilvy earned $1,400,000; Casey earned $850,000.)

Mayakoba Golf Classic

El Camaleon, Riviera Maya, Mexico
Par 35-35–70; 6,923 yards

February 26-March 1
purse, $3,600,000

	SCORES				TOTAL	MONEY
Mark Wilson	66	64	69	68	267	$648,000
J.J. Henry	66	66	69	68	269	388,800
Heath Slocum	68	69	66	67	270	208,800
Kevin Streelman	67	71	68	64	270	208,800
Kevin Na	68	62	72	70	272	144,000
Rich Beem	70	66	72	65	273	105,171.43

	SCORES				TOTAL	MONEY
Jerry Kelly	70	69	66	68	273	105,171.43
Jarrod Lyle	65	71	66	71	273	105,171.43
James Nitties	69	66	69	69	273	105,171.43
Aron Price	69	70	68	66	273	105,171.43
David Toms	70	67	70	66	273	105,171.43
Briny Baird	67	66	67	73	273	105,171.42
Jose Manuel Lara	70	66	69	69	274	72,000
Ted Purdy	69	70	68	67	274	72,000
Cameron Beckman	66	69	68	72	275	57,600
Glen Day	72	70	64	69	275	57,600
Brendon de Jonge	69	70	69	67	275	57,600
Corey Pavin	67	68	69	71	275	57,600
Scott Verplank	67	71	65	72	275	57,600
Harrison Frazar	70	70	67	70	277	36,315
Brian Gay	68	70	71	68	277	36,315
Steve Marino	70	68	69	70	277	36,315
Nick O'Hern	72	70	68	67	277	36,315
Greg Owen	67	71	65	74	277	36,315
Scott Piercy	66	69	69	73	277	36,315
Kevin Stadler	70	72	66	69	277	36,315
Y.E. Yang	69	70	69	69	277	36,315
Notah Begay	68	70	71	69	278	21,960
Jason Day	68	71	72	67	278	21,960
Jason Dufner	68	69	70	71	278	21,960
Joe Durant	72	67	70	69	278	21,960
Dudley Hart	67	71	72	68	278	21,960
Shigeki Maruyama	67	72	66	73	278	21,960
John Merrick	68	68	70	72	278	21,960
Chris Riley	65	68	69	76	278	21,960
Bo Van Pelt	63	69	67	79	278	21,960
Gary Woodland	69	72	63	74	278	21,960
Bill Haas	73	65	74	67	279	14,400
Charles Howell	68	72	69	70	279	14,400
Kent Jones	70	72	66	71	279	14,400
Jose de Jesus Rodriguez	70	69	70	70	279	14,400
Scott Sterling	67	71	68	73	279	14,400
Vaughn Taylor	69	69	72	69	279	14,400
Tim Wilkinson	70	67	69	73	279	14,400
Dean Wilson	68	71	67	73	279	14,400
Peter Lonard	69	69	73	69	280	10,488
Patrick Sheehan	69	69	72	70	280	10,488
Jay Williamson	69	70	71	70	280	10,488
Mark Brooks	68	74	67	72	281	8,658
Chad Campbell	71	66	69	75	281	8,658
Brian Davis	70	70	70	71	281	8,658
Gonzalo Fernandez	73	66	74	68	281	8,658
John Huston	67	70	70	74	281	8,658
Tom Lehman	70	68	70	73	281	8,658
Chez Reavie	70	70	69	72	281	8,658
Tag Ridings	72	69	71	69	281	8,658
Billy Andrade	69	71	69	73	282	8,064
Jesper Parnevik	73	69	71	69	282	8,064
Brett Quigley	70	72	73	67	282	8,064
Colt Knost	75	66	72	70	283	7,884
Chris Stroud	68	71	71	73	283	7,884
Ricky Barnes	70	72	71	71	284	7,704
Greg Chalmers	67	70	78	69	284	7,704
Omar Uresti	76	66	72	70	284	7,704
Chris DiMarco	69	70	74	72	285	7,344
J.P. Hayes	66	75	73	71	285	7,344
John Rollins	72	70	71	72	285	7,344
Esteban Toledo	72	67	72	74	285	7,344
Peter Tomasulo	69	72	69	75	285	7,344

	SCORES				TOTAL	MONEY
James Vargas	72	70	69	74	285	7,344
Aaron Watkins	69	71	72	73	285	7,344
Bryce Molder	72	69	73	72	286	7,020
Dicky Pride	72	68	68	78	286	7,020
Michael Letzig	69	70	74	74	287	6,912
David Mathis	70	71	76	71	288	6,840
Olin Browne	69	72	74	75	290	6,732
Casey Wittenberg	69	72	75	74	290	6,732
Nathan Green	72	68	79	77	296	6,624

Honda Classic

PGA National, Champion Course, Palm Beach Gardens, Florida
Par 35-35–70; 7,158 yards

March 5-8
purse, $5,600,000

	SCORES				TOTAL	MONEY
Y.E. Yang	68	65	70	68	271	$1,008,000
John Rollins	69	68	68	67	272	604,800
Ben Crane	70	65	71	68	274	380,800
Jeff Klauk	69	68	67	71	275	268,800
Robert Allenby	66	68	72	70	276	196,700
Fredrik Jacobson	72	67	67	70	276	196,700
Will MacKenzie	67	67	72	70	276	196,700
Scott Piercy	72	66	73	65	276	196,700
Jason Dufner	72	66	68	71	277	145,600
Jeff Overton	67	67	70	73	277	145,600
D.A. Points	69	69	74	65	277	145,600
Charlie Wi	67	73	65	72	277	145,600
Greg Owen	72	69	71	66	278	90,222.23
Scott Verplank	73	70	69	66	278	90,222.23
Alex Cejka	71	66	70	71	278	90,222.22
Harrison Frazar	72	65	71	70	278	90,222.22
Sergio Garcia	67	72	71	68	278	90,222.22
Davis Love	73	69	69	67	278	90,222.22
Rory McIlroy	70	68	71	69	278	90,222.22
Brett Quigley	71	67	67	73	278	90,222.22
Kevin Streelman	70	68	70	70	278	90,222.22
Mark Calcavecchia	74	67	65	73	279	53,760
Greg Chalmers	73	64	71	71	279	53,760
Ernie Els	73	70	70	66	279	53,760
Brandt Jobe	70	70	70	69	279	53,760
James Nitties	70	67	70	72	279	53,760
Michael Allen	69	71	69	71	280	39,760
Spencer Levin	72	68	70	70	280	39,760
David Mathis	68	68	73	71	280	39,760
John Merrick	69	69	70	72	280	39,760
John Senden	69	73	71	67	280	39,760
Brad Adamonis	70	73	70	68	281	30,320
Angel Cabrera	67	75	71	68	281	30,320
Tim Herron	72	69	74	66	281	30,320
Steve Marino	69	70	71	71	281	30,320
George McNeill	71	72	70	68	281	30,320
Brendon Todd	74	69	66	72	281	30,320
Casey Wittenberg	71	72	67	71	281	30,320
Briny Baird	72	69	71	70	282	22,960
Lucas Glover	71	70	72	69	282	22,960
Todd Hamilton	72	70	71	69	282	22,960
Kent Jones	68	71	70	73	282	22,960
Matt Kuchar	71	70	68	73	282	22,960
Woody Austin	70	73	67	73	283	16,184

	SCORES				TOTAL	MONEY
Darren Clarke	70	71	68	74	283	16,184
Erik Compton	69	69	73	72	283	16,184
Brendon de Jonge	72	70	72	69	283	16,184
Chris DiMarco	72	70	73	68	283	16,184
Jeff Maggert	70	70	69	74	283	16,184
Scott McCarron	72	71	70	70	283	16,184
Nick O'Hern	73	69	69	72	283	16,184
Tadd Fujikawa	71	71	73	69	284	12,805.34
Shaun Micheel	70	71	73	70	284	12,805.34
Chris Riley	68	75	73	68	284	12,805.34
Stewart Cink	67	71	72	74	284	12,805.33
Robert Garrigus	72	70	68	74	284	12,805.33
Brian Gay	72	69	72	71	284	12,805.33
Justin Leonard	70	73	70	71	284	12,805.33
John Mallinger	69	74	69	72	284	12,805.33
Ryan Palmer	73	66	74	71	284	12,805.33
Leif Olson	73	70	69	73	285	12,152
Nicholas Thompson	69	71	74	71	285	12,152
David Berganio, Jr.	71	69	70	76	286	11,984
Miguel Angel Jimenez	70	73	70	74	287	11,648
Michael Letzig	70	71	75	71	287	11,648
Chris Stroud	69	72	69	77	287	11,648
Johnson Wagner	71	71	74	71	287	11,648
Tim Wilkinson	71	71	73	72	287	11,648
Boo Weekley	72	71	72	73	288	11,312
Marc Leishman	73	70	71	75	289	11,200
Bart Bryant	70	73	73	75	291	11,032
Carl Pettersson	72	69	73	77	291	11,032
Brian Bateman	69	73	75		217	10,640
Derek Fathauer	73	69	75		217	10,640
Nathan Green	69	71	77		217	10,640
Rocco Mediate	73	67	77		217	10,640
Gary Woodland	72	70	75		217	10,640
Steve Lowery	72	71	75		218	10,304
J.J. Henry	71	70	78		219	10,192

WGC - CA Championship

Doral Golf Resort & Spa, Blue Course, Miami, Florida   March 12-15
Par 36-36–72; 7,266 yards   purse, $8,500,000

	SCORES				TOTAL	MONEY
Phil Mickelson	65	66	69	69	269	$1,400,000
Nick Watney	66	67	67	70	270	820,000
Jim Furyk	68	68	69	67	272	470,000
Jeev Milkha Singh	65	71	68	70	274	360,000
Camilo Villegas	67	68	69	71	275	275,000
Oliver Wilson	67	70	72	66	275	275,000
Thomas Aiken	74	66	71	65	276	192,500
Soren Kjeldsen	70	66	69	71	276	192,500
Justin Leonard	69	69	68	71	277	142,500
Rod Pampling	66	69	71	71	277	142,500
Kenny Perry	70	64	71	72	277	142,500
Tiger Woods	71	70	68	68	277	142,500
Soren Hansen	74	69	64	71	278	97,142.86
Prayad Marksaeng	65	70	72	71	278	97,142.86
Sean O'Hair	67	70	74	67	278	97,142.86
Ian Poulter	69	67	73	69	278	97,142.86
Steve Stricker	69	70	70	69	278	97,142.86
Charley Hoffman	68	70	67	73	278	97,142.85

	SCORES				TOTAL	MONEY
Alvaro Quiros	72	64	69	73	278	97,142.85
Luke Donald	69	70	68	72	279	80,142.86
Ernie Els	70	71	68	70	279	80,142.86
Padraig Harrington	66	71	71	71	279	80,142.86
Louis Oosthuizen	67	69	73	70	279	80,142.86
Justin Rose	73	70	68	68	279	80,142.86
James Kingston	66	74	67	72	279	80,142.85
Rory McIlroy	68	66	72	73	279	80,142.85
Tim Clark	71	71	69	69	280	74,000
Robert Allenby	69	71	72	69	281	72,000
Ben Curtis	71	69	71	70	281	72,000
Davis Love	70	71	70	70	281	72,000
Briny Baird	70	68	71	73	282	68,500
Paul Casey	71	66	72	73	282	68,500
Sergio Garcia	72	72	68	70	282	68,500
Robert Karlsson	71	70	72	69	282	68,500
Dustin Johnson	70	66	71	76	283	64,000
Martin Kaymer	73	68	70	72	283	64,000
Pat Perez	70	68	72	73	283	64,000
Carl Pettersson	74	69	69	71	283	64,000
Mike Weir	71	69	70	73	283	64,000
Stephen Ames	72	70	71	71	284	58,500
Ken Duke	71	75	67	71	284	58,500
Richard Finch	72	72	69	71	284	58,500
Peter Hanson	70	74	72	68	284	58,500
Ryuji Imada	70	71	69	74	284	58,500
Geoff Ogilvy	73	69	70	72	284	58,500
Mark Brown	73	71	68	73	285	52,000
Darren Clarke	74	71	71	69	285	52,000
Ross Fisher	71	69	72	73	285	52,000
Shingo Katayama	70	70	72	73	285	52,000
Garth Mulroy	70	70	72	73	285	52,000
Andres Romero	67	71	77	70	285	52,000
D.J. Trahan	77	71	66	71	285	52,000
Chad Campbell	72	70	70	74	286	46,000
Zach Johnson	70	72	72	72	286	46,000
Hunter Mahan	71	74	68	73	286	46,000
Rory Sabbatini	69	74	74	69	286	46,000
Vijay Singh	69	72	71	74	286	46,000
Anthony Kim	71	69	72	75	287	43,000
K.J. Choi	73	73	72	70	288	41,500
Stewart Cink	73	73	69	73	288	41,500
Stuart Appleby	71	71	69	78	289	39,550
Dudley Hart	71	75	73	70	289	39,550
Kevin Sutherland	74	76	68	71	289	39,550
Boo Weekley	69	75	75	70	289	39,550
Lee Westwood	71	71	78	69	289	39,550
Retief Goosen	65	76	73	76	290	38,125
Lin Wen-tang	75	70	70	75	290	38,125
Graeme McDowell	73	74	70	73	290	38,125
Adam Scott	71	76	72	71	290	38,125
Trevor Immelman	74	76	72	69	291	37,375
John Rollins	76	71	71	73	291	37,375
Bubba Watson	72	71	74	75	292	37,000
Richard Sterne	70	76	72	75	293	36,750
Y.E. Yang	73	70	73	78	294	36,500
Miguel Angel Jimenez	69	72	76	78	295	36,250
Azuma Yano	77	71	76	73	297	36,000
Billy Mayfair	75	72	75	76	298	35,625
Henrik Stenson	69	73	73	83	298	35,625
Pablo Larrazabal	76	71	75	77	299	35,250
Aaron Baddeley	75				DQ	

Puerto Rico Open

Trump International Golf Club, Rio Grande, Puerto Rico
Par 36-36–72; 7,569 yards

March 12-15
purse, $3,500,000

	SCORES				TOTAL	MONEY
Michael Bradley	67	69	68	70	274	$630,000
Jason Day	66	68	70	71	275	308,000
Brett Quigley	68	71	69	67	275	308,000
Bart Bryant	67	68	73	68	276	154,000
Greg Chalmers	68	70	70	68	276	154,000
J.P. Hayes	71	68	71	68	278	121,625
John Merrick	70	72	70	66	278	121,625
Jeff Overton	69	72	70	68	279	108,500
Joe Durant	71	72	67	70	280	91,000
Kent Jones	69	69	70	72	280	91,000
Jerry Kelly	70	68	73	69	280	91,000
D.A. Points	70	68	72	70	280	91,000
Jonathan Byrd	68	72	73	68	281	58,187.50
Alex Cejka	68	69	74	70	281	58,187.50
Lee Janzen	69	70	73	69	281	58,187.50
Derek Lamely	66	71	77	67	281	58,187.50
Bryce Molder	67	69	72	73	281	58,187.50
Patrick Sheehan	71	70	71	69	281	58,187.50
Chris Smith	71	71	68	71	281	58,187.50
Jay Williamson	71	70	67	73	281	58,187.50
Ronnie Black	69	68	74	71	282	31,150
Robert Damron	70	71	74	67	282	31,150
Jay Delsing	70	72	71	69	282	31,150
Tommy Gainey	72	70	72	68	282	31,150
Charles Howell	69	69	77	67	282	31,150
Greg Kraft	71	71	70	70	282	31,150
Paul Stankowski	69	72	70	71	282	31,150
Scott Sterling	69	69	74	70	282	31,150
Omar Uresti	71	67	70	74	282	31,150
Matt Weibring	70	70	74	68	282	31,150
Tadd Fujikawa	70	68	75	70	283	19,850
Cliff Kresge	67	69	72	75	283	19,850
Troy Matteson	68	69	75	71	283	19,850
Shaun Micheel	71	71	71	70	283	19,850
Greg Owen	71	67	77	68	283	19,850
Corey Pavin	69	69	73	72	283	19,850
Aron Price	70	71	68	74	283	19,850
Rich Beem	70	73	72	69	284	14,700
Carlos Franco	76	67	70	71	284	14,700
Robert Garrigus	70	68	74	72	284	14,700
Ted Purdy	71	69	73	71	284	14,700
Alan Wagner	73	69	72	70	284	14,700
Charles Warren	70	73	71	70	284	14,700
Eric Axley	72	70	72	71	285	9,363.85
Jason Gore	74	69	71	71	285	9,363.85
Matt Jones	70	64	79	72	285	9,363.85
John Mallinger	69	70	74	72	285	9,363.85
Ryan Moore	72	71	72	70	285	9,363.85
Tom Scherrer	71	70	71	73	285	9,363.85
Brandt Snedeker	69	74	72	70	285	9,363.85
Kevin Stadler	67	75	72	71	285	9,363.85
Felipe Aguilar	71	71	69	74	285	9,363.84
Michael Allen	69	74	69	73	285	9,363.84
David Berganio, Jr.	71	71	70	73	285	9,363.84
Estanislao Goya	69	67	74	75	285	9,363.84
Manuel Villegas	72	71	69	73	285	9,363.84
Kris Blanks	72	70	69	75	286	7,700

	SCORES				TOTAL	MONEY
Mark Brooks	70	71	74	71	286	7,700
Glen Day	72	67	76	71	286	7,700
John Huston	71	70	73	72	286	7,700
Colt Knost	71	67	73	75	286	7,700
Neal Lancaster	70	73	72	71	286	7,700
Andy Matthews	73	68	72	73	286	7,700
Rick Price	69	72	76	70	287	7,385
Casey Wittenberg	69	72	77	69	287	7,385
Tyler Aldridge	69	73	73	73	288	7,210
Ricky Barnes	69	71	76	72	288	7,210
Guy Boros	74	68	72	74	288	7,210
Notah Begay	70	72	75	72	289	6,930
Derek Fathauer	74	69	74	72	289	6,930
Robin Freeman	71	72	72	74	289	6,930
Jarrod Lyle	71	70	72	76	289	6,930
Bo Van Pelt	74	67	75	73	289	6,930
Scott Gutschewski	72	69	74	75	290	6,685
Rocco Mediate	68	70	75	77	290	6,685
Matthew Borchert	71	70	78	73	292	6,545
Jimmy Walker	72	71	75	74	292	6,545

Transitions Championship

Innisbrook Resort & Golf Club, Copperhead Course,
Tampa Bay, Florida
Par 36-35–71; 7,340 yards

March 19-22
purse, $5,400,000

	SCORES				TOTAL	MONEY
Retief Goosen	69	68	69	70	276	$972,000
Charles Howell	71	66	71	69	277	475,200
Brett Quigley	73	68	68	68	277	475,200
Mathew Goggin	67	74	70	67	278	223,200
Steve Stricker	69	67	73	69	278	223,200
Charlie Wi	68	73	68	69	278	223,200
Steve Flesch	71	67	72	69	279	180,900
Stuart Appleby	70	67	71	72	280	151,200
Tom Lehman	68	69	68	75	280	151,200
Kevin Na	70	72	71	67	280	151,200
Bo Van Pelt	71	72	71	66	280	151,200
Rich Beem	71	67	71	72	281	105,840
Jonathan Byrd	67	70	71	73	281	105,840
Matt Kuchar	72	68	69	72	281	105,840
Nick Watney	69	67	74	71	281	105,840
Mark Wilson	68	71	74	68	281	105,840
Jason Dufner	71	71	70	70	282	83,700
Kenny Perry	67	74	71	70	282	83,700
Stephen Ames	66	74	72	71	283	58,725
Briny Baird	70	71	71	71	283	58,725
Charley Hoffman	74	68	69	72	283	58,725
Trevor Immelman	68	70	70	75	283	58,725
Troy Matteson	69	68	72	74	283	58,725
Ryan Moore	70	72	71	70	283	58,725
Jeff Overton	69	70	73	71	283	58,725
Kevin Sutherland	69	71	75	68	283	58,725
Bill Lunde	70	71	73	70	284	37,530
John Mallinger	69	73	71	71	284	37,530
Rocco Mediate	72	71	74	67	284	37,530
D.A. Points	73	69	70	72	284	37,530
Aron Price	74	69	72	69	284	37,530
Kirk Triplett	73	70	72	69	284	37,530

	SCORES				TOTAL	MONEY
Woody Austin	69	73	69	74	285	29,160
Richard S. Johnson	69	72	72	72	285	29,160
Jeff Klauk	71	70	71	73	285	29,160
Heath Slocum	71	69	70	75	285	29,160
David Toms	68	73	68	76	285	29,160
Ken Duke	71	70	74	71	286	23,760
Billy Mayfair	72	70	73	71	286	23,760
Nick O'Hern	69	73	71	73	286	23,760
D.J. Trahan	68	72	72	74	286	23,760
Joe Durant	73	67	69	78	287	19,440
Steve Lowery	70	70	73	74	287	19,440
Joe Ogilvie	71	66	73	77	287	19,440
Tom Pernice, Jr.	70	72	71	74	287	19,440
Brendon de Jonge	68	75	72	73	288	14,688
Brian Gay	71	69	78	70	288	14,688
J.J. Henry	69	68	76	75	288	14,688
Ryuji Imada	72	71	73	72	288	14,688
Michael Letzig	69	73	74	72	288	14,688
David Mathis	71	72	71	74	288	14,688
Cameron Beckman	69	72	74	74	289	12,466.29
Matt Bettencourt	70	73	72	74	289	12,466.29
Spencer Levin	70	73	77	69	289	12,466.29
Alvaro Quiros	70	72	75	72	289	12,466.29
Jim Furyk	65	78	72	74	289	12,466.28
John Huston	70	73	69	77	289	12,466.28
Boo Weekley	71	72	70	76	289	12,466.28
Eric Axley	71	71	72	76	290	11,826
Chris Couch	70	73	72	75	290	11,826
Steve Elkington	69	74	72	75	290	11,826
Tim Herron	70	70	72	78	290	11,826
Tommy Armour	73	69	76	73	291	11,340
Ben Crane	68	74	73	76	291	11,340
Jonathan Kaye	73	68	72	78	291	11,340
Scott McCarron	69	69	77	76	291	11,340
Rory Sabbatini	71	72	76	72	291	11,340
Brad Adamonis	71	71	77	73	292	10,908
Jason Bohn	74	68	76	74	292	10,908
Bart Bryant	72	70	74	76	292	10,908
Ryo Ishikawa	69	73	75	76	293	10,692
Will MacKenzie	70	71	75	78	294	10,584
Nathan Green	68	74	83	79	304	10,476

Arnold Palmer Invitational

Bay Hill Club & Lodge, Orlando, Florida
Par 35-35–70; 7,157 yards

March 26-29
purse, $6,000,000

	SCORES				TOTAL	MONEY
Tiger Woods	68	69	71	67	275	$1,080,000
Sean O'Hair	67	65	71	73	276	648,000
Zach Johnson	72	69	68	69	278	408,000
Pat Perez	70	70	70	69	279	236,250
John Senden	70	69	73	67	279	236,250
Scott Verplank	70	69	71	69	279	236,250
Nick Watney	67	71	73	68	279	236,250
Daniel Chopra	68	71	72	69	280	174,000
Jason Gore	65	70	74	71	280	174,000
Kenny Perry	70	71	72	67	280	174,000
Robert Allenby	71	65	74	71	281	123,000
Ben Crane	70	69	75	67	281	123,000

	SCORES				TOTAL	MONEY
Lucas Glover	71	71	69	70	281	123,000
Padraig Harrington	70	68	73	70	281	123,000
Kevin Na	69	70	76	66	281	123,000
Webb Simpson	70	71	70	70	281	123,000
Bob Estes	74	67	71	70	282	84,000
Ryuji Imada	70	66	73	73	282	84,000
Lee Janzen	67	71	73	71	282	84,000
Brandt Snedeker	73	70	67	72	282	84,000
Vaughn Taylor	70	68	74	70	282	84,000
Chad Campbell	68	74	69	72	283	57,600
Charles Howell	71	68	74	70	283	57,600
Hunter Mahan	67	71	74	71	283	57,600
George McNeill	70	72	72	69	283	57,600
James Nitties	70	71	74	68	283	57,600
Corey Pavin	72	70	70	72	284	44,400
Jeev Milkha Singh	71	68	74	71	284	44,400
Mark Wilson	67	71	74	72	284	44,400
Stewart Cink	70	71	72	72	285	36,450
Mathew Goggin	70	72	71	72	285	36,450
Tim Herron	66	72	74	73	285	36,450
Cliff Kresge	74	68	71	72	285	36,450
Justin Rose	75	67	73	70	285	36,450
Johnson Wagner	69	75	72	69	285	36,450
Retief Goosen	74	71	72	69	286	28,875
Paul Goydos	74	70	74	68	286	28,875
Steve Lowery	69	71	77	69	286	28,875
Steve Marino	73	68	75	70	286	28,875
Brian Gay	68	74	72	73	287	21,600
J.J. Henry	68	71	79	69	287	21,600
J.B. Holmes	73	69	72	73	287	21,600
Trevor Immelman	71	73	71	72	287	21,600
Tom Lehman	72	73	72	70	287	21,600
Graeme McDowell	71	69	73	74	287	21,600
Heath Slocum	69	75	72	71	287	21,600
Mike Weir	71	72	72	72	287	21,600
Chris DiMarco	73	70	71	74	288	15,480
Rocco Mediate	68	76	70	74	288	15,480
Jeff Overton	66	73	75	74	288	15,480
David Toms	71	73	71	73	288	15,480
Stuart Appleby	67	72	80	70	289	13,851.43
Tommy Armour	70	74	76	69	289	13,851.43
Brad Faxon	70	72	75	72	289	13,851.43
Jerry Kelly	69	73	76	71	289	13,851.43
D.A. Points	73	70	73	73	289	13,851.43
Marc Turnesa	72	73	74	70	289	13,851.43
Peter Lonard	72	72	77	68	289	13,851.42
Bill Haas	70	75	76	69	290	13,080
Todd Hamilton	72	68	75	75	290	13,080
Jeff Klauk	74	70	76	70	290	13,080
Bill Lunde	72	73	72	73	290	13,080
Vijay Singh	74	70	77	69	290	13,080
Louis Oosthuizen	72	71	76	73	292	12,660
Boo Weekley	72	70	73	77	292	12,660
Aaron Baddeley	75	68	76	74	293	12,300
Richard S. Johnson	70	74	76	73	293	12,300
Skip Kendall	68	73	75	77	293	12,300
Kevin Streelman	71	72	76	74	293	12,300
Brian Davis	71	73	76	75	295	11,940
Oliver Wilson	72	70	78	75	295	11,940
Woody Austin	72	72	76	76	296	11,760
Bart Bryant	71	74	75	79	299	11,640

Shell Houston Open

Redstone Golf Club, Tournament Course, Humble, Texas   April 2-5
Par 36-36–72; 7,457 yards   purse, $5,700,000

		SCORES			TOTAL	MONEY
Paul Casey	66	70	69	72	277	$1,026,000
J.B. Holmes	71	69	68	69	277	615,600
(Casey defeated Holmes on first playoff hole.)						
Fred Couples	68	69	68	74	279	296,400
Nick O'Hern	72	71	66	70	279	296,400
Henrik Stenson	70	67	72	70	279	296,400
Tommy Armour	66	70	72	72	280	178,410
Jason Bohn	69	71	66	74	280	178,410
Hunter Mahan	71	69	72	68	280	178,410
John Mallinger	75	65	70	70	280	178,410
Geoff Ogilvy	67	69	69	75	280	178,410
Ryan Moore	70	68	67	76	281	131,100
Nicholas Thompson	65	75	71	70	281	131,100
Lee Westwood	69	70	68	74	281	131,100
Jonathan Byrd	67	70	70	75	282	96,900
Brian Davis	71	69	68	74	282	96,900
Ernie Els	75	66	71	70	282	96,900
Robert Karlsson	70	71	66	75	282	96,900
D.A. Points	66	72	72	72	282	96,900
Kevin Na	73	68	70	72	283	64,328.58
Justin Leonard	68	70	69	76	283	64,328.57
Steve Marino	69	73	71	70	283	64,328.57
Rory McIlroy	67	73	74	69	283	64,328.57
Ryan Palmer	70	72	72	69	283	64,328.57
Kevin Sutherland	69	71	68	75	283	64,328.57
Bo Van Pelt	70	67	68	78	283	64,328.57
Brian Gay	69	73	68	74	284	42,180
Padraig Harrington	72	67	68	77	284	42,180
Anthony Kim	72	68	70	74	284	42,180
Shaun Micheel	71	72	68	73	284	42,180
Ted Purdy	71	69	73	71	284	42,180
Stuart Appleby	70	68	71	76	285	29,691.82
Bart Bryant	71	72	69	73	285	29,691.82
Ben Curtis	70	72	71	72	285	29,691.82
Lucas Glover	74	68	66	77	285	29,691.82
Dudley Hart	68	72	73	72	285	29,691.82
Brandt Jobe	73	69	69	74	285	29,691.82
Jarrod Lyle	71	68	71	75	285	29,691.82
John Merrick	71	72	68	74	285	29,691.82
Scott Verplank	68	70	71	76	285	29,691.82
John Senden	65	71	71	78	285	29,691.81
Chris Stroud	68	75	71	71	285	29,691.81
Camilo Villegas	69	72	72	73	286	18,842.58
J.J. Henry	72	71	70	73	286	18,842.57
Martin Kaymer	71	70	70	75	286	18,842.57
Colt Knost	66	70	69	81	286	18,842.57
Marc Leishman	68	73	71	74	286	18,842.57
Michael Letzig	71	71	69	75	286	18,842.57
Scott Piercy	66	71	69	80	286	18,842.57
Chad Campbell	72	71	72	72	287	14,402
John Huston	72	70	70	75	287	14,402
Vaughn Taylor	67	72	71	77	287	14,402
Charley Hoffman	71	72	69	76	288	13,224
Peter Lonard	73	69	68	78	288	13,224
Davis Love	73	69	72	74	288	13,224
John Rollins	68	73	72	75	288	13,224
Justin Rose	68	74	73	73	288	13,224

	SCORES				TOTAL	MONEY
Webb Simpson	71	71	71	75	288	13,224
Briny Baird	65	73	71	80	289	12,483
Daniel Chopra	72	71	66	80	289	12,483
Steve Elkington	71	71	69	78	289	12,483
Paul Goydos	71	71	71	76	289	12,483
Charles Howell	71	68	71	79	289	12,483
Heath Slocum	73	67	73	76	289	12,483
Alex Cejka	73	69	73	75	290	11,799
Brendon de Jonge	73	69	71	77	290	11,799
Robert Garrigus	71	68	73	78	290	11,799
Scott McCarron	68	73	72	77	290	11,799
Tom Pernice, Jr.	70	72	71	77	290	11,799
Brendon Todd	71	71	69	79	290	11,799
Billy Mayfair	70	72	74	75	291	11,229
James Nitties	66	72	75	78	291	11,229
Greg Norman	71	69	70	81	291	11,229
Tim Wilkinson	68	75	75	73	291	11,229
Bob Estes	70	73	74	75	292	10,887
Kirk Triplett	72	69	74	77	292	10,887
David Berganio, Jr.	68	73	72	81	294	10,716
Jason Dufner	68	73	75	79	295	10,545
Sergio Garcia	69	71	74	81	295	10,545

Masters Tournament

Augusta National Golf Club, Augusta, Georgia — April 9-12
Par 36-36–72; 7,435 yards — purse, $7,000,000

	SCORES				TOTAL	MONEY
Angel Cabrera	68	68	69	71	276	$1,350,000
Chad Campbell	65	70	72	69	276	660,000
Kenny Perry	68	67	70	71	276	660,000
(Cabrera defeated Campbell on first and Perry on second playoff hole.)						
Shingo Katayama	67	73	70	68	278	360,000
Phil Mickelson	73	68	71	67	279	300,000
Steve Flesch	71	74	68	67	280	242,813
John Merrick	68	74	72	66	280	242,813
Steve Stricker	72	69	68	71	280	242,813
Tiger Woods	70	72	70	68	280	242,813
Jim Furyk	66	74	68	73	281	187,500
Hunter Mahan	66	75	71	69	281	187,500
Sean O'Hair	68	76	68	69	281	187,500
Tim Clark	68	71	72	71	282	150,000
Camilo Villegas	73	69	71	69	282	150,000
Todd Hamilton	68	70	72	73	283	131,250
Geoff Ogilvy	71	70	73	69	283	131,250
Aaron Baddeley	68	74	73	69	284	116,250
Graeme McDowell	69	73	73	69	284	116,250
Nick Watney	70	71	71	73	285	105,000
Stephen Ames	73	68	71	74	286	71,400
Paul Casey	72	72	73	69	286	71,400
Ryuji Imada	73	72	72	69	286	71,400
Trevor Immelman	71	74	72	69	286	71,400
Anthony Kim	75	65	72	74	286	71,400
Sandy Lyle	72	70	73	71	286	71,400
Rory McIlroy	72	73	71	70	286	71,400
Ian Poulter	71	73	68	74	286	71,400
Justin Rose	74	70	71	71	286	71,400
Rory Sabbatini	73	67	70	76	286	71,400
Stuart Appleby	72	73	71	71	287	46,575

	SCORES				TOTAL	MONEY
Ross Fisher	69	76	73	69	287	46,575
Dustin Johnson	72	70	72	73	287	46,575
Larry Mize	67	76	72	72	287	46,575
Vijay Singh	71	70	72	74	287	46,575
Ben Curtis	73	71	74	70	288	38,625
Ken Duke	71	72	73	72	288	38,625
Padraig Harrington	69	73	73	73	288	38,625
Robert Allenby	73	72	72	72	289	33,000
Luke Donald	73	71	72	73	289	33,000
Sergio Garcia	73	67	75	74	289	33,000
Henrik Stenson	71	70	75	73	289	33,000
Bubba Watson	72	72	73	73	290	29,250
Lee Westwood	70	72	70	79	291	27,750
Dudley Hart	72	72	73	76	293	25,500
D.J. Trahan	72	73	72	76	293	25,500
Miguel Angel Jimenez	70	73	78	73	294	21,850
Kevin Sutherland	69	76	77	72	294	21,850
Mike Weir	68	75	79	72	294	21,850
Rocco Mediate	73	70	78	77	298	19,200
Andres Romero	69	75	77	77	298	19,200

Out of Final 36 Holes

Fred Couples	73	73	146	Zach Johnson	70	80	150
Ernie Els	75	71	146	Drew Kittleson	78	72	150
Retief Goosen	75	71	146	Bernhard Langer	70	80	150
Jose Maria Olazabal	71	75	146	Louis Oosthuizen	73	77	150
Adam Scott	71	75	146	Brandt Snedeker	76	74	150
Jeev Milkha Singh	71	75	146	Mathew Goggin	74	77	151
Richard Sterne	72	74	146	Lin Wen-tang	77	74	151
Stewart Cink	69	78	147	Mark O'Meara	75	76	151
Robert Karlsson	73	74	147	Chez Reavie	75	76	151
Martin Kaymer	71	76	147	Craig Stadler	77	74	151
Soren Kjeldsen	76	71	147	Billy Mayfair	77	75	152
Greg Norman	70	77	147	Alvaro Quiros	78	75	153
Reinier Saxton	75	72	147	Prayad Marksaeng	70	84	154
Y.E. Yang	73	74	147	Pat Perez	75	79	154
Briny Baird	73	75	148	Carl Pettersson	75	79	154
K.J. Choi	76	72	148	Steve Wilson	79	75	154
Soren Hansen	72	76	148	Michael Campbell	80	75	155
Justin Leonard	75	73	148	Danny Lee	74	81	155
Jack Newman	72	76	148	Fuzzy Zoeller	79	76	155
Oliver Wilson	73	75	148	Ben Crenshaw	73	83	156
Boo Weekley	73	76	149	Tom Watson	74	83	157
Ian Woosnam	74	75	149	Raymond Floyd	79	79	158
Ryo Ishikawa	73	77	150	Gary Player	78	83	161

(Professionals who did not complete 72 holes received $5,000.)

Verizon Heritage

Harbour Town Golf Links, Hilton Head Island, South Carolina
Par 36-35–71; 6,973 yards

April 16-19
purse, $5,700,000

	SCORES				TOTAL	MONEY
Brian Gay	67	66	67	64	264	$1,026,000
Briny Baird	69	72	65	68	274	501,600
Luke Donald	73	70	65	66	274	501,600
Todd Hamilton	68	66	71	70	275	250,800
Lee Janzen	65	70	69	71	275	250,800

	SCORES				TOTAL	MONEY
Jose Maria Olazabal	68	71	70	67	276	198,075
Tim Wilkinson	71	67	65	73	276	198,075
Tim Petrovic	68	70	69	70	277	165,300
Rory Sabbatini	70	68	73	66	277	165,300
Matt Weibring	70	70	69	68	277	165,300
Woody Austin	70	73	66	69	278	136,800
Paul Casey	73	70	69	66	278	136,800
Tommy Armour	70	68	74	67	279	94,762.50
Alex Cejka	64	71	72	72	279	94,762.50
Bob Estes	68	71	69	71	279	94,762.50
Spencer Levin	72	72	66	69	279	94,762.50
Steve Marino	71	73	67	68	279	94,762.50
Bo Van Pelt	73	70	66	70	279	94,762.50
Boo Weekley	69	72	70	68	279	94,762.50
Dean Wilson	69	74	68	68	279	94,762.50
Aaron Baddeley	75	68	67	70	280	59,280
Tom Lehman	70	69	68	73	280	59,280
Davis Love	70	67	69	74	280	59,280
Jeff Maggert	68	75	66	71	280	59,280
Scott Verplank	72	66	73	69	280	59,280
Ben Crane	73	69	71	68	281	43,035
Jason Dufner	70	73	69	69	281	43,035
Ken Duke	69	70	71	71	281	43,035
Lucas Glover	74	68	70	69	281	43,035
Chris Couch	73	69	70	70	282	33,874.29
Mathew Goggin	73	70	72	67	282	33,874.29
Scott Piercy	69	70	75	68	282	33,874.29
Vaughn Taylor	71	72	69	70	282	33,874.29
Trevor Immelman	66	74	71	71	282	33,874.28
Nick O'Hern	72	70	68	72	282	33,874.28
Ted Purdy	67	71	72	72	282	33,874.28
Tim Clark	72	70	69	72	283	22,230
Charles Howell	69	74	70	70	283	22,230
Fredrik Jacobson	76	68	69	70	283	22,230
Zach Johnson	70	71	70	72	283	22,230
Steve Lowery	73	71	68	71	283	22,230
Bill Lunde	73	69	72	69	283	22,230
George McNeill	71	71	71	70	283	22,230
Greg Owen	69	71	74	69	283	22,230
Jeev Milkha Singh	71	69	71	72	283	22,230
Nicholas Thompson	73	71	69	70	283	22,230
Camilo Villegas	70	72	71	70	283	22,230
Jose Coceres	74	67	67	76	284	14,036.25
Joe Durant	73	71	71	69	284	14,036.25
Ernie Els	68	71	73	72	284	14,036.25
Nathan Green	70	71	70	73	284	14,036.25
Greg Kraft	72	72	69	71	284	14,036.25
Matt Kuchar	71	70	73	70	284	14,036.25
Justin Leonard	70	73	67	74	284	14,036.25
Peter Lonard	72	71	68	73	284	14,036.25
Brad Adamonis	74	68	71	72	285	12,939
Mark Wilson	72	69	74	70	285	12,939
Tommy Gainey	71	68	73	74	286	12,597
Stephen Leaney	68	74	72	72	286	12,597
Rory McIlroy	72	71	72	71	286	12,597
Shaun Micheel	72	68	71	75	286	12,597
Stewart Cink	72	70	72	73	287	12,198
Colt Knost	74	68	72	73	287	12,198
Charlie Wi	71	70	70	76	287	12,198
Cliff Kresge	68	75	74	71	288	11,799
Rod Pampling	68	68	74	78	288	11,799
Brett Quigley	72	72	67	77	288	11,799
Heath Slocum	72	68	70	78	288	11,799

	SCORES				TOTAL	MONEY
Jonathan Byrd	70	73	73	73	289	11,400
Brendon de Jonge	72	72	73	72	289	11,400
Chris DiMarco	72	71	74	72	289	11,400
Michael Allen	72	72	70	76	290	11,058
Michael Letzig	73	71	74	72	290	11,058
Aron Price	68	73	73	76	290	11,058
Charley Hoffman	70	69	72	80	291	10,830
Glen Day	71	73	76	72	292	10,716
Will MacKenzie	73	71	76	74	294	10,602
Robert Garrigus	70	74	75	77	296	10,488

Zurich Classic

TPC Louisiana, Avondale, Louisiana
Par 36-36–72; 7,341 yards

April 23-26
purse, $6,300,000

	SCORES				TOTAL	MONEY
Jerry Kelly	68	66	69	71	274	$1,134,000
Charles Howell	68	69	70	68	275	470,400
Rory Sabbatini	70	67	71	67	275	470,400
Charlie Wi	66	70	71	68	275	470,400
Steve Marino	70	68	68	70	276	239,400
David Toms	68	68	72	68	276	239,400
Steve Stricker	68	73	69	67	277	203,175
Aaron Watkins	70	68	69	70	277	203,175
Jason Dufner	68	73	69	68	278	176,400
Roland Thatcher	68	70	70	70	278	176,400
Joe Ogilvie	70	69	69	71	279	151,200
Tim Petrovic	70	69	73	67	279	151,200
Bob Estes	73	69	68	70	280	111,300
Jeff Overton	68	72	68	72	280	111,300
Rod Pampling	68	71	68	73	280	111,300
Ian Poulter	71	66	72	71	280	111,300
John Rollins	69	67	71	73	280	111,300
Boo Weekley	72	68	71	69	280	111,300
Brian Davis	70	70	70	71	281	76,356
Lucas Glover	72	71	66	72	281	76,356
Charley Hoffman	69	66	77	69	281	76,356
Greg Owen	70	68	72	71	281	76,356
Y.E. Yang	69	70	71	71	281	76,356
Greg Chalmers	69	73	67	73	282	48,746.25
K.J. Choi	72	66	71	73	282	48,746.25
Paul Goydos	69	70	73	70	282	48,746.25
Martin Laird	68	70	71	73	282	48,746.25
Troy Matteson	71	64	75	72	282	48,746.25
D.A. Points	69	71	71	71	282	48,746.25
Kevin Stadler	70	67	71	74	282	48,746.25
Nicholas Thompson	70	70	70	72	282	48,746.25
Jason Day	69	71	71	72	283	38,115
Webb Simpson	70	71	70	72	283	38,115
Daniel Chopra	71	72	70	71	284	30,476.25
Chris DiMarco	73	70	70	71	284	30,476.25
John Mallinger	70	73	71	70	284	30,476.25
Scott Piercy	71	69	70	74	284	30,476.25
Aron Price	73	70	71	70	284	30,476.25
John Senden	70	72	70	72	284	30,476.25
Darron Stiles	73	67	69	75	284	30,476.25
Jay Williamson	67	73	77	67	284	30,476.25
Eric Axley	67	71	76	71	285	20,826
David Mathis	72	65	74	74	285	20,826

	SCORES				TOTAL	MONEY
John Merrick	67	69	72	77	285	20,826
Ryan Moore	68	71	75	71	285	20,826
Scott Verplank	70	73	71	71	285	20,826
Jimmy Walker	70	73	69	73	285	20,826
Charles Warren	67	73	71	74	285	20,826
Nathan Green	67	72	71	76	286	16,128
Parker McLachlin	67	69	78	72	286	16,128
Matt Bettencourt	70	70	74	73	287	14,663.25
Harrison Frazar	72	70	72	73	287	14,663.25
Todd Hamilton	73	70	75	69	287	14,663.25
Jeff Klauk	71	72	74	70	287	14,663.25
Michael Letzig	72	71	73	71	287	14,663.25
James Oh	71	72	74	70	287	14,663.25
Scott Sterling	70	73	72	72	287	14,663.25
Kevin Streelman	73	69	75	70	287	14,663.25
Steve Allan	76	67	72	73	288	13,671
Dudley Hart	70	71	77	70	288	13,671
Ryan Palmer	70	73	69	76	288	13,671
Kenny Perry	69	70	71	78	288	13,671
Brett Quigley	72	69	69	78	288	13,671
Chris Riley	73	70	72	73	288	13,671
Woody Austin	71	68	72	78	289	13,167
Jarrod Lyle	69	70	78	72	289	13,167
George McNeill	69	74	69	78	290	12,852
Rick Price	71	71	74	74	290	12,852
Ted Purdy	70	73	76	71	290	12,852
Matt Jones	72	69	73	77	291	12,600
Wil Collins	72	71	78	74	295	12,411
Lee Janzen	70	71	78	76	295	12,411

Quail Hollow Championship

Quail Hollow Club, Charlotte, North Carolina
Par 36-36–72; 7,442 yards

April 30-May 3
purse, $6,500,000

	SCORES				TOTAL	MONEY
Sean O'Hair	69	72	67	69	277	$1,170,000
Lucas Glover	68	71	68	71	278	572,000
Bubba Watson	71	65	72	70	278	572,000
Tiger Woods	65	72	70	72	279	312,000
Jonathan Byrd	72	72	70	66	280	212,875
Jason Dufner	67	71	71	71	280	212,875
Phil Mickelson	67	71	75	67	280	212,875
Tim Petrovic	71	70	71	68	280	212,875
Ian Poulter	71	70	70	69	280	212,875
Ted Purdy	70	69	72	69	280	212,875
Jim Furyk	71	66	73	71	281	129,071.43
Retief Goosen	68	68	72	73	281	129,071.43
Fredrik Jacobson	71	70	70	70	281	129,071.43
Martin Kaymer	71	70	69	71	281	129,071.43
Boo Weekley	71	70	72	68	281	129,071.43
Y.E. Yang	72	71	66	72	281	129,071.43
Zach Johnson	70	67	68	76	281	129,071.42
George McNeill	69	68	70	75	282	87,750
Shaun Micheel	74	69	73	66	282	87,750
David Toms	71	71	67	73	282	87,750
Charles Warren	69	71	71	71	282	87,750
Matt Bettencourt	72	71	71	69	283	58,592.86
Bill Haas	69	71	71	72	283	58,592.86
Hunter Mahan	68	72	75	68	283	58,592.86

	SCORES				TOTAL	MONEY
Rocco Mediate	72	70	72	69	283	58,592.86
Camilo Villegas	71	67	74	71	283	58,592.86
Davis Love	70	69	70	74	283	58,592.85
Nick Watney	71	71	69	72	283	58,592.85
Cameron Beckman	73	71	72	68	284	44,200
Ross Fisher	73	67	69	75	284	44,200
Bo Van Pelt	69	71	71	73	284	44,200
Ben Curtis	74	70	71	70	285	35,966.67
Cliff Kresge	69	72	72	72	285	35,966.67
Geoff Ogilvy	71	73	68	73	285	35,966.67
John Senden	71	72	73	69	285	35,966.67
Jeff Klauk	69	71	70	75	285	35,966.66
Joe Ogilvie	71	72	69	73	285	35,966.66
Michael Allen	70	73	72	71	286	27,300
Brian Davis	72	71	72	71	286	27,300
Ken Duke	70	72	73	71	286	27,300
Danny Lee	71	69	70	76	286	27,300
Steve Marino	67	72	74	73	286	27,300
Tom Pernice, Jr.	72	69	77	68	286	27,300
Brendon de Jonge	72	69	67	79	287	21,450
Mathew Goggin	71	71	74	71	287	21,450
John Huston	73	71	69	74	287	21,450
Robert Allenby	67	74	77	70	288	16,921.67
Anthony Kim	70	69	78	71	288	16,921.67
Will MacKenzie	70	74	71	73	288	16,921.67
Kevin Sutherland	71	72	75	70	288	16,921.67
Martin Laird	74	70	70	74	288	16,921.66
Brendon Todd	70	70	72	76	288	16,921.66
Robert Karlsson	70	69	78	72	289	14,906.67
Jonathan Kaye	70	72	74	73	289	14,906.67
Chris Stroud	73	69	78	69	289	14,906.67
Steve Wheatcroft	70	73	77	69	289	14,906.67
Kent Jones	72	70	71	76	289	14,906.66
Jeff Overton	70	71	73	75	289	14,906.66
Steve Lowery	73	71	73	73	290	14,300
Jeff Maggert	68	70	75	77	290	14,300
Peter Tomasulo	74	69	73	74	290	14,300
Chad Campbell	72	70	73	76	291	13,910
David Mathis	70	73	72	76	291	13,910
John Rollins	70	74	76	71	291	13,910
Trevor Immelman	73	70	76	74	293	13,520
Pat Perez	74	70	76	73	293	13,520
Aron Price	71	73	78	71	293	13,520
Brad Faxon	74	69	80	71	294	13,195
Parker McLachlin	73	71	74	76	294	13,195
Mark Calcavecchia	69	74	74	78	295	12,870
Steve Flesch	69	74	78	74	295	12,870
Bill Lunde	72	72	74	77	295	12,870
Gary Woodland	70	74	76	76	296	12,610
Rich Beem	71	73	76	82	302	12,480

The Players Championship

TPC Sawgrass, Ponte Vedra Beach, Florida
Par 36-36–72; 7,220 yards

May 7-10
purse, $9,500,000

	SCORES				TOTAL	MONEY
Henrik Stenson	68	69	73	66	276	$1,710,000
Ian Poulter	67	68	75	70	280	1,026,000
John Mallinger	66	71	74	70	281	551,000

	SCORES				TOTAL	MONEY
Kevin Na	71	66	74	70	281	551,000
Ben Crane	65	73	72	72	282	346,750
Brian Davis	71	69	71	71	282	346,750
Jim Furyk	68	74	71	69	282	346,750
Tiger Woods	71	69	70	73	283	294,500
Aaron Baddeley	71	71	76	66	284	237,500
Alex Cejka	66	67	72	79	284	237,500
Tim Clark	72	69	74	69	284	237,500
Vijay Singh	71	72	74	67	284	237,500
David Toms	67	70	77	70	284	237,500
Robert Allenby	73	66	75	71	285	147,250
Angel Cabrera	72	65	77	71	285	147,250
Paul Casey	70	69	76	70	285	147,250
Daniel Chopra	75	65	72	73	285	147,250
Jeff Klauk	71	72	71	71	285	147,250
Matt Kuchar	72	72	73	68	285	147,250
Camilo Villegas	67	72	75	71	285	147,250
Mike Weir	72	72	73	68	285	147,250
Tommy Armour	74	70	70	72	286	79,325
Woody Austin	72	72	68	74	286	79,325
Ben Curtis	71	72	69	74	286	79,325
Sergio Garcia	71	73	73	69	286	79,325
Retief Goosen	67	72	71	76	286	79,325
Geoff Ogilvy	70	72	73	71	286	79,325
Kenny Perry	73	71	68	74	286	79,325
Scott Piercy	71	72	74	69	286	79,325
Justin Rose	70	71	72	73	286	79,325
Steve Stricker	71	71	71	73	286	79,325
Jason Dufner	67	70	77	73	287	53,770
Zach Johnson	72	71	70	74	287	53,770
Justin Leonard	70	69	75	73	287	53,770
Billy Mayfair	70	74	69	74	287	53,770
Kevin Sutherland	73	67	72	75	287	53,770
Jonathan Byrd	67	72	71	78	288	39,900
Luke Donald	74	70	71	73	288	39,900
Charley Hoffman	70	69	76	73	288	39,900
Jeff Overton	71	67	75	75	288	39,900
Tim Petrovic	68	70	75	75	288	39,900
John Rollins	68	76	70	74	288	39,900
John Senden	72	69	72	75	288	39,900
Bubba Watson	67	75	72	74	288	39,900
Ernie Els	73	69	73	74	289	28,595
Ryuji Imada	72	70	75	72	289	28,595
Richard S. Johnson	66	72	74	77	289	28,595
Michael Letzig	71	68	74	76	289	28,595
Stephen Ames	70	71	75	74	290	23,211.67
Jason Bohn	72	71	74	73	290	23,211.67
Padraig Harrington	72	72	74	72	290	23,211.67
Nick O'Hern	68	73	75	74	290	23,211.67
Fredrik Jacobson	70	73	72	75	290	23,211.66
Scott Verplank	67	74	73	76	290	23,211.66
Brad Adamonis	67	76	74	74	291	21,470
Martin Kaymer	71	73	69	78	291	21,470
Phil Mickelson	73	71	71	76	291	21,470
Heath Slocum	75	69	71	76	291	21,470
Mark Wilson	69	72	75	75	291	21,470
Rocco Mediate	73	71	74	74	292	20,710
Chez Reavie	70	72	75	75	292	20,710
Johnson Wagner	69	73	72	78	292	20,710
Michael Allen	71	70	74	78	293	20,330
Steve Flesch	75	69	74	76	294	20,045
Jeev Milkha Singh	68	74	76	76	294	20,045
Cameron Beckman	72	72	73	78	295	19,665

	SCORES				TOTAL	MONEY
John Merrick	70	72	74	79	295	19,665
Pat Perez	72	72	74	78	296	19,285
Jeff Quinney	73	70	75	78	296	19,285
Ryan Moore	71	68	75	84	298	19,000
K.J. Choi	73	69	77		219	18,430
Nathan Green	74	69	76		219	18,430
Robert Karlsson	74	70	75		219	18,430
Martin Laird	71	72	76		219	18,430
Hunter Mahan	73	71	75		219	18,430
Stewart Cink	70	73	77		220	17,765
Bob Estes	75	68	77		220	17,765
Graeme McDowell	71	73	77		221	17,480
Fred Funk	73	71	78		222	17,005
Dustin Johnson	72	72	78		222	17,005
Steve Marino	72	72	78		222	17,005
Rod Pampling	70	73	79		222	17,005

Valero Texas Open

La Cantera Golf Club, San Antonio, Texas
Par 35-35–70; 6,896 yards

May 14-17
purse, $6,100,000

	SCORES				TOTAL	MONEY
Zach Johnson	68	67	60	70	265	$1,098,000
James Driscoll	67	69	67	62	265	658,800
(Johnson defeated Driscoll on first playoff hole.)						
Paul Goydos	63	65	69	69	266	353,800
Bill Haas	67	67	67	65	266	353,800
Brian Davis	65	67	69	66	267	214,262.50
Fredrik Jacobson	66	66	68	67	267	214,262.50
Marc Leishman	64	69	66	68	267	214,262.50
Justin Leonard	63	68	67	69	267	214,262.50
Stephen Ames	66	67	68	67	268	170,800
Charley Hoffman	70	69	63	66	268	170,800
Todd Fischer	70	67	64	69	270	125,050
Mathias Gronberg	66	65	69	70	270	125,050
Jonathan Kaye	71	68	63	68	270	125,050
Scott Sterling	68	63	69	70	270	125,050
Garrett Willis	68	70	65	67	270	125,050
Mark Wilson	67	72	67	64	270	125,050
Kris Blanks	70	65	70	66	271	79,822.86
Brandt Jobe	70	65	70	66	271	79,822.86
Scott McCarron	70	67	67	67	271	79,822.86
James Nitties	68	69	66	68	271	79,822.86
Patrick Sheehan	68	68	68	67	271	79,822.86
Bob Estes	67	70	66	68	271	79,822.85
Frank Lickliter	69	68	65	69	271	79,822.85
Tim Herron	68	71	68	65	272	47,198.75
Dustin Johnson	74	65	62	71	272	47,198.75
Bill Lunde	73	65	67	67	272	47,198.75
Shaun Micheel	67	72	63	70	272	47,198.75
Paul Stankowski	70	69	67	66	272	47,198.75
Scott Verplank	67	70	67	68	272	47,198.75
Jimmy Walker	70	66	68	68	272	47,198.75
Matt Weibring	67	70	65	70	272	47,198.75
Tim Clark	67	69	67	70	273	32,330
J.J. Henry	66	70	66	71	273	32,330
Kent Jones	67	65	70	71	273	32,330
Matt Jones	67	69	72	65	273	32,330
Jeff Maggert	64	70	73	66	273	32,330

		SCORES			TOTAL	MONEY
Greg Owen	65	68	68	72	273	32,330
Corey Pavin	66	72	66	69	273	32,330
Kevin Stadler	67	68	68	70	273	32,330
Mark Brooks	71	68	65	70	274	22,570
Wil Collins	67	69	68	70	274	22,570
Marco Dawson	68	68	69	69	274	22,570
Lee Janzen	66	68	69	71	274	22,570
David Peoples	72	67	68	67	274	22,570
Martin Piller	69	70	64	71	274	22,570
Charlie Wi	68	71	64	71	274	22,570
Eric Axley	72	67	68	68	275	15,176.80
Briny Baird	68	66	69	72	275	15,176.80
Chris DiMarco	72	66	67	70	275	15,176.80
Harrison Frazar	67	69	68	71	275	15,176.80
Robert Gates	73	64	67	71	275	15,176.80
John Mallinger	67	64	72	72	275	15,176.80
Troy Matteson	72	66	68	69	275	15,176.80
Aron Price	69	66	70	70	275	15,176.80
Ted Purdy	64	67	71	73	275	15,176.80
Vaughn Taylor	70	68	69	68	275	15,176.80
Bart Bryant	70	66	69	71	276	13,664
Greg Chalmers	69	67	70	70	276	13,664
J.P. Hayes	71	62	74	69	276	13,664
Chad Campbell	68	69	72	68	277	13,298
Jay Williamson	69	68	70	70	277	13,298
Gary Woodland	67	70	69	71	277	13,298
David Duval	66	69	72	71	278	12,993
Carlos Franco	71	66	70	71	278	12,993
Jason Gore	70	69	67	73	279	12,749
Rocco Mediate	69	70	68	72	279	12,749
Matt Bettencourt	68	71	69	72	280	12,383
Scott Gutschewski	71	66	69	74	280	12,383
Richard S. Johnson	71	68	68	73	280	12,383
Charles Warren	70	66	70	74	280	12,383
Nathan Green	70	69	66	76	281	12,017
Anthony Kim	69	69	70	73	281	12,017
Tag Ridings	69	66	74	73	282	11,834
Matthew Loving	72	67	72	72	283	11,712
Billy Andrade	72	67	71	76	286	11,590

HP Byron Nelson Championship

TPC Four Seasons Resort, Irving, Texas
Par 35-35–70; 7,166 yards

May 21-24
purse, $6,500,000

		SCORES			TOTAL	MONEY
Rory Sabbatini	68	64	65	64	261	$1,170,000
Brian Davis	68	65	66	64	263	702,000
D.A. Points	68	66	65	65	264	442,000
Dustin Johnson	68	65	66	66	265	286,000
Scott McCarron	66	69	68	62	265	286,000
John Mallinger	67	65	65	70	267	234,000
John Senden	71	68	65	64	268	217,750
Briny Baird	69	64	67	69	269	182,000
Fred Couples	69	66	67	67	269	182,000
Marc Leishman	68	70	63	68	269	182,000
Jeff Maggert	71	66	65	67	269	182,000
James Nitties	65	68	68	69	270	149,500
Glen Day	69	66	65	71	271	125,666.67
Danny Lee	69	67	69	66	271	125,666.67

	SCORES				TOTAL	MONEY
Kevin Streelman	67	69	64	71	271	125,666.66
Greg Chalmers	68	69	69	66	272	91,185.72
Robert Garrigus	70	66	69	67	272	91,185.72
Vijay Singh	70	67	69	66	272	91,185.72
Justin Leonard	75	63	66	68	272	91,185.71
Steve Marino	69	69	66	68	272	91,185.71
George McNeill	69	67	66	70	272	91,185.71
Mike Weir	66	71	66	69	272	91,185.71
Rod Pampling	72	67	69	65	273	48,777.09
Chris Riley	71	68	68	66	273	48,777.09
Jimmy Walker	71	68	69	65	273	48,777.09
Tim Wilkinson	69	67	70	67	273	48,777.09
Tommy Armour	67	71	68	67	273	48,777.08
Alex Cejka	69	69	67	68	273	48,777.08
Ken Duke	65	69	71	68	273	48,777.08
Charley Hoffman	71	66	65	71	273	48,777.08
Michael Letzig	68	68	67	70	273	48,777.08
Bryce Molder	68	68	66	71	273	48,777.08
Ted Purdy	74	65	66	68	273	48,777.08
Charlie Wi	73	66	64	70	273	48,777.08
James Driscoll	67	66	69	72	274	32,743.75
Steve Flesch	70	69	69	66	274	32,743.75
Joe Ogilvie	69	70	68	67	274	32,743.75
Greg Owen	68	71	68	67	274	32,743.75
Brad Adamonis	66	70	69	70	275	26,000
Kris Blanks	68	71	66	70	275	26,000
Matt Kuchar	70	69	68	68	275	26,000
Martin Laird	72	67	68	68	275	26,000
David Mathis	72	67	67	69	275	26,000
John Rollins	72	66	68	69	275	26,000
Ben Crane	71	68	71	66	276	18,218.58
Chris DiMarco	67	69	72	68	276	18,218.57
Harrison Frazar	73	66	71	66	276	18,218.57
Nathan Green	70	69	66	71	276	18,218.57
Charles Howell	66	69	68	73	276	18,218.57
Jeff Klauk	72	66	69	69	276	18,218.57
Hunter Mahan	71	68	67	70	276	18,218.57
Brian Bateman	69	70	66	72	277	14,933.75
Mark Calcavecchia	68	70	75	64	277	14,933.75
Colt Knost	67	72	67	71	277	14,933.75
Davis Love	73	64	69	71	277	14,933.75
Troy Matteson	68	69	71	69	277	14,933.75
Nicholas Thompson	73	66	64	74	277	14,933.75
Matt Weibring	67	69	71	70	277	14,933.75
Jay Williamson	68	71	71	67	277	14,933.75
Ricky Barnes	69	70	69	70	278	14,040
Todd Hamilton	71	67	71	69	278	14,040
J.J. Henry	71	68	66	73	278	14,040
Cliff Kresge	70	69	74	65	278	14,040
Y.E. Yang	69	67	69	73	278	14,040
Robert Allenby	67	67	70	75	279	13,455
Notah Begay	73	65	70	71	279	13,455
Bob Heintz	68	70	73	68	279	13,455
Jesper Parnevik	67	68	69	75	279	13,455
David Berganio, Jr.	72	65	72	71	280	13,000
Jonathan Byrd	68	70	66	76	280	13,000
Kent Jones	67	70	74	69	280	13,000
Shaun Micheel	72	67	70	72	281	12,740
Aaron Watkins	67	71	69	76	283	12,610
James Oh	71	68	74	74	287	12,480

Crowne Plaza Invitational

Colonial Country Club, Fort Worth, Texas
Par 35-35–70; 7,204 yards

May 28-31
purse, $6,200,000

		SCORES			TOTAL	MONEY
Steve Stricker	63	63	69	68	263	$1,116,000
Tim Clark	63	64	66	70	263	545,600
Steve Marino	66	67	62	68	263	545,600
(Stricker defeated Clark and Marino on second playoff hole.)						
Jason Day	65	65	65	69	264	297,600
Paul Casey	66	67	66	66	265	248,000
Woody Austin	63	68	67	68	266	215,450
Vijay Singh	64	64	69	69	266	215,450
Ian Poulter	66	69	65	68	268	192,200
Jim Furyk	68	69	67	65	269	161,200
Zach Johnson	69	67	64	69	269	161,200
Kevin Na	66	68	66	69	269	161,200
Kevin Sutherland	66	67	68	68	269	161,200
Luke Donald	68	65	67	70	270	112,840
Tom Lehman	68	69	66	67	270	112,840
Justin Leonard	66	68	64	72	270	112,840
Jeff Overton	69	67	65	69	270	112,840
Charlie Wi	67	70	66	67	270	112,840
Sean O'Hair	65	64	70	72	271	83,700
Corey Pavin	71	69	66	65	271	83,700
Ted Purdy	69	65	66	71	271	83,700
John Senden	68	67	67	69	271	83,700
Jason Bohn	69	65	68	70	272	59,520
Stewart Cink	71	66	68	67	272	59,520
J.J. Henry	71	68	67	66	272	59,520
Nick O'Hern	69	69	66	68	272	59,520
Mark Wilson	67	71	66	68	272	59,520
Stephen Ames	68	68	67	70	273	42,160
James Driscoll	69	64	70	70	273	42,160
Harrison Frazar	67	69	66	71	273	42,160
Brian Gay	68	71	70	64	273	42,160
Matt Kuchar	70	68	65	70	273	42,160
Hunter Mahan	69	67	68	69	273	42,160
David Toms	67	72	65	69	273	42,160
Brian Davis	69	68	70	67	274	30,645.72
Justin Rose	69	69	70	66	274	30,645.72
Rory Sabbatini	71	69	69	65	274	30,645.72
Tim Herron	71	65	66	72	274	30,645.71
Ryan Palmer	69	63	70	72	274	30,645.71
Kenny Perry	64	72	68	70	274	30,645.71
Scott Verplank	70	68	68	68	274	30,645.71
Bob Estes	71	66	68	70	275	22,940
Lucas Glover	70	65	66	74	275	22,940
Brandt Jobe	71	69	66	69	275	22,940
George McNeill	68	70	68	69	275	22,940
Kevin Streelman	68	70	66	71	275	22,940
Matt Bettencourt	69	70	68	69	276	16,337
Michael Bradley	70	67	73	66	276	16,337
Bart Bryant	70	68	67	71	276	16,337
Ben Crane	71	68	70	67	276	16,337
Chris DiMarco	69	71	67	69	276	16,337
Charley Hoffman	73	67	65	71	276	16,337
Fredrik Jacobson	68	70	66	72	276	16,337
Danny Lee	69	67	71	69	276	16,337
Dudley Hart	74	66	68	69	277	14,136
Anthony Kim	69	68	68	72	277	14,136
James Nitties	67	68	70	72	277	14,136

	SCORES				TOTAL	MONEY
Tom Pernice, Jr.	69	67	70	71	277	14,136
Heath Slocum	69	71	68	69	277	14,136
Jason Dufner	69	71	65	73	278	13,516
Rocco Mediate	67	70	69	72	278	13,516
Geoff Ogilvy	70	67	67	74	278	13,516
Greg Owen	68	69	69	72	278	13,516
Bo Van Pelt	71	69	69	69	278	13,516
Tommy Armour	67	72	68	72	279	12,958
Carl Pettersson	71	68	69	71	279	12,958
Adam Scott	68	71	69	71	279	12,958
Mike Weir	69	67	72	71	279	12,958
Derek Fathauer	68	69	70	73	280	12,524
Richard S. Johnson	71	69	70	70	280	12,524
Rod Pampling	73	66	67	74	280	12,524
Ryuji Imada	69	68	73	71	281	12,152
Chez Reavie	72	68	70	71	281	12,152
John Rollins	70	67	71	73	281	12,152
John Merrick	71	68	71	75	285	11,904
Ken Duke	71	69	71		211	11,780
Mark Brooks	71	69	72		212	11,594
Aron Price	67	72	73		212	11,594
Joe Ogilvie	67	73	73		213	11,408
Mark Calcavecchia	68	72	74		214	11,284

Memorial Tournament

Muirfield Village Golf Club, Dublin, Ohio
Par 36-36–72; 7,265 yards

June 4-7
purse, $6,000,000

	SCORES				TOTAL	MONEY
Tiger Woods	69	74	68	65	276	$1,080,000
Jim Furyk	67	70	71	69	277	648,000
Jonathan Byrd	69	68	71	72	280	348,000
Mark Wilson	68	70	69	73	280	348,000
Matt Bettencourt	71	68	68	75	282	219,000
Matt Kuchar	73	67	71	71	282	219,000
Davis Love	72	68	69	73	282	219,000
Stewart Cink	68	72	72	71	283	180,000
Ernie Els	70	70	71	72	283	180,000
Will MacKenzie	70	73	73	68	284	150,000
Geoff Ogilvy	72	74	63	75	284	150,000
Mike Weir	69	69	75	71	284	150,000
K.J. Choi	73	70	72	70	285	126,000
Daniel Chopra	72	69	73	72	286	90,133.34
Jerry Kelly	72	72	75	67	286	90,133.34
Nick Watney	73	71	74	68	286	90,133.34
Chris DiMarco	73	67	73	73	286	90,133.33
Luke Donald	64	76	72	74	286	90,133.33
Ryuji Imada	70	69	74	73	286	90,133.33
Dustin Johnson	73	68	72	73	286	90,133.33
Michael Letzig	72	70	69	75	286	90,133.33
Hunter Mahan	74	69	70	73	286	90,133.33
Alex Cejka	73	68	73	73	287	55,200
Steve Marino	68	72	73	74	287	55,200
Kevin Sutherland	69	75	73	70	287	55,200
Bubba Watson	71	71	70	75	287	55,200
Woody Austin	75	70	73	70	288	40,800
Jason Day	67	73	75	73	288	40,800
Mathew Goggin	73	73	70	72	288	40,800
Rod Pampling	69	71	74	74	288	40,800

	SCORES				TOTAL	MONEY
Kenny Perry	72	73	75	68	288	40,800
Charl Schwartzel	72	68	77	71	288	40,800
Steve Stricker	70	74	73	71	288	40,800
Kevin Na	71	72	73	73	289	33,150
Camilo Villegas	71	74	73	71	289	33,150
Troy Matteson	69	73	71	77	290	28,260
Jose Maria Olazabal	74	74	68	74	290	28,260
Jeff Overton	76	69	71	74	290	28,260
Ted Purdy	67	79	75	69	290	28,260
Richard Sterne	74	71	74	71	290	28,260
Robert Allenby	72	76	68	75	291	22,800
Ben Curtis	71	71	72	77	291	22,800
Steve Flesch	73	75	74	69	291	22,800
Y.E. Yang	73	72	74	72	291	22,800
Lucas Glover	75	69	72	76	292	18,600
Tom Lehman	71	74	74	73	292	18,600
Johnson Wagner	69	74	76	73	292	18,600
Charley Hoffman	71	72	76	74	293	15,264
Lee Janzen	72	73	75	73	293	15,264
Jeff Quinney	75	72	74	72	293	15,264
Webb Simpson	73	71	73	76	293	15,264
D.J. Trahan	73	74	69	77	293	15,264
Martin Kaymer	71	76	72	75	294	13,890
Tom Pernice, Jr.	71	74	73	76	294	13,890
Ian Poulter	75	71	74	74	294	13,890
John Senden	71	74	74	75	294	13,890
*Reinier Saxton	69	75	72	78	294	
David Duval	71	74	74	76	295	13,320
Zach Johnson	71	73	75	76	295	13,320
Marc Leishman	74	74	70	77	295	13,320
Steve Lowery	76	71	71	77	295	13,320
Nicholas Thompson	69	75	78	73	295	13,320
Paul Casey	73	70	75	78	296	12,660
Tim Herron	75	73	76	72	296	12,660
George McNeill	76	69	75	76	296	12,660
Nick O'Hern	73	73	76	74	296	12,660
Brett Quigley	74	73	78	71	296	12,660
Chez Reavie	71	74	72	79	296	12,660
Mark Brooks	75	73	76	75	299	12,120
Bill Haas	74	72	77	76	299	12,120
Jeff Klauk	76	71	79	73	299	12,120
Stuart Appleby	72	74	76	78	300	11,820
D.A. Points	75	70	75	80	300	11,820
Scott McCarron	74	74	82	71	301	11,580
Marc Turnesa	72	73	78	78	301	11,580
Erik Compton	72	75	74	81	302	11,340
Rocco Mediate	73	70	81	78	302	11,340

St. Jude Classic

TPC Southwind, Memphis, Tennessee
Par 35-35–70; 7,244 yards

June 11-14
purse, $5,600,000

	SCORES				TOTAL	MONEY
Brian Gay	64	66	66	66	262	$1,008,000
Bryce Molder	69	63	65	70	267	492,800
David Toms	67	66	69	65	267	492,800
Paul Goydos	72	64	64	68	268	231,466.67
John Senden	69	66	69	64	268	231,466.67
Robert Allenby	67	64	68	69	268	231,466.66

	SCORES				TOTAL	MONEY
Jason Dufner	68	67	69	65	269	180,600
Graeme McDowell	66	71	69	63	269	180,600
Woody Austin	67	66	68	69	270	162,400
Jeff Overton	68	67	70	66	271	145,600
Heath Slocum	71	63	67	70	271	145,600
Kevin Stadler	69	66	70	67	272	123,200
Brendon Todd	73	65	68	66	272	123,200
Rich Beem	66	68	69	70	273	95,200
Ben Crane	69	68	66	70	273	95,200
Harrison Frazar	69	65	73	66	273	95,200
Nathan Green	70	66	70	67	273	95,200
Aron Price	73	66	66	68	273	95,200
Jason Bohn	69	67	69	69	274	70,280
Lee Janzen	68	71	68	67	274	70,280
Roland Thatcher	70	70	66	68	274	70,280
Matt Weibring	70	66	68	70	274	70,280
Brad Adamonis	68	72	67	68	275	48,440
Guy Boros	67	66	70	72	275	48,440
Jason Day	70	65	71	69	275	48,440
Bob Estes	69	67	66	73	275	48,440
Michael Letzig	70	67	69	69	275	48,440
David Mathis	68	69	69	69	275	48,440
Cameron Beckman	68	71	71	66	276	32,648
Ronnie Black	72	68	67	69	276	32,648
Tim Clark	70	67	69	70	276	32,648
Retief Goosen	68	67	71	70	276	32,648
Marc Leishman	69	68	69	70	276	32,648
Brett Quigley	69	66	72	69	276	32,648
Tag Ridings	68	69	68	71	276	32,648
Chris Riley	72	68	68	68	276	32,648
Vaughn Taylor	67	65	69	75	276	32,648
Camilo Villegas	68	67	75	66	276	32,648
Michael Bradley	70	67	69	71	277	24,080
Fredrik Jacobson	67	69	67	74	277	24,080
Brian Vranesh	73	66	72	66	277	24,080
Robert Garrigus	69	70	70	69	278	19,600
Bill Lunde	71	66	69	72	278	19,600
Loren Roberts	67	67	73	71	278	19,600
Patrick Sheehan	68	69	71	70	278	19,600
Vance Veazey	67	68	71	72	278	19,600
Ricky Barnes	67	69	73	70	279	15,792
Chris Stroud	66	70	69	74	279	15,792
Wil Collins	73	67	72	68	280	13,294.40
Glen Day	69	69	70	72	280	13,294.40
Bob Heintz	70	65	73	72	280	13,294.40
Jerry Kelly	67	68	72	73	280	13,294.40
Cliff Kresge	71	69	69	71	280	13,294.40
James Nitties	70	67	71	72	280	13,294.40
Nick O'Hern	72	68	72	68	280	13,294.40
Jose Maria Olazabal	66	70	74	70	280	13,294.40
Marc Turnesa	70	69	72	69	280	13,294.40
Omar Uresti	70	70	70	70	280	13,294.40
John Daly	72	68	71	70	281	12,096
Chris DiMarco	69	68	71	73	281	12,096
Jason Gore	72	65	72	72	281	12,096
Peter Lonard	71	68	70	72	281	12,096
Phil Mickelson	68	70	68	75	281	12,096
Paul Stankowski	71	68	69	73	281	12,096
Scott Verplank	68	69	71	73	281	12,096
J.J. Henry	70	70	68	74	282	11,648
Derek Fathauer	68	71	72	72	283	11,480
David Gossett	70	70	75	68	283	11,480
Greg Chalmers	68	69	76	71	284	11,144

	SCORES				TOTAL	MONEY
Mathias Gronberg	66	70	72	76	284	11,144
Tim Herron	68	71	78	67	284	11,144
Jarrod Lyle	68	69	73	74	284	11,144
John Merrick	72	66	76	73	287	10,808
Jimmy Walker	65	72	82	68	287	10,808
Jay Delsing	70	70	71	77	288	10,640
Dicky Pride	69	69	79	72	289	10,528

U.S. Open Championship

Bethpage State Park, Black Course, Farmingdale, New York   June 18-22
Par 35-35–70; 7,426 yards   purse, $7,500,000
(Event completed on Monday—rain.)

	SCORES				TOTAL	MONEY
Lucas Glover	69	64	70	73	276	$1,350,000
Phil Mickelson	69	70	69	70	278	559,830
David Duval	67	70	70	71	278	559,830
Ricky Barnes	67	65	70	76	278	559,830
Ross Fisher	70	68	69	72	279	289,146
Tiger Woods	74	69	68	69	280	233,350
Soren Hansen	70	71	70	69	280	233,350
Hunter Mahan	72	68	68	72	280	233,350
Henrik Stenson	73	70	70	68	281	194,794
Rory McIlroy	72	70	72	68	282	154,600
Matt Bettencourt	75	67	71	69	282	154,600
Sergio Garcia	70	70	72	70	282	154,600
Ryan Moore	70	69	72	71	282	154,600
Stephen Ames	74	66	70	72	282	154,600
Mike Weir	64	70	74	74	282	154,600
Anthony Kim	71	71	71	70	283	122,128
Retief Goosen	73	68	68	74	283	122,128
Ian Poulter	70	74	73	67	284	100,308
Michael Sim	71	70	71	72	284	100,308
Peter Hanson	66	71	73	74	284	100,308
Graeme McDowell	69	72	69	74	284	100,308
Bubba Watson	72	70	67	75	284	100,308
Lee Westwood	72	66	74	73	285	76,422
Steve Stricker	73	66	72	74	285	76,422
Oliver Wilson	70	70	71	74	285	76,422
Sean O'Hair	69	69	71	76	285	76,422
Vijay Singh	72	72	73	69	286	56,041
Francesco Molinari	71	70	74	71	286	56,041
Azuma Yano	72	65	77	72	286	56,041
J.B. Holmes	73	67	73	73	286	56,041
Johan Edfors	70	74	68	74	286	56,041
Stewart Cink	73	69	70	74	286	56,041
Kevin Sutherland	71	73	73	70	287	47,404
Jim Furyk	72	69	74	72	287	47,404
Camilo Villegas	71	71	72	73	287	47,404
Carl Pettersson	75	68	73	72	288	42,935
*Nick Taylor	73	65	75	75	288	
Adam Scott	69	71	73	75	288	42,935
Todd Hamilton	67	71	71	79	288	42,935
Tim Clark	73	71	74	71	289	38,492
Dustin Johnson	72	69	76	72	289	38,492
*Drew Weaver	69	72	74	74	289	
Billy Mayfair	73	70	72	74	289	38,492
Kenny Perry	71	72	75	72	290	35,536
Thomas Levet	72	72	71	76	291	33,319

	SCORES				TOTAL	MONEY
John Mallinger	71	70	72	78	291	33,319
Rocco Mediate	68	73	79	72	292	27,409
Andres Romero	73	70	77	72	292	27,409
K.J. Choi	72	71	76	73	292	27,409
Tom Lehman	71	73	74	74	292	27,409
Geoff Ogilvy	73	67	77	75	292	27,409
Gary Woodland	73	66	76	77	292	27,409
*Kyle Stanley	70	74	74	75	293	
Jean-Francois Lucquin	73	71	75	75	294	22,501
Andrew McLardy	71	72	75	76	294	22,501
Angel Cabrera	74	69	75	76	294	22,501
Ben Curtis	72	71	74	79	296	21,385
Jeff Brehaut	70	72	81	74	297	20,630
Trevor Murphy	71	69	77	80	297	20,630
Fred Funk	70	74	75	82	301	19,921

Out of Final 36 Holes

Simon Khan	75	70	145	Simon Dyson	78	70	148
David Toms	69	76	145	Douglas Batty	74	74	148
Luke Donald	74	71	145	Matt Kuchar	71	77	148
Martin Laird	74	71	145	Justin Rose	73	75	148
George McNeill	74	71	145	G. Fernandez-Castano	75	73	148
Ryan Blaum	72	73	145	Craig Bowden	74	74	148
Rory Sabbatini	72	73	145	J.P. Hayes	74	74	148
Peter Tomasulo	73	72	145	*Tyson Alexander	73	75	148
Cameron Beckman	76	69	145	Heath Slocum	76	73	149
Martin Kaymer	76	69	145	Stuart Appleby	76	73	149
Miguel Angel Jimenez	77	68	145	Mike Welch	73	76	149
Steve Allan	73	73	146	Steven Conway	80	69	149
Brian Gay	73	73	146	Scott Gutschewski	77	72	149
Raphael Jacquelin	73	73	146	*Ben Martin	72	78	150
Rod Pampling	74	72	146	Darren Clarke	74	76	150
Brandt Snedeker	71	75	146	Kevin Silva	78	72	150
Justin Leonard	71	75	146	Charlie Beljan	78	71	149
James Kamte	74	72	146	*Clark Klaasen	76	74	150
Ryan Spears	73	73	146	Chad Campbell	80	70	150
Angelo Que	77	69	146	John Merrick	73	77	150
Andrew Parr	74	72	146	Paul Casey	75	75	150
Sang Moon Bae	74	72	146	Ben Crane	76	75	151
*Rickie Fowler	78	68	146	Casey Wittenberg	73	78	151
Alvaro Quiros	73	73	146	Boo Weekley	79	72	151
Chris Stroud	76	70	146	Chris Kirk	74	77	151
Nick Watney	73	73	146	Greg Kraft	79	72	151
Bo Van Pelt	73	73	146	Jeev Milkha Singh	78	73	151
Robert Allenby	75	71	146	Josh McCumber	78	73	151
Shawn Stefani	73	73	146	Padraig Harrington	76	76	152
Cortland Lowe	75	71	146	*David Erdy	78	74	152
Nathan Tyler	77	69	146	Clinton Jensen	78	75	153
J.J. Henry	73	74	147	*Drew Kittleson	80	73	153
Zach Johnson	75	72	147	*Bronson Burgoon	74	79	153
Ryuji Imada	75	72	147	Andrew Svoboda	80	74	154
Richard Bland	77	70	147	Darron Stiles	75	79	154
D.J. Trahan	76	71	147	Cameron Yancey	74	80	154
Eduardo Romero	76	71	147	*Vaughn Snyder	76	78	154
James Nitties	78	69	147	David Horsey	81	73	154
Michael Miles	78	69	147	Sean Farren	80	75	155
Charlie Wi	75	72	147	Ernie Els	78	77	155
*Cameron Tringale	70	77	147	*Kyle Peterman	81	75	156
Colby Beckstrom	76	71	147	*Matt Nagy	76	80	156
Ken Duke	76	71	147	Michael Campbell	77	79	156
David Smail	70	77	147	Shintaro Kai	79	78	157
Jose Manuel Lara	77	70	147	Eric Axley	79	80	159

Briny Baird	73	74	147	*Scott Lewis	81	80	161
Charl Schwartzel	77	70	147	*Josh Brock	83	79	162
Kaname Yokoo	77	71	148	Matthew Jones			WD

(Professionals who did not complete 72 holes received $2,000.)

Travelers Championship

TPC River Highlands, Cromwell, Connecticut   June 25-28
Par 35-35–70; 6,844 yards   purse, $6,000,000

	SCORES				TOTAL	MONEY
Kenny Perry	61	68	66	63	258	$1,080,000
Paul Goydos	63	68	63	67	261	528,000
David Toms	65	65	66	65	261	528,000
Ben Curtis	68	64	66	65	263	248,000
Hunter Mahan	66	70	63	64	263	248,000
Ryan Moore	66	65	68	64	263	248,000
Tag Ridings	64	69	65	66	264	193,500
Casey Wittenberg	67	65	65	67	264	193,500
Bo Van Pelt	66	68	64	67	265	168,000
Scott Verplank	67	68	68	62	265	168,000
Lucas Glover	65	71	65	65	266	138,000
Anthony Kim	66	66	67	67	266	138,000
John Merrick	65	67	65	69	266	138,000
Michael Allen	68	65	67	67	267	105,000
D.J. Trahan	66	68	68	65	267	105,000
Bubba Watson	66	68	70	63	267	105,000
Boo Weekley	64	71	67	65	267	105,000
Zach Johnson	67	68	66	67	268	90,000
Greg Chalmers	64	71	68	66	269	75,300
Robert Garrigus	66	69	68	66	269	75,300
Bryce Molder	67	66	67	69	269	75,300
Kyle Stanley	66	67	70	66	269	75,300
J.J. Henry	66	70	68	66	270	57,600
Michael Letzig	70	66	65	69	270	57,600
Chris Riley	67	67	66	70	270	57,600
Kris Blanks	68	66	70	67	271	41,700
Brian Gay	66	68	70	67	271	41,700
Mathew Goggin	65	69	70	67	271	41,700
Will MacKenzie	68	68	66	69	271	41,700
Nick O'Hern	68	68	67	68	271	41,700
Webb Simpson	67	69	70	65	271	41,700
Chris Stroud	71	65	68	67	271	41,700
Johnson Wagner	66	68	70	67	271	41,700
Matt Bettencourt	67	67	69	69	272	28,400
Jason Bohn	67	70	67	68	272	28,400
Brendon de Jonge	70	66	70	66	272	28,400
James Driscoll	68	69	68	67	272	28,400
Nathan Green	69	67	68	68	272	28,400
Justin Leonard	69	66	68	69	272	28,400
Spencer Levin	64	69	67	72	272	28,400
Peter Lonard	67	70	66	69	272	28,400
Jarrod Lyle	67	67	66	72	272	28,400
Sergio Garcia	67	69	71	66	273	20,400
Ryuji Imada	70	67	70	66	273	20,400
Scott McCarron	70	67	70	66	273	20,400
Aaron Watkins	65	67	70	71	273	20,400
Mark Brooks	67	68	71	68	274	16,140
Colt Knost	66	66	69	73	274	16,140
Bill Lunde	67	68	70	69	274	16,140

	SCORES				TOTAL	MONEY
Brandt Snedeker	67	67	69	71	274	16,140
Joe Durant	67	68	68	72	275	13,965
Patrick Sheehan	67	70	67	71	275	13,965
Vijay Singh	66	70	70	69	275	13,965
Kevin Streelman	68	66	68	73	275	13,965
Charles Warren	63	72	69	71	275	13,965
Charlie Wi	66	68	71	70	275	13,965
Jay Williamson	67	68	70	70	275	13,965
Y.E. Yang	65	71	70	69	275	13,965
Ricky Barnes	65	70	72	69	276	13,140
Chad Campbell	67	69	69	71	276	13,140
D.A. Points	65	72	69	70	276	13,140
Aron Price	67	68	70	71	276	13,140
Rich Beem	68	67	72	70	277	12,600
Bob Heintz	68	67	68	74	277	12,600
Luke List	66	69	70	72	277	12,600
Tim Petrovic	68	69	71	69	277	12,600
Gary Woodland	69	67	72	69	277	12,600
Jason Gore	68	68	73	70	279	12,180
Chez Reavie	66	67	73	73	279	12,180
Jerry Kelly	65	70	73	72	280	11,940
Marc Leishman	71	66	72	71	280	11,940
Vaughn Taylor	69	68	72	73	282	11,760
Lee Janzen	66	71	73		210	11,460
Billy Mayfair	70	66	74		210	11,460
Jesper Parnevik	67	70	73		210	11,460
Kevin Sutherland	69	68	73		210	11,460
Tyler Aldridge	69	66	78		213	10,980
Aaron Baddeley	69	68	76		213	10,980
Olin Browne	70	67	76		213	10,980
Chris DiMarco	68	69	76		213	10,980

AT&T National

Congressional Country Club, Bethesda, Maryland
Par 35-35–70; 7,255 yards

July 2-5
purse, $6,000,000

	SCORES				TOTAL	MONEY
Tiger Woods	64	66	70	67	267	$1,080,000
Hunter Mahan	69	69	68	62	268	648,000
Anthony Kim	62	70	68	71	271	408,000
Bryce Molder	64	70	70	68	272	288,000
Lucas Glover	69	66	68	70	273	228,000
Brandt Snedeker	68	70	68	67	273	228,000
Cameron Beckman	68	67	66	73	274	180,750
Jim Furyk	66	67	69	72	274	180,750
Danny Lee	68	67	69	70	274	180,750
Vijay Singh	70	68	70	66	274	180,750
Michael Allen	67	69	65	74	275	127,200
Matt Bettencourt	70	71	66	68	275	127,200
Fred Couples	72	67	68	68	275	127,200
Ryan Moore	69	66	69	71	275	127,200
Kevin Streelman	70	67	71	67	275	127,200
Stuart Appleby	66	69	70	71	276	93,000
Cliff Kresge	70	67	67	72	276	93,000
Davis Love	69	67	70	70	276	93,000
Justin Rose	67	71	69	69	276	93,000
Daniel Chopra	66	68	72	71	277	75,000
Rod Pampling	67	64	71	75	277	75,000
Ryuji Imada	69	69	66	74	278	62,400

	SCORES				TOTAL	MONEY
Ryan Palmer	69	67	71	71	278	62,400
Y.E. Yang	67	71	70	70	278	62,400
Aaron Baddeley	72	68	69	70	279	45,800
Steve Elkington	65	73	71	70	279	45,800
Robert Garrigus	70	68	69	72	279	45,800
Marc Leishman	70	71	67	71	279	45,800
Nick O'Hern	71	70	71	67	279	45,800
Mark Wilson	70	67	70	72	279	45,800
George McNeill	70	66	69	75	280	36,375
Tim Petrovic	68	71	69	72	280	36,375
D.A. Points	64	70	72	74	280	36,375
Charles Warren	73	67	69	71	280	36,375
Scott McCarron	72	65	73	71	281	29,580
Sean O'Hair	69	72	68	72	281	29,580
Joe Ogilvie	69	72	73	67	281	29,580
Webb Simpson	74	67	72	68	281	29,580
Nicholas Thompson	71	70	72	68	281	29,580
Steve Flesch	69	72	71	70	282	24,000
Steve Marino	73	65	68	76	282	24,000
James Nitties	71	67	70	74	282	24,000
Dean Wilson	69	69	72	72	282	24,000
Jason Bohn	72	70	67	74	283	19,200
Chris DiMarco	70	72	74	67	283	19,200
J.J. Henry	76	66	69	72	283	19,200
John Senden	71	70	72	70	283	19,200
Jason Dufner	72	69	71	72	284	15,080
Charley Hoffman	71	69	68	76	284	15,080
Ted Purdy	73	66	69	76	284	15,080
Chez Reavie	70	71	70	73	284	15,080
Boo Weekley	67	69	69	79	284	15,080
Mike Weir	71	71	72	70	284	15,080
Harrison Frazar	69	70	74	72	285	13,560
Nathan Green	71	71	66	77	285	13,560
Peter Lonard	70	70	72	73	285	13,560
David Mathis	71	71	74	69	285	13,560
Rocco Mediate	70	69	72	74	285	13,560
Jeff Quinney	69	73	71	72	285	13,560
Bo Van Pelt	69	72	71	73	285	13,560
Paul Goydos	73	68	74	72	287	12,960
Michael Letzig	68	74	74	71	287	12,960
Bill Lunde	70	68	71	78	287	12,960
Chris Stroud	74	67	75	72	288	12,660
Marc Turnesa	71	69	80	68	288	12,660
Ricky Barnes	70	72	75	72	289	12,300
Notah Begay	70	72	72	75	289	12,300
Troy Matteson	69	71	77	72	289	12,300
Nick Watney	70	72	72	75	289	12,300
Bart Bryant	68	72	73	77	290	11,940
Kevin Stadler	69	73	75	73	290	11,940
*Matt Hill	71	69	75	75	290	
Brian Davis	70	72	74	75	291	11,640
Martin Laird	70	71	76	74	291	11,640
Jeff Maggert	72	70	77	72	291	11,640
James Driscoll	70	70	80	72	292	11,400

John Deere Classic

TPC Deere Run, Silvis, Illinois
Par 35-36–71; 7,257 yards

July 9-12
purse, $4,300,000

	SCORES				TOTAL	MONEY
Steve Stricker	71	61	68	64	264	$774,000
Zach Johnson	69	68	64	66	267	321,066.67
Brandt Snedeker	67	67	68	65	267	321,066.67
Brett Quigley	69	69	62	67	267	321,066.66
J.J. Henry	65	69	66	68	268	156,950
Matt Jones	68	68	63	69	268	156,950
Tim Petrovic	66	67	66	69	268	156,950
Kevin Streelman	70	67	68	64	269	133,300
Aaron Baddeley	68	69	68	65	270	103,200
Cameron Beckman	71	66	64	69	270	103,200
Daniel Chopra	67	70	66	67	270	103,200
Greg Owen	67	67	68	68	270	103,200
Darron Stiles	64	65	70	71	270	103,200
Scott Verplank	70	64	69	67	270	103,200
Chad Campbell	68	67	68	68	271	64,500
Jason Day	66	68	68	69	271	64,500
Charley Hoffman	71	65	66	69	271	64,500
Spencer Levin	67	69	68	67	271	64,500
Peter Lonard	67	69	68	67	271	64,500
George McNeill	67	71	68	65	271	64,500
Chris Stroud	67	68	67	69	271	64,500
Steve Elkington	69	69	65	69	272	48,160
Robert Garrigus	68	70	70	65	273	38,270
Charles Howell	69	69	69	66	273	38,270
Lee Janzen	64	70	66	73	273	38,270
Jerry Kelly	69	64	70	70	273	38,270
Ryan Palmer	70	64	71	68	273	38,270
David Mathis	69	69	69	67	274	31,175
Garrett Willis	69	68	71	66	274	31,175
Todd Hamilton	68	68	70	69	275	27,305
Marc Leishman	68	70	66	71	275	27,305
Bryce Molder	69	69	66	71	275	27,305
Pat Perez	69	68	69	69	275	27,305
Frank Lickliter	69	66	71	70	276	22,188
Ryan Moore	71	67	69	69	276	22,188
Chris Riley	71	67	69	69	276	22,188
Heath Slocum	69	67	70	70	276	22,188
Kyle Stanley	71	66	69	70	276	22,188
Matt Bettencourt	65	70	67	75	277	16,340
Jason Bohn	67	70	69	71	277	16,340
Jason Dufner	71	66	71	69	277	16,340
Ted Purdy	68	70	71	68	277	16,340
Webb Simpson	68	69	68	72	277	16,340
Roland Thatcher	70	68	71	68	277	16,340
Jimmy Walker	71	64	72	70	277	16,340
Dean Wilson	65	70	73	69	277	16,340
*Jack Newman	71	67	69	70	277	
Ken Duke	71	65	72	70	278	11,044.86
Tommy Gainey	69	67	73	69	278	11,044.86
Mathias Gronberg	67	70	69	72	278	11,044.86
Richard S. Johnson	67	68	69	74	278	11,044.86
Johnson Wagner	70	67	73	68	278	11,044.86
Bart Bryant	69	69	65	75	278	11,044.85
Kirk Triplett	67	67	70	74	278	11,044.85
Mark Brooks	69	68	71	71	279	9,847
Brian Davis	67	70	70	72	279	9,847
Davis Love	70	68	68	73	279	9,847

	SCORES				TOTAL	MONEY
Carl Pettersson	70	68	74	67	279	9,847
Kenny Perry	68	68	72	72	280	9,589
D.J. Trahan	71	66	71	72	280	9,589
Jay Williamson	70	68	72	71	281	9,460
Mark Calcavecchia	68	69	68	77	282	9,331
Casey Wittenberg	72	66	70	74	282	9,331
Scott McCarron	68	66	73	76	283	9,202
Matthew Borchert	66	72	72	75	285	9,116
Eric Axley	73	66			139	8,428
Rich Beem	70	69			139	8,428
Michael Bradley	72	67			139	8,428
Bob Estes	70	69			139	8,428
Derek Fathauer	72	67			139	8,428
Harrison Frazar	71	68			139	8,428
Lucas Glover	69	70			139	8,428
Matt Kuchar	71	68			139	8,428
Steve Marino	71	68			139	8,428
Scott Piercy	72	67			139	8,428
Dicky Pride	66	73			139	8,428
Andrew Ruthkoski	68	71			139	8,428
John Senden	70	69			139	8,428
Bo Van Pelt	69	70			139	8,428
Charles Warren	72	67			139	8,428

The Open Championship

See European Tours chapter.

U.S. Bank Championship

Brown Deer Park Golf Course, Milwaukee, Wisconsin   July 16-19
Par 34-36–70; 6,759 yards   purse, $4,000,000

	SCORES				TOTAL	MONEY
Bo Van Pelt	67	68	68	64	267	$720,000
John Mallinger	70	66	66	65	267	432,000
(Van Pelt defeated Mallinger on second playoff hole.)						
Jerry Kelly	69	68	66	65	268	272,000
Dicky Pride	72	69	63	65	269	165,333.34
Jeff Klauk	64	69	69	67	269	165,333.33
Jeff Quinney	67	68	67	67	269	165,333.33
Kris Blanks	70	63	70	67	270	104,250
Brendon de Jonge	70	66	66	68	270	104,250
Jason Gore	66	70	68	66	270	104,250
Spencer Levin	71	68	68	63	270	104,250
Kevin Na	69	65	69	67	270	104,250
Tim Petrovic	68	70	69	63	270	104,250
Chris Riley	67	66	68	69	270	104,250
Omar Uresti	69	67	67	67	270	104,250
Greg Chalmers	64	67	69	71	271	68,000
Tom Pernice, Jr.	70	68	67	66	271	68,000
Casey Wittenberg	71	69	64	67	271	68,000
Steve Flesch	69	65	69	69	272	50,400
Harrison Frazar	70	66	69	67	272	50,400
Skip Kendall	66	70	70	66	272	50,400
Frank Lickliter	66	70	63	73	272	50,400
Corey Pavin	73	67	67	65	272	50,400
Jeff Sluman	69	66	68	69	272	50,400
Scott Hoch	70	67	70	66	273	31,657.15

	SCORES				TOTAL	MONEY
Parker McLachlin	70	68	69	66	273	31,657.15
Michael Letzig	68	67	69	69	273	31,657.14
Steve Lowery	70	68	69	66	273	31,657.14
Jeff Maggert	68	67	66	72	273	31,657.14
Joe Ogilvie	67	71	66	69	273	31,657.14
Loren Roberts	69	69	68	67	273	31,657.14
Joe Durant	67	70	68	69	274	23,720
Nick O'Hern	69	71	68	66	274	23,720
Tag Ridings	66	70	70	68	274	23,720
Johnson Wagner	68	69	67	70	274	23,720
Mark Wilson	68	70	69	67	274	23,720
Cameron Beckman	72	69	67	67	275	18,433.34
George McNeill	69	70	71	65	275	18,433.34
Glen Day	71	67	67	70	275	18,433.33
Brett Quigley	68	72	67	68	275	18,433.33
Kirk Triplett	67	70	68	70	275	18,433.33
Bob Tway	73	64	69	69	275	18,433.33
Brian Davis	73	68	66	69	276	14,400
Carlos Franco	69	71	68	68	276	14,400
Kevin Stadler	69	69	73	65	276	14,400
Chris Stroud	71	67	68	70	276	14,400
Steve Elkington	69	69	67	72	277	11,340
Mark Hensby	67	72	68	70	277	11,340
Scott Sterling	69	71	68	69	277	11,340
Nicholas Thompson	70	71	70	66	277	11,340
Mark Brooks	71	70	70	67	278	9,395.56
Brad Faxon	70	70	67	71	278	9,395.56
Tim Herron	70	69	69	70	278	9,395.56
Stephen Leaney	67	69	70	72	278	9,395.56
Jay Williamson	68	71	70	69	278	9,395.56
Mathias Gronberg	72	68	66	72	278	9,395.55
Lee Janzen	70	68	68	72	278	9,395.55
Matt Jones	71	68	66	73	278	9,395.55
Marc Turnesa	69	65	71	73	278	9,395.55
Ronnie Black	71	70	69	69	279	8,680
Tommy Gainey	67	68	71	73	279	8,680
Jesper Parnevik	73	68	69	69	279	8,680
David Peoples	70	70	70	69	279	8,680
Kevin Streelman	71	67	73	68	279	8,680
Garrett Willis	72	69	67	71	279	8,680
Bill Haas	73	68	70	69	280	8,320
Jonathan Kaye	70	67	73	70	280	8,320
Kyle Stanley	71	66	71	72	280	8,320
Guy Boros	70	69	72	70	281	8,080
Colt Knost	68	71	72	70	281	8,080
John Rollins	71	68	72	70	281	8,080
Heath Slocum	71	70	70	71	282	7,920
Aron Price	70	70	71	72	283	7,840
Cliff Kresge	68	73	71		112	7,760
Troy Matteson	68	70	75		113	7,640
Shaun Micheel	70	71	72		113	7,640
Ryan Helminen	73	68	73		114	7,360
Troy Kelly	69	72	73		114	7,360
Peter Lonard	72	69	73		114	7,360
Leif Olson	69	70	75		114	7,360
Aaron Watkins	71	70	73		114	7,360

RBC Canadian Open

Glen Abbey Golf Club, Oakville, Ontario, Canada
Par 35-37–72; 7,222 yards
(Event completed on Monday—rain.)

July 23-27
purse, $5,100,000

	SCORES				TOTAL	MONEY
Nathan Green	68	65	69	68	270	$918,000
Retief Goosen	65	69	67	69	270	550,800
(Green defeated Goosen on second playoff hole.)						
Jason Dufner	68	63	70	73	274	295,800
Anthony Kim	69	66	66	73	274	295,800
Lee Janzen	68	70	70	67	275	186,150
Jerry Kelly	65	67	72	71	275	186,150
Brandt Snedeker	73	67	67	68	275	186,150
Stephen Ames	68	69	72	67	276	123,037.50
Chris Baryla	69	71	70	66	276	123,037.50
Mark Calcavecchia	71	65	71	69	276	123,037.50
Bob Estes	67	67	68	74	276	123,037.50
Michael Letzig	69	67	66	74	276	123,037.50
Scott McCarron	68	71	67	70	276	123,037.50
Scott Verplank	65	67	71	73	276	123,037.50
Y.E. Yang	69	66	73	68	276	123,037.50
Briny Baird	72	63	70	72	277	69,232.50
Tim Herron	67	68	71	71	277	69,232.50
J.B. Holmes	73	67	67	70	277	69,232.50
Martin Laird	65	69	78	65	277	69,232.50
Bryce Molder	71	69	70	67	277	69,232.50
Chris Riley	68	70	70	69	277	69,232.50
Webb Simpson	71	68	67	71	277	69,232.50
Peter Tomasulo	65	68	72	72	277	69,232.50
Luke Donald	71	69	67	71	278	40,362.86
Jeff Quinney	71	69	65	73	278	40,362.86
Scott Sterling	67	68	72	71	278	40,362.86
Mike Weir	71	67	69	71	278	40,362.86
Mark Wilson	68	71	69	70	278	40,362.86
Pat Perez	67	67	72	72	278	40,362.85
Camilo Villegas	63	71	72	72	278	40,362.85
Joe Durant	65	74	68	72	279	30,243
Corey Pavin	68	70	72	69	279	30,243
Patrick Sheehan	68	70	70	71	279	30,243
Kevin Streelman	72	68	71	68	279	30,243
Dean Wilson	68	70	69	72	279	30,243
Harrison Frazar	68	71	70	71	280	24,543.75
John Merrick	70	68	70	72	280	24,543.75
Leif Olson	68	71	68	73	280	24,543.75
Kevin Sutherland	68	69	70	73	280	24,543.75
Daniel Chopra	70	68	69	74	281	19,380
Ken Duke	66	71	74	70	281	19,380
Steve Elkington	68	71	75	67	281	19,380
Derek Fathauer	66	74	73	68	281	19,380
Scott Piercy	71	69	69	72	281	19,380
Darron Stiles	69	71	68	73	281	19,380
Graham DeLaet	73	66	72	71	282	13,872
Jamie Lovemark	74	66	69	73	282	13,872
Billy Mayfair	69	69	70	74	282	13,872
David Peoples	67	73	76	66	282	13,872
D.A. Points	68	71	66	77	282	13,872
Jimmy Walker	66	70	74	72	282	13,872
Jason Day	70	70	72	71	283	12,240
Kevin Na	63	71	74	76	284	11,934
Nicholas Thompson	73	66	73	72	284	11,934
Frank Lickliter	68	72	72	73	285	11,679

	SCORES			TOTAL	MONEY
Kevin Stadler	70	70	76	69	285	11,679
Brendon de Jonge	67	73	75	71	286	11,526
Jay Williamson	70	68	77	72	287	11,424
Dicky Pride	70	70	76	72	288	11,271
Charles Warren	70	68	69	81	288	11,271
Mike Grob	70	69	75	75	289	11,118
Andres Gonzales	71	69	79	72	291	10,965
Parker McLachlin	66	72	74	79	291	10,965
Jonathan Byrd	72	69			141	10,251
Bob Heintz	70	71			141	10,251
Jeff Klauk	71	70			141	10,251
Cliff Kresge	69	72			141	10,251
Lucas Lee	71	70			141	10,251
Steve Lowery	67	74			141	10,251
David Mathis	71	70			141	10,251
Joe Ogilvie	72	69			141	10,251
Ryan Palmer	69	72			141	10,251
Aron Price	72	69			141	10,251
Omar Uresti	72	69			141	10,251
Bo Van Pelt	74	67			141	10,251

Buick Open

Warwick Hills Golf & Country Club, Grand Blanc, Michigan
Par 36-36–72; 7,127 yards

July 30-August 2
purse, $5,100,000

	SCORES			TOTAL	MONEY
Tiger Woods	71	63	65	69	268	$918,000
Greg Chalmers	66	68	69	68	271	380,800
John Senden	64	66	71	70	271	380,800
Roland Thatcher	70	64	73	64	271	380,800
Y.E. Yang	65	69	71	67	272	204,000
Ben Crane	68	71	65	69	273	177,225
Michael Letzig	67	65	68	73	273	177,225
Woody Austin	68	71	65	70	274	132,600
Bob Heintz	70	68	66	70	274	132,600
John Rollins	68	71	67	68	274	132,600
Vaughn Taylor	65	68	69	72	274	132,600
Brian Vranesh	65	75	67	67	274	132,600
Jimmy Walker	70	64	69	71	274	132,600
J.P. Hayes	68	71	67	69	275	89,250
Justin Leonard	72	67	69	67	275	89,250
Troy Matteson	66	69	72	68	275	89,250
Charles Warren	70	65	68	72	275	89,250
Paul Goydos	66	70	71	69	276	62,074.29
Tim Herron	67	70	70	69	276	62,074.29
Matt Jones	68	68	71	69	276	62,074.29
Neal Lancaster	67	70	70	69	276	62,074.29
Bill Haas	68	68	69	71	276	62,074.28
Bill Lunde	68	65	71	72	276	62,074.28
Billy Mayfair	68	68	69	71	276	62,074.28
Chad Campbell	68	71	68	70	277	41,650
Jim Furyk	69	69	69	70	277	41,650
Tim Petrovic	69	67	70	71	277	41,650
Jason Bohn	68	70	72	68	278	31,790
Jonathan Byrd	69	71	70	68	278	31,790
Jason Day	74	66	68	70	278	31,790
Bob Estes	70	70	71	67	278	31,790
Jason Gore	70	69	71	68	278	31,790
Nathan Green	69	70	71	68	278	31,790

	SCORES				TOTAL	MONEY
James Nitties	65	70	71	72	278	31,790
Scott Piercy	70	70	64	74	278	31,790
Kevin Stadler	67	67	72	72	278	31,790
Kris Blanks	69	68	72	70	279	20,910
Brian Gay	71	69	67	72	279	20,910
Mark Hensby	68	72	68	71	279	20,910
Jeff Klauk	66	70	69	74	279	20,910
Marc Leishman	67	69	68	75	279	20,910
Leif Olson	68	67	71	73	279	20,910
Greg Owen	68	69	70	72	279	20,910
Jeff Quinney	69	67	75	68	279	20,910
Heath Slocum	70	70	70	69	279	20,910
Matt Bettencourt	70	67	65	78	280	13,872
Tom Byrum	67	73	70	70	280	13,872
Kevin Na	69	69	70	72	280	13,872
Brett Quigley	71	69	66	74	280	13,872
Rory Sabbatini	67	69	70	74	280	13,872
Nick Watney	69	69	70	72	280	13,872
Mark Brooks	69	66	71	75	281	11,893.20
Mark Calcavecchia	69	69	73	70	281	11,893.20
Matt Harmon	68	68	70	75	281	11,893.20
Jonathan Kaye	70	67	73	71	281	11,893.20
Tom Pernice, Jr.	67	69	71	74	281	11,893.20
Stuart Appleby	69	67	74	72	282	11,271
Craig Barlow	70	69	73	70	282	11,271
Kent Jones	70	69	72	71	282	11,271
Corey Pavin	66	73	71	72	282	11,271
Chris Stroud	67	71	71	73	282	11,271
Charlie Wi	68	70	70	74	282	11,271
Guy Boros	70	70	73	70	283	10,710
David Duval	69	71	67	76	283	10,710
Steve Lowery	63	75	73	72	283	10,710
Rocco Mediate	68	69	79	67	283	10,710
Darron Stiles	68	71	72	72	283	10,710
Michael Bradley	70	65	76	73	284	10,302
Spencer Levin	70	70	72	72	284	10,302
Aron Price	69	68	74	73	284	10,302
Carlos Franco	71	69	75	70	285	10,098
Patrick Sheehan	69	71	74	74	288	9,996

WGC - Bridgestone Invitational

Firestone Country Club, South Course, Akron, Ohio
Par 35-35–70; 7,472 yards

August 6-9
purse, $8,500,000

	SCORES				TOTAL	MONEY
Tiger Woods	68	70	65	65	268	$1,400,000
Robert Allenby	68	69	69	66	272	665,000
Padraig Harrington	64	69	67	72	272	665,000
Hunter Mahan	68	69	70	66	273	332,000
Angel Cabrera	70	68	68	67	273	332,000
Steve Stricker	67	69	71	67	274	214,333
Stewart Cink	69	69	68	68	274	214,333
Miguel Angel Jimenez	68	72	66	68	274	214,333
Lee Westwood	69	71	70	65	275	160,000
Mike Weir	71	66	69	70	276	145,000
Chad Campbell	71	68	69	69	277	112,500
Oliver Wilson	69	69	68	71	277	112,500
Kenny Perry	69	71	66	71	277	112,500
Jerry Kelly	71	65	69	72	277	112,500

	SCORES			TOTAL	MONEY
Alvaro Quiros	72	65	72	69	278	91,125
Ian Poulter	67	74	67	70	278	91,125
Woody Austin	69	68	69	72	278	91,125
Zach Johnson	67	70	69	72	278	91,125
Y.E. Yang	72	72	69	66	279	83,000
Davis Love	72	66	73	68	279	83,000
Lucas Glover	69	69	68	73	279	83,000
Mathew Goggin	73	71	68	68	280	74,429
Dustin Johnson	70	71	70	69	280	74,429
Darren Clarke	71	70	70	69	280	74,429
Sergio Garcia	68	72	70	70	280	74,429
Pat Perez	70	72	66	72	280	74,429
Geoff Ogilvy	69	71	67	73	280	74,429
David Toms	69	69	69	73	280	74,429
Ernie Els	71	72	70	68	281	67,000
Justin Rose	75	68	69	69	281	67,000
Henrik Stenson	69	72	70	70	281	67,000
Charles Howell	71	72	68	70	281	67,000
Vijay Singh	70	73	67	71	281	67,000
Retief Goosen	71	67	71	72	281	67,000
Tim Clark	66	68	73	74	281	67,000
Anthony Kang	71	76	66	69	282	60,000
Camilo Villegas	70	70	72	70	282	60,000
Anthony Kim	72	68	71	71	282	60,000
Nick Watney	74	68	69	71	282	60,000
Prayad Marksaeng	66	70	72	74	282	60,000
Carl Pettersson	70	70	68	74	282	60,000
J.B. Holmes	70	72	65	75	282	60,000
Ross Fisher	70	71	70	72	283	56,000
Justin Leonard	70	71	70	73	284	55,000
K.J. Choi	74	72	73	66	285	51,500
Graeme McDowell	73	71	71	70	285	51,500
Anders Hansen	73	71	70	71	285	51,500
Luke Donald	70	72	69	74	285	51,500
Nick O'Hern	72	67	71	75	285	51,500
Rory Sabbatini	71	71	68	75	285	51,500
Danny Lee	68	73	75	70	286	46,500
Jim Furyk	73	71	73	69	286	46,500
Christian Cevaer	75	70	71	70	286	46,500
Adam Scott	78	67	71	70	286	46,500
Nick Dougherty	69	71	71	75	286	46,500
Stuart Appleby	74	68	69	75	286	46,500
Scott Verplank	66	69	75	76	286	46,500
Phil Mickelson	70	69	75	73	287	44,250
Boo Weekley	69	69	76	73	287	44,250
Martin Kaymer	72	74	72	70	288	42,750
Thongchai Jaidee	71	74	70	73	288	42,750
Trevor Immelman	70	70	74	74	288	42,750
Soren Hansen	69	71	70	78	288	42,750
Nathan Green	74	71	74	70	289	40,750
Ben Curtis	77	69	72	71	289	40,750
Cameron Beckman	71	71	72	75	289	40,750
Jeev Milkha Singh	70	71	72	76	289	40,750
Soren Kjeldsen	72	70	75	73	290	39,250
Rory McIlroy	75	70	71	74	290	39,250
Sean O'Hair	69	72	76	74	291	38,250
Gonzalo Fernandez-Castano	70	71	73	77	291	38,250
Shingo Katayama	74	72	73	73	292	37,500
Richard Sterne	72	73	71	77	293	37,000
Marc Turnesa	76	75	71	73	295	36,625
Gregory Havret	73	77	70	75	295	36,625
Lam Chih Bing	74	75	75	75	299	36,250
Shane Lowry	78	78	72	72	300	36,000

	SCORES			TOTAL	MONEY
Yuji Igarashi	74	83	73	72	302	35,750
Brian Gay	75	74	76	79	304	35,500

Legends Reno-Tahoe Open

Montreux Golf & Country Club, Reno, Nevada
Par 36-36–72; 7,472 yards

August 6-9
purse, $3,000,000

	SCORES				TOTAL	MONEY
John Rollins	70	62	67	72	271	$540,000
Martin Laird	72	67	66	69	274	264,000
Jeff Quinney	69	69	70	66	274	264,000
Joe Ogilvie	70	68	66	71	275	144,000
Alex Čejka	72	69	68	67	276	109,500
Kevin Na	71	70	67	68	276	109,500
Ryan Palmer	69	68	66	73	276	109,500
Rod Pampling	67	70	73	67	277	93,000
Robert Garrigus	69	67	71	71	278	75,000
J.J. Henry	72	71	65	70	278	75,000
Jonathan Kaye	68	69	73	68	278	75,000
Billy Mayfair	72	72	64	70	278	75,000
Rocco Mediate	70	68	68	72	278	75,000
J.P. Hayes	74	68	70	67	279	54,000
Greg Kraft	72	70	68	69	279	54,000
Marc Leishman	68	68	73	70	279	54,000
Jonathan Byrd	69	72	70	69	280	42,000
Glen Day	74	68	67	71	280	42,000
Matt Jones	71	70	71	68	280	42,000
Chris Riley	72	64	71	73	280	42,000
Charles Warren	75	69	68	68	280	42,000
Steve Elkington	69	71	73	68	281	30,000
Harrison Frazar	75	68	70	68	281	30,000
Tag Ridings	73	68	71	69	281	30,000
Mark Wilson	71	70	68	72	281	30,000
Wil Collins	70	70	72	70	282	20,850
Chris DiMarco	72	69	71	70	282	20,850
Ken Duke	72	72	70	68	282	20,850
Matt Kuchar	72	68	70	72	282	20,850
Steve Lowery	72	72	71	67	282	20,850
James Nitties	69	70	71	72	282	20,850
Ted Purdy	73	68	71	70	282	20,850
Vaughn Taylor	68	69	74	71	282	20,850
Francesco Molinari	73	71	71	68	283	14,828.58
Steve Flesch	71	69	72	71	283	14,828.57
Bob Heintz	73	69	70	71	283	14,828.57
Parker McLachlin	69	69	73	72	283	14,828.57
Shaun Micheel	69	65	73	76	283	14,828.57
Charl Schwartzel	73	70	70	70	283	14,828.57
Matt Weibring	72	70	70	71	283	14,828.57
Jeff Maggert	75	69	73	67	284	12,300
Rich Barcelo	68	69	71	77	285	10,500
Troy Matteson	71	66	76	72	285	10,500
Spike McRoy	71	72	70	72	285	10,500
Chez Reavie	71	71	71	72	285	10,500
Kevin Stadler	72	71	69	73	285	10,500
Michael Allen	72	69	74	71	286	8,070
Jay Delsing	73	71	71	71	286	8,070
Carlos Franco	70	72	77	67	286	8,070
Heath Slocum	73	70	74	69	286	8,070
Troy Kelly	70	71	71	75	287	7,290

	SCORES				TOTAL	MONEY
Nicholas Thompson	77	66	73	71	287	7,290
Matt Bettencourt	72	71	72	73	288	6,756
Kris Blanks	71	69	76	72	288	6,756
Mark Brooks	74	70	74	70	288	6,756
Tommy Gainey	72	70	71	75	288	6,756
Jason Gore	72	70	73	73	288	6,756
Scott McCarron	72	72	73	71	288	6,756
Scott Piercy	71	72	71	74	288	6,756
Patrick Sheehan	71	69	70	78	288	6,756
Brian Vranesh	74	70	73	71	288	6,756
Grant Waite	68	72	73	75	288	6,756
Brendon de Jonge	72	72	72	73	289	6,390
Spencer Levin	68	70	76	75	289	6,390
Tommy Armour	72	70	75	73	290	6,300
Tyler Aldridge	72	72	74	74	292	6,180
Derek Fathauer	75	69	75	73	292	6,180
Aron Price	73	70	75	74	292	6,180
Steve Pate	68	71	77	77	293	6,030
Kirk Triplett	74	70	71	78	293	6,030
Daniel Chopra	72	70	74	78	294	5,940
Eric Axley	70	71	73	81	295	5,880
J.L. Lewis	72	70	75	81	298	5,820

PGA Championship

Hazeltine National Golf Club, Chaska, Minnesota   August 13-16
Par 36-36–72; 7,674 yards   purse, $7,500,000

	SCORES				TOTAL	MONEY
Y.E. Yang	73	70	67	70	280	$1,350,000
Tiger Woods	67	70	71	75	283	810,000
Lee Westwood	70	72	73	70	285	435,000
Rory McIlroy	71	73	71	70	285	435,000
Lucas Glover	71	70	71	74	286	300,000
Martin Kaymer	73	70	71	73	287	233,125
Ernie Els	75	68	70	74	287	233,125
Soren Kjeldsen	70	73	70	74	287	233,125
Henrik Stenson	73	71	68	75	287	233,125
John Merrick	72	72	74	70	288	150,633
Dustin Johnson	72	73	73	70	288	150,633
Zach Johnson	74	73	70	71	288	150,633
Graeme McDowell	70	75	71	72	288	150,633
Francesco Molinari	74	73	69	72	288	150,633
Padraig Harrington	68	73	69	78	288	150,633
Hunter Mahan	69	75	74	71	289	106,567
Vijay Singh	69	72	75	73	289	106,567
Tim Clark	76	68	71	74	289	106,567
Ian Poulter	72	70	76	72	290	81,760
Oliver Wilson	74	72	72	72	290	81,760
Michael Allen	74	71	72	73	290	81,760
Corey Pavin	73	71	71	75	290	81,760
Ross Fisher	73	68	73	76	290	81,760
Robert Allenby	69	75	75	72	291	53,113
K.J. Choi	73	72	73	73	291	53,113
Ben Curtis	73	72	73	73	291	53,113
Scott McCarron	75	72	71	73	291	53,113
Stephen Ames	74	71	70	76	291	53,113
Brendan Jones	71	70	73	77	291	53,113
John Rollins	73	73	68	77	291	53,113
Alvaro Quiros	69	76	69	77	291	53,113

	SCORES				TOTAL	MONEY
Jeff Overton	72	74	75	71	292	40,388
Gonzalo Fernandez-Castano	70	77	73	72	292	40,388
Kevin Sutherland	73	72	74	73	292	40,388
Steve Flesch	74	73	69	76	292	40,388
Soren Hansen	72	76	74	71	293	31,736
Fred Couples	74	74	73	72	293	31,736
Woody Austin	73	73	73	74	293	31,736
Thongchai Jaidee	70	76	73	74	293	31,736
Miguel Angel Jimenez	75	73	71	74	293	31,736
Boo Weekley	74	74	71	74	293	31,736
David Toms	69	75	72	77	293	31,736
Geoff Ogilvy	71	73	78	72	294	21,113
Kenny Perry	74	70	78	72	294	21,113
Rich Beem	71	76	75	72	294	21,113
Luke Donald	71	77	73	73	294	21,113
Chad Campbell	74	73	73	74	294	21,113
Kevin Na	73	75	71	75	294	21,113
Charl Schwartzel	76	70	72	76	294	21,113
Ben Crane	70	75	72	77	294	21,113
Thomas Levet	72	75	76	72	295	16,260
Michael Sim	73	75	76	71	295	16,260
Camilo Villegas	73	73	76	73	295	16,260
Anthony Kim	73	74	71	77	295	16,260
Retief Goosen	77	71	70	77	295	16,260
Ryo Ishikawa	74	74	76	72	296	15,525
Charlie Wi	72	76	75	73	296	15,525
Bob Tway	72	76	74	74	296	15,525
Hiroyuki Fujita	71	74	73	78	296	15,525
Tom Lehman	72	74	76	75	297	15,000
Richard Green	75	73	74	75	297	15,000
John Mallinger	73	71	76	77	297	15,000
J.J. Henry	72	73	80	73	298	14,550
Nathan Green	72	75	76	75	298	14,550
Angel Cabrera	76	70	76	76	298	14,550
Jim Furyk	73	75	73	77	298	14,550
Paul Goydos	70	78	78	73	299	14,050
David Smail	75	73	75	76	299	14,050
Rory Sabbatini	74	70	78	77	299	14,050
Jeev Milkha Singh	74	73	74	78	299	14,050
Justin Leonard	73	75	73	78	299	14,050
Stewart Cink	73	73	72	81	299	14,050
Phil Mickelson	74	74	76	76	300	13,700
Greg Bisconti	75	72	78	76	301	13,600
Sean O'Hair	74	73	82	73	302	13,500
Bob Estes	74	74	77	78	303	13,300
Grant Sturgeon	73	71	80	79	303	13,300
Chris Wood	74	73	77	79	303	13,300
Alastair Forsyth	73	75	75	82	305	13,100

Out of Final 36 Holes

Bubba Watson	84	75	149	Rod Pampling	84	78	152
Davis Love	86	73	149	Brett Quigley	88	74	152
Ryan Palmer	85	74	149	Colin Montgomerie	85	78	153
Marc Turnesa	83	76	149	Jason Dufner	89	74	153
Scott Hebert	82	77	149	Shingo Katayama	85	78	153
Carl Pettersson	82	77	149	Pat Perez	84	79	153
Stuart Appleby	84	75	149	Michael Miles	82	81	153
Sergio Garcia	81	78	149	Darren Clarke	88	76	154
Mathew Goggin	69	80	149	Mark Sheftic	86	78	154
Justin Rose	83	76	149	Paul Azinger	84	80	154
Mark Brooks	84	75	149	Anthony Wall	88	76	154
Aaron Baddeley	86	73	149	Shaun Micheel	86	78	154

Anders Hansen	81	78	149	Will MacKenzie	84	71	155
Brandt Snedeker	85	74	149	Jerry Kelly	87	78	155
Ken Duke	83	77	150	Nick Dougherty	80	75	155
Brian Davis	86	74	150	Mike Weir	84	81	155
Charles Howell	87	73	150	Chris Starkjohann	87	79	156
Andres Romero	85	75	150	Cameron Beckman	88	78	156
Steve Elkington	85	75	150	Todd Lancaster	85	81	156
John Senden	83	77	150	Prayad Marksaeng	86	81	157
Mark Wilson	87	73	150	Mike Small	88	79	157
Charley Hoffman	86	74	150	Steve Schneiter	82	76	158
Briny Baird	86	74	150	Sam Arnold	81	77	158
Nick Watney	85	75	150	Kevin Streelman	86	82	158
Bo Van Pelt	81	79	150	Lee Rinker	88	81	159
Peter Hanson	84	76	150	Michael Campbell	80	79	159
Michael Bradley	80	80	150	Brian Gay	88	81	159
Matt Kuchar	87	73	150	Brian Gaffney	89	80	159
Louis Oosthuizen	82	78	150	Johan Edfors	87	83	160
Tim Weinhart	86	75	151	Tim Petrovic	86	84	160
Ryuji Imada	86	75	151	Adam Scott	82	79	161
Steve Marino	86	75	151	Eric Lippert	88	84	162
Steve Stricker	84	77	151	Ryan Benzel	81	83	164
Steve Webster	86	75	151	Mitch Lowe	84	80	164
D.J. Trahan	82	79	151	Robert Gaus	81	87	168
Craig Thomas	85	76	151	Kevin Roman	87	81	168
Scott Verplank	87	74	151	John Daly			WD
Keith Dicciani	82	80	152	J.B. Holmes			WD

Wyndham Championship

Sedgefield Country Club, Greensboro, North Carolina
Par 35-35–70; 7,130 yards

August 20-23
purse, $5,100,000

	SCORES				TOTAL	MONEY
Ryan Moore	64	65	70	65	264	$936,000
Jason Bohn	68	68	66	62	264	457,600
Kevin Stadler	69	63	66	66	264	457,600
(Moore defeated Bohn on first and Stadler on third playoff hole.)						
Sergio Garcia	67	64	64	70	265	249,600
Michael Allen	68	65	65	68	266	176,280
Fred Couples	66	66	67	67	266	176,280
Justin Rose	65	68	65	68	266	176,280
Brandt Snedeker	64	69	65	68	266	176,280
Kevin Sutherland	71	65	64	66	266	176,280
Bill Haas	62	69	66	70	267	130,000
Steve Marino	67	68	63	69	267	130,000
Chez Reavie	64	67	68	68	267	130,000
Glen Day	69	64	66	70	269	97,500
Charles Howell	68	67	71	63	269	97,500
Jeff Maggert	66	63	71	69	269	97,500
Chris Riley	66	63	66	74	269	97,500
Scott Gutschewski	71	67	64	68	270	68,045.72
David Mathis	70	68	65	67	270	68,045.72
Scott McCarron	66	69	68	67	270	68,045.72
Fredrik Jacobson	68	68	70	64	270	68,045.71
Marc Leishman	67	65	70	68	270	68,045.71
Bryce Molder	68	68	67	67	270	68,045.71
Jeev Milkha Singh	69	64	68	69	270	68,045.71
Jonathan Byrd	66	70	67	68	271	40,235
Ken Duke	66	67	71	67	271	40,235
Lucas Glover	66	68	67	70	271	40,235
Todd Hamilton	67	71	66	67	271	40,235
Tim Herron	68	67	67	69	271	40,235

	SCORES				TOTAL	MONEY
Tim Petrovic	66	68	69	68	271	40,235
Jeff Quinney	70	67	66	68	271	40,235
David Toms	69	68	67	67	271	40,235
Brian Davis	70	65	68	69	272	25,306.67
Jeff Klauk	69	68	66	69	272	25,306.67
Nick O'Hern	69	66	68	69	272	25,306.67
Greg Owen	68	70	66	68	272	25,306.67
Corey Pavin	69	68	66	69	272	25,306.67
Johnson Wagner	66	66	71	69	272	25,306.67
Boo Weekley	65	67	72	68	272	25,306.67
Matt Weibring	68	66	68	70	272	25,306.67
Greg Chalmers	70	68	66	68	272	25,306.66
Rocco Mediate	67	69	69	67	272	25,306.66
Patrick Sheehan	67	67	72	66	272	25,306.66
Darron Stiles	70	66	66	70	272	25,306.66
Matt Bettencourt	69	66	71	67	273	14,497.60
Alex Cejka	67	66	71	69	273	14,497.60
Robert Garrigus	68	67	69	69	273	14,497.60
J.P. Hayes	70	68	66	69	273	14,497.60
Bob Heintz	70	68	67	68	273	14,497.60
Richard S. Johnson	68	70	64	71	273	14,497.60
Joe Ogilvie	67	67	68	71	273	14,497.60
Rod Pampling	69	65	68	71	273	14,497.60
Kevin Streelman	65	68	71	69	273	14,497.60
Mark Wilson	70	65	68	70	273	14,497.60
Daniel Chopra	67	69	68	70	274	11,960
Aron Price	67	67	70	70	274	11,960
D.J. Trahan	67	70	66	71	274	11,960
Brad Faxon	68	68	67	72	275	11,492
Kent Jones	68	68	68	71	275	11,492
Fernando Mechereffe	69	65	70	71	275	11,492
Tom Pernice, Jr.	68	68	69	70	275	11,492
Scott Sterling	67	70	67	71	275	11,492
Bo Van Pelt	66	69	70	70	275	11,492
Rich Beem	67	67	68	74	276	11,128
Brad Adamonis	69	68	68	72	277	10,920
James Driscoll	70	68	67	72	277	10,920
Vaughn Taylor	67	70	68	72	277	10,920
Martin Laird	67	68	69	75	279	10,660
Carl Pettersson	70	65	71	73	279	10,660
Matt Jones	67	69	70	74	280	10,504
Billy Mayfair	69	69	68	75	281	10,400
Kris Blanks	74	62	71		207	9,984
Tommy Gainey	72	66	69		207	9,984
Charley Hoffman	68	70	69		207	9,984
Cliff Kresge	68	69	70		207	9,984
Danny Lee	68	70	69		207	9,984
Brett Quigley	69	69	69		207	9,984
Jimmy Walker	70	67	70		207	9,984
Harrison Frazar	71	67	70		208	9,464
J.J. Henry	69	64	75		208	9,464
Troy Matteson	68	70	70		208	9,464
*Justin Thomas	65	72	71		208	
John Daly	66	70	73		209	9,100
Steve Lowery	69	68	72		209	9,100
John Senden	69	64	76		209	9,100
Jay Williamson	67	70	72		209	9,100
Matthew Borchert	69	68	73		210	8,788
Davis Love	71	67	72		210	8,788

PGA Tour Playoffs for the FedExCup

The Barclays

Liberty National Golf Club, Jersey City, New Jersey
Par 36-35–71; 7,419 yards

August 27-30
purse, $7,500,000

	SCORES				TOTAL	MONEY
Heath Slocum	66	72	70	67	275	$1,350,000
Ernie Els	72	68	70	66	276	495,000
Padraig Harrington	67	75	67	67	276	495,000
Steve Stricker	69	70	68	69	276	495,000
Tiger Woods	70	72	67	67	276	495,000
Fredrik Jacobson	66	72	68	71	277	260,625
Nick Watney	68	73	69	67	277	260,625
Webb Simpson	66	68	72	72	278	232,500
Paul Goydos	65	71	68	75	279	202,500
Ian Poulter	67	72	70	70	279	202,500
Scott Verplank	73	70	68	68	279	202,500
Jason Day	70	73	70	67	280	157,500
Brian Gay	70	72	71	67	280	157,500
Brandt Snedeker	72	75	67	66	280	157,500
Robert Allenby	68	75	69	69	281	120,000
Jim Furyk	69	73	70	69	281	120,000
Dustin Johnson	70	74	73	64	281	120,000
Steve Marino	65	71	68	77	281	120,000
Greg Owen	71	74	65	71	281	120,000
Lee Janzen	68	75	70	69	282	87,375
Hunter Mahan	72	72	68	70	282	87,375
Troy Matteson	71	71	69	71	282	87,375
Y.E. Yang	71	72	68	71	282	87,375
Jonathan Byrd	72	74	67	70	283	63,937.50
Tim Clark	71	70	71	71	283	63,937.50
Bill Haas	72	70	69	72	283	63,937.50
Kevin Na	73	72	71	67	283	63,937.50
Stewart Cink	70	72	71	71	284	53,250
Zach Johnson	70	72	67	75	284	53,250
Matt Kuchar	68	73	68	75	284	53,250
Luke Donald	73	69	73	70	285	39,900
Sergio Garcia	65	76	74	70	285	39,900
Charley Hoffman	66	74	71	74	285	39,900
J.B. Holmes	73	73	69	70	285	39,900
Richard S. Johnson	68	71	73	73	285	39,900
Justin Leonard	68	75	72	70	285	39,900
D.A. Points	70	71	74	70	285	39,900
David Toms	67	75	71	72	285	39,900
Bo Van Pelt	70	74	66	75	285	39,900
Mike Weir	71	71	72	71	285	39,900
Fred Couples	71	76	69	70	286	27,750
Ben Crane	74	73	69	70	286	27,750
Rod Pampling	68	73	69	76	286	27,750
Justin Rose	73	72	69	72	286	27,750
Boo Weekley	75	70	74	67	286	27,750
Chad Campbell	72	75	70	70	287	20,400
Bob Estes	73	74	70	70	287	20,400
Davis Love	70	75	72	70	287	20,400
John Mallinger	74	72	70	71	287	20,400
Tim Petrovic	69	76	74	68	287	20,400
Chris Riley	72	75	70	70	287	20,400
Harrison Frazar	73	71	72	72	288	17,400

	SCORES				TOTAL	MONEY
Jerry Kelly	72	74	76	66	288	17,400
Anthony Kim	75	71	71	71	288	17,400
Phil Mickelson	70	75	74	69	288	17,400
Kenny Perry	71	75	71	71	288	17,400
Kevin Sutherland	69	76	75	68	288	17,400
Cameron Beckman	70	72	74	73	289	16,425
Daniel Chopra	77	69	71	72	289	16,425
James Nitties	71	75	73	70	289	16,425
Adam Scott	75	72	72	70	289	16,425
Kevin Streelman	68	78	69	74	289	16,425
Mark Wilson	72	75	72	70	289	16,425
Bill Lunde	70	73	71	76	290	15,750
John Senden	72	73	71	74	290	15,750
Vaughn Taylor	71	76	69	74	290	15,750
J.J. Henry	72	73	74	72	291	15,300
Brett Quigley	70	77	72	72	291	15,300
Charlie Wi	73	73	73	72	291	15,300
Retief Goosen	70	74	74	74	292	14,850
Charles Howell	76	70	72	74	292	14,850
Ryan Moore	68	78	77	69	292	14,850
Alex Cejka	71	72	77	73	293	14,400
Jeff Overton	72	71	77	73	293	14,400
John Rollins	71	73	73	76	293	14,400
Joe Ogilvie	73	72	78	76	299	14,100
Todd Hamilton	71	74	79	76	300	13,950

Deutsche Bank Championship

TPC Boston, Norton, Massachusetts
Par 36-35–71; 7,207 yards

September 4-7
purse, $7,500,000

	SCORES				TOTAL	MONEY
Steve Stricker	63	72	65	67	267	$1,350,000
Jason Dufner	66	69	68	65	268	660,000
Scott Verplank	65	68	68	67	268	660,000
Angel Cabrera	65	69	70	65	269	310,000
Padraig Harrington	67	67	67	68	269	310,000
Dustin Johnson	68	65	70	66	269	310,000
Geoff Ogilvy	66	68	70	66	270	251,250
Jim Furyk	63	67	73	68	271	217,500
Retief Goosen	65	67	68	71	271	217,500
Sean O'Hair	66	64	70	71	271	217,500
Jerry Kelly	66	69	67	70	272	165,000
Kevin Na	69	66	66	71	272	165,000
John Senden	69	64	70	69	272	165,000
Tiger Woods	70	67	72	63	272	165,000
Bill Haas	69	66	72	66	273	123,750
Matt Kuchar	65	71	68	69	273	123,750
Marc Leishman	70	62	72	69	273	123,750
Kevin Sutherland	68	65	69	71	273	123,750
Jason Day	68	66	72	68	274	94,125
Zach Johnson	68	71	67	68	274	94,125
Justin Leonard	65	68	72	69	274	94,125
Charlie Wi	71	64	72	67	274	94,125
Stephen Ames	67	73	69	66	275	72,000
Jeff Overton	69	66	70	70	275	72,000
Mike Weir	68	65	72	70	275	72,000
Sergio Garcia	70	71	68	67	276	60,000
Charley Hoffman	69	69	70	69	277	53,250
Steve Marino	70	68	71	68	277	53,250

	SCORES				TOTAL	MONEY
Phil Mickelson	71	68	72	66	277	53,250
Pat Perez	70	65	75	67	277	53,250
Mark Wilson	70	69	66	72	277	53,250
Jason Bohn	73	67	69	69	278	43,406.25
Brandt Snedeker	70	70	71	67	278	43,406.25
Kevin Streelman	70	68	71	69	278	43,406.25
Bubba Watson	68	71	71	68	278	43,406.25
Woody Austin	67	70	74	68	279	31,537.50
Greg Chalmers	67	70	74	68	279	31,537.50
Lucas Glover	69	68	72	70	279	31,537.50
Anthony Kim	71	70	67	71	279	31,537.50
Hunter Mahan	73	66	69	71	279	31,537.50
Troy Matteson	66	71	72	70	279	31,537.50
Scott McCarron	70	70	69	70	279	31,537.50
Bryce Molder	67	69	72	71	279	31,537.50
Scott Piercy	67	69	74	69	279	31,537.50
David Toms	67	69	73	70	279	31,537.50
Mathew Goggin	71	69	69	71	280	21,850
Kenny Perry	69	72	69	70	280	21,850
Nick Watney	71	69	71	69	280	21,850
Brian Davis	67	70	73	71	281	18,510
Bob Estes	70	71	71	69	281	18,510
Michael Letzig	68	68	73	72	281	18,510
Davis Love	69	70	71	71	281	18,510
D.A. Points	69	70	73	69	281	18,510
Luke Donald	69	72	72	69	282	17,025
Brian Gay	70	67	73	72	282	17,025
Charles Howell	68	69	71	74	282	17,025
Justin Rose	69	70	77	66	282	17,025
Vijay Singh	67	72	70	73	282	17,025
Boo Weekley	68	69	74	71	282	17,025
Daniel Chopra	67	71	73	72	283	16,500
Briny Baird	73	67	74	70	284	15,975
Jonathan Byrd	67	74	71	72	284	15,975
J.J. Henry	72	68	74	70	284	15,975
Greg Owen	69	69	73	73	284	15,975
Brett Quigley	70	69	71	74	284	15,975
Camilo Villegas	70	69	71	74	284	15,975
Y.E. Yang	71	70	69	75	285	15,450
J.B. Holmes	72	67	71	77	287	15,300
Ben Crane	73	68	78	69	288	15,000
Fredrik Jacobson	70	68	77	73	288	15,000
D.J. Trahan	71	70	76	71	288	15,000
Richard S. Johnson	68	72	75	74	289	14,700
Ryuji Imada	74	66	75	81	296	14,550

BMW Championship

Cog Hill Golf & Country Club, Lemont, Illinois
Par 35-36–71; 7,386 yards

September 10-13
purse, $7,500,000

	SCORES				TOTAL	MONEY
Tiger Woods	68	67	62	68	265	$1,350,000
Jim Furyk	70	70	67	66	273	660,000
Marc Leishman	67	69	68	69	273	660,000
Sean O'Hair	70	68	70	66	274	360,000
Zach Johnson	73	65	70	68	276	300,000
Sergio Garcia	71	68	68	71	278	260,625
Padraig Harrington	68	68	69	73	278	260,625
Kevin Na	72	72	65	70	279	225,000

	SCORES				TOTAL	MONEY
Camilo Villegas	68	74	71	66	279	225,000
Luke Donald	70	69	68	73	280	172,500
Bill Haas	71	68	71	70	280	172,500
Matt Kuchar	71	68	66	75	280	172,500
Brandt Snedeker	69	69	66	76	280	172,500
Mark Wilson	69	66	71	74	280	172,500
Stephen Ames	76	67	69	69	281	127,500
Bo Van Pelt	67	69	72	73	281	127,500
Bubba Watson	69	68	70	74	281	127,500
Steve Marino	66	77	68	71	282	108,750
Rory Sabbatini	66	70	72	74	282	108,750
Ian Poulter	69	71	68	75	283	90,500
John Senden	70	70	66	77	283	90,500
Mike Weir	72	69	71	71	283	90,500
Chad Campbell	70	70	72	72	284	64,875
Stewart Cink	72	74	70	68	284	64,875
Retief Goosen	72	72	71	69	284	64,875
Anthony Kim	69	69	72	74	284	64,875
Kevin Sutherland	75	67	67	75	284	64,875
David Toms	68	71	69	76	284	64,875
Robert Allenby	75	74	67	69	285	53,250
Tim Clark	78	69	73	66	286	43,593.75
Jason Dufner	74	70	69	73	286	43,593.75
Charles Howell	69	72	70	75	286	43,593.75
Fredrik Jacobson	72	71	70	73	286	43,593.75
Dustin Johnson	69	73	71	73	286	43,593.75
Phil Mickelson	71	69	70	76	286	43,593.75
Ryan Moore	71	72	75	68	286	43,593.75
Nick Watney	70	71	73	72	286	43,593.75
Ernie Els	75	67	77	68	287	30,750
Hunter Mahan	73	73	69	72	287	30,750
John Mallinger	68	76	69	74	287	30,750
John Rollins	73	65	74	75	287	30,750
Heath Slocum	70	69	72	76	287	30,750
Scott Verplank	70	75	72	70	287	30,750
Charlie Wi	71	73	72	71	287	30,750
Angel Cabrera	73	75	69	71	288	22,575
Ben Crane	75	69	76	68	288	22,575
Brian Davis	71	70	72	75	288	22,575
Kenny Perry	77	69	70	72	288	22,575
Jerry Kelly	76	73	69	71	289	18,712.50
Justin Leonard	73	69	75	72	289	18,712.50
Davis Love	74	77	67	71	289	18,712.50
Pat Perez	72	71	73	73	289	18,712.50
Nathan Green	73	74	73	70	290	17,550
Steve Stricker	72	73	68	77	290	17,550
Woody Austin	76	72	72	71	291	17,025
Brian Gay	73	71	75	72	291	17,025
Bryce Molder	70	73	71	77	291	17,025
Geoff Ogilvy	68	73	75	75	291	17,025
Jason Bohn	71	74	74	73	292	16,575
Jason Day	71	73	75	73	292	16,575
Jonathan Byrd	69	79	73	72	293	16,125
Charley Hoffman	73	71	72	77	293	16,125
Jeff Overton	72	68	75	78	293	16,125
Webb Simpson	70	74	73	76	293	16,125
Y.E. Yang	71	78	73	75	297	15,750
Lucas Glover	74	75	71	79	299	15,600
Paul Goydos	74	72	73	81	300	15,450
J.B. Holmes	78	73	72	81	304	15,300
Bob Estes	77				WD	

The Tour Championship

East Lake Golf Club, Atlanta, Georgia
Par 35-35–70; 7,154 yards

September 24-27
purse, $7,500,000

	SCORES				TOTAL	MONEY
Phil Mickelson	73	67	66	65	271	$1,350,000
Tiger Woods	67	68	69	70	274	810,000
Sean O'Hair	66	70	70	69	275	517,500
Padraig Harrington	67	69	71	69	276	330,000
Kenny Perry	72	66	64	74	276	330,000
Steve Stricker	70	72	66	69	277	270,000
Jim Furyk	72	68	71	67	278	247,500
Steve Marino	69	71	67	71	278	247,500
Ernie Els	71	66	71	71	279	225,000
Lucas Glover	68	71	72	69	280	202,500
Jerry Kelly	71	67	71	71	280	202,500
John Senden	70	70	69	71	280	202,500
Angel Cabrera	72	67	70	72	281	174,000
David Toms	74	66	70	71	281	174,000
Nick Watney	70	69	71	71	281	174,000
Zach Johnson	70	72	73	67	282	156,000
Geoff Ogilvy	75	73	64	70	282	156,000
Y.E. Yang	71	75	66	71	283	150,000
Stewart Cink	67	72	70	75	284	144,000
Jason Dufner	71	68	73	72	284	144,000
Heath Slocum	73	68	71	72	284	144,000
Scott Verplank	70	71	74	70	285	138,000
Retief Goosen	69	72	72	73	286	135,000
Hunter Mahan	71	73	72	71	287	132,000
Luke Donald	70	71	78	69	288	127,500
Mike Weir	72	72	70	74	288	127,500
Dustin Johnson	69	74	73	73	289	124,500
Brian Gay	72	72	76	72	292	122,250
Marc Leishman	70	74	70	78	292	122,250
Kevin Na	73	70	75	75	293	120,000

Final Standings – PGA Tour Playoffs for the FedExCup

RANK	NAME	FEDEXCUP POINTS	BONUS MONEY
1	Tiger Woods	4,000	$10,000,000
2	Phil Mickelson	2,920	3,000,000
3	Steve Stricker	2,750	2,000,000
4	Jim Furyk	2,437	1,500,000
5	Sean O'Hair	2,200	1,000,000
6	Zach Johnson	2,072	800,000
7	Padraig Harrington	2,050	700,000
8	Heath Slocum	1,855	600,000
9	Kenny Perry	1,450	550,000
10	Scott Verplank	1,245	500,000
11	Jason Dufner	855	300,000
12	Nick Watney	748	290,000
13	Geoff Ogilvy	712	280,000
14	Dustin Johnson	700	270,000
15	Steve Marino	697	250,000
16	Ernie Els	690	245,000
17	Lucas Glover	660	240,000
18	Retief Goosen	640	235,000
19	David Toms	608	230,000
20	Marc Leishman	592	225,000
21	Brian Gay	572	220,000

RANK	NAME	FEDEXCUP POINTS	BONUS MONEY
22	Jerry Kelly	570	215,000
23	Y.E. Yang	565	210,000
24	John Senden	560	205,000
25	Angel Cabrera	558	200,000
26	Kevin Na	545	195,000
27	Hunter Mahan	515	190,000
28	Stewart Cink	505	185,000
29	Mike Weir	467	180,000
30	Luke Donald	457	175,000

PGA Tour Fall Series

Turning Stone Resort Championship

Atunyote Golf Club, Verona, New York
Par 36-36–72; 7,482 yards
(Playoff completed on Monday—darkness.)

October 1-5
purse, $6,000,000

	SCORES				TOTAL	MONEY
Matt Kuchar	67	68	67	69	271	$1,080,000
Vaughn Taylor	67	67	71	66	271	648,000
(Kuchar defeated Taylor on sixth playoff hole.)						
Leif Olson	66	69	68	69	272	348,000
Tim Petrovic	66	71	68	67	272	348,000
John Senden	67	71	68	67	273	228,000
Jimmy Walker	68	69	70	66	273	228,000
Harrison Frazar	75	65	69	65	274	174,600
Rod Pampling	69	69	65	71	274	174,600
Webb Simpson	70	72	67	65	274	174,600
Jeev Milkha Singh	70	72	68	64	274	174,600
Bo Van Pelt	70	66	73	65	274	174,600
Peter Lonard	70	72	70	63	275	126,000
Scott Piercy	70	66	66	73	275	126,000
Rory Sabbatini	73	66	70	66	275	126,000
Fredrik Jacobson	69	67	69	71	276	102,000
Davis Love	71	70	66	69	276	102,000
Justin Rose	69	70	71	66	276	102,000
Scott Gutschewski	68	73	69	67	277	78,240
Charles Howell	69	72	67	69	277	78,240
James Nitties	70	72	67	68	277	78,240
Nick O'Hern	73	70	68	66	277	78,240
D.A. Points	69	69	69	70	277	78,240
Michael Allen	72	67	71	68	278	51,900
Jason Bohn	71	67	70	70	278	51,900
Jonathan Byrd	69	69	67	73	278	51,900
Robert Garrigus	69	70	72	67	278	51,900
Kevin Stadler	68	70	71	69	278	51,900
D.J. Trahan	73	70	69	66	278	51,900
Aaron Baddeley	70	68	73	68	279	38,150
Ben Curtis	71	68	72	68	279	38,150
Dustin Johnson	69	70	69	71	279	38,150
Colt Knost	73	70	68	68	279	38,150
Martin Laird	69	70	69	71	279	38,150
Matt Weibring	70	71	69	69	279	38,150

	SCORES				TOTAL	MONEY
Corey Pavin	71	71	70	68	280	28,328.58
Ben Crane	74	69	69	68	280	28,328.57
Mathias Gronberg	73	69	64	74	280	28,328.57
Will MacKenzie	71	67	70	72	280	28,328.57
Adam Scott	68	70	70	72	280	28,328.57
Brandt Snedeker	71	67	70	72	280	28,328.57
Nicholas Thompson	68	67	69	76	280	28,328.57
Arjun Atwal	71	69	72	69	281	21,000
K.J. Choi	70	70	71	70	281	21,000
Bill Haas	73	69	68	71	281	21,000
Matt Jones	68	72	70	71	281	21,000
Kevin Streelman	70	69	69	73	281	21,000
Greg Chalmers	73	68	69	72	282	15,225
Brendon de Jonge	72	70	71	69	282	15,225
Steve Elkington	73	70	69	70	282	15,225
Richard S. Johnson	72	70	69	71	282	15,225
Troy Matteson	70	67	75	70	282	15,225
Carl Pettersson	72	71	72	67	282	15,225
Chris Stroud	69	71	73	69	282	15,225
Mark Wilson	73	68	71	70	282	15,225
Ken Duke	68	73	69	73	283	13,620
Kent Jones	69	72	71	71	283	13,620
Michael Sim	75	66	72	70	283	13,620
Dean Wilson	73	69	73	68	283	13,620
Stuart Appleby	72	70	70	72	284	13,080
Alex Cejka	71	70	69	74	284	13,080
Ted Purdy	71	70	72	71	284	13,080
Aaron Watkins	74	66	75	69	284	13,080
Casey Wittenberg	70	71	71	72	284	13,080
Nathan Green	72	70	72	71	285	12,480
Bob Heintz	70	70	75	70	285	12,480
Jarrod Lyle	71	68	74	72	285	12,480
Andres Romero	75	67	69	74	285	12,480
Brian Vranesh	71	70	73	71	285	12,480
Matt Bettencourt	72	70	68	76	286	12,060
Aron Price	72	65	71	78	286	12,060
Joe Durant	72	70	72	73	287	11,820
Chris Riley	71	71	71	74	287	11,820
Mark Calcavecchia	72	71	70	75	288	11,580
Roland Thatcher	71	72	74	71	288	11,580
Jason Gore	71	72	74	75	292	11,400

The Presidents Cup

Harding Park Golf Course, San Francisco, California   October 8-11
Par 35-35–70; 7,171 yards

FIRST DAY
Foursomes

Anthony Kim and Phil Mickelson (US) defeated Mike Weir and Tim Clark, 3 and 2.
Adam Scott and Ernie Els (Int'l) defeated Hunter Mahan and Sean O'Hair, 2 and 1.
Vijay Singh and Robert Allenby (Int'l) defeated Lucas Glover and Stewart Cink, 1 up.
Kenny Perry and Zach Johnson (US) defeated Angel Cabrera and Camilo Villegas, 2 up.
Tiger Woods and Steve Stricker (US) defeated Geoff Ogilvy and Ryo Ishikawa, 6 and 4.
Retief Goosen and Y.E. Yang (Int'l) halved with Jim Furyk and Justin Leonard.

POINTS: United States 3½, International 2½

SECOND DAY
Fourballs

Mickelson and Leonard (US) defeated Goosen and Scott, 3 and 2.
Els and Weir (Int'l) defeated Furyk and Kim, 2 up.
Ishikawa and Yang (Int'l) defeated Perry and O'Hair, 4 and 3.
Singh and Clark (Int'l) defeated Glover and Cink, 1 up.
Johnson and Mahan (US) defeated Allenby and Villegas, 2 and 1.
Stricker and Woods (US) defeated Ogilvy and Cabrera, 5 and 3.

POINTS: United States 6½, International 5½

THIRD DAY
Morning Foursomes

Mickelson and O'Hair (US) defeated Goosen and Villegas, 5 and 3.
Leonard and Furyk (US) defeated Els and Scott, 4 and 2.
Allenby and Singh (Int'l) halved with Cink and Mahan.
Woods and Stricker (US) defeated Weir and Clark, 1 up.
Yang and Ishikawa (Int'l) defeated Perry and Johnson, 3 and 2.

THIRD DAY
Afternoon Fourballs

Kim and Furyk (US) defeated Cabrera and Scott, 2 up.
Ogilvy and Allenby (Int'l) defeated Cink and Glover, 2 and 1.
Els and Weir (Int'l) defeated Johnson and Leonard, 5 and 3.
Woods and Stricker (US) defeated Ishikawa and Yang, 4 and 2.
Singh and Clark (Int'l) halved with Mickelson and O'Hair.

POINTS: United States 12½, International 9½

FINAL DAY
Singles

Mahan (US) defeated Villegas, 2 and 1.
Cink (US) defeated Scott, 4 and 3.
Weir (Int'l) halved with Leonard.
Kim (US) defeated Allenby, 5 and 3.
Ogilvy (Int'l) defeated Stricker, 2 and 1.
O'Hair (US) defeated Els, 6 and 4.
Ishikawa (Int'l) defeated Perry, 2 and 1.
Clark (Int'l) defeated Johnson, 4 and 3.
Woods (US) defeated Yang, 6 and 5.
Singh (Int'l) halved with Glover.
Mickelson (US) defeated Goosen, 2 and 1.
Cabrera (Int'l) defeated Furyk, 4 and 3.

TOTAL POINTS: U.S. 19½, International 14½

Justin Timberlake Shriners Hospitals for Children Open

TPC Summerlin, Las Vegas, Nevada
Par 35-36–71; 7,223 yards

October 15-18
purse, $4,200,000

	SCORES				TOTAL	MONEY
Martin Laird	63	67	67	68	265	$756,000
Chad Campbell	67	62	67	69	265	369,600
George McNeill	66	69	63	67	265	369,600
(Laird defeated Campbell on second and McNeill on third playoff hole.)						
Jim Furyk	64	67	73	62	266	184,800
Jeff Klauk	65	67	66	68	266	184,800

	SCORES				TOTAL	MONEY
Charley Hoffman	66	69	64	68	267	151,200
Rickie Fowler	67	64	69	68	268	113,700
Matt Kuchar	66	64	72	66	268	113,700
Ryan Moore	67	63	70	68	268	113,700
Tom Pernice, Jr.	62	69	68	69	268	113,700
Tim Petrovic	65	68	72	63	268	113,700
Andres Romero	68	69	67	64	268	113,700
D.J. Trahan	71	65	65	67	268	113,700
Jason Bohn	66	67	65	71	269	71,400
Greg Chalmers	66	67	67	69	269	71,400
Hunter Mahan	70	63	67	69	269	71,400
Scott Piercy	64	67	65	73	269	71,400
Kevin Streelman	69	67	66	67	269	71,400
Ben Crane	68	65	69	68	270	50,904
Bob Heintz	63	67	68	72	270	50,904
Chris Stroud	69	68	70	63	270	50,904
Matt Weibring	68	68	68	66	270	50,904
Dean Wilson	67	70	66	67	270	50,904
Alex Cejka	66	68	70	67	271	36,960
Fredrik Jacobson	66	69	68	68	271	36,960
Brandt Snedeker	69	66	67	69	271	36,960
Rich Beem	69	64	75	64	272	26,230.91
Tim Clark	69	66	70	67	272	26,230.91
Chris DiMarco	69	68	68	67	272	26,230.91
Brian Gay	66	72	65	69	272	26,230.91
Tim Herron	74	63	66	69	272	26,230.91
Bill Lunde	68	70	68	66	272	26,230.91
Troy Matteson	62	67	70	73	272	26,230.91
Billy Mayfair	68	67	68	69	272	26,230.91
Kyle Stanley	67	69	67	69	272	26,230.91
Roland Thatcher	68	67	70	67	272	26,230.91
Kirk Triplett	65	69	66	72	272	26,230.90
Aaron Baddeley	66	69	69	69	273	16,800
Steve Elkington	70	67	70	66	273	16,800
John Mallinger	72	62	68	71	273	16,800
Parker McLachlin	67	65	70	71	273	16,800
D.A. Points	69	66	69	69	273	16,800
Tag Ridings	70	65	70	68	273	16,800
Chris Riley	73	64	67	69	273	16,800
Mark Wilson	67	66	68	72	273	16,800
J.J. Henry	71	63	74	66	274	13,020
Daniel Chopra	69	68	72	66	275	10,788
Robert Garrigus	65	70	68	72	275	10,788
Mathew Goggin	71	65	71	68	275	10,788
Ernie Gonzalez	75	63	69	68	275	10,788
Nathan Green	68	66	72	69	275	10,788
Greg Owen	66	68	70	71	275	10,788
Johnson Wagner	68	68	73	66	275	10,788
Charles Howell	69	68	69	70	276	9,618
Jerry Kelly	66	69	69	72	276	9,618
Spencer Levin	62	71	68	75	276	9,618
Steve Lowery	68	70	70	68	276	9,618
Stuart Appleby	70	67	70	70	277	9,282
Ryuji Imada	70	66	70	71	277	9,282
Ted Purdy	67	70	71	69	277	9,282
Bo Van Pelt	68	65	72	72	277	9,282
Harrison Frazar	69	69	71	69	278	8,904
Jeff Quinney	68	70	71	69	278	8,904
Jeev Milkha Singh	67	65	75	71	278	8,904
David Toms	66	71	71	70	278	8,904
Jay Williamson	66	71	72	69	278	8,904
Briny Baird	65	71	74	69	279	8,610
Carl Pettersson	69	69	72	69	279	8,610

	SCORES				TOTAL	MONEY
Tommy Armour	68	70	68	75	281	8,442
Cameron Beckman	70	67	73	71	281	8,442
Nick O'Hern	67	69	75	71	282	8,316
Brian Bateman	69	68	72	75	284	8,232
Glen Day	70	68	78	69	285	8,148

Frys.com Open

Grayhawk Golf Club, Raptor Course, Scottsdale, Arizona
Par 35-35–70; 7,125 yards

October 22-25
purse, $5,000,000

	SCORES				TOTAL	MONEY
Troy Matteson	72	61	61	68	262	$900,000
Rickie Fowler	65	64	69	64	262	440,000
Jamie Lovemark	69	64	65	64	262	440,000
(Matteson defeated Fowler and Lovemark on second playoff hole.)						
Tim Clark	68	64	65	67	264	220,000
Bill Lunde	66	67	65	66	264	220,000
Bryce Molder	67	65	70	63	265	173,750
Mike Weir	66	67	71	61	265	173,750
Alex Cejka	67	67	69	64	267	135,000
Ryan Moore	66	65	67	69	267	135,000
Heath Slocum	64	68	68	67	267	135,000
Chris Stroud	67	65	65	70	267	135,000
Nicholas Thompson	66	68	65	68	267	135,000
Ben Crane	66	67	67	68	268	78,100
Tim Herron	68	68	66	66	268	78,100
Martin Laird	67	72	62	67	268	78,100
Justin Leonard	66	64	69	69	268	78,100
Rocco Mediate	67	66	70	65	268	78,100
Nick O'Hern	63	68	67	70	268	78,100
Pat Perez	66	67	68	67	268	78,100
Tom Pernice, Jr.	67	69	68	64	268	78,100
Tim Petrovic	66	71	66	65	268	78,100
Webb Simpson	68	65	64	71	268	78,100
Stephen Ames	66	66	68	69	269	43,250
Robert Garrigus	70	65	65	69	269	43,250
D.A. Points	65	71	67	66	269	43,250
Chez Reavie	70	67	68	64	269	43,250
Chris Riley	70	67	67	65	269	43,250
Andres Romero	68	68	70	63	269	43,250
Greg Owen	65	64	73	68	270	33,250
Carl Pettersson	70	67	65	68	270	33,250
Brett Quigley	68	70	68	64	270	33,250
Bo Van Pelt	67	68	67	68	270	33,250
Chad Campbell	68	67	68	68	271	26,416.67
J.J. Henry	69	67	70	65	271	26,416.67
Spencer Levin	66	71	66	68	271	26,416.67
Arron Oberholser	68	69	66	68	271	26,416.67
Nathan Green	69	66	66	70	271	26,416.66
Bob Heintz	64	73	69	65	271	26,416.66
Ricky Barnes	66	70	71	65	272	18,500
Mark Calcavecchia	71	68	67	66	272	18,500
Steve Elkington	68	71	68	65	272	18,500
Scott McCarron	67	67	70	68	272	18,500
John Merrick	72	65	66	69	272	18,500
Ted Purdy	72	67	64	69	272	18,500
Rory Sabbatini	65	72	68	67	272	18,500
Peter Tomasulo	68	65	70	69	272	18,500
D.J. Trahan	69	64	71	68	272	18,500

	SCORES				TOTAL	MONEY
Kent Jones	71	67	67	68	273	13,350
Ryan Palmer	69	66	68	70	273	13,350
Paul Goydos	66	70	70	68	274	12,060
Matt Jones	67	68	71	68	274	12,060
Jeff Klauk	66	70	70	68	274	12,060
Billy Mayfair	66	70	68	70	274	12,060
Charlie Wi	69	69	68	68	274	12,060
Stuart Appleby	70	65	70	70	275	11,000
Jonathan Byrd	70	66	66	73	275	11,000
Greg Chalmers	70	69	67	69	275	11,000
Brian Davis	70	67	70	68	275	11,000
Chris DiMarco	68	69	69	69	275	11,000
Steve Flesch	69	68	67	71	275	11,000
Jason Gore	70	68	68	69	275	11,000
Tom Lehman	68	65	72	70	275	11,000
John Mallinger	70	68	66	71	275	11,000
Vaughn Taylor	69	66	71	69	275	11,000
Brian Vranesh	68	66	69	72	275	11,000
Matt Bettencourt	69	70	65	72	276	10,300
Fred Couples	67	69	68	72	276	10,300
Mark Wilson	68	67	67	74	276	10,300
Colt Knost	71	66	69	72	278	10,050
Steve Lowery	67	67	76	68	278	10,050
Peter Lonard	69	68	70	72	279	9,850
Johnson Wagner	68	70	72	69	279	9,850
Parker McLachlin	70	68	72	71	281	9,700
Glen Day	70	68	74	70	282	9,600
Brad Faxon	69	69	74	72	284	9,500
Michael Bradley	70	69	73	73	285	9,400
Aron Price	70	69	75	72	286	9,300

Children's Miracle Network Classic

Walt Disney World Resort, Lake Buena Vista, Florida
Magnolia Course: Par 36-36–72; 7,516 yards
Palm Course: Par 36-36–72; 6,957 yards

November 12-15
purse, $4,700,000

	SCORES				TOTAL	MONEY
Stephen Ames	69	70	67	64	270	$846,000
Justin Leonard	68	64	71	67	270	413,600
George McNeill	68	66	69	67	270	413,600
(Ames defeated Leonard on first and McNeill on second playoff hole.)						
Nick O'Hern	68	70	66	67	271	206,800
Justin Rose	65	69	69	68	271	206,800
Mathias Gronberg	68	69	66	69	272	169,200
Brian Davis	72	69	68	64	273	151,575
D.A. Points	71	70	67	65	273	151,575
Zach Johnson	67	70	69	68	274	131,600
Carl Pettersson	71	66	67	70	274	131,600
Jonathan Byrd	70	68	69	68	275	103,400
Bill Haas	68	69	69	69	275	103,400
Jeff Overton	70	68	68	69	275	103,400
Nicholas Thompson	72	69	68	66	275	103,400
Chris DiMarco	68	68	71	69	276	72,850
Tom Lehman	71	67	69	69	276	72,850
Will MacKenzie	67	72	66	71	276	72,850
Joe Ogilvie	70	69	67	70	276	72,850
Jimmy Walker	69	70	68	69	276	72,850
Matt Weibring	68	68	70	70	276	72,850
Kent Jones	70	68	71	68	277	52,640

	SCORES				TOTAL	MONEY
Greg Owen	66	71	70	70	277	52,640
Johnson Wagner	70	68	72	67	277	52,640
Rich Beem	69	73	68	68	278	40,067.50
Ben Crane	71	70	67	70	278	40,067.50
Jeff Maggert	71	69	68	70	278	40,067.50
John Rollins	70	71	67	70	278	40,067.50
Todd Hamilton	74	68	70	67	279	34,780
Charles Howell	70	70	71	69	280	29,240.72
Spencer Levin	71	68	71	70	280	29,240.72
Patrick Sheehan	70	70	69	71	280	29,240.72
Michael Bradley	70	71	72	67	280	29,240.71
Daniel Chopra	68	71	74	67	280	29,240.71
Chez Reavie	68	69	71	72	280	29,240.71
David Toms	73	67	69	71	280	29,240.71
Cameron Beckman	70	68	73	70	281	22,618.75
Brian Gay	68	71	73	69	281	22,618.75
Jeff Quinney	70	71	71	69	281	22,618.75
Jay Williamson	70	71	70	70	281	22,618.75
Jason Bohn	72	70	71	69	282	17,390
Rickie Fowler	66	75	69	72	282	17,390
Tim Herron	70	66	74	72	282	17,390
Ryan Palmer	71	71	70	70	282	17,390
Chris Riley	70	71	73	68	282	17,390
Bo Van Pelt	70	72	69	71	282	17,390
Dean Wilson	75	65	72	70	282	17,390
Ricky Barnes	73	69	71	70	283	12,426.80
Brendon de Jonge	70	72	72	69	283	12,426.80
Harrison Frazar	71	70	69	73	283	12,426.80
Brett Quigley	71	68	70	74	283	12,426.80
Kevin Streelman	70	71	73	69	283	12,426.80
Jeff Klauk	69	72	74	69	284	10,798.25
James Oh	71	71	70	72	284	10,798.25
Tom Pernice, Jr.	69	67	74	74	284	10,798.25
Rod Perry	69	70	73	72	284	10,798.25
Darron Stiles	71	69	71	73	284	10,798.25
D.J. Trahan	70	71	74	69	284	10,798.25
Charles Warren	70	70	72	72	284	10,798.25
Casey Wittenberg	66	71	77	70	284	10,798.25
Kris Blanks	67	70	72	76	285	10,199
Fredrik Jacobson	72	69	69	75	285	10,199
Richard S. Johnson	69	72	71	73	285	10,199
Brandt Snedeker	70	70	72	73	285	10,199
Corey Pavin	69	71	73	73	286	9,823
Aron Price	71	70	71	74	286	9,823
Rick Price	67	73	73	73	286	9,823
Marc Turnesa	72	70	71	73	286	9,823
Briny Baird	71	71	69	76	287	9,588
Peter Lonard	69	70	77	73	289	9,494
Ken Duke	71	71	75	73	290	9,353
Ted Purdy	69	73	74	74	290	9,353

Special Events

Tavistock Cup

Lake Nona Golf & Country Club, Orlando, Florida   March 16-17
Par 36-36–72; 7,215 yards   purse, $3,500,000

FIRST DAY
(Team better ball; 2 points for win, 1 point for tie)

Tiger Woods and John Cook (Isleworth) defeated Chris DiMarco and Henrik Stenson (Lake Nona), 63-64.
Mark O'Meara and Darren Clarke (Isle) defeated Ben Curtis and Mark McNulty (LN), 62-65.
Ian Poulter and Justin Rose (LN) defeated Stuart Appleby and Robert Allenby (Isle), 62-63.
Charles Howell and Nick O'Hern (Isle) defeated Ernie Els and Trevor Immelman (LN), 62-65.
Retief Goosen and Graeme McDowell (LN) defeated J.B. Holmes and Daniel Chopra (Isle), 60-64.

POINTS: Lake Nona 4, Isleworth 6

SECOND DAY
(Singles versus both players on other team; 1 point for win, ½ point for tie)

Immelman 69 and Curtis 69 (LN) versus O'Meara 70 and Cook 71 (Isle).
Goosen 70 and McDowell 66 (LN) versus Appleby 68 and O'Hern 71 (Isle).
Rose 68 and DiMarco 70 (LN) versus Allenby 73 and Holmes 70 (Isle).
Els 69 and McNulty 71 (LN) versus Clarke 68 and Chopra 71 (Isle).
Poulter 69 and Stenson 76 (LN) versus Woods 69 and Howell 69 (Isle).

POINTS: Lake Nona 13, Isleworth 7
TWO-DAY TOTAL: Lake Nona 17, Isleworth 13

(Each member of the Lake Nona team received $100,000; each member of the Isleworth team received $50,000. McDowell received $300,000, and Rose, Appleby and Clarke received $83,333 each for the lowest scores on the second day.)

CVS/Caremark Charity Classic

Rhode Island Country Club, Barrington, Rhode Island   June 22-23
Par 36-35–71; 6,688 yards   purse $1,350,000

	SCORES		TOTAL	MONEY (Team)
David Toms/Nick Price	66	60	126	$300,000
Laura Diaz/Matt Kuchar	69	60	129	200,000
Boo Weekley/Chad Campbell	66	64	130	170,000
Zach Johnson/Nick Watney	67	64	131	140,000
Brett Quigley/Dana Quigley	66	65	131	140,000
Brad Faxon/Juli Inkster	69	63	132	117,500
Billy Andrade/Helen Alfredsson	65	67	132	117,500
Brad Adamonis/Brittany Lincicome	66	67	133	107,500
Davis Love/Morgan Pressel	67	66	133	107,500
Peter Jacobsen/Natalie Gulbis	70	69	139	100,000

PGA Grand Slam of Golf

Port Royal Golf Course, Southampton Parish, Bermuda
Par 36-35–71; 6,824 yards

October 20-21
purse, $1,350,000

	SCORES		TOTAL	MONEY
Lucas Glover	65	66	131	$600,000
Angel Cabrera	70	66	136	300,000
Stewart Cink	67	70	137	250,000
Y.E. Yang	71	70	141	200,000

Kiwi Challenge

Cape Kidnappers Golf Resort, Hawke's Bay, New Zealand
Par 71

November 11-12
purse, $2,000,000

	SCORES		TOTAL	MONEY
Anthony Kim	71	66	137	$1,000,000
Sean O'Hair	68	69	137	500,000
(Kim defeated O'Hair on first playoff hole.)				
Hunter Mahan	73	67	140	300,000
Camilo Villegas	69	72	141	200,000

Callaway Golf Pebble Beach Invitational

Pebble Beach GL: Par 36-36–72; 6,828 yards
Spyglass Hills GC: Par 36-36–72; 6,953 yards
Del Monte GC: Par 36-36–72; 6,365 yards
Pebble Beach, California

November 19-22
purse, $300,000

	SCORES				TOTAL	MONEY
Mark Brooks	70	70	69	67	276	$60,000
D.A. Points	68	70	75	65	278	25,000
Rickie Fowler	68	74	67	69	278	25,000
Bill Lunde	69	75	70	66	280	10,000
Scott Simpson	70	74	68	68	280	10,000
Craig Bowden	71	68	73	69	281	8,000
Matt Bettencourt	67	71	72	71	281	8,000
Cameron Beckman	71	71	72	68	282	6,300
Mina Harigae	70	74	70	68	282	6,300
Shane Bertsch	70	72	71	69	282	6,300
Bryce Molder	69	71	70	72	282	6,300
Parker McLachlin	69	74	72	68	283	5,000
Chez Reavie	73	75	68	68	284	4,250
Dan Forsman	70	73	71	70	284	4,250
Tom Purtzer	67	81	71	66	285	4,100
Manny Villegas	75	69	75	67	286	3,700
Jim Thorpe	67	72	74	73	286	3,700
Russ Cochran	74	76	68	69	287	3,300
John Cook	66	77	74	70	287	3,300
Jeff Gove	70	80	71	68	289	2,900
Nicholas Thompson	70	74	74	71	289	2,900
Olin Browne	66	76	72	75	289	2,900
Justin Bolli	71	78	70	71	290	2,600
Mark Murphy	72	72	73	73	290	2,600
J.J. Henry	71	74	70	75	290	2,600
Tom Gillis	71	78	71	71	291	2,300
Dave Schultz	73	74	73	71	291	2,300

	SCORES				TOTAL	MONEY
Matt Every	71	78	74	69	292	2,200
Kevin Sutherland	72	72	75	73	292	2,200
Rob Grube	71	74	78	71	294	2,050
Andrew Magee	74	77	72	71	294	2,050
Tommy Armour	71	80	70	73	294	2,050
Cody Eberl	69	73	76	76	294	2,050
Brock Mackenzie	70	80	70	75	295	2,000
Morris Hatalsky	70	72	74	79	295	2,000
Mike Small	75	76	71	74	296	1,980
Rocco Mediate	71	76	70	80	297	1,960
Perry Parker	76	72	72	78	298	1,940
Steve Wheatcroft	73	73	74	81	301	1,920
Cary Cozby	72	79	72	85	308	1,900
Aron Price	71	79	69		WD	1,800

Chevron World Challenge

Sherwood Country Club, Thousand Oaks, California
Par 36-36–72; 7,027 yards

December 3-6
purse, $5,750,000

	SCORES				TOTAL	MONEY
Jim Furyk	70	71	67	67	275	$1,350,000
Graeme McDowell	71	69	66	70	276	800,000
Padraig Harrington	69	68	70	70	277	450,000
Lee Westwood	71	67	69	70	277	450,000
Stewart Cink	70	73	68	68	279	243,750
Zach Johnson	68	70	74	67	279	243,750
Sean O'Hair	71	67	71	70	279	243,750
Ian Poulter	68	69	71	71	279	243,750
Y.E. Yang	70	65	71	74	280	195,000
Steve Stricker	71	74	71	65	281	190,000
Paul Casey	75	69	74	64	282	182,500
Kenny Perry	72	65	72	73	282	182,500
Lucas Glover	74	67	70	75	286	175,000
Martin Kaymer	73	72	72	71	288	162,500
Anthony Kim	71	74	73	70	288	162,500
Camilo Villegas	73	69	74	72	288	162,500
Mike Weir	73	70	73	72	288	162,500
Justin Leonard	72	74	72	73	291	150,000

The Shark Shootout

Tiburon Golf Course, Naples, Florida
Par 36-36–72; 7,288 yards

December 11-13
purse, $3,000,000

	SCORES			TOTAL	MONEY (Each)
Jerry Kelly/Steve Stricker	-6	-7	-13	-26	$375,000
J.B. Holmes/Kenny Perry	-2	-10	-13	-25	161,666
Justin Leonard/Scott Verplank	-6	-6	-13	-25	161,666
Chad Campbell/Tim Clark	-5	-5	-15	-25	161,666
Steve Flesch/Dustin Johnson	-5	-7	-11	-23	91,250
Ross Fisher/Ian Poulter	-4	-6	-13	-23	91,250
Chris DiMarco/Rickie Fowler	-3	-7	-10	-20	82,500
Mark Calcavecchia/Brian Gay	-3	-3	-12	-18	77,500
Graeme McDowell/Boo Weekley	-1	-7	-10	-18	77,500
Brad Faxon/Matt Kuchar	1	-10	-9	-18	77,500
Zach Johnson/Nick Price	-1	-7	-8	-16	72,500
George McNeill/Jeff Sluman	-3	-2	-10	-15	70,000

Nationwide Tour

Panama Digicel Championship

Panama Golf Club, Panama City, Panama
Par 35-35–70; 7,102 yards

February 5-8
purse, US$600,000

	SCORES				TOTAL	MONEY
Vance Veazey	67	69	68	69	273	US$108,000
Garrett Willis	70	69	68	66	273	64,800
(Veazey defeated Willis on second playoff hole.)						
Jeff Gove	69	68	68	70	275	40,800
Henrik Bjornstad	69	67	71	69	276	26,400
Jim Herman	67	70	68	71	276	26,400
Rich Barcelo	69	69	71	68	277	19,425
Bryan DeCorso	73	68	66	70	277	19,425
Rafael Gomez	67	68	71	71	277	19,425
Len Mattiace	72	69	64	72	277	19,425
Scott Gardiner	69	71	73	65	278	15,000
John Riegger	72	68	70	68	278	15,000
Dustin Risdon	70	71	67	70	278	15,000
Camilo Benedetti	68	69	68	74	279	10,600
Clodomiro Carranza	67	76	67	69	279	10,600
Justin Hicks	71	72	64	72	279	10,600
Skip Kendall	67	69	74	69	279	10,600
Neal Lancaster	70	68	70	71	279	10,600
Chris Smith	68	70	68	73	279	10,600
Jeff Gallagher	74	68	67	71	280	7,530
Kevin Johnson	67	70	70	73	280	7,530
Esteban Toledo	68	70	68	74	280	7,530
Brennan Webb	72	69	67	72	280	7,530
D.J. Brigman	69	71	68	73	281	5,280
Matt Every	70	73	73	65	281	5,280
Steve LeBrun	74	69	67	71	281	5,280
Jon Mills	71	69	71	70	281	5,280
Alex Prugh	69	69	71	72	281	5,280
Michael Sim	68	71	69	73	281	5,280

Moonah Classic

See Australasian Tour chapter.

HSBC New Zealand PGA Championship

See Australasian Tour chapter.

Michael Hill New Zealand Open

See Australasian Tour chapter.

Chitimacha Louisiana Open

Le Triomphe Country Club, Broussard, Louisiana
Par 36-35–71; 7,004 yards

March 26-29
purse, $550,000

	SCORES				TOTAL	MONEY
Bubba Dickerson	71	64	69	70	274	$99,000
Brian Vranesh	70	69	69	66	274	59,400
(Dickerson defeated Vranesh on first playoff hole.)						
Chris Anderson	70	71	67	67	275	23,512.50
Matt Bettencourt	66	71	73	65	275	23,512.50
Jonas Blixt	68	72	66	69	275	23,512.50
Matthew Borchert	68	69	70	68	275	23,512.50
Geoffrey Sisk	71	65	72	67	275	23,512.50
Vance Veazey	70	69	67	69	275	23,512.50
Drew Laning	68	66	72	70	276	13,200
Bob May	68	70	71	67	276	13,200
Garth Mulroy	67	68	72	69	276	13,200
Michael Sims	64	72	71	69	276	13,200
Scott Sterling	67	69	68	72	276	13,200
Darron Stiles	66	71	71	68	276	13,200
Steve Allan	70	68	67	72	277	7,988.75
Kris Blanks	69	72	69	67	277	7,988.75
Miguel Angel Carballo	68	70	70	69	277	7,988.75
Scott Gardiner	70	67	71	69	277	7,988.75
Neal Lancaster	67	68	72	70	277	7,988.75
Ted Schulz	69	68	70	70	277	7,988.75
Roger Tambellini	69	71	68	69	277	7,988.75
Brennan Webb	73	66	69	69	277	7,988.75
Guy Boros	69	70	69	70	278	4,972
David Branshaw	72	66	69	71	278	4,972
Chad Collins	70	67	71	70	278	4,972
Josh Teater	69	66	74	69	278	4,972
Esteban Toledo	70	68	71	69	278	4,972

Stonebrae Classic

TPC San Francisco Bay at Stonebrae, Hayward, California
Par 36-35–71; 7,188 yards

April 2-5
purse, $600,000

	SCORES				TOTAL	MONEY
Michael Sim	71	64	67	64	266	$108,000
John Kimbell	69	70	65	68	272	52,800
Cameron Percy	73	67	64	68	272	52,800
Matt Every	69	63	71	71	274	26,400
Martin Piller	74	67	63	70	274	26,400
Craig Barlow	68	72	67	69	276	19,425
Andrew Buckle	71	72	67	66	276	19,425
Nick Flanagan	72	68	67	69	276	19,425
Jeff Gallagher	70	68	69	69	276	19,425
Ryan Armour	71	69	65	72	277	16,200
David Branshaw	72	70	68	68	278	13,200
Wil Collins	71	69	70	68	278	13,200
Chad Ginn	67	72	65	74	278	13,200
Craig Kanada	71	71	65	71	278	13,200
Doug LaBelle	73	70	65	71	279	9,900
Dustin Risdon	69	73	62	75	279	9,900
Brian Smock	68	69	69	73	279	9,900
Omar Uresti	73	71	68	67	279	9,900
Todd Demsey	65	71	71	73	280	8,400

		SCORES			TOTAL	MONEY
Jeff Brehaut	74	68	68	71	281	6,500
Josh Broadaway	73	67	72	69	281	6,500
Brad Elder	72	71	67	71	281	6,500
Bob May	72	68	72	69	281	6,500
Clay Ogden	69	69	70	73	281	6,500
Andrew Scott	71	66	71	73	281	6,500

Athens Regional Foundation Classic

Jennings Mill Country Club, Athens, Georgia
Par 36-36–72; 7,004 yards

April 16-19
purse, $550,000

		SCORES			TOTAL	MONEY
Patrick Sheehan	66	69	71	68	274	$99,000
Michael Sim	68	71	72	63	274	59,400
(Sheehan defeated Sim on first playoff hole.)						
Darron Stiles	71	68	70	66	275	37,400
Rich Barcelo	66	73	67	71	277	20,735
Bob Burns	74	63	67	73	277	20,735
Garth Mulroy	70	73	69	65	277	20,735
John Riegger	73	69	69	66	277	20,735
Daniel Summerhays	71	70	67	69	277	20,735
Skip Kendall	68	70	69	71	278	15,400
Cameron Percy	69	72	66	71	278	15,400
Blake Adams	73	66	70	70	279	13,200
Tjaart van der Walt	70	69	69	71	279	13,200
Bobby Clampett	72	71	69	68	280	11,000
Paul Gow	69	69	71	71	280	11,000
Jeff Brehaut	69	71	72	69	281	8,800
Joe Daley	68	73	70	70	281	8,800
Kevin Johnson	71	71	70	69	281	8,800
Kevin Kisner	66	75	70	70	281	8,800
Michael Sims	69	69	72	71	281	8,800
Oskar Bergman	68	73	72	69	282	6,407.50
Brad Elder	70	72	66	74	282	6,407.50
Jeff Gallagher	71	70	69	72	282	6,407.50
Garrett Willis	72	72	72	66	282	6,407.50
Jonas Blixt	72	72	71	68	283	4,546.67
Neal Lancaster	68	72	71	72	283	4,546.67
Jon Mills	74	69	72	68	283	4,546.67
Martin Piller	70	71	72	70	283	4,546.67
David Branshaw	67	73	70	73	283	4,546.66
Len Mattiace	70	73	73	67	283	4,546.66

South Georgia Classic

Kinderlou Forest Golf Club, Valdosta, Georgia
Par 36-36–72; 7,781 yards

April 23-26
purse, $625,000

		SCORES			TOTAL	MONEY
Garth Mulroy	69	66	71	69	275	$112,500
Chris Tidland	69	69	68	70	276	67,500
Garrett Willis	68	70	73	67	278	42,500
Kyle Reifers	70	67	72	70	279	27,500
Chris Smith	69	68	74	68	279	27,500
Marco Dawson	68	69	73	70	280	20,937.50
Bradley Iles	70	69	71	70	280	20,937.50

	SCORES				TOTAL	MONEY
Jon Mills	68	72	72	68	280	20,937.50
Oskar Bergman	70	71	68	72	281	15,000
Paul Claxton	69	71	69	72	281	15,000
Jay Delsing	68	70	71	72	281	15,000
Kevin Johnson	67	71	72	71	281	15,000
Won Joon Lee	71	67	71	72	281	15,000
Dustin White	72	69	70	70	281	15,000
Rich Barcelo	69	70	73	70	282	10,000
Henrik Bjornstad	71	64	73	74	282	10,000
Chad Ginn	72	71	71	68	282	10,000
Tyler Leon	71	68	69	74	282	10,000
Michael Sims	68	71	72	71	282	10,000
Andrew Buckle	69	70	71	73	283	7,541.67
Kevin Kisner	69	70	74	70	283	7,541.67
Guy Boros	70	69	71	73	283	7,541.66
Brad Elder	69	68	73	74	284	5,500
Tripp Isenhour	72	69	71	72	284	5,500
Andrew Johnson	71	72	72	69	284	5,500
J.J. Killeen	68	70	72	74	284	5,500
Jin Park	70	70	71	73	284	5,500
Brian Smock	69	72	72	71	284	5,500

BMW Charity Pro-Am

Thornblade Club, Greer, South Carolina:
Par 35-36–71; 6,669 yards
Bright's Creek Golf Club, Mill Spring, North Carolina
Par 36-36–72; 7,435 yards
Carolina Country Club, Spartanburg, South Carolina
Par 36-36–72; 6,877 yards

May 14-17
purse, $700,000

	SCORES				TOTAL	MONEY
Michael Sim	68	65	62	69	264	$126,000
Fabian Gomez	63	68	67	66	264	75,600
(Sim defeated Gomez on first playoff hole.)						
Blake Adams	66	68	64	69	267	40,600
D.J. Brigman	66	67	70	64	267	40,600
Dustin Bray	64	76	65	63	268	26,600
Jeff Gove	65	65	70	68	268	26,600
Geoffrey Sisk	66	69	67	67	269	22,575
Roger Tambellini	66	68	71	64	269	22,575
Chris Anderson	63	72	68	67	270	18,200
Garrett Osborn	67	70	67	66	270	18,200
Alex Prugh	71	69	65	65	270	18,200
B.J. Staten	69	67	65	69	270	18,200
Ryan Armour	69	72	63	67	271	12,366.67
Craig Bowden	65	70	72	64	271	12,366.67
Hunter Haas	68	69	68	66	271	12,366.67
Scott Parel	71	62	74	64	271	12,366.67
Chris Tidland	71	67	65	68	271	12,366.66
Steve Wheatcroft	68	67	68	68	271	12,366.66
Rich Barcelo	72	68	67	65	272	8,190
Scott Dunlap	65	67	72	68	272	8,190
Tom Gillis	67	69	68	68	272	8,190
Kevin Johnson	67	69	70	66	272	8,190
Jason Knutzon	70	65	72	65	272	8,190
Esteban Toledo	65	72	70	65	272	8,190
Alex Aragon	66	70	71	66	273	5,040
Steve Friesen	72	66	69	66	273	5,040
Craig Kanada	68	70	67	68	273	5,040

	SCORES				TOTAL	MONEY
Ian Leggatt	67	68	69	69	273	5,040
Garth Mulroy	72	67	67	67	273	5,040
Cameron Percy	69	74	64	66	273	5,040
Chris Smith	66	67	71	69	273	5,040
Tjaart van der Walt	66	70	70	67	273	5,040
Vance Veazey	68	67	71	67	273	5,040
Jhonattan Vegas	70	64	72	67	273	5,040

Rex Hospital Open

TPC Wakefield Plantation, Raleigh, North Carolina
Par 35-36–71; 7,257 yards

May 28-31
purse, $525,000

	SCORES				TOTAL	MONEY
Kevin Johnson	65	69	65	67	266	$94,500
Jeff Gallagher	64	69	69	64	266	56,700
(Johnson defeated Gallagher on first playoff hole.)						
David Mathis	66	69	67	67	269	35,700
Chris Baryla	72	67	63	68	270	21,700
D.J. Brigman	68	67	68	67	270	21,700
Chad Collins	68	70	64	68	270	21,700
Jeff Gove	71	67	65	68	271	15,815.63
Skip Kendall	65	70	70	66	271	15,815.63
Jim McGovern	70	66	65	70	271	15,815.62
Cameron Percy	70	66	66	69	271	15,815.62
Justin Bolli	69	68	67	68	272	12,075
Josh Broadaway	64	70	68	70	272	12,075
Justin Hicks	69	65	69	69	272	12,075
Scott Gardiner	70	63	76	64	273	7,886.67
Fabian Gomez	72	66	67	68	273	7,886.67
Hunter Haas	67	68	69	69	273	7,886.67
Ian Leggatt	72	66	68	67	273	7,886.67
Major Manning	72	63	71	67	273	7,886.67
Andrew Svoboda	68	71	65	69	273	7,886.67
Chad Ginn	66	68	69	70	273	7,886.66
Josh Teater	67	71	64	71	273	7,886.66
Grant Waite	68	67	67	71	273	7,886.66
Adam Bland	66	70	66	72	274	4,746
Gary Christian	67	68	68	71	274	4,746
Tom Gillis	66	71	67	70	274	4,746
Garth Mulroy	72	67	66	69	274	4,746
Roger Tambellini	69	69	68	68	274	4,746

Melwood Prince George's County Open

The Country Club at Woodmore, Mitchellville, Maryland
Par 36-36–72; 7,059 yards

June 4-7
purse $675,000

	SCORES				TOTAL	MONEY
Mathias Gronberg	68	69	67	65	269	$121,500
Justin Bolli	69	68	68	70	275	59,400
Robert Damron	72	66	70	67	275	59,400
Esteban Toledo	70	68	72	66	276	32,400
Oskar Bergman	69	66	69	73	277	25,650
Tom Scherrer	66	68	71	72	277	25,650
Jeff Curl	72	64	72	70	278	21,037.50
David Peoples	69	69	67	73	278	21,037.50

		SCORES			TOTAL	MONEY
Cameron Percy	64	68	74	72	278	21,037.50
Ryan Armour	69	69	70	71	279	17,550
Michael Sim	66	71	69	73	279	17,550
Craig Bowden	70	69	70	71	280	12,065.63
Gary Christian	71	68	70	71	280	12,065.63
Marco Dawson	71	69	69	71	280	12,065.63
Matt Hansen	72	66	70	72	280	12,065.63
Chris Baryla	73	67	71	69	280	12,065.62
Adam Bland	68	68	73	71	280	12,065.62
Kevin Johnson	69	68	70	73	280	12,065.62
J.L. Lewis	72	69	69	70	280	12,065.62
Michael Clark	74	67	70	70	281	7,077.86
Gavin Coles	71	67	71	72	281	7,077.86
Brent Delahoussaye	70	69	71	71	281	7,077.86
David McKenzie	70	69	70	72	281	7,077.86
Sal Spallone	69	70	71	71	281	7,077.86
Todd Demsey	65	72	72	72	281	7,077.85
Chad Ginn	70	67	69	75	281	7,077.85

Knoxville Open

Fox Den Country Club, Knoxville, Tennessee
Par 36-36–72; 7,110 yards

June 11-14
purse, $525,000

		SCORES			TOTAL	MONEY
Kevin Johnson	67	65	68	68	268	$94,500
Bradley Iles	67	68	70	63	268	56,700
(Johnson defeated Iles on second playoff hole.)						
Blake Adams	63	70	71	65	269	30,450
David McKenzie	65	65	67	72	269	30,450
Jason Schultz	69	70	65	66	270	19,950
Tjaart van der Walt	65	68	71	66	270	19,950
Dustin Risdon	67	64	73	68	272	17,587.50
Alex Prugh	67	68	73	65	273	15,225
Brian Stuard	69	69	66	69	273	15,225
Esteban Toledo	68	69	68	68	273	15,225
Ryan Armour	67	69	72	66	274	10,762.50
Keoke Cotner	72	67	70	65	274	10,762.50
David Morland	66	69	70	69	274	10,762.50
Chris Nallen	70	66	70	68	274	10,762.50
Cameron Percy	67	70	70	67	274	10,762.50
John Riegger	70	65	70	69	274	10,762.50
Alex Aragon	69	65	69	72	275	7,612.50
Craig Bowden	69	67	67	72	275	7,612.50
Scott Dunlap	66	73	67	69	275	7,612.50
Tom Scherrer	65	70	71	69	275	7,612.50
Henrik Bjornstad	67	71	70	68	276	5,130
Gary Christian	67	65	73	71	276	5,130
Marco Dawson	67	67	75	67	276	5,130
Tom Gillis	68	66	74	68	276	5,130
Jeff Gove	67	70	72	67	276	5,130
Dave Schultz	69	70	69	68	276	5,130
Josh Teater	69	69	69	69	276	5,130

Fort Smith Classic

Hardscrabble Country Club, Fort Smith, Arkansas
Par 35-35–70; 6,783 yards

June 18-21
purse, $550,000

	SCORES				TOTAL	MONEY
Jason Enloe	64	65	71	65	265	$99,000
Chris Tidland	67	62	68	68	265	59,400
(Enloe defeated Tidland on first playoff hole.)						
Justin Bolli	68	66	65	67	266	26,400
Gavin Coles	63	66	70	67	266	26,400
Wil Collins	67	69	66	64	266	26,400
Brian Smock	68	66	66	66	266	26,400
Josh Broadaway	67	68	68	64	267	18,425
Alex Prugh	70	65	68	65	268	16,500
Phil Tataurangi	62	71	66	69	268	16,500
Andrew Buckle	67	68	65	69	269	14,850
Omar Uresti	70	66	69	65	270	13,750
Kris Blanks	67	65	71	68	271	10,450
Jonas Blixt	70	66	74	61	271	10,450
Matt Every	72	68	66	65	271	10,450
Scott Gardiner	67	68	70	66	271	10,450
Doug LaBelle	68	68	70	65	271	10,450
Dustin Risdon	65	68	67	71	271	10,450
Ian Leggatt	68	72	67	65	272	8,250
Keoke Cotner	67	72	69	65	273	7,425
Jim Rutledge	70	69	67	67	273	7,425
Jay Delsing	68	68	68	70	274	6,160
Trevor Dodds	71	67	68	68	274	6,160
Fran Quinn	69	67	69	69	274	6,160
Hunter Haas	68	70	68	69	275	4,431.43
Garrett Osborn	67	67	73	68	275	4,431.43
Michael Putnam	71	69	68	67	275	4,431.43
John Riegger	66	71	69	69	275	4,431.43
Jason Schultz	70	70	66	69	275	4,431.43
Brendan Steele	70	70	65	70	275	4,431.43
Bob May	70	68	67	70	275	4,431.42

Nationwide Tour Players Cup

Pete Dye Golf Club, Bridgeport, West Virginia
Par 36-36–72; 7,308 yards

June 25-28
purse, $600,000

	SCORES				TOTAL	MONEY
Tom Gillis	71	66	66	70	273	$108,000
Cameron Percy	70	69	69	68	276	52,800
Roger Tambellini	69	70	69	68	276	52,800
Jonas Blixt	69	72	67	69	277	28,800
Chris Baryla	72	66	68	72	278	22,800
Ron Whittaker	67	71	68	72	278	22,800
Craig Barlow	71	65	71	72	279	18,075
Jeff Gove	69	67	68	75	279	18,075
Michael Putnam	72	69	70	68	279	18,075
Kyle Reifers	70	70	64	75	279	18,075
Bob May	69	69	71	71	280	15,000
Todd Demsey	72	69	69	71	281	13,800
Blake Adams	72	68	71	71	282	10,920
Won Joon Lee	73	68	64	77	282	10,920
Brian Stuard	67	71	71	73	282	10,920
Josh Teater	69	70	71	72	282	10,920

	SCORES			TOTAL	MONEY
Jhonattan Vegas	72	69	65	76	282	10,920
Michael Arnaud	71	70	67	75	283	8,100
Fabian Gomez	69	69	72	73	283	8,100
Han Seung-su	71	68	66	78	283	8,100
David Peoples	69	65	72	77	283	8,100
Garrett Osborn	70	72	70	72	284	6,480
Adam Short	71	71	75	67	284	6,480
Chris Anderson	69	72	73	71	285	4,536
Scott Brown	74	69	71	71	285	4,536
Jay Delsing	70	70	73	72	285	4,536
Chris Kirk	72	70	69	74	285	4,536
Jon Mills	69	70	69	77	285	4,536
Jim Rutledge	70	73	71	71	285	4,536
Sal Spallone	75	68	71	71	285	4,536
Andrew Svoboda	70	69	71	75	285	4,536
Chris Tidland	74	69	68	74	285	4,536
Esteban Toledo	69	71	71	74	285	4,536

Ford Wayne Gretzky Classic

Georgian Bay Club, Clarksburg, Ontario
Par 35-36–72; 7,139 yards
Raven Golf Club at Lora Bay, Thornbury, Ontario
Par: 36-35–71; 7,112

July 9-12
purse, $800,099

	SCORES			TOTAL	MONEY
Roger Tambellini	64	66	66	69	265	$144,017.82
Blake Adams	68	68	64	69	269	86,410.69
Craig Barlow	67	69	68	66	270	54,406.73
Chris Anderson	67	68	67	69	271	33,070.76
D.J. Brigman	66	70	70	65	271	33,070.76
Garth Mulroy	67	66	65	73	271	33,070.76
Craig Bowden	65	71	67	69	272	25,803.20
David Branshaw	67	66	67	72	272	25,803.19
Jon Mills	70	69	66	68	273	21,602.68
Josh Broadaway	67	69	67	70	273	21,602.67
Dustin Risdon	68	69	66	70	273	21,602.67
Justin Bolli	66	68	72	68	274	16,202.01
Cameron Percy	69	69	67	69	274	16,202.01
Kyle Reifers	61	72	71	70	274	16,202
Brian Stuard	68	68	67	71	274	16,202
Brenden Pappas	65	72	70	68	275	13,601.68
Dustin White	72	66	70	68	276	12,001.49
Alex Prugh	70	67	67	72	276	12,001.48
Danny Wax	67	70	68	71	276	12,001.48
Jason Enloe	64	69	74	70	277	8,993.12
Ryan Armour	67	71	68	71	277	8,993.11
Bubba Dickerson	67	69	68	73	277	8,993.11
John Kimbell	69	68	69	71	277	8,993.11
Joseph Sykora	69	67	71	70	277	8,993.11
Byron Smith	70	66	72	70	278	6,240.78
Paul Claxton	67	66	71	74	278	6,240.77
Gavin Coles	70	68	67	73	278	6,240.77
J.J. Killeen	65	69	74	70	278	6,240.77
Fran Quinn	68	69	69	72	278	6,240.77
Matthew Richardson	68	67	70	73	278	6,240.77

Cox Classic

Champions Run, Omaha, Nebraska
Par 35-36–71; 7,145 yards

July 23-26
purse, $725,000

	SCORES				TOTAL	MONEY
Rich Barcelo	69	62	68	65	264	$130,500
Tom Gillis	65	67	67	66	265	78,300
Brent Delahoussaye	64	67	68	67	266	49,300
J.J. Killeen	63	66	71	67	267	34,800
Jonas Blixt	64	65	69	70	268	26,462.50
Matt Every	62	68	70	68	268	26,462.50
Michael Sim	66	65	67	70	268	26,462.50
Blake Adams	67	65	69	68	269	22,475
David Branshaw	66	68	70	66	270	17,400
Fabian Gomez	66	70	65	69	270	17,400
Billy Horschel	67	66	72	65	270	17,400
Brian Smock	64	67	72	67	270	17,400
Chris Tidland	70	65	65	70	270	17,400
Steve Wheatcroft	67	67	68	68	270	17,400
Camilo Benedetti	67	66	70	68	271	11,962.50
Tadd Fujikawa	64	67	69	71	271	11,962.50
Justin Hicks	68	65	70	68	271	11,962.50
Garrett Osborn	69	64	70	68	271	11,962.50
Chad Collins	66	69	72	65	272	8,482.50
Stuart Deane	69	68	66	69	272	8,482.50
Bubba Dickerson	67	66	68	71	272	8,482.50
Scott Gardiner	68	66	72	66	272	8,482.50
Derek Lamely	68	69	67	68	272	8,482.50
Geoffrey Sisk	69	63	72	68	272	8,482.50
Jon Mills	69	66	71	67	273	5,530.72
Kyle Reifers	65	68	73	67	273	5,530.72
B.J. Staten	68	67	71	67	273	5,530.72
Andrew Buckle	68	66	71	68	273	5,530.71
Hunter Haas	68	65	68	72	273	5,530.71
Bob May	67	66	69	71	273	5,530.71
Garrett Willis	68	66	71	68	273	5,530.71

Nationwide Children's Hospital Invitational

The OSU Golf Club, Scarlet Course, Columbus, Ohio
Par 36-35–71; 7,141 yards

July 30-August 2
purse, $775,000

	SCORES				TOTAL	MONEY
Derek Lamely	71	69	68	65	273	$139,500
*Rickie Fowler	69	66	70	68	273	
(Lamely defeated Fowler on second playoff hole.)						
Tom Gillis	69	68	69	71	277	57,866.67
Dave Schultz	67	68	65	77	277	57,866.67
Gavin Coles	68	68	67	74	277	57,866.66
Blake Adams	71	70	69	68	278	29,450
Steve Wheatcroft	67	71	69	71	278	29,450
Justin Hicks	72	69	71	67	279	24,993.75
Chris Tidland	68	68	70	73	279	24,993.75
*Morgan Hoffmann	70	69	70	70	279	
Scott Gardiner	72	70	69	69	280	18,600
Jeff Gove	70	71	71	68	280	18,600
Won Joon Lee	70	72	71	67	280	18,600
Dustin Risdon	74	66	69	71	280	18,600
Jim Rutledge	69	70	74	67	280	18,600

	SCORES				TOTAL	MONEY
Jhonattan Vegas	70	70	70	70	280	18,600
Jonas Blixt	73	68	71	69	281	11,625
Chad Collins	69	70	73	69	281	11,625
Joe Daley	68	67	71	75	281	11,625
Jon Mills	68	74	68	71	281	11,625
Scott Parel	67	70	70	74	281	11,625
Alex Prugh	72	70	71	68	281	11,625
B.J. Staten	71	69	75	66	281	11,625
Justin Bolli	66	74	72	70	282	7,502
Brad Elder	71	71	66	74	282	7,502
Brian Stuard	71	71	71	69	282	7,502
Andrew Svoboda	71	70	71	70	282	7,502
Phil Tataurangi	67	70	72	73	282	7,502

Preferred Health Systems Wichita Open

Crestview Country Club, Wichita, Kansas
Par 35-36–71; 6,886 yards

August 6-9
purse, $550,000

	SCORES				TOTAL	MONEY
Chris Tidland	67	68	68	65	268	$99,000
Chad Collins	66	67	66	70	269	48,400
Dave Schultz	66	69	67	67	269	48,400
Steven Taylor	65	70	72	64	271	24,200
Jhonattan Vegas	64	67	66	74	271	24,200
Paul Claxton	70	68	68	66	272	19,800
Blake Adams	66	69	67	71	273	17,737.50
Chris Baryla	67	69	73	64	273	17,737.50
Henrik Bjornstad	67	67	72	68	274	13,750
Brandon Brown	68	71	66	69	274	13,750
Scott Gardiner	69	69	70	66	274	13,750
Alex Prugh	68	69	69	68	274	13,750
Michael Sims	68	70	69	67	274	13,750
David Hearn	69	67	72	67	275	9,900
Justin Hicks	65	68	71	71	275	9,900
Joey Lamielle	64	73	71	67	275	9,900
Alistair Presnell	69	70	71	66	276	7,443.34
Jerod Turner	69	71	68	68	276	7,443.34
Miguel Angel Carballo	66	71	68	71	276	7,443.33
Stuart Deane	65	69	72	70	276	7,443.33
Jim Herman	68	71	67	70	276	7,443.33
Luke List	70	67	67	72	276	7,443.33
Will Dodson	67	71	70	69	277	5,280
David McKenzie	65	71	69	72	277	5,280
Fran Quinn	69	71	69	68	277	5,280

Price Cutter Charity Championship

Highland Springs Country Club, Springfield, Missouri
Par 36-36–72; 7,060 yards

August 13-16
purse, $625,000

	SCORES				TOTAL	MONEY
Justin Bolli	65	67	69	66	267	$112,500
Chad Collins	64	64	70	70	268	55,000
Derek Lamely	65	66	72	65	268	55,000
John M. Kelly	68	64	69	68	269	30,000
Henrik Bjornstad	65	68	67	70	270	22,812.50

	SCORES				TOTAL	MONEY
Garrett Osborn	71	63	67	69	270	22,812.50
Dave Schultz	71	63	64	72	270	22,812.50
Camilo Benedetti	66	70	66	69	271	18,750
Scott Gardiner	66	64	71	70	271	18,750
Craig Barlow	68	65	71	68	272	14,375
David Branshaw	65	69	70	68	272	14,375
Paul Gow	66	72	67	67	272	14,375
Chris Nallen	65	67	69	71	272	14,375
Brendan Steele	65	65	72	70	272	14,375
Jay Delsing	67	68	67	71	273	10,312.50
Will Dodson	67	69	66	71	273	10,312.50
Dustin Risdon	66	69	71	67	273	10,312.50
Garrett Willis	67	68	69	69	273	10,312.50
Bubba Dickerson	68	68	70	68	274	7,843.75
J.J. Killeen	69	67	70	68	274	7,843.75
Brian Stuard	68	67	69	70	274	7,843.75
Roger Tambellini	65	67	72	70	274	7,843.75
Ben Bates	68	71	66	70	275	5,650
Paul Claxton	66	69	70	70	275	5,650
David McKenzie	68	66	71	70	275	5,650
Troy Merritt	69	67	71	68	275	5,650
Ron Whittaker	70	65	68	72	275	5,650

Christmas in October Classic

Nicklaus Golf Club at LionsGate, Overland Park, Kansas
Par 36-35–71; 7,251 yards

August 20-23
purse, $625,000

	SCORES				TOTAL	MONEY
Michael Sim	65	67	65	67	264	$112,500
Josh Teater	67	70	63	66	266	67,500
Michael Clark	68	69	68	63	268	42,500
Blake Adams	66	69	68	66	269	30,000
Chad Collins	70	65	68	67	270	25,000
Hunter Haas	65	70	66	70	271	20,937.50
Sal Spallone	70	67	67	67	271	20,937.50
Steve Wheatcroft	66	67	67	71	271	20,937.50
Brad Fritsch	70	68	69	65	272	16,250
Tom Gillis	64	68	68	72	272	16,250
Jon Mills	71	69	67	65	272	16,250
Justin Smith	69	72	66	65	272	16,250
Jeff Brehaut	66	71	69	67	273	12,083.34
Scott Gardiner	69	68	68	68	273	12,083.33
David McKenzie	68	69	67	69	273	12,083.33
Craig Bowden	68	70	70	66	274	8,767.86
Joe Daley	68	66	70	70	274	8,767.86
Jason Knutzon	69	69	71	65	274	8,767.86
Brian Stuard	69	70	68	67	274	8,767.86
Chris Tidland	69	69	68	68	274	8,767.86
Paul Claxton	63	69	72	70	274	8,767.85
Garrett Osborn	65	73	65	71	274	8,767.85
Steven Alker	70	70	71	64	275	5,097.23
Tjaart van der Walt	68	72	70	65	275	5,097.23
Henrik Bjornstad	71	70	66	68	275	5,097.22
Gary Christian	70	68	68	69	275	5,097.22
Gavin Coles	68	73	67	67	275	5,097.22
Matt Hendrix	67	70	68	70	275	5,097.22
Bob Sowards	69	70	66	70	275	5,097.22
Chris Thompson	72	68	68	67	275	5,097.22
Kyle Thompson	69	69	66	71	275	5,097.22

Northeast Pennsylvania Classic

Elmhurst Country Club, Moscow, Pennsylvania
Par 35-35–70; 6,810 yards

August 27-30
purse, $525,000

		SCORES			TOTAL	MONEY
Gary Christian	68	70	63	64	265	$94,500
Mathias Gronberg	68	68	65	64	265	56,700
(Christian defeated Gronberg on ninth playoff hole.)						
Henrik Bjornstad	66	67	67	67	267	35,700
Chris Tidland	69	66	65	69	269	25,200
Tom Gillis	68	71	65	66	270	16,045.32
Garrett Osborn	66	68	69	67	270	16,045.32
Guy Boros	67	64	68	71	270	16,045.31
Kevin Chappell	67	66	68	69	270	16,045.31
David McKenzie	69	65	69	67	270	16,045.31
Peter Tomasulo	67	69	65	69	270	16,045.31
Omar Uresti	69	69	65	67	270	16,045.31
Ron Whittaker	71	66	66	67	270	16,045.31
Craig Bowden	70	70	66	65	271	9,000
Martin Flores	66	71	64	70	271	9,000
Matt Hendrix	70	69	68	64	271	9,000
Cameron Percy	73	65	68	65	271	9,000
Patrick Sheehan	67	71	68	65	271	9,000
Roger Tambellini	72	67	66	66	271	9,000
Garrett Willis	71	68	67	65	271	9,000
Ryan Armour	66	72	68	66	272	5,505
Justin Bolli	67	71	66	68	272	5,505
Jeff Gove	70	70	68	64	272	5,505
Paul Gow	71	69	66	66	272	5,505
Kevin Johnson	70	68	68	66	272	5,505
Jon Mills	71	67	70	64	272	5,505
Jim Rutledge	68	70	68	66	272	5,505

Mexico Open

El Bosque Golf Club, Leon, Mexico
Par 36-36–72; 6,834 yards

September 3-6
purse, $650,000

		SCORES			TOTAL	MONEY
Troy Merritt	69	68	67	69	273	$117,000
Adam Bland	69	70	70	64	273	70,200
(Merritt defeated Bland on first playoff hole.)						
Matthew Richardson	69	69	70	67	275	44,200
Andrew Buckle	73	68	65	70	276	28,600
Garth Mulroy	68	67	69	72	276	28,600
Steven Bowditch	74	70	66	67	277	23,400
Henrik Bjornstad	71	71	71	65	278	19,581.25
Matt Every	74	69	65	70	278	19,581.25
Matt Hendrix	75	69	66	68	278	19,581.25
Derek Lamely	72	71	67	68	278	19,581.25
Kevin Chappell	71	65	73	70	279	16,250
Camilo Benedetti	71	68	68	73	280	14,950
Steve Allan	72	69	68	72	281	13,650
Sal Spallone	72	72	71	67	282	11,700
Josh Teater	71	69	71	71	282	11,700
Jose Trauwitz	72	69	70	71	282	11,700
Bob May	70	71	73	69	283	9,425
Alistair Presnell	70	75	71	67	283	9,425
Brendan Steele	73	68	70	72	283	9,425

	SCORES				TOTAL	MONEY
Brian Stuard	71	67	73	72	283	9,425
Martin Flores	79	67	69	69	284	7,540
Brennan Webb	72	72	71	69	284	7,540
Miguel Angel Carballo	72	66	77	70	285	6,240
Cameron Percy	72	73	70	70	285	6,240
Michael Putnam	71	73	73	68	285	6,240

Utah Championship

Willow Creek Country Club, Sandy, Utah
Par 35-36–71; 7,104 yards

September 10-13
purse, $550,000

	SCORES				TOTAL	MONEY
Josh Teater	65	67	64	68	264	$99,000
Tyler Aldridge	69	68	65	66	268	59,400
Andrew Buckle	64	69	68	68	269	26,400
Matt Jones	69	67	65	68	269	26,400
John Kimbell	66	65	66	72	269	26,400
Steve Wheatcroft	67	65	68	69	269	26,400
Jhonattan Vegas	68	66	66	70	270	17,737.50
Garrett Willis	68	64	69	69	270	17,737.50
Kevin Chappell	70	67	65	69	271	15,950
Craig Bowden	65	65	68	74	272	13,200
Jeff Gove	70	67	62	73	272	13,200
Jon Mills	66	67	69	70	272	13,200
Dave Schultz	69	63	71	69	272	13,200
Chris Baryla	70	67	67	69	273	9,350
Oskar Bergman	69	70	64	70	273	9,350
Kris Blanks	70	68	65	70	273	9,350
David McKenzie	64	70	70	69	273	9,350
B.J. Staten	69	67	68	69	273	9,350
Tom Johnson	69	65	69	71	274	7,700
Fran Quinn	68	65	69	73	275	6,636.67
Kyle Thompson	68	68	71	68	275	6,636.67
Patrick Sheehan	73	66	64	72	275	6,636.66
Joe Daley	66	68	72	70	276	5,500
Troy Kelly	66	70	69	71	276	5,500
Camilo Benedetti	67	70	69	71	277	4,195.72
Miguel Angel Carballo	71	67	69	70	277	4,195.72
Daniel Summerhays	69	66	75	67	277	4,195.72
Shane Bertsch	68	69	69	71	277	4,195.71
Bubba Dickerson	72	66	68	71	277	4,195.71
Michael Putnam	71	65	68	73	277	4,195.71
Tom Scherrer	66	70	69	72	277	4,195.71

Albertsons Boise Open

Hillcrest Country Club, Boise, Idaho
Par 36-35–71; 6,698 yards

September 17-20
purse, $725,000

	SCORES				TOTAL	MONEY
Fran Quinn	68	65	68	69	270	$130,500
Blake Adams	63	65	71	72	271	78,300
Ewan Porter	68	71	69	65	273	42,050
B.J. Staten	68	67	70	68	273	42,050
Troy Kelly	68	69	68	69	274	25,465.63
Skip Kendall	66	69	70	69	274	25,465.63

	SCORES				TOTAL	MONEY
Bradley Iles	68	67	69	70	274	25,465.62
Roger Tambellini	70	68	64	72	274	25,465.62
Craig Bowden	70	65	68	72	275	18,125
Steven Bowditch	72	67	66	70	275	18,125
Andrew Buckle	69	68	66	72	275	18,125
Tom Gillis	73	66	65	71	275	18,125
Brian Smock	71	66	67	71	275	18,125
Ricky Barnes	69	67	70	70	276	13,050
Jonas Blixt	69	64	68	75	276	13,050
Jeff Gove	69	70	67	70	276	13,050
Oskar Bergman	68	71	68	70	277	8,330.91
Fabian Gomez	67	68	72	70	277	8,330.91
Jonathan Kaye	64	71	70	72	277	8,330.91
Won Joon Lee	68	68	68	73	277	8,330.91
James Oh	69	68	69	71	277	8,330.91
Leif Olson	69	63	73	72	277	8,330.91
Patrick Sheehan	65	71	70	71	277	8,330.91
Esteban Toledo	67	70	69	71	277	8,330.91
Tjaart van der Walt	68	67	69	73	277	8,330.91
Steve Wheatcroft	68	67	70	72	277	8,330.91
Lucas Lee	70	69	64	74	277	8,330.90

WNB Golf Classic

Midland Country Club, Midland, Texas
Par 36-36–72; 7,354 yards

September 24-27
purse, $525,000

	SCORES				TOTAL	MONEY
Garrett Willis	64	69	67	68	268	$94,500
Chad Collins	69	68	70	62	269	56,700
Jin Park	69	69	67	66	271	30,450
Darron Stiles	69	66	70	66	271	30,450
Keoke Cotner	69	69	65	69	272	19,950
Esteban Toledo	68	67	71	66	272	19,950
Tom Gillis	68	68	70	67	273	14,212.50
Hunter Haas	70	68	69	66	273	14,212.50
J.J. Killeen	70	66	66	71	273	14,212.50
John Kimbell	68	72	69	64	273	14,212.50
Brendan Steele	66	68	68	71	273	14,212.50
Steven Taylor	67	68	71	67	273	14,212.50
Jerod Turner	67	67	69	70	273	14,212.50
Ryan Armour	69	70	65	70	274	8,925
Fabian Gomez	66	68	72	68	274	8,925
David Hearn	66	68	72	68	274	8,925
Jason Schultz	69	64	70	71	274	8,925
Chris Tidland	68	71	68	67	274	8,925
Gary Christian	72	67	67	69	275	6,363
Bob May	66	70	71	68	275	6,363
Garth Mulroy	70	66	71	68	275	6,363
Fran Quinn	64	67	74	70	275	6,363
Patrick Sheehan	69	71	70	65	275	6,363
Oskar Bergman	69	66	70	71	276	4,690
Justin Hicks	68	71	70	67	276	4,690
Martin Piller	69	71	67	69	276	4,690

Soboba Classic

Country Club at Soboba Springs, San Jacinto, California
Par 36-35–71; 7,101 yards

October 1-4
purse, $1,000,000

	SCORES				TOTAL	MONEY
Jerod Turner	68	66	66	69	269	$180,000
Derek Lamely	68	69	62	72	271	108,000
Brian Stuard	68	67	64	74	273	58,000
Tyrone van Aswegen	68	67	69	69	273	58,000
J.J. Killeen	69	67	67	71	274	40,000
Craig Bowden	67	68	67	73	275	34,750
Cameron Percy	70	68	67	70	275	34,750
Scott Gardiner	73	66	68	69	276	29,000
Justin Hicks	71	66	70	69	276	29,000
Brendan Steele	68	69	68	71	276	29,000
Jeff Hart	70	67	65	75	277	23,000
Bob May	69	71	68	69	277	23,000
Michael Sims	72	69	68	68	277	23,000
Kevin Chappell	69	68	70	71	278	18,000
Chad Collins	71	68	70	69	278	18,000
Michael Putnam	67	74	66	71	278	18,000
Jay Delsing	68	73	69	69	279	16,000
Jeff Gove	71	68	70	71	280	13,040
Paul Gow	72	69	66	73	280	13,040
Won Joon Lee	73	68	67	72	280	13,040
Justin Smith	70	70	68	72	280	13,040
Sal Spallone	69	69	71	71	280	13,040
Henrik Bjornstad	73	66	70	72	281	8,350
Andrew Buckle	73	67	69	72	281	8,350
Garth Mulroy	68	68	68	77	281	8,350
Garrett Osborn	67	70	72	72	281	8,350
Brenden Pappas	69	72	68	72	281	8,350
Steve Pate	69	68	68	76	281	8,350
Alistair Presnell	70	67	67	77	281	8,350
Garrett Willis	68	69	71	73	281	8,350

Chattanooga Classic

Black Creek Club, Chattanooga, Tennessee
Par 36-36–72; 7,040 yards

October 8-11
purse, $500,000

	SCORES				TOTAL	MONEY
Chris Baryla	66	68	65	70	269	$90,000
Troy Kelly	69	67	69	65	270	54,000
David Branshaw	71	66	67	67	271	26,000
Cameron Percy	72	66	68	65	271	26,000
Vance Veazey	74	65	67	65	271	26,000
Roberto Castro	66	71	67	68	272	15,650
Marco Dawson	69	69	67	67	272	15,650
Kyle Reifers	69	65	67	71	272	15,650
Josh Teater	67	67	69	69	272	15,650
Jerod Turner	70	70	67	65	272	15,650
Adam Bland	68	70	69	66	273	11,000
Justin Bolli	71	67	65	70	273	11,000
Bryan DeCorso	70	69	68	66	273	11,000
Tommy Gainey	71	69	65	68	273	11,000
Blake Adams	68	70	69	67	274	8,250
Skip Kendall	76	65	63	70	274	8,250
Scott Parel	68	71	69	66	274	8,250

	SCORES				TOTAL	MONEY
Esteban Toledo	67	69	69	69	274	8,250
Jeff Brehaut	69	68	69	69	275	5,850
Scott Dunlap	72	66	69	68	275	5,850
Hunter Haas	69	67	67	72	275	5,850
Luke List	69	68	71	67	275	5,850
Patrick Sheehan	70	69	67	69	275	5,850
Tyrone van Aswegen	65	70	69	71	275	5,850
Wil Collins	67	69	69	71	276	4,000
Todd Demsey	64	67	73	72	276	4,000
Doug LaBelle	69	69	66	72	276	4,000
Ian Leggatt	66	72	69	69	276	4,000
Jason Schultz	68	68	68	72	276	4,000

Miccosukee Championship

Miccosukee Golf & Country Club, Miami, Florida
Par 35-36–71; 7,200 yards

October 15-18
purse, $625,000

	SCORES				TOTAL	MONEY
Chad Collins	69	66	69	70	274	$112,500
Won Joon Lee	67	67	71	71	276	46,666.67
Brian Smock	66	69	70	71	276	46,666.67
Justin Smith	66	67	71	72	276	46,666.66
Fabian Gomez	70	68	68	71	277	23,750
Bradley Iles	68	68	70	71	277	23,750
Josh Broadaway	66	68	70	74	278	20,156.25
Derek Lamely	68	69	72	69	278	20,156.25
Joe Affrunti	70	68	70	71	279	16,875
Patrick Sheehan	68	71	71	69	279	16,875
Steve Wheatcroft	68	69	70	72	279	16,875
Roberto Castro	74	66	69	71	280	12,250
Gavin Coles	70	69	68	73	280	12,250
Tommy Gainey	71	69	68	72	280	12,250
Darron Stiles	68	69	70	73	280	12,250
Josh Teater	70	66	71	73	280	12,250
Michael Sim	70	70	69	72	281	9,062.50
Michael Sims	71	66	68	76	281	9,062.50
Brian Stuard	67	72	74	68	281	9,062.50
Jhonattan Vegas	72	66	74	69	281	9,062.50
Ian Leggatt	67	72	73	70	282	6,291.67
Luke List	70	69	72	71	282	6,291.67
Cameron Percy	67	69	73	73	282	6,291.67
Brendan Steele	66	72	72	72	282	6,291.67
Keegan Bradley	70	70	68	74	282	6,291.66
Geoffrey Sisk	69	67	71	75	282	6,291.66

Nationwide Tour Championship

Daniel Island Club, Ralston Course, Charleston, South Carolina
Par 36-36–72; 7,446 yards

October 22-25
purse, $1,000,000

	SCORES				TOTAL	MONEY
Matt Every	70	63	67	67	267	$180,000
Michael Sim	64	70	67	69	270	108,000
Josh Teater	69	67	69	70	275	58,000
Steve Wheatcroft	69	69	65	72	275	58,000
Cameron Percy	69	65	70	72	276	38,000

	SCORES				TOTAL	MONEY
Esteban Toledo	71	67	67	71	276	38,000
Chris Baryla	69	70	70	68	277	29,100
Craig Bowden	71	70	70	66	277	29,100
Chad Collins	69	69	70	69	277	29,100
Tom Gillis	75	66	70	66	277	29,100
Fabian Gomez	70	65	72	70	277	29,100
Blake Adams	69	73	70	67	279	22,000
Dustin Risdon	70	72	70	67	279	22,000
Justin Bolli	67	71	72	70	280	17,000
David Branshaw	70	71	69	70	280	17,000
Brian Smock	72	70	68	70	280	17,000
Brian Stuard	76	67	69	68	280	17,000
Jerod Turner	72	64	70	74	280	17,000
J.J. Killeen	72	71	69	69	281	13,500
Alistair Presnell	70	69	73	69	281	13,500
Won Joon Lee	70	67	72	73	282	11,600
Garth Mulroy	76	69	71	66	282	11,600
Henrik Bjornstad	70	71	69	73	283	9,350
Mathias Gronberg	69	69	70	75	283	9,350
Justin Hicks	71	71	68	73	283	9,350
Martin Piller	71	72	71	69	283	9,350

Canadian Tour

Corona Mazatlan Classic Mexican PGA Championship

El Cid Golf & Country Club, Mazatlan, Mexico
Par 36-36–72; 6,623 yards

April 23-26
purse, US$125,000

	SCORES				TOTAL	MONEY
Mauricio Molina	70	72	66	69	277	US$20,000
Andy Matthews	69	71	67	70	277	12,000
(Molina defeated Matthews on first playoff hole.)						
Stephen Dartnall	72	68	67	71	278	7,500
Mike Mezei	68	73	71	67	279	4,521
Manuel Inman	73	66	71	69	279	4,521
Stuart Anderson	70	71	70	68	279	4,521
Jose de Jesus Rodriguez	70	69	70	70	279	4,521
John Ellis	68	71	67	73	279	4,521
Eugene Smith	68	71	67	73	279	4,521
Ryan Yip	72	67	74	67	280	2,875
Mitch Tasker	73	71	69	67	280	2,875
Liam Kendregan	68	72	71	69	280	2,875
Robert Gates	69	70	70	71	280	2,875
Wes Heffernan	69	72	67	72	280	2,875
Ricardo Carrillo	75	69	70	67	281	1,938
Aaron Goldberg	69	75	71	66	281	1,938
Cesar Coello	74	71	67	69	281	1,938

	SCORES				TOTAL	MONEY
Andrew Parr	70	66	75	70	281	1,938
George Bradford	72	73	66	70	281	1,938
Javier Quevedo	71	67	70	73	281	1,938
Tom Stankowski	69	69	73	71	282	1,500
Brian Benedictson	69	70	72	71	282	1,500
Jordan Krantz	72	71	67	72	282	1,500
Octavio Gonzalez	73	67	72	71	283	1,375
Chris Wall	69	76	68	71	284	1,228
Brett Lederer	72	70	74	68	284	1,228
Lee Curry	73	72	67	72	284	1,228
Rob Grube	69	74	68	73	284	1,228

Times Colonist Open

Uplands Golf Club, Victoria, British Columbia
Par 35-35–70; 6,315 yards

June 4-7
purse, C$200,000

	SCORES				TOTAL	MONEY
Byron Smith	68	69	66	64	267	C$32,000
Jim Rutledge	67	68	69	66	270	19,200
*Brady Johnson	67	69	66	68	270	
Brock Mackenzie	69	71	67	65	272	8,680
Ryan Yip	70	68	66	68	272	8,680
Ryan Carter	72	67	64	69	272	8,680
Richard Scott	66	67	68	71	272	8,680
John Ellis	70	68	64	70	272	8,680
Robert Gates	66	68	69	70	273	6,200
Chris Wall	72	67	68	67	274	5,000
Mike Grob	70	69	67	68	274	5,000
Richard Gilkey	68	68	69	69	274	5,000
Andy Matthews	66	68	71	69	274	5,000
Wes Heffernan	66	70	68	70	274	5,000
George Coetzee	69	65	73	68	275	3,700
Greg Machtaler	65	71	70	69	275	3,700
Darren Griff	71	69	69	67	276	2,917
Eric Wang	69	66	72	69	276	2,917
Barrett Jarosch	70	68	68	70	276	2,917
Stuart Anderson	73	65	67	71	276	2,917
Brian Unk	69	67	68	72	276	2,917
Chris Griffin	68	65	70	73	276	2,917
Anthony Rodriguez	70	70	69	68	277	2,153
Erik Olson	70	67	70	70	277	2,153
Brad Heaven	68	71	68	70	277	2,153
Tim Wood	68	70	69	70	277	2,153
Jose de Jesus Rodriguez	71	69	66	71	277	2,153
Justin Smith	65	71	68	73	277	2,153

City of Surrey Invitational

Hazelmere Country Club, South Surrey, British Columbia
Par 36-36–72; 6,806 yards

June 11-14
purse, C$150,000

	SCORES				TOTAL	MONEY
Mike Grob	66	71	68	67	272	C$24,000
Graham DeLaet	69	69	68	68	274	14,400
James Lepp	69	69	71	69	278	7,400
Zack Shriver	71	69	68	70	278	7,400

	SCORES				TOTAL	MONEY
Yohann Benson	69	69	66	74	278	7,400
Jeffrey Rangel	71	71	72	65	279	4,680
Bryn Parry	73	70	69	67	279	4,680
Tim Wood	69	72	71	67	279	4,680
Ryan Carter	73	68	67	71	279	4,680
Brad Heaven	71	67	67	74	279	4,680
J.C. Deacon	72	67	72	69	280	3,075
Andres Gonzales	68	70	71	71	280	3,075
Ryan Thornberry	67	71	71	71	280	3,075
Aaron Goldberg	72	68	69	71	280	3,075
Chris Wall	73	67	68	72	280	3,075
Jose de Jesus Rodriguez	68	70	69	73	280	3,075
Lee Curry	68	72	74	67	281	2,014
Matt Johnston	75	67	69	70	281	2,014
Matt Marshall	71	70	70	70	281	2,014
Liam Kendregan	73	66	71	71	281	2,014
Jaime Gomez	72	68	70	71	281	2,014
Wes Heffernan	70	69	70	72	281	2,014
Adam Short	69	71	64	77	281	2,014
Steve Conway	75	67	71	69	282	1,541
Byron Smith	76	68	68	70	282	1,541
Ciaran McMonagle	72	71	69	70	282	1,541
Tommy Barber	69	73	68	72	282	1,541

ATB Financial Classic

Sirocco Golf Club, Calgary, Alberta
Par 36-36–72; 7,185 yards

June 25-28
purse, C$150,000

	SCORES				TOTAL	MONEY
Graham DeLaet	72	64	67	64	267	C$24,000
Byron Smith	72	68	63	68	271	14,400
Scott Gibson	70	68	66	69	273	9,000
Mauricio Molina	67	67	73	67	274	7,200
Stuart Anderson	67	69	66	73	275	6,000
Josh Geary	70	69	70	67	276	5,175
Garrett Frank	67	66	71	72	276	5,175
Andrew Parr	69	71	67	70	277	4,650
Richard Scott	73	70	67	68	278	4,200
Josh Habig	71	67	66	74	278	4,200
Hugo Leon	75	66	71	67	279	2,978.57
George Coetzee	70	74	67	68	279	2,978.57
Liam Kendregan	72	71	67	69	279	2,978.57
Jae Woo Im	70	70	69	70	279	2,978.57
Eugene Smith	70	69	69	71	279	2,978.57
Mike Grob	72	66	69	72	279	2,978.57
Jim Lemon	70	70	67	72	279	2,978.57
Bryn Parry	71	68	72	69	280	1,907.14
Jason D'Amore	72	70	69	69	280	1,907.14
Wes Heffernan	71	71	68	70	280	1,907.14
Russell Surber	71	68	71	70	280	1,907.14
Danny Sahl	68	73	69	70	280	1,907.14
Tom Stankowski	67	70	72	71	280	1,907.14
Tyler Harris	72	71	63	74	280	1,907.14
Brett Lederer	71	67	75	68	281	1,473.75
Andy Matthews	76	67	70	68	281	1,473.75
Andrew Smeeth	70	68	73	70	281	1,473.75
Ryan Horn	72	70	66	73	281	1,473.75

Telus Edmonton Open

Glendale Golf & Country Club, Edmonton, Alberta
Par 36-36—72; 6,911 yards

July 2-5
purse, C$150,000

	SCORES				TOTAL	MONEY
James Hahn	68	71	67	66	272	C$24,000
Jim Rutledge	67	67	72	66	272	14,400
(Hahn defeated Rutledge on first playoff hole.)						
Graham DeLaet	67	67	70	70	274	8,100
Andrew Parr	74	65	67	68	274	8,100
Barrett Jarosch	70	67	75	64	276	5,700
Rob Grube	71	68	71	66	276	5,700
Mauricio Molina	70	69	72	66	277	4,800
Brian Unk	70	70	69	68	277	4,800
Richard Scott	72	71	68	67	278	3,750
Brent Schwarzrock	67	72	71	67	278	3,750
George Coetzee	67	70	70	71	278	3,750
Wes Heffernan	68	72	69	69	278	3,750
Derek Gillespie	71	72	69	67	279	2,475
Russell Surber	71	72	70	66	279	2,475
Scott Gibson	72	69	69	69	279	2,475
Robert Gates	65	75	70	69	279	2,475
Liam Kendregan	66	71	70	72	279	2,475
Hugo Leon	69	67	71	72	279	2,475
Scott Gibson	72	69	69	69	279	2,475
Robert Gates	65	75	70	69	279	2,475
Mitchell Gillis	71	69	71	69	280	1,875
Ryan Yip	68	71	72	69	280	1,875
Matt McQuillan	69	70	70	71	280	1,875
Tyler Harris	68	71	70	71	280	1,875
Jon Turcott	66	73	72	70	281	1,545
Danny Sahl	67	72	68	74	281	1,545
Yohann Benson	70	67	75	69	281	1,545

Saskatchewan Open

Dakota Dunes, Saskatoon, Saskatchewan
Par 36-36—72; 7,301 yards

July 9-12
purse, C$150,000

	SCORES				TOTAL	MONEY
Andres Gonzales	70	69	72	63	274	C$24,000
Hugo Leon	70	67	73	65	275	11,700
Scott Gibson	69	64	75	67	275	11,700
George Coetzee	70	63	73	71	277	7,200
Brent Schwarzrock	74	69	70	66	279	6,000
Jeffrey Rangel	72	69	72	68	281	4,680
Zack Shriver	73	71	69	68	281	4,680
J.C. Deacon	73	67	72	69	281	4,680
Liam Kendregan	68	70	72	71	281	4,680
Yohann Benson	74	64	72	71	281	4,680
Rob Grube	74	68	77	63	282	3,075
Garrett Frank	73	69	75	65	282	3,075
Matt McQuillan	72	70	72	68	282	3,075
Aaron Goldberg	69	67	76	70	282	3,075
Luke Hickmott	71	69	72	70	282	3,075
Alan McLean	70	70	70	72	282	3,075
Jim Lemon	75	69	75	64	283	2,014
Robert Gates	73	67	77	66	283	2,014
Kris Wasylowich	73	68	76	66	283	2,014

	SCORES				TOTAL	MONEY
Jon McLean	69	70	77	67	283	2,014
Mark Kitts	71	69	75	68	283	2,014
Ryan Yip	71	73	72	67	283	2,014
Todd Halpen	72	68	70	73	283	2,014
Jason Anthony	71	72	75	66	284	1,509
Brady Stockton	69	67	81	67	284	1,509
Ryan Thomas	70	72	74	68	284	1,509
Ryan Thornberry	68	71	73	72	284	1,509
James Hahn	67	67	78	72	284	1,509

Canadian Tour Players Cup

Pine Ridge Golf Club, Winnipeg, Manitoba   July 16-19
Par 36-35–71; 6,622 yards   purse, C$200,000

	SCORES				TOTAL	MONEY
Graham DeLaet	69	72	66	69	276	C$32,000
Ryan Horn	68	72	68	69	277	13,600
Byron Smith	71	64	70	72	277	13,600
Lucas Lee	71	69	64	73	277	13,600
John Ellis	69	71	67	71	278	8,000
Derek Gillespie	70	70	68	71	279	6,900
Mark Leon	74	65	67	73	279	6,900
Mitchell Gillis	72	69	69	70	280	5,800
Luke Hickmott	67	71	70	72	280	5,800
Ryan Thornberry	68	68	73	71	280	5,800
George Coetzee	72	67	69	73	281	4,800
Rob Oppenheim	66	73	68	74	281	4,800
Andy Walker	69	73	69	71	282	4,000
Andres Gonzales	69	73	68	72	282	4,000
Mark Warman	70	73	71	69	283	3,300
Wes Heffernan	69	69	76	69	283	3,300
Tyler Harris	70	71	70	72	283	3,300
Barrett Jarosch	69	74	68	72	283	3,300
Marc Peterson	71	73	70	70	284	2,700
Brad Fritsch	68	73	64	79	284	2,700
Andy Matthews	73	72	71	69	285	2,400
Lee Curry	73	71	68	73	285	2,400
Eric Wang	69	73	70	73	285	2,400
Garrett Sapp	72	72	70	72	286	2,012
Michael Gligic	72	72	70	72	286	2,012
Clayton Rask	72	72	69	73	286	2,012
Marc Lawless	71	73	69	73	286	2,012
Alan McLean	71	70	71	74	286	2,012

RBC Canadian Open

See U.S. PGA Tour section.

Roxul Jane Rogers Championship

Greystone Golf Club, Milton, Ontario
Par 35-36–71; 6,837 yards

August 6-9
purse, C$125,000

	SCORES				TOTAL	MONEY
Ryan Yip	73	68	68	69	278	C$20,000
Jeff Cuzzort	72	72	67	67	278	9,750
Trey Denton	66	72	69	71	278	9,750
(Yip defeated Cuzzort on first and Denton on third playoff hole.)						
James Love	69	74	66	70	279	6,000
Clint Rice	68	75	70	68	281	4,542
Jim Lemon	69	68	70	74	281	4,542
Richard Lee	71	72	63	75	281	4,542
Mike Grob	76	67	70	70	283	3,500
Andrew Parr	70	71	70	72	283	3,500
Kent Eger	70	68	72	73	283	3,500
Jim Seki	64	71	73	75	283	3,500
Brad Heaven	75	66	75	68	284	2,625
Tyler Harris	74	71	69	70	284	2,625
Tom Stankowski	72	71	68	73	284	2,625
Scott Gibson	71	69	73	74	287	2,125
Tim Wood	67	71	74	75	287	2,125
Brian McCann	74	71	68	74	287	2,125
Reg Millage	75	73	69	71	288	1,813
Clayton Rask	71	67	76	74	288	1,813
Andy Walker	76	69	71	73	289	1,594
Lucas Lee	73	71	70	75	289	1,594

Desjardins Montreal Open

Saint-Raphael Golf Club, Montreal, Quebec
Par 36-36–72; 7,050 yards

August 20-23
purse, C$200,000

	SCORES				TOTAL	MONEY
Stuart Anderson	70	65	65	63	263	C$32,000
Clayton Rask	63	68	69	67	267	19,200
Hugo Leon	68	60	69	71	268	12,000
Matt McQuillan	69	65	69	66	269	8,266.67
Graham DeLaet	71	65	66	67	269	8,266.67
Ryan Williams	68	64	68	69	269	8,266.67
Andy Matthews	69	69	65	67	270	6,200
Scott Hawley	72	63	67	68	270	6,200
Garrett Sapp	69	66	67	68	270	6,200
*M. Bussieres	66	71	69	65	271	
Tyler Harris	67	68	69	67	271	4,150
Brock Mackenzie	68	69	67	67	271	4,150
Matt Johnston	70	69	65	67	271	4,150
Yohann Benson	68	65	69	69	271	4,150
Ryan Yip	69	65	68	69	271	4,150
Andy Walker	67	68	67	69	271	4,150
Wes Heffernan	70	67	64	70	271	4,150
Russell Surber	68	64	68	71	271	4,150
J.C. Deacon	71	67	71	63	272	2,660
Garrett Frank	67	70	70	65	272	2,660
Rob Oppenheim	69	67	69	67	272	2,660
Trey Denton	72	66	66	68	272	2,660
Alex Coe	67	68	66	71	272	2,660
Robert Gates	68	65	74	66	273	2,200
Steve Conway	70	65	68	70	273	2,200
Ryan Horn	71	68	64	70	273	2,200

Seaforth Country Classic

Seaforth Golf Club, Seaforth, Ontario
Par 36-35–71; 6,027 yards

August 27-30
purse, C$125,000

	SCORES				TOTAL	MONEY
Brian Unk	64	65	63	64	256	C$20,000
James Hahn	63	63	69	64	259	12,000
Ryan Yip	63	65	67	66	261	7,500
Jason D'Amore	67	64	70	63	264	6,000
Jae Woo Im	67	66	66	66	265	5,000
Scott Gibson	67	65	66	68	266	4,500
Wes Heffernan	63	66	70	68	267	4,000
Stephen Gangluff	66	66	67	68	267	4,000
Liam Kendregan	64	67	72	66	269	3,375
Mitchell Gillis	64	68	70	67	269	3,375
Kent Eger	64	67	70	68	269	3,375
Randall Hutchinson	69	68	69	64	270	2,450
Jim Seki	69	64	70	67	270	2,450
Nemanja Savic	65	69	69	67	270	2,450
Jaime Gomez	68	70	65	67	270	2,450
Clint Rice	68	68	66	68	270	2,450
Garrett Sapp	68	70	68	65	271	1,812.50
Scott Hawley	65	67	71	68	271	1,812.50
Brett Lederer	68	69	65	69	271	1,812.50
Brock Mackenzie	69	66	65	71	271	1,812.50
Andrew Johnson	65	68	72	67	272	1,437.50
Adam Short	68	67	69	68	272	1,437.50
Mark Leon	64	70	69	69	272	1,437.50
Brad Tilley	64	72	67	69	272	1,437.50
J.C. Deacon	65	70	66	71	272	1,437.50

Canadian Tour Championship

St. Catharines Golf Club, St. Catharines, Ontario
Par 36-36–72; 6,792 yards

September 3-6
purse, C$250,000

	SCORES				TOTAL	MONEY
James Love	68	68	66	67	269	C$40,000
Lucas Lee	65	66	68	70	269	24,000
(Love defeated Lee on first playoff hole.)						
Jim Rutledge	66	69	69	66	270	12,333.33
James Hahn	65	72	65	68	270	12,333.33
Alan McLean	69	68	63	70	270	12,333.33
Wes Heffernan	70	68	64	69	271	8,625
Scott Gibson	66	65	69	71	271	8,625
Mitchell Gillis	69	68	68	67	272	7,000
Marc Lawless	71	65	69	67	272	7,000
Luke Hickmott	68	67	66	71	272	7,000
Graham DeLaet	65	66	70	71	272	7,000
Matt Marshall	69	70	68	66	273	4,750
Conner Robbins	68	71	68	66	273	4,750
Andy Walker	68	69	69	67	273	4,750
Stephen Gangluff	68	68	69	68	273	4,750
Josh Geary	71	68	67	67	273	4,750
Andrew Parr	67	67	65	74	273	4,750
Andy Matthews	64	67	76	67	274	3,406.25
Brian Benedictson	69	68	70	67	274	3,406.25
Rob Oppenheim	67	69	68	70	274	3,406.25
Rob Grube	69	66	68	71	274	3,406.25

	SCORES				TOTAL	MONEY
Clayton Rask	63	72	71	69	275	2,691.67
Tyler Harris	69	67	70	69	275	2,691.67
Hoyt McGarity	70	67	69	69	275	2,691.67
J.C. Deacon	72	66	67	70	275	2,691.67
Ryan Carter	69	70	66	70	275	2,691.67
Yohann Benson	69	64	71	71	275	2,691.67

Iberostar Riviera Maya Open

Iberostar Playa Paraiso Golf Club, Riviera Maya, Mexico   September 24-27
Par 36-36–72; 6,683 yards   purse, US$100,000

	SCORES				TOTAL	MONEY
Rafael Gomez	69	67	64	76	276	US$16,000
Antonio Maldonado	68	73	65	71	277	9,600
Scott Gibson	74	67	69	70	280	6,000
John Douma	71	73	68	69	281	4,800
Brock Mackenzie	71	73	71	67	282	3,800
David Jackson	71	71	68	72	282	3,800
Hoyt McGarity	73	72	69	69	283	3,100
Paulo Pinto	72	76	66	69	283	3,100
Liam Kendregan	70	69	73	71	283	3,100
Jae Woo Im	74	72	70	68	284	2,600
Mitchell Gillis	74	71	68	71	284	2,600
Matt Marshall	73	70	70	72	285	2,200
Darren Griff	72	69	67	77	285	2,200
Andy Matthews	73	71	74	68	286	1,650
Jon McLean	68	73	74	71	286	1,650
Andrew Johnson	69	71	75	71	286	1,650
James Allenby	71	72	72	71	286	1,650
Ryan Panichpakdee	69	70	75	72	286	1,650
Garrett Frank	73	68	71	74	286	1,650
Ricardo Carrillo	69	73	74	71	287	1,275
Brady Schnell	71	72	71	73	287	1,275
Oliver Tubb	73	75	72	68	288	1,054.29
Matt McQuillan	73	71	75	69	288	1,054.29
Efren Serna, Jr.	77	70	71	70	288	1,054.29
Josh Habig	71	70	73	74	288	1,054.29
Joseph Greiner	70	68	75	75	288	1,054.29
Ryan Yip	69	71	73	75	288	1,054.29
Mauricio Molina	71	67	74	76	288	1,054.29

Riviera Nayarit Classic

Punta Mita Club de Golf, Pacifico Course, Nayarit, Mexico   October 1-4
Par 36-36–72; 7,014 yards   purse, US$125,000

	SCORES				TOTAL	MONEY
James Hahn	72	64	65	68	269	US$20,000
Eduardo Herrera	68	67	68	69	272	12,000
Jose Trauwitz	70	68	67	69	274	6,750
Darren Griff	71	66	68	69	274	6,750
Andy Walker	70	72	66	67	275	4,750
Matt Marshall	68	68	70	69	275	4,750
Jon McLean	69	73	68	66	276	3,750
Oscar Serna	65	72	72	67	276	3,750
Brock Mackenzie	69	69	70	68	276	3,750

	SCORES				TOTAL	MONEY
Paulo Pinto	66	71	66	73	276	3,750
Josh Habig	70	70	70	67	277	2,750
Derek Oakey	69	70	72	66	277	2,750
Cody Slover	71	71	66	69	277	2,750
Oscar Fraustro	65	71	69	72	277	2,750
Brady Schnell	68	71	71	68	278	2,000
Jason D'Amore	70	67	72	69	278	2,000
Wes Heffernan	68	71	70	69	278	2,000
Marc Peterson	71	69	69	69	278	2,000
Lucas Lee Brazil	70	69	67	72	278	2,000
Craig Matthew	69	68	72	70	279	1,531
Hoyt McGarity	71	71	67	70	279	1,531
David Jackson	68	74	69	68	279	1,531
Kent Eger	67	69	70	73	279	1,531
Justin Regier	67	74	70	69	280	1,284
Mike Mezei	68	68	75	69	280	1,284
Antonio Maldonado	69	71	69	71	280	1,284
Matt McQuillan	71	69	68	72	280	1,284

Tour de las Americas (South America)

Abierto Internacional de Antioquia

Club Deportivo El Rodeo Sede La Macarena,
Medellin, Colombia
Par 36-36–72; 6,792 yards

March 12-15
purse, US$130,000

	SCORES				TOTAL	MONEY
Peter Gustafson	69	69	68	66	272	US$30,043
Daniel Altamirano	65	69	69	70	273	13,777
Jesus Amaya	68	69	72	66	275	8,541
David Vanegas	65	75	69	68	277	4,901
Daniel Barbetti	74	70	68	66	278	3,342
Alvaro Pinedo	70	72	68	68	278	3,342
Julio Zapata	66	73	66	73	278	3,342
Eduardo Herrera	70	69	70	71	280	2,727
Manuel Merizalde	70	73	66	71	280	2,727
Cesar Monasterio	68	72	67	73	280	2,727
Julian Etulain	76	69	70	66	281	2,024
Jose Garrido Manuel	77	70	66	68	281	2,024
Oscar Alvarez	71	70	71	69	281	2,024
Luciano Giometti	68	72	70	71	281	2,024
Fredrik Widmark	74	67	73	68	282	1,500
Mario Hurtado	72	68	72	71	283	1,350
Alejandro Villavicencio	71	70	69	73	283	1,350
Fernando Figueroa	76	69	70	69	284	1,298
Francisco Ojeda	69	71	75	69	284	1,298
Sebastian Saavedra	76	67	71	70	284	1,298
Julio Noguera	76	69	68	71	284	1,298
Edgar Gomez	71	72	69	72	284	1,298

Club Colombia Masters

Country Club de Bogota, Bogota, Colombia
Par 36-36–72; 7,109 yards

March 19-22
purse, US$200,000

	SCORES				TOTAL	MONEY
Alan Wagner	68	71	68	68	275	US$32,000
Edoardo Molinari	69	67	68	72	276	22,050
Julien Guerrier	69	70	69	69	277	14,030
Jamie Moul	73	71	68	66	278	11,000
Julio Zapata	69	70	68	71	278	11,000
Benjamin Alvarado	71	69	70	70	280	6,667
Lloyd Kennedy	70	70	72	68	280	6,667
Julien Quesne	71	73	67	69	280	6,667
Daniel Barbetti	72	71	68	70	281	4,600
Dan Olsen	73	67	67	74	281	4,600
Alfredo Adrian	71	71	72	68	282	3,700
Oscar Floren	71	71	70	70	282	3,700
Soren Juul	71	67	72	72	282	3,700
Manuel Villegas	72	70	69	71	282	3,700
Juan Pablo Abbate	71	70	70	72	283	2,406
Pablo Acuna	68	75	67	73	283	2,406
Louis de Jager	70	70	73	70	283	2,406
Fabian Gomez	71	72	68	72	283	2,406
Ramiro Goti	69	75	69	70	283	2,406
Peter Gustafsson	69	75	68	71	283	2,406
Rob Harris	71	72	66	74	283	2,406
Juan Hoyos	72	71	69	71	283	2,406
Julio Noguera	71	73	68	71	283	2,406
Gareth Shaw	69	74	69	71	283	2,406
Mark Tullo	70	70	69	74	283	2,406

Campeonato Abierto del Centro

Cordoba Golf Club, Cordoba, Argentina
Par 35-36–71; 6,824 yards

April 16-19
purse, US$52,000

	SCORES				TOTAL	MONEY
Fabian Gomez	72	67	66	68	273	US$9,025
Ricardo Gonzalez	66	70	76	65	277	5,253
Angel Cabrera	70	69	70	69	278	3,409
Julio Zapata	67	72	69	71	279	2,709
Andres Romero	72	70	69	69	280	2,291
Federico Cabrera	74	74	67	68	283	2,011
Daniel Vancsik	74	68	68	74	284	1,815
Estanislao Goya	77	72	70	66	285	1,397
Clodomiro Carranza	74	73	70	68	285	1,397
Franco Barrera	69	74	73	69	285	1,397
Emilio Dominguez	69	72	73	71	285	1,397
Eduardo Argiro	74	73	70	69	286	1,057
Daniel Barbetti	74	72	70	71	287	936
Rafael Gomez	68	77	71	71	287	936
Sebastian Fernandez	74	68	72	74	288	886
Hector Ortega	71	71	71	75	288	886
Luis Romero	74	69	69	76	288	886
Mauricio Molina	74	72	75	68	289	800
Alfonso Barrera	73	76	70	70	289	800
Ramiro Goti	71	76	71	71	289	800

TLA Players Championship Acapulco

Fairmont Pierre Marques, Acapulco, Mexico
Par 36-36–72; 6,855 yards

April 24-26
purse, US$70,000

	SCORES			TOTAL	MONEY
Eduardo Herrera	68	65	67	200	US$12,600
Jaime Clavijo	64	65	71	200	7,980
(Herrera defeated Clavijo on second playoff hole.)					
Julian Etulain	70	66	68	204	5,600
Max Alverio	72	69	65	206	4,060
Manuel Merizalde	69	70	67	206	4,060
Ramon Bescansa	68	68	71	207	2,660
Rafael Ponce Orces	66	66	75	207	2,660
Fernando Figueroa	68	72	68	208	1,890
Alvaro Pinedo	70	67	71	208	1,890
Nick Ayala	69	69	71	209	1,680
Joaquin Estevez	74	69	67	210	1,312
Federico Cabrera	73	70	67	210	1,312
Daniel Barbetti	68	73	69	210	1,312
Alfredo Adrian	72	69	69	210	1,312
Daniel Altamirano	66	73	71	210	1,312
Miguel Guzman	66	70	74	210	1,312
Julio Zapata	68	76	67	211	1,017
Clark Burroughs	71	71	69	211	1,017
Cipriano Castro	69	70	72	211	1,017
Juan Berastegui	70	68	73	211	1,017

Copa Mitsubishi Tres Diamantes

Barquisimeto Golf Club, Barquisimeto, Venezuela
Par 36-35–71; 6,644 yards

May 21-24
purse, US$35,000

	SCORES				TOTAL	MONEY
Paulo Pinto	66	71	71	66	274	US$7,200
Diego Larrazabal	66	68	72	71	277	4,560
Julian Etulain	72	73	64	70	279	3,200
Juan Berastegui	73	69	72	66	280	2,320
Juan Hoyos	70	69	73	68	280	2,320
Manuel Merizalde	69	70	71	71	281	1,680
Miguel Martinez	73	74	66	69	282	1,360
Otto Solis	74	74	65	70	283	1,176
Tomas Argonz	73	73	65	72	283	1,176
Oscar Alvarez	76	70	69	69	284	946
Daniel Barbetti	74	70	69	71	284	946
Jaime Clavijo	72	66	74	72	284	946
Alfredo Adrian	70	71	70	73	284	946
Carlos Larrain	70	72	76	68	286	816
*Jose Daniel Ortega	78	72	66	71	287	
Raul Sanz	78	71	68	71	288	776
Vicente Teran	73	72	76	70	291	676
Denis Meneghini	72	74	74	71	291	676
Carlos Maestre	76	70	70	75	291	676
Wolmer Murillo	74	74	68	75	291	676

Venezuela Open Canal I

Lagunita Country Club, Caracas, Venezuela
Par 35-35–70; 6,909 yards

June 24-27
purse, US$60,000

	SCORES				TOTAL	MONEY
Daniel Barbetti	71	64	67	68	270	US$10,800
Raul Fretes	67	68	68	69	272	5,820
Jesus Amaya	64	68	70	70	272	5,820
Agustin Jauretche	68	68	70	67	273	3,480
Miguel Martinez	74	65	66	68	273	3,480
Tomas Argonz	72	68	69	65	274	2,280
Rodolfo Gonzalez	67	68	70	69	274	2,280
Alfredo Adrian	73	64	71	67	275	1,764
Juan Ignacio Gil	68	69	68	70	275	1,764
Juan Berastegui	68	66	74	68	276	1,380
Jose Manuel Garrido	68	67	73	68	276	1,380
Ramon Franco	72	68	67	69	276	1,380
Manuel Merizalde	66	71	70	69	276	1,380
Alessandro Fabietti	67	68	70	71	276	1,380
Fernando Posada	68	70	71	68	277	1,134
Oswaldo Villada	71	69	67	70	277	1,134
Paulo Pinto	68	71	72	67	278	984
Sergio Gabriel Acevedo	72	67	71	68	278	984
Pedro Martinez	71	69	68	70	278	984
*Alejandro Garmendia	70	69	72	68	279	
Ramiro Goti	73	68	67	71	279	834
Francisco Ojeda	70	71	67	71	279	834
*Felipe Velasquez	68	68	71	72	279	

Abierto Internacional Ciudad de Bucaramanga

Club Campestre de Bucaramanga: 36-36–72
Ruitoque Golf & Country Club: 35-36–71
Bucaramanga, Colombia

July 2-5
purse, US$50,000

	SCORES				TOTAL	MONEY
Oscar Alvarez	66	68	67	72	273	$9,000
Jose Manuel Garrido	69	67	72	67	275	4,850
Eduardo Herrera	67	70	67	71	275	4,850
Francisco Ojeda	73	69	65	71	278	2,900
Oswaldo Villada	69	68	68	73	278	2,900
Manuel Merizalde	70	72	66	71	279	1,900
Rodrigo Castaneda	66	70	71	72	279	1,900
Juan Echeverry	74	69	69	68	280	1,470
Oscar Patino	68	69	71	72	280	1,470
Jesus Amaya	73	71	69	69	282	1,200
Mario Hurtado	73	66	73	70	282	1,200
Hector Ortega	72	70	67	73	282	1,200
Alvaro Pinedo	70	70	70	73	283	1,020
Gustavo Acosta	72	69	68	74	283	1,020
Daniel Barbetti	73	73	62	75	283	1,020
Santiago Rivas	72	72	69	71	284	870
Rafael Romero	75	71	67	71	284	870
Rafael Ponce	72	71	67	74	284	870
Juan Ignacio Gil	74	72	71	68	285	720
Tomas Argonz	80	66	70	69	285	720
Fernando Posada	75	68	72	70	285	720

Abierto Internacional de Golf Copa Sura

Club Deportivo El Rodeo Sede Medellin, Medellin, Colombia — July 16-19
Par 36-36–72; 6,792 yards — purse, US$45,000

		SCORES			TOTAL	MONEY
Jose Manuel Garrido	69	67	73	71	280	US$9,000
Edgar Gomez	70	64	73	73	280	5,700
(Garrido defeated Gomez on first playoff hole.)						
Jesus Osmar	71	68	72	70	281	4,000
Diego Larrazabal	74	70	69	70	283	3,200
Jesus Rivas	66	76	74	69	285	2,350
Daniel Barbetti	67	71	75	72	285	2,350
Julian Etulain	70	76	74	66	286	1,610
Agustin Jauretche	70	70	75	71	286	1,610
Juan Martin Hoyos	75	71	73	68	287	1,370
Ramon Franco	70	76	72	69	287	1,370
Alfredo Adrian	72	71	75	70	288	1,220
Manuel Merizalde	79	70	69	71	289	1,045
Mario Hurtado	72	72	73	72	289	1,045
Oscar Patino	73	69	71	76	289	1,045
Luis Romero	74	70	69	76	289	1,045
*Miguel Echavarria	70	67	83	70	290	
Raul Fretes	74	71	71	74	290	920
David Vanegas	73	65	74	78	290	920
Gustavo Acosta	75	74	72	70	291	770
Oscar Alvarez	68	74	77	72	291	770
Jesus Amaya	68	70	75	78	291	770
Paulo Pinto	68	75	77	72	292	662
Rodrigo Castaneda	73	73	74	72	292	662
*Alejandro Velasquez	72	69	78	73	292	
Luciano Giometti	72	72	72	76	292	662
Juan Ignacio Gil	72	75	69	76	292	662

Abierto de Chile

Club de Golf Los Leones, Santiago, Chile — October 8-12
Par 36-36-72; 6,902 yards — purse, US$30,000

		SCORES			TOTAL	MONEY
Agustin Jauretche	69	71	70	69	279	US$7,000
*Matias Dominguez	71	73	67	69	280	
Paulo Pinto	69	69	67	76	281	4,000
Tomas Argonz	71	71	71	69	282	2,750
Nicolas Geyger	72	72	69	69	282	2,750
Julian Etulain	72	72	69	70	283	2,000
Sergio Gabriel Acevedo	72	71	73	68	284	1,333
Miguel Angel Rodriguez	71	74	71	68	284	1,333
Luciano Giometti	74	70	71	69	284	1,333
Sebastian Fernandez	69	72	77	67	285	875
Roy McKenzie	70	70	74	71	285	875
*Guillermo Pereira	69	73	76	68	286	
Benjamin Alvarado	74	69	72	71	286	800
Gustavo Acosta	68	71	73	75	287	725
Christian Leon	68	71	70	78	287	725
Raul Fretes	71	73	73	71	288	625
Tomas Dominguez	73	70	73	72	288	625
Ramon Franco	70	75	72	72	289	550
Juan Ignacio Gil	71	73	76	70	290	500
*Andres Jabalquinto	67	71	76	76	290	

Abierto Hacienda Chicureo Copa BCI

Club Hacienda Chicureo, Santiago, Chile
Par 36-36-72; 7,323 yards

October 13-18
purse, US$30,000

	SCORES				TOTAL	MONEY
Luciano Giometti	68	67	69	76	280	US$7,000
Raul Fretes	72	71	68	71	282	3,250
Miguel Guzman	69	72	69	72	282	3,250
Francisco Valdez	67	74	73	69	283	2,150
Emilio Dominguez	73	71	68	71	283	2,150
Santiago Russi	72	72	69	71	284	1,400
Sebastian Salem	71	71	70	72	284	1,400
Paulo Pinto	71	69	75	72	287	1,000
Christian Leon	69	75	70	75	289	900
Cristian Espinoza	72	71	72	75	290	775
Miguel Angel Rodriguez	68	75	69	78	290	775
Mark Tullo	73	73	74	71	291	600
Julio Noguera	71	77	70	73	291	600
Mauricio Molina	72	73	73	73	291	600
Francisco Cerda	69	75	74	73	291	600
Marco Ruiz	71	71	74	75	291	600
Agustin Jauretche	73	71	77	71	292	400
Sebastian Fernandez	74	70	76	72	292	400
Julian Etulain	71	74	74	73	292	400
Gustavo Acosta	69	76	72	75	292	400

Carlos Franco Invitational

Carlos Franco Country Club, Asuncion, Paraguay
Par 36-36–72; 7,100 yards

November 5-8
purse, US$30,000

	SCORES				TOTAL	MONEY
Agustin Jauretche	71	72	68	69	280	US$5,100
Rodolfo Gonzalez	68	75	70	68	281	2,600
Fabrizio Zanotti	68	73	71	69	281	2,600
Miguel Guzman	70	73	71	71	285	1,275
Walter Alberto Miranda	74	70	70	71	285	1,275
Sergio Gabriel Acevedo	73	70	71	71	285	1,275
Julio Zapata	73	69	70	73	285	1,275
Mauricio Molina	74	73	70	69	286	900
Miguel Fernandez	68	74	75	70	287	780
Joaquin Estevez	68	75	72	72	287	780
Martin Monguzzi	73	70	76	69	288	705
Paulo Pinto	73	71	73	71	288	705
Eduardo Argiro	74	70	72	73	289	660
Cesar Monasterio	74	73	76	67	290	605
Sebastian Saavedra	69	77	74	70	290	605
Matias O'Curry	72	74	70	74	290	605
Nilson Cabrera	79	69	72	71	291	555
Nelson Lautaro Ledesma	77	70	72	72	291	555
Francisco Ojeda	70	76	71	74	291	555
Juan Carlos Fortlage	72	73	74	74	293	527

Roberto de Vicenzo Classic

San Eliseo Golf & Country Club, Buenos Aires, Argentina
Par 36-36–72

November 18-21
purse, US$35,000

	SCORES				TOTAL	MONEY
Fabian Gomez	71	71	68	69	279	US$5,789
Sebastian Fernandez	69	72	68	72	281	3,421
Mauricio Molina	73	72	66	73	284	2,289
Cesar Agustin Costilla	71	70	72	72	285	1,763
Rodolfo Gonzalez	71	70	76	72	289	1,408
Miguel Guzman	70	72	74	73	289	1,408
Diego Ortiz	72	72	74	72	290	1,184
Martin Velazquez	71	72	76	72	291	1,033
Roberto Coceres	72	73	71	75	291	1,033
Miguel Angel Rodriguez	73	77	73	69	292	850
Luciano Giometti	73	71	72	76	292	850
Miguel Fernandez	70	74	77	72	293	737
Juan Ignacio Gil	73	76	72	72	293	737
Emilio Dominguez	76	73	71	73	293	737
Francisco Ojeda	71	75	77	72	295	659
Cesar Monasterio	73	70	74	78	295	659
Gustavo Rojas	69	78	74	75	296	620
David Ferreyra	72	76	73	75	296	620
Juan Carlos Fortlage	73	75	76	73	297	566
Martin Monguzzi	74	76	73	74	297	566
Omar Rolando Solis	74	71	76	76	297	566
Eduardo Argiro	75	72	74	76	297	566
Julio Eduardo Nunez	74	77	69	77	297	566

Torneo de Maestros

Olivos Golf Club, Buenos Aires, Argentina
Par 36-35–71; 6,740 yards

December 3-6
purse, US$91,900

	SCORES				TOTAL	MONEY
Tom Lehman	71	66	67	70	274	US$14,526
Daniel Vancsik	73	70	71	65	279	7,717
Miguel Angel Carballo	71	73	68	67	279	7,717
Roberto Coceres	74	68	70	69	281	4,615
Peter Gustafsson	73	70	67	71	281	4,615
Ian Legatt	71	68	73	71	283	3,193
Ricardo Gonzalez	69	72	69	73	283	3,193
Daniel Altamirano	71	67	74	72	284	2,512
Juan Pablo Abbate	74	69	72	70	285	2,209
Nicolas Geyger	79	68	71	68	286	1,988
*Emiliano Grillo	71	74	71	71	287	
Luciano Giometti	71	74	72	71	288	1,755
Fabrizio Zanotti	76	72	69	71	288	1,755
Emilio Dominguez	73	75	71	70	289	1,474
Paulo Pinto	77	74	70	69	290	1,198
Lucas Juncos	75	76	70	69	290	1,198
Rodolfo Gonzalez	72	74	73	71	290	1,198
Sebastian Fernandez	73	71	74	72	290	1,198
Andres Fabian Romero	74	74	68	74	290	1,198
Sergio Gabriel Acevedo	71	72	72	75	290	1,198
Sebastian Saavedra	76	69	69	76	290	1,198

Visa Open de Argentina

Nordelta Golf Club, Buenos Aires, Argentina

December 10-13
purse, US$80,000

Par 36-36–72

	SCORES				TOTAL	MONEY
Cesar Agustin Costilla	68	71	69	74	282	US$16,660
Paulo Pinto	71	74	72	66	283	8,680
Julio Zapata	72	71	71	69	283	8,680
Sandro Piaget	73	67	76	69	285	5,000
Peter Gustafsson	70	71	73	72	286	3,870
Scott Dunlap	71	69	70	76	286	3,870
Sebastian Salem	73	74	68	73	288	3,000
Julian Etulain	68	76	73	72	289	2,500
Raul Fretes	70	71	75	75	291	2,240
Mauricio Molina	70	72	77	73	292	1,920
Andres Fabian Romero	71	70	70	81	292	1,920
Miguel Angel Carballo	66	77	78	72	293	1,720
Angel Cabrera	73	74	76	71	294	1,474
Juan Ignacio Gil	75	73	74	72	294	1,474
Daniel Barbetti	77	73	70	74	294	1,474
Vicente Fernandez	75	72	73	74	294	1,474
Cesar Monasterio	75	71	72	76	294	1,474
*Emiliano Grillo	70	67	78	79	294	
Carlos Franco	72	76	75	72	295	1,265
Dan Olsen	75	69	77	74	295	1,265

European Tours

Joburg Open

See African Tours chapter.

The Royal Trophy

See Asia/Japan Tours chapter.

Abu Dhabi Golf Championship

Abu Dhabi Golf Club, Abu Dhabi, United Arab Emirates
Par 36-36–72; 7,510 yards

January 15-18
purse, €1,475,158

	SCORES				TOTAL	MONEY
Paul Casey	69	65	63	70	267	€245,122.43
Martin Kaymer	68	68	65	67	268	127,741.93
Louis Oosthuizen	67	69	68	64	268	127,741.93
Anthony Wall	67	67	69	67	270	73,537.46
Johan Edfors	66	69	69	67	271	52,652.82
Padraig Harrington	71	66	68	66	271	52,652.82
Rory McIlroy	66	69	71	65	271	52,652.82
Sergio Garcia	70	71	67	64	272	34,856.76
Danny Willett	71	66	68	67	272	34,856.76
Bradley Dredge	71	69	66	67	273	27,257.89
Peter Hanson	67	71	66	69	273	27,257.89
Francesco Molinari	67	69	71	66	273	27,257.89
Phillip Archer	71	71	67	65	274	23,090.76
Thongchai Jaidee	69	70	69	66	274	23,090.76
Robert Allenby	71	68	69	67	275	19,884.53
Rafael Cabrera-Bello	68	69	69	69	275	19,884.53
Anders Hansen	70	67	69	69	275	19,884.53
Soren Hansen	71	66	71	67	275	19,884.53
Graeme Storm	69	64	69	73	275	19,884.53
Mark Foster	70	69	68	69	276	16,423.37
Stephen Gallacher	74	66	65	71	276	16,423.37
Paul Lawrie	73	70	68	65	276	16,423.37
Peter Lawrie	73	70	69	64	276	16,423.37
Gary Murphy	69	72	69	66	276	16,423.37
Brett Rumford	68	67	71	70	276	16,423.37
Pelle Edberg	72	67	67	71	277	13,751.51
Richard Green	68	65	76	68	277	13,751.51
Alvaro Quiros	69	71	70	67	277	13,751.51
Jyoti Randhawa	71	70	67	69	277	13,751.51
Jeev Milkha Singh	74	67	70	66	277	13,751.51
Marc Warren	70	69	70	68	277	13,751.51
Robert-Jan Derksen	68	72	69	69	278	11,765.99
Simon Dyson	71	68	69	70	278	11,765.99
Jean-Baptiste Gonnet	68	72	72	66	278	11,765.99
Ricardo Gonzalez	72	67	69	71	279	11,030.62
*Danny Lee	68	70	73	68	279	
Oliver Fisher	67	69	69	75	280	10,148.17
Ross Fisher	75	67	70	68	280	10,148.17
Colin Montgomerie	72	67	70	71	280	10,148.17
Rod Pampling	70	72	71	67	280	10,148.17
Oliver Wilson	69	71	70	70	280	10,148.17
Mark Brown	72	69	70	70	281	8,677.42

	SCORES				TOTAL	MONEY
Alastair Forsyth	75	66	69	71	281	8,677.42
Pablo Larrazabal	71	69	72	69	281	8,677.42
Mikael Lundberg	66	69	73	73	281	8,677.42
Jarmo Sandelin	67	75	69	70	281	8,677.42
Michael Jonzon	74	69	72	67	282	7,500.82
Damien McGrane	70	72	70	70	282	7,500.82
Robert Rock	67	75	71	69	282	7,500.82
Jamie Donaldson	69	72	71	71	283	5,883
Gonzalo Fernandez-Castano	71	71	71	70	283	5,883
Ignacio Garrido	67	70	73	73	283	5,883
Trevor Immelman	72	69	71	71	283	5,883
Thomas Levet	69	74	71	69	283	5,883
Andrew McLardy	68	70	72	73	283	5,883
Chapchai Nirat	70	72	71	70	283	5,883
Scott Strange	73	66	72	72	283	5,883
David Dixon	70	69	73	72	284	4,559.32
Magnus A. Carlsson	72	71	75	67	285	4,265.17
Soren Kjeldsen	72	69	71	73	285	4,265.17
Hennie Otto	73	66	73	73	285	4,265.17
Aaron Baddeley	72	71	73	70	286	3,676.87
Martin Erlandsson	71	71	75	69	286	3,676.87
Shiv Kapur	72	70	77	67	286	3,676.87
Gary Orr	75	68	72	71	286	3,676.87
Simon Wakefield	71	72	71	72	286	3,676.87
Paul McGinley	69	73	74	71	287	3,235.65
David Drysdale	72	70	74	72	288	3,015.04
Mads Vibe-Hastrup	72	71	72	73	288	3,015.04
Nick Dougherty	74	69	74	72	289	2,794.42
Chinnarat Phadungsil	72	70	72	76	290	2,684.12
Alejandro Canizares	73	69	73	76	291	2,204.50
Daniel Vancsik	72	69	78	72	291	2,204.50

Commercialbank Qatar Masters

Doha Golf Club, Doha, Qatar
Par 36-36–72; 7,388 yards

January 22-25
purse, €1,882,982

	SCORES				TOTAL	MONEY
Alvaro Quiros	69	67	64	69	269	€314,400.01
Louis Oosthuizen	67	65	69	71	272	163,844.01
Henrik Stenson	66	72	66	68	272	163,844.01
Damien McGrane	69	69	70	67	275	94,321.51
Miguel Angel Jimenez	66	71	70	69	276	73,004.85
Maarten Lafeber	68	70	66	72	276	73,004.85
Andrew Coltart	66	69	70	72	277	43,689.72
Simon Dyson	72	70	69	66	277	43,689.72
Gonzalo Fernandez-Castano	69	72	67	69	277	43,689.72
Sergio Garcia	70	70	67	70	277	43,689.72
Chapchai Nirat	69	69	69	70	277	43,689.72
Aaron Baddeley	68	72	67	71	278	29,852.76
Paul Broadhurst	68	70	69	71	278	29,852.76
Anders Hansen	67	72	68	71	278	29,852.76
Hennie Otto	73	69	69	67	278	29,852.76
Johan Edfors	72	67	69	71	279	24,485.86
Niclas Fasth	70	71	70	68	279	24,485.86
Stephen Gallacher	72	69	69	69	279	24,485.86
Brett Rumford	67	69	73	70	279	24,485.86
Jeev Milkha Singh	70	72	70	67	279	24,485.86
Robert Dinwiddie	67	73	68	72	280	20,467.77
Retief Goosen	69	73	67	71	280	20,467.77

	SCORES				TOTAL	MONEY
Alexander Noren	72	71	66	71	280	20,467.77
Charl Schwartzel	69	72	69	70	280	20,467.77
Adam Scott	73	70	70	67	280	20,467.77
Anthony Wall	70	70	70	70	280	20,467.77
Nick Dougherty	68	72	71	70	281	17,638.12
Thomas Levet	71	70	68	72	281	17,638.12
Andrew McLardy	70	69	70	72	281	17,638.12
Lee Westwood	67	73	67	74	281	17,638.12
Bradley Dredge	74	67	70	71	282	14,902.80
Ernie Els	70	71	73	68	282	14,902.80
Soren Hansen	72	71	70	69	282	14,902.80
Peter Hanson	72	69	71	70	282	14,902.80
Martin Kaymer	71	72	71	68	282	14,902.80
Rod Pampling	70	68	74	70	282	14,902.80
Robert-Jan Derksen	71	72	69	71	283	12,450.44
Richard Finch	73	67	74	69	283	12,450.44
David Howell	71	71	73	68	283	12,450.44
Mikko Ilonen	71	71	71	70	283	12,450.44
Robert Karlsson	68	72	71	72	283	12,450.44
Marcel Siem	72	71	72	68	283	12,450.44
Gregory Bourdy	73	71	73	67	284	10,752.65
Markus Brier	70	71	72	71	284	10,752.65
Jean-Francois Lucquin	71	73	71	69	284	10,752.65
Magnus A. Carlsson	70	71	71	73	285	9,432.15
Paul Lawrie	72	71	72	70	285	9,432.15
Ross McGowan	73	66	75	71	285	9,432.15
Rory McIlroy	76	68	70	71	285	9,432.15
Stephen Dodd	70	72	74	70	286	7,545.72
Ross Fisher	71	71	76	68	286	7,545.72
Peter Hedblom	69	71	75	71	286	7,545.72
Francesco Molinari	72	70	71	73	286	7,545.72
Jyoti Randhawa	71	70	72	73	286	7,545.72
Mads Vibe-Hastrup	73	71	69	73	286	7,545.72
Raphael Jacquelin	71	73	70	73	287	6,036.58
Danny Willett	73	71	71	72	287	6,036.58
Mikael Lundberg	72	71	72	73	288	5,564.97
Gary Murphy	71	71	73	73	288	5,564.97
Thomas Bjorn	70	73	73	73	289	5,187.68
Scott Strange	72	71	74	72	289	5,187.68
Joakim Haeggman	73	70	71	76	290	4,810.40
Pablo Larrazabal	73	71	73	73	290	4,810.40
Jarmo Sandelin	68	75	77	71	291	4,433.11
Oliver Wilson	69	73	74	75	291	4,433.11
Graeme Storm	72	72	77	71	292	4,055.83
Steve Webster	72	71	75	74	292	4,055.83
Jamie Donaldson	70	73	73	77	293	3,772.86
Alvaro Velasco	76	68	75	78	297	3,584.22

Dubai Desert Classic

Emirates Golf Club, Dubai, United Arab Emirates
Par 35-37–72; 7,301 yards

January 29-February 1
purse, €1,930,002

	SCORES				TOTAL	MONEY
Rory McIlroy	64	68	67	70	269	€323,514.99
Justin Rose	68	66	69	67	270	215,674.07
Henrik Stenson	68	65	71	67	271	121,514.17
Paul Casey	68	68	68	68	272	82,432.94
Robert Karlsson	65	71	71	65	272	82,432.94
Martin Kaymer	70	67	68	67	272	82,432.94

	SCORES				TOTAL	MONEY
Miguel Angel Jimenez	72	70	67	66	275	47,266.30
Louis Oosthuizen	68	65	68	74	275	47,266.30
Scott Strange	69	71	66	69	275	47,266.30
Anthony Wall	70	68	68	69	275	47,266.30
Sergio Garcia	70	66	73	67	276	34,551.95
Richard Green	71	63	69	73	276	34,551.95
Ross Fisher	72	69	67	69	277	29,828.56
Colin Montgomerie	70	70	70	67	277	29,828.56
Alvaro Quiros	70	68	75	64	277	29,828.56
Bradley Dredge	73	68	71	66	278	25,671.32
Anders Hansen	71	71	65	71	278	25,671.32
Jeev Milkha Singh	69	68	72	69	278	25,671.32
Oliver Wilson	71	68	73	66	278	25,671.32
Robert-Jan Derksen	70	69	70	70	279	22,905.23
Thomas Levet	73	67	66	73	279	22,905.23
Per-Ulrik Johansson	69	73	70	68	280	21,643.50
Alexander Noren	67	71	70	72	280	21,643.50
Gonzalo Fernandez-Castano	66	70	73	73	282	18,731.82
Mark Foster	69	74	66	73	282	18,731.82
Peter Hanson	71	67	72	72	282	18,731.82
Mikko Ilonen	70	72	72	68	282	18,731.82
Graeme McDowell	70	72	72	68	282	18,731.82
Francesco Molinari	71	71	72	68	282	18,731.82
Gary Murphy	75	68	68	71	282	18,731.82
Charl Schwartzel	69	72	72	69	282	18,731.82
Simon Dyson	71	68	73	71	283	15,286.33
Martin Erlandsson	69	72	69	73	283	15,286.33
Gregory Havret	67	68	72	76	283	15,286.33
Jean-Francois Lucquin	72	68	72	71	283	15,286.33
Andrew McLardy	70	72	72	70	284	13,781.96
Gary Orr	71	70	71	72	284	13,781.96
Hennie Otto	69	73	69	73	284	13,781.96
Mark Brown	70	73	73	69	285	12,229.06
Raphael Jacquelin	69	70	71	75	285	12,229.06
Maarten Lafeber	74	69	70	72	285	12,229.06
Simon Wakefield	73	70	69	73	285	12,229.06
Lee Westwood	70	70	73	72	285	12,229.06
Stephen Dodd	71	69	73	73	286	10,676.17
Jyoti Randhawa	73	68	73	72	286	10,676.17
Brett Rumford	73	70	72	71	286	10,676.17
Magnus A. Carlsson	71	71	73	72	287	9,317.38
Richard Finch	71	71	71	74	287	9,317.38
Alastair Forsyth	71	70	75	71	287	9,317.38
Thongchai Jaidee	70	71	73	73	287	9,317.38
Ricardo Gonzalez	70	71	76	71	288	8,152.71
Michael Jonzon	67	72	76	73	288	8,152.71
*Matthew Turner	70	72	71	75	288	
Paul Broadhurst	70	70	72	77	289	7,182.15
Darren Clarke	74	69	72	74	289	7,182.15
Graeme Storm	68	70	77	74	289	7,182.15
S.S.P. Chowrasia	74	69	73	74	290	6,211.59
Alvaro Velasco	69	71	77	73	290	6,211.59
Paul Waring	67	73	77	74	291	5,823.36
Felipe Aguilar	72	71	76	73	292	5,338.08
Alejandro Canizares	72	71	74	75	292	5,338.08
Christian Cevaer	73	70	76	73	292	5,338.08
Gareth Maybin	70	70	77	75	292	5,338.08
Jarmo Sandelin	71	72	78	72	293	4,852.80
Michael Lorenzo-Vera	73	68	77	76	294	4,561.63
Lee Slattery	69	74	76	75	294	4,561.63
Paul Lawrie	68	75	74	79	296	4,270.47
Daniel Vancsik	70	72	82	77	301	4,076.35

Maybank Malaysian Open

See Asia/Japan Tours chapter.

Johnnie Walker Classic

See Australasian Tour chapter.

Madeira Islands Open BPI - Portugal

Porto Santo Golfe, Porto Santo, Portugal
Par 35-36–71; 6,983 yards

March 19-22
purse, €704,182

	SCORES				TOTAL	MONEY
Estanislao Goya	68	68	69	73	278	€116,660
Callum Macaulay	74	74	67	64	279	77,770
Wil Besseling	69	72	70	69	280	39,410
Damien McGrane	66	72	70	72	280	39,410
Anthony Wall	72	69	73	67	281	29,680
Michael Hoey	69	66	75	72	282	24,500
Thomas Aiken	72	69	71	71	283	19,250
Joakim Haeggman	66	70	75	72	283	19,250
David Drysdale	72	72	71	69	284	14,840
Jan-Are Larsen	71	71	76	66	284	14,840
Jose Manuel Lara	71	76	69	69	285	12,880
Jean-Baptiste Gonnet	69	75	71	71	286	11,340
Jose-Filipe Lima	72	74	69	71	286	11,340
Jarmo Sandelin	72	74	69	71	286	11,340
Carlos Rodiles	73	65	71	79	288	9,870
Marcel Siem	75	70	73	70	288	9,870
Inder Van Weerelt	75	72	71	70	288	9,870
Marc Cayeux	73	72	71	73	289	8,855
Carl Suneson	68	72	78	71	289	8,855
Rafael Cabrera-Bello	76	72	69	73	290	8,143.33
Scott Drummond	71	71	76	72	290	8,143.33
Santiago Luna	69	78	73	70	290	8,143.33
Richard Bland	78	64	75	74	291	6,965
Gary Boyd	72	76	70	73	291	6,965
Paul Broadhurst	70	72	78	71	291	6,965
David Horsey	73	73	72	73	291	6,965
James Kamte	76	71	73	71	291	6,965
Michael McGeady	69	67	77	78	291	6,965
Ake Nilsson	73	74	71	73	291	6,965
Ulrich van den Berg	74	69	78	70	291	6,965
Andrew Butterfield	68	73	75	76	292	5,450
Robert Coles	74	74	72	72	292	5,450
Stuart Davis	70	71	76	75	292	5,450
Klas Eriksson	74	74	73	71	292	5,450
Niclas Fasth	71	70	76	75	292	5,450
Alexandre Rocha	74	70	75	73	292	5,450
Alvaro Velasco	69	74	74	75	292	5,450
Liam Bond	75	69	77	72	293	4,550
Clodomiro Carranza	74	69	76	74	293	4,550
Bradley Dredge	72	74	76	71	293	4,550
Branden Grace	72	72	77	72	293	4,550
Birgir Hafthorsson	73	70	78	72	293	4,550
Jesus Maria Arruti	70	75	75	74	294	3,780
Javier Colomo	71	74	80	69	294	3,780
Garry Houston	71	73	80	70	294	3,780
Per-Ulrik Johansson	72	73	75	74	294	3,780
Roope Kakko	74	72	75	73	294	3,780
John E. Morgan	74	74	73	73	294	3,780

	SCORES				TOTAL	MONEY
Jeppe Huldahl	76	72	72	75	295	3,150
Ricardo Santos	74	73	74	74	295	3,150
Antonio Sobrinho	75	73	74	73	295	3,150
Ignacio Garrido	75	68	72	81	296	2,730
Jean Van de Velde	71	72	73	80	296	2,730
Martin Wiegele	76	69	75	76	296	2,730
Adilson da Silva	72	76	75	74	297	2,310
Matthew Mills	73	70	79	75	297	2,310
Iain Pyman	76	70	75	76	297	2,310
Nuno Campino	79	69	77	73	298	1,925
Gary Clark	71	73	79	75	298	1,925
Julien Clement	77	71	74	76	298	1,925
Rafa Echenique	77	69	79	73	298	1,925
Richard McEvoy	70	75	71	82	298	1,925
Anthony Snobeck	75	69	74	80	298	1,925
Francois Delamontagne	76	71	79	73	299	1,540
Christian Nilsson	71	75	77	76	299	1,540
Phillip Price	75	73	77	74	299	1,540
Michele Reale	71	73	78	77	299	1,540
Nathan Smith	75	72	78	74	299	1,540
Richie Ramsay	73	74	78	75	300	1,330
Petter Bocian	78	69	80	74	301	1,170
Carlos Del Moral	74	72	74	81	301	1,170
David Griffiths	72	74	81	75	302	1,045.50
Costantino Rocca	72	76	79	75	302	1,045.50
Paul Waring	69	74	80	81	304	1,041

Open de Andalucia

Real Club de Golf, Seville, Spain
Par 36-36–72; 7,140 yards

March 26-29
purse, €998,170

	SCORES				TOTAL	MONEY
Soren Kjeldsen	68	72	62	72	274	€166,660
David Drysdale	70	67	66	74	277	111,110
Francesco Molinari	72	68	68	70	278	56,300
Graeme Storm	70	66	73	69	278	56,300
Alastair Forsyth	74	64	68	73	279	42,400
Andrew Coltart	68	73	69	70	280	30,000
Rhys Davies	75	67	68	70	280	30,000
Marcel Siem	68	67	73	72	280	30,000
Thomas Aiken	70	72	69	70	281	21,200
John E. Morgan	70	73	69	69	281	21,200
Chris Doak	66	73	74	69	282	17,233.33
Anders Hansen	72	70	71	69	282	17,233.33
Soren Hansen	75	69	69	69	282	17,233.33
Thomas Bjorn	68	70	71	74	283	13,557.14
Carlos Del Moral	70	67	69	77	283	13,557.14
Stephen Dodd	68	72	72	71	283	13,557.14
Gonzalo Fernandez-Castano	68	70	71	74	283	13,557.14
Ignacio Garrido	71	71	69	72	283	13,557.14
Miguel Angel Jimenez	74	65	73	71	283	13,557.14
Thomas Levct	70	71	70	72	283	13,557.14
Markus Brier	70	71	71	72	284	11,150
Raul Quiros	70	69	71	74	284	11,150
Miles Tunnicliff	70	71	71	72	284	11,150
Fabrizio Zanotti	72	71	69	72	284	11,150
Jose Manuel Lara	69	73	68	75	285	10,250
Inder Van Weerelt	74	70	68	73	285	10,250
Marcus Higley	71	71	74	70	286	9,800

	SCORES				TOTAL	MONEY
Matthew Millar	70	70	75	72	287	9,200
Ake Nilsson	70	70	71	76	287	9,200
Alexandre Rocha	75	67	73	72	287	9,200
Felipe Aguilar	74	66	72	76	288	8,150
Per-Ulrik Johansson	73	68	72	75	288	8,150
Colin Montgomerie	67	72	75	74	288	8,150
Christian Nilsson	71	69	71	77	288	8,150
Jamie Donaldson	69	75	70	75	289	7,000
Peter Hanson	72	72	74	71	289	7,000
Michael Jonzon	69	68	76	76	289	7,000
Jan-Are Larsen	70	70	72	77	289	7,000
Carl Suneson	70	71	73	75	289	7,000
Steve Webster	73	70	75	71	289	7,000
Birgir Hafthorsson	69	73	75	73	290	5,800
David Howell	72	70	75	73	290	5,800
Simon Khan	72	70	73	75	290	5,800
Pablo Larrazabal	71	67	76	76	290	5,800
Jean-Francois Lucquin	67	69	76	78	290	5,800
Steven O'Hara	67	76	73	74	290	5,800
Jesus Maria Arruti	69	72	76	74	291	4,700
Nick Dougherty	72	71	72	76	291	4,700
Bradley Dredge	70	73	76	72	291	4,700
Jarmo Sandelin	70	70	73	78	291	4,700
Danny Willett	74	68	73	76	291	4,700
Jeppe Huldahl	71	68	76	77	292	3,900
Miguel Angel Martin	71	70	75	76	292	3,900
Simon Wakefield	70	73	73	76	292	3,900
Gregory Bourdy	72	69	73	79	293	3,500
Niclas Fasth	72	71	73	78	294	3,133.33
Gregory Havret	70	74	76	74	294	3,133.33
Anthony Wall	75	69	77	73	294	3,133.33
Christian Cevaer	71	70	75	79	295	2,750
Stuart Davis	73	70	79	73	295	2,750
Callum Macaulay	74	70	78	73	295	2,750
Marco Ruiz	69	73	73	80	295	2,750
Seve Benson	70	74	75	77	296	2,350
Wil Besseling	73	70	78	75	296	2,350
Francois Delamontagne	70	74	71	81	296	2,350
David Lynn	72	71	73	80	296	2,350
Pelle Edberg	73	69	76	81	299	2,100
Carlos Rodiles	71	72	79	79	301	2,000
Barry Lane	75	69	77	85	306	1,900

Estoril Open de Portugal

Oitavos Dunes, Cascais, Portugal
Par 36-35–71; 6,893 yards

April 2-5
purse, €1,261,205

	SCORES				TOTAL	MONEY
Michael Hoey	66	76	69	66	277	€208,330
Gonzalo Fernandez-Castano	70	72	68	67	277	138,880
(Hoey defeated Fernandez-Castano on third playoff hole.)						
Francesco Molinari	71	71	68	68	278	78,250
Paul Broadhurst	71	68	67	73	279	53,083.33
Jamie Donaldson	71	69	67	72	279	53,083.33
Mikael Lundberg	70	72	67	70	279	53,083.33
Gregory Bourdy	69	73	69	69	280	28,950
Alastair Forsyth	67	73	69	71	280	28,950
Paul Lawrie	71	69	68	72	280	28,950
David Lynn	69	73	65	73	280	28,950

	SCORES			TOTAL	MONEY
Steve Webster	68	72	71	69	280	28,950
Carlos Del Moral	67	71	71	72	281	17,805.56
Francois Delamontagne	71	73	66	71	281	17,805.56
David Dixon	69	73	68	71	281	17,805.56
Rafa Echenique	74	70	71	66	281	17,805.56
David Horsey	68	74	71	68	281	17,805.56
Michael Jonzon	72	71	70	68	281	17,805.56
Maarten Lafeber	72	71	64	74	281	17,805.56
Callum Macaulay	70	70	72	69	281	17,805.56
Ross McGowan	64	73	71	73	281	17,805.56
Andrew Coltart	71	72	71	68	282	13,375
Stuart Davis	70	69	74	69	282	13,375
Chris Doak	68	70	73	71	282	13,375
Pelle Edberg	70	73	73	66	282	13,375
Jose Manuel Lara	69	75	67	71	282	13,375
Robert Rock	69	72	71	70	282	13,375
Patrik Sjoland	70	73	67	72	282	13,375
Mark Brown	73	68	69	73	283	11,500
Jean-Baptiste Gonnet	72	72	69	70	283	11,500
Hennie Otto	69	73	75	66	283	11,500
Thomas Bjorn	69	73	71	71	284	10,025
Christian Cevaer	70	72	75	67	284	10,025
Niclas Fasth	71	71	71	71	284	10,025
Jean-Francois Lucquin	74	68	73	69	284	10,025
Andrew McLardy	69	73	73	69	284	10,025
Phillip Archer	72	69	69	75	285	8,375
Richard Bland	70	70	74	71	285	8,375
Rhys Davies	71	73	73	68	285	8,375
Simon Dyson	67	72	73	73	285	8,375
Marcus Higley	70	73	73	69	285	8,375
Pablo Martin	72	69	70	74	285	8,375
Simon Wakefield	70	73	71	71	285	8,375
David Drysdale	71	71	76	68	286	6,125
Stephen Gallacher	70	73	74	69	286	6,125
Ricardo Gonzalez	69	75	76	66	286	6,125
Stuart Manley	75	66	73	72	286	6,125
John E. Morgan	70	72	73	71	286	6,125
Wade Ormsby	69	74	72	71	286	6,125
Jarmo Sandelin	73	70	72	71	286	6,125
Lee Slattery	72	72	72	70	286	6,125
Miles Tunnicliff	69	70	74	73	286	6,125
Mads Vibe-Hastrup	70	74	65	77	286	6,125
Chris Wood	74	70	69	73	286	6,125
Wil Besseling	71	73	72	71	287	3,833.33
Estanislao Goya	75	69	75	68	287	3,833.33
Garry Houston	69	73	71	74	287	3,833.33
Paul McGinley	70	74	72	71	287	3,833.33
Phillip Price	72	70	75	70	287	3,833.33
Jean-Francois Remesy	74	70	70	73	287	3,833.33
Ricardo Santos	68	74	76	69	287	3,833.33
Alessandro Tadini	70	72	73	72	287	3,833.33
Inder Van Weerelt	72	72	70	73	287	3,833.33
Rafael Cabrera-Bello	72	69	69	78	288	2,875
Michael Curtain	70	74	71	73	288	2,875
David Frost	71	71	71	75	288	2,875
Joakim Haeggman	73	70	73	72	288	2,875
Gregory Havret	69	75	76	68	288	2,875
Daniel Vancsik	68	71	74	76	289	2,500
Mark Foster	68	74	75	73	290	2,332.50
Antonio Sobrinho	69	75	76	70	290	2,332.50
Marc Cayeux	72	72	78	69	291	1,875
Emanuele Canonica	72	72	73	75	292	1,869
Federico Colombo	70	74	75	73	292	1,869

	SCORES				TOTAL	MONEY
Birgir Hafthorsson	69	75	76	72	292	1,869
Tiago Cruz	71	72	78	72	293	1,863
Nuno Campino	70	74	79	72	295	1,860

Volvo China Open

See Asia/Japan Tours chapter.

Ballantine's Championship

See Asia/Japan Tours chapter.

Open de Espana

PGA Golf Catalunya, Girona, Spain
Par 36-36–72; 7,172 yards

April 30-May 3
purse, €2,000,000

	SCORES				TOTAL	MONEY
Thomas Levet	64	67	71	68	270	€333,330
Fabrizio Zanotti	71	70	66	65	272	222,220
Thomas Bjorn	70	67	71	66	274	112,600
Peter Lawrie	68	66	71	69	274	112,600
Charl Schwartzel	67	73	69	69	278	84,800
Rafael Cabrera-Bello	70	67	74	68	279	65,000
Marcel Siem	67	70	72	70	279	65,000
Gregory Bourdy	71	71	72	66	280	44,933.33
David Horsey	72	70	72	66	280	44,933.33
Jose Manuel Lara	65	73	71	71	280	44,933.33
Stephen Dodd	69	69	69	74	281	33,500
Soren Hansen	63	70	76	72	281	33,500
Francesco Molinari	69	70	70	72	281	33,500
Jarmo Sandelin	66	75	69	71	281	33,500
Stuart Davis	72	65	67	78	282	28,800
Oskar Henningsson	70	73	72	67	282	28,800
Paul Broadhurst	70	69	70	74	283	24,200
Carlos Del Moral	73	71	70	69	283	24,200
Jean-Baptiste Gonnet	72	70	74	67	283	24,200
David Lynn	69	73	70	71	283	24,200
Ross McGowan	71	71	73	68	283	24,200
Matthew Millar	69	75	71	68	283	24,200
Alvaro Quiros	72	68	76	67	283	24,200
Alejandro Canizares	67	69	74	74	284	19,600
Niclas Fasth	75	69	65	75	284	19,600
Mark Foster	69	72	70	73	284	19,600
Alfredo Garcia-Heredia	74	69	72	69	284	19,600
Soren Kjeldsen	69	72	74	69	284	19,600
Michael Lorenzo-Vera	70	74	68	72	284	19,600
Chris Wood	66	70	79	69	284	19,600
John Daly	70	72	74	69	285	14,709.09
Estanislao Goya	75	69	67	74	285	14,709.09
Marcus Higley	71	69	73	72	285	14,709.09
Miguel Angel Jimenez	69	74	68	74	285	14,709.09
Jean-Francois Lucquin	68	71	73	73	285	14,709.09
Santiago Luna	69	71	73	72	285	14,709.09
Paul McGinley	70	67	73	75	285	14,709.09
Steven O'Hara	72	72	73	68	285	14,709.09
Raul Quiros	68	75	70	72	285	14,709.09
Robert Rock	73	70	71	71	285	14,709.09
Steve Webster	74	68	72	71	285	14,709.09

	SCORES				TOTAL	MONEY
Sion E. Bebb	69	71	73	73	286	11,800
Gary Orr	68	72	74	72	286	11,800
Daniel Vancsik	68	75	75	68	286	11,800
Paul Lawrie	68	72	80	67	287	10,600
Pedro Linhart	71	69	72	75	287	10,600
Pablo Martin	68	72	71	76	287	10,600
Fredrik Andersson Hed	71	71	76	70	288	9,400
Gonzalo Fernandez-Castano	72	69	73	74	288	9,400
*Juan Francisco Sarasti	73	69	68	78	288	
Alessandro Tadini	71	71	77	69	288	9,400
Magnus A. Carlsson	71	69	74	75	289	7,800
Christian Cevaer	72	67	78	72	289	7,800
Rafa Echenique	73	71	71	74	289	7,800
Pelle Edberg	69	74	72	74	289	7,800
Jordi Garcia Pinto	73	71	68	77	289	7,800
James Kamte	73	71	72	74	290	6,266.67
Jose-Filipe Lima	68	74	70	78	290	6,266.67
Miles Tunnicliff	72	70	74	74	290	6,266.67
Stephen Gallacher	71	70	78	72	291	5,400
Pablo Larrazabal	71	70	74	76	291	5,400
Jan-Are Larsen	67	76	73	75	291	5,400
Iain Pyman	68	76	69	78	291	5,400
Graeme Storm	69	71	77	74	291	5,400
Bradley Dredge	72	71	73	76	292	4,600
Gary Murphy	70	74	77	71	292	4,600
Manuel Quiros	69	74	80	69	292	4,600
Callum Macaulay	65	76	76	76	293	4,100
Phillip Price	73	71	72	77	293	4,100
Andrew McLardy	72	72	78	72	294	3,725
Ake Nilsson	70	73	73	78	294	3,725

BMW Italian Open

Royal Park I Roveri, Torino, Italy   May 7-10
Par 36-35–71; 7,222 yards   purse, €1,297,620

	SCORES				TOTAL	MONEY
Daniel Vancsik	68	65	69	65	267	€216,660
John Daly	69	69	69	66	273	96,940
Raphael Jacquelin	67	70	68	68	273	96,940
Robert Rock	72	65	68	68	273	96,940
Thomas Aiken	68	70	66	70	274	55,120
Thomas Bjorn	71	67	68	69	275	42,250
Francesco Molinari	68	69	73	65	275	42,250
Julien Clement	70	67	69	70	276	25,805
Robert Dinwiddie	72	67	68	69	276	25,805
Alastair Forsyth	73	68	67	68	276	25,805
Roope Kakko	71	64	68	73	276	25,805
Gareth Maybin	64	70	70	72	276	25,805
Peter O'Malley	74	68	64	70	276	25,805
Alejandro Canizares	70	69	69	69	277	19,110
Robert-Jan Derksen	73	66	73	65	277	19,110
Richic Ramsay	67	70	70	70	277	19,110
Michael McGeady	71	68	68	71	278	16,510
Edoardo Molinari	70	69	69	70	278	16,510
Ake Nilsson	68	69	69	72	278	16,510
Marco Soffietti	72	69	67	70	278	16,510
Branden Grace	69	70	72	68	279	14,495
Anders Hansen	73	65	70	71	279	14,495
Andrew McLardy	74	64	69	72	279	14,495

	SCORES				TOTAL	MONEY
Lee Slattery	72	69	71	67	279	14,495
Mark Foster	70	71	68	71	280	12,155
Marcus Fraser	73	67	72	68	280	12,155
Chris Gane	71	70	68	71	280	12,155
*Matteo Manassero	71	70	72	67	280	
Alan McLean	71	69	67	73	280	12,155
Wade Ormsby	70	71	74	65	280	12,155
Charl Schwartzel	70	72	70	68	280	12,155
Alessandro Tadini	72	68	73	67	280	12,155
Fabrizio Zanotti	68	70	73	69	280	12,155
Marc Cayeux	69	69	76	67	281	9,376.25
Christian Cevaer	67	72	70	72	281	9,376.25
Shiv Kapur	68	73	70	70	281	9,376.25
David Lynn	71	68	70	72	281	9,376.25
Gary Murphy	70	72	70	69	281	9,376.25
Gary Orr	72	68	68	73	281	9,376.25
Alvaro Quiros	71	69	71	70	281	9,376.25
Inder Van Weerelt	69	69	72	71	281	9,376.25
Phillip Archer	71	70	70	71	282	7,670
Stephen Dodd	70	71	75	66	282	7,670
Mathias Gronberg	74	68	70	70	282	7,670
Soren Hansen	74	67	72	69	282	7,670
Anthony Wall	68	67	77	70	282	7,670
Wil Besseling	72	69	74	68	283	6,110
Gary Clark	72	70	68	73	283	6,110
David Frost	76	66	68	73	283	6,110
Jose Manuel Lara	71	69	69	74	283	6,110
John Mellor	69	73	70	71	283	6,110
Patrik Sjoland	72	65	76	70	283	6,110
Andrew Tampion	70	67	70	76	283	6,110
Fredrik Andersson Hed	72	70	71	71	284	4,550
Matteo Delpodio	68	72	70	74	284	4,550
Gregory Havret	69	70	69	76	284	4,550
Jose-Filipe Lima	73	69	72	70	284	4,550
Gareth Paddison	70	72	69	73	284	4,550
Garry Houston	68	73	71	73	285	3,705
Mikko Ilonen	69	71	75	70	285	3,705
Gary Lockerbie	69	69	72	75	285	3,705
Chinnarat Phadungsil	70	69	73	73	285	3,705
Sion E. Bebb	73	68	73	72	286	3,185
Birgir Hafthorsson	70	65	76	75	286	3,185
Marcus Higley	67	70	72	77	286	3,185
Ulrich van den Berg	68	74	70	74	286	3,185
Benn Barham	73	67	78	69	287	2,730
Jonathan Caldwell	71	68	75	73	287	2,730
Marc Warren	74	67	75	71	287	2,730
Brett Rumford	68	69	74	77	288	2,470

The 3 Irish Open

Co. Louth Golf Club, Baltray, Drogheda, Ireland
Par 37-35–72; 7,063 yards

May 14-17
purse, €3,000,000

	SCORES				TOTAL	MONEY
*Shane Lowry	67	62	71	71	271	
Robert Rock	66	65	69	71	271	€500,000
(Lowry defeated Rock on third playoff hole.)						
Johan Edfors	64	70	68	71	273	333,330
Nick Dougherty	66	67	73	69	275	168,900
Marc Warren	67	69	71	68	275	168,900

	SCORES				TOTAL	MONEY
Alastair Forsyth	67	68	71	70	276	127,200
Roope Kakko	66	67	76	69	278	105,000
Thomas Levet	67	66	73	73	279	82,500
Brett Rumford	73	66	72	68	279	82,500
Richard Bland	71	68	71	70	280	60,800
Anthony Wall	72	68	71	69	280	60,800
Chris Wood	69	67	76	68	280	60,800
Jamie Donaldson	66	65	78	72	281	51,600
Darren Clarke	71	68	73	70	282	43,300
Rafa Echenique	69	67	75	71	282	43,300
David Horsey	70	67	78	67	282	43,300
Pablo Martin	70	65	77	70	282	43,300
Andrew McLardy	69	66	77	70	282	43,300
Oliver Wilson	66	68	76	72	282	43,300
Rafael Cabrera-Bello	67	69	79	68	283	34,980
Anders Hansen	68	68	76	71	283	34,980
Thongchai Jaidee	69	70	72	72	283	34,980
Michael Lorenzo-Vera	69	69	73	72	283	34,980
Graeme Storm	70	69	76	68	283	34,980
Thomas Bjorn	71	67	73	73	284	30,300
Stephen Dodd	70	67	74	73	284	30,300
Gary Murphy	70	69	75	70	284	30,300
Louis Oosthuizen	68	69	78	69	284	30,300
Lee Slattery	67	69	75	73	284	30,300
Soren Kjeldsen	67	67	78	73	285	25,800
Pablo Larrazabal	68	70	76	71	285	25,800
Paul Lawrie	66	66	77	76	285	25,800
Gary Orr	68	67	74	76	285	25,800
Lee Westwood	68	66	77	74	285	25,800
Paul Broadhurst	71	69	73	73	286	21,600
David Drysdale	69	68	80	69	286	21,600
Shiv Kapur	66	71	76	73	286	21,600
Simon Khan	72	68	74	72	286	21,600
Charl Schwartzel	72	67	72	75	286	21,600
Mads Vibe-Hastrup	72	68	77	69	286	21,600
David Carter	71	69	73	74	287	17,100
Simon Dyson	71	68	80	68	287	17,100
Martin Erlandsson	68	72	73	74	287	17,100
Niclas Fasth	71	68	78	70	287	17,100
Marcus Fraser	69	71	76	71	287	17,100
Peter Hedblom	68	72	77	70	287	17,100
Raphael Jacquelin	71	66	75	75	287	17,100
Maarten Lafeber	69	70	77	71	287	17,100
Colin Montgomerie	70	65	72	80	287	17,100
Robert-Jan Derksen	69	69	73	77	288	12,300
Ross Fisher	70	67	77	74	288	12,300
Sam Little	72	66	78	72	288	12,300
Rory McIlroy	69	68	76	75	288	12,300
Jose Maria Olazabal	71	67	75	75	288	12,300
Jarmo Sandelin	70	70	74	74	288	12,300
Patrik Sjoland	73	67	73	75	288	12,300
Soren Hansen	71	68	79	71	289	9,225
Damien McGrane	69	71	75	74	289	9,225
Alexander Noren	70	70	79	70	289	9,225
Marcel Siem	69	68	78	74	289	9,225
S.S.P. Chowrasia	74	66	79	71	290	7,950
Gregory Havret	70	66	79	75	290	7,950
Jose Manuel Lara	67	68	77	78	290	7,950
Paul Waring	72	67	80	71	290	7,950
Julien Clement	67	70	75	79	291	7,050
Steve Webster	70	68	77	76	291	7,050
Emanuele Canonica	69	70	77	76	292	6,450
Paul McGinley	71	68	77	76	292	6,450

	SCORES				TOTAL	MONEY
Gary Lockerbie	69	70	77	77	293	6,000
Wil Besseling	69	66	79	80	294	5,700
*Pedro Figueiredo	72	67	78	79	296	
Michael Jonzon	71	69	78	81	299	5,470

BMW PGA Championship

Wentworth Club, Virginia Water, Surrey, England
Par 35-37–72; 7,320 yards

May 21-24
purse, €4,553,916

	SCORES				TOTAL	MONEY
Paul Casey	69	67	67	68	271	€750,000
Ross Fisher	68	73	67	64	272	500,000
Soren Kjeldsen	69	69	68	69	275	281,700
Stephen Dodd	71	68	70	67	276	225,000
Rory McIlroy	72	70	65	71	278	190,800
Ben Curtis	69	70	73	67	279	135,000
Charl Schwartzel	68	72	68	71	279	135,000
Anthony Wall	67	71	72	69	279	135,000
Thomas Levet	70	71	68	71	280	100,800
Thomas Aiken	72	67	74	68	281	90,000
Gonzalo Fernandez-Castano	67	77	70	68	282	80,100
Martin Kaymer	72	70	70	70	282	80,100
Nick Dougherty	73	71	67	72	283	69,150
Graeme McDowell	75	71	68	69	283	69,150
Alessandro Tadini	74	71	69	69	283	69,150
Thomas Bjorn	73	73	70	68	284	58,410
Simon Dyson	74	69	68	73	284	58,410
Jean-Francois Lucquin	70	72	72	70	284	58,410
Alvaro Quiros	69	71	73	71	284	58,410
Robert Rock	71	74	69	70	284	58,410
Markus Brier	70	74	72	69	285	45,450
Paul Broadhurst	73	72	68	72	285	45,450
Robert-Jan Derksen	71	74	69	71	285	45,450
Ernie Els	73	73	70	69	285	45,450
Richard Green	72	74	68	71	285	45,450
Anders Hansen	72	70	71	72	285	45,450
Soren Hansen	73	70	71	71	285	45,450
Alexander Noren	69	71	72	73	285	45,450
Paul Waring	75	71	70	69	285	45,450
Marc Warren	72	66	71	76	285	45,450
Fabrizio Zanotti	70	75	71	69	285	45,450
Jamie Donaldson	70	71	73	72	286	36,000
Robert Karlsson	69	74	72	71	286	36,000
Paul Lawrie	72	71	70	73	286	36,000
Benn Barham	72	73	72	70	287	30,600
Luke Donald	74	72	71	70	287	30,600
Niclas Fasth	68	74	73	72	287	30,600
Alastair Forsyth	70	75	75	67	287	30,600
Shiv Kapur	73	72	70	72	287	30,600
Francesco Molinari	77	68	70	72	287	30,600
Colin Montgomerie	69	73	69	76	287	30,600
Lee Slattery	70	72	74	71	287	30,600
Marcus Fraser	71	73	70	74	288	24,750
David Horsey	67	71	74	76	288	24,750
Thongchai Jaidee	71	74	70	73	288	24,750
Miguel Angel Jimenez	68	70	74	76	288	24,750
Brett Rumford	71	73	72	72	288	24,750
Robert Dinwiddie	73	73	74	69	289	20,700
Pelle Edberg	72	69	77	71	289	20,700

	SCORES				TOTAL	MONEY
Mark Foster	72	70	73	74	289	20,700
Pablo Larrazabal	73	67	73	76	289	20,700
Darren Clarke	74	71	74	71	290	18,000
Pablo Martin	72	73	72	73	290	18,000
Seve Benson	73	72	77	69	291	14,940
Scott Drummond	69	74	74	74	291	14,940
Estanislao Goya	74	71	70	76	291	14,940
Peter Hanson	71	74	74	72	291	14,940
Andres Romero	71	72	76	72	291	14,940
Anton Haig	72	69	81	70	292	12,150
Sam Little	71	73	74	74	292	12,150
Jose Maria Olazabal	74	70	74	74	292	12,150
Marcel Siem	71	75	75	71	292	12,150
Miles Tunnicliff	73	70	73	76	292	12,150
Phillip Archer	72	74	76	71	293	10,125
Alejandro Canizares	71	73	77	72	293	10,125
Ignacio Garrido	73	70	75	75	293	10,125
Jyoti Randhawa	73	73	78	69	293	10,125
Francois Delamontagne	73	73	78	70	294	8,583.33
Mikko Ilonen	74	71	71	78	294	8,583.33
Simon Wakefield	75	69	74	76	294	8,583.33
Raphael Jacquelin	70	76	76	73	295	6,750
John Daly	73	71	77	75	296	6,742.50
Ricardo Gonzalez	70	76	75	75	296	6,742.50
David Howell	76	69	73	78	296	6,742.50
Peter O'Malley	74	72	73	77	296	6,742.50
Johan Edfors	74	72	75	76	297	6,735
Barry Lane	68	78	83	70	299	6,732
Anthony Kang	69	76	76	80	301	6,729

European Open

London Golf Club, Ash, Kent, England
Par 36-36–72; 7,257 yards

May 28-31
purse,€2,043,589

	SCORES				TOTAL	MONEY
Christian Cevaer	67	70	70	74	281	€341,220.01
Gary Orr	71	72	68	71	282	152,669.41
Alvaro Quiros	71	70	69	72	282	152,669.41
Steve Webster	69	72	70	71	282	152,669.41
Stephen Dodd	75	70	70	68	283	73,294.06
Jeev Milkha Singh	67	69	71	76	283	73,294.06
Chris Wood	69	73	68	73	283	73,294.06
Ben Curtis	68	73	75	68	284	43,915.02
Marcus Fraser	69	70	72	73	284	43,915.02
Soren Hansen	69	75	67	73	284	43,915.02
Jose Manuel Lara	70	68	74	72	284	43,915.02
Rory McIlroy	69	73	68	75	285	35,213.91
David Drysdale	72	71	72	71	286	31,460.48
Sergio Garcia	69	75	74	68	286	31,460.48
Martin Kaymer	71	72	72	71	286	31,460.48
Robert Karlsson	68	74	75	70	287	28,253.02
Louis Oosthuizen	68	75	70	74	287	28,253.02
Carlos Del Moral	70	75	71	72	288	23,293.95
Johan Edfors	71	74	71	72	288	23,293.95
Branden Grace	69	75	74	70	288	23,293.95
Simon Khan	67	76	74	71	288	23,293.95
Michael Lorenzo-Vera	67	69	77	75	288	23,293.95
Shaun Micheel	71	71	74	72	288	23,293.95
Chapchai Nirat	69	76	68	75	288	23,293.95

	SCORES				TOTAL	MONEY
Richie Ramsay	74	70	68	76	288	23,293.95
Anthony Wall	68	69	76	75	288	23,293.95
Bradley Dredge	72	69	76	72	289	18,835.34
Anders Hansen	65	73	78	73	289	18,835.34
Roope Kakko	69	76	72	72	289	18,835.34
Peter Lawrie	67	71	79	72	289	18,835.34
Lee Westwood	70	75	74	70	289	18,835.34
Markus Brier	72	72	76	70	290	15,442.64
Chris Doak	68	72	76	74	290	15,442.64
Jamie Donaldson	68	70	74	78	290	15,442.64
Klas Eriksson	71	74	73	72	290	15,442.64
Gonzalo Fernandez-Castano	68	76	75	71	290	15,442.64
Oliver Fisher	71	71	75	73	290	15,442.64
Mikael Lundberg	70	75	74	71	290	15,442.64
Thomas Bjorn	70	74	76	71	291	12,488.65
Estanislao Goya	69	72	75	75	291	12,488.65
David Horsey	68	75	73	75	291	12,488.65
Jean-Francois Lucquin	67	77	73	74	291	12,488.65
Graeme McDowell	70	73	74	74	291	12,488.65
Graeme Storm	68	76	72	75	291	12,488.65
Alessandro Tadini	67	75	74	75	291	12,488.65
Gregory Bourdy	71	70	72	79	292	9,212.94
Niclas Fasth	71	72	75	74	292	9,212.94
Mark Foster	73	72	73	74	292	9,212.94
Ignacio Garrido	71	70	79	72	292	9,212.94
Shiv Kapur	67	74	75	76	292	9,212.94
Paul Lawrie	73	71	73	75	292	9,212.94
Paul McGinley	70	75	74	73	292	9,212.94
Steven O'Hara	71	74	74	73	292	9,212.94
Jyoti Randhawa	66	73	79	74	292	9,212.94
Peter Hanson	66	73	79	75	293	6,469.53
Colin Montgomerie	70	74	74	75	293	6,469.53
Taco Remkes	70	73	77	73	293	6,469.53
Brett Rumford	75	70	74	74	293	6,469.53
Daniel Vancsik	69	71	76	77	293	6,469.53
Magnus A. Carlsson	71	74	68	81	294	5,425.40
Ricardo Gonzalez	69	73	73	79	294	5,425.40
Pablo Larrazabal	70	74	79	71	294	5,425.40
Sam Little	66	75	76	77	294	5,425.40
Jean-Baptiste Gonnet	71	73	75	76	295	4,708.84
Callum Macaulay	71	72	71	81	295	4,708.84
Paul Waring	70	75	72	78	295	4,708.84
Ross McGowan	70	71	78	79	298	4,299.37
Anton Haig	68	73	79	79	299	3,992.27
Marcel Siem	67	76	78	78	299	3,992.27

Celtic Manor Wales Open

Celtic Manor Resort, Newport, Wales
Par 36-35–71; 7,378 yards

June 4-7
purse, €2,073,926

	SCORES				TOTAL	MONEY
Jeppe Huldahl	69	71	68	67	275	€343,086
Niclas Fasth	71	68	71	66	276	228,724
Ignacio Garrido	68	69	71	69	277	128,863.10
Gary Lockerbie	69	70	74	65	278	95,103.44
Danny Willett	73	66	72	67	278	95,103.44
Simon Dyson	74	65	70	70	279	57,844.30
Oliver Fisher	72	69	71	67	279	57,844.30
Richard Green	68	71	71	69	279	57,844.30

	SCORES			TOTAL	MONEY
Jeev Milkha Singh	69	68	73	69	279	57,844.30
Gregory Bourdy	70	70	70	70	280	35,818.18
Richie Ramsay	68	67	76	69	280	35,818.18
Paul Waring	71	68	70	71	280	35,818.18
Chris Wood	72	69	70	69	280	35,818.18
Fabrizio Zanotti	67	71	72	70	280	35,818.18
Klas Eriksson	70	72	69	70	281	29,642.63
Paul McGinley	68	71	71	71	281	29,642.63
Fredrik Andersson Hed	70	67	75	70	282	26,143.15
Rhys Davies	73	69	71	69	282	26,143.15
Miguel Angel Jimenez	70	70	72	70	282	26,143.15
Alan McLean	66	73	76	67	282	26,143.15
Mark Foster	69	69	72	73	283	23,261.23
Simon Khan	69	73	71	70	283	23,261.23
David Lynn	69	73	72	69	283	23,261.23
Peter Lawrie	69	72	74	69	284	21,717.34
Santiago Luna	73	69	71	71	284	21,717.34
Thongchai Jaidee	74	70	74	67	285	19,555.90
Pablo Larrazabal	67	73	71	74	285	19,555.90
Robert Rock	68	68	74	75	285	19,555.90
Lee Slattery	68	73	74	70	285	19,555.90
Bernd Wiesberger	72	70	74	69	285	19,555.90
Magnus A. Carlsson	70	69	72	75	286	16,262.28
Marc Cayeux	70	69	77	70	286	16,262.28
Ross Fisher	70	66	75	75	286	16,262.28
Jose Manuel Lara	69	72	75	70	286	16,262.28
Callum Macaulay	68	71	76	71	286	16,262.28
Gary Orr	68	73	72	73	286	16,262.28
Chris Doak	72	69	74	72	287	13,586.21
Nick Dougherty	66	72	70	79	287	13,586.21
Jean-Baptiste Gonnet	69	68	76	74	287	13,586.21
Branden Grace	70	72	74	71	287	13,586.21
Colin Montgomerie	69	69	78	71	287	13,586.21
Wade Ormsby	69	72	74	72	287	13,586.21
Thomas Bjorn	66	73	74	75	288	11,115.99
Scott Drummond	74	70	74	70	288	11,115.99
Richard Finch	71	68	73	76	288	11,115.99
Marcus Fraser	69	70	73	76	288	11,115.99
Corey Pavin	72	72	71	73	288	11,115.99
Marcel Siem	74	68	77	69	288	11,115.99
John Bickerton	69	70	75	75	289	9,057.47
Stephen Dodd	72	67	76	74	289	9,057.47
Marcus Higley	72	72	73	72	289	9,057.47
Jyoti Randhawa	72	72	74	71	289	9,057.47
Benn Barham	69	72	78	71	290	7,033.26
Bradley Dredge	74	70	71	75	290	7,033.26
Maarten Lafeber	68	76	76	70	290	7,033.26
Christian Nilsson	71	71	77	71	290	7,033.26
Chapchai Nirat	73	69	75	73	290	7,033.26
Iain Pyman	72	72	72	74	290	7,033.26
Sion E. Bebb	75	69	74	73	291	5,249.22
Robert Dinwiddie	71	71	75	74	291	5,249.22
Peter Hedblom	72	67	76	76	291	5,249.22
Eirik Tage Johansen	75	69	74	73	291	5,249.22
Shiv Kapur	73	67	74	77	291	5,249.22
Jean Francois Lucquin	70	72	74	75	291	5,249.22
Taco Remkes	67	75	78	71	291	5,249.22
Scott Strange	72	72	77	70	291	5,249.22
Andrew Oldcorn	76	68	73	75	292	4,322.88
Jonathan Caldwell	72	72	74	75	293	4,014.11
Joakim Haeggman	72	72	75	74	293	4,014.11
Michael Curtain	71	72	74	77	294	3,419.54
David Frost	66	76	75	77	294	3,419.54

	SCORES				TOTAL	MONEY
Alfredo Garcia-Heredia	72	71	84	70	297	3,085
Mark Brown	70	73	81	75	299	3,080.50
Tim Dykes	68	75	78	78	299	3,080.50
Birgir Hafthorsson	69	73	79	79	300	3,076

Saint-Omer Open

Aa Saint-Omer Golf Club, Lumbres, France
Par 36-35–71; 6,845 yards

June 18-21
purse, €606,237

	SCORES				TOTAL	MONEY
Christian Nilsson	68	69	65	69	271	€100,000
Jose-Filipe Lima	69	71	69	68	277	66,660
Javier Colomo	73	71	71	66	281	28,500
Lorenzo Gagli	71	71	68	71	281	28,500
Richard McEvoy	72	74	68	67	281	28,500
Ake Nilsson	71	71	68	71	281	28,500
Sion E. Bebb	70	72	67	73	282	15,480
James Morrison	67	69	70	76	282	15,480
Andrew Tampion	69	70	73	70	282	15,480
Stuart Manley	71	71	70	71	283	10,440
Edoardo Molinari	73	71	69	70	283	10,440
Steven O'Hara	72	70	72	69	283	10,440
Inder Van Weerelt	73	73	71	66	283	10,440
Kane Webber	70	71	74	68	283	10,440
Matthew Cort	73	71	68	72	284	7,687.50
Adam Gee	70	69	71	74	284	7,687.50
Anthony Grenier	75	70	70	69	284	7,687.50
Jamie McLeary	75	69	70	70	284	7,687.50
Wade Ormsby	70	65	74	75	284	7,687.50
Alessandro Tadini	70	73	69	72	284	7,687.50
Simon Wakefield	74	66	70	74	284	7,687.50
Peter Whiteford	69	76	68	71	284	7,687.50
Fredrik Andersson Hed	65	73	71	76	285	6,240
Chris Doak	72	70	71	72	285	6,240
Andreas Hogberg	69	75	70	71	285	6,240
Jan-Are Larsen	73	71	69	72	285	6,240
Eric Ramsay	75	71	68	71	285	6,240
Peter Baker	73	69	69	75	286	5,000
Andrew Butterfield	71	73	73	69	286	5,000
Carlos Del Moral	67	74	73	72	286	5,000
Mark Haastrup	72	73	68	73	286	5,000
Andrew McArthur	70	72	73	71	286	5,000
George Murray	71	73	67	75	286	5,000
Chinnarat Phadungsil	73	69	69	75	286	5,000
Ricardo Santos	71	73	69	73	286	5,000
Anthony Snobeck	71	71	75	69	286	5,000
Francois Calmels	71	74	70	72	287	3,960
Branden Grace	71	75	72	69	287	3,960
Julien Grillon	75	71	71	70	287	3,960
Santiago Luna	74	72	71	70	287	3,960
Ben Mason	74	72	71	70	287	3,960
Carlos Rodiles	71	74	71	71	287	3,960
Tony Carolan	66	73	73	76	288	3,120
Thomas Feyrsinger	69	72	76	71	288	3,120
Peter Gustafsson	76	69	72	71	288	3,120
Matthew Millar	71	69	70	78	288	3,120
Cesar Monasterio	75	70	72	71	288	3,120
Gareth Paddison	70	73	70	75	288	3,120
John Parry	73	70	75	70	288	3,120

	SCORES				TOTAL	MONEY
Martin Wiegele	70	72	72	74	288	3,120
Ben Evans	68	74	73	74	289	2,400
Birgir Hafthorsson	76	68	70	75	289	2,400
Kasper Linnet Jorgensen	69	74	77	69	289	2,400
Dennis Kupper	71	73	72	73	289	2,400
Adrien Bernadet	73	73	75	69	290	2,040
Garry Houston	74	72	72	72	290	2,040
Christophe Brazillier	76	70	72	73	291	1,800
Greig Hutcheon	75	71	73	72	291	1,800
Benoit Teilleria	74	72	72	73	291	1,800
Julien Clement	74	71	75	72	292	1,590
Michael Curtain	66	79	74	73	292	1,590
Chris Gane	72	73	75	72	292	1,590
Mikko Korhonen	69	77	75	71	292	1,590
Kalle Brink	70	75	75	73	293	1,350
Alfredo Garcia-Heredia	72	73	71	77	293	1,350
Lam Chih Bing	72	73	74	74	293	1,350
Unho Park	75	68	72	78	293	1,350
Matthew Zions	73	73	75	73	294	1,200
Peter Kaensche	74	72	76	74	296	1,046.67
Cedric Menut	74	71	73	78	296	1,046.67
Jean-Francois Remesy	75	71	76	74	296	1,046.67
Jamie Moul	72	74	76	75	297	895.50
Rolf Muntz	74	71	74	78	297	895.50
Daniel Denison	72	73	75	78	298	891
Robert Coles	74	72	74	80	300	886.50
Iain Pyman	71	72	72	85	300	886.50
Andre Bossert	72	73	77	79	301	882
Jonathan Caldwell	73	73	71		DQ	

BMW International Open

Golfclub Munchen Eichenreid, Munich, Germany
Par 36-36–72; 7,023 yards

June 25-28
purse, €2,003,000

	SCORES				TOTAL	MONEY
Nick Dougherty	69	65	68	64	266	€333,330
Rafa Echenique	68	69	68	62	267	222,220
Retief Goosen	64	68	67	71	270	125,200
Felipe Aguilar	69	70	66	66	271	78,700
David Drysdale	70	64	68	69	271	78,700
Miguel Angel Jimenez	69	67	70	65	271	78,700
Graeme Storm	70	70	64	67	271	78,700
Shiv Kapur	71	66	70	65	272	50,000
Richard Green	71	68	68	66	273	36,466.67
James Kingston	67	69	67	70	273	36,466.67
Soren Kjeldsen	68	65	70	70	273	36,466.67
Bernhard Langer	68	68	65	72	273	36,466.67
Thomas Levet	68	67	70	68	273	36,466.67
Danny Willett	67	68	71	67	273	36,466.67
Rory McIlroy	71	67	69	67	274	29,400
Magnus A. Carlsson	73	68	66	68	275	27,000
Niclas Fasth	67	73	72	63	275	27,000
David Lynn	67	70	71	67	275	27,000
Bradley Dredge	72	69	66	69	276	24,400
Peter Lawrie	69	68	70	69	276	24,400
Paul Broadhurst	69	70	65	73	277	22,000
S.S.P. Chowrasia	69	70	70	68	277	22,000
Pelle Edberg	71	69	66	71	277	22,000
Anders Hansen	69	69	69	70	277	22,000

	SCORES				TOTAL	MONEY
Thongchai Jaidee	69	66	74	68	277	22,000
Maarten Lafeber	67	70	70	71	278	19,900
Gary Orr	70	70	67	71	278	19,900
Andrew Coltart	67	71	71	70	279	18,700
Peter Hedblom	70	69	69	71	279	18,700
John Bickerton	70	70	70	70	280	16,600
Johan Edfors	71	69	70	70	280	16,600
Oliver Fisher	68	69	71	72	280	16,600
Scott Strange	70	68	70	72	280	16,600
Chris Wood	71	69	71	69	280	16,600
Markus Brier	69	71	70	71	281	13,400
Robert-Jan Derksen	69	71	71	70	281	13,400
Stephen Dodd	68	69	72	72	281	13,400
Louis Oosthuizen	69	69	69	74	281	13,400
Chinnarat Phadungsil	69	69	73	70	281	13,400
Marco Ruiz	73	67	68	73	281	13,400
Henrik Stenson	68	72	72	69	281	13,400
Richard Sterne	72	68	71	70	281	13,400
Fabrizio Zanotti	72	69	68	72	281	13,400
Max Kramer	71	69	73	69	282	11,200
Steven O'Hara	71	70	70	71	282	11,200
Carlos Del Moral	70	71	76	66	283	9,800
Marcus Fraser	67	74	73	69	283	9,800
Hennie Otto	72	69	73	69	283	9,800
Phillip Price	67	72	69	75	283	9,800
Anthony Wall	74	66	70	73	283	9,800
Gregory Bourdy	67	71	71	75	284	7,400
Luke Donald	70	68	73	73	284	7,400
Klas Eriksson	70	71	69	74	284	7,400
Gary Lockerbie	72	68	69	75	284	7,400
Jarmo Sandelin	68	71	71	74	284	7,400
Lee Slattery	70	70	72	72	284	7,400
Bernd Wiesberger	70	70	72	72	284	7,400
Kenneth Ferrie	69	72	73	71	285	5,700
Richard Finch	66	71	73	75	285	5,700
Jean-Baptiste Gonnet	70	70	69	76	285	5,700
Gareth Maybin	71	68	74	72	285	5,700
Seve Benson	70	71	70	75	286	5,000
Gonzalo Fernandez-Castano	69	71	74	72	286	5,000
Gary Murphy	71	70	72	73	286	5,000
Joakim Haeggman	72	67	76	72	287	4,600
Phillip Archer	69	72	74	74	289	4,200
Scott Drummond	71	69	73	76	289	4,200
Colin Montgomerie	70	71	72	76	289	4,200
Michael Hoey	70	71	71	80	292	3,800
Barry Lane	68	73	78	74	293	3,650
Michael Jonzon	70	71	78	78	297	3,000

Open de France ALSTOM

Le Golf National, Paris, France
Par 36-35–71; 7,300 yards

July 2-5
purse, €4,047,916

	SCORES				TOTAL	MONEY
Martin Kaymer	62	72	69	68	271	€666,660
Lee Westwood	68	68	70	65	271	444,440
(Kaymer defeated Westwood on first playoff hole.)						
Ian Poulter	72	69	66	67	274	250,400
Anders Hansen	69	72	68	66	275	184,800
Peter Hanson	65	70	70	70	275	184,800

	SCORES				TOTAL	MONEY
Kenneth Ferrie	70	68	71	67	276	112,400
Richard Green	68	67	70	71	276	112,400
Soren Hansen	68	71	72	65	276	112,400
Paul Waring	66	70	68	72	276	112,400
Gareth Maybin	69	71	71	67	278	74,133.33
Scott Strange	65	72	71	70	278	74,133.33
Danny Willett	68	71	70	69	278	74,133.33
Alejandro Canizares	67	72	71	69	279	55,500
Rafa Echenique	65	67	70	77	279	55,500
Ricardo Gonzalez	67	74	69	69	279	55,500
Soren Kjeldsen	70	71	69	69	279	55,500
Damien McGrane	70	72	69	68	279	55,500
Colin Montgomerie	69	74	65	71	279	55,500
Charl Schwartzel	68	66	72	73	279	55,500
Graeme Storm	69	72	67	71	279	55,500
Magnus A. Carlsson	69	71	71	69	280	44,600
Nick Dougherty	66	76	69	69	280	44,600
Peter Hedblom	73	70	71	66	280	44,600
Peter Lawrie	71	71	71	67	280	44,600
Phillip Archer	69	73	67	72	281	38,600
Seve Benson	70	67	68	76	281	38,600
Francois Delamontagne	75	68	70	68	281	38,600
Miguel Angel Jimenez	67	73	73	68	281	38,600
Jose Manuel Lara	70	72	71	68	281	38,600
Francesco Molinari	67	70	71	73	281	38,600
Darren Clarke	73	69	68	72	282	31,600
Gonzalo Fernandez-Castano	70	72	69	71	282	31,600
David Horsey	72	71	68	71	282	31,600
Thongchai Jaidee	65	75	68	74	282	31,600
Pablo Larrazabal	67	73	74	68	282	31,600
Daniel Vancsik	72	67	72	71	282	31,600
Robert-Jan Derksen	67	71	68	77	283	26,800
Gary Lockerbie	68	75	70	70	283	26,800
Gary Orr	73	70	67	73	283	26,800
Richard Sterne	70	70	69	74	283	26,800
Steve Webster	69	65	74	75	283	26,800
Paul Broadhurst	73	69	71	71	284	21,600
Niclas Fasth	71	72	71	70	284	21,600
Mark Foster	69	74	70	71	284	21,600
Marcus Fraser	68	74	72	70	284	21,600
Paul Lawrie	67	74	71	72	284	21,600
David Lynn	69	74	69	72	284	21,600
Chapchai Nirat	70	72	71	71	284	21,600
Alvaro Quiros	72	71	65	76	284	21,600
David Drysdale	67	76	71	71	285	16,800
Ignacio Garrido	74	66	73	72	285	16,800
Raphael Jacquelin	72	70	70	73	285	16,800
Shane Lowry	69	72	71	73	285	16,800
Jean-Francois Lucquin	70	72	69	75	286	13,600
Miguel Angel Martin	72	71	73	70	286	13,600
Ross McGowan	69	72	74	71	286	13,600
Jose Maria Olazabal	74	69	72	71	286	13,600
Thomas Bjorn	70	70	77	70	287	11,800
Jean Van de Velde	67	75	71	74	287	11,800
Benn Barham	68	74	73	73	288	10,000
John Bickerton	65	77	75	71	288	10,000
Jamie Donaldson	69	71	68	80	288	10,000
Alastair Forsyth	72	69	76	71	288	10,000
James Kingston	71	70	72	75	288	10,000
Barry Lane	70	71	74	73	288	10,000
Marc Warren	68	72	71	77	288	10,000
Philip Golding	71	72	73	73	289	8,200
Steven O'Hara	71	72	70	76	289	8,200

	SCORES				TOTAL	MONEY
Thomas Levet	67	73	75	75	290	7,600
Gregory Bourdy	69	71	71	80	291	6,432.33
Robert Rock	70	70	76	75	291	6,432.33
Oliver Wilson	72	69	71	79	291	6,432.33
Pablo Martin	71	72	72	77	292	5,994
Hennie Otto	74	67	73	79	293	5,989.50
Mads Vibe-Hastrup	68	75	75	75	293	5,989.50
S.S.P. Chowrasia	69	73	77	76	295	5,983.50
Sam Little	67	75	75	78	295	5,983.50
Paul Nilbrink	73	69	79	75	296	5,979

Barclays Scottish Open

Loch Lomond Golf Club, Glasgow, Scotland
Par 36-35–71; 7,149 yards

July 9-12
purse, €3,512,475

	SCORES				TOTAL	MONEY
Martin Kaymer	69	65	66	69	269	€579,339.98
Gonzalo Fernandez-Castano	65	70	64	72	271	301,911.44
Raphael Jacquelin	67	72	66	66	271	301,911.44
Soren Kjeldsen	67	68	67	70	272	160,593.04
Adam Scott	66	67	73	66	272	160,593.04
Retief Goosen	68	63	69	73	273	112,971.30
Nick Watney	67	68	71	67	273	112,971.30
Ross Fisher	69	67	71	67	274	82,382.15
Lee Westwood	73	66	64	71	274	82,382.15
Martin Laird	65	70	69	71	275	69,520.80
Richard Sterne	70	69	67	70	276	61,873.51
Steve Webster	71	70	67	68	276	61,873.51
Ernie Els	69	69	67	72	277	52,314.40
Brian Gay	70	69	65	73	277	52,314.40
Miguel Angel Jimenez	69	70	67	71	277	52,314.40
Geoff Ogilvy	69	70	66	72	277	52,314.40
Jamie Donaldson	69	68	65	76	278	44,956.78
Kenneth Ferrie	67	68	74	69	278	44,956.78
David Lynn	70	72	65	71	278	44,956.78
Angel Cabrera	69	70	69	71	279	39,348.77
Rod Pampling	68	71	67	73	279	39,348.77
Graeme Storm	65	76	71	67	279	39,348.77
Camilo Villegas	69	67	73	70	279	39,348.77
Oliver Wilson	74	65	70	70	279	39,348.77
Seve Benson	70	72	69	69	280	33,022.38
Mark Foster	68	68	72	72	280	33,022.38
Marcus Fraser	68	66	69	77	280	33,022.38
Soren Hansen	67	68	73	72	280	33,022.38
Paul Lawrie	68	72	68	72	280	33,022.38
Damien McGrane	71	68	73	68	280	33,022.38
Anthony Wall	70	69	69	72	280	33,022.38
Thomas Levet	70	71	69	71	281	27,808.32
Jose Maria Olazabal	71	69	69	72	281	27,808.32
Ian Poulter	69	72	68	72	281	27,808.32
Gregory Bourdy	72	70	69	71	282	24,332.28
Richard Green	64	72	73	73	282	24,332.28
Jean-Francois Lucquin	70	71	66	75	282	24,332.28
Francesco Molinari	67	73	68	74	282	24,332.28
Peter O'Malley	74	66	69	73	282	24,332.28
Brett Rumford	68	69	73	72	282	24,332.28
Darren Clarke	69	69	68	77	283	20,508.64
Gregory Havret	67	70	72	74	283	20,508.64
Graeme McDowell	70	72	71	70	283	20,508.64

	SCORES				TOTAL	MONEY
Paul McGinley	65	71	75	72	283	20,508.64
Mads Vibe-Hastrup	69	67	71	76	283	20,508.64
Thomas Aiken	69	66	76	73	284	16,337.39
Stuart Appleby	70	68	72	74	284	16,337.39
Markus Brier	69	69	73	73	284	16,337.39
Pablo Martin	69	72	71	72	284	16,337.39
Rory McIlroy	68	71	72	73	284	16,337.39
Colin Montgomerie	73	69	69	73	284	16,337.39
Gary Orr	70	68	71	75	284	16,337.39
Chris Doak	72	68	69	76	285	12,166.14
Scott Drummond	70	71	72	72	285	12,166.14
David Drysdale	67	73	72	73	285	12,166.14
Thongchai Jaidee	69	70	69	77	285	12,166.14
Alvaro Velasco	71	70	75	69	285	12,166.14
Alejandro Canizares	70	69	76	71	286	9,559.11
James Kingston	69	72	67	78	286	9,559.11
Gary Lockerbie	69	73	73	71	286	9,559.11
Andrew McLardy	68	72	73	73	286	9,559.11
Louis Oosthuizen	70	69	70	77	286	9,559.11
Scott Strange	70	72	74	70	286	9,559.11
Ross McGowan	67	72	75	73	287	7,994.89
Miles Tunnicliff	70	72	72	73	287	7,994.89
Boo Weekley	71	70	72	74	287	7,994.89
John Bickerton	72	69	71	76	288	6,798.55
Paul Broadhurst	71	71	74	72	288	6,798.55
Jason McCreadie	70	67	74	77	288	6,798.55
Alexander Noren	70	71	74	73	288	6,798.55
Sam Little	70	72	72	75	289	5,214
Oliver Fisher	73	68	72	77	290	5,208
Shane Lowry	69	71	71	79	290	5,208
Lee Slattery	71	70	73	76	290	5,208
Michael Lorenzo-Vera	70	72	75	74	291	5,202
Nick Dougherty	71	71	74	76	292	5,199
S.S.P. Chowrasia	73	69	75	76	293	5,196

The Open Championship

Turnberry, Ailsa Course, Ayrshire, Scotland
Par 35-35–70; 7,204 yards

July 16-19
purse, €4,857,633

	SCORES				TOTAL	MONEY
Stewart Cink	66	72	71	69	278	€866,557.54
Tom Watson	65	70	71	72	278	519,934.52
(Cink defeated Watson 14-20 in four-hole playoff.)						
Lee Westwood	68	70	70	71	279	294,629.56
Chris Wood	70	70	72	67	279	294,629.56
Luke Donald	71	72	70	67	280	181,399.38
Mathew Goggin	66	72	69	73	280	181,399.38
Retief Goosen	67	70	71	72	280	181,399.38
Thomas Aiken	71	72	69	69	281	104,449.07
Ernie Els	69	72	72	68	281	104,449.07
Soren Hansen	68	72	74	67	281	104,449.07
Richard S. Johnson	70	72	69	70	281	104,449.07
Justin Leonard	70	70	73	68	281	104,449.07
Ross Fisher	69	68	70	75	282	58,810.37
Thongchai Jaidee	69	72	69	72	282	58,810.37
Miguel Angel Jimenez	64	73	76	69	282	58,810.37
*Matteo Manassero	71	70	72	69	282	
Francesco Molinari	71	70	71	70	282	58,810.37
Jeff Overton	70	69	76	67	282	58,810.37

	SCORES				TOTAL	MONEY
Andres Romero	68	74	73	67	282	58,810.37
Justin Rose	69	72	71	70	282	58,810.37
Henrik Stenson	71	70	71	70	282	58,810.37
Camilo Villegas	66	73	73	70	282	58,810.37
Boo Weekley	67	72	72	71	282	58,810.37
Angel Cabrera	69	70	72	72	283	41,979.90
Peter Hanson	70	71	72	70	283	41,979.90
Oliver Wilson	72	70	71	70	283	41,979.90
Mark Calcavecchia	67	69	77	71	284	33,919.54
John Daly	68	72	72	72	284	33,919.54
James Kingston	67	71	74	72	284	33,919.54
Soren Kjeldsen	68	76	71	69	284	33,919.54
Kenichi Kuboya	65	72	75	72	284	33,919.54
Davis Love	69	73	73	69	284	33,919.54
Nick Watney	71	72	71	70	284	33,919.54
Jim Furyk	67	72	70	76	285	27,152.14
Martin Kaymer	69	70	74	72	285	27,152.14
Graeme McDowell	68	73	71	73	285	27,152.14
Richard Sterne	67	73	75	70	285	27,152.14
Nick Dougherty	70	70	73	73	286	22,126.10
Sergio Garcia	70	69	76	71	286	22,126.10
Thomas Levet	71	73	71	71	286	22,126.10
Steve Marino	67	68	76	75	286	22,126.10
Vijay Singh	67	70	75	74	286	22,126.10
Branden Grace	67	72	73	75	287	18,125.50
Paul McGinley	71	71	70	75	287	18,125.50
Bryce Molder	70	73	67	77	287	18,125.50
Anthony Wall	68	72	75	72	287	18,125.50
Paul Casey	68	76	74	70	288	15,309.18
Gonzalo Fernandez-Castano	69	72	73	74	288	15,309.18
Zach Johnson	70	71	77	70	288	15,309.18
Paul Lawrie	71	73	76	68	288	15,309.18
Rory McIlroy	69	74	74	71	288	15,309.18
Robert Allenby	70	74	73	72	289	12,983.92
Darren Clarke	71	71	78	69	289	12,983.92
Johan Edfors	71	73	72	73	289	12,983.92
David Howell	68	73	72	76	289	12,983.92
Billy Mayfair	69	73	73	74	289	12,983.92
Kenny Perry	71	72	75	71	289	12,983.92
Graeme Storm	72	72	74	71	289	12,983.92
Steve Stricker	66	77	70	76	289	12,983.92
Paul Broadhurst	70	72	74	74	290	12,074.04
David Drysdale	69	73	75	73	290	12,074.04
Tom Lehman	68	74	74	74	290	12,074.04
Kevin Sutherland	69	73	73	75	290	12,074.04
Ryuji Imada	74	69	79	69	291	11,785.18
Fredrik Andersson Hed	71	70	78	73	292	11,496.33
Stuart Appleby	71	72	76	73	292	11,496.33
Padraig Harrington	69	74	76	73	292	11,496.33
Sean O'Hair	68	75	75	74	292	11,496.33
J.B. Holmes	68	70	75	80	293	11,207.48
Fredrik Jacobson	70	72	77	76	295	11,034.17
Mark O'Meara	67	77	77	74	295	11,034.17
Paul Goydos	72	72	77	82	303	10,860.85
Daniel Gaunt	76	67	79	82	304	10,745.31

Out of Final 36 Holes

Ben Curtis	65	80			145	3,697.31
Josh Geary	70	75			145	3,697.31
Todd Hamilton	75	70			145	3,697.31
Anders Hansen	68	77			145	3,697.31
Peter Hedblom	71	74			145	3,697.31

	SCORES		TOTAL	MONEY
Charley Hoffman	71	74	145	3,697.31
Colin Montgomerie	71	74	145	3,697.31
Adam Scott	71	74	145	3,697.31
D.J. Trahan	68	77	145	3,697.31
Mike Weir	67	78	145	3,697.31
Tiger Woods	71	74	145	3,697.31
Peter Baker	74	72	146	3,061.84
K.J. Choi	74	72	146	3,061.84
Tim Clark	71	75	146	3,061.84
Ben Crane	71	75	146	3,061.84
Ryo Ishikawa	68	78	146	3,061.84
Anthony Kim	73	73	146	3,061.84
Matt Kuchar	70	76	146	3,061.84
Martin Laird	74	72	146	3,061.84
Louis Oosthuizen	70	76	146	3,061.84
Elliot Saltman	70	76	146	3,061.84
John Senden	66	80	146	3,061.84
Briny Baird	72	75	147	3,061.84
Mark Brown	71	76	147	3,061.84
Rhys Davies	73	74	147	3,061.84
James Driscoll	76	71	147	3,061.84
David Duval	71	76	147	3,061.84
Richard Green	71	76	147	3,061.84
Rod Pampling	74	73	147	3,061.84
Rory Sabbatini	74	73	147	3,061.84
Charl Schwartzel	71	76	147	3,061.84
David Toms	72	75	147	3,061.84
Ikeda Yuta	76	71	147	3,061.84
Gaganjeet Bhullar	71	77	148	2,744.10
Markus Brier	71	77	148	2,744.10
David Higgins	73	75	148	2,744.10
Charles Howell	73	75	148	2,744.10
Raphael Jacquelin	75	73	148	2,744.10
Sandy Lyle	75	73	148	2,744.10
Prayad Marksaeng	73	75	148	2,744.10
Gary Orr	73	75	148	2,744.10
Alvaro Quiros	71	77	148	2,744.10
Robert Rock	73	75	148	2,744.10
Bubba Watson	73	75	148	2,744.10
Stephen Ames	72	77	149	2,744.10
Rafa Echenique	72	77	149	2,744.10
Brian Gay	73	76	149	2,744.10
Lucas Glover	72	77	149	2,744.10
*Stephan Gross, Jr.	74	75	149	
Liang Wen-chong	77	72	149	2,744.10
Richie Ramsay	77	72	149	2,744.10
David Smail	70	79	149	2,744.10
Brandt Snedeker	72	77	149	2,744.10
Azuma Yano	75	74	149	2,744.10
Chad Campbell	73	77	150	2,426.36
Ken Duke	71	79	150	2,426.36
Tomohiro Kondo	71	79	150	2,426.36
Terry Pilkadaris	68	82	150	2,426.36
Steve Surry	69	81	150	2,426.36
Tim Wood	73	77	150	2,426.36
Marc Cayeux	75	76	151	2,426.36
Sir Nick Faldo	78	73	151	2,426.36
Richard Finch	73	78	151	2,426.36
Jeremy Kavanagh	74	77	151	2,426.36
Hunter Mahan	72	79	151	2,426.36
Carl Pettersson	74	77	151	2,426.36
Tim Stewart	74	77	151	2,426.36
Thomas Haylock	74	78	152	2,426.36

	SCORES		TOTAL	MONEY
Damien McGrane	78	74	152	2,426.36
Greg Norman	77	75	152	2,426.36
Lloyd Saltman	75	77	152	2,426.36
Geoff Ogilvy	75	78	153	2,426.36
Bruce Vaughan	78	75	153	2,426.36
Dustin Johnson	78	76	154	2,426.36
Koumei Oda	76	78	154	2,426.36
Ian Poulter	75	79	154	2,426.36
Daniel Wardrop	75	80	155	2,426.36
Michael Wright	77	79	156	2,426.36
Oliver Fisher	79	78	157	2,426.36
Pablo Larrazabal	79	81	160	2,426.36
Peter Ellebye	77	84	161	2,426.36
Jaco Ahlers	83	79	162	2,426.36
Michael Campbell	78	88	WD	

SAS Masters

Barseback Golf & Country Club, Malmo, Sweden
Par 36-37–73; 7,665 yards

July 23-26
purse, €1,011,916

	SCORES				TOTAL	MONEY
Ricardo Gonzalez	68	68	77	69	282	€166,660
Jamie Donaldson	71	72	73	68	284	111,110
Jeppe Huldahl	72	70	70	74	286	62,600
Martin Erlandsson	70	70	72	76	288	32,114.29
Marcus Fraser	72	69	70	77	288	32,114.29
Oskar Henningsson	70	72	73	73	288	32,114.29
Marcus Higley	72	71	70	75	288	32,114.29
Jacob Olesen	73	72	75	68	288	32,114.29
Lee Slattery	67	70	75	76	288	32,114.29
Nathan Smith	75	71	71	71	288	32,114.29
Danny Willett	71	72	76	70	289	18,400
Robert Dinwiddie	74	70	75	71	290	15,480
Joakim Haeggman	74	70	72	74	290	15,480
Soren Kjeldsen	72	71	75	72	290	15,480
Gareth Maybin	72	73	72	73	290	15,480
Christian Nilsson	72	71	73	74	290	15,480
Pelle Edberg	72	73	73	73	291	12,100
Klas Eriksson	69	78	73	71	291	12,100
Niclas Fasth	72	71	73	75	291	12,100
Jean-Baptiste Gonnet	73	71	70	77	291	12,100
Estanislao Goya	69	74	75	73	291	12,100
David Lynn	73	73	71	74	291	12,100
Jesper Parnevik	74	71	72	74	291	12,100
Richard S. Johnson	74	70	75	73	292	10,400
Mikael Lundberg	73	74	70	75	292	10,400
Richie Ramsay	70	70	77	75	292	10,400
Marc Cayeux	74	69	76	74	293	8,750
Robert-Jan Derksen	77	71	71	74	293	8,750
Maarten Lafeber	72	75	75	71	293	8,750
Pablo Larrazabal	69	71	74	79	293	8,750
Peter Lawrie	73	71	75	74	293	8,750
Wade Ormsby	72	72	70	79	293	8,750
Joel Sjoholm	73	72	71	77	293	8,750
Anders Sjostrand	72	69	75	77	293	8,750
Alejandro Canizares	71	74	70	79	294	7,300
John Mellor	76	70	77	71	294	7,300
Brett Rumford	70	75	74	75	294	7,300
James Driscoll	73	74	73	75	295	6,500

	SCORES				TOTAL	MONEY
Mikko Ilonen	75	72	73	75	295	6,500
Sam Little	72	75	69	79	295	6,500
Gary Murphy	71	74	75	75	295	6,500
Steve Webster	71	73	76	75	295	6,500
Francois Delamontagne	73	75	75	73	296	5,400
Simon Dyson	75	72	73	76	296	5,400
Johan Edfors	74	73	74	75	296	5,400
Mattias Eliasson	73	72	75	76	296	5,400
Michael Hoey	72	74	74	76	296	5,400
Raphael Jacquelin	76	69	73	78	296	5,400
Phillip Archer	75	73	76	73	297	4,400
Callum Macaulay	73	72	74	78	297	4,400
Pablo Martin	69	75	74	79	297	4,400
Alvaro Velasco	77	70	75	75	297	4,400
Fredrik Andersson Hed	74	72	75	77	298	3,500
Ignacio Garrido	73	72	78	75	298	3,500
Peter Hanson	74	73	75	76	298	3,500
Damien McGrane	73	71	76	78	298	3,500
Alessandro Tadini	74	74	73	77	298	3,500
Richard Bland	74	72	77	76	299	2,850
Magnus A. Carlsson	71	71	79	78	299	2,850
Simon Khan	74	74	76	75	299	2,850
Peter O'Malley	74	70	77	78	299	2,850
Rafael Cabrera-Bello	74	74	75	77	300	2,400
Michael Campbell	78	70	73	79	300	2,400
Andrew Coltart	76	71	74	79	300	2,400
Ake Nilsson	75	73	75	77	300	2,400
Marcel Siem	71	74	80	75	300	2,400
Antti Ahokas	74	73	79	75	301	1,804.50
Bradley Dredge	76	72	80	73	301	1,804.50
Will MacKenzie	73	74	76	78	301	1,804.50
Joakim Rask	75	73	74	79	301	1,804.50
Robert Rock	73	73	76	79	301	1,804.50
Bernd Wiesberger	74	72	78	77	301	1,804.50
Per Barth	75	73	72	82	302	1,491
Henrik Stenson	73	74	79	76	302	1,491
Fabrizio Zanotti	78	70	76	78	302	1,491
Niklas Bruzelius	78	70	77	78	303	1,485
Chris Doak	74	73	78	80	305	1,482
Branden Grace	70	78	81	80	309	1,479

Moravia Silesia Open

Prosper Golf Resort, Celadna, Czech Republic   July 30-August 2
Par 36-36–72; 7,155 yards   purse, €2,003,000

	SCORES				TOTAL	MONEY
Oskar Henningsson	70	71	67	67	275	€333,330
Sam Little	70	67	70	70	277	173,710
Steve Webster	66	70	69	72	277	173,710
Marc Cayeux	71	71	70	66	278	84,933.33
Ignacio Garrido	67	70	69	72	278	84,933.33
Graeme Storm	68	68	70	72	278	84,933.33
Jose Manuel Lara	68	70	73	68	279	55,000
Gareth Maybin	73	66	68	72	279	55,000
Robert-Jan Derksen	67	70	71	72	280	42,400
Estanislao Goya	65	75	70	70	280	42,400
John Bickerton	66	71	72	73	282	32,680
David Drysdale	72	72	67	71	282	32,680
Callum Macaulay	68	72	71	71	282	32,680

	SCORES			TOTAL	MONEY
Patrik Sjoland	69	71	73	69	282	32,680
Lee Slattery	71	72	70	69	282	32,680
Santiago Luna	70	69	72	72	283	28,200
Markus Brier	70	73	68	73	284	24,960
Simon Dyson	76	66	69	73	284	24,960
Mark Foster	72	71	71	70	284	24,960
Miguel Angel Jimenez	71	71	69	73	284	24,960
Fabrizio Zanotti	68	71	71	74	284	24,960
Magnus A. Carlsson	72	71	70	72	285	20,800
Robert Dinwiddie	71	70	70	74	285	20,800
Martin Erlandsson	71	74	66	74	285	20,800
Maarten Lafeber	69	68	76	72	285	20,800
Stuart Manley	73	69	71	72	285	20,800
Danny Willett	70	70	75	70	285	20,800
Chris Wood	71	70	71	73	285	20,800
Jeppe Huldahl	68	75	71	72	286	17,800
Matthew Millar	70	70	73	73	286	17,800
Daniel Vancsik	72	71	70	73	286	17,800
Christian Cevaer	74	69	71	73	287	15,750
David Frost	72	70	74	71	287	15,750
Damien McGrane	73	71	70	73	287	15,750
Richie Ramsay	71	68	70	78	287	15,750
Michael Hoey	71	71	68	78	288	14,200
Michael Lorenzo-Vera	68	75	71	74	288	14,200
Marc Warren	71	74	69	74	288	14,200
Carlos Del Moral	73	71	71	74	289	12,000
Francois Delamontagne	67	72	71	79	289	12,000
Jamie Donaldson	71	71	72	75	289	12,000
Raphael Jacquelin	71	73	69	76	289	12,000
Thomas Levet	69	74	70	76	289	12,000
David Lynn	76	69	69	75	289	12,000
Steven O'Hara	71	73	72	73	289	12,000
Jyoti Randhawa	72	73	68	76	289	12,000
Bradley Dredge	70	71	73	76	290	9,200
David Horsey	74	71	71	74	290	9,200
Shiv Kapur	75	67	73	75	290	9,200
Simon Khan	73	71	71	75	290	9,200
Mikael Lundberg	70	74	73	73	290	9,200
Alan McLean	74	71	69	76	290	9,200
Benn Barham	72	73	71	75	291	7,400
Alejandro Canizares	70	74	72	75	291	7,400
Alexandre Rocha	72	73	70	76	291	7,400
Jean-Baptiste Gonnet	72	73	73	74	292	6,600
John Mellor	73	72	73	75	293	5,700
Robert Rock	71	74	71	77	293	5,700
Miles Tunnicliff	72	73	73	75	293	5,700
Inder Van Weerelt	75	69	75	74	293	5,700
Simon Wakefield	73	70	71	79	293	5,700
Kane Webber	71	74	75	73	293	5,700
Fredrik Andersson Hed	75	70	71	78	294	4,900
Brett Rumford	74	71	75	74	294	4,900
Barry Lane	71	74	71	79	295	4,300
Jonathan Lomas	72	72	76	75	295	4,300
Ake Nilsson	72	71	75	77	295	4,300
Nathan Smith	71	72	77	75	295	4,300
Scott Drummond	73	70	78	75	296	3,725
Roope Kakko	72	71	75	78	296	3,725
Felipe Aguilar	71	72	80	78	301	3,000

KLM Open

Kennemer Golf & Country Club, Zandvoort, Netherlands

August 20-23

Par 36-34–70; 6,626 yards

purse, €1,793,300

	SCORES				TOTAL	MONEY
Simon Dyson	67	67	68	63	265	€300,000
Peter Hedblom	66	66	64	69	265	156,340
Peter Lawrie	65	68	65	67	265	156,340
(Dyson defeated Hedblom and Lawrie on first playoff hole.)						
Damien McGrane	67	67	68	64	266	90,000
Darren Clarke	65	67	67	68	267	69,660
Jamie Donaldson	66	68	66	67	267	69,660
Bradley Dredge	66	67	69	66	268	54,000
Terry Pilkadaris	69	65	66	69	269	45,000
Niclas Fasth	69	68	67	66	270	40,320
Ignacio Garrido	66	69	69	67	271	34,560
Alexander Noren	72	66	64	69	271	34,560
Marcus Fraser	69	69	65	69	272	29,160
Oskar Henningsson	67	66	69	70	272	29,160
Barry Lane	68	68	65	71	272	29,160
Andrew Coltart	68	69	69	67	273	23,062.50
Klas Eriksson	67	68	71	67	273	23,062.50
Martin Erlandsson	70	67	73	63	273	23,062.50
Richard Green	69	67	69	68	273	23,062.50
Michael Lorenzo-Vera	68	71	66	68	273	23,062.50
Shane Lowry	66	68	71	68	273	23,062.50
Alessandro Tadini	68	67	66	72	273	23,062.50
Fabrizio Zanotti	74	64	65	70	273	23,062.50
Markus Brier	67	69	65	73	274	19,260
Jean-Baptiste Gonnet	71	67	67	69	274	19,260
Paul Lawrie	66	68	69	71	274	19,260
Felipe Aguilar	68	71	67	69	275	16,020
Carlos Del Moral	67	67	70	71	275	16,020
Kenneth Ferrie	66	67	67	75	275	16,020
David Lynn	68	68	68	71	275	16,020
Gareth Maybin	67	68	69	71	275	16,020
Paul McGinley	64	70	70	71	275	16,020
Wade Ormsby	66	67	71	71	275	16,020
Phillip Price	66	72	68	69	275	16,020
Richie Ramsay	69	68	66	72	275	16,020
Alejandro Canizares	72	63	68	73	276	12,060
Rafa Echenique	69	69	73	65	276	12,060
Ricardo Gonzalez	70	68	70	68	276	12,060
Marcus Higley	71	63	67	75	276	12,060
David Horsey	73	66	68	69	276	12,060
Garry Houston	67	70	67	72	276	12,060
Eirik Tage Johansen	70	64	70	72	276	12,060
Shiv Kapur	71	68	69	68	276	12,060
Mikael Lundberg	70	69	69	68	276	12,060
Benn Barham	71	68	69	69	277	9,900
Christian Cevaer	70	66	67	74	277	9,900
Mark Foster	69	68	73	67	277	9,900
Mark Brown	68	71	68	71	278	7,920
Jorge Campillo	65	71	74	68	278	7,920
Emanuele Canonica	70	67	72	69	278	7,920
Robert-Jan Derksen	70	66	70	72	278	7,920
David Drysdale	72	65	72	69	278	7,920
Simon Khan	68	71	68	71	278	7,920
Sam Little	70	67	63	78	278	7,920
Ross McGowan	70	67	71	70	278	7,920
Gary Orr	64	73	71	71	279	5,940
Guido van der Valk	71	67	71	70	279	5,940

	SCORES				TOTAL	MONEY
Chris Wood	71	68	68	72	279	5,940
Simon Wakefield	69	68	71	72	280	5,400
Peter O'Malley	69	70	71	71	281	5,130
Graeme Storm	71	67	74	69	281	5,130
Michael Jonzon	69	69	74	70	282	4,680
Callum Macaulay	66	73	71	72	282	4,680
Miles Tunnicliff	70	69	70	73	282	4,680
Sion E. Bebb	71	67	67	78	283	4,320
Jeppe Huldahl	69	69	76	70	284	4,140
Phillip Archer	74	64	78	69	285	3,870
Ulrich van den Berg	69	68	73	75	285	3,870
David Dixon	72	66	81	70	289	3,600

Johnnie Walker Championship

Gleneagles Hotel, Perthshire, Scotland
Par 36-36–72; 7,316 yards

August 27-30
purse, €1,603,154

	SCORES				TOTAL	MONEY
Peter Hedblom	72	68	68	67	275	€269,895.15
Martin Erlandsson	74	70	70	62	276	179,926.25
Gregory Havret	68	76	67	67	278	91,171.88
Paul Lawrie	67	69	73	69	278	91,171.88
Gary Orr	73	71	71	64	279	68,662.31
Gregory Bourdy	70	69	71	70	280	45,504.97
Jamie Donaldson	69	71	70	70	280	45,504.97
Shiv Kapur	69	70	72	69	280	45,504.97
Steven O'Hara	68	76	66	70	280	45,504.97
Soren Hansen	69	70	71	72	282	29,027.64
Raphael Jacquelin	72	69	71	70	282	29,027.64
Danny Lee	71	70	72	69	282	29,027.64
David Lynn	76	68	71	67	282	29,027.64
Damien McGrane	72	72	71	68	283	24,290.91
Graeme Storm	69	74	70	70	283	24,290.91
David Carter	74	70	70	70	284	21,861.82
Ricardo Gonzalez	70	71	71	72	284	21,861.82
Gary Murphy	73	69	73	69	284	21,861.82
Richard Bland	72	72	67	74	285	18,116.97
Francois Delamontagne	73	69	70	73	285	18,116.97
David Dixon	76	68	74	67	285	18,116.97
Chris Doak	72	72	74	67	285	18,116.97
Michael Jonzon	70	69	72	74	285	18,116.97
Daniel Vancsik	69	69	74	73	285	18,116.97
Danny Willett	69	71	73	72	285	18,116.97
Fabrizio Zanotti	72	70	70	73	285	18,116.97
Pelle Edberg	72	71	75	68	286	15,141.33
Joakim Haeggman	72	70	72	72	286	15,141.33
John E. Morgan	70	71	78	67	286	15,141.33
Oliver Wilson	73	68	74	71	286	15,141.33
Jonathan Caldwell	72	66	76	73	287	12,793.21
Bradley Dredge	75	67	73	72	287	12,793.21
Colin Montgomerie	76	68	72	71	287	12,793.21
Jose Maria Olazabal	71	68	77	71	287	12,793.21
Richie Ramsay	71	73	74	69	287	12,793.21
Anthony Wall	69	75	72	71	287	12,793.21
Richard Finch	73	70	75	70	288	11,011.88
Maarten Lafeber	71	67	73	77	288	11,011.88
Pablo Larrazabal	70	72	72	74	288	11,011.88
Ross McGowan	74	68	74	72	288	11,011.88
Bernd Wiesberger	71	72	76	70	289	10,202.18

	SCORES				TOTAL	MONEY
Alan McLean	69	73	74	74	290	9,554.42
Chinnarat Phadungsil	70	70	76	74	290	9,554.42
Patrik Sjoland	70	72	76	72	290	9,554.42
Christian Cevaer	69	75	73	74	291	8,096.97
Jean-Baptiste Gonnet	73	71	75	72	291	8,096.97
Simon Khan	70	72	76	73	291	8,096.97
Ake Nilsson	68	73	78	72	291	8,096.97
Alexandre Rocha	72	69	77	73	291	8,096.97
Inder Van Weerelt	73	71	76	71	291	8,096.97
Scott Arnold	71	72	80	69	292	6,315.64
Michael Curtain	72	70	75	75	292	6,315.64
Stephen Dodd	73	70	76	73	292	6,315.64
Mikko Ilonen	71	71	76	74	292	6,315.64
Eirik Tage Johansen	72	70	74	76	292	6,315.64
Simon Dyson	76	68	75	74	293	5,074.10
Stephen Leaney	71	71	78	73	293	5,074.10
Alexander Noren	69	74	74	76	293	5,074.10
Gareth Maybin	69	73	78	74	294	4,615.27
Wade Ormsby	68	73	78	75	294	4,615.27
Phillip Archer	71	69	76	79	295	4,291.39
Pablo Martin	72	71	71	81	295	4,291.39
Marcus Fraser	70	73	74	79	296	4,048.49
Gary Lockerbie	72	72	79	78	301	3,886.55
Wil Besseling	73	70	84	75	302	3,724.61

Omega European Masters

Crans-sur-Sierre Golf Club, Crans Montana, Switzerland
Par 36-35–71; 6,822 yards

September 3-6
purse, €1,996,350

	SCORES				TOTAL	MONEY
Alexander Noren	65	70	63	66	264	€333,330
Bradley Dredge	68	65	68	65	266	222,220
Ross McGowan	67	67	68	65	267	125,200
Miguel Angel Jimenez	65	68	69	67	269	100,000
Thongchai Jaidee	65	71	67	67	270	84,800
Charl Schwartzel	67	68	65	71	271	70,000
Simon Dyson	63	71	73	65	272	48,700
David Howell	68	69	68	67	272	48,700
Rory McIlroy	67	71	70	64	272	48,700
Angelo Que	69	65	68	70	272	48,700
Paul Broadhurst	72	67	68	66	273	34,466.67
Ignacio Garrido	68	71	67	67	273	34,466.67
Thaworn Wiratchant	71	68	67	67	273	34,466.67
Felipe Aguilar	70	66	68	70	274	29,400
Julien Clement	69	67	71	67	274	29,400
Edoardo Molinari	70	67	69	68	274	29,400
Estanislao Goya	70	68	72	65	275	26,400
Paul McGinley	66	68	70	71	275	26,400
Gregory Bourdy	68	72	68	68	276	23,650
David Dixon	69	69	68	70	276	23,650
Michael Lorenzo-Vera	69	68	70	69	276	23,650
Christian Nilsson	65	70	74	67	276	23,650
Mark Foster	70	70	70	67	277	19,900
Maarten Lafeber	71	68	66	72	277	19,900
*Matteo Manassero	68	70	69	70	277	
Pablo Martin	70	66	73	68	277	19,900
Peter O'Malley	68	71	70	68	277	19,900
Graeme Storm	69	66	70	72	277	19,900
Lee Westwood	71	67	73	66	277	19,900

		SCORES			TOTAL	MONEY
Danny Willett	65	71	72	69	277	19,900
Oliver Wilson	70	68	69	70	277	19,900
Thomas Aiken	68	64	75	71	278	14,920
Robert Dinwiddie	74	66	67	71	278	14,920
Rafa Echenique	71	69	66	72	278	14,920
Jean-Baptiste Gonnet	68	72	70	68	278	14,920
David Lynn	68	70	72	68	278	14,920
Graeme McDowell	68	70	71	69	278	14,920
Jyoti Randhawa	70	68	70	70	278	14,920
Brett Rumford	62	73	72	71	278	14,920
Alessandro Tadini	69	68	69	72	278	14,920
Chris Wood	66	72	65	75	278	14,920
Benn Barham	70	66	73	70	279	12,000
Danny Lee	71	67	73	68	279	12,000
Francesco Molinari	67	72	70	70	279	12,000
Andres Romero	65	70	72	72	279	12,000
Peter Hanson	74	65	71	70	280	10,600
Luke List	70	69	67	74	280	10,600
Marcel Siem	67	70	69	74	280	10,600
Seve Benson	71	69	71	70	281	8,600
Rafael Cabrera-Bello	70	70	71	70	281	8,600
Johan Edfors	66	69	69	77	281	8,600
Anthony Kang	71	69	71	70	281	8,600
Callum Macaulay	68	72	68	73	281	8,600
Chapchai Nirat	68	67	74	72	281	8,600
Jeev Milkha Singh	68	69	70	74	281	8,600
Scott Drummond	72	67	72	71	282	6,450
David Drysdale	70	70	73	69	282	6,450
Ricardo Gonzalez	67	72	69	74	282	6,450
Gary Orr	69	71	72	70	282	6,450
Darren Clarke	69	68	74	72	283	5,600
David Horsey	70	70	72	71	283	5,600
Shiv Kapur	68	69	73	73	283	5,600
Richard Bland	71	68	73	72	284	5,000
Louis Oosthuizen	69	71	71	73	284	5,000
Anthony Wall	69	71	77	67	284	5,000
Gareth Maybin	70	68	76	71	285	4,600
Gregory Havret	68	71	74	75	288	4,400
Gary Lockerbie	73	67	78	71	289	4,200
Michael Campbell	69	71	76	76	292	3,900
Mads Vibe-Hastrup	69	69	73	81	292	3,900

Mercedes-Benz Championship

Golf Club Gut Larchenhof, Cologne, Germany
Par 36-36–72; 7,289 yards

September 10-13
purse, €2,000,000

		SCORES			TOTAL	MONEY
James Kingston	67	69	70	69	275	€320,000
Anders Hansen	70	68	70	67	275	220,000
(Kingston defeated Hansen on first playoff hole.)						
Simon Dyson	68	70	68	70	276	101,516.67
Soren Hansen	65	71	70	70	276	101,516.67
Peter Hanson	70	68	67	71	276	101,516.67
Henrik Stenson	70	68	69	71	278	64,000
Anthony Wall	69	70	68	71	278	64,000
David Drysdale	67	70	73	69	279	47,000
Lee Westwood	70	69	72	68	279	47,000
Alex Cejka	70	72	68	70	280	38,400
Rod Pampling	71	72	69	68	280	38,400

	SCORES				TOTAL	MONEY
Francesco Molinari	68	71	69	73	281	32,400
Marcel Siem	70	70	72	69	281	32,400
Chris Wood	66	69	73	73	281	32,400
Darren Clarke	70	70	70	72	282	28,200
Scott Drummond	71	69	74	68	282	28,200
Graeme McDowell	70	72	70	70	282	28,200
Felipe Aguilar	72	69	71	71	283	24,080
Ross Fisher	67	69	78	69	283	24,080
Ricardo Gonzalez	71	71	69	72	283	24,080
Peter Hedblom	71	70	70	72	283	24,080
Jeev Milkha Singh	72	74	68	69	283	24,080
Markus Brier	69	73	73	69	284	19,000
Niclas Fasth	70	67	72	75	284	19,000
Estanislao Goya	74	69	70	71	284	19,000
Raphael Jacquelin	70	72	70	72	284	19,000
Bernhard Langer	71	75	70	68	284	19,000
Paul Lawrie	68	71	69	76	284	19,000
Gareth Maybin	76	73	67	68	284	19,000
Alexander Noren	71	72	70	71	284	19,000
Hennie Otto	73	71	72	68	284	19,000
Scott Strange	67	68	74	75	284	19,000
Steve Webster	76	67	74	67	284	19,000
Johan Edfors	78	71	69	67	285	14,200
Soren Kjeldsen	69	69	71	76	285	14,200
Thomas Levet	70	71	73	71	285	14,200
Paul McGinley	72	68	72	73	285	14,200
Colin Montgomerie	72	69	71	73	285	14,200
Christian Nilsson	69	76	70	70	285	14,200
Graeme Storm	69	68	78	70	285	14,200
Thomas Bjorn	76	71	70	69	286	11,400
Jamie Donaldson	74	70	71	71	286	11,400
Thongchai Jaidee	75	72	71	68	286	11,400
Anthony Kang	71	71	72	72	286	11,400
Prayad Marksaeng	71	68	74	73	286	11,400
Robert Rock	70	72	75	69	286	11,400
Daniel Vancsik	69	72	69	76	286	11,400
David Howell	71	74	72	70	287	9,400
Jose Maria Olazabal	74	68	73	72	287	9,400
Charl Schwartzel	76	72	68	71	287	9,400
Stephen Dodd	69	74	71	74	288	8,400
Nick Dougherty	69	76	75	68	288	8,400
Christian Cevaer	71	72	73	73	289	7,200
Gonzalo Fernandez-Castano	73	70	75	71	289	7,200
Kenneth Ferrie	72	78	70	69	289	7,200
Alvaro Quiros	72	73	73	71	289	7,200
Richard Finch	69	72	73	76	290	6,000
Shane Lowry	75	72	72	71	290	6,000
Mikael Lundberg	78	73	69	70	290	6,000
Thomas Aiken	74	69	73	75	291	5,300
Florian Fritsch	74	71	71	75	291	5,300
Trevor Immelman	70	74	72	75	291	5,300
Louis Oosthuizen	69	76	72	74	291	5,300
Damien McGrane	72	72	76	72	292	4,700
Danny Willett	72	70	71	79	292	4,700
Gregory Havret	77	72	73	72	294	4,400
John Bickerton	74	73	75	73	295	4,000
Gregory Bourdy	72	76	70	77	295	4,000
Miguel Angel Jimenez	70	74	77	74	295	4,000
Pablo Larrazabal	70	73	80	73	296	3,650
Oskar Henningsson	73	70	79	76	298	3,425
Michael Hoey	76	77	74	71	298	3,425
Fabrizio Zanotti	77	75	71	76	299	3,200
Alastair Forsyth	74	75	74	77	300	3,050

	SCORES				TOTAL	MONEY
Jeppe Huldahl	76	78	71	78	303	2,900
Michael Campbell	77	79	76	73	305	2,750
Mark Brown	75	75	75	82	307	2,600
S.S.P. Chowrasia	79	81	74	77	311	2,450

Austrian Golf Open

Fontana Golf Club, Vienna, Austria
Par 35-36–71; 7,066 yards

September 17-20
purse, €989,970

	SCORES				TOTAL	MONEY
Rafael Cabrera-Bello	71	67	66	60	264	€166,660
Benn Barham	63	66	67	69	265	111,110
Soren Hansen	67	67	65	68	267	62,600
Richard Bland	68	70	65	66	269	50,000
Louis Oosthuizen	69	67	65	69	270	42,400
Seve Benson	69	68	68	66	271	28,100
Richard Green	65	66	69	71	271	28,100
Pablo Martin	66	68	70	67	271	28,100
Simon Wakefield	68	70	67	66	271	28,100
David Dixon	68	67	71	66	272	17,925
Pelle Edberg	68	65	71	68	272	17,925
David Horsey	67	67	71	67	272	17,925
Damien McGrane	71	67	67	67	272	17,925
Alex Cejka	69	68	71	65	273	14,700
Gary Murphy	68	67	72	66	273	14,700
Brett Rumford	64	71	68	70	273	14,700
Markus Brier	68	67	69	70	274	12,700
Chris Gaunt	66	67	72	69	274	12,700
Jean-Baptiste Gonnet	65	70	69	70	274	12,700
Joost Luiten	67	67	76	64	274	12,700
David Drysdale	69	68	67	71	275	11,000
Martin Erlandsson	67	68	73	67	275	11,000
Michael Lorenzo-Vera	66	69	70	70	275	11,000
Patrik Sjoland	69	68	69	69	275	11,000
Marc Warren	68	68	71	68	275	11,000
Bradley Dredge	72	64	70	70	276	9,650
Scott Drummond	64	68	72	72	276	9,650
David Lynn	67	68	72	69	276	9,650
Marco Ruiz	70	68	70	68	276	9,650
Phillip Archer	65	71	75	66	277	7,811.11
Magnus A. Carlsson	67	68	72	70	277	7,811.11
Mark Foster	65	68	75	69	277	7,811.11
Ignacio Garrido	71	68	69	69	277	7,811.11
David Howell	69	69	66	73	277	7,811.11
Ross McGowan	67	70	74	66	277	7,811.11
Inder Van Weerelt	72	66	68	71	277	7,811.11
Alvaro Velasco	66	74	69	68	277	7,811.11
Mads Vibe-Hastrup	69	70	68	70	277	7,811.11
Matthew Cort	68	68	69	73	278	5,800
Stephen Dodd	71	68	71	68	278	5,800
Klas Eriksson	69	69	70	70	278	5,800
Gregory Havret	69	67	72	70	278	5,800
Raphael Jacquelin	67	71	70	70	278	5,800
Paul Lawrie	68	70	71	69	278	5,800
Thomas Levet	68	70	70	70	278	5,800
Gary Lockerbie	68	71	71	68	278	5,800
Jean-Francois Lucquin	70	69	71	68	278	5,800
Steven O'Hara	69	71	74	64	278	5,800
Wil Besseling	68	67	74	70	279	4,400

	SCORES				TOTAL	MONEY
Marc Cayeux	71	67	70	71	279	4,400
Maarten Lafeber	70	67	70	72	279	4,400
Alan McLean	72	67	72	68	279	4,400
Callum Macaulay	66	74	68	72	280	3,900
Rafa Echenique	69	70	71	71	281	3,500
Richie Ramsay	72	68	72	69	281	3,500
Alexandre Rocha	70	70	74	67	281	3,500
Iain Pyman	70	65	71	76	282	3,050
Lee Slattery	67	73	70	72	282	3,050
Terry Pilkadaris	71	69	69	74	283	2,900
Sam Walker	72	68	71	73	284	2,800
Alessandro Tadini	68	70	72	75	285	2,700
Birgir Hafthorsson	73	66	73	74	286	2,550
Cesar Monasterio	71	68	73	74	286	2,550
Ulrich van den Berg	72	68	72	75	287	2,400
Jarmo Sandelin	68	70	73	77	288	2,300
*Lukas Nemecz	71	68	82	74	295	

The Vivendi Trophy with Seve Ballesteros

Saint-Nom-la-Breteche Golf Club, Paris, France   September 24-27
Par 36-35–71; 6,919 yards

FIRST DAY
Fourballs

Graeme McDowell and Rory McIlroy (GB&I) defeated Soren Kjeldsen and Alvaro Quiros, 4 and 3.
Anthony Wall and Chris Wood (GB&I) defeated Henrik Stenson and Robert Karlsson, 6 and 5.
Simon Dyson and Oliver Wilson (GB&I) defeated Soren Hansen and Peter Hanson, 3 and 2.
Anders Hansen and Francesco Molinari (Eur) defeated Robert Rock and Steve Webster, 4 and 3.
Miguel Angel Jimenez and Gonzalo Fernandez-Castano (Eur) defeated Ross Fisher and Nick Dougherty, 2 and 1.

POINTS: Great Britain & Ireland 3, Europe 2

SECOND DAY
Fourballs

Dyson and Wilson (GB&I) defeated Stenson and Quiros, 2 and 1.
Dougherty and Fisher (GB&I) defeated Hanson and Soren Hansen, 3 and 2.
Anders Hansen and Molinari (Eur) defeated McDowell and McIlroy, 3 and 1.
Fernandez-Castano and Karlsson (Eur) defeated Rock and Webster, 1 up.
Wall and Wood (GB&I) defeated Jimenez and Kjeldsen, 3 and 2.

POINTS: Great Britain & Ireland 6, Europe 4

THIRD DAY
Morning Greensomes

McIlroy and McDowell (GB&I) defeated Stenson and Hanson, 2 and 1.
Rock and Dougherty (GB&I) defeated Karlsson and Fernandez-Castano, 5 and 4.
Fisher and Wood (GB&I) defeated Anders Hansen and Molinari, 1 up.
Jimenez and Quiros (Eur) defeated Dyson and Wilson, 1 up.

POINTS: Great Britain & Ireland 9, Europe 5

THIRD DAY
Afternoon Foursomes

McIlroy and McDowell (GB&I) defeated Soren Hansen and Kjeldsen, 2 and 1.
Stenson and Hanson (Eur) halved with Dougherty and Webster.
Fisher and Wood (GB&I) defeated Anders Hansen and Molinari, 3 and 2.
Rock and Wilson (GB&I) defeated Quiros and Jimenez, 1 up.

POINTS: Great Britain & Ireland 12½, Europe 5½

FINAL DAY
Singles

Wall (GB&I) halved with Quiros when Wall withdrew due to injury.
McIlroy (GB&I) defeated Stenson, 1 up.
McDowell (GB&I) defeated Karlsson, 3 and 2.
Jimenez (Eur) defeated Fisher, 3 and 1.
Soren Hansen (Eur) defeated Webster, 4 and 2.
Kjeldsen (Eur) defeated Dyson, 3 and 1.
Rock (GB&I) defeated Fernandez-Castano, 1 up.
Anders Hansen (Eur) defeated Dougherty, 7 and 6.
Wood (GB&I) halved with Hanson.
Molinari (Eur) defeated Wilson, 5 and 4.

TOTAL POINTS: Great Britain & Ireland 16½, Europe 11½

Alfred Dunhill Links Championship

St. Andrews Old Course: Par 36-36–72; 7,279 yards   October 1-5
Carnoustie Championship Course: Par 36-36–72; 7,412 yards   purse, €3,242,641
Kingsbarns Golf Links: Par 36-36–72; 7,160 yards
St. Andrews & Fife, Scotland
(Event completed on Monday—high winds.)

	SCORES				TOTAL	MONEY
Simon Dyson	68	66	68	66	268	€540,440.10
Rory McIlroy	68	65	69	69	271	281,640.30
Oliver Wilson	69	67	70	65	271	281,640.30
Rafael Cabrera-Bello	70	68	65	69	272	149,810
Richie Ramsay	67	66	70	69	272	149,810
Ross McGowan	66	68	71	68	273	113,492.40
Darren Clarke	68	68	67	71	274	89,172.62
Luke Donald	72	65	64	73	274	89,172.62
Gregory Bourdy	73	67	67	68	275	57,487.39
Francois Delamontagne	71	67	67	70	275	57,487.39
Kenneth Ferrie	69	66	69	71	275	57,487.39
Ricardo Gonzalez	70	71	68	66	275	57,487.39
Gary Lockerbie	69	71	67	68	275	57,487.39
Paul McGinley	69	67	69	70	275	57,487.39
Lee Westwood	73	67	66	69	275	57,487.39
Peter Hanson	72	64	75	65	276	43,775.65
Raphael Jacquelin	67	71	68	70	276	43,775.65
Jose Manuel Lara	67	68	69	72	276	43,775.65
Paul Broadhurst	70	67	72	68	277	36,780.81
David Dixon	68	67	73	69	277	36,780.81
Michael Hoey	67	66	70	74	277	36,780.81
Simon Khan	74	70	67	66	277	36,780.81
Brett Rumford	68	71	70	68	277	36,780.81
Graeme Storm	69	69	72	67	277	36,780.81
Marc Warren	70	69	71	67	277	36,780.81
Richard Bland	72	67	71	68	278	28,405.53
Carlos Del Moral	69	69	71	69	278	28,405.53

	SCORES				TOTAL	MONEY
Johan Edfors	70	68	70	70	278	28,405.53
Ernie Els	72	72	66	68	278	28,405.53
Padraig Harrington	70	70	72	66	278	28,405.53
Mikko Ilonen	70	64	70	74	278	28,405.53
James Kamte	69	69	70	70	278	28,405.53
Sam Little	68	71	67	72	278	28,405.53
Graeme McDowell	69	70	68	71	278	28,405.53
Steven O'Hara	71	66	74	67	278	28,405.53
Ignacio Garrido	68	71	71	69	279	22,049.96
Joakim Haeggman	73	69	68	69	279	22,049.96
Miguel Angel Jimenez	74	67	68	70	279	22,049.96
Damien McGrane	71	71	68	69	279	22,049.96
Francesco Molinari	71	68	69	71	279	22,049.96
Dale Whitnell	69	69	73	68	279	22,049.96
Thomas Bjorn	64	74	72	70	280	17,186
Bradley Dredge	72	69	69	70	280	17,186
Mark Foster	71	70	68	71	280	17,186
Soren Hansen	71	69	71	69	280	17,186
Thongchai Jaidee	70	69	73	68	280	17,186
Callum Macaulay	72	73	67	68	280	17,186
Marcel Siem	70	71	70	69	280	17,186
Alessandro Tadini	69	70	73	68	280	17,186
Danny Willett	71	67	70	72	280	17,186
Gareth Maybin	66	73	71	71	281	13,619.09
Wade Ormsby	70	66	73	72	281	13,619.09
Marc Cayeux	70	70	71	71	282	10,412.48
Graham DeLaet	70	68	74	70	282	10,412.48
Brad Faxon	74	67	71	70	282	10,412.48
Alastair Forsyth	70	64	77	71	282	10,412.48
Richard Green	72	69	69	72	282	10,412.48
Keith Horne	70	70	70	72	282	10,412.48
Trevor Immelman	71	67	72	72	282	10,412.48
Hennie Otto	70	70	72	70	282	10,412.48
Daniel Vancsik	70	71	70	71	282	10,412.48
Michael Jonzon	72	73	67	71	283	7,944.47
Soren Kjeldsen	70	71	70	72	283	7,944.47
Gary Murphy	71	72	69	71	283	7,944.47
Alvaro Quiros	72	68	70	73	283	7,944.47
Wallace Booth	72	65	75	72	284	6,809.55
David Lynn	73	66	73	72	284	6,809.55
Brett Quigley	72	71	69	72	284	6,809.55
Lam Chih Bing	69	69	74	73	285	6,161.02
Lee Slattery	68	71	72	76	287	5,911.06

Madrid Masters

Centro Nacional de Golf, Madrid, Spain
Par 36-36–72; 7,242 yards

October 8-11
purse, €1,506,741

	SCORES				TOTAL	MONEY
Ross McGowan	66	66	60	71	263	€250,000
Mikko Ilonen	74	63	63	66	266	166,660
David Drysdale	66	65	69	67	267	93,900
Gareth Maybin	70	68	68	64	270	63,700
Gary Murphy	67	65	70	68	270	63,700
Alexander Noren	71	67	67	65	270	63,700
Ignacio Garrido	74	63	67	67	271	38,700
Anthony Wall	66	67	70	68	271	38,700
Danny Willett	66	67	66	72	271	38,700
Jorge Campillo	67	66	68	71	272	24,814.29

	SCORES				TOTAL	MONEY
Emanuele Canonica	67	65	69	71	272	24,814.29
Luke Donald	71	69	65	67	272	24,814.29
Miguel Angel Jimenez	70	68	66	68	272	24,814.29
Gary Lockerbie	68	70	68	66	272	24,814.29
Michael Lorenzo-Vera	69	66	64	73	272	24,814.29
Fabrizio Zanotti	71	65	65	71	272	24,814.29
Sergio Garcia	64	67	71	71	273	19,050
Damien McGrane	67	71	68	67	273	19,050
Francesco Molinari	69	68	69	67	273	19,050
Alvaro Salto	69	67	68	69	273	19,050
Raphael Jacquelin	69	69	65	71	274	17,175
Marcel Siem	67	68	71	68	274	17,175
Paul Broadhurst	71	66	70	68	275	14,700
Bradley Dredge	69	69	69	68	275	14,700
Niclas Fasth	70	69	64	72	275	14,700
Oliver Fisher	65	74	66	70	275	14,700
David Lynn	67	70	70	68	275	14,700
Louis Oosthuizen	69	67	71	68	275	14,700
Charl Schwartzel	71	69	68	67	275	14,700
Alessandro Tadini	68	67	72	68	275	14,700
Alvaro Velasco	72	67	67	69	275	14,700
Seve Benson	70	69	68	69	276	11,640
Alejandro Canizares	72	67	66	71	276	11,640
Scott Drummond	68	70	67	71	276	11,640
Simon Khan	68	68	69	71	276	11,640
Phillip Price	70	69	67	70	276	11,640
Gonzalo Fernandez-Castano	69	70	66	72	277	9,900
David Horsey	66	71	69	71	277	9,900
Barry Lane	68	71	68	70	277	9,900
Pablo Martin	70	67	71	69	277	9,900
Alvaro Quiros	71	67	66	73	277	9,900
Paul Waring	69	69	73	66	277	9,900
Richard Bland	72	67	70	69	278	7,500
Rafael Cabrera-Bello	70	67	71	70	278	7,500
Stephen Dodd	70	69	69	70	278	7,500
Peter Hedblom	69	68	71	70	278	7,500
Maarten Lafeber	69	70	67	72	278	7,500
Peter Lawrie	69	67	72	70	278	7,500
Sam Little	68	70	68	72	278	7,500
Santiago Luna	70	70	68	70	278	7,500
Manuel Quiros	62	73	70	73	278	7,500
Jarmo Sandelin	72	67	72	67	278	7,500
Gregory Bourdy	69	67	72	71	279	4,912.50
Robert-Jan Derksen	69	69	70	71	279	4,912.50
Pelle Edberg	71	68	70	70	279	4,912.50
Jeppe Huldahl	69	71	71	68	279	4,912.50
Paul Lawrie	70	70	69	70	279	4,912.50
Shane Lowry	71	63	73	72	279	4,912.50
Jose Maria Olazabal	75	65	69	70	279	4,912.50
Lee Slattery	68	68	76	67	279	4,912.50
Magnus A. Carlsson	70	69	73	68	280	3,750
Francois Delamontagne	70	66	71	73	280	3,750
Michael Jonzon	71	69	71	69	280	3,750
Daniel Vancsik	70	69	72	69	280	3,750
Marc Warren	70	68	71	71	280	3,750
Mark Brown	68	72	71	70	281	3,300
Thongchai Jaidee	71	67	74	70	282	3,150
Luis Claverie	69	71	69	74	283	2,925
Steven O'Hara	71	68	72	72	283	2,925
Robert Dinwiddie	72	66	74	72	284	2,495
Michael Hoey	69	69	72	74	284	2,495
Carlos Del Moral	69	69	72	75	285	2,247
Jean-Francois Lucquin	70	69	77	73	289	2,244

Portugal Masters

Oceanico Victoria Golf Course, Vilamoura, Portugal
Par 35-37–72; 7,231 yards

October 15-18
purse, €2,994,530

	SCORES				TOTAL	MONEY
Lee Westwood	66	67	66	66	265	€500,000
Francesco Molinari	63	66	68	70	267	333,330
Padraig Harrington	69	62	71	67	269	187,800
Peter Hanson	71	65	66	68	270	138,600
Marcel Siem	67	69	67	67	270	138,600
Johan Edfors	69	66	68	68	271	75,400
Retief Goosen	68	64	64	75	271	75,400
Alexander Noren	70	70	69	62	271	75,400
Justin Rose	65	70	70	66	271	75,400
Charl Schwartzel	65	65	71	70	271	75,400
Danny Willett	69	68	66	68	271	75,400
Robert-Jan Derksen	68	67	67	70	272	47,475
Scott Drummond	68	69	68	67	272	47,475
Oliver Fisher	67	67	68	70	272	47,475
Anthony Wall	68	67	70	67	272	47,475
Francois Delamontagne	69	69	71	64	273	40,500
Louis Oosthuizen	69	69	68	67	273	40,500
Alvaro Quiros	68	65	71	69	273	40,500
Marcus Fraser	70	67	71	66	274	34,028.57
Ricardo Gonzalez	69	67	70	68	274	34,028.57
Peter Hedblom	69	70	66	69	274	34,028.57
Mikko Ilonen	71	69	70	64	274	34,028.57
Thongchai Jaidee	73	67	67	67	274	34,028.57
Robert Rock	70	68	72	64	274	34,028.57
Oliver Wilson	67	70	64	73	274	34,028.57
Alejandro Canizares	71	68	66	70	275	28,950
Bradley Dredge	66	70	69	70	275	28,950
Gareth Maybin	69	67	65	74	275	28,950
Paul McGinley	70	69	68	68	275	28,950
Stephen Dodd	71	64	70	71	276	24,128.57
Simon Khan	66	68	71	71	276	24,128.57
James Kingston	71	64	67	74	276	24,128.57
Shane Lowry	70	65	71	70	276	24,128.57
Rory McIlroy	69	70	71	66	276	24,128.57
Colin Montgomerie	68	71	69	68	276	24,128.57
Steve Webster	71	67	71	67	276	24,128.57
Paul Broadhurst	70	68	71	68	277	20,400
Ben Curtis	68	68	72	69	277	20,400
Peter Lawrie	68	68	65	76	277	20,400
Pablo Martin	66	66	68	77	277	20,400
Darren Clarke	69	68	70	71	278	18,000
David Lynn	71	67	66	74	278	18,000
Taco Remkes	71	68	70	69	278	18,000
Paul Waring	69	71	66	72	278	18,000
Rafael Cabrera-Bello	71	67	68	73	279	14,400
Ignacio Garrido	69	71	69	70	279	14,400
Jean-Baptiste Gonnet	68	70	72	69	279	14,400
Raphael Jacquelin	71	69	74	65	279	14,400
Shiv Kapur	69	70	71	69	279	14,400
Jose-Filipe Lima	67	70	72	70	279	14,400
Damien McGrane	69	67	70	73	279	14,400
Miles Tunnicliff	68	68	70	73	279	14,400
Miguel Angel Jimenez	70	70	66	74	280	10,500
Pablo Larrazabal	70	68	67	75	280	10,500
Phillip Price	68	72	71	69	280	10,500
Jarmo Sandelin	72	68	71	69	280	10,500
Marc Warren	68	67	73	72	280	10,500

	SCORES				TOTAL	MONEY
Mads Vibe-Hastrup	66	73	68	74	281	9,000
Alastair Forsyth	65	68	77	72	282	8,550
Ross McGowan	69	71	71	71	282	8,550
Simon Dyson	70	67	75	71	283	7,800
Gary Lockerbie	73	67	74	69	283	7,800
Fabrizio Zanotti	71	69	74	69	283	7,800
Thomas Bjorn	72	67	72	73	284	6,900
Estanislao Goya	70	66	72	76	284	6,900
Daniel Vancsik	70	70	74	70	284	6,900
Anders Hansen	69	71	69	76	285	6,300
John Bickerton	69	69	76	72	286	6,000
Shaun Micheel	70	70	73	76	289	5,700

Castello Masters Costa Azahar

Club de Campo del Mediterraneo, Castellon, Spain
Par 36-35–71; 7,111 yards

October 22-25
purse, €2,029,865

	SCORES				TOTAL	MONEY
Michael Jonzon	64	68	65	67	264	€333,330
Martin Kaymer	63	67	68	67	265	173,710
Christian Nilsson	69	66	65	65	265	173,710
Sergio Garcia	63	68	67	69	267	100,000
Maarten Lafeber	71	67	64	66	268	84,800
Robert Allenby	64	66	71	68	269	65,000
Soren Hansen	70	68	65	66	269	65,000
Darren Clarke	68	70	67	65	270	42,900
Andrew Coltart	70	64	69	67	270	42,900
Peter Hanson	66	68	66	70	270	42,900
Sam Hutsby	65	68	66	71	270	42,900
Jamie Donaldson	71	67	65	68	271	33,300
Colin Montgomerie	70	69	64	68	271	33,300
Shiv Kapur	67	65	70	70	272	28,800
Jose Maria Olazabal	65	67	70	70	272	28,800
Anthony Wall	68	67	69	68	272	28,800
Fabrizio Zanotti	70	67	69	66	272	28,800
David Drysdale	68	68	66	71	273	24,866.67
David Horsey	67	71	70	65	273	24,866.67
Pablo Larrazabal	71	70	68	64	273	24,866.67
Oliver Fisher	68	69	71	66	274	22,300
Joakim Haeggman	68	71	69	66	274	22,300
John E. Morgan	66	68	72	68	274	22,300
Richie Ramsay	71	69	68	66	274	22,300
Benn Barham	68	66	70	71	275	18,700
Emanuele Canonica	65	69	73	68	275	18,700
Robert-Jan Derksen	71	66	68	70	275	18,700
Branden Grace	74	64	68	69	275	18,700
Jarmo Sandelin	70	66	70	69	275	18,700
Alessandro Tadini	65	72	68	70	275	18,700
Miles Tunnicliff	67	67	72	69	275	18,700
Daniel Vancsik	70	62	72	71	275	18,700
Felipe Aguilar	69	69	70	68	276	14,628.57
Robert Dinwiddie	69	70	67	70	276	14,628.57
Bradley Dredge	70	69	68	69	276	14,628.57
Ignacio Garrido	67	68	70	71	276	14,628.57
Robert Karlsson	72	67	68	69	276	14,628.57
Mads Vibe-Hastrup	72	68	66	70	276	14,628.57
Marc Warren	72	65	70	69	276	14,628.57
Richard Bland	70	69	68	70	277	11,600
Rafa Echenique	67	73	68	69	277	11,600

	SCORES			TOTAL	MONEY
Alfredo Garcia-Heredia	73	68	67	69	277	11,600
Paul Lawrie	70	69	71	67	277	11,600
Mikael Lundberg	69	70	68	70	277	11,600
Manuel Quiros	69	71	71	66	277	11,600
Justin Rose	68	71	66	72	277	11,600
Charl Schwartzel	68	70	68	71	277	11,600
Paul Broadhurst	70	64	75	69	278	8,200
Marc Cayeux	71	70	70	67	278	8,200
Scott Drummond	70	66	70	72	278	8,200
Johan Edfors	70	70	69	69	278	8,200
Gonzalo Fernandez-Castano	68	69	68	73	278	8,200
Estanislao Goya	71	70	68	69	278	8,200
Joost Luiten	70	69	68	71	278	8,200
Marcel Siem	71	70	67	70	278	8,200
Danny Willett	71	66	68	73	278	8,200
Magnus A. Carlsson	72	69	69	69	279	5,600
Eduardo De La Riva	71	68	72	68	279	5,600
Klas Eriksson	70	71	73	65	279	5,600
Santiago Luna	68	69	72	70	279	5,600
Taco Remkes	69	71	70	69	279	5,600
Simon Wakefield	70	69	65	75	279	5,600
Paul Waring	70	71	69	69	279	5,600
Alejandro Canizares	74	67	67	72	280	4,400
Pablo Martin	67	71	70	72	280	4,400
Matthew Millar	70	71	70	69	280	4,400
Gary Murphy	70	70	72	68	280	4,400
Wade Ormsby	72	66	73	69	280	4,400
Rafael Cabrera-Bello	73	67	72	69	281	3,725
Andrew McLardy	70	70	70	71	281	3,725
Federico Cabrera	71	70	72	69	282	2,994
Pelle Edberg	69	70	69	74	282	2,994
Gary Lockerbie	70	71	71	70	282	2,994
John Mellor	73	68	73	68	282	2,994
Pedro Oriol	71	70	71	70	282	2,994
Francis Valera	73	68	74	68	283	2,985
Wil Besseling	72	68	70	74	284	2,980.50
Eirik Tage Johansen	73	68	72	71	284	2,980.50
Bernd Wiesberger	71	65	76	73	285	2,976
Anton Haig	71	67	73	78	289	2,973

Barclays Singapore Open

See Asia/Japan Tours chapter.

Volvo World Match Play

Finca Crotesin Golf Club, Casares, Spain   October 29-November 1
Par 37-35–72; 7,380 yards   purse, €3,250,000

ROUND ROBIN PLAY
Group A
Scott Strange defeated Paul Casey, 1 up.
Anthony Kim defeated Retief Goosen, 4 up.
Anthony Kim defeated Paul Casey, 3 up.
Retief Goosen defeated Scott Strange, 1 up.
Retief Goosen defeated Paul Casey, 1 up.
Scott Strange defeated Anthony Kim, 3 up.

Group B

Sergio Garcia defeated Oliver Wilson, 1 up.
Robert Allenby defeated Martin Kaymer, 1 up.
Sergio Garcia halved with Robert Allenby.
Oliver Wilson defeated Martin Kaymer, 1 up.
Robert Allenby defeated Oliver Wilson, 2 up.
Sergio Garcia defeated Martin Kaymer, 4 up.

Group C

Simon Dyson defeated Henrik Stenson, 3 up.
Angel Cabrera defeated Rory McIlroy, 5 up.
Henrik Stenson defeated Angel Cabrera, 2 up.
Rory McIlroy defeated Simon Dyson, 2 up.
Angel Cabrera defeated Simon Dyson, 7 up.
Rory McIlroy defeated Henrik Stenson, 4 up.

Group D

Jeev Milkha Singh defeated Lee Westwood, 6 up.
Ross Fisher defeated Camilo Villegas, 2 up.
Lee Westwood defeated Ross Fisher, 2 up.
Camilo Villegas defeated Jeev Milkha Singh, 3 up.
Lee Westwood halved with Camilo Villegas.
Ross Fisher defeated Jeev Milkha Singh, 1 up.

SEMI-FINALS

Kim defeated Allenby, 5 and 4.
Fisher defeated Cabrera, 39 holes.

PLAYOFF FOR THIRD-FOURTH PLACE

Allenby defeated Cabrera, 19 holes.

FINAL

Fisher defeated Kim, 4 and 3.

PRIZE MONEY: Fisher €750,000; Kim €450,000; Allenby €250,000; Cabrera €200,000; McIlroy, Strange, Villegas, Wilson €150,000 each; Garcia, Goosen, Stenson, Westwood €130,000 each; Casey, Dyson, Kaymer, Singh €120,000 each.

JBWere Masters

See Australasian Tour chapter.

UBS Hong Kong Open

See Asia/Japan Tours chapter.

Dubai World Championship

Jumeirah Golf Estates, Earth Course,
Dubai, United Arab Emirates
Par 36-36–72; 7,675 yards

November 19-22
purse, €4,955,642

	SCORES				TOTAL	MONEY
Lee Westwood	66	69	66	64	265	€830,675.17
Ross McGowan	71	66	66	68	271	553,781.23
Rory McIlroy	68	69	69	67	273	323,963.32
Padraig Harrington	68	69	69	68	274	224,282.30
Geoff Ogilvy	70	69	68	67	274	224,282.30
Alexander Noren	70	69	67	69	275	162,094.63
Sergio Garcia	71	67	69	69	276	139,553.42

	SCORES				TOTAL	MONEY
Adam Scott	68	73	67	68	276	139,553.42
Peter Hanson	72	71	66	69	278	114,633.17
Miguel Angel Jimenez	72	68	69	69	278	114,633.17
Ian Poulter	71	74	68	65	278	114,633.17
Louis Oosthuizen	71	66	71	71	279	99,681.02
Thomas Aiken	68	70	70	72	280	89,712.92
Robert Allenby	65	72	73	70	280	89,712.92
Jeev Milkha Singh	70	72	68	70	280	89,712.92
Bradley Dredge	70	71	68	72	281	67,783.09
Retief Goosen	69	71	69	72	281	67,783.09
Liang Wen-chong	68	70	73	70	281	67,783.09
Camilo Villegas	66	71	73	71	281	67,783.09
Anthony Wall	71	71	70	69	281	67,783.09
Oliver Wilson	71	72	70	68	281	67,783.09
Johan Edfors	69	70	71	72	282	56,319.78
Jamie Donaldson	73	70	69	71	283	52,581.74
Thomas Levet	73	69	68	73	283	52,581.74
Henrik Stenson	71	71	70	71	283	52,581.74
Scott Strange	73	67	73	70	283	52,581.74
Anders Hansen	73	69	70	72	284	47,348.48
Gareth Maybin	71	69	74	70	284	47,348.48
Graeme Storm	78	66	67	73	284	47,348.48
Gregory Bourdy	71	71	73	70	285	40,086.01
Rafael Cabrera-Bello	71	67	75	72	285	40,086.01
Raphael Jacquelin	70	73	72	70	285	40,086.01
James Kingston	73	73	67	72	285	40,086.01
Soren Kjeldsen	73	69	71	72	285	40,086.01
Graeme McDowell	76	70	71	68	285	40,086.01
Francesco Molinari	72	68	71	74	285	40,086.01
Luke Donald	73	72	71	70	286	33,393.14
Simon Dyson	70	73	70	73	286	33,393.14
Gonzalo Fernandez-Castano	70	73	74	69	286	33,393.14
Thongchai Jaidee	70	74	70	72	286	33,393.14
Martin Kaymer	71	71	72	72	286	33,393.14
David Drysdale	72	73	73	69	287	27,412.28
Niclas Fasth	73	72	73	69	287	27,412.28
Ross Fisher	73	71	70	73	287	27,412.28
Peter Lawrie	71	70	76	70	287	27,412.28
Alvaro Quiros	69	75	73	70	287	27,412.28
Richard Sterne	72	71	74	70	287	27,412.28
Chris Wood	66	78	68	75	287	27,412.28
Nick Dougherty	69	72	73	74	288	23,425.04
Ernie Els	74	74	70	71	289	21,431.42
Robert Rock	74	70	69	76	289	21,431.42
Justin Rose	72	75	73	69	289	21,431.42
Charl Schwartzel	74	72	74	70	290	19,437.80
Soren Hansen	73	73	73	72	291	16,945.77
Peter Hedblom	75	72	73	71	291	16,945.77
Damien McGrane	74	70	76	71	291	16,945.77
Steve Webster	75	73	73	70	291	16,945.77
Danny Willett	76	70	73	76	295	14,952.15

Alfred Dunhill Championship

See African Tours chapter.

South African Open Championship

See African Tours chapter.

Challenge Tour

Club Colombia Masters

See American Tours chapter.

Tusker Kenya Open

Muthaiga Golf Club, Nairobi, Kenya
Par 36-35–71; 7,141 yards

April 16-19
purse, €184,662

	SCORES				TOTAL	MONEY
Gary Boyd	67	64	71	69	271	€28,800
Andrew Butterfield	67	70	70	68	275	16,200
Philip Golding	74	70	66	65	275	16,200
David Hewan	70	66	72	69	277	10,800
Victor Riu	69	71	68	70	278	9,000
Carl Suneson	69	67	72	71	279	7,200
Oscar Floren	71	73	66	70	280	5,760
Robert Coles	69	72	71	69	281	4,680
Chris Gane	73	70	69	69	281	4,680
Peter Gustafsson	68	76	68	70	282	3,456
Lee S. James	70	68	71	73	282	3,456
Ally Mellor	73	72	67	70	282	3,456
Martin Rominger	67	74	71	70	282	3,456
Sam Walker	74	71	71	66	282	3,456
Trevor Fisher, Jr.	71	67	71	74	283	2,610
Edoardo Molinari	71	71	69	72	283	2,610
Julien Quesne	71	71	70	71	283	2,610
Andrew Willey	73	70	69	71	283	2,610
Kalle Brink	74	71	69	70	284	1,811.25
Francois Calmels	71	74	66	73	284	1,811.25
Tyrone Ferreira	71	71	75	67	284	1,811.25
Jerome Forestier	72	70	69	73	284	1,811.25
Julien Grillon	70	71	70	73	284	1,811.25
Jan-Are Larsen	71	71	73	69	284	1,811.25
Andrew Marshall	67	72	73	72	284	1,811.25
Richard McEvoy	70	71	70	73	284	1,811.25

Moroccan Classic

Pullman El Jadida Royal Golf & Spa, El Jadida, Morocco
Par 36-36–72; 6,848 yards

April 30-May 3
purse, €144,396

	SCORES				TOTAL	MONEY
Robert Coles	69	67	71	68	275	€22,400
Matthew Zions	71	68	74	66	279	15,400
Julien Quesne	69	71	71	70	281	9,800
Ben Evans	71	70	70	71	282	7,700
Andrew Willey	70	75	69	68	282	7,700
Andrew McArthur	73	68	69	73	283	5,600
Olivier David	72	70	71	71	284	4,200
Stefano Reale	74	68	71	71	284	4,200

	SCORES				TOTAL	MONEY
Tiago Cruz	70	71	71	73	285	2,884
Anders Schmidt Hansen	70	71	75	69	285	2,884
Steven Jeppesen	70	75	69	71	285	2,884
Michele Reale	72	73	69	71	285	2,884
Joel Sjoholm	69	71	73	72	285	2,884
Julien Clement	68	74	68	76	286	2,240
Andreas Hogberg	73	71	71	71	286	2,240
Johan Wahlqvist	71	74	66	75	286	2,240
Thomas Feyrsinger	70	74	71	72	287	1,767.50
David Griffiths	77	71	67	72	287	1,767.50
Jamie Moul	69	71	75	72	287	1,767.50
George Murray	70	74	71	72	287	1,767.50
Johan Skold	69	71	71	77	288	1,372
Kyron Sullivan	69	76	74	69	288	1,372
Benoit Teilleria	73	68	72	75	288	1,372
Julien Guerrier	73	71	76	69	289	1,274
Alex Haindl	72	72	73	72	289	1,274
Dominique Nouailhac	72	69	74	74	289	1,274
Tom Whitehouse	70	74	75	70	289	1,274

Allianz Open Cotes d'Armor Bretagne

Golf Blue Green, Pleneuf Val Andre, France
Par 35-35–70; 6,435 yards

May 14-17
purse, €154,410

	SCORES				TOTAL	MONEY
Lee S. James	65	70	71	68	274	€24,000
Florian Fritsch	65	73	66	70	274	16,500
(James defeated Fritsch on first playoff hole.)						
John Parry	67	68	72	70	277	10,500
Mikko Korhonen	69	72	71	66	278	9,000
Thomas Feyrsinger	69	69	70	72	280	7,500
Julien Guerrier	66	69	71	75	281	4,150
Steven Jeppesen	65	70	75	71	281	4,150
Nicolas Joakimides	69	72	70	70	281	4,150
Lloyd Kennedy	69	74	71	67	281	4,150
Jan-Are Larsen	67	71	72	71	281	4,150
Andrew Marshall	70	68	70	73	281	4,150
Nicolas Colsaerts	68	73	71	70	282	2,775
Jose-Filipe Lima	68	70	70	74	282	2,775
Andrew Butterfield	75	69	67	72	283	2,400
Dominique Nouailhac	70	68	73	72	283	2,400
Nathan Smith	70	74	69	70	283	2,400
*Victor Dubuisson	66	77	67	74	284	
Joel Sjoholm	66	74	66	78	284	2,025
Andrew Tampion	68	68	73	75	284	2,025
Robert Coles	66	76	71	72	285	1,587
Anders Schmidt Hansen	67	74	73	71	285	1,587
Garry Houston	75	69	69	72	285	1,587
Bruno-Teva Lecuona	70	72	73	70	285	1,587
Eric Ramsay	68	71	72	74	285	1,587
Lars Brovold	70	73	68	75	286	1,380
*Alexandre Kaleka	68	71	76	71	286	
Ben Mason	71	70	72	73	286	1,380
Julien Quesne	67	69	72	78	286	1,380

Piemonte Open

Golf Club La Mandria, Torino, Italy
Par 36-36–72; 6,947 yards

May 20-23
purse, €150,885

	SCORES				TOTAL	MONEY
Edoardo Molinari	67	67	66	70	270	€24,000
Gary Boyd	71	67	67	69	274	16,500
Benjamin Hebert	70	69	68	69	276	9,750
Lloyd Kennedy	73	67	68	68	276	9,750
Andrew Butterfield	69	71	67	71	278	6,750
Gregory Molteni	72	66	71	69	278	6,750
Jean-Nicolas Billot	72	70	67	70	279	4,200
Robert Coles	68	72	73	66	279	4,200
Jan-Are Larsen	67	69	72	71	279	4,200
Nicolas Colsaerts	68	73	71	68	280	3,300
Francois Calmels	70	71	72	68	281	2,775
Charles-Edouard Russo	71	71	70	69	281	2,775
Marco Soffietti	68	71	71	71	281	2,775
Roland Steiner	69	73	69	70	281	2,775
Juan Abbate	73	71	69	70	283	2,250
Olivier David	68	73	71	71	283	2,250
Florian Fritsch	71	71	70	71	283	2,250
Carlos Rodiles	68	71	74	71	284	1,875
Mark Tullo	72	72	70	70	284	1,875
Julien Clement	71	71	74	69	285	1,487.50
Matteo Delpodio	74	70	66	75	285	1,487.50
Julien Guerrier	70	72	70	73	285	1,487.50
Gareth Paddison	73	68	73	71	285	1,487.50
Julien Quesne	71	69	72	73	285	1,487.50
Matthew Zions	73	69	69	74	285	1,487.50

Telenet Trophy

Royal Waterloo, La Marache Course, Lasne, Belgium
Par 36-36–72; 6,968 yards

May 28-31
purse, €154,410

	SCORES				TOTAL	MONEY
Francois Calmels	67	69	70	70	276	€24,000
Carlos Rodiles	67	71	75	65	278	13,500
Sam Walker	70	69	73	66	278	13,500
Simon Thornton	70	70	72	67	279	8,250
Mark Tullo	71	70	70	68	279	8,250
Stuart Manley	66	69	71	74	280	5,400
Andrew Tampion	71	68	71	70	280	5,400
Nicolas Colsaerts	73	67	72	69	281	3,700
Richard McEvoy	69	71	68	73	281	3,700
Tom Whitehouse	69	75	67	70	281	3,700
Andrew Butterfield	70	67	71	74	282	2,625
Andrew McArthur	70	72	69	71	282	2,625
Dominique Nouailhac	69	70	70	73	282	2,625
Pasi Purhonen	68	72	73	69	282	2,625
Charles-Edouard Russo	74	67	72	69	282	2,625
Roland Steiner	70	70	69	73	282	2,625
Juan Abbate	70	71	73	69	283	1,674.38
Fredrik Andersson Hed	73	70	68	72	283	1,674.38
Julien Clement	71	70	70	72	283	1,674.38
Robert Coles	71	67	73	72	283	1,674.38
Peter Gustafsson	74	71	69	69	283	1,674.38
Colm Moriarty	73	72	72	66	283	1,674.38

	SCORES				TOTAL	MONEY
Bjorn Pettersson	71	70	74	68	283	1,674.38
James Ruth	71	71	69	72	283	1,674.38
Christoph Gunther	72	72	68	72	284	1,335
Birgir Hafthorsson	71	73	69	71	284	1,335
Michael Jurgensen	74	70	68	72	284	1,335
Andrew Marshall	70	75	72	67	284	1,335

Karnten Golf Open

Golfclub Klagenfurt-Seltenheim, Klagenfurt, Austria
Par 36-36–72; 6,939 yards

June 4-7
purse, €142,646

	SCORES				TOTAL	MONEY
Christoph Gunther	68	63	75	62	268	€22,400
Florian Fritsch	65	67	70	67	269	12,600
Carlos Rodiles	65	65	71	68	269	12,600
Markus Brier	68	66	70	69	273	7,700
Edoardo Molinari	71	66	66	70	273	7,700
Clodomiro Carranza	67	70	70	68	275	4,666.67
Adam Gee	69	63	72	71	275	4,666.67
Martin Wiegele	68	70	71	66	275	4,666.67
Julien Guerrier	66	71	73	66	276	3,220
Jan-Are Larsen	71	68	68	69	276	3,220
Jesus Maria Arruti	74	67	70	66	277	2,660
Mark Laskey	71	70	67	69	277	2,660
Jacob Olesen	70	68	67	72	277	2,660
Juan Abbate	73	65	72	68	278	1,970
Jean-Nicolas Billot	68	70	70	70	278	1,970
Marco Crespi	66	70	70	72	278	1,970
Mikko Korhonen	69	69	70	70	278	1,970
James Morrison	68	69	74	67	278	1,970
John Parry	68	65	74	71	278	1,970
Matthew Zions	70	67	72	69	278	1,970
Louis de Jager	70	68	69	72	279	1,372
Jamie McLeary	75	67	68	69	279	1,372
Robin Swane	69	73	67	70	279	1,372
Olivier David	69	72	71	68	280	1,274
Tyrone Ferreira	70	71	71	68	280	1,274
Jordi Garcia Pinto	68	71	73	68	280	1,274
Peter Lepitschnik	69	71	72	68	280	1,274

Challenge of Ireland

The Champions Club, Moyvalley Hotel & Country Club,
Co. Kildare, Ireland
Par 36-36–72; 7,370 yards

June 11-14
purse, €156,100

	SCORES				TOTAL	MONEY
Robert Coles	68	69	74	67	278	€24,000
Nicolas Colsaerts	70	66	74	68	278	16,500
(Coles defeated Colsaerts on third playoff hole.)						
Peter Baker	68	72	71	68	279	9,750
Peter Whiteford	71	68	72	68	279	9,750
Peter Kaensche	68	71	70	71	280	7,500
Michael Curtain	73	69	68	71	281	6,000
Francois Calmels	72	68	69	73	282	3,625
Rhys Davies	71	67	72	72	282	3,625

	SCORES				TOTAL	MONEY
Dennis Kupper	72	71	72	67	282	3,625
Ake Nilsson	67	68	76	71	282	3,625
Eric Ramsay	74	69	68	71	282	3,625
Steve Surry	75	69	72	66	282	3,625
Jonathan Caldwell	68	68	73	74	283	2,475
Andrew Marshall	70	71	67	75	283	2,475
Colm Moriarty	70	70	72	71	283	2,475
Sam Walker	72	70	71	70	283	2,475
Peter Gustafsson	70	69	73	72	284	1,893.75
Mark Haastrup	70	70	73	71	284	1,893.75
James Hepworth	70	71	74	69	284	1,893.75
Guy Woodman	69	74	73	68	284	1,893.75
Pablo Del Grosso	73	73	69	70	285	1,485
Mikko Korhonen	70	73	70	72	285	1,485
Juan Abbate	72	74	71	69	286	1,350
Petter Bocian	74	72	69	71	286	1,350
Clodomiro Carranza	70	72	70	74	286	1,350
Florian Fritsch	72	74	70	70	286	1,350
Niklas Lemke	72	71	70	73	286	1,350
Jacob Olesen	71	72	72	71	286	1,350
Damian Ulrich	72	70	72	72	286	1,350

Saint-Omer Open

See European Tour section.

The Princess

Bastad Golf Club, Bastad, Sweden
Par 36-35–71; 6,703 yards

June 25-28
purse, €305,760

	SCORES				TOTAL	MONEY
Andrew Butterfield	62	69	67	73	271	€48,000
Richard McEvoy	70	67	69	66	272	27,000
Carlos Rodiles	66	69	71	66	272	27,000
Christoph Gunther	67	69	69	68	273	18,000
Antti Ahokas	68	68	68	70	274	12,200
Sion E. Bebb	65	71	70	68	274	12,200
Roland Steiner	67	69	70	68	274	12,200
Robert Coles	66	70	72	67	275	7,050
Andrew McArthur	68	71	69	67	275	7,050
Nicolas Meitinger	70	70	67	68	275	7,050
George Murray	71	68	69	67	275	7,050
Colm Moriarty	72	67	69	68	276	5,550
Lloyd Saltman	69	70	69	68	276	5,550
Fredrik Andersson Hed	65	67	74	71	277	4,650
Tony Carolan	66	72	69	70	277	4,650
Joonas Granberg	71	67	71	68	277	4,650
Julien Guerrier	69	71	69	68	277	4,650
Jose-Filipe Lima	68	67	71	72	278	3,650
Edoardo Molinari	71	71	71	65	278	3,650
Martin Rominger	69	72	68	69	278	3,650
Anders Schmidt Hansen	73	69	71	66	279	2,940
Anders Sjostrand	67	73	71	68	279	2,940
Carl Suneson	68	74	69	68	279	2,940
Juan Abbate	68	72	70	70	280	2,670
Francois Calmels	69	73	71	67	280	2,670
Ben Evans	69	72	70	69	280	2,670
Peter Gustafsson	69	72	71	68	280	2,670

Jiyai Shin led the LPGA money list and was Rolex Rookie of the Year.

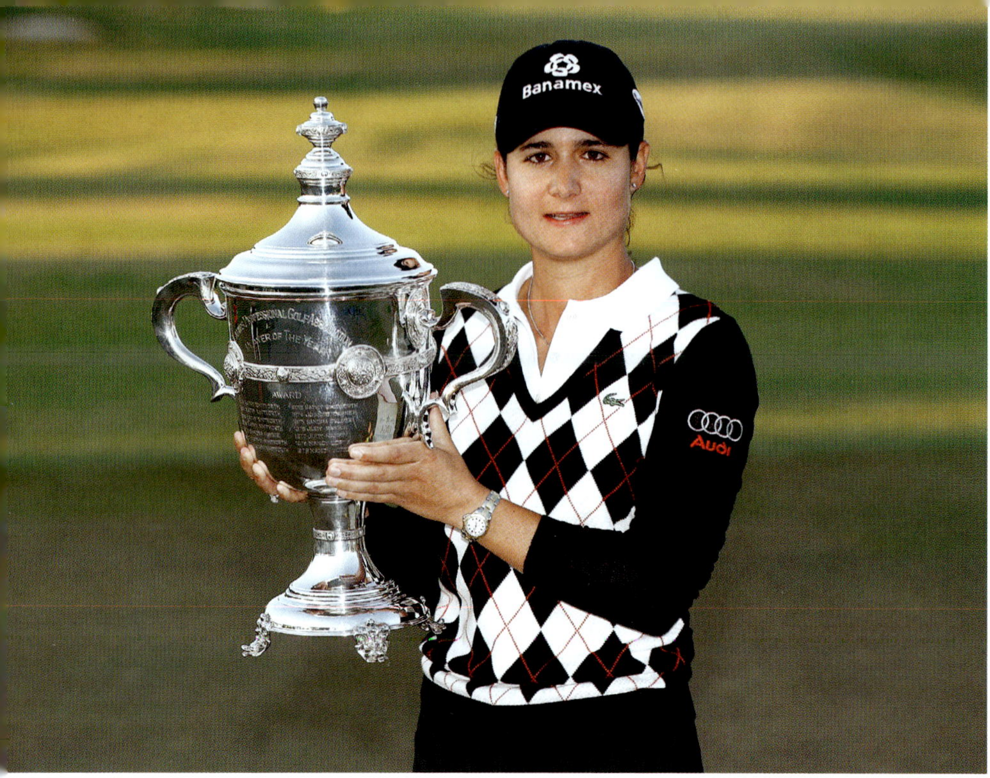

Scott Halleran/Getty Images

Lorena Ochoa won three times and was fourth on the LPGA money list.

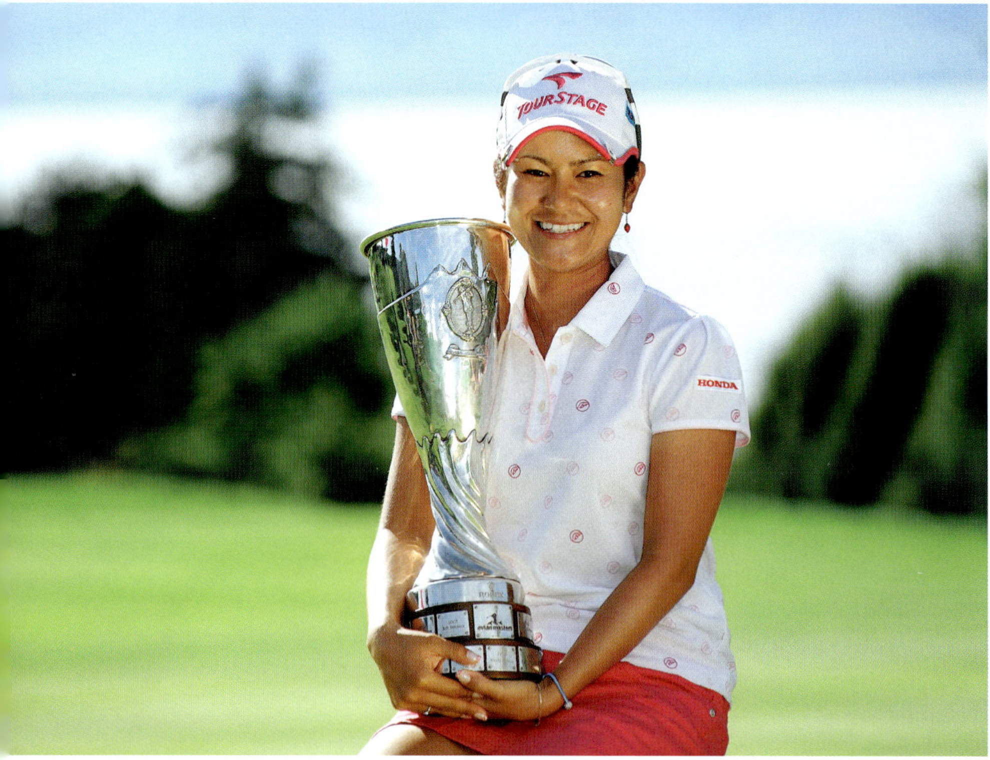

Stuart Franklin/Getty Images

Ai Miyazato placed third on the money list and won the Evian Masters.

Cristie Kerr was second on the money list.

Suzann Pettersen won the Canadian Open.

Yani Tseng was No. 5 on the Rolex Rankings.

Na Yeon Choi won in California and Korea.

Anna Nordqvist won the McDonald's LPGA.

Eun-Hee Ji took the U.S. Women's Open.

Angela Stanford was 10th on the money list.

Brittany Lincicome won the year's first major.

Catriona Matthew won at Royal Lytham.

The Americans celebrated a victory in the Solheim Cup.

In-Kyung Kim claimed the Dubai Masters.

Paula Creamer was ninth on the money list.

Michelle Wie won her first LPGA title.

Bernhard Langer won four times and led the Champions Tour money list.

Jay Haas was the Senior Players champion.

John Cook was third on the money list.

Loren Roberts won The Senior Open.

Andy Bean was seventh on the money list.

Jeff Sluman defended at Pebble Beach.

Fred Funk won the U.S. Senior Open.

Michael Allen was the Senior PGA champion.

Nick Price had one Champions victory.

Sam Torrance led the European money list.

	SCORES				TOTAL	MONEY
Zane Scotland	67	68	74	71	280	2,670
Simon Thornton	72	66	68	74	280	2,670

Credit Suisse Challenge

Wylihof Golf Club, Luterbach, Switzerland
Par 36-37–73; 7,202 yards

July 2-5
purse, €142,310

	SCORES				TOTAL	MONEY
Peter Baker	70	71	66	67	274	€22,400
Florian Praegant	74	68	66	67	275	15,400
Edoardo Molinari	72	69	68	67	276	9,800
Roland Steiner	70	70	69	70	279	8,400
Jorge Campillo	74	69	67	70	280	5,250
Tony Carolan	70	69	71	70	280	5,250
Adam Gee	73	67	71	69	280	5,250
John Parry	69	67	72	72	280	5,250
Andrew Butterfield	73	70	67	71	281	2,884
Anders Schmidt Hansen	72	71	67	71	281	2,884
Lloyd Kennedy	71	72	66	72	281	2,884
George Murray	71	69	72	69	281	2,884
Nathan Smith	71	68	68	74	281	2,884
Liam Bond	71	72	68	71	282	2,310
Julien Quesne	69	69	71	73	282	2,310
Garry Houston	71	72	71	69	283	1,761.67
Lee S. James	68	75	73	67	283	1,761.67
Jan-Are Larsen	74	69	72	68	283	1,761.67
Andrew Marshall	72	70	69	72	283	1,761.67
Carl Suneson	69	70	73	71	283	1,761.67
Martin Wiegele	72	71	70	70	283	1,761.67
Francois Calmels	72	73	68	71	284	1,316
Daniel Denison	72	70	70	72	284	1,316
Niklas Lemke	73	70	73	68	284	1,316
Nicolas Meitinger	69	72	72	71	284	1,316
Gareth Paddison	74	71	70	69	284	1,316

Allianz EurOpen de Lyon

Golf du Gouverneur, Monthieux, France
Par 36-35–71; 7,014 yards

July 9-12
purse, €155,460

	SCORES				TOTAL	MONEY
Alexandre Kaleka	63	67	70	68	268	€24,000
Anders Schmidt Hansen	64	67	69	69	269	16,500
*Victor Dubuisson	67	70	69	67	273	
Marcus Higley	71	68	65	69	273	9,750
Florian Praegant	67	68	72	66	273	9,750
Francois Calmels	68	68	69	69	274	7,500
Christophe Brazillier	69	67	71	68	275	6,000
Jesus Maria Arruti	68	69	71	68	276	4,200
Garry Houston	66	73	67	70	276	4,200
Andrew Willey	70	69	67	70	276	4,200
Sion E. Bebb	70	70	67	70	277	2,800
Tony Carolan	65	70	70	72	277	2,800
Robert Coles	72	65	74	66	277	2,800
Philip Golding	67	68	72	70	277	2,800
Richard McEvoy	69	70	71	67	277	2,800

	SCORES				TOTAL	MONEY
Edoardo Molinari	68	71	72	66	277	2,800
Julien Guerrier	73	68	68	69	278	1,827.86
Christoph Gunther	67	69	70	72	278	1,827.86
James Heath	69	71	69	69	278	1,827.86
Ben Mason	66	70	72	70	278	1,827.86
Gareth Paddison	66	73	71	68	278	1,827.86
Carlos Rodiles	70	65	72	71	278	1,827.86
Peter Whiteford	71	68	70	69	278	1,827.86
Liam Bond	70	66	75	68	279	1,320
Stuart Davis	69	73	67	70	279	1,320
Anthony Grenier	65	71	71	72	279	1,320
Julien Grillon	67	73	68	71	279	1,320
Rolf Muntz	67	70	72	70	279	1,320
John Parry	69	68	70	72	279	1,320
Julien Quesne	71	66	71	71	279	1,320
Charles-Edouard Russo	69	69	68	73	279	1,320
Anthony Snobeck	66	72	73	68	279	1,320

SWALEC Wales Challenge

Vale Hotel Golf & Spa Resort, Cardiff, Wales
Par 36-36–72; 7,266 yards

July 23-26
purse, €152,475

	SCORES				TOTAL	MONEY
Rhys Davies	77	68	70	71	286	€24,000
James Morrison	73	72	70	71	286	16,500
(Davies defeated Morrison on third playoff hole.)						
Andreas Hogberg	70	77	72	68	287	10,500
Matthew Cort	68	75	73	72	288	7,500
Greig Hutcheon	69	76	71	72	288	7,500
Steve Surry	71	71	73	73	288	7,500
Julien Quesne	74	73	72	70	289	4,800
*James Frazer	75	72	70	73	290	
Chris Gane	72	75	71	72	290	3,700
Colm Moriarty	74	74	71	71	290	3,700
Richard Treis	70	73	70	77	290	3,700
Jorge Campillo	72	71	71	77	291	2,925
Soren Juul	76	74	70	71	291	2,925
Julien Grillon	74	72	73	73	292	2,475
Peter Kaensche	73	77	69	73	292	2,475
Jamie McLeary	73	74	71	74	292	2,475
Tom Whitehouse	77	70	73	72	292	2,475
Steven Jeppesen	75	73	72	73	293	1,950
Roland Steiner	76	72	72	73	293	1,950
Peter Whiteford	72	77	72	72	293	1,950
Christophe Brazillier	74	76	70	74	294	1,509
Nicolas Colsaerts	73	72	75	74	294	1,509
*Oliver Farr	73	71	77	73	294	
Garry Houston	74	74	73	73	294	1,509
Dennis Kupper	75	74	69	76	294	1,509
Ricardo Santos	78	72	69	75	294	1,509

Scottish Hydro Challenge

Macdonald Spey Valley Golf Club, Aviemore, Scotland
Par 35-36–71; 7,100 yards

July 30-August 2
purse, €203,300

	SCORES				TOTAL	MONEY
Jamie McLeary	69	67	72	68	276	€32,000
Edoardo Molinari	69	71	67	71	278	22,000
Peter Whiteford	70	70	70	69	279	14,000
Peter Baker	68	72	72	69	281	11,000
Carlos Rodiles	70	74	71	66	281	11,000
Sion E. Bebb	68	74	69	71	282	5,533.33
Gary Boyd	75	71	68	68	282	5,533.33
Scott Jamieson	70	68	73	71	282	5,533.33
James Ruebotham	71	69	68	74	282	5,533.33
Steve Surry	76	69	73	64	282	5,533.33
Mark Tullo	72	68	73	69	282	5,533.33
Nicolas Colsaerts	72	69	75	67	283	3,800
Adrien Bernadet	74	71	70	69	284	3,400
Julien Grillon	73	68	72	71	284	3,400
James Morrison	75	71	67	71	284	3,400
Lorenzo Gagli	70	74	66	75	285	2,700
Ben Mason	68	72	72	73	285	2,700
Kyron Sullivan	71	71	71	72	285	2,700
Simon Thornton	72	69	71	73	285	2,700
Julien Guerrier	67	75	71	73	286	2,300
Rhys Davies	72	73	70	72	287	1,900
Adam Gee	73	70	71	73	287	1,900
Garry Houston	70	72	73	72	287	1,900
Alexandre Kaleka	70	72	72	73	287	1,900
Rikard Karlberg	71	73	70	73	287	1,900
Reinier Saxton	73	68	70	76	287	1,900

SK Golf Challenge

Linna Golf Club, Vanajanlinna, Finland
Par 36-36–72; 7,245 yards

August 6-9
purse, €179,095

	SCORES				TOTAL	MONEY
Nicolas Colsaerts	70	71	70	66	277	€28,000
Rhys Davies	66	76	69	66	277	15,750
Julien Guerrier	71	68	67	71	277	15,750
(Colsaerts defeated Davies and Guerrier on second playoff hole.)						
Jose-Filipe Lima	70	68	72	68	278	10,500
Robert Coles	71	69	68	71	279	7,116.67
Richard McEvoy	71	71	66	71	279	7,116.67
Jacob Olesen	67	73	66	73	279	7,116.67
Roope Kakko	71	69	67	73	280	4,900
Antti Ahokas	66	74	71	70	281	3,718.75
Garry Houston	70	73	70	68	281	3,718.75
Julien Quesne	73	68	67	73	281	3,718.75
Mark Tullo	71	72	67	71	281	3,718.75
Oscar Floren	69	74	66	73	282	2,975
Andrew McArthur	70	75	67	70	282	2,975
Alexandre Rocha	72	70	70	70	282	2,975
Clodomiro Carranza	71	74	73	65	283	2,450
Joonas Granberg	72	72	69	70	283	2,450
Rikard Karlberg	73	69	72	69	283	2,450
Chris Gane	70	70	74	70	284	1,894.38
Iain Pyman	70	74	72	68	284	1,894.38

	SCORES				TOTAL	MONEY
Peter Whiteford	71	71	70	72	284	1,894.38
Andrew Willey	76	70	71	67	284	1,894.38
Ben Evans	70	72	72	71	285	1,645
Lorenzo Gagli	74	72	69	70	285	1,645
Niklas Lemke	70	75	68	72	285	1,645

Trophee du Golf de Geneve

Golf Club de Geneve, Geneva, Switzerland
Par 36-36–72; 6,727 yards

August 13-16
purse, €210,000

	SCORES				TOTAL	MONEY
Julien Quesne	63	69	71	66	269	€24,400
Edoardo Molinari	70	68	64	68	270	18,100
Peter Baker	68	67	69	67	271	11,000
Julien Guerrier	71	68	66	66	271	11,000
Gary Boyd	72	66	66	69	273	7,467
James Morrison	67	67	69	70	273	7,467
Alan Wagner	71	71	65	66	273	7,467
Nicolas Colsaerts	66	71	68	69	274	6,000
John Parry	68	68	67	72	275	5,033
Sam Walker	72	67	68	68	275	5,033
Matthew Zions	66	73	66	70	275	5,033
Rhys Davies	71	68	68	69	276	4,350
Sion E. Bebb	66	71	70	70	277	3,950
Julien Clement	69	68	66	74	277	3,950
Andrew McArthur	69	73	64	71	277	3,950
Jose-Filipe Lima	71	70	68	70	279	3,550
Anders Schmidt Hansen	73	65	70	74	282	3,068
Lee S. James	69	69	72	72	282	3,068
Richard McEvoy	69	70	71	72	282	3,068
Mark Tullo	74	68	68	72	282	3,068
Alexandre Kaleka	69	69	72	73	283	2,730

DHL Wroclaw Open

Toya Golf & Country Club, Wroclaw, Poland
Par 35-35–70; 6,903 yards

August 27-30
purse, €143,276

	SCORES				TOTAL	MONEY
Eric Ramsay	61	68	65	69	263	€22,400
Andrew Butterfield	66	66	66	67	265	12,600
Richard McEvoy	66	66	68	65	265	12,600
Oscar Floren	71	68	64	64	267	7,000
Nathan Smith	68	65	68	66	267	7,000
Steven Tiley	66	69	64	68	267	7,000
Nicolas Colsaerts	68	64	66	70	268	3,920
David Griffiths	71	65	65	67	268	3,920
Christoph Gunther	68	68	67	65	268	3,920
Nicolas Meitinger	67	68	67	67	269	2,940
John Parry	67	68	66	68	269	2,940
Chris Gane	67	67	66	70	270	2,590
Jacob Olesen	69	64	71	66	270	2,590
Lorenzo Gagli	67	66	67	71	271	2,240
Ben Mason	70	67	64	70	271	2,240
Steve Surry	66	72	65	68	271	2,240
Gary Boyd	66	70	69	67	272	1,505

	SCORES				TOTAL	MONEY
Scott Jamieson	67	62	69	74	272	1,505
Mikko Korhonen	68	67	70	67	272	1,505
Jan-Are Larsen	67	66	69	70	272	1,505
Victor Riu	67	67	74	64	272	1,505
Sebastian Saavedra	64	70	70	68	272	1,505
Ricardo Santos	66	69	67	70	272	1,505
Kyron Sullivan	66	69	69	68	272	1,505
Jerome Theunis	70	67	66	69	272	1,505
Martin Wiegele	68	66	66	72	272	1,505

Fred Olsen Challenge de Espana

Tecina Golf, La Gomera, Canary Islands, Spain
Par 36-35–71; 6,937 yards

September 3-6
purse, €150,000

	SCORES				TOTAL	MONEY
Rhys Davies	65	70	65	67	267	€24,000
Steven Jeppesen	65	63	72	68	268	16,500
Luis Claverie	69	67	65	68	269	9,750
Pedro Oriol	69	68	66	66	269	9,750
Jesus Maria Arruti	65	65	71	69	270	6,100
Stuart Davis	67	70	69	64	270	6,100
Charles-Edouard Russo	67	67	70	66	270	6,100
Jorge Campillo	68	70	66	67	271	3,700
Steven Tiley	69	69	67	66	271	3,700
Martin Wiegele	67	70	66	68	271	3,700
Clodomiro Carranza	66	71	67	68	272	2,850
Chris Gane	66	70	67	69	272	2,850
Mark Haastrup	68	67	66	71	272	2,850
Louis de Jager	69	66	69	69	273	2,400
James Morrison	67	69	66	71	273	2,400
Zane Scotland	67	71	66	69	273	2,400
Javier Colomo	66	68	71	69	274	1,950
Johan Skold	67	72	64	71	274	1,950
Daniel Wardrop	67	70	68	69	274	1,950
Raphael De Sousa	66	73	66	70	275	1,509
Stuart Manley	68	65	68	74	275	1,509
Richard McEvoy	70	66	66	73	275	1,509
Benjamin Miarka	66	70	69	70	275	1,509
Michele Reale	73	68	65	69	275	1,509
Sion E. Bebb	68	63	73	72	276	1,335
Francisco Cea	66	74	67	69	276	1,335
Nicolas Meitinger	67	72	69	68	276	1,335
Craig Smith	69	68	71	68	276	1,335

Dutch Futures

Golfclub Houtrak, Halfweg, Netherlands
Par 36-36–72; 7,013 yards

September 10-13
purse, €150,000

	SCORES				TOTAL	MONEY
Nicolas Colsaerts	69	66	67	69	271	€24,000
Andrew McArthur	71	68	66	70	275	13,500
Julien Quesne	69	68	69	69	275	13,500
Andrew Butterfield	68	67	70	71	276	8,250
Jose-Filipe Lima	69	70	70	67	276	8,250
Gary Boyd	70	67	70	70	277	4,650

	SCORES				TOTAL	MONEY
Thomas Feyrsinger	72	70	68	67	277	4,650
Edoardo Molinari	68	69	66	74	277	4,650
George Murray	70	69	68	70	277	4,650
Liam Bond	72	68	68	70	278	3,150
Carl Suneson	67	69	69	73	278	3,150
Christophe Brazillier	67	69	71	72	279	2,850
Colm Moriarty	70	71	66	73	280	2,550
Steven Tiley	69	71	67	73	280	2,550
*Willem Vork	68	71	72	69	280	
Bernd Wiesberger	68	71	67	74	280	2,550
Sion E. Bebb	70	70	67	74	281	2,025
Chris Gane	73	69	69	70	281	2,025
Marcus Higley	70	71	71	69	281	2,025
Matthew Zions	68	71	75	67	281	2,025
Adrien Bernadet	73	70	70	69	282	1,449.38
Robert Coles	69	71	73	69	282	1,449.38
Matthew Cryer	69	72	70	71	282	1,449.38
Rhys Davies	69	68	74	71	282	1,449.38
David Griffiths	69	72	70	71	282	1,449.38
Ben Mason	65	71	76	70	282	1,449.38
Bjorn Pettersson	69	71	74	68	282	1,449.38
Kyron Sullivan	69	72	67	74	282	1,449.38

Kazakhstan Open

Zhailjau Golf Resort, Almaty, Kazakhstan
Par 36-36–72; 7,197 yards

September 17-20
purse, €405,600

	SCORES				TOTAL	MONEY
Edoardo Molinari	67	67	66	68	268	€64,000
Chris Gane	70	66	68	67	271	44,000
Gary Boyd	63	71	71	69	274	24,000
Peter Gustafsson	69	67	67	71	274	24,000
Gareth Paddison	69	67	72	66	274	24,000
Andrew Marshall	71	63	71	70	275	16,000
Sion E. Bebb	74	66	68	68	276	12,000
Julien Quesne	71	67	67	71	276	12,000
Daniel Denison	70	69	66	72	277	9,600
Julien Clement	67	69	71	71	278	8,133.33
Peter Whiteford	68	67	71	72	278	8,133.33
Matthew Zions	68	69	72	69	278	8,133.33
Rhys Davies	72	68	65	74	279	6,600
Oscar Floren	66	72	71	70	279	6,600
Scott Jamieson	74	67	68	70	279	6,600
Martin Wiegele	69	70	68	72	279	6,600
Ben Evans	69	72	70	69	280	5,050
Soren Juul	72	69	66	73	280	5,050
Mikko Korhonen	71	68	70	71	280	5,050
Ben Mason	69	70	70	71	280	5,050
Adam Gee	72	68	69	72	281	3,760
Jacob Olesen	72	68	73	68	281	3,760
Sebastian Saavedra	70	68	70	73	281	3,760
Lloyd Saltman	67	72	71	71	281	3,760
Simon Thornton	69	66	74	72	281	3,760
Alan Wagner	73	67	68	73	281	3,760
Julio Zapata	74	66	69	72	281	3,760

ECCO Tour Championship

Holstebro Golfklub, Jutland, Denmark
Par 35-36–71; 7,044 yards
(Event shortened to 54 holes—rain.)

October 1-4
purse, €182,052

	SCORES			TOTAL	MONEY
Jose-Filipe Lima	70	69	72	211	€28,800
Edoardo Molinari	69	69	74	212	19,800
Roope Kakko	70	69	75	214	12,600
Fredrik Andersson Hed	75	69	72	216	10,800
John Parry	71	69	77	217	9,000
Nicolas Colsaerts	76	70	72	218	5,256
Stuart Davis	71	75	72	218	5,256
Anders Sjostrand	71	71	76	218	5,256
Carl Suneson	71	71	76	218	5,256
Peter Whiteford	75	73	70	218	5,256
Adrien Bernadet	77	70	73	220	3,330
Mark Haastrup	75	72	73	220	3,330
Cesar Monasterio	73	74	73	220	3,330
Nathan Smith	74	74	72	220	3,330
Florian Fritsch	76	73	72	221	2,352.86
Julien Guerrier	75	73	73	221	2,352.86
*Andreas Hartoe	74	71	76	221	
Stuart Manley	71	71	79	221	2,352.86
Richard McEvoy	72	73	76	221	2,352.86
Gareth Paddison	76	72	73	221	2,352.86
Julien Quesne	76	70	75	221	2,352.86
Sam Walker	74	73	74	221	2,352.86
Federico Colombo	73	72	77	222	1,656
Daniel Denison	76	72	74	222	1,656
Adam Gee	72	72	78	222	1,656
Peter Gustafsson	73	74	75	222	1,656
*Joachim Hansen	71	74	77	222	
Alexandre Kaleka	73	76	73	222	1,656
Wilhelm Schauman	76	72	74	222	1,656
Anthony Snobeck	78	70	74	222	1,656

Allianz Golf Open Grand Toulouse

Golf de Toulouse-Seilh, Seilh, France
Par 36-36–72; 6,924 yards

October 8-11
purse, €152,100

	SCORES				TOTAL	MONEY
John Parry	66	68	70	63	267	€24,000
Jose-Filipe Lima	68	68	66	67	269	16,500
Peter Baker	69	68	66	67	270	9,000
Federico Colombo	67	65	71	67	270	9,000
Nicolas Colsaerts	69	62	74	65	270	9,000
Charles-Edouard Russo	64	69	69	69	271	5,000
Roland Steiner	67	65	69	70	271	5,000
Peter Whiteford	65	68	70	68	271	5,000
Antti Ahokas	64	69	67	72	272	2,914.29
Liam Bond	67	67	71	67	272	2,914.29
Robert Coles	68	67	67	70	272	2,914.29
*Victor Dubuisson	69	69	66	68	272	
Stuart Manley	65	71	69	67	272	2,914.29
Julien Quesne	68	66	71	67	272	2,914.29
Carl Suneson	70	67	66	69	272	2,914.29

	SCORES				TOTAL	MONEY
Sam Walker	66	70	67	69	272	2,914.29
Jonathan Caldwell	67	72	66	68	273	2,100
Oscar Floren	70	67	68	68	273	2,100
Martin Wiegele	65	72	65	71	273	2,100
Julien Clement	72	64	66	72	274	1,623.75
Mikko Korhonen	68	67	71	68	274	1,623.75
Richard McEvoy	67	71	70	66	274	1,623.75
Matthew Zions	64	67	72	71	274	1,623.75
Andrew Butterfield	67	71	69	68	275	1,410
Jamie Moul	67	69	72	67	275	1,410
Ake Nilsson	67	66	72	70	275	1,410

Italian Federation Cup

Olgiata Golf Club, Rome, Italy
Par 36-36–72; 6,966 yards

October 21-24
purse, €150,450

	SCORES				TOTAL	MONEY
Edoardo Molinari	66	67	68	66	267	€24,000
Nicolas Colsaerts	68	66	66	68	268	16,500
Rhys Davies	66	68	67	71	272	10,500
Stuart Manley	70	70	67	66	273	9,000
Fredrik Andersson Hed	69	68	64	73	274	7,500
Benjamin Hebert	74	67	67	67	275	5,400
Simon Thornton	65	69	70	71	275	5,400
Peter Gustafsson	70	66	70	70	276	4,200
Ally Mellor	72	69	66	70	277	3,450
Thorbjorn Olesen	70	68	66	73	277	3,450
Scott Jamieson	68	70	69	71	278	2,775
Julien Quesne	71	69	67	71	278	2,775
Charles-Edouard Russo	70	66	72	70	278	2,775
Joel Sjoholm	69	69	67	73	278	2,775
Jonathan Caldwell	69	70	71	69	279	2,250
Robert Coles	69	68	73	69	279	2,250
Andrew Tampion	68	68	71	72	279	2,250
Chris Gane	69	71	69	71	280	1,825
Mark Haastrup	66	70	71	73	280	1,825
John Parry	71	70	69	70	280	1,825
Gary Boyd	70	70	69	72	281	1,455
Peter Kaensche	73	70	70	68	281	1,455
James Morrison	73	68	68	72	281	1,455
Iain Pyman	71	70	66	74	281	1,455
Federico Colombo	73	67	70	72	282	1,305
Oscar Floren	71	70	71	70	282	1,305
Alexandre Kaleka	69	74	68	71	282	1,305
Victor Riu	67	72	73	70	282	1,305
Ricardo Santos	69	70	69	74	282	1,305
Kyron Sullivan	74	69	72	67	282	1,305

Apulia San Domenico Grand Final

San Domenico Golf Club, Puglia, Italy
Par 34-37–71; 7,031 yards

October 28-31
purse, €300,000

	SCORES				TOTAL	MONEY
Peter Whiteford	70	73	69	67	279	€51,500
Andrew Tampion	70	66	75	68	279	34,200
(Whiteford defeated Tampion on first playoff hole.)						
Rhys Davies	71	69	69	71	280	19,300
Fredrik Andersson Hed	72	73	68	69	282	14,300
Andrew McArthur	70	70	70	72	282	14,300
Alexandre Kaleka	70	69	73	71	283	12,000
Edoardo Molinari	74	71	69	71	285	11,100
Gary Boyd	72	73	69	72	286	9,433.33
Steven Jeppesen	72	71	71	72	286	9,433.33
Alan Wagner	74	72	69	71	286	9,433.33
Francois Calmels	71	74	72	71	288	6,660
Oscar Floren	72	71	72	73	288	6,660
Chris Gane	70	75	72	71	288	6,660
Peter Gustafsson	71	69	75	73	288	6,660
Roland Steiner	75	72	73	68	288	6,660
Sam Walker	76	71	74	68	289	4,800
James Morrison	76	70	74	70	290	4,150
John Parry	76	73	75	66	290	4,150
Nicolas Colsaerts	76	72	70	73	291	3,460
Julien Guerrier	70	75	72	74	291	3,460
Eric Ramsay	77	73	72	69	291	3,460
Martin Wiegele	72	70	76	73	291	3,460
Matthew Zions	75	72	75	69	291	3,460
Andrew Butterfield	70	74	73	75	292	3,050
Robert Coles	76	67	75	74	292	3,050

Asian Tour

The Royal Trophy

Amata Springs Country Club, Bangkok, Thailand
Par 36-36–72; 7,322 yards

January 9-11

FIRST DAY
Foursomes

Paul Lawrie and Soren Hansen (Europe) defeated Ryo Ishikawa and Toru Taniguchi, 2 and 1.
Charlie Wi and Liang Wen-chong (Asia) defeated Paul McGinley and Pablo Larrazabal,
2 up.
Hideto Tanihara and S.K. Ho (Asia) defeated Nick Dougherty and Oliver Wilson, 1 up.
Thongchai Jaidee and Prayad Marksaeng (Asia) defeated Niclas Fasth and Johan Edfors,
5 and 4.

POINTS: Asia 3, Europe 1

SECOND DAY
Fourballs

Ishikawa and Taniguchi (Asia) halved with Hansen and Lawrie.
Wi and Liang (Asia) defeated Dougherty and Wilson, 3 and 2.
Tanihara and Ho (Asia) defeated Fasth and Edfors, 2 and 1.
Thongchai and Prayad (Asia) defeated Larrazabal and McGinley, 4 and 2.

POINTS: Asia 6½, Europe 1½

THIRD DAY
Singles

Ishikawa (Asia) halved with Hansen.
Lawrie (Europe) defeated Liang, 3 and 2.
Dougherty (Europe) defeated Wi, 1 up.
Prayad (Asia) defeated Larrazabal, 5 and 4.
Wilson (Europe) defeated Tanihara, 3 and 2.
Edfors (Europe) defeated Ho, 5 and 4.
Taniguchi (Asia) defeated Fasth, 7 and 6.
Thongchai (Asia) defeated McGinley, 5 and 4.

TOTAL POINTS: Asia 10, Europe 6

Asian Tour International

Suwan Golf & Country Club, Bangkok, Thailand
Par 71; 7,125 yards

February 5-8
purse, US$300,000

	SCORES				TOTAL	MONEY
James Kamte	71	63	68	66	268	US$47,550
Tetsuji Hiratsuka	64	68	67	71	270	32,550
Marcus Both	63	68	72	68	271	13,890
Prom Meesawat	69	68	68	66	271	13,890
Juvic Pagunsan	67	71	65	68	271	13,890
Unho Park	65	69	66	71	271	13,890
Wu Ashun	67	71	71	63	272	7,620
Mark Purser	68	66	71	67	272	7,620

	SCORES				TOTAL	MONEY
Rahil Gangjee	65	69	68	70	272	7,620
Atthaphon Prathummanee	68	68	71	66	273	5,910
Simon Griffiths	68	71	71	64	274	4,806
Mo Joong-kyung	66	70	73	65	274	4,806
Gavin Flint	67	69	70	68	274	4,806
Iain Steel	72	63	70	69	274	4,806
Ted Oh	68	66	69	71	274	4,806
Noh Seung-yul	68	66	75	66	275	4,140
Kodai Ichihara	66	69	74	67	276	3,720
Prayad Marksaeng	71	68	68	69	276	3,720
Tim Stewart	69	69	68	70	276	3,720
Danny Chia	67	69	69	71	276	3,720
Andrew Dodt	67	69	74	67	277	3,285
John Parry	73	67	71	66	277	3,285
Adam Groom	67	70	72	68	277	3,285
Matthew Griffin	71	66	69	71	277	3,285
Darren Beck	72	66	70	70	278	2,880
Rhys Davies	69	66	71	72	278	2,880
Hirotaro Naito	67	66	73	72	278	2,880
Tatsuya Sato	74	64	69	71	278	2,880
Frankie Minoza	69	71	68	70	278	2,880

Maybank Malaysian Open

Saujana Golf & Country Club, Kuala Lumpur, Malaysia
Par 36-36–72; 6,971 yards

February 12-15
purse, US$2,000,000

	SCORES				TOTAL	MONEY
Anthony Kang	74	66	64	67	271	US$333,330
David Horsey	71	68	69	64	272	133,055
Jyoti Randhawa	71	69	66	66	272	133,055
Miles Tunnicliff	71	70	63	68	272	133,055
Prayad Marksaeng	69	70	65	68	272	133,055
Gareth Maybin	69	69	69	66	273	70,000
Louis Oosthuizen	70	71	68	65	274	51,600
Liang Wen-chong	65	71	67	71	274	51,600
Alexander Noren	63	71	69	71	274	51,600
Adam Blyth	66	70	66	73	275	40,000
James Kamte	70	72	68	66	276	33,500
Johan Edfors	69	71	68	68	276	33,500
Noh Seung-yul	62	73	71	70	276	33,500
Danny Chia	66	65	74	71	276	33,500
Nick Dougherty	66	70	72	69	277	29,400
Raphael Jacquelin	74	69	73	62	278	25,960
Klas Eriksson	68	75	69	66	278	25,960
Angelo Que	73	70	69	66	278	25,960
Ross McGowan	70	70	71	67	278	25,960
Simon Dyson	71	66	73	68	278	25,960
Jose Manuel Lara	68	74	70	67	279	20,800
Mark Foster	69	71	71	68	279	20,800
Shingo Katayama	69	71	71	68	279	20,800
Martin Erlandsson	73	68	70	68	279	20,800
Juvic Pagunsan	67	73	70	69	279	20,800
Phillip Archer	69	69	70	71	279	20,800
Simon Griffiths	70	66	71	72	279	20,800
Peter Lawrie	72	68	67	72	279	20,800
Shiv Kapur	70	69	66	74	279	20,800
Marcus Fraser	72	67	71	70	280	17,200
Thongchai Jaidee	69	72	69	70	280	17,200
Scott Barr	71	67	70	72	280	17,200

	SCORES				TOTAL	MONEY
Anthony Kim	78	65	71	67	281	15,250
Darren Beck	71	69	70	71	281	15,250
Maarten Lafeber	73	68	69	71	281	15,250
Stephen Leaney	70	69	69	73	281	15,250
Kodai Ichihara	69	73	71	69	282	13,800
Rafael Cabrera-Bello	70	72	70	70	282	13,800
Jean-Francois Lucquin	65	72	74	71	282	13,800
Tony Carolan	70	72	74	67	283	12,400
Richard Finch	70	71	71	71	283	12,400
Prom Meesawat	70	69	73	71	283	12,400
Mikael Lundberg	68	73	68	74	283	12,400
Chris Rodgers	74	69	73	68	284	10,800
Ignacio Garrido	71	71	73	69	284	10,800
Jason Knutzon	70	73	71	70	284	10,800
Lu Wei-chih	72	71	66	75	284	10,800
Mitchell Brown	68	72	74	71	285	9,200
Marcel Siem	70	73	71	71	285	9,200
S. Siva Chandhran	72	70	71	72	285	9,200
Hendrik Buhrmann	70	71	70	74	285	9,200
Mars Pucay	69	70	77	70	286	8,000
Chapchai Nirat	71	72	70	73	286	8,000
David Frost	70	70	78	69	287	6,800
Sam Little	74	69	74	70	287	6,800
Wil Besseling	74	67	73	73	287	6,800
Pelle Edberg	75	67	69	76	287	6,800
Chawalit Plaphol	69	74	78	67	288	5,600
Neven Basic	75	68	76	69	288	5,600
Shaaban Hussin	71	72	75	70	288	5,600
Gavin Flint	72	71	73	72	288	5,600
David Bransdon	72	68	74	74	288	5,600
Jarmo Sandelin	70	73	72	74	289	4,800
Simon Khan	70	72	72	75	289	4,800
Oliver Fisher	69	70	74	76	289	4,800
Robert Rock	73	67	78	72	290	4,200
Frankie Minoza	72	70	72	76	290	4,200
Anton Haig	71	70	72	77	290	4,200
Kim Kyung-tae	72	71	74	74	291	3,725
S.S.P. Chowrasia	69	74	75	73	291	3,725
Scott Hend	73	70	74	75	292	2,997.43
Ross Bain	68	75	72	77	292	2,997.43
Rhys Davies	67	76	77	73	293	2,991.64
David Gleeson	72	71	74	78	295	2,987.78

Johnnie Walker Classic

See Australasian Tour chapter.

Enjoy Jakarta Indonesia Open

New Kuta Golf Resort, Bali, Indonesia
Par 36-36–72; 7,328 yards

February 26-March 1
purse, US$1,250,000

	SCORES				TOTAL	MONEY
Thongchai Jaidee	71	69	67	69	276	US$208,330
Steve Webster	69	69	72	68	278	93,210
Simon Dyson	68	71	70	69	278	93,210
Alexander Noren	69	73	66	70	278	93,210
Rafael Cabrera-Bello	71	72	71	65	279	48,375
Richard Bland	72	71	66	70	279	48,375

	SCORES			TOTAL	MONEY
Simon Khan	68	76	68	68	280	32,250
Jyoti Randhawa	74	70	66	70	280	32,250
Simon Griffiths	70	70	69	71	280	32,250
Noh Seung-yul	69	76	70	66	281	24,000
Jason Knutzon	72	70	70	69	281	24,000
Ignacio Garrido	70	71	74	67	282	19,781.25
Anthony Kang	70	71	70	71	282	19,781.25
Marcus Fraser	69	73	70	70	282	19,781.25
Jeppe Huldahl	73	66	70	73	282	19,781.25
Gaurav Ghei	72	68	74	69	283	15,937.50
Bryan Saltus	70	72	72	69	283	15,937.50
Pelle Edberg	74	71	69	69	283	15,937.50
Daniel Chopra	73	71	70	69	283	15,937.50
Digvijay Singh	69	72	71	71	283	15,937.50
Scott Drummond	71	69	69	74	283	15,937.50
Michael Hoey	71	73	73	67	284	12,812.50
Darren Beck	71	71	72	70	284	12,812.50
Juvic Pagunsan	71	74	69	70	284	12,812.50
Angelo Que	64	76	73	71	284	12,812.50
Lu Wei-chih	71	70	71	72	284	12,812.50
Gary Murphy	70	72	71	71	284	12,812.50
Tony Carolan	68	74	71	71	284	12,812.50
Ross McGowan	69	71	69	75	284	12,812.50
Danny Willett	70	74	73	68	285	10,937.50
Jamie Donaldson	68	71	71	75	285	10,937.50
Magnus A. Carlsson	71	74	74	67	286	8,909.09
Brett Rumford	70	73	74	69	286	8,909.09
Bernd Wiesberger	72	73	72	69	286	8,909.09
Chawalit Plaphol	71	71	74	70	286	8,909.09
Kim Kyung-tae	73	68	74	71	286	8,909.09
Andrew Coltart	73	71	71	71	286	8,909.09
Rhys Davies	69	73	73	71	286	8,909.09
Rory Hie	70	72	72	72	286	8,909.09
Sam Little	73	70	71	72	286	8,909.09
Frankie Minoza	74	69	70	73	286	8,909.09
Gavin Flint	70	72	71	73	286	8,909.09
Wade Ormsby	74	71	73	69	287	7,125
Richie Ramsay	68	76	72	71	287	7,125
Gaganjeet Bhullar	74	71	71	71	287	7,125
Joakim Haeggman	71	74	73	70	288	5,750
Miles Tunnicliff	69	71	77	71	288	5,750
Andrew Dodt	68	75	73	72	288	5,750
Zaw Moe	73	71	71	73	288	5,750
Zhang Lian-wei	69	74	71	74	288	5,750
Ted Oh	73	67	73	75	288	5,750
Gary Lockerbie	71	72	69	76	288	5,750
Chapchai Nirat	70	72	71	75	288	5,750
Mardan Mamat	74	71	72	72	289	4,250
Oliver Fisher	71	74	72	72	289	4,250
Chinnarat Phadungsil	70	71	72	76	289	4,250
James Kamte	72	71	70	76	289	4,250
Neven Basic	75	70	70	75	290	3,750
Seve Benson	70	73	74	74	291	3,500
Antonio Lascuna	68	73	75	75	291	3,500
Mark Foster	72	71	73	75	291	3,500
Scott Strange	73	71	76	72	292	3,187.50
Markus Brier	71	74	73	74	292	3,187.50
Marcel Siem	76	68	78	71	293	2,875
Jean Van de Velde	71	72	81	69	293	2,875
S.S.P. Chowrasia	70	73	77	73	293	2,875
John Bickerton	71	74	72	77	294	2,625
Alessandro Tadini	74	71	74	76	295	2,500
Taco Remkes	70	73	77	78	298	2,375

Singha Thailand Open

Laguna Phuket Golf Club, Phuket, Thailand
Par 35-35–70; 6,896 yards

March 5-8
purse, US$500,000

	SCORES				TOTAL	MONEY
Jyoti Randhawa	68	68	62	65	263	US$79,250
Rhys Davies	65	64	69	67	265	54,250
Lu Wei-chih	65	68	68	65	266	30,500
Wu Ashun	67	67	67	66	267	22,575
S.S.P. Chowrasia	66	62	70	69	267	22,575
Daniel Chopra	67	69	69	63	268	15,750
Yasin Ali	70	68	66	64	268	15,750
Mardan Mamat	66	67	69	67	269	11,775
Kodai Ichihara	68	66	68	67	269	11,775
Mark Purser	68	69	70	63	270	7,744.44
Anthony Kang	67	70	68	65	270	7,744.44
Himmat Rai	65	72	68	65	270	7,744.44
Thongchai Jaidee	69	70	64	67	270	7,744.44
Chapchai Nirat	64	69	69	68	270	7,744.44
Gaganjeet Bhullar	64	66	71	69	270	7,744.44
Keith Horne	65	69	68	68	270	7,744.44
Unho Park	64	71	66	69	270	7,744.44
Juvic Pagunsan	70	65	65	70	270	7,744.44
Anirban Lahiri	68	67	72	64	271	5,866.67
Mo Joong-kyung	65	71	69	66	271	5,866.67
Udorn Duangdecha	66	66	70	69	271	5,866.67
Angelo Que	67	67	71	67	272	5,475
Kim Dae-hyun	70	64	69	69	272	5,475
Jbe' Kruger	68	67	72	66	273	4,725
Iain Steel	69	66	71	67	273	4,725
Varut Chomchalam	69	67	70	67	273	4,725
Rory Hie	69	68	69	67	273	4,725
Tetsuji Hiratsuka	66	70	69	68	273	4,725
Tim Stewart	65	67	69	72	273	4,725
David Bransdon	66	65	69	73	273	4,725
Prom Meesawat	71	64	66	72	273	4,725

SAIL Open

Classic Golf Resort, New Delhi, India
Par 36-36–72; 7,114 yards

March 18-21
purse, US$300,000

	SCORES				TOTAL	MONEY
Chapchai Nirat	62	62	65	67	256	US$47,550
Gaganjeet Bhullar	67	64	66	70	267	25,425
Richard Moir	66	67	66	68	267	25,425
Thammanoon Srirot	67	68	67	67	269	12,420
Keith Horne	68	67	64	70	269	12,420
Mark Purser	65	63	72	69	269	12,420
Chris Gaunt	70	66	67	67	270	8,130
Wisut Artjanawat	65	64	72	69	270	8,130
Rory Hie	67	70	67	67	271	5,975
Ross Bain	67	68	66	70	271	5,975
Antonio Lascuna	65	67	67	72	271	5,975
George Coetzee	68	68	70	66	272	4,897.50
Ashok Kumar	67	68	67	70	272	4,897.50
Thaworn Wiratchant	69	69	65	70	273	4,500
Kodai Ichihara	70	70	66	68	274	3,966
Jason Norris	68	68	71	67	274	3,966

	SCORES				TOTAL	MONEY
Amandeep Johl	68	69	69	68	274	3,966
Will Yanagisawa	68	66	69	71	274	3,966
Prom Meesawat	68	65	68	73	274	3,966
Kiradech Aphibarnrat	72	68	66	69	275	3,240
Mardan Mamat	65	67	73	70	275	3,240
Siddikur	68	70	68	69	275	3,240
Vikrant Chopra	72	68	68	67	275	3,240
Unho Park	70	67	68	70	275	3,240
Shiv Kapur	68	66	69	72	275	3,240
Mars Pucay	67	66	70	72	275	3,240

Black Mountain Masters

Black Mountain Golf Club, Hua Hin, Thailand
Par 36-36–72; 7,184 yards

March 26-29
purse, US$500,000

	SCORES				TOTAL	MONEY
Johan Edfors	64	68	71	68	271	US$79,250
Prayad Marksaeng	70	72	67	64	273	42,375
Chris Rodgers	70	68	67	68	273	42,375
Anirban Lahiri	69	70	67	68	274	24,650
Gaganjeet Bhullar	71	71	70	63	275	17,333.33
Chapchai Nirat	69	68	71	67	275	17,333.33
Thongchai Jaidee	71	69	67	68	275	17,333.33
Darren Beck	69	66	75	67	277	9,464.29
John Parry	74	69	66	68	277	9,464.29
Angelo Que	68	73	67	69	277	9,464.29
Noh Seung-yul	66	71	70	70	277	9,464.29
Lu Wei-chih	71	71	66	69	277	9,464.29
Peter Cooke	67	70	70	70	277	9,464.29
Jason King	68	68	69	72	277	9,464.29
Will Yanagisawa	70	71	71	66	278	6,483.33
Prom Meesawat	70	69	72	67	278	6,483.33
Andrew Dodt	71	72	68	67	278	6,483.33
Frankie Minoza	67	68	75	68	278	6,483.33
Kiradech Aphibarnrat	69	69	71	69	278	6,483.33
Keith Horne	68	71	68	71	278	6,483.33
Juvic Pagunsan	71	73	68	67	279	5,400
Neven Basic	67	74	70	68	279	5,400
Wu Ashun	69	69	70	71	279	5,400
Kodai Ichihara	72	69	67	71	279	5,400
Chris Gaunt	67	73	66	73	279	5,400

Ballantine's Championship

Pinx Golf Club, Jeju Island, South Korea
Par 36-36–72; 7,345 yards

April 23-26
purse, US$2,900,000

	SCORES				TOTAL	MONEY
Thongchai Jaidee	66	71	77	70	284	US$457,249.62
Kang Sung-hoon	69	71	76	68	284	238,285.84
Gonzalo Fernandez-Castano	65	74	76	69	284	238,285.84
(Thongchai defeated Kang and Fernandez-Castano on first playoff hole.)						
Seve Benson	69	70	78	69	286	107,956.63
Rafael Cabrera-Bello	68	72	76	70	286	107,956.63
Ernie Els	68	74	73	71	286	107,956.63
Robert-Jan Derksen	66	69	75	76	286	107,956.63

	SCORES				TOTAL	MONEY
Peter Lawrie	70	75	76	66	287	61,637.25
Danny Willett	69	76	73	69	287	61,637.25
Mardan Mamat	69	70	77	71	287	61,637.25
Terry Pilkadaris	75	68	74	71	288	45,953.58
Choi Ho-sung	69	72	76	71	288	45,953.58
Jason Knutzon	67	74	75	72	288	45,953.58
Pablo Martin	69	69	74	76	288	45,953.58
Brett Rumford	68	73	76	72	289	37,860.27
Scott Barr	68	72	76	73	289	37,860.27
Kang Wook-soon	68	69	77	75	289	37,860.27
Kang Kyung-nam	66	73	75	75	289	37,860.27
Richard Bland	73	72	78	67	290	31,989.18
Graeme Storm	72	68	78	72	290	31,989.18
Mark Brown	65	73	78	74	290	31,989.18
Choi Gwang-soo	71	70	74	75	290	31,989.18
Mikko Ilonen	68	73	74	75	290	31,989.18
Lu Wei-chih	70	75	77	69	291	28,532.38
Rick Kulacz	71	71	77	72	291	28,532.38
Francois Delamontagne	72	72	71	76	291	28,532.38
Gareth Maybin	70	72	78	72	292	25,651.71
Kim Hyung-tae	68	72	82	70	292	25,651.71
Zane Scotland	70	73	76	73	292	25,651.71
Andrew Dodt	72	68	76	76	292	25,651.71
Nick Dougherty	71	72	77	73	293	22,771.03
Felipe Aguilar	69	72	78	74	293	22,771.03
Wu Ashun	69	75	80	69	293	22,771.03
Jose-Filipe Lima	72	72	76	74	294	19,478.83
Marcus Fraser	70	75	75	74	294	19,478.83
Klas Eriksson	71	74	76	73	294	19,478.83
Alessandro Tadini	67	71	84	72	294	19,478.83
Lee Westwood	71	73	76	74	294	19,478.83
Iain Steel	70	73	80	71	294	19,478.83
Markus Brier	71	72	81	70	294	19,478.83
Andrew Tschudin	70	75	75	75	295	16,186.64
Chris Wood	75	70	76	74	295	16,186.64
Hong Soon-sang	68	74	78	75	295	16,186.64
Simon Dyson	69	75	78	73	295	16,186.64
Barry Lane	71	74	78	72	295	16,186.64
Noh Seung-yul	71	69	80	76	296	13,443.14
Oskar Henningsson	73	72	77	74	296	13,443.14
Robert Dinwiddie	67	73	82	74	296	13,443.14
Paul McGinley	73	72	78	73	296	13,443.14
Chawalit Plaphol	68	74	82	72	296	13,443.14
Branden Grace	69	70	81	77	297	11,797.04
Lam Chih Bing	68	72	80	78	298	10,425.29
Henrik Stenson	68	74	81	75	298	10,425.29
Prom Meesawat	71	73	81	73	298	10,425.29
Fred Couples	69	76	81	72	298	10,425.29
Mo Joong-kyung	70	73	77	79	299	9,053.54
Kim Hyung-sung	69	76	78	77	300	8,230.49
Wil Besseling	71	74	80	75	300	8,230.49
Lin Wen-tang	73	71	81	75	300	8,230.49
Lin Wen-hong	69	70	84	78	301	7,270.27
Pablo Larrazabal	72	72	79	78	301	7,270.27
Scott Drummond	70	75	81	75	301	7,270.27
Inder Van Weerelt	70	74	83	74	301	7,270.27
Kwon Myung-ho	72	72	82	76	302	6,584.40
Ted Oh	70	75	80	78	303	6,035.69
Rhys Davies	70	73	82	78	303	6,035.69
Jeppe Huldahl	71	74	86	72	303	6,035.69
Thaworn Wiratchant	71	74	81	78	304	5,234.42
Gaurav Ghei	69	74	84	77	304	5,234.42
Fabrizio Zanotti	71	74	83	76	304	5,234.42

	SCORES				TOTAL	MONEY
Digvijay Singh	73	71	82	79	305	4,115.25
Eirik Tage Johansen	73	72	84	77	306	4,111.33
Peter Hedblom	72	72	87	77	308	4,107.40
Somkiat Srisanga	73	72	89	87	321	4,103.48

GS Caltex Maekyung Open

Nam Seoul Country Club, Seoul, South Korea
Par 36-36–72; 6,962 yards

May 14-17
purse, US$470,000

	SCORES				TOTAL	MONEY
Bae Sang-moon	71	70	70	70	281	US$93,312.60
Ted Oh	68	68	75	70	281	58,320.37
(Bae defeated Oh on second playoff hole.)						
Kim Dae-sub	71	73	70	69	283	25,660.96
Kim Jong-duk	67	74	73	69	283	25,660.96
*Byun Jin-jae	69	70	74	71	284	
Kim Hyung-sung	70	68	75	71	284	16,329.70
Kang Kyung-nam	71	72	69	72	284	16,329.70
Noh Seung-yul	74	72	72	67	285	9,564.54
Son Hyun-ho	72	69	74	70	285	9,564.54
S.K. Ho	67	72	75	71	285	9,564.54
Lam Chih Bing	70	70	72	73	285	9,564.54
Lee Seung-ho	72	69	72	72	285	9,564.54
Jbe' Kruger	76	69	72	69	286	6,590.20
Scott Barr	72	68	75	71	286	6,590.20
Kim Kyung-tae	72	70	72	72	286	6,590.20
Kim Dae-hyun	73	69	69	75	286	6,590.20
*Kim Meen-whee	77	68	72	71	288	
Kwon Myung-ho	72	74	75	67	288	5,883.88
Park Sang-hyun	71	73	73	71	288	5,883.88
Kang Kwon-il	74	69	74	71	288	5,883.88
Kang Wook-soon	72	71	75	71	289	4,950.75
Heo Won-kyoung	75	70	73	71	289	4,950.75
Kim Do-hoon I	71	75	73	70	289	4,950.75
Iain Steel	71	73	75	70	289	4,950.75
Kim Wi-joong	73	71	75	70	289	4,950.75
Jang Ik-jae	72	71	74	72	289	4,950.75
Bang Doo-hwan	72	75	74	68	289	4,950.75
*Jeong Youn-jin	69	71	76	73	289	
*Lee Kyoung-hoon	74	70	72	73	289	
Kang Min-woong	74	68	74	73	289	4,950.75
Park Hyo-won	68	69	76	76	289	4,950.75

Indonesia President Invitational

Damai Indah Golf Club, BSD Course, Jakarta, Indonesia
Par 36-36–72; 7,120 yards

July 23-26
purse, US$400,000

	SCORES				TOTAL	MONEY
Gaganjeet Bhullar	69	68	62	67	266	US$63,400
Adam Blyth	67	66	67	68	268	43,400
Thammanoon Srirot	67	70	66	66	269	24,400
Ted Oh	68	67	66	69	270	19,720
Bae Sang-moon	76	64	64	68	272	14,980
Artemio Murakami	69	67	68	68	272	14,980
Noh Seung-yul	72	68	66	67	273	10,160

	SCORES				TOTAL	MONEY
Darren Beck	66	73	69	65	273	10,160
Marcus Both	66	70	68	69	273	10,160
Lu Wei-chih	70	71	65	68	274	7,040
Scott Hend	70	69	68	67	274	7,040
Kim Dae-hyun	69	67	69	69	274	7,040
Lee Sung	67	67	71	69	274	7,040
Jason King	74	68	65	68	275	5,520
Antonio Lascuna	68	68	70	69	275	5,520
Chris Rodgers	69	67	70	69	275	5,520
Rick Kulacz	72	71	66	66	275	5,520
Thaworn Wiratchant	66	66	71	72	275	5,520
Son Joon-eob	73	65	68	70	276	4,630
David Gleeson	69	73	68	66	276	4,630
Pasi Purhonen	66	70	72	68	276	4,630
Matthew Griffin	73	70	69	64	276	4,630
Simon Griffiths	68	71	71	68	278	4,260
Jay Bayron	71	72	69	66	278	4,260
James Kamte	69	71	67	72	279	3,552
Juvic Pagunsan	74	67	68	70	279	3,552
Tony Carolan	71	68	71	69	279	3,552
Lu Wen-teh	70	70	70	69	279	3,552
Kao Bo-song	69	72	69	69	279	3,552
Lien Lu-sen	71	71	68	69	279	3,552
Mardan Mamat	74	65	70	70	279	3,552
Lam Chih Bing	70	72	71	66	279	3,552
Peter Cooke	69	68	69	73	279	3,552
Rahil Gangjee	70	73	69	67	279	3,552

Brunei Open

Empire Hotel & Country Club, Bandar Seri Begawa, Brunei   July 30-August 2
Par 35-36–71; 7,013 yards   purse, US$300,000

	SCORES				TOTAL	MONEY
Darren Beck	71	67	68	65	271	US$47,550
Boonchu Ruangkit	65	71	64	71	271	25,425
Gaganjeet Bhullar	67	71	64	69	271	25,425
(Beck defeated Boonchu on second and Bhullar on third playoff hole.)						
David Gleeson	66	69	69	68	272	14,790
Juvic Pagunsan	68	68	68	69	273	9,682.50
Lu Chien-soon	65	71	67	70	273	9,682.50
Mardan Mamat	65	71	67	70	273	9,682.50
Scott Barr	66	67	69	71	273	9,682.50
Shaaban Hussin	67	68	69	70	274	5,746.50
Thammanoon Srirot	74	65	67	68	274	5,746.50
Kodai Ichihara	71	64	68	71	274	5,746.50
Jay Bayron	69	65	67	73	274	5,746.50
Ted Oh	64	70	68	73	275	4,617
C. Muniyappa	69	72	62	72	275	4,617
Jbe' Kruger	69	71	70	66	276	4,140
Piya Swangarunporn	68	71	68	69	276	4,140
Gavin Flint	64	68	74	70	276	4,140
Wu Ashun	69	69	72	67	277	3,485
Kwanchai Tannin	69	72	69	67	277	3,485
Anirban Lahiri	67	73	70	67	277	3,485
Siddikur	68	69	70	70	277	3,485
Zhang Lian-wei	69	71	68	69	277	3,485
Mars Pucay	69	68	71	69	277	3,485
Steven Tiley	66	71	72	69	278	2,970
Mo Joong-kyung	67	69	71	71	278	2,970

	SCORES				TOTAL	MONEY
Thaworn Wiratchant	68	67	73	70	278	2,970
Wisut Artjanawat	67	65	72	74	278	2,970
Keith Horne	70	69	68	71	278	2,970

Worldwide Holdings Selangor Masters

Seri Selangor Golf Club, Kuala Lumpur, Malaysia
Par 36-35–71; 7,002 yards

August 5-8
purse, US$300,000

	SCORES				TOTAL	MONEY
Rick Kulacz	68	71	71	63	273	US$47,550
Kiradech Aphibarnrat	65	70	69	70	274	32,550
Mark Purser	69	71	69	67	276	18,300
James Kamte	66	70	72	69	277	14,790
Gaurav Ghei	71	67	72	68	278	10,400
Noh Seung-yul	67	68	73	70	278	10,400
Kodai Ichihara	71	69	68	70	278	10,400
Bae Sang-moon	69	69	72	69	279	7,530
Iain Steel	66	72	74	68	280	6,255
Mitchell Brown	68	69	72	71	280	6,255
Chinnarat Phadungsil	69	75	70	67	281	4,927.50
Kim Dae-hyun	73	65	76	67	281	4,927.50
Angelo Que	71	74	69	67	281	4,927.50
Shaaban Hussin	67	69	72	73	281	4,927.50
Mardan Mamat	72	71	70	69	282	4,230
C. Muniyappa	71	74	66	71	282	4,230
David Gleeson	72	70	71	70	283	3,605
Mo Joong-kyung	70	71	71	71	283	3,605
Andrew Dodt	69	70	71	73	283	3,605
Scott Barr	76	67	76	64	283	3,605
Scott Hend	69	71	69	74	283	3,605
S. Siva Chandhran	69	68	69	77	283	3,605
Muhammad Munir	73	66	75	70	284	3,015
Sattaya Supupramai	71	70	74	69	284	3,015
Juvic Pagunsan	69	74	72	69	284	3,015
Lu Chien-soon	71	66	73	74	284	3,015
Lu Wen-teh	72	70	69	73	284	3,015
Bryan Saltus	73	69	68	74	284	3,015

Queen's Cup

Santiburi Samui Country Club, Koh Samui, Thailand
Par 35-36–71; 6,853 yards

August 13-16
purse, US$300,000

	SCORES				TOTAL	MONEY
Chinnarat Phadungsil	66	65	70	67	268	US$47,550
Kim Dae-hyun	68	67	68	68	271	21,880
Udorn Duangdecha	70	67	67	67	271	21,880
Yoshinobu Tsukada	68	66	66	71	271	21,880
Thammanoon Srirot	69	67	70	66	272	11,235
Keith Horne	74	66	64	68	272	11,235
Kiradech Aphibarnrat	65	71	70	67	273	8,730
M. Sasidaran	72	67	67	68	274	7,530
Anirban Lahiri	71	68	66	70	275	6,600
Rick Kulacz	68	67	69	72	276	5,662.50
Mars Pucay	68	68	67	73	276	5,662.50
Sung Mao-chang	66	69	73	69	277	5,061

	SCORES				TOTAL	MONEY
Kao Bo-song	76	65	66	71	278	4,734
*Huang Choo-tze	71	69	74	65	279	
Mark Purser	68	70	71	70	279	4,230
Himmat Rai	71	66	72	70	279	4,230
Varut Chomchalam	71	70	69	69	279	4,230
Jbe' Kruger	66	70	70	73	279	4,230
Vuttipong Puangkaew	69	71	76	64	280	3,705
Thaworn Wiratchant	72	68	68	72	280	3,705
Danny Chia	71	63	72	75	281	3,510
Chris Rodgers	70	68	75	69	282	3,375
Michael Light	71	69	70	72	282	3,375
Kodai Ichihara	71	72	73	67	283	3,105
Steven Tiley	68	71	73	71	283	3,105
Boonchu Ruangkit	72	70	71	70	283	3,105
Tony Carolan	72	65	73	73	283	3,105

Macau Open

Macau Golf & Country Club, Macau
Par 35-36–71; 6,624 yards

September 10-13
purse, US$500,000

	SCORES				TOTAL	MONEY
Thaworn Wiratchant	67	68	66	68	269	US$79,250
Gaganjeet Bhullar	71	69	69	66	275	54,250
Matthew Griffin	72	72	69	65	278	27,575
Keith Horne	67	71	70	70	278	27,575
Yoshinobu Tsukada	72	70	71	66	279	18,725
Lin Wen-hong	68	67	71	73	279	18,725
Scott Barr	74	70	68	68	280	10,471.43
Rick Kulacz	76	67	69	68	280	10,471.43
Lin Wen-tang	68	71	72	69	280	10,471.43
Taichiro Kiyota	70	71	70	69	280	10,471.43
Zhang Lian-wei	73	68	70	69	280	10,471.43
Tetsuji Hiratsuka	70	70	71	69	280	10,471.43
Andrew Dodt	67	67	73	73	280	10,471.43
Chris Rodgers	70	68	75	68	281	6,758.33
Tim Stewart	70	74	69	68	281	6,758.33
Rafael Ponce	73	69	70	69	281	6,758.33
Marcus Both	71	73	67	70	281	6,758.33
Wu Ashun	69	68	73	71	281	6,758.33
Lam Chih Bing	70	69	70	72	281	6,758.33
Antonio Lascuna	68	72	72	70	282	5,550
Rohan Blizard	74	70	70	68	282	5,550
Artemio Murakami	73	69	69	71	282	5,550
Gavin Flint	68	72	70	72	282	5,550
Angelo Que	68	68	71	75	282	5,550
Gary Simpson	75	67	70	71	283	4,950
Hsu Mong-nan	70	73	72	68	283	4,950
Jean Van de Velde	70	67	70	76	283	4,950

Asia-Pacific Panasonic Open

See Japan Tour section.

Mercuries Taiwan Masters

Taiwan Golf & Country Club, Taipei, Taiwan
Par 36-36–72; 6,923 yards

October 1-4
purse, US$500,000

		SCORES			TOTAL	MONEY
Lin Wen-tang	71	66	71	72	280	US$100,000
Lu Wen-teh	71	71	68	73	283	60,000
Udorn Duangdecha	65	69	73	77	284	35,000
Lin Keng-chi	70	73	69	73	285	25,000
Chan Yih-shin	67	69	79	74	289	20,000
Lu Chien-soon	69	73	73	75	290	17,500
Wu Ashun	72	72	76	71	291	12,500
Danny Chia	71	72	74	74	291	12,500
Hsu Mong-nan	72	70	73	76	291	12,500
Lu Wei-chih	73	74	74	71	292	8,250
Gavin Flint	69	73	74	76	292	8,250
S. Siva Chandhran	73	76	68	75	292	8,250
Sattaya Supupramai	75	70	69	78	292	8,250
Jason King	79	70	69	75	293	6,750
Thaworn Wiratchant	74	71	72	76	293	6,750
Peter Cooke	73	72	73	76	294	6,125
Hsieh Chin-sheng	71	73	73	77	294	6,125
Lin Chie-hsiang	74	73	74	74	295	5,500
Ben Leong	76	67	78	74	295	5,500
Lin Wen-hong	73	71	79	72	295	5,500
Kodai Ichihara	78	70	74	74	296	4,920
Wisut Artjanawat	71	75	76	74	296	4,920
Hsieh Tung-shu	73	75	72	76	296	4,920
Airil Rizman	72	74	73	77	296	4,920
Kwanchai Tannin	71	66	79	80	296	4,920

Hero Honda Indian Open

DLF Golf & Country Club, New Delhi, India
Par 36-36–72; 7,156 yards

October 8-11
purse, US$1,250,000

		SCORES			TOTAL	MONEY
C. Muniyappa	66	69	71	70	276	US$198,125
Lee Sung	65	70	72	69	276	135,625
(Muniyappa defeated Lee on first playoff hole.)						
Anirban Lahiri	72	71	71	64	278	63,041.67
Kwanchai Tannin	68	69	71	70	278	63,041.67
Marcus Both	69	71	67	71	278	63,041.67
Ashok Kumar	71	71	68	70	280	39,375
Digvijay Singh	68	68	71	73	280	39,375
Gavin Flint	73	71	69	69	282	26,500
Keith Horne	67	71	73	71	282	26,500
Antonio Lascuna	69	71	70	72	282	26,500
Harendra Gupta	68	72	67	75	282	26,500
Udorn Duangdecha	71	72	68	72	283	19,343.75
Mukesh Kumar	71	68	70	74	283	19,343.75
Adam Blyth	64	72	72	75	283	19,343.75
Jbe' Kruger	70	68	70	75	283	19,343.75
Danny Chia	71	72	72	69	284	16,500
Gaganjeet Bhullar	73	71	68	72	284	16,500
Unho Park	67	72	71	74	284	16,500
Scott Hend	69	70	74	72	285	14,875
Siddikur	74	71	67	73	285	14,875
Shamim Khan	70	73	74	69	286	13,312.50

	SCORES				TOTAL	MONEY
Daniel Chopra	67	72	75	72	286	13,312.50
Simon Griffiths	73	72	69	72	286	13,312.50
Iain Steel	70	73	69	74	286	13,312.50
Mars Pucay	70	67	73	76	286	13,312.50
Jason King	66	73	71	76	286	13,312.50

Iskandar Johor Open

Royal Johor Country Club, Johor, Malaysia
Par 36-36–72; 6,984 yards
(Event shortened to 54 holes—rain.)

October 22-25
purse, US$1,000,000

	SCORES			TOTAL	MONEY
K.J. Choi	68	64	64	196	US$158,500
Chapchai Nirat	69	65	66	200	108,500
Retief Goosen	69	70	62	201	55,150
Himmat Rai	64	67	70	201	55,150
Kiradech Aphibarnrat	72	68	64	204	37,450
Kodai Ichihara	66	69	69	204	37,450
Juvic Pagunsan	70	68	67	205	27,100
Mars Pucay	69	65	71	205	27,100
Anirban Lahiri	69	69	68	206	17,900
Lin Wen-hong	69	69	68	206	17,900
Noh Seung-yul	69	68	69	206	17,900
Tim Stewart	69	73	64	206	17,900
Chang Tse-peng	65	68	73	206	17,900
Darren Beck	68	64	74	206	17,900
Rahil Gangjee	69	67	71	207	14,400
Chris Rodgers	70	68	70	208	13,500
Jason Norris	72	65	71	208	13,500
Antonio Lascuna	70	70	69	209	11,616.67
Thaworn Wiratchant	70	70	69	209	11,616.67
Prayad Marksaeng	70	69	70	209	11,616.67
Pariya Junhasavasdikul	68	70	71	209	11,616.67
Chinnarat Phadungsil	68	69	72	209	11,616.67
Chan Yih-shin	65	72	72	209	11,616.67
David Bransdon	71	69	70	210	10,050
Lam Chih Bing	71	68	71	210	10,050
Gaganjeet Bhullar	69	69	72	210	10,050
Mardan Mamat	70	72	68	210	10,050

Barclays Singapore Open

Sentosa Golf Club, Singapore
Par 36-35–71; 7,300 yards

October 29-November 1
purse, US$5,000,000

	SCORES				TOTAL	MONEY
Ian Poulter	66	64	72	72	274	US$833,330
Liang Wen-chong	69	68	68	70	275	555,550
Scott Hend	72	66	69	69	276	281,500
Adam Scott	72	71	65	68	276	281,500
Charl Schwartzel	72	68	68	69	277	179,000
Anders Hansen	68	71	68	70	277	179,000
Graeme McDowell	71	65	67	74	277	179,000
Niclas Fasth	69	67	71	71	278	125,000
Kenichi Kuboya	70	70	67	72	279	94,100
Marcus Both	72	71	67	69	279	94,100

	SCORES			TOTAL	MONEY
Andrew Dodt	69	68	70	72	279	94,100
Thomas Levet	68	68	73	70	279	94,100
Kodai Ichihara	68	68	71	72	279	94,100
Phil Mickelson	69	71	69	71	280	67,785.71
Thongchai Jaidee	73	67	71	69	280	67,785.71
Justin Rose	72	70	70	68	280	67,785.71
Sam Hutsby	69	70	69	72	280	67,785.71
Gaganjeet Bhullar	71	67	73	69	280	67,785.71
Juvic Pagunsan	74	69	69	68	280	67,785.71
Ernie Els	67	69	72	72	280	67,785.71
Marc Warren	73	69	67	72	281	56,500
Alexander Noren	70	69	72	70	281	56,500
Daniel Chopra	70	65	74	72	281	56,500
Chapchai Nirat	73	67	72	70	282	49,000
Lin Wen-tang	69	70	68	75	282	49,000
Estanislao Goya	74	68	72	68	282	49,000
Ross McGowan	69	69	70	74	282	49,000
Peter Lawrie	71	66	71	74	282	49,000
Soren Kjeldsen	69	67	75	71	282	49,000
Chan Yih-shin	67	68	75	72	282	49,000
Bae Sang-moon	73	68	70	72	283	38,928.57
Mardan Mamat	72	69	71	71	283	38,928.57
Richard Green	68	73	72	70	283	38,928.57
Keith Horne	74	68	70	71	283	38,928.57
Richard Finch	71	68	70	74	283	38,928.57
Ted Oh	70	73	70	70	283	38,928.57
Prayad Marksaeng	73	70	70	70	283	38,928.57
Tony Carolan	74	67	73	70	284	32,500
Gregory Bourdy	73	67	70	74	284	32,500
Lam Chih Bing	69	69	72	74	284	32,500
Steve Webster	71	72	69	72	284	32,500
Padraig Harrington	74	69	72	69	284	32,500
Jyoti Randhawa	69	72	72	72	285	29,000
Rod Pampling	72	69	72	72	285	29,000
Miguel Angel Jimenez	74	67	69	76	286	26,500
Mikko Ilonen	74	67	75	70	286	26,500
James Kingston	74	66	72	74	286	26,500
Soren Hansen	71	71	68	77	287	23,500
Danny Lee	71	72	72	72	287	23,500
Guido van der Valk	72	71	72	72	287	23,500
Jeppe Huldahl	75	66	75	72	288	20,500
Felipe Aguilar	68	73	76	71	288	20,500
Jason Knutzon	75	67	77	69	288	20,500
Terry Pilkadaris	73	70	74	72	289	17,500
Graeme Storm	74	69	76	70	289	17,500
Zaw Moe	71	72	73	73	289	17,500
Martin Rominger	74	68	77	71	290	14,750
Scott Barr	71	71	75	73	290	14,750
Darren Clarke	73	69	73	75	290	14,750
Kenneth Ferrie	71	72	75	72	290	14,750
Oskar Henningsson	69	73	69	80	291	12,750
Jean-Francois Lucquin	71	72	72	76	291	12,750
Andrew Coltart	70	73	75	73	291	12,750
Thaworn Wiratchant	71	72	72	76	291	12,750
Daniel Vancsik	70	71	74	77	292	11,000
Nick Redfern	71	70	76	75	292	11,000
Christian Cevaer	71	72	76	73	292	11,000
Lu Wei-chih	70	72	74	77	293	10,000
Mitchell Brown	75	68	76	75	294	9,500

WGC - HSBC Champions

Sheshan International Golf Club, Shanghai, China
Par 36-36–72; 7,143 yards

November 5-8
purse, US$7,000,000

	SCORES				TOTAL	MONEY
Phil Mickelson	69	66	67	69	271	$1,200,000
Ernie Els	70	71	68	63	272	675,000
Ryan Moore	66	69	70	68	273	430,000
Rory McIlroy	73	68	70	63	274	315,000
Nick Watney	64	70	70	71	275	250,000
Tiger Woods	67	67	70	72	276	190,000
Martin Kaymer	66	74	69	67	276	190,000
Lee Westwood	70	71	65	71	277	147,500
Alvaro Quiros	69	66	76	66	277	147,500
Anthony Kim	67	69	72	70	278	99,571.43
Francesco Molinari	73	67	70	68	278	99,571.43
Retief Goosen	71	71	68	68	278	99,571.43
Geoff Ogilvy	72	74	65	67	278	99,571.43
Pat Perez	68	69	75	66	278	99,571.43
Soren Kjeldsen	69	72	71	66	278	99,571.43
Daisuke Maruyama	72	69	74	63	278	99,571.43
Ryo Ishikawa	72	67	70	70	279	78,000
Koumei Oda	70	69	72	68	279	78,000
Jyoti Randhawa	68	70	70	72	280	72,000
Thongchai Jaidee	71	69	70	70	280	72,000
Matt Kuchar	68	72	72	68	280	72,000
Alexander Noren	70	71	71	68	280	72,000
Robert Allenby	73	69	70	69	281	66,000
Sergio Garcia	75	70	69	67	281	66,000
Brian Gay	69	69	72	72	282	61,333.33
Camilo Villegas	70	69	73	70	282	61,333.33
Padraig Harrington	74	69	72	67	282	61,333.33
Shane Lowry	66	74	71	72	283	58,000
Ross Fisher	70	70	72	71	283	58,000
Simon Dyson	72	69	72	70	283	58,000
Mark Brown	71	74	71	68	284	55,500
Peter Hanson	72	72	75	65	284	55,500
Lin Wen-tang	67	72	70	76	285	51,000
James Kingston	70	70	75	70	285	51,000
Chapchai Nirat	71	74	70	70	285	51,000
Jeev Milkha Singh	73	72	70	70	285	51,000
Scott Strange	71	72	74	68	285	51,000
Y.E. Yang	72	71	75	67	285	51,000
Shingo Katayama	75	68	77	65	285	51,000
Jason Dufner	69	71	73	74	287	45,000
Henrik Stenson	69	72	74	72	287	45,000
Rod Pampling	69	72	75	71	287	45,000
Garth Mulroy	69	72	76	70	287	45,000
Liang Wen-chong	73	73	73	68	287	45,000
Ricardo Gonzalez	74	71	70	73	288	40,333.33
Oliver Wilson	71	72	73	72	288	40,333.33
Rory Sabbatini	74	68	76	70	288	40,333.33
Gonzalo Fernandez-Castano	73	73	72	70	288	40,333.33
Greg Chalmers	72	74	73	69	288	40,333.33
Ian Poulter	72	69	79	68	288	40,333.33
Yuta Ikeda	73	73	71	72	289	38,000
Stewart Cink	71	74	75	69	289	38,000
Prayad Marksaeng	81	69	70	69	289	38,000
Martin Laird	72	74	73	71	290	36,500
Jerry Kelly	71	75	74	70	290	36,500
Christian Cevaer	73	77	71	69	290	36,500
Michael Jonzon	72	74	73	72	291	35,000

	SCORES				TOTAL	MONEY
Steve Marino	77	70	74	70	291	35,000
Thomas Levet	77	77	72	65	291	35,000
Richard Sterne	74	73	72	73	292	33,750
Lam Chih Bing	71	74	75	72	292	33,750
Sean O'Hair	74	71	76	72	293	32,750
Nathan Green	79	77	72	65	293	32,750
Jeppe Huldahl	76	72	73	73	294	31,750
Mark Murless	71	76	79	68	294	31,750
Danny Lee	74	71	76	74	295	30,750
Zhang Lian-wei	73	70	80	72	295	30,750
Thomas Aiken	74	78	73	71	296	29,750
Anthony Kang	75	76	76	69	296	29,750
Daniel Vancsik	74	74	74	76	298	28,500
Peter Hedblom	77	71	76	74	298	28,500
Wu Ashun	74	71	83	70	298	28,500
Jean Hugo	78	76	74	71	299	27,500
C. Muniyappa	74	69	78	79	300	26,500
Nick Dougherty	68	80	76	76	300	26,500
Gaganjeet Bhullar	74	76	76	74	300	26,500
Wu Wei-huang	74	78	75	74	301	25,500
Paul Casey	67	73	70		WD	

UBS Hong Kong Open

Hong Kong Golf Club, Fanling, Hong Kong
Par 34-36–70; 6,702 yards

November 12-15
purse, US$2,500,000

	SCORES				TOTAL	MONEY
Gregory Bourdy	64	67	63	67	261	US$416,660
Rory McIlroy	66	68	65	64	263	277,770
Francesco Molinari	66	68	66	64	264	140,750
Robert-Jan Derksen	63	68	65	68	264	140,750
Raphael Jacquelin	66	68	68	64	266	96,750
Ian Poulter	68	66	68	64	266	96,750
Peter Lawrie	66	68	66	67	267	75,000
Simon Dyson	68	67	67	66	268	62,500
Scott Strange	68	65	70	66	269	53,000
David Dixon	64	69	69	67	269	53,000
Liang Wen-chong	66	65	72	67	270	39,035.71
Scott Drummond	69	67	68	66	270	39,035.71
Mark Foster	65	69	69	67	270	39,035.71
Thongchai Jaidee	64	71	68	67	270	39,035.71
Darren Clarke	69	67	67	67	270	39,035.71
Charl Schwartzel	65	66	71	68	270	39,035.71
Danny Chia	67	66	68	69	270	39,035.71
Rory Sabbatini	65	67	71	68	271	30,562.50
David Howell	69	66	67	69	271	30,562.50
Graeme McDowell	67	68	66	70	271	30,562.50
Miguel Angel Jimenez	68	69	63	71	271	30,562.50
Simon Khan	67	70	71	64	272	26,000
S.S.P. Chowrasia	65	69	73	65	272	26,000
Simon Yates	70	68	67	67	272	26,000
Pablo Larrazabal	68	67	68	69	272	26,000
Jyoti Randhawa	66	69	67	70	272	26,000
Marcus Both	70	67	65	70	272	26,000
Lin Wen-tang	64	69	67	72	272	26,000
Kiradech Aphibarnrat	68	67	71	67	273	20,785.71
Lam Chih Bing	71	67	69	66	273	20,785.71
Anders Hansen	68	70	68	67	273	20,785.71
Christian Cevaer	71	67	67	68	273	20,785.71

	SCORES				TOTAL	MONEY
Colin Montgomerie	69	69	67	68	273	20,785.71
Andrew McLardy	68	68	67	70	273	20,785.71
Y.E. Yang	66	67	69	71	273	20,785.71
Jeev Milkha Singh	71	67	70	66	274	16,250
Rhys Davies	65	69	71	69	274	16,250
Rahil Gangjee	67	70	68	69	274	16,250
Zhang Lian-wei	67	69	69	69	274	16,250
Jean-Francois Lucquin	69	68	68	69	274	16,250
Markus Brier	70	68	67	69	274	16,250
Jason Knutzon	68	67	69	70	274	16,250
Tony Carolan	65	71	68	70	274	16,250
Mardan Mamat	68	68	68	70	274	16,250
Ignacio Garrido	67	70	68	70	275	13,250
Airil Rizman	68	66	70	71	275	13,250
Lu Wei-chih	65	69	69	72	275	13,250
Shiv Kapur	68	68	72	68	276	11,750
Andrew Dodt	69	68	71	68	276	11,750
Chinnarat Phadungsil	66	66	75	69	276	11,750
Mars Pucay	68	67	73	69	277	10,500
Jamie Donaldson	69	69	70	69	277	10,500
Juvic Pagunsan	67	70	71	70	278	9,750
Graeme Storm	68	67	76	68	279	8,500
Chapchai Nirat	70	65	72	72	279	8,500
Iain Steel	68	70	68	73	279	8,500
Lee Westwood	66	70	69	74	279	8,500
Darren Beck	68	70	72	70	280	7,375
Pablo Martin	69	69	71	71	280	7,375
Bradley Dredge	66	71	73	71	281	6,875
*Shun Yat Jason Hak	70	67	72	72	281	
Kodai Ichihara	65	73	71	72	281	6,875
Chawalit Plaphol	71	67	72	73	283	6,375
Anthony Kang	69	66	74	74	283	6,375
Udorn Duangdecha	62	74	75	73	284	6,000
Wang Ter-chang	66	72	77	77	292	5,750

Johnnie Walker Cambodian Open

Phokeethra Country Club, Siem Reap, Cambodia
Par 36-36–72; 7,226 yards

November 19-22
purse, US$300,000

	SCORES				TOTAL	MONEY
Marcus Both	70	69	73	67	279	US$47,550
Shaaban Hussin	71	67	72	70	280	32,550
Mardan Mamat	74	70	70	67	281	15,130
Shiv Kapur	70	67	74	70	281	15,130
Annop Tangkamolprasert	68	69	70	74	281	15,130
Will Yanagisawa	71	67	75	69	282	8,810
Pariya Junhasavasdikul	68	70	72	72	282	8,810
Craig Smith	69	66	71	76	282	8,810
Lam Chih Bing	73	72	69	69	283	5,746.50
Somchai Pongpaew	71	67	75	70	283	5,746.50
Bryan Saltus	73	70	69	71	283	5,746.50
Jbe' Kruger	72	70	69	72	283	5,746.50
Anirban Lahiri	70	71	75	68	284	4,423.50
Anthony Kang	71	75	70	68	284	4,423.50
Nakul Vichitryuthasastr	75	67	71	71	284	4,423.50
Varut Chomchalam	71	68	72	73	284	4,423.50
Rhys Davies	74	71	72	68	285	3,605
Pijit Petchkasem	72	69	74	70	285	3,605
Vikrant Chopra	69	71	75	70	285	3,605

	SCORES				TOTAL	MONEY
Artemio Murakami	68	69	76	72	285	3,605
Chawalit Plaphol	71	71	70	73	285	3,605
Udorn Duangdecha	72	68	71	74	285	3,605
Adam Groom	74	71	72	69	286	2,970
Marvin Dumandan	74	71	72	69	286	2,970
David Gleeson	67	71	78	70	286	2,970
Neven Basic	69	73	72	72	286	2,970
Blair Wilson	74	71	69	72	286	2,970
Atthaphon Prathummanee	68	73	71	74	286	2,970
Sattaya Supupramai	71	70	68	77	286	2,970

Omega Mission Hills World Cup

Mission Hills Golf Club, Olazabal Course, Shenzhen, China
Par 36-36–72; 7,251 yards

November 26-29
purse, US$5,500,000

	SCORES				TOTAL
ITALY—$1,700,000					
Edoardo Molinari/Francesco Molinari	64	66	61	68	259
IRELAND—$725,000					
Graeme McDowell/Rory McIlroy	58	68	64	70	260
SWEDEN—$725,000					
Robert Karlsson/Henrik Stenson	64	65	62	69	260
ENGLAND—$308,000					
Ian Poulter/Ross Fisher	66	69	63	64	262
JAPAN—$230,000					
Hiroyuki Fujita/Ryuji Imada	62	71	64	69	266
AUSTRALIA—$200,000					
Stuart Appleby/Robert Allenby	68	70	62	67	267
GERMANY—$128,000					
Alex Cejka/Martin Kaymer	66	71	66	65	268
KOREA—$128,000					
Charlie Wi/Y.E. Yang	64	75	61	68	268
SOUTH AFRICA—$128,000					
Rory Sabbatini/Richard Sterne	65	70	62	71	268
UNITED STATES—$128,000					
Nick Watney/John Merrick	67	72	67	62	268
WALES—$128,000					
Stephen Dodd/Jamie Donaldson	66	68	64	70	268
CHILE—$80,000					
Hugo Leon/Martin Ureta	69	67	65	70	271
VENEZUELA—$80,000					
Alfredo Adrian/Jhonattan Vegas	67	67	65	72	271
DENMARK—$68,000					
Soren Kjeldsen/Soren Hansen	66	70	66	70	272
INDIA—$68,000					
Jyoti Randhawa/Jeev Milkha Singh	67	68	65	72	272

	SCORES	TOTAL

PHILIPPINES—$62,000
Mars Pucay/Angelo Que   68   72   64   69   273

SINGAPORE—$62,000
Lam Chih Bing/Mardan Mamat   66   70   66   71   273

THAILAND—$62,000
Prayad Marksaeng/Thongchai Jaidee   67   70   67   69   273

ARGENTINA—$58,000
Estanislao Goya/Rafael Echenique   61   75   64   74   274

FRANCE—$55,000
Christian Cevaer/Thomas Levet   67   73   67   69   276

NEW ZEALAND—$55,000
Danny Lee/David Smail   67   68   70   71   276

CHINA—$50,000
Zhang Lian-wei/Liang Wen-chong   65   71   68   73   277

TAIWAN—$50,000
Lin Wen-tang/Lu Wei-chih   67   74   67   69   277

PAKISTAN—$50,000
Muhammad Munir/Muhammad Shabbir   69   75   64   69   277

CANADA—$46,000
Graham DeLaet/Stuart Anderson   64   74   65   76   279

BRAZIL—$44,000
Rafael Barcellos/Ronaldo Francisco   68   75   68   69   280

SPAIN—$42,000
Gonzalo Fernandez-Castano/Sergio Garcia   69   71   67   74   281

SCOTLAND—$40,000
David Drysdale/Alastair Forsyth   69   73   64   78   284

The King's Cup

Singha Park Golf Club, Khon Kaen, Thailand
Par 36-36—72; 7,546 yards

December 3-6
purse, US$300,000

	SCORES				TOTAL	MONEY
Chan Yih-shin	64	73	67	70	274	US$47,550
Simon Yates	71	69	66	68	274	25,425
Nick Redfern	74	66	68	66	274	25,425
(Chan defeated Yates and Redfern on second playoff hole.)						
Harmeet Kahlon	71	67	72	66	276	13,545
Prayad Marksaeng	70	70	71	65	276	13,545
Kim Dae-hyun	70	68	73	66	277	8,810
Anirban Lahiri	66	72	71	68	277	8,810
Rahil Gangjee	74	64	68	71	277	8,810
Mark Purser	68	75	65	71	279	6,600
Matthew Griffin	72	69	69	70	280	5,910
Thongchai Jaidee	70	73	71	67	281	5,238
Neven Basic	73	68	70	70	281	5,238
*Vasin Sripattranusorn	71	70	71	70	282	
Ross Bain	69	69	71	73	282	4,734
Pavit Tangkamolprasert	70	71	75	67	283	4,410

	SCORES				TOTAL	MONEY
Digvijay Singh	70	73	69	71	283	4,410
Artemio Murakami	70	75	70	69	284	3,877.50
Thaworn Wiratchant	71	70	73	70	284	3,877.50
Thammanoon Srirot	73	68	71	72	284	3,877.50
Corey Harris	69	70	73	72	284	3,877.50
Pornpong Phatlum	73	67	75	70	285	3,420
C. Muniyappa	67	73	74	71	285	3,420
Lin Wen-hong	67	71	74	73	285	3,420
Toni Karjalainen	75	70	75	66	286	3,150
Pongthep Jaewchumnanchao	73	73	73	67	286	3,150
Baek Seuk-hyun	73	71	74	68	286	3,150

OneAsia Tour

Volvo China Open

Beijing CBD International Golf Club, Beijing, China
Par 35-37–72; 7,321 yards

April 16-19
purse, US$2,200,000

	SCORES				TOTAL	MONEY
Scott Strange	70	73	69	68	280	US$366,660
Gonzalo Fernandez-Castano	71	70	68	72	281	244,440
Mark Brown	71	77	65	69	282	113,667
Richard Finch	71	71	66	74	282	113,667
Ashley Hall	75	71	65	71	282	113,667
David Dixon	72	73	67	71	283	71,500
Stephen Dodd	74	71	70	68	283	71,500
Markus Brier	67	73	71	73	284	49,427
Paul McGinley	74	67	75	68	284	49,427
Chapchai Nirat	69	71	72	72	284	49,427
Kurt Barnes	76	70	73	66	285	35,948
Rafael Cabrera-Bello	73	71	72	69	285	35,948
Andrew Coltart	74	73	72	66	285	35,948
Simon Dyson	69	73	70	73	285	35,948
Graeme Storm	72	71	70	72	285	35,948
Choi Ho-sung	70	68	75	73	286	29,700
Branden Grace	72	73	71	70	286	29,700
Aaron Townsend	73	71	70	72	286	29,700
Pablo Martin	75	73	71	68	287	27,280
Carlos Del Moral	72	72	72	72	288	24,904
Marcus Fraser	74	73	70	71	288	24,904
Thongchai Jaidee	70	75	71	72	288	24,904
Gareth Maybin	76	70	70	72	288	24,904
David McKenzie	68	74	71	75	288	24,904
Francois Delamontagne	72	73	72	72	289	21,560
Liang Wen-chong	72	74	70	73	289	21,560
Michael Lorenzo-Vera	73	72	75	69	289	21,560
Colin Montgomerie	73	73	70	73	289	21,560
Bernd Wiesberger	73	73	74	69	289	21,560
Kang Kyung-nam	76	70	73	71	290	18,920
Craig Scott	71	74	73	72	290	18,920

	SCORES				TOTAL	MONEY
Inder Van Weerelt	74	69	74	73	290	18,920
Scott Drummond	75	70	71	75	291	16,544
Klas Eriksson	72	75	72	72	291	16,544
James Kingston	73	73	71	74	291	16,544
Brett Rumford	74	72	74	71	291	16,544
Fabrizio Zanotti	76	70	75	70	291	16,544
Pelle Edberg	75	71	76	70	292	13,200
Johan Edfors	74	72	72	74	292	13,200
Jean-Baptiste Gonnet	71	77	70	74	292	13,200
Eirik Tage Johansen	74	72	73	73	292	13,200
Maarten Lafeber	71	74	76	71	292	13,200
Damien McGrane	72	74	78	68	292	13,200
Moon Kyong-jun	73	74	73	72	292	13,200
Peter O'Malley	71	75	74	72	292	13,200
Anthony Snobeck	75	73	73	71	292	13,200
Song Ki-joon	71	75	71	75	292	13,200
Richard Bland	76	71	72	74	293	9,020
Nick Dougherty	68	79	71	75	293	9,020
Chris Gaunt	74	74	72	73	293	9,020
David Gleeson	74	73	69	77	293	9,020
Peter Hedblom	76	71	77	69	293	9,020
Matthew Millar	70	77	72	74	293	9,020
Chinnarat Phadungsil	70	74	74	75	293	9,020
Jean Van de Velde	74	74	72	73	293	9,020
Chris Wood	72	74	73	74	293	9,020
Felipe Aguilar	73	73	75	73	294	6,380
Wil Besseling	72	76	74	72	294	6,380
Gregory Bourdy	74	72	75	73	294	6,380
Paul Waring	72	76	73	73	294	6,380
Wu Ashun	74	72	74	74	294	6,380
Martin Erlandsson	76	71	75	73	295	5,280
Jung Jae-hoon	75	71	76	73	295	5,280
Alexandre Rocha	73	75	72	75	295	5,280
Miles Tunnicliff	74	74	69	78	295	5,280
Simon Wakefield	76	69	73	77	295	5,280
Heo Won-kyung	72	72	75	77	296	4,400
Brad Kennedy	72	73	74	77	296	4,400
Michael Long	73	75	74	74	296	4,400
Rafa Echenique	72	74	76	76	298	4,020
Zhang Lian-wei	73	74	78	75	300	3,300
Kim Wi-joong	75	72	80	76	303	3,296
Jun Zhou	76	72	86	76	310	3,292

Kolon-Hana Bank Korea Open

Woo Jeong Country Club, Cheonan, South Korea
Par 36-35–71; 7,185 yards

September 10-13
purse, US$817,000

	SCORES				TOTAL	MONEY
Bae Sang-moon	71	71	65	67	274	US$366,660
Kim Dae-sub	67	70	69	69	275	79,804
Kim Kyung-tae	68	70	72	68	278	40,716
Rory McIlroy	71	68	67	72	278	40,716
Michael Wright	67	66	76	70	279	26,058
Jung Jae-hoon	70	68	70	71	279	26,058
Song Ki-joon	69	70	71	71	281	21,579
Kim Dae-hyun	67	68	75	71	281	21,579
Kang Sung-hoon	72	68	74	68	282	17,507
Park Jae-bum	73	66	71	72	282	17,507
Azuma Yano	70	75	70	68	283	12,275

	SCORES				TOTAL	MONEY
Kwon Myung-ho	70	74	70	69	283	12,275
Lee Seung-ho	71	69	73	70	283	12,275
Kang Kyung-sool	67	71	72	73	283	12,275
Song Tae-hoon	76	69	71	68	284	8,346
Kang Ji-man	74	68	73	69	284	8,346
Hwang Inn-choon	69	72	73	70	284	8,346
Kang Kyung-nam	69	69	74	72	284	8,346
Ryo Ishikawa	70	69	72	73	284	8,346
Park Young-soo	71	70	75	69	285	7,328
Choi In-sik	74	69	72	70	285	7,328
Kim Hyung-sung	70	70	73	72	285	7,328
Hyun Jeong-yup	71	69	72	73	285	7,328
Park Do-kyu	70	72	75	69	286	6,497
Choi Joon-woo	69	66	81	70	286	6,497
Jang Ik-jae	72	70	73	71	286	6,497
Kang Wook-soon	75	69	71	71	286	6,497
Noh Seung-yul	70	75	67	74	286	6,497

Midea China Classic

Royal Orchid International Golf Club, Shunde, Guangzhou, China
Par 36-35–71; 6,889 yards

October 15-18
purse, US$500,000

	SCORES				TOTAL	MONEY
Liang Wen-chong	69	65	68	68	270	US$90,000
Zhang Lian-wei	71	71	63	69	274	
Peter Wilson	72	69	70	64	275	
Matthew Millar	70	69	71	65	275	
Michael Long	69	70	68	68	275	
Brad Andrews	71	69	70	66	276	
Kong Wei-hai	72	70	67	67	276	
Andrew Martin	69	65	69	73	276	
Craig Scott	65	72	68	73	278	
Anthony Brown	69	70	71	69	279	
Tsai Chi-huang	69	70	70	71	280	
Stephen Leaney	67	69	71	73	280	
Wu Ashun	70	69	68	73	280	
Li Chao	72	71	71	67	281	
Gyoung Yoon Yu	76	69	70	67	282	
Richard Backwell	71	70	71	70	282	
C.J. Gatto	74	71	67	70	282	
Jun Feng Liu	67	74	69	72	282	
Martin Pettigrew	76	69	71	67	283	
Peter Nolan	69	72	74	68	283	
Eom Jae-woong	74	69	71	69	283	
Jun Bum Park	70	66	77	70	283	
Justin Maker	72	69	72	70	283	
*Huang Wen-yi	69	68	72	74	283	

Australian Open

See Australasian Tour chapter.

Australian PGA Championship

See Australasian Tour chapter.

Omega China Tour

Dell Championship

Orient Golf & Country Club, Xiamen
Par 36-35–72; 7,047 yards

March 19-22
purse, RMB1,000,000

		SCORES			TOTAL	MONEY
Wu Wei-huang	66	67	70	71	274	RMB180,000
Zhou Jun	69	75	66	68	278	90,000
Wu Ashun	69	68	69	72	278	90,000
Shang Lei	71	71	68	70	280	25,937.50
C.J. Gatto	70	72	66	72	280	25,937.50
Eom Jae-woong	69	70	71	71	281	18,750
Zhang Lian-wei	71	70	72	69	282	17,812.50
Goh Kun-yang	77	67	69	69	282	17,812.50
Lu Wen-teh	70	73	72	69	284	16,875
Kong Wei-hai	70	69	74	72	285	16,125
Lin Keng-chi	70	69	72	74	285	16,125
Chen Jian	67	81	67	71	286	15,625
He Shaocai	74	72	68	72	286	15,625
Su Dong	69	75	73	70	287	15,125
Li Chao	72	69	73	73	287	15,125
Liu Anda	71	74	73	70	288	14,625
Liu Guojie	71	75	72	70	288	14,625
Fan Zhipeng	75	71	71	72	289	14,250
Ye Xiong-hui	73	74	74	69	290	13,625
Yang Sheng-qin	73	72	73	72	290	13,625
Lee Joung-wook	75	74	68	73	290	13,625
*Zhang Xinjun	75	73	68	74	290	

Sofitel Zhongshan IGC Open

Zhongshan International Golf Club, Nanjing
Par 36-36–72; 7,189 yards

April 23-26
purse, RMB1,200,000

		SCORES			TOTAL	MONEY
Kurt Barnes	69	70	73	72	284	RMB225,000
Wisut Artjanawat	74	69	74	68	285	135,000
Zhang Lian-wei	69	70	72	75	286	75,000
Liu Guojie	76	68	73	72	289	33,000
Yuan Hao	71	69	76	74	290	26,250
Eom Jae-woong	76	72	71	72	291	21,750
Ye Xiong-hui	74	67	75	75	291	21,750
Craig Scott	74	69	72	76	291	21,750
*Zhang Xinjun	75	71	75	73	294	
Pariya Junhasavasdikul	76	74	71	74	295	19,050
Wu Kang-chun	70	72	78	75	295	19,050
Lu Wen-teh	73	72	75	75	295	19,050
Peter Wilson	75	74	71	75	295	19,050
Cui Qiang	72	73	76	76	297	17,700
Liao Guiming	76	74	70	77	297	17,700
Yuan Zheng	79	73	73	72	297	17,700
Lu Chien-soon	78	74	73	72	297	17,700

	SCORES				TOTAL	MONEY
Li Chao	79	73	73	72	297	17,700
Qiu Zhifeng	72	73	80	73	298	16,650
Lee Joung-wook	74	74	82	68	298	16,650

Luxehills Golf Championship

Luxehills International Country Club, Chengdu
Par 36-36–72; 7,335 yards

June 11-14
purse, RMB1,000,000

		SCORES			TOTAL	MONEY
Chen Jian	66	73	68	70	277	RMB180,000
Rowan Beste	72	65	71	69	277	120,000
(Chen defeated Beste on second playoff hole.)						
Lu Wen-teh	71	71	67	70	279	60,000
Liao Guiming	68	71	70	71	280	30,000
Kurt Barnes	69	75	68	69	281	19,750
Wu Wei-huang	68	75	67	71	281	19,750
Josh Lane	65	73	75	69	282	17,250
Anthony Brown	69	71	71	71	282	17,250
Tsai Chi-huang	71	73	67	71	282	17,250
Yuan Hao	73	72	66	71	282	17,250
*Wei Wei	67	70	71	75	283	
Zhou Jun	68	75	69	72	284	15,500
Wu Kang-chun	67	73	72	73	285	15,500
Liu Guojie	69	72	71	73	285	15,500
Lee Joung-wook	73	74	72	66	285	15,500
Ye Xiong-hui	72	75	69	70	286	14,125
Zhou Xunshu	67	75	72	72	286	14,125
Xu Qin	69	68	74	75	286	14,125
Liang Dingfeng	72	74	72	68	286	14,125
Li Chao	72	72	73	70	287	12,875
Goh Kun-Yang	72	72	71	72	287	12,875
Lucas Bates	70	76	69	72	287	12,875
Wong Woon-man	72	72	71	72	287	12,875
Zhang Cheng-wei	66	75	73	73	287	12,875
Tristan Lambert	68	72	73	74	287	12,875

Dongfeng Nissan Teana Open

Anji King Valley Country Club, Hangzhou
Par 36-36–72; 7,151 yards

June 18-21
purse, RMB700,000

		SCORES			TOTAL	MONEY
Thaworn Wiratchant	70	68	63	67	268	RMB130,000
Eom Jae-woong	67	66	68	68	269	70,000
Li Chao	70	67	69	65	271	40,000
Kurt Barnes	63	68	71	71	273	20,000
Lu Wen-teh	69	70	67	68	274	14,500
Pariya Junhasavasdikul	69	67	69	69	274	14,500
He Shaocai	69	69	70	69	277	13,000
*Choo Tze Huang	70	70	71	68	279	
Josh Lane	70	73	68	68	279	11,768.75
Brad Andrews	71	68	68	72	279	11,768.75
Rowan Beste	71	71	65	72	279	11,768.75
Yuan Hao	64	70	72	73	279	11,768.75
Lin Wen-hong	71	76	67	66	280	10,762.50
Su Dong	71	69	72	68	280	10,762.50

	SCORES				TOTAL	MONEY
*Han Ren	67	70	72	71	280	
Anthony Brown	66	71	71	72	280	10,762.50
*Huang Wenyi	68	68	71	73	280	
Fan Zhipeng	68	72	74	67	281	10,325
Liang Dingfeng	74	69	67	72	282	10,062.50
Liu Junfeng	67	72	69	74	282	10,062.50

Japan Tour

Token Homemate Cup

Token Tado Country Club, Nagoya, Mie
Par 35-36–71; 7,081 yards

April 16-19
purse, ¥130,000,000

	SCORES				TOTAL	MONEY
Koumei Oda	69	70	67	68	274	¥26,000,000
Kim Jong-duck	70	68	69	67	274	13,000,000
(Oda defeated Kim on second playoff hole.)						
Yuta Ikeda	73	68	69	65	275	7,540,000
Steven Conran	69	70	68	68	275	7,540,000
Craig Parry	69	66	75	66	276	4,723,333
Shigeki Maruyama	70	68	70	68	276	4,723,333
Brendan Jones	66	72	68	70	276	4,723,333
Yudai Maeda	69	72	70	66	277	3,679,000
Hiroyuki Fujita	73	67	69	68	277	3,679,000
Kunihiro Kamii	72	69	68	68	277	3,679,000
Tetsuya Haraguchi	65	73	71	69	278	3,146,000
Takamasa Yamamoto	70	70	71	68	279	2,444,000
Taichiro Kiyota	68	71	69	71	279	2,444,000
Mitsuhiro Tateyama	72	67	69	71	279	2,444,000
Masao Nakajima	73	67	68	71	279	2,444,000
Kenichi Kuboya	72	68	68	71	279	2,444,000
Kiyoshi Miyazato	73	70	70	67	280	1,911,000
Kim Hyung-sung	73	68	67	72	280	1,911,000
Brandt Jobe	75	68	67	71	281	1,437,428
Toshinori Muto	74	69	67	71	281	1,437,428
Yui Ueda	70	66	73	72	281	1,437,428
Ryuichi Oda	70	68	71	72	281	1,437,428
Masanori Kobayashi	76	67	70	68	281	1,437,428
Hidemasa Hoshino	72	67	69	73	281	1,437,428
Kazuhiro Yamashita	71	70	66	74	281	1,437,428

Tsuruya Open

Yamanohara Golf Club, Kawanishi, Hyogo
Par 35-36–71; 6,770 yards
(Event shortened to 54 holes—rain.)

April 23-26
purse, ¥120,000,000

	SCORES			TOTAL	MONEY
Masaya Tomida	68	66	64	198	¥18,000,000
David Smail	69	64	67	200	9,000,000
Tomohiro Kondo	68	67	66	201	5,220,000
Yui Ueda	63	67	71	201	5,220,000
Kenichi Kuboya	72	64	69	205	3,138,750
Steven Conran	69	67	69	205	3,138,750
Akio Sadakata	68	67	70	205	3,138,750
Kaname Yokoo	67	68	70	205	3,138,750
Koumei Oda	69	69	68	206	2,088,000
Nobuhiro Masuda	70	67	69	206	2,088,000
Hiroo Kawai	70	67	69	206	2,088,000
Taichiro Kiyota	70	66	70	206	2,088,000
Hideto Tanihara	71	65	70	206	2,088,000
Shingo Katayama	68	66	72	206	2,088,000
Wayne Perske	71	66	70	207	1,503,000
Ryuichi Oda	69	68	70	207	1,503,000
Shigeru Nonaka	73	68	67	208	1,284,000
Kazuhiko Hosokawa	72	69	67	208	1,284,000
Brendan Jones	67	69	72	208	1,284,000
Han Lee	69	71	69	209	909,000
Tatsunori Nukaga	69	71	69	209	909,000
Kouki Idoki	70	69	70	209	909,000
Tadahiro Takayama	72	67	70	209	909,000
Kazuhiro Yamashita	76	64	69	209	909,000
Shigeki Maruyama	70	68	71	209	909,000
Yasuharu Imano	74	69	66	209	909,000
Shintaro Kai	69	67	73	209	909,000

The Crowns

Nagoya Golf Club, Wago Course, Togo, Aichi
Par 35-35–70; 6,531 yards

April 30-May 3
purse, ¥120,000,000

	SCORES				TOTAL	MONEY
Tetsuji Hiratsuka	67	66	64	66	263	¥24,000,000
Kenichi Kuboya	68	67	70	65	270	12,000,000
Prayad Marksaeng	73	66	69	64	272	6,960,000
Taichi Teshima	67	70	66	69	272	6,960,000
Steven Conran	68	68	72	66	274	4,185,000
Shigeki Maruyama	73	68	67	66	274	4,185,000
S.K. Ho	67	71	68	68	274	4,185,000
Hiroyuki Fujita	64	71	66	73	274	4,185,000
Hiroshi Iwata	67	69	70	69	275	3,024,000
David Smail	71	67	66	71	275	3,024,000
Toru Suzuki	70	67	66	72	275	3,024,000
Takao Nogami	65	69	69	72	275	3,024,000
Hideto Tanihara	68	71	70	67	276	2,154,000
Masaya Tomida	70	72	67	67	276	2,154,000
Frankie Minoza	65	71	69	71	276	2,154,000
Ryuichi Oda	68	70	66	72	276	2,154,000
Daisuke Maruyama	68	69	73	67	277	1,612,800
Brendan Jones	71	70	69	67	277	1,612,800
Masanori Kobayashi	69	72	67	69	277	1,612,800

	SCORES				TOTAL	MONEY
Liang Wen-chong	69	72	67	69	277	1,612,800
Shingo Katayama	67	69	70	71	277	1,612,800
Akio Sadakata	72	70	70	66	278	1,100,571
Kim Kyung-tae	69	73	69	67	278	1,100,571
Hirofumi Miyase	70	71	69	68	278	1,100,571
Naoya Sugiyama	68	67	72	71	278	1,100,571
Shigemasa Higaki	70	72	65	71	278	1,100,571
Kunihiro Kamii	67	70	69	72	278	1,100,571
Keiichiro Fukabori	70	67	68	73	278	1,100,571

Mitsubishi Diamond Cup

Oarai Golf Club, Oarai, Ibaraki
Par 36-36–72; 7,190 yards

May 28-31
purse, ¥150,000,000

	SCORES				TOTAL	MONEY
Takashi Kanemoto	72	76	68	67	283	¥30,000,000
Brendan Jones	73	74	67	69	283	15,000,000
(Kanemoto defeated Jones on third playoff hole.)						
Prayad Marksaeng	68	78	71	68	285	10,200,000
Hiroshi Iwata	69	80	70	67	286	6,200,000
Taichi Teshima	73	77	69	67	286	6,200,000
Kaname Yokoo	68	80	70	68	286	6,200,000
Kim Hyung-tae	72	76	75	64	287	4,762,500
Toru Taniguchi	71	76	71	69	287	4,762,500
Satoru Hirota	66	79	75	68	288	4,080,000
Tommy Nakajima	72	75	69	72	288	4,080,000
Yuta Ikeda	71	78	70	71	290	3,330,000
Tomohiro Kondo	73	74	71	72	290	3,330,000
Kim Kyung-tae	66	80	71	73	290	3,330,000
Tadahiro Takayama	69	79	75	68	291	2,360,000
Masamichi Uehira	72	74	76	69	291	2,360,000
Nobuo Serizawa	68	80	73	70	291	2,360,000
Keiichiro Fukabori	69	79	73	70	291	2,360,000
Kiradech Aphibarnrat	71	76	73	71	291	2,360,000
Norio Shinozaki	72	79	69	71	291	2,360,000
Shingo Katayama	71	78	75	68	292	1,830,000
Chawalit Plaphol	71	72	73	76	292	1,830,000
Toshimitsu Izawa	72	76	75	70	293	1,342,500
S.K. Ho	70	80	73	70	293	1,342,500
Ryuichi Oda	75	76	71	71	293	1,342,500
Kiyoshi Murota	74	75	73	71	293	1,342,500
Eddie Lee	71	77	77	68	293	1,342,500
Michio Matsumura	72	76	71	74	293	1,342,500
Shintaro Kai	72	74	72	75	293	1,342,500
Tetsuya Haraguchi	69	75	74	75	293	1,342,500

UBS Japan Golf Tour Championship

Shishido Hills Country Club, Kasama, Ibaraki
Par 36-35–71; 7,280 yards

June 4-7
purse, ¥150,000,000

	SCORES				TOTAL	MONEY
Yuji Igarashi	67	67	72	70	276	¥30,000,000
Toru Suzuki	70	66	71	70	277	10,800,000
Jang Ik-jae	70	64	71	72	277	10,800,000
David Smail	67	69	69	72	277	10,800,000

	SCORES				TOTAL	MONEY
Naoya Takemoto	71	67	71	69	278	6,000,000
Frankie Minoza	67	68	73	71	279	5,175,000
Kazuhiro Yamashita	68	69	69	73	279	5,175,000
Yusaku Miyazato	74	71	69	66	280	4,245,000
Kunihiro Kamii	73	68	70	69	280	4,245,000
Toshinori Muto	72	69	67	72	280	4,245,000
Koumei Oda	69	72	71	69	281	3,060,000
Kiradech Aphibarnrat	71	71	69	70	281	3,060,000
Naoya Sugiyama	71	71	69	70	281	3,060,000
Michio Matsumura	70	72	68	71	281	3,060,000
Ryuichi Oda	69	70	69	73	281	3,060,000
Tomohiro Kondo	69	69	75	69	282	2,148,000
Hiroo Kawai	71	70	72	69	282	2,148,000
Tetsuya Haraguchi	70	74	68	70	282	2,148,000
Yoshinobu Tsukada	69	71	71	71	282	2,148,000
Yuta Ikeda	68	70	66	78	282	2,148,000
Kenichi Kuboya	70	70	73	70	283	1,770,000
Liang Wen-chong	70	70	76	68	284	1,342,500
Taichi Teshima	74	71	71	68	284	1,342,500
Eddie Lee	70	75	71	68	284	1,342,500
Kaname Yokoo	74	67	74	69	284	1,342,500
Azuma Yano	71	71	72	70	284	1,342,500
Kim Hyung-sung	72	70	71	71	284	1,342,500
Hur In-hoi	77	67	69	71	284	1,342,500
Nobuhiro Masuda	71	70	71	72	284	1,342,500

Japan PGA Championship

Eniwa Country Club, Eniwa, Hokkaido
Par 35-35–70; 7,134 yards

June 11-14
purse, ¥130,000,000

	SCORES				TOTAL	MONEY
Yuta Ikeda	65	67	69	65	266	¥26,000,000
Mitsuhiro Tateyama	66	72	65	70	273	13,000,000
Ryuichi Oda	69	70	67	69	275	8,840,000
Norio Shinozaki	65	72	68	71	276	6,240,000
Tomohiro Kondo	71	69	70	67	277	5,200,000
Brendan Jones	67	70	72	69	278	4,680,000
Toru Suzuki	68	72	70	69	279	3,293,875
Kim Kyung-tae	69	70	70	70	279	3,293,875
Kaname Yokoo	66	72	72	69	279	3,293,875
Kazuhiro Yamashita	67	70	70	72	279	3,293,875
Eddie Lee	67	70	73	69	279	3,293,875
Shintaro Kai	68	68	73	70	279	3,293,875
Nobuhito Sato	69	74	69	67	279	3,293,875
Hideto Tanihara	74	69	67	69	279	3,293,875
Kazunori Suzuki	73	67	68	72	280	2,041,000
S.K. Ho	70	69	72	69	280	2,041,000
Hiroyuki Fujita	71	67	70	72	280	2,041,000
Michio Matsumura	71	71	70	68	280	2,041,000
Shigeru Nonaka	66	74	71	70	281	1,482,000
Toshinori Muto	72	68	70	71	281	1,482,000
Makoto Inoue	70	70	68	73	281	1,482,000
Kunihiro Kamii	68	73	71	69	281	1,482,000
Brandt Jobe	68	70	75	68	281	1,482,000
Azuma Yano	71	72	70	68	281	1,482,000
Yoshikazu Haku	69	71	71	71	282	1,092,000
Shigeki Maruyama	71	70	68	73	282	1,092,000
Kiyoshi Murota	70	71	72	69	282	1,092,000
Satoru Hirota	72	71	69	70	282	1,092,000

Gateway to the Open Mizuno Open Yomiuri Classic

Yomiuri Country Club, West Course, Nishinomiya, Hyogo
Par 36-36–72; 7,230 yards

June 25-28
purse, ¥130,000,000

	SCORES				TOTAL	MONEY
Ryo Ishikawa	69	65	68	73	275	¥26,000,000
David Smail	70	72	64	72	278	13,000,000
Kenichi Kuboya	67	71	70	71	279	6,760,000
Tomohiro Kondo	72	70	67	70	279	6,760,000
Kim Hyung-sung	67	66	72	74	279	6,760,000
Koumei Oda	72	70	68	70	280	4,485,000
Hideto Tanihara	71	72	67	70	280	4,485,000
Shigeru Nonaka	70	69	72	70	281	3,815,500
Brendan Jones	73	70	68	70	281	3,815,500
Hiroo Kawai	70	68	74	70	282	3,406,000
Steven Jeffress	74	70	70	69	283	2,561,000
Mitsuhiro Tateyama	72	66	75	70	283	2,561,000
Kaname Yokoo	67	75	71	70	283	2,561,000
Hiroyuki Fujita	71	71	71	70	283	2,561,000
Kunihiro Kamii	74	69	70	70	283	2,561,000
Toru Suzuki	72	71	69	71	283	2,561,000
Taichiro Kiyota	72	68	72	72	284	1,747,200
Takao Nogami	69	70	72	73	284	1,747,200
Makoto Inoue	70	73	67	74	284	1,747,200
Yoshinobu Tsukada	69	68	72	75	284	1,747,200
Prayad Marksaeng	69	67	69	79	284	1,747,200
Taichi Teshima	74	69	71	71	285	1,222,000
Hidemasa Hoshino	67	69	77	72	285	1,222,000
Azuma Yano	73	73	68	71	285	1,222,000
Ryuichi Oda	69	73	71	72	285	1,222,000
Kiradech Aphibarnrat	72	73	71	69	285	1,222,000
Nobuhiro Masuda	71	70	71	73	285	1,222,000

Nagashima Shigeo Invitational Sega Sammy Cup

North Country Golf Club, Chitose, Hokkaido
Par 36-36–72; 7,115 yards

July 23-26
purse, ¥130,000,000

	SCORES				TOTAL	MONEY
Hiroyuki Fujita	69	68	69	66	272	¥26,000,000
Kouki Idoki	68	67	68	70	273	13,000,000
Toru Taniguchi	68	71	69	66	274	7,540,000
Katsumasa Miyamoto	68	66	72	68	274	7,540,000
Shigeru Nonaka	73	69	66	67	275	4,940,000
Taigen Tsumagari	68	69	70	68	275	4,940,000
Shingo Katayama	71	68	69	68	276	3,973,666
Paul Sheehan	67	73	67	69	276	3,973,666
Takeshi Kajikawa	68	69	69	70	276	3,973,666
Ryo Ishikawa	72	70	68	67	277	3,146,000
Taichi Teshima	71	71	68	67	277	3,146,000
Lee Seong-ho	74	66	68	69	277	3,146,000
Tetsuji Hiratsuka	73	69	69	67	278	2,333,500
Bio Kim	69	70	70	69	278	2,333,500
Tomohiro Kondo	71	67	71	69	278	2,333,500
Kim Hyung-sung	72	67	67	72	278	2,333,500
Koumei Oda	72	69	70	68	279	1,747,200
Kim Jong-duck	67	70	72	70	279	1,747,200
Kiyoshi Murota	73	66	70	70	279	1,747,200
Masaya Tomida	71	71	66	71	279	1,747,200

	SCORES				TOTAL	MONEY
Kiyotaka Inoue	69	72	67	71	279	1,747,200
Daisuke Maruyama	70	69	72	69	280	1,192,285
Brendan Jones	73	66	72	69	280	1,192,285
Kazuhiko Hosokawa	68	68	75	69	280	1,192,285
Hiroshi Iwata	71	70	71	68	280	1,192,285
Norihiko Furusho	72	68	69	71	280	1,192,285
Hidemasa Hoshino	72	65	71	72	280	1,192,285
Tommy Nakajima	68	71	69	72	280	1,192,285

Sun Chlorella Classic

Otaru Country Club, Otaru, Hokkaido
Par 36-36–72; 7,535 yards

July 30-August 2
purse, ¥150,000,000

	SCORES				TOTAL	MONEY
Ryo Ishikawa	65	68	71	67	271	¥30,000,000
Brendan Jones	66	70	71	65	272	15,000,000
Yuta Ikeda	70	70	68	67	275	10,200,000
Shingo Katayama	70	69	70	67	276	6,200,000
Taigen Tsumagari	67	68	73	68	276	6,200,000
Kazuhiro Yamashita	66	68	72	70	276	6,200,000
Azuma Yano	72	70	67	69	278	4,950,000
Yusaku Miyazato	74	70	69	68	281	4,091,250
Kim Hyung-sung	68	71	71	71	281	4,091,250
Satoshi Tomiyama	68	72	69	72	281	4,091,250
Hiroyuki Fujita	72	70	66	73	281	4,091,250
Nobuyuki Okuwa	69	71	71	71	282	3,330,000
Ryutaro Nagano	69	72	74	68	283	2,780,000
Hidemasa Hoshino	72	73	69	69	283	2,780,000
Han Lee	69	70	74	70	283	2,780,000
Tetsuya Haraguchi	74	72	69	69	284	2,280,000
Kunihiro Kamii	68	78	68	70	284	2,280,000
Nobuhiro Masuda	72	70	72	70	284	2,280,000
Masaya Tomida	71	74	71	69	285	1,950,000
Tatsunori Nukaga	73	72	66	74	285	1,950,000
Kenichi Kuboya	74	71	71	70	286	1,650,000
Michio Matsumura	71	70	74	71	286	1,650,000
Shunta Maeawakura	70	75	70	71	286	1,650,000
Taichi Teshima	74	71	71	71	287	1,230,000
Brandt Jobe	72	71	73	71	287	1,230,000
Kouki Idoki	73	72	72	70	287	1,230,000
Mitsuhiro Tateyama	72	69	73	73	287	1,230,000
Hur In-hoi	74	72	68	73	287	1,230,000
Kim Kyung-tae	72	74	73	68	287	1,230,000
Yuki Ishikawa	67	73	72	75	287	1,230,000

Kansai Open Golf Championship

Takarazuka Golf Club, Hyogo
Par 36-35–71; 6,682 yards

August 20-23
purse, ¥50,000,000

	SCORES				TOTAL	MONEY
Hiroyuki Fujita	69	66	61	68	264	¥10,000,000
Tetsuji Hiratsuka	65	69	66	66	266	4,200,000
Tomohiro Kondo	67	67	64	68	266	4,200,000
Mitsuhiro Tateyama	67	68	69	64	268	2,400,000
Kunihiro Kamii	67	65	69	68	269	2,000,000

	SCORES				TOTAL	MONEY
Masaya Tomida	62	69	65	74	270	1,800,000
Taichiro Kiyota	68	69	70	65	272	1,421,000
Kim Do-hoon	69	67	69	67	272	1,421,000
Kazuhiro Yamashita	71	70	64	67	272	1,421,000
Yasuharu Imano	70	66	67	69	272	1,421,000
Kim Hyung-sung	69	70	64	69	272	1,421,000
Katsumasa Miyamoto	74	66	66	68	274	1,060,000
Yoshinobu Tsukada	71	68	65	70	274	1,060,000
Yudai Maeda	70	71	68	66	275	835,000
Hideto Tanihara	72	71	65	67	275	835,000
Achi Sato	69	68	70	68	275	835,000
Toru Suzuki	68	67	69	71	275	835,000
Sushi Ishigaki	69	72	68	67	276	590,000
Kaname Yokoo	69	72	68	67	276	590,000
Katsunori Kuwabara	71	69	69	67	276	590,000
Kiyoshi Miyazato	65	74	68	69	276	590,000
Mamo Osanai	68	73	66	69	276	590,000
Takeshi Kajikawa	69	73	64	70	276	590,000
S.K. Ho	73	70	70	63	276	590,000
Hirofumi Miyase	69	68	73	67	277	440,000
Koumei Oda	65	69	73	70	277	440,000

Vana H Cup KBC Augusta

Keya Golf Club, Shima, Fukuoka
Par 36-36–72; 7,146 yards

August 27-30
purse, ¥110,000,000

	SCORES				TOTAL	MONEY
Yuta Ikeda	69	66	69	63	267	¥22,000,000
Yasuharu Imano	69	66	69	63	267	11,000,000
(Ikeda defeated Imano on second playoff hole.)						
Ryo Ishikawa	65	66	71	66	268	7,480,000
Hideto Tanihara	70	64	72	66	272	5,280,000
Toru Taniguchi	68	65	72	68	273	3,996,666
Azuma Yano	67	69	69	68	273	3,996,666
Tetsuya Haraguchi	64	70	70	69	273	3,996,666
Nobuyuki Okuwa	67	71	69	67	274	2,888,600
Kazuhiro Yamashita	68	67	70	69	274	2,888,600
Prayad Marksaeng	71	65	68	70	274	2,888,600
Hirofumi Miyase	67	69	68	70	274	2,888,600
Jun Kikuchi	69	69	65	71	274	2,888,600
Koumei Oda	70	68	71	66	275	1,800,857
Brandt Jobe	66	72	71	66	275	1,800,857
Ryutaro Nagano	71	70	67	67	275	1,800,857
Kiradech Aphibarnrat	71	67	74	63	275	1,800,857
Yoshinobu Tsukada	69	71	67	68	275	1,800,857
Toshinori Muto	69	67	69	70	275	1,800,857
Hiroyuki Fujita	67	67	69	72	275	1,800,857
Tetsuji Hiratsuka	71	63	73	69	276	1,254,000
Taichi Teshima	70	67	70	69	276	1,254,000
Shingo Katayama	70	67	69	70	276	1,254,000
Tomohiro Kondo	73	67	64	72	276	1,254,000
Masaya Tomida	68	69	73	67	277	946,000
Michio Matsumura	69	71	70	67	277	946,000
Jang Ik-jae	71	70	70	66	277	946,000
Yusaku Miyazato	70	68	69	70	277	946,000
Akinori Tani	68	66	72	71	277	946,000

Fujisankei Classic

Fujizakura Country Club, Fujikawaguchiko, Yamanashi
Par 35-36–71; 7,397 yards

September 3-6
purse, ¥110,000,000

	SCORES				TOTAL	MONEY
Ryo Ishikawa	69	65	68	70	272	¥22,000,000
Daisuke Maruyama	72	71	65	69	277	11,000,000
Koumei Oda	69	73	68	68	278	7,480,000
Kaname Yokoo	72	70	70	68	280	4,840,000
Katsumasa Miyamoto	68	72	71	69	280	4,840,000
Shingo Katayama	70	68	75	68	281	3,511,750
Yuta Ikeda	72	71	69	69	281	3,511,750
Tomohiro Kondo	72	67	70	72	281	3,511,750
Toshinori Muto	71	65	71	74	281	3,511,750
Kunihiro Kamii	73	67	68	74	282	2,772,000
Kenichi Kuboya	69	66	69	78	282	2,772,000
Kouki Idoki	65	71	72	75	283	2,442,000
Yudai Maeda	71	70	71	72	284	2,112,000
Tetsuya Haraguchi	73	70	67	74	284	2,112,000
Taigen Tsumagari	74	68	74	69	285	1,580,857
Michio Matsumura	76	66	74	69	285	1,580,857
Yasuharu Imano	69	73	74	69	285	1,580,857
Brendan Jones	75	70	67	73	285	1,580,857
Koichiro Kawano	72	72	68	73	285	1,580,857
Hirofumi Miyase	72	71	69	73	285	1,580,857
Gregory Meyer	71	70	70	74	285	1,580,857
Azuma Yano	74	71	69	72	286	1,089,000
Yoshinobu Tsukada	73	71	69	73	286	1,089,000
Kazuhiko Hosokawa	71	69	72	74	286	1,089,000
Shinichi Yokota	70	70	71	75	286	1,089,000

ANA Open

Sapporo Golf Club, Wattsu Course, Kitahiroshima, Hokkaido
Par 36-36–72; 7,063 yards

September 17-20
purse, ¥110,000,000

	SCORES				TOTAL	MONEY
Toru Taniguchi	67	67	66	72	272	¥22,000,000
Kim Kyung-tae	70	68	69	69	276	7,920,000
Tommy Nakajima	67	69	69	71	276	7,920,000
Kazuhiro Yamashita	69	69	67	71	276	7,920,000
Hideto Tanihara	69	73	65	70	277	4,400,000
Kiyoshi Murota	70	69	69	70	278	3,795,000
Yusaku Miyazato	69	71	68	70	278	3,795,000
Kiradech Aphibarnrat	72	69	70	69	280	3,113,000
Eddie Lee	68	69	72	71	280	3,113,000
Daisuke Maruyama	71	68	67	74	280	3,113,000
Han Lee	70	71	71	69	281	2,552,000
Shigeki Maruyama	71	68	69	73	281	2,552,000
Tomohiro Kondo	69	74	71	68	282	1,914,000
Katsumasa Miyamoto	72	69	71	70	282	1,914,000
Hur In-hoi	72	69	70	71	282	1,914,000
Koumei Oda	66	75	69	72	282	1,914,000
Azuma Yano	66	71	72	73	282	1,914,000
Hirofumi Miyase	73	68	73	69	283	1,430,000
Ryo Ishikawa	68	70	74	71	283	1,430,000
Kouki Idoki	74	68	69	72	283	1,430,000
Yuta Ikeda	72	70	69	72	283	1,430,000
Shingo Katayama	70	71	72	71	284	1,008,857

	SCORES				TOTAL	MONEY
Jang Ik-jae	70	70	72	72	284	1,008,857
Gregory Meyer	72	70	70	72	284	1,008,857
Kaname Yokoo	70	71	71	72	284	1,008,857
Taichi Teshima	69	71	70	74	284	1,008,857
Takashi Kanemoto	67	70	72	75	284	1,008,857
Katsumune Imai	68	71	69	76	284	1,008,857

Asia-Pacific Panasonic Open

Joyo Country Club, Joyo, Kyoto
Par 36-35–71; 7,064 yards

September 24-27
purse, ¥150,000,000

	SCORES				TOTAL	MONEY
Daisuke Maruyama	69	66	67	74	276	¥30,000,000
Yuta Ikeda	68	73	67	72	280	11,850,000
Liang Wen-chong	68	70	69	73	280	11,850,000
Kim Kyung-tae	70	70	66	74	280	11,850,000
Kim Hyung-sung	68	68	71	75	282	6,300,000
Tadahiro Takayama	70	72	70	71	283	5,250,000
Unho Park	71	69	73	71	284	4,200,000
Yuji Igarashi	67	75	70	72	284	4,200,000
Scott Hend	72	71	72	70	285	2,408,571
Michio Matsumura	71	74	72	68	285	2,408,571
Ted Oh	70	72	70	73	285	2,408,571
Koumei Oda	68	75	69	73	285	2,408,571
Noh Seung-yul	67	74	70	74	285	2,408,571
Toshinori Muto	74	64	70	77	285	2,408,571
Yusaku Miyazato	75	69	64	77	285	2,408,571
Kazuhiro Yamashita	75	69	72	70	286	1,537,500
Ryo Ishikawa	73	72	69	72	286	1,537,500
Toru Taniguchi	68	72	73	73	286	1,537,500
Jyoti Randhawa	72	68	70	76	286	1,537,500
Tetsuji Hiratsuka	71	71	73	72	287	1,252,500
Paul Sheehan	72	72	72	71	287	1,252,500
Lam Chih Bing	66	72	74	75	287	1,252,500
Hideto Tanihara	71	71	70	75	287	1,252,500
Kiyoshi Miyazato	69	74	69	75	287	1,252,500
Toru Suzuki	73	64	74	76	287	1,252,500

Coca-Cola Tokai Classic

Miyoshi Country Club, West Course, Miyoshi, Aichi
Par 36-36–72; 7,310 yards

October 1-4
purse, ¥120,000,000

	SCORES				TOTAL	MONEY
Ryo Ishikawa	71	68	66	69	274	¥24,000,000
Takeshi Kajikawa	71	70	65	69	275	12,000,000
Shingo Katayama	68	70	69	70	277	6,960,000
Yuta Ikeda	64	74	68	71	277	6,960,000
Yasuharu Imano	71	71	69	67	278	4,800,000
Michio Matsumura	69	73	70	67	279	4,140,000
Katsumasa Miyamoto	66	72	71	70	279	4,140,000
Koumei Oda	69	69	71	71	280	3,660,000
Daisuke Maruyama	68	68	76	69	281	3,144,000
David Smail	71	71	70	69	281	3,144,000
Masamichi Uehira	70	72	68	71	281	3,144,000
Shinichi Yokota	70	72	72	68	282	2,334,000

	SCORES			TOTAL	MONEY
Jang Ik-jae	71	70	70	71	282	2,334,000
Han Lee	67	76	69	70	282	2,334,000
Hiroyuki Fujita	69	74	67	72	282	2,334,000
Kim Hyung-tae	69	74	72	68	283	1,770,000
Toru Taniguchi	71	69	73	70	283	1,770,000
Yudai Maeda	73	71	68	71	283	1,770,000
Yusaku Miyazato	69	68	71	75	283	1,770,000
Ryuji Imada	72	68	74	70	284	1,416,000
Taigen Tsumagari	70	75	71	68	284	1,416,000
Ryuichi Oda	68	72	72	72	284	1,416,000
Azuma Yano	71	71	74	69	285	1,064,000
Hiroshi Iwata	68	75	74	68	285	1,064,000
Dinesh Chand	73	70	72	70	285	1,064,000
Kiyoshi Miyazato	70	70	74	71	285	1,064,000
Steven Conran	70	71	73	71	285	1,064,000
Kouki Idoki	70	69	70	76	285	1,064,000

Canon Open

Totsuka Country Club, Yokohama, Kanagawa
Par 36-36–72; 7,167 yards
(Event shortened to 54 holes—rain.)

October 8-11
purse, ¥150,000,000

	SCORES			TOTAL	MONEY
Yuta Ikeda	64	72	64	200	¥22,500,000
Tomohiro Kondo	68	70	66	204	9,450,000
Han Lee	69	66	69	204	9,450,000
Kenichi Kuboya	65	68	72	205	5,400,000
Hiroshi Iwata	70	70	67	207	4,087,500
Tetsuya Haraguchi	66	70	71	207	4,087,500
Azuma Yano	67	69	71	207	4,087,500
Tatsunori Nukaga	72	68	68	208	2,538,750
Hiromichi Kubo	70	71	67	208	2,538,750
Kim Kyung-tae	68	72	68	208	2,538,750
Brendan Jones	71	69	68	208	2,538,750
Tetsuji Hiratsuka	68	70	70	208	2,538,750
Shigeki Maruyama	66	72	70	208	2,538,750
Michio Matsumura	68	68	72	208	2,538,750
David Smail	69	67	72	208	2,538,750
Kazuhiro Yamashita	69	67	72	208	2,538,750
Yoshinobu Tsukada	68	72	69	209	1,335,000
Mamo Osanai	72	69	68	209	1,335,000
Katsumasa Miyamoto	68	72	69	209	1,335,000
Shingo Katayama	69	71	69	209	1,335,000
Shinichi Akiba	71	68	70	209	1,335,000
Tatsuhiko Takahashi	71	67	71	209	1,335,000
Toshinori Muto	69	68	72	209	1,335,000
Takao Nogami	67	69	73	209	1,335,000
Liang Wen-chong	74	69	66	209	1,335,000

Japan Open Championship

Musashi Country Club, Royooka Course, Iruma, Saitama
Par 36-36–72; 7,083 yards

October 15-18
purse, ¥200,000,000

			SCORES		TOTAL	MONEY
Ryuichi Oda	74	70	71	67	282	¥40,000,000
Ryo Ishikawa	70	76	65	71	282	18,700,000
Yasuharu Imano	73	69	70	70	282	18,700,000
(Oda defeated Ishikawa and Imano on second playoff hole.)						
Hiroyuki Fujita	69	72	75	69	285	9,200,000
Hirofumi Miyase	72	70	74	69	285	9,200,000
Kenichi Kuboya	70	75	73	69	287	5,650,000
Shintaro Kai	72	74	72	69	287	5,650,000
Hidemasa Hoshino	72	75	66	74	287	5,650,000
David Smail	71	71	72	73	287	5,650,000
Kaname Yokoo	71	72	76	69	288	3,300,000
Masaya Tomida	75	70	73	70	288	3,300,000
Brendan Jones	73	70	73	72	288	3,300,000
Hideto Tanihara	75	69	72	72	288	3,300,000
Tetsuji Hiratsuka	75	71	72	71	289	2,295,000
Han Lee	69	72	76	72	289	2,295,000
Taichi Teshima	69	75	72	73	289	2,295,000
Azuma Yano	70	75	70	74	289	2,295,000
Prayad Marksaeng	73	72	75	70	290	1,950,000
Yuta Ikeda	74	75	71	70	290	1,950,000
Tetsuya Haraguchi	76	69	75	71	291	1,715,000
Katsunori Kuwabara	73	73	74	71	291	1,715,000
Sushi Ishigaki	70	74	74	73	291	1,715,000
Ryutaro Nagano	69	75	73	74	291	1,715,000
Kunihiro Kamii	76	72	72	72	292	1,600,000
Yuji Igarashi	69	76	76	72	293	1,480,000
Kazuhiko Hosokawa	74	71	74	74	293	1,480,000
Shingo Katayama	72	70	76	75	293	1,480,000
Tomohiro Kondo	71	72	74	76	293	1,480,000
Kazuhiro Yamashita	68	76	72	77	293	1,480,000

Bridgestone Open

Sodegaura Country Club, Chiba
Par 36-36–72; 7,138 yards

October 22-25
purse, ¥150,000,000

			SCORES		TOTAL	MONEY
Yuta Ikeda	67	67	71	65	270	¥30,000,000
Kenichi Kuboya	69	68	68	67	272	15,000,000
Shingo Katayama	70	65	69	69	273	10,200,000
Hiroshi Iwata	72	68	68	67	275	7,200,000
Masaya Tomida	70	72	70	64	276	5,700,000
Yusaku Miyazato	73	70	68	65	276	5,700,000
Katsunori Kuwabara	70	67	71	69	277	4,421,250
Ryuichi Oda	70	67	68	72	277	4,421,250
Masanori Kobayashi	71	67	67	72	277	4,421,250
Kaname Yokoo	68	71	64	74	277	4,421,250
Koumei Oda	68	66	74	70	278	3,180,000
Brandt Jobe	70	72	69	67	278	3,180,000
Toru Suzuki	68	67	73	70	278	3,180,000
Hideto Tanihara	71	71	66	70	278	3,180,000
Tetsuji Hiratsuka	69	70	67	73	279	2,580,000
Satoru Hirota	71	72	70	67	280	2,212,500
Azuma Yano	71	68	75	66	280	2,212,500

	SCORES				TOTAL	MONEY
Yui Ueda	73	71	67	69	280	2,212,500
Tetsuya Haraguchi	71	70	70	69	280	2,212,500
Ryo Ishikawa	71	71	72	67	281	1,650,000
Shinichi Yokota	72	69	72	68	281	1,650,000
Kim Hyung-tae	70	70	72	69	281	1,650,000
*Shunsuke Sonoda	72	73	67	69	281	
Toshimitsu Izawa	69	73	70	69	281	1,650,000
Hiroyuki Fujita	67	73	71	70	281	1,650,000

Mynavi ABC Championship

ABC Golf Club, Kato, Hyogo
Par 36-36–72; 7,217 yards

October 29-November 1
purse, ¥150,000,000

	SCORES				TOTAL	MONEY
Toru Suzuki	70	67	66	71	274	¥30,000,000
Takashi Kanemoto	75	68	71	65	279	15,000,000
Azuma Yano	66	74	72	68	280	8,700,000
Hiroyuki Fujita	69	68	71	72	280	8,700,000
Tatsunori Nukaga	72	72	70	67	281	6,000,000
Kazuhiro Yamashita	76	67	70	69	282	5,175,000
Ryo Ishikawa	68	69	72	73	282	5,175,000
Kim Hyung-sung	66	73	70	74	283	4,402,500
Hidemasa Hoshino	66	69	75	73	283	4,402,500
Tomohiro Kondo	69	74	74	67	284	3,930,000
Shingo Katayama	69	74	71	71	285	3,330,000
Brandt Jobe	69	72	71	73	285	3,330,000
Kiyoshi Miyazato	71	72	69	73	285	3,330,000
S.K. Ho	69	74	73	70	286	2,360,000
Kim Kyung-tae	72	72	72	70	286	2,360,000
Kiradech Aphibarnrat	69	72	76	69	286	2,360,000
Shintaro Kai	69	69	73	75	286	2,360,000
Katsumasa Miyamoto	68	72	71	75	286	2,360,000
Toyokazu Fujishima	71	71	69	75	286	2,360,000
Satoru Hirota	71	76	69	71	287	1,770,000
Hirofumi Miyase	69	73	72	73	287	1,770,000
Yusaku Miyazato	73	70	71	73	287	1,770,000
Koumei Oda	75	70	72	71	288	1,298,571
Hiroo Kawai	73	71	72	72	288	1,298,571
Kunihiro Kamii	73	72	72	71	288	1,298,571
Taichi Teshima	70	72	76	70	288	1,298,571
Hideto Tanihara	75	71	68	74	288	1,298,571
Jang Ik-jae	73	71	70	74	288	1,298,571
Takamasa Yamamoto	73	70	69	76	288	1,298,571

The Championship by Lexus

Otone Country Club, Bando, Ibaraki
Par 36-35–71; 7,011 yards

November 5-8
purse, ¥150,000,000

	SCORES				TOTAL	MONEY
Toshinori Muto	68	65	71	64	268	¥30,000,000
Kim Kyung-tae	66	67	69	69	271	15,000,000
Shigeki Maruyama	66	68	68	70	272	10,200,000
Toru Suzuki	71	70	67	65	273	7,200,000
Wayne Perske	66	69	69	71	275	6,000,000
Azuma Yano	70	67	73	67	277	4,975,000

	SCORES				TOTAL	MONEY
Toyokazu Fujishima	69	71	68	69	277	4,975,000
Nobuhiro Masuda	71	69	67	70	277	4,975,000
Makoto Inoue	71	69	67	71	278	4,230,000
Katsunori Kuwabara	67	71	69	72	279	3,930,000
Toru Taniguchi	71	72	70	67	280	3,480,000
David Smail	68	69	71	72	280	3,480,000
Hirofumi Miyase	69	76	68	68	281	2,780,000
Brandt Jobe	72	70	71	68	281	2,780,000
Hidemichi Tanaka	70	71	71	69	281	2,780,000
Satoru Hirota	69	72	71	70	282	2,280,000
Tetsuji Hiratsuka	70	74	72	66	282	2,280,000
Kim Hyung-sung	66	69	73	74	282	2,280,000
Kaname Yokoo	70	72	72	69	283	1,455,000
Masaya Tomida	67	75	71	70	283	1,455,000
Akio Sadakata	71	70	73	69	283	1,455,000
Sushi Ishigaki	72	70	73	68	283	1,455,000
Eddie Lee	72	70	70	71	283	1,455,000
Steven Jeffress	72	68	71	72	283	1,455,000
Dinesh Chand	72	72	71	68	283	1,455,000
Tadahiro Takayama	71	71	69	72	283	1,455,000
Hiroyuki Fujita	71	72	68	72	283	1,455,000
Shintaro Kai	69	71	69	74	283	1,455,000
Kazuhiro Yamashita	67	68	73	75	283	1,455,000
Hideto Tanihara	73	67	67	76	283	1,455,000

Mitsui Sumitomo Visa Taiheiyo Masters

Taiheiyo Club, Gotemba Course, Gotemba, Shizuoka
Par 36-36–72; 7,246 yards

November 12-15
purse, ¥150,000,000

	SCORES				TOTAL	MONEY
Yasuharu Imano	69	65	68	73	275	¥30,000,000
Han Lee	72	68	68	69	277	12,600,000
Kenichi Kuboya	67	71	68	71	277	12,600,000
Ryo Ishikawa	68	71	70	69	278	6,600,000
Kaname Yokoo	69	67	70	72	278	6,600,000
Michio Matsumura	71	69	69	70	279	4,788,750
Ryuichi Oda	70	70	69	70	279	4,788,750
Toru Suzuki	72	67	70	70	279	4,788,750
Taigen Tsumagari	68	68	70	73	279	4,788,750
Ryuji Imada	69	72	69	70	280	3,330,000
Hirofumi Miyase	71	71	67	71	280	3,330,000
Wayne Perske	72	71	71	66	280	3,330,000
Hidemichi Tanaka	73	66	69	72	280	3,330,000
Makoto Inoue	70	68	72	70	280	3,330,000
Daisuke Maruyama	73	69	68	71	281	2,430,000
Shigeki Maruyama	71	72	68	70	281	2,430,000
Masao Nakajima	70	68	67	76	281	2,430,000
Yudai Maeda	71	71	69	71	282	1,770,000
Koumei Oda	72	71	67	72	282	1,770,000
*Yoshinori Fujimoto	73	71	71	67	282	
Katsumasa Miyamoto	72	66	70	74	282	1,770,000
Shigeru Nonaka	67	71	72	72	282	1,770,000
Hideto Tanihara	70	76	68	68	282	1,770,000
Tadahiro Takayama	69	69	73	71	282	1,770,000
Yusaku Miyazato	69	67	71	75	282	1,770,000

Dunlop Phoenix

Phoenix Country Club, Miyazaki
Par 36-35–71; 7,010 yards

November 19-22
purse, ¥200,000,000

	SCORES				TOTAL	MONEY
Edoardo Molinari	70	66	69	66	271	¥40,000,000
Robert Karlsson	70	68	68	65	271	20,000,000
(Molinari defeated Karlsson on second playoff hole.)						
Hirofumi Miyase	69	72	69	67	277	11,600,000
Shane Lowry	73	68	69	67	277	11,600,000
Eddie Lee	75	69	68	66	278	7,600,000
Tadahiro Takayama	69	68	71	70	278	7,600,000
Hiroyuki Fujita	71	72	70	66	279	5,476,666
Shigeki Maruyama	72	70	69	68	279	5,476,666
Steven Conran	69	70	71	69	279	5,476,666
Ryuichi Oda	68	68	72	71	279	5,476,666
Daisuke Maruyama	71	70	68	70	279	5,476,666
Kim Kyung-tae	70	69	69	71	279	5,476,666
Shingo Katayama	68	70	72	70	280	3,840,000
Michio Matsumura	68	73	68	71	280	3,840,000
Yusaku Miyazato	72	69	71	69	281	3,048,000
Kaname Yokoo	70	71	75	65	281	3,048,000
Masaya Tomida	69	70	70	72	281	3,048,000
Yudai Maeda	70	65	73	73	281	3,048,000
Kenichi Kuboya	65	70	71	75	281	3,048,000
David Smail	71	71	70	70	282	2,440,000
Katsumasa Miyamoto	70	69	69	74	282	2,440,000
Koumei Oda	70	70	74	69	283	2,120,000
Ryo Ishikawa	71	70	71	71	283	2,120,000
Kiyoshi Miyazato	68	71	73	72	284	1,760,000
Makoto Inoue	70	74	68	72	284	1,760,000
Hidemasa Hoshino	74	72	70	68	284	1,760,000
Norio Shinozaki	70	74	67	73	284	1,760,000

Casio World Open

Kochi Kuroshio Country Club, Geisei, Kochi
Par 36-36–72; 7,300 yards

November 26-29
purse, ¥200,000,000

	SCORES				TOTAL	MONEY
Koumei Oda	67	65	70	65	267	¥40,000,000
Ryo Ishikawa	68	66	68	68	270	20,000,000
Tetsuji Hiratsuka	67	67	70	68	272	13,600,000
Ryuichi Oda	69	70	69	65	273	8,266,666
Tomohiro Kondo	68	69	67	69	273	8,266,666
Katsumasa Miyamoto	67	67	69	70	273	8,266,666
Kiradech Aphibarnrat	70	70	65	69	274	6,113,333
Kaname Yokoo	69	67	70	68	274	6,113,333
Shigeki Maruyama	67	65	70	72	274	6,113,333
Azuma Yano	68	70	68	69	275	5,240,000
Akio Sadakata	71	70	69	66	276	4,240,000
Shingo Katayama	66	68	74	68	276	4,240,000
Kim Kyung-tae	71	69	69	67	276	4,240,000
Tadahiro Takayama	69	70	69	68	276	4,240,000
Hideto Tanihara	72	70	68	67	277	3,140,000
Brendan Jones	69	71	70	67	277	3,140,000
Hidemasa Hoshino	70	70	70	67	277	3,140,000
Yusaku Miyazato	65	69	73	70	277	3,140,000
Yuta Ikeda	69	70	70	69	278	2,440,000

	SCORES				TOTAL	MONEY
Shintaro Kai	71	71	66	70	278	2,440,000
Hiroo Kawai	69	68	71	70	278	2,440,000
Toyokazu Fujishima	68	69	70	71	278	2,440,000
Shigeru Nonaka	70	70	70	69	279	2,040,000
Kim Hyung-tae	71	71	68	70	280	1,640,000
Taichiro Kiyota	69	70	72	69	280	1,640,000
Taichi Teshima	72	66	71	71	280	1,640,000
Kiyoshi Miyazato	69	69	71	71	280	1,640,000
Tatsunori Nukaga	68	71	70	71	280	1,640,000
Toru Taniguchi	68	68	72	72	280	1,640,000
S.K. Ho	69	67	72	72	280	1,640,000

Golf Nippon Series JT Cup

Tokyo Yomiuri Country Club, Tokyo
Par 35-35–70; 7,016 yards

December 3-6
purse, ¥130,000,000

	SCORES				TOTAL	MONEY
Shigeki Maruyama	70	67	70	64	271	¥40,000,000
Kim Kyung-tae	69	70	64	68	271	15,000,000
(Maruyama defeated Kim on fourth playoff hole.)						
Kazuhiro Yamashita	73	69	68	63	273	10,000,000
Tomohiro Kondo	71	67	70	66	274	5,808,291
Brendan Jones	69	71	68	66	274	5,808,291
Jeev Milkha Singh	71	69	65	70	275	4,768,291
Toru Taniguchi	73	67	71	66	277	4,061,957
Koumei Oda	74	68	68	67	277	4,061,957
Toshinori Muto	70	69	66	72	277	4,061,957
Kenichi Kuboya	75	70	66	67	278	3,234,291
Masaya Tomida	69	70	71	68	278	3,234,291
Azuma Yano	70	70	68	70	278	3,234,291
Hiroyuki Fujita	69	70	72	68	279	2,584,292
Ryuichi Oda	71	72	68	68	279	2,584,292
Hirofumi Miyase	71	73	68	68	280	2,259,292
Katsumasa Miyamoto	70	73	69	68	280	2,259,292
Kaname Yokoo	74	70	73	64	281	1,999,292
Shingo Katayama	73	75	66	67	281	1,999,292
Ryo Ishikawa	78	72	67	66	283	1,778,292
Daisuke Maruyama	70	70	72	71	283	1,778,292
Yasuharu Imano	73	69	71	71	284	1,622,292
Toru Suzuki	72	74	70	69	285	1,518,292
David Smail	74	76	69	68	287	1,362,292
Yuta Ikeda	78	69	68	72	287	1,362,292
Tetsuji Hiratsuka	72	73	74	73	292	1,258,292

Australasian Tour

Subaru Victorian Open

Spring Valley Golf Club, Clayton, Victoria
Par 71; 6,738 yards

January 29-February 1
purse, A$110,000

	SCORES				TOTAL	MONEY
Ashley Hall	68	65	72	69	274	A$16,500
Craig Scott	71	70	65	70	276	9,075
Scott Laycock	68	68	69	71	276	9,075
Aaron Townsend	70	68	70	69	277	5,005
Paul Sheehan	68	70	71	68	277	5,005
Cameron Percy	68	68	72	70	278	3,465
David Diaz	74	69	68	67	278	3,465
Peter Senior	68	72	69	69	278	3,465
Andrew McKenzie	74	66	69	71	280	2,695
Adam Porker	73	68	69	71	281	1,925
Andre Stolz	66	73	69	73	281	1,925
Craig Spence	68	65	73	75	281	1,925
David Lutterus	70	70	69	72	281	1,925
James McLean	66	71	72	72	281	1,925
Terry Pilkadaris	71	71	68	71	281	1,925
Chris Downes	69	67	73	73	282	1,309
Gareth Paddison	68	72	67	75	282	1,309
Marcus Cain	70	69	72	71	282	1,309
Michael Brennan	75	68	68	71	282	1,309
Steve Collins	70	72	68	72	282	1,309
Adam Bland	73	66	73	71	283	1,155
David McKenzie	68	68	77	70	283	1,155
Heath D'Altera	66	66	76	75	283	1,155
Joshua Carmichael	71	71	67	74	283	1,155
Kevin Conlong	74	69	71	70	284	1,067
Rohan Blizard	72	67	67	78	284	1,067
Ryan Haywood	70	68	73	73	284	1,067
Tim Wise	74	69	70	71	284	1,067

Cellarbrations Victorian PGA Championship

Sanctuary Lakes Resort, Melbourne, Victoria
Par 36-36-72; 7,038 yards

February 5-8
purse, A$110,000

	SCORES				TOTAL	MONEY
Andre Stolz	68	67	69	67	271	A$16,500
Stuart Bouvier	66	67	73	67	273	10,670
Adam Bland	69	70	69	66	274	6,875
Cameron Percy	71	68	67	68	274	6,875
Alistair Presnell	69	64	77	65	275	4,372.50
Scott Laycock	65	70	75	65	275	4,372.50
Andrew Bonhomme	65	68	74	69	276	3,685
Brad Kennedy	69	67	70	71	277	3,080
Gareth Paddison	70	67	71	69	277	3,080
*Bryden MacPherson	70	68	68	72	278	
Luke Hickmott	61	70	78	70	279	2,291.67
Paul Sheehan	69	68	72	70	279	2,291.67
Stephen Dartnall	69	66	72	72	279	2,291.67

	SCORES				TOTAL	MONEY
Chris Gaunt	69	67	75	69	280	1,650
David McKenzie	68	70	69	73	280	1,650
Heath Reed	74	65	69	72	280	1,650
Michael Brennan	73	67	71	69	280	1,650
Peter Senior	70	69	72	69	280	1,650
Brad McIntosh	73	65	72	71	281	1,265
Matthew Ecob	68	67	75	71	281	1,265
Michael Long	71	69	70	71	281	1,265
Terry Price	70	69	72	71	282	1,188
Josh Younger	73	67	71	72	283	1,155
Leigh McKechnie	71	67	71	74	283	1,155
Adam Crawford	68	71	69	76	284	1,100
Andrew McKenzie	70	66	76	72	284	1,100
Richard Gallichan	72	67	76	69	284	1,100

Johnnie Walker Classic

The Vines Resort & Country Club, Perth, Western Australia
Par 36-36–72; 7,101 yards

February 19-22
purse, £1,250,000

	SCORES				TOTAL	MONEY
*Danny Lee	67	68	69	67	271	
Hiroyuki Fujita	67	68	70	67	272	A$300,198.31
Felipe Aguilar	68	68	68	68	272	300,198.31
Ross McGowan	70	67	65	70	272	300,198.31
Raphael Jacquelin	70	68	66	69	273	122,242.65
John Bickerton	66	70	66	71	273	122,242.65
Adam Blyth	68	68	71	67	274	79,378.34
Lee Westwood	66	73	68	67	274	79,378.34
Michael Sim	69	69	67	69	274	79,378.34
Paul Casey	71	68	70	66	275	51,595.92
Markus Brier	70	68	70	67	275	51,595.92
Taichiro Kiyota	68	70	69	68	275	51,595.92
Ignacio Garrido	67	68	70	70	275	51,595.92
Nick Dougherty	73	66	70	67	276	37,421.21
Mardan Mamat	65	71	72	68	276	37,421.21
Graeme Storm	73	64	73	66	276	37,421.21
Tony Carolan	65	72	71	68	276	37,421.21
Pelle Edberg	70	67	74	65	276	37,421.21
Peter Senior	70	67	69	70	276	37,421.21
Robert-Jan Derksen	64	72	69	71	276	37,421.21
Ian Poulter	68	69	71	69	277	30,362.21
Andrew Dodt	70	66	70	71	277	30,362.21
Francesco Molinari	68	71	72	66	277	30,362.21
Niclas Fasth	70	69	67	71	277	30,362.21
Tim Wood	69	72	68	69	278	26,327.15
Colin Montgomerie	67	70	72	69	278	26,327.15
Peter Hedblom	73	66	70	69	278	26,327.15
Chris Gaunt	68	69	71	70	278	26,327.15
Anthony Kim	68	68	75	67	278	26,327.15
Bae Sang-moon	70	70	65	73	278	26,327.15
David Smail	70	71	69	69	279	21,961.34
Alexander Noren	68	69	73	69	279	21,961.34
Peter O'Malley	73	68	70	68	279	21,961.34
Won Joon Lee	71	70	66	72	279	21,961.34
Terry Pilkadaris	70	66	68	75	279	21,961.34
Craig Parry	71	69	69	71	280	17,727.83
Brad Kennedy	71	68	70	71	280	17,727.83
Anthony Wall	70	70	69	71	280	17,727.83
David McKenzie	68	73	69	70	280	17,727.83

	SCORES				TOTAL	MONEY
Seve Benson	70	67	71	72	280	17,727.83
Michael Jonzon	71	68	69	72	280	17,727.83
Damien McGrane	66	68	72	74	280	17,727.83
Peter Lawrie	67	70	69	74	280	17,727.83
Gareth Maybin	68	70	68	74	280	17,727.83
Scott Hend	68	72	71	70	281	14,552.70
Clint Rice	67	71	73	70	281	14,552.70
Andrew Coltart	72	69	72	68	281	14,552.70
Anthony Kang	67	67	77	71	282	12,700.53
Marcus Fraser	70	71	70	71	282	12,700.53
David Howell	70	68	74	70	282	12,700.53
Jose Manuel Lara	71	70	74	67	282	12,700.53
Scott Laycock	68	71	70	74	283	10,054.59
Richard Finch	69	70	71	73	283	10,054.59
Gary Lockerbie	69	69	72	73	283	10,054.59
Brett Rumford	71	70	70	72	283	10,054.59
Simon Khan	68	73	72	70	283	10,054.59
Alistair Presnell	72	68	73	70	283	10,054.59
Andre Stolz	69	67	72	76	284	7,937.83
Phillip Price	68	70	73	73	284	7,937.83
James Kamte	73	67	74	70	284	7,937.83
David Frost	73	64	70	78	285	7,011.75
Mikko Ilonen	72	65	75	73	285	7,011.75
Magnus A. Carlsson	71	67	74	73	285	7,011.75
Marcel Siem	72	69	73	71	285	7,011.75
Richie Ramsay	68	73	76	70	287	6,350.27
Darren Beck	70	70	78	71	289	6,085.67
Benn Barham	68	72	82	70	292	5,821.08
Kim Hyung-sung	68	71	77	77	293	5,424.18
Anton Haig	69	72	79	73	293	5,424.18
Michael Long	74	67	77	76	294	5,027.30
Robert Dinwiddie	71	70	70		DQ	4,847.37

Moonah Classic

Moonah Links, Fingal, Victoria
Par 36-36–72; 7,241 yards

February 26-March 1
purse, US$600,000

	SCORES				TOTAL	MONEY
Alistair Presnell	72	67	72	68	279	A$166,153.86
Peter O'Malley	68	70	72	70	280	94,153.85
Michael Sim	69	67	76	70	282	62,307.70
Terry Pilkadaris	70	67	76	70	283	36,000
Skip Kendall	77	67	69	70	283	36,000
Adam Bland	71	70	71	71	283	36,000
Daniel Summerhays	68	70	73	72	283	36,000
Phil Tataurangi	73	71	71	69	284	22,707.69
Paul Sheehan	73	71	69	71	284	22,707.69
Martin Piller	73	71	69	71	284	22,707.69
Steven Conran	71	67	74	72	284	22,707.69
David Smail	71	68	71	74	284	22,707.69
Ryan Haller	73	71	72	69	285	14,473.84
Fran Quinn	72	67	75	71	285	14,473.84
Gareth Paddison	74	68	72	71	285	14,473.84
Dustin White	73	66	72	74	285	14,473.84
Miguel Angel Carballo	68	68	71	78	285	14,473.84
Andrew Tschudin	71	69	73	73	286	10,257.69
Hunter Haas	68	70	74	74	286	10,257.69
Alex Prugh	73	68	71	74	286	10,257.69
Richie Gallichan	71	68	70	77	286	10,257.69

	SCORES				TOTAL	MONEY
Jason Enloe	71	69	76	71	287	8,241.75
Kyle Reifers	69	74	73	71	287	8,241.75
Steve Friesen	75	68	72	72	287	8,241.75
Stephen Dartnall	72	68	74	73	287	8,241.75
Brenden Pappas	71	69	73	74	287	8,241.75
Leigh McKechnie	71	72	70	74	287	8,241.75
Craig Spence	71	73	68	75	287	8,241.75

HSBC New Zealand PGA Championship

Clearwater Resort, Christchurch, New Zealand
Par 36-36–72; 7,122 yards

March 5-8
purse, US$600,000

	SCORES				TOTAL	MONEY
Steven Alker	69	70	67	67	273	US$113,684.26
Josh Geary	72	65	71	67	275	53,526.34
David Smail	68	71	68	68	275	53,526.34
Henrik Bjornstad	71	70	68	67	276	26,105.27
Ryan Hietala	71	67	69	69	276	26,105.27
Michael Sim	71	66	72	67	276	26,105.27
Gavin Coles	70	68	71	68	277	17,842.11
Steve Friesen	69	67	69	72	277	17,842.11
Jason Norris	73	65	70	69	277	17,842.11
Josh Teater	67	68	75	67	277	17,842.11
*Danny Lee	71	67	69	70	277	
Kurt Barnes	64	71	71	72	278	12,631.58
Craig Bowden	69	68	70	71	278	12,631.58
Gareth Paddison	67	68	74	69	278	12,631.58
Anthony Brown	72	69	70	68	279	9,145.27
Matthew Griffin	69	68	72	70	279	9,145.27
Peter O'Malley	69	67	73	70	279	9,145.27
Geoffrey Sisk	72	67	71	69	279	9,145.27
Brian Stuard	70	68	70	71	279	9,145.27
Chad Ginn	71	69	74	66	280	6,831.58
Brad Kennedy	71	67	74	68	280	6,831.58
Craig Parry	71	68	71	70	280	6,831.58
Joe Daley	70	70	71	70	281	5,974.74
Alistair Presnell	67	74	70	70	281	5,974.74
Peter Senior	69	71	71	70	281	5,974.74
Paul Sheehan	70	71	71	69	281	5,974.74
Andre Stolz	67	74	72	68	281	5,974.74

Michael Hill New Zealand Open

The Hills Golf Club, Queenstown, New Zealand
Par 36-36–72; 7,243 yards

March 12-15
purse, US$600,000

	SCORES				TOTAL	MONEY
Alex Prugh	65	71	69	64	269	A$165,087.18
Martin Piller	67	69	68	68	272	93,549.40
Jim Herman	68	73	65	68	274	61,907.69
Andrew Bonhomme	73	69	68	66	276	32,406
Craig Parry	72	70	65	69	276	32,406
Jeff Gove	71	63	72	70	276	32,406
Josh Geary	72	65	68	71	276	32,406
Peter Senior	68	73	67	68	276	32,406
Stephen Dartnall	67	69	72	68	276	32,406

		SCORES			TOTAL	MONEY
Adam Bland	68	71	71	67	277	20,483.04
Jason Norris	69	65	71	72	277	20,483.04
Richard Johnson	70	72	65	70	277	20,483.04
Chad Collins	68	73	69	68	278	12,519.11
David McKenzie	68	72	70	68	278	12,519.11
Henrik Bjornstad	70	67	68	73	278	12,519.11
Joe Daley	75	68	68	67	278	12,519.11
Matt Every	71	68	68	71	278	12,519.11
Michael Wright	73	67	69	69	278	12,519.11
Steve Friesen	69	68	71	70	278	12,519.11
Steven Alker	68	67	72	71	278	12,519.11
Todd Demsey	65	73	70	70	278	12,519.11
Jonas Blixt	68	71	67	73	279	9,110.37
Michael Long	72	70	68	69	279	9,110.37
Roger Tambellini	74	67	67	71	279	9,110.37
David Smail	74	67	70	69	280	7,497.71
Drew Laning	69	68	69	74	280	7,497.71
Kevin Johnson	73	69	72	66	280	7,497.71
Marcus Fraser	71	72	66	71	280	7,497.71

John Hughes Geely WA Open

Cottesloe Golf Club, Swanbourne, Western Australia
Par 36-36–72; 6,633 yards

October 22-25
purse, A$110,000

		SCORES			TOTAL	MONEY
Michael Curtain	71	68	66	67	272	A$16,500
Kim Felton	71	68	69	68	276	10,450
Adam Blyth	70	69	71	67	277	5,390
Anthony Brown	68	67	71	71	277	5,390
Michael Hendry	66	68	71	72	277	5,390
Steven Jones	70	70	68	69	277	5,390
Craig Scott	72	71	71	66	280	3,272.50
Craig Spence	68	69	73	70	280	3,272.50
Andrew Bonhomme	71	67	69	74	281	2,438.33
*Brady Watt	69	73	74	65	281	
David Diaz	71	69	73	68	281	2,438.33
Martin Doyle	65	72	74	70	281	2,438.33
*Matt Jager	68	70	71	72	281	
Ashley Hall	71	68	74	69	282	1,796.67
*Brody Ninyette	72	68	72	70	282	
Clint Rice	67	70	74	71	282	1,796.67
Joshua Carmichael	72	72	68	70	282	1,796.67
Ben Wharton	70	71	70	72	283	1,402.50
Chris Downes	74	69	69	71	283	1,402.50
Ryan Haywood	70	73	67	73	283	1,402.50
Tim Wise	69	71	72	71	283	1,402.50
Brad Shilton	70	71	73	70	284	1,221
Jarrod Moseley	73	71	69	71	284	1,221
Leigh McKechnie	73	70	69	72	284	1,221
Adam Stephens	72	69	73	71	285	1,100
Damian Chatterley	74	69	73	69	285	1,100
Jason Shinc	70	71	74	70	285	1,100
Justin Maker	70	69	71	75	285	1,100
Michael Long	70	71	77	67	285	1,100
Scott Laycock	71	73	72	69	285	1,100
Stuart Bouvier	69	70	71	75	285	1,100

Laurance Scrap Metals WA PGA Championship

Bunbury Golf Club, Clifton Park, Western Australia   October 29-November 1
Par 36-36–72; 6,640 yards   purse, A$110,000

	SCORES				TOTAL	MONEY
Andrew Bonhomme	70	72	70	69	281	A$16,500
David Diaz	69	70	74	69	282	9,075
Hamish Robertson	68	70	70	74	282	9,075
Michael Curtain	68	67	79	69	283	5,005
Scott Laycock	71	70	69	73	283	5,005
Adam Crawford	71	72	70	71	284	3,657.50
Andre Stolz	74	69	69	72	284	3,657.50
Damian Chatterley	72	68	68	77	285	2,731.67
Jason Norris	71	70	70	74	285	2,731.67
Peter Wilson	67	71	74	73	285	2,731.67
Ben Wharton	71	73	67	75	286	1,897.50
Jason Shine	72	73	68	73	286	1,897.50
Michael Foster	71	72	71	72	286	1,897.50
Steve Collins	67	71	72	76	286	1,897.50
Ashley Hall	65	77	74	71	287	1,372.80
Craig Scott	71	74	70	72	287	1,372.80
Kim Felton	74	71	71	71	287	1,372.80
Leighton Lyle	69	71	71	76	287	1,372.80
Michael Long	73	73	72	69	287	1,372.80
John Onions	72	71	75	71	289	1,204.50
Shaun Harmer	72	64	77	76	289	1,204.50
Anthony Brown	74	70	71	75	290	1,122
*Brenton Haines	74	71	70	75	290	
Neil Sarkies	71	74	72	73	290	1,122
Nick Cullen	69	70	76	75	290	1,122
Tigh Van-Leeuwen	69	77	72	72	290	1,122
Timothy Wood	73	72	69	76	290	1,122

Cellarbrations Queensland PGA Championship

City Golf Club, Toowoomba, Queensland   November 5-8
Par 35-35-70   purse, A$110,000

	SCORES				TOTAL	MONEY
Steven Bowditch	64	64	63	69	260	A$16,500
Clint Rice	67	69	66	64	266	10,450
Michael Hendry	70	65	64	68	267	7,700
Michael Wright	68	68	67	66	269	5,500
Brad McIntosh	71	61	68	70	270	4,510
Adam Blyth	69	64	66	72	271	3,657.50
Steve Collins	64	68	69	70	271	3,657.50
Eddie Barr	64	69	66	73	272	2,731.67
Jason Norris	67	66	68	71	272	2,731.67
Marcus Cain	68	69	67	68	272	2,731.67
Bradley Andrews	69	68	66	70	273	1,826
Kurt Carlson	69	67	69	68	273	1,826
Michael Choi	67	68	68	70	273	1,826
Rowan Beste	69	68	69	67	273	1,826
Ryan Haywood	70	67	67	69	273	1,826
Andrew Bonhomme	68	72	65	69	274	1,430
Aaron Pike	69	71	66	69	275	1,260.60
Edward Stedman	67	68	71	69	275	1,260.60
Euan Walters	68	68	69	70	275	1,260.60
Justin Maker	71	69	67	68	275	1,260.60

	SCORES				TOTAL	MONEY
Richard Backwell	69	66	67	73	275	1,260.60
Grant Moorhead	70	66	65	75	276	1,133
Michael Foster	71	67	63	75	276	1,133
Sam Brazel	71	68	69	68	276	1,133
Scott Laycock	66	71	68	71	276	1,133

JBWere Masters

Kingston Heath Golf Club, Melbourne, Victoria
Par 36-36–72; 7,059 yards

November 12-15
purse, A$1,500,000

	SCORES				TOTAL	MONEY
Tiger Woods	66	68	72	68	274	A$270,000
Greg Chalmers	68	69	69	70	276	153,000
Francois Delamontagne	71	70	68	69	278	86,625
Jason Dufner	70	67	71	70	278	86,625
James Nitties	66	71	69	73	279	60,000
Adam Scott	71	71	69	69	280	51,000
Cameron Percy	67	72	69	72	280	51,000
Stuart Appleby	69	70	71	71	281	43,500
Alejandro Canizares	73	72	69	68	282	37,000
Craig Scott	71	72	70	69	282	37,000
Klas Eriksson	71	73	66	72	282	37,000
Alistair Presnell	72	73	66	72	283	28,500
Ashley Hall	69	69	72	73	283	28,500
Bernd Wiesberger	72	67	72	73	284	23,700
Rod Pampling	71	70	70	73	284	23,700
Michael Sim	70	71	69	74	284	23,700
Aaron Baddeley	73	68	76	68	285	17,643.75
Leigh McKechnie	73	71	69	72	285	17,643.75
Seve Benson	71	71	70	73	285	17,643.75
Tim Wilkinson	71	71	67	76	285	17,643.75
Steve Jones	72	75	70	69	286	14,400
Pelle Edberg	71	73	71	71	286	14,400
Steven Bowditch	71	68	75	72	286	14,400
Mathew Goggin	68	70	74	74	286	14,400
Scott Laycock	72	68	70	76	286	14,400
Adam Bland	72	75	73	67	287	11,100
Heath Reed	77	68	74	68	287	11,100
Craig Spence	72	75	72	68	287	11,100
Kurt Barnes	70	73	75	69	287	11,100
Richard Bland	71	73	73	70	287	11,100
Richard Green	72	71	72	72	287	11,100
Geoff Ogilvy	72	73	71	72	288	8,850
David McKenzie	70	72	73	73	288	8,850
Matthew Griffin	71	75	69	73	288	8,850
Manny Villegas	70	68	76	74	288	8,850
Craig Parry	70	76	73	70	289	7,050
Ewan Porter	71	76	70	72	289	7,050
Peter O'Malley	71	74	71	73	289	7,050
Michael Long	71	75	70	73	289	7,050
Gary Murphy	71	73	71	74	289	7,050
Branden Grace	66	75	73	75	289	7,050
Rick Kulacz	69	76	69	75	289	7,050
Wade Ormsby	71	69	73	76	289	7,050
Aaron Townsend	75	72	74	69	290	4,800
Matthew Millar	71	76	72	71	290	4,800
Lee Slattery	69	74	75	72	290	4,800
John Senden	73	69	75	73	290	4,800
Andrew Tampion	71	75	71	73	290	4,800

	SCORES				TOTAL	MONEY
Andre Stolz	71	74	70	75	290	4,800
Peter Nolan	68	72	74	76	290	4,800
Ryan Haller	70	74	76	71	291	2,962.50
Paul Sheehan	73	72	74	72	291	2,962.50
Doug Holloway	67	74	77	73	291	2,962.50
Peter Wilson	73	73	72	73	291	2,962.50
Michael Wright	73	73	71	74	291	2,962.50
Sam Little	71	71	73	76	291	2,962.50
Marcus Fraser	74	73	76	69	292	2,415
*Matthew Giles	74	69	77	72	292	
Marc Leishman	72	73	74	73	292	2,415
Terry Pilkadaris	75	72	72	73	292	2,415
Adam Groom	73	70	75	74	292	2,415
Callum Macaulay	75	71	71	75	292	2,415
Andrew Bonhomme	73	74	73	73	293	2,295
Anthony Brown	72	72	72	77	293	2,295
Josh Younger	72	73	71	77	293	2,295
Terry Price	73	72	80	69	294	2,205
Miles Tunnicliff	74	72	75	73	294	2,205
Jason Norris	73	74	71	76	294	2,205
Mahal Pearce	71	68	77	79	295	2,115
Aaron Pike	74	73	72	77	296	2,070
Rohan Blizard	69	76	77	75	297	2,040
Frank Power	74	70	76	78	298	1,995
Andrew Tschudin	73	72	74	79	298	1,995
Damien Jordan	69	78	79	73	299	1,935
Simon Furneaux	73	74	77	75	299	1,935
Kim Felton	76	71	77	76	300	1,890
Ryan Hammond	75	72	77	78	302	1,860

Cellarbrations NSW PGA Championship

Wollongong Golf Club, Wollogong, New South Wales
Par 35-35-70

November 19-22
purse, A$110,000

	SCORES				TOTAL	MONEY
Aaron Townsend	67	61	65	66	259	A$16,500
Scott Arnold	68	67	61	66	262	9,075
Michael Wright	66	62	64	70	262	9,075
Peter Wilson	65	64	65	70	264	5,500
Michael Hendry	64	70	64	67	265	4,180
Josh Lane	70	61	66	68	265	4,180
*Brendan Smith	65	66	66	68	265	
Rudi Bezuidenhout	69	62	68	67	266	3,465
Ben Wharton	67	65	70	65	267	2,731.66
Michael Long	66	66	68	67	267	2,731.66
Aaron Pike	64	65	66	72	267	2,731.66
Brad Andrews	70	65	69	64	268	1,980
Mathew Holten	69	69	64	66	268	1,980
Luke Hickmott	68	62	66	72	268	1,980
Brent McCullough	69	64	68	68	269	1,490.50
Josh Carmichael	69	63	68	69	269	1,490.50
Brad McIntosh	67	67	66	69	269	1,490.50
Gene Saunders	70	64	65	70	269	1,490.50
Steve Collins	67	69	67	67	270	1,276
Ryan Haller	69	66	67	68	270	1,276
Grant Scott	68	65	69	69	271	1,168.20
Nick Cullen	67	70	65	69	271	1,168.20
Craig Scott	67	66	68	70	271	1,168.20
Steven Jeffress	71	64	66	70	271	1,168.20
Kurt Barnes	68	70	62	71	271	1,168.20

NSW Open

Vintage Golf Resort, Hunter Valley, New South Wales
Par 71

November 26-29
purse, A$135,000

	SCORES				TOTAL	MONEY
Leigh McKechnie	70	72	70	69	281	A$20,250
James Nitties	65	68	73	76	282	12,825
Scott Arnold	66	80	71	66	283	9,450
Mark Purser	66	73	74	71	284	6,142.50
Jason Norris	70	71	64	79	284	6,142.50
Craig Scott	67	70	76	73	286	3,807
Andrew Bonhomme	68	71	74	73	286	3,807
Brad McIntosh	70	72	71	73	286	3,807
Simon Furneaux	70	73	70	73	286	3,807
Rohan Blizard	71	70	67	78	286	3,807
Matthew Guyatt	72	71	74	70	287	2,328.75
Marcus Cain	69	74	72	72	287	2,328.75
Doug Holloway	65	74	75	73	287	2,328.75
Heath Reed	65	74	71	77	287	2,328.75
Scott Adland	74	69	72	73	288	1,764
Richie Gallichan	71	72	71	74	288	1,764
Tim Wilkinson	70	73	70	75	288	1,764
Andrew McKenzie	68	75	74	72	289	1,487.25
Anthony Brown	70	72	74	73	289	1,487.25
Peter Wilson	68	75	73	73	289	1,487.25
Steve Collins	71	75	70	73	289	1,487.25
Brent McCullough	67	74	73	75	289	1,487.25
Troy Kennedy	72	71	69	77	289	1,487.25
Justin Maker	72	71	74	73	290	1,309.50
Steven Horstmann	68	76	72	74	290	1,309.50
Ricky Schmidt	75	69	70	76	290	1,309.50
Michael Light	70	75	69	76	290	1,309.50
Andre Stolz	70	74	68	78	290	1,309.50
Aaron Pike	68	70	72	80	290	1,309.50

Australian Open

New South Wales Golf Club, Sydney, New South Wales
Par 36-36–72; 6,921 yards

December 3-6
purse, A$1,500,000

	SCORES				TOTAL	MONEY
Adam Scott	68	66	67	72	273	A$270,000
Stuart Appleby	66	66	71	75	278	153,000
Bryce Molder	70	72	72	68	282	77,750
Michael Long	69	75	68	70	282	77,750
Nick O'Hern	69	68	71	74	282	77,750
Michael Sim	71	70	71	71	283	54,000
Cameron Percy	74	75	66	69	284	44,000
Rod Pampling	74	71	70	69	284	44,000
Jarrod Lyle	69	68	74	73	284	44,000
Peter O'Malley	69	74	70	72	285	35,250
David Oh	68	73	69	75	285	35,250
Terry Pilkadaris	71	70	76	69	286	24,600
Chris Campbell	71	69	73	73	286	24,600
Tim Wilkinson	73	67	72	74	286	24,600
Richard Green	73	71	67	75	286	24,600
Scott Strange	72	70	68	76	286	24,600
James Nitties	67	72	70	77	286	24,600
Henry Epstein	76	72	72	67	287	17,025

	SCORES				TOTAL	MONEY
Craig Parry	80	67	69	71	287	17,025
Leigh McKechnie	70	72	74	71	287	17,025
Michael Brennan	69	73	75	71	288	15,300
Brad Kennedy	75	70	70	73	288	15,300
Greg Chalmers	70	72	72	74	288	15,300
Paul Sheehan	74	74	72	69	289	13,087.50
Stephen Allan	68	77	74	70	289	13,087.50
Paul Gow	78	69	69	73	289	13,087.50
Mathew Goggin	73	71	71	74	289	13,087.50

Australian PGA Championship

Hyatt Regency Resort, Coolum Beach, Queensland
Par 71; 6,852 yards

December 10-13
purse, A$1,500,000

	SCORES				TOTAL	MONEY
Robert Allenby	70	68	66	66	270	A$270,000
John Senden	73	67	67	67	274	127,125
Scott Strange	67	70	68	69	274	127,125
Marc Leishman	70	71	66	68	275	72,000
Nick O'Hern	70	70	69	67	276	57,000
Michael Sim	71	70	65	70	276	57,000
Rod Pampling	73	69	70	65	277	42,375
Stuart Appleby	67	69	73	68	277	42,375
Josh Geary	70	73	66	68	277	42,375
Geoff Ogilvy	70	66	70	71	277	42,375
Mathew Goggin	70	72	68	68	278	33,000
Chan Shih-ching	68	70	71	70	279	27,500
Matthew Griffin	67	68	73	71	279	27,500
Adam Scott	68	70	68	73	279	27,500
Jason Norris	69	67	76	68	280	18,825
Kyle Stanley	71	71	70	68	280	18,825
Bryce Molder	73	69	70	68	280	18,825
Brad Kennedy	76	66	69	69	280	18,825
Chris Campbell	72	67	71	70	280	18,825
Stephen Dartnall	68	73	69	70	280	18,825
Aron Price	74	69	67	70	280	18,825
Scott Laycock	76	66	68	71	281	15,150
Cameron Percy	72	69	67	73	281	15,150
Mahal Pearce	73	70	69	70	282	13,087.50
Paul Sheehan	73	68	69	72	282	13,087.50
Anthony Brown	71	71	68	72	282	13,087.50
Greg Chalmers	68	70	67	77	282	13,087.50
Heath Reed	70	75	69	69	283	9,814.28
Adam Crawford	71	71	70	71	283	9,814.28
Gavin Flint	71	71	70	71	283	9,814.28
Marcus Both	70	72	69	72	283	9,814.28
Brett Rumford	70	70	70	73	283	9,814.28
Stephen Leaney	71	70	69	73	283	9,814.28
Michael Curtain	73	65	71	74	283	9,814.28

African Tours

Joburg Open

Royal Johannesburg & Kensington Golf Club,
Johannesburg, South Africa
Par 36-35–71; 7,590 yards

January 8-11
purse, €1,174,350

	SCORES				TOTAL	MONEY
Anders Hansen	71	68	64	66	269	R2,256,089
Andrew McLardy	65	68	69	68	270	1,636,910
David Drysdale	65	66	71	69	271	984,992.80
Danny Willett	67	66	71	68	272	596,879.06
Tyrone van Aswegen	69	65	70	68	272	596,879.06
Charl Schwartzel	68	71	63	70	272	596,879.06
Richard McEvoy	69	65	72	67	273	359,171.26
David Dixon	68	69	68	68	273	359,171.26
Joakim Haeggman	69	68	66	70	273	359,171.26
Estanislao Goya	70	69	69	66	274	266,887.50
Louis Oosthuizen	71	66	67	70	274	266,887.50
Charl Coetzee	68	67	75	65	275	201,233.17
Richard Sterne	71	66	70	68	275	201,233.17
Jaco Van Zyl	67	70	69	69	275	201,233.17
Taco Remkes	67	70	69	69	275	201,233.17
Graham DeLaet	72	66	68	69	275	201,233.17
Michael Hoey	64	68	72	71	275	201,233.17
James Kamte	69	69	66	71	275	201,233.17
Thomas Aiken	69	69	66	71	275	201,233.17
Brett Liddle	67	70	69	70	276	162,742.06
Jean Hugo	67	72	67	70	276	162,742.06
Rafael Cabrera-Bello	65	69	70	72	276	162,742.06
Jeppe Huldahl	67	73	71	66	277	145,186.80
Anthony Snobeck	72	64	70	71	277	145,186.80
Oliver Bekker	67	65	73	72	277	145,186.80
Klas Eriksson	69	69	67	72	277	145,186.80
Retief Goosen	70	68	65	74	277	145,186.80
Steven Jeppesen	63	76	72	67	278	121,599.02
Jan-Are Larsen	66	69	75	68	278	121,599.02
Gary Lockerbie	69	68	72	69	278	121,599.02
Brandon Pieters	68	71	70	69	278	121,599.02
James Kingston	71	69	67	71	278	121,599.02
Lorenzo Gagli	70	67	69	72	278	121,599.02
Martin Maritz	66	72	68	72	278	121,599.02
Maarten Lafeber	66	72	72	69	279	106,755
Carlos Del Moral	69	66	72	72	279	106,755
Alan McLean	71	65	71	72	279	106,755
Martin Wiegele	68	72	72	68	280	91,097.60
Chris Gane	70	70	71	69	280	91,097.60
James Morrison	67	68	74	71	280	91,097.60
Bernd Wiesberger	72	64	73	71	280	91,097.60
Mikko Korhonen	69	69	71	71	280	91,097.60
Dion Fourie	68	70	71	71	280	91,097.60
Jesus Maria Arruti	74	65	70	71	280	91,097.60
Gary Clark	72	67	68	73	280	91,097.60
Eirik Tage Johansen	73	65	75	68	281	71,170
Andre Bossert	70	69	74	68	281	71,170
Carl Suneson	67	73	72	69	281	71,170
Cameron Johnston	72	66	73	70	281	71,170
Doug McGuigan	69	71	70	71	281	71,170

	SCORES				TOTAL	MONEY
John Mellor	72	67	70	72	281	71,170
Hennie Otto	67	73	75	67	282	55,512.60
Phillip Archer	69	70	73	70	282	55,512.60
Darren Fichardt	68	70	73	71	282	55,512.60
Tyrone Ferreira	68	72	70	72	282	55,512.60
Antti Ahokas	72	64	72	74	282	55,512.60
Wallie Coetsee	72	64	76	71	283	41,990.30
Alexandre Rocha	67	71	74	71	283	41,990.30
Edoardo Molinari	65	71	74	73	283	41,990.30
Alfredo Garcia-Heredia	65	71	73	74	283	41,990.30
Iain Pyman	71	69	69	74	283	41,990.30
Michiel Bothma	70	70	69	74	283	41,990.30
Simon Griffiths	73	64	71	75	283	41,990.30
Keith Horne	68	70	70	75	283	41,990.30
Raphael Jacquelin	71	65	78	70	284	29,352.77
T.C. Charamba	70	67	77	70	284	29,352.77
Ulrich van den Berg	70	70	73	71	284	29,352.77
Christopher Doak	68	70	74	72	284	29,352.77
Jake Roos	69	69	73	73	284	29,352.77
Chris Wood	69	70	72	73	284	29,352.77
Carlos Rodiles	69	71	71	73	284	29,352.77
Kevin Stone	69	70	71	74	284	29,352.77
Bobby Lincoln	68	72	73	72	285	21,273.36
Kasper Linnet Jorgensen	68	72	74	72	286	21,195.72
Neil Cheetham	73	67	73	73	286	21,195.72
Michele Reale	66	74	73	73	286	21,195.72
David Carter	67	72	73	75	287	21,118.08
Mike Curtis	74	65	75	74	288	21,059.85
Sam Little	72	68	74	74	288	21,059.85
John E. Morgan	69	70	72	78	289	21,001.62
Edrich Jansen	70	70	73	77	290	20,962.80
Gregory Molteni	73	65	77	76	291	20,923.98
Henrik Nystrom	68	72	79	73	292	20,885.16

Africa Open

East London Golf Club, East London, South Africa
Par 36-36–72; 6,740 yards

January 15-18
purse, R5,000,000

	SCORES				TOTAL	MONEY
Retief Goosen	66	70	66	65	267	R792,500
Branden Grace	69	68	66	65	268	343,250
Michael Hoey	68	68	66	66	268	343,250
Darren Fichardt	65	68	67	68	268	343,250
Darren Clarke	67	65	66	70	268	343,250
James Kingston	66	67	65	73	271	177,000
Mark Murless	71	68	69	64	272	147,500
Richard Sterne	72	67	61	73	273	123,000
Ulrich van den Berg	70	67	67	70	274	98,500
Charl Schwartzel	65	73	65	71	274	98,500
Angel Cabrera	62	68	72	72	274	98,500
Graham DeLaet	63	74	64	74	275	83,500
Steve van Vuuren	71	66	70	69	276	76,000
Alex Haindl	66	67	72	71	276	76,000
Brandon Pieters	71	68	70	68	277	68,500
Jaco Van Zyl	73	66	70	68	277	68,500
Marc Cayeux	68	66	69	74	277	68,500
Keith Horne	71	67	68	72	278	62,250
Christiaan Basson	69	70	65	74	278	62,250
Louis de Jager	69	73	69	68	279	55,600

	SCORES				TOTAL	MONEY
Tyrone Mordt	70	73	66	70	279	55,600
Deane Pappas	67	70	69	73	279	55,600
Warren Abery	67	68	70	74	279	55,600
Dawie Van der Walt	68	68	69	74	279	55,600
Louis Moolman	70	71	69	70	280	49,500
Trevor Fisher, Jr.	74	69	67	70	280	49,500
Grant Muller	69	67	71	73	280	49,500
Garth Mulroy	70	72	70	69	281	45,000
Martin Maritz	69	73	69	70	281	45,000
Paulo Pinto	68	69	73	71	281	45,000

Dimension Data Pro-Am

Gary Player Country Club: Par 36-36–72; 7,831 yards
Lost City Golf Course: Par 36-36–72; 6,983 yards
Sun City, South Africa

January 22-25
purse, R1,800,000

	SCORES				TOTAL	MONEY
Deane Pappas	65	66	69	68	268	R285,300
James Kamte	72	67	70	67	276	207,000
Dawie Van der Walt	65	73	72	67	277	124,560
Peter Karmis	69	69	73	68	279	88,380
Jbe' Kruger	70	68	73	69	280	63,720
Jake Roos	71	72	66	71	280	63,720
Martin Maritz	65	73	68	74	280	63,720
Garth Mulroy	67	72	75	67	281	41,580
David Drysdale	70	72	68	71	281	41,580
Branden Grace	70	71	74	67	282	33,750
Marc Cayeux	74	68	68	72	282	33,750
Adilson da Silva	72	72	68	71	283	26,460
George Coetzee	70	73	71	69	283	26,460
Jaco Van Zyl	72	68	73	70	283	26,460
Brandon Pieters	72	68	71	72	283	26,460
Ulrich van den Berg	69	72	70	72	283	26,460
Lindani Ndwandwe	66	72	71	74	283	26,460
Justin Walters	72	68	74	70	284	22,020
Bradley Davison	73	68	74	69	284	22,020
Darren Fichardt	67	69	73	75	284	22,020
Neil Cheetham	71	66	75	73	285	19,980
Neil Schietekat	69	73	76	67	285	19,980
Trevor Fisher, Jr.	73	64	74	74	285	19,980
Tyrone van Aswegen	66	71	76	73	286	17,550
Christiaan Basson	75	66	73	72	286	17,550
Grant Muller	73	72	70	71	286	17,550
Mark Murless	71	72	73	70	286	17,550
Keith Horne	66	72	73	75	286	17,550
Kevin Stone	66	74	71	75	286	17,550
Jaco Ahlers	69	74	70	74	287	14,940
Cameron Johnston	73	68	72	74	287	14,940
Bobby Lincoln	68	73	73	73	287	14,940
Doug McGuigan	71	69	75	72	287	14,940
Jean Hugo	71	73	72	71	287	14,940

Nashua Masters

Wild Coast Sun Country Club, Port Edward, Natal
Par 35-35–70; 6,351 yards

January 29-February 1
purse, R1,200,000

		SCORES			TOTAL	MONEY
Darren Fichardt	66	67	65	65	263	R190,200
Marc Cayeux	66	66	65	67	264	138,000
Branden Grace	68	70	68	62	268	63,840
Tyrone van Aswegen	70	66	65	67	268	63,840
Jaco Van Zyl	68	69	64	67	268	63,840
Titch Moore	66	70	65	68	269	42,480
Charl Coetzee	71	70	65	64	270	32,460
Alan Michell	68	67	69	66	270	32,460
Bradford Vaughan	68	72	66	65	271	23,640
Thomas Aiken	67	70	68	66	271	23,640
Lindani Ndwandwe	69	69	65	68	271	23,640
Michiel Bothma	69	68	70	65	272	18,390
Andre Bossert	71	69	67	65	272	18,390
Warren Abery	69	69	66	68	272	18,390
Adilson da Silva	69	67	67	69	272	18,390
Chris Williams	68	70	70	65	273	15,540
Louis Moolman	70	68	69	66	273	15,540
Nic Henning	70	67	69	67	273	15,540
David Drysdale	67	66	67	73	273	15,540
Clinton Whitelaw	68	69	70	67	274	13,720
Mark Murless	70	69	68	67	274	13,720
Doug McGuigan	68	70	66	70	274	13,720
Robert Wiederkehr	73	68	67	67	275	12,780
Justin Walters	68	71	67	69	275	12,780
Ricky Lee	66	68	75	67	276	11,700
Christiaan Basson	69	67	72	68	276	11,700
Mark Williams	75	65	68	68	276	11,700
Riaan de Bruyn	66	68	71	71	276	11,700

Vodacom Championship

Pretoria Country Club, Pretoria, South Africa
Par 36-36–72; 7,063 yards

February 12-15
purse, R2,650,000

		SCORES			TOTAL	MONEY
Anders Hansen	69	70	66	65	270	R420,025
Charl Schwartzel	69	65	70	70	274	244,065
Graham DeLaet	70	68	65	71	274	244,065
Charl Coetzee	66	76	66	67	275	119,780
Titch Moore	69	66	69	71	275	119,780
Brandon Pieters	69	69	70	68	276	79,058.33
Alan McLean	71	69	68	68	276	79,058.33
Jaco Ahlers	68	66	72	70	276	79,058.33
Jean Hugo	69	69	72	67	277	50,217.50
Branden Grace	69	70	69	69	277	50,217.50
Thomas Aiken	73	69	66	69	277	50,217.50
Michiel Bothma	64	71	69	73	277	50,217.50
Trevor Fisher, Jr.	70	68	74	66	278	38,623.75
Mark Murless	70	69	71	68	278	38,623.75
Adilson da Silva	69	74	67	68	278	38,623.75
Louis de Jager	67	70	70	71	278	38,623.75
Ulrich van den Berg	75	65	69	70	279	33,058.75
Divan van den Heever	71	69	69	70	279	33,058.75
Tjaart van der Walt	67	70	71	71	279	33,058.75

	SCORES				TOTAL	MONEY
Darren Fichardt	69	71	66	73	279	33,058.75
Neil Schietekat	69	71	72	68	280	29,415
Dawie Van der Walt	68	71	72	69	280	29,415
Jake Roos	70	68	71	71	280	29,415
James Kingston	68	75	71	67	281	26,632.50
Andrew Curlewis	70	70	69	72	281	26,632.50
Deane Pappas	69	69	70	73	281	26,632.50
Bradford Vaughan	68	71	69	73	281	26,632.50

Telkom PGA Championship

The Country Club, Johannesburg, South Africa
Par 36-36–72; 7,512 yards

February 19-22
purse, R2,750,000

	SCORES				TOTAL	MONEY
Jaco Van Zyl	70	68	66	66	270	R435,875
Graham DeLaet	68	73	66	64	271	253,275
Trevor Fisher, Jr.	69	68	69	65	271	253,275
Jean Hugo	65	69	69	70	273	124,300
Thomas Aiken	65	71	66	71	273	124,300
Branden Grace	67	68	72	67	274	71,885
Anders Hansen	69	70	68	67	274	71,885
George Coetzee	69	70	67	68	274	71,885
Louis de Jager	69	67	69	69	274	71,885
Charl Coetzee	69	68	68	69	274	71,885
James Kingston	69	66	71	69	275	46,108.33
Michiel Bothma	68	70	68	69	275	46,108.33
Marc Cayeux	68	67	67	73	275	46,108.33
Dion Fourie	66	71	70	69	276	39,050
Kevin Stone	69	69	69	69	276	39,050
Peter Karmis	69	66	71	70	276	39,050
Keith Horne	72	67	73	65	277	33,715
Adilson da Silva	72	66	70	69	277	33,715
Jake Roos	72	68	68	69	277	33,715
Merrick Bremner	69	71	67	70	277	33,715
Titch Moore	68	69	69	71	277	33,715
Willie van der Merwe	71	72	68	67	278	29,700
Alan McLean	72	68	69	69	278	29,700
Tyrone Ferreira	69	67	70	72	278	29,700
Andrew Curlewis	69	71	71	68	279	26,812.50
Deane Pappas	70	71	69	69	279	26,812.50
Tyrone van Aswegen	68	68	72	71	279	26,812.50
Hennie Otto	67	70	70	72	279	26,812.50

Vodacom Business Origins of Golf - Bloemfontein

Bloemfontein Golf Club, Bloemfontein, South Africa
Par 36-36–72; 7,302 yards

April 1-3
purse, R480,000

	SCORES			TOTAL	MONEY
Trevor Fisher, Jr.	69	67	65	201	R76,080
Willie van der Merwe	71	67	64	202	46,800
Jean Hugo	65	67	70	202	46,800
Jaco Van Zyl	64	66	73	203	30,240
Titch Moore	70	65	69	204	20,400
Ryan Tipping	68	65	71	204	20,400
Hendrik Buhrmann	68	69	68	205	15,120

	SCORES			TOTAL	MONEY
Ross Wellington	69	69	68	206	11,460
Jake Roos	70	68	68	206	11,460
Alex Haindl	68	70	68	206	11,460
Adilson da Silva	68	69	69	206	11,460
James Kamte	65	73	69	207	9,120
Merrick Bremner	68	68	71	207	9,120
Divan van den Heever	70	64	73	207	9,120
Mark Murless	72	69	67	208	7,248
Jaco Ahlers	72	68	68	208	7,248
Neil Schietekat	68	71	69	208	7,248
Tyrone van Aswegen	69	69	70	208	7,248
Louis de Jager	69	69	70	208	7,248
Grant Muller	69	69	70	208	7,248
Clinton Whitelaw	72	65	71	208	7,248
Dean Lambert	72	70	67	209	5,844
Steve Basson	68	71	70	209	5,844
Oliver Bekker	68	70	71	209	5,844
David Hewan	71	67	71	209	5,844

SAA Pro-Am Invitational - Prince's Grant

Prince's Grant Golf Estate, KwaZulu-Natal, South Africa
Par 36-36–72; 6,775 yards

April 30-May 2
purse, R500,000

	SCORES			TOTAL	MONEY
Adilson da Silva	68	67	68	203	R79,250
Anton Haig	70	67	67	204	48,750
Darren Fichardt	68	66	70	204	48,750
Jbe' Kruger	73	68	64	205	27,500
Keith Horne	70	68	67	205	27,500
Desvonde Botes	66	70	71	207	16,166.66
Andre Cruse	70	66	71	207	16,166.66
Darryn Lloyd	65	70	72	207	16,166.66
Shaun Norris	70	69	69	208	12,250
Neil Cheetham	70	69	70	209	10,875
Willie van der Merwe	70	69	70	209	10,875
Cameron Johnston	71	73	66	210	9,262.50
Keenan Davidse	75	68	67	210	9,262.50
Albert Pistorius	70	69	71	210	9,262.50
Divan van den Heever	68	70	72	210	9,262.50
Charl Coetzee	72	72	67	211	7,250
Trevor Fisher, Jr.	74	70	67	211	7,250
Jake Roos	72	71	68	211	7,250
Warren Abery	71	72	68	211	7,250
Tyrone van Aswegen	73	70	68	211	7,250
Johan du Buisson	72	69	70	211	7,250
Christiaan Basson	69	71	71	211	7,250
Oliver Bekker	73	69	70	212	5,966.66
Ryan Thompson	70	70	72	212	5,966.66
Brett Liddle	67	73	72	212	5,966.66

Samsung Royal Swazi Sun Open

Royal Swazi Sun Country Club, Mbabane, Swaziland
Par 36-36–72; 6,715 yards

May 6-9
purse, R750,000

	POINTS				TOTAL	MONEY
Jaco Van Zyl	14	18	15	18	65	R118,875
T.C. Charamba	12	10	21	10	53	69,900
Tyrone van Aswegen	11	16	17	9	53	69,900
Titch Moore	4	22	16	5	47	37,875
Tyrone Ferreira	9	12	9	16	46	31,800
Theunis Spangenberg	15	13	4	13	45	24,937.50
Josh Cunliffe	4	12	19	10	45	24,937.50
Oliver Bekker	6	12	13	13	44	18,825
Grant Muller	7	8	13	15	43	14,589.50
Charl Coetzee	7	8	15	13	43	14,589.50
Shaun Norris	15	10	8	10	43	14,589.50
Jean Hugo	10	10	16	7	43	14,589.50
Trevor Fisher, Jr.	11	10	8	13	42	12,229
Dean Lambert	12	9	14	5	40	11,479
Jake Roos	14	5	9	9	37	11,104
Louis de Jager	7	10	13	6	36	10,729
Willie van der Merwe	0	11	15	9	35	10,166.50
Warren Abery	7	8	10	10	35	10,166.50
Christiaan Basson	5	11	6	12	34	9,679
George Coetzee	11	10	8	4	33	9,229
Neil Schietekat	13	7	10	3	33	9,229
Jbe' Kruger	11	11	1	9	32	8,741.50
Wallie Coetsee	2	13	8	9	32	8,741.50
Merrick Bremner	8	7	10	6	31	8,291.50
Chris Williams	2	7	14	8	31	8,291.50

Nashua Golf Challenge

Gary Player Country Club: Par 36-36–72; 7,831 yards
Lost City Golf Course: Par 36-36–72; 6,983 yards
Sun City, South Africa

May 14-16
purse, R500,000

	SCORES			TOTAL	MONEY
Doug McGuigan	66	70	73	209	R79,250
Tyrone van Aswegen	69	68	74	211	57,500
Jaco Van Zyl	70	73	69	212	28,500
Oliver Bekker	70	69	73	212	28,500
James Kamte	70	68	74	212	28,500
Neil Schietekat	73	63	76	212	28,500
Christiaan Basson	71	65	77	213	15,750
Desvonde Botes	73	70	71	214	13,000
Chris Williams	71	70	73	214	13,000
Adilson da Silva	73	72	70	215	10,312.50
Andrew Curlewis	68	74	73	215	10,312.50
Keith Horne	73	68	74	215	10,312.50
Jake Roos	71	69	75	215	10,312.50
Theunis Spangenberg	72	73	71	216	9,000
Mohamed Tayob	72	73	72	217	8,350
Warren Abery	69	75	73	217	8,350
Albert Pistorius	75	70	73	218	7,230
Andre Cruse	72	71	75	218	7,230
Grant Muller	72	71	75	218	7,230
Hendrik Buhrmann	71	70	77	218	7,230
Brandon Pieters	71	69	78	218	7,230

	SCORES			TOTAL	MONEY
Neil Cheetham	73	76	71	220	6,087.50
Darren Holder	71	74	75	220	6,087.50
Merrick Bremner	76	67	77	220	6,087.50
Wallie Coetsee	73	69	78	220	6,087.50

Vodacom Business Origins of Golf - Pretoria

Pretoria Country Club, Pretoria, South Africa — May 20-22
Par 36-36–72; 7,063 yards — purse, R480,000

	SCORES			TOTAL	MONEY
Brandon Pieters	65	67	72	204	R76,080
Darren Fichardt	68	67	70	205	55,200
Dean Lambert	72	69	66	207	38,400
Grant Muller	69	72	67	208	19,872
Keenan Davidse	68	73	67	208	19,872
Mark Murless	68	72	68	208	19,872
Desvonde Botes	68	72	68	208	19,872
Chris Williams	67	69	72	208	19,872
Peter Karmis	72	72	65	209	11,760
Adilson da Silva	70	70	70	210	10,440
Christiaan Basson	70	70	70	210	10,440
Tyrone van Aswegen	67	71	73	211	9,600
Brett Liddle	68	73	71	212	8,656
Jaco Ahlers	68	73	71	212	8,656
Doug McGuigan	70	69	73	212	8,656
Ulrich van den Berg	69	74	70	213	7,656
Andre Cruse	70	71	72	213	7,656
Louis de Jager	75	68	71	214	6,560
Jbe' Kruger	73	69	72	214	6,560
Oliver Bekker	73	69	72	214	6,560
Louis Moolman	70	72	72	214	6,560
Attie Schwartzel	71	69	74	214	6,560
Ockie Strydom	71	69	74	214	6,560
Lindani Ndwandwe	71	72	72	215	5,424
Jaco Van Zyl	71	70	74	215	5,424
Jean Hugo	68	71	76	215	5,424
Mohamed Tayob	71	67	77	215	5,424

Lombard Insurance Classic

Royal Swazi Sun Country Club, Mbabane, Swaziland — June 5-7
Par 36-36–72; 6,715 yards — purse, R500,000

	SCORES			TOTAL	MONEY
Peter Karmis	65	74	59	198	R79,250
Jaco Van Zyl	69	67	66	202	57,500
Jbe' Kruger	70	69	66	205	40,000
Andrew Curlewis	70	71	65	206	19,291.66
Darryn Lloyd	67	73	66	206	19,291.66
Oliver Bekker	67	73	66	206	19,291.66
Clinton Whitelaw	70	70	66	206	19,291.66
Shaun Norris	71	67	68	206	19,291.66
Christiaan Basson	68	69	69	206	19,291.66
Neil Schietekat	71	66	70	207	10,875
Bradford Vaughan	65	70	72	207	10,875
Jaco Ahlers	69	70	69	208	9,262.50

	SCORES			TOTAL	MONEY
Warren Abery	73	65	70	208	9,262.50
Keith Horne	65	73	70	208	9,262.50
Darren Fichardt	69	69	70	208	9,262.50
Titch Moore	68	71	70	209	7,662.50
Brett Liddle	69	68	72	209	7,662.50
Chris Williams	71	65	73	209	7,662.50
Jean Hugo	67	69	73	209	7,662.50
P.H. McIntyre	72	70	68	210	6,450
Desvonde Botes	70	70	70	210	6,450
Keenan Davidse	68	71	71	210	6,450
Ryan Cairns	70	69	71	210	6,450
Josh Cunliffe	68	71	71	210	6,450
Adilson da Silva	72	68	71	211	5,450
Dean Lambert	70	69	72	211	5,450
Grant Muller	66	71	74	211	5,450
Mark Murless	67	70	74	211	5,450

Vodacom Business Origins of Golf - Fancourt

Fancourt, Montagu Course, George, South Africa
Par 36-36–72; 7,342 yards
(Event shortened to 36 holes—rain.)

June 24-26
purse, R480,000

	SCORES		TOTAL	MONEY
Brandon Pieters	72	69	141	R76,080
Clinton Whitelaw	73	69	142	55,200
Callie Swart	70	73	143	38,400
Oliver Bekker	74	70	144	30,240
Darren Fichardt	72	73	145	18,640
Grant Muller	71	74	145	18,640
Attie Schwartzel	70	75	145	18,640
Jaco Ahlers	75	71	146	10,760
Albert Pistorius	75	71	146	10,760
Jbe' Kruger	75	71	146	10,760
Warren Abery	75	71	146	10,760
Bradford Vaughan	74	72	146	10,760
Adilson da Silva	74	72	146	10,760
Jacques Blaauw	76	71	147	7,563.42
Brett Liddle	76	71	147	7,563.42
Reggie Adams	76	71	147	7,563.42
Ryan Tipping	75	72	147	7,563.42
Theunis Spangenberg	77	70	147	7,563.42
Jaco Van Zyl	74	73	147	7,563.42
Callie Burger	73	74	147	7,563.42
Peter Karmis	76	72	148	6,192
Andrew Curlewis	75	73	148	6,192
Josh Cunliffe	74	74	148	6,192
Christiaan Basson	76	73	149	5,328
Johan du Buisson	77	72	149	5,328
David Hewan	75	74	149	5,328
Jean Hugo	75	74	149	5,328
Prinavin Nelson	74	75	149	5,328

Suncoast Classic

Durban Country Club, Durban, South Africa
Par 36-36–72; 6,732 yards

August 6-8
purse, R500,000

	SCORES			TOTAL	MONEY
Louis de Jager	68	68	71	207	R79,250
Chris Swanepoel	67	71	71	209	57,500
Adilson da Silva	70	71	69	210	28,500
Titch Moore	69	70	71	210	28,500
T.C. Charamba	65	74	71	210	28,500
Jean Hugo	71	66	73	210	28,500
Lindani Ndwandwe	75	68	68	211	14,750
Hendrik Buhrmann	67	75	69	211	14,750
Willie van der Merwe	71	73	68	212	10,700
Andrew Curlewis	72	71	69	212	10,700
Divan van den Heever	70	73	69	212	10,700
Peter Karmis	73	69	70	212	10,700
Ryan Cairns	73	64	75	212	10,700
Josh Cunliffe	73	72	68	213	8,566.66
Desvonde Botes	73	69	71	213	8,566.66
Jaco Van Zyl	71	67	75	213	8,566.66
Theunis Spangenberg	71	73	70	214	7,362.50
Dion Fourie	68	74	72	214	7,362.50
Grant Veenstra	68	73	73	214	7,362.50
Don Black	72	68	74	214	7,362.50
Ulrich van den Berg	71	74	70	215	6,700
Tyrone Mordt	69	76	71	216	5,668.75
Toto Thimba, Jr.	72	73	71	216	5,668.75
Steve van Vuuren	72	72	72	216	5,668.75
Vaughn Groenewald	74	70	72	216	5,668.75
Prinavin Nelson	70	74	72	216	5,668.75
Neil Cheetham	74	69	73	216	5,668.75
Brandon Pieters	71	72	73	216	5,668.75
Keenan Davidse	72	70	74	216	5,668.75

Vodacom Business Origins of Golf - Erinvale

Erinvale Golf Estate, Somerset West, South Africa
Par 36-36–72; 7,116 yards
(First round cancelled—rain.)

August 12-14
purse, R480,000

	SCORES		TOTAL	MONEY
Jaco Ahlers	64	71	135	R76,080
Ulrich van den Berg	67	68	135	55,200
(Ahlers defeated van den Berg on first playoff hole.)				
Jaco Van Zyl	71	65	136	38,400
Doug McGuigan	69	69	138	26,400
Reggie Adams	67	71	138	26,400
Chris Swanepoel	71	68	139	15,520
Andrew Curlewis	70	69	139	15,520
Dewald Smit	67	72	139	15,520
Ockie Strydom	72	68	140	10,560
Christiaan Basson	70	70	140	10,560
Desvonde Botes	69	71	140	10,560
Titch Moore	68	72	140	10,560
Steve Basson	70	71	141	8,656
Francois van Vuuren	70	71	141	8,656
Grant Muller	66	75	141	8,656
Louis Moolman	73	69	142	7,088

	SCORES			TOTAL	MONEY
Brandon Pieters	72	70		142	7,088
Nic Henning	72	70		142	7,088
Trevor Fisher, Jr.	75	67		142	7,088
Divan van den Heever	69	73		142	7,088
Alex Haindl	76	66		142	7,088
Adilson da Silva	71	72		143	5,740.80
Mike Curtis	71	72		143	5,740.80
Bradford Vaughan	70	73		143	5,740.80
Des Terblanche	69	74		143	5,740.80
Steve van Vuuren	69	74		143	5,740.80

Telkom PGA Pro-Am

Centurion Country Club, Pretoria, South Africa
Par 36-36–72; 7,328 yards

August 19-21
purse, R450,000

	SCORES			TOTAL	MONEY
Jaco Van Zyl	68	70	66	204	R71,325
T.C. Charamba	68	73	68	209	51,750
Jbe' Kruger	69	71	70	210	32,175
Tyrone Mordt	67	70	73	210	32,175
Desvonde Botes	69	74	68	211	19,125
Christiaan Basson	69	72	70	211	19,125
Dewald Smit	72	72	68	212	14,175
Louis Moolman	69	70	74	213	12,375
Jean Hugo	73	71	70	214	10,200
Brandon Pieters	71	72	71	214	10,200
Hennie Otto	70	73	71	214	10,200
Dion Fourie	73	72	70	215	8,775
Cameron Johnston	69	71	75	215	8,775
David Hewan	73	74	69	216	7,710
Louis de Jager	73	72	71	216	7,710
Des Terblanche	70	72	74	216	7,710
Tyrone Ferreira	71	77	69	217	6,885
Keith Horne	72	73	72	217	6,885
Trevor Fisher, Jr.	72	76	70	218	5,709.37
Warren Abery	75	72	71	218	5,709.37
Peter Karmis	73	74	71	218	5,709.37
Neil Schietekat	71	76	71	218	5,709.37
Thabang Simon	73	74	71	218	5,709.37
Clinton Whitelaw	74	72	72	218	5,709.37
Andre Cruse	71	74	73	218	5,709.37
Brett Liddle	75	70	73	218	5,709.37

Zambia Open

Ndola Golf Club, Ndola, Zambia
Par 37-36–73; 7,079 yards

August 28-30
purse, R800,000

	SCORES			TOTAL	MONEY
Jbe' Kruger	69	68	67	204	R126,800
Titch Moore	65	73	69	207	92,000
Mark Murless	70	72	68	210	43,813.33
Ryan Tipping	68	72	70	210	43,813.33
Desvonde Botes	67	71	72	210	43,813.33
Jean Hugo	70	71	70	211	22,720
Tyrone Ferreira	73	67	71	211	22,720

	SCORES			TOTAL	MONEY
Bradford Vaughan	69	69	73	211	22,720
Merrick Bremner	71	67	73	211	22,720
Farayi Chitengwa	71	73	68	212	13,630
Ignatius Mketekete	70	71	71	212	13,630
Adilson da Silva	70	70	72	212	13,630
Anton Haig	70	69	73	212	13,630
Andrew Odoh	66	73	73	212	13,630
Neil Schietekat	65	70	77	212	13,630
Christiaan Basson	73	71	69	213	10,864
Vaughn Groenewald	70	72	71	213	10,864
David Hewan	73	72	68	213	10,864
T.C. Charamba	72	68	73	213	10,864
Ryan Cairns	69	75	70	214	9,460
P.H. McIntyre	74	70	70	214	9,460
Nic Henning	72	70	72	214	9,460
Jacques Blaauw	72	69	73	214	9,460
Oliver Bekker	69	71	74	214	9,460
Ross Wellington	70	74	71	215	8,364
Niki Ferrari	73	72	70	215	8,364
Irvin Mazibuko	69	72	74	215	8,364
Anil Shah	76	71	68	215	8,364

SAA Pro-Am Invitational - Randpark

Randpark Golf Club, Johannesburg, South Africa
Par 36-36–72; 7,670 yards

September 3-5
purse, R500,000

	SCORES			TOTAL	MONEY
Ryan Tipping	69	70	69	208	R79,250
Chris Swanepoel	71	73	64	208	57,500
(Tipping defeated Swanepoel on second playoff hole.)					
Jbe' Kruger	71	73	65	209	31,666.66
Brandon Pieters	71	69	69	209	31,666.66
Tyrone Mordt	73	64	72	209	31,666.66
Merrick Bremner	72	70	68	210	16,166.66
Alex Haindl	69	71	70	210	16,166.66
Jaco Van Zyl	72	68	70	210	16,166.66
Jean Hugo	70	73	68	211	11,000
Josh Cunliffe	70	72	69	211	11,000
Tyrone Ferreira	69	72	70	211	11,000
P.G. Van Zyl	69	71	71	211	11,000
Desvonde Botes	73	72	67	212	9,500
Louis Calitz	73	73	67	213	8,775
Dean Lambert	75	67	71	213	8,775
Divan van den Heever	74	71	69	214	7,520
Roberto Lupini	72	72	70	214	7,520
Omar Sandys	71	73	70	214	7,520
Ulrich van den Berg	71	71	72	214	7,520
Callie Swart	74	67	73	214	7,520
Dion Fourie	76	70	69	215	5,887.50
Ashley Roestoff	73	72	70	215	5,887.50
Riaan de Bruyn	76	69	70	215	5,887.50
Dewald Smit	72	72	71	215	5,887.50
Ryan Cairns	74	70	71	215	5,887.50
Hendrik Buhrmann	76	68	71	215	5,887.50
Prinavin Nelson	72	72	71	215	5,887.50
Vaughn Groenewald	74	70	71	215	5,887.50

Vodacom Business Origins of Golf - Selborne

Selborne Hotel Spa & Golf Estate, KwaZulu-Natal, South Africa September 16-18
Par 36-36–72; 6,607 yards purse, R480,000

	SCORES			TOTAL	MONEY
Darren Fichardt	65	66	67	198	R76,080
Jbe' Kruger	68	69	68	205	46,800
Keenan Davidse	70	67	68	205	46,800
Adilson da Silva	70	70	67	207	30,240
Jaco Ahlers	65	74	69	208	18,640
Peter Karmis	70	67	71	208	18,640
Thabang Simon	69	68	71	208	18,640
Tyrone Mordt	71	70	68	209	11,920
Jean Hugo	68	70	71	209	11,920
Reggie Adams	66	68	75	209	11,920
Ryan Tipping	71	69	70	210	9,840
Andrew Curlewis	69	69	72	210	9,840
Mark Murless	71	70	70	211	8,880
Christiaan Basson	70	68	73	211	8,880
T.C. Charamba	69	67	76	212	8,208
Desvonde Botes	68	71	74	213	7,656
Alex Haindl	66	68	79	213	7,656
Trevor Fisher, Jr.	67	77	70	214	6,324
Danie van Niekerk	73	70	71	214	6,324
Andre Cruse	70	72	72	214	6,324
Cameron Johnston	71	70	73	214	6,324
Doug McGuigan	69	72	73	214	6,324
Prinavin Nelson	68	72	74	214	6,324
Lindani Ndwandwe	71	69	74	214	6,324
Jaco Van Zyl	71	67	76	214	6,324

SAA Pro-Am Invitational - Paarl

Paarl Golf Club, Paarl, Western Cape, South Africa October 1-3
Par 36-36–72; 6,880 yards purse, R500,000

	SCORES			TOTAL	MONEY
Prinavin Nelson	68	69	68	205	R79,250
Desvonde Botes	71	68	67	206	57,500
Chris Swanepoel	73	66	68	207	31,666.66
Jacques Blaauw	75	64	68	207	31,666.66
Trevor Fisher, Jr.	68	69	70	207	31,666.66
Clinton Whitelaw	80	62	66	208	19,000
Jaco Van Zyl	74	68	67	209	14,750
Divan van den Heever	72	67	70	209	14,750
Ryan Cairns	72	69	69	210	10,700
Doug McGuigan	73	68	69	210	10,700
Louis de Jager	72	69	69	210	10,700
Brandon Pieters	75	65	70	210	10,700
Tyrone Ferreira	71	67	72	210	10,700
Juan Langeveld	73	69	69	211	8,375
Peter Karmis	80	64	67	211	8,375
Ulrich van den Berg	73	68	70	211	8,375
Christiaan Basson	77	67	67	211	8,375
Wayne Westner	72	72	68	212	7,350
Neil Schietekat	72	68	72	212	7,350
Bradford Vaughan	71	71	71	213	6,333.33
Francois Olivier	70	72	71	213	6,333.33
Des Terblanche	76	68	69	213	6,333.33

	SCORES			TOTAL	MONEY
Alex Haindl	72	70	71	213	6,333.33
Andre Cruse	75	69	69	213	6,333.33
Albert Pistorius	69	70	74	213	6,333.33

Vodacom Business Origins of Golf - Final

Simola Golf Estate, Kysna, Southern Cape, South Africa   October 7-9
Par 36-36–72; 7,003 yards   purse, R480,000

	SCORES			TOTAL	MONEY
Brandon Pieters	70	69	69	208	R76,080
Jaco Van Zyl	69	73	67	209	46,800
Doug McGuigan	73	66	70	209	46,800
Tyrone Ferreira	70	71	69	210	30,240
Darren Fichardt	71	72	68	211	17,280
Trevor Fisher, Jr.	67	72	72	211	17,280
Andrew Curlewis	69	70	72	211	17,280
Mark Murless	70	68	73	211	17,280
Alex Haindl	70	73	69	212	11,760
Ulrich van den Berg	73	70	71	214	10,440
Des Terblanche	72	71	71	214	10,440
Prinavin Nelson	72	74	69	215	8,678.40
Ryan Cairns	71	73	71	215	8,678.40
Titch Moore	72	72	71	215	8,678.40
Jacques Blaauw	71	73	71	215	8,678.40
Alan Michell	75	68	72	215	8,678.40
Divan van den Heever	66	72	78	216	7,488
Clinton Whitelaw	72	73	72	217	7,200
Brett Liddle	74	73	71	218	6,432
Steve Basson	73	72	73	218	6,432
Ryan Tipping	72	73	73	218	6,432
P.G. Van Zyl	71	71	76	218	6,432
Derick Petersen	70	71	77	218	6,432
Theunis Spangenberg	73	73	73	219	5,142.85
David Hewan	69	76	74	219	5,142.85
Jaco Ahlers	68	77	74	219	5,142.85
Neil Cheetham	73	72	74	219	5,142.85
Nic Henning	75	69	75	219	5,142.85
Grant Veenstra	72	71	76	219	5,142.85
Kevin Stone	69	73	77	219	5,142.85

BMG Classic

Glendower Golf Club, Gauteng, South Africa   October 16-18
Par 36-36–72; 7,564 yards   purse, R500,000

	SCORES			TOTAL	MONEY
Graham DeLaet	68	69	68	205	R79,250
Jeff Inglis	73	69	64	206	57,500
Louis de Jager	65	76	66	207	31,666.66
Jacques Blaauw	70	71	66	207	31,666.66
Brandon Pieters	68	69	70	207	31,666.66
Neil Cheetham	72	66	70	208	19,000
Trevor Fisher, Jr.	69	72	68	209	14,750
Doug McGuigan	68	72	69	209	14,750
Marc Cayeux	68	73	69	210	10,416.66
Jaco Van Zyl	71	69	70	210	10,416.66

	SCORES			TOTAL	MONEY
Tyrone Ferreira	70	70	70	210	10,416.66
Alex Haindl	70	73	67	210	10,416.66
Oliver Bekker	71	69	70	210	10,416.66
Shaun Norris	67	70	73	210	10,416.66
Warren Abery	71	70	70	211	8,166.66
James Kamte	71	69	71	211	8,166.66
Titch Moore	71	69	71	211	8,166.66
Merrick Bremner	71	70	71	212	6,833.33
Theunis Spangenberg	70	71	71	212	6,833.33
Mike Curtis	71	71	70	212	6,833.33
Grant Muller	69	73	70	212	6,833.33
Bradford Vaughan	72	71	69	212	6,833.33
Albert Pistorius	67	76	69	212	6,833.33
Ulrich van den Berg	69	72	72	213	5,550
Ryan Cairns	75	66	72	213	5,550
Christiaan Basson	72	70	71	213	5,550
Prinavin Nelson	71	69	73	213	5,550
Andre Cruse	71	72	70	213	5,550

Highveld Classic

Witbank Golf Club, Witbank, South Africa
Par 36-36–72; 6,772 yards

October 23-25
purse, R500,000

	SCORES			TOTAL	MONEY
Lindani Ndwandwe	62	66	69	197	R79,250
Alex Haindl	63	67	67	197	57,500
(Ndwandwe defeated Haindl on first playoff hole.)					
Doug McGuigan	65	69	64	198	40,000
Alan McLean	68	66	65	199	31,500
Brandon Pieters	66	69	66	201	23,500
Jacques Blaauw	65	71	66	202	13,214.28
Darren Fichardt	68	68	66	202	13,214.28
Ulrich van den Berg	65	70	67	202	13,214.28
Warren Abery	68	67	67	202	13,214.28
Neil Cheetham	67	67	68	202	13,214.28
Grant Muller	66	68	68	202	13,214.28
Trevor Fisher, Jr.	69	64	69	202	13,214.28
Prinavin Nelson	67	69	67	203	9,016.66
Gerhard Trytsman	72	63	68	203	9,016.66
Ryan Tipping	67	66	70	203	9,016.66
Adilson da Silva	67	69	68	204	7,816.66
P.G. Van Zyl	67	69	68	204	7,816.66
Merrick Bremner	70	65	69	204	7,816.66
Desvonde Botes	68	69	68	205	6,950
Keenan Davidse	68	67	70	205	6,950
Andre Cruse	69	71	65	205	6,950
Jean Hugo	68	70	68	206	6,325
Chris Swanepoel	70	69	67	206	6,325
Michiel Bothma	76	62	69	207	5,550
Thabang Simon	67	71	69	207	5,550
Louis de Jager	68	68	71	207	5,550
David Hewan	70	69	68	207	5,550
Nic Henning	64	70	73	207	5,550

Platinum Classic

Mooinooi Golf Club, Rustenburg, South Africa
Par 36-36–72; 6,835 yards

October 29-31
purse, R550,000

	SCORES			TOTAL	MONEY
Darren Fichardt	70	65	66	201	R87,175
Titch Moore	65	68	69	202	63,250
Grant Muller	66	70	67	203	39,325
Alan McLean	65	66	72	203	39,325
Steve Basson	71	67	66	204	18,535
Adilson da Silva	67	70	67	204	18,535
Ryan Cairns	67	70	67	204	18,535
Teboho Sefatsa	68	67	69	204	18,535
Branden Grace	66	67	71	204	18,535
Trevor Fisher, Jr.	67	70	68	205	11,055
Warren Abery	65	72	68	205	11,055
Jbe' Kruger	63	73	69	205	11,055
Thomas Aiken	67	69	69	205	11,055
Doug McGuigan	66	69	70	205	11,055
Shaun Norris	68	73	65	206	8,800
Danie van Niekerk	69	69	68	206	8,800
Oliver Bekker	65	72	69	206	8,800
Jean Hugo	66	69	71	206	8,800
Mark Murless	74	67	66	207	7,645
Nic Henning	65	72	70	207	7,645
Michiel Bothma	68	67	72	207	7,645
Neil Schietekat	70	70	68	208	6,820
Andre Cruse	71	66	71	208	6,820
Vaughn Groenewald	70	67	71	208	6,820
Josh Cunliffe	69	71	69	209	6,215
Bradford Vaughan	70	70	69	209	6,215

MTC Namibia PGA Championship

Rossmund Golf Club, Swakopmund, Namibia
Par 36-36–72; 6,686 yards

November 12-15
purse, R1,000,000

	SCORES				TOTAL	MONEY
Hennie Otto	72	70	72	66	280	R158,500
Titch Moore	75	66	70	69	280	115,000
(Otto defeated Moore on first playoff hole.)						
Brandon Pieters	70	76	68	68	282	54,766.66
Adilson da Silva	70	70	71	71	282	54,766.66
Tjaart van der Walt	70	71	70	71	282	54,766.66
Christiaan Basson	73	68	73	69	283	28,400
Vaughn Groenewald	70	71	72	70	283	28,400
Tyrone Mordt	66	70	73	74	283	28,400
Willie van der Merwe	68	77	64	74	283	28,400
Bradford Vaughan	71	70	73	70	284	19,900
Marc Cayeux	75	70	70	70	285	16,881
Henk Alberts	69	71	74	71	285	16,881
Josh Cunliffe	72	74	68	71	285	16,881
Ulrich van den Berg	72	70	71	72	285	16,881
Charl Coetzee	71	76	72	67	286	13,826
Jacques Blaauw	72	70	73	71	286	13,826
Warren Abery	73	70	71	72	286	13,826
Des Terblanche	74	72	68	72	286	13,826
Merrick Bremner	72	73	65	76	286	13,826
Ryan Tipping	74	70	72	71	287	11,826

	SCORES				TOTAL	MONEY
Neil Cheetham	68	72	75	72	287	11,826
Andre Cruse	71	71	72	73	287	11,826
Ignatius Mketekete	67	70	75	75	287	11,826
Doug McGuigan	69	69	72	77	287	11,826
Shaun Norris	72	70	73	73	288	10,606
Desvonde Botes	76	69	69	74	288	10,606
Alan McLean	68	71	74	75	288	10,606

Coca-Cola Championship

The Montagu, Fancourt, George, South Africa
Par 36-36–72; 7,342 yards

November 24-26
purse, R550,000

	SCORES			TOTAL	MONEY
Christiaan Basson	70	65	68	203	R89,870
Louis Oosthuizen	74	67	66	207	51,397.50
Andrew Curlewis	71	63	73	207	51,397.50
Dion Fourie	69	68	71	208	27,885
Willie van der Merwe	71	71	67	209	23,430
Grant Muller	73	71	67	211	19,497.50
Titch Moore	71	70	70	211	19,497.50
Warren Abery	71	73	68	212	16,348.75
Tyrone Mordt	70	71	71	212	16,348.75
Brandon Pieters	70	69	73	212	16,348.75
Bradford Vaughan	68	71	73	212	16,348.75
Jaco Ahlers	68	74	71	213	14,300
Alex Haindl	73	70	71	214	13,585
Merrick Bremner	75	68	73	216	12,925
Ulrich van den Berg	75	71	71	217	11,770
Clinton Whitelaw	69	74	74	217	11,770
Neil Schietekat	69	72	76	217	11,770
Ryan Tipping	74	72	72	218	10,890
Dawie Van der Walt	72	73	74	219	10,560
Doug McGuigan	73	70	76	219	10,560
Chris Swanepoel	75	78	67	220	10,175
Brett Liddle	73	73	75	221	9,845
Prinavin Nelson	70	73	78	221	9,845
Charl Coetzee	79	68	75	222	9,515
Lindani Ndwandwe	71	78	74	223	9,295

Gary Player Invitational

The Links, Fancourt, George, South Africa
Par 36-37–73; 7,579 yards

November 27-29
purse, R250,000

	SCORES		TOTAL	MONEY (Each)
Angel Cabrera/Tony Johnstone	66	65	131	R62,500
Bill Longmuir/Omar Sandys	68	66	134	31,250
John Bland/Tjaart van der Walt	63	71	134	31,250
Retief Goosen/Gary Player	70	65	135	
Garth Mulroy/Bertus Smit	66	69	135	
Thomas Aiken/Vincent Tshabalala	67	71	138	
Mark McNulty/Henrietta Zuel	69	70	139	
Sandra Gal/Bobby Jones	76	72	148	

Nedbank Affinity Cup

Lost City Golf Course, Sun City, South Africa
Par 36-36–72; 7,637 yards

November 30-December 2
purse, R550,000

	SCORES			TOTAL	MONEY
Jake Roos	71	66	67	204	R87,175
Albert Pistorius	69	68	67	204	53,625
Mark Murless	66	66	72	204	53,625
(Roos defeated Pistorius on first and Murless on second playoff hole.)					
Warren Abery	67	73	66	206	30,250
Des Terblanche	65	67	74	206	30,250
Thabang Simon	68	69	70	207	20,900
Andrew Curlewis	72	68	69	209	16,225
Jaco Ahlers	71	68	70	209	16,225
Charl Coetzee	71	70	69	210	12,466.66
Bradford Vaughan	68	70	72	210	12,466.66
Tyrone Mordt	69	69	72	210	12,466.66
Prinavin Nelson	70	72	69	211	9,123.88
Alan Michell	73	69	69	211	9,123.88
Andre Cruse	73	69	69	211	9,123.88
Neil Cheetham	70	71	70	211	9,123.88
T.C. Charamba	70	71	70	211	9,123.88
Brandon Pieters	71	70	70	211	9,123.88
Desvonde Botes	71	69	71	211	9,123.88
Chris Williams	69	70	72	211	9,123.88
Omar Sandys	67	71	73	211	9,123.88
Peter Karmis	73	70	69	212	7,095
Keenan Davidse	66	72	74	212	7,095
Justin Walters	71	67	74	212	7,095
Willie van der Merwe	75	68	70	213	6,325
Neil Schietekat	71	70	72	213	6,325
Clinton Whitelaw	74	67	72	213	6,325

Nedbank Golf Challenge

Gary Player Country Club, Sun City, South Africa
Par 36-36–72; 7,831 yards

December 3-6
purse, US$4,385,000

	SCORES				TOTAL	MONEY
Robert Allenby	68	70	68	71	277	$1,200,000
Henrik Stenson	70	68	70	69	277	600,000
(Allenby defeated Stenson on third playoff hole.)						
Tim Clark	69	72	68	69	278	350,000
Ross Fisher	73	69	66	70	278	350,000
Retief Goosen	69	68	67	75	279	275,000
Angel Cabrera	71	67	68	75	281	260,000
Nick Watney	73	73	63	73	282	250,000
Luke Donald	72	71	68	72	283	240,000
Robert Karlsson	70	72	71	71	284	230,000
Hunter Mahan	70	71	72	73	286	220,000
Richard Sterne	72	75	70	75	292	210,000
Rory McIlroy	73	76			WD	200,000

Alfred Dunhill Championship

Leopard Creek Country Club, Malelane, South Africa
Par 35-37–72; 7,249 yards

December 10-13
purse, €1,000,000

	SCORES				TOTAL	MONEY
Pablo Martin	68	63	71	69	271	R1,753,010
Charl Schwartzel	67	69	68	68	272	1,271,900
Anders Hansen	68	70	68	68	274	765,352
Richard Sterne	72	66	72	66	276	429,404.50
Dale Whitnell	70	68	72	66	276	429,404.50
Robert Rock	69	68	70	69	276	429,404.50
Gareth Maybin	68	70	67	71	276	429,404.50
Shiv Kapur	68	71	68	70	277	242,582.66
Michael Lorenzo-Vera	71	69	66	71	277	242,582.66
Damien McGrane	67	70	68	72	277	242,582.66
Ignacio Garrido	72	71	65	70	278	197,974
Garth Mulroy	68	73	72	66	279	173,642
Gregory Bourdy	67	70	72	70	279	173,642
Ulrich van den Berg	64	72	71	72	279	173,642
Pelle Edberg	65	71	72	72	280	154,287
Edoardo Molinari	66	69	72	73	280	154,287
Julien Guerrier	70	70	74	67	281	129,540.25
Shane Lowry	67	71	74	69	281	129,540.25
James Kingston	68	70	72	71	281	129,540.25
Michiel Bothma	72	70	67	72	281	129,540.25
James Kamte	69	71	68	73	281	129,540.25
Dawie Van der Walt	68	70	69	74	281	129,540.25
Sion E. Bebb	67	70	69	75	281	129,540.25
Ernie Els	68	67	69	77	281	129,540.25
Warren Abery	72	71	72	67	282	107,835
Jamie Elson	71	70	72	69	282	107,835
Andrew Coltart	70	72	70	70	282	107,835
Darren Fichardt	67	72	67	76	282	107,835
Adilson da Silva	71	67	75	70	283	94,231.20
Alan McLean	67	74	72	70	283	94,231.20
Andrew Curlewis	71	68	70	74	283	94,231.20
Ariel Canete	68	68	70	77	283	94,231.20
Jacques Blaauw	71	68	66	78	283	94,231.20
Keith Horne	75	68	72	69	284	87,374
Joost Luiten	70	70	73	72	285	81,844
Mikko Ilonen	70	71	71	73	285	81,844
Rafael Cabrera-Bello	69	68	74	74	285	81,844
Markus Brier	72	68	71	74	285	81,844
David Dixon	70	68	79	69	286	71,890
Oliver Bekker	69	74	72	71	286	71,890
Deane Pappas	74	69	72	71	286	71,890
Bradford Vaughan	69	74	71	72	286	71,890
Steve Basson	70	70	71	75	286	71,890
Steven Jeppesen	71	70	77	69	287	58,618
Titch Moore	66	73	76	72	287	58,618
Eirik Tage Johansen	67	73	75	72	287	58,618
Dion Fourie	71	70	72	74	287	58,618
Michael Hoey	73	69	71	74	287	58,618
Grant Muller	71	71	71	74	287	58,618
Doug McGuigan	70	73	68	76	287	58,618
Benn Barham	68	73	77	70	288	44,240
Fabrizio Zanotti	72	71	74	71	288	44,240
Mark Haastrup	72	70	73	73	288	44,240
Richard McEvoy	68	70	76	74	288	44,240
Tjaart van der Walt	67	75	71	75	288	44,240
Charl Coetzee	74	69	68	77	288	44,240
Peter Whiteford	69	74	73	73	289	34,839

	SCORES				TOTAL	MONEY
Kenneth Ferrie	72	68	74	75	289	34,839
Carl Suneson	71	68	73	77	289	34,839
Vaughn Groenewald	71	68	71	79	289	34,839
Richard Finch	69	74	77	70	290	30,415
Louis de Jager	69	73	77	71	290	30,415
James Ruth	72	71	76	71	290	30,415
Hendrik Buhrmann	72	71	73	74	290	30,415
Nic Henning	69	71	77	74	291	27,650
Jarmo Sandelin	69	74	75	74	292	26,544
Peter Baker	74	69	76	74	293	24,885
Rhys Davies	71	72	74	76	293	24,885
Josh Cunliffe	73	70	75	77	295	23,226

South African Open Championship

Pearl Valley Golf Estates, Paarl, Western Cape, South Africa
Par 36-36–72; 7,319 yards

December 17-20
purse, €1,000,000

	SCORES				TOTAL	MONEY
Richie Ramsay	67	75	68	65	275	R1,769,811
Shiv Kapur	71	68	69	67	275	1,284,090
(Ramsay defeated Kapur on first playoff hole.)						
Anders Hansen	66	69	72	69	276	772,687.20
Fredrik Andersson Hed	71	68	68	70	277	504,703.20
Edoardo Molinari	68	69	69	71	277	504,703.20
Darren Fichardt	73	71	68	66	278	362,336.70
Pablo Martin	65	68	72	73	278	362,336.70
Soren Hansen	70	72	70	67	279	224,213.28
Michael Jonzon	68	75	69	67	279	224,213.28
Michiel Bothma	68	73	68	70	279	224,213.28
Chris Swanepoel	72	69	68	70	279	224,213.28
James Kingston	72	66	69	72	279	224,213.28
Pelle Edberg	76	69	68	67	280	169,723.20
Alejandro Canizares	69	67	74	70	280	169,723.20
Gregory Bourdy	69	74	70	68	281	152,974.20
Richard Bland	73	72	66	70	281	152,974.20
Louis Oosthuizen	68	69	73	71	281	152,974.20
Richard Sterne	71	69	74	68	282	136,597.40
Jacques Blaauw	69	75	69	69	282	136,597.40
Scott Dunlap	72	70	70	70	282	136,597.40
Branden Grace	72	70	74	67	283	120,592.80
David Drysdale	75	70	68	70	283	120,592.80
Adilson da Silva	69	69	74	71	283	120,592.80
Damien McGrane	69	72	71	71	283	120,592.80
Simon Khan	73	71	68	71	283	120,592.80
Charl Schwartzel	77	68	70	69	284	103,843.80
Andrew Coltart	74	67	73	70	284	103,843.80
Marc Cayeux	73	72	68	71	284	103,843.80
Thomas Aiken	69	71	71	73	284	103,843.80
Jean Hugo	72	69	70	73	284	103,843.80
Robert Rock	71	74	71	69	285	91,561.20
George Coetzee	74	67	74	70	285	91,561.20
David Hewan	77	68	69	71	285	91,561.20
Dawie Van der Walt	65	73	74	73	285	91,561.20
Keith Horne	71	72	73	70	286	78,162
Gareth Maybin	75	68	72	71	286	78,162
John Bickerton	73	70	72	71	286	78,162
Carlos Rodiles	70	71	73	72	286	78,162
Grant Muller	72	72	70	72	286	78,162
Richard McEvoy	71	69	73	73	286	78,162

	SCORES				TOTAL	MONEY
Callum Macaulay	70	69	73	74	286	78,162
Michael Hoey	70	70	70	76	286	78,162
Rafael Cabrera-Bello	79	65	74	69	287	64,762.80
Gary Murphy	75	69	71	72	287	64,762.80
Andre Cruse	72	71	71	73	287	64,762.80
Jbe' Kruger	72	71	69	75	287	64,762.80
Markus Brier	71	74	72	71	288	51,363.60
Martin Erlandsson	64	74	78	72	288	51,363.60
Richard Finch	68	71	76	73	288	51,363.60
Carl Suneson	71	70	74	73	288	51,363.60
*Dylan Frittelli	69	74	72	73	288	
Jaco Van Zyl	76	67	72	73	288	51,363.60
Louis Moolman	70	74	71	73	288	51,363.60
Brandon Pieters	74	69	70	75	288	51,363.60
Sam Hutsby	71	73	69	75	288	51,363.60
Oliver Bekker	72	72	73	72	289	39,081
Joost Luiten	73	69	73	74	289	39,081
Rhys Davies	73	70	72	74	289	39,081
Mikael Lundberg	74	70	73	73	290	35,172.90
Fredrik Ohlsson	71	73	71	75	290	35,172.90
Oskar Henningsson	74	70	73	74	291	30,706.50
Paul Waring	73	72	72	74	291	30,706.50
Ulrich van den Berg	69	73	74	75	291	30,706.50
Steve Basson	73	70	73	75	291	30,706.50
Dion Fourie	71	72	72	76	291	30,706.50
Peter Karmis	70	73	70	78	291	30,706.50
Garth Mulroy	72	72	72	76	292	26,798.40
Alan McLean	69	73	79	73	294	24,565.20
Peter Whiteford	73	72	75	74	294	24,565.20
*J.G. Claassen	74	69	75	76	294	
Kenneth Ferrie	71	70	75	78	294	24,565.20
James Morrison	72	73	74	77	296	22,332
Lindani Ndwandwe	72	73	75	78	298	16,749
T.C. Charamba	73	72	73	81	299	16,698.75
Doug McGuigan	70	75	72	82	299	16,698.75
James Kamte	70	74	77	79	300	16,648.51
Thabang Simon	75	70	74	82	301	16,615.01
Tyrone Ferreira	71	71	79	81	302	16,581.51
Marco Ruiz	74	70	79	81	304	16,548.01
*Ryan Dreyer	73	72	76	87	308	

Women's Tours

HSBC LPGA Brasil Cup

Itanhanga Golf Club, Rio de Janeiro, Brazil
Par 36-36–72; 6,447 yards

January 24-25
purse, $500,000

	SCORES		TOTAL	MONEY
Catriona Matthew	69	69	138	$100,000
Kristy McPherson	71	72	143	75,000
Angela Park	72	75	147	40,000
Laura Diaz	75	73	148	35,000
Allison Fouch	74	75	149	31,250
Jimin Kang	76	73	149	31,250
Carin Koch	75	75	150	26,250
Louise Friberg	78	72	150	26,250
Candy Hanneman	74	78	152	20,000
Christina Kim	75	77	152	20,000
Leta Lindley	81	71	152	20,000
Eun-Hee Ji	75	78	153	15,500
Karen Stupples	78	75	153	15,500
Jill McGill	75	80	155	14,000
*Patricia Carvalho	79	76	155	

SBS Open

Turtle Bay Resort, Palmer Course, Kahuku, Oahu, Hawaii
Par 36-36–72; 6,560 yards

February 12-14
purse, $1,200,000

	SCORES			TOTAL	MONEY
Angela Stanford	65	71	70	206	$180,000
Michelle Wie	66	70	73	209	108,332
Na Yeon Choi	71	72	69	212	69,690
Angela Park	69	68	75	212	69,690
Ai Miyazato	72	70	71	213	44,484
Yani Tseng	66	75	72	213	44,484
Sarah Lee	73	72	69	214	29,755
Cristie Kerr	70	75	69	214	29,755
Brittany Lang	71	70	73	214	29,755
Natalie Gulbis	74	71	70	215	20,948
Jane Park	72	73	70	215	20,948
Eun-Hee Ji	73	71	71	215	20,948
Jee Young Lee	71	72	72	215	20,948
Taylor Leon	69	74	72	215	20,948
Candie Kung	73	73	70	216	15,539
Johanna Mundy	74	71	71	216	15,539
Hee-Kyung Seo	72	71	73	216	15,539
Paula Creamer	70	73	73	216	15,539
Vicky Hurst	70	71	75	216	15,539
Stephanie Louden	74	74	69	217	12,930
Hee-Won Han	70	75	72	217	12,930
Stacy Lewis	71	70	76	217	12,930
Momoko Ueda	68	71	78	217	12,930
Kristy McPherson	72	73	73	218	11,536
Janice Moodie	71	74	73	218	11,536
Morgan Pressel	73	76	70	219	9,905

	SCORES			TOTAL	MONEY
Meaghan Francella	72	76	71	219	9,905
Pat Hurst	75	72	72	219	9,905
Laura Diaz	70	76	73	219	9,905
Kyeong Bae	67	79	73	219	9,905
Anja Monke	72	73	74	219	9,905

Honda LPGA Thailand

Siam Country Club, Chonburi, Thailand
Par 36-36–72; 6,477 yards

February 26-March 1
purse, $1,450,000

	SCORES				TOTAL	MONEY
Lorena Ochoa	71	69	68	66	274	$217,500
Hee Young Park	79	64	69	65	277	139,852
Paula Creamer	68	70	67	73	278	101,453
Stacy Prammanasudh	75	70	73	63	281	70,826
Brittany Lang	68	69	71	73	281	70,826
Mika Miyazato	73	67	72	70	282	51,684
Yani Tseng	70	71	74	68	283	36,561
Sophie Gustafson	70	73	70	70	283	36,561
Helen Alfredsson	68	72	73	70	283	36,561
Angela Stanford	68	71	73	71	283	36,561
Sun Young Yoo	74	70	72	68	284	27,756
Teresa Lu	72	69	72	71	284	27,756
Na Yeon Choi	73	72	70	70	285	24,349
Jiyai Shin	75	69	71	70	285	24,349
Juli Inkster	71	75	71	69	286	20,521
Nicole Castrale	69	74	73	70	286	20,521
Eun-Hee Ji	73	67	75	71	286	20,521
Karen Stupples	72	71	71	72	286	20,521
Jee Young Lee	73	72	72	70	287	17,611
Cristie Kerr	74	70	70	73	287	17,611
Karrie Webb	71	71	69	76	287	17,611
Shanshan Feng	76	70	75	67	288	15,486
Lindsey Wright	74	74	70	70	288	15,486
Ai Miyazato	71	70	74	73	288	15,486
Morgan Pressel	70	68	76	74	288	15,486
Natalie Gulbis	71	71	74	73	289	13,821
Laura Diaz	73	68	72	76	289	13,821
Melissa Reid	74	75	71	70	290	12,037
Minea Blomqvist	73	68	79	70	290	12,037
Angela Park	76	73	70	71	290	12,037
Jane Park	72	71	76	71	290	12,037
*Moriya Jutanugarn	73	72	72	73	290	
Kristy McPherson	68	72	76	74	290	12,037

HSBC Women's Champions

Tanah Merah Country Club, Garden Course, Singapore
Par 36-36–72; 6,547 yards

March 5-8
purse, $2,000,000

	SCORES				TOTAL	MONEY
Jiyai Shin	72	73	66	66	277	$300,000
Katherine Hull	70	69	66	74	279	182,956
Angela Park	67	76	69	68	280	106,010
Paula Creamer	67	71	72	70	280	106,010
Angela Stanford	69	72	66	73	280	106,010

	SCORES				TOTAL	MONEY
Lorena Ochoa	69	73	69	70	281	57,930
Jane Park	67	71	73	70	281	57,930
Sun Young Yoo	71	69	68	73	281	57,930
Karrie Webb	74	69	73	66	282	42,572
Mi Hyun Kim	71	68	70	73	282	42,572
Cristie Kerr	73	71	70	69	283	36,310
Yani Tseng	72	71	69	71	283	36,310
Se Ri Pak	69	72	72	71	284	32,854
Meena Lee	72	70	71	72	285	28,347
Suzann Pettersen	72	70	71	72	285	28,347
Eun-Hee Ji	69	73	70	73	285	28,347
Amy Yang	73	69	69	74	285	28,347
Jee Young Lee	73	74	71	68	286	23,489
Song-Hee Kim	72	70	74	70	286	23,489
Momoko Ueda	71	73	71	71	286	23,489
Seon Hwa Lee	68	74	73	71	286	23,489
Jimin Kang	72	73	70	72	287	21,035
Juli Inkster	72	70	69	76	287	21,035
Karen Stupples	73	74	67	74	288	19,483
Lindsey Wright	72	69	72	75	288	19,483
Laura Diaz	75	73	72	69	289	17,048
In-Kyung Kim	71	74	74	70	289	17,048
Michele Redman	70	72	74	73	289	17,048
Anja Monke	73	70	72	74	289	17,048
Ai Miyazato	68	72	72	77	289	17,048

MasterCard Classic Honoring Alejo Peralta

BosqueReal Country Club, Mexico City, Mexico   March 20-22
Par 36-36–72; 6,887 yards   purse, $1,300,000

	SCORES			TOTAL	MONEY
Pat Hurst	68	70	68	206	$195,000
Lorena Ochoa	65	73	69	207	103,325
Yani Tseng	68	69	70	207	103,325
Song-Hee Kim	70	69	69	208	67,210
Cristie Kerr	72	72	67	211	54,096
Ji Young Oh	69	74	70	213	37,922
Eun-Hee Ji	67	70	76	213	37,922
Na Yeon Choi	67	70	76	213	37,922
Katie Futcher	74	72	68	214	26,774
Jee Young Lee	73	70	71	214	26,774
Suzann Pettersen	69	71	74	214	26,774
Heather Young	74	70	71	215	20,917
Seon Hwa Lee	69	74	72	215	20,917
Sun Young Yoo	70	70	75	215	20,917
Grace Park	69	71	75	215	20,917
Il Mi Chung	74	72	70	216	16,086
Meena Lee	73	72	71	216	16,086
Teresa Lu	72	72	72	216	16,086
Kristy McPherson	70	73	73	216	16,086
Lindsey Wright	70	73	73	216	16,086
Se Ri Pak	70	69	77	216	16,086
Giulia Sergas	75	72	70	217	12,786
Silvia Cavalleri	73	73	71	217	12,786
Vicky Hurst	72	73	72	217	12,786
Louise Stahle	72	72	73	217	12,786
Jane Park	71	71	75	217	12,786
Brittany Lang	68	74	75	217	12,786
Sandra Gal	75	74	69	218	10,508

	SCORES				TOTAL	MONEY
Mika Miyazato	70	78	70		218	10,508
Kris Tamulis	74	73	71		218	10,508
Carolina Llano	73	74	71		218	10,508

J Golf Phoenix LPGA International

Papago Golf Club, Phoenix, Arizona
Par 36-36–72; 6,711 yards

March 26-29
purse, $1,500,000

	SCORES				TOTAL	MONEY
Karrie Webb	70	68	69	67	274	$225,000
Jiyai Shin	69	71	66	70	276	139,583
In-Kyung Kim	68	68	71	70	277	101,258
Yani Tseng	72	72	67	67	278	70,689
Suzann Pettersen	69	69	70	70	278	70,689
Song-Hee Kim	70	69	73	67	279	51,584
Angela Park	70	71	70	69	280	40,504
Eun-Hee Ji	69	70	70	71	280	40,504
Cristie Kerr	69	72	71	69	281	32,479
Ai Miyazato	71	70	70	70	281	32,479
Lindsey Wright	72	72	70	69	283	26,001
Sun Young Yoo	73	70	70	70	283	26,001
Na On Min	73	69	70	71	283	26,001
Brittany Lang	73	70	67	73	283	26,001
Lorena Ochoa	72	72	70	70	284	19,614
Marcy Hart	71	73	70	70	284	19,614
Kristy McPherson	72	71	70	71	284	19,614
Inbee Park	69	74	70	71	284	19,614
Na Yeon Choi	74	68	71	71	284	19,614
Angela Stanford	73	67	73	71	284	19,614
Karin Sjodin	73	71	70	71	285	16,354
Se Ri Pak	72	72	70	71	285	16,354
Helen Alfredsson	74	68	71	72	285	16,354
Hee Young Park	75	74	69	68	286	15,131
Silvia Cavalleri	70	73	73	71	287	14,329
Irene Cho	70	73	73	71	287	14,329
Jimin Kang	74	73	74	67	288	12,743
Louise Stahle	71	71	74	72	288	12,743
Sophie Gustafson	73	68	75	72	288	12,743
Jee Young Lee	72	71	72	73	288	12,743

Kraft Nabisco Championship

Mission Hills Country Club, Dinah Shore Course,
Rancho Mirage, California
Par 36-36–72; 6,673 yards

April 2-5
purse, $2,000,000

	SCORES				TOTAL	MONEY
Brittany Lincicome	66	74	70	69	279	$300,000
Cristie Kerr	71	68	70	71	280	161,853
Kristy McPherson	68	70	70	72	280	161,853
Lindsey Wright	70	71	71	70	282	105,281
Suzann Pettersen	71	72	74	66	283	77,036
Meaghan Francella	72	73	69	69	283	77,036
Christina Kim	69	69	75	72	285	58,034
Karrie Webb	73	72	72	69	286	44,167
Pat Hurst	71	71	73	71	286	44,167

	SCORES				TOTAL	MONEY
Katherine Hull	69	74	71	72	286	44,167
Jimin Kang	71	70	71	74	286	44,167
Sun Young Yoo	70	78	73	66	287	31,841
Lorena Ochoa	73	73	72	69	287	31,841
Michele Redman	72	73	72	70	287	31,841
Angela Stanford	67	75	74	71	287	31,841
Helen Alfredsson	72	70	72	73	287	31,841
Yani Tseng	69	75	75	69	288	25,542
Paula Creamer	70	72	77	69	288	25,542
Brittany Lang	67	80	71	70	288	25,542
Jee Young Lee	69	80	72	68	289	23,624
*Alexis Thompson	72	72	77	69	290	
Jiyai Shin	72	76	71	71	290	22,392
Song-Hee Kim	69	78	72	71	290	22,392
*Tiffany Joh	71	75	73	71	290	
Nicole Castrale	71	75	73	72	291	20,372
Sakura Yokomine	72	73	74	72	291	20,372
Allison Fouch	76	73	69	73	291	20,372
Hee-Won Han	75	73	72	72	292	18,540
In-Kyung Kim	70	73	75	74	292	18,540
Momoko Ueda	76	72	75	70	293	15,835
Janice Moodie	75	73	74	71	293	15,835
Young Kim	76	71	75	71	293	15,835
Seon Hwa Lee	74	77	69	73	293	15,835
Candie Kung	72	73	74	74	293	15,835
Jane Park	74	76	68	75	293	15,835
Eun-Hee Ji	75	72	76	71	294	12,891
Ji Young Oh	67	78	78	71	294	12,891
Wendy Ward	75	72	74	73	294	12,891
Yuri Fudoh	71	76	73	74	294	12,891
Morgan Pressel	74	73	76	72	295	10,703
Se Ri Pak	71	75	77	72	295	10,703
*Azahara Munoz	71	74	77	73	295	
Na Yeon Choi	75	75	71	74	295	10,703
Alena Sharp	76	69	74	76	295	10,703
Joo Mi Kim	73	70	76	76	295	10,703
Hye Jung Choi	73	75	76	72	296	9,244
Natalie Gulbis	71	75	74	76	296	9,244
Jennifer Rosales	73	79	75	70	297	8,114
Gwladys Nocera	76	74	77	70	297	8,114
Giulia Sergas	74	76	76	71	297	8,114
Angela Park	74	78	73	72	297	8,114
Mi Hyun Kim	73	77	75	72	297	8,114
Soo-Yun Kang	78	74	74	72	298	6,984
Hee Young Park	75	76	75	72	298	6,984
Teresa Lu	72	76	76	74	298	6,984
Rachel Hetherington	75	76	77	71	299	6,265
Moira Dunn	70	79	77	73	299	6,265
Inbee Park	71	79	74	75	299	6,265
Shi Hyun Ahn	75	69	78	77	299	6,265
Ji-Hee Lee	69	82	76	74	301	5,547
Becky Morgan	72	78	76	75	301	5,547
Laura Diaz	76	76	73	76	301	5,547
Il Mi Chung	75	77	76	74	302	5,136
Heather Young	75	77	78	73	303	4,931
Stacy Lewis	73	78	78	74	303	4,931
Sophie Gustafson	72	79	77	75	303	4,931
Michelle Wie	71	81	81	71	304	4,674
Diana D'Alessio	72	76	77	79	304	4,674
Ai Miyazato	75	76	76	78	305	4,519
Silvia Cavalleri	74	77	76	79	306	4,417

Corona Championship

Tres Marias Golf Club, Morelia, Michoacan, Mexico
Par 36-37–73; 6,539 yards

April 23-26
purse, $1,300,000

		SCORES			TOTAL	MONEY
Lorena Ochoa	65	65	69	68	267	$195,000
Suzann Pettersen	69	64	67	68	268	120,655
Na Yeon Choi	66	69	69	70	274	87,527
Wendy Ward	71	68	66	70	275	67,709
Cristie Kerr	70	70	66	70	276	49,544
Yani Tseng	69	66	71	70	276	49,544
Brittany Lang	69	68	70	70	277	33,139
Seon Hwa Lee	72	68	69	68	277	33,139
Morgan Pressel	71	67	67	72	277	33,139
Vicky Hurst	70	71	69	68	278	25,762
Michelle Wie	66	71	72	69	278	25,762
Jimin Jeong	69	73	66	71	279	23,120
Ai Miyazato	69	70	72	70	281	21,666
Eva Dahllof	73	71	71	67	282	19,201
Jill McGill	68	71	72	71	282	19,201
Karrie Webb	70	67	72	73	282	19,201
Shi Hyun Ahn	73	68	69	73	283	15,269
Nicole Castrale	70	69	70	74	283	15,269
Irene Cho	70	67	68	78	283	15,269
Sandra Gal	67	74	70	72	283	15,269
Teresa Lu	72	71	70	70	283	15,269
Kristy McPherson	68	68	73	74	283	15,269
Anna Nordqvist	67	74	67	75	283	15,269
Kyeong Bae	70	72	72	70	284	12,848
Heather Young	74	71	72	67	284	12,848
Mindy Kim	72	73	68	72	285	11,032
Sarah Lee	67	70	71	77	285	11,032
Jee Young Lee	72	68	70	75	285	11,032
Stacy Lewis	70	72	69	74	285	11,032
Alena Sharp	72	68	73	72	285	11,032
Eunjung Yi	67	71	74	73	285	11,032

Michelob Ultra Open

Kingsmill Resort & Spa, River Course, Williamsburg, Virginia
Par 36-35–71; 6,315 yards

May 7-10
purse, $2,200,000

		SCORES			TOTAL	MONEY
Cristie Kerr	69	63	66	70	268	$330,000
In-Kyung Kim	68	64	67	71	270	202,680
Song-Hee Kim	69	63	68	71	271	130,385
Lindsey Wright	65	69	64	73	271	130,385
Wendy Ward	72	64	67	70	273	91,548
Shiho Oyama	69	66	70	69	274	74,902
Angela Stanford	68	68	70	69	275	58,813
Natalie Gulbis	70	65	68	72	275	58,813
Ai Miyazato	71	65	72	68	276	49,380
Lorena Ochoa	64	65	74	74	277	44,941
Teresa Lu	69	72	67	70	278	37,755
Juli Inkster	71	67	70	70	278	37,755
Seon Hwa Lee	67	70	70	71	278	37,755
Il Mi Chung	69	70	67	72	278	37,755
Michelle Wie	70	67	73	69	279	29,073
Amy Yang	67	74	68	70	279	29,073

	SCORES				TOTAL	MONEY
Allison Hanna-Williams	71	67	69	72	279	29,073
Hee-Won Han	66	69	72	72	279	29,073
Na Yeon Choi	67	68	70	74	279	29,073
Jiyai Shin	70	68	76	66	280	22,499
Kyeong Bae	74	66	73	67	280	22,499
Becky Morgan	73	69	70	68	280	22,499
Jimin Kang	71	70	71	68	280	22,499
Young Kim	70	69	71	70	280	22,499
Nicole Castrale	71	67	69	73	280	22,499
Yani Tseng	71	64	72	73	280	22,499
Shanshan Feng	70	67	69	74	280	22,499
Katherine Hull	69	71	74	67	281	17,444
Meena Lee	73	70	70	68	281	17,444
Kris Tamulis	68	70	70	73	281	17,444
Sarah Lee	66	71	71	73	281	17,444
Minea Blomqvist	66	71	70	74	281	17,444

Sybase Classic

Upper Montclair Country Club, Clifton, New Jersey
Par 36-36–72; 6,413 yards

May 14-17
purse, $2,000,000

	SCORES				TOTAL	MONEY
Ji Young Oh	66	69	69	70	274	$300,000
Suzann Pettersen	65	70	69	74	278	184,708
Michelle Wie	70	69	68	73	280	118,824
Paula Creamer	70	69	68	73	280	118,824
In-Kyung Kim	68	73	70	70	281	83,430
Hee Young Park	67	74	67	74	282	62,699
Brittany Lincicome	64	69	72	77	282	62,699
Louise Stahle	73	68	72	70	283	45,339
Amy Hung	70	72	70	71	283	45,339
Candie Kung	71	69	69	74	283	45,339
Momoko Ueda	71	71	71	71	284	36,658
Helen Alfredsson	62	76	72	74	284	36,658
M.J. Hur	74	71	72	68	285	29,529
Karin Sjodin	73	72	69	71	285	29,529
Natalie Gulbis	70	72	70	73	285	29,529
Jiyai Shin	69	71	71	74	285	29,529
Moira Dunn	71	69	70	75	285	29,529
Ai Miyazato	73	68	69	76	286	25,079
Lorena Ochoa	71	71	72	73	287	22,855
Sandra Gal	70	69	75	73	287	22,855
Song-Hee Kim	72	67	74	74	287	22,855
Russy Gulyanamitta	73	69	69	76	287	22,855
Yani Tseng	71	71	74	72	288	17,945
Jee Young Lee	69	71	76	72	288	17,945
Becky Lucidi	72	70	72	74	288	17,945
Katherine Hull	67	73	73	75	288	17,945
Young Kim	71	70	72	75	288	17,945
Meg Mallon	70	73	70	75	288	17,945
Paige Mackenzie	72	71	75	70	288	17,945
Karrie Webb	70	69	72	77	288	17,945
Brittany Lang	68	74	69	77	288	17,945

LPGA Corning Classic

Corning Country Club, Corning, New York
Par 36-36–72; 6,223 yards

May 21-24
purse, $1,500,000

	SCORES				TOTAL	MONEY
Yani Tseng	68	70	62	67	267	$225,000
Paula Creamer	66	72	65	65	268	119,509
Soo-Yun Kang	65	69	65	69	268	119,509
Mika Miyazato	70	67	62	70	269	77,738
Song-Hee Kim	67	68	69	67	271	48,539
Ai Miyazato	69	70	64	68	271	48,539
Vicky Hurst	70	69	63	69	271	48,539
Sandra Gal	65	69	68	69	271	48,539
Angela Stanford	69	69	67	67	272	28,865
Jimin Jeong	66	69	69	68	272	28,865
Karine Icher	64	66	74	68	272	28,865
Mikaela Parmlid	67	67	68	70	272	28,865
Seon Hwa Lee	67	67	68	70	272	28,865
Hee Young Park	64	73	69	67	273	19,624
Natalie Gulbis	68	70	66	69	273	19,624
Meredith Duncan	69	67	68	69	273	19,624
Mi Hyun Kim	69	67	68	69	273	19,624
Helen Alfredsson	67	69	68	69	273	19,624
Lindsey Wright	67	69	67	70	273	19,624
Suzann Pettersen	67	68	68	70	273	19,624
Katherine Hull	68	69	65	71	273	19,624
Jiyai Shin	68	71	67	68	274	15,339
Cristie Kerr	68	71	65	70	274	15,339
In-Kyung Kim	69	69	65	71	274	15,339
Hee-Won Han	65	67	71	71	274	15,339
Michelle Wie	73	67	68	67	275	12,666
Momoko Ueda	72	67	69	67	275	12,666
Brittany Lang	70	68	68	69	275	12,666
Meena Lee	67	72	66	70	275	12,666
Na Yeon Choi	66	68	68	73	275	12,666
Minea Blomqvist	65	70	66	74	275	12,666

LPGA State Farm Classic

Panther Creek Country Club, Springfield, Illinois
Par 36-36–72; 6,746 yards

June 4-7
purse, $1,700,000

	SCORES				TOTAL	MONEY
In-Kyung Kim	69	68	69	65	271	$255,000
Se Ri Pak	66	68	72	66	272	157,384
Hee-Won Han	69	69	70	65	273	91,193
Jee Young Lee	66	69	72	66	273	91,193
Angela Stanford	70	67	69	67	273	91,193
Eun-Hee Ji	70	72	69	63	274	42,509
Paula Creamer	69	71	69	65	274	42,509
Ai Miyazato	73	68	65	68	274	42,509
Amy Hung	71	66	69	68	274	42,509
Suzann Pettersen	68	66	72	68	274	42,509
Cristie Kerr	69	69	66	70	274	42,509
Jiyai Shin	69	67	69	70	275	30,157
Anna Rawson	71	71	69	65	276	27,400
Helen Alfredsson	72	63	71	70	276	27,400
Anna Grzebien	71	70	71	65	277	23,666
Yani Tseng	69	72	70	66	277	23,666

	SCORES				TOTAL	MONEY
Karine Icher	70	72	66	69	277	23,666
Song-Hee Kim	71	69	72	66	278	19,502
Karen Stupples	69	68	75	66	278	19,502
Eunjung Yi	72	67	72	67	278	19,502
Meaghan Francella	69	68	73	68	278	19,502
Joo Mi Kim	70	68	71	69	278	19,502
Kristy McPherson	69	66	69	74	278	19,502
Haeji Kang	74	68	70	67	279	16,458
Shanshan Feng	69	70	71	69	279	16,458
Seon Hwa Lee	69	68	72	70	279	16,458
Mikaela Parmlid	70	70	73	67	280	14,096
Christina Kim	72	68	71	69	280	14,096
Natalie Gulbis	68	72	69	71	280	14,096
Amy Yang	69	69	71	71	280	14,096
Kris Tamulis	67	68	74	71	280	14,096

McDonald's LPGA Championship

Bulle Rock Golf Course, Havre de Grace, Maryland   June 11-14
Par 36-36–72; 6,641 yards   purse, $2,000,000

	SCORES				TOTAL	MONEY
Anna Nordqvist	66	70	69	68	273	$300,000
Lindsey Wright	70	68	69	70	277	182,956
Jiyai Shin	73	68	69	68	278	132,721
Kyeong Bae	70	69	72	68	279	102,670
Angela Stanford	70	71	70	69	280	68,948
Nicole Castrale	65	72	74	69	280	68,948
Kristy McPherson	70	70	70	70	280	68,948
Na Yeon Choi	68	71	70	72	281	49,584
Song-Hee Kim	73	72	68	69	282	39,441
Amy Yang	68	74	70	70	282	39,441
Stacy Lewis	68	72	71	71	282	39,441
Jin Young Pak	69	71	69	73	282	39,441
Brandie Burton	73	71	72	67	283	32,854
Inbee Park	70	72	73	69	284	29,949
Irene Cho	72	75	65	72	284	29,949
Paula Creamer	74	70	71	70	285	25,041
Shi Hyun Ahn	73	70	72	70	285	25,041
In-Kyung Kim	72	74	68	71	285	25,041
Katherine Hull	69	69	76	71	285	25,041
Sophie Gustafson	69	74	70	72	285	25,041
Natalie Gulbis	72	75	69	70	286	21,836
Hee-Won Han	70	69	73	74	286	21,836
Maria Hjorth	71	75	72	69	287	18,105
Michelle Wie	70	74	73	70	287	18,105
Eun-Hee Ji	74	69	73	71	287	18,105
Allison Hanna-Williams	72	74	69	72	287	18,105
Mindy Kim	74	69	72	72	287	18,105
Paige Mackenzie	68	77	69	73	287	18,105
Lorena Ochoa	72	69	73	73	287	18,105
Yani Tseng	73	71	69	74	287	18,105
Beth Bader	73	73	74	68	288	13,147
Young Kim	72	74	71	71	288	13,147
Michele Redman	72	73	72	71	288	13,147
Cristie Kerr	76	70	70	72	288	13,147
Soo-Yun Kang	73	71	72	72	288	13,147
Na Ri Kim	71	73	72	72	288	13,147
Ashleigh Simon	68	74	74	72	288	13,147
Heather Bowie Young	75	70	70	73	288	13,147

	SCORES				TOTAL	MONEY
Seon Hwa Lee	74	71	76	68	289	10,017
Ji Young Oh	73	74	71	71	289	10,017
Janice Moodie	74	73	70	72	289	10,017
Mika Miyazato	72	74	70	73	289	10,017
Brittany Lang	72	72	72	73	289	10,017
Juli Inkster	73	71	73	73	290	8,214
M.J. Hur	71	72	74	73	290	8,214
Anna Grzebien	74	73	69	74	290	8,214
Kris Tschetter	70	72	73	75	290	8,214
Minea Blomqvist	73	69	70	78	290	8,214
Karrie Webb	72	70	76	73	291	6,937
Sandra Gal	71	71	76	73	291	6,937
Stacy Prammanasudh	73	71	72	75	291	6,937
Sun Young Yoo	73	74	68	76	291	6,937
Johanna Mundy	73	73	73	73	292	6,110
Chella Choi	71	72	76	73	292	6,110
Eunjung Yi	73	74	69	76	292	6,110
Moira Dunn	68	74	74	76	292	6,110
Helen Alfredsson	74	71	76	72	293	5,034
Il Mi Chung	74	73	72	74	293	5,034
Karin Sjodin	70	77	72	74	293	5,034
Wendy Doolan	72	73	74	74	293	5,034
Candie Kung	72	72	75	74	293	5,034
Taylor Leon	72	72	75	74	293	5,034
Momoko Ueda	76	71	70	76	293	5,034
Aree Song	68	73	74	78	293	5,034
Se Ri Pak	72	74	74	74	294	4,357
Jee Young Lee	75	72	72	75	294	4,357
Marcy Hart	71	72	75	76	294	4,357
Becky Morgan	71	71	73	79	294	4,357
Carin Koch	74	72	74	75	295	4,057
Katie Futcher	71	71	74	79	295	4,057
Meaghan Francella	69	76	75	76	296	3,907
Jamie Hullett	73	71	76	76	296	3,907
Teresa Lu	76	70	73	77	296	3,907
Karine Icher	75	72	76	74	297	3,806
Julieta Granada	75	72	75	76	298	3,760
Marisa Baena	70	74	78	77	299	3,712
Jackie Gallagher-Smith	72	75	74	82	303	3,665

Wegmans LPGA

Locust Hill Country Club, Pittsford, New York
Par 35-37–72; 6,365 yards

June 25-28
purse, $2,000,000

	SCORES				TOTAL	MONEY
Jiyai Shin	65	68	67	71	271	$300,000
Yani Tseng	73	69	70	66	278	158,960
Kristy McPherson	67	69	76	66	278	158,960
Haeji Kang	68	75	65	71	279	84,906
Mika Miyazato	69	72	67	71	279	84,906
Stacy Lewis	68	67	70	74	279	84,906
Cristie Kerr	75	65	71	69	280	50,607
Meaghan Francella	71	68	71	70	280	50,607
Sun Young Yoo	71	67	69	73	280	50,607
Brittany Lincicome	70	75	67	69	281	35,629
Michelle Wie	69	68	75	69	281	35,629
In-Kyung Kim	71	71	68	71	281	35,629
Mindy Kim	69	68	71	73	281	35,629
Sandra Gal	64	73	69	75	281	35,629

	SCORES				TOTAL	MONEY
Sarah Kemp	69	70	73	70	282	25,392
Ai Miyazato	72	69	70	71	282	25,392
Anna Grzebien	70	71	70	71	282	25,392
Ji Young Oh	69	72	68	73	282	25,392
Brittany Lang	73	66	70	73	282	25,392
Lindsey Wright	71	68	67	76	282	25,392
Morgan Pressel	68	66	70	78	282	25,392
M.J. Hur	68	73	72	70	283	21,185
Alena Sharp	70	70	69	74	283	21,185
Stacy Prammanasudh	71	71	72	70	284	17,870
Amy Yang	69	73	72	70	284	17,870
Karrie Webb	72	71	70	71	284	17,870
Se Ri Pak	69	71	73	71	284	17,870
Karen Stupples	69	72	71	72	284	17,870
Na Yeon Choi	69	72	70	73	284	17,870
Wendy Ward	70	72	68	74	284	17,870

Jamie Farr Owens Corning Classic

Highland Meadows Golf Club, Sylvania, Ohio — July 2-5
Par 34-37–71; 6,428 yards — purse, $1,400,000

	SCORES				TOTAL	MONEY
Eunjung Yi	68	66	61	71	266	$210,000
Morgan Pressel	64	68	67	67	266	126,385
(Yi defeated Pressel on first playoff hole.)						
Michelle Wie	65	69	70	64	268	73,231
Seon Hwa Lee	70	63	68	67	268	73,231
Song-Hee Kim	64	71	64	69	268	73,231
Yani Tseng	68	68	65	68	269	42,902
Suzann Pettersen	65	69	67	68	269	42,902
Lindsey Wright	66	68	71	65	270	29,753
Nicole Castrale	70	66	67	67	270	29,753
Lorena Ochoa	67	68	67	68	270	29,753
Mikaela Parmlid	69	70	62	69	270	29,753
Allison Fouch	70	70	66	65	271	21,450
Helen Alfredsson	67	70	66	68	271	21,450
Wendy Ward	70	66	67	68	271	21,450
Janice Moodie	67	69	67	68	271	21,450
Sarah Kemp	68	63	70	70	271	21,450
Anna Nordqvist	67	70	69	66	272	16,884
Allison Hanna-Williams	67	68	70	67	272	16,884
Cristie Kerr	66	71	66	69	272	16,884
Jiyai Shin	66	67	68	71	272	16,884
Eun-Hee Ji	68	69	71	65	273	14,531
Se Ri Pak	70	67	70	66	273	14,531
Shi Hyun Ahn	68	72	65	68	273	14,531
Natalie Gulbis	68	65	69	71	273	14,531
Karine Icher	68	69	70	67	274	12,490
Hee-Won Han	69	66	72	67	274	12,490
Kyeong Bae	70	64	73	67	274	12,490
Inbee Park	66	71	68	69	274	12,490
Katherine Hull	68	69	70	68	275	10,656
Birdie Kim	69	67	71	68	275	10,656
Rachel Hetherington	72	66	68	69	275	10,656
Jennifer Rosales	71	69	65	70	275	10,656

U.S. Women's Open

Saucon Valley Country Club, Bethlehem, Pennsylvania
Par 36-35–71; 6,740 yards

July 9-12
purse, $3,250,000

	SCORES				TOTAL	MONEY
Eun-Hee Ji	71	72	70	71	284	$585,000
Candie Kung	71	77	68	69	285	350,000
In-Kyung Kim	72	72	72	70	286	183,568
Cristie Kerr	69	70	72	75	286	183,568
Brittany Lincicome	72	72	73	70	287	122,415
Paula Creamer	72	68	79	69	288	99,126
Ai Miyazato	74	74	71	69	288	99,126
Suzann Pettersen	74	71	72	71	288	99,126
Na Yeon Choi	68	74	76	71	289	76,711
Kyeong Bae	75	73	69	72	289	76,711
Hee Young Park	70	74	72	73	289	76,711
Song-Hee Kim	74	69	75	72	290	66,769
Jiyai Shin	72	75	76	68	291	59,428
*Jennifer Song	72	74	73	72	291	
Sun Ju Ahn	75	71	72	73	291	59,428
Morgan Pressel	74	75	69	73	291	59,428
Lindsey Wright	74	70	77	71	292	42,724
Jimin Kang	76	71	74	71	292	42,724
Laura Davies	72	75	73	72	292	42,724
Akiko Fukushima	76	72	72	72	292	42,724
Meaghan Francella	73	72	74	73	292	42,724
Nicole Castrale	74	71	74	73	292	42,724
Anna Grzebien	73	77	69	73	292	42,724
Jean Reynolds	69	72	74	77	292	42,724
Teresa Lu	76	69	70	77	292	42,724
He Yong Choi	77	74	74	68	293	27,420
*Jessica Korda	72	77	75	69	293	
Inbee Park	75	71	77	70	293	27,420
*Alison Lee	75	72	76	70	293	
Juli Inkster	78	73	72	70	293	27,420
Anna Nordqvist	71	75	75	72	293	27,420
Lorena Ochoa	69	79	73	72	293	27,420
Sun Young Yoo	72	74	72	76	294	22,603
Maria Hernandez	74	72	77	72	295	20,702
*Alexis Thompson	71	73	78	73	295	
Kristy McPherson	71	74	77	73	295	20,702
Amy Yang	75	71	75	74	295	20,702
Karrie Webb	75	72	74	74	295	20,702
Louise Friberg	75	72	73	75	295	20,702
Michele Redman	77	73	76	70	296	16,924
Sandra Gal	75	71	77	73	296	16,924
Misun Cho	76	74	73	73	296	16,924
Young Kim	71	75	76	74	296	16,924
*Azahara Munoz	72	76	74	74	296	
Brittany Lang	75	74	73	74	296	16,924
Ji Young Oh	76	71	74	75	296	16,924
Momoko Ueda	72	77	72	75	296	16,924
Stacy Lewis	78	73	76	70	297	13,481
Shanshan Feng	74	74	76	73	297	13,481
Hee-Kyung Seo	75	73	73	76	297	13,481
Maria Jose Uribe	75	76	69	77	297	13,481
Christina Kim	72	76	79	71	298	10,736
Karen Stupples	73	75	78	72	298	10,736
Amanda Blumenherst	75	76	73	74	298	10,736
Hye Jung Choi	72	75	75	76	298	10,736
Giulia Sergas	75	67	76	80	298	10,736

	SCORES				TOTAL	MONEY
Haeji Kang	73	78	77	71	299	9,173
Mika Miyazato	75	76	76	72	299	9,173
Stacy Prammanasudh	73	75	78	73	299	9,173
Yuri Fudoh	73	71	80	75	299	9,173
Cindy Lacrosse	76	75	76	73	300	8,365
Ji-Hee Lee	77	72	77	74	300	8,365
Meena Lee	72	79	75	74	300	8,365
Becky Morgan	75	76	73	76	300	8,365
Allison Fouch	75	75	77	74	301	7,985
*Allie White	74	73	78	76	301	
Mina Harigae	77	72	80	73	302	7,788
Karine Icher	76	74	79	73	302	7,788
Jennie Lee	75	76	78	75	304	7,590
*Candace Schepperle	73	78	76	79	306	
Carolina Llano	73	77	78	79	307	7,458
Lisa Ferrero	77	74	84	77	312	7,323

Evian Masters

See Ladies European Tour section.

Ricoh Women's British Open

See Ladies European Tour section.

The Solheim Cup

Rich Harvest Farms, Sugar Grove, Illinois   August 21-23
Par 36-37–73; 6,670 yards

FIRST DAY
Morning Fourballs

Paula Creamer and Cristie Kerr (US) defeated Suzann Pettersen and Sophie Gustafson, 1 up.
Helen Alfredsson and Tania Elosegui (Europe) defeated Angela Stanford and Juli Inkster, 1 up.
Brittany Lang and Brittany Lincicome (US) defeated Laura Davies and Becky Brewerton, 5 and 4.
Catriona Matthew and Maria Hjorth (Europe) halved with Morgan Pressel and Michelle Wie.

POINTS: United States 2½, Europe 1½

Afternoon Foursomes

Christina Kim and Natalie Gulbis (US) defeated Suzann Pettersen and Sophie Gustafson, 4 and 2.
Becky Brewerton and Gwladys Nocera (Europe) defeated Angela Stanford and Nicole Castrale, 3 and 1.
Maria Hjorth and Anna Nordqvist (Europe) defeated Kristy McPherson and Brittany Lincicome, 3 and 2.
Paula Creamer and Juli Inkster (US) defeated Catriona Matthew and Janice Moodie, 2 and 1.

POINTS: United States 4½, Europe 3½

SECOND DAY
Morning Fourballs

Kim and Wie (US) defeated Alfredsson and Elosegui, 5 and 4.
Diana Luna and Matthew (Europe) halved with Lang and Stanford.

Nordqvist and Pettersen (Europe) defeated Castrale and Kerr, 1 up.
Hjorth and Nocera (Europe) defeated Lincicome and McPherson, 1 up.

POINTS: United States 6, Europe 6

Afternoon Foursomes

Gustafson and Moodie (Europe) defeated Creamer and Inkster, 4 and 3.
McPherson and Pressel (US) defeated Alfredsson and Pettersen, 2 up.
Brewerton and Nocera (Europe) defeated Gulbis and Kim, 5 and 4.
Kerr and Wie (US) defeated Hjorth and Nordqvist, 1 up.

POINTS: United States 8, Europe 8

THIRD DAY
Singles

Creamer (US) defeated Pettersen, 3 and 2.
Stanford (US) defeated Brewerton, 5 and 4.
Wie (US) defeated Alfredsson, 1 up.
Lang (US) halved with Davies.
Inkster (US) halved with Nocera.
Matthew (Europe) defeated McPherson, 3 and 2.
Lincicome (US) defeated Gustafson, 3 and 2.
Luna (Europe) defeated Castrale, 3 and 2.
Kim (US) defeated Elosegui, 2 up.
Kerr (US) halved with Hjorth.
Pressel (US) defeated Nordqvist, 3 and 2.
Gulbis (US) halved with Moodie.

TOTAL POINTS: United States 16, Europe 12

Safeway Classic

Pumpkin Ridge Golf Club, Ghost Creek Course,
North Plains, Oregon
Par 37-35–72; 6,546 yards

August 28-30
purse, $1,700,000

	SCORES			TOTAL	MONEY
M.J. Hur	69	69	65	203	$255,000
Suzann Pettersen	68	68	67	203	136,465
Michele Redman	67	69	67	203	136,465
(Hur defeated Redman on first and Pettersen on second playoff hole.)					
Michelle Wie	68	71	66	205	72,891
Ai Miyazato	67	68	70	205	72,891
Seon Hwa Lee	65	70	70	205	72,891
Anna Nordqvist	65	69	72	206	48,931
Paige Mackenzie	70	71	66	207	38,827
Christina Kim	68	70	69	207	38,827
Angela Stanford	66	71	70	207	38,827
Hee Young Park	74	65	69	208	32,475
Jill McGill	72	71	66	209	26,846
Maria Hjorth	70	71	68	209	26,846
Russy Gulyanamitta	71	67	71	209	26,846
Jeong Jang	68	70	71	209	26,846
Natalie Gulbis	68	69	72	209	26,846
Sarah Lee	72	68	70	210	21,535
Eun-Hee Ji	70	70	70	210	21,535
Jennifer Rosales	68	70	72	210	21,535
Sandra Gal	75	69	67	211	17,877
Julieta Granada	73	69	69	211	17,877
Candie Kung	66	76	69	211	17,877

	SCORES			TOTAL	MONEY
Young Kim	70	71	70	211	17,877
Amy Hung	73	67	71	211	17,877
Cristie Kerr	69	70	72	211	17,877
Beth Bader	64	73	74	211	17,877
Rachel Hetherington	76	68	68	212	13,633
Stacy Lewis	72	72	68	212	13,633
Kristy McPherson	71	73	68	212	13,633
Mika Miyazato	69	73	70	212	13,633
Momoko Ueda	70	71	71	212	13,633
Stacy Prammanasudh	66	73	73	212	13,633
Sophie Gustafson	71	67	74	212	13,633

CN Canadian Women's Open

Priddis Greens Golf & Country Club, Calgary, Alberta, Canada
Par 35-36–71; 6,435 yards

September 3-6
purse, $2,750,000

	SCORES				TOTAL	MONEY
Suzann Pettersen	65	68	66	70	269	$412,500
Momoko Ueda	67	72	70	65	274	157,477
Morgan Pressel	71	71	66	66	274	157,477
Ai Miyazato	69	69	69	67	274	157,477
Karrie Webb	69	68	68	69	274	157,477
Angela Stanford	70	65	69	70	274	157,477
In-Kyung Kim	69	68	69	69	275	78,371
Vicky Hurst	71	71	67	67	276	65,195
Anna Nordqvist	68	71	70	67	276	65,195
Jiyai Shin	72	65	77	63	277	47,530
Song-Hee Kim	71	62	77	67	277	47,530
Juli Inkster	69	72	68	68	277	47,530
Kristy McPherson	71	67	69	70	277	47,530
Sophie Gustafson	69	68	70	70	277	47,530
Lorena Ochoa	66	68	72	71	277	47,530
Amy Yang	70	70	71	67	278	37,035
M.J. Hur	68	67	74	69	278	37,035
Cristie Kerr	72	69	68	70	279	33,707
Anna Rawson	64	73	72	70	279	33,707
Stacy Prammanasudh	68	71	74	67	280	30,793
Carin Koch	68	74	68	70	280	30,793
Sun Young Yoo	69	66	73	72	280	30,793
Michele Redman	70	71	70	70	281	28,575
Na Yeon Choi	74	67	75	66	282	26,008
Maria Hjorth	73	69	70	70	282	26,008
Inbee Park	68	74	69	71	282	26,008
Catriona Matthew	68	66	75	73	282	26,008
Paula Creamer	69	71	74	69	283	22,655
Janice Moodie	71	65	75	72	283	22,655
Rachel Hetherington	70	72	67	74	283	22,655

P&G Beauty NW Arkansas Championship

Pinnacle Country Club, Rogers, Arkansas
Par 36-35–71; 6,244 yards

September 11-13
purse, $1,800,000

	SCORES			TOTAL	MONEY
Jiyai Shin	70	70	64	204	$270,000
Sun Young Yoo	69	67	68	204	143,063
Angela Stanford	66	69	69	204	143,063
(Shin defeated Yoo and Stanford on second playoff hole.)					
Shi Hyun Ahn	71	68	66	205	83,981
Song-Hee Kim	65	68	72	205	83,981
Taylor Leon	71	68	67	206	61,284
Hye Jung Choi	68	69	70	207	48,119
Na Yeon Choi	71	65	71	207	48,119
Becky Morgan	72	69	67	208	40,402
Seon Hwa Lee	74	68	67	209	33,092
Ai Miyazato	72	68	69	209	33,092
Hee Young Park	68	72	69	209	33,092
Helen Alfredsson	69	69	71	209	33,092
Hee-Won Han	72	68	70	210	23,968
Natalie Gulbis	71	69	70	210	23,968
Paula Creamer	70	70	70	210	23,968
Sandra Gal	64	76	70	210	23,968
Na Ri Kim	70	67	73	210	23,968
M.J. Hur	69	68	73	210	23,968
Yani Tseng	68	68	74	210	23,968
Moira Dunn	70	71	70	211	18,385
Stacy Lewis	73	67	71	211	18,385
Paige Mackenzie	69	70	72	211	18,385
Wendy Ward	69	69	73	211	18,385
Stacy Prammanasudh	68	70	73	211	18,385
Jane Park	67	70	74	211	18,385
*Kelli Shean	76	67	69	212	
Kyeong Bae	69	74	69	212	14,015
Joo Mi Kim	73	69	70	212	14,015
Young Kim	70	70	72	212	14,015
Eun-Hee Ji	67	73	72	212	14,015
Eunjung Yi	70	69	73	212	14,015
Cristie Kerr	69	70	73	212	14,015
Michelle Wie	69	70	73	212	14,015
Pat Hurst	66	71	75	212	14,015

Samsung World Championship

Torrey Pines Golf Course, South Course,
San Diego, California
Par 36-36–72; 6,721 yards

September 17-20
purse, $1,000,000

	SCORES				TOTAL	MONEY
Na Yeon Choi	71	67	63	71	272	$250,000
Ai Miyazato	68	68	68	69	273	157,250
Jiyai Shin	66	69	68	74	277	106,925
Paula Creamer	69	69	70	71	279	56,620
Lorena Ochoa	67	69	72	71	279	56,620
Sophie Gustafson	67	70	75	70	282	37,765
Cristie Kerr	72	66	73	72	283	31,470
Song-Hee Kim	66	72	78	70	286	26,437
Suzann Pettersen	71	72	70	73	286	26,437
Yani Tseng	75	66	70	75	286	26,437

	SCORES				TOTAL	MONEY
Angela Stanford	72	74	71	71	288	19,535
Anna Nordqvist	71	74	72	71	288	19,535
Catriona Matthew	74	68	73	73	288	19,535
Brittany Lincicome	70	70	73	75	288	19,535
Juli Inkster	68	74	74	74	290	15,363
Karrie Webb	73	72	70	75	290	15,363
Kristy McPherson	73	72	70	75	290	15,363
Lindsey Wright	73	72	74	72	291	13,905
In-Kyung Kim	72	73	73	76	294	13,270
Eun-Hee Ji	78	73	72	75	298	12,635

CVS/pharmacy LPGA Challenge

Blackhawk Country Club, Danville, California
Par 37-35–72; 6,185 yards

September 24-27
purse, $1,100,000

	SCORES				TOTAL	MONEY
Sophie Gustafson	65	69	66	68	268	$165,000
Lorena Ochoa	68	67	65	72	272	100,395
Amy Yang	72	67	69	66	274	64,584
Sun Young Yoo	73	64	69	68	274	64,584
Amanda Blumenherst	70	71	67	67	275	37,835
Maria Hjorth	69	66	72	68	275	37,835
Angela Stanford	67	70	69	69	275	37,835
Katherine Hull	72	68	68	68	276	27,208
Reilley Rankin	70	69	73	65	277	21,642
Catriona Matthew	71	70	69	67	277	21,642
Christina Kim	70	73	65	69	277	21,642
Morgan Pressel	71	69	67	70	277	21,642
Anna Grzebien	69	71	69	69	278	16,489
Natalie Gulbis	73	66	70	69	278	16,489
Vicky Hurst	71	67	70	70	278	16,489
Paula Creamer	71	67	69	71	278	16,489
Mikaela Parmlid	68	71	70	70	279	13,961
Leta Lindley	70	71	66	72	279	13,961
Sandra Gal	70	72	73	65	280	12,642
Karrie Webb	68	75	69	68	280	12,642
Brittany Lang	71	70	69	70	280	12,642
Shanshan Feng	68	67	75	71	281	11,762
Brittany Lincicome	72	70	70	70	282	11,323
In-Kyung Kim	73	72	69	69	283	9,557
Pat Hurst	73	67	74	69	283	9,557
Juli Inkster	71	72	70	70	283	9,557
Na Ri Kim	67	76	70	70	283	9,557
Candie Kung	73	70	69	71	283	9,557
Alena Sharp	70	72	69	72	283	9,557
Yani Tseng	69	70	71	73	283	9,557
Sophia Sheridan	67	72	71	73	283	9,557

Navistar LPGA Classic

Robert Trent Jones Golf Trail, Senator Course, Prattville, Alabama
Par 36-36–72; 6,546 yards

October 1-4
purse, $1,300,000

	SCORES				TOTAL	MONEY
Lorena Ochoa	66	68	66	70	270	$195,000
Michelle Wie	66	70	72	66	274	101,453
Brittany Lang	68	68	68	70	274	101,453
Yani Tseng	71	63	71	70	275	59,554
Janice Moodie	64	72	68	71	275	59,554
Beth Bader	70	69	70	67	276	39,917
Maria Hjorth	69	68	68	71	276	39,917
Sophie Gustafson	70	65	72	70	277	28,864
Allison Fouch	68	70	68	71	277	28,864
Ji Young Oh	71	69	65	72	277	28,864
Vicky Hurst	72	69	70	67	278	20,656
Na Yeon Choi	67	72	70	69	278	20,656
Hye Jung Choi	68	68	72	70	278	20,656
Pat Hurst	67	70	70	71	278	20,656
Giulia Sergas	69	65	72	72	278	20,656
Sandra Gal	68	69	66	75	278	20,656
Mindy Kim	75	68	66	70	279	16,353
Cristie Kerr	71	73	64	71	279	16,353
Morgan Pressel	69	72	70	69	280	14,550
Young Kim	74	70	66	70	280	14,550
Kris Tamulis	71	72	67	70	280	14,550
Sarah Jane Smith	72	71	66	71	280	14,550
Shi Hyun Ahn	72	72	69	68	281	12,538
Katherine Hull	67	75	70	69	281	12,538
Ashleigh Simon	69	70	72	70	281	12,538
Stacy Prammanasudh	70	69	71	71	281	12,538
Jennifer Rosales	69	72	71	70	282	10,735
Christina Kim	68	73	70	71	282	10,735
Alena Sharp	67	71	73	71	282	10,735
Paige Mackenzie	69	71	70	72	282	10,735
*Alexis Thompson	65	69	74	74	282	

Hana Bank-Kolon Championship

Sky 72 Golf Club, Oceans Course, Incheon, South Korea
Par 36-36–72; 6,409 yards

October 30-November 1
purse, $1,700,000

	SCORES			TOTAL	MONEY
Na Yeon Choi	68	71	67	206	$255,000
Maria Hjorth	68	72	67	207	136,819
Yani Tseng	69	70	68	207	136,819
Ran Hong	70	71	69	210	88,997
Song-Hee Kim	69	72	71	212	71,633
Jiyai Shin	67	76	70	213	58,609
Brittany Lang	73	73	68	214	41,461
Anna Nordqvist	70	73	71	214	41,461
Se Ri Pak	70	72	72	214	41,461
Inbee Park	70	71	73	214	41,461
Bo-Mee Lee	73	74	68	215	29,543
Juli Inkster	70	76	69	215	29,543
Momoko Ueda	70	75	70	215	29,543
Jee Young Lee	70	72	73	215	29,543
Hee Young Park	72	74	70	216	21,446
Sandra Gal	71	75	70	216	21,446

	SCORES			TOTAL	MONEY
M.J. Hur	71	74	71	216	21,446
Hee-Kyung Seo	70	75	71	216	21,446
In-Kyung Kim	72	70	74	216	21,446
Ae-Ree Pyun	71	71	74	216	21,446
Meena Lee	69	73	74	216	21,446
Vicky Hurst	67	75	74	216	21,446
Catriona Matthew	67	79	71	217	17,540
Seon Hwa Lee	70	75	72	217	17,540
Lindsey Wright	70	79	69	218	15,672
Paula Creamer	72	74	72	218	15,672
Meaghan Francella	66	79	73	218	15,672
Jimin Kang	67	73	78	218	15,672
Ha Neul Kim	70	77	72	219	13,111
So Yeon Ryu	71	74	74	219	13,111
Hye-Youn Kim	71	73	75	219	13,111
Ji Young Oh	70	72	77	219	13,111
Eun-Hee Ji	70	71	78	219	13,111

Mizuno Classic

See Japan LPGA Tour section.

Lorena Ochoa Invitational

Guadalajara Country Club, Guadalajara, Mexico
Par 36-36–72; 6,638 yards

November 12-15
purse, $1,100,000

	SCORES				TOTAL	MONEY
Michelle Wie	70	66	70	69	275	$220,000
Paula Creamer	67	69	71	70	277	113,794
Morgan Pressel	72	68	71	67	278	65,936
Jiyai Shin	67	66	74	71	278	65,936
Cristie Kerr	69	70	67	72	278	65,936
Lorena Ochoa	71	69	72	69	281	38,627
Song-Hee Kim	65	72	70	74	281	38,627
Mariajo Uribe	67	72	74	70	283	24,900
Catriona Matthew	68	75	69	71	283	24,900
M.J. Hur	70	70	72	71	283	24,900
Brittany Lang	69	70	72	72	283	24,900
In-Kyung Kim	71	74	65	73	283	24,900
Yani Tseng	72	68	69	74	283	24,900
Anna Nordqvist	73	69	71	71	284	18,628
Brittany Lincicome	69	70	73	72	284	18,628
Ai Miyazato	71	72	70	72	285	16,240
Sun Young Yoo	73	72	67	73	285	16,240
Suzann Pettersen	72	67	72	74	285	16,240
Na Yeon Choi	74	71	72	70	287	14,579
Kristy McPherson	71	69	71	76	287	14,579
Karrie Webb	73	72	70	73	288	13,831
Juli Inkster	71	75	74	69	289	13,084
Candie Kung	73	69	73	74	289	13,084
Laura Davies	76	69	73	72	290	11,682
Hee-Won Han	71	76	70	73	290	11,682
Ji Young Oh	74	72	71	73	290	11,682
Sophie Gustafson	75	69	73	73	290	11,682
Sophia Sheridan	72	73	73	73	291	9,984
Eun-Hee Ji	68	74	76	73	291	9,984
Seon Hwa Lee	71	73	73	74	291	9,984
Katherine Hull	70	73	74	74	291	9,984

LPGA Tour Championship

Houstonian Golf & Country Club, Richmond, Texas
Par 36-36–72; 6,650 yards
(Event shortened to 54 holes and completed on Monday—rain.)

November 19-23
purse, $1,500,000

	SCORES			TOTAL	MONEY
Anna Nordqvist	70	68	65	203	$225,000
Lorena Ochoa	66	72	67	205	136,902
Na Yeon Choi	70	72	64	206	88,071
Kristy McPherson	69	67	70	206	88,071
Hee Young Park	70	72	67	209	51,593
Song-Hee Kim	73	68	68	209	51,593
Sophie Gustafson	70	71	68	209	51,593
Ai Miyazato	73	68	69	210	32,230
Suzann Pettersen	72	68	70	210	32,230
Yani Tseng	69	71	70	210	32,230
Jiyai Shin	70	67	73	210	32,230
Sun Young Yoo	74	69	68	211	23,910
Jee Young Lee	74	68	69	211	23,910
Cristie Kerr	72	69	70	211	23,910
Heather Bowie Young	69	69	73	211	23,910
Amy Yang	76	68	68	212	19,113
Maria Hjorth	73	69	70	212	19,113
Wendy Ward	72	70	70	212	19,113
Karin Sjodin	70	72	70	212	19,113
Meaghan Francella	71	75	67	213	15,753
Il Mi Chung	76	68	69	213	15,753
Katherine Hull	71	72	70	213	15,753
Katie Futcher	73	69	71	213	15,753
Chella Choi	71	69	73	213	15,753
Taylor Leon	68	72	73	213	15,753

Ladies European Tour

ANZ Ladies Masters
See Australian Ladies Tour section.

Women's Australian Open
See Australian Ladies Tour section.

Comunitat Valenciana European Nations Cup

La Sella Golf Resort, Alicante, Spain
Par 36-36–72; 6,283 yards

April 23-26
purse, €325,000

	SCORES				TOTAL
NETHERLANDS—€77,000 Christel Boeljon/Marjet van der Graaff	66	70	66	68	270
FRANCE—€29,500 Gwladys Nocera/Anne-Lise Caudal	67	68	65	74	274
AUSTRALIA—€29,500 Joanne Mills/Nikki Garrett	65	73	65	71	274
ITALY—€29,500 Giulia Sergas/Veronica Zorzi	69	70	73	62	274
ENGLAND—€19,500 Laura Davies/Lisa Hall	67	74	68	66	275
SPAIN—€18,000 Paula Marti/Tania Elosegui	73	67	68	68	276
UNITED STATES—€16,500 Meg Mallon/Beth Daniel	66	67	73	72	278
SWEDEN—€15,000 Carin Koch/Lotta Wahlin	71	68	69	71	279
WALES—€13,500 Becky Brewerton/Lydia Hall	70	72	69	70	281
IRELAND—€11,500 Rebecca Coakley/Martina Gillen	72	70	69	71	282
DENMARK—€11,500 Iben Tinning/Lisa Holm Sorensen	68	72	73	69	282
FINLAND—€10,000 Ursula Wikstrom/Kaisa Ruuttila	75	69	69	73	286
SCOTLAND—€9,000 Clare Queen/Lynn Kenny	69	76	72	71	288
SWITZERLAND—€7,000 Florence Luscher/Frederique Seeholzer	71	70	72	76	289

	SCORES				TOTAL
NORWAY — €7,000					
Marianne Skarpnord/Lill Kristin Saether	70	76	72	71	289
GERMANY — €7,000					
Martina Eberl/Denise-Charlotte Becker	70	75	73	71	289
RUSSIA — €5,000					
Maria Verchenova/Anastasia Kostina	72	72	73	74	291
BELGIUM — €4,000					
Lara Tadiotto/Ellen Smets	73	76	73	73	295
SLOVAKIA — €1,500					
Zuzana Kamasova/*Veronika Falathova	72	75	73	78	298
AUSTRIA — €2,000					
Eva Steinberger/Nicole Gergely	70	100	71	75	316

Deutsche Bank Ladies Swiss Open

Golf Gerre Losone, Ticino, Switzerland
Par 36-37–73; 6,296 yards

May 14-17
purse, €525,000

	SCORES				TOTAL	MONEY
Marianne Skarpnord	69	71	66	70	276	€78,750
Melissa Reid	71	68	68	70	277	53,287.50
Karen Lunn	73	67	69	69	278	36,750
Emma Zackrisson	67	74	70	69	280	28,350
Georgina Simpson	69	72	71	70	282	20,317.50
Nicole Gergely	70	69	72	71	282	20,317.50
Ursula Wikstrom	69	74	70	70	283	15,750
Gwladys Nocera	72	70	72	70	284	12,442.50
Lisa Hall	68	73	72	71	284	12,442.50
Margherita Rigon	70	73	74	68	285	8,557.50
Iben Tinning	71	76	70	68	285	8,557.50
Nikki Garrett	72	75	69	69	285	8,557.50
Carmen Alonso	71	71	73	70	285	8,557.50
Lee-Anne Pace	71	72	72	70	285	8,557.50
Anna Nordqvist	71	72	71	71	285	8,557.50
Anne-Lise Caudal	70	73	71	71	285	8,557.50
Jenni Kuosa	67	70	75	73	285	8,557.50
Beatriz Recari	72	74	72	68	286	6,864.37
Emma Cabrera-Bello	71	74	72	69	286	6,864.37
Krystle Caithness	71	75	69	71	286	6,864.37
Lill Kristin Saether	69	72	70	75	286	6,864.37

HypoVereinsbank Ladies German Open

Golfpark Gut Hausern, Munich, Germany
Par 36-36–72; 6,204 yards

May 21-24
purse, €300,000

	SCORES				TOTAL	MONEY
Jade Schaeffer	66	72	70	67	275	€45,000
Paula Marti	67	69	66	73	275	30,450
(Schaeffer defeated Marti on first playoff hole.)						
Melissa Reid	68	67	71	70	276	18,600
Martina Eberl	71	65	67	73	276	18,600
Trish Johnson	71	69	67	70	277	12,720

	SCORES				TOTAL	MONEY
Marianne Skarpnord	71	71	68	68	278	9,000
Emma Cabrera-Bello	66	72	71	69	278	9,000
Johanna Westerberg	65	67	74	72	278	9,000
Sophie Walker	70	70	72	67	279	6,720
Anja Monke	71	70	70	70	281	5,560
Tania Elosegui	71	70	69	71	281	5,560
Katharina Schallenberg	71	70	69	71	281	5,560
Beatriz Recari	71	71	73	67	282	4,560
Emma Zackrisson	71	73	70	68	282	4,560
Anna Knutsson	72	71	70	69	282	4,560
Lydia Hall	74	70	66	72	282	4,560
Nikki Garrett	74	70	72	67	283	4,140
Anne-Lise Caudal	70	70	69	74	283	4,140
Anna Tybring	71	70	76	67	284	3,825
Riikka Hakkarainen	71	74	70	69	284	3,825
Ursula Wikstrom	72	72	70	70	284	3,825
Joanne Morley	72	72	69	71	284	3,825

ABN AMRO Ladies Open

Eindhovensche Golf Club, Valkenswaard, Netherlands June 5-7
Par 36-36–72; 6,305 yards purse, €250,000

	SCORES			TOTAL	MONEY
Tania Elosegui	70	68	69	207	€37,500
Diana Luna	66	70	72	208	25,375
Marianne Skarpnord	67	74	69	210	17,500
Becky Brewerton	71	74	66	211	12,050
Jade Schaeffer	73	72	66	211	12,050
Iben Tinning	70	74	68	212	8,125
Veronica Zorzi	72	69	71	212	8,125
Rebecca Hudson	74	73	66	213	5,616.66
Virginie Lagoutte-Clement	73	72	68	213	5,616.66
Stefania Croce	70	71	72	213	5,616.66
Stacy Lee Bregman	72	74	68	214	4,308.33
Denise-Charlotte Becker	70	76	68	214	4,308.33
Frances Bondad	71	74	69	214	4,308.33
*Marieke Nivard	72	74	69	215	
Katharina Schallenberg	72	74	69	215	3,668.75
Michele Thomson	72	74	69	215	3,668.75
Emma Lyons	70	75	70	215	3,668.75
Hazel Kavanagh	68	72	75	215	3,668.75
Johanna Westerberg	73	75	68	216	3,268.75
Lynnette Brooky	72	73	71	216	3,268.75
Sophie Walker	71	74	71	216	3,268.75
Jessica Ji	69	73	74	216	3,268.75

Ladies Open de Portugal

Golden Eagle Golf Club, Rio Maior, Portugal June 12-14
Par 36-36–72; 6,451 yards purse, €200,000

	SCORES			TOTAL	MONEY
Johanna Westerberg	74	72	67	213	€30,000
Tania Elosegui	73	70	70	213	20,300
(Westerberg defeated Elosegui on first playoff hole.)					
Bettina Hauert	73	74	67	214	12,400

	SCORES			TOTAL	MONEY
Becky Brewerton	69	76	69	214	12,400
Jade Schaeffer	74	71	70	215	5,833.33
Florentyna Parker	74	71	70	215	5,833.33
Pamela Feggans	71	73	71	215	5,833.33
Anne-Lise Caudal	70	73	72	215	5,833.33
Iben Tinning	69	74	72	215	5,833.33
Christel Boeljon	72	71	72	215	5,833.33
Paula Marti	74	72	70	216	3,546.66
Nicole Gergely	70	75	71	216	3,546.66
Stefania Croce	71	71	74	216	3,546.66
Lee-Anne Pace	72	73	72	217	3,055
Carmen Alonso	69	75	73	217	3,055
Diana Luna	71	73	73	217	3,055
Lotta Wahlin	68	73	76	217	3,055
Linda Wessberg	74	74	70	218	2,800
Malene Jorgensen	73	74	71	218	2,800
Rebecca Coakley	73	76	70	219	2,436.66
Cecilia Ekelundh	71	76	72	219	2,436.66
Karen Lunn	74	73	72	219	2,436.66
Emma Zackrisson	75	72	72	219	2,436.66
Lynnette Brooky	77	70	72	219	2,436.66
Christine Hallstrom	75	71	73	219	2,436.66

AIB Ladies Irish Open

Portmarnock Hotel & Golf Links, Portmarnock,
Co. Dublin, Ireland
Par 36-36–72; 6,318 yards

June 26-28
purse, €500,000

	SCORES			TOTAL	MONEY
Diana Luna	68	69	68	205	€75,000
Gwladys Nocera	68	72	69	209	37,583.33
Florentyna Parker	70	69	70	209	37,583.33
Sophie Gustafson	71	67	71	209	37,583.33
Krystle Caithness	71	69	70	210	21,200
Melissa Reid	68	70	73	211	17,500
Sophie Giquel	70	74	68	212	15,000
Lee-Anne Pace	71	71	71	213	11,850
Marianne Skarpnord	71	70	72	213	11,850
Sophie Walker	74	72	68	214	8,962.50
Frances Bondad	74	70	70	214	8,962.50
*Jodi Ewart	74	69	71	214	
Becky Brewerton	68	72	74	214	8,962.50
Julie Greciet	67	72	75	214	8,962.50
Tania Elosegui	75	70	70	215	7,450
Lydia Hall	69	74	72	215	7,450
Emma Zackrisson	70	72	73	215	7,450
Johanna Westerberg	72	73	71	216	6,800
Jade Schaeffer	74	70	72	216	6,800
Beatriz Recari	72	71	73	216	6,800

SAS Ladies Masters

Larvik Golfklubb, Larvik, Norway
Par 36-37–73; 6,242 yards

July 2-4
purse, €200,000

	SCORES			TOTAL	MONEY
Diana Luna	67	70	70	207	€30,000
Laura Cabanillas	70	68	70	208	20,300
Iben Tinning	71	71	67	209	7,475
Felicity Johnson	69	72	68	209	7,475
Stephanie Na	70	71	68	209	7,475
Beth Allen	72	68	69	209	7,475
Tania Elosegui	71	69	69	209	7,475
Samantha Head	66	73	70	209	7,475
Lisa Holm Sorensen	62	74	73	209	7,475
Veronica Zorzi	66	68	75	209	7,475
Melissa Reid	67	72	71	210	3,720
Emma Cabrera-Bello	68	74	69	211	3,140
Carmen Alonso	67	75	69	211	3,140
Virginie Lagoutte-Clement	73	69	69	211	3,140
Johanna Westerberg	69	72	70	211	3,140
Becky Brewerton	71	70	70	211	3,140
Trish Johnson	69	70	72	211	3,140
Sophie Giquel	66	73	72	211	3,140
Linda Wessberg	75	70	67	212	2,516.66
Lee-Anne Pace	72	69	71	212	2,516.66
Christel Boeljon	70	71	71	212	2,516.66
Anna Knutsson	72	68	72	212	2,516.66
Rebecca Hudson	68	71	73	212	2,516.66
Marianne Skarpnord	70	69	73	212	2,516.66

Open de Espana Feminino

Panoramica Golf & Country Club, San Jordi, Castellon, Spain
Par 36-36–72; 6,252 yards

July 16-19
purse, €275,000

	SCORES				TOTAL	MONEY
Becky Brewerton	65	69	66	70	270	€41,250
Diana Luna	71	71	69	65	276	18,418.12
Breanne Alicia Loucks	72	69	69	66	276	18,418.12
Emma Cabrera-Bello	70	67	72	67	276	18,418.12
Tania Elosegui	71	69	65	71	276	18,418.12
Johanna Westerberg	69	72	70	66	277	8,250
Frances Bondad	72	67	70	68	277	8,250
Elizabeth Bennett	69	72	67	69	277	8,250
Laura Davies	69	70	73	66	278	5,573.33
Bettina Hauert	69	71	69	69	278	5,573.33
*Carlota Ciganda	65	72	71	70	278	
Marianne Skarpnord	71	69	68	70	278	5,573.33
Lee-Anne Pace	68	70	71	70	279	4,578.75
Sarah Heath	70	67	70	72	279	4,578.75
Veronica Zorzi	71	67	73	70	281	3,976.50
Florentyna Parker	72	70	69	70	281	3,976.50
Stacy Lee Bregman	69	72	67	73	281	3,976.50
Anne-Lise Caudal	68	73	66	74	281	3,976.50
Denise-Charlotte Becker	67	72	67	75	281	3,976.50
*Lucie Andre	70	74	73	65	282	
Stefania Croce	72	71	70	69	282	3,547.50
Julie Tvede	69	73	69	71	282	3,547.50
Caroline Rominger	69	71	70	72	282	3,547.50

Evian Masters

Evian Masters Golf Club, Evians-les-Bains, France
Par 36-36—72; 6,347 yards

July 23-26
purse, €2,430,258

	SCORES				TOTAL	MONEY
Ai Miyazato	69	66	70	69	274	€341,249.80
Sophie Gustafson	71	66	67	70	274	225,507.67
(Miyazato defeated Gustafson on first playoff hole.)						
Meena Lee	69	69	72	65	275	145,069.66
Cristie Kerr	70	68	67	70	275	145,069.66
Helen Alfredsson	70	69	68	70	277	84,984.62
Paula Creamer	70	67	70	70	277	84,984.62
Karrie Webb	69	69	68	71	277	84,984.62
Na Yeon Choi	67	68	72	71	278	55,353.63
Yuko Mitsuka	71	66	71	70	278	55,353.63
In-Kyung Kim	67	69	68	74	278	55,353.63
Mi-Jeong Jeon	70	73	68	68	279	44,754.47
Song-Hee Kim	71	66	72	70	279	44,754.47
Ji-Hee Lee	70	75	68	67	280	37,038.38
Brittany Lang	71	70	68	71	280	37,038.38
Se Ri Pak	72	67	70	71	280	37,038.38
Becky Brewerton	67	68	69	76	280	37,038.38
Momoko Ueda	69	75	68	69	281	30,701.74
Anna Nordqvist	70	70	70	71	281	30,701.74
Stacy Lewis	71	67	71	72	281	30,701.74
Maria Hjorth	70	70	73	69	282	27,408.95
Jiyai Shin	72	70	71	69	282	27,408.95
Ji Young Oh	68	73	69	72	282	27,408.95
Shiho Oyama	74	68	75	66	283	24,045.16
Karine Icher	68	69	77	69	283	24,045.16
Lindsey Wright	74	68	72	69	283	24,045.16
Michelle Wie	73	70	70	70	283	24,045.16
Brittany Lincicome	71	71	72	70	284	20,988.55
Eun-Hee Ji	73	70	68	73	284	20,988.55
Wendy Ward	68	71	70	75	284	20,988.55
Johanna Westerberg	71	74	72	68	285	16,235.29
Hee-Kyung Seo	71	71	74	69	285	16,235.29
Chie Arimura	73	72	72	68	285	16,235.29
Rachel Hetherington	70	74	71	70	285	16,235.29
Catriona Matthew	74	72	69	70	285	16,235.29
Erina Hara	73	71	70	71	285	16,235.29
Natalie Gulbis	71	72	71	71	285	16,235.29
Jin Joo Hong	70	71	72	72	285	16,235.29
Rebecca Hudson	71	71	71	72	285	16,235.29
Hee-Won Han	73	71	68	73	285	16,235.29
Karen Stupples	68	72	75	71	286	12,099.66
Pat Hurst	70	71	74	71	286	12,099.66
Kristy McPherson	72	68	74	72	286	12,099.66
Lorena Ochoa	75	69	69	73	286	12,099.66
Katherine Hull	74	72	74	67	287	10,494.39
Laura Davies	71	73	75	68	287	10,494.39
Leta Lindley	72	72	72	71	287	10,494.39
Giulia Sergas	75	72	72	69	288	9,037.27
Tania Elosegui	73	70	74	71	288	9,037.27
Sun Young Yoo	71	73	72	72	288	9,037.27
Suzann Pettersen	72	71	72	73	288	9,037.27
Jee Young Lee	71	72	72	73	288	9,037.27
Angela Stanford	75	71	74	69	289	7,531.05
Teresa Lu	73	72	74	70	289	7,531.05
Seon Hwa Lee	69	74	73	73	289	7,531.05
Morgan Pressel	70	70	75	74	289	7,531.05
Diana Luna	70	72	72	75	289	7,531.05

	SCORES				TOTAL	MONEY
Amy Yang	74	71	68	76	289	7,531.05
Jeong Jang	72	73	75	70	290	6,420.40
Juli Inkster	74	72	73	71	290	6,420.40
Inbee Park	72	73	72	73	290	6,420.40
Hee Young Park	73	69	76	73	291	5,988.14
Candie Kung	70	74	71	76	291	5,988.14
Jane Park	75	71	80	66	292	5,803
Jade Schaeffer	74	72	76	71	293	5,556.12
Yani Tseng	75	72	74	72	293	5,556.12
Anja Monke	71	74	72	76	293	5,556.12
Anne-Lise Caudal	75	70	74	75	294	5,247.20
Michele Redman	70	72	75	77	294	5,247.20
Caroline Rominger	73	74	75	73	295	5,061.69
Marianne Skarpnord	74	72	78	72	296	4,939.21
Mika Miyazato	71	76	77	74	298	4,877.60
Shi Hyun Ahn	75	71	72	81	299	4,813.90
Maria Verchenova	73	74	77	77	301	4,722.19
Melissa Reid	75	72	77	77	301	4,722.19

Ricoh Women's British Open

Royal Lytham and St. Annes Golf Club, Lancashire, England
Par 35-37–72; 6,308 yards

July 30-August 2
purse, €1,645,098

	SCORES				TOTAL	MONEY
Catriona Matthew	74	67	71	73	285	€235,036
Karrie Webb	77	71	72	68	288	147,336
Hee-Won Han	77	73	69	70	289	76,825
Paula Creamer	74	74	70	71	289	76,825
Ai Miyazato	75	71	70	73	289	76,825
Christina Kim	73	71	71	74	289	76,825
Kristy McPherson	74	74	72	70	290	51,918
Cristie Kerr	76	71	75	69	291	42,797.66
Na Yeon Choi	80	71	70	70	291	42,797.66
Jiyai Shin	77	71	68	75	291	42,797.66
Michelle Wie	73	76	74	69	292	28,590.33
Maria Hjorth	72	76	73	71	292	28,590.33
Giulia Sergas	74	67	78	73	292	28,590.33
Hee Young Park	71	75	73	73	292	28,590.33
Song-Hee Kim	70	73	74	75	292	28,590.33
Mika Miyazato	76	72	69	75	292	28,590.33
Michele Redman	75	75	73	70	293	21,048
Kyeong Bae	73	71	74	75	293	21,048
Jane Park	74	72	72	75	293	21,048
Yani Tseng	74	70	78	72	294	17,890.75
In-Kyung Kim	81	70	70	73	294	17,890.75
Angela Stanford	70	76	74	74	294	17,890.75
Se Ri Pak	76	71	73	74	294	17,890.75
Inbee Park	76	72	76	71	295	16,137
Jeong Jang	79	73	72	72	296	15,172
Shinobu Moromizato	74	73	71	78	296	15,172
Jade Schaeffer	79	71	75	72	297	14,383
Brittany Lincicome	77	73	79	69	298	12,839.20
Teresa Lu	75	76	77	70	298	12,839.20
Vicky Hurst	74	75	77	72	298	12,839.20
Lorena Ochoa	75	77	72	74	298	12,839.20
Katie Futcher	75	77	70	76	298	12,839.20
Sophie Gustafson	74	71	82	72	299	10,524
Sun Young Yoo	79	73	75	72	299	10,524
Sandra Gal	69	80	75	75	299	10,524

	SCORES				TOTAL	MONEY
Becky Morgan	80	71	72	76	299	10,524
Yuri Fudoh	80	73	70	76	299	10,524
Brittany Lang	81	70	71	77	299	10,524
Yuko Mitsuka	71	71	79	78	299	10,524
Katherine Hull	75	77	77	71	300	8,945.50
Allison Hanna	76	76	73	75	300	8,945.50
Morgan Pressel	77	72	76	76	301	7,893
Meena Lee	74	74	76	77	301	7,893
Martina Eberl	75	75	72	79	301	7,893
Marianne Skarpnord	76	69	76	80	301	7,893
Carmen Alonso	75	77	77	73	302	6,314.40
Ursula Wikstrom	74	79	75	74	302	6,314.40
Laura Davies	79	74	75	74	302	6,314.40
Il Mi Chung	76	76	75	75	302	6,314.40
M.J. Hur	76	73	74	79	302	6,314.40
Anna Nordqvist	78	75	75	75	303	4,735.75
Irene Cho	77	73	77	76	303	4,735.75
Samantha Head	74	76	72	81	303	4,735.75
Sarah Lee	75	77	70	81	303	4,735.75
Louise Stahle	77	76	74	77	304	3,683.33
Momoko Ueda	74	76	77	77	304	3,683.33
Jin Young Pak	80	73	74	77	304	3,683.33
Christel Boeljon	79	73	74	79	305	3,245
Eunjang Yi	78	75	73	79	305	3,245
Emma Zackrisson	75	77	76	78	306	2,876.66
Anne-Lise Caudal	75	78	75	78	306	2,876.66
Young Kim	78	71	77	80	306	2,876.66
Reilley Rankin	77	76	78	76	307	2,526
Lee-Anne Pace	75	77	75	80	307	2,526
Kristin Tamulis	78	75	82	73	308	2,315
Vikki Laing	73	80	77	79	309	1,193
Stacy Prammanasudh	75	75	79	81	310	1,193
Shanshan Feng	80	72	77	81	310	1,193
Laura Diaz	76	76	76	82	310	1,193
Karin Sjodin	75	74	79	84	312	1,193
Eun-Hee Ji	76	74	81		DQ	1,193

S4/C Wales Ladies Championship of Europe

Royal St. David Golf Club, Harlech, Wales　　　　　　　　　　　　August 6-9
Par 37-35–72; 6,164 yards　　　　　　　　　　　　　　　　purse, €390,565

	SCORES				TOTAL	MONEY
Karen Stupples	69	71	66	70	276	€60,375
Amy Yang	68	65	71	73	277	40,853.75
Katherine Hull	67	68	75	69	279	28,175
Becky Brewerton	70	67	72	71	280	21,735
Melissa Reid	73	68	74	66	281	15,576.75
Anna Nordqvist	66	71	77	67	281	15,576.75
Carin Koch	70	71	73	68	282	12,075
Diana Luna	73	68	70	72	283	10,062.50
Laura Davies	68	74	72	70	284	8,157.33
Julieta Granada	69	74	69	72	284	8,157.33
Jade Schaeffer	69	68	71	76	284	8,157.33
Iben Tinning	71	70	74	70	285	6,533.91
Gwladys Nocera	71	71	73	70	285	6,533.91
Sophie Giquel	72	71	69	73	285	6,533.91
Ursula Wikstrom	74	69	72	71	286	5,809.41
Breanne Alicia Loucks	72	69	73	72	286	5,809.41
Rebecca Coakley	74	69	71	72	286	5,809.41

	SCORES				TOTAL	MONEY
Becky Morgan	72	72	73	70	287	5,138.58
Nikki Garrett	71	71	74	71	287	5,138.58
Samantha Head	72	71	72	72	287	5,138.58
Johanna Mundy	74	71	70	72	287	5,138.58
Bettina Hauert	74	72	69	72	287	5,138.58
Marjet van der Graaff	72	69	71	75	287	5,138.58

The Solheim Cup

See LPGA Tour section.

Finnair Masters

Helsinki Golf Club, Tali, Finland
Par 34-37–71; 5,916 yards

August 28-30
purse, €200,000

	SCORES			TOTAL	MONEY
Beatriz Recari	65	64	73	202	€30,000
Iben Tinning	66	68	68	202	20,300
(Recari defeated Tinning on first playoff hole.)					
Minea Blomqvist	69	69	68	206	10,070
Becky Brewerton	67	68	71	206	10,070
Marianne Skarpnord	68	67	71	206	10,070
Johanna Westerberg	67	67	72	206	10,070
Nikki Garrett	71	69	67	207	6,000
*Je-Yoon Yang	67	71	69	207	
Caroline Afonso	70	70	68	208	4,310
Maria Boden	73	66	69	208	4,310
Elizabeth Bennett	70	69	69	208	4,310
Virginie Lagoutte-Clement	70	66	72	208	4,310
Nicole Gergely	74	69	66	209	3,373.33
Hazel Kavanagh	72	70	67	209	3,373.33
Karen Lunn	70	67	72	209	3,373.33
Malene Jorgensen	68	74	68	210	3,006.66
*Ariya Jutanugarn	71	68	71	210	
Laura Cabanillas	70	69	71	210	3,006.66
Lee-Anne Pace	67	71	72	210	3,006.66
*Moriya Jutanukarn	70	73	68	211	
Anna Tybring	72	70	69	211	2,640
Lotta Wahlin	74	67	70	211	2,640
Trish Johnson	71	70	70	211	2,640
Lynn Kenny	69	72	70	211	2,640
Julie Tvede	73	68	70	211	2,640

UNIQA Ladies Golf Open

Golfclub Fohrenwald-Wiener, Neustadt, Austria
Par 37-35–72; 6,179 yards

September 10-13
purse, €250,000

	SCORES				TOTAL	MONEY
Linda Wessberg	70	68	70	71	279	€37,500
Laura Davies	67	69	74	69	279	25,375
(Wessberg defeated Davies on second playoff hole.)						
Gwladys Nocera	70	70	71	69	280	13,866.66
Bettina Hauert	68	68	73	71	280	13,866.66
Hazel Kavanagh	68	73	67	72	280	13,866.66

	SCORES				TOTAL	MONEY
Veronica Zorzi	69	70	71	71	281	8,750
Marjet van der Graaff	69	67	72	74	282	7,500
Frances Bondad	74	69	69	71	283	5,925
Melissa Reid	67	74	70	72	283	5,925
Maria Boden	70	71	71	73	285	4,800
Johanna Westerberg	70	68	73	74	285	4,800
Christel Boeljon	71	71	76	68	286	4,058.33
Morgana Robbertze	74	70	71	71	286	4,058.33
Dana Lacey	72	73	70	71	286	4,058.33
Nicole Gergely	71	72	76	68	287	3,556.25
Felicity Johnson	71	71	73	72	287	3,556.25
Caroline Afonso	72	71	71	73	287	3,556.25
Jade Schaeffer	68	70	71	78	287	3,556.25
Virginie Lagoutte-Clement	72	70	77	69	288	3,075
Stefanie Michl	69	77	73	69	288	3,075
Katharina Schallenberg	74	74	70	70	288	3,075
Rebecca Coakley	67	72	78	71	288	3,075
Joanne Mills	76	67	73	72	288	3,075
Anja Monke	70	74	72	72	288	3,075
Smriti Mehra	70	71	71	76	288	3,075

Randstad Open de France

Golf d'Arras, Nord-Pas de Calais, France
Par 36-36–72; 6,195 yards

September 17-20
purse, €300,000

	SCORES				TOTAL	MONEY
Nicole Gergely	71	67	70	67	275	€45,000
Ursula Wikstrom	68	71	69	69	277	30,450
Becky Brewerton	70	67	71	70	278	18,600
Anja Monke	70	69	68	71	278	18,600
Felicity Johnson	70	72	70	67	279	11,610
Lee-Anne Pace	72	68	65	74	279	11,610
Lisa Holm Sorensen	73	69	68	70	280	7,740
Tania Elosegui	74	71	64	71	280	7,740
Rebecca Coakley	72	68	67	73	280	7,740
Samantha Head	69	74	70	68	281	5,760
Stefania Croce	70	71	71	69	281	5,760
Trish Johnson	74	68	71	69	282	4,870
Christel Boeljon	73	69	71	69	282	4,870
Caroline Afonso	71	67	72	72	282	4,870
Tara Delaney	70	69	74	70	283	4,330
Hazel Kavanagh	70	71	72	70	283	4,330
Anna Tybring	69	73	68	73	283	4,330
Melissa Reid	71	71	70	72	284	4,080
Laura Davies	70	74	71	70	285	3,825
Gwladys Nocera	72	68	77	68	285	3,825
Nina Reis	73	72	74	66	285	3,825
Ana Larraneta	70	68	70	77	285	3,825

Tenerife Ladies Open

Golf Costa Adeje, Adeje, Tenerife, Spain
Par 36-36–72; 6,080 yards

September 24-27
purse, €300,000

	SCORES				TOTAL	MONEY
Felicity Johnson	69	72	66	67	274	€45,000
Becky Brewerton	66	69	69	72	276	30,450
Bettina Hauert	69	73	67	72	281	21,000
Melissa Reid	69	75	71	67	282	14,460
Tania Elosegui	71	70	68	73	282	14,460
Laura Davies	72	77	66	69	284	9,750
Anja Monke	65	74	74	71	284	9,750
Karen-Margrethe Juul	69	74	70	72	285	7,500
Joanne Mills	72	73	73	68	286	6,360
Emma Cabrera-Bello	72	71	69	74	286	6,360
Virginie Lagoutte-Clement	71	73	70	73	287	5,520
Caroline Rominger	75	68	75	70	288	4,770
Veronica Zorzi	71	72	74	71	288	4,770
Karen Lunn	72	74	70	72	288	4,770
Beatriz Recari	68	70	73	77	288	4,770
Paula Marti	72	71	70	76	289	4,260
Stefania Croce	68	76	67	78	289	4,260
Christel Boeljon	74	71	71	74	290	4,020
Nina Reis	72	69	72	77	290	4,020
Stefanie Michl	73	74	73	71	291	3,735
Laura Terebey	71	72	75	73	291	3,735
Morgana Robbertze	75	71	72	73	291	3,735
Nicole Gergely	72	72	73	74	291	3,735

Madrid Ladies Masters

Casino Club de Golf Retamares, Madrid, Spain
Par 36-37–73; 6,338 yards

October 1-3
purse, €200,000

	SCORES			TOTAL	MONEY
Azahara Munoz	71	68	64	203	€50,000
Anna Nordqvist	71	69	63	203	21,220
(Munoz defeated Nordqvist on first playoff hole.)					
Anne-Lise Caudal	71	68	66	205	12,400
Emma Cabrera-Bello	68	67	70	205	12,400
Bettina Hauert	70	69	67	206	7,160
Lee-Anne Pace	67	71	68	206	7,160
Rebecca Hudson	68	70	68	206	7,160
Veronica Zorzi	68	65	74	207	5,000
Trish Johnson	68	72	68	208	4,480
Marta Prieto	67	74	68	209	4,000
Nicole Gergely	70	73	67	210	3,680
Diana Luna	70	72	69	211	3,330
Christel Boeljon	68	73	70	211	3,330
Krystle Caithness	71	72	69	212	2,980
Sophie Walker	71	71	70	212	2,980
Tania Elosegui	71	70	71	212	2,980
Florentyna Parker	70	72	71	213	2,720
Linda Wessberg	72	74	67	213	2,720
Melissa Reid	71	70	72	213	2,720
Laura Cabanillas	75	69	70	214	2,520
Breanne Alicia Loucks	70	75	69	214	2,520
Samantha Head	73	74	67	214	2,520

Carta Si Ladies Italian Open

Le Rovedine Milano Golf Club, Milan, Italy
Par 36-36–72; 6,871 yards

October 15-17
purse, €200,000

	SCORES			TOTAL	MONEY
Marianne Skarpnord	68	67	69	204	€30,000
Laura Davies	70	65	69	204	20,300
(Skarpnord defeated Davies on third playoff hole.)					
Tania Elosegui	70	70	66	206	14,000
Nicole Gergely	71	65	71	207	10,800
Gwladys Nocera	69	69	70	208	8,480
Jade Schaeffer	71	72	66	209	6,000
Karen Lunn	71	71	67	209	6,000
Becky Brewerton	69	68	72	209	6,000
Giulia Sergas	70	72	68	210	4,260
Caroline Afonso	67	73	70	210	4,260
Beatriz Recari	71	71	69	211	3,640
Christina Kim	73	67	71	211	3,640
Felicity Johnson	72	71	69	212	3,220
Stefanie Michl	76	66	70	212	3,220
Diana Luna	70	66	76	212	3,220
Jenni Kuosa	73	70	70	213	2,880
Anna Rossi	70	73	70	213	2,880
Veronica Zorzi	74	68	71	213	2,880
Iben Tinning	67	75	71	213	2,880
Anja Monke	74	71	69	214	2,344.44
Florentyna Parker	77	68	69	214	2,344.44
Beth Allen	73	72	69	214	2,344.44
Virginie Lagoutte-Clement	74	71	69	214	2,344.44
Julie Greciet	75	69	70	214	2,344.44
Laura Cabanillas	70	73	71	214	2,344.44
Stacy Lee Bregman	71	72	71	214	2,344.44
Julieta Granada	72	70	72	214	2,344.44
Marjet van der Graaff	73	69	72	214	2,344.44

Suzhou Taihu Ladies Open

Suzhou Taihu International Golf Club, Shanghai, China
Par 36-36–72; 6,299 yards

October 30-November 1
purse, €200,000

	SCORES			TOTAL	MONEY
Bo Mi Suh	69	69	72	210	€30,000
Gwladys Nocera	70	71	70	211	20,300
Pornanong Phatlum	68	74	71	213	14,000
Marianne Skarpnord	72	72	70	214	10,800
Lora Fairclough	70	72	73	215	6,620
Rebecca Coakley	74	68	73	215	6,620
Iben Tinning	72	70	73	215	6,620
Frances Bondad	70	70	75	215	6,620
Virginie Lagoutte-Clement	72	73	71	216	4,480
Li-Ying Ye	72	71	74	217	4,000
Nontaya Srisawang	71	75	72	218	3,355
Minea Blomqvist	69	76	73	218	3,355
Jade Schaeffer	73	72	73	218	3,355
Titiya Plucksataporn	74	69	75	218	3,355
Vikki Laing	78	69	72	219	2,845
Christine Hallstrom	73	72	74	219	2,845
Smriti Mehra	73	69	77	219	2,845
Julieta Granada	70	72	77	219	2,845

	SCORES			TOTAL	MONEY
Georgina Simpson	76	71	73	220	2,490
Jessica Ji	74	71	75	220	2,490
Sophie Giquel	74	71	75	220	2,490
Bronwyn Mullins-Lane	77	71	72	220	2,490
Becky Brewerton	71	73	76	220	2,490
Carmen Alonso	72	68	80	220	2,490

Daishin Securities Tomato Tour Korean Ladies Masters

Cypress Golf & Resort, Jeju Island, South Korea
Par 36-36–72; 6,410 yards
(Playoff completed on Monday—darkness.)

November 6-9
purse, €205,000

	SCORES			TOTAL	MONEY
Hyun-Ji Kim	69	73	73	215	€40,026
So Yeon Ryu	76	69	70	215	19,513
Sarah Lee	69	72	74	215	19,513
(Kim defeated Lee on first and Ryu on second playoff hole.)					
Hee-Kyung Seo	68	74	74	216	10,007
*Se-Young Kim	73	72	72	217	
Rebecca Coakley	72	72	73	217	7,505
Anna Rawson	69	74	74	217	7,505
Jeong-Eun Lee	74	70	74	218	6,004
Hyeon-Ju Lee	77	69	73	219	4,003
Ae-Ree Pyun	70	73	76	219	4,003
Sung Ah Yim	75	69	75	219	4,003
*Jung-Eun Han	71	71	77	219	
Hae-Won Jong	76	72	72	220	2,358
Jade Schaeffer	74	71	75	220	2,358
Bo-Mee Lee	69	76	75	220	2,358
Ji-Hae Jang	74	70	76	220	2,358
Soo-Jin Yang	70	71	79	220	2,358
Bo-Kyung Kim	71	71	78	220	2,358
Young-Ran Jo	75	74	72	221	1,951
Seul-A Yoon	73	75	73	221	1,951
Stephanie Na	72	75	74	221	1,951
So-Young Kim	70	74	77	221	1,951

Omega Dubai Ladies Masters

Emirates Golf Club, Majlis Course, Dubai, United Arab Emirates
Par 35-37–72; 6,412 yards

December 9-12
purse, €500,000

	SCORES				TOTAL	MONEY
In-Kyung Kim	70	65	67	68	270	€75,000
Michelle Wie	69	68	71	65	273	50,750
Maria Hjorth	66	73	67	68	274	35,000
Virginie Lagoutte-Clement	69	72	71	65	277	20,175
Laura Davies	71	69	70	67	277	20,175
Tania Elosegui	72	66	70	69	277	20,175
Anna Nordqvist	72	68	65	72	277	20,175
Gwladys Nocera	71	69	68	70	278	12,500
Melissa Reid	73	68	69	69	279	10,133.33
Jade Schaeffer	72	72	66	69	279	10,133.33
Amy Yang	68	70	70	71	279	10,133.33
Catriona Matthew	71	68	71	70	280	8,600
Caroline Afonso	72	70	72	67	281	8,050

	SCORES			TOTAL	MONEY
Sophie Gustafson	72	69	70	71	282	7,700
Felicity Johnson	74	71	70	68	283	7,325
Marjet van der Graaff	71	73	70	69	283	7,325
Christina Kim	72	70	74	68	284	6,900
Titiya Plucksataporn	68	71	73	72	284	6,900
Karen Stupples	71	70	75	69	285	6,225
Becky Morgan	75	67	72	71	285	6,225
Minea Blomqvist	69	72	72	72	285	6,225
Rebecca Coakley	72	71	70	72	285	6,225
Lee-Anne Pace	75	70	68	72	285	6,225
Vikki Laing	72	69	69	75	285	6,225

Japan LPGA Tour

Daikin Orchid Ladies

Ryukyu Golf Club, Nanjo, Okinawa
Par 36-36–72; 6,415 yards

March 6-8
purse, ¥80,000,000

	SCORES			TOTAL	MONEY
Yuko Mitsuka	70	66	72	208	¥14,400,000
Ayako Uehara	69	69	72	210	6,320,000
Erina Hara	70	71	69	210	6,320,000
Tamie Durdin	69	71	71	211	3,440,000
Mi-Jeong Jeon	70	72	69	211	3,440,000
Sakura Yokomine	68	75	68	211	3,440,000
Hiromi Mogi	74	68	69	211	3,440,000
Bo-Bae Song	68	76	67	211	3,440,000
Yukari Baba	75	68	69	212	1,696,000
Yuri Fudoh	72	71	69	212	1,696,000
Nikki Campbell	71	73	68	212	1,696,000
Miho Koga	71	72	70	213	1,328,000
*Mamiko Higa	73	69	71	213	
Yuko Saitoh	73	71	69	213	1,328,000
Tomoko Kusakabe	74	69	70	213	1,328,000
Ji-Woo Lee	73	72	69	214	968,000
Ah-Reum Hwang	71	73	70	214	968,000
Hyun-Ju Shin	71	74	69	214	968,000
Mayumi Nakajima	72	74	68	214	968,000
Kuniko Maeda	73	69	72	214	968,000
Maiko Wakabayashi	72	73	69	214	968,000

Yokohama Tire PRGR Cup

Tosa Country Club, Konan, Kochi
Par 36-36–72; 6,262 yards
(Final round cancelled—rain.)

March 20-22
purse, ¥80,000,000

	SCORES		TOTAL	MONEY
Ayako Uehara	64	71	135	¥10,800,000
Midori Yoneyama	72	68	140	4,740,000
Ah-Reum Hwang	70	70	140	4,740,000
Yayoi Arasaki	69	72	141	3,300,000
Miho Koga	73	68	141	3,300,000
Mika Takushima	74	68	142	1,800,000
Kaori Aoyama	71	71	142	1,800,000
Shinobu Moromizato	71	71	142	1,800,000
Ji-Hee Lee	71	71	142	1,800,000
Sakura Yokomine	74	68	142	1,800,000
Tomomi Hirose	74	69	143	1,086,000
Yuko Saitoh	73	70	143	1,086,000
Mayumi Nakajima	72	72	144	936,000
Namika Omata	72	72	144	936,000
Mayu Hattori	74	70	144	936,000
Eun-A Lim	76	69	145	674,000
So-Hee Kim	73	72	145	674,000
Michiko Hattori	74	71	145	674,000
Rui Yokomine	74	71	145	674,000
Hyun-Ju Shin	72	73	145	674,000
Mi-Jeong Jeon	73	72	145	674,000

Yamaha Ladies Open

Katsuragi Golf Club, Yamana Course, Fukuroi, Shizuoka
Par 36-36–72; 6,485 yards

April 3-5
purse, ¥80,000,000

	SCORES			TOTAL	MONEY
Ah-Reum Hwang	73	67	65	205	¥14,400,000
Ji-Woo Lee	72	71	70	213	5,813,333
Erina Hara	73	68	72	213	5,813,333
Julie Lu	74	70	69	213	5,813,333
Yuko Mitsuka	73	73	69	215	4,000,000
Junko Omote	72	72	72	216	3,200,000
Mi-Jeong Jeon	73	69	75	217	1,657,600
Ritsuko Ryu	73	72	72	217	1,657,600
Nikki Campbell	73	74	70	217	1,657,600
Hyun-Ju Shin	71	74	72	217	1,657,600
Bo-Bae Song	72	73	72	217	1,657,600
Hiromi Mogi	75	71	71	217	1,657,600
Kuniko Maeda	71	75	71	217	1,657,600
Yasuko Satoh	73	72	72	217	1,657,600
Kaori Aoyama	73	73	71	217	1,657,600
Ayako Uehara	72	73	72	217	1,657,600
Sakurako Mori	72	75	71	218	936,000
So-Hee Kim	74	71	73	218	936,000
Mie Nakata	71	70	77	218	936,000
Itsumi Okada	74	72	73	219	752,000
Midori Yoneyama	70	76	73	219	752,000
Yuko Saitoh	75	72	72	219	752,000
Tomoko Kusakabe	76	71	72	219	752,000

Studio Alice Ladies Open

Hanayashiki Golf Club, Yokawa Course, Miki, Hyogo
Par 36-36—72; 6,504 yards

April 10-12
purse, ¥60,000,000

	SCORES			TOTAL	MONEY
Sakura Yokomine	71	73	68	212	¥10,800,000
Mi-Jeong Jeon	69	72	71	212	5,280,000
(Yokomine defeated Jeon on second playoff hole.)					
Rui Kitada	69	73	71	213	4,200,000
Ji-Woo Lee	74	72	68	214	3,300,000
Ji-Hee Lee	72	72	70	214	3,300,000
Yukari Baba	77	68	70	215	2,100,000
Bo-Bae Song	72	70	73	215	2,100,000
Ai Miyazato	69	72	74	215	2,100,000
Chie Arimura	72	75	70	217	1,278,000
Shinobu Moromizato	72	73	72	217	1,278,000
Eun-A Lim	75	68	74	217	1,278,000
Nobuko Kizawa	76	71	71	218	1,014,000
Natsu Nagai	71	74	73	218	1,014,000
Erina Hara	76	69	73	218	1,014,000
Jiyai Shin	74	75	70	219	804,000
*Asako Fujimoto	74	71	74	219	
Hyun-Ju Shin	73	71	75	219	804,000
Mie Nakata	71	72	76	219	804,000
Da-Ye Na	73	69	77	219	804,000
Julie Lu	75	73	72	220	610,000
Michiko Hattori	77	70	73	220	610,000
Yuko Saitoh	73	72	74	220	610,000

Life Card Ladies

Kumamoto Airport Country Club, Kikuyo, Kumamoto
Par 36-36—72; 6,468 yards

April 17-19
purse, ¥70,000,000

	SCORES			TOTAL	MONEY
Ji-Hee Lee	68	72	73	213	¥12,600,000
Sakura Yokomine	73	68	73	214	6,160,000
Erina Hara	76	69	70	215	4,550,000
Yuko Mitsuka	73	70	72	215	4,550,000
Yuri Fudoh	73	72	71	216	3,150,000
Kaori Aoyama	76	71	69	216	3,150,000
Jiyai Shin	72	69	77	218	2,275,000
Kurumi Dohi	73	74	71	218	2,275,000
Mie Nakata	73	74	72	219	1,435,000
Kumiko Kaneda	76	76	67	219	1,435,000
Li-Ying Ye	80	65	74	219	1,435,000
Momoko Ueda	74	70	75	219	1,435,000
Chie Arimura	73	76	72	221	1,015,000
Tomoko Kusakabe	74	73	74	221	1,015,000
Yuko Saitoh	75	73	73	221	1,015,000
Mayumi Nakajima	75	72	74	221	1,015,000
Na-Ri Lee	73	75	73	221	1,015,000
Ikue Asama	74	73	74	221	1,015,000
Ji-Woo Lee	73	73	76	222	718,666
Yayoi Arasaki	75	73	74	222	718,666
Nachiyo Ohtani	75	72	75	222	718,666

Fujisankei Ladies Classic

Kawana Hotel Golf Club, Fuji Course, Ito, Shizuoka
Par 36-36–72; 6,464 yards
(Event shortened to 36 holes—high winds.)

April 24-26
purse, ¥80,000,000

	SCORES		TOTAL	MONEY
Tamie Durdin	68	69	137	¥10,800,000
Jiyai Shin	70	70	140	5,400,000
Sakura Yokomine	68	74	142	3,330,000
Ami Shiozaki	67	75	142	3,330,000
Kuniko Maeda	70	72	142	3,330,000
Shinobu Moromizato	70	72	142	3,330,000
Yuko Mitsuka	71	72	143	2,100,000
Akiko Fukushima	71	73	144	1,650,000
Akane Iijima	73	71	144	1,650,000
Ah-Reum Hwang	73	72	145	1,148,000
Miho Koga	71	74	145	1,148,000
Chie Arimura	65	80	145	1,148,000
*Asako Fujimoto	71	74	145	
Michie Ohba	72	74	146	852,000
Julie Lu	69	77	146	852,000
Tomoko Kusakabe	69	77	146	852,000
Ji-Hee Lee	70	76	146	852,000
*Makoto Takemura	68	78	146	
Bo-Bae Song	73	73	146	852,000
Yuriko Ohtsuka	69	77	146	852,000
Sakurako Mori	71	75	146	852,000

Crystal Geyser Ladies

Keiyo Country Club, Chiba
Par 36-36–72; 6,355 yards

May 1-3
purse, ¥70,000,000

	SCORES			TOTAL	MONEY
Chie Arimura	67	70	70	207	¥12,600,000
Sakura Yokomine	68	73	69	210	6,160,000
Yuko Saitoh	68	69	75	212	4,550,000
Mie Nakata	68	71	73	212	4,550,000
Michie Ohba	72	72	69	213	3,150,000
Akane Iijima	66	75	72	213	3,150,000
Miho Koga	70	72	72	214	2,450,000
Yuri Fudoh	71	73	71	215	1,750,000
Mi-Jeong Jeon	70	69	76	215	1,750,000
Ikue Asama	73	70	72	215	1,750,000
Hiromi Takesue	71	76	69	216	1,169,000
Nachiyo Ohtani	72	73	71	216	1,169,000
Junko Omote	71	69	76	216	1,169,000
Maiko Wakabayashi	73	71	72	216	1,169,000
Ah-Reum Hwang	69	71	76	216	1,169,000
Yuko Mitsuka	70	73	74	217	854,000
Yun-Jye Wei	72	71	74	217	854,000
Momoko Ueda	72	70	75	217	854,000
Bo-Bae Song	69	73	75	217	854,000
*Makoto Takemura	71	72	75	218	
Hiroko Yamaguchi	74	71	73	218	623,000
Shinobu Moromizato	70	74	74	218	623,000
Michiko Hattori	70	73	75	218	623,000
Erina Hara	72	74	72	218	623,000
Kurumi Dohi	75	71	72	218	623,000

	SCORES			TOTAL	MONEY
Itsumi Okada	76	70	72	218	623,000
So-Hee Kim	74	70	74	218	623,000
Hiromi Mogi	72	72	74	218	623,000
Momoyo Yamazaki	74	72	72	218	623,000

World Ladies Championship Salonpas Cup

Ibaraki Golf Club, Tsukubamirai, Ibaraki
Par 36-36–72; 6,553 yards

May 7-10
purse, ¥120,000,000

	SCORES				TOTAL	MONEY
Shinobu Moromizato	69	70	67	69	275	¥24,000,000
Mi-Jeong Jeon	68	69	72	65	276	10,200,000
Paula Creamer	71	68	72	67	276	10,200,000
Akiko Fukushima	68	68	72	69	277	6,840,000
Ji-Hee Lee	68	71	74	65	278	5,532,000
Sakura Yokomine	73	67	71	68	279	4,740,000
Tamie Durdin	69	71	70	68	280	3,408,000
Hyun-Ju Shin	68	73	71	69	280	3,408,000
Yukari Baba	69	72	70	70	280	3,408,000
Li-Ying Ye	72	69	70	73	284	2,352,000
Chie Arimura	70	71	69	68	286	1,780,000
Yuri Fudoh	72	71	72	71	286	1,780,000
Kaori Aoyama	71	73	74	76	286	1,780,000
Yuko Mitsuka	72	74	70	71	287	1,476,000
Bo-Bae Song	73	68	75	71	287	1,476,000
Maiko Wakabayashi	70	68	74	75	287	1,476,000
Miho Koga	73	70	73	72	288	1,230,000
Kyoko Furuya	72	71	72	73	288	1,230,000
Hiroko Yamaguchi	71	73	76	70	289	1,052,000
Tomoko Kusakabe	75	73	71	69	289	1,052,000
Junko Omote	74	70	73	72	289	1,052,000
Eun-A Lim	73	70	74	72	289	1,052,000
Julie Lu	75	73	69	72	289	1,052,000
Ah-Reum Hwang	69	72	73	75	289	1,052,000

Vernal Ladies

Fukuoka Century Golf Club, Asakura, Fukuoka
Par 36-36–72; 6,594 yards

May 15-17
purse, ¥100,000,000

	SCORES			TOTAL	MONEY
Yuko Saitoh	67	70	74	211	¥18,000,000
Eun-A Lim	68	72	74	214	7,266,666
Miho Koga	73	70	71	214	7,266,666
Yuri Fudoh	71	67	76	214	7,266,666
Yuko Mitsuka	68	71	76	215	5,000,000
Sakura Yokomine	68	71	77	216	3,750,000
Chie Arimura	69	71	76	216	3,750,000
Ayako Uehara	74	69	74	217	3,000,000
Mi-Jeong Jeon	73	68	77	218	2,126,666
Nobuko Kizawa	71	71	76	218	2,126,666
Nikki Campbell	74	71	73	218	2,126,666
Ji-Hee Lee	70	70	79	219	1,680,000
Saiki Fujita	75	73	71	219	1,680,000
Ji-Woo Lee	78	66	75	219	1,680,000
Hyun-Ju Shin	71	73	76	220	1,380,000

	SCORES			TOTAL	MONEY
Yukari Baba	71	71	78	220	1,380,000
Namika Omata	71	70	79	220	1,380,000
Na-Ri Lee	75	71	75	221	1,050,000
Akiko Fukushima	78	71	72	221	1,050,000
Miki Saiki	74	71	76	221	1,050,000
So-Hee Kim	67	73	81	221	1,050,000

Chukyo TV Bridgestone Ladies

Chukyo Golf Club, Ishino Course, Toyota, Aichi
Par 36-36–72; 6,421 yards

May 22-24
purse, ¥70,000,000

	SCORES			TOTAL	MONEY
Eun-A Lim	69	71	69	209	¥12,600,000
Yuko Mitsuka	67	71	71	209	6,160,000
(Lim defeated Mitsuka on third playoff hole.)					
Yukari Baba	74	70	68	212	4,200,000
Akiko Fukushima	70	72	70	212	4,200,000
Na Zhang	70	72	70	212	4,200,000
Akane Iijima	71	71	71	213	2,100,000
Mika Takushima	71	72	70	213	2,100,000
Ayako Uehara	72	71	70	213	2,100,000
Mi-Jeong Jeon	70	75	68	213	2,100,000
Miki Saiki	75	69	69	213	2,100,000
Chie Arimura	69	75	70	214	1,169,000
Maiko Wakabayashi	69	71	74	214	1,169,000
Sakura Yokomine	71	72	71	214	1,169,000
Ji-Woo Lee	73	71	70	214	1,169,000
Kumiko Kaneda	69	73	73	215	924,000
Ah-Reum Hwang	71	71	73	215	924,000
Rikako Morita	74	69	72	215	924,000
Na-Ri Lee	73	72	71	216	749,000
Li-Ying Ye	76	69	71	216	749,000
Mayumi Shimomura	74	72	71	217	595,000
Yui Kawahara	74	71	72	217	595,000
Hiromi Takesue	71	73	73	217	595,000
Julie Lu	73	73	71	217	595,000
Ji-Hee Lee	75	72	70	217	595,000
Kyoko Furuya	71	71	75	217	595,000
Tamie Durdin	70	72	75	217	595,000
*Hiroko Ayada	77	71	69	217	
Erina Hara	72	71	74	217	595,000

Kosaido Ladies Golf Cup

Chiba Kosaido Country Club, Ichihara, Chiba
Par 36-36–72; 6,365 yards

May 29-31
purse, ¥60,000,000

	SCORES			TOTAL	MONEY
Sakura Yokomine	68	64	71	203	¥10,800,000
Chie Arimura	67	68	70	205	5,400,000
Shinobu Moromizato	73	67	66	206	3,900,000
Maiko Wakabayashi	70	66	70	206	3,900,000
Rui Kitada	71	68	68	207	3,000,000
Yuko Mitsuka	70	69	69	208	2,400,000
Miki Saiki	70	70	69	209	1,800,000
Hyun-Ju Shin	71	69	69	209	1,800,000

	SCORES			TOTAL	MONEY
Ji-Woo Lee	69	70	70	209	1,800,000
So-Hee Kim	68	73	69	210	1,084,800
Hiromi Takesue	69	67	74	210	1,084,800
Akane Iijima	71	70	69	210	1,084,800
Keiko Sasaki	74	70	66	210	1,084,800
Maria Iida	72	67	71	210	1,084,800
Yuuki Ichinose	71	69	71	211	846,000
*Makoto Takemura	71	70	70	211	
Saiki Fujita	75	66	70	211	846,000
Ah-Reum Hwang	71	69	71	211	846,000
Mika Takushima	72	70	70	212	624,000
Megumi Shimokawa	69	70	73	212	624,000
Bo-Bae Song	72	71	69	212	624,000
Momoyo Yamazaki	72	71	69	212	624,000
Kaori Yamamoto	73	68	71	212	624,000
Ji-Hee Lee	73	70	69	212	624,000

Resort Trust Ladies

The Country Club, Koga, Shiga
Par 36-36–72; 6,611 yards

June 5-7
purse, ¥70,000,000

	SCORES			TOTAL	MONEY
Mi-Jeong Jeon	72	65	65	202	¥12,600,000
Akiko Fukushima	71	70	68	209	6,300,000
Yuko Mitsuka	69	73	71	213	4,900,000
Erina Hara	73	73	68	214	3,850,000
Rikako Morita	74	71	69	214	3,850,000
Tomomi Hirose	76	71	68	215	2,100,000
Shinobu Moromizato	71	72	72	215	2,100,000
Li-Ying Ye	71	70	74	215	2,100,000
Miki Saiki	76	68	71	215	2,100,000
Maiko Wakabayashi	71	72	72	215	2,100,000
Sakura Yokomine	71	77	68	216	1,232,000
Yukari Baba	71	72	73	216	1,232,000
Bo-Bae Song	72	74	70	216	1,232,000
*Asako Fujimoto	74	73	69	216	
Nikki Campbell	77	68	71	216	1,232,000
Kuniko Maeda	76	69	72	217	882,000
Mayumi Nakajima	72	75	70	217	882,000
Na Zhang	74	73	70	217	882,000
So-Hee Kim	73	72	72	217	882,000
Miho Koga	76	72	69	217	882,000
Tamie Durdin	73	75	69	217	882,000

We Love Kobe Suntory Ladies Open

Rokko Kokusai Golf Club, Kobe, Hyogo
Par 36-36–72; 6,457 yards

June 11-14
purse, ¥100,000,000

	SCORES				TOTAL	MONEY
Shinobu Moromizato	69	70	69	68	276	¥18,000,000
Li-Ying Ye	74	68	68	66	276	8,800,000
(Moromizato defeated Ye on second playoff hole.)						
Rui Kitada	72	68	70	69	279	7,000,000
Sakura Yokomine	71	71	70	68	280	6,000,000
Hiromi Mogi	73	68	69	72	282	5,000,000

	SCORES				TOTAL	MONEY
Tamie Durdin	75	67	72	69	283	3,750,000
Yuko Mitsuka	71	73	70	69	283	3,750,000
Yuri Fudoh	72	73	72	67	284	2,125,000
Saiki Fujita	73	67	72	72	284	2,125,000
Na-Ri Lee	72	71	69	72	284	2,125,000
*Ha-Na Jang	68	71	73	72	284	
Nobuko Kizawa	73	70	70	71	284	2,125,000
Chie Arimura	73	68	68	75	284	2,125,000
Maiko Wakabayashi	72	68	67	77	284	2,125,000
Tomoko Kusakabe	70	73	70	72	285	1,500,000
Mai Arai	73	72	69	71	285	1,500,000
Rikako Morita	69	70	71	76	286	1,060,000
Ai Miyazato	75	70	70	71	286	1,060,000
Ah-Reum Hwang	76	70	71	69	286	1,060,000
Bo-Bae Song	74	69	69	74	286	1,060,000
Kumiko Kaneda	73	71	71	71	286	1,060,000
Nikki Campbell	70	69	74	73	286	1,060,000
Akiko Fukushima	73	71	72	70	286	1,060,000
Ji-Hee Lee	73	71	68	74	286	1,060,000

Nichirei PGM Ladies

Miho Golf Club, Miho, Ibaraki
Par 36-36–72; 6,402 yards
(Event shortened to 36 holes—rain.)

June 19-21
purse, ¥80,000,000

	SCORES		TOTAL	MONEY
Sakura Yokomine	69	67	136	¥10,800,000
Chie Arimura	67	71	138	5,400,000
Miho Koga	69	70	139	3,600,000
Mi-Jeong Jeon	68	71	139	3,600,000
Rikako Morita	67	72	139	3,600,000
Ji-Hee Lee	74	66	140	2,100,000
Natsu Nagai	72	68	140	2,100,000
Li-Ying Ye	71	69	140	2,100,000
Tomomi Hirose	73	68	141	1,233,000
Chiharu Yamaguchi	73	68	141	1,233,000
Yuriko Ohtsuka	70	71	141	1,233,000
Mai Arai	67	74	141	1,233,000
Yukari Baba	73	69	142	936,000
Saiki Fujita	72	70	142	936,000
Yuuki Ichinose	71	71	142	936,000
Bo-Bae Song	70	72	142	936,000
Chiaki Takahashi	74	69	143	675,600
Yui Kawahara	73	70	143	675,600
Midori Yoneyama	72	71	143	675,600
So-Hee Kim	72	71	143	675,600
Na-Ri Lee	72	71	143	675,600

Promise Ladies

Madame J Golf Club, Kato, Hyogo
Par 36-36–72; 6,528 yards

June 26-28
purse, ¥80,000,000

	SCORES			TOTAL	MONEY
Shinobu Moromizato	64	70	64	198	¥14,400,000
Ji-Hee Lee	67	68	68	203	7,040,000

	SCORES			TOTAL	MONEY
Sakura Yokomine	70	69	65	204	5,600,000
Saiki Fujita	71	69	66	206	4,800,000
Miki Saiki	69	71	67	207	4,000,000
Yuri Fudoh	71	71	66	208	3,000,000
Mi-Jeong Jeon	69	70	69	208	3,000,000
Chie Arimura	72	68	69	209	1,766,400
Rui Kitada	70	69	70	209	1,766,400
Yuko Mitsuka	70	67	72	209	1,766,400
Yui Kawahara	66	70	73	209	1,766,400
Junko Omote	71	67	71	209	1,766,400
Rikako Morita	71	70	69	210	1,296,000
Ai Nishikawa	69	70	72	211	1,016,000
Aoi Nagata	71	68	72	211	1,016,000
Mikiyo Nishizuka	70	73	68	211	1,016,000
Yuko Saitoh	73	70	68	211	1,016,000
Miho Koga	70	69	72	211	1,016,000
Eun-A Lim	71	68	72	211	1,016,000
So-Hee Kim	71	72	70	213	720,000
Tamie Durdin	70	71	72	213	720,000
Mayu Hattori	71	72	70	213	720,000

Meiji Chocolate Cup

Sapporo Kokusai Country Club, Kita-Hiroshima, Hokkaido
Par 36-36–72; 6,518 yards

July 10-12
purse, ¥90,000,000

	SCORES			TOTAL	MONEY
Mi-Jeong Jeon	71	68	68	207	¥16,200,000
Midori Yoneyama	69	71	73	213	6,540,000
Yuko Mitsuka	73	69	71	213	6,540,000
Miho Koga	74	70	69	213	6,540,000
Erina Hara	70	72	72	214	4,050,000
Da-Ye Na	72	69	73	214	4,050,000
Na-Ri Lee	75	71	69	215	2,475,000
Rikako Morita	76	70	69	215	2,475,000
Saiki Fujita	76	63	76	215	2,475,000
Nikki Campbell	77	69	69	215	2,475,000
Esther Lee	74	71	71	216	1,593,000
Mayu Hattori	69	74	73	216	1,593,000
Keiko Sasaki	76	67	73	216	1,593,000
Natsu Nagai	73	73	71	217	1,233,000
Chie Arimura	74	70	73	217	1,233,000
Junko Omote	76	70	71	217	1,233,000
Sakura Yokomine	74	71	72	217	1,233,000
Akane Iijima	73	74	70	217	1,233,000
Akane Azuma	74	70	74	218	858,000
Yui Kawahara	76	70	72	218	858,000
Yuriko Ohtsuka	73	71	74	218	858,000
Toshimi Kimura	76	72	70	218	858,000
Shinobu Moromizato	72	74	72	218	858,000
Hiromi Mogi	75	73	70	218	858,000

Stanley Ladies

Tomei Country Club, Susono, Shizuoka
Par 36-36–72; 6,542 yards
(Event shortened to 45 holes—fog.)

July 17-19
purse, ¥90,000,000

	SCORES			TOTAL	MONEY
Chie Arimura	67	67	34	168	¥16,200,000
Yuko Saitoh	72	65	35	172	7,920,000
Na-Ri Lee	72	68	34	174	6,300,000
Nikki Campbell	72	69	34	175	4,950,000
Nozomi Sato	71	68	36	175	4,950,000
Midori Yoneyama	70	72	34	176	3,375,000
So-Hee Kim	70	70	36	176	3,375,000
*Asako Fujimoto	71	72	34	177	
Maiko Suzuki	71	72	34	177	1,854,000
Rui Kitada	69	73	35	177	1,854,000
Junko Omote	70	72	35	177	1,854,000
Da-Ye Na	70	72	35	177	1,854,000
Eun-A Lim	71	71	35	177	1,854,000
Mika Takushima	71	71	35	177	1,854,000
Shinobu Moromizato	74	67	36	177	1,854,000
Erika Kikuchi	74	70	34	178	1,020,000
Hiromi Mogi	66	77	35	178	1,020,000
Rikako Morita	74	69	35	178	1,020,000
Maiko Wakabayashi	73	69	36	178	1,020,000
Hiromi Takesue	74	68	36	178	1,020,000
Natsu Nagai	67	74	37	178	1,020,000
Kaori Aoyama	72	69	37	178	1,020,000
Kuniko Maeda	69	71	38	178	1,020,000
Ji-Woo Lee	68	70	40	178	1,020,000

AXA Ladies

Mitsui Kanto Tomakomai Golf Club, Tomakomai, Hokkaido
Par 36-36–72; 6,375 yards

August 7-9
purse, ¥80,000,000

	SCORES			TOTAL	MONEY
Momoko Ueda	68	69	68	205	¥14,400,000
Chie Arimura	68	70	67	205	6,320,000
Ji-Hee Lee	66	71	68	205	6,320,000
(Ueda defeated Arimura on first and Lee on second playoff hole.)					
Rikako Morita	69	69	68	206	4,800,000
So-Hee Kim	69	67	71	207	3,600,000
Hiromi Takesue	68	71	68	207	3,600,000
Jiyai Shin	69	68	71	208	2,800,000
Shinobu Moromizato	75	66	68	209	1,862,000
Eun-A Lim	72	67	70	209	1,862,000
Yui Kawahara	70	70	69	209	1,862,000
Miho Koga	69	68	72	209	1,862,000
Tomoko Kusakabe	70	70	70	210	1,168,000
Nikki Campbell	71	71	68	210	1,168,000
Hyun-Ju Shin	66	70	74	210	1,168,000
Yuko Mitsuka	66	74	70	210	1,168,000
Michie Ohba	70	71	69	210	1,168,000
Sakura Yokomine	70	66	74	210	1,168,000
Bo-Bae Song	73	71	67	211	808,000
Hiromi Mogi	71	68	72	211	808,000
Na-Ri Lee	74	66	71	211	808,000

NEC Karuizawa 72

Karuizawa 72 Golf Club, Karuizawa, Nagano
Par 36-36–72; 6,637 yards

August 14-16
purse, ¥60,000,000

	SCORES			TOTAL	MONEY
Chie Arimura	66	71	69	206	¥10,800,000
Shinobu Moromizato	68	74	66	208	5,280,000
Mi-Jeong Jeon	67	72	70	209	4,200,000
Yuko Mitsuka	69	69	72	210	3,600,000
Momoko Ueda	70	73	68	211	3,000,000
Miki Saiki	75	69	68	212	2,100,000
Kumiko Kaneda	74	70	68	212	2,100,000
Tomoko Kusakabe	69	71	72	212	2,100,000
Eun-A Lim	71	72	70	213	1,350,000
Yuri Fudoh	71	71	71	213	1,350,000
Miho Koga	72	72	70	214	1,098,000
Saiki Fujita	73	70	71	214	1,098,000
Hiroko Fukushima	68	76	71	215	948,000
Midori Yoneyama	71	71	73	215	948,000
Rikako Morita	74	72	69	215	948,000
Chieko Amanuma	72	72	72	216	686,000
Nikki Campbell	73	72	71	216	686,000
*Fumika Kawagishi	74	72	70	216	
Hiromi Takesue	71	75	70	216	686,000
Hiromi Mogi	73	71	72	216	686,000
Ji-Woo Lee	73	72	71	216	686,000
So-Hee Kim	72	75	69	216	686,000

CAT Ladies

Daihakone Country Club, Hakone, Kanagawa
Par 36-37–73; 6,648 yards

August 21-23
purse, ¥70,000,000

	SCORES			TOTAL	MONEY
Shinobu Moromizato	69	71	68	208	¥12,600,000
Miho Koga	69	70	70	209	6,160,000
Yukari Baba	70	72	68	210	4,550,000
Akiko Fukushima	70	70	70	210	4,550,000
Mayu Hattori	74	71	66	211	2,916,666
Ji-Hee Lee	70	72	69	211	2,916,666
Sakura Yokomine	70	71	70	211	2,916,666
Eun-A Lim	70	70	72	212	2,100,000
Kaori Aoyama	71	72	70	213	1,575,000
Esther Lee	71	70	72	213	1,575,000
Akane Iijima	69	76	69	214	1,120,000
Maiko Wakabayashi	70	75	69	214	1,120,000
Miki Saiki	72	73	69	214	1,120,000
Rui Kitada	73	72	69	214	1,120,000
Hiroko Yamaguchi	74	69	71	214	1,120,000
Nobuko Kizawa	73	72	71	216	875,000
Mayumi Shimomura	73	70	73	216	875,000
Ji-Woo Lee	74	73	70	217	700,000
Mi-Jeong Jeon	74	73	70	217	700,000
Na-Ri Lee	72	76	69	217	700,000

Yonex Ladies

Yonex Country Club, Nagaoka, Niigata
Par 36-36–72; 6,304 yards

August 28-30
purse, ¥60,000,000

	SCORES			TOTAL	MONEY
Mi-Jeong Jeon	68	65	66	199	¥10,800,000
Yukari Baba	70	68	66	204	5,280,000
Saiki Fujita	70	70	67	207	3,060,000
Eri Terasawa	67	71	69	207	3,060,000
Shinobu Moromizato	67	71	69	207	3,060,000
Mayu Hattori	71	67	69	207	3,060,000
Miho Koga	69	68	70	207	3,060,000
Tomomi Hirose	67	71	70	208	1,800,000
Bo-Bae Song	68	71	70	209	1,350,000
Toshimi Kimura	69	69	71	209	1,350,000
Hiromi Mogi	70	72	68	210	1,068,000
Chie Arimura	71	71	68	210	1,068,000
Chiharu Tsunekawa	73	68	69	210	1,068,000
Ji-Hee Lee	69	73	69	211	858,000
Sakura Yokomine	70	72	69	211	858,000
Sakurako Mori	69	71	71	211	858,000
Na-Ri Lee	67	72	72	211	858,000
Midori Yoneyama	73	70	69	212	606,000
Hiroko Yamaguchi	67	75	70	212	606,000
Saori Ikushima	73	69	70	212	606,000
Yuri Fudoh	71	71	70	212	606,000
Miki Saiki	69	72	71	212	606,000
Michie Ohba	72	66	74	212	606,000

Golf 5 Ladies

Mizunami Country Club, Mizunami, Gifu
Par 36-36–72; 6,514 yards

September 4-6
purse, ¥60,000,000

	SCORES			TOTAL	MONEY
Shinobu Moromizato	67	69	66	202	¥10,800,000
Miki Saiki	74	65	65	204	4,360,000
Chie Arimura	68	70	66	204	4,360,000
Sakura Yokomine	65	71	68	204	4,360,000
Hyun-Ju Shin	69	70	67	206	2,700,000
Eun-A Lim	69	70	67	206	2,700,000
Miho Koga	67	69	71	207	2,100,000
Nobuko Kizawa	72	70	66	208	1,344,000
Hiromi Mogi	69	70	69	208	1,344,000
Yuko Saitoh	68	69	71	208	1,344,000
Mi-Jeong Jeon	68	68	72	208	1,344,000
Yui Kawahara	68	68	72	208	1,344,000
Yukari Baba	68	72	69	209	1,020,000
Toshimi Kimura	71	70	69	210	900,000
Julie Lu	70	70	70	210	900,000
Maiko Wakabayashi	68	70	72	210	900,000
Akane Iijima	73	69	69	211	669,600
Ayako Uehara	73	69	69	211	669,600
Na-Ri Lee	70	70	71	211	669,600
Kumiko Kaneda	70	69	72	211	669,600
Kurumi Dohi	67	71	73	211	669,600

Japan LPGA Championship Konica Minolta Cup

Seki Country Club, Seki, Gifu
Par 36-36–72; 6,632 yards

September 10-13
purse, ¥140,000,000

	SCORES				TOTAL	MONEY
Shinobu Moromizato	72	67	70	73	282	¥25,200,000
Mi-Jeong Jeon	76	70	73	69	288	12,320,000
Maria Iida	72	70	72	75	289	8,400,000
Chie Arimura	70	73	74	72	289	8,400,000
Yukari Baba	71	71	69	78	289	8,400,000
Rikako Morita	76	75	71	69	291	4,550,000
Erika Kikuchi	75	71	72	73	291	4,550,000
Miho Koga	78	72	70	71	291	4,550,000
Nikki Campbell	77	69	74	71	291	4,550,000
Na-Ri Lee	72	73	73	74	292	2,454,666
Sakura Yokomine	72	72	76	72	292	2,454,666
Ayako Uehara	68	73	74	77	292	2,454,666
Kurumi Dohi	72	74	72	75	293	2,002,000
Yuri Fudoh	77	72	75	69	293	2,002,000
Hiromi Takesue	76	72	70	76	294	1,344,000
Momoko Ueda	76	71	74	73	294	1,344,000
Kaori Aoyama	77	70	71	76	294	1,344,000
Miki Saiki	71	78	69	76	294	1,344,000
Hiromi Mogi	77	74	74	69	294	1,344,000
Hyun-Ju Shin	75	72	75	72	294	1,344,000
Bo-Bae Song	73	71	69	81	294	1,344,000
Eun-Hye Lee	75	73	73	73	294	1,344,000

Munsingwear Ladies Tokai Classic

Minami Aichi Country Club, Minami, Aichi
Par 36-36–72; 6,458 yards

September 18-20
purse, ¥80,000,000

	SCORES			TOTAL	MONEY
Sakura Yokomine	66	65	68	199	¥14,400,000
Yuri Fudoh	63	69	68	200	7,040,000
Maiko Wakabayashi	65	67	70	202	5,600,000
Kaori Aoyama	71	65	67	203	4,400,000
Chie Arimura	67	67	69	203	4,400,000
Yukari Baba	65	70	70	205	3,200,000
Erina Hara	65	71	71	207	2,400,000
Ji-Hee Lee	67	71	69	207	2,400,000
Mi-Jeong Jeon	70	69	68	207	2,400,000
Hyun-Ju Shin	69	70	69	208	1,560,000
Miho Koga	70	71	67	208	1,560,000
Ah-Reum Hwang	70	70	69	209	1,360,000
Akiko Fukushima	69	69	71	209	1,360,000
Kaori Yamamoto	68	71	70	209	1,360,000
Ayako Uehara	73	68	69	210	1,120,000
So-Hee Kim	68	71	71	210	1,120,000
Namika Omata	72	70	68	210	1,120,000
Mikiyo Nishizuka	70	69	72	211	811,428
Yasuko Satoh	69	73	69	211	811,428
Junko Omote	70	70	71	211	811,428
Li-Ying Ye	72	67	72	211	811,428
Hiromi Mogi	71	69	71	211	811,428
Nikki Campbell	69	69	73	211	811,428
Yuki Ichinose	69	71	71	211	811,428

Miyagi TV Cup Dunlop Ladies Open

Rifu Golf Club, Rifu, Miyagi
Par 36-36–72; 6,554 yards

September 25-27
purse, ¥60,000,000

	SCORES			TOTAL	MONEY
Chie Arimura	70	65	71	206	¥10,800,000
Momoko Ueda	67	69	72	208	5,280,000
Sakura Yokomine	70	70	71	211	4,200,000
Ji-Hee Lee	71	72	69	212	3,000,000
Yuko Mitsuka	71	70	71	212	3,000,000
Hiromi Mogi	69	73	70	212	3,000,000
Yuki Ichinose	69	71	73	213	2,100,000
Kaori Aoyama	71	73	70	214	1,800,000
Miho Koga	72	71	72	215	1,500,000
Yun-Jye Wei	67	79	70	216	1,167,000
Miki Saiki	71	75	70	216	1,167,000
Na-Ri Lee	71	75	71	217	954,000
Maria Iida	73	70	74	217	954,000
Bo-Bae Song	72	71	74	217	954,000
Eun-Hye Lee	72	71	74	217	954,000
Mayumi Nakajima	70	72	75	217	954,000
Hyun-Ju Shin	73	74	71	218	744,000
Mayu Hattori	71	75	72	218	744,000
Midori Yoneyama	73	72	74	219	654,000
Kim Bo-Kyung	72	75	73	220	564,000
Tamie Durdin	72	76	72	220	564,000
Natsu Nagai	73	71	76	220	564,000
Yayoi Arasaki	70	72	78	220	564,000
Kaori Nakamura	71	76	73	220	564,000
Shinobu Moromizato	72	74	74	220	564,000

Japan Women's Open

Abiko Golf Club, Abiko, Chiba
Par 36-36–72; 6,559 yards

October 1-4
purse, ¥140,000,000

	SCORES				TOTAL	MONEY
Bo-Bae Song	69	69	71	68	277	¥28,000,000
Sakura Yokomine	70	68	74	65	277	15,400,000
(Song defeated Yokomine on first playoff hole.)						
Ai Miyazato	73	71	68	68	280	10,780,000
Shinobu Moromizato	72	70	70	69	281	7,000,000
Yuri Fudoh	70	70	72	70	282	5,880,000
Miki Saiki	71	71	70	71	283	3,955,000
Akiko Fukushima	68	70	71	74	283	3,955,000
Mika Miyazato	67	68	70	78	283	3,955,000
Miho Koga	70	74	68	71	283	3,955,000
Nikki Campbell	71	69	76	69	285	2,200,800
Momoko Ueda	71	72	69	73	285	2,200,800
Saiki Fujita	70	73	68	74	285	2,200,800
Mayu Hattori	70	76	70	69	285	2,200,800
Yukari Baba	67	73	72	73	285	2,200,800
Eun-A Lim	68	74	71	73	286	1,478,400
Akane Iijima	74	73	68	71	286	1,478,400
*Harukyo Nomura	73	69	70	74	286	
Hiromi Mogi	73	73	69	71	286	1,478,400
Ji-Woo Lee	76	70	69	71	286	1,478,400
Mi-Jeong Jeon	73	72	68	73	286	1,478,400

Sankyo Ladies Open

Akagi Country Club, Kiryu, Gunma
Par 36-36–72; 6,462 yards

October 9-11
purse, ¥100,000,000

	SCORES			TOTAL	MONEY
Ai Miyazato	74	70	68	212	¥18,000,000
Mi-Jeong Jeon	66	73	74	213	7,900,000
Mayu Hattori	69	73	71	213	7,900,000
Michie Ohba	70	74	71	215	5,500,000
Ji-Hee Lee	75	69	71	215	5,500,000
Sakura Yokomine	71	73	72	216	3,500,000
Rui Kitada	72	72	72	216	3,500,000
Yun-Jye Wei	74	71	71	216	3,500,000
Nikki Campbell	76	69	72	217	2,250,000
Akane Iijima	70	70	77	217	2,250,000
Julie Lu	74	74	70	218	1,730,000
Chie Arimura	71	73	74	218	1,730,000
Miho Koga	71	74	73	218	1,730,000
Yuko Mitsuka	80	70	69	219	1,530,000
Miki Saiki	78	73	69	220	1,380,000
Mika Takushima	72	72	76	220	1,380,000
Sakurako Mori	75	72	74	221	1,130,000
Hiromi Takesue	73	75	73	221	1,130,000
Mayumi Shimomura	74	71	76	221	1,130,000
Momoko Ueda	77	72	73	222	910,000
Seiko Watanabe	73	76	73	222	910,000
Momoyo Yamazaki	76	70	76	222	910,000

Fujitsu Ladies

Tokyu Seven Hundred Club, Chiba
Par 36-36–72; 6,588 yards

October 16-18
purse, ¥80,000,000

	SCORES			TOTAL	MONEY
Nikki Campbell	69	69	69	207	¥14,400,000
Ai Miyazato	69	69	69	207	7,040,000
(Campbell defeated Miyazato on fourth playoff hole.)					
Akane Iijima	70	65	73	208	4,800,000
Miki Saiki	70	65	73	208	4,800,000
Yukari Baba	68	68	72	208	4,800,000
Tamie Durdin	69	70	70	209	3,200,000
Eun-A Lim	70	71	69	210	2,800,000
Shinobu Moromizato	70	71	70	211	2,200,000
Miho Koga	71	69	71	211	2,200,000
Aoi Nagata	71	69	72	212	1,536,000
Yuri Fudoh	73	68	71	212	1,536,000
Asako Fujimoto	71	70	72	213	1,152,000
Mikiyo Nishizuka	70	70	73	213	1,152,000
Ah-Reum Hwang	70	70	73	213	1,152,000
Julie Lu	69	72	72	213	1,152,000
Chie Arimura	69	72	72	213	1,152,000
Yun-Jye Wei	72	72	69	213	1,152,000
Esther Lee	72	72	69	213	1,152,000
Yumiko Yoshida	69	73	72	214	792,000
Kaori Ohe	72	70	72	214	792,000

Masters Golf Club Ladies

Masters Golf Club, Miki, Hyogo
Par 36-36–72; 6,510 yards

October 23-25
purse, ¥123,000,000

	SCORES			TOTAL	MONEY
Jiyai Shin	70	70	68	208	¥22,140,000
Yuko Mitsuka	71	68	69	208	9,717,000
Akiko Fukushima	70	65	73	208	9,717,000
(Shin defeated Fukushima and Mitsuka on first playoff hole.)					
Ji-Hee Lee	71	69	70	210	6,150,000
Chie Arimura	72	67	71	210	6,150,000
Shinobu Moromizato	67	69	74	210	6,150,000
Miki Saiki	70	73	70	213	2,718,300
Hiromi Mogi	70	72	71	213	2,718,300
Kuniko Maeda	72	70	71	213	2,718,300
Sakura Yokomine	68	73	72	213	2,718,300
Ayako Uehara	69	71	73	213	2,718,300
Stacy Lewis	70	70	73	213	2,718,300
Eun-A Lim	69	69	75	213	2,718,300
Yukari Baba	70	68	75	213	2,718,300
Akane Iijima	75	70	69	214	1,562,100
Miho Koga	72	72	70	214	1,562,100
Mayu Hattori	73	71	70	214	1,562,100
Mi-Jeong Jeon	73	70	71	214	1,562,100
Bo-Bae Song	73	73	69	215	1,164,400
Yui Kawahara	73	72	70	215	1,164,400
Michie Ohba	72	69	74	215	1,164,400

Hisako Higuchi IDC Otsuka Ladies

Musashigaoka Golf Club, Hanno, Saitama
Par 36-36–72; 6,561 yards

October 30-November 1
purse, ¥70,000,000

	SCORES			TOTAL	MONEY
Mi-Jeong Jeon	65	71	67	203	¥12,600,000
Michie Ohba	69	66	69	204	5,530,000
Chie Arimura	69	65	70	204	5,530,000
Bo-Bae Song	69	70	67	206	3,237,500
Akane Iijima	67	71	68	206	3,237,500
Eun-Hye Lee	72	66	68	206	3,237,500
Mayu Hattori	68	68	70	206	3,237,500
Junko Omote	70	69	68	207	1,925,000
Yuko Mitsuka	71	68	68	207	1,925,000
Yuko Shiroto	69	70	69	208	1,365,000
Ji-Hee Lee	71	67	70	208	1,365,000
Rui Kitada	71	70	68	209	1,225,000
Hiromi Mogi	69	68	72	209	1,225,000
Ah-Reum Hwang	69	71	70	210	1,050,000
Tamie Durdin	68	70	72	210	1,050,000
Akiko Fukushima	70	67	73	210	1,050,000
*Miho Mori	74	68	69	211	
Shinobu Moromizato	70	70	71	211	910,000
Julie Lu	69	72	71	212	770,000
Maiko Wakabayashi	65	74	73	212	770,000
Yun-Jye Wei	67	71	74	212	770,000

Mizuno Classic

Kinetetsu Kashikojima Country Club, Shima, Mie
Par 36-36–72; 6,506 yards

November 6-8
purse, ¥137,438,000

	SCORES			TOTAL	MONEY
Bo-Bae Song	68	65	68	201	¥18,900,000
Lorena Ochoa	71	69	64	204	8,704,710
Hee Young Park	67	69	68	204	8,704,710
Brittany Lang	66	70	68	204	8,704,710
Yani Tseng	69	69	67	205	4,001,760
Inbee Park	70	66	69	205	4,001,760
Jiyai Shin	69	67	69	205	4,001,760
Mi-Jeong Jeon	68	68	69	205	4,001,760
Momoko Ueda	68	68	70	206	2,553,210
Rui Kitada	69	66	71	206	2,553,210
In-Kyung Kim	69	65	72	206	2,553,210
Maria Hjorth	71	69	67	207	1,938,330
Sakura Yokomine	71	69	67	207	1,938,330
Eun-A Lim	70	68	69	207	1,938,330
Song-Hee Kim	69	67	71	207	1,938,330
Akane Iijima	70	64	73	207	1,938,330
Na Yeon Choi	72	68	68	208	1,525,680
Miki Saiki	69	70	69	208	1,525,680
Jee Young Lee	69	68	71	208	1,525,680
Ai Miyazato	69	67	72	208	1,525,680
Candie Kung	71	69	69	209	1,338,120
Anna Nordqvist	73	65	71	209	1,338,120
Hyun-Ju Shin	69	68	72	209	1,338,120
Vicky Hurst	68	69	72	209	1,338,120
Sun Young Yoo	74	68	68	210	1,150,470
Lindsey Wright	72	69	69	210	1,150,470
Ah-Reum Hwang	70	68	72	210	1,150,470
Hee-Won Han	69	68	73	210	1,150,470
Amy Yang	74	68	69	211	890,190
Mayu Hattori	71	69	71	211	890,190
Karrie Webb	70	70	71	211	890,190
Shi Hyun Ahn	73	66	72	211	890,190
Li-Ying Ye	71	68	72	211	890,190
Kyeong Bae	71	68	72	211	890,190
Nobuko Kizawa	67	72	72	211	890,190
Eunjung Yi	69	69	73	211	890,190

Itoen Ladies

Great Island Club, Chonan, Chiba
Par 36-36–72; 6,619 yards

November 13-15
purse, ¥90,000,000

	SCORES			TOTAL	MONEY
Sakura Yokomine	67	70	69	206	¥16,200,000
Ayako Uehara	69	70	71	210	7,920,000
Miho Koga	70	71	70	211	6,300,000
Yuki Ichinose	71	70	72	213	5,400,000
Kaori Aoyama	72	71	71	214	3,750,000
Tamie Durdin	69	73	72	214	3,750,000
Chie Arimura	71	71	72	214	3,750,000
Yun-Joo Jeong	73	71	71	215	2,700,000
Mi-Jeong Jeon	68	70	78	216	2,250,000
Yuriko Ohtsuka	74	73	70	217	1,692,000
Hyun-Ju Shin	74	73	70	217	1,692,000

	SCORES			TOTAL	MONEY
Tomoko Kusakabe	70	74	73	217	1,692,000
Hiromi Takesue	71	75	72	218	1,368,000
Na-Ri Lee	71	76	71	218	1,368,000
Akane Iijima	72	73	73	218	1,368,000
Hiromi Mogi	70	74	74	218	1,368,000
Yayoi Arasaki	76	71	72	219	1,008,000
Shinobu Moromizato	71	73	75	219	1,008,000
Yuko Mitsuka	70	72	77	219	1,008,000
Yui Kawahara	70	70	79	219	1,008,000

Daioseishi Elleair Ladies Open

Elleair Golf Club, Mitoyo, Kagawa
Par 36-36–72; 6,408 yards

November 20-22
purse, ¥90,000,000

	SCORES			TOTAL	MONEY
Chie Arimura	67	62	67	196	¥16,200,000
*Harukyo Nomura	67	66	71	204	
Rui Kitada	70	67	68	205	7,110,000
Yuko Mitsuka	68	69	68	205	7,110,000
Nikki Campbell	66	70	70	206	4,162,500
Mayu Hattori	72	66	68	206	4,162,500
Momoko Ueda	67	71	68	206	4,162,500
Michie Ohba	71	68	67	206	4,162,500
Ah-Reum Hwang	68	69	70	207	2,005,200
Yuri Fudoh	70	68	69	207	2,005,200
Ji-Hee Lee	67	70	70	207	2,005,200
Shinobu Moromizato	68	71	68	207	2,005,200
Toshimi Kimura	68	66	73	207	2,005,200
Maria Iida	70	68	70	208	1,368,000
Kuniko Maeda	70	68	70	208	1,368,000
Julie Lu	69	69	70	208	1,368,000
Mayumi Shimomura	72	68	68	208	1,368,000
Yukari Baba	66	72	71	209	1,098,000
Bo-Bae Song	72	67	70	209	1,098,000
Miho Koga	70	71	69	210	882,000
Hyun-Ju Shin	70	71	69	210	882,000
Mikiyo Nishizuka	69	71	70	210	882,000
Miki Saiki	69	69	72	210	882,000

Japan LPGA Tour Championship Ricoh Cup

Miyazaki Country Club, Miyazaki
Par 36-36–72; 6,508 yards

November 26-29
purse, ¥100,000,000

	SCORES				TOTAL	MONEY
Sakura Yokomine	69	71	73	69	282	¥25,000,000
Shinobu Moromizato	73	69	70	71	283	9,837,500
Ji-Hee Lee	72	70	71	70	283	9,837,500
Akane Iijima	74	69	65	75	283	9,837,500
Mayu Hattori	75	68	68	72	283	9,837,500
Ai Miyazato	74	69	71	70	284	5,380,000
Momoko Ueda	69	70	75	70	284	5,380,000
Yukari Baba	72	68	74	71	285	3,880,000
Miho Koga	71	71	71	73	286	2,410,000
Chie Arimura	73	70	71	72	286	2,410,000
Bo-Bae Song	73	71	68	76	288	1,710,000

	SCORES				TOTAL	MONEY
Miki Saiki	74	71	69	75	289	1,410,000
Eun-A Lim	70	73	71	75	289	1,410,000
Mi-Jeong Jeon	72	70	74	74	290	1,110,000
Nikki Campbell	73	73	71	74	291	920,000
Tamie Durdin	72	75	77	69	293	770,000
Akiko Fukushima	76	74	73	70	293	770,000
Ayako Uehara	72	75	72	75	294	620,000
Rui Kitada	76	72	77	71	296	530,000
Ah-Reum Hwang	72	76	74	75	297	500,000

The Kyoraku Cup

Ryukyu Golf Club, Nanjo, Okinawa
Par 73; 6,150 yards

December 4-5
purse, ¥58,500,000

FIRST ROUND

So Yeon Ryu (Korea) defeated Yuri Fudoh, 72-74.
Jeong-Eun Lee (Korea) defeated Akiko Fukushima, 73-74.
Bo-Bae Song (Korea) defeated Miho Koga, 66-72.
Mi-Jeong Jeon (Korea) defeated Erina Hara, 72-74.
Ji-Hee Lee (Korea) defeated Momoko Ueda, 68-71.
Miki Saiki (Japan) defeated Eun-A Lim, 71-74.
Eun-Hee Ji (Korea) defeated Ai Miyazato, 70-72.
Hee-Kyung Seo (Korea) defeated Sakura Yokomine, 68-70.
Na Yeon Choi (Korea) defeated Yukari Baba, 69-73.
Jiyai Shin (Korea) defeated Ayako Uehara, 71-72.
In-Kyung Kim (Korea) defeated Chie Arimura, 70-72.
Shinobu Moromizato (Japan) defeated Bo-Mee Lee, 67-71.

POINTS: Korea 20, Japan 4

FINAL ROUND

Jeong-Eun Lee (Korea) halved with Yuri Fudoh, 72-72.
Akiko Fukushima (Japan) defeated In-Kyung Kim, 69-73.
Bo-Mee Lee (Korea) defeated Yuko Saitoh, 70-72.
Yukari Baba (Japan) defeated So Yeon Ryu, 72-73.
Bo-Bae Song (Korea) defeated Miho Koga, 68-70.
Momoko Ueda (Japan) defeated Sun Young Yoo, 65-69.
Ai Miyazato (Japan) defeated Eun-A Lim, 64-71.
Sakura Yokomine (Japan) defeated Mi-Jeong Jeon, 71-74.
Hee-Kyung Seo (Korea) defeated Chie Arimura, 71-72.
Eun-Hee Ji (Korea) defeated Miki Saiki, 71-75.
Ayako Uehara (Japan) defeated Na Yeon Choi, 71-72.
Shinobu Moromizato (Japan) defeated Jiyai Shin, 71-73.

TOTAL POINTS: Korea 29, Japan 19

(Each member of the Korean team received ¥3,000,000; each member of the Japanese team received ¥1,500,000.)

Australian Ladies Tour

Peugeot Kangaroo Valley ALPG Classic

Kangaroo Valley Resort, Kangaroo Valley, New South Wales
Par 71; 6,066 yards

January 12-13
purse, A$40,000

	SCORES		TOTAL	MONEY
Karen Lunn	70	70	140	A$6,000
Susie Mathews	68	74	142	4,200
Shani Waugh	75	69	144	2,566.67
Mianne Bagger	72	72	144	2,566.67
Nikki Garrett	73	71	144	2,566.67
Cherie Byrnes	75	70	145	1,500
Sarah Kemp	70	75	145	1,500
Sunny Park	75	71	146	1,133.33
Vicky Thomas	72	74	146	1,133.33
Rachel Bailey	70	76	146	1,133.33
Rebecca Coakley	70	78	148	905
Carlie Bridge	75	73	148	905
Jenny Lee	74	74	148	905
Joanne Mills	73	75	148	905
Sarah Nicholson	73	76	149	720
Tamara Hyett	75	75	150	640
Carmen Railton	79	72	151	500
Heidi McCulkin	78	73	151	500
Lisa Jean	75	76	151	500
Rebecca Green	75	76	151	500
Bree Turnbull	74	77	151	500
Stacey Tate	73	78	151	500

Xstrata Coal Branxton Golf Club Pro-Am

Branxton Golf Club, Hunter Valley, New South Wales
Par 36-36-72; 5,658 yards

January 17-18
purse, A$25,000

	SCORES		TOTAL	MONEY
Rachel Bailey	70	72	142	A$3,600
Nancy Harvey	70	73	143	2,340
Laura Davies	69	74	143	2,340
Shani Waugh	72	73	145	1,560
Lisa Jean	74	72	146	1,080
Tamara Beckett	74	72	146	1,080
Joanne Mills	71	75	146	1,080
Rebecca Coakley	68	79	147	714
Angela Harris	77	70	147	714
Wendy Hawkes	75	72	147	714
Kasey Henshaw	72	75	147	714
Vicky Thomas	73	76	149	528
Jane Kim	74	75	149	528
Sarah Kemp	74	75	149	528
Stacey Tate	76	74	150	392
Tamara Hyett	76	74	150	392
Katy Jarochowicz	76	74	150	392

	SCORES			TOTAL	MONEY
Carmen Hajjar	76	75		151	324
Vikki Tutt	75	76		151	324
Mianne Bagger	74	78		152	233.14
Verity Knight	78	74		152	233.14
Sarah Nicholson	77	75		152	233.14
Cherie Byrnes	77	75		152	233.14
Sunny Park	77	75		152	233.14
Carlie Bridge	73	79		152	233.14
Rebecca Green	76	76		152	233.14

LG Bing Lee Women's NSW Open

Oatlands Golf Club, Sydney, New South Wales
Par 36-36–72; 6,008 yards

January 23-25
purse, A$125,000

	SCORES			TOTAL	MONEY
Sarah Oh	65	67	69	201	A$18,750
Katherine Hull	69	67	68	204	12,500
Susie Mathews	74	65	69	208	8,500
Nikki Campbell	67	74	68	209	5,750
Nikki Garrett	65	73	71	209	5,750
Sarah-Jane Smith	68	71	71	210	4,625
Marianne Skarpnord	72	68	71	211	3,412.50
Sarah Kemp	71	68	72	211	3,412.50
Mollie Fankhauser	70	70	71	211	3,412.50
Laura Davies	70	69	72	211	3,412.50
Jenny Lee	66	71	74	211	3,412.50
Kate Combes	69	72	71	212	2,337.50
Carlie Bridge	71	71	70	212	2,337.50
Kirsty S. Taylor	68	73	72	213	2,062.50
Joanne Mills	71	73	70	214	1,781.25
Cherie Byrnes	74	71	69	214	1,781.25
Sarah Nicholson	73	70	72	215	1,459.38
Frances Bondad	72	70	73	215	1,459.38
Rachel Bailey	71	74	70	215	1,459.38
Gwladys Nocera	67	70	78	215	1,459.38

New Zealand Women's Open

Clearwater Resort, Christchurch, New Zealand
Par 36-36–72; 6,222 yards

January 30-February 1
purse, A$117,000

	SCORES			TOTAL	MONEY
Gwladys Nocera	71	68	69	208	A$17,550
Katherine Hull	65	73	76	214	7,605
Nikki Garrett	72	71	71	214	7,605
Bobea Park	73	67	74	214	7,605
Sarah Kemp	73	67	74	214	7,605
Sarah Oh	68	67	80	215	3,802.50
Mollie Fankhauser	70	75	70	215	3,802.50
Lee-Anne Pace	70	72	74	216	2,925
Martina Eberl	71	73	73	217	2,574
Joanne Mills	74	74	71	219	2,340
Vicky Thomas	72	74	74	220	1,852.50
Wendy Doolan	71	72	77	220	1,852.50
Sarah-Jane Smith	73	73	74	220	1,852.50
*Cecilia Cho	69	73	79	221	

	SCORES			TOTAL	MONEY
Yuki Sakurai	74	73	74	221	1,544.40
Sarah Nicholson	71	75	76	222	1,411.02
Johanna Westerberg	71	73	78	222	1,411.02
Julie Tvede	73	72	77	222	1,411.02
*Caroline Bon	73	74	75	222	
Dana Lacey	74	75	73	222	1,411.02
Becky Morgan	72	78	72	222	1,411.02

ANZ Ladies Masters

Royal Pines Resort, Ashmore, Queensland
Par 35-37–72; 6,443 yards

February 5-8
purse, A$600,000

	SCORES				TOTAL	MONEY
Katherine Hull	69	67	68	68	272	A$90,000
So Yeon Ryu	71	68	71	67	277	50,400
Tamie Durdin	70	71	66	70	277	50,400
Sarah Kemp	73	68	69	68	278	23,025
Yani Tseng	71	72	69	66	278	23,025
Mollie Fankhauser	70	70	68	70	278	23,025
Gwladys Nocera	69	73	69	67	278	23,025
Lindsey Wright	71	70	71	67	279	13,200
Jiyai Shin	69	69	72	69	279	13,200
Anna Rawson	71	70	70	69	280	10,290
Nikki Garrett	72	70	71	67	280	10,290
Ai Miyazato	71	70	70	70	281	8,850
Becky Brewerton	67	73	70	71	281	8,850
Rachel Hetherington	70	73	71	68	282	7,680
Marianne Skarpnord	67	72	72	71	282	7,680
Stacy Lee Bregman	68	73	72	70	283	7,006.50
Nikki Campbell	69	65	78	71	283	7,006.50
Linda Wessberg	72	72	67	72	283	7,006.50
Anne-Lise Caudal	72	72	70	69	283	7,006.50
Frances Bondad	70	70	73	71	284	5,860
Nina Reis	75	68	72	69	284	5,860
*Rebecca Flood	69	69	75	71	284	
Sarah Oh	70	72	76	66	284	5,860
Bobea Park	71	72	71	70	284	5,860
Hee-Kyung Seo	72	69	72	71	284	5,860
Kristie Smith	73	62	75	74	284	5,860
Titiya Plucksataporn	74	68	70	72	284	5,860
Melissa Reid	74	69	72	69	284	5,860
Lee-Anne Pace	67	70	76	71	284	5,860

Women's Australian Open

Metropolitan Golf Club, Melbourne, Victoria
Par 36-37–73; 6,562 yards

February 12-15
purse, A$500,000

	SCORES				TOTAL	MONEY
Laura Davies	74	76	67	68	285	A$75,000
Tania Elosegui	69	72	75	70	286	50,000
Chang Hee Lee	69	70	75	73	287	26,833.33
He Yong Choi	72	73	71	71	287	26,833.33
Melissa Reid	76	72	70	69	287	26,833.33
Karrie Webb	66	75	75	74	290	15,875
Katherine Hull	76	74	70	70	290	15,875

	SCORES				TOTAL	MONEY
Clare Queen	70	75	72	74	291	9,850
Marianne Skarpnord	71	71	76	73	291	9,850
Lisa Hall	74	73	74	70	291	9,850
Hye Youn Kim	70	73	75	73	291	9,850
Nikki Campbell	79	70	73	69	291	9,850
Georgina Simpson	73	68	77	74	292	6,600
Diana D'Alessio	72	76	69	75	292	6,600
Christel Boeljon	74	71	72	75	292	6,600
Alison Walshe	77	69	69	78	293	6,016.67
Sarah Oh	74	75	73	71	293	6,016.67
Anne-Lise Caudal	74	75	69	75	293	6,016.67
Nikki Garrett	73	75	71	75	294	5,250
Joanne Mills	74	69	76	75	294	5,250
Lynn Kenny	72	72	75	75	294	5,250
Gwladys Nocera	79	73	71	71	294	5,250
Susie Mathews	74	71	74	75	294	5,250
Becky Brewerton	75	73	76	70	294	5,250
Rebecca Hudson	72	74	71	77	294	5,250

Senior Tours

Mitsubishi Electric Championship

Hualalai Golf Course, Ka'upulehu-Kona, Hawaii
Par 36-36–72; 7,053 yards

January 23-25
purse, $1,800,000

	SCORES			TOTAL	MONEY
Bernhard Langer	64	66	68	198	$315,000
Andy Bean	67	66	66	199	196,000
Jay Haas	65	66	70	201	132,000
Mark McNulty	69	66	67	202	104,750
Jeff Sluman	65	67	70	202	104,750
John Cook	68	67	68	203	80,000
Gil Morgan	68	69	66	203	80,000
Brad Bryant	64	65	75	204	64,500
Loren Roberts	71	65	68	204	64,500
Mark James	69	66	70	205	57,000
Hale Irwin	65	67	74	206	47,000
Tom Kite	66	69	71	206	47,000
Mark Wiebe	70	65	71	206	47,000
Ben Crenshaw	68	71	68	207	37,000
Jerry Pate	67	68	74	209	30,000
Craig Stadler	72	65	72	209	30,000
Tom Watson	69	67	73	209	30,000
D.A. Weibring	69	71	69	209	30,000
Andy North	70	68	72	210	24,000
Tom Purtzer	69	70	71	210	24,000
Curtis Strange	71	67	72	210	24,000
Jim Thorpe	69	70	71	210	24,000
Bobby Wadkins	70	69	71	210	24,000
Allen Doyle	69	72	70	211	20,000
R.W. Eaks	66	71	74	211	20,000
Lonnie Nielsen	72	65	74	211	20,000
Gary Player	70	71	71	212	17,500
Mike Reid	68	74	70	212	17,500
Bruce Lietzke	69	72	73	214	15,500
Eduardo Romero	73	69	72	214	15,500
Bruce Vaughan	70	71	73	214	15,500

Allianz Championship

Old Course at Broken Sound, Boca Raton, Florida
Par 36-36–72; 6,807 yards

February 13-15
purse, $1,700,000

	SCORES			TOTAL	MONEY
Mike Goodes	67	68	66	201	$255,000
Fulton Allem	66	70	66	202	149,600
Bernhard Langer	64	73	67	204	122,400
Mark James	67	69	69	205	83,866.67
Gil Morgan	69	65	71	205	83,866.67
Tom Jenkins	67	67	71	205	83,866.66
Andy Bean	69	69	68	206	49,640
Russ Cochran	67	71	68	206	49,640
David Edwards	69	71	66	206	49,640
Dan Forsman	71	65	70	206	49,640

	SCORES			TOTAL	MONEY
Larry Mize	67	69	70	206	49,640
John Cook	71	70	66	207	32,640
John Harris	67	75	65	207	32,640
Morris Hatalsky	70	72	65	207	32,640
Jerry Pate	64	71	72	207	32,640
Eduardo Romero	72	69	66	207	32,640
Don Pooley	71	68	69	208	27,200
Jay Haas	72	65	72	209	23,970
Mark McNulty	72	69	68	209	23,970
Bruce Vaughan	69	70	70	209	23,970
Ben Crenshaw	73	71	66	210	16,830
Vicente Fernandez	69	71	70	210	16,830
Bruce Fleisher	70	73	67	210	16,830
Gene Jones	73	70	67	210	16,830
Mark O'Meara	71	71	68	210	16,830
Nick Price	69	69	72	210	16,830
Loren Roberts	72	72	66	210	16,830
Joey Sindelar	71	69	70	210	16,830
Robert Thompson	71	69	70	210	16,830
Jim Thorpe	70	71	69	210	16,830

ACE Group Classic

TPC Treviso Bay, Naples, Florida
Par 36-36–72; 7,005 yards

February 20-22
purse, $1,600,000

	SCORES			TOTAL	MONEY
Loren Roberts	70	71	68	209	$240,000
Gene Jones	70	70	70	210	140,800
Ben Crenshaw	71	72	68	211	88,000
Bernhard Langer	70	72	69	211	88,000
James Mason	74	67	70	211	88,000
Don Pooley	68	73	70	211	88,000
Brad Bryant	73	69	71	213	48,800
Mike Goodes	70	73	70	213	48,800
Nick Price	75	71	67	213	48,800
Joey Sindelar	71	73	69	213	48,800
Bruce Fleisher	73	70	71	214	35,200
Wayne Levi	69	73	72	214	35,200
Jeff Sluman	75	69	70	214	35,200
Mike McCullough	71	71	73	215	30,400
Dan Forsman	70	72	74	216	26,400
Sandy Lyle	71	73	72	216	26,400
Blaine McCallister	76	74	66	216	26,400
Jerry Pate	72	72	72	216	26,400
Scott Hoch	80	72	65	217	19,936
Tom Jenkins	76	71	70	217	19,936
Tom Kite	73	72	72	217	19,936
John Morse	71	75	71	217	19,936
Lonnie Nielsen	71	71	75	217	19,936
Fulton Allem	70	75	73	218	15,296
Andy Bean	77	70	71	218	15,296
David Edwards	75	74	69	218	15,296
Fred Funk	76	76	66	218	15,296
Denis O'Sullivan	71	75	72	218	15,296
Bob Gilder	73	83	63	219	11,340
Jay Haas	69	76	74	219	11,340
Gary Koch	71	75	73	219	11,340
Tom McKnight	76	72	71	219	11,340
Joe Ozaki	77	70	72	219	11,340

	SCORES			TOTAL	MONEY
Bobby Wadkins	75	72	72	219	11,340
Tom Wargo	72	74	73	219	11,340
Denis Watson	77	74	68	219	11,340

Toshiba Classic

Newport Beach Country Club, Newport Beach, California
Par 35-36–71; 6,584 yards

March 6-8
purse, $1,700,000

	SCORES			TOTAL	MONEY
Eduardo Romero	66	68	68	202	$255,000
Mark O'Meara	67	66	70	203	136,000
Joey Sindelar	68	72	63	203	136,000
David Eger	70	67	68	205	73,440
Fred Funk	69	67	69	205	73,440
Tom Jenkins	69	67	69	205	73,440
Tim Simpson	68	70	67	205	73,440
Denis Watson	67	68	70	205	73,440
Bernhard Langer	65	68	73	206	44,200
Jeff Sluman	69	68	69	206	44,200
Bobby Wadkins	69	69	68	206	44,200
Jim Thorpe	69	68	70	207	34,566.67
Bruce Vaughan	69	71	67	207	34,566.67
Sandy Lyle	70	67	70	207	34,566.66
John Cook	69	67	72	208	25,670
Dan Forsman	72	71	65	208	25,670
Bob Gilder	66	73	69	208	25,670
Morris Hatalsky	70	67	71	208	25,670
Gene Jones	68	69	71	208	25,670
Joe Ozaki	71	74	63	208	25,670
Robert Thompson	70	69	69	208	25,670
Nick Price	72	69	68	209	17,097.15
Tom Watson	68	72	69	209	17,097.15
Keith Fergus	70	69	70	209	17,097.14
Tom Kite	70	70	69	209	17,097.14
Mike McCullough	70	68	71	209	17,097.14
D.A. Weibring	71	67	71	209	17,097.14
Fuzzy Zoeller	70	70	69	209	17,097.14
Andy Bean	68	70	72	210	13,430
Hal Sutton	76	69	65	210	13,430
Mark Wiebe	74	66	70	210	13,430

AT&T Champions Classic

Valencia Country Club, Valencia, California
Par 36-36–72; 6,973 yards

March 13-15
purse, $1,600,000

	SCORES			TOTAL	MONEY
Dan Forsman	72	67	66	205	$240,000
Don Pooley	70	65	70	205	140,800
(Forsman defeated Pooley on first playoff hole.)					
Jay Haas	67	69	70	206	115,200
Fulton Allem	69	71	67	207	78,933.34
Ben Crenshaw	68	72	67	207	78,933.33
Joey Sindelar	64	70	73	207	78,933.33
Ken Green	71	68	69	208	57,600
Bernhard Langer	68	72	69	209	48,000

	SCORES			TOTAL	MONEY
Tom Purtzer	65	75	69	209	48,000
Jeff Sluman	69	70	71	210	41,600
David Edwards	67	75	69	211	35,200
Bruce Lietzke	68	70	73	211	35,200
Robert Thompson	69	70	72	211	35,200
Andy Bean	69	72	71	212	28,000
Jerry Pate	70	71	71	212	28,000
Tim Simpson	69	69	74	212	28,000
Bobby Wadkins	70	72	70	212	28,000
Bob Gilder	70	73	70	213	20,068.58
Fred Funk	72	69	72	213	20,068.57
Gene Jones	70	72	71	213	20,068.57
Dana Quigley	74	69	70	213	20,068.57
Mark Wiebe	70	70	73	213	20,068.57
Ian Woosnam	73	72	68	213	20,068.57
Fuzzy Zoeller	69	74	70	213	20,068.57
David Eger	70	72	72	214	14,592
Gary Hallberg	69	75	70	214	14,592
Morris Hatalsky	73	70	71	214	14,592
Scott Hoch	71	71	72	214	14,592
Loren Roberts	72	70	72	214	14,592
John Cook	68	74	73	215	11,306.67
Hale Irwin	69	74	72	215	11,306.67
Wayne Levi	69	73	73	215	11,306.67
Eduardo Romero	70	75	70	215	11,306.67
Tom McKnight	71	68	76	215	11,306.66
Joe Ozaki	74	73	68	215	11,306.66

Cap Cana Championship

Punta Espanda Golf Club, Cap Cana, Dominican Republic   March 27-29
Par 36-36–72; 7,260 yards   purse, $2,100,000

	SCORES			TOTAL	MONEY
Keith Fergus	68	68	67	203	$315,000
Andy Bean	71	68	65	204	168,000
Mark O'Meara	71	65	68	204	168,000
Joey Sindelar	70	68	67	205	126,000
Gene Jones	72	66	68	206	100,800
Bernhard Langer	70	73	64	207	79,800
Mark McNulty	70	68	69	207	79,800
R.W. Eaks	71	70	67	208	67,200
John Cook	69	73	67	209	56,700
Gil Morgan	72	68	69	209	56,700
Brad Bryant	71	73	66	210	44,625
Jay Haas	70	70	70	210	44,625
Nick Price	68	74	68	210	44,625
Eduardo Romero	68	68	74	210	44,625
Fulton Allem	75	65	71	211	33,642
Scott Hoch	70	71	70	211	33,642
Tom Jenkins	68	73	70	211	33,642
Tom Purtzer	74	68	69	211	33,642
Craig Stadler	70	69	72	211	33,642
Ronnie Black	70	71	71	212	26,880
Bruce Vaughan	71	67	74	212	26,880
David Eger	67	75	71	213	21,595
Dan Forsman	72	73	68	213	21,595
James Mason	73	71	69	213	21,595
Lonnie Nielsen	73	70	70	213	21,595
Joe Ozaki	70	71	72	213	21,595

	SCORES			TOTAL	MONEY
Tim Simpson	68	70	75	213	21,595
Phil Blackmar	70	72	72	214	16,632
Gary Hallberg	73	68	73	214	16,632
John Harris	75	69	70	214	16,632
Don Pooley	72	67	75	214	16,632
Jim Thorpe	71	72	71	214	16,632

Outback Steakhouse Pro-Am

TPC Tampa Bay, Lutz, Florida
Par 35-36–71; 6,783 yards

April 17-19
purse, $1,700,000

	SCORES			TOTAL	MONEY
Nick Price	66	67	71	204	$255,000
Larry Nelson	65	71	70	206	150,450
Loren Roberts	71	69	67	207	102,283.34
Lonnie Nielsen	68	69	70	207	102,283.33
Hal Sutton	74	64	69	207	102,283.33
Jay Haas	68	68	72	208	81,600
Mike McCullough	67	69	73	209	61,200
John Cook	69	72	69	210	44,880
Bruce Fleisher	69	72	69	210	44,880
Larry Mize	69	71	70	210	44,880
Mark O'Meara	73	68	69	210	44,880
Jim Thorpe	71	71	68	210	44,880
David Eger	69	71	71	211	32,300
Bernhard Langer	70	72	69	211	32,300
Tom Wargo	70	70	71	211	32,300
Scott Hoch	70	73	69	212	25,602
Gene Jones	72	72	68	212	25,602
Mark McNulty	67	72	73	212	25,602
Joey Sindelar	72	70	70	212	25,602
Fuzzy Zoeller	70	72	70	212	25,602
Andy Bean	71	72	70	213	17,995.72
Dan Forsman	73	70	70	213	17,995.72
Mike Goodes	71	73	69	213	17,995.72
Jeff Sluman	72	70	71	213	17,995.71
Des Smyth	72	69	72	213	17,995.71
Craig Stadler	76	69	68	213	17,995.71
Bobby Wadkins	71	70	72	213	17,995.71
Phil Blackmar	71	71	72	214	13,464
R.W. Eaks	72	73	69	214	13,464
Gil Morgan	71	71	72	214	13,464
Tim Simpson	70	73	71	214	13,464
Robert Thompson	71	74	69	214	13,464

Liberty Mutual Legends of Golf

Westin Savannah Harbor Resort & Spa, Savannah, Georgia
Par 36-36–72; 7,087 yards

April 24-26
purse, $2,600,000

	SCORES			TOTAL	MONEY (Team)
Bernhard Langer/Tom Lehman	61	66	62	189	$450,000
Jeff Sluman/Craig Stadler	63	65	61	189	265,000
(Langer and Lehman defeated Sluman and Stadler on second playoff hole.)					
Loren Roberts/Mark Wiebe	64	61	65	190	198,000
John Cook/Joey Sindelar	63	63	64	190	198,000

	SCORES			TOTAL	MONEY (Team)
Tom Kite/Gil Morgan	68	62	62	192	133,000
Des Smyth/Mark James	68	62	62	192	133,000
Andy Bean/Jerry Pate	66	64	63	193	102,000
Mark O'Meara/Nick Price	63	64	66	193	102,000
Fred Funk/Scott Hoch	65	66	63	194	82,000
John Jacobs/Fuzzy Zoeller	61	67	66	194	82,000
Tom Watson/Andy North	66	64	65	195	69,500
Dan Forsman/Tom Purtzer	66	62	67	195	69,500
Bruce Fleisher/Tom Jenkins	65	67	64	196	57,666.66
Jay Haas/Ben Crenshaw	67	63	66	196	57,666.66
Sandy Lyle/Ian Woosnam	62	68	66	196	57,666.66
David Eger/Mark McNulty	66	65	66	197	49,500
Larry Nelson/Jim Thorpe	67	65	65	197	49,500
R.W. Eaks/Bob Gilder	66	67	65	198	43,500
Brad Bryant/Lonnie Nielsen	70	63	65	198	43,500
Mike Goodes/D.A. Weibring	64	68	67	199	36,000
Keith Fergus/Greg Norman	66	66	67	199	36,000
Allen Doyle/Dana Quigley	67	66	66	199	36,000
Morris Hatalsky/Don Pooley	70	64	65	199	36,000
Tim Simpson/Bruce Vaughan	70	66	64	200	31,000
Hubert Green/Leonard Thompson	66	67	68	201	29,000
Ken Green/Mike Reid	67	70	64	201	29,000
Jay Sigel/Dave Stockton	66	67	69	202	27,000
Eduardo Romero/Denis Watson	66	70	69	205	25,500
Blaine McCallister/Larry Mize	66	70	69	205	25,500
Bobby Wadkins/Lanny Wadkins	69	69	68	206	24,000
Gibby Gilbert/J.C. Snead	69	69	71	209	23,000

Regions Charity Classic

Robert Trent Jones Golf Trail at Ross Bridge, Hoover, Alabama   May 15-17
Par 36-36–72; 7,473 yards   purse, $1,700,000
(Event shortened to 36 holes—rain.)

	SCORES		TOTAL	MONEY
Keith Fergus	66	66	132	$255,000
Gene Jones	69	66	135	149,600
Joe Ozaki	69	67	136	122,400
Jay Don Blake	70	67	137	65,571.43
Brad Bryant	72	65	137	65,571.43
Tom Jenkins	68	69	137	65,571.43
Tom McKnight	67	70	137	65,571.43
Loren Roberts	68	69	137	65,571.43
Jim Thorpe	67	70	137	65,571.43
Larry Mize	66	71	137	65,571.42
Morris Hatalsky	70	68	138	33,028.58
Phil Blackmar	69	69	138	33,028.57
Dan Forsman	65	73	138	33,028.57
Joey Sindelar	69	69	138	33,028.57
Hal Sutton	66	72	138	33,028.57
Bruce Vaughan	70	68	138	33,028.57
Denis Watson	69	69	138	33,028.57
Bruce Fleisher	68	71	139	21,322.86
Bob Gilder	70	69	139	21,322.86
James Mason	70	69	139	21,322.86
Larry Nelson	70	69	139	21,322.86
Tim Simpson	70	69	139	21,322.86
Gil Morgan	67	72	139	21,322.85
Lonnie Nielsen	68	71	139	21,322.85

	SCORES		TOTAL	MONEY
Andy Bean	70	70	140	14,185.56
Jay Haas	71	69	140	14,185.56
Tom Kite	71	69	140	14,185.56
Bernhard Langer	71	69	140	14,185.56
Tom Purtzer	69	71	140	14,185.56
Fred Funk	68	72	140	14,185.55
Mike Goodes	69	71	140	14,185.55
Gary Koch	72	68	140	14,185.55
Fuzzy Zoeller	68	72	140	14,185.55

Senior PGA Championship

Canterbury Golf Club, Beachwood, Ohio
Par 34-36–70; 6,895 yards

May 21-24
purse, $2,000,000

	SCORES				TOTAL	MONEY
Michael Allen	74	66	67	67	274	$360,000
Larry Mize	69	69	71	67	276	216,000
Bruce Fleisher	71	70	69	67	277	136,000
Tom Watson	72	72	70	66	280	96,000
Chris Starkjohann	71	68	72	70	281	65,500
Fred Funk	71	71	69	70	281	65,500
Gil Morgan	71	68	70	72	281	65,500
Jeff Sluman	70	68	70	73	281	65,500
Dan Forsman	70	70	74	68	282	46,200
Jay Haas	71	74	68	69	282	46,200
Mark James	69	71	72	70	282	46,200
James Mason	71	73	68	70	282	46,200
Tim Simpson	70	71	68	73	282	46,200
Mark O'Meara	76	70	69	68	283	33,000
Eduardo Romero	73	72	68	70	283	33,000
Tom Kite	69	70	69	75	283	33,000
John Cook	73	69	73	69	284	24,000
Scott Hoch	66	72	76	70	284	24,000
Tom Purtzer	66	72	74	72	284	24,000
Bernhard Langer	68	70	73	73	284	24,000
Mark McNulty	72	69	70	73	284	24,000
John Morse	69	72	74	70	285	16,500
Tom Lehman	75	68	74	68	285	16,500
Andy Bean	74	72	72	67	285	16,500
Keith Fergus	73	69	72	71	285	16,500
Joe Ozaki	75	67	69	74	285	16,500
Joey Sindelar	69	72	69	75	285	16,500
Gene Jones	75	69	72	70	286	12,500
Loren Roberts	73	74	68	71	286	12,500
Kiyoshi Murota	73	71	70	72	286	12,500
Don Pooley	74	69	68	75	286	12,500
Jay Don Blake	70	69	71	76	286	12,500
Bill Britton	75	70	70	72	287	10,250
Bob Cameron	72	73	73	69	287	10,250
Russ Cochran	70	71	73	73	287	10,250
James Blair	71	72	71	73	287	10,250
Jeff Roth	74	73	69	72	288	7,886
Mike Goodes	75	71	71	71	288	7,886
Gary Hallberg	69	74	71	74	288	7,886
Kirk Hanefeld	75	70	73	70	288	7,886
Ian Woosnam	71	72	75	70	288	7,886
Ross Drummond	70	66	76	76	288	7,886
Dana Quigley	69	75	77	67	288	7,886
Walter Hall	72	73	70	74	289	6,000

	SCORES				TOTAL	MONEY
Lonnie Nielsen	76	69	73	71	289	6,000
Mike Reid	74	71	73	71	289	6,000
Mark Wiebe	72	73	74	70	289	6,000
Chip Beck	73	73	74	69	289	6,000
John Harris	72	74	70	74	290	4,725
Hal Sutton	71	76	70	73	290	4,725
Bobby Wadkins	75	71	72	72	290	4,725
Greg Norman	73	72	73	72	290	4,725
Bob Tway	75	72	70	74	291	4,275
Bill Longmuir	77	70	72	72	291	4,275
Juan Quiros	72	75	73	71	291	4,275
Sam Torrance	70	71	80	70	291	4,275
Ron Streck	73	74	68	77	292	4,125
Allen Doyle	72	74	73	73	292	4,125
Bob Gilder	71	74	71	77	293	3,908
Roger Chapman	74	68	73	78	293	3,908
Costantino Rocca	72	75	70	76	293	3,908
Dave Stockton	70	73	72	78	293	3,908
Hale Irwin	70	74	73	76	293	3,908
Wayne Grady	71	72	74	76	293	3,908
Robert Gibbons	71	73	75	74	293	3,908
Tom McKnight	72	73	75	73	293	3,908
Mike Smith	75	71	75	72	293	3,908
Tom Wargo	74	73	72	75	294	3,763
Vicente Fernandez	76	71	73	74	294	3,763
Brad Bryant	73	67	78	78	296	3,688
John Jacobs	70	73	76	77	296	3,688
Ronnie Black	75	71	76	74	296	3,688
Ken Green	72	74	76	74	296	3,688
Jim Woodward	72	75	76	77	300	3,625
Jon Fiedler	72	74	80	76	302	3,600
Jim White	74	73	75	83	305	3,575
Fred Gibson	73	74	78	83	308	3,550

Principal Charity Classic

Glen Oaks Country Club, West Des Moines, Iowa
Par 35-36–71; 6,877 yards

May 29-31
purse, $1,725,000

	SCORES			TOTAL	MONEY
Mark McNulty	68	69	66	203	$258,750
Fred Funk	68	69	66	203	138,000
Nick Price	68	67	68	203	138,000
(McNulty defeated Price on second and Funk on fourth playoff hole.)					
Mark Wiebe	68	68	69	205	103,500
David Eger	69	69	68	206	82,800
John Cook	70	73	64	207	53,475
Morris Hatalsky	72	70	65	207	53,475
Loren Roberts	71	70	66	207	53,475
Tom Jenkins	72	68	67	207	53,475
Tom Kite	68	70	69	207	53,475
Bruce Summerhays	72	67	68	207	53,475
Jeff Sluman	68	71	69	208	35,075
Mike Reid	72	66	70	208	35,075
Joey Sindelar	69	67	72	208	35,075
Phil Blackmar	71	71	67	209	30,188
Jay Don Blake	70	71	68	209	30,188
Jerry Pate	70	72	68	210	22,992
Jim Colbert	70	72	68	210	22,992
Bob Gilder	72	70	68	210	22,992

	SCORES			TOTAL	MONEY
Gene Jones	72	69	69	210	22,992
Lonnie Nielsen	67	72	71	210	22,992
Larry Nelson	68	71	71	210	22,992
Jay Haas	72	67	71	210	22,992
Tom Wargo	75	69	67	211	15,417
Bruce Vaughan	67	74	70	211	15,417
Dan Forsman	71	70	70	211	15,417
Brad Bryant	71	69	71	211	15,417
Hale Irwin	70	69	72	211	15,417
Craig Stadler	72	67	72	211	15,417
Hal Sutton	70	68	73	211	15,417
Tim Simpson	68	70	73	211	15,417

Triton Financial Classic

The Hills Country Club, Austin, Texas
Par 36-36–72; 6,879 yards

June 5-7
purse, $1,600,000

	SCORES			TOTAL	MONEY
Bernhard Langer	65	69	67	201	$240,000
Mark O'Meara	68	69	70	207	140,800
Dana Quigley	68	71	69	208	115,200
Larry Mize	68	72	69	209	78,933.34
Scott Hoch	69	69	71	209	78,933.33
Gene Jones	69	66	74	209	78,933.33
John Cook	69	73	69	211	46,720
Fred Funk	72	71	68	211	46,720
Jay Haas	70	68	73	211	46,720
Tom Kite	68	70	73	211	46,720
John Morse	71	68	72	211	46,720
Dan Forsman	71	69	72	212	31,600
Mark James	68	71	73	212	31,600
Mark McNulty	69	75	68	212	31,600
Joey Sindelar	72	69	71	212	31,600
Chip Beck	71	71	71	213	26,400
Leonard Thompson	73	70	70	213	26,400
Loren Roberts	71	72	71	214	24,000
Fulton Allem	73	71	71	215	19,936
Olin Browne	71	73	71	215	19,936
Vicente Fernandez	76	69	70	215	19,936
Mike McCullough	67	73	75	215	19,936
Tim Simpson	71	74	70	215	19,936
David Eger	66	78	72	216	15,640
Jerry Pate	70	73	73	216	15,640
Jeff Sluman	68	69	79	216	15,640
Mark Wiebe	68	74	74	216	15,640
Dave Eichelberger	74	72	71	217	11,626.67
John Harris	73	73	71	217	11,626.67
Gil Morgan	71	76	70	217	11,626.67
Don Pooley	74	70	73	217	11,626.67
Tom Purtzer	73	74	70	217	11,626.67
Dave Stockton	70	73	74	217	11,626.67
Gary Hallberg	73	70	74	217	11,626.66
Morris Hatalsky	71	72	74	217	11,626.66
Lonnie Nielsen	74	67	76	217	11,626.66

Dick's Sporting Goods Open

En-Joie Golf Course, Endicott, New York
Par 37-35–72; 6,974 yards

June 26-28
purse, $1,650,000

	SCORES			TOTAL	MONEY
Lonnie Nielsen	66	66	63	195	$247,500
Ronnie Black	69	63	66	198	132,000
Fred Funk	64	65	69	198	132,000
Brad Bryant	68	68	65	201	99,000
Dan Forsman	70	68	65	203	68,200
Jay Haas	66	68	69	203	68,200
John Morse	69	67	67	203	68,200
Gary Hallberg	67	66	71	204	49,500
Mike Hulbert	67	68	69	204	49,500
Mike Goodes	70	65	70	205	36,630
Tom Kite	67	70	68	205	36,630
Larry Mize	68	69	68	205	36,630
Nick Price	70	66	69	205	36,630
Joey Sindelar	68	69	68	205	36,630
Scott Hoch	70	67	69	206	24,915
Tom Jenkins	68	69	69	206	24,915
Mark McNulty	70	69	67	206	24,915
Eduardo Romero	69	63	74	206	24,915
Jim Thorpe	70	71	65	206	24,915
Gary Trivisonno	71	67	68	206	24,915
D.A. Weibring	67	69	70	206	24,915
Andy Bean	67	68	72	207	18,645
Jeff Sluman	68	67	72	207	18,645
Don Pooley	69	71	68	208	15,085.72
Hal Sutton	68	72	68	208	15,085.72
Bruce Vaughan	72	68	68	208	15,085.72
Chip Beck	73	68	67	208	15,085.71
Russ Cochran	71	71	66	208	15,085.71
David Ogrin	69	68	71	208	15,085.71
Scott Simpson	70	68	70	208	15,085.71

3M Championship

TPC Twin Cities, Blaine, Minnesota
Par 36-36–72; 7,100 yards

July 10-12
purse, $1,750,000

	SCORES			TOTAL	MONEY
Bernhard Langer	67	68	65	200	$262,500
Andy Bean	65	69	67	201	154,000
Scott Hoch	67	69	66	202	126,000
Tom Kite	69	67	67	203	105,000
Nick Price	65	68	71	204	77,000
Steve Thomas	73	64	67	204	77,000
Dan Forsman	67	71	67	205	56,000
Larry Mize	71	67	67	205	56,000
Mark O'Meara	71	70	64	205	56,000
Gene Jones	66	68	72	206	45,500
Ronnie Black	67	74	66	207	40,250
Mark McNulty	70	70	67	207	40,250
John Cook	71	68	69	208	33,250
David Edwards	70	71	67	208	33,250
Jay Haas	71	69	68	208	33,250
David Eger	72	71	66	209	27,168.75
Bruce Fleisher	69	73	67	209	27,168.75

	SCORES			TOTAL	MONEY
Dana Quigley	71	69	69	209	27,168.75
Jeff Sluman	72	70	67	209	27,168.75
Chip Beck	71	70	69	210	22,400
Brad Bryant	70	71	69	210	22,400
R.W. Eaks	70	71	70	211	16,838.89
Mike Goodes	68	71	72	211	16,838.89
Morris Hatalsky	71	75	65	211	16,838.89
John Jacobs	70	74	67	211	16,838.89
Mark James	71	69	71	211	16,838.89
Tom Jenkins	73	69	69	211	16,838.89
James Mason	74	69	68	211	16,838.89
Don Pooley	71	73	67	211	16,838.89
Fuzzy Zoeller	70	68	73	211	16,838.88

The Senior Open Championship

See European Senior Tour section.

U.S. Senior Open

Crocked Stick Golf Club, Carmel, Indiana
Par 36-36–72; 7,316 yards

July 30-August 2
purse, $2,600,000

	SCORES				TOTAL	MONEY
Fred Funk	68	67	68	65	268	$470,000
Joey Sindelar	66	68	70	70	274	280,000
Russ Cochran	72	72	64	68	276	175,152
Greg Norman	66	70	68	73	277	110,441
Loren Roberts	68	71	74	64	277	110,441
Mark O'Meara	70	69	68	72	279	83,165
Scott Simpson	68	72	68	71	279	83,165
Robin Freeman	70	68	71	71	280	69,762
Tom Lehman	68	70	72	70	280	69,762
Olin Browne	72	75	68	66	281	61,528
*Tim Jackson	66	67	73	76	282	
Brad Bryant	68	71	71	72	282	57,684
Dan Forsman	66	71	71	75	283	50,902
Jay Haas	70	70	71	72	283	50,902
Andy Bean	67	74	75	67	283	50,902
Bruce Vaughan	68	70	71	75	284	42,871
Jeff Sluman	69	74	71	70	284	42,871
Larry Mize	73	73	71	67	284	42,871
Eduardo Romero	73	70	70	72	285	37,290
John Cook	73	69	72	71	285	37,290
*Bryan Norton	73	73	69	70	285	
Steve Haskins	73	70	69	74	286	29,604
Mark Wiebe	70	71	72	73	286	29,604
Bob Tway	70	69	74	73	286	29,604
Bernhard Langer	73	71	73	69	286	29,604
Ian Woosnam	72	72	74	68	286	29,604
Joe Ozaki	71	71	76	68	286	29,604
David Edwards	72	74	71	70	287	21,355
Gene Jones	72	75	70	70	287	21,355
Jerry Courville	71	73	74	69	287	21,355
Gil Morgan	75	69	74	69	287	21,355
Jim Thorpe	71	69	74	74	288	17,480
Hale Irwin	78	67	70	73	288	17,480
Tom Jenkins	73	73	70	72	288	17,480
Ronnie Black	73	73	70	72	288	17,480

	SCORES				TOTAL	MONEY
Tim Simpson	70	72	72	75	289	14,677
R.W. Eaks	72	69	74	74	289	14,677
Mike Goodes	70	70	75	74	289	14,677
Mike Reid	73	71	73	72	289	14,677
Craig Stadler	75	72	71	71	289	14,677
Mark McNulty	73	73	72	71	289	14,677
Fulton Allem	67	76	76	70	289	14,677
Keith Fergus	73	72	69	76	290	11,893
David Eger	71	70	74	75	290	11,893
Bob Gilder	71	71	75	73	290	11,893
Tom Watson	71	72	75	72	290	11,893
Don Pooley	71	71	75	74	291	10,379
Bobby Wadkins	71	75	72	73	291	10,379
John Ross	74	70	73	75	292	9,115
Bruce Fleisher	74	73	71	74	292	9,115
Hal Sutton	73	74	72	73	292	9,115
Chip Beck	74	71	75	73	293	7,894
Denis Watson	72	73	77	71	293	7,894
Tsukasa Watanabe	71	74	76	72	293	7,894
Bruce Lietzke	75	72	76	71	294	7,494
John Harris	68	75	75	77	295	7,221
Dana Quigley	71	75	74	75	295	7,221
Jim Woodward	75	72	74	75	296	6,890
Steve Thomas	73	73	78	72	296	6,890
*Bert Atkinson	72	75	78	72	297	
Graham Banister	72	75	73	81	301	6,680
Kevin Marion	75	72	85	78	310	6,545

JELD-WEN Tradition

Crosswater Club at Sunriver Resort, Sunriver, Oregon   August 20-23
Par 36-36–72; 7,683 yards   purse, $2,600,000

	SCORES				TOTAL	MONEY
Mike Reid	70	67	66	69	272	$392,000
John Cook	69	67	68	68	272	231,000
(Reid defeated Cook on first playoff hole.)						
Brad Bryant	62	72	67	73	274	190,000
Larry Mize	69	67	70	69	275	158,000
Fred Funk	68	67	73	69	277	108,600
Loren Roberts	65	71	71	70	277	108,600
Tom Watson	67	74	69	67	277	108,600
Morris Hatalsky	71	71	70	67	279	75,566.67
Don Pooley	72	71	68	68	279	75,566.67
Tom Lehman	67	71	70	71	279	75,566.66
Gene Jones	74	65	71	70	280	52,050
Tom Kite	70	70	71	69	280	52,050
Gil Morgan	70	71	72	67	280	52,050
Mark O'Meara	69	71	68	72	280	52,050
Eduardo Romero	69	68	70	73	280	52,050
Jeff Sluman	71	72	69	68	280	52,050
Keith Fergus	70	69	72	70	281	37,895
Mike Goodes	70	73	68	70	281	37,895
Jay Haas	73	72	68	68	281	37,895
Bernhard Langer	71	70	70	70	281	37,895
David Eger	71	72	71	68	282	29,575
Bruce Fleisher	69	69	71	73	282	29,575
Craig Stadler	71	67	72	72	282	29,575
Bob Tway	72	70	71	69	282	29,575
Allen Doyle	70	72	68	73	283	25,350

	SCORES				TOTAL	MONEY
Mark McNulty	69	71	73	70	283	25,350
Andy Bean	69	73	71	71	284	22,100
R.W. Eaks	68	71	73	72	284	22,100
Lonnie Nielsen	70	67	74	73	284	22,100
Hal Sutton	69	71	70	74	284	22,100
Ben Crenshaw	72	68	71	74	285	17,160
Mike McCullough	69	73	70	73	285	17,160
Joe Ozaki	76	70	71	68	285	17,160
Tom Purtzer	72	72	72	69	285	17,160
Scott Simpson	76	70	66	73	285	17,160
Jim Thorpe	68	72	72	73	285	17,160
Bruce Vaughan	71	70	73	71	285	17,160
Hale Irwin	68	73	72	73	286	14,040
Tim Simpson	73	71	69	73	286	14,040
Dan Forsman	73	71	71	72	287	13,260
Russ Cochran	72	73	70	73	288	12,220
Mark James	70	75	74	69	288	12,220
Mark Wiebe	72	72	73	71	288	12,220
Olin Browne	76	70	73	70	289	10,660
James Mason	73	71	72	73	289	10,660
Larry Nelson	69	73	75	72	289	10,660
Ronnie Black	77	70	71	72	290	9,100
Tom Jenkins	75	73	71	71	290	9,100
Joey Sindelar	74	76	73	67	290	9,100
Bob Gilder	73	74	74	71	292	7,072
Sandy Lyle	75	77	71	69	292	7,072
Jerry Pate	73	76	71	72	292	7,072
Bobby Wadkins	77	72	71	72	292	7,072
Denis Watson	73	74	72	73	292	7,072
Bruce Lietzke	75	70	74	75	294	5,980
Peter Jacobsen	77	73	72	74	296	5,720
Fulton Allem	73	73	76	75	297	5,200
Isao Aoki	77	74	73	73	297	5,200
Graham Marsh	74	73	74	76	297	5,200
John Harris	73	78	77	71	299	4,550
Bruce Summerhays	80	72	72	75	299	4,550
Dave Eichelberger	76	76	77	71	300	4,160
Tom Wargo	75	72	81	73	301	3,770
Fuzzy Zoeller	80	75	73	73	301	3,770
Dana Quigley	77	73	74	78	302	3,380
Lanny Wadkins	74	81	76	73	304	3,120
Gary Player	78	79	76	77	310	2,860
Vicente Fernandez	75	77	75		WD	

Boeing Classic

TPC Snoqualmie Ridge, Snoqualmie, Washington
Par 36-36–72; 7,264 yards

August 28-30
purse, $1,800,000

	SCORES			TOTAL	MONEY
Loren Roberts	68	65	65	198	$270,000
Mark O'Meara	66	69	64	199	158,400
Dan Forsman	69	67	66	202	118,800
Bernhard Langer	69	66	67	202	118,800
Hal Sutton	71	70	63	204	86,400
Craig Stadler	70	66	69	205	72,000
Mark James	71	69	67	207	64,800
Mark McNulty	68	65	75	208	57,600
John Cook	69	69	71	209	48,600
Jeff Sluman	72	69	68	209	48,600

	SCORES			TOTAL	MONEY
David Eger	75	65	70	210	37,080
Bob Gilder	70	71	69	210	37,080
Nick Price	69	70	71	210	37,080
Robert Thompson	72	71	67	210	37,080
Bobby Wadkins	72	70	68	210	37,080
Tom Kite	69	73	69	211	27,945
Eduardo Romero	76	68	67	211	27,945
Tim Simpson	73	67	71	211	27,945
Mark Wiebe	72	71	68	211	27,945
Brad Bryant	71	70	71	212	22,320
R.W. Eaks	70	71	71	212	22,320
Larry Mize	73	72	67	212	22,320
Jay Don Blake	73	70	70	213	18,450
Mike Goodes	79	66	68	213	18,450
Don Pooley	69	72	72	213	18,450
Scott Simpson	71	72	70	213	18,450
Olin Browne	74	71	69	214	13,995
Gary Hallberg	71	72	71	214	13,995
Hale Irwin	70	70	74	214	13,995
Tom Jenkins	74	67	73	214	13,995
Sandy Lyle	71	72	71	214	13,995
James Mason	69	74	71	214	13,995
Denis Watson	76	71	67	214	13,995
Fuzzy Zoeller	71	74	69	214	13,995

Walmart First Tee Open

Pebble Beach Golf Links: Par 35-37–72; 6,822 yards
Del Monte Golf Course: Par 36-36–72; 6,357 yards
Monterey Peninsula, California

September 4-6
purse, $2,100,000

	SCORES			TOTAL	MONEY
Jeff Sluman	65	73	68	206	$315,000
Gene Jones	68	70	70	208	184,800
Tom Lehman	71	65	73	209	138,600
Mark O'Meara	67	67	75	209	138,600
Olin Browne	66	73	71	210	86,800
David Eger	68	73	69	210	86,800
Loren Roberts	66	66	78	210	86,800
Fred Funk	69	71	71	211	57,750
Tom Jenkins	72	66	73	211	57,750
Mark McNulty	68	70	73	211	57,750
Tom Watson	70	69	72	211	57,750
John Cook	68	71	73	212	44,100
Gary Hallberg	69	72	71	212	44,100
Tom Kite	67	72	74	213	38,850
Scott Simpson	68	74	71	213	38,850
Keith Fergus	70	75	69	214	33,600
Andy North	69	71	74	214	33,600
Joe Ozaki	73	70	71	214	33,600
Lonnie Nielsen	72	70	73	215	28,665
Nick Price	68	72	75	215	28,665
Fulton Allem	75	69	72	216	21,256.67
Andy Bean	72	70	74	216	21,256.67
Mike Goodes	71	71	74	216	21,256.67
John Jacobs	73	73	70	216	21,256.67
Jerry Pate	71	74	71	216	21,256.67
Tim Simpson	71	69	76	216	21,256.67
Allen Doyle	71	69	76	216	21,256.66
Bob Gilder	69	68	79	216	21,256.66

	SCORES			TOTAL	MONEY
Mark Wiebe	70	70	76	216	21,256.66
Michael Allen	69	73	75	217	14,201.25
Chip Beck	70	72	75	217	14,201.25
Russ Cochran	72	75	70	217	14,201.25
R.W. Eaks	71	71	75	217	14,201.25
Bruce Lietzke	73	68	76	217	14,201.25
Gil Morgan	72	71	74	217	14,201.25
Jim Thorpe	72	72	73	217	14,201.25
Bobby Wadkins	72	72	73	217	14,201.25

Greater Hickory Classic

Rock Barn Golf & Spa, Conover, North Carolina
Par 35-37–72; 7,046 yards

September 18-20
purse, $1,750,000

	SCORES			TOTAL	MONEY
Jay Haas	62	71	65	198	$262,500
Andy Bean	67	68	65	200	140,000
Russ Cochran	67	68	65	200	140,000
Nick Price	66	67	68	201	94,500
Hal Sutton	67	69	65	201	94,500
Mark McNulty	67	69	67	203	63,000
Jeff Sluman	67	69	67	203	63,000
Bob Tway	69	67	67	203	63,000
David Frost	68	68	69	205	45,500
Gene Jones	68	68	69	205	45,500
Larry Nelson	69	68	68	205	45,500
David Eger	70	68	68	206	30,865.63
Dan Forsman	67	70	69	206	30,865.63
Tom Jenkins	66	72	68	206	30,865.63
James Mason	71	69	66	206	30,865.63
Olin Browne	70	67	69	206	30,865.62
Fred Funk	69	67	70	206	30,865.62
Gil Morgan	65	70	71	206	30,865.62
Scott Simpson	70	67	69	206	30,865.62
Mark Wiebe	67	71	69	207	23,100
Brad Bryant	70	67	71	208	18,112.50
John Cook	71	69	68	208	18,112.50
Lonnie Nielsen	68	68	72	208	18,112.50
Jerry Pate	66	74	68	208	18,112.50
Tim Simpson	70	67	71	208	18,112.50
Craig Stadler	71	67	70	208	18,112.50
Bruce Vaughan	68	72	68	208	18,112.50
Bobby Wadkins	67	70	71	208	18,112.50
Joe Ozaki	70	66	73	209	14,175
Chris Starkjohann	68	70	71	209	14,175

SAS Championship

Prestonwood Country Club, Cary, North Carolina
Par 36-36–72; 7,137 yards

September 25-27
purse, $2,100,000

	SCORES			TOTAL	MONEY
Tom Pernice, Jr.	67	67	69	203	$315,000
David Frost	69	68	67	204	168,000
Nick Price	68	68	68	204	168,000
Dan Forsman	67	68	70	205	126,000

	SCORES			TOTAL	MONEY
Andy Bean	68	70	68	206	81,900
Olin Browne	72	66	68	206	81,900
Russ Cochran	66	69	71	206	81,900
Denis Watson	66	69	71	206	81,900
Keith Fergus	71	71	65	207	50,400
Larry Mize	67	70	70	207	50,400
Loren Roberts	70	71	66	207	50,400
D.A. Weibring	68	70	69	207	50,400
Mark Wiebe	70	68	69	207	50,400
Tom Jenkins	68	74	66	208	36,750
Tom Purtzer	69	70	69	208	36,750
Jim Thorpe	67	71	70	208	36,750
Bob Tway	70	68	70	208	36,750
Ronnie Black	70	69	70	209	27,846
Fred Funk	70	71	68	209	27,846
Tom Lehman	72	69	68	209	27,846
Don Pooley	72	68	69	209	27,846
Joey Sindelar	67	69	73	209	27,846
Brad Bryant	71	69	70	210	21,525
Tom Kite	71	68	71	210	21,525
Wayne Levi	70	73	67	210	21,525
Bobby Wadkins	68	70	72	210	21,525
Chip Beck	68	71	72	211	18,690
Scott Simpson	68	71	72	211	18,690
Phil Blackmar	71	69	72	212	15,210
R.W. Eaks	67	69	76	212	15,210
Bob Gilder	72	70	70	212	15,210
Lonnie Nielsen	73	70	69	212	15,210
Mark O'Meara	71	67	74	212	15,210
Jerry Pate	69	73	70	212	15,210
Tim Simpson	69	71	72	212	15,210

Constellation Energy Senior Players Championship

Baltimore Country Club, East Course, Timonium, Maryland   October 1-4
Par 35-35–70; 7,037 yards   purse, $2,700,000

	SCORES				TOTAL	MONEY
Jay Haas	66	70	67	64	267	$405,000
Tom Watson	66	68	64	70	268	237,600
Loren Roberts	70	67	65	71	273	178,200
Mark Wiebe	69	67	66	71	273	178,200
John Cook	69	68	65	72	274	118,800
Bernhard Langer	72	65	69	68	274	118,800
Phil Blackmar	71	70	64	70	275	91,800
Fred Funk	71	68	69	67	275	91,800
Mark O'Meara	70	69	68	69	276	67,500
Nick Price	69	69	69	69	276	67,500
Mike Reid	68	72	68	68	276	67,500
Tim Simpson	69	69	69	69	276	67,500
Keith Fergus	70	69	69	69	277	52,650
Morris Hatalsky	70	69	66	72	277	52,650
Andy Bean	69	73	65	71	278	40,770
Jay Don Blake	70	70	70	68	278	40,770
Dan Forsman	68	72	68	70	278	40,770
Gary Hallberg	74	68	69	67	278	40,770
Hale Irwin	72	67	68	71	278	40,770
Gene Jones	71	68	67	72	278	40,770
Joey Sindelar	69	71	70	68	278	40,770
Mark James	69	71	68	71	279	30,510

	SCORES				TOTAL	MONEY
Lonnie Nielsen	65	73	70	71	279	30,510
David Eger	70	74	69	67	280	24,685.72
David Frost	71	76	66	67	280	24,685.72
Larry Nelson	72	69	68	71	280	24,685.72
Ronnie Black	72	68	67	73	280	24,685.71
Mike Goodes	70	69	68	73	280	24,685.71
Jeff Sluman	74	68	66	72	280	24,685.71
Fuzzy Zoeller	69	72	67	72	280	24,685.71
Sandy Lyle	67	73	66	75	281	19,440
Eduardo Romero	68	74	69	70	281	19,440
Bob Tway	68	68	73	72	281	19,440
Olin Browne	70	72	71	69	282	17,010
Don Pooley	72	71	71	68	282	17,010
Bruce Vaughan	72	68	71	71	282	17,010
Chip Beck	72	71	68	72	283	14,580
Robin Freeman	71	69	73	70	283	14,580
Scott Simpson	69	71	71	72	283	14,580
Robert Thompson	69	75	68	71	283	14,580
Fulton Allem	69	70	69	76	284	12,960
Russ Cochran	75	71	69	69	284	12,960
Allen Doyle	72	70	71	72	285	11,340
R.W. Eaks	73	75	69	68	285	11,340
Joe Ozaki	71	68	74	72	285	11,340
Tom Purtzer	71	73	69	72	285	11,340
Kirk Hanefeld	74	69	70	73	286	8,640
Tom Kite	74	69	72	71	286	8,640
James Mason	77	70	70	69	286	8,640
Larry Mize	70	73	70	73	286	8,640
Jerry Pate	77	67	72	70	286	8,640
Craig Stadler	71	65	70	80	286	8,640
Brad Bryant	73	73	71	70	287	6,210
Bruce Lietzke	74	68	69	76	287	6,210
Blaine McCallister	72	70	73	72	287	6,210
Gil Morgan	71	71	74	71	287	6,210
Jim Thorpe	72	72	70	73	287	6,210
Bruce Summerhays	76	68	69	75	288	5,265
Hal Sutton	74	72	68	74	288	5,265
Bob Gilder	71	69	70	79	289	4,725
John Morse	71	74	72	72	289	4,725
Walter Hall	73	71	74	72	290	4,050
Mark W. Johnson	73	76	68	73	290	4,050
Des Smyth	72	74	74	70	290	4,050
Ben Crenshaw	75	71	69	76	291	3,105
John Harris	71	74	71	75	291	3,105
Chris Starkjohann	74	71	70	76	291	3,105
Steve Thomas	75	74	69	73	291	3,105
Donnie Hammond	79	67	71	75	292	2,457
Tom McKnight	76	69	75	72	292	2,457
Tom Jenkins	72	75	72	75	294	2,214
Denis Watson	76	71	74	76	297	2,052
Bobby Wadkins	72	72	75	80	299	1,890
Mike Hulbert	79	73	71	80	303	1,782
Mike McCullough	73	78	74	79	304	1,674
Wayne Grady	81	70	74	81	306	1,566
Bruce Fleisher	69	69	71		WD	
D.A. Weibring	74				WD	

Administaff Small Business Classic

The Woodlands Country Club, The Woodlands, Texas
Par 36-36–72; 7,018 yards

October 16-18
purse, $1,700,000

	SCORES			TOTAL	MONEY
John Cook	65	72	68	205	$255,000
Jay Haas	70	66	71	207	136,000
Bob Tway	67	70	70	207	136,000
Bernhard Langer	68	71	69	208	83,866.67
Tom Lehman	69	71	68	208	83,866.67
Dan Forsman	64	71	73	208	83,866.66
Olin Browne	69	70	70	209	54,400
Russ Cochran	68	71	70	209	54,400
Tom Watson	69	68	72	209	54,400
David Frost	74	70	66	210	40,800
Gene Jones	69	67	74	210	40,800
Mark Wiebe	67	69	74	210	40,800
Fuzzy Zoeller	70	74	67	211	34,000
Keith Fergus	68	73	71	212	28,900
Bob Gilder	74	68	70	212	28,900
Mark James	71	70	71	212	28,900
Don Pooley	72	73	67	212	28,900
Nick Price	67	74	71	212	28,900
Andy Bean	71	72	70	213	21,802.50
Fred Funk	72	72	69	213	21,802.50
Bruce Lietzke	68	71	74	213	21,802.50
Craig Stadler	73	68	72	213	21,802.50
David Eger	69	71	74	214	17,850
Mark O'Meara	72	70	72	214	17,850
Jim Thorpe	69	72	73	214	17,850
Fulton Allem	74	68	73	215	15,130
Tom Kite	71	75	69	215	15,130
Loren Roberts	70	73	72	215	15,130
Joey Sindelar	69	74	72	215	15,130
John Morse	73	71	72	216	11,754.29
Mike Reid	69	75	72	216	11,754.29
Jeff Sluman	73	73	70	216	11,754.29
Hal Sutton	73	72	71	216	11,754.29
Jay Don Blake	67	72	77	216	11,754.28
Allen Doyle	71	72	73	216	11,754.28
Jack Ferenz	71	72	73	216	11,754.28

AT&T Championship

Oak Hills Country Club, San Antonio, Texas
Par 35-36–71; 6,670 yards

October 23-25
purse, $1,700,000

	SCORES			TOTAL	MONEY
Phil Blackmar	72	67	64	203	$255,000
Andy Bean	67	67	70	204	124,666.67
Tom Kite	67	69	68	204	124,666.67
Jay Haas	68	67	69	204	124,666.66
John Cook	68	71	66	205	81,600
Hale Irwin	71	67	68	206	68,000
Keith Fergus	69	71	67	207	54,400
Bernhard Langer	70	68	69	207	54,400
Scott Simpson	68	69	70	207	54,400
Russ Cochran	66	68	74	208	39,100
Mike Goodes	68	72	68	208	39,100

	SCORES			TOTAL	MONEY
Jeff Sluman	69	67	72	208	39,100
Jim Thorpe	70	69	69	208	39,100
Chip Beck	70	69	70	209	29,750
David Frost	73	69	67	209	29,750
Tom Jenkins	72	71	66	209	29,750
Craig Stadler	68	74	67	209	29,750
Dan Forsman	69	71	70	210	23,247.50
Morris Hatalsky	71	71	68	210	23,247.50
James Mason	69	71	70	210	23,247.50
Mark O'Meara	67	70	73	210	23,247.50
Peter Jacobsen	72	73	66	211	15,997
Gene Jones	71	71	69	211	15,997
Gil Morgan	71	71	69	211	15,997
John Morse	69	72	70	211	15,997
Loren Roberts	71	72	68	211	15,997
Jeff Roth	69	73	69	211	15,997
Tim Simpson	68	69	74	211	15,997
Joey Sindelar	73	70	68	211	15,997
Bruce Vaughan	72	69	70	211	15,997
Mark Wiebe	71	71	69	211	15,997

Charles Schwab Cup Championship

Sonoma Golf Club, Sonoma, California
Par 36-36–72; 7,103 yards

October 29-November 1
purse, $2,500,000

	SCORES				TOTAL	MONEY
John Cook	68	62	67	69	266	$442,000
Russ Cochran	69	66	68	68	271	255,000
Brad Bryant	68	67	69	69	273	195,500
Jeff Sluman	66	69	70	68	273	195,500
Phil Blackmar	66	67	72	69	274	141,000
Bernhard Langer	72	65	70	68	275	106,000
Loren Roberts	70	73	66	66	275	106,000
Tom Watson	69	64	71	71	275	106,000
Eduardo Romero	67	71	70	68	276	83,000
Jay Haas	71	68	70	68	277	63,583.34
Tom Jenkins	71	66	71	69	277	63,583.34
Mark McNulty	69	71	68	69	277	63,583.33
Larry Mize	71	66	68	72	277	63,583.33
Gil Morgan	70	68	69	70	277	63,583.33
Lonnie Nielsen	70	67	69	71	277	63,583.33
Mark O'Meara	70	70	71	67	278	48,500
Mark Wiebe	69	69	71	69	278	48,500
Andy Bean	72	71	73	63	279	42,500
Dan Forsman	72	69	67	71	279	42,500
Tom Kite	73	69	72	66	280	39,000
Mike Goodes	72	69	69	71	281	37,000
Gene Jones	70	70	71	71	282	35,000
Mike Reid	72	69	70	72	283	33,000
Nick Price	72	72	68	72	284	31,000
Fred Funk	71	69	74	71	285	28,000
Don Pooley	75	69	72	69	285	28,000
Keith Fergus	75	68	72	72	287	26,000
David Eger	72	70	73	76	291	25,000
Joey Sindelar	70	68			WD	

European Senior Tour

Aberdeen Brunei Senior Masters

Empire Hotel & Country Club, Brunei
Par 35-36–71; 6,840 yards

February 27-March 1
purse, €314,315

	SCORES			TOTAL	MONEY
Mike Cunning	69	67	70	206	€47,194.46
Jimmy Heggarty	73	68	67	208	31,462.98
Giuseppe Cali	70	69	70	209	17,849.99
Bob Cameron	67	69	73	209	17,849.99
Katsuyoshi Tomori	70	70	69	209	17,849.99
Chung Chun-hsing	69	72	69	210	10,697.41
Sandy Lyle	72	69	69	210	10,697.41
Glenn Ralph	70	68	72	210	10,697.41
Sam Torrance	71	69	70	210	10,697.41
Doug Johnson	73	64	74	211	7,865.74
David Merriman	70	65	76	211	7,865.74
John Chillas	73	70	69	212	6,040.89
Seiji Ebihara	70	68	74	212	6,040.89
Stewart Ginn	70	72	70	212	6,040.89
Noel Ratcliffe	73	69	70	212	6,040.89
Costantino Rocca	72	66	74	212	6,040.89
Choi Sang-ho	69	74	70	213	5,034.08
Graham Banister	73	69	72	214	3,751.09
Bob Boyd	70	72	72	214	3,751.09
Ross Drummond	68	72	74	214	3,751.09
David Good	71	72	71	214	3,751.09
Jeff Hall	69	72	73	214	3,751.09
Juan Quiros	72	70	72	214	3,751.09
Emilio Rodriguez	74	70	70	214	3,751.09
Boonchu Ruangkit	70	70	74	214	3,751.09
Kevin Spurgeon	69	73	72	214	3,751.09

DGM Barbados Open

Royal Westmoreland Resort, St. James, Barbados
Par 36-36–72; 6,972 yards

March 18-20
purse, €160,105

	SCORES			TOTAL	MONEY
Sam Torrance	65	63	74	202	€25,234.63
Angel Franco	70	67	69	206	16,823.08
Mike Harwood	68	72	70	210	11,776.16
Horacio Carbonetti	72	70	69	211	8,428.36
Nick Job	70	71	70	211	8,428.36
Alan Tapie	73	71	68	212	6,729.23
Ross Drummond	69	69	75	213	5,131.04
Bill Longmuir	71	71	71	213	5,131.04
Martin Poxon	70	69	74	213	5,131.04
Des Smyth	74	69	70	213	5,131.04
Jerry Bruner	72	70	72	214	3,574.91
Delroy Cambridge	71	72	71	214	3,574.91
Glenn Ralph	72	67	75	214	3,574.91

	SCORES			TOTAL	MONEY
David J. Russell	71	73	70	214	3,574.91
Gordon J. Brand	68	73	74	215	2,944.04
Luis Carbonetti	72	72	71	215	2,944.04
Giuseppe Cali	71	71	74	216	2,691.70
Bobby Lincoln	71	76	70	217	2,523.46
Bob Cameron	70	75	73	218	2,226.26
Jose Maria Canizares	74	73	71	218	2,226.26
Andrew Murray	71	73	74	218	2,226.26

Son Gual Mallorca Senior Open

Son Gual Golf, Palma, Mallorca, Spain　　　　　　　　　　May 8-10
Par 36-36–72; 6,941 yards　　　　　　　　　　　　　purse, €299,700

	SCORES			TOTAL	MONEY
Mark James	70	70	66	206	€45,000
Eamonn Darcy	71	70	65	206	30,000
(James defeated Darcy on third playoff hole.)					
Roger Chapman	68	70	71	209	21,000
Mike Cunning	73	72	65	210	16,500
Angel Franco	71	72	68	211	12,120
Bobby Lincoln	70	70	71	211	12,120
Kevin Spurgeon	70	71	70	211	12,120
Gordon Brand, Jr.	74	70	68	212	8,250
Horacio Carbonetti	71	70	71	212	8,250
Carl Mason	71	70	71	212	8,250
Ian Woosnam	73	68	71	212	8,250
Gordon J. Brand	72	74	67	213	5,925
Delroy Cambridge	67	75	71	213	5,925
John Chillas	70	74	69	213	5,925
Peter Mitchell	72	71	70	213	5,925
Jerry Bruner	69	72	73	214	4,657.50
Ross Drummond	71	72	71	214	4,657.50
Tony Johnstone	73	69	72	214	4,657.50
Sam Torrance	74	71	69	214	4,657.50
Torsten Giedeon	71	70	74	215	3,522
Mike Harwood	72	69	74	215	3,522
Jose Rivero	79	68	68	215	3,522
Jean Pierre Sallat	74	68	73	215	3,522
Alan Tapie	73	71	71	215	3,522

Irish Seniors Open

Ballybunion Golf Club, Co. Kerry, Ireland　　　　　　　　June 5-7
Par 36-35–71; 6,506 yards　　　　　　　　　　　　　purse, €349,284

	SCORES			TOTAL	MONEY
Ian Woosnam	74	70	67	211	€52,500
Bob Boyd	72	68	71	211	35,000
(Woosnam defeated Boyd on third playoff hole.)					
Roger Chapman	67	71	74	212	21,875
Tony Johnstone	71	74	67	212	21,875
Emilio Rodriguez	72	74	67	213	15,820
Gordon J. Brand	71	72	71	214	12,600
Giuseppe Cali	72	72	70	214	12,600
Eamonn Darcy	73	72	69	214	12,600
Ross Drummond	72	76	67	215	9,800

	SCORES			TOTAL	MONEY
Glenn Ralph	69	74	73	216	8,750
Jose Rivero	72	74	70	216	8,750
Peter Mitchell	74	73	70	217	7,700
John Bland	72	75	71	218	6,650
Gordon Brand, Jr.	73	78	67	218	6,650
Mike Harwood	72	78	68	218	6,650
Horacio Carbonetti	69	77	73	219	5,433.75
John Chillas	76	76	67	219	5,433.75
Seiji Ebihara	71	80	68	219	5,433.75
Des Smyth	69	77	73	219	5,433.75
Delroy Cambridge	70	79	71	220	4,109
Angel Franco	78	68	74	220	4,109
Stewart Ginn	76	74	70	220	4,109
David J. Russell	75	75	70	220	4,109
Katsuyoshi Tomori	70	76	74	220	4,109

Jersey Seniors Classic

La Moye Golf Club, Jersey, Channel Isles
Par 36-36–72; 6,581 yards

June 12-14
purse, €160,091

	SCORES			TOTAL	MONEY
Delroy Cambridge	69	70	68	207	€24,394.27
Mike Clayton	64	73	70	207	16,262.84
(Cambridge defeated Clayton on third playoff hole.)					
Katsuyoshi Tomori	69	69	70	208	11,383.98
Angel Franco	72	65	72	209	8,147.68
Kevin Spurgeon	68	69	72	209	8,147.68
Roger Chapman	68	75	67	210	6,179.88
Ross Drummond	73	71	66	210	6,179.88
Carl Mason	73	68	70	211	4,662.01
Costantino Rocca	73	67	71	211	4,662.01
Des Smyth	72	67	72	211	4,662.01
Gordon J. Brand	74	68	70	212	3,350.14
Bob Cameron	71	73	68	212	3,350.14
Seiji Ebihara	73	68	71	212	3,350.14
Guillermo Encina	68	73	71	212	3,350.14
Tony Johnstone	71	67	74	212	3,350.14
Mike Harwood	71	69	73	213	2,764.69
Horacio Carbonetti	72	71	71	214	2,520.74
Ian Woosnam	70	71	73	214	2,520.74
John Chillas	69	73	73	215	2,085.71
Mike Cunning	72	66	77	215	2,085.71
Domingo Hospital	70	68	77	215	2,085.71
Simon Owen	72	70	73	215	2,085.71

Ryder Cup Wales Seniors Open

Royal Porthcawl Golf Club, Mid Glamorgan, Wales
Par 36-36–72; 6,796 yards

June 19-21
purse, €588,230

	SCORES			TOTAL	MONEY
Bertus Smit	74	68	69	211	€88,234.50
David Merriman	73	70	72	215	58,823
Ross Drummond	72	72	72	216	30,911.49
Bobby Lincoln	75	69	72	216	30,911.49
Des Smyth	74	69	73	216	30,911.49

	SCORES			TOTAL	MONEY
Ian Woosnam	75	67	74	216	30,911.49
John Bland	78	72	68	218	18,823.36
Jerry Bruner	72	70	76	218	18,823.36
Nick Job	76	74	68	218	18,823.36
Seiji Ebihara	76	69	74	219	13,529.29
Domingo Hospital	76	69	74	219	13,529.29
Glenn Ralph	78	72	69	219	13,529.29
Katsuyoshi Tomori	77	74	68	219	13,529.29
John Chillas	79	70	71	220	9,999.91
Tony Johnstone	72	75	73	220	9,999.91
Carl Mason	75	71	74	220	9,999.91
Simon Owen	77	68	75	220	9,999.91
Kevin Spurgeon	72	73	75	220	9,999.91
Gordon J. Brand	75	71	75	221	7,329.35
Bob Cameron	69	80	72	221	7,329.35
Roger Chapman	82	71	68	221	7,329.35
Jimmy Heggarty	80	69	72	221	7,329.35
Costantino Rocca	71	81	69	221	7,329.35

De Vere Collection PGA Seniors Championship

De Vere Slaley Hall, Hunting Course, Northumberland, England   June 25-28
Par 36-36–72; 7,036 yards   purse, €294,470

	SCORES				TOTAL	MONEY
Carl Mason	73	70	67	69	279	€47,115.20
Angel Franco	69	72	73	68	282	26,084.15
Christopher Williams	72	70	71	69	282	26,084.15
Gordon Brand, Jr.	69	73	71	70	283	15,665.80
Nick Job	76	71	68	68	283	15,665.80
Roger Chapman	74	71	72	68	285	10,294.67
John Chillas	74	69	71	71	285	10,294.67
Jimmy Heggarty	74	69	72	71	286	8,033.14
Jerry Bruner	75	73	70	69	287	7,020.17
Bob Cameron	71	73	72	72	288	5,229.79
Mike Cunning	73	72	71	72	288	5,229.79
Ross Drummond	76	71	71	70	288	5,229.79
Seiji Ebihara	75	71	74	68	288	5,229.79
George Ryall	74	74	71	69	288	5,229.79
Kevin Spurgeon	70	73	74	71	288	5,229.79
Ian Woosnam	73	75	71	69	288	5,229.79
Horacio Carbonetti	75	76	69	69	289	3,654.37
Bobby Lincoln	71	73	74	71	289	3,654.37
Juan Quiros	71	78	70	70	289	3,654.37
Mike Williams	74	72	73	70	289	3,654.37

The Senior Open Championship

Sunningdale Golf Club, Old Course, Berkshire, England   July 23-26
Par 35-35–70; 6,616 yards   purse, €1,414,914

	SCORES				TOTAL	MONEY
Loren Roberts	66	68	67	67	268	€222,777.53
Fred Funk	64	65	72	67	268	116,118.20
Mark McNulty	69	67	68	64	268	116,118.20
(Roberts defeated Funk on first and McNulty on third playoff hole.)						
Bernhard Langer	72	67	65	65	269	66,847.38

	SCORES				TOTAL	MONEY
Sam Torrance	67	65	71	67	270	56,640.27
Larry Mize	69	70	64	68	271	43,440.21
Greg Norman	67	69	64	71	271	43,440.21
Tom Kite	67	68	69	69	273	27,509.78
Don Pooley	70	66	69	68	273	27,509.78
Bruce Vaughan	70	69	65	69	273	27,509.78
Denis Watson	68	68	66	71	273	27,509.78
Tom Watson	67	69	70	67	273	27,509.78
Michael Allen	70	65	71	68	274	20,089.51
Tony Johnstone	68	71	66	69	274	20,089.51
Sandy Lyle	68	70	69	67	274	20,089.51
Scott Simpson	68	69	69	68	274	20,089.51
Denis O'Sullivan	68	71	70	67	276	17,569.50
Joey Sindelar	69	72	67	68	276	17,569.50
Russ Cochran	69	70	71	67	277	15,763.84
Mike Goodes	71	71	67	68	277	15,763.84
Jay Haas	66	71	68	72	277	15,763.84
Gene Jones	74	67	67	69	277	15,763.84
Ian Woosnam	68	69	70	70	277	15,763.84
Jeff Sluman	69	70	69	70	278	14,400.07
David Eger	69	71	67	72	279	13,496.53
Kirk Hanefeld	72	71	68	68	279	13,496.53
Mark O'Meara	69	70	68	72	279	13,496.53
Gordon J. Brand	68	68	73	71	280	11,978.88
Curt Byrum	68	75	69	68	280	11,978.88
Gary Koch	70	70	69	71	280	11,978.88
Chris Williams	66	76	66	72	280	11,978.88
Fulton Allem	70	72	73	66	281	10,204.75
Andy Bean	70	72	67	72	281	10,204.75
Gordon Brand, Jr.	68	71	71	71	281	10,204.75
Mike Donald	71	70	70	70	281	10,204.75
Wayne Grady	70	72	71	68	281	10,204.75
Noel Ratcliffe	71	72	71	67	281	10,204.75
Olin Browne	68	73	72	69	282	8,696.51
Sir Nick Faldo	70	70	69	73	282	8,696.51
Juan Quiros	72	71	68	71	282	8,696.51
Eduardo Romero	70	71	71	70	282	8,696.51
Bertus Smit	69	71	70	72	282	8,696.51
Ben Crenshaw	73	70	65	75	283	7,552.98
Bob Gilder	72	70	70	71	283	7,552.98
Mark James	70	69	68	76	283	7,552.98
Kevin Spurgeon	72	70	68	73	283	7,552.98
Joe Ozaki	71	70	72	71	284	6,663.56
Mike Reid	72	71	70	71	284	6,663.56
Mark Wiebe	71	68	70	75	284	6,663.56
Ronnie Black	71	71	71	72	285	5,280.03
Philip Blackmar	68	72	74	71	285	5,280.03
Delroy Cambridge	71	73	73	68	285	5,280.03
Gary Hallberg	74	68	71	72	285	5,280.03
Morris Hatalsky	72	67	73	73	285	5,280.03
Doug Johnson	70	69	70	76	285	5,280.03
Costantino Rocca	74	70	72	69	285	5,280.03
Robert Thompson	70	74	68	73	285	5,280.03
Jerry Bruner	67	74	68	77	286	3,640.61
Luis Carbonetti	73	70	68	75	286	3,640.61
Tom Lehman	70	73	73	70	286	3,640.61
John Morse	72	71	72	71	286	3,640.61
Andrew Murray	69	74	71	72	286	3,640.61
Tim Simpson	73	71	71	71	286	3,640.61
*Paul Simson	71	69	72	74	286	
Des Smyth	66	74	74	72	286	3,640.61
Bobby Wadkins	73	70	70	73	286	3,640.61
Manuel Pinero	70	74	70	73	287	2,978.84

	SCORES				TOTAL	MONEY
Stewart Ginn	71	72	72	73	288	2,724.72
Lonnie Nielsen	72	71	71	74	288	2,724.72
Tom Purtzer	73	71	73	71	288	2,724.72
Giuseppe Cali	71	73	72	73	289	2,280.01
Bob Cameron	70	72	74	73	289	2,280.01
Graham Marsh	70	74	70	75	289	2,280.01
Glenn Ralph	70	73	73	73	289	2,280.01
Philippe Dugeny	71	69	76	74	290	1,898.83
Angel Fernandez	70	71	76	73	290	1,898.83
Craig Stadler	74	69	73	76	292	1,708.24
Bobby Lincoln	72	72	82		DQ	1,391.60

Bad Ragaz PGA Seniors Open

Golf Club Bad Ragaz, Bad Ragaz, Switzerland
Par 35-35–70; 6,183 yards

August 7-9
purse, €220,407

	SCORES			TOTAL	MONEY
John Bland	65	69	65	199	€33,000
Bob Boyd	65	65	69	199	22,000
(Bland defeated Boyd on second playoff hole.)					
Sam Torrance	72	63	65	200	15,400
Doug Johnson	66	67	69	202	12,100
Bill Longmuir	70	65	68	203	8,426
Andrew Murray	70	70	63	203	8,426
Juan Quiros	70	66	67	203	8,426
Chris Williams	72	67	64	203	8,426
Giuseppe Cali	71	68	65	204	4,644.44
Roger Chapman	68	70	66	204	4,644.44
Mike Clayton	66	68	70	204	4,644.44
Eamonn Darcy	67	70	67	204	4,644.44
Guillermo Encina	69	73	62	204	4,644.44
Bobby Lincoln	68	68	68	204	4,644.44
Denis O'Sullivan	69	66	69	204	4,644.44
Emilio Rodriguez	72	63	69	204	4,644.44
Katsuyoshi Tomori	67	66	71	204	4,644.44
Gordon Brand, Jr.	65	68	72	205	2,834.33
Torsten Giedeon	68	70	67	205	2,834.33
Jeff Hall	68	67	70	205	2,834.33
Mike Harwood	64	69	72	205	2,834.33
Noel Ratcliffe	69	66	70	205	2,834.33
Bertus Smit	67	67	71	205	2,834.33

Cleveland Golf/Srixon Scottish Senior Open

Fairmont St. Andrews, Fife, Scotland
Par 36-36–72; 6,848 yards

August 21-23
purse, €262,094

	SCORES			TOTAL	MONEY
Glenn Ralph	71	67	70	208	€39,353.51
Bob Cameron	69	68	72	209	22,300.32
Luis Carbonetti	69	69	71	209	22,300.32
Peter Senior	70	70	71	211	14,429.62
Roger Chapman	71	69	72	212	11,176.40
Carl Mason	71	68	73	212	11,176.40
Gordon Brand, Jr.	71	69	73	213	9,444.84
Tony Johnstone	71	70	73	214	7,870.70

	SCORES			TOTAL	MONEY
Bill Longmuir	72	73	69	214	7,870.70
Stephen Bennett	74	72	70	216	6,034.21
Angel Franco	73	75	68	216	6,034.21
Torsten Giedeon	73	71	72	216	6,034.21
Andrew Murray	72	72	72	216	6,034.21
Giuseppe Cali	74	71	72	217	4,591.24
Ross Drummond	69	70	78	217	4,591.24
Peter Mitchell	73	71	73	217	4,591.24
Ian Woosnam	71	72	74	217	4,591.24
Bob Boyd	71	78	69	218	3,478.85
Eamonn Darcy	74	75	69	218	3,478.85
Jose Rivero	73	73	72	218	3,478.85
Des Smyth	72	76	70	218	3,478.85
Mike Williams	76	76	66	218	3,478.85

Travis Perkins plc Senior Masters

Woburn Golf Club, Duke's Course, Milton Keynes, England   September 4-6
Par 35-37–72; 6,896 yards   purse, €285,510

	SCORES			TOTAL	MONEY
Tony Johnstone	69	71	66	206	€42,781.50
Peter Senior	69	67	71	207	28,521
Jose Rivero	72	70	69	211	19,964.70
Chris Williams	75	67	71	213	15,686.55
Sam Torrance	71	74	69	214	12,891.49
Mike Clayton	72	71	72	215	9,697.14
Domingo Hospital	70	73	72	215	9,697.14
Bill Longmuir	70	76	69	215	9,697.14
David Merriman	72	69	74	215	9,697.14
Jerry Bruner	74	72	70	216	6,845.04
Nick Job	78	70	68	216	6,845.04
Manuel Pinero	73	72	71	216	6,845.04
Costantino Rocca	69	75	73	217	5,704.20
Gordon J. Brand	72	71	75	218	5,276.39
Bob Cameron	75	73	70	218	5,276.39
Luis Carbonetti	74	71	74	219	4,295.26
Guillermo Encina	70	73	76	219	4,295.26
Marc Farry	74	75	70	219	4,295.26
Angel Franco	71	71	77	219	4,295.26
Bertus Smit	73	74	72	219	4,295.26

Casa Serena Open

Casa Serena Golf, Prague, Czech Republic   September 18-20
Par 35-36–71; 6,776 yards   purse, €600,000

	SCORES			TOTAL	MONEY
Peter Mitchell	67	67	66	200	€90,000
Glenn Ralph	70	68	65	203	51,000
Peter Senior	64	69	70	203	51,000
Ian Woosnam	67	69	68	204	33,000
Bob Cameron	69	67	69	205	22,980
Nick Job	68	67	70	205	22,980
Bernhard Langer	67	68	70	205	22,980
Carl Mason	66	71	68	205	22,980
Domingo Hospital	66	71	70	207	16,800

	SCORES			TOTAL	MONEY
Torsten Giedeon	70	69	69	208	13,320
Mike Harwood	68	71	69	208	13,320
Noel Ratcliffe	66	68	74	208	13,320
David J. Russell	68	73	67	208	13,320
Des Smyth	70	67	71	208	13,320
Gordon J. Brand	67	71	71	209	10,500
Gordon Brand, Jr.	68	70	71	209	10,500
Jerry Bruner	67	72	71	210	9,020
Jose Rivero	72	67	71	210	9,020
Chris Williams	68	71	71	210	9,020
Bob Boyd	72	68	71	211	7,230
Mike Cunning	72	68	71	211	7,230
Marc Farry	67	72	72	211	7,230
Bill Longmuir	71	70	70	211	7,230

Benahavis Senior Masters

La Quinta Golf & Country Club, Marbella, Spain
Par 35-36–71; 6,424 yards

October 16-18
purse, €180,000

	SCORES			TOTAL	MONEY
Carl Mason	66	72	68	206	€27,000
Gordon Brand, Jr.	71	67	68	206	18,000
(Mason defeated Brand on second playoff hole.)					
Ross Drummond	67	69	71	207	12,600
Andrew Murray	68	71	69	208	9,018
Des Smyth	70	72	66	208	9,018
Bob Cameron	68	69	72	209	6,120
Eamonn Darcy	73	67	69	209	6,120
Angel Fernandez	72	68	69	209	6,120
Glenn Ralph	72	69	68	209	6,120
Tony Johnstone	68	69	73	210	4,680
Manuel Moreno	69	71	71	211	3,825
Manuel Pinero	72	71	68	211	3,825
David J. Russell	73	72	66	211	3,825
Bertus Smit	70	70	71	211	3,825
Roger Chapman	70	70	72	212	2,883.60
John Hoskison	71	71	70	212	2,883.60
Juan Quiros	69	72	71	212	2,883.60
Jose Rivero	68	70	74	212	2,883.60
George Ryall	73	67	72	212	2,883.60
Matt Briggs	70	73	71	214	2,304
Domingo Hospital	73	72	69	214	2,304

OKI Castellon Senior Tour Championship

Club de Campo del Mediterraneo, Castellon, Spain
Par 36-36–72; 6,818 yards

November 6-8
purse, €400,000

	SCORES			TOTAL	MONEY
Mike Harwood	65	72	66	203	€64,433
Angel Franco	64	70	72	206	42,955.33
Sam Torrance	67	71	69	207	30,068.73
Carl Mason	68	71	69	208	23,625.43
Jerry Bruner	67	72	70	209	19,415.81
Bob Cameron	71	70	69	210	15,463.92
Domingo Hospital	71	69	70	210	15,463.92

	SCORES			TOTAL	MONEY
Jose Rivero	69	71	70	210	15,463.92
Nick Job	70	71	70	211	11,168.38
Denis O'Sullivan	68	68	75	211	11,168.38
Des Smyth	66	77	68	211	11,168.38
Bill Longmuir	71	68	73	212	8,483.68
Juan Quiros	71	68	73	212	8,483.68
Glenn Ralph	70	70	72	212	8,483.68
Chris Williams	72	70	70	212	8,483.68
Mike Clayton	70	70	73	213	7,302.41
John Chillas	69	72	73	214	6,872.85
Mike Cunning	72	65	78	215	5,695.88
Tony Johnstone	71	74	70	215	5,695.88
Peter Mitchell	69	75	71	215	5,695.88
Manuel Pinero	70	72	73	215	5,695.88
Ian Woosnam	72	72	71	215	5,695.88

Mauritius Commercial Bank Open

Constance Belle Mare Plage, Mauritius
Par 36-36–72; 6,584 yards

December 11-13
purse, €230,000

	SCORES			TOTAL	MONEY
Kevin Spurgeon	71	67	72	210	€34,500
Gordon J. Brand	72	70	69	211	23,000
Angel Franco	70	72	70	212	14,375
Sam Torrance	74	71	67	212	14,375
John Bland	72	70	71	213	8,809
Bob Boyd	73	69	71	213	8,809
Mike Cunning	74	72	67	213	8,809
David Frost	70	70	73	213	8,809
Roger Chapman	70	73	71	214	6,210
Ricky Willison	72	72	70	214	6,210
Jerry Bruner	75	69	71	215	5,060
Ross Drummond	71	72	72	215	5,060
Doug Johnson	68	77	70	215	5,060
Nick Job	71	69	76	216	4,255
David Merriman	74	69	73	216	4,255
Peter Dahlberg	71	70	76	217	3,570.75
Peter Mitchell	68	73	76	217	3,570.75
Glenn Ralph	67	74	76	217	3,570.75
George Ryall	75	74	68	217	3,570.75
Bob Cameron	74	71	73	218	2,852
Bill Longmuir	72	71	75	218	2,852
Denis O'Sullivan	77	69	72	218	2,852

Japan Senior Tour

Fancl Classic

Susono Country Club, Susono, Shizuoka
Par 36-36–72; 6,851 yards

August 21-23
purse, ¥60,000,000

	SCORES			TOTAL	MONEY
Tateo Ozaki	68	68	67	203	¥15,000,000
Tsukasa Watanabe	70	69	66	205	5,400,000
Masahiro Kuramoto	73	66	66	205	5,400,000
Tommy Nakajima	69	67	70	206	2,550,000
Atsushi Murota	63	70	73	206	2,550,000
Hiroshi Ueta	71	70	66	207	2,100,000
Takashi Miyoshi	70	70	68	208	1,650,000
Nobumitsu Yuhara	69	69	70	208	1,650,000
Katsunari Takahashi	73	67	69	209	1,320,000
Hajime Meshiai	72	71	67	210	1,106,000
Hikaru Emoto	72	70	68	210	1,106,000
Noboru Sugai	69	68	73	210	1,106,000
Tomohiro Maruyama	72	71	68	211	858,600
Takaaki Fukuzawa	71	69	71	211	858,600
Gohei Sato	70	69	72	211	858,600
Yoshio Fumiyama	71	68	72	211	858,600
Takeru Shibata	72	67	72	211	858,600
David Ishii	72	71	69	212	750,000
Masami Ito	70	74	69	213	675,000
Keiji Teshima	72	72	69	213	675,000
Shuichi Sano	73	70	70	213	675,000
Boonchu Ruangkit	72	70	71	213	675,000

Komatsu Open

Komatsu Country Club, Komatsu, Ishikawa
Par 36-36–72; 6,932 yards

September 10-12
purse, ¥60,000,000

	SCORES			TOTAL	MONEY
Tomohiro Maruyama	70	67	72	209	¥12,000,000
Masami Ito	68	71	70	209	4,140,000
Boochu Ruangkit	69	70	70	209	4,140,000
David Ishii	68	69	72	209	4,140,000
(Maruyama won on first playoff hole.)					
Ikuo Shirahama	73	69	68	210	1,849,500
Tommy Nakajima	68	73	69	210	1,849,500
Katsunari Takahashi	69	71	70	210	1,849,500
Yuji Takagi	68	72	70	210	1,849,500
Shuichi Sano	70	74	68	212	1,386,000
Yoshinori Mizumaki	69	71	72	212	1,386,000
Masahiro Kuramoto	72	72	69	213	1,176,000
Kiyoshi Murota	71	72	70	213	1,176,000
Yoshio Fumiyama	71	71	71	213	1,176,000
Tsukasa Watanabe	71	72	72	215	1,020,000
Chen Tze-chung	73	73	70	216	760,666
Shinji Ikeuchi	75	70	71	216	760,666

	SCORES			TOTAL	MONEY
Seiji Ebihara	72	72	72	216	760,666
Koji Okuno	73	71	72	216	760,666
Hikaru Emoto	75	69	72	216	760,666
Katsuyoshi Tomori	68	75	73	216	760,666
Noboru Sugai	72	71	73	216	760,666
Nobumitsu Yuhara	72	71	73	216	760,666
Akiyoshi Omachi	75	68	73	216	760,666

Japan PGA Senior Championship Tamahome Cup

Ito Golf Club, Fukuoka
Par 36-35–71; 6,758 yards

September 24-27
purse, ¥50,000,000

	SCORES				TOTAL	MONEY
Kiyoshi Murota	68	68	67	66	269	¥10,000,000
Tateo Ozaki	68	66	71	70	275	5,000,000
Norikazu Kawakami	70	71	71	66	278	3,500,000
Tommy Nakajima	75	69	68	67	279	2,500,000
Kimpachi Yoshimura	70	70	70	71	281	1,616,666
Nobumitsu Yuhara	70	71	69	71	281	1,616,666
Seiji Ebihara	74	67	68	72	281	1,616,666
Tsukasa Watanabe	71	72	71	68	282	1,200,000
David Ishii	70	71	70	71	282	1,200,000
Hiroshi Ueda	69	71	74	69	283	1,025,000
Nichito Hashimoto	74	69	71	69	283	1,025,000
Yoshinori Mizumaki	69	72	67	76	284	950,000
Taisei Inagaki	69	73	71	72	285	875,000
Katsunari Takahashi	71	70	70	74	285	875,000
Noboru Sugai	71	76	73	66	286	680,000
Masahiro Kuramoto	71	74	73	68	286	680,000
Katsuyoshi Tomori	75	68	72	71	286	680,000
Shinji Ikeuchi	71	73	71	71	286	680,000
Yoshinori Ichioka	75	72	68	71	286	680,000
Gohei Sato	69	72	72	73	286	680,000

Fujifilm Senior Championship

Hirakawa Country Club, Chiba
Par 36-36–72; 7,094 yards
(Event shortened to 36 holes.)

October 1-3
purse, ¥70,000,000

	SCORES		TOTAL	MONEY
Hajime Meshiai	67	72	139	¥14,000,000
Masami Ito	69	71	140	5,250,000
Tateo Ozaki	68	72	140	5,250,000
Katsunari Takahashi	69	72	141	2,660,000
Katsuyoshi Tomori	68	73	141	2,660,000
Noboru Sugai	72	70	142	1,750,000
Ikuo Shirahama	71	71	142	1,750,000
Koji Okuno	72	71	143	1,435,000
Nobumitsu Yuhara	71	72	143	1,435,000
Yoshinori Mizumaki	73	71	144	1,124,000
Tsukasa Watanabe	72	72	144	1,124,000
Noboru Fujiike	71	73	144	1,124,000
Masahiro Kuramoto	71	73	144	1,124,000
Tommy Nakajima	71	73	144	1,124,000
Keisuke Goi	70	74	144	1,124,000

	SCORES				TOTAL	MONEY
Chen Tze-ming	69	75			144	1,124,000
David Ishii	71	74			145	857,500
Yutaka Hagawa	70	75			145	857,500
Kimpachi Yoshimura	74	72			146	738,500
Yukio Noguchi	74	72			146	738,500
Shinji Ikeuchi	73	73			146	738,500
Taisei Inagaki	71	75			146	738,500

Japan Senior Open Championship

Biwako Country Club, Shiga
Par 36-36–72; 6,946 yards

October 29-November 1
purse, ¥80,000,000

	SCORES				TOTAL	MONEY
Tsukasa Watanabe	73	68	66	73	280	¥16,000,000
Tateo Ozaki	72	69	70	70	281	6,320,000
Kiyoshi Murota	70	69	71	71	281	6,320,000
Katsunari Takahashi	67	73	70	71	281	6,320,000
Yoshinori Mizumaki	69	71	72	70	282	3,360,000
Tommy Nakajima	72	71	68	76	287	2,800,000
Larry Nelson	71	75	77	65	288	2,240,000
Hiroshi Ueda	75	68	72	73	288	2,240,000
Hajime Meshiai	71	72	74	73	290	1,640,000
Masahiro Kuramoto	72	71	72	75	290	1,640,000
Yoshinori Ichioka	71	71	76	74	292	1,192,000
Katsuyoshi Tomori	75	74	71	72	292	1,192,000
Gary Hallberg	72	74	70	76	292	1,192,000
David Ishii	75	73	67	77	292	1,192,000
Nobumitsu Yuhara	72	74	72	75	293	944,000
Noboru Fujiike	73	77	74	70	294	800,000
Yutaka Hagawa	71	73	77	73	294	800,000
*Toshiki Sakiyama	73	75	73	73	294	
Koji Okuno	73	75	72	74	294	800,000
Teruo Nakamura	78	68	72	76	294	800,000
Masami Ito	77	71	70	76	294	800,000

Handa Cup Philanthropy Senior Open

Skyway Country Club, Chiba
Par 36-36–72; 6,824 yards

November 12-15
purse, ¥110,000,000

	SCORES				TOTAL	MONEY
Ian Woosnam	75	70	68	71	284	¥25,000,000
Gohei Sato	74	69	73	71	287	12,100,000
Yutaka Hagawa	71	72	74	71	288	6,050,000
Yoshinori Mizumaki	73	70	70	75	288	6,050,000
Masahiro Kuramoto	71	71	72	74	288	6,050,000
Hajime Meshiai	73	71	74	71	289	3,850,000
Tsunemi Nakajima	75	70	72	74	291	3,300,000
Ikuo Shirahama	74	74	71	74	293	2,860,000
Toyotake Nakao	71	72	76	75	294	2,530,000
Hiroshi Ueda	77	73	72	73	295	2,200,000
Katsunari Takahashi	75	75	75	71	296	1,870,000
Tomohiro Maruyama	80	71	72	73	296	1,870,000
Tsukasa Watanabe	76	71	77	72	296	1,870,000
Tateo Ozaki	75	75	77	70	297	1,485,000
Katsuyoshi Tomori	75	75	76	71	297	1,485,000

	SCORES				TOTAL	MONEY
Sam Torrance	81	73	69	74	297	1,485,000
Hiromi Ogino	72	74	76	75	297	1,485,000
Sandy Lyle	73	79	74	72	298	1,074,562
Yoshio Fumiyama	77	75	71	75	298	1,074,562
Masami Ito	75	75	74	74	298	1,074,562
Kazuo Kanayama	74	75	72	77	298	1,074,562
Hisashi Nakase	75	74	73	76	298	1,074,562
Yasuzo Hagiwara	76	72	77	73	298	1,074,562
Nobumitsu Yuhara	76	72	74	76	298	1,074,562
Tadayoshi Kusano	72	73	79	74	298	1,074,562